COMPARATIVE
Animal Physiology

C. LADD PROSSER

PROFESSOR OF PHYSIOLOGY, UNIVERSITY OF ILLINOIS

FRANK A. BROWN, JR.

PROFESSOR OF BIOLOGY, NORTHWESTERN UNIVERSITY

Second Edition, Illustrated

W. B. SAUNDERS COMPANY

PHILADELPHIA   LONDON

PREFACE

This is the second edition of a survey of Comparative Animal Physiology, first published in 1950. The book is intended to serve two purposes: (1) as a text in courses at the upper-class undergraduate and first-year graduate level, and (2) as a reference book for beginning investigators and for others who wish to check the principal references in certain physiological fields. An increased effort has been made in this new edition to present a unified picture of comparative physiology, to supply summarizing sections, and to emphasize general principles.

Tables of data are less extensive than in the first edition; they present representative entries for older material and more detailed entries for data published since 1950. The reference lists are highly selected; they include what are considered to be permanent contributions made prior to 1950 and are more complete for recent publications. However, the reference lists are no substitute for a literature search and are intended to help investigators begin such a search. Review papers are indicated with an asterisk. In the interest of economy, titles of references are condensed. Many statements, particularly those common to standard textbooks, are not documented.

Certain factual background is assumed on the part of the reader. It is assumed that the elementary principles of physiology, both of cells and of organisms, are known. Acquaintance with the principal phyla and classes of animals is also assumed. An attempt is made to identify animals named generically by common names or class. Elementary knowledge of organ function as presented in general mammalian and human physiology courses is assumed, but an appropriate presentation of each function system in mammals is given. The boundary between cellular and comparative physiology is not sharp, and some discussion of cellular function is presented, particularly when comparative applications are possible.

In addition to presenting certain biological principles, comparative physiology makes important contributions to ecology and animal phylogeny. This book is organized on a function-system basis. The first two thirds deals with environment-organism interaction and the rest with effector and integrative systems. The index is intended to provide necessary references to various kinds of environment, and to different kinds of animals so that ecologists and biologists concerned with a particular group of animals may find the information they desire.

The help of many specialists in reading portions of the manuscript is acknowledged. Particular thanks are extended to: V. T. Bowen, T. H. Bullock, J. B. Case, Russell Close, Hallowell Davis, V. Dethier, G. S. Fraenkel, Jean Hanson, Sanford Hart, R. Hungate, W. H. Johnson, Donald Kennedy, S. W. Kuffler, C. Manwell, Richard Nystrom, Betty Roots, William J. Rutter, H. Schöne, Ralph Smith, B. L. Strehler, Garth Thomas, H. M. Webb, P. A. Wright, and E. Zuckerkandl.

One of us (C.L.P.) wishes to record his special gratitude to his wife, Hazel B. Prosser, whose help in bibliographic search and manuscript preparation, with unfailing enthusiasm, has made possible the completion of this book.

C. Ladd Prosser
Frank A. Brown, Jr.

CONTENTS

Chapter 11

CHEMORECEPTION 319

C. L. Prosser

Chapter 12

PHOTORECEPTION 335

F. A. Brown, Jr., and C. L. Prosser

Chapter 13

CIRCULATION OF BODY FLUIDS .. 386

C. L. Prosser

Chapter 14

MUSCLE AND ELECTRIC ORGANS.. 417

C. L. Prosser

Chapter 15

AMOEBOID MOVEMENT 468

C. L. Prosser

Chapter 16

CILIA 475

F. A. Brown, Jr.

Chapter 17

TRICHOCYSTS AND NEMATOCYSTS 485

F. A. Brown, Jr.

Chapter 18

BIOLUMINESCENCE 489

F. A. Brown, Jr.

Chapter 19

CHROMATOPHORES AND
COLOR CHANGE 502

F. A. Brown, Jr.

Chapter 20

ENDOCRINE MECHANISMS 538

F. A. Brown, Jr.

Chapter 21

NERVOUS SYSTEMS 587

C. L. Prosser

Chapter 1

INTRODUCTION

The science of physiology is the analysis of function in living organisms. One of the prerequisites for its study is a knowledge of morphology. Physiology is a synthetic science which applies physical and chemical methods to biology.

The Fields of Physiology. For practical purposes, physiology can be divided into three categories, as follows.

Cellular Physiology. Cellular or general physiology treats of those basic characteristics common to most living organisms. A vast amount of biochemical evolution occurred in protoplasm before multicellular organisms appeared, and cells are exceedingly complicated in their functional organization. In any cell— yeast, muscle fiber, or leaf parenchyma cell —the fundamental properties of differential permeability, oxidative enzyme activity, role of nucleotides, nuclear-cytoplasmic interaction, and many other properties are much the same. At the cellular level all organisms have more in common than in difference, and this basic similarity should form the starting point for evolutionary theory. Cellular specialization has led to some diversity of cell types and has often brought with it the loss of one function with emphasis on another. In this sense, one may speak of a comparative physiology of the cells in one organism. The characters treated in cellular physiology are nearly universal and are extremely stable with respect to the environment; these characters will not be discussed in this book.

Physiology of Special Groups. The physiology of special groups of organisms treats of functional characteristics in particular kinds of plants and animals. Traditionally, the basic animal physiology is human and mammalian physiology, and this science provides the rational basis for much of medicine and animal husbandry. The physiology of higher plants is equally specialized and important as a basis for plant agriculture. Insect physiology, fish physiology, and the physiology of parasites are rapidly growing fields.

Comparative Physiology. Comparative physiology treats of organ function in a wide range of groups of organisms. Comparative animal physiology integrates and coordinates functional relationships which transcend special groups of animals. It is concerned with the ways in which diverse organisms perform similar functions. Genetically dissimilar organisms may show striking similarities in characteristics and response to the same environmental stimulus. Closely related animals frequently react very differently to their surroundings. While other branches of physiology use such variables as light, temperature, oxygen tension, and hormone balance, comparative physiology uses, in addition, species or animal type as a variable for each function. Physiological homologies and analogies are as real as morphological ones, and their analysis leads to unique kinds of biological generalizations.

Phylogeny. The physiology of any animal group reflects the history of that group. The phylogenist uses data of paleontology when it is available but relies also on taxonomy and comparative morphology. Since we cannot carry out physiological experiments on fossils, it is important to learn how far functional analogy and homology agree with morphological evidence for animal relationships. Functional evidence exists for preadaptation, parallel evolution, convergence and divergence, embryonic retention, and other evolutionary trends. Similar methods have been used for a given function by different animals, and, conversely, similar animals may use diverse methods for the same function.

Some zoologists favor a polyphyletic "tree," by which most phyla arose nearly simultaneously. A more widely accepted scheme is

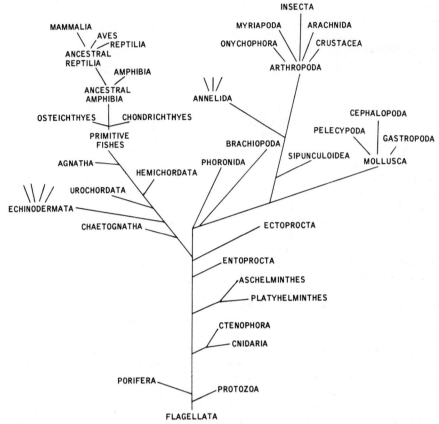

FIGURE 1. Phylogenetic tree of the animal kingdom. (Modified from Hyman, L. H.: The Invertebrates:
Protozoa through Ctenophora. McGraw-Hill Book Co.)

shown in Figure 1.[3] There is disagreement regarding details, and some controversial phyla are omitted from the figure. Flagellates are the most primitive of protozoans, and other modern protozoans and sponges are off-shoots from the direct phylogenetic line. At the level of primitive acoelomate worms there diverged the Platyhelminthes, Nemathelminthes, and other lower worms. At this level there occurred a bifurcation which resulted in two important parallel lines. On the one side are the annelids, arthropods, and molluscs; on the other side, the echinoderms and chordates. The cephalopods show the greatest specialization among the molluscs, the insects among the arthropods, and the birds and mammals among the chordates. In general, embryological differences have been used to distinguish different lines. The annelid-arthropod-mollusc groups show determinate cleavage, i.e., the blastomeres arrange themselves in a stereotyped pattern and there is little intercellular interaction, each cell having a fixed prospective role, whereas in the echino-

derms and chordates cleavage is indeterminate. In the former group, mesoderm formation begins with a particular cell in the blastula which starts two lateral mesodermal bands; in the echinoderm-chordates, mesoderm arises as an outpouching from the archenteron, i.e., from endoderm. In the annelid-arthropod line the coelom is hollowed out from mesodermal bands, while in echinoderms and chordates the coelom pushes out from the archenteron. In the annelid-arthropod-mollusc line the blastopore gives rise to the mouth, and the anus is opened secondarily at the opposite end, whereas in the echinoderm-chordates the blastopore becomes the anus and the mouth opens secondarily. Deviations from these embryological characteristics are known and may be explicable as recent modifications. It is of interest to note physiological agreement and disagreement with the preceding phylogenetic scheme.

Speciation.   There are several species concepts and no one of them can apply to all organisms with their various types of reproduction.[5] The typological concept makes use of stable distinctive characters, usually morphological, not necessarily adaptive, and it is most useful in classification. The characters of cellular physiology are too universal to be used in classification; certain other physiological characters may distinguish large groups—classes, phyla, or groups of phyla; still other functional characters, particularly those associated with specific proteins, are restricted to small taxonomic groups. Many physiological characters are very sensitive to the environment, hence are unstable taxonomically. Some of the physiological characters which have been analyzed genetically are based on multiple factors, and frequently adaptive characters have large safety factors and parallel or alternate functional paths. It is doubtful that physiological characters can be used extensively to characterize species although they are supplementary, and some pairs of species are physiologically isolated but morphologically indistinguishable.

The most useful concept of a species is of a population or series of populations within which there can be a flow of genes in either space or time. Continuous series of populations of an animal—in clines, circles, and the like—are single species even though the terminal populations may be incapable of cross-breeding if brought together. Actually, in nature many breeding populations are very restricted, and hybridization between "species" is more common than is sometimes recognized. Populations which remain distinct when sympatric, i.e., do not cross-breed even though living together, are clearly different species. When two populations are spatially separated (allopatric) there may develop isolating differences which keep them reproductively separated if they come together later in geological time.

A biological definition of species includes all those factors which restrict gene flow to a specific population or group of populations.[6] Reproductive isolation may result from morphological differences, seasonal or diurnal habits, chromosomal, hormonal, and behavioral differences, physiological and psychological incompatibility, and ecological separation. The adaptations which initially fit separated populations to the physical factors in their different environments provide primary isolation; with climatic or geographic change these adaptations may not be necessary and the populations may come together.

Then secondary isolation, e.g., behavior, prevents gene flow between sympatric species. Since no two species occupy identical ecological niches or have the same geographic ranges, a complete description of physiological adaptation, including behavior, should serve to describe species.[6]

The physiological description of species has rarely been attempted; it requires a combination of field and laboratory observations which are possible for very few organisms. First there must be a description of physiological variation in natural populations in terms of critical characters, a statistical analysis of adaptive capacity. Second, such variation as is found must be analyzed for the genetic component and that which is environmentally determined; this requires cross-acclimation, transplantation, and breeding experiments. Finally, an analysis of physiological mechanisms underlying the varying characters is needed.[4]

Ecology. Where an animal lives is related to where its ancestors lived. There is no simple way to summarize all of the environmental factors influencing an organism, but we may distinguish four main habitats—marine, fresh-water, terrestrial, and endoparasitic. Each of these has been extensively subdivided by zoogeographers, marine biologists, and ecologists. The animals in different environments are confronted with different problems; conversely, in the same environment different animals solve a given problem in different ways.

The comparative physiologist considers the organism as played upon by a variety of environmental factors—water, inorganic ions, organic food, oxygen and carbon dioxide, light, high and low frequency mechanical waves, pressure, gravity, ionizing and other radiation, and temperature. Comparative physiologists are concerned with the adaptive responses to these environmental factors. In addition, an animal is influenced in its environment by other organisms—plants and animals. Consideration of the biotic environment leads to the study of animal behavior.

The range of a species is determined through natural selection by its limits of tolerance. One environmental factor, e.g., salinity, may limit the distribution of one group; another factor, e.g., temperature, may limit a different group. Over an ecological range, individuals may vary within limits set by their genotype; a phenotype results from the combination of genetic and environmental factors.

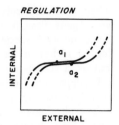

FIGURE 2. Diagrams representing internal state as function of external condition for a given parameter. Two degrees of acclimation indicated as a_1 and a_2. Solid lines lie within the range of normal tolerance; broken lines lie within the range tolerated for brief periods only. In the pattern of conformity, the variations of the internal state correspond with the external variations. In the pattern of regulation, the internal state is somewhat independent of the external.

Criteria of Physiological Variation.*

Among the most useful criteria of functional differences among animals are tests under environmental stresses; long-term survival is determined more by extremes in nature than by means. Most of the following stress tests can be applied for a number of environmental factors:[5]

1. Survival tests at environmental limits, for example, median lethal values for heat, cold, salinity, dilution, and oxygen supply. Survival data must be accompanied by knowledge of the acclimation state and must be obtained over such a time that the cause of death is uniform. Lethal levels may be plotted as a function of acclimation level to provide a "tolerance polygon."[2]

2. Environmental limits for reproduction. Embryos are often more sensitive to stresses than are adults, yet completion of full life cycles is what counts in nature.

3. Recovery from a deviated state.[1] Animals tend toward certain "norms," and when deviated, as by excess hydration or dehydration, heating or cooling, they may compensate, or on removal of the stress they may

* *Acclimation* refers to the compensatory change in an organism under maintained deviation of a single environmental factor (usually in the laboratory). If acclimation is complete, a measured rate function is the same under one environmental condition as under another. *Acclimatization* refers to those compensatory changes in an organism undergoing multiple natural deviations of milieu—climatic, physical, and biotic.

Adaptation is a general term referring to any alteration or response of an organism which favors survival in a changed environment. Physiological adaptation refers to *conformity* and *regulation* of internal state as well as compensation by long-term acclimation or acclimatization.

return in a definite pattern to the original "norm." The rate of return is characteristic for a particular kind of animal.

4. Rate functions. Rates may be measured for movements and for metabolism, for various enzymatic reactions as a function of environmental stresses. These yield curves such as those for temperature characteristics.

5. Behavior. This includes taxic responses, selection of "preferred" environments in gradients, and also complex behavior, such as courtship, mating, and rearing of young.

6. Internal state as a function of the environment.[4] Some animals change internally to conform to the environment, for example, poikilotherms in varying temperature. Others maintain relative internal constancy in a changing environment; they regulate, for example, homeotherms. Measurements of conformity and regulation can be extended to all the physical factors of the environment. In general, conformers tolerate wide internal variation but narrow environmental limits, whereas regulators tolerate only narrow internal variation but a wider environmental range (Fig. 2). Acclimation can shift the tolerated internal limits for a conformer; it can change the critical limits for either failure or activation of homeostatic controls in a regulator. Both patterns, conformity and regulation, are homeostatic in the sense of permitting survival in a changing environment, and most animals show combinations of the two patterns.*

Time Course of Environmental Effects.

Animals show a temporal pattern of response to a suddenly applied environmental stress (Fig. 3). First there is stimulation leading to a shock reaction, overshoot of a rate function, or behavioral response. This response is usually measured in seconds or minutes. Then follows a stabilized state which is the period

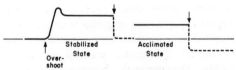

FIGURE 3. Time course of change of a rate function under environmental stress. Stress applied at first arrow (bottom) leads to overshoot for seconds or minutes, then to stabilized rate (hours). Upon removal of stress (second arrow), direct recovery ensues. If stress persists (days and weeks), some compensation is usually reached in state of acclimation during which the organism changes so that return to the original environmental condition (arrow 3) leads to undershoot of rate.

of relative constancy during which rate functions are usually measured. This period of stabilization may last for minutes or hours. If the stress persists for days or weeks most animals enter a state of compensation or acclimation. In perfect compensation the rate function is the same at each environmental condition. If an organism in the stabilized state is returned from the stress to the original environment, its rate function returns directly; if an organism in the state of compensation is returned, the rate function goes beyond its original level, indicating that the animal is in an altered physiological state. If a changed environment persists long—for a lifetime—there may be nongenetic effects carried to successive generations, as by cytoplasmic transmission and particularly by behavioral continuity. Finally, over many generations, selection of adapted genotypes results in physiologically different populations in two environments.

Plan for Study of Comparative Physiology. Animals do not react to a complex environmental situation with a single organ system. The organism as a whole is not equal to the sum of its parts, and out of the whole organism emerge unique characteristics not present in any of the parts when isolated. It is important, therefore, to examine the relation between components of the environment and whole organisms, and to analyze the interactions in terms of organ and cell physiology. The plan of this book is to consider the reactions of animals to specific variations in a series of environmental factors and then to consider effector and coordinating mechanisms in general. The diverse facts of comparative physiology can be integrated as homologies and analogies and as adaptive mechanisms, particularly as they throw light on animal relationships, speciation, and distribution.

For the applied biologist, comparative physiology has practical applications in describing the physiology of economically important animals. For the ecologist, it helps the understanding of restriction of plants and animals to particular habitats. For the medical physiologist, the comparative viewpoint places man in his proper biological perspective. For the general biologist, it provides meaning to natural variation, and general principles which can be reached only with *kind* of organism as a variable.

REFERENCES

1. ADOLPH, E., Physiological Regulations. Lancaster, Pa., Cattell Press, 1943, 502 pp.
2. FRY, F. E. J., Publ. Ontario Fish. Res. Lab. *68*: 1-62, 1947. Theory of physiological adaptation.
3. HYMAN, L. H., The Invertebrates: Protozoa through Ctenophora. New York, McGraw Hill Book Co., 1940, 726 pp.
4. PROSSER, C. L., Biol. Rev. *30*: 229-262, 1955. Physiological variation in animals.
5. PROSSER, C. L., *in* The Species Problem, edited by E. Mayr. Washington, A.A.A.S., 1957, pp. 339-369.
6. PROSSER, C. L., Am. Scientist *47*: 536-550, 1959; *in* Evolution after Darwin, edited by S. Tax. University of Chicago Press, 1960, vol. 1, pp. 569-594.

Chapter 2

WATER: OSMOTIC BALANCE

INTRODUCTION

Water is an essential constituent of all living things; it is the universal biological solvent, the continuous phase in which most of the cellular reactions of metabolism occur, and the most necessary to life of all environmental constituents. Life undoubtedly began in a watery medium. Numerous exits from water to land have been made in the course of evolution, but only a few groups of animals have been successful in maintaining themselves out of water. Each group which has made the exit from water has used its own set of adaptations to life in air, some being more successful than others. Insects have made the exit more complete than have other animals, and a few insects return to water for part of their life cycle. All other animals, including birds and mammals, return to a watery medium at least for embryonic life.

One problem of animal life is to maintain inside the organism just the proper amount of water—not too much, not too little. Terrestrial animals must retain and use what water is available; fresh-water animals must exclude water to prevent self-dilution; some marine and parasitic animals are in osmotic conformity with their medium, whereas others are more dilute and have the problem of taking in enough water while living in a plenitude of it. The environmental range with respect to water, from fresh water through the sea to salt lakes, from humid swamps to dry deserts, is far greater than the tolerated range of concentrations of body fluids; hence animals must have a variety of mechanisms for regulating their osmotic balance.

Physical Considerations. The water content of a solution, either within an animal or outside, gives little indication of the actual water activity (in a thermodynamic sense, the effective water concentration). The effective concentration of all solutes, or osmotic con-centration, is often expressed in *osmoles*, that is, the total number of moles of particles per liter of solvent. *Osmolal concentration* is given by the colligative properties, which are dependent on the total number of solute particles independent of size or chemical nature of the dissolved material. Any one of the colligative properties can be calculated from any of the others; the higher the concentration of solute, the greater are the osmotic pressure, the lowering of vapor pressure, the elevation of the boiling point, and the depression of the freezing point of the solution. The osmotic pressure is that pressure necessary to prevent entry of water across a semipermeable membrane (one which permits solvent only to pass) into a solution. Strictly semipermeable membranes rarely if ever exist in living organisms; otherwise there would be no exchange of solutes, and cells are rarely if ever bathed by pure water; hence *osmotic pressure* is a less useful concept *per se* than *osmotic concentration*.

Of the methods for measurement of osmotic concentration, the osmotic pressure is useful for organic solutes although elaborate precautions are necessary to ensure a really semipermeable membrane. Two vapor pressure methods are sometimes used. (1) A drop of solution of unknown concentration may be placed in a capillary separated by air from drops of a known concentration on either side; the ends are sealed with petrolatum and, according to whether the unknown is more or less concentrated, the drop will lose or gain in size. (2) A drop of unknown concentration may be placed on one junction of a thermocouple, a drop of known solution on the other junction, and the changes in temperature due to evaporation and condensation from one junction to the other may then be recorded. Vapor pressure is lowered in proportion to the mole fraction of solute.

The most commonly used method for determining osmoconcentration is measurement of *freezing-point lowering*, Δ. This can be done with large samples by an immersion thermometer, following the supercooling and ultimate plateau temperature of freezing. More commonly with small samples the melting point is observed by placing a thermometer (Beckman type) beside a capillary containing a drop of frozen unknown immersed in a medium which is allowed to warm slowly and the temperature of disappearance of the last crystal (viewed with a microscope) is recorded. By Gross' method, drops of the unknown (0.01 ml) are placed in capillaries which are sealed with petrolatum and mounted on a rack along with others containing known NaCl concentrations. The rack is immersed in a dish of brine cooled by dry ice, polaroids are placed below and above the dish to make the crystals of ice more visible, and from the times of melting, the unknown solutions can be expressed in terms of equivalent NaCl concentrations. Good stirring and a slow rate of rise of the brine temperature are essential.

Since the colligative properties depend on the total number of solute particles, the osmotic concentration (C) of non-electrolyte will be the same as its molal concentration. Dilute solutions behave ideally like gases; hence by analogy the osmotic pressure (π) equals the osmolal concentration (C) multiplied by the gas constant (R) (R = 0.082 liter atmosphere/°C/mole) and the absolute temperature (T),

$$\pi = C\,R\,T.$$

For electrolytes the osmotic concentration will exceed the molal concentration by some quantity (i), the *isotonic coefficient*. The osmotic concentration (C) of an electrolyte is given by the product of (i) and the molal concentration (c) of the electrolyte; hence for electrolytes

$$\pi = i\,c\,R\,T.$$

The isotonic coefficient represents the sum of the activity coefficients of all the solutes. Weak electrolytes in dilute solutions are completely dissociated but (i) is less than 2 for a univalent salt and less than 3 for one which dissociates into 3 ions because of interaction between the ions. Also (i) decreases as the concentration increases up to a critical level, and then increases again. Unfortunately, biological solutions cannot be regarded as infinitely dilute and (i) must be determined for each concentration of electrolyte being used.

A 1 osmolal aqueous solution freezes at −1.86°C; therefore the lowering of the freezing point is $\Delta = -1.86$ i c. Since an osmolal solution has an osmotic pressure (π) of 22.4 atmospheres,

$$\pi = \Delta\frac{22.4}{1.86} = 12.06\,\Delta.$$

For practical purposes osmotic concentrations are usually given as osmolal (or milliosmolal), as lowering of the freezing point, or in equivalent NaCl concentration (millimolal). A few representative values from Bureau of Standards tables for NaCl follow:

% NaCl	Molality	i	Δ (°C)
4.08	0.7	1.806	−2.38
2.92	0.5	1.81	−1.69
1.75	0.3	1.83	−1.02
1.17	0.2	1.84	−0.68
0.58	0.1	1.87	−0.34

Patterns of Biological Response to Osmotic Conditions. One solution is said to be isosmotic with another if they have equal osmotic concentrations. An *isotonic* solution is one in which a cell (or organism) does not change its volume. An *isosmotic* solution of substance to which a cell is permeable, but which is initially absent from the cell, is not isotonic. Hence the term isosmotic is preferable in referring to equal osmotic concentrations. Similarly a *hypoosmotic* solution is more dilute and a *hyperosmotic* one more concentrated than a comparison solution.

Nearly all fresh-water and terrestrial plants, by virtue of their cellulose walls and active plasma membranes, maintain their cellular constituents, particularly their vacuolar sap, at concentrations higher than those of the fluids which bathe their tissues. The cells are continually more concentrated than the tissue fluids and hence turgid. In desert plants osmotic pressures of some 50 atmospheres may be attained between cell and extracellular water, and the osmotic pressure of cells of xerophytes exceeds that of mesophytes when they are grown under similar conditions. In animals, inelastic cell walls are absent and, while the outer gel cytoplasm maintains some turgidity, the intracellular concentration is approximately the same as that in extracellular fluid. Excised tissues in isosmotic saline may swell, particularly at low temperature and in anoxia; water is gained which is then lost on return to higher temperature and adequate oxygen. This has been interpreted as indicating a normal active extrusion of water and a maintained hypertonicity inside the cells.[153, 189] A better interpretation seems to be that under unfavorable conditions autolysis and increased permeability to ions lead to increased intracellular concentrations and altered salt distribution, hence swelling, and that under more favorable conditions ions are being actively extruded.[47, 55, 149] Also, in organs where active transport of water had been postulated there is increasing evidence that the transport can be explained by secretion and/or reabsorption of solutes accompanied by water movements. Hence in multicellular animals intracellular and extracellular fluids are usually isosmotic, and regulation of osmotic concentration occurs not in single cells, as in plants, but in the organism as a whole.

The *water content* of tissues differs greatly with type of tissue, age, metabolic activity, and a variety of environmental conditions. A few typical values are:

	percentage water		percentage water
plants		animals	
tip of growing shoots	91—93	jellyfish	95—98
leaves	75—85	mammal (total)	63—68
stems	50—60	muscle	75
stored wheat	5—10	fat	10
		skeleton	35
		earthworm	84
		insect	
		adult	45—65
		larva	58—90

The water content gives very little indication of osmotic properties. A jellyfish with a water content of 95 per cent or more has a higher osmotic concentration than a fish which is only 70 per cent water but which contains relatively more organic material and less electrolytes. Similarly, the density or *specific gravity* of a solution is not a direct function of osmotic concentration, but depends on the nature of the solute, its concentration, the temperature, and barometric pressure.

There are numerous variations in osmotic properties of animals with season, age, nutrition, reproductive and molting cycles, and geographic races. In the following account an attempt is made to select comparable material, but it must be emphasized that measured values of osmoconcentration for a given species may differ with conditions of acclimation, and there may be genetic variation upon which natural selection can operate.

The range of environmental osmotic conditions tolerated by animals is great; the tolerated range of internal osmoconcentrations is much less. (See Table 1 for representative habitats and animals.)

The ocean is the ancestral animal home.

The total osmotically effective concentration of the ocean has increased only slightly since the earliest appearance of life. The water of midocean is now equivalent to a 3.5 per cent salt solution, smaller seas and bays are diluted by inflow of fresh water, and in estuaries and river mouths brackish water merges with fresh. In seas such as the Mediterranean, where evaporation is high, the salinity exceeds that of the ocean. Fresh-water dilutions of ocean water are often expressed as per cent sea water, and *salinity* or total salt content in parts per thousand ($^0/_{00}$). An average sea water may be as follows: 100 per cent S.W. = salinity 34.5 $^0/_{00}$ = Δ of $-1.88°C$ = sp. gr. at $10°C$ 1.0215 = chlorinity 18.8 $^0/_{00}$ = osmolarity 1.01.

Any water with a salinity less than 0.5 $^0/_{00}$ ($\Delta = -0.05°$) may be considered as fresh. We shall refer to any water between fresh and 30 $^0/_{00}$ as brackish although ecologists recognize at least four intermediate ranges each with its animal and plant communities.

Animals and plants which are restricted to a narrow range of salinity, usually to full sea water, are called *stenohaline*; those which are tolerant of a variety of salinities are *euryhaline*. Many exits have been made from the ocean to fresh water and from water to land, and many separate reinvasions of water. Nature is carrying out experiments in osmotic adaptation which we can observe at the present time, and species may be determined by the range of osmotic lability of a population. All phyla and most classes of animals have representatives in the marine habitat; some animals have remained in the ancestral home, some have returned to it. Members of fewer phyla have ventured into brackish water, and comparatively few meet the demands imposed by fresh water for osmoregulation. Some animals have invaded land directly from the ocean, others through the avenues of estuarine and fresh water. The parasitic habit has been assumed by marine, fresh-water, and soil-dwelling groups. Evidence regarding the osmotic limitation to distribution of a group of animals can be obtained by observing the responses to *osmotic stress*.

There are two extreme patterns of response to osmotic stress. Animals may be osmotically labile (dependent) and their body-fluid concentration may change with the medium; these are *osmoconformers*. Other animals are osmotically stable (independent), and when the medium changes, the internal concentration remains relatively constant; these are *osmoregulators*. The terms *poikilosmotic* and

TABLE 1.   TYPICAL VALUES OF OSMOCONCENTRATION IN LOWERING OF FREEZING POINT FOR AQUATIC ENVIRONMENTS AND FOR ANIMALS*

Medium	$\Delta_o °C$	Animal	$\Delta_i °C$
Fresh water	—0.01	Fresh-water mussel	—0.08
		Pelomyxa	—0.14
		Fresh-water fish	—0.50 to —0.55
		Frog	—0.45
		Crayfish	—0.82
		Earthworm	—0.3 to —0.4
Brackish water	—0.2 to —0.5	Mammal	—0.55 to —0.58
		Insects	
		larvae	—0.5 to —1.0
		adults	—0.9 to —1.2
Sea water	—1.85	Marine fish	—0.65 to —0.7
		Marine invertebrates	—1.8 to —1.85
		Marine elasmobranchs	—1.85 to —1.92
Salt lakes 50-250 $^0/_{00}$	—13.5 to —15°	Brine shrimp (Artemia)	—1.2 to —1.6

* Δ_o = freezing point of medium.
Δ_i = freezing point of body fluid.

homoiosmotic are often applied respectively to conforming and regulating animals. There are, of course, all gradations between the extremes of lability and constancy; an animal may conform osmotically in one concentration range and regulate in another. Osmotic changes may bring about gain or loss of water and thus volume changes; if salt transfer also occurs, the volume is kept constant when the animal's concentration changes with the medium. Osmoconformers tolerate wider variation in internal osmoconcentrations, while osmoregulators can withstand a wider environmental range.

Animals tend to maintain an "optimum" osmotic concentration for a given environment. Many species, upon return to normal environment after a period of dehydration, take up water, and after a period of hydration, lose water, until the osmoconcentration reaches the "optimum" for the particular animal.[2, 5] The time course of recovery from the deviated state of water balance may be characteristic of a given species. Detailed accounts of the older literature on osmoregulation have been given[19, 128] and representative values of osmoconcentrations tabulated[8] (Table 1). We shall confine this discussion to ecological and phylogenetic implications and to current views regarding adaptive mechanism. Osmotic phenomena involve movement not only of water but also of solutes and since the principal osmotic solutes are salts, some consideration will be given to *ion regulation* along with water balance.

OSMOTIC CONFORMERS

Limited Volume Regulation. *Marine Eggs and Protozoa.* Most marine inverte-brates are isosmotic, that is, their internal concentration corresponds to that outside. The limitation to the distribution of all osmolabile animals is probably the dilution at which their protoplasmic organization can still permit basal metabolic functions. The simplest osmotic conformity is found in many marine and parasitic invertebrates which are permeable to water and which gain or lose water according to the concentration of the medium. An organism which is a simple osmometer swells or shrinks in proportion to its total solute concentration and is bounded by a membrane permeable to water only; thus there is no volume regulation. In all living cells, however, there is probably some ionic exchange. Animals which come closest to being true osmometers are the eggs of marine invertebrates, particularly echinoderms and annelids. When the volume of a marine invertebrate egg is measured in different dilutions and concentrations of sea water, the cell approaches the relation: pressure (π) $\times$ volume (V) = a constant (K), (π V = K). In very dilute sea water the marine egg does not swell as much as would be expected if it followed the gas laws in proportionality of volume and pressure (Fig. 4). The explanation of this deviation seems to be that a certain portion of the cell volume is osmotically inactive; this portion consists of large organic molecules which occupy a greater relative volume than inorganic salts. When a correction is made for this osmotically inactive volume (b) it is found that π (V — b) = K. The osmotically inactive volume is 7.3 per cent of the initial cell volume in unfertilized *Arbacia* eggs, 27.4 per cent in fertilized eggs.[217] A second explanation of

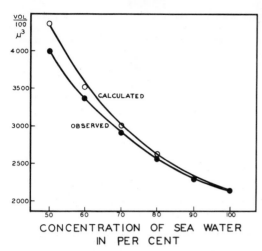

FIGURE 4. Volumes of fertilized *Arbacia* eggs as a function of dilution of sea water as per cent normal sea water. ● observed volumes. ○ volumes calculated from gas laws. (From Lucké, B., and McCutcheon, M.: Physiol. Rev., vol. 12.)

the failure of cells to swell as much as predicted in dilute media might be leakage of salt, i.e., failure of the semipermeable nature of the membrane. Salt leakage apparently is negligible over the range of rapid reversible changes, but it may be important in extreme dilutions where injury occurs. The permeability to water as indicated by the rates of swelling and shrinking is increased markedly on fertilization. The rate of swelling is less than the rate of shrinking, that is, the egg is more permeable to outward than to inward movement of water.

Both marine and endoparasitic Protozoa are usually isosmotic with their medium. The flagellate *Noctiluca* is isosmotic but may have a lower specific gravity than sea water owing to the presence of considerable amounts of a salt, probably ammonium chloride, of lower specific gravity than NaCl.[1] Several gregarines from the gut of mealworms swell and shrink according to the tonicity of the medium; they have a high glycogen content which may cause as much as 70 to 80 per cent of their volume to be osmotically inactive.

Multicellular Animals. Osmotic conformity with poor volume regulation is shown by numerous marine invertebrates. The unsegmented sipunculid worms survive well in either dilute or concentrated sea water. The body weight of phascolosoma (*Golfingia* = phascolosoma) decreases or increases on transfer to high or low concentrations, reaches equilibrium in a few hours, and holds for at least 2 days. On return to normal sea water

(S.W.) the original volume is approached; approximately 23 per cent of the body volume is osmotically inactive.[4] From the rate of weight changes of worms with gut and nephridia tied off, inward permeability of the body wall to water is found to be greater than the outward permeability.[4] However, in another sipunculid, *Dendrostomum,* after a small weight change (e.g., in S.W. diluted or concentrated by less than 20 per cent) there may be some volume recovery in 4 to 6 days (Fig. 5). Thus, with time there is salt exchange, more by gut and nephridia than by body wall, and limited volume regulation.[84] When salt solutions are injected, volume changes correspond to those on immersion, and some days later there may occur volume recovery accompanied by salt movement.

Various Degrees of Volume Regulation: Molluscs, Echinoderms. Some molluscs also show very slow volume regulation. The nudibranch, *Doris,* swells rapidly in dilute sea water, and remains swollen for at least 24 hours, although there may be slight volume decrease at 48 hours. In another gastropod, *Onchidium,* water permeability greatly exceeds salt permeability so that there is little volume regulation.[53] The gastropod, *Aplysia,* on transfer to 75 per cent S.W. gains weight for 2 or 3 hours but then recovers, and if transferred back to 100 per cent S.W. it loses weight, indicating that it had lost salt during its volume recovery (Fig. 5).[28] Recent experiments[239] indicate damage to *Aplysia* even in 80 per cent S.W., while in 95 per cent S.W. the blood salinity does not fall in 5 hours quite to that of the medium; O_2 consumption is increased briefly after transfer from one salinity to another.

Mytilus edulis, the common mussel, is found in sea water (e.g., the North Sea at salinity 30 $^o/_{oo}$), in brackish water (as in the Baltic, at 15 $^o/_{oo}$), and even at dilutions as great as 4 to 6 $^o/_{oo}$ (Finnish Bay).[202, 203] The hemolymph concentration conforms to that of the medium as follows:

Δ_o	Δ_1
—0.94	—0.95
—0.77	—0.77
—0.37	—0.37

If bivalves are transferred directly from full to dilute sea water (*Mytilus, Crassostrea,* or *Modiolus*) the valves remain closed for variable periods, and with the valves closed a marine pelecypod can survive and maintain hemolymph undiluted for many days, or the hemolymph may become diluted very gradually (*Scrobicularia*). However, if the valves are forced open, there is weight gain, rapid dilution, and little volume regulation during 2 days. Only such molluscan species as *Mytilus* can live indefinitely in dilutions of some 50 per cent. In *Mytilus* the tissue and hemolymph chloride concentrations become reduced in dilute sea water; hence swelling is less than if no salt were lost.[128] In dilute sea water (15 $^0/_{00}$) the *Mytilus* oxygen consumption is lower than in normal sea water, the ciliary activity is less, the heart rate less, and heat resistance reduced; elevated O_2 consumption is found, however, in the isolated gills,[202, 203] as follows:

Animals	Ciliary rate (mm/sec)	O_2 consumed by gills (mm^3 O_2/100 mg dry wt/hr)
North Sea animals in 30 $^0/_{00}$	0.68	82
North Sea animals in 15 $^0/_{00}$	0.51	144
Baltic animals in 30 $^0/_{00}$	0.44	84
Baltic animals in 15 $^0/_{00}$	0.51	141

Individuals growing in low salinities (Baltic) are smaller than those of the same

age in full sea water. These observations by Schlieper together with older data indicate that those few marine bivalves, which like *Mytilus* are euryhaline, are osmoconformers but that in dilute sea water they are living under considerable stress. Bivalves from deep water, where salinity variations are small, show less tolerance of salinity change than do estuarine and littoral species. The osmotic differences among populations from different regions are environmentally induced, that is, a population acclimated to a new salinity comes to be like a population native to that habitat. Limpets from the high intertidal zone are more tolerant of reduced salinity than those from lower intertidal regions.[13] *Cardium lamarcki* can tolerate salinities of 5 $^0/_{00}$, *C. edule* not lower than 20 $^0/_{00}$.[166]

An octopus is isosmotic and excretes 6 to 10 per cent of body weight per 24 hours as urine which is of importance in ionic regulation.[143]

The echinoderms are entirely marine and conform osmotically to the medium; indeed in all except holothurians the ambulacral fluid is essentially sea water. The holothurian *Caudina* swells in dilute sea water, but the increase is much less than if the body wall were semipermeable, and volume changes persist for at least 4 days.[124] Echinoids, asteroids, and ophiuroids, because of their exoskeletons, cannot swell much. Starfish put into 55 per cent sea water increased in weight by 32 per

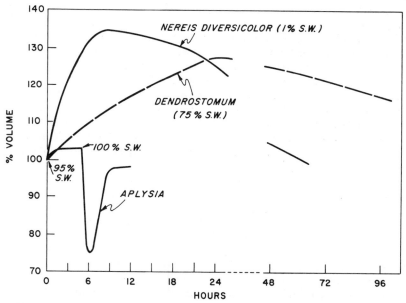

FIGURE 5. Percentage change in volume of several osmoconforming animals when transferred at zero time to the dilutions of sea water indicated. *Nereis* data,[107] *Dendrostomum*,[84] *Aplysia*.[239]

cent within 4 hours and they showed no recovery of weight within 50 hours. *Asterias rubens* is unable to survive such dilution as *Mytilus edulis* and in the Baltic reaches its limit at 8 $^0/_{00}$; also *Asterias* cannot be transported directly from the North Sea to the Baltic. When compared with *Asterias* living in 30 $^0/_{00}$ sea water, *Asterias* in 15 $^0/_{00}$ has a soft integument, increased water content, lessened tolerance of high temperature, and its metabolism is reduced.[32, 126, 202, 203] Hence *Asterias* is stenohaline.

Despite the fact that marine jellyfish are composed of only 3 to 5 per cent solids the osmotic concentration of the jelly disc is essentially the same as that of the ocean where they occur.[33] Their tolerance of dilution of the medium is limited; corals and ctenophores may tolerate 20 per cent reduction in salinity.[103] The blood of ascidians, *Ascidia, Molgula,* is approximately isosmotic with the ocean and conforms to the medium over a range from 40 to 140 per cent S.W.; *Molgula* urine is isosmotic or slightly hyperosmotic over the same range.

LIMITED OSMOREGULATION

Polychaetes. Some polychaete annelids show osmotic lability and swell in dilute media,[18] as follows for *Arenicola:*[201]

Δ_o	Δ_1	habitat
—0.29	—0.28 to 0.30	dilute sea water
—0.75	—0.75 to 0.76	Kiel Canal
—1.72	—1.70	Helgoland

In England, the limit for *Arenicola* is 12 $^0/_{00}$.[226] *Perinereis cultrifera* became swollen in 20 per cent sea water and showed no return to its original volume for 60 hours.[18]

Nereid polychaetes form a series of increasing volume regulation and tolerance of dilute medium: *Perinereis cultrifera<Nereis pelagica<Neanthes virens<Nereis diversicolor<Neanthes lighti.* The first two species are stenohaline marine; *Neanthes virens* can regulate its volume down to 3 to 8 $^0/_{00}$; *Nereis diversicolor* occurs in England at 5 to 4 $^0/_{00}$ and in Finland at 4 $^0/_{00}$, and can live in the laboratory below 1 $^0/_{00}$ (to 1.4 per cent sea water), while *Neanthes lighti* can live in fresh water (0.09 $^0/_{00}$ in Lake Merced).[227, 228] The limiting dilution for *Nereis diversicolor* in Finland appears to be due to reduced dilution-tolerance at low temperatures, probably for reproduction, since larvae are more sensitive than adult worms

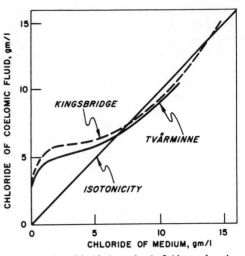

FIGURE 6. Chloride in coelomic fluid as a function of chloride in the medium for *Nereis diversicolor* from Millport (Scotland), and from Tvarminne (Finland).[226]

to dilution of the medium.[187] In dilute sea water *N. diversicolor* remains hyperosmotic to its medium but is not able to maintain the same blood concentration as in sea water (Fig. 6).[226] O_2 consumption increases initially on transfer to dilute sea water, partly because of muscular resistance to swelling.[18] In dilute sea water osmotic and volume regulation fails if cyanide is added, if O_2 is much reduced, or if the medium lacks calcium.[18] Tracer methods show a faster Cl^- exchange and a threefold greater water permeability in *Neanthes virens* than in *Nereis diversicolor,* and much greater Na^+ permeability in *Perinereis cultrifera* than in *Nereis diversicolor.*[74] When *N. diversicolor* is in very dilute sea water, its permeability to ions and water is less than in sea water, and, furthermore, it absorbs Cl^- actively from the medium.[107] Probably the nephridia produce a blood-hypoosmotic urine when *N. diversicolor* is in a dilute medium. *Neanthes lighti* often occurs in brackish water, tolerates fresh water, and reproduces viviparously, not by shedding eggs and sperm as do the marine and strictly brackish worms.[228]

In polychaetes there are, therefore, several levels of osmoregulation. Some, such as *Arenicola* and *Perinereis,* conform in concentration to their environment, swell in dilute media, and show little volume regulation. Others, like *Nereis diversicolor,* show weak but definite osmotic and volume regulation in dilute media and can live in dilute brackish water; they have restricted permeability to salts and water, they absorb ions from a dilute medium and may form a dilute urine. Finally, *Neanthes lighti* can survive and reproduce in fresh water.

Regulation by Water Storage. The flatworm *Gunda* (now *Procerodes*) *ulvae* lives in intertidal zones where it may be alternately exposed for several hours twice each day to fresh water and then to undiluted sea water. In soft tap water *Gunda* swells rapidly and dies within 48 hours, but in diluted sea water or stream water containing significant calcium, swelling is retarded. Other substances than calcium salts fail to retard swelling.[244] In dilute sea water, water passes to the parenchyma, which swells, then it collects in vacuoles in endodermal cells lining the gut. Thus body volume is kept relatively constant and other body cells are kept from becoming diluted.[18] Oxygen consumption is elevated at equilibrium in dilute sea water, and in anaerobic conditions or in cyanide swelling is greater than normal. The vacuoles remain while the worm is in dilute sea water, but some active process, either decreased permeability or increased excretion (but not by way of the gut), prevents further volume increase.

A VARIETY OF ADAPTATIONS: AQUATIC CRUSTACEA

Poikilosmotic Marine Crustaceans. Numerous marine crabs, especially those found in deep sea water, are poikilosmotic with good volume regulation. For example, *Maja,* a spider crab usually occurring at 15 to 100 fathoms, survives only a few hours in sea water diluted by more than about 20 per cent.[216] When placed in dilute sea water (80 per cent S.W.) *Maja* swells initially, but within 3 hours the weight decreases because of loss of salt and accompanying water. By the time the weight is back to normal the osmoconcentration of the blood is the same as that of the diluted medium. Conversely, when put into a more concentrated medium, *Maja* gains salts, and the hemolymph concentration conforms to the external concentration. Numerous other marine crustaceans behave similarly—*Palinurus, Portunas, Cancer antennarius, Lophopanopeus, Speocarcinus, Hyas,* and *Pagurus.*[128] An interesting osmolabile crustacean is *Lernaeocera branchialis,* a copepod parasitic on codfish.[155a] The fish blood is hypoosmotic (equivalent to 1.443 per cent NaCl), and while the copepod is attached to its host it also is hypoosmotic to the sea water (equivalent to 2.0 to 2.8 per cent NaCl), but when separated from the host it becomes isosmotic with the sea water (3.5 per cent saline). A barnacle, *Balanus balanoides,* remains closed in air and when bathed by dilute (50 per cent) sea water; opening is initiated by bathing with salt solution, particularly solutions containing calcium.[16] A lobster is isosmotic with the medium and produces isosmotic urine which differs ionically from blood.[39]

Limited Hyperosmotic Regulation: Shore Crabs. A number of crabs show a limited ability to remain hyperosmotic in dilute sea water although they are poikilosmotic in sea water and higher salinities. These are shore crabs which venture to varying degrees into fresh-water inlets. Some of these

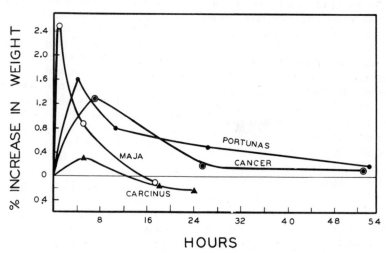

FIGURE 7. Percentage gain in weight by crabs transferred to dilute sea water at zero time. *Maja* in 75 per cent sea water, *Carcinus* in 75 per cent sea water,[216] *Portunus* in 66 per cent sea water, *Cancer* in 66 per cent sea water.[102]

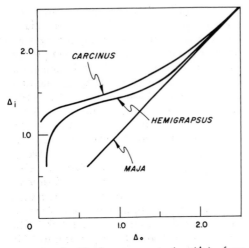

FIGURE 8. Blood osmoconcentration (Δ_i) of several marine crustacea as a function of environmental osmoconcentration. *Carcinus* data,[57, 201] *Maja*,[57] *Hemigrapsus*.[106]

genera can be contrasted with the poikilosmotic sea crabs. When placed in 66 per cent sea water, *Cancer* recovers its volume more slowly than *Maja* (Fig. 7). In a hyperosmotic medium the blood of the shore crab *Eriphia* reached that of the medium only after 72 hours, whereas *Maja* reached the same concentration in 12 hours[216] (Fig. 8). When the marine *Portunus* and *Hyas* were placed in sea water containing some iodine as a tracer, the blood reached 98 per cent and 76 per cent of the medium concentration in 2½ hours while the blood of *Cancer* and *Carcinus* had only 10 to 15 per cent as high a concentration in the same time.[101] Hence the permeability of the gills and carapace of the shore crabs to both water and salts both inward and outward is much less than in marine crabs. In addition, the antennary glands appear to excrete more urine in a dilute medium than in isosmotic sea water.

The shore crabs of the genus *Carcinus* occur from depths of a few fathoms, through tidal pools, to estuaries of dilution down to approximately one-third sea water. *Carcinus* is isosmotic in high salinities, may be slightly hyperosmotic in 100 per cent sea water, and in diluted sea water it is hyperosmotic.[57] When moved from normal sea water into a diluted solution it swells hardly at all, and its blood concentration comes to a new equilibrium in about 12 hours. When transferred to 50 per cent sea water the weight increase in 2½ hours was ten times greater with the excretory pores plugged than with them open.

Apparently the gills are not impermeable to water, but the kidneys excrete it, as follows:[150]

Urine output (ml/24 hr/ 50 gm body wt)	Salinity of medium (%)
5.1	3.3
6.3	1.62
8.5	1.57

There was greater weight increase with both mouth and excretory pores plugged than with only the latter closed; hence some water must be eliminated by the mouth.[16] The urine eliminated in normal sea water may be hyperosmotic, isosmotic, or hypoosmotic to the blood; thus this urine serves mainly in ionic rather than in osmotic regulation. In dilute sea water the urine is slightly hypoosmotic to the blood but is more concentrated than the medium.[150]

Iodine tracer experiments show *Carcinus* to have a very low permeability to this ion, both incoming and outgoing. In dilute media *Carcinus* consumes more oxygen than in normal sea water, in contrast to *Maja* which consumes less oxygen when diluted. Also, in dilute sea water *Carcinus* appears to absorb chloride actively, probably by the gills, into its more concentrated blood. Thus, three mechanisms play a part in osmoregulation of *Carcinus* in a dilute medium: low permeability to water and salts, increased fluid output, particularly of urine, and active salt absorption from the medium.[150]

Hyperosmotic regulation has been examined in numerous other crustaceans which survive well in brackish water. *Pachygrapsus crassipes,* a Pacific Coast shore crab, is normally slightly hypoosmotic to sea water; however, the blood concentration nearly doubles just before a molt and is at a minimum in the paper-shell stage[17] (Fig. 9). *Pachygrapsus'* urine is slightly hypoosmotic to the hemolymph when the animal is in a diluted medium.[176] The blue crab *Callinectes* is often found far up rivers where the salinity limit may be as low as 0.045 to 0.18 °/oo.[152] The break point of the blood-medium curve is toward higher salinities for crabs collected in full sea water than for those collected in dilute sea water, but acclimation to sea water of the crabs from dilute water shifts their curves toward higher levels.[10] Reproduction appears to take place only in regions of higher salinities. *Carcinus* embryos develop over the range 28 to 40 °/oo; adults tolerate a much wider range.[187]

Adaptive behavior has not been much examined in crustaceans, but an African marine crab, *Jasus*, has receptors on the antennules which respond to dilute sea water.[127]

In none of the hyperosmotically regulating crabs has a complete balance sheet of inflow and outflow of water and salt been possible; hence knowledge of the mechanisms of hyperosmotic regulation in shore crabs and of what limits their penetration into truly fresh water remains incomplete. Undoubtedly, extrarenal routes of excretion remain to be discovered.

Regulation in Both Fresh and Sea Water: Eriocheir, Gammarus. In *Eriocheir sinensis*, the wool-handed crab of Northern Europe, hyperosmotic regulation is so good that the crab matures in fresh-water rivers; however, it returns in the autumn to the sea to breed. When this crab is transferred to different salinities there are no volume changes and uptake of tracer iodine is only a small per cent of that by marine crabs;[150] hence its permeability to water and ions is exceedingly low. The blood concentration in fresh water is only slightly less ($\Delta_i = -1.22°$) than in the North Sea ($\Delta_o = -1.66°$)[201] (Fig. 9). The urine output in fresh water is low (only 3 to 5 ml/day from a 60 gm crab), and urine may be slightly hyperosmotic to the blood irrespective of the medium. Chloride and ammonia losses are the same with excretory pores closed as with them open.[215] *Eriocheir* absorbs salt from very dilute solution against a concentration gradient. No difference in metabolism in salt or fresh water was detected.[216] Isolated gills filled with blood having a sodium concentration of 300 mM absorb sodium from a medium of sodium concentration of 8 mM; this

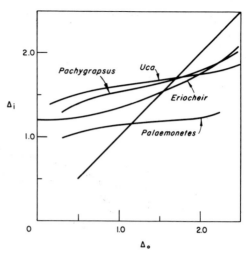

FIGURE 9. Blood osmoconcentration (Δ_i) of several hyperosmotically and hypoosmotically regulating crustaceans as a function of environmental osmoconcentration (Δ_o). Data for *Uca*,[83, 106] *Pachygrapsus*,[106, 176] *Eriocheir*,[215] Palaemonetes.[155]

active absorption of sodium is inhibited by inhibitors of respiratory enzymes and of cholinesterase.[122] In *Eriocheir*, then, the kidneys have no osmoregulating function but do function in ion regulation. The crab is able to live in fresh water because of its low salt and water permeability and the ability of its gills to absorb sodium chloride. Possible extrarenal routes of water excretion have not been investigated. The African fresh-water crab, *Potamon*, resembles *Eriocheir* in excreting small amounts of a blood-isosmotic urine and actively absorbing sodium and potassium.[219]

The genus *Gammarus* has marine, brackish, and fresh-water species. Some species are

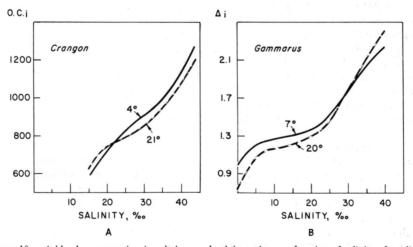

FIGURE 10. *A*, blood concentration in relative conductivity units as a function of salinity of medium for *Crangon crangon*, adapted to 4°C and to 21°C.[35] *B*, blood osmoconcentration Δ_i as a function of salinity of the medium for *Gammarus duebeni* adapted to 7° and to 20°C.[118]

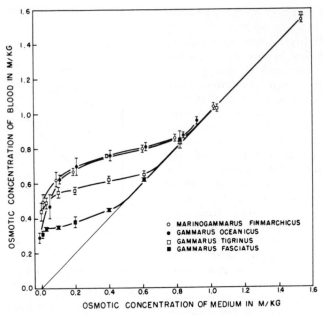

FIGURE 11.   Osmoconcentration of blood as a function of the osmoconcentration of sea water in four species of gammarids.[246]

restricted in salinity range while others are more tolerant. *Gammarus duebeni* is tolerant of a wide range of salinities and temperatures—the Black Sea, fresh ponds in England, and warm springs of Iceland. Temperature and salinity tolerance are reciprocally related in that optimal salinities (8 to 20 $^0/_{00}$) can be tolerated at temperature extremes; extreme salinities (high or low) are tolerated only at optimal temperatures (4 to 16°C), and hyperosmotic regulation is better at low than at high temperatures (Fig. 10B). When transferred from sea water to dilute media, marine species of *Gammarus* show hyperosmotic regulation at higher blood concentrations, but their regulation fails at higher environmental concentrations than in brackish or fresh-water species (Fig. 11). Evidently the mechanism activated in hyperosmotic regulation as the medium is diluted is active salt uptake.[246]

The isopod *Gnorimosphaeroma oregonensis* occurs in two races—one in fresh and brackish, the other in sea water; the first shows better hyperosmotic regulation, and no intergrades were found.[184]

The preceding examples are of groups of crustaceans in which penetration from sea to fresh water is not complete and in which the most important adaptation appears to be active absorption of salts.

Hypoosmotic Regulation: Land Crabs, Shrimps, Brine Shrimps. A few of the crustaceans which regulate hyperosmotically also regulate hypoosmotically, that is, they can maintain the blood concentration lower than the medium. Their blood-medium curves show varying degrees of flatness out to limiting concentrations at each end (Fig. 9). *Pachygrapsus crassipes* lives among rocks above low tide; the fiddler crab, *Uca,* spends long periods in air on sand and mud flats, and the land or coconut crab of the South Pacific, *Birgus,* can be drowned by immersion. Hypoosmotic regulation has also been found in the Australian rock crab, *Leptograpsus,* and the mangrove flat crab, *Heloecius.*[58] The ghost crab, *Ocypode,* maintains blood chloride relatively constant (378 mM) over a wide range, but its regulation fails at below 120 and above 600 mM Cl$^-$ in the medium.[66] A terrestrial hermit crab, *Coenobita perlatus,* in the presence of water spends 90 per cent of the time out of water, and five times more time in sea water than in fresh.[85] Hypoosmotic regulation is also found in *Eriocheir* and in several shrimps and prawns —*Palaemonetes, Crago*—which remain submerged and are never naturally exposed to high salinities. Also hypoosmotic regulation, of obvious adaptive value, occurs in *Artemia,* the brine shrimp, and probably in other phyllopods in saline lakes.

Hypoosmotic crabs like *Uca* can live longer in air, and during desiccation their blood concentration increases less than does that of isosmotic crabs like *Hemigrapsus.*[106] The urine of *Pachygrapsus* is isosmotic with the blood when in hyperosmotic sea water; hence the antennary glands are not hyperosmotic regulators in this animal.[176] However, in *Uca* the urine may be slightly blood-hyperosmotic both in 100 per cent S.W. and in 75 per cent S.W.[83] A desiccated *Pachygrapsus* put into concentrated (140 per cent) sea water shows net active uptake of water; also in air it may secrete water outward into the branchial chamber.[85] In both *Pachygrapsus* and *Uca* in 175 per cent S.W. the urine concentration of magnesium is much higher and that of sodium lower than when they are in 100 per cent sea water. Extrarenal excretion of sodium and water is indicated, mainly by the gills and partly by the stomach. Tissue storage of salts may permit short-term adjustments in blood concentrations. *Birgus* drinks fresh water and will place water in its gill chamber without becoming immersed in it.[85] The mangrove crab, *Goniopsis,* leaves water only to feed, and the kidneys filter enough fluid for Cl^- excretion and may reabsorb water; the land crab *Gecarcinus,* however, must excrete chloride extrarenally.[66] The gills of the ghost crab *Ocypode* contain secretory cells.[66]

Palaemonetes varians is normally isosmotic with 70 per cent sea water and hence hypoosmotic in normal sea water. Its urinary output increases in both dilute and concentrated sea water:[155, 159, 160]

Medium	Urine output (in % body wt/hr)
5% S.W.	1.63
50% S.W.	0.15
100% S.W.	0.42

However, the urine (in *Palaemon,* which resembles *Palaemonetes*) is isosmotic with the blood at all concentrations and in concentrated sea water the urine sodium concentration does not decrease as in the land crabs.

Palaemonetes varians lives in brackish and saline ponds (0.38 to 1.0 $^0/_{00}$ Cl), *P. longirostris* in greater dilutions (0.67 $^0/_{00}$ Cl), and *P. antennarius* in fresh water. Much salt is lost via the urine, and in fresh water active salt absorption is necessary.

	Δ_i	Δ_u	Δ_o	Urine flow (in % body wt/hr)
P. varians	1.05	1.01	.11	1.63 in 5-10% sea water
P. longirostris	.95	.9	.07	1.82 in 5-10% sea water
P. antennarius	.75	.67	.01	2.5 in fresh water

The meaning of hypoosmotic regulation in such crabs as *Eriocheir* is not apparent. In *Uca, Pachygrapsus,* and *Birgus* it has been suggested that such regulation is an adaptation to evaporation from the branchial chamber.[106] Yet the branchial fluid is less than 3 per cent of the body volume; hence the salts contained in it would not put much stress on the blood.[85] The crab in air may secrete fluid into the gill chamber; hence with a low initial blood concentration and lower evaporation the elevation of the blood would not be so great as in isosmotic crabs. The hypoosmotic regulation by prawns in sea water suggests that hypotonicity is normally of some unknown advantage. In *Crangon* the blood-medium curves (by conductivity measurement) cross so that at 15 $^0/_{00}$ a decrease in temperature causes a decrease in blood concentration while at 25 $^0/_{00}$ a decrease in temperature elicits an increase in blood concentration (Fig. 10*A*).[35] However, *Crangon* is more resistant to osmotic variation at relatively low temperatures (5 to 10°) than at 20°, but below 3°C the osmotic resistance decreases as the temperature approaches 0. In Holland these shrimps migrate in the spring toward dilute waters inshore and in the autumn toward the higher salinity of the North Sea. They are unable to live in brackish estuarine waters of low salinity in winter because their osmoregulation breaks down at temperatures below 3°C.

Artemia, the brine shrimp, thrives in Great Salt Lake at 22 per cent salinity, and in salterns where sodium chloride is precipitating. It lives also in sea water as dilute as 0.26 per cent NaCl and requires that the principal salt be NaCl.[50] *Artemia* is normally hypoosmotic but is not a perfect regulator (Fig. 12). The blood is hypoosmotic to media more concentrated than 25 per cent sea water. The permeability to water and salts is low as compared with some other microcrustaceans, and *Artemia* obtains water by swallowing and absorbing the water. The osmoconcentration of the gut fluid is greater than that of the hemolymph in all sea water concentrations, but the gut fluid concentration is less than that of a concentrated medium. The sodium and chloride in the gut fluid are less than in the hemolymph; hence sodium chloride and water are being absorbed from the gut, leaving other salts to be voided from the intestine. The epithelia of the first ten gills actively excrete NaCl into a hyperosmotic medium, and may absorb it from a dilute medium. Thus the gut is the principal organ

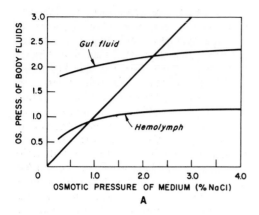

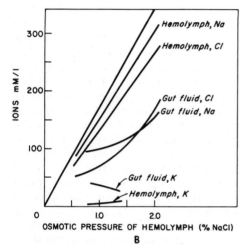

FIGURE 12. *A, Artemia*: osmotic concentration of gut fluid and hemolymph in different salinities, indicated in per cent NaCl.[50] *B, Artemia*: Na$^+$, Cl$^-$, and K$^+$ in hemolymph and gut fluid at different osmotic concentrations of hemolymph.[50]

ARTEMIA

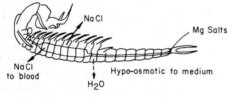

FIGURE 13. *Artemia*: main paths of ion and water movement. Solid arrows indicate active, and broken arrows passive, movement.

of water balance; the gills, of NaCl balance (Fig. 13).

Hyperosmotic Regulation: Fresh-Water Crustaceans. Fresh-water crustaceans have relatively high hemolymph osmoconcentrations. Blood of the Italian crab *Telphusa fluviatilis* has a Δ_i of $-1.17°$ and the Δ_i of

the crayfish *Cambarus* or *Astacus* in fresh water is usually about $-0.80°$. When crayfish are put into dilute sea water (50 per cent S.W.) the blood concentration rises and they continue to be hyperosmotic, but in higher concentrations than this the blood is isosmotic. Crayfish have been kept for a month in 66 per cent sea water and for 3 months in 50 per cent sea water, but they are not normally found in very brackish water. In isosmotic saline there is no weight change in crayfish, either with or without antennary glands plugged, but in more dilute media there is an increase in weight (5.5 per cent of body weight in 48 hours) when the excretory pores are plugged, and in hyperosmotic media a weight loss. Apparently crayfish are not impermeable. Permeability to iodide as a tracer salt is low but not so low as in *Eriocheir*.

The urine output of crayfish in fresh water averages about 0.175 per cent of body weight per hour, an excretion volume not much higher than in many marine crustaceans.[159]

Crustacean	Medium	*Urine output* (in % wt/hr)
Maja	S.W.	0.125
Cancer	S.W.	0.125 to 0.416
Eriocheir	F.W.	0.175
Carcinus	S.W.	0.416
Cambarus and Astacus	F.W.	0.158 to 0.217

However the crayfish urine is very dilute:[215]

	Δ *f.p.*			*Cl* (in mM/l)	
medium	*blood*	*urine*		*blood*	*urine*
0.018	0.81	0.09		195	10

When salt is added to the medium the urine concentration increases; in isosmotic solutions the urine output approaches zero.

In no condition has a crayfish been observed to excrete a salt-free urine. A 50 gm crayfish loses 600 mM of Cl$^-$ daily. Some salt is normally obtained from food, but crayfish can be kept for weeks without food. Krogh[128] washed out crayfish in distilled water for 3 days, and when they were then put into 0.02 Ringer solution they took up chloride initially at the rate of 2.3 mM/hr even though the external concentration was 2 mM and the internal 100 mM. This rate of uptake is slightly less than shown by *Eriocheir*. Crayfish actively absorb Br$^-$; they take up Cl$^-$ from KCl; Na$^+$ and Cl$^-$ from NaCl; and Na$^+$ from Na$_2$SO$_4$. The absorption of Na$^+$ is regulated according to both internal and external concentrations; the minimum equilibrium concentration is 0.04 mM NaCl.[219]

The difference in chloride content of urine and blood suggests either that salt is reabsorbed into the blood or that water is secreted by the kidney. The crayfish kidney consists first of a coelomic sac penetrated by blood vessels and sinuses and lined by a single epithelial layer (Fig. 14). Then follow the green tubular labyrinth, a spongelike structure, and a long (3 cm.) nephridial canal. The canal empties into the urinary bladder. The blood supply, opening from vessels into hemocoel spaces, is rich to all parts except the bladder.[165] The nephridial tubule in the fresh-water *Gammarus pulex* is longer than in the marine *Gammarus locusta*,[216] and in a lobster the nephridial canal is not well differentiated from the large labyrinth tubules.[165] Thus the entire crustacean kidney is, in principle, like one unit of the vertebrate kidney. Peters[165] removed fluid from each region of the crayfish kidney and obtained chloride concentrations as follows:

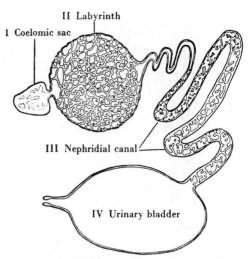

FIGURE 14. Diagram of crayfish kidney. (Modified from Krogh, A.: Osmotic Regulation in Aquatic Animals. Cambridge University Press, and Peters, H.: Ztschr. Morph. Oecol., vol. 30.)

	blood	coelomic sac	main labyrinth
Cl⁻ mM/l	196	198	209

	end of labyrinth	nephridial canal	bladder
Cl⁻ mM/l	212	90	10

It is postulated that the fluid from the coelomic sac and labyrinth may be a blood filtrate, essentially isosmotic with the blood, and that in the nephridial canal chloride and other solutes may be reabsorbed, leaving a dilute urine to enter the bladder. Further evidence for filtration and reabsorption comes from the fact that inulin, a substance widely used to ascertain glomerular filtration rates in vertebrates, is at a higher concentration in the dilute urine than in the blood of crayfish but is at the same concentration in the lobster, where the urine is isosmotic. In the lobster[39] and crayfish[185] glucose in the blood is high but essentially zero in the urine, but after phlorhizin (which in mammals poisons the glucose-absorbing mechanism) glucose in lobster and crayfish urine equals that in blood.

There is also evidence for secretion by the crayfish kidney. The epithelial cells of the coelomic and tubules contain large vacuoles which can be seen being extruded from the tubule cells. These vacuoles are lacking when crayfish are kept in saline but reappear in fresh water. The labyrinth cells can accumulate and secrete certain dyes.[138] This evidence argues for filtration-reabsorption as well as tubular secretion by vacuolation. Cells of the distal tubule (crayfish) show under electron microscopy extensive folding of the basal membrane and a smooth distal (lumen) surface; hence active transport must occur on the

blood side (Fig. 15). Labyrinth cells have a brush border of microvilli and also large protruding vacuoles.[22]

Potts[174] has calculated the osmotic work done to maintain hypertonicity of various degrees. For any animal entering brackish water from sea water the reduction in blood concentration below sea water is far more important than the production of a blood-hypoosmotic urine; however, in fresh water, reduction of urine concentration to approach that of the medium would effect a further reduction in osmotic work. Potts' calculation for a crayfish follows:

Concentration (osmols/l)			Urine volume (ml/hr/60 gm)
blood	urine	medium	
0.42	0.124	0.0065	0.095

If the blood and urine were at sea-water concentration and the medium were fresh water, osmotic work to the extent of 1.31 cal/hr/60 gm would be expended; whereas reducing the blood to 0.42 osmol/l and putting out a blood-isosmotic urine would reduce the work to 0.098 cal/hr/60 gm. If the urine were also reduced to equivalent of the medium the value would be 0.023 cal/hr.

By its low permeability to water and salts and by two energy-requiring processes—salt reabsorption or water secretion in the kidney, and active salt absorption by the gills—the crayfish is able to maintain a high internal concentration while living in fresh water (Fig. 16).

In summary, the aquatic crustaceans range

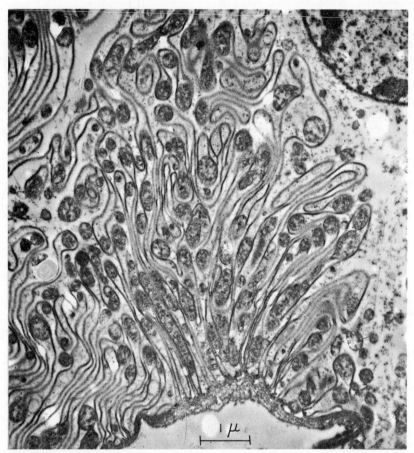

FIGURE 15. Crayfish kidney. Electron micrograph of basal section of cell of distal tubule (nephridial canal); membranous lamellae extending from basement membrane (below) to nuclear region (upper right).[22]

from osmoconforming marine crabs with volume and ion (but not osmotic) regulation, through shore crabs with limited hyperosmotic regulation, to fresh-water forms with good hyperosmotic control. In addition, some crustaceans can live in either fresh or marine environments, and some, like the land crabs and shrimps, show good hypoosmotic regula-

CRAYFISH

Salts
to blood   H₂O

NaCl

Dilute
Urine
                        Hyperosmotic
                        to medium

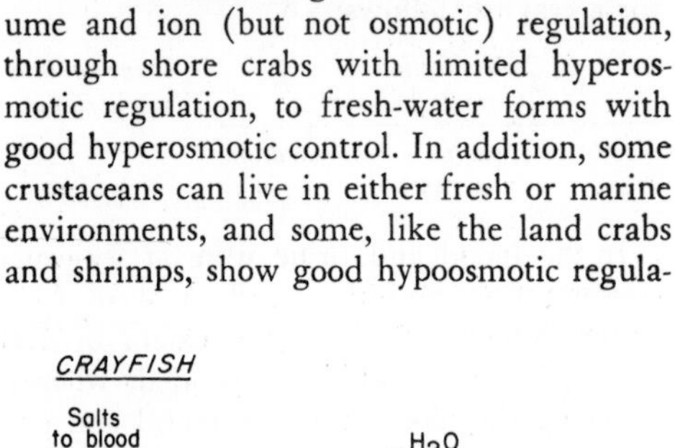

FIGURE 16. Crayfish. Diagrammatic representation of the main paths of ion and water movement in osmoregulation. Broken arrow indicates passive, and solid arrows active, movement.

tion; the brine shrimp carries hypoosmotic regulation to the extreme. Numerous mechanisms permit varied osmotic patterns, particularly variations in surface permeability to water and salts, active extrarenal (gill) absorption of salts from fresh water, and excretion of salts into hyperosmotic media, specific absorption from stomach, and salt storage in tissues. The kidneys are more important in ionic than in osmotic regulation, and in some fresh-water crabs they put out an isosmotic urine while in crayfish the urine is very dilute. It is probable that the first requisite in migration from the sea to fresh water was capacity for active absorption of salts, and that dilution of body fluids and excretion of blood-hypoosmotic urine came later.

ADAPTATION TO SEA WATER, FRESH WATER, AND TO THE ENDOPARASITIC ENVIRONMENT: PROTOZOA

Protozoa are a diverse group of animals which are so small that direct measurement of the osmotic concentration of their cytoplasm or excretory fluid is difficult. Indirect evidence indicates, however, that marine and parasitic Protozoa have no osmotic problem, in that they are isosmotic with their medium and the only water they eliminate is that coming from food. All fresh-water Protozoa, however, must be hyperosmotic to their medium; the evidence is good that in them the contractile vacuole eliminates excess water load.

Some protozoan species can readily with-stand transfer to extreme concentrations of the medium, from distilled water to concentrated sea water; others are extremely limited in their osmotic tolerance. *Amoeba lacerata* can live in either fresh or sea water. *Paramecium woodruffi* and *Paramecium calkinsi* can be adapted to sea water, but *Paramecium caudatum* only with great difficulty.[75] Of the flagellates, *Astasia* is more tolerant of high salinity than *Euglena*. Three species of *Euplotes* which occur in fresh water and in 2.5 and 4.0 per cent salinity are of diminishing size in that order. From one of these, *E. vassus*, clones were isolated which differed in ability to withstand transfer to high salinity lakes.[79]

Osmolar Concentration and Volume Regulation. The water balance of various Protozoa has been estimated from volume changes and vacuolar output in media of different concentrations, particularly of non-electrolytes, to which the cells are virtually impermeable. The volume of *Amoeba proteus* and of *Pelomyxa carolinensis* has been measured by putting them into capillaries; *Amoeba mira* and *A. lacerata* become spherical; the peritrichous ciliates *Rhabdostyla brevipes*, *Zoothamnium marinum*, and *Cothurnia curvula* and the suctorian *Discophrya piriformis* (*Podophrya*) are sufficiently symmetrical that volume can be calculated. In general, the marine and brackish-water forms, *Amoeba mira*, *A. lacerata*, and *Cothurnia*, showed good volume regulation within a few hours of transfer while the fresh-water *Amoeba proteus*, *Pelomyxa*, and *Rhabdostyla* and the marine *Zoothamnium* failed to return to their original volume for at least some hours after transfer.

Values of osmotic concentration of the cytoplasm even of the same species vary greatly according to different investigators. The large rhizopod *Pelomyxa carolinensis* gave by vapor pressure measurements a concentration equivalent to 54.5 mM NaCl (103 mosM),[136] and by volume measurements 94 mosM (recalculated in reference[136]). By measurement

of minimal contractile vacuole output the cytoplasmic concentration was estimated for *Discophrya* to be 40 to 50 mosM[120] and by vapor pressure measurement on *Spirostomum* to equal 26 mM NaCl (89 mosM).[168] Thus it can be concluded that fresh-water Protozoa are dilute as compared with most other animals but that they are hyperosmotic to their medium.

Entrance of Water. Permeability to water as measured by osmotic swelling is usually given in volume of water entering per unit of cell surface in a given time for an osmotic gradient, which may be expressed as mol/ml, or osmotic pressure in atmospheres or in cm of H_2O. A pressure difference of 1 atmosphere at $27°C$ corresponds to a concentration gradient of $1/24,000$ mol/cm^3.[52] An osmotic permeability value in μ^3/μ^2 atm sec may be converted to cm^3/cm^2 sec, cm H_2O by dividing by 10.34 (since 1 atm = 1034 cm H_2O). Permeability constants obtained with D_2O or H_2O^{18} are given in the units of diffusion constants which reduce to cm/sec. When converted to the same units (by multiplying osmotic constants by 0.13) the values obtained osmotically are larger than those by diffusion methods.[52] Some values of water diffusion constants are given on p. 27; osmotic values in ml/cm^2, cm H_2O, sec (from references 220 and 248 and other sources) follow:*

Amoeba proteus[145]	0.42×10^{-10}
Pelomyxa[24]	0.29×10^{-10}
Pelomyxa[136] (= Chaos)	0.275×10^{-10}
Fresh-water peritrichous ciliates[120]	0.27×10^{-9}
Marine peritrichous ciliates[120]	0.11×10^{-9}
Arbacia egg	0.40×10^{-9}
Human erythrocytes	0.92×10^{-8}
Frog ovarian eggs	0.89×10^{-8}
Frog body cavity eggs	0.01×10^{-8}
Lamprey eggs (fresh)[87]	0.77×10^{-10}
Lamprey eggs (7 hr development)[87]	0.048×10^{-10}
Capillaries of cat muscle	2.5×10^{-8}
Capillaries of frog mesentery	$56. \times 10^{-8}$
Capillaries of frog glomerulus	$220. \times 10^{-8}$
Gastric mucosa	0.08×10^{-8}
Necturus kidney tubule	0.15×10^{-7}
Aquatic dipteran (Sialis) larvae[218]	0.134×10^{-9}

Rhizopods have a lower water permeability than ciliates, but all values for Protozoa are low compared with those for aquatic eggs and for blood cells. Permeability of the pellicle in fresh-water Protozoa is evidently low but not negligible.

On the basis of the observed permeability to heavy water and the computed surface area

---

* There is recent evidence that, at least in ciliates, D_2O penetrates less rapidly than does H_2O.[121a]

it is calculated that in *Pelomyxa* some thirteen times the cell volume passes in and out by exchange per hour, but that of this only the equivalent of 2 per cent of the cell volume is osmotic, or the amount which must be eliminated by the contractile vacuole per hour.[136] This is in fair agreement with previously observed values of 3.8 per cent of the volume evacuated per hour.[24]

In addition to entrance of water across the body surface, quantities of water enter with food, and in ciliates the cytopharynx membrane appears to be more permeable than the rest of the body surface. In fresh-water peritrichs the water taken up by food vacuoles may be 8 to 20 per cent of the output of the contractile vacuole and in *Paramecium* 30 per cent. In a suctorian, *Tokophrya infusorium,* the vacuolar output increased sixfold during feeding.[195] A suctorian may eat a prey equal to its own volume; it discards approximately half, puts out a fifth as increased contractile vacuolar volume, and the remainder increases the body size by about a third.[120] In the marine *Amoeba mira* there is virtually no vacuolar output in the nonfeeding state, but large vacuoles appear when the animal begins to feed.[98] Also, some water is obtained by oxidation of food.

In *Paramecium* the contractile vacuole activity increases not only during feeding but also when water is merely pumped toward the mouth. In addition, the vacuoles are less active when the animals are swimming and the peristome is partly closed. A group of parasitic ciliates, the Ophryoscolecidae from the stomach of cattle, are able to close the oral passage; when this is done the pulsation of their contractile vacuole is greatly slowed.

Function of the Contractile Vacuoles. Evidence that the contractile vacuole functions in osmotic regulation comes from the distribution of vacuoles among Protozoa in different habitats as follows:[120]

may well eliminate certain ions differentially.

Further evidence for osmotic function of the contractile vacuole comes from its output of fluid under different conditions. Both volume and pulsation frequency must be measured to get the total water excretion, and measurements must be made in such a way that experimental procedure does not influence the rate. Fresh-water Protozoa eliminate more fluid by their contractile vacuoles than do the marine or endoparasitic in natural media.[120] The time required to eliminate a quantity of water equal in volume to the body of the animal for fifteen fresh-water species (except one) ranged between 4.1 and 53 minutes, whereas for four marine species it was 2¾ to 4¾ hours, and for one endoparasitic ciliate (measured in fresh water) it was 4 hours.

In experimental media the vacuolar output is influenced by tonicity. *Amoeba mira* can live in distilled water or in concentrated sea water, and the average size of the amoebae is not significantly different in the two media. When actively feeding, the rate of output by vacuoles, which are derived from food vacuoles, increases with increased dilution of the medium. *Vahlkampfia calkinsi,* a parasitic amoeba, cultured in sea water on agar had no contractile vacuole; when transferred to a similar agar culture with tap water, one or more vacuoles developed and pulsated regularly. A marine ciliate, *Amphileptus gutta,* showed a 21 per cent increase in vacuolar rate in 70 per cent S.W. and formed additional vacuoles in 60 per cent sea water.[110] In several marine peritrichs transferred to dilute sea water the vacuolar rate initially increased much, then settled down at a higher level than it was in 100 per cent S.W.; the increase in output was prevented by adding a nonpenetrating nonelectrolyte of proper concentration.

Numerous fresh-water Protozoa show re-

Class	Fresh water	Marine	Endoparasitic
Sarcodina			
(Rhizopoda)	present	present in few	absent
Flagellata	present	present in many	absent from most
Ciliata	present	present in most	present in many
Sporozoa			absent

In marine and parasitic Protozoa the contractile vacuole eliminates water of a nonosmotic source, i.e., water from food and metabolic water; in addition, some water may be required in the elimination of specific salts. Nothing is known of ionic regulation in marine Protozoa, and the contractile vacuoles

duced vacuolar activity when put into dilute sea water. When *Amoeba verrucosa* was cultured in increasing concentrations of sea water the vacuolar pulsations slowed and no vacuole was seen when the animals were in 50 per cent S.W.; when fresh water was added, the vacuole reappeared. Fresh-water peritrichous ciliates put into dilute sea water showed considerable slowing of pulsations of the vacuoles, and pulsations stopped in sea water more concentrated than 12 per cent. When *Paramecium* is first put into a hyperosmotic solution the body becomes flattened as water is withdrawn, but later it recovers normal shape. In *Paramecium caudatum* the vacuolar output varied as follows:[92]

Medium (% NaCl solution)	Vacuolar output (in equivalents of body vol per hr)
0	4.8
0.5	1.38
0.75	1.08
1.0	0.16

Cultures of *Paramecium woodruffi* and *Paramecium calkinsi* were established in several dilutions of sea water. After 5 months the average intervals between pulsations of the contractile vacuoles in *Paramecium woodruffi* were as follows:[75]

% S.W.	Seconds
0	13
25	22
50	32
75	47
100	65

Paramecium calkinsi showed an average interval of 23 seconds at all concentrations.

There may be specific salt effects in addition to tonicity. For example, in *Paramecium caudatum*[62] in glucose solution of $\Delta = -0.075°$ the contractile vacuoles pulsated at 2.4 to 4.1/min, whereas in Ringer solution of the same osmotic concentration the rate was 3.8 to 4.7/min and in $CaCl_2$ it was 4.2 to 7.2/min. Evidently the contractile vacuoles of Protozoa have an osmoregulating function, but other factors besides tonicity of the external medium may affect the amount of fluid excreted.

Mechanisms of Filling and Emptying Contractile Vacuoles. Usually a contractile vacuole is formed when numerous small vacuoles or vesicles fuse; these may arise in a given region or in various parts of the cell. In some, particularly ciliates, there are canals of various shapes which fill and empty into the contractile vacuole. During the period of filling, or diastole, the viscosity of the cytoplasm in the vicinity of the contracile vacuole is low, while at the time of emptying, or systole, viscosity is high. The contractile vacuole membrane resembles the plasma membrane in holding back solutes such as some dyes. Contractile vacuoles have been kept intact after removal from the cell.

There are four theories of the filling of contractile vacuoles: (1) hydrostatic pressure, (2) secretion of water, (3) secretion of solute with subsequent diffusion of water, (4) enclosure of cytoplasmic fluid by a membrane, followed by reabsorption of solutes. These could be resolved if a method were available for removing the contents of a vacuole and measuring its osmotic concentration.

The hydrostatic pressure theory proposes that fluid filters across the vacuole membrane in proportion to the difference between the hydrostatic pressure and the colloid osmotic pressure of the cytoplasm. In *Spirostomum* a hydrostatic pressure of 4 cm H_2O and a colloid osmotic pressure of 2 cm H_2O were measured.[168] That protozoan cells have some turgidity is indicated by the variety of their shapes. However, as Kitching points out, the hydrostatic pressure would be no less if water were squeezed into a vacuole contained inside the cell; hence this hypothesis can hardly apply.

Secretory work is done in contractile vacuole production. Evidence for this comes from the use of respiratory inhibitors.[120] When the marine peritrich, *Cothurnia,* was transferred to 12.5 per cent sea water the volume increased and vacuolar output rose; when cyanide was added the vacuolar output declined nearly to zero and the cell volume increased (Fig. 17). Fresh-water species reacted to cyanide and other respiratory inhibitors by similar near cessation of vacuolar pulsation and increase of volume.

Secretion is further evidenced by the association of granules with vacuole formation. Mitochondria or mitochondria-like granules occur around contractile vacuoles in *Amoeba proteus,* and there is a rough correlation between vacuole activity and number of granules. Osmium-staining bodies occur near the vacuoles of many ciliates,[78] and electron micrographs show Golgi canals opening into a vacuole,[194] or small vesicles fusing.[156] There is little doubt that oxidative secretion is involved in filling the contractile vacuole, but whether secretion of solute or water or reabsorption of solute occurs remains to be demonstrated.

Kitching favors the hypothesis that water or very dilute solution is secreted. Nonfeeding Protozoa often continue to put out quantities of water for days in a dilute medium. When the bailing out of water is stopped, the cells swell.

An alternative hypothesis is that solute is secreted first, that the membrane is more

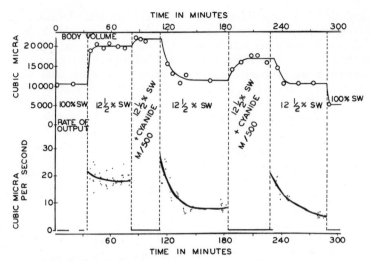

FIGURE 17. Body volume in cubic micra, and excretory output of contractile vacuole in the marine peritrich *Cothurnia*; successively in: normal sea water, 12.5 per cent sea water, 12.5 per cent sea water plus cyanide, 12.5 per cent sea water, and normal sea water.[120]

permeable to water and that water then enters as the vacuole swells. By crushing an *Amoeba lacerata* under a coverslip, free vacuoles have been obtained; these swell or shrink according to the concentration of the medium.[98] Calculations based on the assumption of secretion of a substance similar to an amino acid in size and density show that the amount of such substance needed to satisfy the vacuolar needs would be 1.1×10^{-9} cm³/hr or 0.05 per cent of the body volume/hr. Actually *Pelomyxa* has been shown to decrease in size during starvation by 0.333 per cent of its volume per hour.[24] The marked increase in vacuolar output on feeding may result from osmotic filling due to added waste solute. It is possible, therefore, that sufficient solute could be secreted to permit osmotic filling of the contractile vacuole. Contrary evidence is the fact that vacuoles fill at a constant or accelerating rate.

Electron micrographs show a layer of small vesicles around a growing vacuole, mitochondria outside the vesicles in *Amoeba*,[156] and many vesicles near the limiting membrane of the vacuole in a ciliate.[194] It is possible that these vesicles surround cytoplasmic fluid, that solutes are reabsorbed, and thus a dilute "urine" formed by a negative pinocytosis.

The filling, the frequency of pulsation, and the emptying of protozoan vacuoles may be interrelated but brought about by quite different processes. A sudden decrease in temperature causes a temporary fall in vacuolar rate and an increase in diameter, while a rise in temperature causes a temporary increase in rate but decrease in vacuole volume

so that the cell swells initially. Temperature may affect secretion of fluid, ultimate vacuole diameter, and frequency of discharge differently. When animals are moved from one concentration of nonelectrolyte (sucrose) to another there is a time lag before the new vacuolar rate is reached; this lag increases if the medium is highly dilute or concentrated. Small changes in cell volume may be important in controlling vacuolar output and the gel-sol relations, and emptying may require contraction of the gel.

When the suctorian *Discophrya* is subjected to hydrostatic pressure of about 2500 lb/in² there is expansion of the pellicle as indicated by visible creasing, increase in vacuole frequency, and decrease in vacuole volume. At high pressures which are known to cause solation (100,000 lb/in²) the vacuole output diminishes and the cell rounds up.[97, 120] The structural organization of contractile proteins, the cell size, gel-sol ratio, and osmotic concentration each may have some part in regulating vacuolar frequency, size, and systole.

The species differences in water and salt permeability, the striking differences in adaptability among three species of *Paramecium*, the irregularity of pulsations of vacuoles of marine forms in dilute media, the complex effects of temperature and pressure, and the differences in reactions in different solutes indicate that control of contractile vacuoles is not simply osmotic although an important function of contractile vacuoles is osmotic regulation. The process of filling may not be the same in all Protozoa in all media. Many questions will be answered when direct measurements, both on the vacuole contents at different stages of filling and on the cytoplasm, are possible.

PARASITIC HELMINTHS

Intestinal parasites may be subjected to considerable variations in medium from time to time, and limited evidence indicates varying degrees of osmotic regulation. A cestode, *Cysticercus tenuicollis*, from the abdominal cavity of sheep is approximately isosmotic with its milieu but can maintain some hypertonicity and hypotonicity under experimental conditions; it shows small volume changes in dilute media. A fish tapeworm, *Schistocephalus*, also has an osmotic concentration similar to that of the host, $\Delta = -0.44°$. Trematodes have not been much investigated osmotically; *Fasciola hepatica* is said to be hyperosmotic to the bile of its host.

More information exists regarding ascarids. *Ascaris lumbricoides* is normally hypoosmotic to intestinal fluid:[96]

	Δ	Cl^- (mM/l)
Ascaris lumbricoides	$-0.655°C$	52
Pig intestinal fluid	$-0.869°C$	66

The variation of intestinal fluid in both osmotic and chloride concentration is much greater than the variation of the *Ascaris* body fluid; hence there must be osmotic and ionic regulation by the worm. Specimens of *Ascaris* gain weight in a dilute medium, less if their gut is closed by ligation; hence the body wall is somewhat permeable to water. Chloride must be actively excreted. Ascaris' osmotic concentration varies with that of the medium over a range up to the concentration of the normal intestinal fluid, but it is always above the medium. The role of excretory organs in osmotic and ionic regulation is unknown for *Ascaris*. The excretory ampullae of third stage larvae of *Nippostrongylus* and *Ancylostoma* are observed to pulsate much more frequently in dilute than in concentrated media.[245] More accurate data are needed regarding the salt and water exchange of various parasitic worms with and without excretory organs. It is probable that many degrees of regulation will be discovered among them.

REGULATION IN FRESH-WATER SPONGES, COELENTERATES, FLAT-WORMS, AND MOLLUSCS

How fresh-water sponges and coelenterates keep from swelling to the bursting point is not well known. Fresh-water sponges appear to eliminate water by contractile vacuoles in amoebocytes and choanocytes; marine sponges lack contractile vacuoles.[77] The osmotic concentration of cells of the fresh-water sponge *Spongilla* in summer is low (25 to 30 mM NaCl) but at the time of gemmulation the concentration rises (110 mM NaCl).[259]

Cells of isolated tentacles of *Hydra viridis* and *Pelmatohydra oligactis* showed a steady decrease in volume when in sucrose more concentrated than 0.04 M. Permeability to water of endodermal cells of a hydra is about 0.6 and of ectoderm 0.27 $\mu^3/\mu^2/atm/min$.[134] In diluted sea water of salinity 2.5 $^0/_{00}$ hydra body cells were shrunken; in distilled water they were swollen. The body cells must be rather dilute (about 17 mM) but definitely hyperosmotic to the medium. Endoderm cells of *Hydra* contain vacuoles which resemble those seen in cells lining the gut of many turbellarians. The vacuoles in *Hydra* are not seen to contract, and in distilled water the body cells separate and the animal disintegrates. The mechanism of hyperosmotic regulation in fresh-water coelenterates is unknown. Some brackish-water hydrozoans, *Cordylophora*, can grow in dilute sea water and even in fresh water; the surface-volume ratio of tentacles and hydranth body diminishes in dilute medium, and endodermal cells change from broad and flat to narrow and long with the change from sea to fresh water.[119] Presumably cell surface is involved in osmotic regulation.

Osmoregulation in free-living fresh-water flatworms has not been much investigated. *Planaria* and *Dendrocoelum* gain weight in distilled water and lose it in physiological saline. A turbellarian (*Gyratrix hermaphroditus*) has a well-developed protonephridial system when it occurs in fresh water but this is degenerate in brackish and salt-water specimens.[129] It seems probable that the excretory system gets rid of osmotic water.

Fresh-water bivalve molluscs such as *Anodonta* have a very low blood concentration ($\Delta_i = -0.08°C$, or approximately 0.042 osmolar). In solutions of sea water more concentrated than $\Delta_o = -0.1$, *Anodonta* loses weight.[67] Anesthetized specimens and specimens chilled to 4 to 5°C gain weight in fresh water. Hence *Anodonta* is permeable to water and excretes a dilute urine which may amount to 50 per cent of body volume per day.[143] Fluid from the pericardial cavity passes through the nephrostome into the kidney. The blood is under a hydrostatic pressure of about 6 cm H_2O and the colloid osmotic pressure of the blood is some 3.8 mm H_2O.[169] Hence there might be filtration through the wall of the heart into the pericardial cavity. From inulin clearance a filtration of 1 to 1.3 ml/hr/100 gm body wt is obtained, and from body weight loss a slightly larger value. The urine concentration is 0.0236 osmols/l, about half that of blood.[174] Fluid drawn from the kidney is lower in chloride and calcium but higher in protein and nonprotein nitrogen than the blood. Hence the kidney absorbs some salt, but still much is lost in the urine. To compensate, *Anodonta* and *Unio* can actively absorb chloride and sodium from approximately millimolar solutions, but they cannot reduce the concentration below about 0.1 mM.[128] The hypothesis of filtration and reabsorption may be questioned on the anatomical basis that the kidneys receive a rich supply of blood returning from visceral sinuses and the hydrostatic pressure in the postrenal sinus may be high in comparison to that in the pericardium. Potts[174] calculated that if *Anodonta* in fresh water had a blood concentration equal to that of sea water it would do osmotic work to the extent of 62 cal/hr/100 gm. At its low blood concentration, however, thirtyfold lower than sea water, the osmotic work is reduced by 2500 times; by reducing the urine nearly to the concentration of the medium a further reduction of nearly two more times in osmotic work results and this osmoregulation is only 1.2 per cent of total metabolism. Hence the fresh-water bivalve, one of the most dilute of all multicellular animals, is remarkably efficient osmotically.[128, 151]

REGULATION BY EXCLUSION OF WATER

Eggs of Marine Fish and of Fresh-Water Animals. The eggs of marine invertebrates swell and shrink to correspond with changes in the medium. The eggs of marine teleosts, on the other hand, are hypoosmotic to sea water, whereas all fresh-water eggs are hyperosmotic to their medium. Some means must be provided to maintain the osmotic gradients prior to the development of excretory organs.

The egg of the marine killifish *Fundulus* has an internal concentration corresponding to $\Delta = -0.76°$, less than half that of the surrounding sea water, and when placed in different dilutions of sea water there is little change in freezing point. The chloride content of embryos of several marine teleosts is one-fifth to one-half that of sea water.[128] In the *Fundulus* egg striking changes occur at fertilization. An internal hydrostatic pressure of as much as 150 mm Hg can be recorded, the electrical resistance of the egg membrane rises from 3450 ohms/cm² in the unactivated egg to 13,290 ohms/cm² on activation.[112-114] The outer inelastic chorion prevents swelling. Between the chorion and the egg is the perivitelline space occupied by clear colloid which swells by imbibition and causes the egg proper to shrink and to be under hydrostatic pressure. If the egg is put into hypertonic sucrose or salt solutions there is a transient fall in pressure and slight swelling of the true egg until the perivitelline material comes into equilibrium with the medium. Apparently the chorion is permeable to water and solutes, but the vitelline membrane is virtually impermeable. Kao suggests that the colloid osmotic pressure of the perivitelline material compresses the egg so that membrane pores are vanishingly small.[112-114]

Eggs of fresh-water fish likewise have a very low permeability. In the trout *Salmo* the embryo has a Δ_i of -0.43 to $-0.49°$, whereas the Δ of the perivitelline material is $-0.02°C$.[232] During the first hour after oviposition the eggs become impermeable to water and salts; the barrier is the vitelline membrane, and impermeability remains as long as this is intact and calcium is present in the medium.[232] By heavy water exchange and osmotic gradients no permeability of the trout egg to water could be demonstrated.[175] The ovarian eggs of the zebra fish *Brachydanio* had an osmotic permeability sixty times greater than the shed eggs. The water permeability of eggs of brook lampreys (*Lampetra planeri*) decreased eighteenfold as development began.[87] Ovarian eggs of the lamprey are in osmotic equilibrium with peritoneal fluid (110 mM NaCl); during development the egg concentration is reduced to equivalent to 30 to 40 mM NaCl; at hatching it equals 80 mM, and in a few days rises to the adult level.

In frog eggs the osmotic concentration falls from about equivalent to 120 mM NaCl at the time of laying to 80 mM at the time the blastopore closes, because of initial swelling followed by reduced permeability.[128] Similarly, eggs of *Daphnia* and of *Limnaea* initially swell, then become relatively impermeable to water.[128]

Diffusion permeability constants (cm/sec) as measured by diffusion of D_2O or H_2O^{18} for various eggs and other cells follow (modified from references 52, 136, 154, and 175) (see p. 21 for osmotic constants):

frog ovarian eggs	0.128×10^{-3}
frog body cavity egg	0.075×10^{-3}
zebra fish ovarian egg	0.068×10^{-3}
zebra fish,	
shed, nondeveloping egg	0.036×10^{-3}
human erythrocytes	$5.3 \ \ \times 10^{-3}$
Pelomyxa	$0.25 \ \times 10^{-4}$
Amoeba	$0.21 \ \times 10^{-4}$
frog gastric mucosa	$0.48 \ \times 10^{-4}$

It is concluded that, whereas marine invertebrate eggs become more permeable on fertilization, eggs of marine and fresh-water fish and probably of most fresh-water animals become virtually impermeable to water and salts. This protection against osmotic stress, at least in vertebrate eggs, appears due to reduced pore size in the vitelline membrane.

TRANSITIONS BETWEEN FRESH-WATER AND MARINE LIFE: FISHES

The origin of vertebrate animals is obscure. All prochordates are marine, and the phylum Chordata doubtless arose from marine ancestors. *Amphioxus* has protonephridial excretory organs. Some Agnatha are entirely marine (the hagfishes), while others are predominantly fresh-water (lampreys). There is disagreement as to whether the earliest and now extinct fish (Ostracoderms and Placoderms) lived in fresh water,[190] brackish estuaries, or in the sea.[188] Fresh-water origin of fish is suggested by the dilute blood of all modern bony fish and the low salt content of blood of cartilaginous fish, and also by the glomerular kidney, which is well adapted for excreting a hypoosmotic urine. Irrespective of their origin, Osteichthyes and Chondrichthyes evidently migrated from fresh water to the sea in the Cretaceous. Many modern fish (teleosts) have reinvaded fresh water, whereas a few others (holosteans) have lived continuously in fresh water. Numerous migrations have occurred and certain marine fish are not now independent of fresh water; some, like salmon (anadromous), return to fresh water to spawn. Conversely, others, like the eels (catadromous), breed in the ocean and reach maturity as adults in fresh water.

Osteichthyes (Teleosts). In river mouths some fish such as *Fundulus* occur in either fresh or brackish regions, both as young and as adults; others such as the menhaden and gray squeteague go into fresh water when young; still others such as winter flounders are rarely found in fresh water.[144] Fresh-water fish such as carp can be transferred slowly to dilute sea water, and they regulate their blood concentration up to an isosmotic medium[57] but do not survive long at the higher concentrations.

In fresh-water fish the blood has a concentration of 130 to 170 milliosmolar and the urine is copious but dilute. The following data are for the gar pike:[221]

Medium Δ_o	Blood Δ_i	Urine Δ_u	Urine volume (ml/kg/day)
-0.03	-0.57	-0.08	200 to 400

Fresh-water fish drink little, but accumulations of suspended material in the gut indicate they do some drinking. The skin is relatively impermeable to water, but some enters by gills and oral membranes (see Fig. 19).

The inward stream of water through the gill and oral membranes provides a water load and the kidneys of fresh-water fish have nephrons with well-developed glomeruli which normally filter a considerable volume. As the filtrate passes down the tubules most of the salts are absorbed, leaving a dilute urine. However, the urine is not so dilute as the external medium, hence salt loss must be compensated. Part of the salt comes from food. A second part of the needed salt is absorbed from the medium by secretory cells on the gills, as shown by use of a chamber which separates the water bathing the anterior part from that bathing the posterior part of the fish. Salt is lost to distilled water by gills as well as by kidneys. Chloride can be absorbed from very dilute solutions; a roach, *Leuciscus,* took up chloride from 0.042 mM solution and a goldfish, *Carassius,* could reduce the Cl^- concentration from 1 mM to 0.02 mM. Ordinary chlorinated tap water contains about 0.3 mM of Cl^- per liter and pond water somewhat less. The ruffle, *Acerina,* and the perch, *Perca,* lost salt in all solutions tested, hence these species must depend upon food to replace lost salt.[128]

In the ocean the problem is to conserve water and exclude salt, and the water-excreting glomerular kidney is a liability. The blood of marine teleosts is not much more concentrated than that of fresh-water fish ($\Delta_i = -0.7°$), hence a mechanism for maintaining a high degree of hypotonicity is necessary. The urine is scanty, 2.5 to 4 ml/kg/24 hours in sculpin and toadfish. The urine is always hypoosmotic to the blood, and there is no relation between urine flow and Cl^- content. Smith[224] found, by the use of dyes

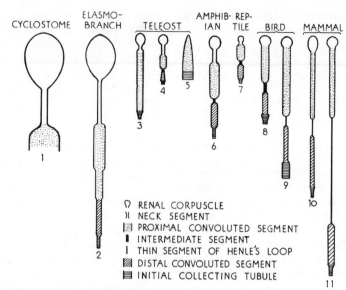

FIGURE 18. Schematic representation of the kidney unit (nephron) of various vertebrates[141] (elasmo-branch[115]): *1*, cyclostome *Bdellostoma stouti*, *2*, elasmobranch, *3*, teleost *Myoxocephalus octodecimspinosus*, *4*, teleost *Ameiurus nebulosus*, *5*, teleost *Opsanus tau*, *6*, amphibian *Rana catesbiana*, *7*, reptile *Chrysemys marginata*, *8*, bird *Gallus domesticus*, *9*, bird *Gallus domesticus*, *10*, mammal *Lepus cuniculus* (rabbit).

and a divided chamber, that marine fish, unlike fresh-water ones, swallow large quantities of water. Dilute gastric secretion rich in potassium is added in the stomach. As the sea water passes down the intestine, water is absorbed and also some salts, more Na^+ and Cl^- than Mg^{++} and $SO_4^=$. The osmotic concentration decreases down the gut, hence relatively more salt is absorbed than water, as shown for *Lophius*:[221]

	Δ	Na^+	K^+	Ca^{++}	Mg^{++}	Cl^-	$SO_4^=$ (mM/l)
sea water	−1.33°		4.6	8.0	35	350	26
anterior intestine	−1.04	143	77.	15.2	60	90	94
posterior intestine	−0.83	128	37.	18.8	92	72	122
urine	−0.64 (−0.55)		7.6	14.8	75	161	36
blood	−0.66						

Some of the sea salts, particularly Mg^{++} and $SO_4^=$, are lost in feces; the urine salts are also largely Mg^{++}, Ca^{++}, $SO_4^=$, and phosphate, while most of the Na^+, K^+, and Cl^- must be excreted extrarenally. Normally such fish as the sculpin, goosefish, and haddock show zero or low Cl^- in their urine, but, with handling, the fish become diuretic, and Cl^-, Mg^{++}, $SO_4^=$, and phosphate in the urine are increased. Nitrogenous wastes are largely given off through the gills. An eel or sculpin *(Myoxocephalus)* may swallow 40 to 200 ml S.W./kg/day, and if marine fish are prevented from drinking they cannot long survive. Some Arctic fish living near the sur-

face where ice is forming have blood which freezes at −1.5°C in winter and at the higher temperature of −0.8°C in summer. The blood solute which increases in winter is organic and is unidentified.[214]

In view of the reduced urine output it is not surprising to find less well-developed kidneys in marine teleosts than in fresh-water fish[141] (Fig. 18). In the toadfish, *Opsanus tau*, and the goosefish, *Lophius*, for example, glomeruli are absent in adults although there may be pseudoglomeruli in the young fish. In the toadfish the urine flow is only 2.5 ml/kg/day as compared with 300 ml/kg/day in a fresh-water catfish. The typical marine teleostean kidney also lacks the distal convoluted segment in the tubules. Even in those marine fish with glomeruli, the filtration rate is low.

Excretion by an aglomerular kidney is essentially tubular secretion. This kidney can excrete $MgHPO_4$, sulfate, chloride, uric acid, and creatinine and can concentrate numerous dyes such as phenol red. It is unable to excrete glucose, even at high blood levels and after phlorhizin. Inulin is not excreted by an aglomerular kidney. In *Lophius* with a plasma $\Delta_i = -0.67$ and $\Delta_u = -0.57$ the urine is essentially free of chloride, but there may be a hundredfold concentration of Mg^{++}, Ca^{++}, and $SO_4^=$ above blood concentrations.[70, 72] Perfusion of the *Lophius* kidney shows an increase in urine output up to a constant pressure of about 150 mm H_2O; hence the secretory system is sensitive to blood pressure; however, excretion occurs at 30 to 40 mm H_2O or half the colloid osmotic pressure (85 mm H_2O); therefore water must be actively secreted or at least carried along with secreted salts.[37]

That the gills are the route of extrarenal NaCl excretion was clearly shown by perfusion of a heart-gill preparation of an eel.[128] Chloride is secreted outward into sea water containing nearly three times as much Cl^- as the blood. When the concentration of the perfusion fluid was increased the Cl^- transported outward increased; at low internal concentration the secretion stopped. In the epithelium of the gills of *Fundulus* (and *Anguilla*) are osmophilic, mitochondria-rich secretory cells which appear to eliminate Cl^- when the fish is in sea water and to take in chloride in fresh water. In sea water these cells have a large distal vesicle which gives a positive histochemical test for Cl^-; in fresh water the osmophilia and alkaline phosphatase increase.[48, 80] The pseudobranchs may have this function,[48] or not.[161]

Many fish can live in either fresh or salt water. The curves relating internal to external concentration are relatively flat. The blood of salmon in the sea freezes at $-0.762°$, while the blood of salmon at their fresh-water spawning grounds freezes at $-0.668°$. Thus the king salmon blood is diluted by only 12 per cent on going to its breeding territory. The fry of chum salmon are more resistant to high salinity than are coho salmon, and the chum return to the sea as fry while the coho remain in fresh water a year or more.[30] Chum fry show lower cruising speed in sea water than in fresh water.[99] Arctic char, *Salvelinus alpinus,* in summer in the ocean have $\Delta_i = -0.81°$; in the winter in fresh water, $\Delta_i = -0.61°$. The blood chloride of *Salvelinus* in equilibrium with fresh water is 149.7 mM; with sea water 191.4 mM.[99] The brown trout, *Salmo trutta,* of England or of America, when fully acclimated to either fresh or sea water, has essentially the same blood concentration ($\Delta = -0.65°$).[81]

The killifish, *Fundulus heteroclitus,* lives well in either fresh or sea water. Acclimation in body density is accomplished in 6 hours on going into sea water and in 24 hours on going into fresh water; the body density decline in fresh water is due largely to increase in gas volume in the swim bladder; also, blood chloride concentration may drop by 30 per cent.[31] Some workers found hypophysectomized *Fundulus* to live normally in fresh water; others[38] state that it fails to survive long in fresh water and the blood chloride falls rapidly. Injections of neurohypophyseal hormone into catfish and carp have no effect on water balance, and hypophysectomized eels tolerate changes from sea water to fresh.[68] Yet in other marine and fresh-water fish cytological examination shows depletion of neurosecretory cells of the hypothalamus in hyperosmotic medium, and replenishment of secretory granules in dilute medium. Hence the possible role of the neurohypophysis in water balance of fish remains uncertain. The thyroid appears to be activated in migrations from sea to fresh water and may be important in osmoregulation.[14] The starry flounder, *Platichthys stellatus,* is euryhaline; in sea water it consumes more oxygen and shows more thyroid activity than in fresh water.[95]

Both American and European eels breed in the Sargasso Sea of the mid-Atlantic, then the young fish migrate to fresh water where they mature. The blood of *Anguilla vulgaris* is hypotonic in sea water and hypertonic in fresh water. Recorded freezing points of the blood are for eels in sea water, -0.69 to $-0.73°$, and for eels in fresh water $-0.61°$ to $-0.62°$.[34, 57]

A starving *Anguilla* in either fresh or sea water lost about 0.3 per cent of its weight per day. When the esophagus was blocked an eel died in sea water after a 12 per cent loss of weight in 3 days, whereas in fresh water it lived well but lost 0.7 per cent of its weight per day. Thus the eel does not drink fresh water but does drink sea water.[128] The kidney of *Anguilla* has glomeruli, also a distal segment, and in fresh water its kidneys function like the kidneys of typical fresh-water fish. In addition, it has a very low skin and gill permeability to chloride and water. In the sea the gills actively excrete Cl^-; in fresh water the gills are not very effective chloride absorbers.

The European stickleback, *Gasterosteus aculeatus,* occurs in two interbreeding subspecies, *gymnurus* which is predominantly a fresh-water fish, and *trachurus* which lives in the brackish water of river mouths.[93] Both forms show good osmotic and chloride regulation. *Trachurus* has a higher number of lateral scale plates and fewer vertebrae than *gymnurus*, but complete intergradation and cross-fertility are found between the two extremes. From mixed egg populations in different salinities more of the *gymnurus* type survived in low concentrations, but more *trachurus* in high salinities. The salinity relations are affected by temperature in that the *gymnurus* type at 15° and 19° has a decreased number of fin rays when reared at increasing salinities, while the *trachurus* has an increased number of fin rays at increasing salinities. Here then is a genetic linkage of labile morphological characters with temperature and salinity dependence; natural selection favors the two extremes.[93] The physiological bases for the differences have not been examined.

Agnatha (Cyclostomes).   The myxinoids (hagfishes) are exclusively marine; they are essentially isosmotic with their medium, and inorganic salts comprise 99 per cent of osmotically active solutes; *Myxine* shows much ionic regulation.[186] A Pacific hagfish, *Polistotrema*, is isosmotic over a range of medium from 85 to 116 per cent sea water, but when handled it becomes hyperosmotic.[146]

Petromyzonts (lampreys), on the other hand, are either anadromous or exclusively

planeri in fresh water is lower than in *fluviatilis*:[87]

	Osmolar concentration of serum (equiv. mM NaCl)	Urine output (ml/gm/day)
Lampetra planeri	113	1.3
Lampetra fluviatilis	143	0.3

When put into sea water at osmoconcentrations equal to or greater than the blood the ammocoetes and adults of *planeri* and the adults of *fluviatilis* are unable to regulate hypoosmotically although the ammocoetes of *fluviatilis* do well in sea water. If the *fluviatilis* adults which have returned to fresh water to spawn are transferred to sea water like that where they developed, they die; therefore the mechanism of maintaining hypotonicity has been lost.[87, 147] The cyclostomes present striking differences in osmoregulation between species and at different stages in their life cycle, and they deserve more detailed investigation.

Chondrichthyes (Elasmobranchs).   Elasmobranch fishes, sharks, and rays are today largely marine although paleontological evidence indicates that they were once more abundant in fresh water. They are unique among fishes in that their blood osmoconcentration is higher than that of their environment, even the sea. This is shown in the following representative data compiled by Smith:

Species	Δ_o	Δ_{Serum}	Δ_{Urine}	Blood Cl (mM/l)	Urea (mM/l)
Raja stabuliforis	−1.85	−1.93	−1.68	273	2010
Squalus acanthias	−1.33	−1.62		234	1490
Pristis microdon	0.0	−1.02	−0.10	170	780
Torpedo marmorata					1450-1840
Scyllium canicula					2080-2640
Raja laevis				255	320

fresh water, and blood osmoconcentrations of *Petromyzon* $\Delta_i = -0.48°$ in fresh water and $\Delta_i = -0.59°$ in sea water have been reported.[69] In fresh water *Petromyzon* actively absorbs chloride salts, but if the temperature is low (1 to 3°) the absorbing mechanism is slowed to the point that salts are lost; its urine output at 18° is 45 per cent body weight per day; both loss and uptake of salt are rapid.[252] In Britain the anadromous *Lampetra fluviatilis* has been compared with the freshwater *Lampetra planeri*. When excretory papillae were ligated, *planeri* gained several times more water than *fluviatilis*; in fact, *planeri* is more permeable to water than are teleosts. The blood osmoconcentration in

The salt concentration of the plasma of both marine and fresh-water elasmobranchs is of the same order as that in fresh-water teleosts, but the osmotic fraction due to NaCl is only 41 to 47 per cent of the total.[57] Most of the osmotic concentration is made up by retention of huge quantities of urea in all body tissues and fluids. Thus the elasmobranch can maintain the same osmotic gradient in sea water as in fresh water and continue to excrete a blood hypoosmotic urine. Reabsorption of urea by the dogfish kidney varies according to plasma urea concentration and is independent of glucose and water reabsorption; the exact site in the renal tubules is not known.[115] Isolated tubules can secrete phenol red and some other substances (e.g., para-aminohippuric acid).[73] The skin and gills are relatively impermeable to urea and the young are provided with urea, either by viviparity or by placement in an impermeable egg case containing urea which lasts until they can develop their own mechanism for conserving it. Smith[222] compared elasmobranchs living in fresh and brackish water in southeastern Asia and found that for a doubling of osmotic concentration in a series from fresh to salt water species the urea increased by nearly 100 per cent and the serum Cl^- by only 60 per cent. The ability of individual rays and dogfish to adapt to changed tonicity of the medium is not great. The urine output is low in marine elasmobranchs, and the urine is concentrated but hypoosmotic to the blood. Magnesium, phosphate and sulfate are excreted by the kidneys. The NaCl gained from sea water and food is secreted by *Squalus* (dogfish) by the rectal gland in fluid isosmotic with the blood but twice as concentrated in NaCl, and containing virtually no Ca^{++}, Mg^{++}, or urea.[40]

In all fish (except myxinoids) the kidneys put out a blood hypoosmotic urine as do fresh water animals. However, by reduced urine flow, by loss of glomeruli in a few marine forms, by extrarenal active salt excretion, and in elasmobranchs by maintaining hyperosmotic blood rich in urea, life in the sea has been possible. Copious urine made by a filtration-reabsorption mechanism, usually coupled with active absorption of salts from the medium, permits a steep osmotic gradient in fresh water (Fig. 19). Only the myxinoid cyclostomes among vertebrates are isosmotic with the sea by virtue of high salt concentration.

THE TRANSITION TO LAND

Amphibia. Some Amphibia are permanently aquatic; others spend at least a part of their life on land. Eggs are normally laid in water or in a very moist environment. Moisture-conserving adaptations used by various Amphibia which do not lay their soft-coated eggs in pond water are the deposition of eggs in leaf mold, in foam, in holes in the ground, between leaves which form a cup to collect moisture; a few have direct development without metamorphosis. The rate of water uptake by tadpoles just after hatching is several times greater than by adults. Some desert Amphibia develop rapidly and the adults burrow underground. A few frogs are known to breed in brackish water,[162] but none are truly marine.

The water content is similar in terrestrial and aquatic anurans, but the tolerable water loss on desiccation decreases in the order: fossorial $>$ terrestrial $>$ semiaquatic $>$ aquatic:[234, 235]

Species	Habitat	% weight loss tolerated (for 20-gm animals)
Scaphiopus hammondi	fossorial	50
Rana pipiens	semiaquatic	46
Rana clamitans	aquatic	39

The tolerated percentage loss of water is less in large than in small individuals. In *Rana pipiens* after dehydration to different amounts and return to water the rate of gain or rehydration increases rapidly for small amounts of dehydration and approaches a limit of about 12 per cent of body weight per hour; after excessive hydration (by injecting water) the rate of loss of water or return

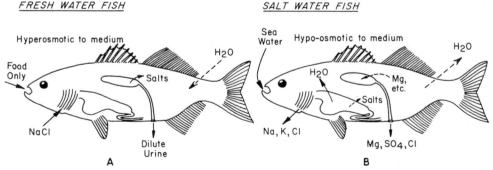

FIGURE 19. Schematic representation of main paths of ion and water movement in osmoregulation of fresh-water bony fish, *A*, and marine bony fish, *B*. Solid arrows—active transport. Broken arrows—passive transport.

to normal water load is slower than the rate of rehydration and is a linear function of excess water load.[2]

The blood of a frog is hyperosmotic to pond water; the urine is hypoosmotic to the blood and more copious in a dilute than in a concentrated medium:[33]

Δ_o	Δ_i	Δ_u
—0.07	—0.44 to —0.56	—0.17

When a frog is placed in dilute sea water the blood remains hyperosmotic and the urine concentration increases proportionately more than the blood but is still blood-hypoosmotic.

The osmotic behavior of frogs has been extensively studied and reviewed.[2, 128] If the cloaca of a frog is tied shut and the frog is left in pond or tap water, the body weight increases; when the cloaca is later untied, urine is voided and the weight falls to the original value. When the concentration of the medium is increased, either by salt or sugar, the rate of gain of weight is decreased, and in hyperosmotic solutions weight is lost. Adolph calculated that at 20°, water equivalent to 31 per cent of the body weight can enter and be excreted every 24 hours.[3] This is only a small fraction of what would enter a true osmometer of similar concentration and surface. A skinless frog gains weight faster than a normal one. If the brain is destroyed or lesions made in the midbrain or anterior medulla, but are not made in the spinal cord, the rate of water intake increases by as much as four to five times. Slime secretion may be one factor decreasing skin permeability to water. The skin gives limited protection against loss of water by evaporation in air. At 100 per cent humidity at 20°, one-fifth of the heat produced in the metabolism of the frog is lost as latent heat of evaporation; since the frog is continually at a higher temperature than saturated air it could never take up water from the air, but it can from moist surfaces.[3] However, water loss by way of the skin is reduced in high humidity, and below 94 per cent humidity more heat is lost by evaporation than is produced by metabolism. In fresh water or in hypoosmotic solutions frogs, like fresh-water fish, do not drink water, but they do absorb it through the skin; in hyperosmotic solutions (140 mM NaCl) they have been observed to drink, and they produce a concentrated but blood-hypoosmotic urine.[108, 109]

A frog, like a fish, excretes blood-hypo-osmotic but never a salt-free urine. The salt is partly made good by food and the ability for selective salt absorption by the skin is well developed. When frogs which have been kept in distilled water for several days and have lost some body salts are put back into tap water or dilute Ringer solution, an active uptake of salt occurs. In tap water or 0.01 Ringer solution, chloride was taken up at the rate of 0.05 mM/hr/cm^2 body surface.[128] Chloride is absorbed with Na$^+$ from NaCl solutions but without the cation from KCl, NH$_4$Cl, and CaCl$_2$; Br$^-$ but not I$^-$ is absorbed. The mechanisms for absorption of Na$^+$ and Cl$^-$ are separate, and in isolated skin the Cl$^-$ transporting system disappears while the Na$^+$ transporting system remains and seems to be responsible for the skin potential.[237]

In addition to salt replacement by food and selective absorption, amphibians have a well-developed ability to retain salts by their kidneys. The kidneys of *Rana* and *Necturus* have been favorable objects of study because of the small number of relatively large nephrons. The glomeruli lie in a layer close to the mesial border of the kidney. Beyond each glomerulus is a ciliated neck, then the thick-walled proximal tubule, then a narrow intermediate tubule, and finally the distal tubule which empties into a collecting tube (Fig. 18). Blood supplies to glomeruli and tubules are separate.

The amount of glomerular filtration is ascertained from the "clearance" of some substance which is neither reabsorbed, stored, nor secreted by the tubules. Clearance of a nonreabsorbed substance is given by:

$$C = \frac{U\,V}{P}$$

where C = ml of protein-free plasma filtered per unit of time, U = urine concentration of the substance being measured, V = the volume of urine formed in the given time, and P = concentration of the substances in plasma water. For all substances which are filtered in the glomeruli but are neither reabsorbed nor secreted by the renal tubules, the clearance equals the filtration rate; for substances which are to some extent reabsorbed (Na$^+$ or Cl$^-$) the clearance is less than the filtration, whereas substances secreted by tubules (e.g., p-aminohippuric acid, PAH) have clearance greater than unity. Several substances (e.g., K$^+$) are both reabsorbed and secreted, and the clearance alone cannot show how they are handled by the renal tubules. In frogs, creatinine and inulin have been used to measure filtration rate, and values of about 30 ml/kg/hr obtained under normal conditions. Creatinine clearances range from 10 ml/kg/hr at low urine flows (5 ml/kg/hr) to 22 ml/kg/hr at high urine flows (17 ml/kg/hr).[71]

Richards and his associates collected fluid from various regions of a nephron by micropipette and analyzed each fluid. In both frog and *Necturus* the glomerular fluid has essentially the same sugar and chloride concentrations as the blood plasma; it is free of the normal blood proteins.[223, 243] These findings support the view that the glomerular fluid is an ultrafiltrate from the plasma, i.e., contains the blood solutes except for protein. The filtration pressure is the difference between the blood pressure (29 mm Hg) and the colloid (protein) osmotic pressure (7.7 mm Hg) of the blood. The chloride content decreases along the distal tubule, hence chloride reabsorption must occur in that segment. Glucose diminishes in concentration early in the proximal tubule; after injection of the drug phlorhizin the glucose is not reabsorbed and actually increases in concentration because of water reabsorption so that the reducing power of fluid at the distal end of the proximal tubule is above that in the plasma. Water and salt may be reabsorbed all along the tubule, both in the distal and in the proximal portion. Acidification of the urine occurs in the distal tubules. From the proximal tubule, salt and water are reabsorbed with no osmotic change; the distal tubule removes salt but has low water permeability, hence the urine is hypotonic. Antidiuretic hormone (ADH) from the posterior pituitary increases water permeability of the distal tubule, and hence it increases urine concentration and decreases its volume.[196, 200] Water may be reabsorbed not only by the tubules but also from the bladder, particularly in dehydrated toads.[64] The water reabsorption in *Necturus* is sufficient to account for the doubling of the concentration of urea. In the bullfrog, however, water reabsorption is insufficient, that is, the urea clearance is seven to ten times higher than the filtration rate; therefore some urea must be secreted by tubule cells.[206] Urea can also be secreted by the tubules when the renal arteries are ligated and only the renal portal circulation remains. The tubules of pronephros, mesonephros, and metanephros of the developing frog can concentrate phenol red.[105] *Necturus* urine is normally hypoosmotic to the blood, but in dehydration sufficient water can be reabsorbed to produce blood-isosmotic urine; water moves with an osmotic gradient and when NaCl is absorbed water goes with it.[248]

Water balance in amphibians is largely under control of a polypeptide hormone from the neurohypophysis. This hormone is similar to mammalian ADH or antidiuretic hormone in favoring water retention. It increases skin permeability to water, enhancing water absorption by dehydrated frogs; in this respect it is most effective on toads, less on frogs and scarcely at all on aquatic amphibians.[63] Toad tadpoles are unaffected by pituitary injections, but adult toads respond with increased water uptake at 1/2000 to 1/200 the dose effective for frogs.[193] In isolated frog skins bathed by Ringer solution on the inside and water on the outside the inflow of water was increased by pituitary hormone from 0.0045 to 0.0267 ml/cm²/hr.[198] The hormone also increases the potential existing across isolated skin[76] and increases active absorption of Na^+.[108, 109] Pituitary extract also increases the osmotic movement of water across the bladder, and comparison of various synthetic neurohypophyseal hormones indicates that arginine vasotocin may be the active agent in amphibians[196, 197] (see p. 546).

Hypophysectomized toads *(Bufo bufo)* show unimpaired ability to absorb water according to degree of hydration.[108, 109] The pituitary hormones, although found in other classes of vertebrates (including cyclostomes), appear to increase the skin permeability to water only in amphibians. Injections caused increase in water uptake according to the following order of species:[230] *Necturus maculosus* < *Rana clamitans* < *Rana pipiens* < *Bufo americanus*. Independence of a water medium is in the same order.

Urine flow is reduced by the neurohypophyseal hormone by two means: by a reduction in filtration, due to constriction of glomerular arterioles, and mainly by increasing the tubular reabsorption of water. The dose needed to reduce urine flow is one-tenth that needed to enhance skin permeability. Also, the neurohypophyseal hormone increases absorption of water from the bladder. Adrenocortical hormones increase the uptake of Na^+ and Cl^-, whereas the pituitary hormone favors water retention.[198, 199] It is postulated that salt is actively reabsorbed by the kidney tubule and with it some water; under action of the neurohypophyseal hormone the permeability to water is enhanced so that water leaves the tubule osmotically and isosmotic urine may result.

In a study of taste responses of the frog

tongue, a water taste was discovered.[260] Fresh water on the tongue initiates a massive discharge of nerve impulses from certain taste receptors. It is suggested that this water taste may serve reflexly to keep the mouth closed and prevent drinking. It may also function in detection of the salinity of a medium. Whether the frog has brain osmoreceptors is not known.

The mechanisms of osmoregulation in Amphibia can be summarized as follows: Water enters osmotically but at a retarded rate, owing to low permeability of the normal skin. The water which does enter is excreted as a copious dilute urine. Salt is lost in the urine, and to a less amount by the skin. This salt loss is made good by food and by active absorption from pond or tap water. Also salt loss is minimized by active reabsorption in

under natural conditions an earthworm is always in a semidesiccated state. The normal water content of *Lumbricus terrestris* is about 85 per cent body weight. In dry air an earthworm can survive a loss of 50 to 80 per cent of the body water.[191] *Allolobophora* is more tolerant of desiccation than *Pheretima* or *Eisnia fetida.*[82] Water passes out of a worm after excess hydration more quickly than it is taken in after dehydration. Earthworms orient toward a moist and away from a dry surface. In air the body surface is kept moist by excreted water and upon irritation coelomic fluid is extruded through the dorsal pores.

The osmotic concentration of body fluids varies according to the state of hydration. Representative values of freezing-point depression and chloride are as follows:

	Coelomic fluid		Blood		Urine	
	Δ	Cl⁻	Δ	Cl⁻	Δ	Cl⁻
		mg %		mg %		mg %
Lumbricus terrestris[177]						
(From tapwater)	−0.31	270	−0.29	217	−0.06	20
Pheretima posthuma[15]	−0.28 to −0.31		−0.4 to −0.5	50	−0.05 to −0.65	3.7

the kidney tubules, and to a less amount in the bladder, of chloride which filters through the glomeruli. There also may be passive water reabsorption, which largely accounts for increased urine concentration of some waste products that are not reabsorbed; under some conditions tubular secretion of specific substances such as urea may occur. The neurohypophysis limits urine volume as a first response to drying and increases the skin inward permeability to water. Of these mechanisms at least four require expenditure of energy: maintenance of low skin permeability, active salt absorption by the skin, tubular reabsorption against a concentration gradient, and tubular secretion of specific substances.

Invertebrates Restricted to Moist Air.
Earthworms. There are many fresh-water annelids—the Hirudinea and Oligochaeta; earthworms are adapted to life in moist soil where osmotic stress is intermediate between that of fresh water and air. Soil-dwelling earthworms can survive well in aerated fresh water or in moist air; some species, however, avoid immersion. Adaptive mechanisms of water balance in earthworms have been examined in detail.[2, 177] When an earthworm is transferred from soil to tap water it absorbs water equivalent to as much as 15 per cent of its initial weight in about 5 hours. Water-adapted worms removed from aerated fresh water to moist soil or air lose water. Hence

When placed in different dilutions of Ringer solution *Lumbricus* showed increased total osmoconcentration (coelomic fluid) so that it remained hyperosmotic even when the medium increased threefold in concentration over tapwater; thus the worm is a good hyperosmotic regulator. In the same experiment the chloride concentration in coelomic fluid was maintained relatively constant and significantly below that of the more concentrated medium. At all concentrations of the medium the urine was blood-hypoosmotic.[177]

There are various types of nephridia in earthworms, some large and occurring as one pair per segment, others small and very numerous in each segment. The best known nephridia are open to the coelom by a ciliated funnel, the nephrostome, but there are many which are closed internally (Fig. 20). Some worms, e.g., *Pheretima posthuma*, from dry soils in India have some nephridia which empty into the intestine whereas others (e.g., *Lumbricus, Eutyphoeus*) have all of the nephridia emptying externally.[15]

Coelomic fluid enters the nephrostomes under the force of ciliary beat. Dyes and breakdown products from hemoglobin may accumulate in tubular epithelium. There is good evidence for reabsorption of some materials as the fluid passes down the nephridial tubule. There may also be secretion; certainly in those worms lacking nephrostomes urine must be formed by secretion. Nephridial excretion of urine by earthworms in tapwater is 2 to 2.5 per cent of the body weight per hour.[15] The urine chloride concentration was 7.7 per cent of the coelomic fluid chloride concentration in *Lumbricus,* and 4.6 per cent in *Pheretima.* In *Pheretima* the blood glucose was 100 mg per 100 ml, but no glucose was found in coelomic fluid or urine. Samples of fluid removed from various parts of a nephridium show that reduction in concentration occurs largely in the distal wide tube, partly in the middle tube, and not at all in the proximal narrow tube.[177] The functional analogy of the nephridium to the vertebrate nephron is clear. When nephridia are isolated in hypoosmotic media, vesicles appear in marginal cells; hence there may be some excretion by vacuoles;[191] in addition, ciliary activity of the nephrostome is enhanced in dilute medium.

The salts which are lost in the hypoosmotic urine of worms in water are replaced from food and by active absorption.[238] Leeches which have lost some of their body salts by living in distilled water for 2 weeks absorb from 0.01 Ringer solution as much as 0.48 mM salt per gm body weight during the first half hour of immersion.[128]

Snails. Terrestrial snails can live in somewhat drier places than earthworms. Their water balance has not been much investigated. In *Helix* the blood concentration varies with activity and humidity; the blood concentration of an active snail is given as equivalent to 0.5 per cent NaCl ($\Delta_i = -0.30$).[111] In the giant African snail *Achatina fulica,* the freezing point of the blood is $-0.46°$

and of urine $-0.28°$, and urine is formed at the rate of 5 per cent of body weight per hour.[142, 143] Inulin appears in the urine at the same concentration as in the blood, but glucose is apparently reabsorbed and phenol red is concentrated. If back pressure on the kidney is increased urine flow stops, suggesting filtration reabsorption through blood vessels in the kidney and by kidney tubules.[143] Osmotic concentration is apprehended in the pedal ganglion of a slug as indicated by action potentials with nearly the same sensitivity as in mammalian brain osmoreceptors.[116]

High-Humidity Arthropods. A number of arthropods are intermediate between oligochaetes and insects in their water relations. These include the onychophorans, isopods, myriapods, and spiders. They can be characterized by greater evaporative water loss than occurs from most insects as illustrated in the following:

Percentage body weight lost per half hour by evaporation in dry air[148, 250]

	% at 24°C		% at 30°C
earthworm	37.0	Rhodnius nymph	0.04
Peripatus	14.5	Nematus larva	0.16
centipede	15.5		
sowbug	8.5		

The onychophoran *Peripatopsis* lacks mechanism for restraint of water loss from its tracheae and actually loses water twice as fast as an earthworm, forty times as fast as a smooth-skinned caterpillar, and eighty times as fast as a cockroach.[140] *Peripatopsis* selects a high humidity region in a gradient; it has hygroreceptors both on antennae and on the

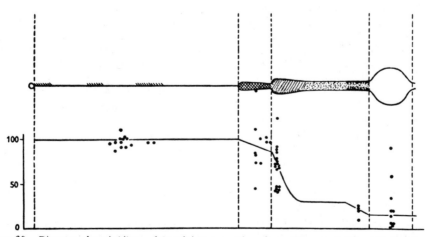

FIGURE 20. Diagram of nephridium of *Lumbricus terrestris* and osmotic concentration of urine (equated to Ringer as 100) from different regions of nephridium. (From Ramsey, J. A.: J. Exp. Biol., vol. 26.)

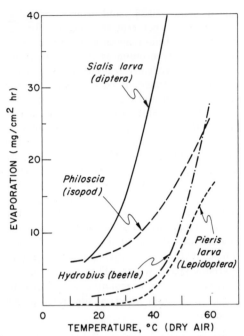

FIGURE 21. Evaporation in mg H_2O/cm² surface/hour in dry air, at increasing temperatures. Insects: beetle *Hydrobius*;[97] mayfly *Sialis*; butterfly *Pieris*;[58] isopods *Philoscia* (or of *Porcellio*);[58] spiders *Lycosa* and *Tegenaria*.[52]

	Δ_i	*Habitat*
Ligia	−2.15°C	marine littoral
Oniscus	−1.04	
Armadillidium	−1.18	terrestrial
Porcellio	−0.30	
Asellus	−0.50	fresh-water

rest of the body.[42] *Peripatus* loses water half as fast as an earthworm, twice as fast as a centipede, and twenty times as fast as a millipede. Restriction to a damp environment may account for the lack of successful radiation of the Onychophora.[148]

Isopods occur in sea water, fresh water, and on land. Terrestrial isopods lose water more readily and are more restricted to a moist environment than are myriapods.[59, 60] The respiratory pleopods of isopods present extensive moist surfaces. A sowbug, *Porcellio scaber*, loses by evaporation a greater percentage of its water than either earthworm or insect[41] (Fig. 21); the sowbug goes to a region of high humidity in a gradient. *Ligia oceanica* is a marine isopod which lives between rocks at high tide level and above. Kept in sea water it may be hyperosmotic ($\Delta_i = -2.15$, $\Delta_o = -1.98$). In dilute sea water it shows good hyperosmotic regulation and maintains relatively constant osmoconcentration over the range from 50 to 100 per cent sea water.[157] When kept on filter paper soaked in distilled water the Δ_i fell to −1.44 and if desiccated the Δ_i was found to be −3.48. This is in marked contrast to isopods and myriapods living in a fresh-water or moist air environment:

The isopods differ from insects in that evaporative water loss increases linearly with rising temperature and decreasing humidity, that is, with increasing saturation deficit, instead of showing a "critical" temperature. This is partly due to the lack of a waxy cuticle in isopods (Fig. 21). Also the respiratory surfaces lose much more than do spiracles, five to fifteen times more per unit of surface than the rest of the body surface. Unlike insects, most isopods absorb no water from moist air but take up water by either mouth or anus.[61, 229] Many terrestrial isopods roll into balls, clump together, and tend to aggregate in moist regions. Of four genera of isopods the most nocturnal and photonegative loses most water by transpiration: *Philosia* > *Oniscus* > *Porcellio* > *Armadillidium*.[45] Isopods form a series of increasing success in air from the Ligiidae to the Armadillidiidae.

Spiders are much better adapted for life in dry air than are isopods and diplopods; for example, at 30°C three species of spider evaporated an average of only 0.6 mg H_2O/cm²/hr as compared with over 4 mg H_2O/cm²/hr from *Porcellio* (isopod) (Fig. 21).[51] Spiders respire mainly by book-lungs but may also have simple tracheae; if the book-lungs are kept open the evaporative loss is doubled. When the temperature is raised there is little increase in evaporative loss up to about 40°, above which evaporation increases sharply; abrasion by an inert dust increases evaporative loss. These effects indicate a waxy protective layer over the cuticle and in this respect spiders resemble insects and ticks and differ from isopods and diplopods which lack the waxy epicuticle. Spiders can drink water held in soil by capillarity.[158]

INSECTS AND ARACHNIDS

Insects are essentially terrestrial animals, but some members of several orders have invaded fresh water, at least for larval life. There are some dipteran larvae occurring in salt lakes, and a few in brackish and sea water.

Aquatic Insects. A brackish-water species of Corixidae or water boatman (*Sigura lugubris*) has been compared with two fresh-water species (*Sigura distincta* and *Sigura forrarum*). The curves relating internal and external concentrations resemble similar curves for fresh-water Crustacea. *Sigura lugubris* has relatively constant osmoconcentration between 0.1 and 1.5 per cent salinity; it regulates less well above and below this range. The fresh-water species regulate well at greater dilutions, but blood concentration rises more at increasing external concentrations than does that of *lugubris*.

The hemolymph of various aquatic insects is similar in osmotic concentration to that of fresh-water crayfish. Insects differ from other animals in the small fraction of their osmotic pressure due to chlorides and the large fraction due to organic substances, particularly amino acids. In mammalian plasma Cl^- constitutes two-thirds of the anions, in a silkworm only 12 to 18 per cent, and in larvae of the botfly only 7 per cent.[131] The chlorides in the body fluids of larvae of *Culex* and *Aedes* account for only 35 to 40 per cent of the total osmoconcentration,[251] in *Drosophila* 20 per cent.[262] Larvae of Odonata have blood concentration equivalent to 0.88 to −1.01 per cent NaCl, of which chlorides account for half; in different media the chloride varied, but other solutes and total osmoconcentration were relatively constant.[213] In a neuropteran larva, *Sialis lutaria,* blood chloride declined when the larvae were kept in distilled or tap water, and nonprotein nitrogen (NPN) fractions (largely amino acids) tended to compensate; in dilute salt solutions the blood chloride increased and NPN fell, with the result that blood osmoconcentration remained relatively constant.[20]

Osmoregulation in dipteran larvae, particularly mosquitoes and midges, has been extensively studied.[19, 128, 178, 251] The anal papillae function in osmotic regulation. Isolated papillae swell in tap water and constrict in Ringer solution. If an *Aedes argenteus* larva is ligated ahead of the opening of the malpighian tubes into the gut and then put into hyperosmotic glucose, the hind part shrinks, whereas without the ligature the whole larva shrinks. If the ligation is behind the opening of the malpighian tubes and the larva is placed in fresh water the posterior part becomes swollen while the anterior part does not. By several such ligation experiments Wigglesworth found that larvae normally swallow little water, that the anal papillae are the region most permeable to water, and that water is excreted by the malpighian tubes. When *Aedes argenteus* larvae are transferred to various salinities a constant internal osmoconcentration is maintained in external concentrations lower than or equivalent to

0.65 per cent NaCl; in media of higher concentration the body fluid conforms to the environment. By gradual acclimation the larvae can be made to live in sea water dilutions equivalent to 1.4 per cent NaCl. The anal papillae of *Culex pipiens* larvae reared in 0.65 per cent NaCl are very small; in 0.006 per cent NaCl they are larger; when the larvae are reared in distilled water the anal papillae are very large, and the epithelial cells may become vacuolated (Fig. 22). The anal papillae of *Aedes detritus* larvae in Algerian ponds of a salinity equivalent to 1.2 to 10 per cent NaCl are smaller than those of larvae of *Aedes aegyptii* from fresh water.[251] Salt absorption by anal papillae is inhibited by anticholinesterases.[123] Salt-absorbing papillae occur in *Culex, Aedes, Libellula, Aeschna,* and *Chironomus.* Aquatic larvae of a beetle, *Helodes,* absorb chloride mainly by the gut, partly by anal papillae.[236]

In larvae of the trichopteran *Limnophilus* reared in a salinity equivalent to 0.01 per cent NaCl, the osmotic concentration of the body fluid was equivalent to 0.031 to 0.048 per cent NaCl, that of fluid from the malpighian tubes was similar (0.031 to 0.66 per cent NaCl)

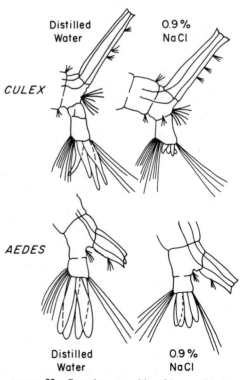

FIGURE 22. Posterior extremities of larvae of Culex and Aedes showing variation in size of anal papillae when larvae are reared in distilled water or in 0.9 per cent NaCl.[251]

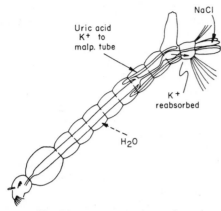

AEDES MOSQUITO LARVA

FIGURE 23. Diagram representing main paths of movement of ions and water in osmoregulation of mosquito larva. Passive entrance of water, active uptake of NaCl from medium, active reabsorption of potassium from hindgut.

whereas rectal urine was very dilute (equivalent to 0.000 to 0.009 per cent NaCl). Ramsay[178] examined fluids from various regions of the intestine of mosquito larvae. In a fresh-water species, *Aedes aegypti*, the intestinal fluid is isosmotic to hemolymph, and after the rectal epithelium absorbs salts the fluid is strongly hypoosmotic. Conversely, in a larva of *A. detritus* living in diluted sea water the blood-isosmotic intestinal fluid is made hyperosmotic in the rectum:[178]

	Equivalent % NaCl		
	Rectal fluid	Body fluid	Intestinal fluid
A. aegypti (in distilled H_2O)	0.07	0.63	0.57
A. detritus (in S.W.)	3.5	0.93	1.2

The malpighian tubes form a fluid which is lower in sodium than the hemolymph, but of the same osmoconcentration. Water and salt reabsorption then occur in the rectal epithelium.

Sialis larvae are unlike the mosquito larvae in that there is no special mechanism for ion absorption, hence no region which is very water permeable; the cuticle has low permeability, as demonstrated with heavy water. Also the excretory fluid is not so hypoosmotic to the blood as in the fresh-water mosquito larva; the conductivity of rectal fluid in *Sialis* is 65 per cent of that of the blood. However, the excretory fluid contains no detectable chloride, low sodium and potassium but considerable amounts of ammonium bicarbonate.[218] If the blood chloride is doubled in

concentration, some appears in the excretory fluid.

In summary: In both *Sialis* and mosquito larvae amino acids constitute a large part of the osmotically active solutes of the blood; in the mosquito larvae blood sodium chloride is maintained by active absorption by anal papillae and by salt reabsorption in the rectum (Fig. 23), whereas in *Sialis* salts are absorbed from the gut, the entire body surface is relatively impermeable, and chloride is kept from the excretory fluid by the malpighian tubes.

Larvae of the dipteran genus Ephydra live in saline lakes and are markedly hypoosmotic. In a medium equivalent to 8 per cent NaCl the hemolymph is maintained at a concentration equal to 1 per cent NaCl and there is only a small decrease in blood concentration when in distilled water. As in Artemia, these dipteran larvae must be very impermeable to both water and salts.[231a]

Two sibling species of *Anopheles* are morphologically similar although their eggs are distinguishable and hybrids are sterile; one, *A. gambiae,* develops in fresh water, the other, *A. melas,* normally breeds in brackish water but can develop in concentrations as high as 150 per cent sea water.[20, 233]

Terrestrial Insects and Arachnids.
Terrestrial insects have very successfully solved the problems of life in dry air. Their water content varies widely according to species and stage in life cycle (50 to 70 per cent water). The osmotic concentration of the hemolymph varies widely but tends to be higher than for aquatic insects and for terrestrial animals restricted to high humidities:

		Δ_1
Arachnids	Scorpion	−1.125
	Spider	−0.894
Insects: Terrestrial	Carabus intricatus	−0.94
	Tenebrio molitor (larva)	−1.165
	Mantis religiosa	−0.885
	Ephestia elatella (larva)	−1.122
	Drosophila (larva)	−0.70
Insects: Aquatic	Mosquito larvae	−0.65

As in the aquatic insects amino acids constitute an unusually large fraction and chlorides a small fraction of the osmotically active solutes in the blood; for example, in larvae of *Drosophila melanogaster* amino acids contribute 30 per cent and chloride only 10 per cent of the total.[262]

The principal loss of water from insects is by evaporation; a mammal may have a surface to volume ratio of 0.5 whereas in an insect the relative amount of surface to volume may be 50.[21] One avenue of evaporative loss is the spiracles, and most insects keep these closed between respiratory movements. Those lacking spiracular control have higher rates of water loss. When the spiracles are forcibly kept open, as by exposure to CO_2 or in activity, the water loss is increased many times.[250]

The insect integument is a complex structure of chitin, tanned proteins, waxes, polyphenols, and cement.[182] The number and position of the wax layers relative to the tanned protein varies in different groups as does the thickness and degree of hardening. In general, the low water evaporation (1 to 3 mg $H_2O/cm^2/hr$ in dry air)[250] depends on the cuticular wax. The permeability constant for water of wax and cuticle is some two thousand-fold less than that of red blood cells. Aquatic insects in air tend to lose more water by evaporation than do terrestrial insects: *Limophilus* larva 11, *Corixa* 2, adult *Hydrobius* 0.3, *Tenebrio* pupae 0.02 mg/cm^2/hr at 20°C.[97] Water loss is increased by abrasion of the cuticle, by removal of wax by appropriate lipid solvents, and by changing the physical properties of the wax by raising its temperature. As the temperature rises the water loss increases, gradually at small temperature increases, and then more steeply[61, 250] (Fig. 21). This has been interpreted as due to a critical temperature of melting of the wax; however, there may be a wide range of "melting," and there is probably no sharp transition temperature.[97] At high temperatures death may be due to desiccation rather than to temperature *per se*. High humidity retards the evaporative loss at elevated temperatures.

A unique property of insects and ticks which is poorly understood is their ability to absorb water from an atmosphere which is humid but less than saturated. This water absorption, which occurs only in living metabolizing animals, has been demonstrated in a variety of orders of insects as well as in ticks.[21, 36] It occurs with spiracles covered,[36] and some soil insects can absorb water from the soil. One hypothesis is that the wax layer makes the tanned cuticle asymmetric with respect to water movement;[21] tanned gelatin with wax on one side can show similar asymmetrical uptake of water.

Lost water is replaced by drinking and from food. Also some insects, such as clothes moths, wax moth larvae, and various grain eaters, get sufficient water metabolically from oxidation of food. At low humidity, larvae of flour moths and beetles eat more relative to size, yet grow more slowly.

The loss of water by excretion is kept low by rectal reabsorption of water from the fluid secreted into the malpighian tubules (Fig. 24). Ramsay's observations on mosquito larvae indicated rectal reabsorption of ions in fresh water and of water in sea water. Malpighian tubules (from the stick insect *Dixippus*) isolated in saline produce a slightly hypoosmotic fluid which differs in ionic composition from the hemolymph. Secretion of urine by the malpighian tubes is stopped if the hydrostatic pressure in the lumen is raised above 20 cm H_2O.[179]

The blood-sucking bug, *Rhodnius*, during the first 2 to 3 hours after a meal rids itself by urine of three-quarters of the water consumed. Rectal urine at this time is isosmotic with the hemolymph ($\Delta_u = -0.65°$).[249] Thereafter the urine becomes cloudy with uric acid crystals. In the upper part of the malpighian tubes a clear alkaline fluid is secreted, in the lower tube the urine becomes acid, the tube becomes packed with uric acid crystals, and the rectal urine has twice the osmotic concentration of the hemolymph ($\Delta_u = -1.43°$). Wigglesworth interpreted these observations by postulating water reabsorption in both the lower malpighian tubes and the rectum.[249] Blood-sucking ticks excrete water and salts by the coxal glands as a blood-hypoosmotic fluid.[61]

Another adaptive mechanism in osmotic regulation is the behavioral tendency to select a region of "preferred" humidity in a gradient. Slightly desiccated animals tend to go to higher humidities and hydrated ones to drier air (*Blatta*, *Ptinus*,[61] *Drosophila*[163]). *Tribolium* at 27°C can distinguish between 95 per cent and 100 per cent relative humidity (R.H.), but not such small differences in the range 40 to 55 per cent R.H.[253]

Hygroreceptors are widely distributed in insects. In *Tenebrio* they are on the antennae and in *T. confusa* and *T. destructor* hygroscopic discrimination is possible only if peg organs on antennal segments 7 to 11 are present; *T. castaneum* has receptors on the maxillary palpi.[192] In *Drosophila*, *Aedes*, *Blatella*, and *Oncopeltus*[9] the antennae contain hygroreceptors.

Humidity preferences may be important in the distribution of many insects. For example, the tropical forest mosquitoes *Anopheles bellator* and *A. homunculus* overlap for part of their ranges in the forest canopy, but

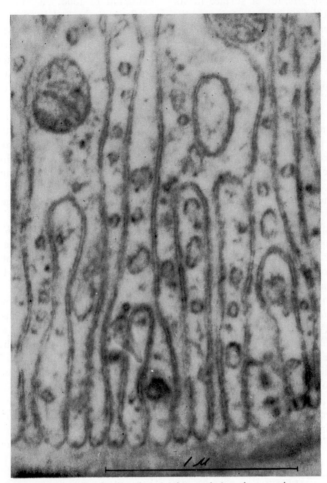

FIGURE 24. Electron micrograph of cells of malpighian tubules of a grasshopper to show extensive infolding of proximal membrane of secretory cells around lumen. (From Beams, H. W., Tahmisian, T. N., and Devine, C. L.: J. Biophys. Biochem. Cytol., vol. 1.)

bellator rises higher in the evening and descends less far down in the day because of its greater tolerance of low humidity.[171] Of two *Drosophila* genera, one, *D. persimilis,* occupies a colder, wetter range than *D. pseudoobscura.* Mosquitoes select different salt solutions for oviposition, probably by salt taste receptors located on tarsi and tibiae. Some chemoreceptor hairs of flies serve for water taste.[255] Activity of tsetse flies is greater in dry than in moist air, apparently under stimulation from thoracic spiracular sense endings.

In summary: Insects have become more independent of environmental water than any other group (except desert mammals). This they have accomplished by reduction in respiratory water loss, by a waxy cuticle which is relatively impervious to water, by some poorly understood mechanism for absorbing water from the atmosphere, by containing amino acids rather than salts as the principal blood solutes, by producing a blood-hyperosmotic excretory fluid as a result of the remarkable reabsorption by the rectum, and by excreting nitrogen as uric acid (Chapter 6). Some aquatic insects actively absorb ions; in none has active outward secretion of ions been shown, a possible explanation of the absence of insects from the sea.

REPTILES AND BIRDS

Reptiles are more independent of a moist environment than Amphibia because of protection by horny scales against surface evaporation, and because in most reptile groups the eggs are cleidoic (boxed-in) or else the animals are viviparous. A lizard lacking skin loses water by evaporation as fast as an intact newt.

The water content of tissues of desert reptiles is as high as or higher than that of mammals.[117] The blood osmoconcentration in reptiles is generally somewhat higher than in amphibians. Freezing point data for blood and urine of representative reptiles are given at bottom of page.[26, 221]

The renal corpuscles of most reptiles are poorly vascularized; the blood supply is better in turtles and crocodiles than in snakes and lizards. Many land turtles have a lobed bladder, and the possibility of water reabsorption there has not been investigated. The amount of urine excreted by reptiles is small, and urine of snakes and lizards may be solid or semisolid; the site of water reabsorption is unknown; it may be the cloaca. In the alligator the urine flow is 0.4 to 1.2 ml/kg/hr as compared with 1.5 to 20.0 ml in *Rana*, and in the alligator glomerular filtration is 1.5 to 3.4 ml/kg/hr, compared with 2.8 to 40 ml in the frog.[141] A lizard, *Trachysaurus*, hydrated, formed 5.7 ml urine/kg/hr, and dehydrated, only 0.24 ml urine/kg/hr.[26]

The principal loss of water from land reptiles must be by way of the lungs, and desert reptiles get most of their water from food. Lizards and snakes have been observed to drink to compensate for a water deficit, whereas frogs take up water through the skin. A subspecies of water snake living in salt marshes will not drink salt water, while the fresh-water subspecies will drink it and succumb.[167]

Marine reptiles—turtles, crocodiles, snakes and lizards—have special glands in the head with openings in lachrymal or nasal ducts which resemble the salt glands of marine birds. The secretion of the salt gland of a loggerhead turtle has been found to be a concentrated NaCl solution.[210]

In bird as in reptiles there is very little recent information about kidney function. Cloacal urine may be a viscous paste of uric acid crystals. However, there is some question as to whether most of the water reabsorption occurs in the cloaca, in the lower intestine, or in the kidney.[231] Data for hens are given at top of page.

Ureteral urine is viscous and contains large amounts of urates which precipitate on cooling; the blood uric acid is reported as not exceeding 0.091 per cent, whereas the ureteral urate concentration may be 0.2 to 0.7 per

Plasma osmoconcentration (equiv. NaCl) (mEq)	Urine osmoconcentration (equiv. NaCl) (mEq)
161	177 (ureteral)
181	232 (cloacal)

Glomerular filtration	Urine output
1.22 ml/kg/min	25-70 ml/kg/day

cent.[258] The osmoconcentration of ureteral urine is higher after water deprivation and after injection of neurohypophyseal hormone; hence considerable water reabsorption must occur in the kidney, and antidiuretic hormone has some effect. However, the bird pituitary gland contains a different antidiuretic hormone from that of the rat, as tested on the rat. Creatinine and uric acid may be secreted by the tubules of bird kidneys.[225]

The osmoconcentration of hens' eggs is less than that of the blood, and the yolk has an osmoconcentration similar to the white. Embryonic blood gradually increases in concentration during incubation.[100]

Salt-marsh subspecies of Savannah sparrows drink more sea water than northern migratory subspecies, but decrease their consumption when given water of increased salt concentration, while the migrators increase their drinking.[43] Respiratory loss of water is relatively greater in small birds than in large, and water availability may be critical for desert birds.

Marine birds—sea gulls, cormorants, pelicans—have nasal glands which excrete hyperosmotic sodium chloride. Stimulation of secretion is by an increase in blood salt or osmoconcentration. The intake and excretion during 8 hours of a cormorant fed 60 gm of fish and 3 gm of NaCl were as follows:[211]

	Cl mEq	Na mEq	K mEq	H_2O ml
Intake	54	54	4	50
Cloacal elimination	27.5	25.6	2.66	108.9
Nasal elimination	26.1	23.8	.31	51.4

In the nasal salt gland the cells have the plasma membrane multiply folded and are capable of a high degree of secretion of

Reptile	Habitat	Δ_o	Δ_i	Δ_u
Caretta rempi	sea water	−1.85	−0.66	−0.64
Emys europea	fresh water		−0.44	−0.10
Testudo graeca	land		−0.60	−0.19
Natrix natrix (grass snake)			−0.68	−0.22
Trachysaurus (dehydrated desert lizard)			−0.65	−0.62

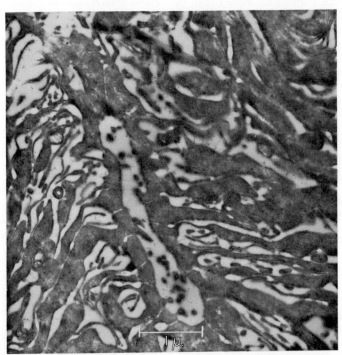

FIGURE 25.   Electron micrograph of portion of lumen and surrounding secretory cells of salt gland of Leach's petrel (*Ocenodroma leucor hoa*). Fixation, hypertonic osmic acid to demonstrate continuity of epicytoplasmic spaces between basal infoldings of the cell, which communicate via tiny pores with the lumen. (Courtesy of W. L. Doyle.)

$NaCl^{56}$ (Fig. 25). The salt gland excretes NaCl, the kidney $MgSO_4$ from swallowed sea water; nasal secretion requires less water than renal excretion of the same amount of salt.

MAMMALS

Regulation of water balance in mammals permits them to live in moist or dry air, in fresh or salt water, and over a wide range of environmental temperatures. The most important osmotic advance made over all other vertebrates is in the kidney tubules, which permit the production of a markedly blood-hyperosmotic urine. In numerous mammals complete balance records of water intake and outgo have been made.

In man, for example, the daily water loss for a 70-kg individual is 600 to 2000 ml by the kidneys, 50 to 200 ml by feces, 350 to 700 ml by insensible evaporation from the skin, 50 to 400 ml by sweat, and 350 to 400 ml from the lungs. A lactating mother may lose an additional 900 ml as milk. Thus the total normal daily loss may range from 1 to more than 9 liters, depending on temperature, exercise, state of hydration, and other factors. This loss must be made up by water drunk, water in food, and metabolic water. Most of the common mammals have a plasma concentration which is about 0.30 osmolar (equivalent to 0.95 per cent NaCl) ($\Delta_i = -0.8°$). In man the urine concentration varies greatly with body water load but is usually about 0.65 osmolar and the maximum urine concentration in thirsting man is reported as 1.4 osmolar ($\Delta_u = -2.6°$).[256] The permeability of the skin of mammals to water is extremely low, a fact of particular importance in aquatic mammals. However, many mammals use water evaporation either by sweat glands or by panting as a means of cooling, and this loss may become critical in some environments. For man, loss of 10 per cent of the body water causes serious illness and for mice, loss of 30 per cent of body water results in death.[86] Insensible evaporation may comprise 10 per cent of the water loss. Conversely, man in water may take up water by the skin, mostly by imbibition by the stratum corneum; some of this water reaches the blood.[29]

The limit of urine dilution in man is 50 mosM, and the limit of concentration is 1400 mosM; a desert rat can produce urine of 5000 mosM.[27, 256] Data on mechanism of control of urine concentration have been obtained by micropuncture analysis of tubular fluid,[242] by stopping urine flow for a given period by back-pressure in the ureter with analysis of successive portions following release,[139] and by analysis of slices of kidney at different levels.[254] Those mammals which can produce the most concentrated urine have the longest loops of Henle (long papilla).[96, 205]

Glomerular filtration under "normal" conditions of the kidney in a dog is about 4.3 ml/min/kg body weight; in an average young man it is 127 ml/min (corrected to 1.73 M^2 body surface). This means that the equivalent of the total extracellular fluid of the body is reworked by the kidney about sixteen times each day.[223, 225] In man 1100 l plasma circulated per day in the glomeruli yields 180 l filtrate; of this 178.5 l is resorbed, leaving 1.5 l/day of urine.[90] The filtrate is protein free but contains all smaller plasma solutes in proportions determined by the Donnan equilibrium or ionic balancing of the plasma proteins. Filtration in the glomerulus is largely determined by the difference between the hydrostatic (blood) pressure and the colloid osmotic pressure of the serum

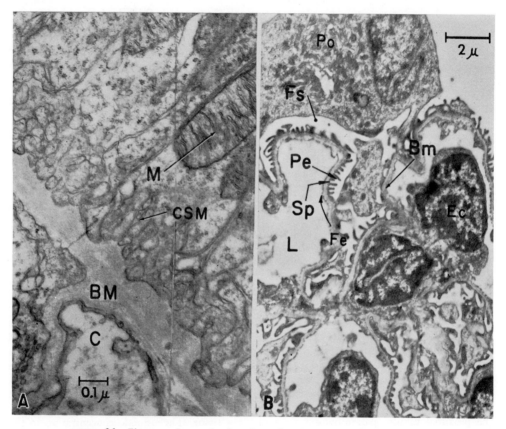

FIGURE 26. Electron micrograph of portions of rat kidney. (From B. V. Hall.)

A, section of basal portion of proximal tubule.

    M   = mitochondrion of tubule cell
    CSM = infolding of basal portion of surface membrane of proximal tubule cell
    BM   = basement membrane
    C   = capillary lumen

B, section of glomerulus.

    L   = lumen of capillary
    Ec   = endothelial cell
    Po   = podocyte (epithelial cell of visceral layer of Bowman's capsule)
    Fs   = filtration space
    Bm   = basement membrane
    Pe   = pedicel
    Sp   = interpedicellar slit-pore
    Fe   = fenestrated attenuated endothelium (lamina fenestrata)

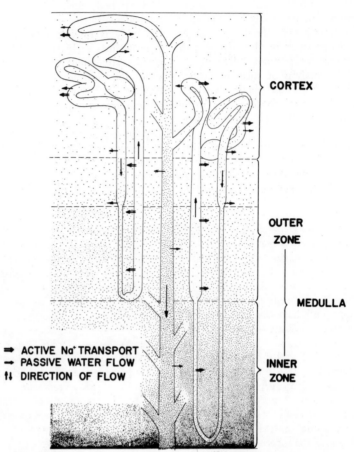

CORTEX

OUTER ZONE

MEDULLA

INNER ZONE

⇒ ACTIVE Na⁺ TRANSPORT
→ PASSIVE WATER FLOW
↑↓ DIRECTION OF FLOW

FIGURE 27. Diagram of two renal nephrons of mammalian kidney; one with the long loop and the other with the short loop of Henle. Osmoconcentration in regions of kidney indicated by density of dots. (From B. Schmidt-Nielsen.)

proteins. The size of protein molecule which is retained is set by a complicated system of slit pores. The fluid passes through pores in the endothelial cells, permeable basement membrane, and emerges between processes of covering cells (podocytes) on the lumen side of the capsule (Fig. 26). Of these filtered solutes the sugar is reabsorbed actively in the proximal tubule: paraminohippuric acid (PAH) is excreted in this region. The fluid in the proximal tubule is isosmotic with plasma.

In the loop of Henle the tonicity of the fluid increases steadily toward the papilla and decreases again in the ascending limb toward the cortex. In the early distal convolutions the fluid is distinctly hypotonic to the plasma.

The loops of Henle act as countercurrent multiplier systems in which diffusion, combined with active transport of sodium, results in a higher osmoconcentration of the entire papilla than of the cortex.[205] Flow is in opposite directions in the ascending and descend-

ing arms of a loop, sodium is moved actively out of the ascending and passively into the descending loop, that is, it can be cycled within the loop. Active Na^+ absorption takes place in the thick and possibly also in the thin ascending limb of the loop of Henle. This creates an osmotic gradient between the fluid in the ascending limb and the surrounding tissue. The osmotic concentration in the descending limb rises through diffusion of water out of the tubule to the hypertonic interstitium and through the diffusion of Na^+ into the descending limb. The exchange and the osmotic gradient between the two limbs of the loop of Henle in which fluid flows in opposite directions (the countercurrent multiplier system) create an increasing osmotic concentration in tubules, capillaries, and interstitium, from outer through inner zone of the medulla (Fig. 27).

In water diuresis the hypotonic fluid in the early distal convolutions remains hypotonic throughout the distal convolutions and throughout the collecting duct because of low permeability of these structures to water. However, in antidiuresis, when antidiuretic hormone is present in the blood, the permeability of the distal convolution and collecting ducts increases, water diffuses out of the distal convoluted tubules, and the fluid becomes isosmotic to the blood by the time it enters the collecting ducts. As the collecting duct fluid passes down through the increasingly hypertonic environment in the medulla, water diffuses out of the collecting duct, making the final urine practically isotonic to the renal papilla and hypertonic to the blood.

Substances such as creatinine may be secreted by the tubules in goat, rat, apes, and man but not in dog, seal, rabbit, and cat.[247]

There is also some reabsorption from the bladder.[132] Epithelial cells of the proximal tubule show prominent Golgi apparatus, mitochondria, and extensive lamellae of the basal membrane; the cells of the loop of Henle are thin and have microvilli on the lumen edge; distal tubule cells have long prominent mitochondria and very few microvilli; collecting tubule cells have many vesicles, some projecting into the lumen.[180]

The water-retaining principles (ADH) are polypeptides produced by the supraoptic (paraventricular) nucleus of the hypothalamus; they pass along the infundibular stalk to the neurohypophysis where they are stored. Mammalian extract is many times more effective on rat kidney and less effective on frogs than the extracts of nonmammalian vertebrates.[91]

The neurohypophyseal principles of mammals are oxytocin and vasopressin. Pig and hippopotamus vasopressin differs from that of other mammals (including peccary) in containing lysine instead of arginine in the side chain (page 546). In birds (fowl), amphibians (frog), and marine fish (Pollachius) the active polypeptides are oxytocin and arginine vasotocin, the latter being the principal ADH and consisting of the oxytocin ring and vasopressin side chain. The cyclostome Petromyzon has arginine vasotocin and little or no oxytocin; the elasmobranch Squalus has an unidentified polypeptide. Vasopressin is evidently restricted to mammals.[170, 197]

The blood level of ADH in mammals is controlled reflexly by osmoreceptors located anteromedially in the hypothalamus (anterior to mammillary bodies) and responding to small (1 to 2 per cent) changes in plasma osmoconcentration.[240] Intracarotid perfusion of hypertonic NaCl reduces urine flow. Increased

blood concentration elicits liberation of ADH and reduces urine volume. Injection of as small an amount of hyperosmotic saline as 0.005 to 0.01 ml of 2 to 3 per cent NaCl into the paraventricular nucleus of a goat elicits polydipsia (excessive drinking), followed in about 2 hours by polyuria. Electrical stimulation of this area of the brain indicates separate centers for the drinking and the antidiuretic response. Increased electrical activity is recorded from the supraoptic nucleus after intracarotid injection of hyperosmotic solutions.[241]

Water taste receptors on the tongue have been identified in dog, pig, and cat; laboratory rats lack water taste, and rabbits give a delayed response.[133, 261] Increase of body water load dilutes the blood and reflexly results in diuresis in proportion to the load; repeated loading by mouth results in adaptation —prompter water excretion. Thirst is a complex sensation which involves stimulation of brain osmoreceptors, general tissue dehydration, and to less extent dryness of the mouth.[256]

Water restriction imposes severe stress on desert mammals. Water balance measurements in terms of intake and output (particularly evaporative loss) showed decreasing turnover in three small rodents: Blarina which is subterranean > Peromyscus from the forest floor > Microtus from dry grassy prairie.[44] A similar series of water requirements exists for five races of Peromyscus from xeric and mesic habitats.[135] In an Australian marsupial, Setonyx, the average urine production changed from 25 ml/hr and a mean concentration of 456 mosM/l in the wet season to 3 ml/hr and a concentration of 1163 mosM/l in the dry season.[25]

Kangaroo rats (Dipodymys) as described by the Schmidt-Nielsens illustrate water-conserving mechanisms in the extreme.[204, 207, 208] These animals remain by day in the burrows where the relative humidity reduces the evaporative loss from the lungs by 25 per cent as compared with outside air. When dry air is inspired the evaporative loss from the lungs is only 0.54 mg H_2O/ml O_2 used, as compared with 0.84 in man or 0.94 mg H_2O in a laboratory rat. When fed on relatively dry grain at humidities above 10 per cent R.H. without access to drinking water, the kangaroo rats showed no sign of negative water balance and apparently used the water of oxidation of food, which amounted to 73.4 mg H_2O/100 cal energy. The water of oxidation of various foods is:

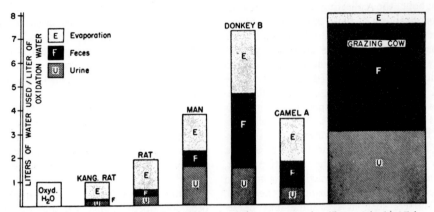

FIGURE 28.   Relative water loss by various routes in different mammals. (From Schmidt-Nielsen, B., Schmidt-Nielsen, K., Haupt, T. R., and Jarnum, S. A.: Am. J. Physiol., vol. 185.)

	gm H_2O/gm food	gm H_2O/kcal
fat	1.07	0.113
carbohydrate	0.556	0.133
protein	0.396	0.092

The relative efficiency of kangaroo rat and laboratory white rat follows:[208, 212]

loss in gm H_2O/100 cal food
metabolized at 22 mg H_2O/l air

	Feces	Urine	Evapo-ration	Total loss	Oxidative intake
white rat	4	5	14	23	13
kangaroo rat	0.63	3.4	3.4	8	13

The kangaroo rat can concentrate urine to a urine/plasma (U/P) osmolal ratio of 18 as compared with 4 in man. The normal blood level of ADH in *Dipodomys* is much higher than in laboratory rats. A beaver, which has short loops of Henle only, shows a maximum urine osmolality of 600; a rabbit, with both short and long loops of Henle, 1500; and a desert rodent *Psammomys*, with long loops only, a maximum concentration of 6000 osmolal.

Maximum renal concentrating capacities of different mammals have been summarized:[25, 256]

Maximum concentrations observed

	Δ_u (°C)	mEq Cl^-/l urine
pollock whale	−1.8 to −2.5	
dog	−3.5 to −4.3	400
man	−2.2 to −2.75	370
seal	−3.9 to −4.5	500
rat		
laboratory	4.8	760
kangaroo	−10.4 to −10.9	(1500)
camel	−4.6 to −5.9	
cat	−4.0 to −6.0	
chicken	−1.0	

The urea U/P ratio of the kangaroo rat may be 400, as compared with 170 in man and 200 in a white rat. Even at low urea ratios, the urea/inulin clearance is greater than unity; hence urea may be excreted by the kidney tubules. In mammals on a high protein diet there may be some tubular secretion of urea.

In larger mammals the loss of water by skin evaporation and from the lungs parallels resting metabolism. The sweat glands are under control of the autonomic nervous system, and in man active sweating begins when the air temperature reaches about 86° F. (Chapter 9). Loss of water by the skin is necessary for temperature control, but blood is diverted to the skin from other areas and the body loses salt. A man walking in the desert at 110°F loses 1 quart of water per hour; sweating increases by 20 gm per hour for each 1°F rise in air temperature.[6] During such exposure an exercising man does not voluntarily drink enough water to restore his water balance, and if water loss exceeds 12 per cent of body weight in dry heat, man collapses. A dog suffers more in the heat than man because a dog loses water only, not salt, and hence the blood concentration rises. In panting, cooling and oxygenation are associated, and a panting dog may lose so much CO_2 that it develops alkalosis. A burro has many sweat glands, but its sweat contains little salt; therefore the blood chloride rises during work in the heat.

Camels tolerate loss of more than twice as much of the body water (30 per cent) as most laboratory animals.[209, 212] A camel has low urine output (one-third that of the donkey), and fecal and evaporative losses of water are small (Fig. 28). The maximal urine concentration recorded by the Schmidt-Nielsens for a thirsty camel was 3.17 osmolar (Δ_u = −5.9°). Camels put out much less water for evaporative cooling than other large mammals (p. 269). A camel kept 16 days without water, then given water, drank 40 liters in 10 minutes, enough to rehydrate its tissues.[209]

Marine mammals have blood only a little more concentrated than that of land mammals. The urine of marine mammals can be more concentrated than sea water:[33, 128, 173]

Marine mammal	Δ_i	Δ_u
whale (*Delphinus phocaena*)	−0.74	
whale (*Balaenoptera borealis*)		−2.46
dolphin (*Tursiops tursio*)	−0.83	−2.3
seal (*Phoca foetida*)	−0.70	−0.75 to −4.5

The concentration of blood of two marine birds is about the same as that of the mammals ($\Delta_i = -0.64$ to -0.69).

Water balance has been calculated for the seal *Phoca vitulina* by Irving.[104] No water is lost for temperature regulation; hence the only loss is by lungs, feces, and urine. The balance corresponding to 100 calories equivalent of food follows:

	H_2O intake (gm)		H_2O loss (gm)
food	1000	lung	106
oxidative water	121	feces	200
		urine (difference between intake and output)	815

The food (1250 gm of herring) would yield urea and salt sufficient to give 800 ml of urine a freezing point of −2.7°C. In fasting seals the Δ_u was −1.95°, whereas after a meal of herring the concentration increased to $\Delta_u = $ −1.98 to −3.6°. The magnesium and chloride of the urine and intestinal residue are so low that it is unlikely that any sea water is swallowed. Marine mammals living on fish, which are hypoosmotic to the ocean, appear to get ample water from their food to keep the blood more dilute than the ocean.

Krogh[128] extended the calculation to the walrus and whalebone whales, which feed largely on marine invertebrates that are more concentrated than fish and more concentrated than the blood of the mammals themselves. Less water might be lost from the lungs in the whale because it extracts more of the oxygen and thus does not need to saturate so much air. Assuming a little less water loss by feces than in the seal, the kidney could excrete the salt and urea with the water available from its food and produce urine within the observed concentration range. These calculations are based on assumptions regarding composition of food, absence of drinking, and water loss by various routes, all of which need to be determined.

Mammalian urine can be more concentrated than sea water; hence the body should be able to extract some water from sea water and excrete the salts. A kangaroo rat can get along well when it drinks sea water.[207] In man the utilization of sea water seems to be limited not by the kidneys but by the action of the salts on the gastrointestinal system. For rats the lethal dose of sea water, 16 per cent of the body weight, is the same whether given by stomach or intraperitoneally, and death evidently results from cellular dehydration.[7] Cats on high protein and fat diet put out very concentrated urine and can survive indefinitely on sea water.[257] The ability to use sea water is here closely related to the concentrating capacity of the kidney.

Mammals are aquatic during embryonic life. As adults they have very low surface permeability to water although they may use evaporation from sweat secretion or respiratory surface for cooling. They can excrete a urine which is very dilute in water diuresis or is strongly hyperosmotic to the blood. The primitive water-excreting kidney has evolved into a filtration-reabsorption and secretion system which can excrete waste products with little loss of water. Mammals which live in the desert or in the sea have no unique mechanisms but merely differ quantitatively from mammals which are less versatile in coping with water deficit or surfeit.

CONCLUSIONS

When animals are arranged according to their osmotic performance (Table 2), certain correlations with their distribution and taxonomic relationships are apparent. Many of the differences between animals from various habitats are differences in the degree of development of a capacity rather than in the specific kind of capacity. Success in the ocean may accompany either osmotic lability or osmotic stability.

Most marine invertebrates conform to the sea in their blood concentration. The only ocean animals in which a sharp gradient is maintained are marine vertebrates. A few crustaceans find some unknown advantage in being hypoosmotic. Elasmobranch fishes which retain urea have a gradient in the same direction as in fresh water. In other marine vertebrates (except hagfishes) some method of salt excretion exists and the blood is hypoosmotic to the sea. Marine teleosts ex-

TABLE 2. OSMOTIC PERFORMANCE

Osmotic characteristics	Principal mechanisms	Examples
Osmotic conformity	Poor volume regulation	Marine invertebrate eggs
		Sipunculids
	Volume regulation by salt exchange	Marine molluscs, Maja
		Nereis pelagica
		N. cultrifera
Limited osmoregulation	Low permeability; salt reabsorption in nephridia(?), salt uptake	N. diversicolor
	Water storage in endodermal cells	Gunda = Procerodes
Fair osmoregulation in hypotonic media	Selective absorption of salts from medium, kidney reabsorption or secretion, low permeability	Carcinus
Regulation in hypertonic and in hypotonic media except at extremes	Hypoosmotic regulation by extrarenal salt secretion; salt storage	Uca, Pachygrapsus
Unlimited regulation in hypotonic media	Hypotonic copious urine, salt reabsorption or water secretion in kidney, active salt uptake, low surface permeability	Crayfish
		Fresh-water teleosts
		Amphibia
	Water impermeability	Fresh-water embryos
		Marine fish eggs
Maintenance of hypertonicity in all media	Urea retention	Elasmobranchs
Regulation in hypertonic media	Extrarenal salt excretion, reduced kidney output	Marine teleosts
	Excretion by gill and gut	Artemia
Regulation in moist air and fresh water	Low skin permeability, salt absorption from medium, salt reabsorption in kidney	Earthworm
		Frog
Regulation in dry air	Low permeable cuticle; hypertonic urine by rectal reabsorption, water absorption from air	Insects
	Hypertonic urine, water reabsorption in kidney	Birds and mammals
	Salt secretion by nasal gland	Marine birds

crete salt against a gradient by their gills; marine mammals produce concentrated urine. One important reason why insects and amphibians have not extensively invaded salt water may be their lack of mechanisms for secreting salt outward; this is surprising in view of the capacity of some of them for absorbing salt actively against a gradient. Osmoconcentration of blood is usually maintained by salts, but in insects a large fraction is by amino acids, in elasmobranchs by urea, and in some winter-hardened fish and insects by other organic solutes.

As the water becomes more dilute in estuaries or bays receiving much fresh-water inflow, species drop out in order of decreasing ability to regulate hyperosmotically. Which mechanisms fail or what processes are modified as dilutions become more extreme differ in different kinds of animals.

Success in fresh water requires osmotic regulation of such order that a high concentration of body fluids can be maintained against an extreme osmotic gradient. Such regulation requires active mechanisms for (1) low permeability to water, (2) water elimination, (3) salt retention, and (4) salt replacement.

Fresh-water animals differ from the marine in degree of development of these regulating mechanisms. Reduction of osmotic work comes from great reduction of osmotic concentration of blood and further reduction in urine concentration, but with dilution of tissue fluids come metabolic restrictions. Copious water elimination is necessary in all fresh-water animals except in very water-impermeable eggs. Marine protozoans put into fresh water develop vacuoles or increase the output of vacuole systems already present. Marine Crustacea which can live in brackish water increase their urine output in the more dilute media. Fresh-water fish excrete a copious urine, whereas in some marine fish the kidney is reduced to a set of simple tubules. But nowhere is there an animal which can excrete pure water; hence there must be mechanisms for salt retention and salt replacement. Low salt permeability is found in many animals, both marine and fresh-water. Salt reabsorption occurs in those marine animals whose kidneys function in the conservation of certain useful salts, but the capacity for salt reabsorption is much more highly developed in fresh-water animals, as in the long tubules of the kidneys of fresh-water crustaceans and vertebrates. Salt may be replaced from food or by active absorption from dilute solutions. In some insects there are anal papillae for salt absorption; frogs take up salt against a gradient by their skin; in many fresh-water crustaceans and fish the gills appear to secrete salt inward. It is probable that in the evolutionary invasion of fresh water, at least by crustaceans, active salt uptake preceded dilution of blood and excretion of dilute urine.

Ability to live in salinities greater than sea water requires the ability to maintain hypotonicity. This the brine shrimp can do, also the crabs which spend much time out of water, and numerous shrimps and prawns, for which there seems to be some advantage in hypotonicity. In marine teleosts hypotonicity is maintained by salt excretion from the gills; in crustaceans both gills and stomach function in this.

Success on land (air) requires protection against loss of water from the body surfaces and from the respiratory membranes and against excessive loss of water by excretion. The only truly successful land animals are higher arthropods (arachnids, myriapods, and insects) and higher vertebrates (reptiles, birds, and mammals). All other animals are largely restricted to an environment which is at least moist. Life in soil is osmotically similar to but less rigorous than life in fresh water. The land arthropods have a chitinous coat. In the vertebrates protection against surface drying is afforded by skin, horny scales, feathers, and hair. The insects have been the most successful in minimizing surface evaporation, and have a thin waxy cuticle of such unique properties that it not only largely prevents evaporation but can actually take up water from a moist atmosphere. All of the successful land animals also have protection against loss of water from their respiratory surfaces. Lack of such protection keeps some groups (Onychophora, land Isopoda, Amphibia) restricted to a moist environment. All of the successful land dwellers seem able to retain water by excreting a concentrated waste fluid. This is functionally comparable to salt secretion by the gills of marine fish, but probably no marine animals except mammals excrete a blood-hyperosmotic urine. Many land insects excrete nitrogenous wastes in solid or semisolid form and reabsorb water in the posterior digestive tract. The renal tubules of mammals, and to a less extent of birds, concentrate urine beyond blood levels. In marine birds, probably in some others, a nasal gland excretes concentrated NaCl solution. In amphibians and mammals control of osmotic water balance by hypophyseal hormones has been well demonstrated. Some land animals, particularly insects, have surface moisture receptors and seek out an "optimum" humidity.

The lability of osmotic characters is illustrated by the fact that many animal groups have representatives in atypical environments —polychaetes in fresh water and soil, sponges and medusae in fresh water, hermit crabs on land, dipteran larvae in the ocean, amphibians in deserts. Closely related snails dwell in salt, brackish and fresh water and on land. Some fish breed in the sea and mature in fresh water, others migrate in the reverse direction. Thus the quantitative differences in response to osmotic stress seem to be more important than the qualitative differences. The limits of the quantitative differences may vary with stage in the life cycle and may determine the range of a species.

When populations of a species from different parts of its range are compared, they often differ markedly in osmotic concentration, in the shape of their blood-medium curves, and in their tolerances. However, by gradual acclimation marked changes in osmotic properties can be induced. In osmoconformers like *Mytilus* and *Asterias* and in osmoregulators like *Callinectes* and *Nereis diversicolor* the differences between high and low salinity populations seem to be environmentally induced, but genetic differences cannot yet be excluded. Other closely related animals (races, subspecies, or species) do differ genetically in their osmotic capacities. This is best documented in the sticklebacks *Gasterosteus gymnurus* and *trachurus,* in saline clones of *Euplotes vassus,* in closely related nereids, and in *Anopheles bellator* and *homunculus.*

Mechanisms of osmotic regulation are complex. They often involve several organ systems and are under nervous and endocrine control. They may be linked with respiratory function, for example, in spiracle closure in insects, and with temperature regulation as in heat regulation in mammals. Among many cold-blooded animals the effects of temperature and salinity are interdependent. The linkage between "optimal" temperature and salinity has been demonstrated in the stickleback, in *Mytilus, Asterias, Crangon,* and gammarids. Behavioral responses to moisture are widespread and are based on special sense cells—saline detectors in crabs, barnacles, limpets, and salmon; hygroreceptors and water taste in insects and earthworms; water taste in frogs and mammals; osmosensitive neurons in slug ganglia and in mammalian hypothalamus.

The role of excretory organs in osmoregulation seems to follow a general pattern which is reasonably well understood only in the vertebrates. Kidneys are present in osmotically conforming invertebrates, and in these animals they function in ionic regulation. However, even here the pattern is of some sort of filtration followed by specific reabsorption and supplemented by active secretion. The fluid initially separated from body fluids, whether by nephrostomes in annelid nephridia, by the coelomosac and labyrinth of a crayfish, by the malpighian tubes of an insect or the glomerulus of a vertebrate kidney, is isosmotic with body fluids. Then specific solutes, sugar, certain ions, and even water may be reabsorbed in the tubules or lower gut through which the urine passes. Whenever any solute is absorbed water must accompany it. The vertebrate kidney seems not derived from any existing invertebrate organ; it is well suited for water elimination; in the aglomerular fish the secretory function of the tubules is all that remains. Possible tubular secretion in the invertebrates has scarcely been considered.

Active transport of ions is better demonstrated in osmoregulation than in other body functions. Ion secretion may be outward, as in the gills of marine fish, in rectal glands of dogfish, or in salt glands of birds, and possibly in gills of hypoosmotic crabs. Salt secretion may be inward, as in surface membranes of fresh-water crustaceans, fish and amphibians, anal papillae of dipteran larvae, and in many kidneys. The nature of enzyme systems which may mediate active ion movement is not known. There is no proved instance of active transport of water in the absence of either solute transport or osmotic gradient. It is unnecessary now to postulate cellular hypertonicity in tissues of animals and its maintenance by active water extrusion. Examples of apparent water transport are found in the filling of contractile vacuoles, the reabsorption of water from the collecting tubules of the mammalian kidney under the influence of antidiuretic hormone, and water reabsorption in the insect rectum. The ability of many insects to absorb water from the atmosphere indicates a remarkable water selectivity, which is probably not under enzymatic control. Where extrarenal excretory routes supplement renal ones, sodium chloride and sometimes potassium are excreted extrarenally, and magnesium, calcium, phosphate, and sulfate are excreted by the kidney—as by land crabs, marine teleosts, and sea birds; brine shrimps excrete NaCl by the gills, magnesium salts by the gut.

In a survey of osmoregulation one is impressed by the lability of regulating mechanisms and at the same time the general patterns of regulation so commonly found. By more intensive study of those animals in which certain functions are quantitatively better developed, it may be possible to get a better understanding not only of osmotic factors which limit animal distribution but also of cellular transport of ions and water.

REFERENCES

1. Adcock, E. M., J. Exp. Biol. *17*: 449-463, 1940. Permeability of gregarines.
2. *Adolph, E. F., Physiological Regulations. Lancaster, Pa., Jacques Cattell Press, 1943, 502 pp.
3. *Adolph, E. F., Biol. Rev. *8*: 222-246, 1933. Exchange of water in frog.
4. Adolph, E. F., J. Cell. Comp. Physiol. *9*: 117-135, 1937. Osmotic swelling of *Phascolosoma*.
5. *Adolph, E. F., Am. J. Physiol. *184*: 18-28, 1956. Nature of adaptation.
6. Adolph, E. F., et al., Physiology of Man in the Desert. New York, Interscience Publishers, 1947, 357 pp.
7. Albrecht, C. B., Am. J. Physiol. *163*: 370-385, 1950. Toxicity of sea water to mammals.
8. *Albritton, E. C., ed., Standard Values in Blood. Philadelphia, W. B. Saunders Co., 1952.
9. Andersen, L. W., and Ball, H. J., Ann. Ent. Soc. Am. *52*: 277-284, 1959. Identification of hygroreceptors, milkweed bug.
10. Anderson, J. D., and Prosser, C. L., Biol. Bull. *105*: 369, 1953. Osmotic variation in populations of Callinectes.
11. Andersson, B., Acta physiol. scand. *28*: 188-201, 1953. Effects of saline injected into hypothalamus.
12. Andersson, B., and Zotterman, Y., Acta physiol. scand. *20*: 95-100, 1950. Water taste in frog.
13. Arnold, D. C., J. Mar. Biol. Assn. U. K. *36*: 121-128, 1957. Response of limpets to different salinities.
14. Baggerman, B., Arch. Néerl. Zool. *12*: 105-317, 1957. Migrations of sticklebacks.
15. Bahl, K. N., Quart. J. Micr. Sci. *76*: 559-572, 1934; *85*: 343-389, 1945; *Biol. Rev. *22*: 109-147, 1947. Function of nephridia in earthworms.
16. Barnes, H., and Barnes, M., Veroff. Inst. Meeresforsch. Bremerhaven *5*: 160-164, 1958. Ion stimulation in barnacles.
17. Baumberger, J. P., and Olmsted, J. M. D., Physiol. Zool. *1*: 531-544, 1928. Osmotic changes in crabs during molt cycle.
18. Beadle, L. C., J. Exp. Biol. *8*: 211-227, 1931;

*Reviews

11: 382-396, 1934; 14: 56-70, 1937. Volume and osmotic control in *Nereis* and *Gunda*.

19. *BEADLE, L. C., Ann. Rev. Physiol. 19: 329-358, 1957. Comparative physiology of osmoregulation.

20. BEADLE, L. C., and SHAW, J., J. Exp. Biol. 27: 96-109, 1950. Blood chloride and nonprotein nitrogen in larvae of *Sialis*.

21. BEAMENT, J. W. L., Symp. Soc. Exp. Biol. 8: 94-117, 1954. Water movement through insect cuticle.

22. BEAMS, H. W., ANDERSON, E., and PRESS, N., Cytologia 21: 50-57, 1956; Proc. Iowa Acad. Sci. 63: 681-685, 1956. Electron microscopy of crayfish kidney.

23. BEAMS, H. W., TAHMISIAN, T. N., and DEVINE, C. L., J. Biophys. Biochem. Cytol. 1: 197-202, 1955. Electron microscopy of malpighian tubule of grasshopper.

24. BELDA, W. H., The Salesianum 37: 68-81, 125-134, 1942; 38: 17-24, 1943. Contractile vacuole function in *Pelomyxa*.

25. BENTLEY, P. J., J. Physiol. 127: 1-10, 1955. Water balance in a marsupial.

26. BENTLEY, P. J., J. Physiol. 145: 37-47, 1959. Water and electrolyte balance, lizard *Trachysaurus*.

27. *BERLINER, R. W., LEVINSKY, N. G., DAVIDSON, D. G., and EDEN, M., Am. J. Med. 24: 730-744, 1958. Mechanism of production of hyperosmotic urine in mammals.

28. BETHE, A., Pflüg. Arch. ges. Physiol. 221: 344-362, 1929; 234: 629-644, 1934. Permeability of marine invertebrates to water and salts.

29. BEUTTNER, K. J. K., J. Appl. Physiol. 14: 261-268, 269-276, 1959. Uptake of water by human skin.

30. BLACK, V. S., J. Fish. Res. Bd. Canada 8: 164-176, 1951. Osmotic changes in salmon fry, in fresh to sea water.

31. *BLACK, V. S., *in* The Physiology of Fishes, edited by M. E. Brown. New York, Academic Press, vol. 1, Chap. 4. Osmotic relations in fish.

32. BOCK, K. J., and SCHLIEPER, C., Kieler Meeresforsch. 9: 201-221, 1953. Properties of tissues of starfish from different salinities.

33. BOTTAZZI, F., Erg. Physiol. 7: 161-402, 1908. Freezing points and conductivities of body fluids.

34. BOUCHER-FIREZ, S., Ann. Inst. Oceanog. Monaco 15: 217-327, 1935. Experiments on the blood chemistry of eels.

35. BROEKEMA, M. M., Arch. Néerl. Zool. 6: 1-100, 1941. Migration and osmotic behavior of shrimp *Crangon*.

36. BROWNING, T. O., J. Exp. Biol. 31: 331-340, 1954. Water balance in ticks.

37. BRULL, L., and CUYPERS, Y., J. Mar. Biol. Assn. U. K. 33: 733-738, 1954. Kidney function in *Lophius*.

38. BURDEN, C. E., Biol. Bull. 110: 8-24, 1956. Pituitary regulation of water balance in *Fundulus*.

39. BURGER, J. W., Biol. Bull. 113: 207-223, 1957. Kidney function in *Homarus*.

40. BURGER, J. W., and HESS, W. N., Science 131: 670-671, 1960. Salt secretion by rectal gland of dogfish.

41. BURSELL, E., J. Exp. Biol. 32: 238-255, 1955. Transpiration of terrestrial isopods.

42. BURSELL, E., and EWER, D. W., J. Exp. Biol. 26: 335-353, 1950. Behavior in humidity gradient, *Peripatopsis*.

43. CADE, T. J., and BARTHOLOMEW, G. A., Physiol. Zool. 32: 230-237, 1959. Use of sea water by Savannah sparrows.

44. CHEW, R. M., Ecol. Monog. 21: 215-225, 1951. Water exchange of small mammals.

45. CLOUDSLEY-THOMPSON, J. L., J. Exp. Biol. 33: 576-582, 1956. Transpiration from isopods.

46. CONWAY, E. J., and GEOGHEGAN, H., J. Physiol. 130: 427-445, 1955. Autolytic changes in stored mammalian tissues.

47. CONWAY, E. J., and McCORMACK, J. I., J. Physiol. 120: 1-14, 1953. Intracellular and extracellular osmotic concentrations, mammalian tissues.

48. COPELAND, D. E., J. Morph. 87: 369-380. Chloride cells in fish gills.

49. COPELAND, D. E., and DALTON, A. J., J. Biochem. Biophys. Cytol. 5: 393-366, 1959. Chloride cells in fish gills.

50. CROGHAN, P. C., J. Exp. Biol. 35: 213-218, 219-233, 243-249, 1958. Osmotic and ionic regulation in *Artemia*.

51. DAVIES, M. E., and EDNEY, E. B., J. Exp. Biol. 29: 571-582, 1952. Water loss from spiders.

52. *DAVSON, H., Textbook of General Physiology, 2nd Ed. Boston, Little Brown & Co., 1959, p. 218-233, 420-479. Water and ion permeability, kidney function.

53. DEKHUYZEN, M. C., Arch. Néerl. Physiol. 5: 563-571, 1921. Osmotic relations in Sipunculus.

54. D'ERRICO, G., Beitr. Chem. Physiol. und Path. 9: 453-469, 1907. Urine concentration in hens.

55. DEYRUP, I., J. Gen. Physiol. 36: 739-750; Am. J. Physiol. 175: 349-352, 1953. Fluid exchange by mammalian tissue slices.

56. DOYLE, W. L., To be published. Electron microscopy of salt gland of birds.

57. *DUVAL, M., Ann. Inst. Oceanog. Monaco 2: 1-231, 1925. Osmotic relations in aquatic animals.

58. EDMONDS, E., Proc. Linn. Soc. N. S. Wales 60: 233-247, 1935. Osmotic relations in marine crustaceans.

59. EDNEY, E. B., Nature 164: 321-322, 1949; J. Exp. Biol. 28: 91-115, 1951. Water loss from land isopods.

60. *EDNEY, E. B., Biol. Rev. 29: 185-219, 1954. Wood lice and the land habitat.

61. *EDNEY, E. B., Water Relations of Terrestrial Arthropods. Cambridge University Press, 1957, 108 pp.

62. EISENBERG, E., Arch. Biol. 35: 441-464, 1925. Function of contractile vacuole in Paramecium.

63. ELIASSEN, E., and JORGENSEN, C. B., Acta physiol. scand. 23: 143-151, 1951. Osmotic stress and water balance in anurans.

64. EWER, R. F., J. Exp. Biol. 27: 40-49, 1950; 29: 173-177, 429-439, 1952. Effects of pituitary extracts on water balance in toads.

65. FLEMISTER, L. J., Biol. Bull. 115: 180-200, 1958; 116: 37-48, 1959. Ion regulation by gill and kidney of land and marsh crabs.

66. FLEMISTER, L. J., and FLEMISTER, S. C., Biol.

Bull. *101*: 259-273, 1951. Ion regulation by gill and kidney of land and marsh crabs.

67. FLORKIN, M., Bull. Acad. Roy. Belg., Cl. Sci. *24*: 143-146, 1938. Osmotic concentration in blood of Anodonta.

68. *FONTAINE, M., Mem. Soc. Endocrinol. *5*: 69-82, 1956. Hormonal control of water and salt balance in fish.

69. FONTAINE, M., and KOCH, H., J. de physiol. *42*: 287-318, 1950. Effects of salinities on fish.

70. FORSTER, R. P., J. Cell. Comp. Physiol. *42*: 487-509, 1953. Renal function in marine teleosts.

71. FORSTER, R. P., J. Cell. Comp. Physiol. *12*: 213-222, 1938; *20*: 55-69, 1942. Creatinine clearance in frogs.

72. FORSTER, R. P., and BERGLUND, F., J. Gen. Physiol. *39*: 349-359, 1956. Renal function in aglomerular teleost, Lophius.

73. FORSTER, R. P., SPERBER, I., and TAGGART, J. V., J. Cell. Comp. Physiol. *44*: 315-318, 1954. Dye transport by kidney slices, marine teleosts and elasmobranchs.

74. FRETTER, V., J. Mar. Biol. Assn. U. K. *34*: 151-160, 1955. Uptake of radio sodium by nereid polychaetes.

75. FRISCH, J. A., Arch. Protist. *93*: 38-71, 1939; Anat. Rec. *89*: 571, 1944. Contractile vacuole function in *Paramecium*.

76. FUHRMAN, F. A., and USSING, H. H., J. Cell. Comp. Physiol. *38*: 109-130, 1951. Effect of pituitary hormones on isolated frogskin.

77. GATENBY, J. B., J. Roy. Micr. Soc. *74*: 133-161, 1954. Contractile vacuoles and Golgi apparatus in sponges.

78. GATENBY, J. B., DALTON, A. J., and FELIX, N. D., Nature *176*: 301-302, 1955. Golgi apparatus and contractile vacuoles of Protozoa.

79. GAUSE, G. F., J. Exp. Zool. *87*: 85-100, 1951; Quart. Rev. Biol. *17*: 99-114, 1942. Genetic variants in osmoregulating Protozoa.

80. GETMAN, H. C., Biol. Bull. *99*: 439-445, 1950. Chloride cells in eel.

81. GORDON, M. S., Biol. Bull. *112*: 28-33, 1957. Osmoregulation in Arctic char and brown trout.

82. GRANT, W. C., Ecology *36*: 400-407, 1955. Tolerance of water loss in earthworms.

83. GREEN, J. W., HARSCH, M., BARR, L., and PROSSER, C. L., Biol. Bull. *116*: 76-87, 1959.

84. GROSS, W. J., J. Exp. Biol. *31*: 402-423, 1954. Osmotic responses of sipunculid, *Dendrostomum*.

85. GROSS, W. J., Am. Nat. *89*: 205-222, 1955; Biol. Bull. *112*: 248-257, 1957. Physiol. Zool. *33*: 21-28, 1960. Responses to osmotic stress in crabs of terrestrial habit.

86. HALL, F. G., Biol. Bull. *42*: 31-51, 1922. Tolerance of desiccation in mammals.

87. HARDISTY, M. W., Nature *174*: 360-361; J. Exp. Biol. *33*: 431-447, 1956; *34*: 237-251, 1957. Osmotic regulation in larval and adult lampreys.

88. HARVEY, H. W., The Chemistry and Fertility of Sea Waters. Cambridge University Press, 1955, 224 pp. Constants for normal sea water.

89. *HEIDERMANNS, C., Handbuch der Zoologie 8, Teil 4, No. 8, 1-62, 1956. Mammalian kidney functioning.

90. *HEINZE, E., and NETTER, H., Handbuch der Zoologie, 8, Teil 4, No. 9, 1-46, 1956. Water balance in mammals.

91. HELLER, H., J. Physiol. *100*: 125-141, 1941; Experientia *6*: 368-376, 1950. Pituitary water balance hormones from different vertebrates.

92. HERFS, A., Arch. Protist. *44*: 227-260, 1922. Contractile vacuole in different salinities.

93. HEUTS, M. J., J. Genetics *49*: 183-191, 1949; Evolution *1*: 89-102, 1947. Racial differences in osmotic behavior of sticklebacks, *Gasterosteus*.

94. HEVESY, G., HOFER, E., and KROGH, A., Scand. Arch. Physiol. *72*: 199-214, 1935. Permeability of skin of frogs to water.

95. HICKMAN, C. P., Canad. J. Zool. *37*: 997-1060, 1960. Osmoregulation in starry flounder.

96. HOBSON, A. D., STEPHENSON, W., and BEADLE, L. C., J. Exp. Biol. *29*: 1-21, 1952. Effect of environmental salinity on body fluids of *Ascaris*.

97. HOLDGATE, M. W., and SEAL, M., J. Exp. Biol. *33*: 82-106; 107-118, 1956. Water loss through cuticle of insects.

98. HOPKINS, D. L., Biol. Bull. *90*: 158-176, 1946. Responses of contractile vacuoles in *Amoeba*.

99. HOUSTON, A. H., Canad. J. Zool. *37*: 591-605, 1959; *37*: 729-748, 1959. Behavior of salmon fry in different salinities; control of blood ions in different salinities, steelhead trout.

100. HOWARD, E., J. Cell. Comp. Physiol. *50*: 451-470, 1958. Osmotic and ion concentrations in chick embryos.

101. HUF, E., Pflüg. Arch. ges. Physiol. *237*: 240-250, 1936. Effects of hydrostatic pressure on water permeability of body surface of Crustacea.

102. HUKUDA, K., J. Exp. Biol. *9*: 61-68, 1932. Volume changes in marine animals.

103. HYKES, A. V., C. R. Soc. Biol. Paris *103*: 355-358, 1930. Salinity tolerance of ctenophores.

104. IRVING, L., Fisher, K. C., and McINTOSH, F. G., J. Cell. Comp. Physiol. *6*: 387-391, 1935. Water balance in seals.

105. JAFFEE, O. C., J. Cell. Comp. Physiol. *44*: 347-363, 1954. Excretion by kidney of developing frog.

106. JONES, L. L., J. Cell. Comp. Physiol. *18*: 79-92, 1941. Osmotic regulation in crabs.

107. JORGENSEN, C. B., and DALES, R. P., Physiol. Comp. Oecol. *4*: 357-374, 1957. Volume and osmotic regulation in nereid polychaetes.

108. JORGENSEN, C. B., and ROSENKILDE, P., Biol. Bull. *110*: 306-309, 1956; Endocrinology *59*: 601-610, 1956. Stimulation of sodium and water uptake in toads by ADH.

109. KALMAN, S. M., and USSING, H. N., J. Gen. Phys. *38*: 361-370, 1955. Stimulation of sodium uptake in toads by ADH.

110. KALMUS, H., Arch. Protist. *66*: 409-420, 1929. Contractile vacuole responses in a marine ciliate.

111. KAMADA, T., J. Exp. Biol. *10*: 75-78, 1933. Osmotic concentration of blood of snail.

112. KAO, C. Y., J. Gen. Physiol. *40*: 91-105, 107-119, 1956. Properties of membrane of developing Fundulus eggs.

113. KAO, C. Y., and CHAMBERS, R., J. Exp. Biol. *31*: 139-149, 1954. Internal hydrostatic pressure in relation to the medium in developing Fundulus eggs.

114. KAO, C. Y., CHAMBERS, R., and CHAMBERS, E. L.,

J. Cell. Comp. Physiol. *44*: 447-461, 1954. Internal hydrostatic pressure and permeability of the chorion in developing Fundulus eggs.

115. KEMPTON, R. T., Biol. Bull. *104*: 45-56, 1953. Physiology of dogfish kidney.

116. KERKUT, G. A., and TAYLOR, B. J. R., J. Exp. Biol. *33*: 493-501, 1956. Responses of pedal ganglion of slug to osmotic change.

117. KHALIL, F., and ABDEL-MESSEIH, G., J. Exp. Zool. *125*: 407-414, 1954. Water content of desert reptiles and mammals.

118. KINNE, O., Kieler Meeresforsch. *9*: 126-133, 134-150, 1952; Zool. Jahrb., Abt. Syst. *82*: 405-424, 1954; Zeitschr. Wiss. Zool. *157*: 427-491, 1953; Zool. Jahrb., Abt. Physiol. *64*: 183-206, 1953; Veroff. Inst. Meeresforsch. Bremerhavn *6*: 177-202, 1959. Systematics, ecology, and osmotic regulation in different salinities and temperatures, *Gammarus*.

119. KINNE, O., Zool. Jahrb., Abt. allg. *67*: 407-486, 1958; *in* Physiological Adaptation, edited by C. L. Prosser. Am. Physiol. Soc. 1958, pp. 92-106. Responses of hyroids to salinity and temperature.

120. KITCHING, J. A., J. Exp. Biol. *13*: 11-27, 1936; Biol. Rev. *13*: 403-444, 1938; J. Exp. Biol. *28*: 204-214, 1951; *29*: 363-371, 1952; *31*: 56-67, 68-75, 76-83, 1954; Symp. Soc. Exp. Biol. *8*: 63-75, 1954. Effects of respiratory inhibitors on and mechanisms of filling and emptying in contractile vacuoles of ciliates.

121. *KITCHING, J. A., Symp. Soc. Exp. Biol. *8*: 63-75, 1954; Protoplasmatologia *3*, D—3a, 1-54. Properties of contractile vacuoles in Protozoa.

121a. KITCHING, J. A., and PADFIELD, J. E., J. Exp. Biol. *37*: 73-82, 1960. Permeability of ciliates to heavy water.

122. KOCH, H. J., *in* Recent Developments in Cell Physiology, edited by J. A. Kitching. New York, Academic Press, 1954, pp. 15-27. Effects of enzyme inhibitors on sodium transport by crab gill.

123. KOCH, H. J., J. Exp. Biol. *15*: 152-160, 1938. Salt absorption by *Aedes*.

124. KOIZUMI, T., Sci. Rep. Tohoku Univ., Ser. IV, *7*: 259-311, 1932. Exchange of water and electrolytes in the holothurian Caudina.

125. KORR, I., J. Cell. Comp. Physiol. *13*: 175-193, 1939. Osmotic function of chicken kidney.

126. KOWALSKI, R., Kieler Meeresforsch. *11*: 201-213, 1955. Effects of salinity on starfish.

127. KRIJGSMAN, B. J., and KRIJGSMAN, N. E., Ztschr. vergl. Physiol. *37*: 78-81, 1954. Osmoreception in a marine crab.

128. *KROGH, A., Osmotic Regulation in Aquatic Animals. Cambridge University Press, 1939, 242 pp.

129. KROMHOUT, G. A., J. Morph. *72*: 167-177, 1943. Protonephridia of turbellarians.

130. LEES, A. D., J. Exp. Biol. *23*: 379-410, 1947. Transpiration, epicuticle, water balance, ticks.

131. LEVENBOOK, L., Biochem. J. *47*: 336-346, 1950. Blood composition Gastrophilus larva.

132. LEVINSKY, N. G., and BERLINER, R. W., Am. J. Physiol. *196*: 549-553, 1959. Absorption from mammalian bladder.

133. LILJESTRAND, G., and ZOTTERMAN, Y., Acta physiol. scand. *32*: 291-303, 1954. Water taste in mammals.

134. LILLY, S. J., J. Exp. Biol. *32*: 423-439, 1955. Osmoregulation in *Hydra*.

135. LINDEBORG, R. G., Contr. Lab. Vert. Biol. Univ. Mich. *58*: 1-32, 1952. Water requirements of different rodents.

136. LOVTRUP, S., and PIGON, A., C. R. Lab. Carlsberg Ser. Chim. *28*: 1-36, 1951.

137. MALOEUF, N. S. R., Ztschr. vergl. Physiol. *25*: 1-28, 1938. Osmotic adjustment in Mytilus and Asterias.

138. MALUF, N. S. R., Zool. Jahrb., Abt. allg. *59*: 515-534, 1939; J. Gen. Physiol. *24*: 151-167, 1940; Biol. Bull. *81*: 134-148, 1941. Anatomy of kidney, uptake of salts, urine formation, in crayfish.

139. MALVIN, R. L., WILDE, W. S., and SULLIVAN, L. P., Am. J. Physiol. *194*: 135-142, 1958; *197*: 177-180, 1959. Localization of nephron transport by stop-flow analysis.

140. MANTON, S. M., and RAMSAY, J. A., J. Exp. Biol. *14*: 470-472, 1937. Water loss from the onychophoran, Peripatopsis.

141. MARSHALL, E. K., Physiol. Rev. *14*: 133-159, 1934. Comparative physiology of the vertebrate kidney.

142. MARTIN, A. W., STEWART, D. M., and HARRISON, F. M., J. Cell. Comp. Physiol. *44*: 345, 1954. Excretion in *Achatina*.

143. *MARTIN, A. W., *in* Recent Advances in Invertebrate Physiology, edited by B. Scheer. University of Oregon Press, 1957, pp. 247-276. Ann. Rev. Physiol. *20*: 225-242, 1958. Renal function in invertebrates.

144. MASSMAN, W. H., Ecology *35*: 75-78, 1954. Distribution of fish in fresh and brackish water.

145. MAST, S. O., and FOWLER, C., J. Cell. Comp. Physiol. *6*: 151-167, 1935. Volume measurement, water permeability, *Amoeba proteus*.

146. McFARLAND, W. N., and MUNZ, F. W., Biol. Bull. *114*: 348-356, 1958. Osmotic properties of hagfish *Polistotrema*.

147. MORRIS, R., J. Exp. Biol. *33*: 235-248, 1956. Osmoregulation of lampern *(Lampetra)* during spawning migrations.

148. MORRISON, P. R., Biol. Bull. *91*: 181-188, 1946. Water loss by *Peripatus*.

149. MUDGE, G. H., Am. J. Physiol. *165*: 113-127, 1951; *167*: 206-223, 1951. Active transport of ions and water by rabbit kidney slices.

150. NAGEL, H., Ztschr. vergl. Physiol. *21*: 468-491, 1934. Osmoregulation in crustaceans.

151. *NEEDHAM, J., Chemical Embryology. Cambridge University Press, 1931, pp. 777-945; Biol. Rev. *13*: 225-251, 1937. Evolution of osmotic function.

152. ODUM, H., Bull. Mar. Sci. Gulf & Carib. *3*: 134-156, 1955. *Callinectes* in dilute brackish water.

153. OPIE, E. L., Harvey Lect. *50*: ('54-'55) 292-315, 1956. Intracellular and extracellular osmoconcentrations, liver.

154. PAGANELLI, C. V., and SOLOMON, A. K., J. Gen. Physiol. *41*: 259-277, 1957. Exchange of tritiated water across red cell membranes.

155. PANIKKAR, N. K., Nature *144*: 866-867, 1939. Osmotic behavior of Palaemonetes.

155a. PANIKKAR, N. K., and SPROSTON, N. G., Parasitology *33*: 214-223, 1941. Osmoconcentration of a parasitic copepod.

156. PAPPUS, G. D., and BRANDT, P., J. Biophys. Biochem. Cytol. *4*: 485-487, 1958. Electron microscopy of contractile vacuole in *Amoeba*.

157. PARRY, G., J. Exp. Biol. *30*: 567-574, 1953. Osmotic and ionic regulation in isopod *Ligia*.

158. PARRY, G., J. Exp. Biol. *31*: 218-227, 1954. Drinking of soil water by spiders.

159. PARRY, G., J. Exp. Biol. *31*: 601-613, 1954; *32*: 408-422, 1955. Urine production by *Palaemonetes*.

160. PARRY, G., J. Exp. Biol. *34*: 417-423, 1957. Osmoregulation of fresh-water prawns.

161. PARRY, G., Nature *183*: 1248-1249, 1959. Chloride cells in fish gills.

162. PEARSE, A. S., The Migrations of Animals from Sea to Land. Duke University Press, 1936, 176 pp.

163. PERTTUNEN, V., and ERKHILA, H., Nature *169*: 78, 1952. Humidity reactions, *Drosophila*.

164. PERTTUNEN, V., and SYRJÄMÄKI, J., Ann. Entomol. Fenn. *24*: 78-83, 1958. Humidity reactions and antennal receptors, *Drosophila*.

165. PETERS, H., Ztschr. Morph. Oecol. *30*: 355-381, 1935. Structure and function of excretory organs, crayfish and lobster.

166. PETERSEN, G. H., Nature *181*: 356-357, 1958. Salinity tolerance of two species of *Cardium*.

167. PETTUS, D., Copeia 1958, 207-211. Behavior differences between brackish- and fresh-water snakes.

168. PICKEN, L. E. R., J. Exp. Biol. *13*: 387-392, 1936. Osmotic concentration of cytoplasm of Spirostomum.

169. PICKEN, L. E. R., J. Exp. Biol. *14*: 20-34, 1937. Urine formation, fresh-water molluscs.

170. PICKERING, B. T., and HELLER, H.: Nature *184*: 1463, 1959. Identification of active ADH principle in cold-blooded vertebrates.

171. PITTENDRIGH, C. S., Evolution *4*: 43-63, 64-78, 1950. Humidity behavior and distribution of two species of *Anopheles*.

172. PITTENDRIGH, C. S., *in* Behavior and Evolution, edited by A. Rowe and G. Simpson. Yale University Press, 1958, pp. 300-416. Separation, two species of *Drosophila* by humidity behavior.

173. Portier, P., J. Physiol. Path. Gén. *12*: 202-208, 1910. Osmotic concentrations of blood of marine birds and mammals.

174. POTTS, W. T. W., J. Exp. Biol. *31*: 614-617, 618-630, 1954. Urine production in *Anodonta*: energetics of osmotic regulation in brackish and fresh-water animals.

175. PRESCOTT, D. M., and ZEUTHEN, E., Acta physiol. scand. *28*: 77-94, 1953. Water permeability of fresh-water eggs.

176. PROSSER, C. L., GREEN, J. W., and CHOW, T. J., Biol. Bull. *109*: 99-107, 1955. Ionic regulation in *Pachygrapsus*.

177. RAMSAY, J. A., J. Exp. Biol. *26*: 46-56, 65-75, 1949. Osmotic relations and hypotonic urine formation, *Lumbricus*.

178. RAMSAY, J. A., J. Exp. Biol. *27*: 145-157, 1950; *28*: 62-73, 1951. Osmoregulation and excretion, mosquito larvae.

179. RAMSAY, J. A., J. Exp. Biol. *31*: 104-113, 1954; *32*: 200-216, 1955. Excretion of ions and water by malpighian tubes of *Dixippus*.

179a. REMANE, A., and SCHLIEPER, C., Die Biologie des Brackwassers. Stuttgart, Schweizerbartsche, 1958, 348 pp.

180. RHODIN, J., Internat. Rev. Cytol. *7*: 485-534, 1958; Am. J. Med. *24*: 661-675, 1958. Electron microscopy of kidney tubules.

181. RIBBANDS, C. R., Ann. Trop. Med., Parasitol. *38*: 87-99, 1944. Salinity differences, two species of *Anopheles*.

182. *RICHARDS, A. G., The Integument of Arthropods, University of Minnesota Press, 1951, 441 pp.

183. RICHARDS, G., CLAUSEN, M. B., and SMITH, M., J. Cell. Comp. Physiol. *42*: 395-414, 1953. Permeability of arthropod cuticle.

184. RIEGEL, J. A., Biol. Bull. *116*: 272-284, 1959. Salinity differences, two species sphaeromid isopods.

185. RIEGEL, J. A., and KIRSCHNER, L. B., Biol. Bull. *118*: 296-307, 1960. Inulin and glucose excretion by crayfish.

186. ROBERTSON, J. D., J. Exp. Biol. *31*: 424-442, 1954. Blood composition of fish.

187. ROBERTSON, J. D., *in* Physiology of Invertebrate Animals, edited by B. Scheer. University of Oregon Press, 1957, pp. 229-246. Ion balance in invertebrates.

188. ROBERTSON, J. D., Biol. Rev. *32*: 156-187, 1957. Habitat of the early vertebrates.

189. ROBINSON, J. R., Proc. Roy. Soc. London, *B, 137*: 378-402, 1950; *140*: 135-144, 1952; Biol. Rev. *28*: 158-194, 1953; Symp. Soc. Exp. Biol. *8*: 42-62, 1954. Evidence for active transport of water from tissue cells.

190. ROMER, A. S., and GROVE, B. H., Am. Midl. Nat. *16*: 805-856, 1935. Habitat of early vertebrates.

191. ROOTS, B. I., J. Exp. Biol. *32*: 765-774, 1955; *33*: 29-44, 1956. Water relations of earthworms.

192. ROTH, L. M., and WILLIS, E. R., J. Exp. Zool. *116*: 527-570; *117*: 451-488, 1951; *118*: 337-362, 1951; J. Morphol. *91*: 1-14, 1952. Hygroreceptors and humidity responses of *Tenebrio, Tribolium, Aedes,* and *Blatella*.

193. ROWLANDS, A., J. Exp. Biol. *31*: 151-160, 1954. Effects of pituitary on water uptake, toad.

194. RUDZINSKA, M. A., J. Biophys. Biochem. Cytol. *4*: 195-202, 1958. Electron microscopy of contractile vacuoles of a suctorian.

195. RUDZINSKA, M. A., and CHAMBERS, R., Biol. Bull. *100*: 49-58, 1951. Contractile vacuole activity in a suctorian.

196. SAWYER, W. H.: Am. J. Physiol. *164*: 44-48, 1950; *189*: 564-568, 1957. Effects of pituitary principles on water permeability and excretion, amphibians.

197. SAWYER, W. H., Endocrinology *66*: 112-120, 1960; Nature *184*: 1464, 1959; Fed. Proc. *19*: 167, 1960. Identification of active ADH principle in cold-blooded vertebrates.

198. SAWYER, W. H., *in* The Neurohypophysis, edited by H. Heller. New York, Academic Press, 1957, pp. 171-180. Mechanism of action of hypophys-

eal hormones from various vertebrates on amphibian kidney.

199. SAWYER, W. H., and SAWYER, M. R., Physiol. Zool. *25*: 84-98, 1952. Mechanism of action of hypophyseal hormones from various vertebrates on amphibian kidney.

200. SAWYER, W. H., TRAVIS, D. F., and LEVINSKY, N. G., Am. J. Physiol. *163*: 364-369, 1950. Effects of pituitary principles on water permeability and excretion, amphibians.

201. *SCHLIEPER, C., Biol. Rev. *10*: 334-359, 1935; Ztschr. vergl. Physiol. *9*: 478-514, 1929. Osmotic regulation in aquatic animals.

202. SCHLIEPER, C., Die Naturwiss. *40*: 538-539, 1953; Kieler Meeresforsch. *11*: 22-33, 1955. Physiological adjustment of tissues of *Mytilus* from different salinities.

203. SCHLIEPER, C., and KOWALSKI, R., Kieler Meeresforsch. *12*: 154-165, 1956; *8*: 3-20, 1957. Physiological adjustment of tissues of *Mytilus* from different salinities.

204. SCHMIDT-NIELSEN, B., Am. J. Physiol. *170*: 45-56, 1952. Urea excretion by tubules of kangaroo rats.

205. *SCHMIDT-NIELSEN, B., Physiol. Rev. *38*: 139-168, 1958; Fed. Proc. *15*: 163, 1956. Countercurrent principle in kidney function; urea excretion.

206. SCHMIDT-NIELSEN, B., and FORSTER, R. P., J. Cell. Comp. Physiol. *44*: 233-246, 1954. Dehydration and temperature effects on renal function in frog.

207. SCHMIDT-NIELSEN, B., and SCHMIDT-NIELSEN, K., Am. J. Physiol. *160*: 291-294, 1950; J. Cell. Comp. Physiol. *38*: 165-186, 1951. Water balance in kangaroo rats.

208. SCHMIDT-NIELSEN, B., and SCHMIDT-NIELSEN, K., Ecology *31*: 75-85, 1950; Am. J. Physiol. *162*: 31-36, 1950. Evaporative water loss from desert mammals.

209. SCHMIDT-NIELSEN, B., SCHMIDT-NIELSEN, K., HOUPT, T. R., and JARNUM, S. A., Am. J. Physiol. *185*: 185-194, 1955. Water balance, camel.

210. SCHMIDT-NIELSEN, K., and FÄNGE, R., Nature *182*: 783-785, 1958. Salt glands in marine reptiles.

211. SCHMIDT-NIELSEN, K., JORGENSEN, C. B., and OSAKI, H., Am. J. Physiol. *193*: 101-107, 1958. Excretion by salt gland of birds.

212. *SCHMIDT-NIELSEN, K., and SCHMIDT-NIELSEN, B., Physiol. Rev. *32*: 135-166, 1952. Water metabolism of desert mammals. Also *in* Biology of Deserts, edited by J. L. Cloudsley-Thompson. Institute of Biology, London, 1954, p. 73.

213. SCHOFFENIELS, E., Arch. Internat. Physiol. *58*: 1-4, 1950. Osmotic concentration and chlorides in dragonfly nymphs.

214. SCHOLANDER, P. F., *et al.*, J. Cell. Comp. Physiol. *49*: 5-24, 1957. Osmoconcentration in arctic fish.

215. SCHOLLES, W., Ztschr. vergl. Physiol. *19*: 552-554, 1933. Ionic regulation in *Astacus* and *Eriocheir*.

216. SCHWABE, E., Ztschr. vergl. Physiol. *19*: 183-236, 1933. Osmoregulation in crabs.

217. SHAPIRO, H., J. Gen. Physiol. *32*: 43-51, 1948. Osmotically inactive volume in sea urchin eggs.

218. SHAW, J., J. Exp. Biol. *32*: 353-384, 1955. Ionic and water balance in aquatic larvae of *Sialis*.

219. SHAW, J., J. Exp. Biol. *36*: 126-144, 157-176, 1959. Osmoregulation in fresh-water crayfish and crab, *Astacus,* and *Potamon*.

220. SIDEL, V. W., and SOLOMON, A. K., J. Gen. Physiol. *41*: 243-257, 1957. Penetration of water into erythrocytes.

221. *SMITH, H. W., Quart. Rev. Biol. *7*: 1-26, 1932. Evolution of fish kidneys.

222. *SMITH, H. W., Biol. Rev. *11*: 49-82, 1936. Osmotic function of retained urea in elasmobranchs.

223. *SMITH, H. W., The Kidney. New York, Oxford University Press, 1951, 1049 pp.

224. *SMITH, H. W., From Fish to Philosopher. Boston, Little, Brown & Co., 1953, 264 pp.

225. *SMITH, H. W., Principles of Renal Physiology. Oxford University Press, 1956, 237 pp.

226. SMITH, R. I., Biol. Bull. *108*: 326-345, 1955; *109*: 453-474, 1955; J. Mar. Biol. Assn. U.K. *34*: 33-46, 1955; *35*: 81-104, 1956. Chloride regulation of *Nereis diversicolor* from different salinities and localities.

227. SMITH, R. I., Biol. Bull. *105*: 335-347, 1953. Distribution of *Neanthes lighti*.

228. *SMITH, R. I., (Roscoff Symposium) Union Internat. Sci. Biol. Ser. B., No. 24; Biologie comparée des espèces marines 93-107, 1958. Adaptations of nereid worms to different salinities.

229. SPENCER, J. O., and EDNEY, E. B., J. Exp. Biol. *31*: 491-496, 1954. Absorption of water by land isopods.

230. STEGGERDA, F. R., Proc. Soc. Exp. Biol. Med. *36*: 103-106, 1937. Effect of Pituitrin on water uptake by amphibians.

231. *STURKIE, P. D., Avian Physiology. Ithaca, N. Y., Comstock Press, 1954, Chapt. 13, pp. 206-228. Excretion in birds.

231a. SUTCLIFFE, D. W., Nature *187*: 331-332, 1960. Osmoregulation in aquatic dipteran larvae.

232. SVETLOV, P., Arch. Entwick. *114*: 771-785, 1929. Osmoconcentration of fish embryos.

233. THOMSON, R. C. M., Bull. Ent. Res. *36*: 185-252, 1945. Selection of saline breeding places by *Anopheles*.

234. THORSON, T. B., Ecology *36*: 100-116, 1955; Copeia 230-236, 1956. Distribution of amphibians as correlated with tolerance of desiccation.

235. THORSON, T. B., and SVIHLA, A., Ecology *24*: 374-381, 1943. Distribution of amphibians as correlated with tolerance of desiccation.

236. TREHERNE, J. E., Trans. Roy. Ent. Soc. London *105*: 117-130, 1954. Osmoregulation in aquatic larvae of beetles.

237. *USSING, H. H., Adv. Enzymol. *13*: 21-65, 1952. Permeability of amoebae and frog skin to water.

238. VAN BRINK, J. M., and RIETSEMA, J., Physiol. Comp. Oecol. *1*: 348-351, 1949. Active absorption of chloride by *Lumbricus*.

239. VAN WEEL, P. B., Ztschr. vergl. Physiol. *39*: 492-506, 1957. Osmoregulation and volume control in *Aplysia*.

240. VERNEY, E. B., Proc. Roy. Soc. London, *B. 135*: 25-106, 1947. Osmoreceptors, mammals.
241. VON EULER, C., Acta physiol. scand. *29*: 133-136, 1953. Electrical responses of hypothalamus to saline.
242. WALKER, A. M., *et al.,* Am. J. Physiol. *134*: 562-579, 1941. Micropuncture of mammalian kidney tubules.
243. WEARN, J. T., and RICHARDS, S. N., Am. J. Physiol. *71*: 209-227, 1924. Glomerular filtrate of frog.
244. WEIL, E., and PANTIN, C. F. A., J. Exp. Biol. *8*: 73-81, 1931. Adaptations of *Gunda* to salinity.
245. WEINSTEIN, P. P., Exp. Parasitol. *1*: 363-376, 1952. Excretory function in nematode larvae.
246. WERNTZ, H., To be published. Physiological ecology of gammarids.
247. WESSON, L. G., and ANSLOW, U. P., Am. J. Physiol. *170*: 255-269, 1952. Control of urine concentration in mammalian kidney.
248. WHITTEMBURY, G., OKU, D. E., WINDHAGER, E. E., and SOLOMON, A. K., Am. J. Physiol. *197*: 1121-1127, 1959. Water permeability of *Necturus* kidney tubules.
249. WIGGLESWORTH, V. B., J. Exp. Biol. *8*: 411-451, 1931. Excretion in *Rhodnius*.
250. WIGGLESWORTH, V. B., J. Exp. Biol. *21*: 97-114, 1945. Evaporative loss from insects.
251. *WIGGLESWORTH, V. B., J. Exp. Biol. *10*: 16-26, 1933; *15*: 235-247, 1938; Principles of insect physiology. London, Methuen & Co., 1939, 434

pp. Osmotic and ionic control in mosquito larvae.
252. WIKGREN, B. J., Acta Zool. Fennica *71*: 1-102, 1953. Osmotic regulation in lampreys.
253. WILLIS, E. R., and ROTH, L. M., J. Exp. Zool. *115*: 561-587, 1950. Humidity reactions, *Tribolium*.
254. WIRZ, H., HARGISTY, B., and KUHN, W., Acta Helvetica Physiol. *9*: 196-207, 1951. Concentrating mechanism in the mammalian kidney.
255. WOLBARSHT, M. L., Science *125*: 1248, 1957. Water taste in *Phormia*.
256. WOLF, A. V., *in* Thirst, Physiology of the Urge to Drink and Problems of Water Lack. Springfield, Ill., Charles C Thomas, 1958, pp. 340-372.
257. WOLF, A. V., *et al.,* Am. J. Physiol. *196*: 633-641, 1951; *196*: 625-632, 1959. Utilization of sea water by cats.
258. YOUNG, E. G., and Dreyer, N. B., Am. J. Physiol. *49*: 162-180, 1933. Excretion of uric acid by birds.
259. ZEUTHEN, G., Ztschr. vergl. Physiol. *26*: 537-547, 1939. Osmotic concentration of sponges in hibernation.
260. ZOTTERMAN, Y., Acta physiol. scand. *18*: 181-189, 1949; Experientia *6*: 57-58, 1950. Water taste in frog.
261. ZOTTERMAN, Y., Acta physiol. scand. *37*: 60-70, 1956. Water taste in mammals.
262. ZWICKY, K., Ztschr. vergl. Physiol. *36*: 367-390, 1954. Osmotic concentrations in larvae of *Drosophila*.

Chapter 3

INORGANIC IONS

The osmotic concentration of a solution depends on the total number of solute particles irrespective of kind; we shall now consider how animals select particular inorganic ions from their environment. In discussing osmotic mechanisms, some consideration of the most abundant ions in body fluids, the chlorides, was necessary, but the emphasis in ionic regulation is on selection or exclusion of specific elements. Many animals which conform osmotically to their environment regulate ionically; hence ionic regulation is a more general and primitive capacity than osmotic regulation.

There is little relation between abundance and availability of elements, and only indirect correlation between availability and biological utilization. Ninety per cent of protoplasm is composed of carbon, hydrogen, and oxygen. Nitrogen, although present in far greater amount in the atmosphere than is oxygen or carbon, is less used. In large part, the chemical properties of an element determine its biological usefulness. Metals have special uses, and the most abundant elements in the earth's crust, such as silicon and aluminum, have limited biological application. Marine animals tend to accumulate a higher proportion of potassium than sodium from sea water and to exclude magnesium and sulfate, which are abundant sea ions. The concentration of hydrogen ions tends to be higher in body fluids than in surrounding aqueous media. In the following discussion inorganic elements are considered as ions behaving as they would in solutions of comparable concentrations, although in body fluids unknown and variable amounts are bound to organic molecules.

IONS IN INTRACELLULAR AND EXTRACELLULAR FLUIDS

All cells appear to have an inorganic composition different from the fluids which bathe them, that is, cell membranes selectively regulate cytoplasmic ion composition. As examples of isolated cells, sea urchin eggs and red blood cells may be cited (Table 3). Unfertilized sea urchin eggs contain some twenty times more potassium and some nine times less sodium than sea water; the sum of cations is 292 mEq/kg_{H_2O}, of inorganic anions is less than 100 mEq; the necessary anionic balance is given by phosphates and organic anions.[142] Red blood cells usually contain higher concentrations of potassium than the plasma, although in some species (cat and dog) they have relatively more sodium. In some strains of sheep the red cells change from potassium to sodium predominance early in development; this character is inherited in mendelian ratios.[54] Most orders of mammals have high K^+ red cells, Artiodactyla vary, and carnivores tend to have high Na^+ red cells.[182]

In compact tissues of multicellular animals the extracellular space can be estimated by measuring the concentration in a tissue of some substance which does not readily penetrate cells and which is not rapidly excreted or stored. Inulin and thiocyanate have been used. On the assumption that the extracellular concentration is the same as in the plasma, one can calculate the volume such a concentration would occupy in the tissue. For example, the inulin space in a rat kidney is 16.7 per cent and in a guinea pig kidney 21 per cent of the total volume.[40] In some tissues, as striated muscle, the chloride concentration inside cells is very low, and chloride can be readily replaced by other ions like sulfate; in these tissues the chloride space is similar to extracellular space. However, in other tissues, e.g., connective tissues, there is much intracellular chloride. From the total analysis of a muscle and the measurement of the extracellular space, the intracellular concentrations of certain ions can be calculated (Table 3).

In striated muscle and in peripheral nerve of all animals which have been examined the chloride is mainly extracellular, the sodium is lower inside and the potassium much higher inside the fibers. Most of the calcium and magnesium of muscle is inside the fibers. The ratio of calcium inside to that outside in squid and crab nerves is much less than in vertebrate nerves.[92] In frog skeletal muscle calcium is mainly in the A band and excitation is accompanied by an influx of Na^+ and Ca^{++} and an outflux of K^+ (Chapter 14). The sum of the cations is normally in excess of the readily measured anions; this could result from cationic or anionic binding to proteins, the presence of quantities of organic acids (anions), and Donnan equilibrium.

Invertebrate muscles, like most vertebrate muscles and nerves, contain much phosphate, but crustacean and molluscan nerves are low in phosphate and high in organic acids; the free amino acids in *Carcinus* nerve fibers amount to 25 per cent of the dry weight[106] and about 25 per cent of the total osmoconcentration. In muscle of the crustacean, *Nephrops,* organic phosphates constitute more than half the anions and some 10 per cent of the osmoconcentration, amino acids nearly half the osmoconcentration, and trimethylamine oxide 7 per cent.[138] Nerves of marine crustaceans and molluscs have more than 20 per cent of dry weight as aspartic and glutamic acids or other amino acids.[106] In the giant nerve fibers of the squid the total cations amount to 520 mEq/gm; chloride and phosphates 185 mEq; aspartic, glutamic,

TABLE 3. CONCENTRATIONS OF IONS IN TISSUES AND BODY FLUIDS mM/KG EXCEPT WHERE STATED OTHERWISE

Animal	Tissues	Na	K	Ca	Mg	Cl	SO₄	
Sea urchin[142]	unfertilized eggs	52.0	210.0	4.0	11.0	80.0	6.0	
(*Paracentrotus*)								mM/Kg_{H_2O}
	sea water	485.0	10.0	11.0	55.0	566.0	29.0	
Man[150]	red blood cells	10.0	105.0		5.5	80.0		
	serum	143.0	5.0	5.0	2.2	103.0	1.0	
Dog[1, 113, 157]	red blood cells	97.0	8.0		3.7	65.0		
	muscle	24.8	96.0		18.0	16.3		
	liver	33.8	81.3		16.0	33.2		
	serum	150.5	5.3		1.8	108.0		
Rat[41]	whole muscle	26.6	101.4	1.5	11.0	16.3		
	plasma	145.0	6.2	3.1	1.6	116.0		
Frog[41]	whole muscle	23.9	84.6	2.5	11.3	10.5	0.3	
	muscle fiber water	15.5	126.0	3.3	16.7	1.2		mM/l_{H_2O}
	plasma	103.8	2.5	2.0	1.2	74.3	1.9	
Frog[81]	muscle							
	intracellular	9.2	140.0					
	extracellular	120.0	2.5					
Carcinus[146]	whole muscle		120.0	13.8	35.8	54.0		
	muscle fiber	54.0	112.0	5.2	16.9	53.0		
	blood	468.0	12.1	17.5	23.6	524.0		
Squid[113]	nerve		244.0					
	muscle	53.6	113.7			71.0		
	blood	354.0	16.6			469.0		
Eledone[77]	muscle	81.0	101.0	3.7	12.7	93.0		
	blood	425.0	12.2	11.6	57.2	480.0	43.1	
Fresh-water crab[148]	muscle	44.0	111.0			32.0		
(*Potamon*)								
Aplysia[77]	muscle	325.0	47.8	16.7	95.5	378.0		
	blood	492.0	9.7	13.3	49.0	543.0	28.2	
Buccinium[77]	muscle	62.6	82.1	7.8	35.0	121.0		
	blood	413.0	7.7	10.6	42.0		24.9	
Anodonta[77]	muscle	5.2	10.5	5.4	2.5	10.6		
	blood	15.4	0.38	5.3	0.35	10.5	1.5	
Caudina[98]	muscle	191.0	138.0	89.0	39.0	122.0	65.0	
	blood cells	202.0	176.0	6.9	14.5	126.0	131.0	
	plasma	460.0	11.8	10.7	50.5	523.0	29.0	
Nephrops[138]	muscle whole	83.0	167.0	5.2	19.1	109.9	3.1	
	intracellular	27.0	177.0	3.8	20.2	56.0	2.0	mM/Kg_{H_2O}
	blood plasma	504.0	8.6	13.9	10.2			

fumaric, and succinic acids total only 95 mEq; there is present, however, isothionic acid (2-hydroxyethane-sulfonic acid) to the extent of 230 mEq/gm.[96] In muscle there are carbohydrate energy stores, and also adenosine and creatinine or arginine which are used in energy transfer; in many muscles there is carnitine, and in molluscan and crustacean muscles such substances as taurine, betaine, and trimethylamine which contribute osmotically and anionically. In muscles of a fresh-water clam, chloride concentration is only one-third the sum of the cations.[77]

The tendency of cells to accumulate potassium and to exclude sodium and chloride ions is very general in animals and plants. In marine algae the vacuolar sap differs from the cytoplasm, and both differ from sea water in respect to all elements. Root cells of growing plants take up nitrate against a steep concentration gradient. In general, plants do not need Na^+, at least not in such amount as animals, and plants contain more K^+, while in animals the amounts of Na^+ and K^+ are nearly equal. Hence herbivorous animals tend to have a high K^+ diet and carnivorous ones eat relatively more Na^+. A ciliate, *Spirostomum,* concentrates K^+ and actively pumps Na^+ out.[33] Growing cells add and accumulate certain ions, nongrowing cells maintain a steady state in which there is a continuous exchange of ions in and out.

In cellular activity the distribution of ions changes; for example, when a nerve fiber conducts an impulse, potassium moves out and sodium moves in (Chapter 21). The mechanisms by which ionic gradients are maintained across cell membranes is a field of active interest in cellular physiology. In general, some ions such as chloride and potassium tend to distribute themselves passively according to the electrical field, the membrane permeability, and the equilibrium imposed by nonpenetrating protein anions inside the cell. Other ions, such as sodium, are actively transported in one direction (usually outward) in opposition to their normal diffusion gradient. Ions such as potassium, which appear on analytical evidence to be passively distributed, may in fact be actively transported, since their distribution changes when metabolism is slowed. Ionic distribution may be regulated hormonally; the adrenal cortex is important for K-Na balance, and blood of adrenalectomized rats contains more K^+ and less Na^+ than does that of normal rats. Relatively more of cellular Ca^{++} and Mg^{++} is bound than of

univalent cations. Sodium is widely used in animals in maintenance of osmotic pressure and of membrane excitability; high potassium uniformly depresses membrane potentials. Cs^+ and Rb^+ are similar to and can partly substitute for K^+; Li^+ can partly substitute for Na^+. Our present concern, however, is not with ionic regulation at the cellular level, but rather with the ionic concentrations in body fluids of animals as related to their environment.

IONS IN BODY FLUIDS

Sea Water. Since the sea is the ancestral animal home and since sponges and cnidarians and, to some extent, echinoderms use sea water as a body fluid, one might expect a correspondence between sea salts and body fluids. It was formerly believed that the oceans had changed in composition since the Cambrian, and that specialized animals, especially those with closed circulations, might resemble in ionic proportions the ocean at the time their ancestors' circulation became closed. Current evidence is that the composition of the seas has been relatively constant throughout animal evolution. There may have been a small increase in sodium and total salinity in the ocean, but precipitated calcium carbonate is replenished by inflow from rivers.[38, 143, 180]

The ratio of K to Na in material leached from rocks is approximately 1.0, but more K is adsorbed on soil particles. Hence there is much less K than Na in sea water.

Harvey[76] gives a good summary of the chemistry of the sea, and Barnes[7] gives tables which are useful for computing the concentration of each of the common ions at different salinities. As a reference for considering body fluids, the composition of an "average" sea water is given in Table 4. The pH is determined largely by the ratio of H_2CO_3 to HCO_3^- and may be taken as 8.16 in equilibrium with air.

Extracellular Fluids. Ions in body fluids are sometimes presented as concentrations (mol/l_{H_2O}) and sometimes as ratios of abundance to some relatively universal reference such as chloride. The concentrations of different ions in the body fluids of an animal may vary with season and temperature, with physiological state, sex, age, and nutrition; in many animals, particularly ionic conformers, the ions vary with the medium. The total osmoconcentration and the blood conductivity of male *Carcinus* are greater than in females.[61] The blood of a crayfish in May-June

TABLE 4. COMPOSITION OF "AVERAGE" SEA WATER[7, 141]

	$mM/l_{s.w.}$	gm/kg_{H_2O}
Salinity 34.33 $^0/_{00}$ ⎱ 20°C Chlorinity 19 $^0/_{00}$ ⎰		
Sodium	470.2	10.933
Magnesium	53.57	1.317
Calcium	10.23	0.414
Potassium	9.96	0.394
Strontium	0.156	0.014
Chloride	548.3	19.657
Sulfate	28.25	2.744
Bromide	0.828	0.067
Borate as H_3BO_3	0.431	0.027
Bicarbonate	2.344	0.145
Osmotic equivalence ⎰ 0.557 M NaCl ⎱ 0.949 M sucrose		

has a higher concentration of Na^+ and a lower concentration of Ca^{++} than in January-February.[47] Fresh-water brown trout have higher concentrations of blood ions in winter than in summer.[65] The blood of butterflies in the larval stage contains more Mg^{++} and Cl^- but less K^+ and phosphate than the pupae.[26] Hence absolute concentrations of

TABLE 5. CONCENTRATIONS OF IONS IN BODY FLUIDS (MM/L BLOOD EXCEPT WHERE STATED OTHERWISE)

Animal	Na	K	Ca	Mg	Cl	SO_4	Protein (mg/ml)
Marine Invertebrates							
Coelenterate							
Aurelia[136] mM/l_{H_2O}	454	10.2	9.7	51.0	554	14.58	0.4
sea water	459	9.78	10.05	52.5	538	26.55	
Echinoderms							
Marthasterias[136] mM/l_{H_2O}	459	10.8	10.1	51.2	540	26.5	0.6
Holothuria[136] mM/l_{H_2O}	489	10.7	11.0	58.5	573	28.4	0.7
Echinus[136] mM/l_{H_2O}	444	9.6	9.9	50.2	522	34.0	
Sipunculids							
Phascolosoma[136] mM/l_{H_2O}	508	11.5	11.2	38.8	561	26.8	0.9
Annelids							
Aphrodite[136]	456	12.3	10.05	51.7	538	26.5	0.9
Arenicola[136]	459	10.1	10.0	52.4	537	24.4	0.2
Molluscs							
Mytilus[124] mM/l_{H_2O}	502	12.5	12.5	55.6	585	29.4	1.2-1.7
Ostrea	544	14.7	10.9				
Aplysia[77]	492	9.7	13.3	49.0	543	28.2	
Sepia[136] mM/l_{H_2O}	460	23.7	10.75	56.9	589	4.7	109
Arthropods							
Lithodes[138] mM/l_{H_2O}	476	12.4	12.3	52.2	536	24.7	
Nephrops[138] mM/l_{H_2O}	518	7.6	13.8	8.9	520	17.8	42
Palinurus[138] mM/l_{H_2O}	545	10.3	13.4	16.6	557	20.5	
Homarus[29]	472	10	15.6	6.8	470		
Maja[136] mM/l_{H_2O}	500	12.7	13.9	45.2	569	14.3	53
Carcinus[146]	468	12.1	17.5	23.6	524		40
Geocarcinus	539	9.9	25.6	66.7	483	19.9	
Pachygrapsus[126]	465	12.1	11.4	29.2			35
Palaemon[122]	394	7.7	12.6	12.6	430	2.6	
Ligia[121]	586	14	36	21	596	4.5	
Uca[69]	328	11	16	46	537	42	
Fresh-Water Molluscs							
Anodonta mM/l blood[48]	13.9	0.28	11.0	0.31	12.0		(pH 7.5) 3.0
F.W. medium	0.48	0.059	2.7	0.375			
Anodonta[124] mM/l_{H_2O}	15.55	0.487	8.4	0.19	11.7	0.73	

TABLE 5—(*Continued*)

Animal	Na	K	Ca	Mg	Cl	SO$_4$	Protein (mg/ml)
Fresh-Water Crustacea							
Cambarus[115]	146	3.9	8.1	4.3	139		
F.W. medium[115]	0.65	0.01	2.0	0.21	0.48		
Asellus[108]	137	7.4			125		
Nematodes							
Ascaris[80]	129	24.6	5.9	4.9	52.7		
Annelids							
Lumbricus[130, 141a]							
blood	105	8.9			43		
coelomic fluid	83.2	12.4			46		
Insects							
Orthoptera							
Dixippus[128] mEq	8.7	27.5	16.2	145	93	(pH 6.6)	10
Locusta[84]	109	20					
Locusta[49, 58]	60	12	17	25			
Chortophaga adult[11]	109	3.46	2.85	21.5			2.5
Periplaneta[3]	161	7.9	4.0	5.6	144	(pH 7.5)	
Odonata							
Libellula[49, 58]	178	3.8	18.4	12			
Diptera							
Calliphora[49, 58]	140	26	21	34			
Gastrophilus larva[105]	175	11.5	2.84	15.9	14.9	(pH 6.8)	107.5
Tipula larva[49, 58]	85	8.2	12.3	16			
Sialis[147]	109	5	7.5	19	31		
Chironomus larvae[49, 58]	104	2.1	10	15			
Aedes larvae[156]	100	4.2			51.3		
F.W. medium	2	.66			3.9		
Lepidoptera							
Ephestia[49, 58]	33	33	41	51			
Samia pupa[11]	2.59	42	9.4	32.6			42.9
Hymenoptera[49, 58]							
Bombyx[48]	14	46	24	81			60
Apis[49, 58]	11	31	18	21			
Coleoptera							
Leptinotarsa[49, 58]	3.5	55	47	188			
Popillia[110]	20	10	16	39	19		
Vertebrates							
Cyclostomes							
Myxine (S.W.)[137]							
mM/l$_{H_2O}$	558	9.6	6.25	19.4	576	6.6	
Lampetra (F.W.)[137]							
mM/l$_{H_2O}$	119.6	3.2	1.96	2.1	95.9	2.72	
Hagfish Polistotrema	450				500		
Elasmobranchs							
Raja (S.W.)[75]	254	8	6	2.5	255		
Narcine[144]	134	7	12	3	159		.
Rhinobatus[144]	143	12.8	7.3	2	143.6		
Teleosts							
Lophius (S.W.)[27]	185-200	5	6	5	153		
Muraena (S.W.)[137]							
mM/l whole blood	211.8	1.95	3.86	2.42	188.4	5.67	80
Coregonus (S.W.)[137]							
mM/l$_{H_2O}$	140.9	3.81	2.67	1.69	116.8	2.29	41.9
Mackerel[14]	188	9.8			167		35.
Barracuda[14]	215	6.4			189		33.
Sea Water[14]	445	9.8			537		
Brown Trout (F.W.)[65]	149.3	5.1			140.5		
Birds and Mammals							
Chicken[1]	154	6.0	5.6	2.3	122		
White-tailed deer[177]	174	10.4			101		
Rat[39]	145	6.2	3.1	1.6	116		59
Man[99]	145	5.1	2.5	1.2	103	2.5	66
	139	4.2	5.2	1.7	103	1.2	
Dog[1]	150	4.4	5.3	1.8	106	2.0	58

TABLE 6. RATIOS OF BLOOD TO MEDIUM (i/o)

Animal	Na	K	Ca	Mg	Cl	SO₄
Spirostomum[33]	0.4	10.8			0.1	
Holothuria[136]	1.008	1.03	1.02	1.04	1.00	1.00
Phascolosoma[136]	1.04	1.10	1.04	0.69	0.98	0.91
Aphrodite[136]	0.99	1.26	1.0	0.988	1.00	0.999
Arenicola[136]	1.00	1.03	0.998	1.00	0.997	0.92
Carcinus[146]	1.02	0.95	1.23	0.42	0.98	
Carcinus[171]	1.11	1.21	1.27	0.36	0.998	0.572
Palaemon[122]	0.85	0.85	1.05	0.20	0.85	0.10
Pachygrapsus[126]	1.01	1.23	1.14	0.56		
Uca[69]	0.83	1.22	1.33	0.52	0.93	1.91
Homarus[29]	1.07	1.0	1.68	0.133	0.94	
Ligia[121]	1.18	1.30	3.32	0.37	1.03	0.14
Ascaris[80]	1.04	0.92	1.3	0.89	0.86	
Phallusia[137]	0.99	1.00	0.93	0.988	1.036	0.525
Salpa[137]	1.003	1.129	0.959	0.949	1.024	0.649
Myxine[137]	1.10	0.896	0.563	0.335	0.973	0.217
Muraena[137]	0.38	0.16	0.31	0.04	0.29	0.17

elements mean little unless the condition of the animal is stated. However, for reference a few typical recent values are given in Table 5; more detailed tables are given in the first edition of this book and in reference 1.

Deviations from conformity to the aquatic environment are indicated by the ratios of internal to external concentrations of particular ions (Table 6). A more satisfactory way to indicate ionic regulation in marine animals is to compare the blood concentration before and after dialysis against sea water (Table 7). Any differences between dialyzed blood and sea water result from protein binding of ions; differences between normal blood and dialyzed blood indicate regulation by the animal.

Marine Invertebrates. All marine animals have a relatively constant hydrogen ion concentration which is more acid (pH 7.2 to 7.8) than sea water (pH 8.0 to 8.1). Most of the measurements are on body fluids drained in air; hence because of the loss of CO_2 the recorded pH may be a little higher than that

TABLE 7. RATIO OF UNDIALYZED BLOOD TO BLOOD DIALYZED AGAINST SEA WATER
(From Robertson[136] except where indicated)

Animal	Na	K	Ca	Mg	Cl	SO₄
Coelenterate						
Aurelia	0.99	1.05	0.96	0.99	1.03	0.55
Echinoderm						
Marthasterias	1.0	1.12	1.0	0.98	1.0	1.0
Molluscs						
Pecten	0.997	1.97	1.025	0.973	1.00	0.965
Mya	1.008	1.067	1.066	0.99	.999	1.01
Ensis	0.987	1.55	1.076	0.987	.992	0.86
Buccinium	0.973	1.419	1.043	1.028	.996	0.900
Pleurobranchus	1.001	1.171	1.117	0.994	.996	1.017
Eledone	0.973	1.521	1.071	1.027	1.017	0.772
Ostrea	0.995	1.291	1.006	1.023	.998	0.997
Mytilus	1.00	1.347	0.995	0.995	1.005	0.982
Archidoris	0.987	1.281	1.317	1.073	1.002	0.963
Sepia	0.925	2.052	0.905	0.981	1.051	0.221
Crustaceans						
Lithodes	1.03	1.27	1.12	0.97	1.03	1.04
Nephrops	1.13	0.79	1.24	0.167	.99	0.69
Palinurus	1.10	0.98	1.07	0.293	1.01	0.74
Carcinus[171]	1.096	1.176	1.079	0.34	1.036	0.607
Squilla	1.11	1.29	1.08	0.32	1.01	0.82
Eupagurus	1.05	1.30	1.37	0.49	.96	1.35
Maja	1.00	1.25	1.22	0.81	1.02	0.66
Portunus	1.05	1.34	1.11	0.47	.97	0.78
Pachygrapsus	0.94	0.95	0.92	0.24	.87	0.46

inside the animal. Most marine animals maintain their blood 0.5 to 1 pH unit more acid than the sea.

In echinoderms the coelomic fluid in representatives of all classes which have been examined is more similar to sea water than in any other phylum. Their only ionic regulation is a slightly higher K^+ concentration and a higher H^+ concentration than in the medium. Echinoderm body fluids are very similar to sea water, but the ions in echinoderm muscle, body wall, and blood cells are very different (Table 5).

Coelenterates also are limited in their ionic regulation, but the jelly of medusae differs from sea water in having higher K^+ and lower $SO_4^=$. The sipunculid phascolosoma (*Golfingia*) maintains higher K^+ and lower Mg^{++} and $SO_4^=$ in its body fluid than in the medium. This is the more significant because this sipunculid worm has such low salt permeability as to appear semipermeable over some hours (Chapter 2).

In marine pelecypods the blood potassium and calcium are high relative to sea water; gastropods have higher potassium and lower sulfate concentrations; cephalopods have much higher potassium and lower sulfate levels. The few polychaetes which have been analyzed retain relatively high potassium concentrations. The sipunculids, molluscs, and most polychaetes are osmoconformers, yet they have excretory organs which probably function in their limited ionic regulation.

Ascidians show little regulation except very low blood sulfate (*Phallusia, Salpa*, Table 5).[137]

The marine arthropods present a variety of degrees of ionic regulation. Most of them accumulate potassium while in a few, e.g., *Homarus*, potassium is as low as in sea water. Magnesium and sulfate are kept lower than in the medium. The highly active crabs—*Carcinus, Portunas, Pachygrapsus, Nephrops*, and *Palaemon*—have low Mg^{++} (14 to 18 per cent of that in sea water), whereas more sluggish crustaceans—*Maja, Hyas*—have high magnesium concentrations.[138] Most marine crustaceans have Ca^{++} higher than in the ocean, and *Homarus* is remarkable in having more Ca^{++} than K^+ in its blood (Table 5). All Crustacea regulate Mg^{++} and $SO_4^=$ although the hermit crab *Eupagurus* is reported to have more $SO_4^=$ than does sea water. In brackish water, crustaceans maintain about the same proportions of ions as in sea water; the high calcium in the blood is striking; the level varies according to the molt cycle.

Fresh-Water Animals. The ions in all fresh-water animals are necessarily different from the ions of their medium. In crayfish blood all ions are about ten times more concentrated than in mussel blood, except for calcium, which is similar in the two. The ratio of magnesium to calcium is higher in crayfish than in most marine Crustacea. The blood sodium of a crayfish is normally 200 mM/l, in water with a sodium content of 0.4 mM to 2.0 mM/l, and the blood Na increases very little even in a medium of 100 mM/l Na^+. After blood Na^+ has been increased experimentally a crayfish in tap water loses Na^+ rapidly until its "normal" level is reached. How the internal concentration of sodium is controlled so precisely is unknown.[28] In fresh-water pelecypods all elements except calcium are very dilute (Table 5).

Insects. Many insects have high potassium and low sodium concentrations in the hemolymph. It has been suggested that the Na/K ratio is highest (11 to 27) in blood-feeding insects, high (1 to 18) in carnivorous ones, and low (<1) in herbivorous insects.[21] However, in the cockroach this ratio is independent of diet.[161] A silkworm has in its body fluids about the same sodium concentration as the mulberry leaves on which it feeds, but on pupation it loses practically all of its sodium and the pupal tissues contain much potassium but negligible sodium.[160] Florkin and Duchateau have presented evidence that the more ancient orders of insects (Odonata, Orthoptera, some Diptera) have high sodium, low potassium, and relatively low magnesium in their hemolymph, whereas in the more recent groups (Lepidoptera, Coleoptera, Hymenoptera), which evolved with higher plants, the hemolymph potassium is high and sodium low (Table 5). However, the range within single orders is very great, and it seems probable that the Na/K ratio is influenced by the diet as well as by the genotype.

The hemolymph potassium concentration in some insects is so high that it would block conduction in nerves of most animals, but insect nerves are protected by a sheath which is impermeable to potassium.[84] Migratory locusts go on a march when the blood potassium level is reduced, and they fail to march when blood potassium is high, during feeding.[52]

The magnesium content is relatively low in some of those insects with high hemolymph potassium and the ratio Ca/Mg increases in the order: herbivorous$<$omnivorous$<$carnivorous$<$blood-feeding.[34] The pH of the blood of many insects, e.g., Hymenoptera and Lepidoptera, is between 6.4 and 6.8.[78] Insect blood tends to have high amino acid and low Cl^- concentrations (p. 37).

Vertebrates. Vertebrates show less variation in ionic ratios in their blood than many invertebrates, much less variation than insects. The magnesium level is low in vertebrate bloods, and the ratio $(Na^+ + K^+)/(Ca^{++} + Mg^{++})$ is higher in vertebrate bloods than in the body fluids of invertebrates.[57] Many cellular functions vary with the ratio of alkaline metals to alkaline earths.

In marine vertebrates every ion is regulated. The hagfishes are isosmotic with sea water, NaCl accounting for 88 per cent of osmotic solutes, but they show regulation of all ions. The fresh-water lampreys resemble fresh-water bony fish (Table 5).[137] Marine teleosts tend to have higher Mg^{++} and Ca^{++} concentrations than do fresh-water fish. Elasmobranchs resemble teleosts in ionic composition but in addition maintain high urea concentrations.

In summary: The echinoderms show little ionic regulation except slight retention of potassium; coelenterates exclude sulfate; some annelids, molluscs, and crustaceans show limited regulation of potassium, sulfate, and magnesium; the cephalopods and certain marine crustaceans markedly regulate most ions except sodium and chloride. Insects are unique in low blood pH and some of them in high hemolymph potassium concentration. Vertebrates, both aquatic and terrestrial, regulate all ions and have lower plasma magnesium, sulfate, and potassium than marine invertebrates.

RESPONSES TO ALTERATIONS IN THE IONIC MEDIUM

Those animals whose body fluids resemble sea water in concentration are ionic conformers. For example, when the holothurian *Caudina chilensis* was placed in an artificial sea water with disproportionate ionic changes, K^+ increased by three times, Ca^{++} two and one-half times, Cl^- increased, Na^+ and $SO_4^=$ decreased; within 5 days the coelomic fluid conformed in all respects to the new medium.[97] In *Golfingia*, there is regulation of potassium and sulfate; the content of Cl^- in the muscles increased more than did the K^+ when these elements were increased proportionately in the medium.[155]

Hyperosmotic and hypoosmotic regulation may be accompanied by changes in blood ions in different proportions. In *Carcinus*

transferred from S.W. (sea water) to 2/3 S.W. the Na^+, K^+, and Cl^- decreased the least proportionately, that is, the ratio of these to the medium increased and these salts were retained, whereas Mg^{++} and $SO_4^=$ decreased proportionately more and the I/O ratio actually decreased.[171] When Mg^{++} and $SO_4^=$ were increased without an increase in total salinity in artificial S.W. *Carcinus* excreted more of these salts so that their concentration in the blood was not much increased. When *Eriocheir* was transferred from fresh water to sea water the blood protein decreased and Na^+ and Cl^- increased more than K^+ and Ca^{++}.[145] Thus in a dilute medium sodium and potassium are used in preference to Mg^{++} in maintaining hypertonicity. However, *Pachygrapsus* and *Uca* in hyperosmotic sea water showed relatively greater increase in serum Mg^{++} and less increase in Na^+ and K^+ than there was in the medium (see Table 10).[69, 126] The terrestrial hermit crab *Caenobita* tolerated a range of blood Na^+ from 83 to 220 per cent of the normal level.[72]

Ascaris lumbricoides in several culture media showed remarkable constancy of internal K^+, Ca^{++}, and Mg^{++}, and good regulation of Na^+ and Cl^-.[80]

Regulation of blood chloride usually parallels osmotic regulation. In osmotic conformers like *Mytilus,* blood and tissue chlorides rise and fall in proportion to changes in the medium.[101] *Anodonta* kept without food in tapwater for many months lost a little sodium, increased in blood calcium, but remained remarkably constant in Cl^-, K^+, and Mg^{++} concentrations.[58] The crab *Ocypode altricans* maintained its blood chloride at 378 mM/l over a range of external Cl^- from 120 to 600 mM/l.[56] In animals which show hyperosmotic regulation but no hypoosmotic regulation the chloride concentration remains high in dilute media (*Nereis diversicolor,*[154] *Gammarus duebeni,*[13] *Aedes aegypti*).[175] In animals which regulate hypoosmotically, the blood chloride is lower than that in the concentrated media (*Gammarus obtusatus,*[13] *Aedes detritus,*[12] *Uca*[69]).

The preceding evidence indicates that some animals are ion conformers and others ion regulators and that among the regulators some ions are maintained more constant than others when the medium changes. In the vertebrates the ionic ratios tend to be more fixed than in animals with open circulatory systems. The ionic composition of the blood of marine fish is not much different from that of fresh-water fish although tests on marine fish in media with disproportionate changes in ions seem not to have been made.

MECHANISMS OF IONIC REGULATION

Protein Binding and Diffusion Rates. One physical factor which permits concentration differences is the Donnan equilibrium. Some inorganic ions may be held by organic ions of opposite sign (largely anionic proteins) which cannot diffuse across body membranes, thus keeping the concentration of bound ions higher than on the side lacking the nondiffusible substance. Both electrical and osmotic equilibria apply only if some of the protein molecules have more than one ionizing group. The Donnan equilibrium requires that the product of diffusible cations and diffusible anions inside be equal to the product of diffusible cations and diffusible anions outside, as follows for sodium, protein, and chloride:

Inside	Outside
$Na_1^+ Cl_1^-$	$Na_o^+ Cl_o^-$
$Na_1^+ Pr_1^-$	

$$\frac{Na_1}{Na_o} = \frac{Cl_o}{Cl_1} \quad and \quad \begin{array}{c} Na_1 > Na_o \\ Cl_1 < Cl_o \end{array}$$

If the concentration gradient of all ions were maintained by protein binding, the Donnan ratios should hold for all elements, and on dialysis against sea water (for marine bloods) the ionic differences should persist. Table 8 shows that in body fluids, like those of *Aurelia* and *Marthasterias* where the protein is very low, there are no significant differences in ionic composition between dialyzed blood and sea water. In some of the crustaceans, however, where protein concentrations are higher (Table 5) 10 to 20 per cent of calcium is bound to protein, other ions not significantly. However, in all marine animals the differences remaining after dialysis are so small compared with the differences between normal blood and sea water that it can be concluded that protein binding is insignificant as a regulating mechanism.

In addition, when the Donnan ratios for various ions between blood and medium

(I/O) are examined, some of them tend to be similar but others, especially sodium, deviate markedly. As more biological systems are examined—body extracellular fluids in relation to the environment, to secreted fluids, and to intracellular electrolytes—it becomes increasingly evident that the Donnan equilibrium is of minor importance and that active mechanisms for maintaining ionic gradients must be sought.

Another physical factor which might select certain elements is differential diffusion rates through body membranes. Penetration across nonliving surface membranes tends to follow the mobility series: $K > Na > Ca > Mg$; $Cl > SO_4$, and these are in the order of usual retention. Ions may also move in similar series in an electrical gradient. Diffusion *per se* could be effective only so long as the concentration outside was greater than that inside. Accumulation could result if the ion which diffuses in were trapped by complexing with a nondiffusible material inside. Data on dialyzed bloods show protein binding to be slight, and radioactive tracer experiments indicate that the majority of inorganic ions in body fluids are readily exchangeable. However, differential permeability may play some part in regulation; hence the nature of the surface membranes maintained by metabolic activity must be important.

Active Uptake. Metabolically controlled transport can be brought about by enzymatic carriers or by membranes containing specific exchange molecules. The nature of metabolically maintained carrier, whether enzymatic or by exchange, is virtually unknown although models have been proposed.[43] In order that electrical equilibrium be maintained the electrolytes must be absorbed either as neutral molecules or, if as ions, by exchange with another ion of the same sign. The use of tracers has permitted Ussing[167] to develop a method for distinguishing passive flux in and out across a membrane from active transport. Evidence for active absorption of certain elements was discussed in Chapter 2; nearly all animals which can penetrate brackish water from the sea and most fresh-water animals are able to

TABLE 8.   DONNAN RATIOS OF DIALYZED BLOOD TO SEA WATER[136, 138]

Animal	Na	K	Ca	Mg	Cl	SO₄	Protein (mg/ml)
Aurelia	1.00	1.00	1.01	0.998	1.00	1.00	0.4
Marthasterias	1.00	0.99	1.00	1.015	1.00	1.00	0.6
Nephrops	1.01	1.014	1.12	1.03	0.99	0.98	33.0
Palinurus	1.026	1.028	1.185	1.038	0.986	0.985	49.0

extract and concentrate ions from the medium. When a lamprey, *Petromyzon,* is kept cold, the urine volume decreases as does Cl^- excretion, but active absorption decreases more, so Cl^- is lost from the fish.[176] In dilute sea water a lobster may absorb Cl^- by its gills.[29]

Krogh found that a frog can absorb Cl^- with Na^+ from NaCl against a concentration gradient of 1:1000; it can take up Cl^- from NH_4Cl, KCL, or $CaCl_2$. It also absorbs Br^- but takes up I^-, NO_3^-, and CNS^- only by diffusion; Na^+ is actively absorbed but not K^+, NH_4^+, or Ca^{++}. The crab *Eriocheir* actively absorbs Cl^-, Br^-, and CNS^-, but not NO_3^-, I^-, or $SO_4^=$; it absorbs Na^+ and K^+ but not Ca^{++}.[101] Active absorption of ions has been demonstrated in fresh-water molluscs, Daphnia, earthworms, insect larvae, and fish (see p. 26, Chapter 2). Isolated frog skin is electrically positive on the corium side in proportion to the sodium transported to that side; saline solution on the corium side becomes slightly basic, and sodium transport is stopped in absence of oxygen and reduced in absence of potassium.[55, 167] Shore crabs, e.g., *Carcinus* (p. 14), can actively absorb salt from a dilute medium, and a desiccated *Pachygrapsus* can take up water from hyperosmotic 140 per cent sea water.[71]

Isolated gills of *Eriocheir* actively absorb Na^+ and K^+ (with Cl^-), and the two cations are absorbed by independent mechanisms; both respiratory inhibitors and anticholinesterases block the uptake, and they also increase salt loss into water.[95] Sodium transport is also blocked by anticholinesterases in frog skin[94] and in *Chironomus* anal papillae.[95] This may not mean that acetylcholine *per se* is involved, but rather that a cholinesterase-like protein may be important in maintaining ion gradients. *Astacus* absorbs Na^+ from 0.3 mM Na/l; the normal influx in equilibrium at this concentration is 1.5 μM/10 gm body wt/hr. The minimum concentration at which equilibrium is maintained is 0.04 mM/l—at higher concentrations influx reaches a constant level and exceeds outflow.[148] The blood concentration of Na^+ determines the regulation, and above 200 mM Na^+ the excretion increases and absorption decreases, while below 200 mM Na^+ in the blood, urine loss decreases and influx increases. After some Na is depleted by keeping crayfish in distilled water, the active uptake may increase by seven times.[28] Aquatic isopods maintain blood ions even when not fed; hence there must be active uptake.[108]

Larvae of *Aedes aegypti* show a net uptake in addition to passive exchange; mechanisms for absorption of sodium and potassium are separate.[163] In *Aedes* larvae 90 per cent of Na exchange is by the anal papillae, and the transport by a carrier molecule is increased sixfold after feeding.[156] Anal papillae of *Chironomus* are larger in tap water than in salt solutions. Epithelial cells on fish gills which appear to secrete chlorides outward in sea water and to transport chlorides inward in fresh water were described on page 29, Chapter 2.

In a few fresh-water animals active absorption of salt by surface epithelia is absent or negligible. For example, in the eel *Anguilla* and in *Sialis* larva, uptake of salts is by the gut. The importance of selective salt replacement from food is recognized also in animals which have epithelial absorption as well. In terrestrial animals the gut is the only route available.

Excretion. It is less wasteful of energy for an excretory organ to reabsorb a substance which has been filtered in the same concentration as in the blood than it is to absorb this substance from a more dilute fluid.[124] (Refer to p. 19.) Unwanted ions which enter by diffusion or in food may be concentrated in an excretory fluid. Kidneys evolved in marine animals which are isosmotic with their medium but which regulate ionically. The coelenterates and echinoderms lack special excretory organs and they show least ionic regulation. It is reasonable to assume that in annelids, molluscs, and arthropods, kidneys arose and still function in ionic regulation; on migration to fresh water they took over water regulation secondarily. In some, e.g., *Eriocheir* in fresh water, kidneys play no part in osmoregulation. In fishes, kidneys were early used in water regulation, and on migration of teleosts to the sea kidneys were inadequate for ionic regulation, and extrarenal routes developed. The extent to which salts are excreted extrarenally in invertebrate animals is not known. Possibly the contractile vacuole in marine Protozoa has an ion-regulating function.

Evidence for active excretion of selected ions is given by the ratios of urine to plasma concentrations (U/P ratios), and a few selected, recently published values are given in Table 9. These ratios are subject to much variation with dietary changes and the like, but they indicate the efficiency of the kidneys in salt regulation. In most of the marine Crustacea the kidney retains potassium and calcium and eliminates excess magnesium and

TABLE 9.   RATIOS OF CONCENTRATION OF IONS IN URINE TO CONCENTRATION
IN PLASMA (U/P RATIOS)

Animal	Na	K	Ca	Mg	Cl	SO₄
Pheretima (u/coel.fl.)[5]	0.13	0.40	0.54	0.14	0.05	0.71
Sepia[136]	0.79	0.50	0.70	0.68	1.0	2.15
Nephrops[136, 138]	0.98	0.83	0.81	1.30	1.01	1.06
Homarus[136]	0.99	0.91	0.64	1.80	1.01	1.59
Homarus[29]	0.96	0.4-1.0	0.81	1.7	1.01	
Palinurus[136]	0.98	0.65	0.86	1.37	1.01	0.98
Palaemon[122]	0.82	0.86	0.94	6.70	1.06	3.8
Maja[136]	0.99	0.98	0.99	1.07	0.98	2.14
Carcinus[171]	0.95	0.78	0.94	3.90	0.98	2.24
Pachygrapsus[126]	0.70	0.94	1.01	6.1		
Uca[69]	0.84	1.45	1.01	2.35	1.15	1.12
Eriocheir (S.W.)[145]		1.15	0.93	2.17	1.135	
Eriocheir (F.W.)[145]		1.39	0.47	0.22	0.95	
Cambarus[107]	0.46	0.14	0.09	0.45	0.082	
Dixippus[128]	0.45	8.1	0.29	0.17	0.75	
Sygnathus[51]	0.41	0.24	1.85	10.75	1.70	
Lophius[27]	0.94	0.4	1.6-3.3	62.0	1.1	
Ocypode[56]					1.2	
Goniopsis[56]					1.4	
Muraena[51]	0.58	0.12	3.6	26.35	1.75	
Man[70]	1.16	7.5	1.87	2.41	1.63	20-60

especially sulfate. In excess salt loads, as after injection of salts or hyperosmotic sea water, the urinary excretion may not account for all the injected salt. *Pachygrapsus'* kidney is relatively ineffective in regulation of Na^+, K^+, and Ca^{++}, more effective for Mg^{++}[126]

In *Pachygrapsus* and *Uca* kept in hyperosmotic sea water the urine increases in concentration of Mg^{++} and $SO_4^=$ much more than of K^+, Ca^{++}, and Cl^-, and the Na^+ output actually decreases[69, 126] (Table 10). Extrarenal routes of excretion—gills and gut—seem probable. An important avenue of excretion besides gills and kidneys in marine crustaceans is the stomach, from which there may be regurgitation. Phenol red, for example, injected into a lobster appears in much higher concentrations in stomach fluid than in urine,[29] and in *Uca* the stomach fluid may be important in ion excretion.[69] Crab kidneys are important in Mg^{++} and $SO_4^=$ regulation. In the prawn *Palaemon* under excess salt load the sodium in the urine increases less than the Mg^{++}.[122] The lobster kidney actively concentrates Mg^{++} and $SO_4^=$ but not Ca^{++}.[29] In fresh-water crayfish the urine is dilute, but under excess salt load the urine concentration increases markedly. Normally only about 6 per cent of the total Na outflow from a crayfish is by urine. Some is by passive diffusion and 30 per cent is by exchange diffusion across the body surface, particularly the gills. Diffusion outflux increases when loss by urine diminishes at low blood concentra-

tions.[28] *Artemia* excretes much NaCl by its gills.[42] That the ions are excreted each at its own rate, but with some influence of one on another, is shown by alteration of u/s ratios for various ions when crabs are placed in different salinities (Table 10).

The Na^+ and K^+ regulation in several insects has been examined by Ramsey[127-129, 131] by analyses of hemolymph, malpighian tube urine, and intestinal fluid. In general, Na^+ and K^+, particularly potassium, are secreted by the malpighian tubes and are then reabsorbed in varying amounts along with water in either the rectum or lower midgut, with the result that the hemolymph concentrations are maintained. In the bug *Rhodnius* after a blood meal the ratio of malpighian tube urine to plasma for potassium may be 17.7 as compared to 0.75 for sodium. Potassium is secreted against a gradient in the upper tubule; some may be reabsorbed in the proximal tubule with the net effect of eliminating the high potassium content of the meal. In mosquito larvae also, the U/P ratio for tubular potassium is ten times that for sodium, and malpighian fluid is hypoosmotic to blood. Both Na^+ and K^+ are absorbed with Cl^- by the anal gills, but even in a medium of dilute NaCl the U/P ratio for K^+ is greatly in excess of that for Na^+; hence K^+ must be actively transported by the tubule. Rectal absorption tends to keep the hemolymph Na^+ and K^+ constant in different media. In the

TABLE 10.   DISPROPORTIONATE CHANGES IN IONS IN URINE AND BLOOD OF
CRUSTACEANS IN DIFFERENT SALINITIES*

	Medium of S.W.	Osmotic concentration	Na	K	Ca	Mg	Cl	SO₄
Pachygrapsus[126]	50%	urine 0.39	356	10.6	8.4	32.1		
		blood 0.46	313	8.4	8.6	8.9		
		u/s 0.85	1.2	1.3	0.97	4.0		
	100%	urine 0.53	318	11.2	12.0	143.6		
		blood 0.57	465	12.1	11.4	29.2		
		u/s 0.93	0.7	0.94	1.01	6.1		
	170%	urine 0.9	264	17.2	18.6	324.6		
		blood 0.9	668	17.4	12.3	33.1		
		u/s 1.0	0.4	1.0	1.36	7.8		
Uca[69]	100%	urine 0.58	276	16	17	108	622	47
		blood 0.50	328	11	16	46	537	42
		u/s 1.16	0.81	1.45	1.06	2.2	1.15	1.1
	175%	urine 0.68	218	20	20	255	704	120
		blood 0.59	375	15	14	55	574	49
		u/s 1.15	0.58	1.3	0.7	4.64	1.22	2.45
Palaemon[122]	50%	urine	206	7.7	25	67.1	330	3.6
		blood	257	6.7	28.3	22.2	300	2.3
		u/s 1.0	0.80	1.1	0.88	3.0	1.1	1.56
	100%	urine	324	6.6	24	168.6	458	19.8
		blood	394	7.7	25.2	25.2	430	5.2
		u/s 1.0	0.82	0.86	0.95	6.7	1.06	3.7
	120%	urine	432	8.5	29.3	184.5	622	32
		blood	473	10.2	29.9	41.2	494	6.4
		u/s 1.0	0.91	0.83	0.98	4.48	1.26	5.0
Caenobita[71, 72]	F.W. (access to)	urine	461	17.1	26.9	108		
		blood	447	10.5	27.9	65.7		
		u/s	1.01	1.5	0.92	1.3		
	S.W.+ F.W. (access to)	urine	517	14.9	25.7	81.5		
		blood	465	10.5	29.4	61.8		
		u/s	1.07	1.3	0.93	1.6		
	50% S.W. (access to)	urine	728	13.7	32.9	126		
		blood	669	13.6	30.7	114		
		u/s	1.14	2.0	1.04	1.1		

* Osmotic concentrations in equivalent molality of NaCl. Ion concentrations in mM/l. u/s = urine/serum.

stick insect *Dixippus* excretion has been studied *in situ* and in isolated malpighian tubules. The tubules excrete about 0.7 μEq Na$^+$ and 21 μEq K$^+$ per day; analyses of feces show that of these amounts 95 per cent of the Na$^+$ and 80 per cent of the K$^+$ are reabsorbed along with water in the rectum. The tubular secretion of K$^+$ increases more with increased concentration in the medium (artificial hemolymph) than does secretion of Na$^+$ with increased hemolymph Na$^+$. Regulation of hemolymph concentration is less effective after a sudden increase in Na$^+$ or K$^+$ than in *Rhodnius*. In all of these insects, then, there is circulation of cations, mainly potassium, from hemolymph into tubule and back through the hindgut into the hemolymph. Apparently an active flow of fluid, brought about by secretion of potassium, and

with it water, is necessary to eliminate products such as uric acids.

Regulation of ions in vertebrates is primarily excretory. In marine bony fish which swallow sea water some of the divalent salts are voided with feces, others by the urine, while the excess monovalent salts are largely excreted by the secretory epithelium of the gills (p. 29, Chapter 2). This pattern of excretion is found in both glomerular and aglomerular marine fish. Aglomerular fish (*Myoxocephalus*) can excrete a supersaturated solution of $MgHPO_4 \cdot 3H_2O$ in the urine.[123] Perfused aglomerular kidneys of *Lophius* can reduce the plasma magnesium virtually to zero.[27] In freshly caught fish the urine chlorides often approach zero concentration but in the perfused *Lophius* kidney, Cl$^-$ and Na$^+$ are excreted at about plasma levels and potassium at a lower concentration, and high plasma Mg^{++} depresses Ca^{++} excretion.[15] An isolated proximal kidney tubule of the amphibian *Necturus* actively absorbs Na^+; the transport can be blocked by the drugs ouabain and dinitrophenol.[149, 174]

In mammals the kidneys regulate the blood levels of various ions by selective reabsorption.[112, 153] The sequence is as follows: of the filtered sodium about 80 per cent is reabsorbed by passive diffusion (and possibly some active transport) from the proximal tubules, and some is actively absorbed in the thin loop and the distal tubule; chloride goes with the sodium and only a small fraction of the filtered sodium and chloride may be lost in the urine. Potassium is reabsorbed proximally, but some may be secreted distally, according to the blood level. The plasma level of sulfate is relatively low; hence little is reabsorbed and excess $SO_4^=$ is excreted. Calcium is regulated according to the proportion of bound and free ions, and the balance between tissue and plasma calcium is controlled in part by the parathyroid hormone. The stop-flow method supports the preceding picture that in a dog glucose and $HPO_4^=$ are reabsorbed, PAH (para-aminohippuric acid) secreted in proximal segments, Na^+ is actively reabsorbed in the loop of Henle and distal tubule, HCO_3^- increases in the proximal tubule[178] (see p. 44).

Sodium reabsorption in the kidney is regulated by hormones from the adrenal cortex; in adrenocorticoid deficiency an excessive amount of sodium is lost in the urine and with it an osmotically equivalent amount of water. There is disagreement regarding the effects of adrenal cortical hormones on the ionic balance between tissues and plasma. In elasmobranchs (skate) the removal of the inter-renal glands (equivalent to the adrenal cortex) is reported to have no significant effect on blood electrolytes.[75]

The vertebrate kidneys are important also in regulating acid-base balance. Urine is usually acid (pH 4.4 to 5.8), and current evidence for mammals is that in the distal tubule cells CO_2 is converted by carbonic anhydrase to H_2CO_3, which dissociates at once to HCO_3^- and H^+; the latter passes out in exchange for tubular Na^+, which then returns to the plasma as $NaHCO_3$, and the urine in the collecting tube is acid. At high plasma potassium concentration, potassium may compete with H^+ in the Na^+ exchange. If the carbonic anhydrase (C.A.) is inhibited by a sulfanilamide or Diamox (acetazole amide) the urine pH rises because of the excretion of more $NaHCO_3$. The urine of fish is also acid (pH 5.7), and in both dogfish, *Squalus,* and sculpin, *Myoxocephalus,* inhibition of C.A. does not prevent acidification, whereas in the fresh-water catfish *Ameiurus* (*Ictalurus*) and in the frog the C.A. inhibitor results in an alkaline urine.[82] In the alligator the urine is normally alkaline (pH 7.8) as a result of high concentration of NH_4^+ and HCO_3^-, and after C.A. inhibition Cl^- substitutes for HCO_3^- and the urine pH actually decreases.[79] Hence there are several different acidification mechanisms in vertebrate kidneys.

Some extrarenal glands secrete univalent salts, particularly NaCl outward. The gills of marine fish excrete Na^+, K^+, Cl^-, p. 28). The rectal gland of a dogfish, *Squalus,* eliminates NaCl as follows:[30]

| | mosM | mM | | | | | |
		Na	K	Cl	Ca	Mg	urea
Rectal gland secretion	1018	540	7.1	533	>1	>1	14.5
Plasma	1018	286		246			351
Urine	780	337		203			
Sea water	930	440	9.1	495	10	51	

Salt-secreting nasal glands occur in gulls, penguins, cormorants, pelicans, gooneys: the secretion in a gooney contains 829 mM Na^+ and 24 mM K^+.[59] Secretion of NaCl is stimulated by the facial nerve. Enzyme evidence suggests phosphatidic acid as a sodium carrier.[83] The salt glands enlarge when the birds live near and drink sea water. The gland cells show deep infolding of the basal membranes, which provide considerable surface area (Fig. 25).

Ion Storage. In some animals, ions can move into and out of tissues in maintenance of relative constancy of serum concentrations. In *Pachygrapsus*, for example, changes in conductivity of a dilute medium are greater than can be accounted for by changes in blood concentration; it is calculated that the equivalent "solute space" is larger than the blood volume and may correspond to salt stores in tissues.[71] Autoradiographs of *Asellus* show that 20 to 30 per cent of the total body sodium is outside the hemolymph and is mainly in certain organs.[108] In *Astacus* the total equivalent Na space is 47 per cent while the blood volume is 29 per cent of total body weight.[28] Electron micrographs of various tissues of crustaceans, especially muscle, show extensive surface invaginations which may represent fluid compartments separate from true extracellular space. In mammals, univalent ion stores are mobilized under influence of the adrenal cortex. The best known are the calcium stores of the bone which can be depleted on low calcium diet. Such stores might be especially useful for short-term needs, as in an intertidal animal, or under ionic stresses.

Behavior. Many animals have specific salt taste receptors (see Chemoreception, Chapter 11). Also many have a water taste as well as general means of detecting "thirst." Dehydrated terrestrial animals tend to take up water to some equilibrium level. Mammals with a deficiency of adrenocortical hormones drink salt solution in preference to water. Given a choice of water and salt solution, thirsty rats drink more water,[46] but normally hydrated rats select isosmotic salt solution. *Pachygrapsus* selects 100 per cent sea water when given the choice of this or dilutions or higher concentrations of sea water.[71] Crabs which spend most of the time on land appear to regulate blood ions by varying their entrance into water; *Caenobita* spent 90 per cent of the time out of water and visited sea water five times more than they did fresh water.[72] It is probable, therefore, that in many animals behavior contributes to maintenance of appropriate salt balance.

It may be said in summary that active processes in excretion have taken a variety of patterns, active transport outward (secretion), and active transport inward (reabsorption), in combination with filtration. The net result in all animals with kidneys is the regulation of blood level of ions. Both renal and extrarenal active ion transport require oxidative energy. Some animals seem to require cholinesterase for the process, as in the absorption of Na^+ by crab gill, *Chironomus* papillae, and frog skin; others need carbonic anhydrase as in acidification of urine in freshwater fish and mammals. Phosphatides have been suggested as Na^+ carriers; adrenocortical and neurohypophyseal hormones may regulate Na^+ and water permeability of some cells. In insects a potassium circulation by tubular secretion and rectal reabsorption provides the fluid stream for nitrogenous excretion. Usually the transport of each cation is by a different path, yet in land crabs the secretion of sodium by the kidney is inhibited by magnesium. Thus, at present, ionic regulation appears to result from many different transport mechanisms; perhaps the next decade may bring identification of some of the enzymes of active transport.

SECONDARY AND TRACE ELEMENTS

The primary elements in organic compounds are hydrogen, carbon, oxygen, and nitrogen. Coupled with these in many key compounds are phosphorus, and sulfur in a few amino acids, and hence in proteins. Sulfur is of major importance in mucopolysaccharides. Chloride is the common anion which, with bicarbonate, phosphates, and organic acids, provides electrical balance. Calcium is the most common skeletal component. There remain a large number of elements which have special functions in animals. Of the forty-eight well-measured elements in sea water, animals are known to make use of approximately half. Some inorganic compounds are accumulated in inactive tissues, storage excretion.

Some of the minor and trace elements are widely distributed in living matter; others are variable in occurrence. Some elements which, in traces, are necessary for life are toxic in high concentrations. Sporadic distribution of certain elements is not readily understood, and in analyses it is important to distinguish elements concentrated by the animal from those in associated organisms. Extensive tables of the elementary composition of biological material have been given,[35, 103, 166, 173, 179] especially in the monumental work by Vinogradov[169] on which much of the following account is based. Activation analyses are revealing traces of heavy elements which had escaped chemical detection.

Halogens. Chlorine is the common halogen of animals (but not of plants), and it is the most widely dispersed and innocuous anion. Bromine can sometimes be substituted for chlorine, but it is not a normal constituent in most animals. Sea water contains several thousand times more bromine than iodine, yet iodine is more used by animals. In a series of sponges the keratinous species tend to have a higher content of both of these elements and an I/Br molecular ratio of 3.9, whereas nonkeratinous sponges have a lower content and an I/Br ratio of 2.1. Of the alcyonarian corals one group has more bromine than chlorine and another more iodine than chlorine.

Iodine-containing proteins are widely distributed, as in spongin of sponges, in scleroproteins of polychaetes, particularly the keratinous tubes of sabellids, and the integument of arthropods. From these proteins mono-iodotyrosine and diiodotyrosine and the derivative thyroxine can be obtained in many of these invertebrates. However, applied thyroxine has no effects comparable to those in vertebrates.[63, 64, 64a] It has been suggested that iodotyrosines and thyroxine are widely distributed and that only in the vertebrates is the synthesis and release of these active agents from protein localized in an organ like the thyroid.[63, 64, 64a] By use of I^{131} it was shown that in tunicates, e.g., *Ciona*, iodine is bound in the endostyle (larva) and test (adult);[9, 10] autoradiographs in the endostyle show granules resembling thyroid colloid. In *Amphioxus* the endostyle and mucous glands of the gut accumulate iodine and the endostyle has thyroxine activity. The ammocoete larva of lampreys has an endostyle which concentrates iodine into thyroglobulin and hydrolyzes this to thyroxine.[36, 104] Thus these iodine compounds are elaborated in animals which lack thyroids.

Fluorine is present as fluorite in the shell, and fluorine is found in the mantle of certain gastropods (*Archidoris* of family Doriidae). It is concentrated in some sponges.[24] Fluorine is found in traces in vertebrate bone and aids the hardening of dental enamel, but in excess it causes abnormal bone structure.

Metals. The sporadic concentration of various heavy metals has long been noted. Modern nutrition indicates the need for traces of some of these and their enzymatic functions are gradually becoming recognized. Iron is present in heme proteins such as the cytochromes, catalase, and peroxidase in aerobic cells. Heme pigments, hemoglobins, have evolved several times as oxygen carriers in blood (see Chapter 8). The iron content of some snails is high (0.2 to 0.8 per cent dry weight), and the radular teeth of *Patella* contain Fe_2O_3 to the extent of 50 per cent of the ash weight. The blood cells of oysters have granules which stain for iron.[60] Iron may be deposited in a ring of cells around the midgut of Drosophila.[125]

Copper occurs in sea water, about 1 mg/100 l. Some marine molluscs and arthropods concentrate copper to 1 mg/100 ml blood, where it functions in the respiratory pigment hemocyanin (Hcy)[45] (Chapter 8). Concentrations of copper in vertebrates are much lower, but copper appears necessary for the synthesis of hemoglobin, and possibly of cytochrome. Copper is necessary for the enzymes polyphenol oxidase, laccase, ascorbic acid oxidase, and tyrosinase;[111] it is important in the tanning of the cuticular proteins in arthropods. Copper concentrations are high in molluscs and arthropods. In the crab *Maja* the Hcy content of blood is reduced at the time of a molt, and part of the copper lost from the blood is stored in the hepatopancreas to be utilized in resynthesis of Hcy after the molt.[181] In the red pigment, turacin, of touraco feathers, copper may have a concentration of 7 per cent. A man needs 2 mg Cu per day, more while growing, and blood concentration is 0.5 to 1 ppm.[44] Domestic animals living in a region low in soil copper develop numerous deficiency symptoms such as anemia, rough faded hair, and neural lesions.

Zinc is found widely in higher concentrations than copper in animal tissues.[169] It is present in relatively large amounts in bivalve molluscs, especially *Pecten* and *Ostrea* (0.04 per cent dry weight). Octopus urine contains zinc 170 times more concentrated than it is in sea water. Zinc is concentrated in the prostate gland of mammals and is present in ejaculate.[73] Deficiency of Zn leads to defects in feather and skin development of birds.[140] Zinc is an essential component of the enzyme carbonic anhydrase, which catalyzes the hydration of CO_2 in many tissues such as gills, red blood cells, and the vertebrate kidney.[164, 165] Zinc is found also in kidney phosphatase, pancreatic carboxypeptidase, glutamic and lactic dehydrogenases, and also in alcohol dehydrogenase of yeast.

Molybdenum has not often been reported in analyses of marine animals (0.0002 - 0.002 per cent dry),[169] but it is often found when sought. In mammals a trace of molybdenum is needed, an excess is toxic, and it is required for proper utilization of copper. A diet high in molybdenum induces symptoms which can be counteracted by increased copper intake; hence in low Cu^{++} areas the symptoms may in reality be due to Mb^{++} poisoning. Molybdenum plays a part in the function of several flavoproteins and is found in xanthine oxidase.[111, 133, 162]

Cobalt is a constituent of vitamin B_{12} (Chapter 4). Microorganisms need Co for B_{12} synthesis, and many animals require the vitamin. Cobalt-deficient soils are recognized; ruminants require cobalt for the rumen organisms; a sheep needs at least 0.05 mg/day.[114] Milk has some cobalt. Cobalt is one of the very few metals required by *Tetrahymena*, which rapidly accumulates it.[152]

Vanadium is not found in most animals, but it may be concentrated by more than a half million times above sea water level by certain ascidians.[17] Most of it is found in their blood, but some is localized in gut and ovaries. Vanadium is present in the plasma of two families, Cionidae and Diazonidae, and in special blood cells, vanadocytes, in Ascidiidae and Perophoriidae, but it is absent from most other families of tunicates.[172] This metal is in a green pigment which appears to have no respiratory function (see Chapter 8). A *Ciona* which weighs 20 gm may contain 100 μg of vanadium; from the rate of pumping and removal of vanadium it is calculated that *Ciona* could not extract from sea water more than 45 per cent of this amount in a year; hence it seems certain that the vanadium must be obtained by tunicates from particulate matter—plankton and detritus.[62] Why vanadium should be concentrated by these few kinds of animals is a mystery. A given genus of tunicate contains much more vanadium when living in warm waters than in cold; *Ciona* at Roscoff had 1.5 per cent in the ash, *Ciona* from the Gulf of Kola only 0.05 per cent vanadium in the ash.[169] Some individual tunicates (*Phallusia, Molgula*) contain niobium instead of vanadium.[32] Vanadium is concentrated by one mollusc, *Pleurobranchus plumella,* and by a polyzoan, *Plumatella.*[172]

Manganese occurs in traces in many animals (5 to 10 mg per 100 cc. of ash). In oysters the Mn content is high in gills and ovaries, highest at periods of reproductive activity. It is also high in fresh-water bivalves.[60] Manganese may be accumulated by certain Hymenoptera and stored along with other metals in midgut cells.[22] Manganese may function as a cofactor in oxidative phosphorylation, in L-malic dehydrogenase, and is a functional constituent of liver arginase (Chapter 6). In some of these functions magnesium may substitute for manganese. Deficiencies are known in domestic animals, and ducklings require 15 ppm in the diet.[16] Deficiency of magnesium leads to bone defects.

Magnesium is an essential element for all animals. The ciliate *Tetrahymena,* for example, requires Mg but not Ca.[151] In soft tissues magnesium is usually lower in concentration than calcium, but it may be present in greater concentration (as in *Littorina*). Magnesium is the active metal in chlorophyll and is, therefore, found in all green plants. It serves as the cofactor for enzymes in transfer of high-energy phosphate (ATP) in hexokinase, enolase (Chapter 7), and in the activation of muscle contractile proteins (myokinase).

Aluminum is widely distributed in traces, but in molluscs like *Helix* and *Littorina* it may be 0.2 to 0.8 per cent of the ash.[173] No enzymatic function has been assigned to aluminum. Nickel occurs in keratinous tissues, especially feathers; it is present in liver and thymus, and has been reported slightly concentrated in a few molluscs and in at least one sponge.[18] Tin and silver are metals of sea water which have been rarely reported as present in animals. Titanium has been reported in some coelenterates. Lead is widely distributed, more in molluscs (0.05 per cent of ash) than in other animals. Boron occurs widely (0.01 to 0.05 per cent of ash) and in *Helix* in high amounts (0.25 per cent).[173] Selenium has recently been reported as needed in traces by chicks.[166]

Skeletal Elements. *Special Roles of Calcium.* Two basic compounds were used early in evolution as skeletal substances, the oxides of silicon and carbonate of calcium; only the latter are utilized by large animals. Skeletons of protein—spongin, fibroin, conchiolin—have 15 to 18 per cent nitrogen. Chitin (6 per cent N) is widely used, particularly in arthropods, and tunicates have tunicin, a cellulose-like material. Such organic skeletal materials often occur in combination with $CaCO_3$.

Barium is found in traces in many animals, but more is found in *Helix.*[173] It can be deposited in vertebrate bone. One group of deep sea rhizopods, the Xenophyophora, have a skeleton which is a combination of protein with $BaSO_4$. The radiolarian *Acantharia* has a skeleton mainly of celestite ($SrSO_4$).[119] Barium may be stored in some hymenopterans in cells of the midgut; it is not so stored in *Drosophila.*[23]

Silicon is widely used as a supporting material in plants and diatoms; Equisetales and grasses are familiar examples. Among the Protozoa, the Heliozoa have spicules of $SiO_2 \cdot n(H_2O)$; radiolarians have relatively more silicon dioxide than oxides of calcium, magnesium, and iron; and Foraminifera, while mostly calcareous, have some members with much SiO_2. Two groups of sponges, Demospongiae and Hyalospongiae, the siliceous or glass sponges, may have spicules of $SiO_2 \cdot (H_2O)$. Silicon also occurs in significant amounts in a few bryozoan skeletons.

Calcium skeletons are of several sorts. Calcium carbonate is the most extensive skeletal material; this may be amorphous, it may be as calcite, often combined with $MgCO_3$, when it consists of hexagonal crystals and is very stable; it may be as argonite, in rhombic biaxial crystals, sometimes with $SrCO_3$. Calcium also occurs in various phosphates like the apatites ($Ca_3P_2O_8 \cdot CaCO_3$) of vertebrate bone. The shell of gastropods of the family Doriidae contains fluorite.

Foraminiferan shells of $CaCO_3$ constitute vast deposits, many of them associated with petroleum. Coral deposits are primarily $CaCO_3$, but some contain 1 per cent $CaSO_4$ and as much as 10 per cent $MgCO_3$. Corals actively concentrate calcium from sea water, adsorb it on mucopolysaccharides, then combine it with bicarbonate formed from CO_2 by the aid of carbonic anhydrase to constitute the calcium carbonate of the corallum skeleton; the H_2CO_3 produced in the reaction $Ca(HCO_3)_2 \rightarrow CaCO_3 + H_2CO_3$ appears to be used (as CO_2) by the symbiotic algae, the zooxanthellae. Calcification is reduced by inhibitors of carbonic anhydrase and also by removal of the zooxanthellae; hence calcification requires rapid removal of hydrogen.[66, 67]

Brachiopod shells may be 50 per cent $Ca_3(PO_4)_2$ in addition to the carbonate; some of them also have CaF_2. Serpulid worm tubes and the skeletons of echinoderms are primarily $CaCO_3$ with small amounts of sulfates and phosphates and some $MgCO_3$; tropical echinoderms have more skeletal magnesium than arctic species.[35] Molluscan shells are more than 99 per cent $CaCO_3$; pelecypods have varying proportions of calcite and aragonite; gastropods have more aragonite. Shells of pelecypods, and also serpulids, deposited in high temperatures tend to have more aragonite and more strontium; hence crystal analysis of fossils permits some estimate of the temperature of the ancient seas.[109] Among arthropods, barnacle shells are calcite; decapod crustaceans have chitinous exoskeletons in which calcification may be lacking, or may be present with amorphous $CaCO_3$, or as calcite.

Molluscan shells are formed by the activity of the epithelium at the edge of the mantle. First a birefringent protein matrix, the periostracum, is formed, and then $CaCO_3$ is deposited on this. Recent experiments with radiotracer calcium show that, while calcium is taken up rapidly from the gut and distributed by the blood, it can also be taken directly from the water by the mantle cells and deposited as shell.[19, 87, 88, 132] Snails such as

Helix can store amorphous $CaCO_3$ in digestive glands and deposit calcite in the shell. During long periods out of water pelecypods produce metabolic acids which may be buffered by calcium eroded from the shell so that the blood pH remains constant.[50]

Some arthropods calcify the chitinous exoskeleton, others do not. Crabs may store much calcium (often as $Ca_3(PO_4)_2$) in the hepatopancreas before a molt; crayfish may store it in gastroliths. The isopod *Limnoria* molts in two steps, posterior half first; then a large amount of calcium is shifted from the anterior to the posterior half for storage before the anterior half molts.[74] Thus crustaceans have a variety of means of limiting the loss of skeletal calcium in a molt; calcium regulation, at least in crayfish, is controlled by a hormone from the sinus gland (Chapter 20).

In insects, barium and strontium granules appear in cells of malpighian tubules, less frequently in midgut and reproductive cells, apparently as storage granules.[170]

In earthworms the esophageal epithelium of the calciferous glands secretes spherules of $CaCO_3$ crystals. Functions such as providing buffer capacity for the blood have been suggested, but the principal function of calcite secretion by the calciferous glands appears to be storage excretion of excess calcium from food.[135]

In vertebrate bone the ratio of $Ca_3P_2O_8$ to $CaCO_3$ is about 7 in mammals (close to pure dahllite) and is 11 in fish (approaching apatite). Teeth and tusks have some 2 per cent magnesium salts, bones less than 0.3 per cent. Vitamin D regulates the Ca in blood and the mineralizing of bone by aiding absorption from the gut and (together with parathormone) by mobilizing Ca^{++} from bone.

Analyses for strontium of fossils, skeletons, and animal tissues show that the Sr/Ca ratio depends on the medium or food more than on the kind of organism.[119] Analyses of skeletons of some 250 species of marine animals show a tenfold range in Sr/Ca ratios; only in the nudibranchs and madreporarians is the ratio higher than in sea water.[159]

The tissues of aging animals contain more calcium than do those of young animals. Rotifers have more calcium as they age.[102] Mouse livers take up more calcium when old.

In summary: Of the elements which form small organic molecules, only sulfur and phosphorus are widely used, and iodine in limited amount. Metals may complex with proteins; iron and copper occur in transport pigments and important enzymes; other metals such as Zn, Mg, Mn and Co (and possibly Mb) serve as cofactors or occur in compounds with enzymatic action. Other elements occur sporadically, vanadium in large concentrations in some ascidians, Sn, Al, Pb, Cd in traces, and no function is known for them. As skeletal material, organic substances (chitin, protein, cellulose) have been successfully used in many organisms. For greater rigidity silicon and calcium are widely used, strontium and barium rarely. Calcium with its variety of carbonates and phosphates has provided a range of skeletal materials.

INORGANIC LIMITS ON DISTRIBUTION

In the preceding account a number of elements have been indicated as essential for normal growth and function. Marine embryos can get inorganic ions directly from the sea water. In fresh water, however, the egg must have a store of salts to last through much of development.[116] Also for the penetration of rivers by euryhaline animals the presence of certain elements in the water may be more important than the total salinity. Fresh water has been colonized only by those animals which can provide adequate ash in their eggs. Many marine crabs, for example, can live in springs and rivers in which the water is hard and has chloride concentrations in the range 25 to 100 ppm.[118] Requirements of brackish-water animals for specific elements are poorly known; the requirements for embryonic life may be more rigorous than for adults. In fresh-water ponds the pH is important, and acid bogs are unsuited to many animals. Water in ponds in pine barrens is very acid—pH 4 to 4.5; some species of frog embryos can tolerate such acidity, others cannot.[68] Fresh-water sponges are limited to an optimal range of calcium, and different species vary in the lower limit of minerals essential to normal life.[86] Similarly, fresh-water molluscs require a minimal concentration of calcium for normal shell deposition, and they are usually absent from acid ponds. The spring bloom of plankton in fresh-water lakes may be limited by scarcity of dissolved silica. In the sea the plankton blooms are often limited by the paucity of available phosphates and nitrates, and silicates limit diatoms. In the cycle of the sea, these nutrients are converted by phytoplankton near the surface to organic molecules; the organisms sink and decompose, and there is a new crop after the nutrients are restored to the surface waters. In terrestrial animals,

deficiency diseases due to lack of specific metals have been mentioned. In general, animals are rarely limited by lack of specific elements; their food, however, particularly if it consists of planktonic diatoms, may be markedly limited.

BALANCED SALT MEDIA

The preceding sections have considered the relation between animals and their environment with respect to those elements which constitute the bulk of inorganic substances in living systems. The specific functions of the different elements, the antagonisms and interactions among them, comprise a large section of cellular physiology. A proper balance among the different elements is necessary for optimal functioning of organs and for growth and development; the salt requirements for growth may differ from those for maintenance of a tissue. A proper balance of ions is needed for normal irritability, permeability, contractility, and other functional characters of particular tissues. Sodium is required for normal osmotic pressure, and for excitability. Potassium depolarizes excitable membranes. The effects of salts on heart and other muscles are discussed in later chapters.

Numerous culture media have been devised (Protozoa,[93] aquatic animals in general).[117] Lack of success in culturing animals in synthetic media may result from salt imbalance as well as from lack of some specific nutritional factor. Many tissues survive better in a saline to which some proteins such as serum globulins, even from unrelated animals, are added. Requirements for minor elements can be established only by very rigorous chemical controls. In general, the following elements are essential: C, H, O, N, P, S, Ca,

TABLE 11.   SALT MIXTURE FOR
MAMMALIAN DIETS
(U.S. Pharmacopeia XIV, 1950)

Calcium carbonate	68.6	gm
Calcium citrate	308.3	
Calcium biphosphate	112.8	
Magnesium carbonate	35.2	
Magnesium sulfate	38.3	
Potassium chloride	124.7	
Dibasic potassium phosphate	218.8	
Sodium chloride	77.1	
Cupric sulfate	0.08	
Ferric ammonium citrate	15.72	
Manganese sulfate	0.21	
Ammonium alum	0.01	
Potassium iodide	0.04	
Sodium fluoride	0.52	
total	1000	gm

K, Na, Fe, Mg, and Co. An element which is not essential to survival may accelerate growth. For example, magnesium accelerates growth of *Euglena anabaens,* and traces of vanadium stimulate *Chilomonas paramecium. Tetrahymena* needs K, PO_3, Fe, Mg, Cu, Ca, and Co, but not Mo, Mn, or SO_4.[93] *Hydra* requires Ca^{++} in the medium. Many salt mixtures have been devised as part of the diet of nonaquatic animals; one of these is given in Table 11.

Maintenance of excised live tissues is ideally best in plasma. However, for practical pur-

poses solutions are used which simulate normal body fluids with respect to salts. When tissues are first excised, permeability is increased and potassium may leak out of cells. Hence the optimal inorganic medium is not necessarily like plasma. The appropriate balance of elements, particularly between Na and K, also the ratio $(Na + K)/(Ca + Mg)$, is more often reached empirically than by analysis of body fluids. Currently in the design of physiological salines there are added organic compounds, particularly amino acids and metabolic substrates (sugars and organic

TABLE 12.   SELECTED PHYSIOLOGICAL SOLUTIONS
(Quantities in grams for 1 liter solution except where indicated)

Animal	NaCl	KCl	CaCl	MgCl₂	NaHCO₃	Other salts*
Homarus[37]	26.42	1.12	2.78	0.32		$MgSO_4$, 0.49; H_3BO_3, 0.5256 NaOH, 0.192
Carcinus[120]	31.4	1.04	1.4	2.3	NaHCO₃ to pH 7.0	
Carcinus[90]	34.1	0.61	1.11	4.95		Na_2SO_4, 4.05
Squid[81]	26.25	0.75	1.17	5.02	2.16	phosphate buffer, pH 7.6
Squid[91]	27.6	0.74	1.09	2.29		$MgSO_4$, 3.32; phosphate buffer pH 7.6
Artificial Sea Water[141]	28.85	0.811	1.244	2.633		Mg_2SO_4, 3.649
Sea Water[76]	23.48	0.66	1.10	4.98	0.19	Na_2SO_4, 3.92 KBr, 0.096; H_3BO_3, 0.026 $SrCl_2$, 0.024; NaF, 0.003
Skate[4]	16.38	0.89	1.11	0.38		Urea, 21.6; NaH_2PO_4, 0.06
Rhinobatus (Elasmobranch)[144]	8.37	0.95	0.4	0.094		Urea, 20.94; glucose, 0.276
Narcine (Elasmobranch)[144]	7.83	0.52	0.67	0.105		Urea, 12.54; glucose, 0.167
Ascaris[6]	7.5	1.42	0.50	0.42		phosphates to pH 6.7
Insects[3]	9.32	0.77	0.50		0.18	0.01 M NaH_2PO_4
Locust[84]	7.59	0.746	0.22	0.188	0.336	0.78 gm KH_2PO_4
Cockroach[180a]	10.93	1.57	0.85	0.17		
Helix[89]	5.74	0.15	1.1			
Fresh-water mussels	Sea water 4 parts to 100 parts solution					
Crayfish[168]	12.0	0.4	1.5	0.25	0.2	
Fish embryo heart[85]	6.5	0.2	0.10	0.04	0.20	glucose, 1.0; phosphate buffer, pH 6.7
Electrophorus[2]	0.19	0.005 M	0.003 M	0.0015 M		phosphate buffer 0.005 M to pH 6.75
Fresh-water fish[31]	5.9	0.25	0.28		2.1	$MgSO_4 \cdot 7H_2O$, 0.29; KH_2PO_4, 1.6
Frog Ringer[134]	6.5	0.14	0.12		0.20	glucose, 2.0; NaH_2PO_4, 0.01 M
Bird Ringer[14a]	6.8	1.73	0.64		2.45	$MgSO_4$, 0.25; pH 7.4
Mammal Ringer[134]	9.0	0.42	0.24		0.2	pH 7.4
Mammal Tyrode[134]	8.0	0.2	0.2	0.1	1.0	NaH_2PO_4, 0.05 M
Mammal Krebs[100] saline	6.9	0.354	0.282		2.1	$MgSO_4 \cdot 7H_2O$, 0.294; KH_2PO_4, 0.162 gm glucose, 2.0
Mammal Krebs[100] medium	5.56	0.354	0.28		2.1	$MgSO_4 \cdot 7H_2O$, 0.294; KH_2PO_4, 0.162 gm glucose, 2.0 Na pyruvate, 0.542 Na fumarate, 0.745 Na L-glutamate, 0.813

* If glucose is used, it is added just before saline is to be used.

acids). It is probable that physiological salt solutions of the future will be very complex. A few useful solutions are presented in Table 12.

CONCLUSIONS

During chemical evolution certain inorganic ions were bound to organic molecules, and by virtue of their physical properties different ions functioned in specific ways. Primitive cells tended to accumulate some elements and to exclude others, and inorganic ions functioned osmotically, in specific biochemical reactions, in maintaining biopotentials and in establishing membrane excitability. In multicellular organisms, ionic gradients are general between intracellular and extracellular fluids; in particular most cells are higher in K^+, Ca^{++}, Mg^{++}, and $HPO_4^=$, and lower in Na^+ and Cl^- than their medium. The body fluids of marine animals are regulated in increasing degree in the series: echinoderms $<$ coelenterates $<$ sipunculids $<$ annelids; much variation in regulation is found in molluscs and arthropods; the maximum regulation is in marine vertebrates. The first ions to be regulated to concentration lower than the medium were magnesium and sulfate; the first to be retained in higher concentration was potassium. Body fluids of some animals conform to the environment in respect to all common ions, some regulate a few ions, and others regulate all. Active transport of ions must have evolved very early, and excretion or absorption of ions involved kidneys and active gill membranes long before excretory organs took over osmotic or nitrogenous waste control. Certain tissues may store given elements, e.g., Ca^{++} or Cu^{++}, to be used at need, and the level in the blood may be under hormonal regulation.

The ionic composition of an animal may vary according to its medium or diet and may be regulated within genetically determined limits. For example, herbivorous insects tend to have higher blood K^+ than carnivorous ones. Fresh-water animals must have mechanisms for retaining salts, and, since none can excrete pure water, for replenishing salt losses. It may well be that penetration of some marine animals into fresh water is limited more by lack of specific ions than by osmotic concentration; eggs of fresh-water animals must have sufficient stores of ions to last until mechanisms of active uptake develop. Distribution, especially in fresh water and soils, may be limited by availability of skeletal elements, by hydrogen ion concentration, and by occurrence of necessary trace elements.

The culture of aquatic animals, and the maintenance of excised tissues in viable condition, require balanced salt solutions. For marine invertebrates, sea water is a first approximation; blood equivalents are better; for other animals, culture media have been devised empirically. For maintenance of tissues, analyses of blood suggest the composition of media, NaCl is added to make up osmotic concentration, and empirical tests are made; the addition of proteins is gaining favor.

As analytical methods are improved, more elements previously considered nonessential prove to be required in small amounts. Iron and copper are used in pigments; these and several other metals are essential for known enzymes or energy-yielding compounds. Other elements are needed in structural compounds, for instance, calcium and silicon in skeletons. The enzymatic role of still other elements, such as molybdenum, is not yet known. Some ions are accumulated by animals of certain species, e.g., vanadium by some tunicates, with no apparent function. Other elements are retained in certain tissues as a sort of storage excretion.

REFERENCES

1. *ALBRITTON, E. C., ed., Standard Values in Blood. Philadelphia, W. B. Saunders Co., 1952, pp. 117-119. Blood electrolytes.
2. ALTAMIRANO, N., J. Cell. Comp. Physiol. *45*: 249-277, 1955. Physiological saline, electric eel.
3. ASPERN, K. V., and VON ESCH, I., Arch. Néerl. Zool. *11*: 342-360, 1956. Composition of hemolymph in Periplaneta.
4. BABKIN, B. P., ET AL., Contr. Canad. Biol. Fish., N.S. *8*: 209-219, 1933. Saline for Raja.
5. BAHL, K. N., Biol. Rev. *22*: 109-147, 1947. Ionic composition, body fluids, earthworms.
6. BALDWIN, E., and MOYLE, V., J. Exp. Biol. *23*: 277-291, 1947. Physiological saline, *Ascaris*.
7. BARNES, H., J. Exp. Biol. *31*: 582-588, 1954. Tables for ionic composition, sea water.
8. BARNES, H., in Treatise on Marine Ecology and Paleoecology *1*: 297-344, 1957. Distribution of ions in the seas.
9. BARRINGTON, E. J. W., J. Mar. Biol. Assn. U. K. *36*: 1-16, 1957; in Comparative Endocrinology, edited by A. Gorbman. New York, John Wiley & Sons, 1959, pp. 250-265. Iodine in ascidian *Ciona* and in Amphioxus.
10. BARRINGTON, E. J. W., and FRANCHI, L. L., Nature *177*: 432, 1956. Iodine in ascidian *Ciona*.
11. BARSA, M. C., J. Gen. Physiol. *38*: 79-92, 1954. Blood composition, grasshopper and moth.

*Reviews

12. BEADLE, L. C., J. Exp. Biol. *16*: 346-362, 1939. Chloride regulation, mosquito larvae.

13. BEADLE, L. C., and CRAGG, J. B., J. Exp. Biol. *17*: 153-163, 1940. Ionic adaptations, Gammarus.

14. BECKER, E. L., ET AL., Physiol. Zool. *31*: 224-227, 1954. Ions in tissues of fish.

14a. BENZINGER, T., and KREBS, H. A., Klin. Wchnschr. *12*: 1206-1208, 1933. Physiological saline, birds.

15. BERGLUND, F., and FORSTER, R. P., J. Gen. Physiol. *41*: 429-440, 1958. Ion transport, aglomerular kidney, *Lophius.*

16. BERNARD, R., and DEMERS, J. M., Rev. Canad. Biol. *11*: 147-158, 1952. Manganese requirement of ducklings.

17. BERTRAND, D., Bull. Am. Mus. Nat. Hist. *94*: 407-455, 1950. Biogeochemistry of vanadium.

18. BERTRAND, G., and MACHEBOEUF, M., C. R. Acad. Sci. *180*: 1380-1383, 1925. Co and Ni in animals.

19. BEVELANDER, G., Biol. Bull. *102*: 9-15, 1952. Calcification in molluscs.

20. BIALASZEWICZ, K., Arch. Internat. Physiol. *36*: 41-53, 1933. Ion composition of bloods, marine animals.

21. BONÉ, G. J., Ann. Soc. Roy. Zool. Belg. *75*: 123-132, 1944. Sodium-potassium ratio in insect hemolymph.

22. BOWEN, V. T., J. Exp. Zool. *115*: 175-206, 1950. Manganese accumulation, Vespidae.

23. BOWEN, V. T., J. Exp. Zool. *118*: 509-529, 1951. Storage of barium and strontium in insects.

24. BOWEN, V. T., and SUTTON, D., J. Mar. Res. *10*: 153-167, 1951. Mineral constituents of sponges.

25. BOYLE, P. J., and CONWAY, E. J., J. Physiol. *100*: 1-63, 1941. Ions in frog muscle.

26. BRECHER, L., Biochem. Ztschr. *211*: 40-64, 1929. Minerals in butterflies.

27. BRULL, L., and CUYPERS, Y., J. Mar. Biol. Assn. U. K. *34*: 637-642, 1952. Kidney function in *Lophius.*

28. BRYAN, G. W., J. Exp. Biol. *37*: 83-128, 1960. Sodium regulation in the crayfish *Astacus fluviatilis.*

29. BURGER, J. W., Anat. Rec. *122*: 460-461, 1955; Biol. Bull. *113*: 207-223, 1957. Excretion in lobster.

30. BURGER, J. W., and HESS, W. N., Science *131*: 670-671, 1960. Salt secretion by rectal gland, ion balance in *Squalus.*

31. BURNSTOCK, G., J. Physiol. *141*: 35-45, 1958. Saline for fresh-water fish.

32. CARLISLE, O. B., Nature *181*: 933, 1958. Niobium in ascidians.

33. CARTER, L., J. Exp. Biol. *34*: 71-84, 1957. Ions in *Spirostomum.*

34. CLARK, E. W., and CRAIG, R., Physiol. Zool. *26*: 101-107, 1953. Calcium and magnesium in insects.

35. *CLARKE, F. W., and WHEELER, W. C., Prof. Papers, U. S. Geol. Surv. *124*: 1-62, 1922. Minerals in marine invertebrates.

36. CLEMENTS, M., and GORBMAN, A., Biol. Bull. *108*: 258-263, 1955. Iodine in endostyle of lamprey larvae.

37. COLE, W. H., J. Gen. Physiol. *25*: 1-6, 1941. Saline for Homarus.

38. CONWAY, E. J., Proc. Roy. Irish Acad. *48*: 119-159, 1942-1943. The origin of ions in the seas.

39. *CONWAY, E. J., Biol. Rev. *20*: 56-72, 1945. Electrolytes in muscle and plasma; frog, rat.

40. CONWAY, E. J., Internat. Rev. Cytol. *4*: 377-396, 1955. Hypothesis for active ion transport.

41. CONWAY, E. J., and HINGERTY, D., Biochem. J. *42*: 372-376, 1948. Ions in mammalian muscle.

42. CROGHAN, P. C., J. Exp. Biol. *35*: 425-436, 1958. Ionic fluxes in *Artemia.*

43. *DANIELLI, J. F., Symp. Exp. Biol. *8*: 1-14, 1954. Selective active transport of ions.

44. DAVIS, G. K., *in* Copper Metabolism, edited by W. McElroy and B. Glass. New York, Academic Press, 1950, pp. 216-229. Requirement of cattle for copper.

45. *DETHIER, V. G., *in* Copper Metabolism, edited by W. McElroy and B. Glass. New York, Academic Press, 1950, pp. 154-174. Copper in invertebrates.

46. DEUTSCH, J. A., and JONES, A. D., Nature *183*: 1472, 1949. Water-salt preference in rats.

47. DRILHON-COURTOIS, A., Ann. Physiol. *10*: 377-424, 1934. Minerals in crustaceans.

48. DUCHATEAU, G., and FLORKIN, M., Arch. Internat. Physiol. *57*: 459-460, 1950. Ions in blood of *Anodonta.*

49. DUCHATEAU, G., FLORKIN, M., and LECLERCQ, J., Arch. Internat. Physiol. *61*: 518-549, 1953. Ions in insect hemolymph.

50. DUGAL, L. P., J. Cell. Comp. Physiol. *13*: 235-251, 1939. Calcium of shell as buffer in clams.

51. EDWARDS, J. G., and CONDORELLI, L., Am. J. Physiol. *86*: 383-398, 1928. Electrolytes in blood and urine of fish.

52. ELLIS, P. E., and HOYLE, G., J. Exp. Biol. *31*: 271-279, 1954. Ion stimulation of locust marching.

53. EMANUEL, C. F., and MARTIN, A. W., Ztschr. vergl. Physiol. *39*: 226-234, 1956. Ions in octopus urine.

54. EVANS, J. V., ET AL., Proc. Roy. Soc. London B, *148*: 249-262, 1958. Genetic differences in K^+ and Na^+ in red blood cells, sheep.

55. FLEMING, W. R., J. Cell. Comp. Physiol. *49*: 129-152, 1957. Sodium transport by frog skin.

56. FLEMISTER, L. J., and FLEMISTER, S. C., Biol. Bull. *101*: 259-273, 1951. Chloride regulation in *Ocypode.*

57. *FLORKIN, M., Biochemical Evolution, edited and translated by S. Morgulis. New York, Academic Press, 1949, 157 pp.

58. FLORKIN, M., DUCHATEAU, G., and LECLERCQ, J., Arch. Internat. Physiol. *57*: 209-210, 1949; C. R. Soc. Biol. *144*: 977-978, 1950. Ions in insect hemolymph, blood of *Anodonta.*

59. FRINGS, L., Science *128*: 1572, 1958. Salt gland secretion, marine birds.

60. GALTSOFF, P. S., Physiol. Zool. *15*: 210-215, 1942. Metals, particularly manganese, in oysters.

61. GILBERT, A. B., J. Exp. Biol. *36*: 113-119, 1959. Blood conductivity, *Carcinus.*

62. GOLDBERG, E. B., McBLAIR, W., and TAYLOR,

K. M., Biol. Bull. *101*: 84-94, 1951. Uptake of vanadium by tunicates.

63. *GORBMAN, A., Physiol. Rev. *35*: 336-346, 1955. Iodine utilization and evolution of thyroid function.

64. GORBMAN, A., BERG, O., and KOBAYASHI, H., *in* Comparative Endocrinology, edited by A. Gorbman. New York, John Wiley & Sons, 1959, pp. 302-319. Iodine utilization and evolution of thyroidal function.

64a. GORBMAN, A., ET AL., J. Exp. Zool. *127*: 75-87, 1954. Iodine utilization and evolution of thyroid function.

65. GORDON, M. S., J. Exp. Biol. *36*: 227-252, 1959. Ion regulation, brown trout.

66. GOREAU, T. F., Biol. Bull. *116*: 59-75, 1959. Mode of calcium deposition, corals.

67. GOREAU, T. F., and GOREAU, N. I., Biol. Bull. *117*: 239-250, 1959. Mode of calcium deposition, corals.

68. GOSNER, K. L., and BLACK, I., Ecology *38*: 256-262, 1957. Frogs in acid bogs.

69. GREEN, J. W., HARSCH, M., BARR, L., and PROSSER, C. L., Biol. Bull. *116*: 76-87, 1959. Ionic regulation, *Uca*.

70. GREGERSON, M. I., The Kidney, *in* MacLeod's Physiology in Modern Medicine, edited by P. Bard, St. Louis, C. V. Mosby Co., 1941, pp. 1093-1198.

71. GROSS, W. J., Biol. Bull. *112*: 248-257, 1957; *113*: 268-274, 1957; *116*: 248-259, 1959. Ionic regulation, *Pachygrapsus*.

72. GROSS, W. J., and HOLLAND, P. V., Phys. Zool. *33*: 21-28, 1960. Water and ionic regulation in terrestrial crab, *Caenobita*.

73. GUNN, S. A., and GOULD, T. C., Am. J. Physiol. *193*: 505-508, 1958. Role of zinc in reproduction, rat.

74. HARRISON, F. M., and MARTIN, A. W., J. Cell. Comp. Physiol. *43*: 247-256, 1954. Calcium in relation to molt, *Limnoria*.

75. HARTMAN, F. A., ET AL., Physiol. Zool. *14*: 476-486, 1941; *17*: 228-238, 1944. Composition of blood of skate.

76. *HARVEY, T. W., Chemistry and Fertility of Sea Waters. Cambridge University Press, 1955, 274 pp.

77. HAYES, F. R., and PELLUET, D., J. Mar. Biol. Assn. U. K. *26*: 580-589, 1947. Inorganic constituents of molluscs.

78. HEIMPEL, A. M., Canad. J. Zool. *34*: 210-212, 1956. pH of insect blood.

79. HERNANDEZ, T., and COULSON, R. A., Science *119*: 291-292, 1954. Constituents of alligator urine.

80. HOBSON, A. D., ET AL., J. Exp. Biol. *29*: 22-29, 1952. Ions in *Ascaris* and its medium.

81. HODGKIN, A. L., and KATZ, B., J. Physiol. *108*: 37-77, 1949. Physiological saline for squid.

82. HODLER, J., ET AL., Am. J. Physiol. *183*: 155-162, 1955. Urine pH, fish.

83. HOKIN, L. E., and HOKIN, M. R., Nature *184*: 1068-1069, 1959; J. Biol. Chem. *234*: 1381, 1959. Phosphatides in Na transport; bird salt gland.

84. HOYLE, G., Nature *169*: 281-282, 1952. Blood potassium and nerve conduction in insects; physiological saline, insects.

85. HUGNEL, H., Ztschr. vergl. Physiol. *42*: 63-102, 1959. Saline for fish heart.

86. JEWELL, M. E., and BROWN, H. W., Ecology *10*: 427-475, 1929; *20*: 11-28, 1939. Ecology of bog lakes.

87. JODREY, L. H., Biol. Bull. *104*: 398-407, 1953. Calcium deposition in oyster shells.

88. JODREY, L. H., and WILBUR, K. M., Biol. Bull. *108*: 346-358, 1955. Calcium deposition in oyster shells.

89. JULLIEN, A., ET AL., C. R. Soc. Biol. *149*: 723-725, 1955. Ions in *Helix*.

90. KEYNES, R. D., J. Physiol. *113*: 73-98, 1951. *Carcinus* saline.

91. KEYNES, R. D., J. Physiol. *117*: 119-150, 1952. Squid saline.

92. KEYNES, R. D., and LEWIS, P. R., J. Physiol. *134*: 399-407, 1956. Calcium in invertebrate nerves.

93. KIDDER, G. W., DEWEY, V. C., and PARKS, R. E., Physiol. Zool. *24*: 69-75, 1951. Inorganic requirements of *Tetrahymena*.

94. KIRSCHNER, L. B., Nature *172*: 348, 1953; J. Cell. Comp. Physiol. *53*: 85-92, 1959. Cholinesterase and ion transport in frog skin.

95. KOCH, H. J., EVANS, J., and SCHICKS, E., Recent Advances in Cell Physiology, edited by J. Kitching. Symp. Colston Res. Soc. *7*: 15-27, 1954. Ion absorption by gills of *Eriocheir*.

96. KOECHLIN, B. A., Proc. Nat. Acad. Sci. *40*: 60-62, 1954; J. Biophys. Biochem. Cytol. *1*: 511-529, 1955. Isothionic acid in squid axons.

97. KOIZUMI, T., Sci. Rep. Tohoku Univ., ser. IV *7*: 259-311, 1932. Electrolyte exchange in holothurian Caudina.

98. KOIZUMI, T., Sci. Rep. Tohoku Univ., ser. IV *10*: 269-275, 277-286, 1935. Inorganic composition of tissues in the holothurian Caudina, and effects of changes in the medium.

99. KRAMER, B., and TISDALL, F. F., J. Biol. Chem. *47*: 475-481, 1921. Electrolytes in human serum.

100. KREBS, H., Biochim. Biophys. Acta *4*: 249-289, 1950. Serum analyses, physiological saline, mammals.

101. *KROGH, A., Osmotic Regulation in Aquatic Animals. Cambridge University Press, 1939. 242 pp.

102. LANSING, A. I., Biol. Bull. *82*: 392-400, 1942. Calcium and aging in invertebrates.

103. *LEHNINGER, A. L., Physiol. Rev. *30*: 393-429, 1950. Metal ions in enzyme systems.

104. LELOUP, J., J. de Physiol. *47*: 671-677, 1955. Iodine in endostyle of *Lampetra* larvae.

105. LEVENBOOK, L., Biochem. J. *47*: 336-346, 1950. Composition of *Gastrophilus* larva blood.

106. LEWIS, P. R., Biochem. J. *52*: 330-338, 1952. Amino acids in invertebrate nerves.

107. LIENEMANN, L. J., J. Cell. Comp. Physiol. *11*: 149-159, 1938. Ions in blood and urine of crayfish.

108. LOCKWOOD, A. P. M., J. Exp. Biol. *36*: 546-556, 562-565, 1959. Ion regulation in fresh-water isopod, *Asellus*.

109. LOWENSTAM, H. A., Proc. Nat. Acad. Sci. *40*: 39-48, 1954. Composition of carbonate-secreting marine invertebrates.

110. LUDWIG, D., Physiol. Zool. *24*: 329-334, 1951. Composition of blood of Japanese beetle.

111. Mahler, H. R., and Green, D. E., Science 120: 7-12, 1954. Metalloflavoproteins and electron transport.

112. Malvin, R. L., et al., Am. J. Physiol. 195: 549-557, 1958. Ion transport along renal tubule.

113. *Manery, J. F., Physiol. Rev. 34: 334-417, 1954. Water and electrolyte metabolism.

114. *Marston, H. R., Physiol. Rev. 32: 66-121, 1952. Cobalt, copper, and molybdenum in nutrition.

115. McLennan, H., Ztschr. vergl. Physiol. 37: 490-495, 1955. Ions in blood and eggs of crayfish.

116. Needham, J., Biol. Zentbl. 50: 504-509, 1930. Ionic barriers to penetration of marine organisms into fresh water.

117. Needham, J. G., Galtsoff, P. S., Lutz, F. E., and Welch, P. S., Culture Methods for Invertebrate Animals. Ithaca, N. Y., Comstock Publishing Co., 1937, 590 pp.

118. Odum, H. T., Bull. Mar. Sci. Gulf Carib. 3: 134-156, 1953. Invasion of hard waters by marine animals.

119. Odum, H. T., Science 114: 211-213, 1951; Publ. Inst. Mar. Sci. 4: 38-114, 1957. Biochemical deposition of strontium.

120. Pantin, C. F. A., J. Exp. Biol. 11: 11-27, 1934. Saline for Carcinus.

121. Parry, G., J. Exp. Biol. 30: 567-574, 1953. Ionic regulation in isopod Ligia.

122. Parry, G., J. Exp. Biol. 31: 601-613, 1954. Ionic regulation in prawn Palaemon.

123. Pitts, R. F., J. Cell. Comp. Physiol. 4: 389-395, 1934. Urine composition, marine fish.

124. Potts, W. R. W., J. Exp. Biol. 31: 376-385, 1954. Composition of blood, Mytilus and Anodonta.

125. Poulson, D. F., and Bowen, V. T., Exp. Cell. Res. Supp. 2: 161-180, 1952. Accumulation of iron by Drosophila larvae.

126. Prosser, C. L., Green, J. W., and Chow, T. J., Biol. Bull. 109: 99-107, 1955. Ionic balance in Pachygrapsus.

127. Ramsay, J. A., J. Exp. Biol. 29: 110-126, 1952. Sodium and potassium excretion by malpighian tubules of Rhodnius.

128. Ramsay, J. A., J. Exp. Biol. 31: 104-113, 1954; 32: 183-199, 1955; 33: 697-708, 1956. Excretion in stick insect Dixippus.

129. Ramsay, J. A., J. Exp. Biol. 30: 79-89, 1953. Sodium and potassium exchanges, mosquito larvae.

130. Ramsay, J. A., J. Exp. Biol. 26: 46-56, 65-75, 1949. Chloride excretion in earthworms.

131. *Ramsay, J. A., J. Exp. Biol. 30: 358-369, 1953; Symp. Soc. Exp. Biol. 8: 1-15, 1954. Movements of electrolytes in insects and other invertebrates.

131a. Rao, K. P.: Experientia 9: 465, 1953. Effect of intertidal level on calcium deposition in Mytilus.

132. Rao, K. P., and Goldberg, E. D., J. Cell. Comp. Physiol. 43: 283-292, 1954. Utilization of dissolved calcium by Mytilus.

133. Reid, B. L., et al., Proc. Soc. Exp. Biol. Med. 94: 737-740, 1957. Molybdenum in poultry nutrition.

134. Richards, O., ed., Marine Biol. Lab. Formulae and Methods, 1936. Elasmobranch saline.

135. Robertson, J. D., J. Exp. Biol. 13: 279-297, 1939. Calciferous glands of earthworms.

136. Robertson, J. D., J. Exp. Biol. 26: 182-200, 1949; 30: 277-296, 1953. Ionic regulation in marine invertebrates.

137. Robertson, J. D., J. Exp. Biol. 31: 424-442, 1954. Composition of blood of lower chordates.

138. *Robertson, J. D., in Physiology of Invertebrate Animals, edited by B. T. Scheer. University of Oregon Press, 1957, pp. 229-246. Ionic regulation by invertebrates.

139. Robertson, J. D., and Webb, K. A., J. Exp. Biol. 16: 155-177, 1939. Estimation of ions in body fluids of marine animals.

140. Robertson, R. H., and Schaible, P. J., Science 127: 875, 1958. Zinc requirement of chick.

141. Robinson, R. A., J. Mar. Biol. Assn. U. K. 33: 449-455, 1954. Vapor pressure and osmotic equivalence of sea water.

141a. Roots, B., Unpublished data. Ions in earthworm body fluids.

142. Rothschild, L., and Barnes, H., J. Exp. Biol. 30: 534-544, 1953. Inorganic constituents of sea urchin eggs.

143. *Rubey, W. W., Bull. Geol. Soc. America 62: 1111-1148, 1951. Geological history of sea water.

144. Salome Pereira, R., and Sawaya, P., Bol. Fac. Fil. Cien. Univ. Sao Paulo Zool. no. 21, 85-92, 1957. Ions in blood of elasmobranchs.

145. Scholles, W., Ztschr. vergl. Physiol. 19: 522-554, 1933. Ionic regulation in crayfish.

146. Shaw, J., J. Exp. Biol. 32: 383-396, 1955. Ionic regulation in muscle fibers, Carcinus.

147. Shaw, J., J. Exp. Biol. 32: 353-382, 1955. Absorption of ions by larvae of Sialis.

148. Shaw, J., J. Exp. Biol. 36: 145-156, 1959. Ion balance in muscle fibers of a fresh-water crab, Potamon.

149. Shipp, J. C., et al., Am. J. Physiol. 195: 563-570, 1958. Ion transport by kidney tubules of Necturus.

150. Shohl, A. T., Mineral Metabolism. New York, Reinhold Publishing Corp., 1939, 384 pp.

151. Slater, J. V., Physiol. Zool. 25: 283-287, 1952. Magnesium requirement of Tetrahymena.

152. Slater, J. V., Physiol. Zool. 25: 323-332, 1952; Biol. Bull. 112: 390-399, 1957. Influence of accumulation of cobalt in Tetrahymena.

153. *Smith, H. W., Principles of Renal Physiology. New York, Oxford University Press, 1956, 237 pp.

154. Smith, R. I., Biol. Bull. 109: 453-474, 1955. Chloride balance in Nereis diversicolor.

155. Steinbach, H. B., Biol. Bull. 78: 444-453, 1939. Electrolytes in Phascolosoma muscle.

156. Stobbart, R. H., J. Exp. Biol. 36: 641-653, 1959. Sodium regulation in larvae of Aedes aegypti.

157. Sullivan, L. P., et al., Am. J. Physiol. 198: 244-254, 1960. Ion transport along renal tubule.

158. Thomas, I. M., J. Mar. Biol. Assn. U. K. 35: 203-210, 1956. Iodine uptake by Amphioxus.

159. Thompson, T. G., and Chow, T. J., in Papers, Marine Biology and Oceanography, Pergamon, 1956, pp. 20-39. Strontium-calcium ratio in marine organisms.

160. Tobias, J. M., J. Cell. Comp. Physiol. 31: 125-

142, 1948. Potassium, sodium, and water in muscle, nerve, and blood of cockroach.

161. Tobias, J. M., J. Cell. Comp. Physiol. *31*: 143-148, 1948. Potassium and sodium in tissues of silkworm.

162. Totter, J. R., and Comar, C. L., *in* Inorganic Nitrogen Metabolism, edited by W. D. McElroy and B. Glass. Johns Hopkins University Press, 1956, pp. 513-520. Molybdenum in xanthine oxidase.

163. Treherne, J. E., J. Exp. Biol. *31*: 386-401, 1954. Exchange of sodium in larvae of *Aedes*.

164. *Underwood, E. J., *in* Biochemistry and Physiology of Nutrition, edited by G. H. Bourne and G. Kidder. New York, Academic Press, 1953, vol. 2, pp. 427-504. Trace elements.

165. *Underwood, E. J., Trace Elements in Human and Animal Nutrition. New York, Academic Press, 1956, 430 pp.

166. *Underwood, E. J., Ann. Rev. Biochem. *28*: 499-526, 1959. Mineral metabolism.

167. *Ussing, H. H., Symp. Soc. Exp. Biol. *8*: 407-422, 1954. Active transport of inorganic ions.

168. Van Harreveld, A., Proc. Soc. Exp. Biol. Med. *34*: 428-432, 1936. Physiological saline for crayfish.

169. *Vinogradov, A. P., The Elementary Chemical Composition of Marine Organisms. Memoir Sears Found. Mar. Res. II. Yale University Press, 1953, 647 pp.

170. Waterhouse, D. F., Austral. J. Sci. Res. *B, 4*: 144-162, 1951. Barium and strontium in insects.

171. Webb, D. A., Proc. Roy. Soc. London, *B, 129*: 107-136, 1940. Osmotic and ionic regulation in *Carcinus*.

172. Webb, D. A., Publ. Staz. Zool. Napoli *28*: 273-288, 1956. Vanadium in marine invertebrates.

173. *Webb, D. A., and Fearon, W. R., Scient. Proc. Roy. Dublin Soc. *21*: 487-503, 505-539, 1937. Chemical elements in marine animals.

174. Whittenbury, G., et al., Am. J. Physiol. *197*: 1121-1127, 1959. Ion and water movements through *Necturus* kidney tubules.

175. Wigglesworth, V. B., J. Exp. Biol. *15*: 235-247, 1938. Chloride regulation, blood of *Aedes* larvae.

176. Wikgren, B. J., Acta Zool. Fennica *71*: 1-102, 1953. Ion regulation in lampreys.

177. Wilber, C. G., and Robinson, P. F., J. Mammal. *39*: 309-310, 1958. Blood composition of deer.

178. Wilde, W. S., and Malvin, R. L., Am. J. Physiol. *195*: 153-160, 1958. Ion movements along kidney tubule.

179. *Williams, R. J. P., Biol. Rev. *28*: 381-415, 1953. Metal ions in biological systems.

180. Woodring, W. P., Proc. Nat. Acad. Sci. *40*: 219-224, 1954. Paleochemistry.

180a. Yeager, J. F., J. Agric. Res. *59*: 121-137, 1939. Physiological saline, cockroach.

181. Zuckerkandl, E., C. R. Soc. Biol. *151*: 460-463, 676-679, 1957. Copper concentration in hemolymph and hepatopancreas of *Mya*.

182. Zundel, W. S., and Woodbury, D. M., Fed. Proc. *19*: 66, 1960. Sodium and potassium in mammalian erythrocytes.

Chapter 4

NUTRITION

Nutritive patterns show wide variation in what is required in diet from the environment and what an animal can synthesize. Organic nutrients are required in three different orders of magnitude: (1) Energy-yielding compounds must be available in sufficient quantity to permit growth and work, usually in grams per kilogram of body weight daily. (2) Substances such as amino acids, purines, and some lipids are needed in milligram amounts by diet or synthesis within the animal to provide carbon skeletons for more complex organic molecules. (3) Specific growth factors—vitamins, coenzymes—are needed in quantities of micrograms per kilogram of body weight daily. Animals differ greatly from one another in their capacity to use different energy-yielding compounds, to convert compounds of one class of foodstuff to another, and to synthesize the specific dietary substances.

What is a vitamin for one animal may not be a dietary requirement for another. The amino acids which constitute proteins are similar in all organisms, although the proportions vary from one protein to another, and the coenzymes of cellular metabolism, such as the phosphopyridine nucleotides, are similar in all cells. Animals differ as to which amino acids and coenzymes can be synthesized and which must be taken as food. Some special food requirements are associated with physiological specializations of certain animals. Some essential substances may be synthesized by an animal but in insufficient amounts; hence they are required in the diet. Many animals obtain essential nutrients from symbiotic bacteria.

The nutrition of a given animal reflects its microhabitat, although food selection is often more influenced by taste preferences than by nutritive values (Chapter 11). Herbivores, carnivores, omnivores, and dietary specialists usually differ in their digestive capacities (Chapter 5). The basic aspects of nutrition were established before the appearance of animals as we know them, and the evolution of animal nutrition is replete with examples of loss of ability for specific synthesis and subsequent dependence on external sources.

ORIGIN OF NUTRITIVE TYPES

Organisms fall into three classes (Table 13) with respect to sources of energy: (1) Chemotrophic organisms (largely bac-

TABLE 13.   PATTERNS OF MINIMAL NITROGEN AND CARBON REQUIREMENTS[39, 96]

Nitrogen source	Carbon source		
	Chemotrophic (inorganic energy sources)	Phototrophic (CO_2 in light)	Heterotrophic (acetate or other acids or sugars)
Autotrophic NO_3	Fe and S bacteria	Green flagellates, e.g., Euglena gracilis in light Chlamydomonas	Polytoma ocellatum
NH_3			P. uvella Chilomonas paramecium
Mesotrophic (single amino acids)		Euglena deses	Euglena gracilis in dark Strigomonas sp.
Metatrophic (mixture of many amino acids)		E. pisciformis	Ciliates (Tetrahymena) "higher animals"

teria) get their energy from inorganic reactions such as oxidation of iron or sulfur. (2) Phototrophic cells use sunlight in photosynthesis. (3) Heterotrophic organisms oxidize preexisting organic compounds of varying degrees of complexity; some can use lower fatty acids such as acetate but most need sugars or higher carbohydrates. With respect to nitrogen sources, organisms are autotrophic if they can use inorganic nitrogen, nitrate, or ammonia; they are mesotrophic if they can rely on single amino acids (or ammonia and an organic acid); and are metatrophic if they require many amino acids either in compounds or mixtures. All animals except green flagellate protozoans are ultimately dependent on photoautotrophic plants for their carbon sources of energy. Whether flagellates are plants or animals is a matter of definition, but they certainly represent the widest range of nutritional patterns; some are photosynthetic, others heterotrophic, some can use nitrate (*Chlamydomonas, Euglena gracilis*), some ammonia (*Chilomonas*), a few are mesotrophic (*Euglena deses*) or metatrophic (*Euglena pisciformis*);[39] many of them require a few vitamins; parasitic flagellates have highly specialized requirements. Nutritionally flagellates present plant-like and animal-like aspects.

Modern ideas of the origin of life stem from Oparin, and it is postulated that the first organisms were heterotrophic forms which used preexisting compounds; then phototrophs appeared, to be followed by the heterotrophic forms we now know as animals.[7, 14, 148] The age of the earth is placed by geochemists at between 4.5 and 5 billion years. Between 1.5 and 2.5 billion years ago the earth's atmosphere changed from reducing to oxidizing. The earliest fossils are of blue-green algae 1 to 1.5 billion years old, while the earliest Cambrian animal fossils are approximately 0.51 billion years old. The primitive reducing atmosphere contained, according to Urey, nitrogen, hydrogen, water, and some methane and ammonia, but lacked free oxygen. It permitted much radiation, particularly ultraviolet, to reach the earth. It is postulated that in shallow bodies of sea water under the action of high-energy radiation, organic molecules were formed and that these accumulated during a billion or more years.[14] Miller has circulated an aqueous solution of methane, ammonia, and hydrogen through an energy field and within as short a time as a week amino acids, lower fatty

acids, and other organic molecules were found.[105] In the primitive "organic soup," reactions between organic molecules and polymerization of some of these occurred, with the utilization of energy. The energy may have been provided by high energy organophosphates. Metallo-organic compounds probably appeared and iron porphyrins would have been very effective catalysts of energy-yielding oxidations.[19] It would be a short step from iron porphyrins to photochemical reactions and the liberation of oxygen. Polymerization of both nucleic acids and proteins presumably occurred, and it has been shown that artificial peptides tend to coil in an alpha helix as soon as eight to ten members are reached and that polymerization accelerates as coiling proceeds.[57] The amino acids which became incorporated into proteins were L-amino acids. The manner of duplication of macromolecules remains unknown, but it is probable that coacervate droplets containing DNA first duplicated, and that proteins have never self-duplicated in the absence of nucleic acids as templates. Polypeptides have been synthesized by condensation reactions involving addition of single amino acids, but in living cells proteins are formed from mixtures of amino acids by action of a nucleic acid template and without successive additions.

The aggregates of nucleoproteins with capacity for duplication and other proteins capable of enzymatic degradation of organic substances for energy were the first organisms.[57] In these heterotrophic pro-organisms those properties basic to all life evolved—use of high energy phosphate bonds for transferring energy in biological work, stepwise electron transfer in intermediary metabolism, use of metalloproteins to catalyze oxidation, use of L-amino acids in natural proteins, active transport of ions by cell surfaces, the use of certain ions intracellularly and rejection of others, selective permeability of membranes, the control of protein synthesis by nucleic acids, and many other universal properties of living things. Biochemically and biophysically, far more evolution took place before there were living organisms as we know them than since. The time during which chemical evolution occurred was much longer than the time for organic evolution. Perhaps this is the reason the similarity of living organisms is more impressive than their diversity.

As the supply of organic compounds became depleted, mechanisms for synthesizing which had appeared by mutation had selective value, and photoautotrophs plus some chemoautotrophs evolved from heterotrophic pro-organisms. The oxygen of the present atmosphere is derived from photosynthesis, and the present atmosphere filters out much of the short-wave radiation which formerly impinged on the earth; hence suitable conditions for the creation of life existed only during one period in the history of the earth. The transition from anaerobic to aerobic conditions permitted important biochemical changes. In general, the ability to use light or inorganic reactions to provide energy for CO_2 reduction goes with the ability to use nitrate or ammonia (rarely atmospheric nitrogen), and, in contrast, heterotrophic organisms which require fatty acids or sugars also need amino acid nitrogen.

Beginning with the generalized patterns of nutrition in the flagellates, animals show increasing specialization and dependence on environmental sources for nutrients. The type of basic foodstuff used by an animal depends partly on its position in a food chain, for example, the chain from phytoplankton to zooplankton to small fish and large ones. Selection of food plants by insects on the basis of taste is highly specialized, and the nutritive value of sugars is not necessarily correlated with taste preferences.[47] Drosophila species are isolated, in part, by selection of certain strains of yeast as food.[32, 36] Many animals, for example, ruminants and termites, use symbiotic microorganisms not only to synthesize vitamins but to digest basic foodstuffs (Chapter 5). Other organisms such as corals and some flatworms contain photosynthetic zooxanthellae within their tissues and use some products from these as food.

CARBON REQUIREMENTS

Phototrophic green flagellates (chloroflagellates) reduce CO_2 directly in light and use organic acids or sugars for energy in the dark. The colorless flagellates (leucophytes) were derived from green forms, and some species can change color and form according to amount of light. Leucophytes have been cultured extensively on acetate[120] and other organic acids,[146] and they differ specifically as to which acids they can use.[97] Numerous flagellates use lower fatty acids and alcohols but cannot use sugars. *Polytomella caeca,* for example, lacks hexokinase and hence cannot phosphorylate glucose.[97] *P. agilis* can use ethanol, butanol, acetate but not methanol, formate, or citrate.[94] *Prototheca* uses saturated fatty acids up to palmitic, and some alcohols, but not formic acid and not dicarboxylic acids.[8] *Polytoma caeca* can use acids of up to 5 carbons (valerate) but not caproate, yet it can use hexyl alcohol.[155] *Chlamydomonas* uses only the even-numbered fatty acids and even-numbered monohydric alcohols, and lactic and tricarboxylic acids, while the odd-numbered alcohols above C_1 inhibit growth.[27] When *Polytomella uvella* is transferred from an acetate to butyrate medium it increases its ability to oxidize butyrate by six to ten times by a process of enzyme induction;[22] grown without butyrate it loses ability to utilize butyrate.[121] *Chilomonas* uses only even-numbered carbon fatty acids, alcohols, lactic acid, and the acids of the tricarboxylic acid cycle. Odd-numbered acids above C_1 inhibit growth, and there is no use of sugars.[27]

The ciliate *Tetrahymena* can make carbohydrate and fatty acids from acetate.[132] It is commonly cultured with glucose as its principal energy source; it can also use levulose, mannose, and maltose but cannot use some thirteen other sugars, including sucrose.[71] Failure to culture some ciliates in the absence of living food is probably related to protein rather than to carbohydrate requirement.[91]

Parasites are often able to use only foods which have been partly degraded. A number of cestodes, for example, can use only a few monosaccharides but no disaccharides. For example, *Lacistorhynchus* from a dogfish uses glucose and galactose but not mannose, fructose, maltose, sucrose, or lactose.[124] Several insects such as cockroaches, *Tenebrio,* and *Drosophila* have been cultured with glucose as carbohydrate. Some adult insects normally live exclusively on a diet of sugars. Adult honeybees can survive on any of seven sugars which are sweet to them and on six which are tasteless, but they cannot use five others which are tasteless.[150] *Ephestia kuehniella* uses starch and glucose; *Ephestia entella* uses only glucose.[50] Adult blowflies can use all pentoses except fucose and hexoses except sorbose; they can use maltose, sucrose, trehalose, and melezitose well, but use lactose and cellobiose poorly; there is poor correlation between utilization and taste stimulation of the tarsi.[63] Blowflies can live on α-glucosides and α-galactosides but not on other glycosides.[45] Wood-eating insects use various components from the wood (p. 117). Termites appear to be nourished mainly by lower fatty acids formed from cellulose in their digestive tracts by symbiotic flagellates.

The interconversion of carbohydrates, fats, and proteins has been studied more in mammals than in other organisms. Some animal tissues as well as bacteria can fix some CO_2 in the reaction from pyruvic to oxaloacetic acids; it is probable that such CO_2 fixation can occur in most cells. When mice breathe a bit of $C^{14}O_2$, some C^{14} appears in liver glycogen within a few minutes. The normal equilibrium in intermediary metabolism is such that CO_2 fixation is negligible in the over-all carbon economy. Rats can survive on a diet of protein (plus minerals and vitamins), but they then excrete an excess of acetone bodies. Acetate can be substituted for part of the carbohydrate in a rat's diet. Some protein and fat are necessary to provide essential amino acids and fatty acids, but it is possible for mammals (man included) to dispense with dietary carbohydrate. The total requirement of carbon compounds is largely determined by the caloric needs. For an average man these needs may range from 65 Cal/hr when asleep to 500 Cal/hr at strenuous work. The energy yield of the different foodstuffs in kilocalories per gram is approximately 4.1 for protein and carbohydrate and 9.3 for fat.

In summary: Intermediate degradation products of the three classes of basic foodstuffs enter common enzymatic pathways; hence there is some common usage and even interconversion. Such dietary differences as exist among heterotrophs result from differences in digestive enzymes and in enzymes for the initial stages of degradation.

NITROGEN REQUIREMENTS

Relatively few organisms—nitrogen-fixing bacteria and fungi—can utilize atmospheric nitrogen. Most photosynthetic plants can utilize nitrates. For example, blue-green algae (e.g., *Phormidium*)[119] can use NO_3 or ammonia but not nitrogen. Some colorless flagellates (*Astasia* and *Chilomonas*) are unable to use amino acids from the medium but require ammonia as a nitrogen source.[74] *Astasia chattoni* grows well on a medium of ammonia and acetate.[74] Marked strain differences in *Astasia longa* exist.[130] Other flagellates, e.g., some species of *Euglena*, grow on single amino acids;[39] *Strigomonas* sp, a parasitic flagellate from insects, needs the single amino acid methionine but can synthesize it if supplied threonine, cysteine, and serine.[111]

All other animals require mixtures of amino acids. Ruminant mammals make use of symbiotic bacteria which build essential amino acids from ammonia.[95] Other mammals, laboratory and domestic, have been found to utilize small amounts of ammonia if given in addition an adequate mixture of essential amino acids. Experiments with N^{15}-labeled NH_4OH show that *Calliphora* larvae can use some ammonia.[133, 134] It is probable that all animals are able to make use of some ammonium salts.

Many animals—Protozoa, insects, and vertebrates—have been cultured or maintained on mixtures of amino acids as the sole nitrogen source. Some of them need exogenous purine-pyrimidine while others can make these necessary compounds (see p. 89). Cestode worms appear to be unable to utilize whole protein and to use only amino acids; they normally live in a medium rich in amino acids, the intestine of a host. Some ciliates (*Tetrahymena*) do well on amino acids as sole nitrogen sources, while other carnivorous ciliates (*Stylonychia, Euplotes, Colpidium,* and a suctorian) have not been cultured without whole protein or polypeptides.[81, 92] Some amoebae grow better on living than on dead bacteria.[15] It is probable that the apparent requirement of protein or even of living food is not nutritional but has to do with ingestion. *Stylonychia* and *Euplotes* grow well on a diet of *Tetrahymena* grown on a sterile synthetic medium, plus some vitamin supplements.[92] *Artemia* grow on a liquid medium rich in nutrients only to third-stage metanauplii; if starch grains are added to stimulate filter feeding the brine shrimps grow to adults axenically.[122]

SPECIFIC FACTORS IN NUTRITION

In biochemical evolution, certain types of organic compounds came to be essential for protoplasmic structure and function. Synthesis of proteins, carbohydrates, fats, and nucleic acids requires definite structural components. In addition, energy-yielding and synthetic reactions came to be catalyzed by enzymes consisting of proteins plus specific cofactors. Later, specialized functions, often in single or several tissues of certain groups of animals, developed, with unique requirements for specific carbon compounds.

The evolution of the nutrition of special requirements is partly one of the loss of synthetic capacity so that what is a dietary essential for one animal is not for another. Whether a given substance is a dietary essential is often determined by whether or not it is synthesized in sufficient amount by the animal. Frequently, symbiotic microorganisms synthesize the essential nutrient so that the host without the microorganisms needs the "vitamin" but with its normal symbionts does not need it, or the organism, e.g., parasite, may live in a medium rich in essential substances and use exogenous supply exclusively.

Many dietary essentials are needed in larger amounts for growth than for adult maintenance; hence they are called growth factors. Need for an essential nutrient is recognized by retarded growth or by some defect in adults after they have been fed a diet deficient in a given substance. In practice, nutritionists aim first at axenic culture, that is, culture in the absence of cther living organisms, particularly bacteria, yeasts, and protozoans. This usually means supplying a source of protein and carbohydrate plus a sterile extract of yeast, liver, or other complex biological mixture. The next steps are to fractionate the protein and ultimately culture the organism on a mixture of amino acids and to substitute various known vitamins for the tissue extract. The identification of essential amino acids and of specific vitamins has been made for relatively few organisms, yet certain common patterns are emerging and the qualitative requirements for a few ciliates, some parasitic protozoa and helminths, and the insects and vertebrates in general can be predicted with some accuracy.

The quantitative approach to nutrition is made difficult by the fact that a given nutrient is sometimes essential only if some other nutrient is lacking. Precursors may be substituted for an essential nutrient as, may related substances. A compound may spare the need for a more usual nutrient and may or may not completely replace it. Another difficulty is that nutrients must be ingested before they can be utilized, and certain diets might be adequate nutritionally but are not accepted by an animal.

Requirement for a nutrient may first appear in a second generation on a diet lacking it; hence small but sufficient amounts may be carried in the egg for one generation.[60]

A survey of essential nutrients shows some which are required by classes or possibly phyla, and still others which are needed only by certain genera or even species. Most of the so-called essentials are actually used in cellular function by all animals but are synthesized by many, hence are not needed from an exogenous source. Some synthesizing abilities have been retained by all animals; some must have been lost early in animal evolution, others at the establishment of certain phyla; still others have been genetic losses in single species or even strains. Examples will be given of both general and specific requirements.

There is no satisfactory classification of all dietary essentials; they can, however, be grouped according to the way they are used: (1) Some organic compounds are needed because they provide carbon skeletons or essential side groups of organic molecules. These substances are required in relatively large amounts (0.5 to 2 gm/day by human). Usually organic homologues or substances which are similar in some key structure can be substituted for the normal nutrient. The best-known of this category are the essential amino acids. (2) Other dietary essentials are used as coenzymes in specific reactions of intermediary metabolism. These are needed in small amounts (0.1 to 1 mg/day in man), and they may be grouped as water-soluble vitamins. (3) Still other substances are less universally needed and may function only in specialized tissues. Examples are some fat-soluble vitamins. These resemble hormones which have specific target organs. Indeed they may be considered as exogenous hormones. Blood and tissue levels of the coenzyme precursors decrease with increasing body size as does metabolism, while the more specialized vitamins show no such relationship.[10] The need for coenzymes evolved very early and is most widespread; that for amino acids appeared early in animal evolution. The specialized needs often represent substances belonging to a class of compounds used previously for other functions.

Substances Required for Organic Structure

Amino Acid Requirements. During growth, new protein is continually being synthesized. In adult animals the body proteins are being replaced at variable rates; the half-time for replacement of total protein in a rat is 17 days; in a man 80 days.[153] For the synthesis of protein, animals need varying proportions of the twenty common amino acids. In addition, specific amino acids are needed for the synthesis of various nitrogen-containing compounds other than proteins, for example, various amines and glutathione. Certain amino acids are needed, not specifically for their nitrogen, but especially for their carbon skeleton, and analogues can be substituted for some of these, for example, phenylpyruvic acid can be aminated to form phenylalanine and this can go to alanine.

All autotrophic organisms can synthesize each of the twenty normally occurring amino acids, but animals in general (except flagellates) have lost the ability to synthesize some of these. Certain amino acids are essential in the diet whereas others are dispensable; evidently they are synthesized by the animal in sufficient amounts either from ammonia and carbohydrate or from specific amino acid precursors. Some proteins are inadequate nutritionally in that they are deficient in particular essential amino acids. Zein is deficient in tryptophan, lysine, cysteine, and hydroxyproline; human and beef hemoglobins are deficient in isoleucine and rich in methionine, whereas dog hemoglobin is high in isoleucine and lacking in methionine.[153] Beef plasma albumin is deficient in tryptophan, isoleucine, and methionine, rich in lysine and cystine. Egg albumin is low in leucine and glutamic acid; casein is low in glycine. The essential amino acids have been identified by the systematic omission of each from a diet. The cockroach *Blatella* grows well on fibrin or casein, less well on egg albumin and wheat glutin, very poorly on zein, gelatin, and hemoglobin.[89] *Tetrahymena* used proteins of fish meal or egg albumin twice as well as those of soybeans or linseed and used gelatin hardly at all. The order of utilization differed according to nitrogen level in the diet.[43] Wood-eating *Limnoria* appears to use amino acids from fungi infecting the wood.[84]

A few of the dispensable amino acids are particularly stimulating on growth and may be needed as dietary supplements at certain developmental stages. The amounts of each required amino acid are relative rather than absolute because they depend on the balance of other amino acids. Interconversions among the amino acids are numerous and some may be used as precursors of others.[131] An increase of one may cause a deficiency of the next most limiting amino acid. For example, in rats if threonine is added alone to a suboptimal diet, growth is retarded unless tryptophan is also added in proportion; methionine or lysine alone depresses growth; when they are together growth is normal. Similarly, if leucine is added to a 9 per cent casein diet, growth is less than on casein alone, but if isoleucine also is added, normal growth resumes.[42]

Toxicity of single amino acids may be antagonized not only by others but sometimes by certain B vitamins. For example, high methionine in low casein is depressant and counteracted by pyridoxine.[42] Some mutants of the bacteria *E. coli* require certain amino acids at high but not at low temperatures.[113] Natural amino acids are the L-acids, and L-amino acids are generally used much better than D-amino acids. However, there is much variation among amino acids as to whether a D-acid can be used, is indifferent, or is toxic. Statements of essentiality of amino acids must, therefore, be qualified by reference to other dietary components.

With a recognition of the preceding restrictions, Table 14 summarizes recent data on essential and dispensable amino acids. The most striking feature is the similarity in requirements by all animals. Apparently the general pattern of loss of synthetic capacity of some nine (or ten) amino acids was established very early in animal evolution. Superimposed on this general pattern of similar amino acid requirements there are specific requirements for certain animals. Some amino acids are indicated as stimulating growth but are not essential for adult maintenance; pairs of others are indicated as interchangeable. Some animals, e.g., cockroaches, can be cultured through certain stages, but not throughout a full life cycle without a certain acid.

Tetrahymena geleii, strain W, was the first ciliate to be cultured on a synthetic medium of known chemicals, and ten amino acids were required (Table 14). Methionine can be replaced by homocysteine as a sulfur-containing amino acid,[81] and growth is stimulated by serine or glycine. Strain E, however, requires serine, making its total requirement eleven amino acids. Growth is slowed although survival is possible in the absence of arginine; tyrosine spares but cannot replace phenylalanine.[80] Both citrulline and ornithine can spare arginine; some amino acids, e.g., histidine, are toxic in high concentration, while in the absence of serine the need for threonine is increased.[68] The D-isomers of some—threonine, isoleucine, and tryptophan— are not utilized but D-arginine is used.[81] Cysteine and homocysteine can spare methionine for *Tetrahymena*;[40] quantitative needs depend on the balance among amino acids.[61] *Paramecium multimicronucleatum* is similar to *Tetrahymena geleii,* strain E, in amino acid requirements.[75] It has been impossible to culture the carnivorous *Glaucoma scintillans* or *Colpidium campylum* on amino acid mixtures although they do well in a medium of casein and are stimulated by additional specific amino acids in casein. It is probable that

TABLE 14. REQUIREMENTS OF ANIMALS FOR AMINO ACIDS

Protozoa group: *Tetrahymena* Strain W81, *Tetrahymena* Strain E40, *Paramecium*[75], *Crithidia*[82].

Amino acid	Strain W81	Strain E40	Paramecium[75]	Crithidia[82]	Phormia[21,67]	Pseudo-sarcophaga[70]	Musca[20]	Calliphora[133,134]	Drosophila[65,66]	Aedes larva[137]	Hylemya[56]	Blatella[60]	Apis[33]	Caenorhabditis[37]	Salmon[34]	Chinook salmon[62]	Rat[126]	Chicken[4]	Man[2,126]
glycine	−	−	+	−	−	stim	−	−	stim	−(+pupa)	−	−	−	−	−	−	−	stim	−
alanine	−	−	stim	−	−	stim	−	−	stim	−	−	or glut +2nd gen	−	−	−	−	−	−	−
valine	+	+	+	+	+	+	+	+	+	+	+	+2nd gen	+	+	+	+	+	+	+
leucine	+	+	+	+	+	+	+	+	+	+	+pupa	+2nd gen	+	+	+	+	+	+	+
serine	−stim	++	or glyc	−	−	stim	−	−	−	stim	−	−	−	−	−	−	−	−	−
lysine	+	++	+	+	+	+	+	+	+	+	+pupa	+2nd gen	+	+	+	+	+	+	+
isoleucine	+	++	+	+	+	+	+	+	+	+	+	+	+	+	+	+	+	+	+
histidine	+	++	++	++	++	++	++	++	+	++	+3rd instar	+	++	++	++	+	+	+	+growth
arginine	+	++	++	+or cit	++	++	++	++	+or cit	++	+	+fertile	++	++	++	+	+growth	++	+growth
phenylalanine	+	+	+	+	+	+	+	+	+	+	+3rd instar	+eggs	+	+	+	+	+	+	+
tyrosine	−	−	+	+	+	stim	−	−	−	+	−	+eggs	−	+	+	+	−	−	−
tryptophan	+	+	+	+	+	+	+	−	−	+	+	+2nd gen	+	+	+	+	+	+	+
proline	−	−	+	−	−	−	−	−	−	stim	−	−	stim	−	−	−	−	−	−
hydroxyproline	−	−	stim	−	+	−	−	−	−	stim	−	−	−	−	−	−	−	stim	−
glutamic acid	−	−	stim	−	or asp	−	−	−	−	−	−	−	−	−	−	−	−	−	−
aspartic acid	−	−	stim	−	or glut	−	−	−	−	−	−	−	−	−	−	−	−	−	−
threonine	+	+	+	stim	+	+	+	+	+	+	+3rd instar	+2nd gen	+	+	+	+	+	+	+
methionine	+	+	+	+or cyst	+or cyst	+	+	+	+	+	+pupa	stim	stim	+	+	+	+	+	+
cysteine	−	−	+	or meth	or meth	−	−	−		−	−	−	−	−	−	−	−		
cystine	−	−	−	or meth	or meth	−	−	−		−(+pupa)	−	−	−	−	−	−	−	+	+
citrulline		−	or arg	or arg	−	−	−	−	stim or arg	−				−	−	−			

stim = stimulates growth, but not required.
− = not required.
+ = required.
+growth = needed for growth, not maintenance.
+pupa, etc. = needed for certain stages in life cycle.

Glaucoma and *Colpidium* require particulate foodstuffs to initiate formation of food vacuoles, while *Tetrahymena* forms food vacuoles of true solutions.[83] For a trypanosomiid flagellate from mosquitoes, *Crithidia*, phenylpyruvic acid can replace phenylalanine; cysteine, cystathionine, or homocysteine can replace methionine, and citrulline, but not ornithine, can replace arginine.[82]

The soil nematode *Caenorhabditis briggsae* has been cultured axenically, and it needs the same ten amino acids as does a rat although some unknown substance must be supplied from liver protein in addition to the known B vitamins.[37] Tapeworms appear not to use proteins but rather the amino acids from the intestine of the host. *Hymenolepis diminuta* supplied with alpha-ketoglutaric, pyruvic, or oxalacetic acid, plus ammonium ions, can synthesize L-amino acids.[31]

Several insects have been grown on mixtures of amino acids as the sole nitrogen source (Table 14). Larvae of the fly *Calliphora* do not require proline.[133, 134] Larvae of the fly *Phormia* can use either methionine or cystine and either glutamic or aspartic acid.[67] The beetle *Oryzaephilus* needs cystine and glycine but not lysine, while the roach *Blatella* can grow without proline or lysine.[60] In the absence of leucine, isoleucine, and valine, roaches mature but fail to produce viable eggs.[60] *Musca* and *Pseudosarcophaga* both need the same ten amino acids but in different proportions.[70] In onion maggots (*Hylemya antiqua*) lack of several amino acids caused death in the first instar; lack of other amino acids caused death in the third instar, and lack of still other amino acids resulted in death just before pupation.[56] Thus there are evidently quantitative differences in the reserves of some amino acids necessary for different insects. The flour beetle, *Tribolium confusum*, can use D-forms of methionine, phenylalanine, and possibly lysine, but not of other essential amino acids.[54, 88] Strain differences in requirements exist in *Drosophila melanogaster*; for example, in one glycine stimulates growth, in another it is required.[65, 66] Cystine is necessary for emergence of adult mosquitoes, *Aedes aegypti*, and for growth of their larvae either phenylalanine or tyrosine (or both) is necessary.[58] For *Tenebrio* a mixture of amino acids is not yet devised which is as good a nutrient as casein; some, such as threonine, tryptophan, lysine, and phenylalanine, stimulate growth; others, such as leucine, histidine, and isoleucine, when alone depress growth.[87]

The amino acid requirements of mammals have been investigated by omitting various amino acids from a food mixture and observing growth (rat) and weight and nitrogen balance (man, dog).[126] Arginine is synthesized by the rat but not at a rate sufficient for normal growth. Cystine is also needed and can be synthesized if adequate methionine is present. Adult humans require eight amino acids whereas growing rats need ten (Table 14). Infants need histidine and arginine in addition to the eight other amino acids required by adults.[2] Man requires most of the essential amino acids in amounts varying from 0.25 to 1.0 gm per day. In general D-acids cannot be used well, but phenylalanine and methionine can be used in the D-form.[126] Tyrosine is needed by rat and man if the ration is low in phenylalanine. When cystine and tyrosine supply are adequate or high, the amounts of methionine and phenylalanine can be reduced. Chickens require glycine and arginine; citrulline but not ornithine can be substituted for arginine, and tyrosine is needed if the ration is low in phenylalanine.[4] Salmon require the same nine amino acids as mature rats (Table 14).[142]

In conclusion, the basic pattern of requirement of essential amino acids is similar in all animals. Numerous specific differences occur, even for genetic strains. Quantitative requirements depend on the amounts of precursors or on replacement by substances with comparable carbon skeletons.

Choline. Choline, sometimes classed with water-soluble vitamins, provides essential structural components for several syntheses. It is a constituent of lecithin (phosphatidyl choline); it has a quaternary nitrogen, hence is important in such compounds as acetylcholine (see Chapters 13 and 21), and it is an important source of labile methyl groups needed in transmethylation processes.

$$HO - CH_2 - CH_2 - \overset{+}{N} \equiv (CH_3)_3$$

Choline

It is synthesized from methionine and ethanolamine in mammals and as a methyl donor acts via betaine and methionine. On a diet low in protein, particularly in the amino acid methionine, and high in fat, mammals show a requirement for choline, and in choline deficiency, rats have local hemorrhages, fatty liver, and ultimately renal damage. Normally when there is adequate methionine mammals do not need exogenous choline. For many insects, however, choline is an essential needed in relatively large amounts. A cockroach does not make choline from ethanolamine and methionine although it can use betaine (trimethyl glycine) in place of choline.[60, 112] Choline appears to be required by most beetles, probably not by the housefly; it is supplied in relatively large amounts (100 mg/gm) in synthetic diets for *Calliphora*[133, 134] and *Phormia*.[17] In *Drosophila*, choline is needed for pupation and can be replaced by lecithin.[127] Dietary choline is not required by *Tetrahymena*.

Purines and Pyrimidines. Purines and pyrimidines are essential for the synthesis of nucleic acids (RNA and DNA).

Guanine

Most animals appear to synthesize sufficient of these, and purine constituents have been traced from glycine, CO_2, NH_3, and the "1-carbon fragment." Purines and pyrimidines are not vitamins for vertebrates or insects although growth of some insects (e.g., *Musca*,[16] *Drosophila*[127]) is increased when RNA is supplied. In Drosophila adenine and thymine are as effective as RNA. The Oregon strain of *Drosophila melanogaster* fails to develop unless supplied RNA or the pyrimidine, cytidine.[41] Several Protozoa, however, need these important structural compounds. One species of the flagellate *Chlamydomonas* needs the pyrimidine, uracil.[121] The trypanosomid *Crithidia* needs a purine and a pyrimidine; if folic acid in the medium is high there is no need for the pyrimidine, otherwise thymine and methionine must be present.[82] *Tetrahymena* requires both a purine and a pyrimidine. For the purine it needs guanine; adenine and hypoxanthine can spare but not replace guanine and xanthine, and uric acid is ineffective; hence *Tetrahymena* is unable to close the imidazole ring.[81] Of the pyrimidines, *Tetrahymena* needs uracil although cytidine and cytidylic acid can be substituted but cytosine, thymine, and orotic acid cannot. Similarly,

Glaucoma needs guanine although adenine and hypoxanthine are sparing; *Glaucoma* also needs uracil as a pyrimidine (or uracylic acid, cytidine, or cytidylic acid). In *Tetrahymena*, thymine cannot spare uracil but can spare the vitamin folic acid, whereas in *Glaucoma* thymine spares neither uracil nor folic acid. *Stylonychia* or *Euplotes* grown on sterile *Tetrahymena* need a supplement of hypoxanthine and guanine and also a sterol and thiamine; purine metabolism is different in *Stylonychia* and *Tetrahymena*.[80] For *Paramecium multimicronucleatum* the purine need can be supplied by guanine, guanosine, or guanylic acid, not by adenine, and the py-

Uracil

rimidine need by cytidine or uracil, not thymidine.[75, 76] A malaria organism, *Plasmodium knowlesii*, needs purines and pyrimidines for best survival.[145] The requirement of "higher" Protozoa for purines and pyrimidines represents a specialization of these animals.

Essential Fatty Acids. Most animals grow and live well with little or no dietary fat, but since fat is a favorable storage substance it can be interconverted to and from carbohydrate and sometimes to and from protein; fat may be deposited after high caloric intake even when no fat is fed. *Chilomonas* accumulated fat droplets when fed acetate, particularly in the absence of sulfur.[102] In many animals the deposited fat may differ from the food fat in melting point or degree of saturation. The total fat intake can be reduced to very low levels in birds and mammals. Rats on a low fat diet develop hematuria, loss in weight, scaly feet and tail, all of which are then cured by feeding linoleic acid as sodium linoleate, about 30 mg per day.[100] Arachidonic acid but not linolenic acid can also be used by rats.[123]

Linoleic Acid. Man on low fat diet shows a decline in blood concentration of linoleic

$$CH_3(CH_2)_4CH = CH \cdot CH_2 \cdot CH = CH(CH_2)_7COOH$$
Linoleic Acid

acid; apparently man can synthesize more of this acid than can a rat.

Several lepidoptera, e.g., the genus *Ephestia*, the pink bollworm, the rice moth *Corcyra*,[147] and the webworm *Loxostege*,[89] require linoleic acid for successful development, emergence, and normal appearance of the scales. Linoleic acid synthesis has been demonstrated as occurring in *Tenebrio* but not in *Ephestia*.[50] Linoleic acid deficiency in cockroaches is shown by aborted egg-cases and death of second generation nymphs; linolenic acid can substitute in *Ephestia* and bollworm but not in cockroach.[60, 152]

Unsaturated fats function in various ways—structurally and in energy metabolism. Apparently specific ones are needed and a few animals are unable to synthesize enough of unsaturated fatty acids for their needs.

Sterols. Steroids constitute a large class of fused carbon ring compounds, and the most common of animal sterols is cholesterol. This is important in synthesis of fatty acids and of some steroid hormones. Apparently all animals use cholesterol in lipid metabolism, but there are variations in their ability to synthesize it.[69]

or 7-ketocholesterol and some other configurations (Fig. 29).[90] *Drosophila* normally uses yeast ergosterol but can also utilize cholesterol and 7-dehydrocholesterol. The carnivorous *Dermestes* can use only animal sterols—cholesterol or 7-dehydrocholesterol; normal precursors are not used; hence cholesterol synthesis must be blocked at several steps.[23] It appears that the ability to synthesize cholesterol requires specific configurations of the dietary precursors, that herbivorous insects have wider synthetic capacities than carnivorous ones; omnivorous species such as roaches are intermediate.

The snail *Helix* needs a dietary sterol and normally uses sitosterol.[151]

Some ciliates, e.g., *Tetrahymena*, can synthesize their needed sterols and do not require any of the diet. However, *Paramecium aurelia* needs a dietary sterol, and can use several but not those with more than one double bond in A or B rings or with very different side chains from cholesterol.[24] A number of flagellates need a sterol—*Trichomonas columbae*, an intestinal parasite of pigeons—and other trichomonads require cholesterol or a closely related sterol.[18, 80] The colorless euglenoid

Cholesterol

Cholesterol is synthesized in sufficient amount by vertebrates; however, guinea pigs can be cured of a leg stiffness by dietary sterol (stigmasterol).[78] All insects seem to require a dietary sterol, usually cholesterol. Other sterols can be used instead by some insects, especially herbivorous ones.[9, 89] *Bombyx* normally eats plant sitosterol, yet 85 per cent of its body sterol is cholesterol.[89] A cockroach *Blatella* does best on cholesterol but can use several plant sterols and can convert ergosterol to 22-dehydrocholesterol, possibly by symbiotic microorganisms.[23] Larvae of houseflies *Musca* do well on cholesterol or cholesteryl acetate or oleate, half as well on 7-dehydrocholesterol, ergosterol, and stigmasterol, but they cannot use 7-hydroxycholesterol

Peranema trichophorum needs a sterol—cholesterol serves best.[140] A myxomycete, *Labyrinthula vitellum*, needs a steroid, but another species *L. minuta* synthesizes cholesterol in absence of any in its diet.[149]

The sterols constitute much of the unsaponifiable fats, and their identification may be useful in determining the taxonomy of some groups of animals.[13] The principal sterol in insects and vertebrates, where the unsaponifiable portion is less than 7 per cent of total fats, is the 27-carbon cholesterol. In most invertebrates the unsaponifiable formation is greater. Sponges contain a variety including C_{27}, C_{28}, and C_{29} sterols, some of which are unique. Gastropod and pelecypod molluscs contain mainly cholesterol, but pele-

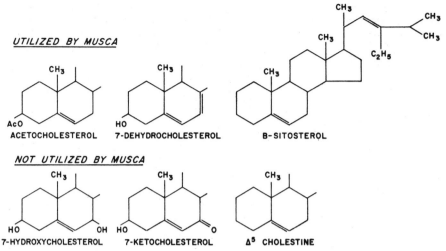

FIGURE 29. Cholesterol modifications.[90]

cypods have various higher melting-point sterols, mostly with 28 carbons. Among echinoderms, the crinoids, ophiuroids, and echinoids have cholesterol, the asteroids and holothurians different compounds, stella-sterols.[13] There may be an evolutionary trend toward reduction in the number of kinds of body sterols.

Essential Nutrients with Enzymatic Functions

Water-Soluble Vitamins. A number of dietary essentials, the water-soluble vitamins, function as coenzymes in specific metabolic reactions which are common to most if not all animal cells. Certain of the water-soluble vitamins are widely required; others can be synthesized (in part or the whole); still other vitamins are required by only a few organisms, which have lost the capacity for synthesizing them. Some vitamins are needed in such small amounts that need has not been demonstrated for all animals, and synthesis has been unjustifiably postulated. The B vitamins will be considered in order of decreasing requirement from the most general to the more specific.

Thiamine. The first B vitamin to be dis-covered was thiamine, active in preventing beriberi in man and polyneuritis in birds. Thiamine plus adenosine triphosphate forms cocarboxylase (diphosphothiamine), an im-portant coenzyme in oxidative decarboxyla-tion of pyruvic acid (see p. 183). Thiamine also functions in other decarboxylations and in interactions between pentose shunt and glucose (p. 182). Thiamine is widely dis-tributed in plant and animal tissues, and probably all cells whether aerobic or anaerobic require it. The thiamine molecule consists of two parts, a pyrimidine and a thiazole moiety:

Thiamine

$$H_3C - C \underset{\underset{\displaystyle C}{\overset{\displaystyle N}{\|}}}{\overset{\displaystyle N}{}} \quad \overset{\displaystyle NH_2}{\underset{\displaystyle C}{C}} \quad HC \overset{\displaystyle S}{\underset{\displaystyle N}{}} C - CH_2 - CH_2OH$$

Pyrimidine   Thiazole

Thiamine occurs in natural waters, both fresh and marine, particularly in regions near where there is bacterial growth; it occurs also in soils.[38] Many bacteria, molds, and some flagellates can synthesize both the pyrimidine and thiazole rings and from these the com-plete thiamine molecule. Some microorgan-isms require either the pyrimidine or the thiazole as nutrient; others need both the pyrimidine and thiazole,[98] and many Protozoa and some molds need the complete thiamine molecule as do all multicellular animals which have been investigated (Table 15). Flagellates vary considerably in their requirement of thiamine. Of the colorless *Polytoma,* one

TABLE 15. REQUIREMENTS OF ANIMALS FOR WATER-SOLUBLE VITAMINS

	Rat[3]	Guinea Pig[125]	Salmon[34]	Chinook salmon[62]	Blatella[60]	Palorus[25]	Lasioderma[116]	Tribolium[101]	Hylemya[56]	Phormia[17]	Musca[16]	Drosophila[11]	Musca[20]	Calliphora[133]	Aedes aegypti[137]	Tenebrio[48]	Caeno-rhabditis[37]	Pseudo-sarcophaga[70]	Paramecium[75]	Tetrahymena[81]	Crithidia[82]
thiamine	+	+	+	+	+	+	+	+	+	+	+	+	+	+	+	+	+	+	+	+	+
cobalamin	+	−	+?	sl+	+eggs	−	+	stim	stim		−	+		−?	+pupa		?	−stim	−	−	+
biotin	+	−	+	+	+eggs	+	+	stim	stim	stim	+	+		+	+	+	?	+	+	−	+
riboflavin	+	+?	+	+	+	+	+	+	+	+	+	+	+	+	+	+	+	+	+	+	+
niacin	+	+	+?	+	+	+	+	+	+	+	+	+	+?	+	+	+	+	+	+	+	+
pyridoxine	+	+	+	+	+	−	+	+	+	+	+	+		+	+pupa	+	+	−	+	+	+
ascorbic acid		+	+	+																+	+
PGA (folic)	+	+	+	+	+eggs	−	+	+	+	+	+growth	+		+	+pupa	+	+	−	+	+	+ or +thymine +threo
α-lipoic							+	stim	stim	−						+				+	+
carnithine						+		stim	stim						stim or choline	+			+	−	
hematin								+	+				RNA					RNA stim			+
pantothenic	+	+	+	+	+	+	+	+	+	+	+	+	+	+	+	+	+	+	+	+	+
choline	+ or cobal. +meth.	+	+	+	+ = betaine	+	+stim	+	+	stim	−(+)	+		+	+stim	+	+	+		−	
cholesterol or other sterol					+		+ or yeast	+	+	+	+	+	+	+	+	+		+	+	+	
purine	−					+		+	+	+	RNA or adenine	+	RNA stim		RNA given			RNA stim	+	+	+
pyrimidine								stim			adenine	+	stim						+	+	
essential fatty acid	−		+	+	+linoleic	−	−			−				−		+			+	+	−
pteridine																					+
inositol	+	−	+?	+	+	−	−				−(+)	+?		−	+?			−		−	
glutathione												+?			+?				+	+?	
PABA	+	−	+	−	+	−	−	+	+	−				−	−		?	−		−	

− = not required.
+ = required.
+pupa, etc. = required for certain stages in life cycle.
stim = stimulates growth, but not required.
? = questionable.
−(+) = uncertain.

TABLE 16. REQUIREMENTS FOR THIAMINE, COBALAMIN, AND BIOTIN BY VARIOUS FLAGELLATES[121]

	Chloro-phyceae of 37 species	Eugleninae of 10 species	Crypto-phyceae of 16 species	Dino-phyceae of 15 species	Chryso-phyceae of 13 species	Bacillario-phyceae of 9 species
thiamine	7+	7+	4+	3+	9+	0+
cobalamin	5+	9+	4+	14+	10+	3+
biotin	0+	0+	0+	1+	3+	0+

species, *caudatum*, requires it while *P. obtusum* does not.[121] Many green flagellates have a thiamine requirement (Table 16). Multiplication of *Chilomonas paramecium* on an acetate-ammonia medium is doubled by the addition of thiamine alone and increased fivefold by thiamine plus iron. *Chilomonas* can synthesize some thiamine if supplied both the pyrimidine and thiazole moieties.[72] All animal flagellates—Trypanosoma, Leishmania, and Strigomonas—need thiamine.[80] *Tetrahymena* also can synthesize thiamine[132] but grows best when it has been added to the medium. Insects need thiamine in small amounts, *Phormia* 3 μg/gm, *Tenebrio* 1 μg/gm diet.[48] Trout need it in amounts of some 0.16 mg/kg body wt/day.[118] For man the recommended amount is 0.5 mg/1000 calories of diet. Many animals (especially insects and mammals) have microorganisms in the digestive tract, for example, in the rumen of sheep and cattle, and these animals do not need thiamine in their diet. In deer, synthesis by symbionts may exceed intake by five to twelve times.[143] Calves reared on synthetic milk, however, require dietary thiamine.

Cobalamin (Vitamin B$_{12}$). Cobalamin has extensive nutritional utilization, but less than thiamine. Vitamin B$_{12}$ is a cobalt-containing compound which occurs in natural waters, often in concentrations of 0.0001 to 0.001 mg/ml. The molecule consists of two portions, a porphyrin-like ring with cobalt, and a nucleotide, ribazole phosphate. It is usually isolated as the cyanide derivative, cyanocobalamin.[137a]

Vitamin B$_{12}$ functions in many ways in the metabolism of 1-carbon fragments. It may function in synthesis of proteins and of methyl compounds.[137a] It is a cofactor for several isomerases, as in conversion of methylmalonic to succinic and in rat liver (via coenzyme A).[61a, 137b] Cobalamin is required by many flagellates, both green photosynthesizing forms and colorless species, and *Euglena*

CYANOCOBALAMIN

gracilis is a sensitive organism for bioassay.[73, 121]

The vitamin B$_{12}$ required by algae and protozoans is normally produced by bacteria, and there is evidence that the availability of this vitamin may be a factor limiting gross productivity in some natural waters.[73, 121]

It may be that cyanocobalamin is an essential nutrient for all animals, but in some the amount needed is so small that it has not been demonstrated, for example, in *Tetrahymena geleii*. Vitamin B$_{12}$ is synthesized by symbiont microorganisms. A roach grows well but does not produce viable eggs without cobalamin.[60] The need for it has not been demonstrated in other insects. In mammals lack of cobalamin results in anemia due to failure of maturation of red blood cells. The vitamin is an antipernicious anemia factor of which about 1 mg/day is needed by man.

Biotin. It functions in CO_2 fixation in bacteria and mammals and is probably involved in oxaloacetate synthesis (see p. 183). Egg yolk is rich in biotin, and egg white contains an antibiotin factor. Biotin is present in natural waters and is required by a few flagellates, some of them green[121] (Table 16). Need for biotin has not been demon-

cytochrome. It is a constituent of Warburg's "yellow enzyme," xanthine oxidase, D-amino acid oxidase, and cytochrome reductase.

$$CH_2 - \overset{\overset{\displaystyle OH}{|}}{\underset{\underset{\displaystyle H}{|}}{C}} - \overset{\overset{\displaystyle OH}{|}}{\underset{\underset{\displaystyle H}{|}}{C}} - \overset{\overset{\displaystyle OH}{|}}{\underset{\underset{\displaystyle H}{|}}{C}} - CH_2OH$$

Riboflavin

strated in *Tetrahymena*. It stimulates growth of flour beetles,[48] and mosquito larvae fail to metamorphose without biotin.[144] It is needed in very small amounts by all insects which have been carefully studied.[85]

Biotin

Biotin is synthesized by symbiotic bacteria in the intestine of many animals. Not enough is synthesized to satisfy the needs of the hamster,[26] but probably enough is produced by symbionts in rabbits.[114] Deficiency of biotin in hens results in high embryonic mortality and skeletal deformities in chicks;[28] chickens are good assay animals. Biotin deficiency can be produced in monkeys, calves, and other experimental mammals by sterilization of the intestinal tract or by feeding the antibiotin factor of egg white. The recommended amount for man is less than 10 μg/day.

Riboflavin. Riboflavin, an alloxazine derivative, functions in flavin mononucleotide (FMN) or flavin adenine dinucleotide (FAD) as the prosthetic group of flavoprotein enzymes which act in cellular respiration between dehydrogenases and either oxygen or

Riboflavin is synthesized by many microorganisms—yeasts, bacteria, and probably flagellates. It stimulates multiplication of *Chilomonas* but is not a dietary requirement.[115] Riboflavin is required by *Tetrahymena*[81] (which, however, can synthesize some)[132] and by numerous insects (Table 15). Some insects (*Lasioderma, Blatella*) appear to get sufficient riboflavin from intestinal symbionts, but others (*Tenebrio, Drosophila*) require it in the diet. Trout need some 0.5 mg of riboflavin per kg body weight per day.[104] Rats deficient in riboflavin develop skin lesions, shedding of hair, and ocular lesions. Fur-bearing mammals such as the fox require riboflavin for normal sleekness and color of fur.[129] Riboflavin is synthesized by intestinal microorganisms in many mammals; hence the true requirement is difficult to establish. Rabbits may excrete in feces ten to fifteen times their intake so they grow well without dietary riboflavin either because of cecal absorption or from eating feces.[114] Ruminants obtain sufficient riboflavin through synthesis by rumen organisms; the rumen contents may contain riboflavin concentrated a hundredfold, and milk may contain ten times as much as the dietary intake by the cow.[103] Calves lacking ruminant organisms require riboflavin in the diet.[154] A true requirement by man is not established although the recommended intake is 1.0 to 1.5 mg/day (Tables 17 and 18).

Niacin (Nicotinic Acid). Nicotinic acid amide (niacinamide) combines with adenine, a pentose and phosphate to form DPN (diphosphopyridine nucleotide or coenzyme I)

TABLE 17. AMOUNTS OF REQUIRED VITAMINS

	Needed Crithidia[82] µg/ml	Recommended Tetrahymena[81] µg/ml	Tenebrio[48] µg/gm dry	Calliphora[133, 134] µg/gm solution	Musca[20] µg/ml	Hylemya[56] µg/ml	Drosophila[127] µg/gm wet	Phormia[17] µg/gm dry
thiamine	0.01	1	25	3	20	1.5	0.2	3
cobalamin						0.04		
biotin	0.0001	0.0005	0.25	0.04		0.02		R
riboflavin	0.015	0.1	12.5	3	0.25	2.4	0.8	5.5
niacin	0.065	0.1	50	35	200	10	1.0	12
pyridoxine	0.019	2	12.5	4	2	30	0.24	4
ascorbic acid							0.20	
PGA (folic)	0.0004		2.5	14		6		0.25
α-lipoic		0.37				0.4 stim		
carnitine			5					
pantothenic	0.046	0.1	25	12	10	6	1.6	12
choline		1	500	100		20		80
cholesterol or other sterol			1000		10	100		
nucleic acid		100						

and TPN (triphosphopyridine nucleotide or coenzyme II), which are coenzymes for many dehydrogenases (see p. 180). Niacin is synthesized from tryptophan by many animals and by symbiotic bacteria. This synthesis has been observed in *Chilomonas,*[138] but *Tetrahymena* and *Colpoda* are incapable of it.[81]

Niacin is required by a variety of insects (e.g., *Blatella*) but is produced by the sym-

Niacin

TABLE 18. RECOMMENDED AMOUNTS OF VITAMINS IN DIETS
(All in µg/kg body wt/day)[3]

	Brook trout	Man (25 yr)	Cat	Young dog	Mature dog	Lab. rat	Germ-free rat	Chicken (half-grown)	Germ-free chicken	Fox mature
thiamine	100-200	25	50	33	18	50	400	110	5000	30
cobalamin		?		1.5	0.55					
biotin	10-26	R					4	7	32	
riboflavin	400-700	25	320	90	44	100	1300	140	2400	50
niacin	3000-4000	250	2300	400	24		5	1100	4000	260
pyridoxine	200-300	15-31		55	22	40	1400	240	1600	30
ascorbic acid		1150					R		160,000	
PGA (folic)	100-200			15	8		400	40	800	5
pantothenic	1000-1300			100	55	360	12,000	173,000	16,000	210
choline				55,000	33,000	40,000		111,000	160,000	
vitamin D		R	0.48	0.5	0.16		1	380	600	
vitamin A		41.5	81	120	59	10	240	120	190	10
vitamin E				2200		1200	25,000	1400	20,000	1200
vitamin K							5	28	4000	
inositol							50		80,000	

R = required; amounts not given.

biotic microorganisms in some of them; hence a nutritional requirement is not always demonstrated (Table 15).[79] *Phormia* cannot use tryptophan for niacin;[17] *Drosophila* needs both. In rats, mice, and men tryptophan is converted to niacin, partly by digestive microorganisms, but largely in the liver, and more niacin than is ingested may be excreted even after the intestinal organisms have been poisoned or after tryptophan has been injected.[77] Calves lacking rumen organisms synthesize sufficient niacin, but niacin-deficient dogs and foxes develop "black tongue" which is cured by feeding nicotinic acid. In man, pellagra results in part from a deficiency of niacin. Pellagra is a complex condition which is common on a diet of corn, the protein of which, zein, is deficient in tryptophan and which may also contain an antiniacin factor. Recommended intake of niacin by man is 10 to 15 mg/day.

Pyridoxine (Pyridoxal, Pyridoxamine). Pyridoxine is a pyridine derivative. Vitamin B_6 can be provided as pyridoxine, pyridoxal, or pyridoxamine.

growth of *Tetrahymena*[81] and *Colpoda*. Pyridoxine is a general requirement for insects except when synthesized by their symbiotic flora (Table 17). The rumen contents of sheep, also the milk of cows, may contain ten times as much pyridoxine as the food; synthesis by rumen organisms[103] is indicated, and also by intestinal bacteria as in humans and in pigs.[106] Pyridoxine-deficient ducklings show retarded growth and anemia. Convulsions appear in extremely deficient rats and pigs, dermatitis in rats, and anemia in dogs, foxes, and pigs. The requirement in the rat is proportional to the protein intake. The human requirement for pyridoxine has not been established.

Pantothenic Acid (Pantoyl-beta-alanine). Pantothenic acid (P.A.) is combined with adenylic acid, 2-mercaptoethylamine, and three phosphates to form coenzyme A which is important in reactions which transfer acyl groups.[5] It is therefore used in transfer of acetyl from pyruvic acid to the tricarboxylic acid cycle and in acetylation of choline to form acetylcholine.

$$HO-CH_2-\underset{\underset{CH_3}{|}}{\overset{\overset{CH_3}{|}}{C}}-\overset{\overset{OH}{|}}{CH}-\overset{\overset{O}{\|}}{C}-\underset{\underset{H}{|}}{N}-CH_2-CH_2-COOH$$

Pantothenic acid

Pyridoxal phosphate is the coenzyme for transamination of alpha-amino acids, hence it is important in protein metabolism. Pyridoxine stimulates growth by, but is not essential for, *Chilomonas*.[115] It must be supplied in relatively large amounts for optimal

Colpidium requires pantothenic acid in twenty times greater concentrations than *Tetrahymena* does.[81] P.A. favors survival of Plasmodium.[145] Insects generally need it even when not depleted of microorganisms (Table 15). Ruminants show marked synthesis by rumen organisms (six to twenty-five times above the concentration in their food), and the vitamin is synthesized by cecal bacteria in rabbits and also in the colon of man. The human requirement has not been established. A striking feature of pantothenate deficiency in rats is hemorrhagic necrosis of the adrenal cortex and reduced adrenocortical function.

Folic Acid (Pteroylglutamic Acid.) Folic acid consists of glutamic acid, *p*-aminobenzoic

Pyridoxine

Folic acid

acid and a substituted pterin. In some cells (yeast and chicken liver) folinic acid (citrovorum factor) occurs, and this substance may be more active as the vitamin than is folic acid.

This vitamin functions in intermediary metabolic reactions involving 1-carbon fragments. Folic acid is required for purine and pyrimidine synthesis, and in *Tetrahymena,* but not *Glaucoma,* thymine can spare the folic acid need.[81, 83] Folic acid action on growth is antagonized by aminopterin which in low concentrations can stop hematopoiesis and growth in mice. Drosophila does not need RNA but does better with it, and if folic acid is low or lacking, more RNA is needed. Folic acid is partly replaced for *Drosophila* by thymine, a purine, or high serine.[127] Folic acid is widely required, probably in all animals in small amounts, but is commonly synthesized by symbiotic microorganisms. Even in man there is good evidence that intestinal bacteria supply much of this vitamin although dietary deficiency may lead to anemia.

α-Lipoic Acid (Thioctic Acid). This is a sulfur-containing acid (6, 8-dithio-n-octanoic acid) which condenses with thiamine to form lipothiamide, which first receives the acyl group from pyruvate in the oxidative decarboxylation of this key intermediate (p. 182). Then the acyl is transferred to coenzyme A with subsequent reduction of DPN. It is interesting that four vitamins, thiamine, α-lipoic acid, pantothenic acid, and niacin, are required in this important part of cellular metabolism.

$$
\begin{array}{l}
\text{S—CH}_2 \\
\quad | \\
\quad \text{CH}_2 \\
\quad | \\
\text{S—CH} \\
\quad | \\
\quad (\text{CH}_2)_4 \\
\quad | \\
\quad \text{COOH}
\end{array}
$$

α-Lipoic acid

α-Lipoic acid is synthesized by most animals and can be obtained from mammalian liver, chick embryos, and the like.[139] Hence, it is not usually needed in the diet. In *Tetrahymena,* however, a factor called protogen long eluded the protozoan nutritionists and turned out to be α-lipoic acid.[81, 132] Requirement of α-lipoic acid has not been demonstrated in insects.

Ascorbic Acid (Vitamin C). Ascorbic

acid, like glutathione, is reversibly oxidized or reduced by many oxidants and reductants; it is not assigned to any known coenzyme. It is involved in oxidation of tyrosine.

$$
\begin{array}{l}
\text{O} = \text{C}\text{——}\!\!\rceil \\
\quad | \qquad\quad | \\
\text{HO — C} \quad\;\; | \\
\quad \| \qquad\quad | \\
\text{HO — C} \qquad | \\
\quad | \qquad\;\; \text{O} \\
\text{H — C}\text{——}\!\!\rfloor \\
\quad | \\
\text{HO — C — H} \\
\quad | \\
\quad \text{CH}_2\text{OH}
\end{array}
$$

Ascorbic acid

Ascorbic acid is widely found in plant and animal tissues and is present in human blood, about 1 mg per 100 ml. It occurs in high concentration in the adrenal cortex, and under various body stresses the cortical ascorbic acid decreases rapidly. Ascorbic acid was early discovered as the antiscurvy vitamin in man, and lack of it results in scattered hemorrhages, particularly of the gums, and in swollen joints. The human requirement is 1.6 mg kg/day.[135] Ascorbic acid is synthesized in sufficient amounts by most vertebrates; it is not needed in the diet of the rat and hamster, but it must be fed to guinea pigs, monkeys, and men. It is synthesized by insects such as honeybee larvae and is not needed in the diet of insects or of ciliate protozoans. However, many of the trypanosomes which are mammalian flagellate blood parasites, such as *Leishmania tropica* and *Trypanosoma cruzi,* require ascorbic acid, while free-living ones, such as *Strigomonas* and *Leptomonas,* do not.[98] *Aedes aegypti* needs glutathione.[137]

Hematin. All aerobic organisms have oxidative enzymes and carriers (cytochromes) which contain iron in a porphyrin ring, in some cases similar to and in others identical with hematin (see Chapter 8). The heme of cytochrome is synthesized by many plants and animals which do not make hemoglobin. Various flagellates parasitic in the blood of birds and mammals and several species of *Leishmania* and *Trypanosoma* require hematin (or its equivalent) when cultured *in vitro.*[96] A parasitic trypanosome from the digestive tract of a mosquito, *Strigomonas fasciculata,* requires hematin, while *S. oncopelti* from hemipterans and *S. parva,* a parasite of flies, do not require it.[98] This is another instance of loss of a synthetic function by a parasite, with increasing dependence on the host. A blood-sucking hemipteran, *Triatoma*, also has nutritional requirement for hematin.[99] Hematin is therefore a vitamin for certain blood-feeding animals.

Carnitine (β-Hydroxybutyrobetaine). Muscles of all animals appear to contain nitrogenous acids such as carnosine, anserine, and carnitine. They may function as anions to balance the excess of inorganic cations present in muscle cells. Carnitine content follows:[46]

Vitamin A₁

Mammal Muscle	1000 μg/gm dry
Mammal Brain	87 μg/gm dry
Wheat	7-14 μg/gm wet
Yeast	35 μg/ gm wet

Carnitine occurs also in other tissues. It is synthesized by virtually all animals, and the only ones known to require it in the diet are grain-eating beetles of the family Tenebrionidae.[51-53] Larvae of the fly *Phormia* convert choline but not betaine to carnitine.[67] Substitution of different compounds shows the essentiality of the quaternary ammonium group separated by 3 carbons from the carboxyl.

$$(CH_3)_3 \equiv \overset{+}{N} - CH_2 - CHOH - CH_2 - COO^-$$
Carnitine

Carnitine is a vitamin for the flour-eating *Tenebrio molitor* and *obscurus*, *Tribolium confusum* and *castaneum*, and *Palorus*, but not for *Gnathocerus*.[46] *Lasioderma* does not need it. *Dermestes* synthesizes much of it, as does *Phormia*.[55, 85, 86] Some preparations of casein contain enough carnitine, and deficiency symptoms failed to develop on a diet lacking zinc as well as carnitine.

Pteridine. A trypanosomid flagellate from mosquitoes, *Crithidia fasciculata*, requires a pteridine for growth. This active compound can be obtained from urine and liver, and need for it has not been demonstrated in other animals;[82, 117] it is a nitrogen storage waste in butterflies (Chapter 6). Another example of highly specialized requirement is the need of the bacterium *Hemophilus parainfluenzae* for putrescine.[64]

Vitamins with Restricted Loci of Action

Fat-Soluble Vitamins. Some of the water-soluble vitamins may have restricted actions in those organisms which need them. Requirement for the fat-soluble vitamins A, D, E, and K appears at present restricted to vertebrates although these or similar compounds are widely found.

Vitamin A. This is known in two forms, vitamin A₁ and A₂.

Two molecules of vitamin A are formed from one of β-carotene which occurs widely in plants. The conversion of β-carotene or a provitamin occurs partly in the liver but mainly in the intestine; the vitamins are stored in the liver, and also in the retina, in both the rods and the pigment cells. The function of vitamins A₁ and A₂ in vision is discussed in Chapter 12, p. 361. Vitamin A₁ occurs in higher vertebrates and marine fish; A₂ is predominant in fresh-water fish. Deficiency in vitamin A results first in night blindness and later in xerophthalmia; in extreme deficiency there may be retarded skeletal growth and lesions of the skin. An excess of dietary vitamin A may be toxic. The dietary requirement depends on the animal's synthetic capacity and the amount of dietary carotenes. The concentration in liver of different animals varies by some thousandfold and is lowest in the guinea pig and highest in the polar bear and seal.[107] No invertebrates have been found to need dietary vitamin A, but many of them contain it. Squid liver contains much vitamin A, and it is used in vision by the squid. In a variety of marine crustaceans—euphausids, amphipods, copepods—90 per cent of the vitamin A is found in the eyes.[44] Carotenoids are made only by plants, but many animals can select and modify those they consume.[59]

Vitamin D. This is a class of substances the most important of which are D_2, or calciferol, formed by ultraviolet irradiation of ergosterol, and D_3 formed by irradiation of 7-dehydrocholesterol. Vitamin D_3 is present in fish liver and is synthesized in the skin of higher animals under the action of sunlight. Birds secrete the precursor in the preen gland, place it on the feathers, where it is activated, and then either eat it or absorb the vitamin directly.[107]

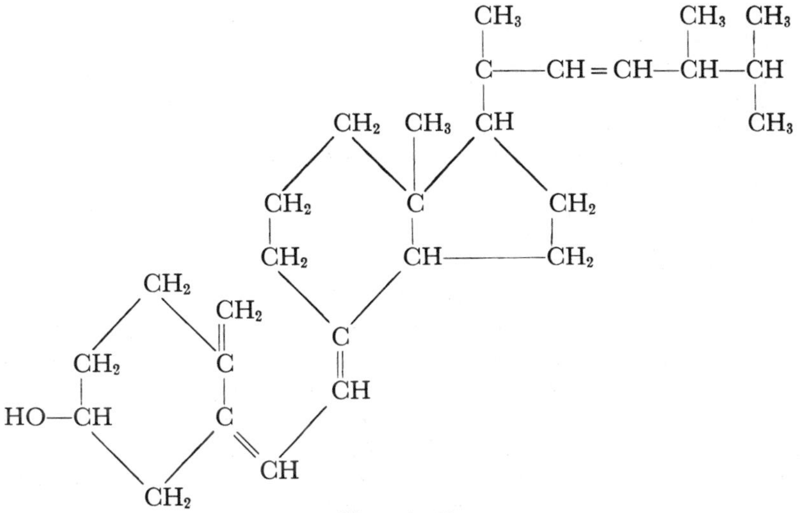

vitamin E results in degeneration of germinal epithelium, production of immobile sperm, and resorption of mammalian embryos. Hepatic necrosis, local hemorrhages, and lesions in the testis have been observed in deficient chickens,[1] tadpoles, and fish.[29] The rabbit and guinea pig are more sensitive than the rat. It is likely that vitamin E is a dietary requirement of all vertebrates. Extracts of heart and skeletal muscle of rats contain α-tocopherol, and the cytochrome reductase of

CH₃ ... (structural formula)

Vitamin D

Vitamin D aids calcium absorption from the digestive tract and with parathormone regulates the blood level of calcium and the mobilization of calcium for mineralization of bone. Deficiency of vitamin D results in rickets in man; in a rat no rickets appears unless there is also an imbalance of calcium and phosphorus in the diet. Mammals are less capable of liver storage of vitamin D than are fish. No form of vitamin D has been found essential for any invertebrate although sterols are widely utilized for other functions.

Vitamin E (Tocopherol). Three tocopherols differ in number and position of substituent methyl groups.

Tocopherol contains a phytol chain as do chlorophyll and vitamin K. Deficiency in

these tissues shows enhanced activity for oxidation of DPNH and succinate when tocopherols are added; the vitamin may be a cofactor for cytochrome reductase in these tissues.[108, 109] In addition, vitamin E may act as a general antioxidant specifically against the auto-oxidation of unsaturated fatty acids by inhibiting peroxidation of unsaturated lipids. In the chicken and rat such substances as methylene blue can counteract manifestations of vitamin E deficiency. A laying hen requires 1.2 mg of α-tocopherol per day.[35] Selenium can sometimes replace vitamin E as an antioxidant.[141]

Vitamin K. Vitamin K occurs in two forms, K_1 and K_2.

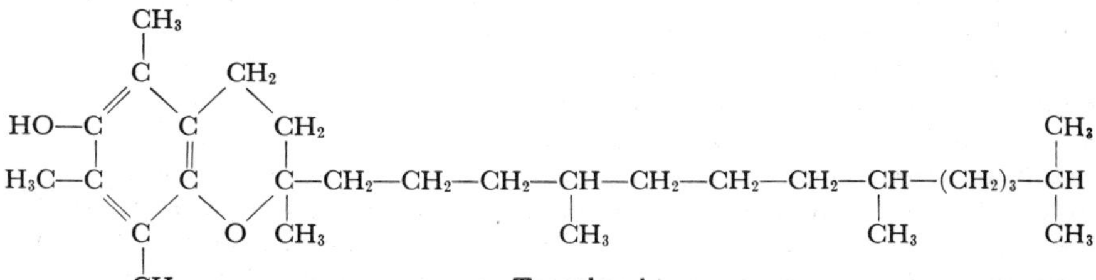

α-Tocopherol

K₁ is 2-methyl-3-phytyl-1,4-naphthoquinone

Vitamin K_1 is commonly obtained from alfalfa; K_2 from fish meal. It has a role in photosynthesis, hence, is widely distributed. It is also similar to a pigment of unknown function in echinoderms, echinochrome. Vitamin K is made by symbiotic microorganisms, and even man seems to absorb enough from intestinal bacteria, although newborn infants may show a deficiency. Chickens are very sensitive to a deficiency and are used for assay. Vitamin K stimulates the formation of prothrombin and is necessary for normal clotting of the blood. Deficiency leads to hemorrhages. The naphthoquinone portion of the molecule has activity similar to that of the entire vitamin.

CONCLUSIONS

The goal of complete culture through several reproductive cycles on a synthetic diet of known chemicals has been achieved with relatively few animals. The discovery of a new growth factor for one animal often aids in discovering the needs for other animals, as for α-lipoic acid = protogen = thioctic acid. Nevertheless, many factors required by specific animals remain to be discovered. Many animals can be cultured on a synthetic medium provided small amounts of extracts from yeast or liver are added.

Examples of the difficulties of axenic culture are shown by the Nemathelminthes and Platyhelminthes. Some tapeworms and parasitic roundworms have been kept alive and have shown some morphogenesis in synthetic media. However, unknown factors seem necessary for completing a life cycle. Better results have been obtained with soil nematodes.[37] For reproduction, they require one or more factors which are found in yeast, liver, or chick embryo extract. These are needed in very small amounts, but a medium containing all known vitamins is inadequate.

One important requirement for nutrition is ingestion. It is probable that many animals have defied culture in solutions of amino acids, sugar, and vitamins because they do not feed on the solution. This may be part of the block to culture of some ciliate protozoans and of parasitic nematodes. A comparable factor in natural nutrition is palatability of food. Feeding often depends on chemical "attraction" or "repellence."

For no other function system is the interdependence of different kinds of organisms so evident as for nutrition. There are food specificities which may be correlated with the complement of digestive enzymes or with taste preferences. There are unknown growth factors derived from tissues of food organisms. Frequently a food derived from a deficient animal is inadequate. For example, planaria grow well on liver from normal guinea pigs but not on liver from guinea pigs deficient in some water-soluble vitamins.[156] *Glaucoma* can live on *Tetrahymena* reared on a synthetic medium except that extra purines must be supplied. There are many quantitative correlations of food requirements with the normal diet. *Phormia* larvae can be fed on pork liver, rich in B vitamins; *Phormia* has much higher vitamin requirements than *Drosophila,* which can be reared on yeast with about one-half to one-eighth the B-vitamin content of pork.[127] Tapeworms cannot utilize protein but must have a supply of amino acids. Flagellates adapt enzymatically from one fatty acid to another. It is probable that some of the correlations between normal diet and requirements are genetic and some represent enzyme inductions.

Many dietary essentials are supplied by contaminant microorganisms. Bark beetles appear to obtain some unknown factor from fungus since they fail to pupate when fed sterile bark. Symbionts may be used for basic foodstuffs as in corals, termites, or ruminants, or for "vitamins" as in many insects and vertebrates. It is difficult to rid many animals of the symbiotic microorganisms in the digestive tract without secondary damage, but unless this is done true vitamin requirements cannot be established. For example, in man and many insects true need for such substances as cobalamin and α-lipoic acid has not been established, if it exists. In nature, the dependence on symbionts is such that the nutritional requirements of the total organism with its associates are very different from the requirements after sterilization. The blood-feeding bug *Rhodnius* depends on symbiotic bacteria to provide adequate supplies of pyridoxine, pantothenate, thiamine, and niacin.[6]

Another complication in establishing quantitative dietary essentials is the synergistic or antagonistic interaction between different nutrients, the presence of precursors for synthesis, the sparing action of one nutrient on another. Frequently the substitutions and antagonisms can be understood in terms of the contribution of specific parts of a molecule to some biochemical reaction, and as the cofactors of intermediary metabolism are better known, the prediction of a complete nutrition for an organism is improved. The synthesis of animal sterols is possible with precursors of certain configurations but not with others which are slightly different.

A striking feature of the science of nutrition is the similarity in requirements by all animals. Some nine amino acids are essential for all animals; certain water-soluble enzymic cofactors seem universally required. Superimposed on the common requirements are those for certain animal groups and still other specialities needed by single species or even genetic strains. The similarity of basic nutritional needs is based on the common enzymic patterns of metabolism which were selected during the period of chemical evolution. The first pro-organisms were heterotrophic, using preformed nutrients and acquiring the enzymes which were continued in use by autotrophic organisms. Heterotrophic animals retained the basic enzymic paths but relied more and more on their food to supply structural molecules and coenzymes. With increasing remoteness from autotrophy the ability to synthesize many commonly required cofactors disappeared. Thus the need for essential amino acids and for many B vitamins is based on an ancient cellular requirement. With the evolution of new chemical systems which did not have the common primitive origin, for example,

the rhodopsin system in vision or the calcified vertebrate bone, variants of compounds which had other functions were used, and the requirement of special nutrients for certain functions in a few animals appeared. A given type of molecule may serve new functional needs. Knowledge of nutrition, therefore, implies an understanding of chemical evolution as it has occurred both before the advent of "living" organisms and since then.

REFERENCES

1. ADAMSTONE, F. B., J. Morphol. *52*: 47-89, 1951; Arch. Pathol. *31*: 603-612, 613-621, 1941. Vitamin E deficiency in chicks.
2. ALBANESE, Z., J. Clin. Nutrit. *1*: 44-51, 1952. Effects of amino-acid deficiencies, rats and man.
3. ALBRITTON, E. C., ed., Standard Values in Nutrition and Metabolism. Philadelphia, W. B. Saunders Co., 1954, Chapters I-VIII.
4. ALMQUIST, H. J., and MECCHI, E., J. Biol. Chem. *135*: 355-356, 1940; J. Nutrit. *28*: 325-331, 1944. Amino acid requirements, chickens.
5. BADDILEY, J., Adv. Enzymol. *16*: 1-22, 1955. Structure of coenzyme A.
6. BAINES, S., J. Exp. Biol. *33*: 533-541, 1956. Role of symbiotic bacteria in nutrition of Rhodnius.
7. BARGHOORN, E. S., Mem. Geol. Soc. Am. *67*: 75-86, 1957. Origin of life.
8. BARKER, H. A., J. Cell. Comp. Physiol. *7*: 73-93, 1935. Metabolism of alga Prototheca.
9. BECK, S. D., and KAPIDIA, G. G., Science *126*: 258-259, 1957. Metabolism of sterols by insects.
10. BEERSTECHER, E., Science *111*: 300-302, 1950. Comparative biochemistry of vitamin function.
11. BEGG, M., J. Exp. Biol. *33*: 142-154, 1956. Water-soluble vitamins for Drosophila larvae.
12. BEGG, M., and ROBERTSON, F. W., J. Exp. Biol. *26*: 380-387, 1950. Nutritional requirements, Drosophila larvae.
13. BERGMAN, W., J. Org. Chem. *12*: 67-75, 1947; J. Mar. Res. *8*: 137-176, 1949; *in* Cholesterol, edited by R. S. Cook, New York, Academic Press, 1958, pp. 435-444. Evolutionary aspects and comparative biochemistry of animal sterols.
14. BLUM, H. F., Time's Arrow and Evolution, Princeton University Press, 1951, 222 pp.
15. BRENT, M., Biol. Bull. *106*: 269-278, 1954. Nutrition of amoeba-flagellate Tetramitus.
16. BROOKES, V. J., and FRAENKEL, G., Physiol. Zool. *31*: 208-223, 1958. Nutrition of housefly, Musca.
17. BRUST, M., and FRAENKEL, G., Physiol. Zool. *28*: 186-204, 1955. Nutrition of larvae of blowfly *Phormia*.
18. CAILLEAU, R., Ann. Inst. Pasteur *59*: 137-181, 293-328, 1937. Nutrition of flagellates.
19. *CALVIN, M., Am. Scientist *44*: 248-263, 1956. Chemical evolution and origin of life.
20. CHANG, J. T., and WANG, M. Y., Nature *181*: 566, 1958. Nutrition of *Musca*.

*Reviews

21. CHELDELIN, V. H., and NEWBURGH, R. W., Ann. New York Acad. Sci. 77: 373-383, 1959. Nutrition of blowfly *Phormia*.

22. CIRILLO, V. P., Proc. Soc. Exp. Biol. Med. 88: 352-354, 1955; J. Protozool. 3: 69-74, 1956. Induced enzyme synthesis in flagellate *Polytoma*.

23. CLARK, A. J., and BLACK, K., J. Biol. Chem. 234: 2583-2588, 2578-2582, 2589-2594, 1959. Sterol requirements and sterol synthesis in insects.

24. CONNER, R. L., and van WAGTENDONK, W. J., J. Gen. Microbiol. 12: 31-36, 1955. Steroid requirement of Paramecium.

25. COOPER, M. I., and FRAENKEL, G., Physiol. Zool. 25: 20-28, 1952. Nutrition of flour beetle *Palorus*.

26. COOPERMAN, J. M., WAISMAN, H. A., and ELVEHJEM, C. A., Proc. Soc. Exp. Biol. Med. 52: 250-254, 1943. Vitamin requirements of hamster.

27. COSGROVE, W. B., and SWANSON, B. K., Physiol. Zool. 25: 287-292, 1952. Culture of *Chilomonas*.

28. COUCH, J. R., et al., Anat. Rec. 100: 29-48, 1948; J. Nutrit. 35: 57-72, 1948; Arch. Biochem. 21: 77-86, 1949. Synthesis, function and requirement for biotin in chickens.

29. CUMMINGS, H. W., Anat. Rec. (suppl) 84: 499, 1942. Vitamin E deficiency in guppies.

30. DA CUNHA, A. B., et al., Ecology 38: 98-106, 1957. Nutritional preferences of *Drosophila* species.

31. DAUGHERTY, J. W., Proc. Soc. Exp. Biol. Med. 85: 288-291, 1954. Use of amino acids and ammonia by tapeworm *Hymenolepis*.

32. DAVIS, G. R. F., Canad. J. Zool. 34: 82-85, 1956. Amino acid requirements, beetle *Orzaephilus*.

33. DE GROOT, A. P., Experientia 8: 192-194, 1952; Physiol. Comp. Oecol. 3: 1-90, 1953. Amino acid requirements of honey bee.

34. DELONG, D. C., et al., Fed. Proc. 15: 549, 1956. Essential amino acids for chinook salmon.

35. DJU, M. Y., et al., Am. J. Physiol. 160: 259-263, 1950. Utilization of tocopherols by laying hens.

36. DOBZHANSKY, T., and DA CUNHA, A. B., Ecology 36: 34-39, 1955. Nutritional preferences of Brazilian species of *Drosophila*.

37. DOUGHERTY, E. C., et al., Ann. New York Acad. Sci. 77: 176-217, 1959. Axenic culture of nematode *Caenorhabditis*.

38. DROOP, M. R., J. Mar. Biol. Assn. U. K. 37: 323-330, 1958. Thiamine requirement in marine and supralittoral protista.

39. DUSI, H., Ann. Inst. Pasteur 50: 550-597, 840-890, 1933. Nutrition of euglenoids.

40. ELLIOTT, A. M., Physiol. Zool. 22: 337-345, 1949; 23: 85-91, 1950. Amino acid and growth-factor requirements, *Tetrahymena*.

41. ELLIS, J. F., Physiol. Zool. 32: 29-39, 1959. Adenine and cytidine requirement in axenic *Drosophila*.

42. ELVEHJEM, C. A., Fed. Proc. 15: 965-970, 1956. Amino acid imbalance.

43. FERNELL, W. R., and ROSEN, G. D., Brit. J. Nutrit. 10: 143-156, 1956. Evaluation of protein quality with *Tetrahymena*.

44. *FISHER, L. R., et al., J. Mar. Biol. Assn. U. K. 31: 229-258, 1952; Biol. Rev. 34: 1-36, 1959. Vitamin A and other carotenoids in invertebrates.

45. FRAENKEL, G., J. Exp. Biol. 17: 18-29, 1940. Utilization of sugars by blowflies.

46. FRAENKEL, G., Physiol. Zool. 24: 20-28, 1952; Biol. Bull. 104: 359-371, 1953; J. Nutrit. 65: 361-395, 1958. Requirements of carnitine by flour beetles, biological distribution of carnitine.

47. *FRAENKEL, G., Science 129: 1466-1470, 1959. Raison d'être of secondary plant substances.

48. *FRAENKEL, G., Ann. New York Acad. Sci. 77: 267-274, 1959. Historical survey of dietary requirements of insects.

49. FRAENKEL, G., and BLEWETT, M., J. Exp. Biol. 20: 28-34, 1943; Biochem. J. 37: 686-692, 692-695, 1943. Food requirements of several insects.

50. FRAENKEL, G., and BLEWETT, M., J. Exp. Biol. 22: 162-171, 172-190, 1946. Nutrition of moth, *Ephestia*.

51. FRAENKEL, G., and CHANG, P., Physiol. Zool. 27: 40-56, 1954. Carnitine requirements and function in *Tenebrio*.

52. FRAENKEL, G., and FRIEDMAN, S., Vitam. & Horm. 15: 73-118, 1957. Carnitine requirements and function in *Tenebrio*.

53. FRAENKEL, G., and LECLERCQ, J., Arch. Internat. Physiol. 64: 601-622, 1956. Carnitine, chemistry and nutritional properties.

54. FRAENKEL, G., and PRINTY, G. E., Biol. Bull. 106: 149-157, 1954. Amino acid requirement of *Tribolium*.

55. FRAENKEL, G., et al., Biochem. J. 35: 712-720, 1941. Sterol requirements of *Dermestes*.

56. FRIEND, W. G., et al., Canad. J. Zool. 34: 152-162, 1956; 35: 535-543, 1957; Ann. New York Acad. Sci. 77: 384-393, 1959. Nutrition of onion maggot *Hylemya*.

57. GAFFRON, H., The Origin of Life, *in* Evolution after Darwin, edited by S. Tax. University of Chicago Press, 1960, vol. I, pp. 39-84.

58. GOLDBERG, L., and DEMEILLON, B., J. Biol. Chem. 43: 379-387, 1948. Protein and amino acid requirements of Aedes larvae.

59. *GOODWIN, T. W., The Comparative Biochemistry of Carotenoids. London, Chapman and Hall, 1952, 356 pp.

60. GORDON, H. T., Ann. New York Acad. Sci. 77: 290-338, 1959. Nutrition of roach Blatella.

61. GORDON, H. T., Ann. New York Acad. Sci. 77: 338-348, 1959. Effect of amino acid balance on growth of Tetrahymena.

61a. GURNANI, S., MISTRY, S. P., and JOHNSON, B. C., Biochem. Biophys. Acta 38: 187-188, 1960. Vitamin B_{12} function.

62. HALVER, J. E., J. Nutrit. 62: 225-243, 1957; 63: 95-105, 1957. Nutrition of chinook salmon.

63. HASSETT, C. C., et al., Biol. Bull. 99: 446-453, 1950. Nutritive value and taste thresholds of carbohydrates for blowfly.

64. HERBST, E. J., and GLINOS, E. B., J. Biol. Chem. 214: 175-184, 1955. Putrescine requirement of *Hemophilus*.

65. HINTON, T., Ann. New York Acad. Sci. 77: 366-372, 1959. Amino acid and growth factor requirements of Drosophila.

66. HINTON, T., et al., Physiol. Zool. 24: 335-353,

1951. Amino acid and growth-factor requirements of Drosophila.

67. Hodgson, E., et al., Canad. J. Zool. 34: 527-531, 1956. Choline substitutes, amino acid requirements, Phormia.

68. Hogg, J. F., and Hogg, A. M., J. Biol. Chem. 192: 131-139, 1951. Amino acid metabolism of Tetrahymena.

69. *Horning, M. G., in Cholesterol, edited by R. Cook. New York, Academic Press, 1958, pp. 445-455. Sterol requirements in insects and protozoans.

70. House, H. L., Canad. J. Zool. 32: 331-365, 1954; Ann. New York Acad. Sci. 77: 394-405, 1959. Nutrition of Pseudosarcophaga, dipteran parasite of spruce budworm.

71. Huddleston, S. M. S., Physiol. Zool. 24: 141-153, 1951. Nutrition of Tetrahymena.

72. Hutchens, J. O., J. Cell. Comp. Physiol. 16: 265-267, 1941. Thiamine requirement of Chilomonas.

73. *Hutner, S. H., and Provasoli, L., in Biochemistry and Physiology of Protozoa, edited by S. H. Hutner and A. Lwoff. New York, Academic Press, 1955, pp. 17-43; Ann. New York Acad. Sci. 56: 852-862, 1953. Vitamin B$_{12}$ and other vitamin requirements of flagellates, especially Euglena gracilis.

74. Jahn, T. L., J. Protozool. 2: 1-5, 1955. Flagellate nutrition.

75. Johnson, W. H., Physiol. Zool. 25: 10-19, 1952; 30: 106-113, 1957. Sterile culture of Paramecium multimicronucleatum, amino acid requirements.

76. *Johnson, W. H., Ann. Rev. Microbiol. 10: 193-212, 1956. Nutrition of Protozoa.

77. Jungulira, P. B., and Schweigert, B. S., J. Biol. Chem. 175: 535-546, 1948. Synthesis of nicotinic acid by rats.

78. Kaiser, E., and Wulzen, A., Arch. Biochem. 31: 326-329, 1951. Sterol as antistiffness factor for guinea pig.

79. Kato, M., and Hamamura, Y., Science 115: 703-704, 1952. Niacin in insects.

80. *Kidder, G. W., Nutrition of invertebrate animals, in Biochemistry and Physiology of Nutrition, edited by G. H. Bourne & J. W. Kidder, 2: 162-196, 1953.

81. Kidder, G. W., and Dewey, V. C., Biol. Bull. 87: 121-133, 1944; 89: 229-241, 1945; Arch. Biochem. 8: 293-301, 1945; 20: 433-443, 1949; 21: 58-65, 66-73, 1949; Proc. Nat. Acad. Sci. 33: 347-356, 1947; 34: 81-88, 566-574, 1948. Amino acid and growth-factor requirements of Tetrahymena.

82. Kidder, G. W., and Dutta, B. N., J. Gen. Microbiol. 18: 621-638, 1958. Nutrition of trypanosomiid flagellate Crithidia.

83. Kidder, G. W., et al., Proc. Soc. Exp. Biol. Med. 86: 685-689, 1954; Arch. Biochem. Biophys. 55: 126-129, 1955. Nitrogen, purine, and pyrimidine requirements of ciliate Glaucoma.

84. Lane, C. E., Ann. New York Acad. Sci. 77: 246-249, 1959; Bull. Mar. Sci. Gulf Carib. 7: 289-296, 1957, in Marine Boring and Fouling Organisms, edited by D. L. Ray. University of Washington Press, 1959, pp. 34-45. Food of Teredo and Limnoria.

85. Leclercq, J., Arch. Internat. Physiol. Biochim. 57: 67-70, 1949. Biotin requirement of Tenebrio.

86. Leclercq, J., Arch. Internat. Physiol. Biochim. 62: 101-108, 1954; 65: 337-346, 1957. Carnitine in nutrition of Tenebrio and Gnathocerus.

87. Leclercq, J., and Huot, L., Arch. Internat. Physiol. Biochim. 66: 473-482, 1958. Replacement of casein by amino acids, Tenebrio.

88. Lemonde, A., and Bernard, R., Rev. Canad. Biol. 10: 96-97, 1951; Canad. J. Zool. 29: 80-83, 1951. Amino acid nutrition of Tribolium.

89. *Levinson, Z. H., Riv. parasitol. 16: 113-138, 189-204, 1955. Nutritional requirements of insects, review.

90. Levinson, Z. H., and Bergman, E. D., Biochem. J. 65: 254-260, 1957. Steroid use and fatty acid synthesis by Musca larvae.

91. Lilly, D. W., Ann. New York Acad. Sci. 56: 910-920, 1953. Nutrition of carnivorous ciliates.

92. Lilly, D. W., et al., Proc. Exp. Biol. Med. 83: 434-438, 1953; J. Protozool. 3: 200-203, 1957; Tr. New York Acad. Sci. ser. 2, 18: 531-539, 1956. Nutrition of carnivorous ciliates, Stylonychia, Euplotes.

93. *Lipke, H., and Fraenkel, G. S., Ann. Rev. Entomol. 1: 17-44, 1956. Insect nutrition, review.

94. Little, P. A., et al., Proc. Soc. Exp. Biol. Med. 78: 510-513, 1952. Culture of flagellate Polytomella.

95. Loosli, J. K., et al., Science 110: 144-145, 1950. Synthesis of amino acids in rumen.

96. *Lwoff, A., L'evolution physiologique: Etude des pertes de fonctions chez les microorganismes, Paris, Hermann, 1944, 308 pp.

97. Lwoff, A., Ann. Inst. Pasteur 61: 580-617, 1938; C. R. Acad. Sci. 205: 630-632, 756-758, 882-884, 1937. Vitamins and growth of flagellates.

98. *Lwoff, M., in Biochemistry and Physiology of Protozoa, edited by A. Lwoff. New York Academic Press, 1951, pp. 129-177. Nutrition of parasitic flagellates.

99. Lwoff, M., and Nicolle, P., C. R. Soc. Biol. 139: 879-881, 1945. Hematin requirement of Triatoma.

100. MacKenzie, C. G., MacKenzie, J. B., and McCollum, E. V., Biochem. J. 33: 935-943, 1939. Growth of rats on low fat diet.

101. Magis, N., Bull. Ann. Soc. Entomol. Belg. 90: 49-58, 1954. Nutritional requirements of Tribolium confusum.

102. Mast, S. O., and Pace, D. M., Protoplasma 23: 297-325, 1936. Role of sulfur in protoplasmic synthesis by Chilomonas.

103. McElroy, L. W., and Goss, H., J. Biol. Chem. 130: 437-438, 1939; J. Nutrit. 20: 527-540, 541-550, 1940. Vitamin synthesis in rumen.

104. McLaren, B. A., et al., Arch. Biochem. 10: 433-441, 1946. Growth requirements of trout.

105. Miller, S. L., J. Am. Chem. Soc. 77: 2351-2361, 1955. Production or organic substances under possible primitive earth conditions.

106. Moller, P., Acta physiol. scand. 23: 47-54, 1951. Pyridoxine nutrition.

107. *Moore, T., *in* Biochemistry and Physiology of Nutrition, edited by G. H. Bourne and J. W. Kidder, *1*: 265-290, 1953. The fat-soluble vitamins.

108. Nason, A., and Donaldson, K. D., Tr. New York Acad. Sci. ser. 2, *20*: 27-50, 1957. Enzymatic role of vitamin E.

109. Nason, A., and Lehman, I. R., Science *122*: 19-22, 1955. Enzymatic role of vitamin E.

110. Nathan, H. A., and Cowperthwaite, J., J. Protozool. *2*: 37-42, 1955. "Crithidia factor."

111. Newton, B. A., J. Gen. Microbiol. *17*: 708-717, 1957. Methionine requirement of flagellate *Strigomonas oncopelti*.

112. Noland, J. L., and Baumann, C. A., Proc. Soc. Exp. Biol. Med. *70*: 198-201, 1949; Ann. Ent. Soc. Am. *44*: 184-188, 1951. Choline and amino acid requirements of *Blatella germanica*.

113. *Oginsky, E. L., and Umbreit, W. W., Introduction to bacterial physiology, San Francisco, Freeman, 1954, 404 pp.

114. Olcese, O., Pearson, P. B., and Schweigert, B. S., J. Nutrit. *35*: 577-590, 1948. Synthesis of B vitamins in rabbits.

115. Pace, D. M., Exp. Med. Surg. *5*: 236-250, 1947. Effects of vitamins on growth of Chilomonas.

116. Pant, N. C., and Fraenkel, G., Biol. Bull. *107*: 420-432, 1954. Role of symbiotic yeasts in two anobiid beetles.

117. Patterson, E. L., *et al.*, J. Am. Chem. Soc. *77*: 3167-3168, 1955. Pteridine requirement of protozoan Crithidia.

118. Phillips, A. M., Tr. Am. Fish. Soc. *76*: 34-45, 1946; *74*: 81-87, 1947. Vitamin requirements of brook trout.

119. Pintner, I. J., and Provasoli, L., J. Gen. Microbiol. *18*: 190-199, 1958. Culture of blue-green alga, Phormidium.

120. *Pringsheim, E. G., Biol. Rev. *16*: 191-204, 1941. Evolution and nutritional interrelations among flagellates.

121. *Provasoli, L., Ann. New York Acad. Sci. *56*: 839-851, 1953; *in* Perspectives in Marine Biology, edited by A. A. Buzzati-Traverso. University of California Press, 1958, pp. 385-403. Ann. Rev. Microbiol. *12*: 279-308, 1958. Nutrition and ecology of algae, particularly flagellate protozoans.

122. Provasoli, L., and Shiraishi, K., Biol. Bull. *117*: 347-355, 1959. Axenic culture of Artemia.

123. Quackenbush, F. W., Kummerow, F. A., and Steenbock, H., J. Nutrit. *24*: 213-224, 1942. Fatty acid nutrition, rats.

124. Reed, C. P., Exp. Parasitol. *6*: 288-293, 1957. Carbohydrate utilization by cestodes.

125. Reid, M. E., Proc. Soc. Exp. Biol. Med. *85*: 547-550, 1954. B-vitamin requirements of guinea pig.

126. *Rose, W. C., Physiol. Rev. *18*: 100-136, 1938; Fed. Proc. *8*: 546-552, 1949. Amino acid requirements in rat and man.

127. Sang, J. H., J. Exp. Biol. *33*: 45-72, 1956; Ann. New York Acad. Sci. *77*: 352-365, 1959. Nutritional requirements of Drosophila.

128. Sarma, P. S., Proc. Soc. Exp. Biol. Med. *58*: 140-141, 1945. Pyridoxine and tryptophan metabolism in rice moth larvae.

129. Schaeffer, A. E., *et al.*, J. Nutrit. *34*: 121-129, 1947; Arch. Biochem. *12*: 349-357, 1947. Nutrition of foxes.

130. Schoenborn, H. W., Physiol. Zool. *25*: 15-19, 1952. Culture requirements of colorless euglenoids.

131. *Scrimshaw, N. S., *et al.*, Ann. Rev. Biochem. *27*: 403-426, 1958. Interrelations among amino acids.

132. Seaman, G. R., J. Biol. Chem. *186*: 97-104, 1950; Proc. Soc. Exp. Biol. Med. *79*: 158-159, 1952; *80*: 308-310, 1952; Physiol. Zool. *26*: 22-28, 1953. Utilization of acetate, nature and function of protogen in *Tetrahymena*.

133. Sedee, D. J. W., Experientia *9*: 142-143, 1953; Acta. Physiol. Pharm. Néerl. *3*: 262-269, 1954.

134. Sedee, D. J. W., *et al.*, Arch. Internat. Physiol. Biochem. *67*: 384-395, 1959. Amino acid and vitamin requirements of blowfly larvae.

135. *Sherman, H. C., The Chemistry of Food and Nutrition. New York, Macmillan Co., 1946, 675 pp.

136. Silverman, P. H., and Levinson, Z. H., Biochem. J. *58*: 291-297, 1954. Lipid requirements of housefly larvae.

137. Singh, K. R. P., and Brown, A. W. A., J. Insect Physiol. *1*: 199-220, 1957. Nutritional requirements of *Aedes aegypti*.

137a. Smith, E. L., Vitamin B$_{12}$, London, Methuen & Co., 1960, 196 pp.

137b. Smith, R. M., and Monty, K. J., Biochem. Biophys. Res. Comm. *1*: 105-109, 1959. Vitamin B$_{12}$ and isomerase reactions.

138. Stokely, P. S., Exp. Cell. Res. *5*: 320-324, 1953. Synthesis of nicotinic acid by *Chilomonas paramecium*.

139. Stokstad, E. L. R., *et al.*, Proc. Soc. Exp. Biol. Med. *92*: 88-91, 1956. Thioctic acid in chick nutrition.

140. Storm, J., and Hutner, S. H., Ann. New York Acad. Sci. *56*: 901-909, 1953. Nutrition of Peranema.

141. Tappel, A., *et al.*, Fed. Proc. *19*: 419, 1960. Antioxidant function of vitamin E.

142. *Tarr, H. L. A., Ann. Rev. Biochem. *27*: 223-244, 1958. Fish nutrition.

143. Teeri, A. E., *et al.*, J. Mammal. *36*: 553-557, 1955. Vitamin excretion, deer.

144. Trager, W., J. Biol. Chem. *176*: 1211-1223, 1948; Biol. Bull. *75*: 75-84, 1938. Culture of mosquito larvae.

145. Trager, W., J. Parasitol. *33*: 345-350, 1947; J. Exp. Med. *92*: 349-365, 1950. Culture of malaria parasite, Plasmodium.

146. *Trager, W., Biol. Rev. *22*: 148-177, 1947; Physiol. Rev. *21*: 1-35, 1941; *in* Insect Physiology, edited by K. D. Roeder. New York, John Wiley & Sons, 1953, Chapter 14, pp. 404-422. Reviews of nutrition of invertebrates, especially insects.

147. Uberoi, N. K., J. Zool. Soc. India *8*: 85-90, 1956. Fatty acids and lipid metabolism of rice moth Corcyta.

148. *Urey, H. C., Proc. Nat. Acad. Sci. *38*: 351-363, 1952. Chemical history of the earth and origin of life.

149. Vishniac, H. S., and Watson, S. W., J. Gen.

Microbiol. *8*: 248-256, 1953; Biochem. Biophys. Acta *26*: 430-431, 1957. Steroid requirement of Labyrinthula.

150. Vogel, B., Ztschr. vergl. Physiol. *14*: 273-347, 1931. Sugar use, honeybee.

151. Wagge, L. E., J. Exp. Zool. *120*: 311-342, 1952. Sterols and calcium metabolism in Helix.

152. Wanderzant, E. S., *et al.*, J. Econ. Entomol. *50*: 606-608, 1957. Dietary fatty acids for pink bollworm.

153. *White, A., Handler, P., Smith, E. L., and Stetten, D., Principles of Biochemistry. New York, McGraw-Hill Book Company, 1954, 1115 pp.

154. Wiese, A. C., *et al.*, J. Nutrit. *33*: 263-270, 1947. Riboflavin deficiency in calves.

155. Wise, D. L., J. Protozool. *2*: 156-158, 1955; *6*: 19-23, 1959. Carbon nutrition, Polytomella.

156. Wulzen, R., and Bahrs, A. M., Physiol. Zool. *4*: 204-213, 1931. Balanced diet for Planaria.

Chapter 5

FEEDING AND DIGESTION

In the carbon cycle of nature, animals depend on plants to provide high-energy carbon compounds through photosynthesis. Some organic compounds, proteins, fats, and many carbohydrates, are widely used as foods; others, celluloses, waxes, and hydrocarbons, are less commonly used. Many animals rely on symbiotic microorganisms to digest foods for which they lack their own enzymes. Most of the major divisions of the animal kingdom have species which feed on a wide variety of foods and other species which specialize in a restricted diet. Food selection is often based on chemoreception (Chapter 11). The nature of feeding mechanisms appears to be determined largely by the habitat and the food available to a particular organism. The form and function of the digestive tract as well are, in most cases, definitely correlated with the types of food used and the feeding mechanism.

FEEDING MECHANISMS

Methods of intake differ according to whether the food is dissolved in natural waters, exists in particulate form, in masses or large particles, or is a liquid. Feeding mechanisms have been classified by Yonge[205] and Nicol,[151a] and a quantitative analysis of filter feeding is given by Jorgensen.[98]

Soluble Food. Natural waters contain dissolved organic material in concentrations of the general order of 2 to 20 mg/l, the amount being greater in regions of much organic detritus. In shallow sea water an average value is 4.5 mg dissolved organic matter per liter, of which 1.5 mg/l may be "protein" or nitrogen-containing organic matter. The dissolved organic matter is far greater in amount than the plankton, which may comprise at most a few tenths of a milligram per liter; the dead particulate matter usually comprises about 1 mg/l. In fresh-water lakes the concentrations are

similar to those in the sea; Wisconsin lakes averaged 16 mg total organic matter per liter, of which 8 per cent was planktonic; of the dissolved organic matter, 75 per cent was carbohydrate and 23 per cent protein.[21] In some Scandinavian lakes the total was 14.3 mg/l, of which phytoplankton constituted 1.7 mg; colloidal matter, 1.0 mg; and dissolved organic matter, 11.6 mg.[114]

The extent to which dissolved organic matter can be used by animals has not been adequately determined. Some Protozoa, e.g., *Tetrahymena,* can be cultured in solutions containing some 4 to 5 gm of nutrients per liter, a concentration far greater than is encountered in natural waters. Endoparasites such as cestodes and parasitic Protozoa can absorb enough from their rich environment that they do not need any special digestive structures. Some coelenterates, ascidians, and molluscs which pump quantities of water have been shown to diminish the organic solutes in filtered water. However, most filter feeders are unable to retain small organic molecules, and under normal conditions aquatic animals eliminate more organic matter than is dissolved in the medium.[114] However, the solitary coral *Fungia* removed, in one hour, some 25 per cent of labeled glucose or tyrosine from 100 ml of solution of concentrations as low as 1 mg/l.[181] Addition of various organic compounds in small amounts to water lacking particulate food has failed to prolong survival of many animals for which it has been tried.[37] The cladoceran *Moina* was unable to live indefinitely and reproduce in a broth solution or filtered bacterial medium, but it prospered when the same medium contained bacteria.[182] There may be some absorption of organic substances, but at present it seems unlikely that dissolved foods are adequate for growth of any aquatic animal except those living in a rich medium such as blood or intestinal fluid. Significance of dissolved organic matter for maintenance is an open question; however, dissolved foods may influence the rate of pumping of water.

Particulate Food. Particulate food consists of detritus particles, organic substances adsorbed on inert particles, dead planktonic cells; it comprises also living phytoplankton, mainly diatoms, flagellates, and bacteria. Particulate organic matter varies with the type of water, geographical latitude, and depth. In surface sea water it may range in quantity from 0.2 to 1.7 mg/l, of which one-tenth may be "protein." The content of particulate organic matter decreases rapidly with increasing depth and at 100 meters may be only 25 μg/l.[98] Phytoplankton varies greatly with season, location, and depth; in inshore sea water it may range in abundance from zero to 700 μg/l; in the open ocean, e.g., Sargasso Sea, values are lower than near the continents. Similarly, in fresh-water lakes phytoplankton may be abundant (2 mg/l) near the surface in the summer. Jorgensen calculated that the phytoplankton is sufficient to provide for maintenance and growth of most filter-feeders but that at certain seasons and in deep waters, filter-feeders must use nonliving organic particles.

Several methods used by animals to collect particles from water follow:

Pseudopodial Feeding. Rhizopods may engulf food particles by means of food cups; they may also take in fluid by pinocytotic vacuoles. Particles are caught on the reticulate pseudopodia of radiolarians and foraminiferans and then brought to the main part of the body for ingestion. Pinocytosis, the engulfing of fluid into small vacuoles, is a widespread cellular phenomenon. Intracellular digestion by food vacuoles is common in Protozoa, Porifera, Coelenterata, and Turbellaria; intracellular digestion takes place in amoebocytic cells in Pelecypods.

Mucoid Feeding. Many animals secrete mucous sheets which filter out particles, which are then eaten by the animals. The tube-dwelling polychaete *Chaetopterus*,[131] also *Nereis* under some conditions,[77] and the echiuroid *Urechis*[131] secrete a mucous net, pump water through it by the activity of posterior appendages, and swallow the sacful of trapped food about every 15 minutes. The nets of *Chaetopterus* retain not only small particles but protein molecules as large as hemocyanin (but not as small as ovalbumin); hence they have a pore size of about 0.004 μ (40Å). No other filter feeders have been shown to retain single large molecules. *Chironomus plumosus* larvae secrete a mucous funnel which is held by a thread in front of the larva in its tube; under favorable conditions a funnel is consumed and replaced every 1½ to 2 minutes.[197] Mucoid filtering and ciliary filtering may both be present in lamellibranchs and ascidians. The gastropod *Crepidula* has two mucous filters, one at the entrance of the mantle cavity and the other over the frontal surface of the gill; these collect food and are periodically rolled up and eaten.[201] Other gastropods with ciliary pumps, such as *Struthiolaria* and *Nemertus*,[144] extrude external mucous films which trap food particles.

Ciliary and Flagellar Feeding. Ciliary mechanisms for fine-particle feeding are found in the ciliate protozoans, sponges, many tubicolous annelids, echiuroids, rotifers, entoprocts, ectoprocts, phoronids, brachiopods, some gastropods, most lamellibranchs, and many tunicates and cephalochordates. Ciliate protozoans carry particles by special ciliary currents to the "mouth," where there is some selection of food. In sponges a water current is generated by flagellated choanocytes; some filtering is done by the epithelial pores, some by the prosopyles between choanocytes where phagocytosis occurs.[105, 192] One-micron particles are retained by the fresh-water sponge *Spongilla,* and the fresh-water *Ephydatia fluviatilis* pumps 1200 times its body volume of water daily.[105]

Lamellibranchs have been extensively studied and three filtering mechanisms have been proposed. Gill filaments bear several sets of cilia which can sort large from small particles and can transport food to the palps; straining may be between the rows of laterofrontal cilia of the gill filaments. Also, the gill epithelium may secrete mucous sheets which capture food.[131] Possibly the gills do the sorting in concentrated suspensions; the mucus, when the food suspension is dilute. Finally, according to observations on small transparent mussels,[186] particles are caught by adhesion to the long laterofrontal cilia, wiped off by the frontal ones and transported to the palps. The labial palps can discriminate food from inedible particles, which are discarded as pseudofeces. For example, oysters reject purple bacteria and retain algae when fed a mixture of the two.[129] The ciliary filter of *Mytilus* keeps back 30 to 40 μ particles, can retain or pass 7 μ particles, and cannot retain particles smaller than 1.5 μ.[186] *Mytilus* retains flagellates, but not graphite particles, of 4 to 5 μ.[97, 99] Oysters usually retain flagellates and other particles larger than 2 to 3 μ, pass particles 1 μ or less. Adult oysters pump some 20 to 50 ml/hr/mg N (about 10 l/oyster); veliger oysters, twenty to thirty times more.[110] Small *Pecten* pump at the rate of 1 l/gm/hr, older ones at 0.7 l/gm/hr.[29] Pumping rates in large *Mytilus* and scallops are somewhat less. A small bivalve, *Lasea,* excludes toxic flagellates, takes others at varying rates, and filters independently of particle size or density of suspension.[11] In the brachiopod *Neothyris* the gill filaments separate inward from outward currents and cilia filter large particles; mucus, smaller ones.[164] In tunicates a ciliary current carries water from the branchial sac through filtering stigmata to the atrial sac; also, mucous sheets in the branchial sac entrap particles.[97, 99] In general, the amount of water which must be pumped for respiratory needs is greater than that needed for food, and bivalves and ascidians commonly pump 10 to 20 l H_2O/ml O_2 consumed. For each ml O_2 the animal needs about 0.8 mg food; hence at 15 l pumped/ml O_2 consumed, each liter of water must contain 0.05 mg utilizable food.[97, 99]

Tentacular and Setose Feeding. Some tube-dwelling polychaetes like *Amphitrite* capture food by ciliated tentacles.[38] In Amphioxus (*Branchiostoma*) lateral cilia of the branchial bars create currents, and cirri around the mouth keep out coarse particles. Copepods produce currents by antennal vibrations, which may beat some 600 to 1620 times/min; particles retained by the setae of maxillae are scraped off by maxillulae and maxillipedes. Particles of 1 to 2 μ are retained by some copepods; 10 μ, by *Calanus*.[137]

Mechanisms for Taking Food Masses. Some burrowing animals swallow inactive food such as mud. Certain holothurians use their tentacles to force mud into their digestive tracts; annelids such as *Lumbricus* and *Arenicola* and sipunculids like Phascolosoma use eversible pharynges; burrowing crustaceans such as *Upogebia* and *Callianassa* use their mouth appendages. The organic content of the mud is utilized and the residue ejected as feces. In *Arenicola,* action of ciliated ridges in the esophagus and peristalsis move ingesta from mouth to rectum in 14 minutes.[103]

The honeybee proventriculus filters pollen so that honey is regurgitated into the crop and pollen passes to the midgut.[9]

Some animals have structures for scraping and boring foodstuffs. Examples are the Aristotle's lantern of echinoids, radular apparatus of some molluscs, boring valves of *Teredo,* and heavy mouth parts of termites.

Prey-feeding mechanisms were classified by Yonge as follows: (1) Structures for seizing only. These include the impaling proboscis of *Didinium,* nematocysts of coelenterate tentacles, the turbellarian pharynx, jawed pharynges of many polychaetes, teeth and radulas of some gastropods. (2) Structures for seizing and masticating. Examples are the jaws and radulas of molluscs, the jaws and other mouth parts of crustaceans, insects, arachnids and myriapods, and the toothed jaws of vertebrates. In the jawed vertebrates the anterior teeth often bite or gnaw, posterior teeth masticate; however, there is much variety, ranging from amphibians and billed birds which chew very little to the ungulates with heavy chewing molars. (3) Structures for seizing followed by external digestion. The sarcodinian *Vampyrella* digests a hole through the walls of the algae on which it feeds. *Asterias'* everted stomach kills and digests its prey. Some carnivorous gastropods, cephalopods, and spiders seize prey and carry out some external digestion.

Mechanisms for Taking Fluid Food. Structures for piercing may be combined with sucking, as in hookworms, leeches, many dipterans, ticks, mites, and cyclostomes. Structures for sucking only are found in suctorian protozoans, nematodes, adult lepidopterans, some flies, and suckling mammals. Tentacles of the suctorian *Podophrya* adhere and apply suction to *Paramecium,* not to *Spirostomum*.[106] Phloem sap is forced into the stylets of aphids by sap pressure, not sucked in.[143] Some homopterans living in the phloem of grasses lack most digestive enzymes and live on dissolved compounds in the plant juices. Some aphids must suck large quantities of plant juices to obtain sufficient protein; the excess sugars are regurgitated with slight modification of the sugar as honeydew.[70]

Use of Symbiotic Organisms. Termites, ruminant mammals, and some other animals maintain in the digestive tract cultures of protozoans and/or bacteria which provide the host with organic compounds and, in ruminants at least, provide protein as well. These will be discussed in a later section. Other animals have associated with them algae, zooxanthellae and zoochlorellae, which may provide nutrients. The giant bivalve *Tridacna* has thick fleshy mantle edges exposed to the sun, and in tissue cells (especially in amoebocytes) are many zooxanthellae. Amoebocytes come and go to the mantle and digest the starch-laden zooxanthellae and transport the products to body tissues. Hyaline structures in the mantle epithelium appear to focus light on the algae, and mantle regions in the shade have few zooxanthellae.[204] A turbellarian, *Convoluta roscoffensis,* has its body cells packed with zoochlorellae; clumps of the worms in intertidal pools are brilliant green. The adult worm has no digestive tract, except for a mouth, and no excretory organs. How the products of photosynthesis are used is unknown.[102]

The extent to which hydroids and corals which contain zooxanthellae use them for food is debated. Yonge[204] found that corals have extracellular proteases, that they feed on plankton organisms, particularly zooplankton, by tentacular and mucous mechanisms, and that when kept in the dark they expel their zooxanthellae. Some kinds of coral live without the algae, but the typical algae are not found outside corals.

In some coral heads the plant biomass exceeds the animal by three times, the filamentous green algae in the coral stems exceeding the zooxanthellae; over a 24-hour period photosynthesis approximately equals respiration, and the algae can provide two thirds of the food energy for the coral.[153] Sea anemones containing zooxanthellae were placed in sea water containing $C^{14}O_2$, and the tagged carbon was evident in the gastrodermis in 18 hours and in all tissues after a few weeks; hence, carbon compounds were transferred from symbiotic algae to the animal tissues.[146] There are considerable species differences, and other corals failed to incorporate much C^{14} when the zooxanthellae fixed it from $C^{14}O_2$.[67] Possibly the algae supply specific growth substances. Amoebocytes of some fresh-water sponges contain algae which may supply sugar to sponge cells.

The use of intestinal symbionts as food is discussed elsewhere (p. 118).

Food Selection. Some animals are omnivorous, others herbivorous, others carnivorous. All show food preferences and even filter feeders select certain food particles from a mixed diet. The stimulus to ingestion in *Hydra* (and *Physalia*)[124] is by reduced glutathione (G-SH), which may come from any live animal.[128] Dead animals are rejected, but dead material may be taken after

it has been treated with a low concentration of reduced G-SH.

Food selection by Protozoa is partly chemical and partly physical and is shown by acceptance or rejection of given foods and by different rates of feeding.[107] Paramecium takes starch grains, but refuses them if they are coated with iodine or thionine. Coelenterates are stimulated to feed by *Daphnia* juice; a nematocyst penetrates the prey, which, pierced, releases stimulating fluid. The presence of particles in the fluid medium increases swallowing by *Artemia*. Amoebae take up dissolved glucose by pinocytosis only if protein (e.g., bovine albumin) is present; true food vacuoles are induced only by particulate food.[28]

Specialization with respect to diet is most highly developed in insects, both carnivorous and herbivorous. The choice of particular food plants by insects is determined not by nutrient value but rather by taste preference; food preferences are partly genetic, partly due to habituation and olfactory conditioning.[43] Food selection will be considered in the chapter on chemoreception. Mud-feeding animals may select different types of mud according to its texture, presumably by mechanoreceptors. Closely related species of animals and even different populations may be kept isolated by highly selective feeding behavior.

MECHANICAL FACTORS IN DIGESTION

The digestive tracts of animals, like the feeding mechanisms, show striking adaptations to the character of the foods and the feeding habits of the organism. The evolution and adaptation of digestive systems have been discussed by Yonge.

Functional Regions of Digestive Tracts. There is much morphological variation according to type of food, but a functional sequence follows: (a) Reception. This region includes the mouth with its associated appendages and cavity. Food selection, primarily by taste, smell, and texture may occur in the reception region; there are often oral glands which secrete a lubricating fluid. Blood-sucking animals (leeches, mosquitoes) usually have an anticoagulant in their salivary secretion; carnivores feeding on live prey may secrete paralyzing toxins; many insects and vertebrates, also *Helix,* secrete salivary carbohydrases, and some carnivorous cephalopods have salivary proteases in addition to poisons and mucus. (b) Conduction and storage.

This occurs in the esophagus and crop, which are often muscular. Digestive glands here are rare although there may be some regurgitation of enzymes into this region. (c). Internal trituration and early digestion. This is the region of gizzards and gastric mills and true stomachs. Special grinding mechanisms occur in rotifers, some annelids, crustaceans and insects, and in birds. The crayfish gastric mill has also a filtering mechanism. Digestive enzymes may be secreted into the stomach by unicellular glands in the lining or by glandular diverticula or ceca. The diverticula may be tubes where intracellular digestion occurs, as in the midgut gland (hepatopancreas) of clams, brachiopods, and starfish. The diverticula may do both intracellular and extracellular digestion, with or without absorption as in arachnids and crustaceans. Or the diverticula may be purely secretory as in cephalopods and prochordates. (d) Final digestion and absorption. This is the anterior intestine or posterior midgut, and it may overlap the preceding region with respect to absorption. Digestion may continue, using enzymes liberated in the preceding region, as in most insects, or many glands may empty into the lumen as in vertebrates. In bees the water is absorbed from the anterior midgut. (e) Feces formation. This region is conspicuous in many terrestrial animals in which an important function is the absorption of water from the fecal material, as in insect hindgut and vertebrate colon. The whole intestine of crustaceans and of most molluscs comprises this region. In pelecypods and many gastropods the undigested material is twisted together with mucus into a fecal string which is moved by ciliary action and peristalsis down the intestine; covering the feces by a mucous coat prevents reingestion by these filter feeders.

Protection of Digestive Epithelia. In animals where digestion is primarily extracellular and where coarse food passes through the digestive tract, the epithelial lining of the lumen is protected. The commonest protection is by mucus secreted from special cells. This is particularly evident in holothurians, gastropods, and vertebrates. A second method of protection is the peritrophic membrane of insects (also some polychaetes). This membrane is less than 0.5 μ thick and has a protein ground substance combined with chitinous fibrils. It covers the food mass, and it may be formed by delamination from the surface of all midgut cells (Orthoptera, Hymenoptera, coleopteran larvae), or it may

be secreted by special cells at the anterior end of the midgut (Diptera, Dermoptera);[141, 200] insects which feed exclusively on liquids lack the peritrophic membrane. The mucus and peritrophic membranes protect against abrasion and against proteolytic enzymes; in addition, living epithelial cells are not permeable to the enzyme molecules and may contain antienzymes. In some digestive sacs, as the stomach of most gastropods and the gizzard of birds, there is a tough resistant lining; foregut and hindgut epithelium of insects is often lined with chitin.

Movement of Food Mass. Food is propelled along the digestive tract at appropriate speed by ciliary action or by muscular activity or by a combination of both. Ciliary activity appears to be the exclusive means of movement through the digestive tract in such organisms as the ectoprocts, entoprocts, and pelecypod molluscs. Muscular activity is involved to a greater or less extent in food propulsion in other animals. Sometimes movement of somatic musculature associated with locomotion serves as an effective force in the propulsion, supplementing the action of poorly developed visceral musculature, as in worms and holothurians. In addition to moving the food, the muscular activity serves to triturate further and to mix the food with digestive fluids.

The initiation of mechanical activity in visceral muscle is generally intrinsic (arthropods, vertebrates, probably cephalopods) although it may be regulated by nervous and endocrine systems. In mammals, for example, sympathetic nerves decrease and the parasympathetics increase motility of the gut. In addition, the digestive tube often contains its own regulating nerve network. The muscles of internal trituration may be striated but those of peristalsis are usually smooth muscle. Properties of these muscles will be considered in Chapter 14.

The time of retention of food in the digestive tract is inversely related to the efficiency of the digestive processes; food passes more rapidly when fed in large amounts than when in small amounts. A blood meal may be retained by a leech for several months. One blood meal lasts the bug *Rhodnius* for one instar, but food passes rapidly through caterpillars and grasshoppers.[202] In fish, several days may be required for digestion (3 days in dogfish).[189] In warm-blood animals digestion is more rapid. Food remains in the human stomach 3 to 4½ hours, carbohydrates remaining a shorter time than proteins; in cattle, food remains in the rumen an average of 61 hours, in the omasum 8 hours, and in the abomasum 3 hours.[46, 157] A delicate balance exists between the kind of food, the rate of digestion, and the rate of propulsion along the digestive tract; part of the regulation may be local and much of it is reflex in nature.

SITE AND SEQUENCE OF DIGESTION

Intracellular or Extracellular. In many animals there is both intracellular and extracellular digestion, but some animals have specialized in one or the other. Intracellular digestion is more primitive.

Autotrophic organisms absorb only simple organic molecules. Some bacteria secrete digestive enzymes such as proteases, which liquefy gelatin; they absorb the products of intermediate size and complete the digestion intracellularly. A few Protozoa are capable of extracellular digestion, but most take in food and digest it in a food vacuole or in the cytoplasm. A food vacuole is extracellular in the sense that the contents are separated from the cytoplasm by a membrane which has very low permeability to many substances such as organic acids. Enzymes are secreted into the food vacuole, and enzymes contained within live ingested food may act autolytically in the vacuole.

In metazoa extracellular digestion is associated with the appearance of mechanisms for internal trituration and the chemical breakdown of small particles or molecular aggregates. Extracellular digestion appears to have evolved first as an adaptation for dealing with large particles in order to reduce them to such size that intracellular digestion could take over; it is a sort of chemical trituration. The evolutionary trend has been toward replacement of intracellular by extracellular digestion.

In sponges digestion is exclusively intracellular. In triclad turbellarians digestion occurs primarily inside the large phagocytic cells lining the gut, while in rhabdocoel worms digestion occurs in the lumen of the gut.[93] In coelenterates intracellular digestion is predominant in the endoderm (*Hydra*) or mesenteric filaments (*Metridium*) or lining of the manubrium (medusae); in addition, the gastrovascular cavity of some coelenterates contains a protease and esterase. Concurrent intracellular and extracellular digestion also occurs in echinoderms, which secrete enzymes upon food while it is still outside the body. Furthermore, amoebocytes are abundant in the lumen of the echinoderm digestive system, and the cells of the pyloric diverticula are phagocytic. The polychaete *Arenicola* has extracellular digestion as well as intracellular digestion in epithelial cells of the stomach and by amoebocytes.[103]

Molluscs show a variety of digestive patterns. In cephalopods, digestion is primarily extracellular in the lumen of the digestive tract. Many gastropods, particularly carnivorous ones and omnivores like *Helix,* have extracellular digestion combined with limited intracellular digestion in the midgut gland. Other gastropods, particularly herbivores, and all lamellibranchs digest primarily intracellularly in amoebocytes and in cells of the midgut gland or diverticula, which may be extensively branched and have many openings to the stomach.[148] In these gastropods and pelecypods the only extracellular digestion appears to be amylase action from the crystalline style. Filtered stomach fluid from the bivalve *Tridacna* showed some digestive action on casein and dipeptides, but the digestion was weaker than the normal breakdown of zooplankton by intact *Tridacna*.[135] Other enzymes than amylase in the lumen appear to come from extruded waste fragments from diverticula cells.[144, 205] Morton argues that the molluscan style originated in trituration and in formation of the fecal string. In primitive molluscs the cilia of the stomach rotate mucous strings, retaining food particles that are removed for intracellular digestion.[145]

Digestion is predominantly extracellular in the annelids, crustaceans, insects, cephalopods, tunicates, and chordates (but not *Amphioxus*). Digestion is extracellular in all classes of vertebrates, but many organs such as liver, spleen, and kidney contain intracellular enzymes which are capable of hydrolyzing foods. The animal groups with extracellular digestion are the most active and by many standards the most successful. They have mechanisms for pulverizing their food and can consume, digest, and eliminate residues more rapidly than do animals with intracellular digestion. Further, the surface required for extracellular digestion is much less extensive, compared with the ramified chambers of digestive diverticula in flatworms, bivalves, gastropods, and echinoderms. Although extracellular digestion has evolved several times, it has not always developed simultaneously for different foods in the same animal.

Sequence of Action of Digestive Enzymes; pH of Digestive Fluids. In some animals with extracellular digestion, various enzymes are secreted together into one chamber, as in the crayfish stomach or insect midgut. Others have a series of chambers with enzymes secreted into them in sequence, as birds and mammals.

Digestive enzymes may be distinguished by their pH optima although these optima are often broad and vary somewhat with different substrates. The pH in a digestive organ does not always correspond with the optima for enzymes acting in it, and the pH at the surface of food particles where hydrolysis occurs may differ from that in the fluid contents in general. The pH in a digestive chamber varies according to whether food is present or not. In most animals the hydrogen ion concentration of the digestive mixture changes regularly during the course of digestion.

Regions of food reception may be nearly neutral. In man the saliva is slightly acid (parotid secretion pH 5.8, mandibular 6.4); in a cow it may be alkaline (pH 8.1 or higher).[174] Saliva of a cockroach has a pH of 6.9, and the pH of the mouth contents of several grasshoppers was 5.5.[23]

In general, the early stages of active digestion are acid and later stages alkaline. In the mammalian stomach the parietal cells secrete HCl to the extent of 0.4 to 0.5 per cent (pH 0.91). When diluted with food, the contents of the stomach range from pH 1.5 to 2.5 in normal humans.[18] The acid of the stomach is bactericidal, kills cells of food which may be alive when swallowed, and may aid in decalcification of food. The acid stomach of vertebrates also facilitates absorption of iron. Stomach acid also facilitates activation of the principal gastric enzyme pepsin and provides an optimum pH for its action. In ruminants the fermentation portions of the stomach are alkaline, and only the abomasum is acid. In birds, the pH of the crop is 4.5 to 5.8, proventriculus 4.4 to 4.9, and gizzard 2.0 to 2.6.[50] The stomach contents in frogs are nearly as acid as in mammals. In the bony fish which have a stomach the gastric pH (3.7) is not so low as in mammals, but elasmobranchs have very acid gastric contents. Stomachless fish swallow food directly into the alkaline intestine.

In no invertebrate is the crop or midgut as acid as the vertebrate stomach. However, in most molluscs the stomach pH is 5.3 to 5.8; in holothurians the foregut pH is 6.5 to 6.8 and the midgut 6.8 to 7.0. The midgut of insects varies according to diet and can be acid in blowfly larvae and alkaline in Lepidoptera and Coleoptera. The midgut tends to be alkaline in phytophagous insects and somewhat acid in carnivorous insects. The pH of the stomach and ceca of a mite was 4 to 5, of the colon 7 to 8.[86] In orthopteran insects the pH of the crop is 5.0 to 6.0.[115] In free-living Protozoa the pH of food vacuoles can be determined if food is stained with appropriate indicators. In general, the food vacuole is initially acid; values of 3.5 to 4.0 have been noted for *Amoeba*[138] and values as acid as 1.4 in *Paramecium*.[138] After a brief period the vacuolar contents become alkaline and digestion proceeds.

The regions of terminal digestion are usually alkaline. The pancreatic and intestinal secretions of mammals have a pH of 7.5 to 8; intestinal contents of fish are also alkaline. A molluscan intestine tends to be at a higher pH than the stomach, and the pH of the hindgut of holothurians is 7.2 to 7.4. Insects are extremely varied; in orthopterans the pH's of the hindgut and midgut are similar and slightly acid. The hindgut of several hymenopteran larvae is distinctly acid.[81] In several Diptera and Lepidoptera the hindgut is neutral or alkaline, and in the silkworm and clothes moth the pH is as high as 9.8 to 9.9.[177] In a few animals, e.g., the polychaete *Sabella,* the midregion of the digestive tract is alkaline and the posterior region acid. Protozoa food vacuoles in late stages of digestion are near neutrality.

STIMULATION OF SECRETION OF DIGESTIVE FLUIDS

When a digestive organ does not contain food there is usually a low-level continuous secretion of fluid which may have a lubricating function and which differs in composition from the secretion during active digestion. In animals which feed most of the time, as in pelecypods with continuous ciliary propulsion of food or in continually browsing scavengers, the flow of digestive fluid must be continuous. However, in most animals feeding is periodic and secretion is elicited to correspond to the presence of food; in starvation there is scanty dilute but continuous secretion. Gland cells can be stimulated directly by food in the digestive lumen, by chemical agents in tissue fluids (hormonally), by nerve impulses, or by all three methods of stimulation.

The control of digestive secretion has been examined very extensively in mammals, but hardly at all in other animals. Gastrointestinal hormones of mammals are reviewed by Grossman.[72] Control of salivary secretion in mammals is entirely nervous. The submaxillary and sublingual glands receive parasympathetic stimulation by the chorda tympani nerve, and the parotid gland by the auriculotemporal nerve; in addition, the salivary glands are innervated from the cervical sympathetics. Both parasympathetic and sympathetic nerves stimulate secretion although the nature of the fluid secreted differs according to the nerves stimulated and the glands activated. Normally there is some continuous secretion, but salivary secretion can be stimulated reflexly by food in the mouth or by other stimuli associated with food by conditioning. The stimulating action of parasympathetics is prevented by atropine, which probably blocks the action of acetylcholine liberated at the nerve endings. Pilocarpine stimulates the glands to secretion of fluid and may increase enzyme synthesis in the submaxillaries.

Secretion of gastric juice is stimulated by the vagus nerve and is antagonized by atropine. The sympathetic nerve may antagonize the vagus and elicit slight mucus secretion. Mechanical stimulation of gastric mucosa elicits secretion. Certain foods, particularly meat, as well as mechanical stimulation, cause the liberation from the mucosa into the blood of a substance which stimulates the parietal cells to secrete HCl. This hormone, gastrin, has some of the properties of histamine.

The vagus has a weak stimulating action on the pancreas. When the acid chyme from the stomach enters the duodenum a hormone is liberated from the intestinal mucosa; this substance, secretin, is carried in the blood and strongly stimulates pancreatic juice secretion. Secretin is a polypeptide having a molecular weight about 5000. It also increases bile secretion by the liver. A second hormone from the intestinal mucosa, pancreozymin, appears to stimulate secretion of the pancreatic enzymes (in contrast to fluid). A third hormone, cholecystokinin, from the upper intestinal mucosa causes smooth muscle of the gallbladder to contract and empty it; the best stimulants for production of cholecystokinin are fat, fatty acids, HCl, and peptones. A fourth intestinal hormone is enterogastrone, which inhibits acid secretion by the stomach; this antagonist of gastrin is elicited by fats. Control of secretion of fluid and of enzymes is separate (saliva, pancreas), and there may be some selective stimulation of specific pancreatic enzymes; this is difficult to understand since isolated zymogen granules contain all three enzymes.[84]

Nervous influences on intestinal secretion are slight or negligible. The intestinal glands respond readily to stimulation of the mucosa, and a hormone from the mucosa, enterocrinin, stimulates secretion of intestinal enzymes. The mucus-secreting cells of the intestine are continually replaced by new cells from the base of the crypts. In summary, a progressive series from nervous to hormonal control is evident. Salivary secretion is entirely nervous; gastric secretion is nervous and hormonal, pancreatic mainly hormonal, and secretion of intestinal fluids and of bile predominantly hormonal.

In birds, secretion of gastric juice by the proventriculus is stimulated by the vagus nerves and also by gastrin. In the frog, gastric secretion is stimulated by reflexes elicited by food in the stomach and by mechanical stimulation of the stomach. There is no evidence for gastrin in the frog.[34] It is not established that any hormones influence normal gastric secretion in amphibians, although histamine and mammalian gastrin are effective when injected.

In elasmobranch fish, as in the frog, the vagus nerve does not affect gastric secretion. The continuous secretion of gastric juice in fasting skates and dogfish is inhibited by epinephrine or by sympathetic nerve impulses but is not altered by stimulating or cutting the parasympathetic nerves. In perfusion experiments both acetylcholine and histamine increase gastric secretion in elasmobranchs. Gastric secretion is under nervous control of the vagus in mammals and birds; in amphibians the sympathetics stimulate, and in elasmobranchs the sympathetics inhibit, gastric secretion. Secretin has been obtained from the small intestine of birds, turtles, frogs,[111] teleosts, and elasmobranchs.[14] Other gastrointestinal hormones have not been looked for in lower vertebrates.

Stimulation of secretion of digestive fluids has not been much studied in invertebrates. In cephalopods the salivary glands are endocrine structures; they also secrete poisons and have some proteolytic function; they are controlled by the nervous system. In the cephalopod stomach, preliminary digestion is by pancreatic enzymes; the hepatic sphincter releases liver juice only during active digestion.[19] In snails and crayfish, secretory activity as seen cytologically is markedly increased after feeding. Rhythmic waves of secretion have been reported for midgut glands of *Helix* and *Astacus*.[112] In the snail *Achatina*[190] and the crab *Atya*[191] no rhythmic waves of secretion occur, but a sequence of secretion and restitution is clearly recognized.

In *Lumbricus,* stimulation of the ventral nerve cord elicits secretion of digestive enzymes in crop and intestine.[82] In the cockroach *Blatella,* secretion of digestive fluids seems to be elicited not by nerves but by secretagogues.[40] Activity of secretory cells of *Dytiscus* is maximal 45 minutes after feeding.[41] A blood-borne agent from fed *Tenebrio* stimulates mitoses in the midgut of starved individuals; during starvation proteases accumulate in midgut cells of *Tenebrio* but, on feeding, enzymes are liberated into the crop.[44] *Corethra* regurgitates digestive juices from midgut to pharynx, probably by a nervous reflex.[66] In these invertebrates, therefore, there is not a clear distinction between direct stimulation by food, by hormones, and by the nervous system. Food is the ultimate stimulus for secretion of digestive fluids in all animals; there is much variation in its mode of action.

DIGESTION OF CARBOHYDRATES

Plants synthesize a vast array of carbohydrates. Animals can break down some of these by their own hydrolytic enzymes, others by symbiotic microorganisms; animals can use some of the simple plant sugars directly, others they synthesize into specific metabolic intermediates. The carbohydrate units or monosaccharides which are commonly used in metabolism are hexoses, less commonly pentoses, and rarely tetroses and trioses.

Classes of Carbohydrates and Their Utilization. Hexoses exist in solution as five or six membered, oxygen-containing rings (furanose and pyranose respectively).

The natural sugars commonly used by animals are D-sugars. However a D-sugar may exist in two isomeric forms, of which the α-form is more strongly dextrorotatory than the β-form. The structure of α-glucose and β-glucose differs in the position of the H and OH on carbon no. 1 (C_1) as follows:

(α-glucose rotation +111°)

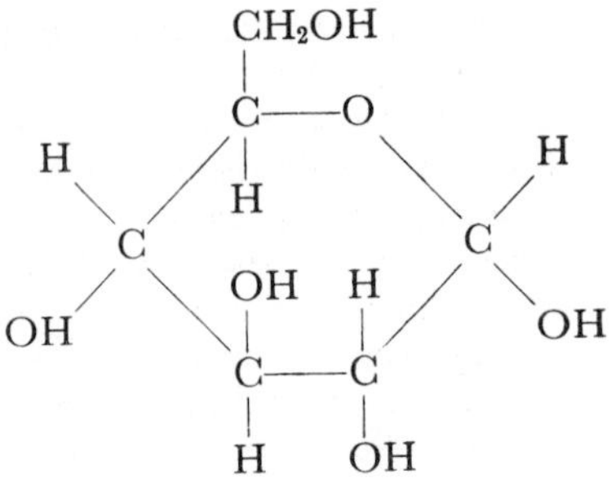

(β-glucose rotation +19°)

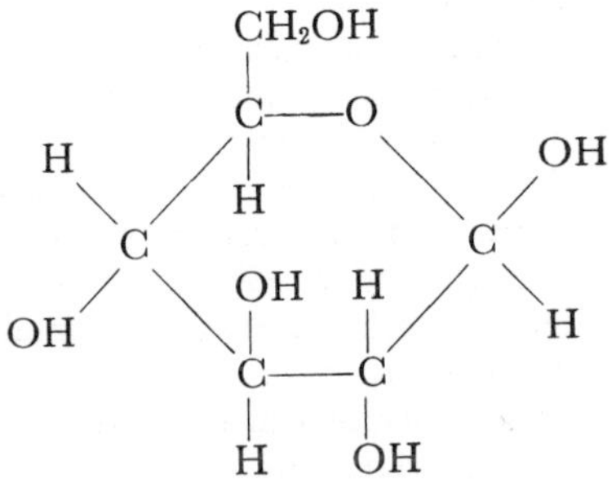

The disaccharide sucrose is represented as shown at the bottom of the page.

Oligosaccharides are intermediate in size between monosaccharides and polysaccharides. Oligosaccharides (disaccharides and trisaccharides and substituted sugars) may be classified according to their products on hydrolysis. Weidenhagen[68, 159, 184, 193] proposed that digestion of oligosaccharides could be

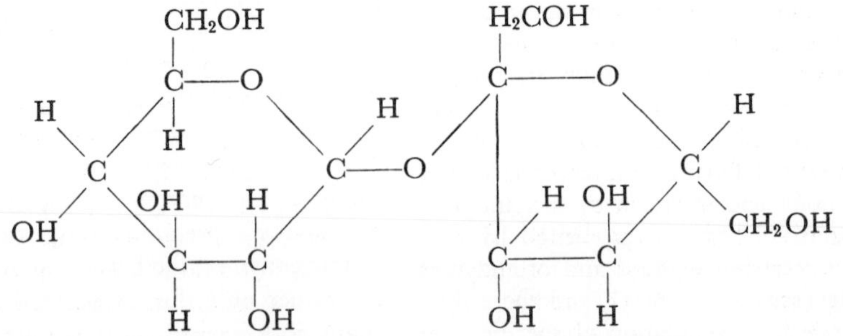

α-D glucopyranosyl   β-D fructofuranoside

accounted for by five enzymes of the following stereospecificity:

(oligosaccharide) and maltose; the dextrin is hydrolyzed by an oligosaccharidase, oligo-1,6-

Class and enzyme	Example	Products of hydrolysis
α-glucosides: (α-glucosidases)	α-maltose ⟶ 2 α-glucose	
	α-methyl glucoside ⟶ α-glucose + methyl alcohol	
	sucrose ⟶ α-glucose + β-fructose	
	(Sucrose can be attacked from the β-fructose or the α-glucose end; yeast invertase is a β-fructofuranosidase; animal sucrase is an α-glucosidase.)	
	melezitose ⟶ α-glucose + turanose ↘ β-fructose + α-glucose	
β-glucosides: (β-glucosidases)	cellobiose ⟶ β-glucose + β-glucose	
	salicin ⟶ β-glucose + saliginin	
	arbutin ⟶ tetramethyl β-glucose + quinol	
	β-gentiobiose ⟶ β-glucose + β-glucose	
	β-methyl glucoside ⟶ β-glucose + methyl alcohol	
α-galactosides: (α-galactosidase)	raffinose ⟶ α-galactose + β-sucrose ↘ α melibiose + β-fructose	
	(Raffinose is a trisaccharide which can go to α-galactose plus sucrose by the enzyme melibiase or to β-fructose plus melibiose by a β-fructofuranosidase.)	
	α-melibiose ⟶ α-galactose + glucose	
	α-methyl galactoside ⟶ α-galactose + methyl alcohol	
β-galactosides: (β-galactosidase)	β-lactose ⟶ β-galactose + α-glucose	
	β-methyl galactoside ⟶ β-galactose + methyl alcohol	
β-fructosides (fructofuranosides): (β-fructosidases)	sucrose ⟶ β-fructose + α-glucose	
	raffinose ⟶ β-fructose + α-melibiose	

An enzyme which acts on sucrose can be distinguished as an α-glucosidase if it also hydrolyzes melezitose or as a β-fructofuranosidase if it also acts on raffinose. Differences in relative specificity within a class are common. In yeasts an enzyme for maltose has been separated from one for α-methyl glucoside; both act on sucrose. Hence, Weidenhagen's hypothesis, while useful, is an oversimplification.

Polysaccharides are highly polymerized carbohydrates which serve for food storage and as structural elements. The most important plant storage product is starch. This consists of amylose, a straight chain of α-1,4 glucosidic links and of amylopectin, a branched compound with α-1,6 bonds at the branch points and 24 to 30 units (α-1,4 links) between branches. Amylopectin is often on the outside of a starch grain and is less easily digested than amylose. Glycogen, the corresponding animal storage polysaccharide, is a mixed α-1,4, α-1,6 linked structure having about 10 glucosyl units between branch points. These polysaccharides are of indefinite molecular weight. In mammals, amylose is broken by α-amylase (pancreatic or salivary) by random cleavage to maltose (87 per cent) and glucose (13 per cent), while amylopectin is cleaved to limit dextrin

glucosidase, and maltose is broken by maltase (an α-glucosidase) to two α-glucose molecules. Thus three enzymes are needed in mammals for digestion of starch.[120] Glycogen can be hydrolyzed by the same amylase that splits starch.

The most important structural polysaccharide of plants is cellulose. This consists of chains of β-glucoside units, is less soluble in aqueous solutions than starch, and is resistant to boiling and mild acid treatment. Many microorganisms and a few metazoa have enzymes which can attack cellulose. The reason most animals are unable to digest cellulose is that their digestive glucosidase and amylase act only on α-glucosidic compounds. Several tunicates (e.g., *Phallusia* and *Molgula*) make their test (coat) of a structural polysaccharide which appears identical to plant cellulose. Cellulose has recently been found by x-ray analysis to occur widely, even in human skin.[161]

Some other plant polysaccharides and associated compounds have been little studied with respect to animal utilization. Lichenin or reserve cellulose is an unbranched substance which is more easily digested than cellulose. Hemicelluloses are smaller molecules formed from cellulose. Xylan is a pentosan which contains the pentose, xylose, and may also contain arabinose and glucuronic acid; it is rarely used by animals. Lignin is an amorphous constituent of plant cell walls which is not digested by animals. Similarly, inulin, a fructosan, and pectin, which contains galacturonic acids, are rarely digested. Chitin is synthesized by some animals and plants; it is a nitrogen-containing compound, which is split by a few animals which have chitinase to acetylglucosamine.

Distribution of Polysaccharidases. *Digestion of Starch.* Enzymes for digesting starch are more widely found than those for any other substrate. All animal amylases appear similar although there are slight differences in pH optima and in activity. Animal amylases are α-amylases (in contrast to emulsin from almonds, a β-amylase); they are activated by chloride ions and lose their activity on dialysis. In the mammalian intestine the three enzymes, pancreatic α-amylase, intestinal α-oligosaccharase, and maltase, act in sequence.[120] The pH optimum of pancreatic and salivary amylase is about 7.0. A salivary amylase is found in man, apes, elephant, and pig; its occurrence is doubtful or slight in rodents, dogs, and several ungulates.[125] Salivary amylase is present in birds and in traces in frogs. All vertebrates have an active pan-

creatic amylase, and amylase is reported in the bile of chickens, sheep, and cattle. In general, amylase is very active in herbivorous and omnivorous animals; in carnivores it may act on food glycogen (Table 19).

Amylase is found in secretions of the midgut, chiefly from the ceca, of many insects, especially the herbivorous. Larvae of some parasitic sarcophid flies and blood-sucking flies lack amylase although they have some maltase and sucrase.[166] The tsetse fly *Glossina* has very weak amylase in the midgut whereas non-blood-sucking *Calliphora* has active amylase in both salivary and midgut glands. Insect salivary amylase, like that of man, is inactivated by dialysis, reactivated by NaCl.[41] The amylase of most insects acts in a slightly acid medium, but an amylase in the silkworm has an optimal pH of 9.6.[177]

Herbivorous molluscs have active extracellular amylase, either in midgut digestive glands (hepatopancreas) or in crystalline style, or in both. The style of lamellibranchs and most herbivorous gastropods is a convenient laboratory source of amylase. In addition, amoebocytes and digestive diverticula of bivalves digest starch, glycogen, and several sugars. The style may be formed rapidly after feeding, even between tides;[144, 145] it

TABLE 19.　DIGESTION OF POLYSACCHARIDES

Animal	Starch	Gly-cogen	Cellu-lose	Chitin	Comments
Soil amoebae[188]	+		+	+	chitinase (1/5 of cellulase strength)
Pelomyxa extract[196]	+	+			
Lumbricus intestine[187]	+	+	sl+	+	also inulin
Strongilocentrotus[123]	+	(its bacteria on agar)			
Mytilus hepatopancreas[56]	+ pH 5.6	+	— pH 6.2-6.5	—	
Teredo[119]	+		+		(in toluene, ∴ not bacteria)
Helix hepatopancreas and clean intestine[53]			—	—	
Helix total digestive extract[101]	+	+	+	+	also pectin, inulin, lichenin
Helix (bacteria from gut)[94]			+	+	
Limnoria enteric glands[163]	+		+		also hemicellulose, not lignin not by bacteria
Porcellio midgut glands[149]	+		—		
Buprestidae[165]	+		+		also pectin
Ctenolepisma (silverfish)[122]	+		+		not bacteria
Scolytidae[155]	+		—		
Lyctidae[155]	+		—		
Bombyx larva and Maja[96] exuvial fluid				+	
Calliphora larva, adult[49]	+		—		
all vertebrates	+	+	—	—	
Myzus (Aphididae)[1]					pectinase

is pushed forward by cilia in the style sac and the tip wears against a gastric shield. The pH optimum for style amylase from a number of lamellibranchs is between 6.0 and 7.0.[1] In carnivorous gastropods the style is absent, and a weak amylase is present in the hepatopancreas.

Amylase has been demonstrated in several Protozoa, particularly in *Pelomyxa*[196] and *Entamoeba*.[83] In coelenterates, amylase acts intracellularly in mesenteric filaments of anthozoans. In annelids, extracellular digestion of starch occurs mainly in the intestine, but some occurs in the crop.

Cellulose Digestion. Most animals which utilize cellulose do so by means of symbiotic microorganisms; a few animals have their own cellulase (Table 19). Digestion of cellulose by putrefactive bacteria and fungi is well known, and some soil amoebae contain cellulase.[188] The economically important wood borers *Teredo* (pelecypod)[119] and *Limnoria* (isopod),[163] and also *Ctenolepisma* (silverfish)[121, 122] and, to less extent, *Lumbricus* (and other earthworms)[187] produce their own cellulases in digestive glands. *Limnoria* digests hemicellulose well, cellulose less well, and lignin not at all.[162a] Complete utilization of cellulose occurs in *Ctenolepisma* if small amounts of organic nitrogen are supplied.[122] *Teredo* utilizes hemicellulose to a less extent than cellulose. The snail *Helix* digests a great variety of foods, and its cellulase has been studied kinetically. Its intestine contains bacteria which in culture liberate a cellulase, but sterile extracts of *Helix* intestine and hepatopancreas fail to digest cellulose.[53] Similar cellulolytic bacteria are found in other land snails but not in aquatic snails. Some cellulose hydrolysis is brought about by extracts of the crystalline style of certain pelecypods, even after bacterial action has been eliminated.[52] Sea urchins (*Strongylocentrotus*) have agar-digesting bacteria in the intestine which aid in the digestion of algae.[123]

Wood contains cellulose, hemicellulose, lignin, starch, and sugars, and the various wood-dwelling insects utilize different compounds. The nutrition of wood-boring insects in general has been summarized[134] for beetles[134] and termites and wood roach.[30, 87, 89] Wood insects can be grouped into the following categories: (1) In some—Lyctidae, powder post beetles, and Bostrychidae—only the stored food, i.e. starch and sugar, is used, and the cellulose is unchanged in the diges-

tive tract. (2) The bark beetles (Scolytidae) consume the cell contents of wood and can also digest hemicelluloses. The cerambycid larva *Phymatodes*[134] can use xylan. (3) Numerous Cerambycidae and Anobiidae and some Buprestidae[165] have cellulase in their own digestive secretions and can attack heartwood. (4) Several groups of insects harbor in their digestive tracts bacteria and flagellate Protozoa which can digest cellulose. Larvae of lamellicorn beetles have in the proctodeal chamber bacteria which can split cellulose. In three families of termites and in the wood-feeding roach *Cryptocercus* the hindgut harbors flagellates which digest cellulose. The protozoa are anaerobic and can be removed by subjecting the hosts to high oxygen pressure or starvation, and after defaunation (but while still possessing bacteria) the termites or roaches die in a few days on the cellulose diet which before defaunation supported them.[89] Particles of wood are engulfed by the protozoans and digested within them. The most important products of flagellate digestion for the termite appear to be fatty acids. For growth and reproduction termites need some nitrogen, such as is present in small amounts in wood; it is probable but not proved that they use their own proteolytic enzymes and that nitrogen is cycled through symbiotic generations.

In ruminants much of the fiber in forage is broken down in the capacious rumen and reticulum by symbiotic bacteria and protozoa. In many nonruminant mammals less complete breakdown of food fibers occurs in colon and cecum. The rumen-reticulum may accommodate contents equal to one-seventh the weight of the whole ruminant animal. Conditions in the great mass of the rumen ingesta are virtually anaerobic and the oxidation-reduction potential is about —0.35 volts. The pH of the sheep rumen is 5.5 to 6.8 during digestion.[39] Starches, glucose, and other soluble carbohydrates are utilized and, in addition, the cellulose, hemicellulose, xylan, and lignin are partially digested. The larger coarser fibers tend to remain in the rumen near the top, but the host periodically regurgitates and remasticates a bolus of this coarse material. Rumination serves to comminute the fibers of less digestible material, and no large fibers are found in normal feces.

The ruminant secretes copious quantities of saliva, the cow as much as 60 l/day; the saliva is alkaline because of a high content of $NaHCO_3$.[175] This neutralizes the fermentation acids in the rumen and gives rise to CO_2. This plus CO_2 and methane from the fermentation may amount to as much as 2 l of gas per minute. Some of this gas is absorbed, but most of it is eliminated by eruction (belching). Oligotrich protozoa of the genera *Diplodinium, Entodinium,* and *Ophryoscolex* avidly digest starch. *Diplodinium* digests cellulose and stores reserve polysaccharide, which is later fermented when the substrate is exhausted.[88, 183] Holotrich protozoa *Isotricha* and *Dasytricha* absorb soluble carbohydrates and convert them into "starch" which they store. After sugars are exhausted the reserve starch is fermented to hydrogen, CO_2, and acetic, butyric, and lactic acids.[5]

Most of the fiber digestion in the rumen is by obligately anaerobic bacteria which occur in numbers up to a billion per ml of rumen contents.[88, 89] Four chief types have been identified and their products obtained in pure cultures: (1) *Bacteroides succinogenes* which produces acetic and succinic acids and fixes CO_2. (2) *Ruminococcus flavefaciens* and *R. albus* which produce H_2, CO_2, ethanol, and formic, acetic, lactic, and succinic acids. (3) *Butyrivibrio fibrisolvens* producing H_2, CO_2, ethanol, and formic, acetic, butyric, and lactic acids. The preceding products have been identified in pure culture.[36, 88] Many noncellulolytic bacteria also occur in the rumen. They act on starch and other fermentable materials in the nonfibrous fraction and attack fermentation products of the fiber-utilizing bacteria; lactic acid is fermented to acetic, propionic, and butyric acids, ethanol to acetic acid, succinic acid to propionic acid, and formic acid to H_2 and CO_2 which are converted to methane.[26] Sheep saliva has no amylase, but the rumen fluid contains amylase from the bacteria. The rumen may contain up to 10 gm per 100 ml of fatty acids compared with 0.25 per cent in the dry food. The final products as measured in rumen contents are CO_2, methane, acetic, propionic, and butyric acids, small amounts of formic, valeric, and caproic acids, but no higher fatty acids.[4, 69] The proportions of these acids, which supply some 70 per cent of the energy requirements of the host, vary according to diet, and recorded values are 41 to 65 per cent acetic acid, 20 to 43 per cent propionic acid, and 15 to 18 per cent butyric acid. Propionic acid is most rapidly absorbed so that it decreases in time in proportion to the others.[69] On a caloric basis butyric acid may

constitute one fifth of the total, but on a mole basis only one eighth.[76] When C^{14}-acetic acid was fed, much of the C^{14} appeared in butyric acid and less in valeric acid, whereas when C^{14}-propionic acid was fed, the labeled C appeared mainly in valeric acid and not at all in butyric acid; hence, a 2-carbon condensation is indicated.[69] The rumen epithelium converts butyric acid to ketones (acetoacetic acid) in vitro.[156] Absorption of water and of the acids occurs mainly in the abomasum. Sheep live normally when their rumen protozoa (but not bacteria) have been eliminated; hence, the function of the Protozoa is in doubt; possibly by storing polysaccharide they tend to maintain a continuous supply of fatty acid. The energy available to ruminants from a given carbohydrate is less than in monogastric mammals, partly because the rumen organisms live at the expense of fermentation energy, the methane is not used by the host, and the fermentation acids do not yield as much energy as the carbohydrates from which they were formed. Ruminant tissues use acetate more readily than do tissues of nonruminants; fatty acids are converted to milk fat, but some acetate must be converted to glucose and galactose to provide milk sugar, lactose.[167]

In addition to providing oxidizable acids to the host, the rumen microorganisms serve as a source of protein; rumen fluid containing bacteria, Protozoa, and indigestible particles passes into the abomasum or true stomach, where the organisms are killed and their digestion starts. The rumen microorganisms can synthesize many of their nitrogenous cell constituents from such simple compounds as urea and, to a less degree, nitrite and ammonia.[126] Some ammonia is absorbed from the rumen and converted to urea in the liver.[139] Thus, ruminants can obtain protein from nonamino nitrogen, and in modern agriculture as much as one third of the nitrogen in animal feeds is supplied as urea. Ruminants can use urea for essential amino acids. Rumen microorganisms can also reduce SO_4 to sulfide, and S^{35} sulfate can be recovered in the amino acids of protein.[126, 127] The ruminant has been compared to a plankton feeder; it maintains its own culture of microorganisms in large numbers and the microbial crop from the rumen is continuously digested.

Analogous mechanisms for fiber utilization have developed in other mammals. The colon of the horse and the cecum of some rodents are less effective than the rumen because the microorganisms grow at a point past the site of action of proteolytic enzymes. A horse digests fiber less completely than a ruminant but much better than a pig. Some Australian marsupials, e.g., the wallaby, with a large sacculated stomach may utilize cellulose by bacterial fermentation to fatty acids much as the ruminants. Bacteria in the cecum of birds digest starch. Pectins have been shown to be broken down in the colon of dog and man.[104] Rabbits may derive some nutrients (in addition to B vitamins) by their coprophagy,[35] and bacteria utilizing only cellulose and cellobiose have been isolated from the rabbit cecum.[75]

Polysaccharides other than starch, glycogen, and cellulose are not much used as animal foods. Lichenin or reserve cellulose is digested by many invertebrates—sponges, earthworms, crayfish, tunicates, *Helix,* and many insects. *Helix* is the most versatile of animals in respect to its utilization of carbohydrates and it is said even to digest inulin; whether its inulase, like its cellulase and chitinase, is of bacterial origin is not known. Cerambycid beetles and *Helix* are reported to use the pentosan, xylan.[159] Chitin is split by chitinase to acetyl-D-glucosamine units (Table 19). Chitinases have been found as digestive enzymes in *Lumbricus,* in soil amoebae, in *Helix* (of bacterial origin); chitinase occurs in the exuvial fluid of some insect larvae and molting crustaceans.[96] The saliva of many kinds of aphids and some leafhoppers contains a pectinase, which may facilitate penetration of plant tissues.[1]

Distribution of Glycosidases. Sugar-digesting enzymes are identified by tests on digestive juices and tissue extracts and by nutrition tests on utilization of different sugars. The number of oligosaccharidases in animals is small compared with those present in plants and microorganisms, and it is probable that several sugars of one stereochemical type are digested by the same enzyme. Table 20 gives the distribution of glycosidases in a few selected animals. Maltase is widely distributed; it attacks other α-glucosides but not necessarily α-methyl glucoside. Maltase often occurs in combination with amylase, as in human saliva, or separately, as in the mammalian intestine or molluscan midgut glands. The pH optimum is usually broad and in the weakly acid range. Mammals and reptiles have an active intestinal maltase, frogs and fish a pancreatic one.

Maltase and sucrase activity go together, and the pH optima are closely similar. It is probable that in animals maltose and sucrose are digested by the same enzyme. In bivalve molluscs the crystalline style liberates amylase while digestion of maltose and other sugars appears to take place inside the wandering amoebocytes;[205] however, some extracellular digestion of sugar has been claimed.[135]

Beta-glucosides are used by *Helix, Limnoria,* crayfish, some insects—*Tenebrio* and cockroach, *Bombyx* larvae[91]—but not others—*Calliphora, Drosophila*; digestive fluid of sowbugs has an active β-glucosidase.[149] There are reports of limited utilization of certain β-glucosides by a few mammals and of lack of digestion of others.[24] As tested on a β-D-glucopuranoside, a β-glucosidase is active in extracts of guinea-pig pancreas, rat kidney, mouse and pig intestine.[32]

Alpha-galactosides are used by some insects but apparently not by mammals. It is probable that raffinose is digested by insects by an α-galactosidase rather than by a β-fructosidase. Among β-galactosides, lactose is digested in mammalian intestines, more in infants than adults, but it is said not to be digested by the intestine of turtle or carp. Lactose is not digested by many crustaceans and insects but is digested by *Helix*. A number of tissues (pancreas, intestine, kidney, liver) of several laboratory mammals contain a β-D-galactosidase.[32] Beta-fructosidases are indicated as present in several invertebrates but not in any vertebrates.

The Weidenhagen hypothesis of distribution of glycosidases by class is useful as a first approximation. Within a class, particularly among α-glycosidases, one substrate may be used but not another. The rare occurrence of cellulases has been correlated with the rarity of active β-glucosidases. There is some indication that animals with their own enzymes for digesting cellulose can also digest β-glucosides. No vertebrate has its own cellulase, but some may digest certain β-glucosides.

Sugar digestion may change with age. Honeybee larvae can use lactose; adult bees cannot. Sucrase first appears in the pharyngeal gland of the worker bee after it starts foraging, and it then increases markedly. Larvae of moths and butterflies have sucrase in addition to lipase and protease in the midgut, whereas those adults which suck nectar have sucrase but no other digestive enzymes, and nonfeeding moths have no digestive enzymes

TABLE 20. DISTRIBUTION OF DIGESTIVE GLYCOSIDASES

Enzyme	Substrate	Entamoeba[88]	Pelomyxa[196]	Helix[20,115]	Cryptobionta[140]	Astacus[116]	Sowbugs Porcellio Armadillidium[149]	Cockroach	Bombyx larval midgut	Calliphora[49,57] adult	Calliphora adult	Calliphora larva	Tenebrio[58] Growth	Tenebrio Enzyme	Drosophila[154] utilization	Stable-fly[27]	Goldfish[170]	Man	Horse	Cattle	Sheep	Dog	Rabbit	Rat
α-glucosidase	maltose	+	+	+	+	+		+		+	+	+	+	+	+		+	+	+	+	+	+	+	+
	melezitose	−			+					+	+	+	+	+	+			+						
	sucrose		+	+	−	+	+	+		+	+	+	sl+	+	+	+	+	+	+	+	+	+	+	+
	α-methyl glucoside				+					+	+	−	−	−	+									
	trehalose											+		+										
	turanose												+	+										
β-glucosidase	cellobiose		+			+	+	+	sl+	−	−	−	+	+	−									
	gentiobiose					+																		
	arbutin			+	+		−gland +juice																	
	β-methyl glucoside				+				+									+		−		+		+
	salicin			+			−gland +juice		+	−	−							−	+	+	+		+	−
α-galactosidase	raffinose		+	+	−		+gland			+	+	+	+	+	+						−		−	
	melibiose			+	−		+gland			+	+	−	−	+	+			−	−	−	−	−	−	−
	α-methyl galactoside			+																				−
β-galactosidase	lactose			+	−	−	−gland			−	−	−		sl+	−			+	+	+	+	+	+	+
	β-methyl galactoside			+				−		−	−		sl+				−	+		+			+	+
β-fructosidase	gentianose	−	+	+?		+	−gland											−	−	−	−	−	−	−
	raffinose			+?		+																		

whatever. Sugar digestion is weak in carnivorous animals. For example, the blood-

digestion is essentially a series of hydrolyses of peptide linkages:

$$-\underset{\underset{H}{|}}{\overset{\overset{R_1}{|}}{C}}-\overset{\overset{O}{\|}}{C}-N-\underset{\underset{H}{|}}{\overset{\overset{H}{|}}{C}}- + HOH \longrightarrow -\underset{\underset{H}{|}}{\overset{\overset{R_1}{|}}{C}}-\overset{\overset{O}{\|}}{C}-OH + H_2N-\underset{\underset{H}{|}}{\overset{\overset{R_2}{|}}{C}}-$$

sucking tsetse fly *Chrysops* has no salivary carbohydrases and has amylase and sucrase only in the posterior midgut, whereas the closely related non-blood-sucking *Calliphora* has amylase in the salivary glands and amylase, maltase, and sucrase in both anterior and posterior midgut.[202] Lactase is present in infant mammals to a greater extent than in adults.

It was formerly believed that in absorption, glucose is phosphorylated by hexokinase as it enters the mucosal cells and that the phosphorylated sugar is broken by phosphatase as it leaves the cell. Glucose is carried in the blood to liver or other storage tissue where it is converted to glycogen. Initial phosphorylation of sugars is indicated by the facts that absorption decreases according to the series of diminishing phosphorylation and that after hexokinase is poisoned with phlorhizin or iodoacetic acid there is reduced absorption of galactose and glucose but not of pentoses. Recent evidence tends to exclude a unified phosphorylation mechanism since some sugars which lack OH groups in position for phosphorylation are absorbed; furthermore, active absorption can be prevented by configurational changes. Even if not phosphorylated, certain sugars are actively transported against a concentration gradient, and those which are actively absorbed (glucose, galactose, α-methylglucoside) compete with each other but not with sugars which are not actively absorbed (mannose, xylose).[100]

Classification of Proteases. Proteases differ in respect to the size of molecule and the groups adjacent to the petide bonds which they attack, and also in respect to optimum pH, presence or absence of a metal, and the effects of activating and inhibiting agents. [42, 61, 63, 64, 178, 206] All proteases act only on compounds of the L-series, i.e., those with naturally occurring amino acids. Activation involves the exposure of some active molecular site, sometimes by removal of the terminal part of a molecule.

Endopeptidases (Proteinases). These enzymes may attack central bonds of proteins and of peptones, as well as certain specific peptides.

PEPSIN. Pepsin acts in an acid medium (pH 1.0 to 5.0) and is inactivated in a neutral or alkaline one. According to Northrup, who has crystallized this and other proteases, pepsin attacks positively charged proteins. It has a molecular weight of 34,000 to 38,000. Pepsin is secreted in vertebrates from the chief cells of the stomach as pepsinogen, which is activated autocatalytically in an acid medium (pH <6). This enzyme attacks peptide bonds with an adjacent aromatic amino acid, e.g., tyrosine or phenylalanine, and to a less extent cysteine; it is particularly effective on a peptide linkage between dicarboxylic and aromatic amino acids if the second carbonyl of the dicarboxylic acid is free and if there is no free amino group near the peptide link as follows:

$$C_6H_5CH_2O-\overset{\overset{O}{\|}}{C}-HN-\underset{\underset{(CH_2)_2}{|}}{\underset{\underset{COOH}{|}}{CH}}-CO-\vdots-HN-\underset{\underset{\langle OH\rangle}{|}}{CH}-CO-HN-CH_2-CO-NH_2$$

carbobenzoxy   glutamyl   pepsin break   tyrosyl   glycinamide

DIGESTION OF PROTEINS

Proteins are digested to their component amino acids which may then be absorbed and built into specific new proteins. Protein

TRYPSIN. Trypsin acts in an alkaline medium (pH 7.0 to 9.0), in which most proteins are negatively charged. It has a molecular weight of 34,000. It is secreted as trypsinogen, which may be activated by a specific enzyme such as intestinal enterokinase, or it may be activated autocatalytically. Trypsin acts on peptide links adjacent to arginine or lysine.

thionine, e.g., glycyl phenylalaninamide; cathepsin C requires SH activation for action on certain proteins such as serum albumin,

$$\text{L alanyl—L arginyl—L leucyl—L tyrosyl—glycyl—L glutamyl}$$

trypsin   chymotrypsin

Specific proteinaceous trypsin inhibitors are found in pancreatic extract, egg white, and soybean extract.

CHYMOTRYPSIN. A series of pancreatic chymotrypsins (at least four) are known, some of which are derivatives of others. The molecular weights range from 27,000 to 40,000. Chymotrypsinogen is activated in an alkaline medium (pH 7.0 to 9.0) in the presence of trypsin. Chymotrypsin acts in an alkaline medium and attacks peptide links with adjacent aromatic amino acids, particularly tyrosine, phenylalanine, tryptophan and, to a less extent, methionine. It is inhibited by organic phosphates such as isopropylfluorophosphate and by benzoyl derivatives of several amino acids.

CATHEPSINS. Several different cathepsins are known as intracellular proteases from mammalian liver, kidney, and spleen. Cathepsins function also extracellularly in many invertebrates. They act best in a weakly acid medium (pH 4.0 to 6.0). According to the classification of mammalian cathepsins by Fruton,[62, 185] cathepsin A resembles pepsin in its substrate requirement, is easily tested on carbobenzoxy-glutamyl tyrosine, requires no activator, and acts at pH 4.0. Cathepsin B resembles trypsin in substrate, is tested on benzoylargininamide, and is activated by a sulfhydryl-reducing compound such as cysteine or HCN. Its pH optimum is 5.0. Cathepsin C resembles pancreatic chymotrypsin in specificity, is tested on carbonyls of tryptophan, tyrosine, phenylalanine, or me-

but not on others such as hemoglobin; its pH optimum is 6.0.[185] Other so-called cathepsins are exopeptidases.

Rennin is an enzyme which clots milk protein (casein). Some proteolytic enzymes have a rennin action. However, there are probably specific rennins, as in the stomach of infants, distinct from pepsin.

Endopeptidases from nonmammals have not been extensively studied with respect to substrate requirements. For practical purposes, proteases with pH optimum 1.5 to 3.0 may be considered as pepsins, those working in an alkaline medium (pH 7.0 to 9.0) as trypsins, and those in weak acid (pH 4.0 to 6.5) as cathepsins. The pH optimum varies with substrate and according to whether the substrate is native or denatured protein. For example, the pH optimum for mammalian trypsin on casein and fibrin is higher than it is on gelatin.

Exopeptidases. These enzymes attack terminal peptide bonds, i.e., substrates with free polar groups, and they normally act on polypeptide products of proteinase action. They generally show broad pH optima in the neutral or weakly alkaline range, and they usually differ from endopeptidases in that they contain a metal or may be activated by one.

CARBOXYPEPTIDASES. A carboxypeptidase removes a terminal amino acid with a free carboxyl group. It is inhibited by a free amino group nearby. A useful substrate is chloracetyltyrosine. Pancreatic carboxypeptidase acts best on peptides containing tyrosine, phenylalanine, or tryptophan, for example:

leucyl   break   glycyl   break   tyrosine

Pancreatic carboxypeptidase has been crystallized; it contains 1 zinc atom per molecule; it has a molecular weight of 34,000.

AMINOPEPTIDASES. An aminopeptidase acts on a peptide bond next to a terminal amino acid with a free amino group. It is inhibited by a free carboxyl nearby. Aminopeptidase from pancreas and intestinal mucosa has an optimum pH at 8.0, and requires manganese.

DIPEPTIDASES. There are numerous dipeptidases which break dipeptides into their constituent amino acids. Glycylglycine dipeptidase is activated by Co^{++} (or Mn^{++}) with which it may chelate; it is specific for glycylglycine and has a pH optimum of 7.6. Intestinal glycyl-1-leucine dipeptidase is activated by Mn, that from the uterus and muscle by Zn; it is inhibited by CN and other metal-binding inhibitors. Prolidase acts on peptide bonds lacking a peptide hydrogen, e.g., glycylproline; it is activated by Mn, has a pH optimum at 7.7, is slightly inhibited by CN^-. Carnosinase acts on carnosine (β-alanylhistidine), is activated by Zn^{++} or Mn^{++}, and is inhibited by CN^- or S^-.

Distribution of Proteases. Proteolytic enzymes have been obtained from tissue extracts and from digestive fluids of many animals. Data obtained prior to 1949 were summarized in the first edition of this book. A few representative examples from that table, together with more recent data, are given in Table 21.

Enzymes extracted from glandular tissue are generally the same as those from the lumen of a digestive organ into which the glands secrete, particularly after activation. However, tissue extracts frequently contain proteolytic enzymes with two pH optima, that is, there are more than one enzyme. Unfortunately, very few enzyme preparations have been tested on the specific substrates, but rather they are identified merely by pH optima.

Trypsins. Trypsins, or at least proteinases with alkaline pH optima, are more widely distributed than any other endoproteases. Trypsin is characteristic of the pancreas of all vertebrates, and an alkaline proteinase is found in most invertebrates. In the pancreas of several fresh-water fish a typical trypsin with alkaline pH optimum and enterokinase activation occurs. In all insects with protein digestion the active enzyme is trypsin. The pH optimum is not necessarily 7.5 to 8.0; in the silkworm it is 9.5, and in several crickets the pH optimum extends from 6.2 to 9. Trypsin occurs in both parasitic and free-living Diptera.[166] Some trypsins are activated by mammalian enterokinase as in several insects (e.g., *Blatta*),[40] *Sepia,* and *Limulus.*[173] Other trypsins, as in *Paramecium,*[138] snail *Murex,*[136] crab *Maja,*[136] *Peripatopsis,*[80] and several insects[160] are not activated by enterokinase. Attempts to find other tissue activators have not been successful. Whether the invertebrate trypsins which are not activated by enterokinase are like vertebrate chymotrypsin can be learned only by tests with specific substrates.

Wool contains the protein keratin which is unique in containing peptides bonded by disulfides. The gut fluid of the clothes moth *Tineola* contains a strong reducing substance which maintains a very low oxidation-reduction potential (-190 to -250 mv) in the midgut (cf. $+10$ to 30 mv in Blatella).[40] The pH of the proteolysis is high (pH 9.5 to 10) as it is also for the silkworm and the wax moth.[177, 200] *Tineola* protease differs from vertebrate trypsin in not being inhibited by sulfhydryl.[160] Dermestid beetles also have a low redox potential but can digest wool at a lower pH than the clothes moth. The reducing conditions in the clothes moth midgut are such that metalloproteins containing metals such as mercury are detoxified by reduction, and the insect can survive very high concentrations of the toxic metal.[198] A collagenase occurs in sheep blowfly larvae, but not in larvae of houseflies or several other insects.[199]

Cathepsins. Proteinases acting in the pH range of 4 to 6.5 are usually considered as cathepsins; some require reducing substances for activation, probably as a result of the requirement for certain functional $-SH$ groups; others do not. They are predominantly intracellular proteinases in vertebrates, but they occur extracellularly as well in invertebrates and they function near cytoplasmic pH values. Cathepsins occur also in digestive juice of some invertebrates; they have been demonstrated in tissue extracts of *Paramecium,*[171] in several snails,[169] and in both gland extracts and stomach juice of the crab *Maja.*[136] Often two pH optima occur, one in weak acid for cathepsin and the other in the alkaline range for a trypsin (e.g., in cephalopod *Polypus*).[171] The tryptic diges-

TABLE 21.   CHARACTERISTICS OF PROTEINASES

Animal	Tissue fluid	Substrate	pH optimum	Activation or inhibition
Protozoa				
Paramecium[171]	extract	casein		no enterokinase
		gelatin	7.4	activation
			4.6	activated by cysteine, HCN
Pelomyxa[85]	cytoplasmic granules	casein	3.75	not activated by cysteine, HCN
Coelenterates				
Pseudoactinia[113]	digestive juice	casein	8.5	(juice pH 6.7-6.8)
	gastric filament	gelatin	8.0	
Madrepore corals[204]	gastric fluid	fibrin	7.1, 8.7	
	mesenteric filaments	fibrin	5.3, 6.5-10	
Annelids				
Sabella[150]	midgut	gelatin	8.0	
Lumbricus[82]	typhlosole	gelatin and casein	5.2-5.7	(slight activation by cysteine)
	intestinal wall		7.7-8.3	
Molluscs				
Octopus[8]	salivary secretion	casein	8.5	
Polypus[171]	hepatopancreas digestive juice	gelatin	4.6	activated by HCN
			7.8	inhibited by HCN
Sepia[168]	liver extract	casein	6.1	
		gelatin	5.6	
	stomach juice	casein	6.8	activated by enterokinase
		gelatin	5.6	
Ostrea[171]	midgut glands	casein	4-4.2, 8-8.5	
		gelatin		
Helix[169]	midgut glands	gelatin	5.5	activated by HCN, H_2S
Achatina[190]	midgut glands	gelatin	5.6	
Mytilus[56]	intracellular	peptone	4.6, 7	
		egg albumin	4.5, 8.2	
Arthropods				
Limulus[173]	hepatopancreas stomach fluid	casein	9	activated by enterokinase inhibited by H_2S
Peripatopsis[80]	saliva	casein, gelatin	7-7.5	no activation by H_2S or enterokinase
Astacus[116]	stomach fluid	casein	6.2, 8.0	(slight at pH 8.0)
		gelatin		
Maja[135]	stomach fluid		6, 8	no CN or H_2S activation
			6-7	no enterokinase activation
Several spiders[158]		gelatin	7-9	
			also pH 2	
Blatella[40]	midgut ceca	casein	8	
Calliphora larvae[49]	gut	azocasein	7.8	
Carabus[173]	crop and midgut	casein	9	
Dragonfly nymph[12]	crop and midgut	edestin	5-5.5	
	anterior intestine	edestin	8.9	
Bombyx larva[177]		gelatin	9.2	
		casein	11.5	
Lucilia[160]		collagen	8.5	
		gelatin	7.6	
Tineola[160]	intestinal extract	casein	9.3	
		gelatin	9.8-10	
Echinoderms				
Distolasterias[171]	pyloric ceca	gelatin	4.8	activated by HCN, H_2S
		gelatin	7.6	inhibited by HCN
Prochordates				
Amphioxus[13]	digestive diverticula	gelatin	8.3	
Chordata				
Acanthias[194]	pancreas	fibrin	8.2	
	stomach	fibrin	2-2.4	
Several teleosts[22]	stomach	gelatin	3	
	pancreas	fibrin	7.7-7.8	
Cyprinus[194]	pancreas	fibrin	8.7	activated by enterokinase
Ophiocephalus[194]	gastric mucosa		1.6, 5.6	
Frog[194]	stomach	fibrin	2.2	
	pancreas		6.8	

tion (presumably combined with dipeptidases) may be inhibited by CN^-, whereas some cathepsins are activated by it; hence activity-pH curves with and without cyanide cross.[171] An earthworm has a cathepsin, with pH optimum 5.2 to 5.8, somewhat activated by cysteine and predominantly in the typhlosole, and also a trypsin, pH optimum 7.7 to 8.3, mainly in intestinal wall.[82] Some invertebrate cathepsins, like cathepsins B and C, are activated by CN or SH (*Paramecium, Pelomyxa,* Starfish, *Polypus*); others (e.g., *Maja*) resemble cathepsin A of vertebrates in not requiring activation by reducing agents. However, the identity of invertebrate cathepsins with vertebrate cathepsins A, B, and C should be checked by peptide substrates.

Pepsins. Pepsin is characteristic of vertebrates only. Prochordates and microphagous cyclostomes lack a stomach and have no peptic digestion. Beginning with the jawed carnivorous fish—elasmobranchs and bony fish—peptic digestion occurs in the stomach.[7] Some teleosts lack a stomach and these have no pepsin, e.g., *Fundulus.* The acid-secreting parietal cells may be located in different regions from the pepsinogen-secreting chief cells. In a frog, pepsin is secreted in the esophagus and upper stomach, HCl in the pyloric end of the stomach. In birds the glandular stomach or proventriculus lies between the crop and grinding gizzard and secretes both HCl and pepsinogen. The gizzard contents are less acid in an adult hen (pH 3.1) than in a young chicken (pH 2.7 in 23-day chick).[194]

Crystalline pepsins from salmon, halibut, and shark differ in specificity from mammalian and avian crystalline pepsins. Pig, sheep, and chicken pepsins are active on benzoyl-1-glutamyl-1-tyrosine, also on zein; crystalline salmon pepsin does not attack these substrates but is highly active on hemoglobin and edestin.[64, 152] A protease with pH optimum of 3 to 4 in combination with pepsin has been reported in gastric mucosa and in gastric juice of several mammals[25, 142] and fish—trout,[117] pike,[25] and Indian *Ophiocephalus.*[132] Crystalline salmon pepsin has two pH optima.[152] By precipitation and electrophoresis of extracts of pig stomach, proteases with two pH optima have been separated;[142] and of the two enzymes from fish stomachs, the one acting at higher pH is enhanced by HCN and H_2S; hence it appears to be a cathepsin.[25] The physiological meaning of the gastric catheptic-like proteases is unknown, but their existence appears to be established.

Extracts of houseflies yielded an enzyme active at pH 1.5 to 3.0 in addition to trypsin,[71] and stable-fly larva midgut protease has a pH optimum of 2.4.[118] A similar acid peak for spider proteases was interpreted as a broad catheptic peak with an intermediate pH dip. Dual peaks for proteases from tissue extracts may indicate multiple enzymes; however, it is difficult to see how enzymes of different pH optima could function in the same digestive fluid unless they act far from their optima. Tests with specific peptide substrates and better ways of characterizing the various "cathepsins" are needed. It is probable that numerous trypsins, pepsins, and cathepsins exist in different animals but that the only true pepsins are vertebrate.

Peptidases. The distribution of exopeptidases was given in the first edition of this book, and little new information has been added. They have a broad pH optimum in the low alkaline range. The principal exopeptidases of mammals have been enumerated above. Carboxypeptidase occurs along with trypsinogen in pancreatic juice; aminopeptidase and dipeptidase from intestinal secretions constitute what was formerly called erepsin. Peptidases have been obtained from various tissues, e.g., leucylaminopeptidase, carboxypeptidase, and a tripeptidase in the pancreas, leucyldipeptidase in intestinal mucosa. In many animals the carboxypeptidase occurs separately and has a different pH optimum from aminopeptidases and dipeptidases. In a starfish the stomach has aminopeptidase and dipeptidases; hepatic ceca have all three.[171] In the snail *Murex* the midgut gland has carboxypeptidase, the digestive tube and esophageal glands a dipeptidase and aminopeptidase. In *Sepia* the pancreas has aminopeptidase and dipeptidase, the liver these plus carboxypeptidase. In a trypanosome the pH optimum of carboxypeptidase is 4.5, of aminopeptidase and dipeptidases about 8.0. In several beetles and crickets the carboxypeptidase is weak compared with the aminopeptidases and dipeptidases.[173] The carnivorous *Didinium* may derive a dipeptidase from its prey, *Paramecium.* Peptidase activity is in the cytoplasmic matrix; proteinase (cathepsin) is associated with granules in *Pelomyxa.*[85] In conclusion, many peptidases occur; carboxypeptidase is often separate from aminopeptidases and dipeptidases. A more precise characterization of invertebrate peptidases is desirable.

DIGESTION OF FATS

Neutral fats consist of higher fatty acids linked to the trihydric alcohol glycerol. Fats may be partially hydrolyzed to monoglycerides and diglycerides or fully hydrolyzed to the alcohol and the fatty acid, as in the following diagram where R refers to the acid chain, as palmitic, stearic, or oleic acid.

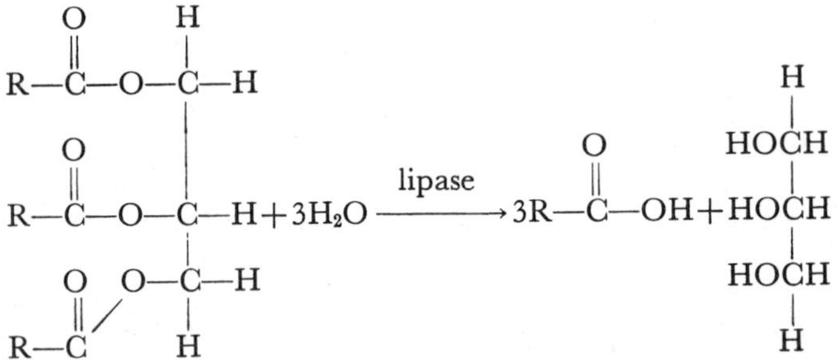

$$
\begin{array}{c}
\text{O} \quad\quad \text{H} \\
\| \quad\quad\quad | \\
\text{R}-\text{C}-\text{O}-\text{C}-\text{H} \\
\\
\text{O} \quad\quad\quad | \\
\| \quad\quad\quad | \\
\text{R}-\text{C}-\text{O}-\text{C}-\text{H}+3\text{H}_2\text{O} \xrightarrow{\text{lipase}} 3\text{R}-\text{C}-\text{OH}+\text{HOCH} \\
\\
\text{O} \quad \text{O}-\text{C}-\text{H} \\
\|/ \quad | \\
\text{R}-\text{C} \quad\quad \text{H}
\end{array}
$$

(right side products)

$$
\begin{array}{c}
\text{H} \\
| \\
\text{HOCH} \\
| \\
\text{HOCH} \\
| \\
\text{H}
\end{array}
$$

Neutral fat (triglyceride) may be absorbed without hydrolysis and may be digested intracellularly, often at some distance from the digestive tract. Lipases hydrolyze the esters of higher fatty acids; esterases hydrolyze esters of shorter acids. The distinction between lipases and esterases is not sharp because neither type of enzyme shows very marked specificity of substrate and both have fairly broad pH optima.

In mammals, pancreatic extract acts on both long chain and short esters; extracts of some other tissues, such as liver, hydrolyze only short esters.[3, 92, 147] Pancreatic lipase is highly active on olive oil; liver esterase scarcely affects this oil, whereas on methylbutyrate liver esterase is several times more active than is pancreatic lipase. Both act on tributyrin, the lipase more than the esterase. Pancreatic lipase is activated by leucylglycylglycine, the esterase is not; the lipase is inhibited by quinine and some other alkaloids, liver esterase by atoxyl and fluoride. Bile salt (taurocholate) accelerates lipase, slightly inhibits liver esterase.[147] Milk contains an esterase active on tributyrin and methylbutyrate but not on olive oil. Mammalian stomach extract contains a lipase which is active on higher triglycerides at pH 7.5 and on lower ones and tributyrin at a lower pH

(5.0 to 6.0). Liver esterase is more effective than gastric esterase on tributyrin in some animals (horse); it is much more effective in birds and about the same in fish.[92] The physiological role of gastric lipase is not clear, although a lipid meal inhibits secretion of gastric acid. The pH optimum of gastric lipase is 6.3 in dog and rabbit, 5.5 in man, 8.6 in horse, 7.9 in pig.[79] Evidently esterases and lipases are distinct even though they overlap in function and both act on tributyrin; mammalian pancreas extract has esterase and lipase, the juice mainly lipase. Most of the digestive lipase of vertebrates is pancreatic lipase. In fish it is difficult to separate pancreatic tissue from the intestinal wall, and extracts of the intestinal wall (plaice) or of intestinal slime (carp) yield a lipase which is active in a weakly alkaline medium.

Bile salts activate pancreatic lipase and also facilitate emulsification of fats, thus increasing the total area of oil-water interface at which lipase can act and favoring absorption of fat droplets. Bile acids appear to decrease from 27-carbon to 24-carbon acids in the vertebrate classes from elasmobranchs to mammals; certain kinds of animals have unique acids.[78] In mammals the principal acid is cholic ($C_{23}H_{39}O_3 \cdot COOH$), and this is coupled with the bases taurine or glycine; in rabbits the main bile acid is deoxycholic, and in the Indian rat *Myocastor* it is nutriacholic acid. *Rana catesbiana,* and the alligator, caiman, and crocodile have trihydroxycoprostanic acid ($C_{26}H_{45}O_3 \cdot COOH$); the Boidae snakes, however, have pythocholic acid ($C_{23}H_{45}O_3 \cdot COOH$). Several teleosts have as the principal bile acid tetrahydroxynorsterocholanic acid ($C_{26}H_{45}O_4 \cdot COOH$). Elasmobranchs have sulfates of the polyhydric alcohol scymnol ($C_{27}H_{46}O_5$) instead of a bile acid.[15] Bile acids are relatively class specific, but certain families and genera have acids peculiar to them. Bile-type acids which reduce the interfacial tension of fats have been observed but not identified in crayfish, lobster, and crabs, but not in *Helix* or holothurians.[195] *Helix* stomach lipase is activated by $CaCl_2$, inhibited by NaF and citrates, and acts in the series tributyrin>methylbutane>tween>tridein.[51] In *Mytilus*, lipase is intracellular, but there may be extracellular esterase.

Fat digestion has been observed in many animals; the distinction between lipase and esterase has not usually been made. In *Pelomyxa*, ingested or injected fat disappears and stained fatty acids can be seen to pass from food vacuoles into the cytoplasm. Fat droplets may be absorbed by cells lining the gastrovascular cavity of *Hydra*. A tissue extract from an actinian contains an esterase which is active on tributyrin but not on olive oil.[113] In molluscs the digestive diverticula (midgut gland) contain a lipase which is active at about pH 7.0 in *Mya*,[205] *Ostrea*, and *Mytilus* and at pH 6 in *Helix*,[205] *Aplysia*, and *Achatina*.[190] When stained fat is fed to mussels and oysters, droplets are found in ciliated epithelium of the stomach, of digestive diverticula, and in amoebocytes; the gastric juice may also hydrolyze some fat.[65] In *Sepia* a lipase (esterase) is found in stomach juice as well as in pancreas; the pH optimum on tributyrin is 6.0 to 6.3.[168] Lipase (pH optimum 7.8 to 8.4) is much more active in the carnivorous leech *Haemopsis* than in the blood sucker *Hirudo;* this enzyme is active in the series tributyrin > ethyl butyrate > olive oil; it is inhibited by quinine and fluoride.[6]

Arthropods make good use of fats. Lipase from the stomach of a crayfish is active on methylbutyrate and olive oil over a wide pH range (5.5 to 7.0), and *Limulus* gastric lipase has a pH optimum at 7.7. The lipases of some crustaceans and several molluscs (*Aplysia, Helix, Octopus*) resemble liver esterases of vertebrates in acting better on lower esters, such as tributyrin and methylbutyrate, than on fats such as olive oil.[195]

Several insects have been shown to have lipases and esterases. In a cockroach the midgut has a lipase which sometimes is regurgitated into the crop; this lipase is active on ethylbutyrate at pH 8.0, and it is not inhibited by quinine.[48] A salivary lipase occurs in larvae of the meat-eating calliphorid fly *Phaenicis*.[166] Various tissues of *Bombyx* larvae cleave the esters tributyrin, methylbutyrate, and cetylacetate, but not olive oil.[55] Extracts of the midgut of larvae of the wax moth *Galleria* are active in an alkaline medium (pH 9.3 to 9.6) in the following order: tributyrin > methylbutyrate > olive oil; quinine and fluoride do not inhibit the activity.[47, 133] The wax moth larva utilizes as much as 38 per cent of the higher fatty acids (C_{24}-C_{30}) of beeswax. Bacteria from the gut of *Galleria* grow on wax, e.g., esters of cerotic acid ($C_{25}H_{51}COOH$). Presumably the bacteria break down the waxes to lower acids which can then be digested by the wax moth larva.[54, 130] The African honey-guide birds also appear to use symbiotic bacteria to break down higher esters of beeswax.[60] It is probable that most arthropod lipases resemble liver esterase, although some arthropods may have both lipase and esterase; more tests with substrates of different acid chain lengths and more tests with inhibitors are needed.

Bile salts emulsify fat to droplets as small as 0.5 μ in diameter, and these can be seen inside epithelial cells.[10] Such intracellular fat droplets are interpreted as neutral fat absorbed directly without hydrolysis and transported via the lacteals to the lymph system, while fatty acids are transported by the hepatic portal system.[59] Other histochemical evidence is that, soon after a fat meal, fatty acid can be stained in absorptive cells, that fat droplets appear later and centrally, hence are probably formed from the absorbed fatty acid. Short-chain fatty acids are absorbed against a concentration gradient, by an energy-requiring process, in intestine *in vitro*.[179] Chemical evidence indicates that triglycerides and diglycerides can be formed from monoglycerides during digestion and that ingested fatty acid may retard fat absorption because of slowing of gastric emptying.[17] In the duodenal fistula of a dog 10 minutes after an olive oil meal the fatty acid concentration amounted to 17 to 34 per cent of total fat and on longer incubation 41 to 76 per cent, while the monoglycerides never exceeded 8 per cent. Thus, triglycerides could amount to only 35 to 40 per cent, and absorption as fatty acid is predominant.[45] In *Periplaneta* fat droplets can be seen in epithelial cells after a meal of fat;[48] lower fatty acid products formed by symbionts in termites and ruminants are readily absorbed. There is evidence, therefore, for some absorption of fatty acids and of triglycerides and diglycerides, but the relative importance of fatty acids seems greater in mammals.

The fat deposited reflects to some extent the type of fat ingested; the melting point of subcutaneous fat in hogs is lower when the hogs are fed oils of low melting point than when they are fed harder fats. Mammals tend to have fewer higher unsaturated fats than do poikilothermic vertebrates; marine fish have a high percentage of higher unsaturated fats.[108, 109] A reptile (python) is intermediate between ungulates and fish; it has in its storage fats a high proportion of oleic acid, less palmitic and stearic.

CORRELATIONS OF DIGESTIVE ENZYMES WITH FOOD HABITS; CONCLUSIONS

Selection of specific foods appears to be primarily on the basis of taste preferences; feeding behavior and feeding mechanisms are correlated in a general way, and digestive enzymes are correlated still more broadly with type of food. Omnivorous animals are equipped with an array of digestive enzymes; herbivores tend to have more active carbohydrases and carnivores stronger proteases. Some herbivores and carnivores are extreme specialists which are adapted enzymatically to single kinds of food.

Phenotypic differences in digestive enzymes are distinct from genotypic differences. Feeding can stimulate not only secretion of enzymes but their synthesis, and diet can induce changes in the proportions of enzymes in individual animals. Rats fed for 3 weeks on a diet predominantly carbohydrate had proportionately more pancreatic amylase than they had on other diets; those fed protein showed a slight increase in proteases, although fat induced no lipase increase.[73] African natives who live on a high carbohydrate diet had twice as much amylase in their saliva as Europeans, and more than natives who were predominantly carnivorous.[180] A single meal of one type of food failed to alter the proportions of enzymes secreted in pancreatic juice of a dog,[74] but alternation between high and low protein for a week increased trypsin activity of the pancreas.

In adult mosquitoes, *Aedes,* any type of food increases synthesis of proteases above the level at starvation, protein more than sugar, and protease activity is increased seventeen to twenty times in adult *Aedes* 18 hours after a blood meal.[176] *Periplaneta* on a diet of wheat bran produces more proteinase than on white bread.[41] If a cockroach is fed one type of food constantly the enzymes for digesting it are depleted.[40] The stable-fly *Stomoxys* increases its trypsin synthesis some 12 hours after a blood meal.[27] In digestive

glands of hornworms fed on potato for 3 days, the amylase activity more than doubled.

The pharyngeal glands of bees have more proteinases in nurses than in foragers and no proteinases in wax bees; the sucrase in thoracic glands is richer in foraging bees than in others, and lipase is found in the postcerebral glands in wax bees only.[90] Foraging bees have much less invertase in early spring and late fall than in midsummer. On a high starch diet the snail *Achatina* has an elevated amylase content in the midgut gland computed on a nitrogen but not on a dry weight basis; proteolytic activity does not increase on a meat diet. The gland changes in its histology according to diet.[162, 190]

Enzymic changes correlated with diet occur during development in many animals. Many adult butterflies and moths have carbohydrases only; as caterpillars they were well provided with enzymes for each class of food. Blowfly larvae have active proteases and weak carbohydrases, the adults have active carbohydrases and weak proteases. Rennin is present in the stomachs of mammalian infants, absent or diminished in adults. Intestinal lactase diminishes with age.

In summary: The synthesis of specific enzymes may be stimulated by appropriate food. Digestive glands may be altered histologically by diet; hence the basis for comparing enzyme activity may change.

There are evidently many genetically determined differences in digestive enzymes according to habit. Animals of closely related species may differ in enzymes according to diet, and adoption of a parasitic way of life may be accompanied by loss of enzymes. Certain leaf-hoppers (*Tetingella*) which live on soluble food in the phloem of plants lack amylase, proteinase, and lipase, while others (*Empoasca*) which live on mesophyll cells have a full set of enzymes.[172] A blood-sucking calliphorid fly, *Apaulina,* has no amylase, trypsin, or butyrase, and weak maltase and sucrase, whereas scavenger species of the same flies have active enzymes for each food class.[166]

Carnivores with strong proteolytic activity but weak carbohydrases are coelenterates, Turbellaria, Asteroidea, cephalopod molluscs, stomatopod crustaceans, and scavenger insects.[205] Many coelenterates lack extracellular amylase; they digest protein in the gastrovascular cavity and may have weak carbohydrases which are intracellular. What specific foodstuffs the corals and anemones derive from symbiotic algae remains to be learned.

Carnivorous carabid beetles and meat-eating blowfly larvae have active proteases but weak carbohydrases. The intestine of the herbivorous carp has more amylase and less proteinase than the intestine of the carnivorous pickerel.[2]

Many gastropod and pelecypod molluscs feed on phytoplankton or larger aquatic plants and in those possessing a crystalline style the only strong extracellular digestion is of starch, as mussels, clams, and oysters.[151a] There is a style in all herbivorous pelecypods; it is vestigial in the carnivorous septibranch bivalves; the style is present in only those herbivorous gastropods which feed by cilia or by slow radular action; in archeogastropods (e.g., *Lunella*) the style is a mucus rod; carnivorous snails have no style. The tunicate *Ciona* has practically no protein digestion but has active carbohydrases.

Food specialists can be more restricted than to meat or vegetable diet. Most spectacular are the wood and plant fiber eaters which digest cellulose by their own enzymes or more usually by symbionts. The use of symbionts has been acquired numerous times —termites, *Helix,* ruminant mammals; ability to produce cellulase is rare among animals— *Teredo,* the isopod *Limnorea.* The clothes moth is able to reduce the disulfide linkages of keratin, making possible digestion of wool; and the wax moth can by aid of symbiotic bacteria utilize beeswax. One fly larva lives in oil wells, digesting insects which fall into the oil and possibly harboring symbiotic bacteria which break down the hydrocarbons. Other specialists rely on digestive enzymes within their food: leeches derive nourishment from a blood meal which slowly autolyzes in the gut. Some parasitic animals appear to have lost most of the essential digestive enzymes and to rely on their host's digestion; trypanosomes and parasitic Platyhelminthes and parasitic insects have fewer enzymes than free-living animals of the same sort.

The animal groups most successful in digestion are not the specialists but the omnivores with a full complement of enzymes, as some snails (Helix), higher crustaceans, many insects, and the vertebrates. Proteins, carbohydrates, and fats are all used by these animals. The various enzymes may be mixed in one chamber as in snails or crustaceans or may be secreted in successive parts of the alimentary tract as in vertebrates.

In general, intracellular digestion is associated with the absence of triturating mechanisms. Phagocytic cells, e.g., lamellibranch amoebocytes and diverticular epithelium, may possess a variety of enzymes. Extracellular digestion is more economical of area of cell surfaces.

Animal hydrolytic enzymes are often very different from corresponding plant enzymes, particularly carbohydrases, and animal enzymes are less varied than are those known in microorganisms. Also, digestive enzymes differ from animal group to group, but these differences are poorly known. Among carbohydrases, stereochemical or group specificity is often marked, and the existence of a given polysaccharidase is usually associated with the presence of an enzyme for corresponding sugars, as cellulase with β-glucosidase or amylase with α-glucosidase. Exceptions to the rule of single enzymes for all members of each class of sugar have been noted.

Proteases occur in the greatest diversity. Distinction among proteases has, in the past, been made largely on the basis of pH optima. Trypsins are most widely distributed although differences exist in activation by enterokinase, and the distinction with respect to substrates, as between trypsin and chymotrypsin, has not been made for nonmammals. Pepsin and an acid stomach are distinctly vertebrate characters which have been lost by several groups of bony fish—Dipnoi—and some cyprinodonts. Amphioxus and the cyclostomes have not acquired a pepsin. The presence of two pH optima, one very acid, in a few invertebrates may indicate properties of one protein rather than the presence of two enzymes. Cathepsins constitute a poorly defined group of enzymes, some activated by reducing agents and others not; some of them are exopeptidases, some occurring intracellularly, others extracellularly. A vertebrate gastric protease acting at pH 4.5 to 6.0 has been frequently reported but not explained.

Distinction between lipases and esterases is based on length of the carbon chain of substrates. Frequently, enzymes which attack only short esters have been incorrectly called lipases.

The pH optimum for a given enzyme is not always the same as the physiological pH at which it functions. Also the pH optimum differs somewhat according to substrate. In general, the early phases of digestion tend to be more acid than later phases.

In summary, food selection and feeding behavior provide one important basis for isolation of groups of animals. General correlations between digestive enzymes and diet have been established, but specific characterization of digestive enzymes of different animals presents many interesting and puzzling questions.

REFERENCES

1. ADAMS, J. B., and McALLAN, J. W., Canad. J. Zool. *34*: 541-543, 1956; *36*: 305-308, 1958. Pectinase in aphids.
2. AL-HUSSAINI, A. H., Quart. J. Micr. *90*: 323-354, 1949. Digestive enzymes in relation to feeding habits, fish.
3. *AMMON, R., and JADOMA, M., *in* The Enzymes, edited by J. B. Sumner and K. Myrback. New York, Academic Press, 1951, vol. 1, pt. 1, ch. 9, pp. 390-442. Esterases and lipases.
4. ANNISON, E. F., Biochem. J. *57*: 400-405, 1954. Acids released in rumen of sheep.
5. *ANNISON, E. F., and LEWIS, D., Metabolism in the Rumen. London, Methuen & Co., 1959, 178 pp.
6. AUTRUM, H., and GRAETZ, E., Ztschr. vergl. Physiol. *21*: 429-439, 1934. Lipases in leeches.
7. BABKIN, B. P., ET AL., J. Biol. Board. Canada *1*: 251-259, 1935. Gastric secretion in elasmobranchs.
8. BACQ, Z. M., and GHIRETTI, F., Publ. Staz. Zool. Napoli *24*: 256-278, 1953. Secretion from Octopus salivary glands.
9. BAILEY, L., J. Exp. Biol. *29*: 310-327, 1952. Separation of honey from pollen by proventriculus of honeybee.
10. BAKER, J. R., J. Micr. Sci. *92*: 79-86, 1951. Fat absorption by intestinal epithelium of mouse.
11. BALLANTINE, D., and MORTON, J., J. Mar. Biol. Assn. U. K. *35*: 241-274, 1956. Filter feeding by *Lasea*.
12. BALLANTINE, R., Anat. Rec. Suppl. 78 (Abstr. no. 11), p. 44, 1940. Proteases of dragonfly nymphs.
13. BARRINGTON, E. J. W., Philosoph. Tr. Roy. Soc. London, B, *228*: 269-311, 1937. Digestive system of Amphioxus.
14. BAYLISS, L. E., and STARLING, E. H., J. Physiol. *29*: 174-180, 1903. Secretin, vertebrates.
15. BERGMANN, M., and PACE, W. T., J. Am. Chem. Soc. *65*: 477-478, 1943. Bile acids of elasmobranchs.
16. *BERGMANN, W., *in* Progress in the Chemistry of Fats and Other Lipids. New York, Academic Press, *1*: 18-69, 1952.
17. BERGSTRÖM, B., Acta physiol. scand. *25*: 291-347, 1952. Mechanism of intestinal fat absorption.
18. BEST, C. H., and TAYLOR, N. B., Physiological Basis of Medical Practice. Baltimore, William Wood & Co., 1942, pp. 695-859. Digestion.
19. BIDDER, A. M., Quart. J. Micr. Sci. *91*: 1-44, 1950. Digestion in squids.
20. BIERRY, H., C. R. Acad. Sci. *152*: 465-468, 904-906, 1911; *156*: 265-267, 1913; Biochem. Ztschr. *44*: 402-471, 1912. Digestion by coelenterates.
21. BIRGE, E. A., and JUDAY, C., Bull. Bur. Fish. *42*: 185-205, 1926. Organic content of freshwater lakes.
22. BODANSKY, M., and ROSE, W. C., Am. J. Physiol.

* Reviews

23. BODINE, J. H., Biol. Bull. *48*: 79-83, 1925. Digestive tract pH, grasshoppers.
24. BOYAJIAN, L. Z., Glycosidases of Human Small Intestine. M.D. essay, Yale University, 1956.
25. BUCHS, S., Ztschr. vergl. Physiol. *36*: 165-175, 1954. Proteases in mammal and fish stomachs.
26. CARROLL, E. J., and HUNGATE, R. E., Appl. Microbiol. *2*: 205-214, 1955. Microorganisms in rumen.
27. CHAMPLAIN, R. A., and FISH, F. W., Ohio J. Sci. *56*: 52-62, 1956. Digestive enzymes of stable fly, *Stomoxys*.
28. CHAPMAN-ANDERSEN, C., and HOLTER, H., Exp. Cell. Res., Suppl. 3, 52-63, 1955. Pinocytosis in amoeba.
29. CHIPMAN, W. A., and HOPKINS, J. D., Biol. Bull. *107*: 80-91, 1954. Filtration by scallop, *Pecten*.
30. CLEVELAND, L. R., Quart. Rev. Biol. *1*: 51-59, 1926; Biol. Bull. *54*: 231-237, 1928. Flagellate symbionts in termites and wood roach *Cryptocercus*.
31. CLEVELAND, L. R., *et al.*, Mem. Am. Acad. Arts Sci. *17*: 185-342, 1934. Flagellate symbionts in termites and wood roach *Cryptocercus*.
32. COHEN, R. B., *et al.*, J. Biol. Chem. *195*: 239-249, 607-614, 1952. Beta-galactosidases.
33. CRANE, R. K., and KRANE, S. M., Biochim. Biophys. Acta *20*: 568-569, 1956; *29*: 30-32, 1958; *31*: 397-401, 1959. Absorption of sugars in intestine.
34. CROMBACH, J. J., *et al.*, Acta Physiol. Pharmacol. Neerl. *7*: 78-92, 1958. Stimulation of pepsin secretion in frogs.
35. *CUTHBERTSON, D. P., and PHILLIPSON, A. T., *in* Biochemistry and Physiology of Nutrition, edited by G. H. Bourne and G. W. Kidder, *2*: 128-161, 1953. Microbiology of digestion.
36. CUTHBERTSON, D. P., Nature *183*: 1644-1646, 1959. Function of rumen.
37. DAKIN, W. J., and DAKIN, C. M. G., J. Exp. Biol. *2*: 293-322, 1925. Inadequacy of dissolved nutrients in natural waters.
38. DALES, R. P., J. Mar. Biol. Assn. U. K. *34*: 55-79, 1955. Feeding and digestion, terebellid polychaetes.
39. DANIELLI, J. F., *et al.*, J. Exp. Biol. *22*: 75-87, 1945. Absorption of fatty acids from rumen.
40. DAY, M. F., and POWNING, R. F., Australian J. Sci. Res. *2*: 175-215, 1949. Digestion in several insects.
41. *DAY, M. F., and WATERHOUSE, D. F., *in* Insect Physiology, edited by K. D. Roeder. New York, John Wiley & Sons, 1953, pp. 273-349. Feeding and digestion in insects.
42. *DESNUELLE, P., Ann. Rev. Biochem. *23*: 55-78, 1954. Proteolytic enzymes.
43. *DETHIER, V. G., Evolution *8*: 33-54, 1954. Evolution of food preferences in phytophagous insects.
44. DODD, R. H., J. Exp. Biol. *33*: 311-324, 1956. Proteolysis in *Tenebrio* and *Dytiscus*.
45. DOWSE, C. M., SAUNDERS, J. A., and SCHOFIELD, B., J. Physiol. *134*: 515-526, 1956. Fat digestion in dog.
46. *DUKES, H. H., The Physiology of Domestic

62: 482-487, 1922. Digestion in elasmobranchs and teleosts.

Animals. Ithaca, N. Y. Comstock Publishing Co., 1942, pp. 217-226. Digestion.

47. DUSPIVA, F., Ztschr. vergl. Physiol. *21*: 632-641, 1934. Digestion of wax by waxmoth.
48. EISNER, T., J. Exp. Biol. *130*: 159-181, 1955. Digestion and absorption of fat by cockroach.
49. EVANS, W. A. L., Exp. Parasitol. *5*: 191-206, 1956; Nature *177*: 478, 1956. Carbohydrate digestion by blowfly.
50. FARNER, D. S., Poultry Sci. *21*: 445-450, 1942. Avian digestive tract, pH.
51. FERRERI, E., Ztschr. vergl. Physiol. *41*: 373-389, 1958. Histochemistry of fat absorption, Helix.
52. FISH, G. R., Nature *175*: 733-734, 1955. Cellulase in mollusc styles.
53. FLORKIN, M., and LOZET, F., Arch. Internat. Physiol. *57*: 201-207, 1949. Bacterial origin of *Helix* cellulase.
54. FLORKIN, M., LOZET, F., and SARLET, H., Arch. Internat. Physiol. *57*: 71-88, 1949. Digestion of wax by *Galleria* larvae.
55. FODOR, P. J., Enzymologia *13*: 66-72, 1948. Lipases and esterases of silkworm.
56. Fox, D. L., and MARKS, G. W., Bull. Scripps Inst. Oceanog. *4*: 29-47, 1936. Digestive enzymes of *Mytilus*.
57. FRAENKEL, G., J. Exp. Biol. *17*: 18-29, 1940. Utilization of sugars by adult blowflies.
58. FRAENKEL, G., J. Cell. Comp. Physiol. *45*: 393-408, 1955. Digestion of sugars by mealworm, *Tenebrio*.
59. *FRAZER, A. C., Physiol. Rev. *20*: 561-581, 1940. Fat absorption in mammals.
60. FRIEDMANN, H., and KERN, J., Quart. Rev. Biol. *31*: 19-30, 1956. Wax-eating by honeyguides (birds).
61. *FRUTON, J. S., Harvey Lect. *51* (1955-56): 64-87, 1957.
62. *FRUTON, J. S., and MYCEK, M. J., Ann. Rev. Biochem. *25*: 57-78, 1956. Proteolytic enzymes.
63. *FRUTON, J. S., and SIMMONDS, S., General Biochemistry, 2d ed. New York, John Wiley & Sons, 1958, chapter 30, pp. 623-749. Metabolic breakdown and synthesis of proteins.
64. FRUTON, J. S., *et al.,* J. Biol. Chem. *136*: 559-560, 1940; *146*: 463-470, 1942; *174*: 851-858, 1948; *194*: 793-805, 1942. Specificity of proteases, particularly cathepsins.
65. GEORGE, W. C., Biol. Bull. *102*: 118-127, 1952. Digestion and absorption of fats in lamellibranchs.
66. GERSCH, M., Experientia *11*: 413-416, 1955. Stimulation of intestinal activity, *Corethra* larvae.
67. GOREAU, T. F., and GOREAU, N. I., Science *131*: 668-669, 1960. Uptake of C^{14} by zooxanthellae in corals.
68. GOTTSCHALK, A., *in* The Enzymes, edited by J. B. Sumner and K. Myrback. New York, Academic Press, 1951, vol. I, pt. 1, pp. 551-582. Glycosidases.
69. GRAY, F. V., *et al.,* J. Exp. Biol. *28*: 74-82, 83-90, 1951; *29*: 54-56, 57-65, 1952. Fermentation in rumen of sheep.
70. GRAY, H. E., and FRAENKEL, G., Phys. Zool. *27*: 56-65, 1954. Honeydew production by aphids.

71. GREENBERG, B., and PARETSKY, D., Ann. Entomol. Soc. America *48*: 46-50, 1955. Protein digestion in housefly.
72. *GROSSMAN, M. I., Physiol. Rev. *30*: 33-90, 1950. Gastrointestinal hormones.
73. GROSSMAN, M. I., GREENGARD, H., and IVY, A. C., Am. J. Physiol. *138*: 676-682, 1943; *141*: 38-41, 1944. Variations in pancreatic secretion with diet.
74. GUTH, P. H., *et al.,* Am. J. Physiol. *187*: 207-223, 1956. Variations in pancreatic enzymes with conditions of stimulation.
75. HALL, E. R., J. Gen. Microbiol. *7*: 350-357, 1952. Utilization of cellulose by rabbits.
76. HALSE, K., and VELLE, U., Acta physiol. scand. *37*: 380-390, 1956. Acid production, rumen of sheep.
77. HARLEY, M. B., Nature *165*: 734-735, 1950. Filter feeding in *Nereis*.
78. HASLEWOOD, G. A. D., *et al.,* Biochem. J. *47*: 584-594, 1950; *49*: 67-72, 1951; *51*: 139-143, 1952; *52*: 583-588, 1953. Bile salts of vertebrates by classes.
79. HAUROWITZ, F., and PETROU, W., Ztschr. Physiol. Chem. *144*: 68-75, 1925. Gastric lipase, pH optimum.
80. HEATLEY, N. G., J. Exp. Biol. *13*: 329-343, 1936. Digestive enzymes of Peripatopsis (Onychophora).
81. HEIMPEL, A. M., Canad. J. Zool. *33*: 99-106, 1955. Acidity of digestive tract, various insects.
82. HERAN, H., Ztschr. vergl. Physiol. *39*: 44-62, 1956. Digestion in earthworms.
83. HILKER, D., *et al.,* Exp. Parasitol. *6*: 459-464, 1957. Starch digestion by *Entamoeba*.
84. HOKIN, L. E., Biochem. Biophys. Acta *18*: 379-388, 1955. Zymogen granules in dog pancreas.
85. HOLTER, H., and LOVTRUP, S., C. R. Lab. Carlsberg, Sér. Chim. *27*: 37-62, 1949. Proteolytic enzymes of amoebae.
86. HUGHES, T. E., Quart. J. Micr. Sci. *91*: 45-61, 1950. Digestion in mites.
87. HUNGATE, R. E., Ann. Entomol. Soc. America *36*: 730-739, 1943; Proc. Texas Acad. Sci. *27*: 91-98, 1944. Cellulose fermentation by flagellates in termites.
88. HUNGATE, R. E., Biol. Bull. *84*: 157-163, 1943. Action of rumen protozoa on cellulose.
89. *HUNGATE, R. E., *in* Biochemistry and Physiology of Protozoa, edited by S. H. Hutner and A. Lwoff. New York, Academic Press, 1955, vol. 2, pp. 159-199. Mutalistic intestinal protozoa.
90. INGLESENT, H., Biochem. J. *34*: 1415-1418, 1940. Enzymes from different worker bees.
91. ITO, T., and TANAKA, M., Biol. Bull. *116*: 95-105, 1959. Beta-glucosidase of midgut of silkworm.
92. ITOH, R., J. Biochem. *33*: 269-276, 1941. Milk esterase and gastric lipase.
93. JENNINGS, J. B., Biol. Bull. *112*: 63-80, 1957. Feeding and digestion in free-living flatworms.
94. JEUNIAUX, C., Arch. Internat. Physiol. *58*: 350-356; *59*: 242-245, 1950; Acad. roy. Belgique Classe des Sciences, Mémoires *28* fasc. 7: 1-45, 1954. Chitinase from intestinal bacteria of *Helix*.
95. JEUNIAUX, C., Arch. Internat. Physiol. Biochem.

64: 583-586, 1956. Chitinase in digestive tube of *Porcellio*.

96. JEUNIAUX, C., and AMANIEU, M., Arch. Internat. Physiol. Biochem. *83*: 94-103, 1955. Chitinase in exuvial fluid of *Bombyx*.

97. JORGENSEN, C. B., J. Mar. Biol. Assn. U.K. *28*: 333-344, 1949; Biol. Bull. *103*: 356-363, 1952. Particle filtration in relation to feeding in molluscs, especially *Mytilus*, and ascidians.

98. *JORGENSEN, C. B., Biol. Rev. *30*: 391-454, 1955. Filter feeding in invertebrates.

99. JORGENSEN, C. B., and GOLDBERG, E. D., Biol. Bull. *105*: 477-489, 1953. Particle filtration in relation to feeding in molluscs, especially *Mytilus*, and ascidians.

100. JORGENSEN, C. R., et al., Fed. Proc. *19*: 130, 1960. Active absorption of sugars.

101. KARRER, K., et al., Helv. Chim. Acta *8*: 792-810, 1925. Cellulase in Helix.

102. KEEBLE, F., Plant-Animals, a Study in Symbiosis. Cambridge University Press, 1910, p. 163.

103. KERMACK, D. M., Proc. Zool. Soc. London *125*: 347-381, 1955. Anatomy and physiology of gut of *Arenicola*.

104. KERTESZ, Z. I., J. Nutrit. *20*: 289-296, 1940. Fate of pectins in digestive tracts, mammals.

105. KILIAN, E. F., Ztschr. vergl. Physiol. *34*: 407-447, 1952. Ingestion and water currents, freshwater sponge.

106. KITCHING, J. A., J. Exp. Biol. *29*: 255-266, 1952. Feeding by suctorian *Podophrya*.

107. *KITCHING, J. A., Protoplasmatologia 3D, *36*: 1-54, 1956. Food vacuoles.

108. KLENK, E., Hoppe-Seylers Ztschr. Physiol. Chem. *221*: 264-270, 1933. Saturation of body fats, vertebrates.

109. KLENK, E., et al., Hoppe-Seylers Ztschr. Physiol. Chem. *232*: 54-63, 1935. Saturation of body fats, vertebrates.

110. KORRINGA, P., Quart. Rev. Biol. *27*: 266-308; 339-365, 1952. Filter feeding in oysters.

111. KOSCHTOJANZ, C. S., et al., Ztschr. vergl. Physiol. *18*: 112-115, 1932. Secretin from lower vertebrates.

112. KRIJGSMAN, B. J., Ztschr. vergl. Physiol. *2*: 264-296; *8*: 187-280, 1928. Digestion in Helix.

113. KRIJGSMAN, B. J., and TALBOT, F. H., Arch. Internat. Physiol. *61*: 277-291, 1953. Digestion in sea anemones.

114. *KROGH, A., Biol. Rev. *6*: 412-442, 1931. Utilization of dissolved foods by aquatic animals.

115. *KRÜGER, P., Ergebn. Physiol. *35*: 538-631, 1933. Review, pH of digestive fluids, lower animals.

116. KRÜGER, P., and GRAETZ, E., Zool. Jahrb. Abt. allg. Zool. Physiol. *45*: 463-514, 1928. Gastric enzymes of crayfish.

117. LABARRE, J., et al., Rev. Canad. Biol. *10*: 140-148, 1951. Proteolytic enzymes in stomach of cod, *Gadus*.

118. LAMBREMONT, E. N., et al., Science *129*: 1484-1485, 1959. Acid protease, fly larvae.

119. LANE, C. E., and GREENFIELD, L. J., J. Biol. Chem. *204*: 669-672, 1953; Bull. Mar. Sci. Gulf and Carib. *2*: 385-392, 1952. Cellulose digestion, use of wood as food, *Teredo*.

120. LARNER, J., et al., J. Biol. Chem. *212*: 9, 1955; *215*: 723-736, 1955; *223*: 709-725, 1956; Arch. Biochem. Biophys. *58*: 252-257, 1955; Biochim.

Biophys. Acta *20*: 53-61, 1956. Intestinal enzymes for digesting starch and oligosaccharides.

121. LASKER, R., J. Ins. Physiol. *3*: 86-91, 1959. Cellulose digestion by silverfish, *Ctenolepisma*.

122. LASKER, R., and GIESE, A. C., J. Exp. Biol. *33*: 542-553, 1956. Cellulose digestion by silverfish, *Ctenolepisma*.

123. LASKER, R., and GIESE, A. C., Biol. Bull. *106*: 328-340, 1954. Nutrition of sea urchin *Strongylocentrotus*.

124. LENHOF, H. M., and SCHNEIDERMANN, H. A., Biol. Bull. *116*: 452-460, 1959. Glutathione stimulation of feeding in *Physalia*.

125. *LENKEIT, W., Ergebn. Physiol. *35*: 573-631, 1933. Salivary secretion, mammals.

126. LEWIS, D., Biochem. J. *56*: 391-399, 1954. Production and absorption of ammonia in rumen of sheep, reduction of sulfate.

127. LEWIS, D., et al., Biochem. J. *66*: 587-592, 1957. Production and absorption of ammonia in rumen of sheep.

128. LOOMIS, W. F., Ann. New York Acad. Sci. *77*: 73-86, 1959. Glutathione stimulation of ingestion in *Hydra*.

129. LOOSANOFF, V. L., Science *110*: 122, 1949. Food selection by oysters.

130. LOZET, F., and FLORKIN, M., Experientia *5*: 402-404, 1949. Intestinal bacteria of *Galleria*.

131. MacGINITIE, C. E., Biol. Bull. *77*: 115-118, 1939; *88*: 107-111, 1945. Feeding methods, *Chaetopterus*, *Urechis*.

132. MAHALANABIS, S. K., and ROYCHANDHURI, B. M., Indian. J. Physiol. *4*: 145-155, 1950. Gastric enzymes of fish.

133. MANKIEWICZ, E., Canad. J. Res. ser. E *27*: 195-201, 1949. Wax digestion by *Galleria* larvae.

134. *MANSOUR, K., and MANSOUR-BEK, J. J., Biol. Rev. *9*: 363-382, 1934. Digestion of wood by insects.

135. MANSOUR-BEK, J. J., Ztschr. vergl. Physiol. *17*: 154-208, 1932; *20*: 343-369, 1933; Enzymologia *12*: 221-231, 1948. Digestive enzymes from *Maja* and *Tridacna*.

136. MANSOUR-BEK, J. J., Ztschr. vergl. Physiol. *20*: 343-369, 1934. Protein digestion Murex.

137. MARSHALL, S. M., and ORR, A. P., J. Mar. Biol. Assn. U. K. *34*: 495-529, 1955. Filter feeding by *Calanus*.

138. MAST, S. O., Biol. Bull. *83*: 173-204, 1942; *92*: 31-72, 1947. Food vacuoles, amoeba, paramecium.

139. McDONALD, I. W., Biochem. J. *51*: 86-90, 1952. Ammonia production in rumen digestion.

140. MEEUSE, B. J. D., and ZEÜGAL, U., Nature *181*: 699-700, 1958. Carbohydrases of *Cryptochiton*.

141. MERCER, E. H., and DAY, M. F., Biol. Bull. *103*: 384-394, 1952. Electron microscopy of peritrophic membranes.

142. MERTEN, R., et al., Hoppe-Seyler's Ztschr. Physiol. Chem. *289*: 173-187, 1952. Gastric cathepsin in pigs.

143. MITTLER, T. E., J. Exp. Biol. *34*: 334-341, 1957. Feeding of aphids.

144. MORTON, J. E., Quart. J. Micr. Sci. *92*: 1-25, 1951; Proc. Malacol. Soc. London *29*: 85-92, 1952; Philosoph. Tr. Roy. Soc. London, B,

239: 89-160, 1955. Morphology and function of digestive systems of molluscs.

145. *MORTON, J. E., J. Mar. Biol. Assn. U. K. *35*: 563-584, 1956; Biol. Rev. *35*: 92-140, 1960. Functions of gut, ciliary feeders, especially molluscs; formation and origin of crystalline style.

146. MUSCATINE, L., and HAND, C., Proc. Nat. Acad. Sci. *44*: 1259-1263, 1958. Transfer of carbon compounds from symbiotic algae to tissues of a coelenterate.

147. NACHLAS, N. M., and SELIGMAN, A. M., J. Biol. Chem. *181*: 343-355, 1949. Specificity of esterases and lipases.

148. NAKAZIMA, M., Jap. J. Zool. *11*: 469-566, 1956. Structure and function of midgut gland of molluscs.

149. NEWCOMER, W. S., Anat. Rec. *113*: 30, 1952; J. Cell. Comp. Physiol. *43*: 79-86, 1954; Physiol. Zool. *29*: 157-162, 1956. Beta-glucosidases of isopods and cockroach.

150. NICOL, E. A. T., Tr. Roy. Soc. Edinburgh, *56*: 537-598, 1930. Feeding and digestion in *Sabella*.

151. NICOL, J. A. C., J. Mar. Biol. Assn. U. K. *38*: 469-476, 1959. Digestion in sea anemones.

151a. NICOL, J. A. C., The Biology of Marine Animals. New York, Interscience Publishers, 1960, pp. 202-279. Feeding and digestion.

152. NORRIS, E. R., et al., J. Biol. Chem. *134*: 443-454, 1940; *204*: 673-681, 1953. Crystalline pepsin from salmon and tuna.

153. ODUM, H. T., and ODUM, E. P., Ecolog. Monog. *25*: 291-320, 1955. Trophic structure and productivity of a coral reef.

154. OHSAWA, W., and TSUKUDA, H., J. Inst. Polytech. Osaka Univ. D. *7*: 163-171, 1956. Utilization of sugars by Drosophila.

155. PARKIN, E. A., J. Exp. Biol. *17*: 364-377, 1940. Digestive enzymes of wood-boring larvae.

156. PENNINGTON, R. J., Biochem. J. *51*: 251-258, 1952; *56*: 410-417, 1954. Utilization of fatty acids from sheep rumen.

157. PHILLIPSON, A. T., J. Physiol. *116*: 84-97, 98-111, 1952. Emptying of stomach of sheep.

158. PICKFORD, G. E., Tr. Connecticut Acad. Arts, Sci. *35*: 33-72, 1942. Digestive enzymes of spiders.

159. *PIGMAN, W. W., Adv. Enzymol. *4*: 41-74, 1944. Classification of glycosidases.

160. POWNING, R. F., DAY, M. F., and IRZKIEWICZ, H., Austral. J. Scientif. Res. *4*: 49-63, 1951. Proteinases of insects.

161. PRESTON, R. D., Symp. Soc. Gen. Physiol., edited by M. Edds. New York, Ronald Press, 1960. Distribution of celluloses in animals.

162. PROSSER, C. L., and VAN WEEL, P., Physiol. Zool. *31*: 171-178, 1958. Changes in enzymes with diet, *Achatina*.

162a. RAY, D. L., in Marine Boring and Fouling Organisms, edited by D. L. Ray. University of Washington Press, 1959, pp. 372-386. Properties of cellulase from *Limnoria*.

163. RAY, D. L., and JULIAN, J. R., Nature *169*: 32-33, 1952. Cellulase in *Limnoria*.

164. RICHARDS, J. R., Nature *164*: 367-368, 1949; J. Morphol. *90*: 65-91, 1952. Ciliary feeding in a brachiopod.

165. RIVNAY, E., Bull. Ent. Res. *36*: 103-119, 1945. Enzymes in root-eating beetle larvae.

166. ROCKSTEIN, M., and KAMAL, A. S., Physiol. Zool. *27*: 65-70, 1954. Digestive enzymes in fly larvae.

167. ROGERS, T. A., Scient. Am. *198*: 34-38, 1958. Metabolism of ruminants.

168. ROMIJN, C., Arch. Néerl. Zool. *1*: 373-431, 1935. Digestive enzymes of cephalopods.

169. ROSEN, B., Ztschr. vergl. Physiol. *21*: 176-187, 1934; *24*: 602-612, 1937. Protein digestion, snails, crustaceans.

170. SARBAHI, D. S., Biol. Bull. *100*: 244-257, 1951. Digestive enzymes in goldfish.

171. SAWANO, E., Tokyo Imp. Univ. Sci. Rep. Ser. IV, *4*: 327-334, 1929; Tokyo Univ. Lit. & Sci., B, *2*: 101-126, 1935; *3*: 221-242, 1938. Proteases from *Ostrea, Polypus,* and *Paramecium*.

172. SAXENA, K. N., Experientia *10*: 383-384, 1954. Feeding and digestion of leafhoppers.

173. SCHLOTTKE, E., Ztschr. vergl. Physiol. *22*: 359-413, 1935; *24*: 210-247, 422-450, 463-492, 1937. Digestion in *Limulus,* various insects.

174. SCHMIDT-NIELSEN, B., Acta physiol. scand. *11*: 104-110, 1946. Salivary pH in man.

175. SCHWARTZ, C., et al., Pflüg. Arch. Physiol. *202*: 475-477, 1924; *213*: 592-594, 1926. Acidity of saliva and gastric juices, domestic animals.

176. SHAMBAUGH, G. F., Ohio J. Sci. *54*: 151-160, 1954. Protease stimulation by foods in adult *Aedes*.

177. SHINODA, O., Jap. J. Biochem. *11*: 345-367, 1930. Digestive enzymes of silkworms.

178. *SMITH, E. L., in Enzymes and Enzyme Systems, edited by J. T. Edsall. Harvard University Press, 1951, pp. 47-76. Specificity and mode of action of peptidases.

179. SMYTH, D. A., and TAYLOR, C. B., J. Physiol. *141*: 73-80, 1958. Active absorption of fatty acids by intestine.

180. SQUIRES, B. T., J. Physiol. *119*: 153-156, 1953. Human salivary amylase in relation to diet.

181. STEPHENS, G., Science *131*: 1532, 1960. Uptake of glucose from solution by coral *Fungia*.

182. STUART, C. A., et al., Physiol. Zool. *4*: 87-100, 1931. Culture of a cladoceran on various diets.

183. SUGDEN, B., J. Gen. Microbiol. *9*: 44-53, 1953. Metabolism of oligotrich protozoa from sheep rumen.

184. *SUMNER, J. B., and MYRBACK, K., eds., The Enzymes. New York, Academic Press, 1951.

185. TALLAN, H. H., JONES, M. E., and FRUTON, J. S., J. Biol. Chem. *194*: 793-805, 1952. Tissue cathepsins.

186. TAMMES, P. M. L., and DRAL, A. D. G., Arch. Néerl. Zool. *11*: 87-112, 1955. Straining of suspensions by mussels.

187. TRACEY, M. V., Nature *167*: 776-777, 1951. Cellulase and chitinase of earthworms.

188. TRACEY, M. V., Nature *175*: 815, 1955. Cellulase and chitinase of soil amoebae.

189. VAN SLYKE, D. D., and WHITE, G. F., J. Biol. Chem. *9*: 209-217, 1911. Protein digestion, in dogfish.

190. VAN WEEL, P. B., Physiol. Comp. Oecol. *2*:

1-19, 1950; Ztschr. vergl. Physiol. *42*: 433-448, 1959. Physiology of midgut gland. *Achatina*.

191. van Weel, P. B., Physiol. Zool. *28*: 40-54, 1955. Histophysiology of midgut gland of crab *Atya*.

192. van Weel, P. B., Physiol. Comp. Oecol. *1*: 110-127, 1949. Feeding by fresh-water sponges.

192a. van Weel, P. B., Ztschr. vergl. Physiol. *42*: 433-448, 1959. Diet, digestion, snail *Achatina*.

193. Veibel, S., *in* The Enzymes, edited by J. Sumner and K. Myrback. New York, Academic Press, 1951, vol. 1, pt. 1, pp. 583-620. Glycosidases.

194. *Vonk, H. J., Biol. Rev. *12*: 245-287, 1937; Adv. Enzymol. *1*: 371-417, 1941. Digestion in lower vertebrates.

195. *Vonk, H. J., Ann. Rev. Physiol. *17*: 483-498, 1955. Comparative physiology: nutrition, feeding, and digestion.

196. Waldner, H., Ztschr. vergl. Physiol. *38*: 334-340, 1956. Glycolytic enzymes of *Pelomyxa*.

197. Walshe, B., Nature *160*: 474, 1947. Feeding by *Chironomus* larvae.

198. Waterhouse, D. F., Australian J. Scient. Res. *B 5*: 143-168, 178-188, 444-459, 1952. Digestion of wool by insects.

199. Waterhouse, D. F., and Irzykiewicz, H. J., Insect Physiol. *1*: 18-22, 1957. Collagenase in larva of blowfly.

200. *Waterhouse, D. F., Australian J. Scient. Res. *B 2*: 428-437, 1949; Ann. Rev. Entomol. *2*: 1-18, 1959. Digestion in insects.

201. Werner, B., Zool. Anz. *146*: 97-113, 1951. Filter feeding in *Crepidula*.

202. *Wigglesworth, V. B., Principles of Insect Physiology, 4th ed., rev. London, Methuen & Co., 1950, 544 pp.

203. Wilson, T. H., and Crane, R. K., Biochim. Biophys. Acta *29*: 30-32, 1958; *31*: 397, 1959. Glucose absorption by intestine.

204. Yonge, C. M., Sci. Rep. Great Barrier Reef Exped., Brit. Mus. *1*: 59-91, 1930; 283-321, 1936; Biol. Rev. *19*: 68-80; Geol. Soc. Am. Mem. *67*: 429-442, 1957. Symbiotic relations between zooxanthellae, corals, and *Tridacna*.

205. *Yonge, C. M., Biol. Rev. *3*: 21-76, 1928; *12*: 87-115, 1937; Tabulae Biologicae. *21*: 1-45, 46-68, 1954. Feeding and digestion in various invertebrates.

206. *Yudkin, W. H., *in* Biochemistry and Physiology of Nutrition, edited by G. H. Bourne and G. W. Kidder. New York, Academic Press, 1953, vol. 2, pp. 230-284. Hydrolytic enzymes.

Chapter 6

NITROGEN EXCRETION

Products of catabolism are excreted from animals by diffusion and by active processes of elimination. Waste carbon dioxide and water are derived from catabolism of all classes of foodstuff. Nitrogenous wastes may come from proteins by way of amino acids, which may be transaminated or deaminated. Nitrogen wastes come also from the purine and pyrimidine bases of nucleic acids, and from miscellaneous nitrogenous compounds. The amount of waste nitrogen is determined by the utilization of protein for energy and by the rate of breakdown and turnover of body cell constituents.

PRODUCTS OF PROTEIN DEGRADATION

Amino Acids. Proteins are hydrolyzed to polypeptides and dipeptides, and these are broken down to their constituent amino acids. The concentration of free amino acids in animal blood is normally low (35 to 55 mg/100 ml of plasma in man);[95] insects, however, rely on amino acids to provide a large portion of their osmotic requirements, hence, have high blood concentrations (p. 37). The loss of amino acids by excretion is negligible in most animals, but some aquatic invertebrate animals excrete considerable amounts of amino acids.

Ammonia. Amino acids undergo deamination which may be either oxidative or hydrolytic, and free ammonia is liberated. Ammonia is a toxic substance, low in concentration in the blood of most animals.

It is formed rapidly in drawn blood of vertebrates, but the amount present *in vivo* in mammals is normally not more than 0.001 to 0.003 mg/100 ml (15 to 60 μmol/l).[11] The concentration of ammonia in the blood of amphibians, reptiles, and fish is higher than in mammals, but it is less than 0.1/100 ml.[32] If the blood ammonia reaches 5 mg/100 ml in rabbits, death results.[8] Many invertebrates appear to be more tolerant of ammonia. Blood ammonia values in mg/100 ml have been reported as 0.4 to 2.4 in *Maja*, 2.8 to 4.8 in *Sepia*,[25] 1.6 to 1.8 in *Homarus*, 0.7 to 2.0 in snails,[35] and 2.3 to 3.0 in the earthworm *Pheretima*.[4] Ammonia increases in the blood of *Hydrophilus* and *Dytiscus* on standing, but not in the blood of crayfish, lobster or snail.[35] Ammonia concentration is low in the blood of *Anodonta* (0.05 mg/100 ml).[36]

Because of its toxicity ammonia must be excreted as rapidly as it is formed, or it must be converted to a less toxic substance. Ammonia is highly soluble in water, is diffusible, and is excreted as ammonia by many animals which have ample water for carrying away excretory products.

In some animals in which ammonia is not an important nitrogenous waste it is important in acid-base balance. In mammals, for example, nearly all the excreted ammonia comes from glutamic acid of the blood and is liberated by glutaminase in the kidney. The amount of glutamine amide nitrogen removed from the blood is increased, and urine NH_3 nitrogen is increased during acidosis, while both quantities are decreased during alkalosis.[74] In metabolic acidosis the renal glutaminase may increase threefold, and the NH_3 formed may increase so much that its concentration in blood leaving the kidney may be higher than in renal arterial blood. When ammonia diffuses out of the kidney distal tubule cells, sodium which has been filtered can exchange for H^+ which then reacts in the tubule lumen with NH_3 to form NH_4^+ (Fig. 30). Thus excretion of ammonia counteracts blood acidosis and conserves alkaline reserve (Na^+).[74] Ammonia is also formed in quantity by putrefactive microorganisms in the cecum and colon of some mammals and is absorbed.[11] A good correlation exists between NH_3 excretion and

135

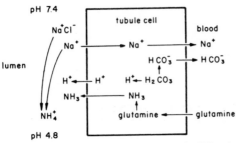

FIGURE 30. Diagram of excretion of NH_3 in acidification of urine.

renal glutaminase in rat, dog, and rabbit; the rabbit is a poor NH_3 producer, excretes only 0.001 to 0.01 mEq NH_3 daily, has low renal glutaminase, and dies when it has reached an acidosis which would not harm a dog, which excretes 10 to 100 mEq daily.[75, 95] In the alligator, alteration of acid excretion occurs without change in urine ammonia.[49]

Glutamine as a source of ammonia and the role of NH_3 excretion in acid-base regulation has not been much investigated in animals in which NH_3 constitutes a large part of the nitrogenous waste. The sculpin *Myoxocephalus* excretes most of its nitrogenous waste as ammonia through the gills; only 14 per cent of this comes from blood NH_3 but the gills have active glutaminase and glutamic acid dehydrogenase; hence the excreted NH_3 is formed in the gills from blood glutamine.[43] In the earthworm *Lumbricus*, food leads to increased acid production, which is neutralized by increase in excreted ammonia.[63]

Ammonia is also formed from urea by the action of urease, an enzyme purified from plants, certain molds, and bacteria and reported from several animals.

Urea. Urea is less toxic and slightly more soluble in water than ammonia. Human blood normally contains 18 to 38 mg of urea per 100 ml; values above about 40 mg/100 ml indicate uremia in man, who can tolerate, however, much higher concentrations. In ruminant animals urea (from their blood) may be used by symbiotic microorganisms in the rumen for protein synthesis; urea is sometimes added to cattle feed as a nitrogen source.

The best-known method of formation of urea from the ammonia of protein breakdown is by the ornithine cycle (Fig. 31). Two mols of ammonia enter the cycle, one via aspartic acid and the other via carbamyl phosphate. One CO_2 and the high energy phosphate from three ATP molecules are used. The ornithine cycle is coupled to the oxidative tricarboxylic acid (TCA) cycle (see p. 184) via α-ketoglutaric and oxaloacetic acids. Separate enzymes are required for each step. Figure 31 shows that aspartic acid is formed by transamination of glutamate (with oxaloacetic); this aspartate condenses with citrulline in the presence of ATP to form argininosuccinate, which is then converted to fumarate and arginine. The fumarate is utilized in the TCA cycle, while arginine is hydrolyzed by arginase to urea and ornithine. Carbamyl phosphate is formed in a complicated single reaction from NH_3, CO_2, and ATP, and carbamyl phosphate reacts with ornithine to form citrulline.

The ornithine cycle has been most studied with mammalian liver, but most of the enzymes occur elsewhere. In addition to liver and kidney, some yeasts and algae have enzymes for formation of argininosuccinate. Mammalian kidney has only traces of arginase and cannot form citrulline from ornithine. In birds, arginase is present only in the kidney, whereas in mammals and in most fish it is in the liver. The richest source of liver arginase is in elasmobranch fish;[9] the arginase concentration in *Helix* is several times greater than in mammalian liver.[6]

Arginase may act on dietary arginine as well as on arginase formed in the ornithine cycle, and in animals lacking the cycle its action in forming urea is exclusively on exogenous arginine, an amino acid with four nitrogens.

Uric Acid. Some animals, particularly birds, terrestrial reptiles, some snails, and insects, convert their ammonia to uric acid. This substance has low toxicity and is relatively insoluble; it can be stored or excreted in crystalline form.

Urea is made in the liver of mammals (dog), uric acid in the liver of birds (goose). Hepatectomy results in increased ammonia and amino acids in the blood of both ureotelic and uricotelic vertebrates. Pigeons make hypoxanthine in the liver and oxidize this by xanthine oxidase to uric acid in the kidney; by contrast, goose liver contains xanthine oxidase. The synthesis of hypoxanthine (and thus uric acid) is more complex than that of urea. Use of C^{13} and C^{14} labels identified the following sources of the components of uric acid (Fig. 32); carbons: 6 from CO_2, 2 and 8 from formate ("one-carbon metabolic fragment"), 4 and 5

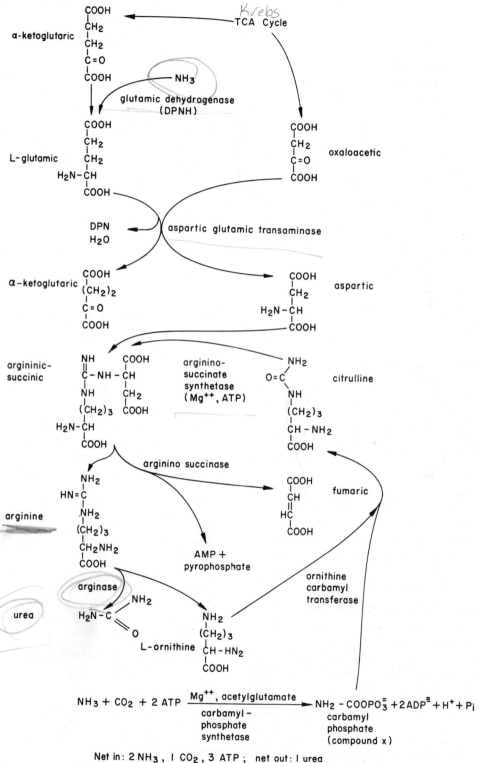

FIGURE 31. Modified ornithine cycle for urea production.[7, 59, 73, 76]

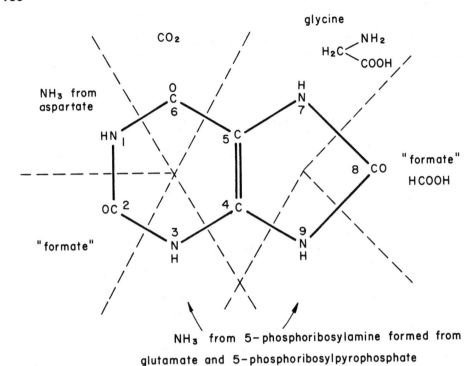

FIGURE 32.   Sources of uric acid components (bird).

from glycine; nitrogens: 7 from glycine, 1 from aspartic, and 3 and 9 from the amide of glutamine. In both urea and uric acid synthesis carbamyl phosphate is used, and glutamic acid as a direct source of NH_3. The over-all reaction in uric acid synthesis is as follows:

$$3\ NH_3 + CO_2 + ATP + glycine + 2\ formate$$
$$\xrightarrow[\text{(ribose-1-phosphate)}]{} hypoxanthine \longrightarrow uric\ acid$$

Guanine. Spiders excrete most of their nitrogen as guanine (2-amino-6-oxypurine), a substance less soluble in water than uric acid. Its method of synthesis is unknown.

PURINE EXCRETION PRODUCTS

Roughly 5 per cent of excretory nitrogen comes from nucleic acid metabolism, which yields principally the purines adenine and guanine. Pyrimidine nitrogen is usually excreted as urea or ammonia.

Purines. Some animals excrete purines without further degradation. In some animals adenine, but not other purines, may be oxidized; guanine is accumulated or excreted as such in the pig, but in most animals it is deaminated. Different enzymes act on the purine adenine and the nucleoside adenosine (adenine-ribose).

Uric Acid. Uric acid is formed as an end-product by oxidative deamination as in Figure 33.

Man and higher apes lack uricase, which oxidizes uric acid; hence they have higher blood concentration than other animals. Gout is associated with high uric acid levels in the blood, but the attacks may be caused by some precursors.[51]

Allantoin. The pyrimidine ring of uric acid may be opened by uricase and allantoin and is formed as in Figure 33.

Allantoic Acid. Further oxidation by allantoinase forms allantoic acid.

Urea. Allantoic acid is broken by allantoicase to glyoxylic acid and urea.

Ammonia. A few animals and many plants possess urease which converts urea to ammonia and carbon dioxide.

MISCELLANEOUS NITROGENOUS COMPOUNDS

Other nitrogenous products are:

Trimethylamine Oxide. This is excreted, especially by marine fish, and by other vertebrates when on a diet rich in trimethylamine.

Hippuric Acid and Ornithuric Acid. Benzoic acid entering in the diet of mammals is removed by combination with glycine to form hippuric acid (benzoylglycine). In

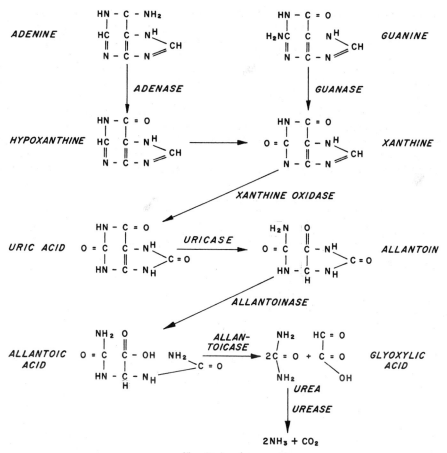

FIGURE 33. Purine decomposition.

birds, benzoic acid combines with ornithine to form ornithuric acid.

Creatine and Creatinine. Creatine is important as an energy storage compound, particularly in muscle. Some creatine is apparently converted to creatinine and excreted, although creatine may also be excreted unchanged.

Pyrimidines. Pyrimidines from nucleic acids may be excreted as such.

Pterines. These nitrogenous pigments deposited in butterfly wings are sometimes regarded as excretory products; certain aspects of pterine synthesis resemble uric acid synthesis.

GENERAL PATTERN OF NITROGEN EXCRETION

In no group of animals is nitrogenous excretion limited to one product. In most animals the total nonprotein nitrogen excreted exceeds the identified components. Those animals which excrete significant amounts of amino acids lose potential metabolites. Animals are called ammonotelic when nitrogen (from proteins) is excreted predominantly in the form of ammonia, ureotelic when urea is the main product, uricotelic when the main product is uric acid. Many animals can produce a given substance even though it may not be the predominant product, that is, they may be ureogenic or uricogenic even though they are not ureotelic or uricotelic.

In general, the correlation between kind of excretory product and availability of water is so good that nitrogen excretion appears to be an important adaptive character. In the series ammonia, urea, uric acid, there is decreasing toxicity. Animals whose eggs are protected against water loss (cleidoic eggs) store nontoxic embryonic waste products, and the adults tend to excrete the same products (e.g., uric acid), whereas animals whose embryos can excrete freely into surrounding water (noncleidoic eggs) excrete products which may be more toxic. Embryonic habitat is one, but not the only, factor determining the kind of nitrogenous excretion. Nitrogen excretion is a labile character, and the excretory pattern may change with stage in the life cycle, availability of water, nutrition, and other influences.

Numerous tabulations of the percentage of total nitrogen excreted by various animals have been presented.[7, 8, 22, 33, 47] The most recent general summary is presented in the Handbook of Biological Data.[1] Table 22 gives certain representative selected values for various groups of animals as well as recently published data.

Ammonotelic Animals. Ammonia is a soluble substance which diffuses readily across most body surfaces into water. Aquatic invertebrate animals excrete a large proportion of their nitrogen as ammonia. In Protozoa the quantity of ammonia excreted varies with diet, stage in culture cycle, and species.[60] Various ciliates and coelenterates have been shown to excrete quantities of ammonia. Echinoderms are ammonotelic, but they also give off considerable amounts of amino acids. *Sipunculus* excretes ammonia predominantly, as do fresh-water leeches. Polychaete worms

TABLE 22.　PER CENT OF NITROGEN EXCRETED IN DIFFERENT FORMS

Animal	NH_3	Urea	Uric acid	Amino	Purine	Other
Protozoa						
Tetrahymena[82]	+ stationary phase					
Paramecium[24]	++ (endogenous)					
Coelenterates						
Actinians[25]	52.7	4.2				
Sipunculids and Annelids						
Sipunculus[25]	50	9.7	0	16.6	4.1	19.4
Aphrodite[8]	80	0.2	0.8			
Lumbricus[22]						
starved	8.6	84.4	0.76			undetermined 7, allantoin trace
fed	72	5	1.4			undetermined 16, allantoin 2
Pheretima[4]	42	50	0	0.6		creatine 7.8
Nematodes						
Nematodirus[77]	40-73	7-11	trace	33-37		
Echinoderms						
Asterias[25]	39.3	11.7	trace	23.8	3.6-10	16-26
Molluscs						
Sepia[25]	67	1.7	2.1	7.8	4.9	
Littorina						
(sea water, summer)[65]	40	12.6	0.8	7	29	
Limnaea						
(fresh water, summer)[65]	42	14	5		39	
Arion (terrestrial)[65]	9.8	0.2	3.3	18	16.6	17-62
Ascidians						
Ciona[44]	87					
Ascidiella[44]	95					
Crustaceans						
Carcinus[25]	68	3	0.7	8.7	3.2	
Astacus[25]	60	11	0.8	10.1	4.4	
Gammarus locusta (marine)[27]	87	0	0	7		
Marinogammarus (marine)[27]	87	0	0	4		2
Orchestia (marine littoral)[27]	70	1	0	11		10
Ligia (marine terrestrial)[27]	83	0	0	6		9
Gammarus pulex (fresh water)[27]	71	10	0	10		7
Asellus aquaticus (fresh water)[27]	62	0	5	10		21
Oniscus acellus (terrestrial)[27]	50	0	4	0		16
Porcellio (terrestrial)[27]	56	0	6	0		18
Armadillidium (terrestrial)[27]	55	1	8	6		30
Insects						
Rhodnius[98] (1 day postfeeding)	0	trace	90-92	0		+ creatine
Attacus[23] (1 day postfeeding)	1-8	trace	80.8	9.5		
Aedes aegypti adult[50]	6.4	11.9	47.3	4.4		19
Culex pipiens[50]	10	7.9	46.9	5.5		20
Sialis larvae[88]	90					

TABLE 22—(*Continued*)

Animal	NH₃	Urea	Uric acid	Amino	Purine	Other	
Fish							
Cyprinus[83]	60	6.2	0.2	6.5			22
Carassius[83]	73.3	9.9					16.8
Lophius[15]	13	1	0.02	3		trimethylamine oxide	19
						creatine	2.8
						creatinine	33
						undetermined	30
Flounder[45]	2.2	17.3	1.2	8.9		trimethylamine oxide	0.4-1
						undetermined	55
						creatinine	23.3
Sculpin[45]	1.6	14.6	0.7	4.2		trimethylamine oxide	23.1
						undetermined	54.6
						creatinine	23.3
Torpedo[25]	1.7	85.3		1.7			
Reptiles							
Testudo leithii[52]	4.2	48.7	33.6	2.4		creatine	1.8
						undetermined	8.4
						creatinine	0.95
Testudo elegans[58]	6.2	8.3	56.1	13.1	3		
Testudo sulcata[52]	2.8	20.2	55	4.4		creatine	1.7
						undetermined	14.9
						creatinine	0.95
Testudo denticulata[58]	6.0	29	6.7	15.6	2.8		
Testudo graeca[58]	4.1	22	51.9	6.6	9.4		
Chrysemys picta[101]	15.3	39	18.8	11.5		undetermined	18.6
Python[3]	8.7		89	2.3			
Black snake (Coluber) embryo[17]	20	60	20				
Phrynosoma[94]	0.6	0	98			creatinine	trace
Amphibians							
Rana catesbiana (adult)[66]	3.2	84	0.4				
(larva)		10					
Bufo (larva)[59]	80						
(adult)	15						
Xenopus (larva)[92]	78	27					
(legs developing)	46	54					
(early adult)	75	25					
Birds							
Hen[66]	3-4	10	87				
Chick embryo (total excretion)	11.2	11.4	77.1				
(calc. from ref. 18, 19) day 1	29	25	46				
day 10	5	31	64				
day 21	11	11	78				
Mammals							
dog 1st 24 hr[96]	14.9	28	1.6			allantoin	13
adult[96]	2.7	88	0.4			allantoin	3.6
man 1st 24 hr[96]	7.6	70	8				
adult[96]	3.5	85	2.2				
cat[46]	4-8	72-84	0.02-0.22			creatinine	10
camel[84]	2.4	68	1.3	1.7		creatinine	10
						creatine	2.1
						undetermined	14.8
leopard[41]	3.2	87.1	0.06	0.86	0.25	allantoin	.52
						creatinine	.88
						creatine	.44
bat[41]	6.0	63.4	0.87	0.96		creatinine	8.5
man[37]	4.8	86.9	0.65			creatinine	3.6
						undetermined	4

are ammonotelic; however, urea and traces of uric acid are reported in *Arenicola* coelomic fluid. The cephalopods *Sepia* and *Octopus* excrete most of their nitrogen as NH_3, and the pelecypods which have been examined, both marine and fresh-water, are largely ammonotelic. The gastropod *Aplysia* is ammonotelic, but excretory products of other gastropods are diverse, as will be shown later. *Helix* kidney and "liver" contain a urease which breaks urea to ammonia; ureases have been reported for some other invertebrates.[48]

Crustaceans give off much amino acid nitrogen, but the predominant excretory product of marine and fresh-water crustaceans is ammonia. The crab *Carcinides* puts out 86 per cent of its excreted N as NH_3.[64]

In crustaceans the body surface, particularly the gills, is permeable to NH_3 and urea; excretion of these substances is not much altered by plugging the excretory pores. The kidneys may excrete dyes and other less diffusible substances, whereas the gills are the chief route for nitrogen excretion. Analysis of the urine of crustaceans is, therefore, inadequate to measure their total nitrogen excretion. Various species of isopods and gammarids are ammonotelic in decreasing amount in the following series: marine > fresh-water > terrestrial.[27] Aquatic insects tend to be ammonotelic; for example, the aquatic larvae of *Sialis* excrete 90 per cent of their nitrogen as NH_3; they have a blood concentration of 0.5 mg per 100 ml and show signs of toxicity at 7 mg per 100 ml; when ligated so as to prevent excretion by the malpighian tubules, nitrogen is stored in some form other than ammonia.[88] Dragon-fly nymphs (*Aeschna*) excrete mainly ammonia whether fed or fasted.[88]

Fresh-water fish are ammonotelic, although they also excrete some urea; most of their nitrogenous wastes diffuse out across the gills and less nitrogen leaves by the urine.

Trimethylamine Oxide. Marine teleosts are confronted by the serious osmotic problem of retaining sufficient water, and they show considerable variation in their pattern of nitrogen excretion. Many of them are ammonotelic but also excrete considerable amounts of urea and miscellaneous nitrogenous products. Some marine teleosts excrete as much as one-third of their nitrogen as trimethylamine oxide (TMO), a soluble non-toxic substance. Trimethylamine is present in muscles of marine fish, absent from muscles of fresh-water fish. Trimethylamine (TMA) is negligible in amount in echinoderms, oysters, *Mytilus,* chitons, gastropods, tunicates, algae, and diatoms, but is abundant in *Cardium,* scallops, octopus, squid, copepods, crabs, and barnacles; it occurs in the serum of dogfish and ratfish, and in teleosts, although less. Salmon and eel contain more trimethylamine oxide in sea water than when in fresh water; salmon in fresh water lack TMO; when in sea water and fed liver they show no increase in TMO, but when fed scallops or salmon meal they increase much in content of TMO. The trimethylamine oxide of fish appears, therefore, not to be endogenous but to come from their food.[10, 68] It would be of interest to know whether sculpins and *Lophius,* which excrete more than a third of their nitrogen as trimethylamine oxide, produce some of it endogenously. The spiny dogfish has a relatively high blood concentration of TMO, and over 90 per cent of that filtered by its kidney is reabsorbed.[21] In the rat, urinary trimethylamine comes from food; excretion of TMO is increased by feeding TMA but not by feeding betaine.[68]

Urea. Some bony fish excrete considerable amounts of urea. Elasmobranch fish are ureotelic, and marine species retain a concentration of 2 to 2.5 per cent of urea in the blood; fresh-water species retain 1 per cent;[9] by the high urea concentration they maintain themselves hyperosmotic to their medium (Chapter 2). All tissues of a dogfish except brain and blood are able to synthesize urea by the same cycle as mammals. Excess urea is excreted, largely through the gills. Dogfish eggs contain a large amount of deposited urea; the embryos early start to synthesize quantities of urea.

Amphibians are ureotelic, at least as adults, and the liver of both frog and toad can synthesize urea. Calculations of glomerular filtration and tubular reabsorption indicate that some urea must be secreted actively by the tubules of some amphibian kidneys.[38] Double perfusion of a bullfrog kidney with labeled urea shows that both reabsorption and secretion go on simultaneously, with secretion in excess.[55] In *Rana catesbiana* the excretion of urea rises steeply at the onset of metamorphosis; the enzyme which cleaves argininosuccinate is rate-limiting, and the ornithine cycle may not be functional in the liver of early tadpoles.[14]

Mammals, including monotremes, are ureotelic. Embryonic wastes diffuse readily into the maternal circulation; embryonic life is aquatic. There is need for conservation of water in adult mammals, however, and urea may be concentrated by as much as a hundred times by the reabsorption of water in the kidney tubules. In desert animals like the kangaroo rat, and possibly in other mammals on high protein and low water intake, there may be active tubular secretion of urea.[78] Ruminants can use urea as an ultimate protein source, and on a low protein diet a camel or sheep can reduce its urea excretion twentyfold and can retain injected urea for use in the rumen.[79-81]

In general, ureotelic animals are not greatly restricted in water supply, yet they do not live in an excess of it as do ammonotelic animals.

Uric Acid. Uricotelic animals usually live in relatively dry environments and develop from protected eggs. Most insects are too restricted in their water supply for them to excrete ammonia, or even urea, in quantity, although some aquatic ones excrete ammonia. The urine formed in the malpighian tubules of insects is rich in uric acid and there may be a mass of uric acid crystals left after absorption of water from the secreted solution (e.g., in mosquitoes).[16] In *Rhodnius,* secretion at pH 7.2 occurs in the proximal part of the malpighian tubule and reabsorption of water and base in the lower tube, leaving crystals of uric acid at pH 6.6.[30, 98] Some insects (Lepidoptera) deposit nitrogenous pigments. During development much nitrogenous waste is lost in the meconium at the time of molt. *Lucilia* larvae accumulate waste granules which are not uric acid, but the pupae accumulate uric acid, which is excreted in the meconium.[93] Many Dipteran larvae excrete allantoin but store uric acid; their pupae make only the allantoin. In a series of Lepidoptera the blood uric acid in pupae was three times greater than in larvae.[28] In larvae of *Prodenia* and *Galleria* uric acid is synthesized in the fat body, there is more in the blood of the fed larvae than in the starved, and urea is not a precursor of uric acid.[2] Some aquatic Hemiptera, Collembola, and the phasmid *Carausius* convert uric acid to allantoin or allantoic acid.[73]

Fresh-water and terrestrial gastropods in general have cleidoic eggs. During development of the egg of *Limnaea* the uric acid content increased from 0.5 mg per 100 ml in the cleavage stages to 1.0 mg per 100 ml when the embryo occupied one-quarter to one-half of the egg case, to 4.5 mg per 100 ml when the egg was about to hatch.[5] In hibernation the nephridium stores uric acid to as much as three-quarters of the organ's weight.[65]

Water conservation is important for lizards and snakes, and their eggs must retain embryonic nitrogenous excretion until hatching. Hence they excrete most of their nitrogen as the relatively insoluble and innocuous uric acid (Table 22). In *Phrynosoma,* the horned toad, the urine is a solid ball of uric acid.

Birds convert most of the ammonia from protein to uric acid. Their urine is a semisolid mass of uric acid crystals. Blood uric acid concentrations are high in uricotelic animals (5 to 20 mg/100 ml in insects,[33, 99] and 5 mg/100 ml in chickens[103]) as compared with blood concentrations in ammonotelic animals (0.73 mg/100 ml in *Chaetopterus,*[100] 0.1 mg in *Arenicola,*[89] 2.3 mg/100 ml in *Homarus,* 2.1 in *Libinia,*[100] and 0.05 to 0.2 mg/100 ml in ureotelic mammals[69]). Hence the distinction between ureotelic and uricotelic metabolism is quantitative, and the presence of uric acid in the blood or coelomic fluid does not necessarily indicate that uric acid excretion is predominant.

Guanine. Many spiders excrete nitrogen predominantly as guanine; in Tarantulae, for example, the malpighian tubules and the cloacal sacs may elaborate guanine crystals, and in the laboratory the spiders may deposit the crystals in culture dishes. The method of formation of guanine from protein nitrogen is unknown. In other animals guanine is degraded along with other purines.

MODIFICATION OF NITROGEN EXCRETION

Animal Groups with Mixed Excretion Patterns. Most reptiles, snakes, and lizards are uricotelic. Turtles, however, can form urea by the ornithine cycle, and they excrete much nitrogen as urea. In addition, their ammonia excretion is significant, and two aquatic species excrete some uric acid (Table 22). Needham argues that the mode of excretion is related to the water supply in embryonic life; since turtles usually lay their eggs in moist sand where diffusion of NH_3 would be too slow to avoid toxicity and yet where storage of uric acid is unnecessary, urea is sufficiently nontoxic. Some species of land turtles (*Testudo*) excrete more urea, some more uric acid, and individual turtles show marked day-to-day variation in the proportions of urea and uric acid.[52] Alligators normally excrete large amounts of

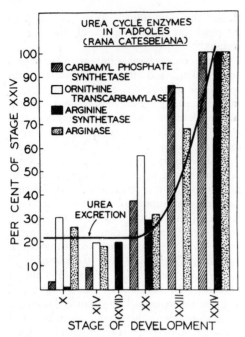

FIGURE 34. Relative amounts of enzymes of ornithine cycle at different stages in development of tadpoles. Metamorphosis at stages XVIII to XXV. (From Brown, G. W., and Cohen, P. P.: *in* Chemical Basis of Development, edited by W. D. McElroy and B. Glass. Academic Press.)

ammonia. Thus reptiles show several excretory patterns.

The gastropods present an interesting series with respect to transition from sea to fresh water to land and accompanying transition toward uric acid excretion.[65, 87] Needham[65] compared the uric acid content in the nephridia of a number of species of operculates; values vary with nutrition and hibernation, but certain general indications follow: The uric acid in the nephridium of marine operculates is very low (2 to 4 mg/gm dry weight). Terrestrial snails, by contrast, contain much uric acid (31 to 1000 mg/gm), whether pulmonates or operculates. A series of littoral snails (*Littorina* species) is intermediate in uric acid concentration (1.5 to 26 mg/gm dry). The fresh-water snails do not form a uniform group; *Hydrobia jenkinsi*, which has entered fresh water from the sea recently, contains little uric acid, whereas *Bythnia*, *Paludina*, and *Limnaea stagnalis* contain much uric acid and probably have penetrated fresh water secondarily from land. Snails are unable to produce urea by the ornithine cycle and produce it only from the arginine of their food; hence their only choice in protein degradation is ammonia or

uric acid. The group merits further study, but the general trend is from ammonia to uric acid excretion as osmotic stress increases. *Littorina* excretes 61 per cent of its nitrogen as NH_3 in the winter, 40 per cent in summer.

Changes in Excretory Pattern with Life Cycle. In Carcinides, nitrogen excretion is much reduced before ecdysis and also before oviposition.[62]

The tadpole of the toad *Bufo* excretes 80 per cent of its nitrogen as ammonia; this amount declines as the tail is absorbed, and the terrestrial adult excretes only 15 per cent as ammonia.[59] In *Xenopus* both tadpole and adult are aquatic and excrete most of their nitrogen as ammonia, but the ratio of ammonia to urea goes through a minimum at metamorphosis.[59, 92] The larvae of the salamander *Triturus* and of the frog *Rana temporaria* excrete some 75 per cent of their nitrogen as ammonia; when the tail is absorbed and forelimbs formed ammonia excretion diminishes to 10 per cent.[59] At the onset of metamorphosis of *Rana catesbiana* all of the enzymes of the ornithine cycle increase rapidly[14] (Fig. 34). Larvae of the newt *Triturus* excrete 75 per cent of their nitrogen as ammonia, 25 per cent as urea; on metamorphosis the ammonia drops to 57 per cent. The terrestrial red eft excretes only 13 per cent as NH_3, 87 per cent as urea; 2 to 3 years later the mature newt returns to water to breed and its ammonia excretion rises to 26 per cent;[61] thus two shifts occur.

Newborn mammals excrete relatively less urea than do adults; in addition, the total nitrogen excretion is much less, probably because of less breakdown of tissues and more anabolism of amino acids.[97]

It was formerly thought that the nitrogen excretion of embryos of snakes and birds went through a sequence from ammonia, through urea, to uric acid. The interpretation of analyses is difficult in that excretory products may be stored in the yolk-sac and allantois, there may be interconversion of compounds, and ammonia and urea may come from several sources. Analyses of black snake, *Coluber*, embryos, yolk, yolk-sac, and albumen suggest that ammonia is excreted initially and may be lost as a gas, that after about 11 days urea is excreted in such amounts that it accounts for 60 per cent of the total nitrogen excreted during incubation, and that urea accumulates in the allantois. After 50 days uric acid is excreted predominantly, while at that time urea may be reabsorbed and converted to NH_3, which is then incorporated into uric acid.[17] Urease was found in the fetal liver and kidney at the time of decline in urea excretion. Labeled urea injected into the viviparous garter snake *Thamnophis* was converted in part to uric acid.[17] In alligator embryos the total ammonia in the egg is relatively constant and there does not appear to be an early stage of NH_3 excretion; rather urea and uric acid are excreted from the beginning.

In the incubating chick embryo, some NH_3 is present initially, but it increases in total, beginning on the tenth day; both urea and uric acid also increase in amount, uric acid much more than urea.[18] As percentage of total nitrogen ammonia declines gradually from the first day, urea rises to a maximum at 6 to 9 days and then declines, while the uric acid increases rapidly from about the eleventh day of incubation. Arginase increases up to the eighteenth day, is uniformly distributed for the first 6 days, and then is more concentrated in kidney and liver.[42] Injection of arginine induces arginase activity.[76] It has been postulated that a ureogenic stage (by the ornithine cycle) precedes uricogenesis and that some urea (and NH_3) may be converted into uric acid. In another study the presence of urease was not confirmed, no increase in total NH_4 was found, arginase appeared uniformly distributed throughout the embryo up to 11 days of incubation, and uric acid was formed from the fifth day when the mesonephros first appears to function.[29, 31] It was suggested that the urea formed in chick embryo is from arginine derived from yolk proteins and that the kidneys excrete only uric acid at all stages. The simple recapitulation of patterns of nitrogen excretion during development as proposed by Needham cannot be accepted but the sequential changes remain unclear.

Changes in Nitrogen Excretion Induced by Diet. *Paramecium* excretes some 91 per cent of nitrogen products as NH_3 when not fed, 55 per cent when fed glycine, and no ammonia when fed starch.[24]

The arginase content of the midgut gland of fed *Helix pomatia* is six times greater than that of the starved snails.[6]

Earthworms excrete quantities of protein, mostly mucus; of the nonprotein nitrogen the different components depend on nutritional state. In freshly collected, well-fed *Lumbricus terrestris* urea constitutes 8 to 15 per cent of excreted nitrogen; during starvation the ammonia excreted via urine decreases and urea increases to 86 per cent in 1 month starvation.[22] *Eisenia foetida* differs from *Lumbricus* in excreting four times as much NH_3 as urea in starvation and in replacing some ammonia excretion by urea when fed.[63] The total excreted nitrogen increases by several times on feeding, an indication of protein metabolism. When arginine was fed to *Lumbricus,* the excretion of both urea and ammonia increased; ornithine but not citrulline increased urea excretion. During a fast the urea content of tissues of *Lumbricus* increases; the arginase increases some ten times, especially in the intestine.[22] *Lumbricus* uses NH_3 to neutralize acid from vegetable food. *Eisenia* uses other means, such as $CaCO_3$.[63]

Excretion by meat-eating insects is influenced by diet. In the bug *Rhodnius,* for example, immediately after a blood meal there is considerable urea; later, uric acid is greatly in excess.[98] Blowfly larvae which are eating meat give off much ammonia; this is probably formed in the gut and hence is not a true metabolic excretory product. At pupation, ammonia excretion stops and uric acid becomes the main product. Some of the uric acid from protein breakdown is converted to allantoin.[13] The nitrogen excreted by adult mosquitoes is 82 per cent uric acid soon after emergence, only 15 per cent uric acid 2 weeks later, but after a blood meal the uric acid rises to 79 per cent of the nitrogen excreted.[90] On a low protein diet camels increase creatinine and decrease urea excretion; man shows a similar trend but to a less degree.[80]

Changes Induced by Water Deprivation. Examples have been cited of animals in which the nitrogen excretion changes from ammonia to urea or uric acid during development on transition from an aquatic to terrestrial habitat; some animals can change their mode of nitrogen excretion as adults.

When the lungfish *Protopterus aethiopicus* is active in fresh water it excretes nearly three times more nitrogen as NH_3 than as urea. When estivating in its mud cocoon, however, it excretes urea which may accumulate to the extent of 1 to 2 per cent of the body weight in a year; muscle urea increases by some seven times. When the fish returns to water, urea is rapidly excreted, and the excretion of ammonia increases to its characteristic high proportion.[83] Evidently the shift from ammonotelic to ureotelic metabolism and back in dipnoans depends on available water, but the effect of enforced starvation accompanying the estivation has not been examined.

A crocodile is normally ammonotelic, but when kept out of water its excretion of urea and uric acid increases.[8] Similarly *Xenopus*, normally ammonotelic in water, produces and stores increasing amounts of urea when kept in air, and reverts to ammonia excretion when returned to water; this reversal is not found in *Rana*.[92]

An Indian amphibious snail (*Pila globosa*)[53] had uric acid in its nephridium as follows:

freshly collected	1.68	mg/gm dry whole nephridium
in moist jar	60	mg/gm (anterior part)
	14	mg/gm (posterior part)
in dry jar	102	mg/gm (anterior part)
	42	mg/gm (posterior part)
returned to water	29.8	mg/gm (anterior part)
	nil	(posterior part)

Thus this snail tends to accumulate uric acid in its nephridium under conditions of estivation.

DISTRIBUTION OF ENZYMES OF PROTEIN BREAKDOWN

Deaminases catalyze the liberation of ammonia from amino acids in animals of all phyla. Urease has been reported from earthworms, *Helix*, and snake embryos; it may have some other role than to convert the urea of purine breakdown to ammonia in ammonotelic animals.

Urea can be formed by the ornithine cycle, by the action of arginase on dietary arginine, by allantoicase on allantoic acid, and by unknown reactions. The ornithine cycle operates in livers of mammals, frogs, and turtles; the cycle is said to be lacking in teleost livers but it functions in elasmobranchs.[9] The ornithine cycle is lacking in adult uricotelic snakes and birds. In invertebrates the ornithine cycle has been indicated, with variations from the mammalian pattern, in the earthworm.[22] Its presence in *Tetrahymena* has been claimed[82] and denied;[26] the small amount of arginase may act on exogenous arginine, and the principal product is NH_3.[26]

Arginase is found in mammalian liver and in lower concentrations in kidney, mammary glands, and testes. Uricotelic birds and snakes lack liver arginase but have it in the kidney;[17, 20, 42] in chick embryos arginase increases up to 18 days of incubation,[18, 19] and the enzyme can be induced by injecting arginine, as it can in rat livers.[76] In fish, the amount of liver arginase is low in cod, salmon, bullhead, and trout, intermediate in herring, and very high in elasmobranchs

(dogfish and skate) and holocephalans (ratfish).

Arginase is low in the hepatopancreas of the ammonotelic *Asterias* and *Carcinus*, and is absent from hepatopancreas of *Mytilus*, *Pecten*, *Buccinium*, and *Littorina*.[5] Freshwater snails have arginase concentrations comparable to those in mammals, whereas in the terrestrial *Helix*, arginase concentrations may be eight times greater than in mammalian liver. However, *Helix* hepatopancreas does not form urea by the ornithine cycle. The arginase concentration in snails parallels the uric acid content of the nephridia. Thus, arginase may be correlated with ureogenesis whether by the ornithine cycle (frogs, mammals, elasmobranchs, earthworms) or by exogenous arginine.

The synthesis of uric acid in birds (and possibly reptiles) is complex but makes use of several steps in common with urea synthesis in other vertebrates. Glutamate-aspartate is used to introduce NH_3 in both, and carbamyl phosphate is also used in both. Both require TCA cycle acids and energy from ATP. Furthermore, uric acid synthesis shares xanthine oxidase with the path of purine degradation. The synthesis of uric acid from NH_3 in insects and snails remains to be elucidated.

DISTRIBUTION OF ENZYMES AND PRODUCTS OF PURINE METABOLISM

A small proportion of the nitrogen excreted by animals comes from purines in nucleic acid metabolism. The amount varies with the diet and is greater with meat than with plant food. Enzymes of purine metabolism differ from those of protein metabolism, even though some of the end-products are the same. An animal may excrete some uric acid from purines, regardless of whether its protein is degraded to ammonia, urea, or uric acid. Purines may be excreted as such, e.g., adenine or guanine, or they may be deaminated to xanthine or hypoxanthine, which is converted to uric acid by xanthine oxidase. If uricase is present, allantoin is then formed; allantoinase converts this to allantoic acid; allantoicase converts this to urea; urea may be broken down to ammonia by urease. Numerous invertebrates—annelids, molluscs, and arthropods—have deaminases of the free bases (adenase and guanase); many vertebrate livers lack adenase but can deaminate the nucleosides by adenosinase and guanosinase. The type of purine breakdown product in different animals has been identified partly by analysis of excretory products and excretory organs and partly by identification of the enzymes in tissues, particularly liver (or hepatopancreas). Detailed summaries of purine products have been presented in references 1, 34, and 54 and in the first edition of this book. A few selected values are given in Table 23, and Figure 35 summarizes results.

In the flatworms and those annelids which have been examined, purines are excreted and enzymes for degrading them are lacking. However, urease has been reported in nematodes.[77]

Many other ammonotelic invertebrates degrade their purine to ammonia. Uricase has been reported in actinians, and uricase and allantoinase in echinoderms. The egg of the sea urchin Strongylocentrotus contains urease, xanthine oxidase, uricase, allantoinase,

and allantoicase.[12] All four enzymes occur in Sipunculus and in the hepatopancreas of Mytilus, crayfish, and lobster. Arginase and xanthine oxidase are found in the midgut gland of Helix and the amphibious snail Pila; arginase is found in nephridia of Helix but not of Pila; in Helix urease and uricase are absent from midgut gland but urease is present in nephridium.[6, 53] Comparison of uricolysis in ammonotelic and uricotelic gastropods would be of interest; apparently among molluscs there is some lability of purine degradation as of protein breakdown.

Terrestrial insects are predominantly uricotelic animals and tend to convert their purines to uric acid or to allantoin. Enzymes degrading uric acid were not found in Hydrophilus, Tenebrio, or Aeschna.[34] Larvae of the blowfly Lucilia convert much of the uric acid from protein to allantoin; uricase is

TABLE 23.   DISTRIBUTION OF URICOLYTIC ENZYMES*

Animal	Tissue	Xanthine oxidase	Uricase	Allantoinase	Allantoicase	Urease
Echinoderms			+	+		
Sea urchin eggs[12]		+	+	+	+	+
Sipunculids		−	+	+	+	+
Planaria	entire	−	−	−	−	
Lumbricus	entire		−	−	−	
also	chloragogue	+				
Hirudo		−		−	−	−
Crustaceans						
Astacus, Homarus	hepatopancreas		+	+	+	+
Molluscs						
Planorbis		+	+	−	−	
Mytilus	hepatopancreas		+	+	+	+
Helix	hepatopancreas	+	−			−
Anodonta	hepatopancreas	sl+	+	+	+	−
Insecta						
Lucilia	eggs, larva, adult		+	−		−
Tenebrionidae		+	−			
Horsefly, blowfly			+			
Cockroach, bee			−			
Prodemia	larva	+	−			
Fish						
Protopterus	liver	+	+	+	+	
Cyprinids, esocids, scombrids	liver		+	+	+	
Salmonids, pleuronectids, anguillids	liver		+	+	−	
Raja	liver		+	+	+	
Amphibians						
Frog	liver		+	+	+	−
Reptiles						
Lacerta		+		−	−	
Testudo		+			−	
Birds (adult)		+	−	−		
Mammals						
Most mammals		+	+	−	−	−
Anthropoids			−	−	−	−

* + indicates presence; − indicates absence.

Detailed references are given in Table 31 in first edition of this book.

Purine N

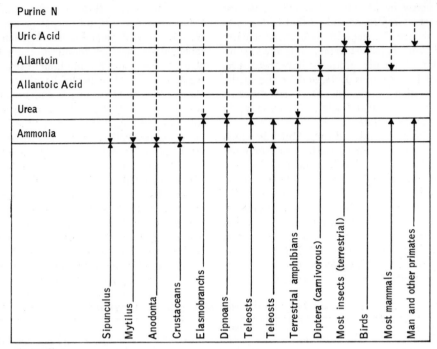

Amino N

FIGURE 35. Principal end products of purine and amino nitrogen degradation. Broken line, purine breakdown; unbroken line, amino breakdown. (Modified from Florkin, M., and Duchateau, G.: Arch. Internat. Physiol., vol. 53.)

absent from the pupae and reappears in the adults.[13] In *Prodemia* and *Galleria* larvae the fat body converts purines into uric acid.[2] Some other insects (hemipterans, orthopterans) excrete allantoin, some allantoic acid.[70]

One cyclostome, *Lampetra fluviatilis,* like the annelids, has no enzymes for degrading purines. The livers of the dipnoan *Protopterus* and the elasmobranch *Raja* degrade their purines to urea. Among teleosts one group has uricase, allantoinase, and allantoicase, whereas another group lacks the allantoicase; the two methods of purine excretion seem unrelated to habitat.

Amphibians degrade purines to urea but not to ammonia. Reptiles, whether ureotelic or uricotelic, excrete their purines as uric acid. Likewise, birds lack uricase and allantoinase. Most mammals have uricase and excrete some allantoin. Man and other anthropoids, however, lack this enzyme and excrete uric acid. Among dogs, Dalmatian coach hounds excrete some eleven times more uric acid and much less allantoin nitrogen than other breeds.[39, 56] This difference results not from any difference in purine metabolism in the liver but from failure to reabsorb filtered uric acid in the kidneys; uric acid clearance even

exceeds that of creatine.[102] Injected uricosuric drugs reduce tubular reabsorption and increase uric acid excretion in non-Dalmatians but not in Dalmatians.

Two evolutionary trends have occurred in purine metabolism:[33] (1) Degradation completely to ammonia requires a chain of enzymes and is accomplished only among a few groups of lower invertebrates. Other animals, both vertebrate and invertebrate, break the chain at various points. The evolutionary trend is toward the elimination of enzymatic steps. (2) The end products of protein and purine catabolism tend to be the same—ammonia, urea, or uric acid. Some uricotelic animals excrete purines as allantoin; exceptions to this biochemical convergence are found, particularly among molluscs, fish, and mammals.

CONCLUSIONS

The form of nitrogenous waste produced by protein catabolism is related to the availability of water during both embryonic and adult life of an animal. Ammonia diffuses freely out of and away from aquatic invertebrates and fish. Where there is some osmotic stress but ample dilution, urea appears, as in amphibians and mammals.

Extreme need for water retention in insects, land gastropods, snakes and lizards, and birds is satisfied by uric acid excretion; this is associated with cleidoic eggs.

In ureotelic mammals, ammonia excretion is one means of regulating acid-base balance, and ammonia is made via glutamic acid; ammonia may also come from blood glutamate in ammonotelic animals and by action of urease in the purine degradation scheme. Production of urea by the ornithine cycle represents an important part of protein catabolism, is coupled to the energy-yielding tricarboxylic cycle, and has been analyzed only in higher vertebrates, particularly in mammalian livers. There are indications that the ornithine cycle operates with some modifications in a few invertebrates, but there is evidence that urea may also be produced by some other routes. Arginase may function only on exogenous arginine in some ammonotelic and uricotelic animals. The ornithine cycle of the liver exists in teleosts and amphibians but seems to have been lost in birds and uricotelic reptiles. The route of formation of uric acid in birds uses a few enzymes in common with ureogenesis and purine degradation and adds numerous others. Trimethylamine oxide is excreted in quantity by many marine fish; in these it comes largely from their invertebrate food, but the possibility of endogenous origin of some of the excreted trimethylamine oxide has not been thoroughly investigated. Miscellaneous nitrogenous products (guanine, creatine, pterines, and the like) are of varying importance in different groups, and in many animals large portions of the nitrogenous products are unidentified.

Embryonic retention of a biochemical trait is shown in nitrogen excretion patterns. Blowfly larvae excrete ammonia before they excrete uric acid; tadpoles produce ammonia before they produce urea. Chicks, alligators, and snakes appear to excrete urea before uric acid, perhaps by different tissues and from different sources.

Such complex sequences as the ornithine cycle and the synthesis of uric acid from ammonia or purines could hardly have evolved at once. Indeed, most of the steps have other functions, and they have probably been combined in many gradual stages. For example, carbamyl phosphate is used in the synthesis of pyrimidine by bacteria and animals. Some bacteria use part of the ornithine cycle for generating ATP. Arginase and urease are widely found in microorganisms, plants, and animals. Arginine is an important amino acid in proteins, and the enzymes for making it participate also in synthesis of muscle phosphagens. Synthesis of uric acid is closely tied to metabolism of the purines, essential constituents of nucleic acids. Thus the process of nitrogen excretion illustrates well the evolutionary principle that new functions are assumed by existent compounds, furnishing a kind of biochemical preadaptation.

Nitrogen excretion is a labile character. It has changed during the evolution of several groups according to their habitat. The best example of phyletic change in form of nitrogenous products is in the gastropods. The marine teleosts excrete more of their nitrogen as urea than do their fresh-water relatives. However, terrestrial isopods have retained ammonia as their principal nitrogenous product, and thus they resemble aquatic isopods and amphipods; perhaps their lack of ability to excrete less toxic materials has restricted land isopods to moist environments.

Nitrogen excretion in individual animals is also modifiable with diet and osmotic stress. The earthworm *Lumbricus* excretes more urea when fed and more ammonia when starved. The pattern is reversed in *Eisenia*. *Rhodnius* and blowfly larvae give off ammonia immediately after feeding, uric acid later. Lungfish store urea during estivation and excrete ammonia when active. In crocodiles, *Xenopus,* and in at least one snail, changes in nitrogenous products have been noted according to whether they are living in water or in air. The urea excretion by a camel may drop fortyfold on a low nitrogen diet.[80]

Several enzymatic routes may lead to the same nitrogenous product. The enzymes for various products may be present in varying degrees and one product may predominate. The relative amount and activity of a given path have some genetic basis; they also depend on the immediate osmotic and nutritional state. The sequence of steps by which the environment induces changes in the enzymes for nitrogen excretion is totally unknown. Added arginine can induce synthesis of arginase.

Purines may be excreted as such or may be degraded through a series of steps which are similar in many animal groups. There is a tendency for the products of protein and of purine catabolism to be the same and for enzymatic steps to be lost as less degraded products (uric acid, allantoin) are excreted.

150 NITROGEN EXCRETION

REFERENCES

1. *ALBRITTON, E. C., ed., Standard Values in Nutrition and Metabolism. Philadelphia, W. B. Saunders Co., 1954, Table 112.

2. ANDERSON, A. D., and PATON, R. L., J. Exper. Zool. *128*: 443-451, 1955. Uric acid synthesis from purines in insects.

3. BACON, R. F., Philippine J. Sci. *4*: 165, 1909. Excretion by python.

4. BAHL, K. N., Quart. J. Micr. Sci. *85*: 343-390, 1945. Excretion in earthworms.

5. BALDWIN, E., Biochem. J. *29*: 252-262, 1935. Arginase in invertebrates.

6. *BALDWIN, E., Biol. Rev. *11*: 247-268, 1935. Uric acid in relation to distribution of snails.

7. *BALDWIN, E., Chap. 4, 43-61, *in* Comparative Biochemistry. Cambridge University Press, 1939, 107 pp.

8. *BALDWIN, E., Dynamic Aspects of Biochemistry, 3rd ed. New York, Macmillan Co., 1959. Chap. 12-14. Products of protein and purine metabolism.

9. BALDWIN, E., Nature *181*: 1591-1592, 1958; Comp. Biochem. Physiol. *1*: 24-37, 1960. Ureogenesis in elasmobranchs.

10. BENOIT, G. J., and NORRIS, E. R., J. Biol. Chem. *158*: 439-442, 1945. Origin of trimethylamine oxide in salmon.

11. *BESSMAN, S. P., *in* Inorganic Nitrogen Metabolism, edited by D. McElroy and B. Glass. New York, Academic Press, 1955, pp. 408-439. Ammonia metabolism in animals.

12. BROOKBANK, J. W., and WHITELEY, A. H., Biol. Bull. *107*: 57-63, 1954. Urease in sea urchin embryos.

13. BROWN, A. W. A., Biochem. J. *32*: 895-902, 903-912, 1938. Nitrogen metabolism, insect *Lucilia*.

14. BROWN, G. W., and COHEN, P. P., *in* Chemical Basis of Development, edited by W. D. McElroy and B. Glass. New York, Academic Press, 1958, pp. 495-513. Biosynthesis of urea in metamorphosing tadpoles.

15. BRULL, L., and NIZET, E., J. Mar. Biol. Assn. U. K. *32*: 321-328, 329-336, 1953. Nitrogenous constituents in blood and urine of fish *Lophius*.

16. *CHAUVIN, R., Physiologie de l'insecte. Institut National Richerche Agriculture, Paris, 1956, pp. 235-261. Nitrogen excretion in insects.

17. CLARK, H., J. Exp. Biol. *30*: 492-501, 1953. Nitrogen excretion by snake embryos.

18. CLARK, H., and FISCHER, D., J. Exp. Zool. *136*: 1-15, 1957. Nitrogen excretion by developing chick embryos.

19. CLARK, H., FISCHER, D., and FLORIO, B., Anat. Rec. *117*: 524, 1953. Nitrogen excretion by developing chick embryos.

20. CLARK, H., and SISKEN, B. F., J. Exp. Biol. *33*: 384-393, 1956. Nitrogen excretion by snake embryos.

21. COHEN, J. J., *et al.,* Am. J. Physiol. *194*: 229-235, 1958. Trimethylamine oxide in dogfish.

22. COHEN, S., and LEWIS, H. B., J. Biol. Chem. *180*: 79-91, 1949; *184*: 479-484, 1950. Nitrogenous metabolism in *Lumbricus*.

23. COURTOIS, A., C. R. Soc. Biol. *101*: 365-366, 1929. Nitrogenous composition of meconium, Lepidoptera.

24. CUNNINGHAM, B., and KIRK, P. L., J. Cell. Comp. Physiol. *18*: 299-316, 1941. Nitrogen excretion of Paramecium.

25. *DELAUNAY, H., Bull. Sta. Biol. Arcachon *24*: 95-214, 1927; Biol. Rev. *6*: 265-301, 1931; Ann. Physiol. Physicochim. Biol. *10*: 695-724, 1934. Reviews of nitrogen excretion.

26. DEWEY, V. C., HEINRICH, M. R., and KIDDER, G. W., J. Protozool. *4*: 211-219, 1957. Absence of urea cycle in *Tetrahymena*.

27. DRESEL, E. B., and MOYLE, V., J. Exp. Biol. *27*: 210-225, 1950. Nitrogen excretion by amphipods and isopods.

28. DRILHON, A., and FLORENCE, G., Bull. Soc. Chim. Biol. *28*: 160-167, 1946. Nitrogen compounds in blood of insects.

29. EAKIN, R. A., and FISHER, J. R., *in* Chemical Basis of Development, edited by W. D. McElroy and B. Glass. New York, Academic Press, 1958, pp. 514-522. Nitrogen excretion in early chick embryos.

30. *EDNEY, E. B., Water Relations of Terrestrial Arthropods. Cambridge University Press, 1957, 108 pp.

31. FISHER, J. R., and EAKIN, R. E., J. Embryol. Exp. Morph. *5*: 215-224, 1957. Nitrogen excretion by chick embryo.

32. FLORKIN, M., Arch. Int. Physiol. *53*: 117-120, 1943. Ammonia in blood.

33. *FLORKIN, M., L'évolution biochemique. Paris, Masson et Cie, 1944, 210 pp. Translated and edited by S. Morgulis. New York, Academic Press, 1949, 157 pp.

34. FLORKIN, M., and DUCHATEAU, G., Arch. Internat. Physiol. *53*: 267-307, 1943. Evolution of purine metabolism; enzymes of purine breakdown in insects.

35. FLORKIN, M., and FRAPPEZ, G., Arch. Internat. Physiol. *50*: 197-202, 1940. Ammonia in animal bloods.

36. FLORKIN, M., and HONET, R., Arch. Internat. Physiol. *47*: 125-132, 1939. Ammonia in Anodonta blood.

37. FOLIN, O., Am. J. Physiol. *13*: 45-65, 1905. Analyses of human urine.

38. FORSTER, R. P., Am. J. Physiol. *179*: 372-377, 1954. Urea excretion by frog.

39. FRIEDMAN, M., and BYERS, S. O., J. Biol. Chem. *175*: 727-735, 1948. Uric acid excretion, Dalmatian dog.

40. FRUTON, J. S., and SIMMONDS, S., General Biochemistry, 2nd Ed. New York, John Wiley & Sons, 1958. Chapter 33, End products of amino acid metabolism.

41. FUSE, N., Jap. J. Med. Sci. II *1*: 103-110, 1925. Nitrogen in urine of various mammals.

42. GOLDIE, M., Physiol. Zool. *32*: 197-209, 1959. Arginase in chick embryo.

43. GOLDSTEIN, L., and FORSTER, R. P., Fed. Proc. *19*: 359, 1960. Ammonia excretion from gills of sculpin *Myxocephalus*.

44. GOODBODY, I., J. Exp. Biol. *34*: 297-305, 1957. Ammonia excretion, ascidians.

45. GRAFFLIN, A. L., and GOULD, R. G., Biol. Bull. *70*: 16-27, 1936. Nitrogen excretion, trimethylamine oxide, sculpin, flounder.

*Reviews

46. HAMMETT, F. S., J. Biol. Chem. *22*: 551-558, 1915. Urinary nitrogen, cat.

47. *HEIDERMANNS, C., Tabul. Biol. *14*: 209-273, 1937. Uric acid in invertebrate tissues.

48. HEIDERMANNS, C., and KIRCHNER-KÜHN, I., Ztschr. vergl. Physiol. *34*: 166-178, 1952. Urease in *Helix*.

49. HERNANDEZ, T., and COULSON, R. A., Science *119*: 291-292, 1954. Carbonic anhydrase inhibitor on urine pH, alligator.

50. IRREVERRE, F., and TERZIAN, L. A., Science *129*: 1358-1359, 1958. Nitrogen excretion, mosquitoes.

51. *KEILIN, J., Biol. Rev. *34*: 265-296, 1959. Uric acid and guanine excretion.

52. KHAHLIL, F., and HAGGAG, G., J. Exp. Zool. *130*: 423-432, 1955. Nitrogen excretion in turtles.

53. LAL, M. B., and SAXENA, B. B., Nature *170*: 1024, 1952. Uricotelism in a snail.

54. LASKOWSKI, M., *in* The Enzymes, edited by J. B. Sumner and K. Myrback. New York, Academic Press, 1951, Vol. 1, part 2, pp. 946-950. Allantoinase and allantoicase.

55. LOVE, J. K., and LIFSON, N., Am. J. Physiol. *193*: 662-668, 1958. Urea secretion by frog kidney.

56. MILLER, G. E., DANZIG, L. S., and TALBOT, J. H., Am. J. Physiol. *164*: 155-158, 1951. Excretion of uric acid, dogs.

57. MORGULIS, S., J. Biol. Chem. *50*: 52-54, 1922. Uric acid in polychaetes.

58. MOYLE, V., Biochem. J. *44*: 581-584, 1949. Nitrogenous excretion, turtles.

59. MUNRO, A. F., Biochem. J. *54*: 29-36, 1953. Ammonia and urea excretion, developing amphibians.

60. NARDONE, R. M., and WILBER, C. G., Proc. Soc. Exp. Biol. Med. *75*: 559-561, 1950. Nitrogen excretion, *Colpidium*.

61. NASH, G., and FANKHAUSER, G., Science *130*: 714-716, 1959. Nitrogen excretion in developing newts.

62. NEEDHAM, A. E., Nature *178*: 595-596, 1956. Nitrogen output in ecdysis, crustaceans.

63. NEEDHAM, A. E., J. Exp. Biol. *34*: 425-446, 1957. Nitrogen excretion by earthworms.

64. NEEDHAM, A. E., Physiol. Comp. Oecol. *4*: 209-239, 1957. Nitrogen excretion in *Carcinides*.

65. NEEDHAM, J., Biochem. J. *29*: 238-251, 1935. Uricotelism and habitat of gastropods.

66. *NEEDHAM, J., Chemical Embryology. Cambridge University Press, 1931, vol. 2, sec. 9, pp. 1055-1145. Nitrogenous wastes of embryos.

67. NEEDHAM, J., Biol. Rev. *13*: 224-251, 1938. Nitrogen excretion in relation to environment.

68. NORRIS, E. R., and BENOIT, G., J. Biol. Chem. *158*: 433-438, 1945. Trimethylamine oxide in marine animals.

69. PETERS, J. P., and VAN SLYKE, D. D., Quantitative Clinical Chemistry. Baltimore, Williams & Wilkins, 1946, vol. 1. Normal values of nitrogen.

70. POISSON, R., and RAZET, P., C. R. Acad. Sci. *234*: 1804-1806, 1952; *237*: 1362-1363, 1953. Nitrogen excretion by insects.

71. RATNER, S., Fed. Proc. *8*: 603-609, 1949; Adv. Enzymol. *15*: 319-387, 1954. Details of the ornithine cycle.

72. RATNER, S., and PETRAK, B., J. Biol. Chem. *191*: 693-705, 1951; *200*: 161-174, 1953; *204*: 95-113, 1953. Details of the ornithine cycle.

73. RAZET, P., C. R. Acad. Sci. *234*: 2566-2568, 1952; *236*: 1304-1306, 1953. Uricolytic enzymes in insects.

74. RECTOR, F. C., SELDIN, D. W., ROBERTS, A. D., and COPENHAVER, J. H., Am. J. Physiol. *179*: 353-358, 1954. Ammonia excretion and urine acidification.

75. RICHTERICH, R., GOLDSTEIN, L., and DEARBORN, E. H., Am. J. Physiol. *192*: 392-400, 1958. Ammonia excretion in mammals.

76. ROEDER, M., J. Cell. Comp. Physiol. *50*: 241-248, 1957. Induction of arginase, chick embryo.

77. ROGERS, W. P., Australian J. Sci. Res. Ser. B, *5*: 210-222, 1952; Exp. Parasitol. *4*: 21-28, 1955. Nitrogen excretion by parasitic nematodes.

78. SCHMIDT-NIELSEN, B., Am. J. Physiol. *170*: 45-56, 1952. Urea excretion, kangaroo rat.

79. SCHMIDT-NIELSEN, B., and OSAKI, H., Am. J. Physiol. *193*: 657-661, 1958. Nitrogen excretion in relation to diet, sheep.

80. SCHMIDT-NIELSEN, B., SCHMIDT-NIELSEN, K., HOUPT, T. R., and JARNUM, S. A., Am. J. Physiol. *188*: 477-484, 1957. Urea excretion in camel.

81. SCHMIDT-NIELSEN, B., *et al.*, Am. J. Physiol. *194*: 221-228, 1958. Nitrogen excretion in relation to diet, sheep.

82. SEAMAN, G. R., J. Protozool. *1*: 207-210, 1954. Urea formation, *Tetrahymena*.

83. SMITH, H. W., J. Biol. Chem. *81*: 727-742, 1929; J. Biol. Chem. *88*: 97-130, 1930. Nitrogen excretion in fish, lungfish.

84. SMITH, H. W., and SILVETTE, H., J. Biol. Chem. *78*: 409-411, 1928. Nitrogen excretion, camels.

85. SONNE, J., J. Biol. Chem. *173*: 69-81, 1949. Nitrogen atom precursors in purines.

86. SONNE, J., *et al.*, J. Biol. Chem. *220*: 369-378, 1956. Nitrogen atom precursors in purines.

87. SPITZER, J. M., Zool. Jahrb., Abt. allg. Zool. Physiol. *57*: 457-496, 1937. Nitrogen excretion and distribution of molluscs.

88. STADDON, B. W., J. Exp. Biol. *32*: 84-94, 1955; *36*: 566-574, 1959. Ammonia excretion, neuropteran larva, Odonata larvae.

89. STRUNK, C., Zool. Jahrb., Abt. allg. Zool. Physiol. *52*: 216-222, 1932. Urea, uric acid in coelomic fluid, Arenicola.

90. TERZIAN, L. A., IRREVERRE, F., and STAHLER, N., J. Insect Physiol. *1*: 221-228, 1957. Nitrogen excretion, adult *Aedes*.

91. UMBREIT, W. W., Metabolic Maps, Minneapolis, Burgess Publishing Co., 1952, p. 232.

92. UNDERHAY, E. E., and BALDWIN, E., Biochem. J. *61*: 544-547, 1955. Nitrogen excretion, tadpoles of *Xenopus*.

93. WATERHOUSE, D. F., Australian J. Sci. Res. Ser. B, *3*: 76-112, 1951. Excretion, malpighian tubules, *Lucilia* larvae.

94. WEESE, A. O., Science *46*: 517-518, 1917. Urinary nitrogen, Phrynosoma.

95. *WHITE, A., HANDLER, P., SMITH, E. L., and STETTIN, D., Principles of Biochemistry, New York, McGraw-Hill Book Co., 1954. Chapters 19 and 20.

96. WHITE, H. L., and ROLF, D., Am. J. Physiol. *169*: 174-179, 1952. Ammonia excretion, mammals.

97. WIDDOWSON, E. M., DICKERSON, J. W. T., and McCANCE, R. A., Biochem. J. *69*: 421-424, 1958. Nitrogen excretion, newborn mammals.

98. WIGGLESWORTH, V. B., J. Exp. Biol. *8*: 411-445, 1931. Uric acid in urine of *Rhodnius*.

99. *WIGGLESWORTH, V. B., Principles of Insect Physiology. London, Methuen & Co., 1939, Chap. 12.

100. WILBER, C. G., J. Cell. Comp. Physiol. *31*: 107-109, 1948. Uric acid in body fluids of marine invertebrate animals.

101. WILEY, F. H., and LEWIS, H. B., Am. J. Physiol. *81*: 692-695, 1927. Nitrogenous excretion in turtle.

102. WOLFSON, W. O., COHN, C., and SHORE, C., J. Exp. Med. *92*: 121-128, 1950. Uric acid secretion, Dalmatian dog.

103. YUNGHERR, I., and MATTERSON, L. D., Proc. 48th Annual Meeting, U. S. Livestock Sanitary Association, 1944, pp. 185-196. Chicken uric acid.

Chapter 7

OXYGEN: RESPIRATION AND METABOLISM

INTRODUCTION

Oxygen is necessary to provide energy for life processes, and the availability of oxygen imposes limits on distribution and survival of animals. Some microorganisms obtain energy exclusively by nonoxidative means, but all higher animals and plants are aerobic, and the few parasites which now can live without oxygen have acquired the ability secondarily.

The terms *respiration* and *metabolism* have several meanings. External respiration refers to those mechanisms by which oxygen is brought into and CO_2 is expelled from the organism; internal respiration or intermediary metabolism refers to the sum of enzymatic reactions, both oxidative and nonoxidative, by which energy is made available for biological work. Metabolism is expressed in terms of oxygen consumed, heat produced, or carbon dioxide liberated.

The early phases of chemical evolution occurred under anaerobic conditions when the earth had a reducing atmosphere. It is probable that the transfer of energy from organic substrates in a stepwise fashion by adenosine triphosphate (ATP) and the enzymes catalyzing anaerobic metabolism, as in glycolysis and fermentation, evolved very early. Some oxygen may have been released from water by photochemical reactions catalyzed by metalloporphyrins, but all of the oxygen in the earth's present atmosphere has come from photosynthesis. The transition from reducing to oxidizing atmosphere occurred over a long period, some 2 billion years ago. The rate of photosynthesis is such that the atmospheric oxygen could all be formed in 2000 years. Aerobic metabolism followed anaerobic and is less universal and more efficient; both must have appeared before there was differentiation of organisms.[10, 200]

EXTERNAL RESPIRATION

Availability of Oxygen. Oxygen which enters across a respiratory surface or into cells where it is used must diffuse *via* an aqueous solution; its availability depends on the concentration immediately outside the organism. The maximum concentration is limited by air, of which oxygen comprises 20.95 per cent (dry air), or exerts 159 mm Hg partial pressure at sea level. The concentration available decreases at high altitudes; normally sea water is nearly in equilibrium with air, and in warm surface waters, both fresh and salt, where there is much photosynthesis, the oxygen concentration may exceed air saturation. At the bottom of ponds and lakes and at certain oceanic depths, oxygen is often scarce. Also the environment of intestinal parasites may be nearly free of oxygen. Concentrations of oxygen are given in per cent or partial pressure of the oxygen in a gas mixture such as air; in milliliters, milligrams, or mols dissolved in a liter of liquid; or, better, the partial pressure in atmospheres (or mm Hg) to which the amount of dissolved oxygen corresponds. The amount of gas corrected to STP dissolved in water is the product of the Bunsen solubility coefficient (α) times the per cent of an atmosphere of the gas in equilibrium with the water.

$$\text{ml } O_2/l = \alpha \left(\frac{\text{atm } O_2}{100} \right)$$

The solubility coefficient decreases with rising temperature and increasing salinity as follows:[158]

Temp. α_{H_2O}	O_2 content in Water (air saturation)	O_2 content: Sea Water (34.96 0/00) (air saturation)
5° C. 0.44	9.22 ml O_2/l (13.2 mg)	6.89 ml O_2/l (9.8 mg)
20° C. 0.031	6.51 ml O_2/l (9.4 mg)	5.05 ml O_2/l (7.8 mg)

153

The diffusion coefficient D (diffusivity) for oxygen is derived from Fick's diffusion equation: $\frac{dv}{dt} = - AD \frac{dc}{dx}$ which states that the amount diffusing in a given time equals the diffusion coefficient D times the area times the concentration gradient over distance x. The units of D are ml/cm^2/cm length/$C_1 - C_2$/ time, which reduces to cm^{2}time^{-1}. The coefficient D increases about 3 per cent per °C rise in temperature. Krogh introduced a diffusion constant K which uses the difference in partial pressure of gas per unit length of liquid phase instead of concentration gradient. Its dimensions are ml/cm^2/cm/atm pressure/time, which reduces to cm^{2}time^{-1} atm. Krogh's K is actually the product of the diffusion coefficient D times the solubility coefficient α. Solubility of oxygen decreases about 1.6 per cent per °C rise, in the range 16 to 25°C; hence the diffusion constant of Krogh increases about 1.4 per cent per °C.[191] At 20°C in water $D_{oxygen} = 2 \times 10^{-5}$ cm^2/sec and $K_{oxygen} = 3.4 \times 10^{-5}$ cm^2/min atm. Diffusion constants (K) given by Krogh for oxygen at 20°C follow:[158]

air	11.0	muscle	0.000014
water	0.000034	chitin	0.000013

It is to be noted that diffusion of oxygen in air is 3,000,000 times what it is in water.[87] Carbon dioxide is twenty-eight times more soluble in water at 20°C than is oxygen; it also forms a hydrate (H_2CO_3) which dissociates as a weak acid; its measured diffusion constant in water is about twenty-five times greater than that of oxygen.[158]

Modes of External Respiration. *Direct Diffusion.* All cell surfaces are permeable to oxygen, even those impermeable to water. In those animals with oxygen transport systems in body fluids certain epithelia have become specialized for external respiration. Where no transport system exists oxygen enters directly by diffusion from the medium into cells where it is used. For a metabolizing organism, availability is limited by the length of the diffusion path. The limiting distance through which oxygen can be supplied at known gradients and rates of use has been calculated for various shapes of cell.[111, 123] For a sphere having $Po_2 = O$ mm Hg only at the center

$$C_o = \frac{A\,r^2}{6\,K}$$

where C_0 is the required oxygen pressure outside the sphere, A the oxygen consumption in ml O_2 per gm per minute, r the radius of the sphere, and K the diffusion constant. In organisms with fairly high metabolic rates, diffusion suffices if the tissue is no more than 1 mm in thickness. However, in animals with tissues more than 0.5 mm distant from an oxygen supply, some supplementary transporting system is necessary unless metabolism is very low.[158]

In Protozoa, Porifera, Coelenterata, many Platyhelminthes, Nematoda, Rotifera, some Annelida, Ectoprocta, and Endoprocta, oxygen is obtained by diffusion directly from the surrounding water. There may be channels through which water passes, the oxygen may diffuse through several cell layers, and transport may be facilitated by cytoplasmic streaming. In animals with circulatory systems the distance of a metabolizing cell from a blood capillary or sinus is limited by the diffusion path.

Integument. Since all cells are permeable to oxygen it can be said that all multicellular animals have some cutaneous respiration. Krogh has shown that integumentary gas exchange is greater than commonly supposed. In many free-living embryos the circulatory system develops well before special organs of respiration, and the blood is oxygenated at the surface. Special respiratory structures occur in many free-swimming embryos.

In most annelids (oligochaetes, hirudineans, some polychaetes) the integument is highly vascular and provides the principal route of exchange. Respiration is integumentary in some sipunculids, some aquatic insects, and numerous other invertebrates. In eels Krogh found cutaneous respiration to provide some 60 per cent of the total oxygen need, and aquatic pulmonate snails obtain about equal amounts of oxygen from water and from air.[158] Blowfly larvae obtain 2.5 to 10 per cent of their oxygen cutaneously.[41, 92]

In frogs the oxygen uptake by the skin is some 50 ml/kg/hr throughout the year, while the uptake by the lungs increases during the spring and summer and is zero during winter hibernation. Carbon dioxide elimination by the skin exceeds that by the lungs at all times of the year, even in midsummer, when it may be 2.2 times the lung loss[69, 158] (Fig. 36). Animals which rely to any extent on integumentary respiration have some means of keeping the body surface moist. Carbon dioxide loss by way of the skin has been reported as 85 per cent of that lost by lungs in a lizard, 1 per cent in man,[86] 7.6 per cent in a rabbit.[157] Much of the exchange from skin in mammals may be due to skin metabolism. In larvae of the fly *Phormia* cutaneous respiration is normally 2.5 per cent of the total.[41]

Gills. Several types of well-vascularized respiratory appendages fall into the category of gills. They are usually aquatic but may be aerial. They are either ciliated and motile or are located in currents of water flow. In fish the countercurrent principle operates (see p. 44); blood in the capillaries flows in opposite direction to water outside the gill surface; this provides rapid oxygen uptake and almost complete saturation as the blood leaves the gill filaments.[158]

Polychaetes have various gill structures, such as parapodia (*Nereis*), gills (*Arenicola*), and branchial tufts (Terebellidae and most Sabellidae), which provide for part of the oxygen uptake. In echinoderms dermal branchiae, or papulae, supplement the tube feet through which most respiratory exchange occurs. The papulae are evaginations of the body wall which bring the slowly moving coelomic fluid in close association with the cilia-stirred external sea water. In molluscan and ascidian gills an orderly flow pattern is provided by rows of cilia (Chapter 16).

Aquatic Crustacea have gills which are usually ventilated by the paddle-like movements of special appendages such as the scaphognathites. Pearse[202] described a series of crabs with increasing ability to remain on land and corresponding reduction of gills. For example, the number of gills in two low tide crabs was 26; in high intertidal species it was 18, and in a beach crab, 12. In the grapsoid land crabs there is not only a reduction in number and size of gills, but branchial tufts are present—vascularized membranous projections into the branchial cavity. Active aquatic crabs have a larger gill area (1367 mm^2/gm in *Callinectes*) than sluggish crabs (748 mm^2/gm in *Libinia*); intertidal crabs have more gill area (624 mm^2/gm in *Uca*) than land crabs (325 mm^2/gm in *Ocypode*).[105] *Birgus* and *Ocypode* need merely moisten their branchial tufts and reduced gills occasionally to survive well on land. In isopods the endopodites of abdominal appendages are essentially gills, (aquatic *Asellus*), and in some terrestrial forms (*Ligia, Oniscus*) these are covered and serve as air-breathing gills or they may lead to trachea-like structures (*Porcellio*).

Numerous aquatic insects have gills through which oxygen passes directly to the profusely branched tracheae. Tracheal gills occur in nymphs of Odonata, Plecoptera, Trichoptera, and Ephemeridae and in larvae of a few beetles. In tube-dwelling trichopteran larvae there are ventilating movements, and the rectal tracheal gills of dragonfly nymphs present an extensive surface for aeration. Damsel-fly nymphs (*Enallagma*) living at low oxygen concentrations have functional tracheal gills,[205] but caddis-fly larvae (*Macronema*) do not show reduced oxygen consumption when their gills are removed. The role of anal papillae of aquatic dipteran larvae which function in ion absorption rather than in respiration has been discussed (Chapter 2).

The gills of cyclostomes and fish are usually covered and are ventilated by breathing movements of mouth and operculum; some fish gills also make limited movements. Mackerel keep the mouth open while swim-

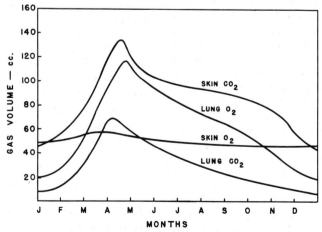

FIGURE 36.   Oxygen and carbon dioxide exchange through the skin and lungs of the frog *Rana temporaria* measured simultaneously throughout the year. (After Dolk, H. E., and Postma, N.: Ztschr. vergl. Physiol., vol. 5.)

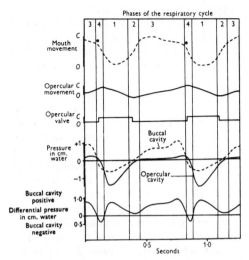

FIGURE 37. Mouth and opercular movement and pressure in buccal and opercular cavities during two respiratory cycles of the roach, *Leuciscus rutilus*. O indicates mouth open and C mouth closed. (From Hughes, G. M., and Shelton, G.: J. Exp. Biol. vol. 35.)

ming, and in experimental conditions those which were swimming had blood 85 per cent saturated with oxygen; the blood of stationary fish was only 11 per cent saturated.[107] Sluggish bottom-dwelling fish have relatively less gill surface than fast pelagic ones.[105] Some swamp teleosts are adapted for breathing air and, like land crabs, they have reduced gill surfaces and modified branchial chambers as *Electrophorus,* or have branchial tufts, as *Anabas.* In one fish, *Lepidosiren,* the gills hypertrophy in the male during the period of care of the young in a nest burrow. The gills of amphibians are functional throughout life in aquatic urodeles, in larvae only of others. In teleosts (tench, roach, and trout) the gills separate buccal from branchial cavities; pressure in the buccal cavity precedes a slight suction in the branchial cavity[127] (Fig. 37). The suction pump is most important for bottom-dwelling species. A similar sequence of pumps occurs in dogfish and skates, but a leopard shark makes no respiratory movements when swimming.[127]

Lungs. A variety of structures are classed as lungs; in all of them the respiratory surface is folded into the body, and virtually all lungs are parts of or are outgrowths from the alimentary tract. Most lungs are aerial, a few are water filled; ventilation and diffusion lungs are distinguished according to the presence or absence of mechanisms for air renewal.

WATER-LUNGS. Among the invertebrates several dissimilar structures serve as respiratory cavities which are alternately filled with or emptied of water. The respiratory trees of holothurians are filled with sea water by cloacal pumping and contractions of the trees themselves, and gas exchanges with the coelomic fluid. Diverticula from the hindgut of the gephyrean worm *Urechis* are filled by pumping action of the cloaca, and respiratory exchange is facilitated by contraction waves in the hindgut.

AIR-LUNGS. All air-lungs present moist surfaces across which oxygen diffuses and from which water can evaporate; hence all are protected against evaporation, and open by small openings to the exterior.

1. Diffusion lungs. Many arachnids, spiders and scorpions have book lungs which open to the exterior by a spiracle and which contain tubes which serve to aerate the blood. An isopod, *Porcellio,* a chilopod *Scutigera,* and the tropical snails Janellidae have a vestibulum into which tubes analogous to tracheae open. Diffusion lungs are best known in pulmonate snails where the mantle cavity is modified as a lung which opens to the exterior by a pneumostome which can be opened or closed according to respiratory conditions. Diffusion is adequate for gas exchange even with gradients of only 1 to 2 mm Hg partial pressure of oxygen.[158] The exposed surface is relatively large, the animals are usually small, and in general the metabolic requirements are low.

2. Gas bladders and lungs of fish. There are two types of gas bladder, the open in physostome teleosts and the closed in the physoclistous fish. The physostomes can gulp air into their bladder, and both types can secrete gas into the bladder. The gas bladder is primarily a hydrostatic organ, but in some fish it contains much oxygen, which can be used in hypoxic conditions. Secretion of gas into the bladder will be discussed on page 189. In lungfish (dipnoans) the lung arises from the floor of the pharynx and may not be homologous with the gas bladder of teleosts. Dipnoans use the lung as the main respiratory organ during long periods out of water.

3. Ventilation lungs. (a) Alimentary mucosa. A number of tropical fish (and also a number from the temperate zone) which inhabit water low in oxygen swallow air and respire by means of the intestinal or gastric mucosa. A variety of respiratory adaptations —suprabranchial air chambers, pharyngeal

and opercular chambers—of tropical fresh-water fish have been described.[194]

b. Alveolar lungs. Lungs of terrestrial vertebrates present a series from the unialveolar lung of the urodele *Proteus*, through amphibians with partitioning septa, to the lungs of birds and mammals with lobules of alveoli. This series increases in respiratory surface and vascularity. Lungs are highly elastic and have smooth muscle fibers in the bronchioles and in their minute subdivisions. The oxygen pressure gradient across the epithelium of a ventilated lung is relatively steep. Two kinds of ventilation are found, a positive-pressure type in which air is forced into the lung by swallowing or buccal movements (as in the frog),[49] and a negative-pressure system in which air is drawn in by increasing the space around the lungs (as in man). During eupnea (normal breathing) in mammals, inspiration is active and expiration largely passive, but some animals—birds and turtles—effect both movements by active muscular contraction. The throat movements of turtles formerly thought to be respiratory are now considered to be olfactory.[188]

Birds have extensive air sacs which are devoid of respiratory epithelium but which may have three or four times the volume of the lungs and which lie above and behind the lungs.[291] These permit a two-way flushing of the lungs so that there is gas exchange during both inspiration and exhalation. Breathing may be increased during flight by synchronization of wing and respiratory movements.

Tracheae. Tracheal respiration carries air directly to the metabolizing cells without blood. Tracheae are found in insects, and also in onychophorans, some spiders, isopods, diplopods, and chilopods. In spiders the distinction between tracheae and lung tubes is not sharp. Tracheal respiration of insects has been described in detail by Wigglesworth[282] and Edwards.[75] Each trachea has an outer epithelium continuous with the hypodermis and an intima continuous with the cuticle which contains radial, spiral, or beadlike taenidia for support. Tracheae usually open by spiracles; some, however, receive oxygen from gills. Single spiracles may serve for both inspiration and expiration, but more usually there are numerous spiracles, some of them (commonly the anterior ones) for inflow and others for outflow of air. The locust *Chortophaga viridifasciata* circulates some 0.222 ml air/gm/min at 28°C.[189] Since the tracheal system combines respiratory with circulatory functions the vital capacity is high, 60 mm^3/

gm in *Dytiscus*.[158] The tracheae branch extensively and open into small tracheoles which may be fluid filled; each tracheole is surrounded by a tracheal cell at its origin as a sort of valve. Tracheoles may penetrate into tissue cells.

Ventilation is accomplished by contraction of body-wall muscles, usually abdominal, and spiracles can be closed or opened according to need. Spiracular movements can occur independently of air pumping. In some insects, the flea for example, spiracles remain partially open all the time. Expiration is an active process, inspiration either active or passive. Many insects have air sacs which, during the interval between inspiration and expiration, build up by compression considerable intratracheal pressure. Valvular structures direct air flow, but at times the direction of flow can reverse.

Aquatic insects have a variety of respiratory adaptations. Cutaneous, rectal, and gill respiration have already been mentioned. Numerous dipteran and coleopteran larvae pierce weed stems and use the contained gases. Others, like *Notonecta* and *Dytiscus*, hold a bubble of air by the aid of hydrofuge hairs (often under the elytra), and the spiracles open into it. As oxygen is used from the bubble, more diffuses in from the water; nitrogen diffuses out only when its partial pressure is greater than the nitrogen pressure in the water. Hence the bubble can transfer many times its volume of oxygen and can last for many hours without renewal.[224, 263, 264] Other aquatic Hemiptera (especially *Amphelocheirus*) and Coleoptera have a dense hair mat with as many as 2.5×10^8 hairs/cm^2. This surface is nonwettable and holds a very thin gas layer or plastron which serves as a permanent physical gill through which oxygen diffuses. The plastron insects, although air-breathing, never need to come to the surface.[263, 264]

OXYGEN CONSUMPTION BY INTACT ANIMALS; MODIFYING AGENTS

Biological literature gives many values of oxygen consumption by various animals, yet metabolic levels are meaningful only for the particular conditions of measurement. Rate of oxygen consumption is influenced by activity, temperature, nutrition, body size, stage in life cycle, season, and time of day, as well as by previous oxygen experience and genetic background. Although they are subject to many necessary qualifications, a few selected values of rates of oxygen consumption measured under relatively normal physiological conditions are useful as a basis for later discussion of modifying factors (Table 24). Detailed tables are found in reference 196 and in the first edition of this book.

Activity. One of the intrinsic modifiers of O_2 consumption most difficult to control is muscular and other activity. By definition, "basal" metabolism represents the oxygen consumption for maintenance only. In man this is measured in a postabsorptive state, in a relaxed but awake subject, usually in mid-morning. For measurements on animals, slight movements are minimized by darkness, quiet, and habituation to the metabolism chamber. Frequently measurements are made

TABLE 24.   OXYGEN CONSUMPTION UNDER APPROXIMATELY NORMAL PHYSIOLOGICAL CONDITIONS

Animals	Body weight (gm)	Oxygen consumption (ml O_2/gm wet wt/hr)	Temperature °C
Mammals			
long tailed shrew[203]	3.6	10.6 (basal) 15.6 (24-hr fed)	
short tailed shrew[203]	21.2	3.4 5.2 (24-hr fed)	
house mouse[203]	17	1.7 3.5 (24-hr fed)	
red backed mouse[193]	21.7	2.27	
laboratory mouse[183]	20	1.69	
laboratory rat[151]	2.82	0.88	
ground squirrel[145]	227	0.95	
guinea pig[193]	460	0.76	
Erinaceus[145]	684	0.738	
Arctomys[145]	1868	0.483	
cat[15]	3000	0.446	
dog[183]	20,000	0.360	
sheep[151]	46,800	0.250	
woman[151]	57,900	0.204	
cow[151]	300,000	0.124	
Birds			
hummingbird[204]	3.8	10.7 (rest) 85 (active)	
swallow[204]	22	6 (active)	
widow bird[204]	9	7 (rest)	
pigeon[291]		1.5 (rest) 42 (active)	
Poikilothermic vertebrates			
trout (Salvelinus)[104]		0.349	15
scup[107]		0.064	20
puffer[107]		0.061	20
toadfish[107]		0.038	20
loach[135]		0.036	15
turtle[14]	3000-4000	0.088	16
alligator[14]	53,000	0.0747	16
rattlesnake[14]	2000-3000	0.068	16
frog[15]	35	0.056	16
Insects			
Chironomus larvae[270]		0.192	
Prodiamessa larvae[109]		0.4-0.6	
Tenebrio larvae		0.182	12
Haemonis (aquatic beetles)[263, 264]		0.381	
Schistocerca (locust)[159]		0.63 (rest) 15 (flight)	
Calliphora adults[262]		1.7	
Various butterflies[290]		0.4-0.7 (rest)	
Crustaceans			
Uca pugilator[75]		0.05	20
Emerita[76]		0.11	20
Homarus[29]		0.50	15
Cambarus[206]		0.10	
Molluscs			
Helicella[149] ⎫	170	0.186	23
Zebrina[149] ⎬snails		0.052	23
Limnea[47] ⎭		0.0114	
Pecten[61]		0.07	20
oysters[154]		0.006	10
Anodonta[60]		0.002	
Mytilus[223]		0.055	

TABLE 24—(Continued)

Animals	Body weight (gm)	Oxygen consumption (ml O_2/gm wet wt/hr)	Temperature °C
Worms			
Nippostrongylus[222]		1.3	
Rotylenchus (nematode)[199]		0.66	
Ascaris[213]		0.50	
Urechis (echiuroid)[117]		0.012	
Enchytraeus[160]		0.03	
Chaetopterus		0.008	
Arenicola[60]		0.031	
Protozoans	Body volume (µl)		
Trypanosoma[32] (rhodesiense)		60.0	
Bresslaua[239]	0.015	7.3	
Tetrahymena[9]		2.85	
Paramecium[129]	0.6	1.3	
Pelomyxa[294]	10.0	0.5	

on curarized or anesthetized animals, but muscle tone varies with level of anesthesia. "Standard" metabolism refers to oxygen consumption measured with minimal motor activity. More constant results are frequently obtained by measuring metabolism at a fixed level of forced activity—swimming, running, flying—which gives at maximum maintained level the "activity" metabolism. When O_2 consumption is measured at different O_2 pressures, the activity metabolism remains constant down to an incipient limiting level; the standard metabolism is constant down to a lower O_2 pressure, which is the level at which there can be no excess activity and below which even the needs of maintenance cannot be met.[94, 95] Actual measurements usually fall between standard and activity metabolism, and true basal conditions are probably never attained, even in measurements on man. Moreover, there is evidence, to be considered later, that activity and rest metabolism may go via different enzymatic paths in many cells.

The increase in oxygen consumption depends on the level of exercise. In man, consumption in exercise may be fifteen to twenty times the resting value; in insects, flight may cause a fiftyfold to two hundredfold increase; active metabolism of fish (trout) may be four times the standard metabolism.[94, 95] Bees and butterflies have been shown to consume 90 l O_2/kg/hr during sustained flight, or fifteen times the bee's body volume in oxygen (ninety times body volume of air) every minute.[158] A series of butterflies consumed 0.4 to 0.7 ml O_2/gm/hr at rest, 40 to 100 ml/gm/hr in flight.[290] In Drosophila the oxygen consumption increased from 28 at rest to 350 mm³/gm/min (at 11,000 wing beats per minute).[46] A desert locust, Schistocerca gregaria, consumed 0.63 ml O_2/gm/hr at rest and 10 to 30 ml O_2/gm/hr in flight.[159] After a period of exercise most animals pay off an accumulated oxygen debt (p. 177). Insects like Drosophila, which metabolize only carbohydrate in activity, accumulate small debts which are paid within a minute or two. In man the contribution of muscle tissue may increase from 20 per cent in basal condition to 80 per cent in exercise.[118]

Active fish such as darters have several times higher metabolic rates than sluggish fish. The activity difference is reflected at the tissue level; excised brain of active fish such as menhaden and mullet had an oxygen consumption (µl O_2/gm wet/min) of 11 to 14; for brain from less active sea bass and croaker it was 7.7 to 9.7, and from sluggish bottom fish, flounder and toadfish, 5.6 to 6.9.[267, 269] Respiration of some dividing cells—Tetrahymena, sea-urchin eggs[293]—shows an increase during the first half of each mitotic step, with a leveling and decrease later. Mytilus edulis consume twice as much oxygen during the active season, June and July, as in the winter, November to January.[39] Measurements on animals in group stimulation frequently give different results from measurements on separate individuals.

Nonmuscular activity is also reflected in metabolic increase. Fresh-water limpets have enhanced metabolism during the reproductive season.[17] Activity is a factor which is difficult to control but which must be recognized in all metabolic measurements.

Rhythmic Fluctuations in Metabolic Rate. Under conditions of controlled temperature, illumination, humidity, and chemical content of medium, metabolic rate fluctuates, often to very substantial degrees, as a function of time. Fluctuations in metabolism, with time, under controlled conditions, contain the same periods as those of the external physical environment. Organisms, in their natural physical environments, possess adaptively adjusted rhythms of their various activities which are reflected in metabolic rate changes. Since their periodic patterns tend to persist even in constant conditions in the laboratory, metabolic rate becomes a function of time in these recurring patterns. The common periods for these persistent recurring patterns of biological activity are the solar day, the lunar day, the synodic month, and the year. Numerous examples of these may be found in reviews.[108, 276] These rhythms appear normally to depend upon the external cycles of such common factors as light, temperature, and ocean tides for establishing their phase relationships relative to the actual times of day, lunar day, phase of moon, and, through photoperiod, time of year, but once the phases are adjusted the actual period lengths of the recurring patterns are independent of these rhythmic changes in light and temperature. Solar and lunar rhythms of metabolism appear to persist indefinitely, with high mean precision in period length, under constant conditions in the laboratory. The lengths of the periods are independent of temperature. In the fiddler crab, *Uca,* for example, O_2 consumption in a persistent daily cycle is 30 to 50 per cent higher at about 6 A.M. than at about 6 P.M., and in a lunar-day cycle it is 30 to 50 per cent higher when the moon is at either its highest or lowest altitude than when it is at the horizon.[276] In constant conditions potato plants not only display indefinitely both significant solar-day and lunar-day periodicity in O_2 consumption, with a synodic monthly periodicity a consequence of their mutual periodic reinforcement, but they display also synodic monthly and annual rhythms of mean daily rate. O_2 consumption is about 20 per cent higher at the third quarter of the moon than at new moon, and about 80 per cent higher in April and May than in October and November.[38]

Metabolic rate fluctuations of organisms, even in constant conditions of ambient temperature and pressure, also reflect importantly and in characteristic manners the large random, weather-related changes in outdoor atmospheric temperature and pressure, though the mediators for these relationships remain to be discovered.[36, 38]

Sex. Metabolic differences between the sexes are widespread and are not always in the same direction. Human males at every age have a higher rate of oxygen consumption than females, and the difference becomes more marked with increasing age; however, the difference disappears when oxygen consumption is calculated for fat-free females.[67] The male housefly *Musca domestica* has a higher O_2 consumption than the female, but in the reproductive phase the female increases metabolism.[75] The O_2 consumption of the male adult silkworm is three times that of the female at high temperature, but this difference diminishes at low temperatures. A male waxmoth, *Galleria,* consumes more O_2 during the first three-fourths of pupal development; the female consumes more than the male later.[58] In *Daphnia,* likewise, the male metabolizes more in early development, and not later. In *Tribolium,* metabolism of the female is greater. Excised muscles of male cockroaches *Periplaneta* consume five times more oxygen at 25°C than do muscles from females.[11] Sex differences in metabolism may represent differences in relative amounts of active tissues; they may result from different muscle tone, and they certainly reflect hormonal effects.

Nutrition. Animals with adequate glycogen and fat reserves maintain a fairly constant level of standard metabolism during a prolonged fast. However, where there are scanty reserves, as in many adult insects and in birds, the metabolism is more dependent on the food intake. Endogenous metabolism of tissues is consistently lower than the metabolism when organic substrates are supplied.

The energy production varies with the nature of the food metabolized, and the caloric value of a liter of oxygen also depends on the food. The respiratory quotient (R.Q.), or ratio of CO_2 produced to O_2 consumed, varies with the metabolite. Absolute values depend on chemical variations, particularly for proteins and fats, but average textbook values follow:

	Carbohydrate	Fat	Protein
Cal/gm	4.199	9.5	4.19
l O_2/gm	0.82	2.03	0.97
l CO_2/gm	0.82	1.43	0.78
R.Q.	1	0.71	0.80
Cal/l O_2	5.0	4.7	4.5

For an R.Q. of 0.75, the caloric value of oxygen is 4.74 Cal/l O_2. Limitations on interpretation of R.Q. will be given on page 186. The ciliate *Tetrahymena* consumes 16 mm³ O_2/mg dry wt/hr without peptone substrate and 77 with it. The flagellate *Astasia* consumed twenty times more oxygen in the presence of acetate than without it. Some proteins increase metabolism out of proportion to their caloric value, that is, they have a specific dynamic action. It must be concluded that the presence or absence of food as well as the kind of food makes considerable difference to values of oxygen consumption.

Body Size. The rate of oxygen consumption is sometimes given per animal, usually per gram or kilogram of body weight (wet or dry), rarely per unit of nitrogen content, and often as some exponential function of body weight. Qo_2 refers to ml O_2 (at STP) consumed/gm dry wt/hr. When large and small adults of a species or when different sized species of the same general type of animal are compared, it is found that the total metabolism of larger animals is higher but that the metabolic rate of the small exceeds that of the large. In general, metabolism is more uniform when expressed as a power function of body size, and many papers have discussed what measure of body size gives most consistency and meaning.[15, 152] If M = total metabolism or O_2 consumed per hour or day, and W = body weight,

then $\quad M = K W^b$

and $\log M = b \log W + \log K$.

The constant b is obtained from the slope of a plot of log oxygen consumption against log weight and K from the Y intercept. For rate of oxygen consumption

$$\log \frac{M}{W} = (b - 1) \log W + \log K.$$

The constant K gives the position of the curve on the metabolism axis and for mammals it has a numerical value of 10 to 12. The constant b gives the rate at which O_2 consumption changes with size; if metabolism is proportional to weight, b = 1; actually b is usually less than 1.0 (Fig. 38). This means that in similar species or during growth, metabolism increases less than body mass. Similar allometry applies to appendage lengths and to many morphological characters.

Body surface follows the same exponential function, and in mammals surface area is given by a constant times $W^{0.66}$. Oxygen consumption in mammals is nearly constant when expressed per $W^{0.73}$. It has been argued that O_2 consumption is closely correlated with surface area because of the greater heat dissipation in small mammals, that is, if a whale produced as much heat per gram as a mouse, its interior temperature would approach the boiling point. This is an over-

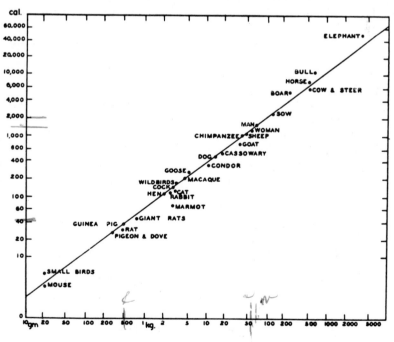

FIGURE 38. Double logarithmic plot of average total heat production and average body weight of birds and mammals. (From Benedict, F. G.: Carnegie Inst. Washington Publ. No. 503.)

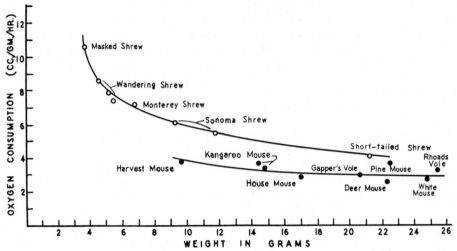

FIGURE 39.   Oxygen consumption of small mammals as a function of body weight. (After Pearson, O. P.: Science, vol. 108.)

simplification in that heat is lost by lungs and other avenues; some birds and mammals function with much of their body surface at very low temperature; body temperature is nonadaptive in that it does not vary with climate, and metabolism follows the same function at different environmental temperatures. The rate of O_2 consumption rises so steeply with small size that it would be virtually impossible for a mammal weighing less than 3.5 gm to obtain sufficient food when active (Fig. 39). A hummingbird consumes some 85 ml O_2/gm/hr in hovering activity

and about 14 when awake but not flying; its reserves are insufficient for this rate of metabolism at night; hence its body temperature drops.[204] In hibernating mammals the O_2 consumption correlates with body weight, not with body surface.[145]

That more than heat relations lies beneath the exponential function of metabolism is shown by the good logarithmic relation between O_2 consumption and weight in poikilotherms (Fig. 40). In an extensive survey Hemmingsen[116] concludes that metabolism = K weight[b] with b not far from 0.73 in poiki-

These Animals must be always active or hibernate (handwritten marginal note)

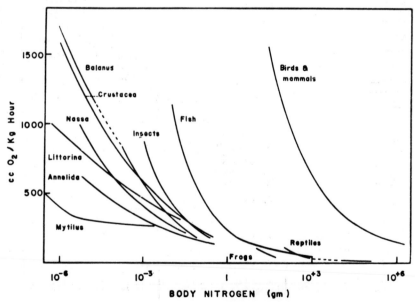

FIGURE 40.   Comparison of metabolic rate of various animals as a function of body nitrogen. (From Zeuthen, E.: C. R. Trav. Lab. Carlsberg. Ser. Chim., vol. 26.)

lotherms, homeotherms, and beech trees! Various poikilotherms show the increase in metabolism with decreasing body weight, but at different positions on the O_2 axis and with slightly different slopes. A series of reptiles and amphibians gives a good straight line b = 0.738. Bertalanffy[19-21] concluded that many poikilotherms—fish, the isopod *Armadillidium*, mussels, *Ascaris*—give a b of 0.66, and that others—some insect larvae and adults—give a b of 1, that is, the metabolism is proportional to weight; while others—as *Planorbis*—are intermediate. He pointed out that the growth pattern of the first group is exponential up to some plateau, of the second it is linear to a critical size before a molt, and of the third it is sigmoid. In some holometabolous insects b approaches 1, while in hemimetabolous insects values tend to be lower.[75]

A correlation of metabolism with type of respiratory mechanism is indicated by Ludwig.[175] In gill breathers—bivalves, prosobranch snails, and the aquatic isopod *Asellus*—O_2 consumption is proportional to surface (length^2); in tracheate insects and pulmonate snails it is proportional to weight (length^3); in animals with two respiratory routes intermediate exponents are recorded—skin and tracheae in *Dixippus*, gill and pseudotracheae in *Porcellio*, or skin and lungs in fresh-water pulmonates (*Zebrina*). Range in b values from 0.45 to 1 was found in pulmonate snails.[17, 18] In tropical fish *Etroplus* the value of b is higher at low temperatures (1 at 0°) and less at high temperatures (0.67 at 35°). However, for *Chironomus* larvae b = 0.7 on a dry weight basis at 10° and 20°.[77] *Artemia* differs somewhat in form according to salinity, and b for those from sea water is 0.88, while for those from brine it is 0.62.[100] In one lizard, *Uta*, b decreases with rising temperature; in another, *Sceloporus*, the trend is reversed.[63]

Zeuthen[294, 295] examined existing data and pointed out that there are numerous relations between metabolism and weight (or nitrogen content). Among unicellular organisms bacteria have a very high oxygen consumption, some as much as 100 to 500 l O_2/kg/hr. Protozoa consume less, for example, *Pelomyxa* is 10^7 to 10^8 larger than *Salmonella* or *Escherichia* and consumes only 0.2 l O_2/kg/hr. The slope for a number of bacteria, flagellates, ciliates, and rhizopods is low: 0.7 based on literature data, 0.55 for three protozoans in the nonfeeding state. Small multicellular poikilotherms—microcrustacea, lower worms, molluscs—give steeper log-log plots. Soil nematodes give b of 0.9.[199] A number of invertebrates containing less than about 1 mg nitrogen (40 mg body weight) have b values averaging 0.95.[294] In larger poikilotherms the slope is less; among a series of Crustacea b dropped from 0.95 to 0.80 at about 1 mg N. *Pachygrapsus* of a wide size range give a b of 0.66. Cockroaches, walking-sticks and tarantulas had b about 0.8;[80] *Mytilus* 0.67.[223] For *Uca pugilator* b = 0.8; *U. minax*, 0.7; and *U. pugnax*, 0.66.[260] When data from fish and amphibia are included the value for large poikilotherms is close to 0.76[294] (0.85 for speckled trout).[136]

Intraspecific measurements indicate that in very early developmental stages (1 mg N) the slope is low (0.7 to 0.8), that later during development b is 0.9 to 1, and that in larger mature individuals it is low again. This sequence was demonstrated well for *Mytilus*[294] and in *Artemia* (Fig. 41).[78] In older mealworms, *Talorchestia*, earthworms, starfish, and frogs the O_2 consumption values deviate from a straight line and may even decline as maximum sizes are reached. A similar triphasic relation is indicated for amphibians[28] and for chickens.[35] Extensive measurements on domestic mammals indicate high b values in early stages, usually up to weaning, and lower b values later. In children the b value is 1.02 at 3 years of age and declines with age. Most metabolism measurements on mammals have been made on young adults.

Interpretations of the size correlations of metabolism are difficult. In unicellular organisms, oxygen consumption is nearly proportional to cell surface, and possibly size is limited by the surface; certainly, large Protozoa have diminishingly low metabolism. Multicellular animals, even of the size of Protozoa, have much higher metabolism, and the O_2 consumption is no longer closely related to external surface; enzymes grow to the limit with body weight. It appears that, above about 40 mg, enzymes increase in activity less than body size and may even decrease as maximum size is reached. A suggested correlation with muscle fiber surface area[62] or possibly a correlation with total cell membranes has not been explored. Zeuthen points out that animals can either be small, grow rapidly, and live intensely or they can be large, grow slowly, and metabolize at a low rate.

One explanation of decreased metabolism with increased body size is the disproportionate increase of tissues of low metabolic rate—

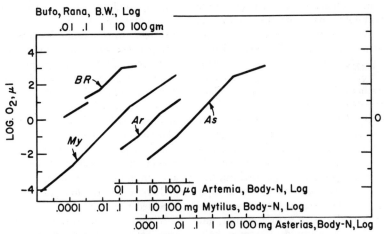

FIGURE 41. Double logarithmic plot of total oxygen consumption per organism per hour as a function of total body nitrogen, during the growth of animals: *BR*, Bufo and Rana; *My*, Mytilus; *Ar*, Artemia; *As*, Asterias. (Modified from Zeuthen, E.: Quart. Rev. Biol., vol. 28.)

skeleton, fat, connective tissues in general. Because of different relative weights of various organs the oxygen consumption of different tissues need not be expected to change with the same exponent of body weight as total metabolism.[183] Respiration and glycolysis of rat skin yield b values slightly less than in the intact rat.[96] In active tissues the enzyme concentrations may not increase in proportion to either tissue or total mass. Striated muscle, which constitutes 35 to 40 per cent of total weight in small animals, less in large ones, is particularly difficult to obtain in thin enough strips for *in vitro* measurements. Oxygen consumption of tissues of rats covering a wide range of size (and age) failed (except diaphragm) to correlate with body size.[19-21] Liver but not kidney slices from birds showed a size correlation.[57] Tissues from nine mammalian species studied in a medium highly fortified with organic substrates gave good summated Qo_2's and showed some correlation with body size but not enough to account for differences in metabolism.[155] For example, the metabolic rate of a horse was 11 per cent of that of a mouse, yet the brain and kidney rates were 47 per cent. The liver Qo_2 of the horse was 13 to 23 per cent of that of the mouse, yet liver Qo_2 was similar in guinea pig, cat, and dog. In a series—mouse, rat, dog—each tissue showed decreasing rate of O_2 consumption but not in proportion to the decrease in total metabolism.[183] Measurements of Qo_2 of liver, brain, and muscle from a number of fish failed to correlate with body size.[267, 269] However, in rats, rabbits, sheep, and steers there is a good correlation between abundance of mitochondria and total metabolism; the total mitochondrial mass is less in a steer than in a rat in proportion to $W^{0.77}$.[250] Cytochrome oxidase of skeletal muscle and liver[161] and total cytochrome c[71] are correlated with body surface ($W^{0.67}$). Succinoxidase and malic dehydrogenase increase in concentration in the series from large to small mammals but not logarithmically.[93] For a series of mammals, b values for liver oxidase were 0.73; for transaminases, 0.25 to 0.54.[170]

In summary: Metabolism is correlated inversely to body weight in all sorts of organisms, the exponential factor varies from 0.55 to 1.0, and there are many causes for this correlation. Influencing the negative exponential correlation are body surface in homeotherms and in unicellular organisms, growth patterns, type of external respiration, increase of enzymes as related to body mass, and disproportionate increase of different tissues. A triphasic relation between metabolism and size appears in comparisons of unicellular, small multicellular, and larger animals, and the same sequence may occur intraspecifically during development.

Development.   In addition to the changes in O_2 consumption as a function of increasing size mentioned in the preceding section, there are other metabolic correlates of life cycle. It is difficult to separate size *per se* from developmental stage. In general, old animals have lower metabolism than young ones, but embryos may respire less and a maximum may occur late in development. A mammalian fetus has a lower rate of O_2 consumption than a newborn. The metabolic peak occurs in man at about the time of weaning, in cattle between weaning and puberty, in swine at puberty, and in horses when mature.[35] In chickens the peak occurs 4 weeks after hatching. A comparable age effect occurs in Protozoa, cultures of which, e.g., *Chilomonas*, decrease in O_2 consumption as they age. The rate of O_2 consumption by embryos of the black snake (*Natrix natrix*) drops precipitately during 5 to 25 days of incubation.[51]

In *Rana* there is a jump in metabolism at the end of gastrulation and in *Amblystoma* somewhat later—just before establishment of circulation.[28] In sea urchin eggs (*Arbacia*) the O_2 consumption increases sevenfold on fertilization, and the increased respiration is CN-sensitive, while that of the unfertilized egg is not. In *Fundulus*, metabolism increases abruptly both at fertilization and when the circulation is established. Other animals—starfish and amphibians—show no increase at fertilization; still others, the clam *Cumingia* and polychaete *Chaetopterus*, show a decrease.

Holometabolous insects show a gradual increase in metabolic rate during larval development, then a rapid drop early in pupal life, followed by a rise prior to emergence as an adult; this U-shaped metabolic curve is found for many insects (*Tenebrio, Drosophila*).[68] During pupal reorganization, extensive changes in enzyme patterns occur; diapausing cecropia pupae are insensitive to certain respiratory poisons. In honeybees, O_2 consumption by pupae is minimal; the queens show greater changes than workers and consume more O_2 at all stages. Hemimetabolous insects show a rise in O_2 consumption just after each molt and a decline during the intermolt, e.g., the milkweed bug *Oncopeltus fasciatus*, and *Rhodnius*.[75, 296]

A most spectacular change in metabolism with the life cycle is the drop during encystment. For example, the O_2 consumption of cysts of a ciliate *Bresslaua* was less than 2 per cent of that in free-swimming individuals.[239] The preceding examples illustrate the need to specify age and stage in life cycle when giving the O_2 consumption of an animal.

Hormones. The effects of endocrines on metabolism are discussed in Chapter 20. Many of the changes mentioned in preceding paragraphs are mediated by hormones. Thyroid extracts increase metabolism in amphibians and mammals but may not in fish and lampreys. Gonadal steroids, however, may increase fish metabolism.[124] The sinus gland of crustaceans may regulate metabolism indirectly; removal of eyestalks from crabs increases their oxygen consumption, and injection of eyestalk extract into crabs whose eyestalks have been removed decreases their O_2 uptake. Crustacean metabolism increases prior to molting.[230] In adult flies (*Calliphora erythrocephala*) removal of the corpora allata decreases O_2 consumption, and implantation of the gland increases it.[262] Metabolic changes are associated with reproductive activity in many animals and are caused indirectly by reproductive hormones.

Races. Most of the preceding differences in metabolism concern changes in individual animals. Racial differences in O_2 consumption in respect to temperature have been noted (Chapter 9). Various laboratory strains of guinea pigs have been observed to differ in O_2 consumption.[219] A strain of the mouse *Peromyscus maniculatus* from the high Sierras has a lower metabolism than a sea-level strain when both strains are maintained under similar conditions.[54] The "killer" strain of *Paramecium aurelia* has a higher metabolic rate than the "sensitive" strain.[248] Differences in metabolism of various ethnic groups of man have frequently been indicated, but these have been questioned because of differences in nutritional history. Genetic differences among different orders of animals of the same class are well illustrated by the differences in activity, size, and temperature regulation which result in the following averages of metabolism in kcal/$gm^{0.73}$/hr: insectivores 30, rodents 17.1, bats 4.5.[193] *Uca pugilator* from Florida have a lower metabolic rate but show more temperature effect than Woods Hole specimens.[65] *Uca pugilator* which lives in sand mud has higher O_2 consumption than *U. minax* which lives among *Spartina* roots.[268] *Uca* in tropical and temperate water differ in metabolic responses to temperature.

Homogenized muscle consumed oxygen in decreasing amount in the series: *Tenebrio* > *Sarcophagus* > *Periplaneta*.[3] The lower metabolism of poikilotherms than of homeotherms is discussed on page 257. For example, the Qo_2 of snail liver is one-tenth that of rat liver.[217]

Most genetic differences in metabolism are correlated with other adaptive differences and can best be considered with specific stresses. Those metabolic differences associated with the stress of low O_2 will be discussed on page 177.

Temperature and CO_2. The effects of temperature on metabolism are discussed in detail in Chapter 9. In general, homeothermic animals have a range of minimal metabolism at neutral air temperatures, and their O_2 con-

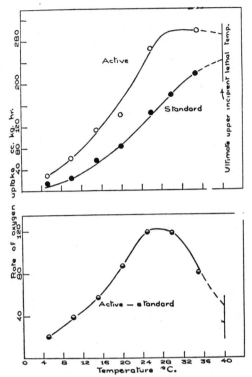

FIGURE 42. Rate of oxygen consumption of young goldfish in activity and under standard conditions at various temperatures. Lower curve gives difference between active and standard metabolism, i.e., energy available for work. (From Fry, F. E. J.: Publ. Ontario Fish Res. Lab., vol. 68.)

sumption increases both when body temperature rises and in the cold. In poikilotherms the metabolism rises and falls with body temperature about two and one-half times per 10°C in the physiological range. Standard metabolism of fish increases continuously with temperature up to lethal levels; active metabolism may either increase to a plateau or pass through a peak at a temperature above which fish are incapable of increased work[94, 95] (Fig. 42). Aquatic poikilothermic animals acclimated to cold tend to have higher metabolic rates at a given temperature than those of the same species acclimated to high temperatures, although at their natural temperatures those in the cold metabolize less than those in warm water. The general effect is to compensate for environmental changes with season and latitude.

The oxygen consumption of many aquatic animals becomes reduced in high CO_2 concentrations. In speckled trout the reduction in active metabolism at elevated CO_2 is greater at 10° than at 20°C, but in bull-

heads the effect of CO_2 is similar at both temperatures.[12]

Salinity. Examples of differences in metabolic rate with salinity changes are given in Chapter 2. For animals of a kind, the O_2 consumption of fresh-water species tends to be higher than of marine species. Those species which are euryhaline (e.g., *Mytilus edulis*) consume more oxygen in dilute brackish water than in sea water; stenohaline animals (e.g., *Asterias*) consume less. Prawns from marine environment increased their O_2 consumption to a maximum in 25 per cent sea water while prawns from brackish water increased to a maximum metabolism in tap water.[212] The O_2 consumption of *Artemi* reared at low salinity is twice that of those from high salinity in small specimens; it is approximately the same in large ones.[78, 100]

Photoperiod can also affect metabolism. *Pachygrapsus* on an 8-hour photoperiod consumed 55 per cent more oxygen than on a 16-hour day.[64] Similar effects have been observed with salmon.

METABOLISM AS RELATED TO ENVIRONMENTAL OXYGEN

The ideal way to distinguish regulation and conformity with respect to oxygen is to measure oxygen concentration (or pressure) in tissues of animals in different environmental oxygen concentrations. Technical difficulties, despite the oxygen electrode, have not permitted such measurements to be made with ease and accuracy. Alternatives are to measure oxygen consumption as a function of environmental oxygen, to measure the partial pressures necessary for loading and unloading the transport pigments, and to test survival time in reduced oxygen.

Conformity and Regulation in Respect to Oxygen. Many animals in reduced environmental oxygen regulate their oxygen consumption down to some critical pressure (P_c) below which their O_2 consumption declines rapidly, i.e., they show a wide range of oxygen independence. In other animals (conformers) the O_2 consumption goes up as the environmental O_2 concentration increases, even toward an atmosphere of O_2; at air saturation these animals do not approach their possible potential use of oxygen. In metabolic regulators the P_c is below air saturation; in conformers P_c is usually not sharp and is well above 155 mm Hg. In some O_2-conforming animals the slope of metabolism-oxygen curves is less steep above air satura-

Mammies are regulators

tion than below; these are intermediate between true regulators and conformers. The position of the metabolism-oxygen curve and the value of critical pressure are influenced by many internal and external factors and are often closely correlated with animal distribution. Below critical pressure, oxygen availability limits metabolism; above P_c something else such as fuel supply or enzyme concentration fixes the metabolic level (Fig. 43).

In oxygen-regulating animals P_c is not necessarily a sharp point, but rather the metabolism-oxygen curve is often hyperbolic, of the form:

$$M = \frac{P}{K_1 + K_2 P}$$

where M is the rate of oxygen consumption, P is partial pressure of O_2, and K_1 and K_2 are constants. When P/M is plotted against P, a straight line results, the slope of which is K_2 and the intercept K_1.[258]

Lists of oxygen-regulating and oxygen-conforming animals have been given.[31, 258] The distinction is not always sharp, and values of P_c refer to a range of O_2 concentration under specific conditions. Frequently, metabolic regulation is found in a population at low density, but at higher animal numbers the metabolism varies with O_2 pressure, probably because diffusion is limiting. Examples of well-established regulators are found in the following groups (critical pressures given as partial pressures of O_2 in mm Hg):

Most Protozoa—*Tetrahymena, Paramecium, Trypanosoma*[33]

Coelenterates—*Hydra* between 10 and 100 per cent O_2 in the gas phase[166]

Annelids—*Tubifex*,[153] *Lumbricus*,[139] the leeches *Glossiphonia* and *Hirudo*,[178] larvae of some polychaetes, P_c = 40 to 50 mm[295]

Echinoderm eggs—*Arbacia*, unfertilized, P_c = 40; fertilized, P_c = 50 mm Hg[258]

A few parasitic worms—*Trichinella*, P_c = 8 mm; *Nematodirus, Haemonchus*;[222] *Rhabditis elegans*, P_c = 121 mm; *Rhabditis strongyloides*, P_c = 58.5 mm[8]

Molluscs—clam *Mya*, P_c = 40 to 50 mm; oyster, P_c = 100 mm; snail *Ancylus*, P_c = 80 mm;[17] snail *Australabrus*, P_c = 30 mm;[34] *Mytilus*, P_c = 50 per cent air saturation

Crustacea—copepod *Calanus*, P_c = 204 ml O_2/l;[182] crayfish, P_c = 40 mm;[120] crab *Pugettia* P_c = 70 mm;[279] *Uca pugilator* and *Uca pugnax*, P_c = 4 mm[260]

Insects—termite *Termopsis*, P_c = 38 mm;[55] diapausing cecropia pupae, P_c = 23 to 28 mm;[231, 233] several chironomid larvae, P_c = 55 to 68 mm[270]

Most aquatic vertebrates P_c = 30 mm Hg

Crucian carp—30 mm Hg at 5°C[25]

All terrestrial vertebrates; probably all terrestrial insects.

Oxygen-conforming animals include those in which the O_2 consumption increases linearly with concentration through air saturation and some animals in which it increases proportionately less in this range than at lower concentrations. Some O_2-conforming animals follow:

Protozoa—*Spirostomum*[252]

Numerous coelenterates—actinians,[117] *Cassiopea*

Free-living worms—*Sipunculus*,[117] *Urechis*, leeches *Piscicola* and *Erpobdella*,[178] *Nereis*[4]

Most parasitic worms—trematodes *Fasciola, Schisto-*

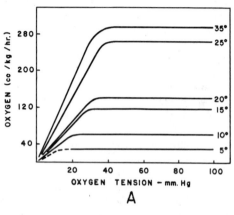

A

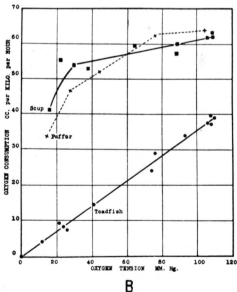

B

FIGURE 43. *A*, standard metabolism of goldfish as a function of partial pressure of oxygen at different temperatures. (From Fry, F. E. J., and Hart, J. S.: Biol. Bull., vol. 94.)

B, oxygen consumption as a function of partial pressure of oxygen in three marine fish. Metabolic regulation in scup and puffer, conformity in toadfish. (From Hall, F. G.: Am. J. Physiol., vol. 88.)

soma, cestode *Diphyllobothrium,* nematodes *Ascaris, Litomosoides, Ascaris,* strongyles larvae[32, 43, 164, 213]

Some molluscs and crustaceans—*Limax, Limulus, Homarus,* series of marine crustaceans[4, 176, 261, 277] daphnid *Simocephalus* fifth instar conforms over environmental range 14.6 to 1.1 cc O_2/l[125]

Echinoderm adults—starfish, sea urchins

Some aquatic insects—*Ephemera,*[91] *Anatopynia, Tanytarsus*[270]

Few vertebrates—toadfish,[107] *Triturus pyrrhogaster,* cutaneous respiration[176]

Relative independence of oxygen may be related to body size. In large animals without special respiratory organs or circulation, long diffusion distance may result in O_2 dependence—actinians, *Sipunculus,* nematodes. When a *Metridium* was cut into pieces it was less O_2 dependent than when intact.[117] The critical pressure is extremely low in Protozoa and is 2.5 mm Hg in *Tetrahymena* where the diffusion path is short.[9] In some species with a circulation the large individuals tend to have higher critical pressures. *Cambarus* weighing 4.3, 9.0, and 17.1 gm showed critical pressures of 32, 48, and 65 mm Hg respectively.[115] *Lymnaea auricularia* is a regulator with P_c of 76 mm Hg, while *Lymnaea pereger* and *L. palustris* are conformers.[18]

Modifiers of Oxygen Dependence. The critical oxygen concentration falls and

The P_c for trout at 20°C is higher for large than for small fish.[136] Because of the lower solubility at high temperature the differences with temperature appear less when oxygen is reported in concentration than in pressure. Maximum cruising speed of the trout parallels the oxygen consumption as a function of environmental oxygen.[99] The P_c of salmon eggs is higher than of the larvae, which consume more O_2.[113] Exposure of salmon eggs to O_2 below air saturation delays development.[2]

Limiting oxygen concentration below which fish are unable to remove oxygen from water parallels P_c's and decreases from active to sluggish fish as follows:[107]

	P_c (mm Hg)		P_c (mm Hg)
Mackerel	70	Sea robin	8.5
Cunner	14.8	Puffer	4.7
Scup	13.1	Tautog	1.6
		Toadfish	0.0

The sluggish toadfish is an O_2 conformer; the others, regulators (Fig. 43B). Under comparable conditions P_c of active metabolism of a goldfish is 80 and of a bullhead 50 mm Hg.[12]

In general, animals from high oxygen environments have higher O_2 consumption at air levels and higher P_c than animals from low oxygen environments. This is illustrated for mayfly nymphs (Fig. 44A) as follows:[91]

Genus	Habitat	O_2 consumption at air saturation (ml O_2/gm/hr)	Critical oxygen level (ml O_2/l)
Baetis	swift streams	2.8	12
Leptophlebia	lake	2.1	2.5
Cloeon	pond	1.3	2

metabolic regulation is more evident in diminished activity and at low temperatures. Activity and standard metabolism have not been separated in many so-called O_2 conformers, and it may be that if motor activity could be excluded they would show critical pressures in the range of air saturation. Active metabolism is more O_2-dependent than standard metabolism. In trout *Salvelinus fontinalis* the oxygen consumption during active swimming is higher at all temperatures than at rest and goes through a maximum at a lower temperature during activity. The P_c and minimum tolerable oxygen concentration are higher as the temperature rises (Fig. 43A):[104]

A similar series of increasing dependence on oxygen is found in comparing larvae from stagnant ditches, ponds, and fast streams (Fig. 45). The stream species are less resistant to hypoxia, have lower thermal tolerance, and their O_2 consumption declines more with low environmental oxygen (Fig. 44B).[270]

Acclimation to low O_2 can make for regulation down to low O_2 concentrations. Chironomid larvae become more independent of environmental oxygen after some hours of adaptation to low O_2 in glass tubes.[270] Also the leech *Erpobdella testacea* from air saturation is an O_2 conformer, but after a few hours at reduced O_2 it regulates its consump-

	5.0°C	24.5°C
P_c activity metabolism	100 mm Hg	150 mm Hg
P_c standard metabolism	30 mm Hg	79 mm Hg
Lethal minimum O_2 concentration	19 mm Hg (3-5°)	45 mm Hg (23°)

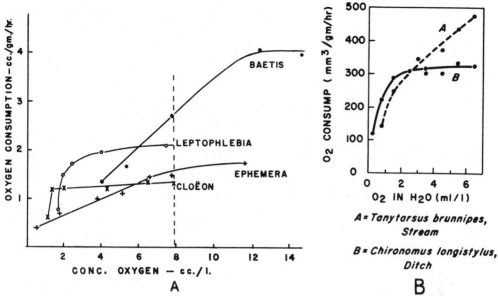

A

B

FIGURE 44. *A,* rate of oxygen consumption as a function of oxygen concentration in the water by mayfly nymphs, showing metabolic regulation in Cloëon and Leptophlebia, and metabolic conformity at levels of air saturation in Baetis and Ephemera. (From Fox, H. M., Wingfield, C. A., and Simmonds, B. G.: J. Exp. Biol., vol. 14.)

B, oxygen consumption as a function of oxygen concentration by two dipteran larvae—a conformer Tanytarsus, and a regulator, Chironomus. (From Wälshe, B. M.: J. Exp. Biol., vol. 25.)

tion down to less than half air saturation.[178] Goldfish acclimated for several days to low oxygen (1/6 air saturation) show a lower P_c and lower standard metabolism than before the acclimation.[207] Life in low oxygen environments does not necessarily result in regulation down to low concentrations; various parasitic helminths living in the same gut differ in their oxygen dependence. Caddis fly (Trichoptera) larvae may require fast streams, not so much because of O_2 concentration as because of agitation of the water. A lake species of the gastropod *Ancylus* is more O_2-conforming than a stream species, the opposite to arthropods.[17] Amphipods from mountain streams are more sensitive to low oxygen than members of species from stagnant pools.

Animals which live in low oxygen and can rely on glycolysis for energy tend to be oxygen conformers. Among the O_2-metabolic-regulating parasites are some blood-dwelling protozoans, *Trypanosoma cruzi, Plasmodium,* and also the nematode *Trichinella* which normally lives in the high oxygen of muscle. Most parasitic helminths are oxygen conformers. Some of these are large—the trematode *Fasciola,* cestode *Diphyllobothrium,* nematode *Ascaris.* However, it is doubtful

that diffusion is critical because minced *Ascaris* as well as intact worms showed O_2 conformity (See reference 32 for summary), and many small parasites such as the nematode *Litomosoides* and *Schistosoma* (only 0.03 mg dry weight) are oxygen dependent[43] (Fig. 46). In aquatic annelids and insects, life in low oxygen tends to favor metabolic regulation and low critical pressures, whereas parasites which make use of anaerobic glycolysis are likely to be oxygen conforming.

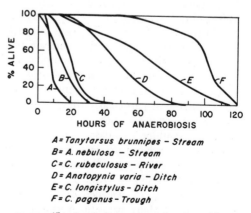

A = Tanytarsus brunnipes – Stream
B = A. nebulosa – Stream
C = C. rubeculosus – River
D = Anatopynia varia – Ditch
E = C. longistylus – Ditch
F = C. paganus – Trough

FIGURE 45. Survival curves as a function of hours of anaerobiosis, in insect larvae from aquatic environments of high oxygen (stream) to low oxygen (trough). (From Wälshe, B. M.: J. Exp. Biol., vol. 25.)

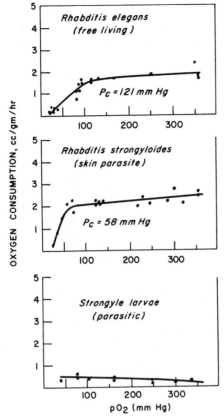

OXYGEN CONSUMPTION, cc/gm/hr

Rhabditis elegans
(free living)

$P_C = 121$ mm Hg

Rhabditis strongyloides
(skin parasite)

$P_C = 58$ mm Hg

Strongyle larvae
(parasitic)

pO₂ (mm Hg)

FIGURE 46. Oxygen consumption of three nematodes as a function of partial pressure of oxygen. (Modified from Bair, T. D.: J. Parasitol., vol. 41.)

Limiting Factors in Critical Oxygen Concentrations. The critical limits of metabolism as a function of environmental oxygen might be imposed at three sites—in metabolizing cells, O_2 transport system, and respiratory epithelium. Cellular limits might be in saturation of oxidative enzymes or in failure of diffusion to provide enough oxygen.

Experiments with sea urchin eggs, bacteria, mammalian heart, and yeast[286] indicate that oxidations catalyzed via the cytochrome system are not oxygen limited at pressures down to about 2.5 mm Hg.[147] On the contrary, other oxidations, particularly those involving flavoprotein oxidases such as D-amino acid oxidase, xanthine oxidase, and glucose oxidase, are reduced to less than half at about 5 per cent oxygen.[164] Lactic acid production (glycolysis) in retina is more sensitive to low O_2 (5 vol per cent) than is respiration.[147] Many parasitic worms which are oxygen conformers lack the cytochrome system.[32, 43] Anaerobic glycolysis is less in aerobic than in anaerobic conditions (Pasteur

effect), and lactic acid production can be stimulated by admitting oxygen to an anaerobic system. A systematic study of O_2 dependence of various enzymes from animals of different degrees of metabolic regulation has not been made. While O_2 pressure needed for saturation of enzymes is probably not often limiting, it cannot be ruled out.

Some invertebrates without an active blood pigment are metabolic conformers, while those with blood pigment, and insects with tracheae, are regulators. A good transport system does not, however, guarantee metabolic regulation. *Carcinus*[117] regulates, but *Homarus*[261] and *Limulus*[4] are conformers. The oxygen conformity of some decapod crustaceans and *Limulus* may be related to the fact that the hemocyanin is normally never fully saturated.[215] (Chapter 8.) The cutaneous respiration of *Triturus pyrrhogaster* is O_2 conforming, while *Triturus viridescens* can get sufficient O_2 above air levels.[176] Most transport pigments become saturated in the presence of an oxygen pressure well below air saturation (Chapter 8). After the pigment (e.g., hemoglobin) is inactivated, the critical pressure may become higher. In an earthworm the O_2 consumption is normally independent of O_2 pressure down to about 3 per cent (22 mm Hg), but when the hemoglobin has been inactivated by CO the metabolism is regulated only down to 8 per cent (60 mm Hg).[139] Maloeuf points out that, in general, unicellular organisms, tracheates, and animals with transport pigments which saturate at low pressures are O_2 regulators.

The third and most important determinant of P_c is the respiratory epithelium and its ability to withdraw or utilize oxygen from the water or air supplied to it. Oxygen utilization may be regulated by circulatory adaptations and by ventilation control.

OXYGEN WITHDRAWAL

If the O_2 consumption is to remain constant as environmental O_2 decreases, the per cent withdrawal or extraction from water or gas in the ventilation organ must increase while the rate of ventilation remains constant, or per cent withdrawal may remain constant while the ventilation increases. If the metabolism is O_2 dependent the ventilation and/or withdrawal decrease in low oxygen. Hazelhoff[114] measured the difference in concentration of O_2 between inflowing and outflowing water in a large number of invertebrates. In those which feed on small particles—mostly filter feeders—there is so much water flow to supply food that the withdrawal of oxygen is small. In sponges the O_2 withdrawal from the circulated water ranges from 10 to 40 per cent and averages about 20 per cent; in pelecypods and ascidians also the per cent withdrawal is low (3 to 10).[114] Oxygen withdrawal of *Mytilus* is 3 per cent at 13°C, 15 per cent at 20°.[223] However, the per cent withdrawal is very sensitive to the needs, e.g., for *Anodonta* and *Mya* in aerated water after a period of anaerobiosis the initial withdrawal exceeded 20 per cent and fell in 4 to 5 hours to 5 to 10 per cent.[60] In *Pecten grandis* the O_2 consumption was fairly constant down to 0.5 to 1.0 ml O_2/l, i.e., the P_c is low, and per cent withdrawal remained about 2 per cent over this range;[61] hence ventilation increased.

In animals with feeding mouthparts the per cent withdrawal of oxygen from water passing over respiratory surfaces is greater. In a series of polychaetes and crustaceans withdrawal averaged 50 per cent.[114] In *Arenicola* it was 30 to 35 per cent both at air and at 5 per cent of air saturation. In a crab, *Calappa,* the per cent withdrawal remained constant or increased slightly as the O_2 decreased from 4 ml/l to 0.4 ml/l.[114] In low environmental oxygen, *Homarus* does not increase ventilation; it does increase the per cent withdrawal presumably by circulatory improvement, but not enough to prevent a gradual decline in O_2 consumption:[261]

O_2 concentration in water (ml/l)	Ventilation (l/hr)
5.78	9.8
3.77	9.51
2.44	9.56

After the environmental oxygen concentration dropped from 6.68 ml/l to 2.1 ml/l, O_2 consumption of a crayfish declined by 33 per cent and the O_2 withdrawal by 14 per cent.[173]

In some marine gastropods O_2 withdrawal is high, about 60 per cent,[114] and in cephalopods even higher. In *Octopus* a reduction of oxygen in the water to one-fourth air saturation caused an increase in per cent withdrawal from 35 to 70 and a fourfold increase in ventilation.[285]

Most fish show good respiratory regulation, fairly constant oxygen withdrawal, and increased ventilation in low oxygen. In eel and trout the O_2 removal is about 80 per cent, and when O_2 is reduced the ventilatory

activity increases greatly.[158] In the puffer *Spheroides,* removal of oxygen remained at 46 per cent over a wide range of oxygen pressure (Fig. 43B); as the temperature rose, the O_2 consumption increased and ventilation increased, but per cent utilization remained constant. The removal of oxygen by fish gills may be more than doubled because of the countercurrents of blood and water, i.e., the blood which leaves the gills contacts water of highest O_2 and lowest CO_2. The relative gill area is much greater in fast than in sluggish fish, 821,000 mm² in a menhaden as compared with 72,870 mm² in a toadfish of comparable size.[105] Trout which have been acclimated to low O_2 survive exposure to lower O_2 concentrations than they did before the acclimation and utilize more of the O_2 in the water.[247]

In comparison with aquatic animals, most mammals extract 2 to 5 per cent of the inspired oxygen. Diving mammals extract more. Air breathers are, in general, independent of O_2 concentration in the range of usual atmospheric pressures, and they compensate for reduction in oxygen by increasing their ventilation.

REGULATION OF OXYGEN CONSUMPTION

Auxiliary External Respiration. Respiration is mainly cutaneous in many animals. A frog's cutaneous loss of CO_2 ex-

Withdrawal (per cent)	O_2 consumption (ml/gm/hr)
30.6	0.045
42.1	0.039
55.1	0.033

ceeds that by the lungs at all seasons, and O_2 uptake by lungs is predominant only in the summer; the lungs are auxiliary to the skin. In eel and amphibians, cutaneous respiration is adequate at low temperatures. The yarrow, a fish of stagnant South American rivers, breathes sufficiently by its gills in water containing 1.3 to 5 ml O_2/l and 8 to 30 ml CO_2/l, but at lower oxygen or higher CO_2 it surfaces, gulps air, and respires by its gas bladder.[44] Tarpons likewise gulp air when the O_2 in water is low. Cutaneous respiration in man may account for 1.9 per cent of O_2 uptake and 2.7 per cent of CO_2 loss; this probably represents the respiration of the skin.[86] An electric eel is normally an air breather with accessory respiratory organs in the mouth, but it can live by skin breathing.[163] A pond loach, *Misgurnus,* shifts from branchial to intestinal breathing (of air) when the oxygen in the water is less than 2 ml/1 (35 mm Hg); cutaneous breathing is one-sixth of total when the fish is in water and one-third to one-half of total when in air.[135] Mayfly nymphs normally remove O_2 from water at air saturation down to 2.4 per cent saturation; after tracheal gills are removed they cannot reduce the oxygen from saturation of below 14.5 per cent; thus the tracheal gills permit survival in low oxygen.[205] Of two polychaetes, *Sabella pavonia* uses its tentacular crown as auxiliary when normal irrigation of its tube is prevented, while *Myxicola infundibulum* uses its crown continually.[278]

Morphological Adaptations and Pigment Synthesis. Frog and salamander tadpoles reared in low oxygen (one-half air saturation) have large, branched, thin walled gills. Similar tadpoles reared in high oxygen concentration (nearly an atmosphere) have small, stubby, thick walled gills.[72] The hemipteran *Rhodnius* increases the growth of tracheae to regions of its body low in oxygen,[283] and aquatic dipteran larvae develop highly branched peripheral tracheoles when kept in water low in oxygen.[282] Increased vital capacity and pulmonary ventilation in men acclimated to high altitudes are due in part to morphological changes. Land crabs have reduced gills and a membranous branchial chamber in contrast to the gills of aquatic crabs.

The function of transport pigments in respiratory regulation will be discussed in Chapter 8. Some pigments function as respiratory stores; others function in transport primarily at low oxygen pressures, and the animal is able to get adequate oxygen at high pressures even if its pigment is inactivated. In *Daphnia, Artemia,* and numerous other small crustaceans hemoglobin is synthesized in considerable amounts when the animals are kept at low oxygen for some days.[88] Similarly birds and mammals at high altitudes synthesize more hemoglobin than at sea level.

Regulation of Ventilation. *Vertebrates.* Mammals meet respiratory stress by increasing their ventilation. The primary impulses for inspiration pass from intrinsically active neurons of the inspiratory portion of the respiratory center to the diaphragm and intercostal muscles, which enlarge the chest cavity when they contract. As the lungs expand, sensory impulses are sent to the brain over vagus afferents which terminate the inspiratory discharge. Exhalation in quiet breathing is largely passive, but may be active. There is reciprocal interaction between inspiratory, expiratory, and tonic (pneumotaxic) centers.[201, 272] The most delicate control of the respiratory center is by the CO_2 concentration in the blood. Carbon dioxide is the primary direct stimulant, although under some conditions decreased blood pH may be effective. In addition, the chemoreceptors of the carotid sinus are sensitive to oxygen lack and come into action in respiratory stress.[289] The carotid sinus receptors may be stimulated when the alveolar O_2 falls below about 100 mm Hg (cats and man acclimated to high altitude) or to 60 mm Hg (dogs and man stimulated acutely).[211] In addition the carotid sinus is stimulated by CO_2 when the alveolar P_{CO_2} rises above about 30 mm Hg.[81] Stimulation of the respiratory center results in increases of both rate and amplitude of ventilation. Thus in birds and mammals carbon dioxide is the first line of respiratory stimulation, and oxygen lack second.

The breathing rate tends to be much faster in small than in large mammals and birds. Quiet breathing (eupnea) may be interrupted by extra or complementary breaths; these are more common in rodents than in carnivores and are rare in large mammals.[187]

In some birds—English sparrow, starling, mallard duck—carbon dioxide stimulates breathing, while in others—muscovy and pekin ducks—it causes apnea, probably by inhibitory reflexes from chemoreceptors in the nasopharynx.[119, 122] In diving mammals and birds the sensitivity of the respiratory center to CO_2 is less than in nondivers.

In reptiles as in mammals, increased CO_2 causes increased rate and to some extent increased amplitude of breathing. The respiratory center of turtles has been considered a prototype for the mammalian center. In amphibians the respiratory center is sensitive to CO_2 and there are *glandula intercarotica,* analogous to the carotid bodies of mammals, which respond when blood oxygen is low.[251]

In aquatic animals in general, carbon dioxide with its high solubility in water rarely accumulates in respiratory stress as in air breathers, and here primary respiratory stimulation is not so much by CO_2 as by low oxygen. The air-breathing electric eel differs from aquatic fish in being CO_2 sensitive.[163] Respiratory centers of elasmobranchs and teleosts are well defined and show autonomous activity; their reflex control is not understood. In dogfish, inhibitory afferents occur in all gill branches of the ninth and tenth cranial nerves; inflation of the pharynx inhibits respiration.[228] Microelectrodes in the brainstem of catfish and crucian carp showed spontaneous activity of an isolated respiratory center dorsal to the trigeminal motor nucleus.[128] Transections of spinal cord and brain in a tench did not affect breathing unless the cut was behind the facial lobe of the medulla.[246] A stickleback, *Gasterosteus*, swims into regions low in oxygen but is then stimulated to increased random movements and respiratory distress.[142] The eel *Anguilla* and a trout *Salmo* remove some 80 per cent of oxygen at air saturation, a smaller percentage at low O_2 concentrations. They may increase ventilation fivefold when the O_2 content of the water falls below 4 ml/l.[158] In a trout the increased activity required for a fourfold increase of ventilation increased the O_2 consumption by 70 per cent, probably by CO_2 stimulation.

Invertebrates (Except Insects). Annelids ventilate by a variety of methods, some by ciliary beating, some by parapodial movement, some tubicolous ones by body-wall contraction. Tube-dwelling polychaetes usually show intermittent ventilatory movements with long pauses between series. These have been described for some thirty families of polychaetes,[172] and analyzed in detail for *Arenicola*.[278] Pumping is by intrinsic rhythms which are modified according to the gases dissolved in the water. In *Nereis*, for example, at low oxygen concentrations (2 ml/l) the pumping movements may become continuous rather than intermittent.

The oligochaetes *Tubifex* and *Limnodrilus* occur in the mud of stagnant pools where oxygen may be very scarce. In ample oxygen no ventilatory movements are necessary; when the oxygen is reduced slightly below air levels the tail waves slowly back and forth; as oxygen is depleted the body extends farther and farther and may reach ten to twelve times its usual length; at very low oxygen tensions corkscrew motions tend to pull upper layers of water down toward the worm, and in complete anoxia the worm

collapses. Carbon dioxide may inhibit the rhythm initiated by oxygen lack. A swamp oligochaete *Alma* living in mud virtually devoid of O_2 carries down air bubbles by the upfolding edges of its vascular hind end.[13] *Alma* remains unaffected by an atmosphere of pure CO_2 for 48 hours. Some polychaetes construct chimneys which permit them to draw in water from upper, better oxygenated levels.

In terrestrial pulmonate snails—*Limax, Helix, Arion*—the opening of the pneumostome is stimulated by CO_2 and in 3 to 5 per cent CO_2 the respiratory aperture remains open;[59] air exchange is by diffusion. Aquatic pulmonates remain submerged for long periods and obtain about the same amount of oxygen from the water cutaneously (0.03 ml/hr) as from the air in the mantle lung (0.026 ml/hr).[97] When the oxygen in the water is high (6.4 ml/l), they remain submerged three times as long as when it is low (1.7 ml/l).[47] *Planorbis* rises to the surface when the lung O_2 gas concentration falls to 1 to 4 per cent; *Limnea* rises when it is 6 to 13 per cent.[97] These snails are relatively insensitive to increased CO_2.

Pelecypods *Mya* and *Anodonta* are stimulated by low O_2 to increased pumping, and after a period of anaerobiosis the velocity of water flow in them is increased by several times. In the cephalopod molluscs, e.g., *Octopus*, ventilation is increased as much as ten times by O_2 lack; CO_2 also increases frequency and amplitude of breathing, and oxygen utilization may reach 80 per cent. Octopus is more sensitive than most aquatic animals to CO_2.[285]

The difference between aquatic and terrestrial animals in sensitivity to low oxygen is well illustrated by a series of isopods and amphipods. As the oxygen was decreased below 50 per cent of air saturation the aquatic species (brackish *Gammarus locusta* and *Idotea* more than marine and fresh-water species) accelerated breathing movements of the pleopods while the semiterrestrial species (*Orchestia gammarellis* and *Ligia italica*) were unaffected; at less than 25 per cent air saturation, paralysis of breathing occurred in both groups.[271]

The metabolism of the lobster *Homarus* is strictly oxygen conforming, and, as O_2 concentration decreases or CO_2 increases, the frequency of respiratory movements is unaltered.[261] The lack of respiratory stimulation by low O_2 is in agreement with observations on *Carcinus* and *Balanus* but not on crayfish. *Astacus* tripled its breathing rate and doubled the ventilation volume when the O_2 dropped from 6.6 to 2.1 ml/l.[173] Carbon dioxide had little effect until after the calcareous carapace was coated with collodion, after which breathing frequency increased proportionately with increase in CO_2 from 5 to 20 per cent.[206] In the crab *Eriocheir*, breathing frequency is inversely proportional to the O_2 concentration; CO_2 in concentrations below 15 ml/l was without effect, but exposure to 20 to 30 ml CO_2/l caused a transient decrease in frequency, followed by stimulation. The transient response was lacking when antennae were removed; hence there may be initial stimulation of antennal receptors followed by stimulation of a respiratory center. *Limulus* does not hyperventilate, but rather the breathing frequency is proportional to O_2 concentration, and in anoxia breathing stops; excess CO_2 also stops breathing. Sensory receptors for O_2 and CO_2 are indicated, and it may be that the respiratory arrest is a protection in foul water.[274] It is of interest that both *Homarus* and *Limulus* are O_2 conformers and show no increased ventilation in low O_2.

The varied responses to respiratory stress in crustaceans (and *Limulus*) are shown in Table 25.

Insects. Most insects make pumping movements which force air through the tracheal system in a given direction; in addition, most of them can open the spiracles by varying amounts independently or in coordination with breathing. Segmental nerve centers (abdominal and mesothoracic and metathoracic) are responsible for the rhythmic ventilation movements. These centers are regulated by thoracic (usually prothoracic) secondary centers. Low concentrations of CO_2 stimulate the spiracles to remain open; slightly higher concentrations stimulate the ganglionic centers to cause more active ventilation; still higher CO_2 (25 per cent) may anesthetize an insect. Spiracles of *Carabus* remain open in 1½ per cent CO_2.[209] Low oxygen also can stimulate ventilation, and it appears to be the primary stimulant in aquatic insects with tracheal gills. In caddis larvae, *Limnophilus*, for example, respiratory movements are accelerated when the O_2 is reduced but not when CO_2 is increased.[89]

In *Periplaneta* the abdominal ganglia can maintain a breathing rhythm, but its rate is slower than when under control of the thoracic centers, and treatment of the exposed thoracic nervous system only with CO_2 is effective in enhancing breathing rhythm.[242] In one mutant of *Drosophila melanogaster* the motor centers are exceptionally sensitive to CO_2 as an anesthetic. The concentration of CO_2 needed to cause opening of spiracles varies greatly with the insect. In flies the CO_2 threshold rises with increasing O_2 concentration; it is probable that both CO_2 and O_2

TABLE 25. RESPONSES TO RESPIRATORY STRESS BY ORGANISMS OF VARIOUS HABITATS*

Animal	Habitat	O_2 decrease	CO_2 excess
Isopods			
Asellus[271]	fresh water	+	0
Idotea[271]	brackish water	++	
Cymodoce[271]	marine	+	
Ligia[271]	semiterrestrial marine	0	0
Gammarids			
Gammarus pulex[271]	fresh water	+	+
Gammarus locusta[271]	brackish	++	transient +
Melita[271]	marine	+	
Orchestia[271]	semiterrestrial marine	0	0
Other crustaceans			
Balanus[140]	marine littoral	0	0
Chirocephalus[140]	fresh water	0	0
Squilla[140]	marine	+	+
Pandalus[140]	marine	+	+
Carcinus[140]	marine	0	0
Homarus[261]	marine	—	—
Eriocheir[158]	fresh water	+	initially —, then +
Astacus[173]	fresh water	+	+
Limulus[274]	marine	—	—

* + stimulation, 0 no effect, — inhibition of ventilation.

chemoreceptors exist.[45] Hive bees are stimulated by low O_2 or high CO_2 to ventilate by fanning.

Continuous records of respiration of some insects, particularly larvae and pupae, show periodic bursts of CO_2 output with more or less continuous O_2 consumption.[231, 233] An adult carabid may show a burst of CO_2 production every 30 seconds and a Sphinx moth pupa once every 24 hours.[208, 209] The increases in O_2 consumption may be much smaller. At 25° C a cecropia pupa shows a burst every 7.3 hours and at 10° every 3 to 4 days[231, 233] (Fig. 47). At high metabolic rates the bursts disappear, and at low levels of metabolism they are accentuated. In low oxygen (below 10 to 15 per cent) or high carbon dioxide (above 10 per cent) the bursts disappear and spiracles remain open. Furthermore, if spiracles are forced open by small tubes, the bursts of CO_2 production disappear.[40] The bursts cannot be due merely to opening of the spiracles in response to CO_2 stimulation, since movement of gaseous CO_2 from inside to outside would not be recorded manometrically. Rather, the periodic opening of the spiracles by lowering the pressure releases bound CO_2 from tissue fluids. The net effect is to diminish loss of water without respiratory impairment.

Diving Animals. Reference has been made to various diving air-breathing poikilotherms—insects, snails, amphibians; each of these can obtain some oxygen from the water. Virtually nothing is known of the physiology of water reptiles. Birds and mammals are dependent on air, and the difference in survival times between divers and nondivers is as striking as the marked relaxation of a diver as compared with the struggling of a nondiver when submerged. A few observed maximum durations of dive selected from data assembled by Irving follow:[131]

Harbor seal (*Phoca vitulina*)	15	minutes
Muskrat (*Ondatra zibethica*)	12	minutes
Beaver (*Castor canadensis*)	15	minutes
Sperm whale (*Physeter macrocephalus*)	1½	hours
Greenland whale (*Balaena* sp.)	1	hour
Finback whale (*Balaenoptera physalus*)	½	hour
Man	2½	minutes

Prolonged diving is made possible by adaptations, which are respiratory, circulatory, and behavioral. The rate of oxygen consumption of diving mammals in air does not differ greatly from that of land mammals; it ranges from 546 ml O_2/kg/hr in the seal down to 180 ml in the manatee, comparable to 250 ml in man.[234, 236] The lung volume is slightly large in some diving mammals (7.4 per cent in seal); in the great whales lung

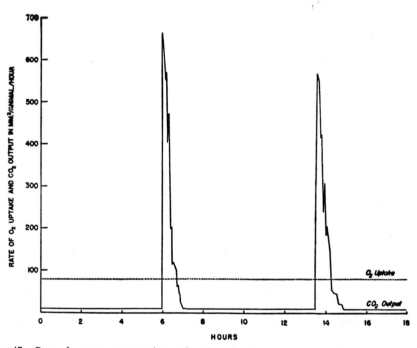

FIGURE 47. Rate of oxygen consumption and carbon dioxide production by *Cecropia pupae*. (From Schneiderman, H. A., and Williams, C.: Biol. Bull., vol. 109.)

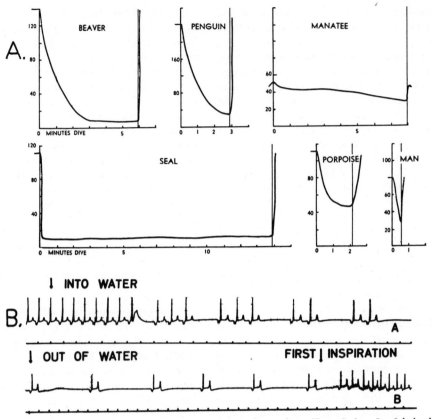

FIGURE 48. *A,* heart rate of several animals during and after a dive. (From Irving, L., Scholander, P. F., and Grinnell, S. W.: J. Cell. Comp. Physiol., vol. 17.) *B,* Electrocardiogram of snake, Tropidonotus, during and after a dive; heart does not recover until breathing resumes. (From Johansen, K.: Am. J. Physiol., vol. 197.)

capacity is only about 2.5 per cent of body volume, compared with 7.7 per cent in man. Tidal air is considerably greater in most divers, as high as 80 per cent of the lung volume in the porpoise, compared with 20 per cent in man.[132] The oxygen capacity of the hemoglobin of a seal is 1.78 ml O_2/gm Hb, compared with 1.23 for man, and the blood volume is about the same—10 to 11 per cent of body weight. The total O_2 capacity of the blood is slightly higher in some diving animals than in man (29.3 vol per cent in the seal) but not in all (17.7 vol per cent in the beaver). The Bohr effect (p. 213) in the blood of diving birds is less than in nondivers; this difference does not occur in mammals.[180] Muscle hemoglobin is high in nearly all diving mammals; seal muscle yields ·7715 mg Hb/100 gm, compared with 1084 mg from beef.[220] The highly pigmented muscle of whales may hold half the body store of oxygen. Tissue fluids appear similar to those in nondivers and cannot constitute important oxygen stores.

Scholander[234, 236] calculated the total oxygen stores of a 29-kg bladdernose seal as 1520 ml. During a 25-minute period at rest this seal consumes about 6250 ml of O_2, which is four or five times as much as the oxygen stores could supply for the dive. The major store, in the blood, is used at a steady reduced rate throughout a dive, while muscle oxygen is used up during the first 5 to 10 minutes, following which the muscles rely on glycolysis. Oxygen utilization during the dive may be only 20 to 25 per cent of the resting rate.[234, 236] In seals the muscle oxygen is some 20 per cent and in whales over 40 per cent of the total O_2 stores.[236]

Lactic acid does not accumulate in the blood to any great amount during the dive, but in the seal *Cystophora* blood lactic acid may rise from 70 mg per 100 ml to 175 mg per 100 ml immediately after the dive. In the early part of a dive, oxygen stores in the muscle are used, supplemented by oxygen from the blood; later, anaerobic processes cause much lactic acid to accumulate in the muscle, from which circulation is virtually excluded. All pinnipeds have a striated sphincter around the posterior vena cava just ahead of the diaphragm. Blood supply to the head may be maintained while supply to the body is occluded. Another important circulatory adaptation is the bradycardia (heart slowing) which has been demonstrated in many diving birds and mammals (including trained human divers) (Fig. 48). In the seal the heart slows from a resting rate of about 80/min to 10/min during a dive; less slowing occurs in a porpoise. The bradycardia is a vagal reflex; the venous sphincter is innervated by the phrenic nerve.[131, 234, 236]

Respiratory sensitivity to carbon dioxide is lower in divers than in nondivers; a high threshold of the respiratory center has been demonstrated in beaver, seal, muskrat, and porpoise.[132] The resting respiratory mechanism is adjusted to a high carbon dioxide tolerance and normal relative apnea, 2 to 4 inspirations per minute in a porpoise, 2 to 3 in a seal. Utilization of inspired oxygen is high; a porpoise weighing 170 kg breathed once a minute, inspired 10 l with each breath and consumed about 1 l of oxygen, a utilization of 10 per cent, or two to three times as efficient as man's. In addition, divers relax when submerged, whereas nondivers increase their oxygen consumption by struggling. Scholander[234, 236] presented evidence that diving animals do not get nitrogen bubbles in their blood when they surface because at depths the lungs are compressed, no air enters them, the alveolar wall probably thickens, circulation is reduced, and hence conditions are unsuitable for gas invasion of the blood.

Diving poikilotherms, e.g., turtles, show bradycardia when held under water. A trout, *Salmo trutta,* shows bradycardia when removed from water, but in water low in O_2, breathing is stimulated and there is no bradycardia.[244a]

heart slowing, and locomotor efficiency. The relative importance of these adaptations varies among the diving mammals.

METABOLIC ADAPTATIONS

Oxygen Debt. If all animals were required to obtain all their energy exclusively by direct aerobic oxidation they would be limited in locomotor activity, and many environments would be closed to them. Actually, most animals can obtain some energy anaerobically and then later oxidize the products as an oxygen debt, and some animals live in environments virtually devoid of oxygen. Some such habitats are the following: soils, particularly in swampy regions and after rain; deep regions of oceans where there is insufficient mixing with the upper layers where oxygen is gained by photosynthesis and diffusion; muddy bottoms and deeper layers of stagnant rivers, ponds, and lakes, and also the upper layers in winter when photosynthesis and inflow are lacking; in the stomach and intestinal tract of host animals, where the oxygen content is usually below 1 per cent, and in the large intestine, where it is often zero. Regions which are less extreme but in which oxygen is at less than its sea-level pressure are saline lakes, warm springs, high mountains, and the various tissues and secretions in which parasites live.

Animals in hibernation tolerate hypoxia for a few hours as compared to minutes when not hibernating (hedgehog).[22]

Life without oxygen is possible if nonoxidative sources of energy are used. Strict anaerobiosis, common among bacteria, is rare among animals, but probably all animals can use some nonoxidative routes of energy production and then either excrete the byproducts or oxidize them. Anaerobic metabolism produces less energy and results in incompletely catabolized products as follows for glucose:

oxidation

$$C_6H_{12}O_6 + 6\,O_2 \rightarrow 6\,CO_2 + 6\,H_2O + 686\;Cal/mol$$

fermentation

$$C_6H_{12}O_6 \rightarrow 2\,CH_3CH_2OH + 2\,CO_2 + 50\;Cal/mol$$
$$\text{(ethyl alcohol)}$$

glycolysis

$$C_6H_{12}O_6 \rightarrow 2\,CH_3CH(OH)COOH + 36\;Cal/mol$$
$$\text{(lactic acid)}$$

The ability of diving mammals to remain submerged is, then, based on several interacting mechanisms: oxygen storage (limited), ability to tolerate oxygen debt in muscles, relative insensitivity of the respiratory center to CO_2 and lactic acid, circulatory shunts,

Fermentation, the production of ethyl alcohol, is not found in animals (except in one trypanosome); however, polyhydric alcohols such as glycerol are formed by a few animals. Glycolysis is usually written as producing lactic acid, but this may be excreted, may be oxidized, or may react to form other compounds. For example, lactic acid in many aerobic animals is postanaerobically oxidized in small part and in large part reconverted to carbohydrate (usually glycogen). Aerobic glycolysis is the reliance on energy from the production of lactic and other acids in the presence of oxygen. In the anaerobic oxidation of acids and other intermediates, carbon dioxide is liberated without any uptake of oxygen. Many glycolyzing parasitic worms produce lactic, valeric, caproic, butyric, and propionic acids and excrete these, even in the presence of oxygen. These worms tolerate high concentrations of these acids and can afford the wasteful means of getting energy because they live in a rich medium. The normal products of rumen bacteria, protozoans, and termite intestinal flagellates are lower fatty acids (Chapter 6). Intestinal parasites often have a mixed metabolism, part glycolytic and part oxidative.

In tolerance of oxygen lack animals range from (1) a few obligatory anaerobes such as the intestinal flagellates of termites, which are poisoned by small amounts of oxygen, through (2) those which often live for long times in a medium nearly devoid of oxygen but which use oxygen when it is supplied, such as some intestinal helminths and mud-dwelling tubificid worms, (3) those which are normally aerobic but which can survive for many hours without oxygen, as frogs, earthworms, cockroaches, aquatic snails, and to a lesser degree diving and hibernating mammals,[249] (4) aerobic animals which are highly dependent on oxygen but which can build up a brief debt, particularly in their muscles, as birds and mammals, many adult insects, and cephalopod molluscs.

In general, those animals with normally high metabolism are less tolerant of oxygen lack than more sluggish forms; eggs and cysts are very resistant, hibernating poikilotherms more resistant than nonhibernating. Slow moving nematodes and mites from seaweed tolerated anoxia for more than 16 hours, fast moving amphipods survived only a few minutes without O_2.[281] Von Brand[31] reviewed anaerobiosis in invertebrates and pointed out that in the same environment, for example, a mammalian gut, one species may be living oxidatively while another is getting its energy by glycolytic routes. A trout, which is very sensitive to O_2 lack, pays back an O_2 debt, but a crucian carp, which

can tolerate anoxia for several hours at 16°C, does not repay an O_2 debt.[25]

Some animals after a period of anaerobiosis show increased oxygen consumption in proportion to, or greater than, the deficit accumulated and excrete none of the acids. Others pay only part of the debt, and still others pay none at all but excrete all the acids which were formed anaerobically. The percentage of a debt paid varies according to whether the acid is all oxidized or is partly reconverted to carbohydrate or is partly excreted, and this varies with the motor activity; hence quantitative measures of debts are difficult to interpret. Among animals which have been shown to pay off large amounts of oxygen debt are the following: the snail *Planorbis*, planarians, earthworms, cockroaches, grasshoppers, *Tenebrio*. The respiratory volume of a turtle is doubled after a 20-minute dive.[188] A clam such as *Mya* consumes extra oxygen for a few hours after a low tide;[61] some lamellibranchs survive out of water for many days; they produce lactic acid which is buffered by the calcium salts of their shell.[73] Some less tolerant animals can develop only a small debt and must repay it in a short time, for example *Drosophila*.[46] After flight the O_2 consumption of butterflies may be elevated for 60 to 90 minutes.[290] Animals which pay off an oxygen debt tend to accumulate more lactic acid during the anaerobiosis than do those which excrete some of the acids. A chub or trout is sensitive to O_2 lack and in exercise accumulates more lactic acid in its blood than a catfish, which tolerates water low in oxygen.

Frequently animals survive long periods of anaerobiosis by relative inactivity, and when oxygen is supplied they become hyperactive, hence consume more oxygen than normally. This change in activity with oxygen supply has been noted in ascarid worms[164] and in larvae of *Chironomus plumosus*.[270] Two intertidal polychaetes showed no O_2 debt. When activity was taken into account *Chironomus plumosus* showed increased O_2 consumption corresponding to only 0.5 per cent of its debt; *Chironomus thummi* on the other hand increased its O_2 consumption by 55 per cent, and *Chironomus bathophilus* had no increase at all after anaerobiosis.[109] *Chironomus thummi* did not reconvert any of its acids to glycogen but oxidized and excreted them. Some parasitic worms *Ascaris* and *Eustrongylides* show a small increase in O_2 consumption after anaerobiosis but excrete most of their acids. *Ascaris* regenerates

TABLES 26.   PARASITES

Predominantly Aerobic			Predominantly Glycolytic		
species	O_2 debt	survival in N_2, days	species	O_2 debt	survival in N_2, days
nematodes			nematodes		
Nippostrongylus			Ascaris		7-9
Litomosoides	none	<1	Nematodirus	(partial anaerobe)	<2
Necator					
			trematodes		
Ancylostoma		21	Fasciola		1.5
Eustrongylides	30%	3	Schistosoma	none	5
			Opisthorchis	(partial anaerobe)	18
			cestode		
			Moniezia		0.5

one twentieth to one tenth of the glycogen consumed.[32]

Other animals show no postanaerobic increase in O_2 consumption, that is, they excrete all of their acid products. *Nereis* and *Urechis* react in this way as do the parasitic nematode *Litomosoides* and trematode *Schistosoma*.[32, 43] Developing salmon eggs show no increase in O_2 consumption after a period in low oxygen.[113]

Postanaerobic metabolism tends to be more sensitive to oxygen pressure than preanaerobic; there is disagreement as to whether this is due to the limits of diffusion in the face of greater demand or whether a different enzyme route is used. *Eustrongylides ignotus* repays 30 per cent of an oxygen debt in 16 to 18 hours; while paying off the debt it is slightly more O_2 dependent, but the P_c is not higher if the postanaerobic measurement is made at a low temperature.[31] Freshwater snails Lymnaeidae and Physidae (*Helisoma* and *Physa*) are sensitive to anaerobiosis and are damaged in less than 6 hours, while the Planorbidae and operculates (*Australorbis* and *Helisoma*) are more resistant, surviving more than 24 hours of anaerobiosis. Both groups show elevated postanaerobic metabolism of variable time course. The more resistant snails accumulate less lactate and recover faster after anaerobiosis, but both groups appear to oxidize all of the lactate produced.[34, 190] However, the postanaerobic metabolism shows the same percentage increase at all pressures,[34] and the change in position of the metabolism-oxygen curve postanaerobically is like that due to high temperature; hence no different enzyme route is indicated.

Lack of a simple correlation between metabolic pattern and resistance to anaerobiosis is illustrated by the data for parasites in Table 26.[32, 43, 222]

It may be concluded that the concept of oxygen debt is highly relative, and the magnitude of debt which can be repaid is variable. Animals which are sensitive to oxygen lack usually pay off some debt; those which tolerate oxygen lack well may pay off a small debt or none at all. In many animals increased activity follows anaerobiosis and this increases O_2 consumption.

Metabolic Pathways. One of the great achievements of modern science is the elucidation of the principal pathways by which energy for biological work is made available from the degradation and transformation of substrates, particularly carbohydrates. In the process of metabolism of energy-yielding substrates (exergonic processes), compounds containing "high energy" bonds (e.g., adenosine triphosphate, ATP) are produced. The cleavage (hydrolysis) of these high energy bonds is then coupled with energy-requiring (endergonic) processes for biological work. High energy compounds (usually ATP) are thus the currency of the metabolic economy of the cell, as follows:

$$(a) \quad ADP + iP \xrightarrow{\text{energy-yielding metabolic pathways}} ATP$$

$$(b) \quad ATP \xrightarrow{\text{biological work}} ADP + iP$$

where ADP = adenosine diphosphate, iP = inorganic phosphate.

The high energy pyrophosphoryl bond of ATP is indicated:

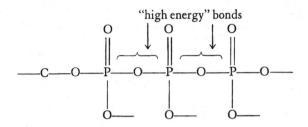

Detailed maps of enzymatic function are presented in various monographs and biochemistry texts,[156, 280] and by testing these pathways we can learn how some animals are able to obtain ample energy anaerobically and how others require oxygen. Oxidation, as dehydrogenation, can occur in the absence of oxygen, as can CO_2 liberation by decarboxylation; the important distinction between anaerobic and aerobic paths is whether the hydrogen acceptor can be reduced by an enzyme which is not part of an oxygen-requiring sequence. The over-all plan is schematized as follows:

High energy bonds may be generated in glycolysis, in the hexose monophosphate shunt, in formation of "active acetyl," and primarily through coupled phosphorylation accompanying oxidation of pyridine nucleotides (DPN, TPN) or flavoproteins through the cytochromes. Each of these metabolic systems can be identified in a variety of animals.

Metabolic pathways have been elucidated mainly in mammalian tissues and in microorganisms. The comparative physiologist is concerned with their applicability to animals which differ in oxygen dependence and in the substrate oxidized. Identification of a given enzyme system in a tissue is by (1) use

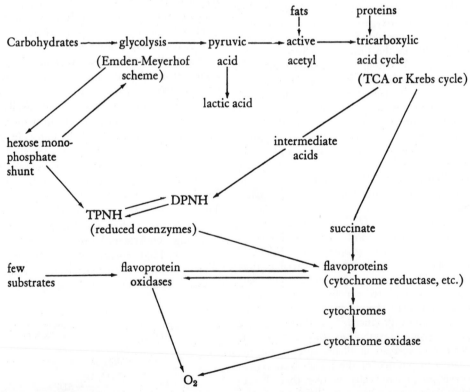

* DPN and TPN (diphosphopyridine and triphosphopyridine nucleotides) are coenzymes which carry hydrogen (protons).

of inhibitors which are more or less specific, (2) increase of O_2 uptake by adding specific intermediates as substrates or by adding electron carriers, (3) identification of carriers (coenzymes, cytochromes, flavoproteins) by spectroscopic or chemical means, and (4) isolation of enzymes.

Glycolytic Systems. The principal steps of the glycolytic path constitute the Emden-Meyerhof scheme; details differ slightly in microorganisms, but the following applies to vertebrate liver:*

and liberates 4, thus resulting in a net gain of 2 ATP per mol glucose. If glycogen is used instead of glucose, as in muscle, only 1 ATP is used and the net gain is 3 ATP for each 6-carbon unit of glycogen metabolized. In addition, hydrogens are transferred to 2 DPN, and these hydrogens are passed on to oxygen via the flavoprotein-cytochrome system, yielding a maximum of 3 $\sim$P (high energy phosphate bonds) each. Hence there is an over-all yield in the formation of 2 molecules of pyruvate of 8 $\sim$P if glucose

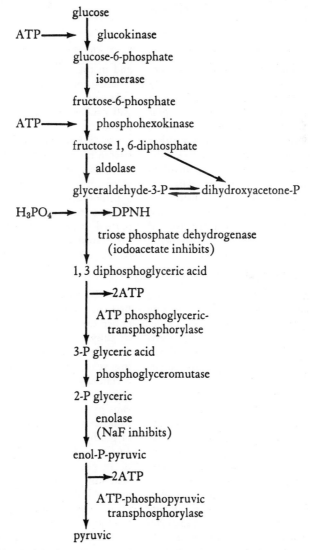

Pyruvic acid can be reduced to lactic acid or it can enter the tricarboxylic acid cycle (p. 183). The glycolytic path uses 2 ATP's

is utilized and 9 in muscle glycolysis of glycogen.

$$C_6H_{12}O_6 + DPN \rightarrow 2\ CH_3COCOOH + DPNH + 2 \sim P$$
$$2\ DPNH + O_2 \rightarrow DPN + 2\ H_2O + 6 \sim P$$

Another anaerobic oxidative chain, the hexose monophosphate shunt, provides a parallel path between glucose-6-phosphate

* Arrows indicate the direction of breakdown; actually all but the first step are reversible.

and fructose-6-phosphate (numbers in parentheses are number of carbons in molecules):

All the enzymes of the glycolytic chain seem to be present in the cestode *Hymenolepis*.[214]

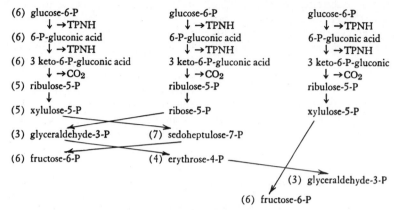

In this shunt from three glucose phosphates are formed two fructose phosphates plus one triose (glyceraldehyde) phosphate (which can be oxidized via DPN) plus CO_2 plus $TPNH_2$ in two steps of reduction of TPN. The xylulose in the shunt can be used in either of two ways to form fructose and glyceraldehyde, (1) by reacting with ribose to yield glyceraldehyde and sedoheptulose with the latter going to erythrose and fructose or (2) by reacting with erythrose to yield glyceraldehyde and fructose. The fructose-6-P and glyceraldehyde-3-P re-enter the glycolytic sequence. The over-all reaction is:

$$3 \, C_6H_{12}O_6\text{-P} + 3 \, TPN \rightarrow 3 \, TPNH_2 + 3 \, CO_2 + 2 \, \text{fructose-6-P} + \text{triose-3-P}$$

Two additional oxidative steps involving TPN are available as compared with the one in glycolysis. The importance of the monophosphate shunt varies in different organisms and in different tissues of a given animal. In mammalian liver one-half of the sugar oxidation utilizes this shunt.

All animals appear to have the enzymes of glycolysis, and probably also the monophosphate shunt, although there may be specific differences in the enzyme proteins. Glycolysis to pyruvic and lactic acids has been demonstrated in muscles of grasshopper, cockroach, oyster, *Thyone,* and *Pecten,* but in the two insects iodoacetate appears not to inhibit, in *Pecten* inhibition is slow, and in *Thyone* and oyster IOA inhibits promptly as in vertebrates.[129] Silkworm midgut contains the enzymes of glycolysis and the pentose shunt.[133] In addition to glycolysis, muscles of the housefly have enzymes for gluconate and ribulose utilization, and pea aphids have enzymes of the hexose monophosphate shunt rather than active hexokinase; hence the shunt is a major pathway in insects.[48, 197]

and in the malaria organism *Plasmodium*.[181] The O_2 consumption of some species of trypanosomes (*T. evansi, equinum, gambiense,* and *rhodesiense*) is much more inhibited by iodoacetate than it is in others (*lewisi, cruzi*).[33] Evidence has been presented for the hexose monophosphate shunt in ascarids, trematodes, cestodes, planarians, and earthworms.[169]

Important variations in glycolytic patterns come at the terminal steps. Pyruvic acid in normal oxidative metabolism is oxidatively decarboxylated to CO_2 and "active acetyl" which then enters the citric acid cycle. In anaerobiosis in the majority of animals the pyruvic is reduced to lactic acid, which is either excreted or in the presence of oxygen is fully oxidized, or partly oxidized and partly reconverted to glycogen. In fermenting yeasts pyruvic acid is decarboxylated to acetaldehyde which can then form either ethanol or acetic acid. In some microorganisms pyruvic can condense with CO_2 to form oxaloacetic acid. In parasitic animals a variety of products are formed. The filarial nematode *Litomosoides carinii* aerobically converts 30 to 45 per cent of the glucose used to lactic acid and 25 to 35 per cent to acetic, while anaerobically 80 per cent goes to lactic and 20 per cent to acetic; it excretes these acids, has no O_2 debt, yet it survives less than a day under anaerobic conditions. On the other hand, the trematode *Schistosoma mansoni* converts 80 per cent of its glucose used to lactic acid whether aerobic or anaerobic; it also incurs no postanaerobic debt and is resistant to anaerobiosis.[43] The liver fluke *Fasciola hepatica* produces volatile fatty acids anaerobically, three times more propionic than acetic acid, and only 4 to 9 per cent lactic;[179] this fluke metabolizes aerobically when oxygen is available. Tapeworms put out lactic acid and some succinic but no volatile higher fatty acids as the nematodes do.[214] The cestode *Hymenolepis* (also *Oochoristica*) produces mainly lactic acid;[214] but higher fatty acids have been reported from *Moniezia*.[30]

Ascaris converts only 2 per cent of the glucose used anaerobically to lactic acid, 1 per cent aerobically;[30] it produces some acetic and propionic acids but mainly three acids of five carbons each—D,L-2-methylbutyric (20 per cent), n-valeric (8 per cent) and cis-2-methylcrotonic acids[43] (not valeric according to Moyle[195]). A heterakis nematode from the fowl excretes in nitrogen, propionic acid,

The trypanosomes show much species variation and von Brand[33] has classified them into four groups, three of which are shown in Table 27.

It may be concluded that the basic pattern of glycolysis, along with phosphorylation and dephosphorylation, is very widespread, that there may be minor enzyme differences, and that the major variation is in the products formed. Why so many parasites excrete various fatty acids is not explained. Excretion of glycerol, particularly by trypanosomes, indicates a similarity to alcoholic fermentation.

Oxidative Systems. In aerobic metabolism the most common fate of pyruvic acid is oxidative decarboxylation by coenzyme A (Co A) to enter the tricarboxylic acid (TCA) (Krebs or citric acid) cycle as follows:

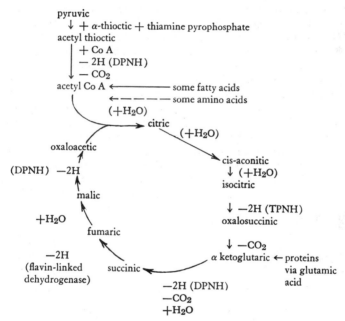

acetic acid, higher fatty acids, and lactic acid, in the proportion 76:28:3:1; its acid ratios in oxygen are similar.[82, 102] The enzymic routes by which parasitic helminths produce higher acids are unknown.

Several protozoans have succinic acid among their glycolytic products. The parasitic *Trichomonas foetus* (which lacks a cytochrome system) produces acetic and succinic acids whether air is present or not, and it is sensitive to IOA inhibition.[225] The free living ciliate *Tetrahymena* also produces succinate when kept anaerobically in the presence of pyruvate and CO_2.[198] It is suggested[243, 244] that in *Trypanosoma cruzi* succinic acid replaces the pyruvic of most cells in forming acetyl Co A.[33]

In the series of steps between pyruvic and citric acids (including the condensation with oxaloacetic), 3 ATP are formed, or 6 per mol of glucose. For each turn of the wheel and oxidation of 1 pyruvic acid, a total of 3 CO_2 molecules is formed and 5 dehydrogenations (by DPN or TPN or a flavin-linked dehydrogenase) occur; 15 high-energy phosphate bonds also are formed, 30 per mol glucose, of which 6 are in the oxidation of pyruvate and 24 in the cycle *per se*. To these are added the net gain of 2 ATP from anaerobic glycolysis plus 6 ATP formed aerobically in the transfer of 2H from DPNH formed in the oxidation of triosephosphate in glycolysis. This means that in aerobic metabolism of

TABLE 27. TRYPANOSOMES

Group	lewisi	congolense	brucei (evansi, equiperdum hippicum)
sugar utilization	low	high	very high
aerobic products	succinic (70%) lactic (15%) acetic, pyruvic	acetic, little succinic, glycerol, pyruvic	pyruvic, glycerol
anaerobic products	succinic (70%) lactic (15%) acetic, pyruvic	succinic, glycerol, acetic (pyruvic)	pyruvic, glycerol
respiratory quotient	high	high	very low
effect of cyanide on O₂ uptake	strong inhibition	moderate inhibition	no inhibition

glucose some 38 high energy phosphates are formed as compared with only 2 in anaerobic glycolysis. The yield of ATP for the oxidative steps of the citric acid cycle is evaluated by measuring the ratio of inorganic phosphorus incorporated to oxygen used; the theoretical P/O ratio for α-ketoglutarate as substrate is 4, for succinate 2, malate 3, and isocitrate 3. Some amino acids can enter the cycle via glutamic acid to α-ketoglutarate; others, by deamination to acetyl-Co A; fats enter through acetyl-Co A.

At each dehydrogenation in the citric acid cycle the reduced coenzymes in the presence of their respective dehydrogenases are then oxidized by the cytochrome system. Succinic dehydrogenase transfers hydrogen directly without DPNH or TPNH.

none which, together with a lipoprotein, constitutes the factor by which electrons are transferred to cytochrome c_1 and c. This factor which couples to the cytochrome c is sensitive to antimycin; cytochrome a (cytochrome oxidase) is inhibited by CO, an inhibition reversed by light; cyanide and azide inhibit principally cytochrome a, while the other cytochromes are little or not affected by these agents. The side chain attached to the benzoquinone ring of coenzyme Q from animals usually contains ten isoprenoid units, but chains of nine units are reported from rat and walleyed pike.[57a, 105a]

A few flavoproteins can transfer hydrogen directly to oxygen, often with the formation of hydrogen peroxide, which is immediately broken down to water and oxygen by cata-

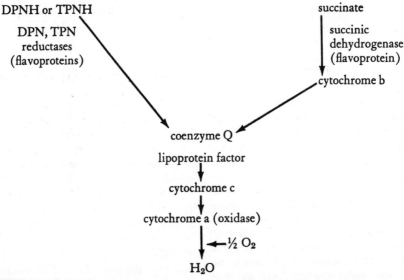

This system is the final common path for many oxidations. The oxidation of DPNH and TPNH and of succinate is by flavoprotein enzymes (specific dehydrogenases). Coenzyme Q is a small molecule, a benzoqui-

lase. These aerobic dehydrogenases which bypass cytochrome include: D-amino acid oxidase, xanthine oxidase, tyrosinase, glycine oxidase, and others.

Numerous dehydrogenases require DPN as

a coenzyme, a few use TPN, and some flavo-proteins do not require either coenzyme. Those oxidative paths utilizing DPN yield more ATP than the TPN-linked paths. Transhydrogenase couples DPN and TPN, as for example:

$$\text{isocitrate} \rightarrow \text{TPNH} \underset{\xrightarrow{\hspace{1.2cm}}}{\overset{\text{transhydrogenase}}{\rightleftharpoons}} \text{DPNH} - - \rightarrow O_2$$

In most cells the enzymes of the TCA cycle and the cytochrome chain are located in mitochondria while those of glycolysis are outside the mitochondria. The mitochondria are, therefore, an important source of energy within cells. Phosphorylation can be decoupled from oxidation by such agents as dinitrophenol and thyroxin.[165]

Some of the inhibitors commonly used in identification of oxidative steps are the following:

carbon monoxide—ferrocytochrome oxidase (reversed by light)
cyanide and azide—ferricytochromes
antimycin A—cytochrome c reductase (coenzyme Q factor)
malonate—competes with succinate for succinic dehydrogenase
Amytal—flavin-linked systems
iodoacetate—phosphoglyceraldehyde dehydrogenase

The citric acid cycle and the cytochrome system usually occur together. Utilization of the intermediate acids can sometimes be demonstrated with cell extracts but not with intact cells, which are not permeable to the compounds. The cycle has been demonstrated in numerous insects[221] (cockroach,[11] house-fly,[48] and others). In his original spectroscopic identification of cytochrome, Keilin found the thoracic muscles of honeybees to be richer than any other tissue; as measured enzymatically cytochrome oxidase of cockroach leg muscle is as active as the best preparations of pigeon breast muscle.[11] In insect flight muscle, the enzymes of the citric acid cycle-cytochrome system are contained in giant mitochondria, sarcosomes which lie between fibrils.[226, 273] TPN is required for oxidative phosphorylation by locust sarcosomes.[216] Cytochrome c and succinate increase O_2 consumption by homogenates of mealworms *Tenebrio*, and the extra succin-oxidase respiration is sensitive to CN^-, unlike endogenous respiration, which is not.[174] Insect blood has TPN-linked L-malic dehydrogenase.[84] *Musca* sarcosomes contain an oxidative chain which is not stimulated by DPN; the cytochrome is also different from that of heart muscle. Cytochrome has been identified from hepatopancreas of *Aplysia, Helix*,[265] and oyster.[144]

In a series of crustaceans, annelids, and molluscs, highest levels of cytochrome were found in the most active muscles. No cytochrome system could be demonstrated in muscles of the snails *Planorbis* and *Lymnaea*; no cytochrome c, in the holothurian *Parastichopus*; flavoproteins were indicated in some polychaetes and molluscs.[185] *Ascaris* has cytochrome oxidase and also an alternate path for DPNH and succinate to molecular O_2, which is insensitive to CN^- and antimycin.[150] The tapeworm *Hymenolepis* contains the enzymes of the TCA cycle and cytochrome system, although an unknown labile step is indicated between succinic dehydrogenase and cytochrome.[214] In the trematode *Fasciola*, cytochrome bands are reported, cyanide inhibits and glutamic and glycerophosphate stimulate O_2 uptake.[106] In some nematodes—*Nematodirus, Ascaridia,* and *Neoaplectana*—the TCA cycle has been demonstrated although *Ascaridia* lives largely anaerobically (liberates succinic acid) and *Nematodirus* partly so.[184] In other nematodes—*Ascaris* and *Litomosoides*—cytochrome and cytochrome oxidase are absent although there is some other cyanide-sensitive oxidase which can oxidize succinic acid directly with H_2O_2 formation.[43, 213] *Schistosoma* has some cytochrome, but it accounts for less than 10 per cent of the oxygen consumption. Thus, animals which are largely anaerobic may or may not have active oxidase systems; in adopting the parasitic life, the trend has been to loss of oxidative enzymes.

Among Protozoa, cyanide inhibition of respiration has been frequently observed. *Tetrahymena* metabolizes the acids of the TCA cycle (in brei but not intact) as does *Paramecium*. When *Tetrahymena* is maintained in 10^{-4} KCN it develops some resistance to 10^{-3} KCN, which normally inhibits its respiration.[186] The endogenous respiration of the amoeba *Mayorella* is inhibited by cyanide but its metabolism of glucose is increased by cyanide at the same concentration.[218] The malaria parasite *Plasmodium gallinacea* uses the TCA cycle; when inside the red cell its oxidation of pyruvate is complete; the free parasite, however, liberates some acetate.[253] Other parasitic protozoans, *Trichomonas (hepatica* and *foetus)*, lack enzymes of the Krebs cycle;[32] *Trichomonas* also lacks the cytochrome system. *Trypanosoma lewisi* and *Strigomonas oncopelti* use the cytochrome system.[225] The trypanosomes which produce pyruvic acid only are cyanide resistant; those which form a series of other acids are cyanide sensitive.[1]

Respiratory Quotients. Some measure of the substrates oxidized and of type of metabolism is given by the respiratory quotient or R.Q. $= \frac{CO_2}{O_2}$. The R.Q. is given as 1.0 for carbohydrate, 0.71 for fat, and 0.79 for protein. Herbivores tend to have higher R.Q.'s than carnivores. The interpretation of R.Q. is more complex than mere identification of foodstuff.

Values higher than 1.0 are found when fat is being formed from carbohydrate; some energy is made available in this process. High R.Q.'s associated with fat deposition have been demonstrated in various parasites, in honeybee queens, in mammals preparatory to hibernation, and in fattening livestock. High R.Q. values are also obtained when animals rely on glycolysis and oxidation of the intermediate acids. In low oxygen environments when there is reliance on glycolysis, R.Q. values are high. Oxidation of pyruvic acid yields an R.Q. of 1.2. In hyperventilating mammals the R.Q. is high.

Low R.Q. values are found when CO_2 is fixed, as by the calcareous shell of a crustacean. Also, CO_2 fixation can occur enzymatically, as by combining with pyruvic acid. Carbon dioxide may be retained in tissues, as in hibernating mammals, and in insects where it is liberated in bursts. Low R.Q. values result from conversion of fat and protein to carbohydrate. Increase in R.Q. with high temperature has been reported for several poikilotherms, and changes at different stages of the life cycle occur in numerous animals. Caution must therefore be used in interpreting R.Q. values.

Alternate Metabolic Pathways. The preceding sections present evidence that a few animals can obtain sufficient energy by anaerobic means but that most of those living in low oxygen utilize some oxygen and are capable of shifting to aerobic metabolism. These animals rely heavily on the glycolytic path and hexose monophosphate shunt; they excrete a variety of acid products although it is unlikely that energy is derived in the conversion of pyruvate to the fatty acids. Many of these animals, particularly parasites, continue to rely to a large extent on glycolysis in the presence of oxygen and to excrete the acids formed. However, many aerobic animals can rely on anaerobic routes temporarily; some excrete the acids formed, others oxidize them or reconvert them to glycogen. In general, those which excrete the intermediate acids are able to survive longer without oxygen.

Aerobically there are parallel transfer systems for hydrogen via DPN, TPN, succinic dehydrogenase, and various flavoproteins. The principal alternatives, however, are between the cytochrome-linked and the noncytochrome-linked oxidases. In very few cells does CN^- or CO inhibition of cytochrome oxidase reduce O_2 consumption to zero. Noncytochrome-linked paths are less well understood than the cytochrome system. There are many examples of enzymatic changes with development and with activity. Unfertilized sea urchin eggs are CN^- resistant, and after fertilization the increased O_2 consumption is CN^- sensitive; however, in reduced oxygen the unfertilized eggs are somewhat cyanide sensitive.[171] Succinate is used by larvae and early pupae of *Tenebrio,* but in late pupae this substance inhibits O_2 consumption by 85 per cent, indicating that respiration of late pupation is by a phenolase system.[174] In *Drosophila* and *Phormia* flight muscles, the turnover of cytochrome c in muscle mitochondria increases with beat frequency.[167] In regenerating *Tubifex* the increased O_2 consumption associated with differentiation is CN^- stable, while the energy for segmentation comes from a CN^- sensitive system.[6] In *Trypanosoma gambiense* the developmental stage (within the insect proventriculus) is CN^- sensitive; the stage in the blood is not.[33] Changes in respiratory quotient also indicate shifts in metabolism with stage in life cycle and with respiratory and nutritional conditions.

Diapausing grasshopper eggs and pupae of cecropia moths are insensitive to CN^- and CO; just before emergence they become sensitive to these inhibitors. The cecropia larvae contain cytochromes a_1, a_3, b, c, and a unique one, cytochrome b_5; the pupal tissues (except muscle) lose cytochromes b and c.[245] Also cytochrome c reductase declines on pupation and reappears just before onset of adult development. The prothoracic gland hormone which initiates preparation for emergence stimulates the synthesis of components of the cytochrome system.[245] The larval heart is blocked by 10^{-3} M CN^-; the adult heart, by 10^{-5} M CN^-; and that of the pupa, by 10^{-2} to 10^{-3} M CN^- after a long time. Also the pupal heart continues to beat for over 3 hours in nitrogen, whereas the adult heart stops in less than 10 minutes.[112] If pupal tissues are treated with dinitrophenol (DNP) the enhanced respiration is CO and azide sensitive, and if the O_2 concentration is reduced to 2 per cent the O_2 consumption is not reduced but is then sensitive to CO. Evidently the resistance to CO and to low O_2 in pupal tissues is due to an excess of cytochrome oxidase relative to cytochrome c.[162]

	At sea level (mm Hg)	At 17,500 feet (mm Hg)
O_2	105	45
CO_2	40	25
water	47	47
nitrogen	568	270
total	760	387

In mammals, especially man, gradual acclimatization at high altitude results in increased pulmonary ventilation, increased lung capacity, increased oxygen capacity of the blood due to increase in numbers of circulating red cells, and increased cardiac output.[192]

Changes in blood gases in man:[130]

	O_2 capacity (mM/l)	Hb (gm/m^3 ml)	Blood CO_2 (mM/l)	P_{CO_2} (mm Hg)
Sea level	9.3	15.3	21.72	40.1
Altitude 14,000 ft.	12.29	20.8	15.87	33.1

In isolated frog nerves the increase in O_2 consumption associated with conduction is inhibited by azide; the resting metabolism, by methylfluoroacetate.[70]

In frog muscle, azide inhibits the metabolism of activity but not of rest. The O_2 consumption associated with division in yeast, and luminescence in luminous bacteria can be separated from the basal O_2 consumption by differential sensitivities to narcotics. Further evidence for separation of oxidative systems is the fact that mitochondria contain all the enzymes of the TCA cycle and cytochrome oxidation, but not the aerobic flavoproteins, lactic dehydrogenase, xanthine dehydrogenase, and the like.

An enzymic pathway may be subject to stimulation, e.g., rats on high sucrose diet show an elevation of glucose-6-phosphatase of liver.

The various paths by which energy can be made available differ greatly in efficiency. Anaerobic glycolysis is wasteful, but it permits animals to survive under hypoxic or anoxic stress. The parallel paths provide a safety mechanism in case one enzyme becomes blocked, and they may provide some metabolic separation of true basal from active metabolism.

ACCLIMATION TO LOW OXYGEN

Prolonged living in low oxygen induces a variety of adaptive responses in different animals. The effects of high altitude result from reduced partial pressure of oxygen rather than from reduced total pressure *per se*.

The respiratory stress of high altitudes is illustrated by the differences in partial pressures of gases in the alveoli of man:

Muscles of the right ventricle become hypertrophied, with an increase in the ratio of heart weight to body weight. The difference between capillary P_{O_2} at sea level and at altitude is thus minimized.[126] There is reduced alkaline reserve, some tissues become more vascular, and myoglobin may increase, but there are no changes in oxygen consumption. Carotid sinus chemoreceptors become more sensitive to low oxygen, so that ventilation is increased.[211, 254] Either no metabolic changes or slightly reduced O_2 consumption has been found in tissues from animals acclimatized to high altitudes.[266] However, higher levels of succinoxidase, increased glycolysis, and ATP-ase are found.[259] Cytochrome c oxidase is increased in some tissues.

Reduction in oxidative metabolism of poikilotherms acclimated to low oxygen was mentioned on page 169. Hibernating mammals (e.g., hedgehogs) can survive several hours of anoxia, and tissues from hibernators are more resistant to low oxygen.[22] Acute exposures to low oxygen inactivate various oxidative enzymes of mammals,[177] yet many invertebrate animals can be transferred from air to anaerobic conditions with no apparent damage.

The increase in circulating blood cells in mammals at high altitudes is largely due to stimulation of the hemopoietic tissues. The plasma of persons from high altitudes or of animals exposed to hypoxia contains an erythropoietic factor, hemopoietin, which stimulates the bone marrow of recipients.[103] In certain invertebrates, stimulation by low oxygen is more marked. *Daphnia, Artemia, Chironomus* larvae, and *Planorbis* synthesize increased amounts of hemoglobin when maintained for a few days in water low in oxygen. They may change from a pale color to bright red. However, *Physa, Tubifex,* and *Arenicola* failed to respond by increasing hemoglobin synthesis. In *Daphnia* and *Conchostraca* not only did the circulating hemoglobin increase but also muscle and ganglionic hemoglobin and tissue cytochrome.[88]

Insects, e.g., *Musca,* build up resistance to repeated decompressions by some unknown mechanism.[121]

Acclimation to low oxygen is mainly in ventilation and transport systems; increases in pigment synthesis and probably in some enzymes have been reported.

TOXICITY OF HIGH OXYGEN CONCENTRATIONS

Death of cells at low oxygen presumably results from their inability to get enough energy to maintain normal molecular structure, especially of cell membranes. Cells can also be killed by high concentrations of oxygen. Termites can be rid of intestinal flagellates by putting them into pure oxygen; 1 atmosphere of O_2 is more toxic to the flagellates at 4 to 5°C than it is at 25°; several atmospheres pressure are more toxic at high temperatures.[53] Cultures of the parasitic protozoan *Trichomonas* grow best in the absence of oxygen and less well as oxygen is supplied, that is, they are facultative aerobes.[138] Some parasitic helminths cannot be maintained at high oxygen concentrations; *Ascaris* dies in 30 to 60 minutes in 100 per cent O_2.[164]

Besides the parasites, some free living animals which normally live in regions low in oxygen are sensitive to atmospheric oxygen. Chironomid larvae (*C. plumosus*), *Tubifex,* and one ostracod (*Heterocypris*) lived best at 4 per cent O_2, a shorter time at 21 per cent (air saturation), and they were killed in 2 to 4 days in 100 per cent oxygen. On the other hand, *Planorbis, Physa, Artemia,* an ostracod, and *Arenicola* did as well at 21 per cent as at 4 per cent, and most of these tolerated 1 atmosphere of oxygen.[90] Paramecia swell and die at 2 atmospheres of O_2.[98] *Tubifex,* like other oligochaetes, regenerates lost segments; this regeneration does not proceed at very low oxygen pressures, yet O_2 above air saturation blocks the differentiation and causes the animals to break apart in a few days; cyanide relieves the toxicity of high oxygen.[6] Thus, mud dwellers and parasites which normally live in low oxygen are more readily damaged by high oxygen than are

animals which live usually at air saturation. The effects are not due to pressure *per se.* Exposure of, pupae of the hymenopteran *Habrobracon* to 1 atmosphere of O_2 for 1 hour or to 2 atmospheres of O_2 for 5 minutes causes cytological damage and reduced metabolism of the emerged adults.[50] Many invertebrates show a transient increase in oxygen consumption when first placed at high pressures.[217]

A pressure of several atmospheres of oxygen may be toxic to mammals; a 5-hour exposure to 6 atmospheres of O_2 is lethal to mice.[98] The toxicity is relieved by reducing agents such as glutathione and cysteine; hence toxic oxidizing radicals or peroxides may have been formed. A similar explanation may apply to the parasites and mud dwellers. Succinic and pyruvic dehydrogenases and triose dehydrogenase are inhibited by high O_2 pressure; catalase, flavoproteins, and lactic and malic dehydrogenases are not; the sensitive enzymes have active —SH prosthetic groups.[66] Most of those animals which are very sensitive to oxygen rely normally to a large extent on glycolysis.

GAS LIBERATION: SWIM BLADDERS

The transfer of oxygen across respiratory membranes into blood is by diffusion gradient, even in the lungs at high altitudes where the pressure is low. However, diffusion by known gradients cannot account for oxygen transfer in a number of examples where some sort of gas secretion is postulated. The rhizopod *Arcella* reduces its specific gravity and rises to the surface of a pond by forming along its margin bubbles of gas which appear to be oxygen.[26] *Hydra oligactis* is also said to rise by secreting gas into a mucous cover.[148] Siphonophores (Portuguese man-of-war) have a large float which, in some, has a pore which can be opened or closed; below the float is a gas gland, from cells of which bubbles have been observed to arise.[134] There is no evidence that the gas differs from air, but it seems certain that it is liberated from the glandular tissue. The floats of some giant kelps contain 5 to 10 per cent carbon monoxide.[27] When various insect larvae molt, their tracheal system is fluid filled, yet gas rapidly replaces the fluid. In the fly *Sciara,* for example, tracheal filling can occur when the larvae are submerged or in high pressures of gas other than oxygen; the gas-filling process is reversible. It is postulated that as fluid is absorbed a negative pressure is created which draws gas from tissue fluids into the tracheae.[41, 146]

The most studied but still unexplained example of gas secretion is in the teleost swim bladder.[83] In physoclists all the gas is secreted, and physostomes when kept submerged are capable of secreting some gas. The primary function of the swim bladder is hydrostatic, regulating the level of the fish in the water, and deep water fish rise and sink according to the gas volume. Another function of the swim bladder is sensory, the amplifying of underwater sounds (Chapter 10); in some fish the swim bladder participates also in sound production. The swim bladder can provide oxygen at times of respiratory stress, as in swamp-dwelling fish.[141] Swim bladders are more commonly found in marine surface and bathypelagic (down to 600 meters) than in bottom fish. Teleost swim bladders are derived from the dorsal gut.

The gas secreted into swim bladders is very different from air. Scholander and his associates[237, 240] have analyzed the gas from many marine fish taken at different depths. The pressure increases about 1 atm per 10 meters of depth; hence gas is secreted against 10 atm pressure at 100 meters depth, and when the fish rises rapidly the gas expands to the point of rupture of the bladder. The bulk of the gas in swim bladders of marine fish is oxygen, there is a trace of CO_2 and more nitrogen than could be accounted for by equilibrium with the water (Fig. 49). In the ocean the nitrogen remains at 0.8 atm at all depths, i.e., at the surface it is 80 per cent or 0.8 atm, at 100 atm it is 0.8 per cent of the total pressure, still 0.8 atm. A swim bladder may have 5 to 15 atm of nitrogen at 900 meters.[143] Thus, not only oxygen but also nitrogen is secreted. In most fresh-water physoclists also the gas is predominantly oxygen. However, in the whitefish the gas may be more than 99 per cent nitrogen, and in other lake physostomes (which are secreting rather than swallowing gas into the air bladder) nitrogen often constitutes more than 90 per cent of the gas;[229, 255, 256] this may be secreted against a hydrostatic pressure of 8 to 15 atmospheres.

One hypothesis for oxygen liberation is that acid produced in the rete mirabile or gas gland causes release of oxygen from hemoglobin by shifting the dissociation curve to the right (Bohr effect) and reducing the maximum saturation (Root effect) (p. 218). Examination of dissociation curves of a va-

riety of deep sea fish shows the hemoglobin to remain saturated at very high O_2 pressures in some and to be relatively insensitive to pH, yet these fish have high pressures of oxygen in their swim bladders.[255, 256] The capillaries of the rete serving the gas gland end in loops with parallel vessels beneath in a countercurrent arrangement so that a steep pressure between bladder and rete could be maintained without loss to the blood, where the gases are at very different pressures and proportions.

Tracer experiments show that the secreted oxygen is derived from oxygen dissolved in the water but that much of the CO_2 is from carbohydrate stores.[235, 238] A gas gland exposed in a living fish can secrete bubbles rich in O_2.[235, 238] In *Fundulus* the secretory epithelium loses glycogen during the several days required to fill the bladder after the gas is removed.[56] The gas gland is rich in carbonic anhydrase, phosphatases, acetylcholine esterase, and dehydrogenases, and secretion is initiated reflexly by posture receptors, since secretion stops after the nerve to the gas gland is cut.[7, 83] Fluid bathing the gland becomes acid in conditions which would be similar to those for oxygen secretion.

The argon/nitrogen ratio in swim bladder gas is the same as in air; hence the nitrogen is probably deposited physically since there is

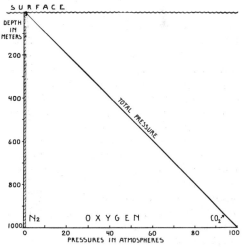

FIGURE 49. Composition of swim bladder gas of fish taken at different depths in the sea. Hatched area is equal to the partial pressure of nitrogen in the sea water. The partial pressure of nitrogen in the swim bladder is represented as the distance to the left of each point and of oxygen to the right of each point out to the total pressure. The CO_2 pressure is less than the thickness of the diagonal line. (From Scholander, P. F., and van Dam, L.: Biol. Bull., vol. 104.)

no likelihood of a chemical reaction involving argon.[257] However, when fish are put into different mixtures of dissolved inert gases, the proportion of the soluble gas argon in the swim bladder is high compared to the insoluble neon and helium. If oxygen were secreted as minute bubbles, inert gases would diffuse into these in proportion to their solubility in tissue fluids; oxygen could then be preferentially reabsorbed, leaving the high pressure of argon and nitrogen.[287]

In summary: Many fish secrete into the swim bladder nearly pure oxygen; others, nearly pure nitrogen; others, mixtures in proportions very different from those in the blood or surrounding medium. Oxygen secretion is not a simple liberation from oxyhemoglobin by acidification, but the cellular mechanism of the secretion remains obscure.

CONCLUSIONS

Oxygen is one environmental constituent which is rarely available in excess; air normally sets the upper limit of oxygen concentration. Many animal adaptations exist, however, which facilitate the acquisition of oxygen when it is scarce. Diffusion is adequate for the respiration of very small organisms, but special ventilation mechanisms appear with increasing body size, and the net effect of gills, lungs, and branched tracheae is to provide extensive absorbing surfaces. Environments low in oxygen are largely aquatic, and aquatic animals have varied ventilatory and metabolic adaptations. In air, oxygen is abundantly available (except at high altitudes), but since oxygen must enter by a moist surface, respiration in terrestrial animals requires breathing mechanisms designed for water conservation. Active transport of oxygen into fish swim bladders is by some unknown mechanism.

A common way of measuring an animal's "efficiency" is to measure its oxygen consumption, often as a function of some environmental variable. Yet it is virtually impossible to state a norm or "basal" value of metabolism. Oxygen consumption increases less than does weight from small to large animals of a kind, that is, like many body dimensions it is an exponential function of weight and the exponent is usually between 0.55 and 1.0. Small multicellular animals have higher exponents than unicellular or large multicellular ones. Metabolism is not directly correlated with any one kind of measurement of size but: (1) External surface area may be important in one-celled

organisms and, for different reasons, in homeotherms. (2) Differences in proportions of "active" and "less active" tissues contribute an undeterminable amount. Furthermore, possible relations of oxygen consumption to (3) growth pattern, (4) total active cell surfaces, and (5) respiratory area need elucidation, and there is evidence that (6) mitochondrial oxidative enzymes have the same relation to body size as does metabolism. A most elusive question is how the delicate relation between increasing size and enzyme activity is adjusted. In addition to size, age, growth, sex, hormonal levels, activity, and a variety of environmental agents affect oxygen consumption.

An important modifier of metabolism is the level of available oxygen. Many animals regulate metabolism over a wide range of oxygen concentrations. In some, the rate depends on oxygen concentration to above the highest values they normally experience—they are oxygen conformers. Factors which make for oxygen conformity are: (1) large size with long diffusion paths, (2) lack of ventilating and/or circulatory systems, (3) inadequate control of ventilation so that O_2 intake does not keep pace with the reduced environmental oxygen, (4) life in a habitat of constant high oxygen where regulation is unnecessary, and (5) life usually in extremely low oxygen so that reliance is placed on anaerobic methods of getting energy. The limiting oxygen concentration below which metabolic regulation fails is most commonly imposed (a) by ventilation and external respiratory surfaces, to lesser degrees (b) by the oxygen saturation of cell enzymes, and (c) by oxygen-transporting pigments and fluids.

Regulation of metabolism in reduced environmental oxygen is partly by ventilation and transport adaptations, which tend to maintain an adequate supply of oxygen, and partly by enzymatic adaptations which provide energy anaerobically. Ventilation is usually under central nervous control; in air breathers it is regulated mainly by the carbon dioxide in blood or air; in aquatic animals, more by the oxygen concentration in water. Central nervous centers may be stimulated directly, or reflexly via respiratory chemoreceptors. Such chemoreceptors in aquatic animals are virtually unexplored. An important safety factor in external respiration is given by multiple routes of O_2 uptake; cutaneous loss of CO_2 is surprisingly large, especially in aquatic animals. In many animals the increased utilization of oxygen in hypoxic stress is partly by ventilation but also by improved circulation. In prolonged hypoxia morphological changes favor increased ventilation and increase in transport pigments.

Enzymatically all animals are able to get some energy without oxygen. A few live without it normally; some require a little oxygen, but even when it is available they rely mainly on aerobic glycolysis; many animals can use anaerobic energy for a brief effort only. The enzymes of glycolysis and the hexose monophosphate shunt are widespread among animals, and these paths differ mainly in quantitative details. Anaerobic liberation of energy is expensive, but this makes no difference to parasites living in a rich organic medium which lacks only oxygen. Toxic acids are formed in glycolysis, but these are readily lost in an aquatic medium, or they may be oxidized; occasionally they may be reconverted to glycogen. Parasites adapted to a semianaerobic life tend to lose oxidative enzymes and to excrete a variety of acids whose production is not understood. Animals which must perform oxidation to survive get their energy stepwise in complex metabolic routes and usually have parallel paths, sometimes converging or diverging, some ending via iron-containing carriers (cytochromes), a few by hydrogen-carrying enzymes direct to oxygen. The oxidative paths of the tricarboxylic acid cycle appear similar in all aerobic metabolism; some variations in cytochromes are known, and some tissues also use noncytochrome paths, presumably flavoproteins. Shifts in metabolic paths with activity, stage in life cycle, availability of oxygen, and under different environmental conditions are poorly known adaptations.

REFERENCES

1. Agrosin, M., and von Brand, T., Exp. Parasitol. 3: 517-524, 1954; 4: 548-563, 1955. Carbohydrate metabolism of trypanosomes.
2. Alderdice, D. F., et al., J. Fish. Res. Board Canada 15: 229-249, 1958. O_2 sensitivity, salmon eggs.
3. Allen, W. R., and Richards, A. G., Canad. J. Zool. 32: 1-8, 1954. O_2 uptake by insect muscle.
4. Amberson, W. R., Biol. Bull. 55: 79-92, 1928. Effects of oxygen tension on metabolism of protozoans and other invertebrates.
5. Amberson, W. R., Mayerson, H. S., and Scott, W. J., J. Gen. Physiol. 7: 171-176, 1924. Effects of oxygen tension on metabolism of protozoans and other invertebrates.

*Reviews

6. Anderson, J. C., Biol. Bull. 111: 179-189, 1956. Relation of metabolism to regeneration in Tubifex.
7. Augustinsson, K-B, and Fänge, R., Acta physiol. scand. 22: 224-230, 1951. Innervation and acetylcholine splitting in air bladder of fish.
8. Bair, T. D., J. Parasitol. 41: 613-623, 1955. Oxygen consumption of nematodes in relation to O_2 pressure.
9. Baker, E. G. S., and Baumberger, J. P., J. Cell. Comp. Physiol. 17: 285-304, 1941. Critical O_2, Tetrahymena.
10. Barghoorn, E. S., Mem. Geol. Soc. America 67: 75-86, 1957. Origin of life.
11. Barron, E. S. G., and Tahmisian, T. N., J. Cell. Comp. Physiol. 32: 57-70, 1948. Metabolism of cockroach muscle.
12. Basu, S. P., J. Fish. Res. Board Canada 16: 175-212, 1959. Active respiration of fish in relation to ambient concentrations of oxygen and carbon dioxide.
13. Beadle, L. C., J. Exp. Biol. 34: 1-10, 1957. Respiration of swamp oligochaete Alma.
14. Benedict, F. G., Carnegie Inst. Washington Publ. 425: 404-517, 1932. Physiology of reptiles.
15. Benedict, F. G., Carnegie Inst. Washington Publ. 503: 1-215, 1938. Vital energetics.
16. Benedict, F. G., and Lee, R. C., Carnegie Inst. Washington Publ. 497: 1-239, 1938. Hibernation and marmot physiology.
17. Berg, K., Hydrobiologia 4: 225-267, 1952. Oxygen consumption by fresh-water snails.
18. Berg, K., Lumbye, J., and Ackleman, K. W., J. Exp. Biol. 35: 43-73, 1958; 36: 690-708, 1959. Oxygen consumption by fresh-water snails and limpets.
19. von Bertalanffy, L., Nature 116: 156, 1949. Am. Naturalist 85: 111-117, 1951. Relation between total and tissue metabolism and body size and growth type.
20. von Bertalanffy, L., and Krywienczyk, J., Am. Naturalist 87: 107-110, 1953. Relation between total metabolism and body size, crustaceans.
21. von Bertalanffy, L., and Pirozynski, W. J., Science 113: 599, 1951; Biol. Bull. 106: 240-256, 1953. Relation between tissue metabolism and body size and growth type.
22. Biorck, G., et al., Acta physiol. scand. 37: 71-83, 1956. Tolerance of anoxia by hibernators.
23. Black, E. C., J. Fish. Res. Board Canada 12: 917-929, 1955; 14: 117-134, 1957. Comparative physiology: fuel of muscle metabolism. Accumulation of lactic acid in blood in exercised fish.
24. *Black, E. C., and Drummond, G. I., Ann. Rev. Physiol. 22: 169-190, 1960. Comparative physiology: fuel of muscle metabolism. Accumulation of lactic acid in blood in exercised fish.
25. Blazka, P., Physiol. Zool. 31: 117-128, 1958. Anaerobic metabolism of fish.
26. Blès, E., Quart. J. Micr. Sci. 72: 527-648, 1929. O_2 secretion, Arcella.
27. Blinks, L., in Manual of Physiology, edited by D. M. Smith. Waltham, Mass., Chronica Bot., 1951, Chapter 14. CO in kelp floats.
28. Boell, E. J., Ann. New York Acad. Sci. 49:

773-800, 1948. Metabolism of amphibian embryos.

29. BOSWORTH, M., O'BRIEN, H., and AMBERSON, W. R., J. Cell. Comp. Physiol. 9: 77-87, 1936. R.Q.; marine animals.

30. VON BRAND, T., Ztschr. vergl. Physiol. 18: 562-595, 1933; Biol. Bull. 92: 162-166, 1947. Metabolism of cestodes and strongyles.

31. VON BRAND, T., Anaerobiosis in Invertebrates. Normandy, Mo., Biodynamica, 1946, pp. 137-278.

32. *VON BRAND, T., Chemical Physiology of Endoparasitic Animals. New York, Academic Press, 1952, Chap. 10, 13, and 14. Respiration of parasites.

33. VON BRAND, T., in Biochemistry and Physiology of Protozoa, edited by A. Lwoff. New York, Academic Press, 1951, vol. 1, pp. 177-234, 434. J. Cell. Comp. Physiol. 29: 33-48, 1947; 45: 421-434, 1955; Zool. Anz. 157: 119-123, 1956. Intermediary metabolism of trypanosomes.

34. VON BRAND, T., et al., Biol. Bull. 98: 266-276, 1950; 104: 301-312, 1953; Physiol. Zool. 28: 35-40, 1955. Postanaerobic and preanaerobic metabolism of snails.

35. BRODY, S., Bioenergetics and Growth. New York, Reinhold Publishing Co., 1945, 1023 pp., Chap. 13-15. Metabolism in relation to body size.

36. BROWN, F. A., Biol. Bull. 115: 81-100, 1958. Solar-day, lunar-day and annual cycle in metabolism.

37. BROWN, F. A., Am. Scientist 47: 147-168, 1959; Science 130: 1535-1544, 1959. Environmental correlates of biological rhythms.

38. BROWN, F. A., BENNETT, M. F., and WEBB, H. M., Proc. Nat. Acad. Sci. 44: 290-296, 1958. Solar-day, lunar-day and annual cycles in metabolism.

39. BRUCE, J. R., Biochem. J. 20: 829-846, 1926. Respiration of Mytilus.

40. BUCK, J. B., in Physiological Triggers, edited by T. H. Bullock. Washington, American Physiological Society, 1957, pp. 72-79. Cyclic CO_2 release by saturnid moth pupae.

41. BUCK, J. B., and KEISTER, M. L., Biol. Bull. 109: 144-163, 1955; Biol. Bull. 105: 402-411, 1953; J. Exp. Biol. 32: 681-691, 1955; Physiol. Zool. 29: 137-146, 1956. Cyclic CO_2 release by saturnid moth pupae; cutaneous and tracheal respiration; tracheal filling, fly larvae.

42. VON BUDDENBROCK, W., and ROHR, G., Ztschr. Allg. Physiol. 20: 111-160, 1923. Respiration of Dixippus.

43. BUEDING, E., J. Exp. Med. 89: 107-130, 1949; Physiol. Rev. 29: 195-218, 1949; J. Gen. Physiol. 33: 475-495, 1950; J. Biol. Chem. 193: 411-423, 1951; 196: 615-627, 1952. Carbohydrate metabolism in parasitic worms.

44. CARTER, G. S., Biol. Rev. 6: 1-35, 1931. Aquatic and aerial respiration in fish.

45. CASE, J. F., J. Cell. Comp. Physiol. 44: 338-339, 1954; Physiol. Zool. 29: 163-172, 1956. CO_2 sense organs on insect spiracles.

46. CHADWICK, L. E., Biol. Bull. 93: 229-239, 1947. R.Q., Drosophila in flight.

47. CHAETUM, E. P., Tr. Am. Micr. Soc. 53: 348-407, 1934. Pulmonate respiration.

48. CHEFURKA, W., Biochim. Biophys. Acta 17: 294-296. Carbohydrate metabolism, Musca muscles.

49. CHERIAN, A. G., Acta Physiol. Pharm. Néerl. 5: 154-168, 1956. Breathing in frog.

50. CLARK, A. M., and HERR, E. B., Biol. Bull. 107: 329-334, 1954; Am. J. Phys. 198: 441-444, 1960. Oxygen toxicity, Habrobracon and Prodenia.

51. CLARK, H., J. Exp. Biol. 30: 502-505, 1953. Metabolism, black snake embryo.

52. CLAUSEN, R. G., Ecology 17: 216-226, 1936. Oxygen consumption, fresh-water fish.

53. CLEVELAND, L. R., and BURKE, A. U., J. Protozool. 3: 74-77, 1956. Oxygen toxicity in symbiotic protozoa.

54. COOK, S. F., and HANNON, J. P., J. Mammal. 35: 553-560, 1954. Metabolic differences between strains of Peromyscus maniculatus.

55. COOK, S. F., and SMITH, R. E., J. Cell. Comp. Physiol. 19: 211-219, 1942. Termite metabolism.

56. COPELAND, D. E., J. Exp. Zool. 120: 203-212, 1952; J. Cell. Comp. Phys. 40: 317-336, 1952. Reflex control and histophysiology of swim bladder.

57. CRANDALL, R. R., and SMITH, A. H., Proc. Soc. Exp. Biol. Med. 79: 345-346, 1952. Tissue metabolism in growing birds.

57a. CRANE, F. L., et al., Biochim. Biophys. Acta 31: 490-501, 1959; 33: 169-185, 1959. Coenzyme Q.

58. CRESCITELLI, F., J. Cell. Comp. Physiol. 6: 351-368, 1935. Respiratory metabolism, bee moth.

59. DAHR, E., Lunds. Univ. Aarsskr. N. F. Avd. 2, 20, no. 10: 1-19, 1924. Lung movements in pulmonate snails.

60. VAN DAM, L., Zool. Anz. 118: 122-128, 1937. External respiration of various invertebrates.

61. VAN DAM, L., Biol. Bull. 107: 192-202, 1954. Active and standard metabolism in scallops.

62. DAVISON, J., Biol. Bull. 109: 407-419, 1955. Metabolism and body size, Anura.

63. DAWSON, W. R., and BARTHOLOMEW, G. A., Physiol. Zool. 29: 40-51, 1956; 31: 100-111, 1958. Metabolic and cardiac responses to temperature in lizards.

64. DEHNEL, P. A., Nature 181: 1415-1417, 1958. Photoperiod and oxygen consumption of crabs.

65. DEMEUSY, N., Biol. Bull. 113: 245-253, 1957. Respiration in Uca.

66. DICKENS, F., Biochem. J. 40: 171-187, 1946. Oxygen poisoning of enzymes.

67. VON DOBELN, W., Acta physiol. scand. 37, suppl. 126: 1-78, 1956. Human metabolism as function of body mass.

68. DOBZHANSKY, T., and POULSEN, D. F., Ztschr. vergl. Physiol. 22: 473-478, 1935. O_2 consumption by Drosophila pupae.

69. DOLK, H. E., and POSTMA, N., Ztschr. vergl. Physiol. 5: 417-444, 1927. Frog respiration.

70. DOTY, R. W., and GERARD, R. W., Am. J. Physiol. 162: 458-468, 1950. Inhibitors of nerve oxygen consumption.

71. DRABKIN, D. L., J. Biol. Chem. 182: 317-333, 1950. Chromoproteins and body size.

72. DRASTICH, L., Ztschr. vergl. Physiol. 2: 632-657, 1925. O_2 pressure and gill size, salamanders.

73. DUGAL, L. P., and IRVING, L., C. R. Soc. Biol.

124: 526-528, 1937. Shell carbonates as buffers, clam.

74. EDMONDS, S. J., Australian J. Mar. Freshw. Res. *8*: 55-63, 1957. Respiration of Sipunculid *Dendrostomum*.

75. *EDWARDS, G. A., Physiol. Comp. Oecol. *2*: 34-50, 1950; *in* Insect Physiology, edited by K. D. Roeder. New York, John Wiley & Sons, 1953, pp. 55-95. Hormone metabolism of *Uca*; insect respiration.

76. EDWARDS, G. A., and IRVING, L., J. Cell. Comp. Physiol. *21*: 169-181, 1943. Temperature and seasonal metabolism of sand crab, *Emerita*.

77. EDWARDS, R. W., J. Exp. Biol. *35*: 383-395, 1958. Metabolism of *Chironomus* larvae, temperature and body size.

78. ELIASSEN, E., Univ. Bergen Årbok Naturvit. Rekke. *11*: 1-65, 1952. O$_2$ consumption of *Artemia* as function of size, season and salinity.

79. ELLENBY, C., J. Exp. Biol. *28*: 492-507, 1951. Body size in relation to O$_2$ consumption and pleopod beat in *Ligia*.

80. ENGER, P. S., and SAVALOV, P., J. Insect Physiol. *2*: 232-233, 1958. Metabolism of tropical arthropods.

81. VON EULER, U. S., *et al.*, Skand. Arch. Phys. *83*: 132-152, 1940. Carotid sinus sensitivity in man and cat.

82. FAIRBAIRN, D., XIX Physiol. Cong. 339, 1953. CO$_2$ fixation by a nematode.

83. FÄNGE, R., Quart. J. Micr. Sci. *99*: 95-102, 1958; Acta physiol. scand. *30*, suppl. 110: 1-133, 1953. Structure and function of gas bladder.

84. FAULKNER, P., Biochem. J. *64*: 430-435, 1956. Malic dehydrogenase, insects.

85. FIELD, J., BELDING, H. S., and MARTIN, A. W., J. Cell. Comp. Physiol. *14*: 143-157, 1939. Relation between tissue and basal metabolism.

86. FITZGERALD, L. R., Physiol. Rev. *37*: 325-336, 1957. Cutaneous respiration in man.

87. FORSTER, R. E., Physiol. Rev. *37*: 391-452, 1957. Respiratory exchange in lungs.

88. FOX, H. M., Proc. Roy. Soc. London, B, *143*: 203-214, 1955. Effect of oxygen on heme concentration in invertebrates.

89. FOX, H. M., and SIDNEY, J., J. Exp. Biol. *30*: 235-237, 1953. Effect of oxygen pressure on breathing in caddis larvae.

90. FOX, H. M., and TAYLOR, A. E. R., Proc. Roy. Soc. London, B, *143*: 214-225, 1955. Oxygen tolerance by aquatic invertebrates.

91. FOX, H. M., WINGFIELD, C. A., and SIMMONDS, B. G., J. Exp. Biol. *14*: 210-218, 1937. O$_2$ consumption by aquatic insects from different environments.

92. FRAENKEL, G., and HERFORD, G. V. B., J. Exp. Biol. *15*: 266-280, 1938. Insect cutaneous respiration.

93. FRIED, G. H., and TIPTON, S. R., Proc. Soc. Exp. Biol. Med. *82*: 531-532, 1953. Oxidative enzymes in relation to body size, mammals.

94. FRY, F. E. J., Publ. Ontario Fish. Res. Lab. *68*: 1-52, 1947. Effects of temperature and oxygen on animal activity.

95. FRY, F. E. J., and HART, J. S., Biol. Bull. *94*: 66-77, 1948. Effects of temperature and oxygen on animal activity.

96. FUHRMAN, F. A., and FUHRMAN, G. J., J. Appl. Physiol. *10*: 219-223, 1957. Skin metabolism in relation to body size.

97. FUSSER, H., and KRUGER, F., Ztschr. vergl. Physiol. *33*: 14-52, 1951. Metabolism of snails.

98. GERSCHMAN, R., *et al.*, Am. J. Physiol. *192*: 563-571, 1958; Science *119*: 623-626, 1954; Am. J. Physiol. *181*: 272-274, 1955; Oxygen toxicity, mice and paramecia.

99. GIBSON, E. S., and FRY, F. E. J., Canad. J. Zool. *32*: 252-260, 1954. O$_2$ consumption of lake trout as function of oxygen pressure.

100. GILCHRIST, B. M., Proc. Roy. Soc. London, B, *143*: 136-146, 1954; Hydrobiologia *8*: 54-65, 1956; *12*: 27-37, 1958. Hemoglobin, oxygen consumption by *Artemia* at different salinities.

101. GILMOUR, D., J. Cell. Comp. Physiol. *15*: 331-342, 1940. Anaerobiosis, termites.

102. GLOCKLIN, V. C., and FAIRBAIRN, D., J. Cell. Comp. Physiol. *39*: 341-356, 1952. Metabolism of nematode from fowls.

103. GORDON, A. S., Physiol. Rev. *39*: 1-40, 1959. Hemopoietin.

104. GRAHAM, J. M., Canad. J. Res. Sec. D *27*: 270-288, 1949. Effects of temperature, oxygen pressure, and activity on metabolism of trout.

105. GRAY, I. E., Biol. Bull. *107*: 219-225, 1954; *112*: 34-42, 1957. Gill area in marine fish and crabs.

105a. GREEN, D. E., and HATEFI, Y., Science *133*: 13-19, 1961. Mitochondrial enzyme systems.

106. VON GREMBERGEN, G., Enzymologia *13*: 241-257, 1949. Oxidative metabolism of trematode *Fasciola*.

107. HALL, F. G., Am. J. Physiol. *88*: 212-218, 1929; Biol. Bull. *61*: 457-461, 1931. O$_2$ withdrawal and consumption by marine fish.

108. *HARKER, J. E., Biol. Rev. *33*: 1-52, 1958. Metabolic rhythms.

109. HARNISCH, O., Zool. Jahrb. Abt. allg. Zool. *64*: 97-111, 1954; Zool. Anz. *139*: 1-12, 1942. Respiration of *Corethra* larvae and chironomids.

110. HARRISON, R. J., and TOMLINSON, J. D. W., Proc. Zool. Soc. London *126*: 205-233, 1956. Circulatory adaptations of diving mammals.

111. HARVEY, E. N., J. Gen. Physiol. *11*: 469-475, 1928. Oxygen diffusion pressure.

112. HARVEY, W. R., and WILLIAMS, C. M., Biol. Bull. *114*: 23-25, 1958. Cyanide sensitivity of silkworm heart.

113. HAYES, F. R., WILMUT, I. R., and LIVINGSTON, D. A., J. Exp. Zool. *116*: 377-395, 1951. O$_2$ consumption of salmon eggs and embryos.

114. HAZELHOFF, E. H., Ztschr. vergl. Physiol. *26*: 306-327, 1938. Oxygen utilization, invertebrates.

115. HELFF, O. M., Physiol. Zool. *1*: 76-96, 1928. Respiratory regulation, crayfish.

116. HEMMINGSEN, A. M., Rep. Steno Hosp. *4*: 7-58, 1950. Relation of standard metabolism to total mass of microorganisms, plants and animals.

117. HENZE, M., Biochem. Ztschr. *26*: 254-278, 1910. Oxyregulation and phylogeny.

118. *HERRINGTON, L. P., Heat Production and Thermal Conductance in Small Animals at Various Temperatures, Reinhold, N. Y., American Institute of Physics, 1941.

119. HIESTAND, W. A., and RANDALL, W. C., J. Cell. Comp. Physiol. *17*: 333-340, 1941. Stimulation of respiratory center of birds.

120. HIESTAND, W. A., and SINGER, J. I., Proc. Indiana Acad. Sci. *43*: 205-210, 1934. Respiratory regulation in leech, crayfish.

121. HIESTAND, W. A., and STEMLER, F. W., Physiol. Comp. Oecol. *2*: 362-370, 1952. Acquired tolerance of insects to anoxia.

122. HIESTAND, W. A., *et al.*, Physiol. Zool. 26: 167-173, 1953. Stimulation of respiratory center of birds.

123. HILL, A. V., Proc. Roy. Soc. London, B, *104*: 39-96, 1929. O_2 and CO_2 diffusivities.

124. HOAR, W. S., Canad. J. Zool. *36*: 113-121, 1958. Thyroxin and gonadal steroids on metabolism of goldfish.

125. HOSHI, T., Sci. Rep. Tohoku Univ. Ser. 4, *20*: 345-355, 1954. Effect of O_2 concentration on metabolism of daphnids.

126. HOUSTON, C. S., and RILEY, R. L., Am. J. Physiol. *149*: 565-588, 1947. Respiratory and circulatory acclimatization to high altitudes.

126a. HUGHES, G. M., J. Exp. Biol. 37: 11-27, 28-45, 1960. Gill ventilation in teleosts and elasmobranchs.

127. HUGHES, G. M., and SHELTON, G., J. Exp. Biol. *35*: 807-823, 1958. Gill ventilation in teleosts.

128. HUKUHARA, T., and OKADA, H., Jap. J. Physiol. 6: 313-320, 1956. Automaticity of respiratory center of fish.

129. HUMPHREY, G. F., Austral. J. Exp. Biol. Med. Sci. *22*: 135-138, 1944; *27*: 353-359, 1949; *31*: 291, 1953; J. Cell. Comp. Physiol. *34*: 323-325, 1949. Intermediary metabolism of molluscs, paramecia, cockroaches.

130. HURTADO, A., *et al.*, Air University Reports on Altitude, U. S. A. F. Reports, 1956, pp. 56-104. Blood chemistry at sea level and high altitudes.

131. *IRVING, L., Physiol. Rev. *19*: 112-133, 1939. Respiration in diving mammals.

132. IRVING, L., SCHOLANDER, P. F., and GRINNELL, S. W., J. Cell. Comp. Physiol. *17*: 145-168, 1941. Porpoise respiration.

133. ITO, I., and HORIE, Y., Arch. Biochem. Biophys. *80*: 174-186, 1959. Carbohydrate metabolism of silkworm midgut.

134. JACOBS, W., Ztschr. vergl. Physiol. *24*: 583-601, 1937. Gas secretion, siphonophores.

135. JEUKEN, M., A Study of Respiration of *Misgurnus fossilis,* the Pond Loach. Ph.D. Thesis, University of Leiden, 1957.

136. JOB, S. V., Pub. Ont. Fish. Res. Lab. *73*: 1-39, 1955. O_2 consumption of speckled trout.

137. JOHANSEN, K., Am. J. Physiol. *197*: 604-606, 1959. Heart activity during diving of snakes.

138. JOHNSON, J. G., J. Parasitol. 28: 369-379, 1942. Oxygen poisoning of *Trichomonas.*

139. JOHNSON, M. L., J. Exp. Biol. *18*: 266-277, 1942. Critical oxygen tension, earthworm.

140. JOHNSON, M. L., J. Exp. Biol. *13*: 467-475, 1936. Respiratory regulation, crustaceans.

141. *JONES, F. R. H., and MARSHALL, N. B., Biol. Rev. *28*: 16-83, 1953. Structure and function of teleost swim bladder.

142. JONES, J. R. E., J. Exp. Biol. 29: 403-415, 1952. Reactions of fish to low oxygen concentration.

143. KANWISHER, J., and EBELING, A., Deep Sea Research *4*: 211-217, 1957. Composition of swim bladder gas.

144. KAWAI, K., Nature *181*: 1468, 1958. Cytochrome system in oysters.

145. KAYSER, C., Arch. Sciences Physiol. *4*: 361-378, 1950. O_2 consumption of cold blooded vertebrates and hibernating and nonhibernating mammals.

146. KEISTER, M. L., J. Morphol. *93*: 573-587, 1953. Pupal respiration in *Phormia.*

147. KEMPNER, W., Cold Spring Harbor Symposium 7: 269-289, 1939. Role of oxygen tension in biological oxidations.

148. KEPNER, W. A., and THOMAS, W. L., Biol. Bull. *54*: 529-533, 1938. Gas secretion by *Hydra.*

149. KIENLE, M. L., and LUDWIG, W., Ztschr. vergl. Physiol. *39*: 103-118, 1956. Metabolism and body size in land snails.

150. KIKUCHI, G., *et al.*, Biochim. Biophys. Acta *36*: 335-342, 1959. Cytochrome system in *Ascaris.*

151. *KLEIBER, M., Physiol. Rev. *27*: 511-541, 1947. Body size and metabolic rate.

152. KLEIBER, M., and COLE, H. H., Am. J. Physiol. *161*: 294-299, 1950. Body size and metabolic rate in two strains of rats.

153. KOENEN, M. L., Ztschr. vergl. Physiol. *33*: 436-456, 1951. Metabolism of *Tubifex* and *Limnodrilus.*

154. KORRINGA, P., Quart. Rev. Biol. 27: 266-308, 339-365, 1952. Metabolism of oysters.

155. KREBS, H. A., Biochim. Biophys. Acta *4*: 249-269, 1950. Body size and tissue respiration.

156. KREBS, H. A., and KORNBERG, H. L., Energy Transformations in Living Matter. Berlin, Springer-Verlag, 1957, 298 pp.

157. KROGH, A., Scand. Arch. Physiol. *15*: 328-419, *16*: 348-357, 1904. Cutaneous respiration, vertebrates.

158. *KROGH, A., Comparative Physiology of Respiratory Mechanisms. University of Pennsylvania Press, 1941. 172 pp.

159. KROGH, A., and WEIS-FOGH, T., J. Exp. Biol. *28*: 344-357, 1951; Tr. Roy. Soc. London, B, *237*: 1-36, 1952. Respiratory exchange in desert locusts.

160. KRÜGER, F., Ztschr. vergl. Physiol. *34*: 1-5, 1952; *37*: 118-127, 1955. Respiratory metabolism in annelids.

161. KUNKEL, H. O., *et al.,* Am. J. Physiol. *186*: 203-206, 1956; J. Biol. Chem. *198*: 229-236, 1952. Cytochrome oxidase in relation to body weight.

162. KURLAND, C. G., and SCHNEIDERMAN, H. A., Biol. Bull. *116*: 136-161, 1959. Respiratory enzymes of silkworm pupae.

163. LANGLEY, L. L., Am. J. Physiol. *159*: 578, 1949. Respiration of electric eel.

164. LASER, H., Proc. Roy. Soc. London, B, *140*: 230-243, 1952. Effect of low oxygen tension on aerobic dehydrogenases.

165. LEHNINGER, A. L., *et al.,* Science *128*: 450-455, 1955. Oxidative phosphorylation.

166. LENHOFF, H. M., and LOOMIS, W. F., J. Exp. Zool. *134*: 171-181, 1957. Respiratory regulation in *Hydra.*

167. LEVENBOOK, L., and WILLIAMS, C. M., J. Gen.

Physiol. *39*: 497-512, 1956. Mitochondria of flight muscles of insects.

168. Levy, R. R., and Schneiderman, H. A., Nature *182*: 491-493, 1958. Analysis of discontinuous respiration, insects.

169. de Ley, J., and Vercruysse, R., Biochim. Biophys. Acta *16*: 615-616, 1955. Carbohydrate metabolism in various worms.

170. Lin, E. C. C., *et al.*, Am. J. Physiol. *196*: 303-306, 1959. Amino acid metabolism in relation to body size and sex.

171. Lindahl, P. E., Ark. Kemi Mineral. och Geol. 14A, paper 12, 1-31, 1940. Cyanide insensitivity of sea urchin eggs.

172. Lindroth, A., Ztschr. vergl. Physiol. *28*: 485-532, 1941. Respiratory regulation, polychaetes.

173. Lindroth, A., Ark. Zool. *30B*: 1-7, 1938. Respiratory regulation, crayfish.

174. Ludwig, D., and Barsa, M. C., Ann. Entomolog. Soc. America *50*: 128-132, 1957. Intermediary metabolism of *Tenebrio*.

175. Ludwig, W., and Krywienczyk, J., Ztschr. vergl. Physiol. *32*: 464-467, 1950; *39*: 84-88, 1956. Metabolism and body size of various animals, especially insects and molluscs.

176. Maloeuf, N. S. R., Ztschr. vergl. Physiol. *25*: 1-28, 29-42, 43-46, 1937. Critical oxygen tensions.

177. Mangebier, W. L., Am. J. Physiol. *177*: 231-235, 1954. Effects of anoxia on respiratory enzymes.

178. Mann, K. H., J. Exp. Biol. *33*: 615-626, 1956. Comparative study of metabolism in leeches.

179. Mansour, T. E., Biochim. Biophys. Acta *34*: 456-464, 1959. Carbohydrate metabolism of liver fluke *Fasciola*.

180. Manwell, C. M., Science *127*: 705-706, 1958. Respiratory adaptations of diving animals.

181. Marshall, P. B., Brit. J. Pharmacol. *3*: 8-14, 1948. Carbohydrate metabolism, *Plasmodium*.

182. Marshall, S. M., *et al.*, J. Mar. Biol. Assn. U. K. *20*: 1-27, 1935. O_2 consumption of copepod *Calanus*.

183. Martin, A. W., and Fuhrman, F., Physiol. Zool. *28*: 18-34, 1955. Summated tissue metabolism in mouse and dog.

184. Massey, V., and Rogers, W. P., Austral. J. Scient. Res., B, *3*: 251-263, 1950. Intermediary metabolism in nematodes.

185. Mattison, A. G. M., Arkiv Zool. *12*: 143-163, 1959. Cytochrome system in invertebrate muscles.

186. McCashland, B. W., J. Protozool. *3*: 131-135, 1956. CN sensitivity of *Tetrahymena*.

187. McCutcheon, F. H., J. Cell. Comp. Physiol. *37*: 447-476, 1951; Fed. Proc. *10*: 87, 1951. Breathing in various mammals.

188. McCutcheon, F. H., Physiol. Zool. *16*: 255-269, 1943. Respiratory mechanisms in turtles.

189. McGovran, E. R., Ann. Ent. Soc. America *24*: 751-761, 1931. Tracheal ventilation, insects.

190. Mehlman, B., and von Brand, T., Biol. Bull. *100*: 199-205, 1951. Anaerobic metabolism of snails.

191. Millington, R. J., Science *122*: 1090, 1955. Diffusion constant and diffusion coefficient.

192. *Mitchell, H. H., and Edman, M., Nutrition and Climatic Stress, with Particular Reference to Man. Springfield, Ill., Charles C Thomas, 1951, Chapter 4. Effects of altitude.

193. Morrison, P. R., J. Cell. Comp. Physiol. *31*: 281-292, 1948. Oxygen consumption, small mammals.

194. Moussa, T. A., J. Morphol. *98*: 125-160, 1956. Air-breathing organs of fish.

195. Moyle, V., and Baldwin, E., Biochem. J. *51*: 504-510, 1952. Volatile acids from *Ascaris*.

196. *National Academy of Sciences, Handbook of Respiration, Philadelphia, W. B. Saunders, 1958, 403 pp.

197. Newburgh, R. W., and Cheldelin, V. H., J. Biol. Chem. *214*: 37-45, 1955. Enzymes in aphids.

198. van Niel, C. B., *et al.*, Proc. Nat. Acad. Sci. *28*: 157-161, 1942. Utilization of carbon compounds by protozoa.

199. Nielsen, C. O., Natura Jutlandica, Aarhus, Denmark *2*: 1-131, 1949. O_2 consumption by nematodes.

200. Nursall, O. R., Nature *183*: 1170-1172, 1959. Relation of oxygen to origin of metazoa.

201. Ondina, D. M., *et al.*, Am. J. Physiol. *198*: 389-392, 1960. Respiratory centers of rat.

202. Pearse, A. S., The Migrations of Animals from Sea to Land. Duke University Press, 1936. Carnegie Institution Washington Tortugas Papers, *391*: 205-223, 1929. Crustacean gills and habitat.

203. Pearson, O. P., Ecology *28*: 127-145, 1947; Science *108*: 44-46, 1948. Energy requirement, shrews and flying squirrels.

204. Pearson, O. P., Condor *52*: 145-152, 1950; Scient. Am. *188*: 69-72, 1953. Metabolism of hummingbirds.

205. Pennak, R. W., and McColl, C. M., J. Cell. Comp. Physiol. *23*: 1-10, 1944. Respiration of damselflies.

206. Peters, F., Ztschr. vergl. Physiol. *25*: 591-611, 1938. Respiratory control, crayfish.

207. Prosser, C. L., *et al.*, Physiol. Zool. *30*: 137-141, 1957. Acclimation to reduced oxygen in goldfish.

208. Punt, A., Physiol. Comp. Oecol. *2*: 59-74, 1950; *4*: 121-131, 1956; *4*: 132-141, 1956. Respiration and cyclic CO_2 production in insects.

209. Punt, A., *et al.*, Biol. Bull. *112*: 108-119, 1957. Respiration and cyclic CO_2 production in insects.

210. Purvis, J. L., Biochim. Biophys. Acta *30*: 440-441, 1958. Transhydrogenase in mitochondria.

211. Rahn, H., and Otis, A. B., Am. J. Physiol. *150*: 202-221, 1947; *157*: 445-462, 1949. Carotid sinus thresholds for low oxygen.

212. Rao, K. P., J. Exp. Biol. *35*: 307-313, 1958. O_2 consumption in relation to size and salinity, prawns.

213. Rathbone, L., Biochem. J. *61*: 574-579, 1955. Intermediary metabolism of *Ascaris*.

214. Read, C. P., J. Exp. Parasitol. *1*: 1-118, 1951; *1*: 353-362, 1952; *5*: 325-344, 1956. Intermediary metabolism of cestodes.

215. Redmond, J. P., J. Cell. Comp. Physiol. *46*: 209-247, 1955. Transport of blood gases in crustaceans.

216. Rees, K. R., Biochem. J. *55*: 470-481, 1953;

58: 196-202, 1954. Oxidative enzymes of hepatopancreas of *Helix* and muscle of *Locusta*.

217. REHREN, E., Zool. Jahrb. Abt. allg. Zool. *65*: 237-266, 1955. Metabolic responses, molluscs and leeches, to oxygen stimulation.

218. REICH, K., Physiol. Zool. *28*: 145-151, 1956. Effects of respiratory inhibitors on amoeba and trypanosomes.

219. RISS, W., Am. J. Physiol. *180*: 530-534, 1955. Metabolic differences, strains of guinea pigs.

220. ROBINSON, D., Science *90*: 276-277, 1939. Oxygen stores during dive, seal.

221. *ROCKSTEIN, M., Ann. Rev. Entomol. *2*: 19-36, 1957. Intermediary metabolism, insects.

222. ROGERS, W. P., Parasitology *39*: 105-109, 302-313, 1949; Austral. J. Sci. Res. *2*: 157-165, 1949. Aerobic metabolism of parasitic nematodes.

223. ROTTHAUWE, H. W., Veroff. Inst. Meeresforsch. Bremerh. *5*: 143-159, 1958. Metabolism of *Mytilus*.

224. DE RUITER, L., *et al.*, Acta Physiol., Pharmacol. Néerl. *2*: 180-213, 1951. Use of "physical gill" by aquatic insects.

225. RYLEY, J. F., Biochem. J. *49*: 577-585, 1951; *59*: 353-361, 361-369, 1955. Anaerobic and aerobic metabolism of parasitic flagellates.

226. SACKTOR, B., J. Gen. Physiol. *35*: 397-407, 1952; Arch. Biochem. Biophys. *45*: 349-365, 1953. Cytochrome c in fly.

227. SACKTOR, B., and BODENSTEIN, D., J. Cell. Comp. Physiol. *40*: 157-161, 1952. Cytochrome c in cockroach.

228. SATCHELL, G. H., J. Exp. Biol. *36*: 62-71, 1959. Respiratory reflexes in dogfish.

229. SAUNDERS, R. L., Canad. J. Zool. *31*: 547-560, 1953. Swim bladder gas of fresh-water physostomes.

230. SCHEER, B. T., *in* Recent Advances in Invertebrate Physiology, edited by B. T. Scheer. University of Oregon Press, 1957, Chapter 12. Hormonal control of metabolism in crustaceans.

231. SCHNEIDERMAN, H. A., Nature *177*: 1169-1171, 1956. Discontinuous respiration in silkworm.

232. SCHNEIDERMAN, H. A., and WILLIAMS, C. M., Biol. Bull. *106*: 210-229, 1954. Metabolism of silkworms during diapause and development.

233. SCHNEIDERMAN, H. A., and WILLIAMS, C. M., Biol. Bull. *109*: 123-143, 1955. Discontinuous respiration in silkworm.

234. SCHOLANDER, P. F., Hvalradets Skrifter no. 22, 1-131, 1940. Respiratory and circulatory adaptations of whales and other diving mammals.

235. SCHOLANDER, P. F., J. Cell. Comp. Physiol. *48*: 523-528, 1956. Oxygen secretion by gas gland of cod.

236. SCHOLANDER, P. F., and IRVING, L., J. Cell. Comp. Physiol. *17*: 169-191, 1941; J. Biol. Chem. *142*: 431, 1942. Respiratory and circulatory adaptations of diving mammals.

237. SCHOLANDER, P. F., and VAN DAM, L., Biol. Bull. *104*: 75-86, 1953; Biol. Bull. *107*: 260-277, 1954. Composition of gases in swim bladder of fish at various depths.

238. SCHOLANDER, P. F., VAN DAM, L., and ENNS, T., J. Cell. Comp. Physiol. *48*: 517-522, 1956. Oxygen secretion by gas gland of cod.

239. SCHOLANDER, P. F., *et al.*, Biol. Bull. *102*: 157-184, 1951. Oxygen consumption of single protozoans.

240. SCHOLANDER, P. F., *et al.*, Biol. Bull. *101*: 178-193, 1951. Composition of gases in swim bladder of fish at various depths.

241. SCHOLANDER, P. F., *et al.*, Science *123*: 59-60, 1955. Nitrogen secretion in swim bladder of whitefish.

242. SCHREUDER, J. E., and DEWILDE, J., Physiol. Comp. Oecol. *2*: 355-361, 1952. Respiratory stimulation by CO_2, cockroach.

243. SEAMAN, G. R., Exp. Parasitol. *2*: 236-241, 1953; *5*: 138-148, 1956. Intermediary metabolism of hemoflagellates.

244. SEAMAN, G. R., and NASCHKE, M. D., J. Biol. Chem. *217*: 1-12, 138-148, 1956. Intermediary metabolism of *Tetrahymena*.

244a. SERFATY, A., and RAYNAUD, P., Hydrobiol. *12*: 38-42, 1958. Bradycardia in carp in air.

245. SHAPPIRIO, D. G., and WILLIAMS, C. M., Proc. Roy. Soc. Lond., B, *147*: 218-232, 233-246, 1957. Cytochrome system in silkworm pupae.

246. SHELTON, G., J. Exp. Biol. *36*: 191-202, 1959. Respiratory center of tench.

247. SHEPARD, M. P., J. Fish. Res. Board Canada *12*: 387-446, 1955. Tolerance of oxygen lack in speckled trout.

248. SIMONSEN, D. H., and VAN WAGTENDONK, W. J., Fed. Proc. *8*: 250-251, 1949. Oxygen consumption and genetic strains, *Paramecium*.

249. *SLATER, W. K., Biol. Rev. *3*: 303-328, 1928. Anaerobiosis.

250. SMITH, R. E., Ann. New York Acad. Sci. *62*: 403-422, 1956. Relation between mitochondrial properties and body size in mammals.

251. SMYTH, D. H., J. Physiol. *95*: 305-327, 1939. Respiratory control by frog.

252. SPECHT, H., J. Cell. Comp. Physiol. *5*: 319-333, 1935. Oxygen consumption by *Spirostomum*.

253. SPECK, J. F., *et al.*, J. Biol. Chem. *164*: 119-144, 1946. Biochemistry of malaria parasite.

254. *STICKNEY, J. C., and VAN LIERE, E. J., Physiol. Rev. *33*: 13-34, 1953. Acclimatization to low oxygen tension.

255. SUNDNES, G., Nature *183*: 986, 1959. Gas secretion in swim bladder of coregonid fish.

256. SUNDNES, G., *et al.*, J. Exp. Biol. *35*: 671-676, 1959. Gas secretion in swim bladder of coregonid fish.

257. TAIT, J. S., Canad. J. Zool. *34*: 58-62, 1957. Nitrogen and argon in salmonoid swim bladders.

258. *TANG, P. S., Quart. Rev. Biol. *8*: 260-274, 1933. O_2 consumption and O_2 pressure.

259. TAPPAN, D. V., *et al.*, School of Aviation Medicine, Randolph A. F. B., Reports 55-98, 1956; Am. J. Physiol. *190*: 93-98, 99-103, 1957. Enzyme changes at high altitudes.

260. TEAL, J. M., Physiol. Zool. *32*: 1-14, 1959. Respiration of marsh crabs.

261. THOMAS, H. J., J. Exp. Biol. *31*: 228-251, 1954. Oxygen uptake of *Homarus*.

262. THOMSEN, E., J. Exp. Biol. *26*: 137-149, 1949. Hormones on metabolism, flies.

263. *THORPE, W. H., Biol. Rev. *25*: 344-390, 1950. Plastron respiration in aquatic insects.

264. THORPE, W. H., and CRISP, D. J., J. Exp. Biol.

26: 219-260, 1949. Plastron respiration in aquatic insects.

265. Tosi, L., and Ghiretti, F., Experientia *15*: 18-19, 1959. Cytochrome, *Aplysia*.

266. Ullrich, W. C., *et al.,* J. Appl. Physiol. *9*: 49-52, 1956. Metabolism of rats at high altitudes.

267. Vernberg, F. J., Biol. Bull. *106*: 360-370, 1954. O$_2$ consumption by tissues of teleosts of different size.

268. Vernberg, F. J., Physiol. Zool. *29*: 227-234, 1956; Biol. Bull. *117*: 589-593, 1959. Metabolism of crustaceans, particularly *Uca,* from different latitudes.

269. Vernberg, F. J., and Gray, I. E., Biol. Bull. *104*: 445-449, 1953. O$_2$ consumption by tissues of teleosts of different size.

270. Wälshe, B. M., J. Exp. Biol. *25*: 35-44, 1948. O$_2$ requirements of chironomid larvae.

271. Wälshe-Maetz, B. M., Nature *169*: 750-751, 1952. Respiratory control in crustaceans.

272. Wang, S. C., *et al.* Am. J. Physiol. *190*: 333-342, 343-349, 1957. Respiratory center of cat.

273. Watanabe, M. E., and Williams, C. M., J. Gen. Physiol. *34*: 675-689, 1951. Enzymes of insect sarcosomes.

274. Waterman, T. H., and Travis, D. F., J. Cell. Comp. Physiol. *41*: 261-290, 1953. Respiratory reflexes, *Limulus*.

275. Webb, H. M., and Brown, F. A., Biol. Bull. *115*: 303-318, 1958. Daily and lunar rhythms of metabolism in *Uca*.

276. *Webb, H. M., and Brown, F. A., Physiol. Rev. *39*: 127-161, 1959. Biological rhythms.

277. van Weel, P. B., *et al.,* Pacific Sci. *8*: 209-218, 1954. O$_2$ consumption by marine crustaceans.

278. Wells, G. P., Proc. Roy. Soc. London, B, *140*: 70-82, 1932; J. Mar. Biol. Assn. U. K. *28*: 447-464, 1949. Respiratory movements in polychaetes, especially *Arenicola*.

279. Weymouth, F. W., *et al.,* Physiol. Zool. *17*: 50-70, 1944. Respiration in relation to body weight, Crustacea.

280. White, A., Handler, P., Smith, E. L., and Stetten, D., Principles of Biochemistry. New York, McGraw-Hill Book Co., 1956, 1117 pp.

281. Wieser, W., and Kanwisher, J., Biol. Bull. *117*: 594-600, 1959. Respiration of seaweed-inhabiting invertebrates.

282. Wigglesworth, V. B., Principles of Insect Physiology, 1939. London, Methuen & Co., 1939, Chap. 9 and 13.

283. Wigglesworth, V. B., Quart. J. Micr. Sci. *95*: 115-137, 1954. Growth of tracheal system in *Rhodnius*.

284. Will, A., Ztschr. vergl. Physiol. *34*: 20-25, 1952. Body size and O$_2$ consumption in isopods.

285. Winterstein, H., Ztschr. vergl. Physiol. *2*: 315-328, 1925. Control of respiration in cephalopods.

286. Winzler, R. J., J. Cell. Comp. Physiol. *17*: 263-276, 1941. Respiration of yeast at low oxygen pressures.

287. Wittenberg, J. B., J. Gen. Physiol. *41*: 783-804, 1958. Secretion of inert gas into fish swim bladder.

288. Wittner, M., J. Protozool. *4*: 24-29, 1957. O$_2$ poisoning, *Paramecium*.

289. Witzler, E., *et al.,* Pflüg. Arch. *261*: 211-218, 1955. Stimulation of carotid sinus by low O$_2$.

290. Zebe, E., Ztschr. vergl. Physiol. *36*: 290-312, 1954. Metabolism, lepidoptera.

291. Zeuthen, E., Kgl. Danske Vidensk-Selskab Biol. Medd. *17*: 1-51, 1942. Ventilation of respiratory tract of birds.

292. Zeuthen, E., C. R. Trav. Lab. Carlsberg, Ser. Chim. *26*: 17-161, 1947. Oxygen consumption of developing animals.

293. Zeuthen, E., Arch. Néerl. Zool. *10*, suppl. 1: 31-52, 1952. Metabolism in relation to cleavage of sea urchin eggs.

294. Zeuthen, E., Quart. Rev. Biol. *28*: 1-12, 1953. O$_2$ uptake as related to size of organisms.

295. *Zeuthen, E., Ann. Rev. Physiol. *17*: 459-482, 1955. Comparative physiology of respiration.

296. Zwicky, K., and Wigglesworth, V. B., Proc. Roy. Entomolog. Soc. London *31*: 153-160, 1956. O$_2$ consumption in molting cycle of *Rhodnius*.

Chapter 8

RESPIRATORY FUNCTIONS OF
BODY FLUIDS*

Whenever a circulatory system transports oxygen from a respiratory surface to body tissues, there is usually a transport pigment in the blood. In only a few sluggish animals can the blood transport enough oxygen in solution without a pigment. In man, for example, oxygen is *dissolved* in the plasma to the extent of 0.3 volumes (vol) per cent; in whole blood 0.24 vol per cent. Actually, arterial blood *contains* over 19 vol per cent of oxygen; 98 per cent of the oxygen in the blood is combined with hemoglobin. In some animals the pigment functions in transport continuously, in some it functions only at low oxygen pressures, and in others it holds a store of oxygen for use in periods of hypoxia. Blood pigments serve additional functions as buffers in the transport of carbon dioxide and as protein for maintaining colloid osmotic pressure of the blood.

All transport pigments contain a metal in an organic complex. Most blood pigments have iron; a few have copper; other pigments are known, but their respiratory function has not been proved. Numerous summaries have been made.[9, 56, 57, 133, 147, 198]

DISTRIBUTION OF PIGMENTS

Hemoglobins. Hemoglobins consist of an iron-porphyrin (heme) coupled to a protein, globin. Porphyrins are widely distributed in nature. Chlorophyll is a magnesium-porphyrin. The iron-porphyrin protein, cytochrome, is found in nearly all aerobic cells. The specific iron-protoporphyrin, heme, is the best known oxygen-carrying pigment. The protein moiety or globin varies considerably in size, amino-acid composition, solubility, and other physical properties from animal to

animal. In fact, it was proposed by Svedberg[182] that the invertebrate hemoglobins are sufficiently different from vertebrate ones to warrant a different name, erythrocruorins. However, all have the same heme, and there is such overlap of properties that all of them are now called hemoglobins.[108]

Hemoglobins occur sporadically in unrelated groups of animals. Their distribution, primarily as identified spectroscopically, follows:

Chordates:
  Vertebrates—All classes have hemoglobin (Hb) in blood corpuscles; red muscles contain myoglobin (muscle hemoglobin or Mb). Pigment is lacking in a few fish—leptocephalan eel larvae, and in three genera of Antarctic fish.[167]

  Mammalian erythrocytes are non-nucleated, circular (except in Camellidae), biconcave; erythrocytes of most other vertebrates are elliptical, nucleated, double convex. In general, the non-nucleated cells are smaller and more numerous than the nucleated ones; the largest red cells occur in amphibians. The hemoglobin content is 12 to 18 gm/100 ml blood in most mammals and birds, 6 to 10 in amphibians and reptiles, 6 to 11 in fish.[1, 69] The average life of a circulating red cell is in days: man 113 to 118, dog 90 to 135, rat 50 to 60, rabbit 50 to 70, chicken 28 to 38, turtle more than 11 months.[17]

  Prochordates—no Hb in *Amphioxus* or most prochordates.

Echinoderms:
  Holothurians—*Thyone, Cucumaria, Molpadia, Caudina*—have hemoglobin in corpuscles.

Annelids:
  Oligochaetes—*Lumbricus, Tubifex*—and hirudineans—*Hirudo, Analastoma*—have Hb dissolved in blood plasma; *Lumbricus* has myoglobin in muscle.

  Polychaetes show a variety of pigments:
  A. Those with a closed circulatory system may have

* Part of the material in this chapter was contributed by Clyde Manwell of the University of Illinois.

1. Hemoglobin in both coelomic fluid cells and in blood plasma—*Terebella*, *Travisia*.

2. Hemoglobin only in blood plasma—Nereidae, *Arenicola*, *Amphitrite*, Cirratulidae, Eunicidae, and others.

3. Chlorocruorin in plasma—Sabellidae, Serpulidae, Chlorhaemidae, Ampharetidae. Some serpulids have both hemoglobin and chlorocruorin together in the plasma.

4. Hemerythrin in blood cells—*Magelona*.

5. No pigment in either blood or coelomic fluid—Syllidae, *Phyllodice*, Aphroditidae, Chaetopteridae, *Lepidonotus*.

B. Polychaetes lacking a functional circulatory system may have

1. Hemoglobin in cells in coelomic fluid—Capitellidae, Glyceridae, *Polycirrus hematodes*, *P. aurantiacus*.

2. No pigment in coelomic fluid—*Polycirrus tenuisetis*, *P. arenivorus*.

Echiuroids: Hemoglobin occurs in coelomic corpuscles in *Urechis*, *Thalassema*, and also in body wall muscles of *Urechis* and *Arhynchite*.

Phoronids: Hb in corpuscles in *Phoronis* and *Phoronopsis*.

Arthropods:

Crustacea—Hemoglobin unknown in Malacostraca, common among Entomostraca.
Anostraca—*Artemia*, Cladocera—*Daphnia*, Notostraca—*Triops*, *Apus*.
Conchostraca, a parasitic copepod, an ostracod, a parasitic cirripede.[63]

Insects—Chironomid larvae, *Gastrophilus* (a dipteran parasite, Hb within tracheal and some other cells).

Molluscs: in corpuscles in a few pelecypods—*Solen*, *Arca*, *Pectunculus*, in plasma of one gastropod, *Planorbis*. Myoglobin in radular muscle of many prosobranch gastropods and chitons.

Nemerteans: In plasma in some, in erythrocytes in others; also in some ganglion cells of *Polia*.

Platyhelminthes: A few parasitic trematodes and rhabdocoeles, *Derostoma*, *Syndesmis*, *Telorchis*.

Nemathelminthes: Hb in pseudocoelic fluid and in hypodermal cells of body wall—*Ascaris*, *Nippostrongylus*, *Eustrongylides*, *Camallanus*.

Protozoa: *Paramecium* and *Tetrahymena* (certain strains).

Plants: Root nodules of some legumes contain Hb, which is formed when plant and bacteria are symbiotic, not when separate.

Hemoglobins may exist extracellularly dissolved in body fluids, or they may be intracellular, in corpuscles or tissue cells, particularly muscle and nerve. Hemoglobin may occur in only a few genera of a phylum, and sporadically in members of unrelated phyla. The hemoglobin type of molecule has evolved many times and there are many different hemoglobins, with different proteins and similar heme.

Chlorocruorins. This pigment, green in dilute solution, contains iron in a different porphyrin from hemoglobin. It occurs in the plasma of at least four families of polychaete worms, particularly the Sabellidae and Serpulidae. Some twenty-one species of Serpulimorpha have been shown to have chlorocruorin, but *Potamilla* has muscle hemoglobin and blood chlorocruorin; in the genus *Spirorbis* the species *borealis* has chlorocruorin, *corrugatus* has blood hemoglobin, and *militaris* neither. The genus *Serpula* has both hemoglobin and chlorocruorin in the blood.[62, 65]

Hemerythrins. A third iron-containing pigment, hemerythrin, occurs in the polychaete worm *Magelona*, in the sipunculid worms Sipunculus, *Dendrostomum*, *Golfingia* (phascolosoma), in the brachiopod *Lingula*, and in some priapulids. Hemerythrin is found in corpuscles, is violet in color, and the iron is not contained in a porphyrin.

Hemocyanins. The pigment which is next in importance to hemoglobin, as judged by its occurrence, is the copper-containing hemocyanin. It is found among molluscs in amphineurans, cephalopods, and some gastropods, among arthropods in many malacostracans and crustaceans; in *Limulus* and a few arachnids. Hemocyanin is a copperprotein without any porphyrin group: it always occurs dissolved in the plasma. Many molluscs, e.g., the snail *Busycon* and the amphineuran *Cryptochiton*, have hemocyanin in the blood and myoglobin in some muscles.

Miscellaneous Pigments. Several other pigments may be mentioned although their function in oxygen transport is doubtful or unproved. Some ascidians contain a vanadium chromogen. Certain cells of echinoids, particularly the eleocytes of the coelomic fluid and gonads, have a red pigment, echinochrome; this is a quinone which contains no metal, and there is no convincing evidence that it has a respiratory function. Actinohematin is a hematoporphyrin in tissues of numerous actinians; it may function in intracellular oxidation.

CHEMISTRY OF TRANSPORT PIGMENTS

Hemoglobins. *General Structure*. Hemoglobins consist of variable numbers of unit molecules, each unit containing one heme and its associated protein. The unit molecular weight (M.W.) is approximately 17 to 18 $\times 10^3$; the blood Hb of higher vertebrates has four units (i.e., M.W. = 68 to 72 $\times 10^3$). Heme is a protoporphyrin, as shown in Figure 50).

The iron content of mammalian hemoglobin is 0.336 per cent and the heme content

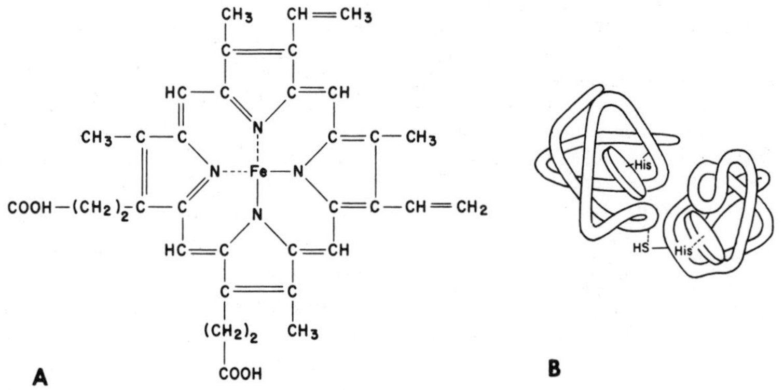

FIGURE 50.　*A*, structural formula of heme. *B*, configuration of two of the subunit chains of hemoglobin as deduced from x-ray diffraction data. Hemes represented as discs connected via histidine to protein. Sulfhydryl (SH) groups are in different planes from the histidine (His). (Modified from Perutz, M. F., *et al.*: Nature, vol. 185.)

is 4 per cent; the iron is normally in the ferrous state. The function of hemoglobin as an oxygen carrier depends on the loose combination of the ferrous iron with oxygen (oxygenation). The iron can be oxidized to the ferric form by strong oxidants, resulting in methemoglobin which is no longer capable of combining reversibly with oxygen. Oxygen combines in the proportion of one molecule per atom of iron. Carbon monoxide can also combine reversibly with hemoglobin and the affinity for CO is usually much greater than for O_2. The exact position of the heme and of the amino acid residue in the protein to which the fifth coordination position of Fe(II) can be bonded is not known with certainty. Pauling has pictured the heme in hemoglobin and myoglobin as being in a crevice in the globin.[143] This view has been challenged by several workers on a variety of chemical and physical grounds;[107] x-ray analysis of crystalline whale myoglobin places the heme at the surface, although inclined slightly.[111] Titration and other data have led to the hypothesis that the heme is attached by imidazole linkages to histidines of the protein, although more acid groups have been suggested. It appears now that the hemes are very near or on the surface, attached to a hydrophobic region of the protein, the iron atom very likely being bound to an imidazole group of a histidine residue.[133]

Deoxygenated ("reduced") hemoglobin has a positive magnetic moment (paramagnetic); this is due to a combination of ionic bonding involving the electron orbitals of the ferrous iron, and to unquenched orbital momenta. Combination of "reduced" hemoglobin with oxygen or carbon monoxide results in a loss of the magnetic moment—i.e.,

it becomes diamagnetic—weakly repulsed in magnetic field as are most chemical compounds; this indicates an absence of unpaired electrons and, thus, covalent bonding in the oxy-state. This change in chemical bonding does not involve gain or loss of entire electrons—i.e., when hemoglobin combines with oxygen it is *not oxidized,* but the valence of the iron remains ferrous. Rather it indicates a change in probability distributions associated with various electrons. Recently a few metal chelates have been found that combine reversibly with oxygen as do hemoglobin and the other respiratory pigments.[133]

The recent intense research on human hemoglobin has revealed much about its structure. The 4-heme human hemoglobin molecule is made up of two equal halves, each of which consists of two different polypeptide chains, one of which is called the α-chain, the other, the β-chain. Fetal hemoglobin of the human differs from the adult hemoglobin only in the β-chains (sometimes called γ-chains in fetal Hb). Some twenty-two abnormal human hemoglobins have been described; some of these differ from each other by as little as one amino acid residue on one of the chains. It is of interest that changing one glutamic acid residue to one valine residue out of the approximately 290 amino acid residues in the 34,000 molecular weight asymmetric unit decreases the solubility of the deoxygenated form of hemoglobin by a hundredfold;[16, 90, 93] this results in the condition known as sickle cell anemia.

Absorption Bands. All heme compounds show characteristic absorption spectra; the midpoints of some of these bands are given in Table 28. Oxygenated hemoglobin has two principal bands, an alpha band in the

TABLE 28. ABSORPTION BANDS OF OXYGENATED, CARBON-MONOXIDE, DEOXYGENATED, AND OXIDIZED (MET) FORMS OF PIGMENT IN Mμ

(SPAN IN Mμ BETWEEN α BANDS OF OXY AND CARBON MONOXIDE HB)

Hemoglobins	oxy Hb		Carbon-monoxide Hb		Span	Deoxy Hb	Met Hb
Vertebrates							
man	576.4		571.0	536	5.4		
	576.9	544.8	570.5	535	6.4	565	630
horse	576.7	543	571.1		5.6	556	
sheep[99]	576.4	540.2					
guinea pig	576.5	539.5					
fowl[79]	576.9		571.8		5.1		
	578	541	571.8		6.2	556	
pigeon	576.3		576		5.3		
lizard	576.2		571.5		4.7		
tortoise	576.6		571.7		4.9		
carp	576.2		571.6		4.6		
Annelids							
Arenicola	574.6	540	569.8		4.8	563	
Lumbricus	575.5		572		3.5		
	576	544	570	535	6.0		
Nephthys[99]	575.1	538.7					
Gephyrean							
Urechis	577	542				552	
Echinoderms							
Cucumaria	579	543	573	535	9	538	
Caudina	577.5	544.2				560	
Arthropods							
Chironomus[188]	578.5	541.8	573.2	538.8	4.3		
	577.7		572.7				
Daphnia	576.6						
Daphnia	577	543	574	539			
Simocephalus	587	542	574	539			
Gastrophilus	581	545	571.5	540.5	9.55	558	637
Molluscs							
Arca	578	541.5				556	
Planorbis	574.6		570.8		3.8		
Nematodes							
Nematodirus[162]	575	541	569	538.8	6.0-6.5	556	
Ascaris	578.4	541.5					
Heterakis[79]	578.3	542	570.0	530	8.3	555	
Ascaris							
perienteric fluid	578.4	541.5					
Ascaris[32] (hypodermis)	579.8	542.5	570.3		9.0-9.5	555	
Gastrophilus					10.0-9.3		
Nippostrongylus	577.7	540.5					
Strongylus	578.1	540				555	637
Paramecium	581	545	574	538	7	555	633
Legume root nodule	574	540	564	538		557	625
Myoglobins							
guinea pig	580	541					
horse heart	582	542	579		3	555	630
Busycon	576	540					
Cryptochiton[72]							
(radular m.)	580	540	(410)				
Chlorocruorin							
Sabella	604	558					
Spirographis	604.8	560	601.8	574		525	
Hemerythrin							
Phascolosoma	408-510					390-410	
Sipunculus[159]	493						
Lingula	470-520						
Hemocyanin							
Octopus	570	355					
Limulus	575-580	U.V.					
Homarus, Busycon	570	U.V.					
Palinurus	558	335					

Detailed references are given in Table 52 in first edition of this book.

yellow and a beta band in the green. Carbon monoxide-hemoglobin also has two bands at shorter wavelengths than oxyHb, and the distance in $m\mu$ (or Å) between the α bands of oxyHb and carbon monoxide Hb is called the span and is characteristic of a given hemoglobin. Deoxygenated hemoglobin has a single broad band in the yellow-green. Methemoglobin shows four absorption bands, two of which, α and β, are most prominent. In addition to these bands there is strong absorption in the violet with peaks (Soret bands) as follows:[101]

Soret absorption bands in $m\mu$

	HbO$_2$	HbCO	Met Hb	Hb
Hemoglobin	414.5	420	406	425
Myoglobin	418	424	407	435

Different hemoglobins show qualitatively the same absorption bands. However, differences in proteins may be seen as shifts of several Å units within a class (Mammalia), and as shifts of several $m\mu$ from one class or phylum to another. Usually the α peak is higher than the β peak, but in some, e.g., *Ascaris* and legume nodule Hb, the β peak is higher.[32, 109] The span between α bands of oxyHb and carbon monoxide Hb is for most hemoglobins 43 to 56 Å units, for muscle hemoglobin (myoglobin) 31 to 36 Å, while for the parasitic fly larva *Gastrophilus* the span is 95 Å and for root nodule hemoglobin it is 100 Å.[198]

In most parasites the hemoglobin has slightly different absorption bands from those of the host, e.g., *Ascaris* in pig and *Gastrophilus* in horse, but *Nematodirus* has bands similar to those of its sheep host.

Globins. Differences in the respiratory proteins are indicated by their solubilities, amino acid composition, isoelectric points, alkaline denaturation, electrophoretic mobilities, molecular size, immunological properties, and oxygen affinity. Within several species, genetic strains differ in amino acid composition of their hemoglobins, and individuals may have a mixture of two or more hemoglobins. Interspecific and intergeneric differences in hemoglobins are also known.

SOLUBILITY AND ALKALINE DENATURATION. In neutral phosphate buffer, horse hemoglobin is more soluble than that of man, cow fetal hemoglobin is six times and sheep twenty times more soluble than the adult hemoglobins, whereas human adult hemoglobin is more soluble than fetal. Denaturation at high pH is much slower in human fetal hemoglobin (HbF) than in the adult hemoglobin (HbA), but in most animals—

sheep, tadpoles, larvae of certain teleosts, and dogfish—the embryonic hemoglobin denatures faster than adult.[100] HbF and HbA can be separated from mixtures by different rates of denaturation. The hemoglobin of *Lumbricus* denatures in alkali in three steps while that of a terebellid polychaete *Eupolymnia* is apparently homogeneous in denaturation. Hb of *Lumbricus* denatures in 23 minutes, that of *Eisenia foetida* in 5 minutes.[131] A turtle, *Pseudemys scripta,* has two hemoglobins; the one of smaller molecular weight denatures in 4 minutes; the larger one, in 120 minutes.[146]

ISOELECTRIC POINT. In general, the vertebrate hemoglobins are isoelectric at pH 6.8 to 7.0 while most invertebrate hemoglobins have isoelectric points between 5.0 and 6.0. However, some fish have low isoelectric points—carp 6.5, toadfish 5.75 to 6.23;[160] cyclostome hemoglobin is isoelectric at pH 5.6 to 5.7.[186] In the turtle *Pseudemys* the lighter hemoglobin is isoelectric at pH 5.7; the heavier one, at 7.2.[146] Some invertebrate hemoglobins have relatively high isoelectric points (*Gastrophilus* 6.2), others low ones (*Arenicola* 4.6).[182] The hemoglobin of root nodule bacteria is isoelectric at pH 4.5.

AMINO ACID COMPOSITION AND SEQUENCE. Numerous analyses give the percentage of various amino acids in different hemoglobins. Some of these are summarized in Table 29. In horse hemoglobin the basic groups are equally divided (40 per cent each) between lysine and histidine while in muscle hemoglobin (Mb) 62 per cent are lysine and 3.0 per cent histidine.[183] HbA has no isoleucine; Mb has 5 per cent.[165] Human HbA and HbF have the same sequence of amino acids in the α chains but differ in the other chains. The invertebrate hemoglobins appear to have relatively less histidine and lysine and more arginine and much more cystine than the vertebrate hemoglobins.[159] Lamprey Hb resembles mammalian Hb in low arginine and high lysine, but resembles invertebrate Hb in low histidine and high cystine.[160]

Weak hydrolysis removes terminal peptides from a protein and, by the use of hydrolyses and amino acid chromatography, the sequence of amino acid residues can be ascertained. The N-terminal sequence in the β chains of four human hemoglobins is as follows:[90, 93]

HbA: val- hist- leuc- thr- pro- glut- glut- lys
HbS: val- hist- leuc- thr- pro- val- glut- lys
HbC: val- hist- leu- thr- pro- lys- glut- lys
HbG: val- hist- leu- thr- pro- leu- glyc- lys

TABLE 29.   DATA IN PERCENTAGE OF TOTAL NITROGEN FOR AMINO ACIDS
MOST COMMONLY DETERMINED

	Horse[183] Hb	Human[165] Hb	Human[175] Hb	Horse[183] myoHb	Lamprey Hb	Arenicola Hb	Glycera Hb	Lumbricus Hb	Spirographis Chlorocruorin	Thunnus (tuna)[138]
							160			
arginine	3.65	4.0	3.3	2.2	3.52	10.04	9.64	10.07	9.64	5.6
histidine	8.71	8.1	8.4	8.5	3.37	4.03	5.39	4.68	2.38	
lysine	8.51	7.98	9.6	15.5	7.51	1.85	4.90	1.73	3.64	
tyrosine	3.03		3.0	2.4						
tryptophan	1.7	2.0	1.5	2.34						
aspartic acid	10.6		11.0	8.2						11.2
glutamic acid	8.15		7.2	16.48						6.7
cystine	0.45			0	4.40	4.08	3.40	1.47	1.64	
cysteine	0.56	0.71		0						
leucine	15.4		14.9	16.8						
isoleucine			0.21							11.7
alanine	7.4		10.2	7.95						
phenylalanine	7.9		7.6	5.09						
valine	9.1		10.6	4.09						
threonine										4.4
serine										4.5
proline										2.4
glycine										4.3

Genetic studies indicate that HbS (sickle) and HbC are mutants of the same locus. Another mutant, HbE, is known for the same genetic locus as HbS.[6] Amino acid composition of hemoglobins A, C and E is similar but not identical.[181] HbF has higher glutamic acid and methionine and lower valine and proline.

IMMUNOLOGY. Immunological tests of hemoglobins show greatest differences between unrelated animals and similarity between species assumed to be closely related. Cetaceans are close to pinnipedes, according to immunological properties of their myoglobins.[111]

ELECTROPHORETIC MOBILITY. Electrophoretic analysis shows species differences in mobility and indicates several types within a given animal. Sheep show two components mixed in the blood: one of these, HbI, is more abundant at sea level; the other, HbII, is more abundant at altitudes, and different breeds of sheep can be distinguished by the proportions of the two hemoglobins.[46] Adult human hemoglobin has 2.5 per cent of a modified form, A_2; in thalassemia patients this fraction is 5.1 per cent.[117] Human 20-week fetuses contain a hemoglobin of slower electrophoretic speed than that in umbilical cord blood (HbF). It is suggested that three hemoglobins are made at different sites—HbP (early or primitive) in mesoblastic cells,

HbF (fetal) in liver, and HbA (adult) in marrow.[118] Among birds, three components were found in chicken and duck, two in twenty species of wild birds, and one in pigeon and penguin.[40, 161] Horse myoglobin has two electrophoretic components;[22] hemoglobin of pig has one; cow, 2; sheep, 2; and buffalo, 2.[184a] Electrophoretic analysis of hemoglobins from a number of reptiles and amphibians shows many with several components. Tadpole and adult frog hemoglobins are distinct. Genera and in some instances species can be distinguished.[35] Several species of fish have one, several two, and one has three Hb's.[29] Confirmation of differences in electrophoretic mobility by other criteria has been made for only a few animals.

MOLECULAR SIZE. Estimates of molecular weight from osmotic pressure measurements on horse hemoglobin yield a mean of 66,400; molecular weights obtained by ultracentrifugation are slightly higher. Representative values of sedimentation constants together with calculated molecular weights where sufficient data were available are given in Table 30. The sedimentation constant (S_{20}) is the sedimentation velocity in cm/sec in a unit centrifugal field at $20\,°C$ in a medium reduced to the viscosity of water.[182] In general, the sedimentation constants (S_{20}) for vertebrate hemoglobins are 4.3 to 4.7×10^{-13} cm and those for invertebrate hemoglobins

TABLE 30.   SEDIMENTATION CONSTANTS, MOLECULAR WEIGHTS, AND
ISOELECTRIC POINTS OF BLOOD PIGMENTS[182]

(Sedimentation constants in parentheses are secondary values)

Pigment	Sedimentation constant (cm x 10^{-13}/ sec/dyne at 20°)	Molecular weight	Isoelectric point	Location of pigment
Hemoglobin				
Mammals				
horse	4.4	68,000	6.9	Corpuscles (non-nuclear)
rabbit	4.4		7.3	
man	4.48		7.0	
hedgehog	4.5		7.49	
myoglobin		17,000	6.78	
Birds				Corpuscles
hen	4.2		7.2	
pigeon	4.4		7.2	
duck	4.4		7.5	
Fish				Corpuscles
Raja clavata	4.3			
Protopterus annectens	4.3		7.2	
Cyprinus carassius	4.4		6.45	
Tautoga onitis	4.2		7.45	
Opsanus tau	4.3		5.7-6.2	
Amphibia				Corpuscles
Salamandra maculosa	4.8 (7.0)			
Rana temporaria	4.5			
Bufo valliceps	4.8 (7.7) (12.5)			
Reptiles				Corpuscles
Chrysemys picta	4.5 (7.0)			
Anguis fragilis	4.8			
Lacerta vivipara	4.6 (7.1)			
Coluber longissimus	4.6		7.43	
Cyclostomes				
Lampetra fluviatilis	1.87	19,100	5.6	Corpuscles
Polistotrema	1.9			
Myxine glutinosa	2.3	23,100		
Leeches				
Hirudo medicinalis	58		5.01	Plasma
Oligochaetes				
Lumbricus terrestris	61	2,946,000	5.28	Plasma
Polychaetes				
Nereis virens	58.6		5.1	Plasma
Arenicola marina	57.4	3,000,000	4.56	Plasma
Pectinaria belgica	54 (12)			Plasma
Glycera xouxii	3.5			Corpuscles
Notomastus latericeus	2.1	36,000	6.0	Corpuscles
Echinoderms—holothurians				
Thyone briareus	2.6	23,600	5.8	Corpuscles
Molluscs—lamellibranchs				
Arca pexata	3.5	33,600	5.6	Corpuscles
Molluscs				
Planorbis corneus	33.7	1,539,000	4.77	Plasma
Crustacea				
Daphnia pulex	16.3			Plasma
Insects				
Chironomus plumosus (larva)	2.0	31,400	5.4	Plasma
Chlorocruorin				
Polychaetes				
Serpula vermicularis	59	about 3,000,000		Plasma
Sabella pavonia	53			Plasma
Hemerythrin				
Sipunculus		66,000	5.85	Corpuscles
Golfingia[123]		119,400		Corpuscles

TABLE 30—(*Continued*)

Pigment	Sedimentation constant (cm x 10^{-13}/ sec/dyne at 20°)	Molecular weight	Isoelectric point	Location of pigment
Hemocyanin				
Molluscs				
Gastropods				
Buccinium undatum	102 (132)		4.61	Plasma
Littorina littorea	99.7 (132)		4.34	Plasma
Busycon canaliculatum	101.7 (130)		4.5	Plasma
Helix pomatia	98.9	6,680,000	5.0	Plasma
Cephalopods				
Decapods				
Loligo vulgaris	56.7			Plasma
Rossia owenii	56.2	3,316,000		Plasma
Octopods				
Octopus vulgaris	49.3	2,785,000		Plasma
Eledone moschata	49.1	2,791,000		Plasma
Arthropods				
Xiphosura				
Limulus polyphemus	34.6 (56.6) (16.1) (5.9)	1,300,000	6.4	Plasma
Crustacea				
Caridea				
Pandalus borealis	17.4	397,000		
Palaemon fabrici	16			
Palinura				
Palinurus vulgaris	16.4	447,000		
Jasus lalandii	17.1		4.65	
Anomura				
Pagurus striatus	16			
Eupagurus bernhardus	17 (22)			
Astacura				
Nephrops norvegicus	24.5	812,000	4.64	
Homarus vulgaris	22.6	803,000	4.95	
Astacus fluviatilis	23.3		4.93	
Brachyura				
Hyas araneus	23			
Maja squinado	27			
Cancer pagurus	23.6 (16.4)		4.65	
Carcinus maenas	23.3 (16.7)			

are much higher. Hemoglobin molecules of amphibians and reptiles tend to be slightly larger than those of mammals, birds, and fishes. In several amphibians two components were observed, and in *Bufo valliceps* three, with S_{20} values of 4.8, 7.7, and 12.5—suggestive of aggregation.[182] Muscle hemoglobin from mammalian heart and skeletal muscle has a M.W. of 17,000, and contains 1 heme per molecule; blood hemoglobin has a molecular weight of nearly 68,000 and has 4 hemes per molecule. Fetal hemoglobin is of the same size as adult. The circulating hemoglobin of cyclostomes has a weight of about 17,000, and its oxygen transport properties indicate it has 1 heme unit.[186] In those invertebrates in which the hemoglobin (erythrocruorin of Svedberg) is in solution in the plasma, the molecular weight is usually greater than 1,000,000. The large size tends to confine the molecules to the circulatory system. Those invertebrates with hemoglobin in corpuscles have smaller molecules. For example, in *Thyone* and *Gastrophilus* the M.W. is about 34,000, and, at least in *Gastrophilus,* there is good evidence for 2 heme units per molecule. Exceptions to the correlation of size with location are found in chironomid larvae where a hemoglobin of low molecular weight is free in the plasma. Myoglobin from the mollusc *Cryptochiton* has in unpurified solution some molecules that function as if they had a molecular weight of 34,000.[129]

When mammalian hemoglobin is treated with certain agents such as urea, it splits into molecules of size corresponding to M.W. 34,000; with more difficulty these halves can be split again.[198] X-ray diffraction data indicate that a molecule of horse hemoglobin is a spheroid 64 Å by 55 Å by 50 Å; the globin units are flat discs with the hemes on the outside.[144] Myoglobin (M.W. 18,000) has dimensions of 40 Å by 35 Å by 23 Å.[111] The heme in each molecular unit is a flat disc surrounded by a single coiled polypeptide chain in an alpha helix.[110] The wet crystals of hemoglobin consist of 50 per cent water, of which one-third is bound to the protein. The crystals of hemoglobin from different species of animals, and also fetal hemoglobin crystals, are of characteristic form.

CARBON MONOXIDE AFFINITY. Another difference between hemoglobins is in their relative affinity for carbon monoxide. The CO affinity relative to that for oxygen is given by $a = \dfrac{HbCO\ pO_2}{HbO_2\ pCO}$. Values have been summarized as follows:[63, 109, 198]

Branchioma (chlorocruorin)	570
Chironomus (hemoglobin)	400
horse	280
man	230
Arenicola	150
Tubifex	40
Planorbis	40
rabbit	40
root nodules (legume)	37
Gastrophilus	0.67
myoglobins	28-51
cytochrome oxidase	0.1

These data show that chlorocruorin has a greater affinity for CO than does any hemoglobin, and that all of the hemoglobins tested (except from *Gastrophilus* and *Ascaris*)[32] have a greater affinity for CO than for O_2. The relative affinity for CO is logarithmically directly related to the span between the absorption bands of oxyHb and COHb[8, 9] for a number of vertebrate, but not for some invertebrate, hemoglobins. Affinity of Hb for nitric oxide is much greater than for CO.[71]

In summary: Heme is similar, but the globins of different species differ widely, and within one species there may be several hemoglobin types. Hemoglobin of cyclostomes is apparently intermediate between that of vertebrates and invertebrates in several respects. Differences in the molecular size of hemoglobins are correlated with location inside or outside of cells; hemoglobins appear to be built of multiples of basic units, each of M.W. of about 17,000. The differences in amino acid composition are reflected in mobilities, solubilities, and modification of absorption bands. The small differences in protein composition also affect oxygen transport.

Chlorocruorin. Chlorocruorin, the green iron-containing blood pigment of sabellid and serpulid worms, has a porphyrin which differs from heme in that on one pyrrole ring a vinyl chain is replaced by a formyl as follows:[53]

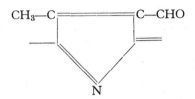

The amino acids of chlorocruorin resemble in proportion those of invertebrate hemoglobins. The close similarity to hemoglobin may explain the fact that some worms have both pigments and that in the same genus one species has chlorocruorin and another has hemoglobin (p. 199). Chlorocruorin, oxychlorocruorin, and carbon monoxide-chlorocruorin have absorption bands about 20 to 25 mµ toward the red compared with analogous hemoglobin bands[61, 65] (Table 28). *Spirorbis* chlorocruorin has a molecular weight of about 3,000,000; this pigment is always in solution in the plasma[182] (Table 29). As with hemoglobin, 2 atoms of oxygen combine with an atom of iron.[61]

Hemerythrin. This pigment contains approximately three times as much iron as hemoglobin—0.9 to 1.0 per cent;[56, 123] however, the iron is directly attached to the protein and there is no porphyrin present. The visible absorption spectra of various hemerythrins lack the sharp bands characteristic of heme derivatives; oxyhemerythrin of sipunculids and of *Priapulus* and *Lingula* possesses a gradually increasing extinction coefficient as the wavelength goes from red to blue, interrupted only by a small maximum at 500 mµ;[49] maxima occur also at 330 and 280 mµ.[123] Deoxygenated hemerythrin has no peak absorption in visible light, but methemerythrin absorbs broadly at 400 to 500 mµ.[114] Any persistence of color of nitrogen-equilibrated hemerythrin is due to methemerythrin, which is often present, especially in preparations of the more unstable hemerythrins, e.g., *Dendrostomum* vascular hemerythrin or *Golfingia* coelomic hemerythrin. The isoelectric point of *Sipunculus* hemerythrin is pH 5.8, and the molecular weight is similar to that of hemoglobin. Older data on *Sipunculus* indicate 12 iron atoms per molecule with a molecular weight of 62 to 66 $\times$ 10^3; recent data on *Golfingia gouldii* hemerythrin indicate a molecular weight almost twice as large (120×10^3), and 19 iron atoms per molecule.[123]

It has been postulated[113] that there are 3 iron atoms per molecule of O_2 combined in oxyhemerythrin, that in the oxygenated state all of the iron is ferric, while in deoxygenated hemerythrin 2 are ferrous and 1 ferric, and that the 2 iron atoms which change valence are attached to the protein by a sulfur-containing amino acid. Difficulties with this hypothesis are based on the following:[133] (1) Only 2 atoms of iron per molecule of O_2 were found by some workers;[24] suggesting that previous preparations may have been contaminated with methemerythrin. (2) In *Sipunculus* hemerythrin the total number of cysteine residues can accommodate only two-fifths of the iron atoms; hence iron must be bound to nonsulfhydryl sites. (3) With ferric atoms there should be some paramagnetism, yet, while deoxygenated hemerythrin is paramagnetic, the oxyhemerythrin had almost no magnetic moment.[116] (4) Changes from ferrous to ferric complexes are not accompanied by such drastic increase in light absorption as is the oxygenation of hemerythrin. The bonding of iron in hemerythrin is not strictly comparable to that observed in simple ferrous-ferric complexes. Manwell[133] has postulated a resonance system, e.g.,

which explains the complex set of data at present in the literature most satisfactorily, as well as accounting for the reversibility of the reaction.

Hemocyanin. In hemocyanin the copper is probably bound directly to the protein of the molecule, and hemocyanin usually constitutes more than 90 per cent of the total blood protein. The blood copper gives a measure of the hemocyanin (Hcy) concentration, which is highest in cephalopods, and lowest in some crustaceans (Table 31).

Hemocyanins are visibly colorless when deoxygenated but have a strong absorption in the ultraviolet with a peak at 280 mμ (the usual protein band). When oxygenated, hemocyanins are blue, have a broad low absorption peak in the visible at about 570 mμ, and absorb nearly 100 times more strongly at 355 mμ.[148]

Hemocyanin molecules are large (Table 30). Molluscan hemocyanins have sedimentation constants corresponding to molecular weights of several million. Crustacean hemocyanin molecular weights are several hundred thousand. A recent value for lobster hemocyanin gives S_{20} of 24.5, corresponding to M.W. of 825,000;[119] from other properties it was deduced that the molecule is an ellipsoid 32.2 mμ in diameter and 7.8 mμ thick.[119] As shown in Table 29, *Pandalus* and *Palinurus* have a sedimentation constant of 16; *Nephrops* and *Homarus*, 23; *Astacus*,

$$Fe(III)—O_2—Fe(III)$$
$$Fe(III)—O_2 \ldots Fe(II) \qquad\qquad Fe(II) \ldots O_2—Fe(III)$$
$$Fe(II) \ldots O_2 \ldots Fe(II)$$

TABLE 31.   COPPER CONTENT OF HEMOCYANIN BLOODS AND PURIFIED HEMOCYANIN

	Cu in blood (mg/100 ml)	Cu in Hcy (purified) %	O_2 capacity of blood in air (vol %)
Cephalopods			
Octopus vulgaris	23.5-28.5	0.25	3.1 - 4.5
Loligo pealei	24.9	0.26	3.8 - 4.5
Gastropods			
Helix pomatia	6.5-11.5	0.24	1.15- 2.2
Busycon canaliculatum		0.245	2.1 - 3.3
Xiphosura			
Limulus polyphemus	8.1	0.173	0.74- 2.7
Crustacea			
Astacus fluviatilis	7.0- 8.0		2.4
Palinurus vulgaris	9.5	0.148	1.4 - 1.8
Homarus vulgaris	9 -10	0.187	4.1 -14.0, 3.0
Cancer pagurus	5 - 6		1.6 - 2.3
Carcinus maenas	9		1.1 - 1.2
Maja squinado	3.5		0.84- 1.75
(Sea water)	0.00001 mg Cu/100 ml		

Detailed references are given in Table 54 in first edition of this book.

Cancer, and *Carcinus* show both values, that is, their molecules are of two aggregation sizes. Hemocyanin from *Limulus* shows four sedimentation constants, the principal one corresponding to a molecular weight of 1,300,000. *Helix pomatia* hemocyanin shows three molecular sizes. According to Svedberg, in each species the larger molecules are aggregates of definite numbers of the smallest. Members of three decapod suborders, the Caridea, Palinura, and Anomura, have S_{20} values of 16 to 17, while in suborders Astacura and Brachyura the main component has $S_{20} = 23$ to 24.[102, 182] Despite the different sizes the hemocyanin of *Limulus* separates electrophoretically into only two components and Hcy of *Busycon* migrates as a single band.

An amino acid analysis of *Helix* hemocyanin shows twice as much cystine and tryptophan, and more arginine than in human hemoglobin (Table 29).

Oxygen combines reversibly with hemocyanin in the proportion of 1 oxygen molecule to 2 copper atoms. Oxygenation of hemocyanin greatly stabilizes the molecule, and, upon oxygenation[133] several crustacean and molluscan hemocyanins show a rise of 2 to 4 degrees in coagulation point, and resistance to denaturation in high urea concentrations.

Bonding of the copper by sulfur has been suggested but not proved.[50, 113, 115] Removal of copper from the molecule may result in some reorganization of secondary and tertiary protein structure, and removal of copper from hemocyanin results in only a fractional increase in the number of —SH groups available for titration. Therefore, at present, the binding of copper in hemocyanin, like the binding of iron in hemerythrin, is not settled. Copper in deoxygenated hemocyanin is in the cuprous condition, as judged by the ability of Cu(I), but not Cu(II), to combine with apohemocyanin to regenerate oxyhemocyanin, and by the colorless condition of deoxygenated hemocyanin. Chemical evidence indicates that half of the copper atoms of oxyhemocyanin are cupric.[115, 176] A resonance system involving a cuprous-oxygen-cupric bridge has been suggested. This has been subsequently modified[133] to include a resonance system involving an additional "species" in which the bonding involves only 3d electrons and not the one 4s of cuprous copper

Hemovanadin. Many ascidians are rich in a green pigment containing vanadium.[191] The vanadium content varies from 0.04 per cent (*Ciona intestinalis*) to 0.186 per cent (*Ascidia mentula*) of the total dry weight. Doubt has been expressed that the ascidians can get their vanadium from sea water, which contains only 0.3 to 0.6 mg/m³; it is likely that they get it from particulate matter (see Chapter 3). Webb[191] found that vanadium is lacking in the more primitive ascidian families, and is present in the plasma of the Cionidae and Diazonidae and in blood cells (vanadocytes) in several families, principally the Ascidiidae and Perophoridae; vanadium pigment is lacking in higher families such as Styelidae and Molgulidae.

The vanadocytes are about 8 μ in diameter and constitute 1.2 per cent of the total blood volume and 60 per cent of blood cells in Ascidiidae. On hemolysis these cells yield the chromogen which contains vanadium and iron in equal amounts.[27, 191] The chromogen appears to consist of a chain of pyrrole rings; it is not a protein and not a porphyrin and may have a molecular weight of around 900. In the ascidian, vanadium is kept in a reduced form by a high concentration of H_2SO_4. Titration of the whole blood showed a total acidity of 0.022 N, and cytolyzed corpuscles showed an acidity of 1.83 N, or 9 per cent H_2SO_4. Hemovanadin kept at pH 2.4 can reduce cytochrome c either with or without oxygen. The oxidation potential of the chromogen is too low for it to be useful physiologically in respiration. Reducing agents are not oxidized more rapidly by air in the presence of vanadocytes than in their absence. Many ascidians lack vanadocytes and yet live in the same habitat with those which have them. The function of this remarkable pigment remains unknown, but it appears that it is not concerned with oxygen transport.

Rates of Association and Dissociation. The rates of loading and unloading of respiratory pigments with oxygen and carbon monoxide have been measured photoelectrically. Half-times for dissociation, that is, times for unloading 50 per cent of oxygen, follow:

hemoglobin	man[140]	0.038 sec. (pH 8.6, 22°)
	sheep[140]	0.028 sec. (pH 8.6, 22°)
	frog[140]	0.02 sec. (pH 8.6, 22°)
	Lumbricus[169]	0.07 sec. (pH 8.0, 23°)

$$Cu(I) \ldots O_2—Cu(II) \qquad Cu(II)—O_2 \ldots Cu(I)$$
$$Cu(I) \ldots O_2 \ldots Cu(I)$$

hemoglobin	Glycera[169]	0.027 sec. (pH 8.6, 28°)
	Ascaris[32]	
	body fluid	220.0 sec. (pH 9.0, 16°)
	body wall	80.0 sec. (pH 6.0, 3°)
hemocyanin	Maja[140]	0.025 sec. (pH 8.6, 22°)
	Limulus[140]	0.075 sec. (pH 8.6, 22°)

Other measurements are given in net velocity constants (actually the combination of the velocity constant for each heme) and insufficient data are published to convert to half-times or the converse. Association velocity constants for hemoglobin in l/mol sec follow:[70, 71]

	oxygen	carbon monoxide
sheep	2.6×10^6 at pH 9.1, 19°	1.8×10^5 at pH 9.2, 19°
Lumbricus	2.3×10^6 at pH 9.2, 20°	4.1×10^5 at pH 9.2, 20°
Arenicola	2.3×10^6 at pH 6.3, 20°	2.9×10^5 at pH 6.3, 20°

When comparable units are used it is found that association is faster than dissociation. The reactions of mammalian myoglobin are faster than those of hemoglobin; the half-time for myoglobin association with oxygen is only 0.0004 sec.[140] The hemoglobins of *Ascaris* are aberrant in being unusually slow in deoxygenation. Hemocyanins are similar in speeds to hemoglobins.

OXYGEN TRANSPORT BY RESPIRATORY PIGMENTS

Functions of Hemoglobins. *Oxygen Capacity.* The first requisite of an oxygen-transport substance is ability to combine reversibly with enough oxygen to supply the needs of the animal. The oxygen capacity is the amount of oxygen carried in blood or in blood cells when they are saturated. Oxygen content is usually expressed as volumes per cent or moles per liter of oxygen in whole blood or cells, and is determined by measuring the amount of oxygen combined after the blood sample is saturated with air. Equilibration with air may not permit saturation if the pigment requires a very high pressure for oxygenation, particularly in the presence of CO_2 and at high temperatures; hence equilibration with pure oxygen is preferable for accurate determination of O_2 capacity. Also some blood cells, particularly nucleated erythrocytes, consume considerable amounts of oxygen, which must be taken into account in the equilibration. The oxygen capacity is proportional to the amount of hemoglobin or other pigment in the blood or blood cells (Fig. 51).

Table 32 gives the oxygen capacity of the blood of a number of animals. The O_2 capacity of the blood of mammals and birds is usually between 15 and 20 volumes per 100 ml. Some, but not all, diving mammals have unusually high oxygen capacities. The llama even at sea level has a high capacity. Among cold-blooded vertebrates the O_2 capacities are lower, usually between 5 and 12 vol per cent. Young animals tend to have lower O_2 ca-

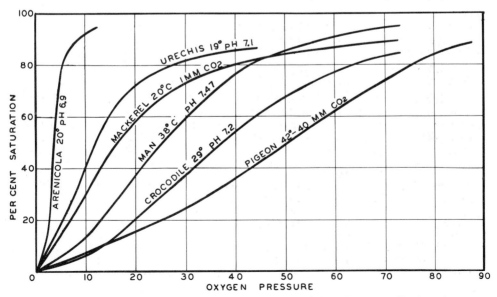

FIGURE 51. Oxygen equilibrium curves in per cent saturation of hemoglobin as a function of oxygen pressure in mm Hg in a variety of animals. (Data assembled by Redfield, A. C.: Biol. Rev., vol. 9.)

TABLE 32.   RESPIRATORY CHARACTERISTICS OF BLOOD

Animal	P_{50} pO_2 in mm Hg	Conditions under which P_{50} is determined	O_2 capacity vol % (ml O_2/100 ml) of Blood	Cells	n
Mammals					
woodchuck[45]	23.8	40 mm 38°			
fox[94]	37	40 mm CO_2 37.5°	21.7	44	
man[13]	27	40 mm CO_2 38° whole blood	20	45.5	2.9
horse[39]	26	41 mm CO_2 pH 7.47 38°	16.7, 14		2.9
sheep[13, 39]	40, 33.5	40 mm CO_2 39°	15.9	41	2.9
fetus[12]	22	pH 7.4 38°			
rabbit	31.6	pH 7.6 38.6°	15.6	30.2	
fetus[12]	28	pH 7.4 38°			
cat[13]	36	pH 6.8 38°	15		
kangaroo rat[74, 170]	49	40 mm CO_2 37° whole blood	17.5		
lab. white rat[170]	56	40 mm CO_2 37° whole blood	18.6		
porpoise[77]	30	46 mm CO_2 38°	20.7		
seal[95]	31	40 mm CO_2 38°	29.3	61.3	
llama[82]	22	43 mm CO_2 38°	23.4		
sea lion[58]	40	44 mm CO_2 38°	19.8	68.0	
horse myoglobin	3.26	pH 7.4 37° solution			1.0
dog[13]	29				
Birds					
pigeon[39]	35	40 mm CO_2 37.5°	20	40	
duck[166]	50	pH 7.1 37.5°	12.3		3
chicken[166]	58	31 mm CO_2 38°	10.5		
goose[190]	37.5	50 mm CO_2 42°	19.8		
Reptiles					
Pseudemys concinna[180]	19.5	40 mm CO_2 25°	6.6-10.8	50	
Chrysemys picta[136]	15	pH 7.4 25.5°			
Crocodilus acutus[38]	38	pH 7.2 29°	8 -10	43	
alligator[38]	28	42 mm CO_2 29°	6.7		
Heloderma[42]	31	37 mm CO_2 20°	10		
Eumeces (lizard)[33]	19	pH 7.2 28°	12.5		
Amphibia					
Rana esculenta adult[156]	13.2	pH 7.22 20°	9.8		2.9
Rana esculenta tadpole	4.6	pH 7.32 20°	7.8		
Amphiuma[178]	28	43 mm CO_2 26°	2.5- 8.4	25	
Fish					
carp[18]	5	1-2 mm CO_2 15°	12.5	37	
catfish[18]	1.4	0-1 mm CO_2 15°	13.3	41	
Rainbow trout[96]	18	1-2 mm CO_2 15°	13.8		
Atlantic salmon[18]	19	1-2 mm CO_2 15°			
sucker[18]	12	1-2 mm CO_2 15°	10.6	33	
eel[155]	12.5	pH 7.3 20° (solution)			1.8
toadfish[163]	14	1 mm CO_2 20°	6.2	32	
scup[163]	6.4	pH 7.38 25°	7.3	23	
sea robin[163]	16	1 mm CO_2 20°	7.66	32	
mackerel[163]	16	1 mm CO_2 20°	15.7		
skate[38]	26	pH 7.8 25°	4.2- 5.7	30	
Squalus[126] adult	16.4	pH 7.3 12°			
fetal	10.6				
Petromyzon[186]	19	pH 6.8 20° solution			1.0
Polistotrema[130]	2-4	pH 7.2 5-15°			1.0
electric eel[192]	12	0 mm CO_2 28°	19.75		
baiara[192]	8	0 mm CO_2 28°	10.22		
hassa[192]	20	0 mm CO_2 28°	18.18		
Protopterus[55]	11	0 mm CO_2			
Bagrus (deep F.W.)[55]	1.5	0 mm CO_2			
Lates (high O_2 F.W.)[55]	17	0 mm CO_2			
Invertebrates					
Urechis[149]	12.3	8.6 mm CO_2 19°	2.2- 6.7	10.17	
Arenicola[99]	3-4	no CO_2 20°			

TABLE 32—(*Continued*)

Animal	P_{50} pO_2 in mm Hg	Conditions under which P_{50} is determined	O_2 capacity vol % (ml O_2/100 ml) of		n
			Blood	Cells	
Arenicola[13]	2-2.5	pH 7.4 18°			6
Arenicola	1.8	pH 7.3 20°	5.7- 8.2		
Arenicola[197]	1.6-2	0 CO_2 20°	2 - 8		
Tubifex[62]	0.6	0 mm CO_2 17°			
Eupolymnia[133]	36	pH 7.2 10-12			1.0
Nephthys[99] vasc. fluid	6	pH 7.4 20°	0.18-0.48		
Nephthys coel. fluid	7.6	pH 7.4 20°			
Lumbricus	4.0	7.3 10°			1.8
Lumbricus[84]	8	pH 7.3, 20°			
Allolobophora[84]	6	pH 7.3 20°			
Alma[14]	2	1 mm CO_2			
Cucumaria miniata[132]	12.5	7.4 10°			1.4
Cryptochiton[129]	18	pH 7.2 10-12°			1.2
Planorbis[121]	7	0 mm CO_2 20°	0.9 -0.15		
Planorbis[199]	3	1-4 mm CO_2 20°			
Daphnia[63]	3.1	pH 7.7 17°			
Ceriodaphnia[63]	0.8	0 mm CO_2 17°			
Chironomus plumosus[188]	0.6	pH 7.7, 0 CO_2 17°	6		
Gastrophilus[109]	4.9	pH 7 39° concentrated solution			
Ascaris[32]	0.05	pH 7 11.5° dilute solution			
Nippostrongylus[162]	0.2	pH 7.4 19°			
Nematodirus[162]	0.05	pH 7.4 19°			
Chlorocruorin					
Sabella (Spirographis)[61]	27	pH 7.7 20°			
Hemerythrin					
Sipunculus[56]	8	.07-80 mm CO_2 19°	1.6	21	
Phascolosoma (Golfingia) (solution)[116]	2.9	6.3 20°			1.37
Hemocyanin					
Sepia[196]	4	.7 mm CO_2 14°	7		
Octopus[196]	5	.7 mm CO_2 14°	3.9-5.0		
Loligo[151]	36	0 mm CO_2 23°	3.8-4.5		
Busycon[151]	6	13.5 mm CO_2 23°	2.1-3.3		
Busycon	15	0 mm CO_2 23°			
Cryptochiton (blood)[129]	18	no Bohr effect			1.0
Helix[121]	12	0-23 mm CO_2 20°	1.1 -2.2		
Limulus[151]	11	0 mm CO_2 23°	.74-2.7		
Panulirus[152]	6.5	pH 7.53 15°	1.99		
	14	pH 7.53 25°			
Homarus[152, 197]	14	0 mm CO_2 25°	1.31		
	102	38 mm CO_2 20°			
Cancer[151]	8	1.5 mm CO_2 15°	1.6-2.3		
Loxorhynchus[152]	15	0 mm CO_2 25°	1.03		
Mytilus[125]			0.318		
Asterias[125]			0.46		
Mussels (fresh-water)[44]			0.70		

pacity than adults; for example, a 5-day-old rat has a capacity of 5.3 vol per cent compared to 19.2 for an adult.[26] In a few fish which inhabit sluggish, acid waters and can resort to air breathing (hassa and electric eel), unusually high O_2 capacities have been reported. O_2 capacity of several shallow water teleosts is higher (19.9 vol per cent average) than for four species of deep water fish (3.4 to 8.4 vol per cent).[174] Active fish like the mackerel tend to have higher O_2 capacities than sluggish ones like the toadfish (Fig. 52). Among the invertebrates the O_2 capacity also corresponds to the amount of respiratory pigment. Individual variation within a species is great. Where there is a significant amount of pigment, as in *Arenicola, Urechis*, and others, the oxygen capacity

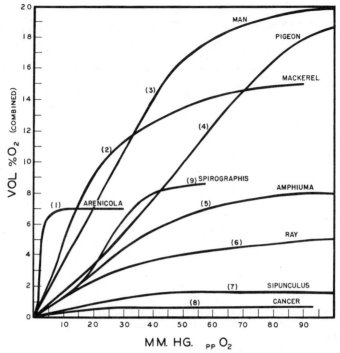

FIGURE 52. Oxygen equilibrium curves in volumes per cent of oxygen combined as a function of partial pressure of oxygen in mm Hg. (1) Arenicola 20°, pH 4.9; (2) mackerel 20°, 1 mm CO_2; (3) man 38°, pH 7.4; (4) pigeon 42°, 40 mm CO_2; (5) *Amphiuma* 20°, 43 mm CO_2; (6) ray 10.4°, pH 7.8; (7) *Sipunculus* 19°, pH 7.7; (8) Cancer 23°, 1 mm CO_2; (9) *Spirographis* 20°, pH 7.7. (Data assembled by Florkin, M.: Ann. Physiol., vol. 10, except data for *Spirographis* from Fox, H. M.: Proc. Roy. Soc. London, B, vol. 111.)

is roughly ten times greater than it would be without the pigment.

Oxygen Equilibrium Curve. In no animal is the blood exposed directly to atmospheric pressure of oxygen (155 mm Hg). Most respiratory pigments become saturated at much lower oxygen pressures. The most important differences among the hemoglobins of different animals are in the partial pressures at which they load and unload oxygen. These pressures determine the range of usefulness of a particular pigment. In man, for example, the blood is exposed in the lungs to oxygen at a partial pressure of approximately 100 mm Hg. When the blood leaves the lungs it carries 19 vol per cent of oxygen at 80 mm Hg, and 98 per cent of its hemoglobin is saturated. In the capillaries the blood passes through tissues where the oxygen pressure is low (5 to 30 mm Hg). Here 25 to 30 per cent of the oxygen is unloaded, and venous blood carries 14 vol per cent of oxygen at about 40 mm Hg.

The relation between the oxygen held by the hemoglobin and the partial pressure of oxygen is best seen by plotting the per cent saturation of the hemoglobin against the partial pressure of oxygen, the oxygen equilibrium curve. For muscle hemoglobin, in which there is 1 heme per molecule, the dissociation curve is a hyperbola; for blood it is usually sigmoid (Fig. 51). The equilibrium curve is given by the approximate equation:

$$Y = \frac{100(p/p_{50})^n}{1 + (p/p_{50})^n}$$

where Y = per cent hemoglobin combined with O_2 or $\dfrac{100\ HbO_2}{(Hb + HbO_2)}$; p = pressure of O_2 in mm Hg. When $\log \dfrac{Y}{100 - Y}$ is plotted against $\log p$ the slope at the point of half-saturation (where $Y = 50$ per cent) gives n, which is a measure of the interaction between hemes (Figs. 58D, 59B, 65B). For myoglobin $n = 1$; for mammalian hemoglobins n is between 2.4 and 2.9; for *Arenicola* Hb $n = 4$ to 6[198] (Table 32). The oxygen affinity of a particular heme on the Hb molecule is influenced by the condition of at least some of the other hemes, whether or not they are combined with oxygen, and by certain groups that combine with hydrogen ions. Change of O_2 affinity of one heme by oxygenation of another affects the physiological properties of the hemoglobin. Such "heme-heme" interactions are usually facilitating and account for the sigmoid equilibrium curve and the value of n, which is greater than one, but less than the number of hemes. The hemes are separated by 20 to 50 Å; hence the heme-heme interactions cannot be the result of direct electronic effects or electrostatic forces but must involve the protein. Apparently all four combining centers in Hb are identical.[2] Dialysis of hemoglobin solutions lowers values of n, as does treatment with SH-poisons.[157]

If a high partial pressure is needed to saturate a pigment, that pigment is said to have a low affinity, whereas if the curve lies at low pressures the pigment has a high O_2 affinity. The affinity for oxygen is expressed as the partial pressure at which half the molecules are oxygenated, or P_{50}; this is more accurately determined than the pressure of loading or saturation. Some selected values of half-saturation pressures are given in Table 32. These are useful in indicating the position of the equilibrium curve but are subject to a number of modifying factors. In mammals P_{50} decreases with increasing body size[170] (Fig. 53).

Modifiers of Oxygen Affinity. SALTS AND DILUTION. The P_{50} for hemoglobin in intact corpuscles is often higher than for the pigment extracted by hemolysis. Furthermore, as a solution of hemoglobin is diluted the curve may move toward lower partial pressures of oxygen.[59] Fetal mammalian hemoglobin shows little or none of the increased O_2 affinity found for adult Hb on hemolysis. The P_{50} for whole sheep blood was 7.2 mm Hg at 6°C; for a hemoglobin solution of approximately the same concentration it

was 5 mm; dilution by ten times lowered the P_{50} to about half.[142] When the solution of Hb is dialyzed with loss of salts, the curve moves back to the right. For the hagfish *Polistotrema* at 18°C, P_{50} is 3.5 mm Hg for cell suspension, and 1.8 mm Hg for Hb solution.[130] The red cells of the holothurian *Cucumaria* show a P_{50} of 12.5 mm Hg; the Hb in solution, 3.84.[132] Changes in shape of the O_2 equilibrium curve and in heme interactions (n) are particularly evident for fish blood (p. 218 and Fig. 58A). Thus both dilution and the presence of salts lower P_{50} of hemoglobin, and observations made on whole blood are not to be compared quantitatively with those on the purified pigment.

CARBON DIOXIDE AND PH. When carbon dioxide enters vertebrate blood, as it does in the capillaries, the affinity of the hemoglobin for oxygen is reduced and the equilibrium curve moves to the right (normal Bohr effect). At high CO_2 pressures, therefore, the oxygen pressure at which hemoglobin becomes saturated with oxygen is higher than it is at low CO_2 pressures. In the tissues, addition of CO_2 facilitates the unloading of oxygen, while in the lungs as CO_2 is given off the uptake of O_2 (oxygenation) is facilitated (Figs. 54, 55). The Bohr effect represents some interaction between oxygenation equilibrium and proton dissociation (acid strength) of hemoglobin. When oxygenation of a heme facilitates the dissociation of a proton from the protein, the Bohr effect is a shifting of the oxygen equilibrium curve in the direction of higher partial pressures of oxygen upon addition of acid. The CO_2 effect may be more than that obtained by changing the pH of the medium.[139]

The magnitude of the Bohr effect in Hb of mammals, tadpoles, and frogs has been

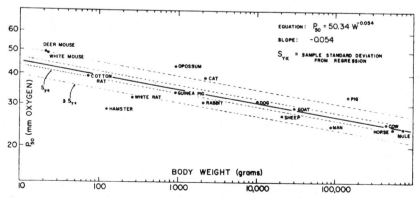

FIGURE 53. P_{50} in mm Hg partial pressure of oxygen for mammals in series of increasing body weight. (From Schmidt-Nielsen, K., and Larimer, J.: Am. J. Physiol., vol. 195.)

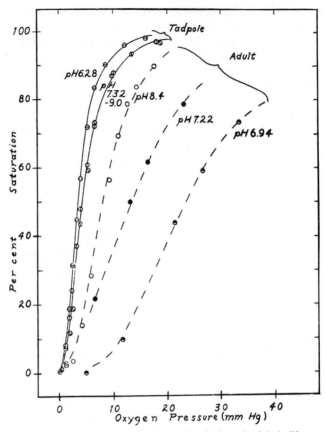

FIGURE 54. Oxygen equilibrium curves of hemoglobin of tadpole and adult bullfrogs. (From Riggs, A.: J. Gen. Physiol., vol. 35.)

correlated with the number of sulfhydryl groups, and the blocking of sulfhydryls by

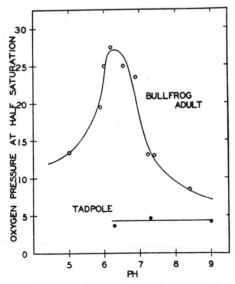

FIGURE 55. P50 of tadpole and adult bullfrog hemoglobin as a function of pH. (From Riggs, A.: J. Gen. Physiol., vol. 35.)

mercurials reduces heme-heme interactions and the Bohr effect.[157, 158] Tadpole Hb binds 0.8 Hg^{++}/mol; adult frog, 5 Hg^{++}/mol; tadpole blood shows no Bohr effect; frog blood, a marked one[156] (Fig. 54, 56). The —SH groups are suggested as possible heme (oxygenation)-linked groups rather than the imidazole groups formerly considered as the oxygenation-linked groups. Silver titration reveals 8 mols of —SH/mol of sheep and human hemoglobin, 10 mols per mol of dog Hb.[15] While the correlation between number of —SH per molecule and the magnitude of the Bohr effect is good, there are some exceptions. Adult human hemoglobin has more —SH than has fetal, but the former has a smaller Bohr effect; this may involve the strength of interaction between two oxygenation-linked groups as well as the total number of —SH groups.[158a] *Arenicola* and *Glycera* hemoglobins have higher —SH numbers than any mammalian hemoglobin yet these have very little (*Arenicola*) or no (*Glycera*) Bohr effect.[133] It is possible that only some of the —SH are the

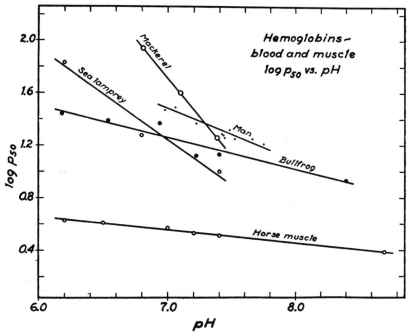

FIGURE 56. Log P_{50} as a function of pH for various hemoglobins. (From Wald, G., and Riggs, A.: J. Gen. Physiol., vol. 35.)

oxygenation-linked groups, even though the total number determines the magnitude of the interaction between the oxygenation-linked groups and the hemes. It has also been postulated that the —SH groups are not the actual site of gain and loss of protons upon oxygenation of mammalian hemoglobin, but that they are adjacent to the actual "linked groups." At present the correlation between number of —SH and magnitude of the Bohr effect is impressive. Manwell[133] has suggested that any proton-binding group in that region of the protein undergoing configurational change during oxygenation would be an oxygenation-linked group; thus in some cases these may be —SH groups, in others imidazoles; this would explain the existence of —SH groups not contributing to the Bohr effect.

The Bohr effect normally results in a steady rise in P_{50} with acidification; it may be lacking, or the P_{50} may go through a maximum as the pH is lowered and in acid solutions decline again (a reverse Bohr effect) (Fig. 56). The magnitude of the Bohr effect may be expressed as the change in P_{50} per unit change in pH or $\Delta \log P_{50}/\Delta$ pH. Some representative values are given in Table 33. In aquatic animals, particularly fish, the CO_2 effect on the equilibrium curve is greater than in terrestrial animals (mammals). This is related to the

TABLE 33.   MAGNITUDE OF BOHR EFFECT IN SHIFT OF P_{50} PER pH UNIT[*] [3, 5, 128, 158a, 186, 198]

$\Delta \log P_{50}/\Delta$pH			
mouse	—0.96	horse hemoglobin	—0.68
guinea pig	—0.79	crocodile	—0.8
rabbit	—0.75	bullfrog	—0.24
dog	—0.65	mackerel	—1.2
man	—0.62	lamprey (Petromyzon)	—0.7
pig	—0.57	Polistotrema	—0.0
cow	—0.52	Arenicola	—0.0
elephant	—0.38	Gastrophilus	—0.0
duck	—0.67	Lumbricus	—0.25
surf scoter	—0.58	Eupolymnia	—0.0
western grebe	—0.45	Spirographis (chlorocruorin)	—0.66
horse myoglobin	—0.10		

[*] Mammalian and bird values measured on hemoglobins at 35 to 37°C, most others at 20 to 26°C.

fact that the normal CO_2 pressure in blood of fish is lower. However, aquatic animals which live in stagnant water usually have hemoglobin which is less sensitive to CO_2 than is that of animals inhabiting fast-moving waters.

The equilibrium curve of myoglobin is nearly independent of pH, and no Bohr effect is found for the hemoglobins of *Urechis, Gastrophilus, Glycera, Cryptochiton, Eupolymnia,* and *Cucumaria*.[133] The Bohr effect is extremely small or absent in hagfish and *Arenicola* (Fig. 59), large in lampreys. Diving birds (e.g., grebe) show less Bohr effect than nondivers. The invertebrates which show little or no Bohr effect must load their pigment with oxygen over a narrow range of O_2 pressures (high or low), and apparently elimination of CO_2 presents no problem to them.

TEMPERATURE. A rise in temperature also shifts the oxygen dissociation curve to the right. If the blood of a frog is warmed to 35° its O_2 dissociation curve is far to the right of man's, whereas at 15° human blood remains saturated at low pressures; hence it would be of little use as a carrier. The temperature effect may be significant for desert reptiles. Both CO_2 and temperature effects are of considerable ecological importance.

Representative Values for O_2 Affinity. A value of P_{50} for a given animal pigment is meaningful only if the state of the pigment, the P_{CO_2} (or pH), and temperature are stated. In Table 29 and Figures 51 to 61 are given some selected data from the very extensive literature in which half-saturation pressures and equilibrium curves are measured under nearly physiological conditions. Figure 52 plots the actual amount of O_2 combined in vol per cent instead of per cent saturation as in Figure 51. These data show that hemoglobins differ greatly in their oxygen affinity, and bloods differ in the amount of oxygen they carry when saturated. Unloading pressures set the upper limit of tissue oxygen pressure and the lower limit of environmental oxygen for function of the hemoglobin.

Muscle hemoglobin has a greater affinity for O_2 than blood Hb and can take oxygen from blood; thus it serves as a transfer system between blood and cell enzymes. When hemoglobin (or myoglobin) is added to a fine filter separating two solutions of different concentrations of oxygen, the rate of diffusion of O_2 is several hundred times greater than in the absence of the pigment, which there-

fore facilitates diffusion.[172] Dog myoglobin becomes only 40 per cent deoxygenated at 5 mm pressure of O_2; blood Hb is 95 per cent deoxygenated at this pressure.[86] Myoglobin has been shown to have a higher O_2 affinity than hemoglobin in mammals, in turtles (*Chrysemys picta*), and in several molluscs. The myoglobin facilitates transfer of oxygen from hemoglobin to cellular enzymes.

In general, avian hemoglobins require higher oxygen pressures than mammals to reach saturation. In ducks and pigeons the difference between oxygen in arterial and venous blood shows utilization of 60 per cent compared with 27 per cent in man, 44 per cent in a turtle, and 66 per cent in the skate *Raja*. Mammals which make quick active movements (mouse, cat) tend to have higher P_{50} values than animals which are slow and steady (dog). The P_{50} of a mouse is 72 mm Hg compared with 24 mm for woodchuck.[60] For mammals there is a tendency for P_{50} values to be higher for small and active animals than for large and sluggish ones. P_{50} varies with body size according to the relation $P_{50} = 50.34\ W^{-0.054}$ (Fig. 53). A high unloading pressure increases the steepness of gradient of O_2 from capillary to tissue. Also most cold-blooded animals have dissociation curves to the left of the curves of warm-blooded animals, that is, the affinity for oxygen of the hemoglobin of aquatic vertebrate animals is greater.

Changes During a Life Cycle. Chemical differences between fetal and adult hemoglobins were mentioned on page 200. The equilibrium curves of goat and sheep fetal hemoglobins in the corpuscles lie well to the left of those of adults, i.e., the fetal hemoglobin becomes oxygenated at much lower pressures (Fig. 57). In solution the difference is less, but the fetal P_{50} still lies to the left of the maternal.[10, 135] In man the equilibrium curve of fetal blood is a little to the left of that of adults, but in salt solution the fetal hemoglobin curve is to the right of that of adults, and after dialysis the two curves are similar.[3, 80] Likewise, in the garter snake (*Thamnophis*) a fetal-maternal shift occurs for Hb in corpuscles although in solution the two curves are superimposable.[133] The meaning of the fetal-maternal difference in P_{50} is that the embryo is adapted to life at lower oxygen pressures. The respiratory properties of the primitive hemoglobin prior to fetal Hb are not yet known.

In incubating chickens the hemoglobin has

a greater affinity for oxygen than it has in the hen; the equilibrium curve moves to the right after hatching,[81] and young birds are more resistant to low oxygen than are older ones. The blood of the bullfrog tadpole becomes saturated with oxygen at lower pressures than does the blood of the adult frog; tadpole P_{50} at pH 7.3 is 4.6 mm Hg compared with 13.2 mm Hg in the adult bullfrog; n is 2.8 for both.[156]

Fetal (or postlarval) hemoglobins also occur in some fishes and elasmobranchs. Metamorphosis of the postlarva of the teleost *Scorpaenichthys* is accompanied by a change in hemoglobin type just as in the metamorphosis of the bullfrog.[126] For most of its 22- to 23-month gestation period the spiny dogfish *Squalus suckleyi* has a fetal Hb with higher O_2 affinity than the adult pigment.[126] An oviparous ray has a transient embryonic hemoglobin of high O_2 affinity during the first few months of development. Hemoglobins of lampreys and their ammocoete larvae are distinguishable electrophoretically. Apparently fetal hemoglobins have appeared several times in vertebrate evolution; hence they must be significant for the success of viviparity. Chemical differences (alkaline denaturation, electrophoresis) have been observed between human fetal and adult Hb, but not between fetal and adult Hb of cat or garter snakes.

The fetal-maternal shift in O_2 affinity is another example of diffusive oxygen transfer systems in which diffusion of O_2 is facilitated by interposing a pigment of intermediate affinity between primary blood at high O_2 partial pressure and tissue at low pressure. In viviparous animals the transfer is from air to maternal blood to fetal blood to fetal tissue. The meaning of the shift in frogs and birds may be associated with the transition from an aquatic embryonic life to air breathing.

Ecological Correlations in Amphibians and Fishes. Those amphibians which spend much of their time on land have oxygen equilibrium curves to the right of the curves for aquatic species, and the loading pressures are higher with greater availability of oxygen. Similarly, in a series of turtles, the terrestrial box turtle has the lowest oxygen affinity ($P_{50} = 28.5$ mm Hg); aquatic turtles have higher O_2 affinities, the P_{50} for the loggerhead turtle being 12 mm Hg.[68] In the sluggish terrestrial *Terrapene* the P_{50} is 11 mm Hg as compared with 32 mm Hg in the active swimmer *Chelydra*.

The properties of the respiratory pigments of fish are important in limiting their distribution. Fish such as trout, which live in regions of high oxygen, require higher oxygen pressures for saturation than do such fish as the catfish and carp whose hemoglobin loads and unloads at low oxygen pressures. Table 32 shows that the oxygen capacity of the blood of these different species is similar despite marked differences in the position of their O_2 equilibrium curves. A carp "surfaces" when O_2 in the water is less than 2 vol per cent; at air saturation the O_2 in arterial blood is 7 to 8 vol per cent and in veins 0.8 to 1; hence there is a steep gradient to the tissues.[97]

In general, those fish which live in relatively stagnant water have a low P_{50}, and the Bohr effect, while it may be considerable percentage-wise, does not put the dissociation curve out of a useful range, whereas in those fish with high P_{50} an increase in CO_2 from 2 to 10 mm Hg may move the equilibrium curve so far to the right that the fish suffocate even in ample oxygen. Thus CO_2, which favors unloading in the tissues, prevents loading in the gills. When the Po_2 was kept at 160 mm Hg, a shiner (*Notropos*) died at 80 mm Hg of CO_2, and a bullhead did not die until the CO_2 reached 338 mm Hg.[21] Addition of CO_2 to a closed vessel containing trout blood may cause the appearance of a bubble of oxygen.[18] A small increase in CO_2 may force a fish with low O_2 affinity to swim into water of very high oxygen, whereas

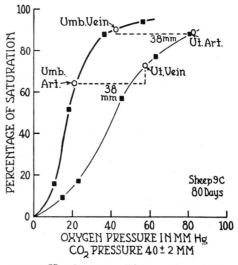

FIGURE 57. Oxygen equilibrium curves of sheep adult (uterine vessels at right) and fetus (umbilical vessels at left). (From Barron, O. H., and Meschia, G.: Cold Spring Harbor Symp., vol. 19.)

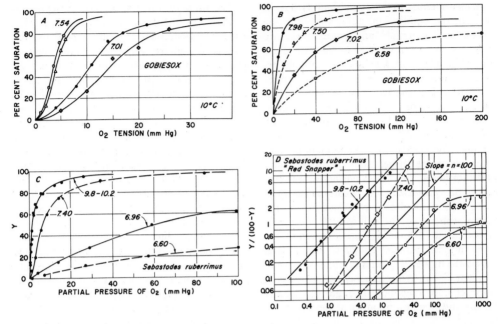

FIGURE 58.   Oxygen equilibrium curves of fish hemoglobins.

A, clingfish *Gobiesox meaendricus,* hemoglobin solutions, 10°C. Measurements at pH 7.54 and 7.01, showing positive Bohr effect; Δ and ✲ for fresh Hb solution, ⊙ and ● for solution stored 48 hours, showing small increase in O_2 affinity, no change in n, and persistent Bohr effect.

B, clingfish erythrocytes at pH 7.98, 7.50, 7.02, and 6.58. Bohr effect similar in cells or in solution, but slope of equilibrium curve hyperbolic for erythrocytes and sigmoid for solution.

C and *D,* erythrocytes of red snapper *Sebastodes ruberrimus.* Linear plot in *C.* Log-log plot in *D.* Measurements at pH 9.8 to 10.2, 7.4, 6.96, and 6.60, showing positive Bohr effect and reduction of saturation at high P_{O_2} (Root effect). *D* shows decrease in heme-heme interactions or n value with acidification. (From Manwell, C.: Unpublished data.)

in fish with high O_2 affinity the CO_2 effect is less significant. Among fresh-water fish the P_{50} of the catfish, carp, and bowfin is not raised above 10 mm Hg of O_2 by 10 mm pressure of CO_2, whereas the P_{50} of the sucker and of three species of trout is raised above 35 mm. Fish such as trout with a low O_2 affinity and great Bohr effect show much greater increases in blood lactic acid on exercise than do catfish and carp, which tolerate low O_2 concentrations and have less Bohr effect.[19] Sensitive marine fish are toadfish, mackerel, and sea robin; elasmobranchs are less affected by CO_2. The effect of CO_2 on the equilibrium curve is similar whether the red cells are intact or hemolyzed in the trout, sea robin, and Atlantic salmon. In other fish such as carp, sucker, tautog, and toadfish, the effect of CO_2 is less on hemolyzed blood than on blood with cells intact.[164]

In many fish, particularly those with large Bohr effects, not only is the equilibrium curve moved to the right by lowered pH, but the curve flattens at less than complete saturation, i.e., the curve changes in shape[163]

(Fig. 58C). This shift downward is termed the Root effect.[171]

In the tautog *Tautoga,* the Root effect or lowering of saturation with acidification occurs in the physiological pH range for erythrocytes, but requires more acid after hemolysis.[164] In addition, at a physiological pH, the oxygen equilibrium curve is hyperbolic for blood cells, but becomes sigmoid on hemolysis. Similar effects are found for the red snapper *Sebastodes* (Fig. 58). However, the clingfish *Gobiesox* blood shows no Root effect, whether hemolyzed or not, although n increased from 1.3 to 2.6 on hemolysis. In *Scorpaenichthys* the presence of Hb in erythrocytes not only suppresses heme-heme interactions, but reduces the Bohr and Root effects as well. In the sea robin *Prionotus* the erythrocyte has little effect on the oxygen equilibrium of Hb. It is of interest that those teleosts with a Root effect at physiological pH's have a swim bladder, whereas those whose Hb lacks a Root effect (*Gobiesox*) or where the erythrocyte suppresses it (*Scorpaenichthys*) lack this structure.[133]

Properties of the blood correlate well with distribution of fish in tropical fresh water. In the South American paku, which is found near waterfalls, addition of 25 mm CO_2 decreased the oxygen saturation by 48 per cent; in three river fish a similar amount of CO_2 reduced the oxygenation by about 25 per cent; in three fish species inhabiting marshy ponds where the water pH was 3.8 to 5.0, the CO_2 effect was small—7 to 13 per cent. The slow-water fish is similar in P_{50} to the fast-water fish, but the blood of the slow-water fish is less affected by CO_2.[192] Similarly, a series of fishes from Uganda showed blood properties correlated with ecology, and the lungfish were the only ones able to live where oxygen was low and CO_2 high.[55]

The blood of some fish is very sensitive also to changes in temperature. A rise in temperature acts like CO_2 to lower the O_2 affinity. In three species of trout the P_{50} rises about 1 mm Hg of oxygen partial pressure with each degree C.[20] At higher temperatures the amount of oxygen dissolved in water is also diminished so that the combined effect on the equilibrium curve and the dissolved oxygen forces the fish to seek cool water.

Invertebrates. In some invertebrates, hemoglobin functions in oxygen transport at atmospheric pressures; in others, only at low pressure; in some it appears to provide an oxygen store for use in periods of respiratory suspension or hypoxia, and in a few no function has been established. The following sorts of evidence are useful in judging whether a respiratory pigment functions in oxygen transport: (1) the position of the oxygen equilibrium curve, i.e., whether the pigment loads and unloads at pressures corresponding to those at the respiratory surface and in tissues; (2) the effect of CO_2, i.e., whether the addition of CO_2 facilitates unloading of O_2 at tissue pressures and, conversely, whether loss of CO_2 aids loading of O_2 at respiratory pressures (Fig. 59); (3) the oxygen capacity of the blood and the difference between the O_2 combined and uncombined with pigment, as compared with the oxygen requirement of the animal; (4) differences between arterial and venous blood in O_2 content, indicating utilization; (5) effect on oxygen consumption of CO, as a result of poisoning or inactivating the pigment at different oxygen pressures. In experimental carbon monoxide poisoning it is important that the maintained combination of the hemoglobin with CO be checked spectroscopically and that the amount of CO used be small enough that there is no interference with tissue respiration.

In annelids, hemoglobin commonly appears to transport oxygen. The oxygen consumption of an earthworm, *Lumbricus,* is reduced by CO poisoning at O_2 partial pressures of 40 mm Hg and higher, but at lower O_2 concentrations where the metabolism is normally low, sufficient O_2 can be supplied without the pigment[98] (Fig. 60a). A rise in temperature from 7° to 20°C shifts the P_{50}

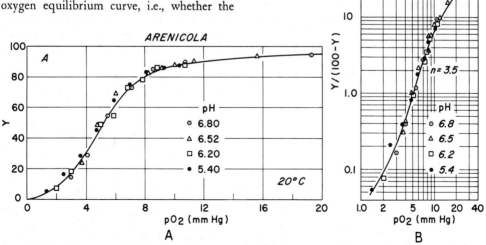

FIGURE 59. Oxygen equilibrium curve for blood of *Arenicola sp. A,* linear plot; *B,* double logarithmic plot. Lack of effect of change in pH. (From Manwell, C.: Unpublished data.)

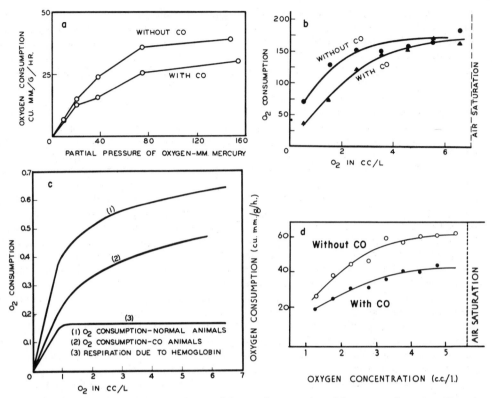

FIGURE 60.   *a*, oxygen consumption by *Lumbricus* as function of partial pressure of oxygen with and without carbon monoxide. (From Johnson, M. L.: J. Exp. Biol., vol. 18.)

    b, oxygen consumption by *Chironomus* as function of Po_2 with and without carbon monoxide. (From Ewer, R. F.: J. Exp. Biol., vol. 18.)

    c, oxygen consumption by *Tubifex* as a function of dissolved oxygen in presence and absence of carbon monoxide. (From Dausend, K.: Ztschr. vergl. Physiol., vol. 14.)

    d, oxygen consumption by *Sabella* (which contains chlorocruorin) with and without carbon monoxide. (From Ewer, R. F., and Fox, H. M.: Proc. Roy. Soc. London, B, vol. 129.)

for Hb of *Allolobophora terrestris* from 0.7 to 6.0 mm Hg (Fig. 61), while in *Lumbricus terrestris* P_{50} is shifted from 2 to 8 mm Hg.[84] An African oligochaete, *Alma emini,* lives in

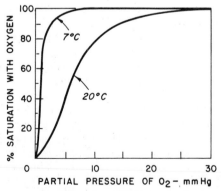

FIGURE 61.   Oxygen equilibrium curve for hemoglobin of earthworm Allolobophora at two temperatures. (From Haughton, T. M., *et al.*: J. Exp. Biol., vol. 35.)

swamps where the mud more than a few millimeters down is anaerobic; the Hb is saturated at less than 2 mm Hg and is unaffected by CO_2 up to 200 mm Hg of CO_2.[14] The hemoglobin of the aquatic oligochaete *Tubifex* is half saturated at 0.6 mm Hg, but *in vivo* the bands of oxyHb disappear when the O_2 in the water outside reaches about 10 mm Hg.[62] In the presence of CO the respiration is reduced about one-third that at higher pressures (above 35 mm Hg), and by a lesser amount at lower pressures[31] (Fig. 60c). Two-thirds of the normal O_2 requirement is supplied by O_2 in solution in the body fluid, and there must exist an extremely steep gradient from water to tissues. In these oligochaetes, therefore, Hb transports O_2, particularly at the higher partial pressures of the normal range of O_2 and at steep gradients. In three species of leeches with Hb, the O_2 consumption was reduced by CO at 20 per cent and 10 per cent but not at 3 per cent, while two species which lack Hb were unaffected by CO; the standard metabolism of those without Hb was higher than of those with it.[177]

In the polychaete *Nereis diversicolor,* inactivation of Hb by CO reduces O_2 consumption by about 50 per cent at high concentrations (7.5 ml O_2/l) and blocks all consumption at 3.3 ml O_2/l;[103] hence Hb is particularly important at low oxygen. Intertidal burrowing polychaetes have higher P_{50}'s than do aquatic and some terrestrial oligochaetes. The P_{50} of *Eupolymnia* is 36 mm Hg as compared with 3.5 to 4.8 for *Lumbricus*.[131] Several species of *Arenicola* show moderately high O_2 affinities—P_{50} of 1.8 mm Hg and complete saturation at 5 to 10 mm Hg of O_2.[197] *Arenicola* hemoglobin could provide an O_2 store which would last not more than 21 minutes, much less than the low-tide period.[99] In *Nephthys* the P_{50} of blood Hb is 5.5 mm Hg and of coelomic fluid Hg 7.5. The interstitial water in sand outside the worms (*Arenicola* and *Nephthys*) averaged 6.7 mm Hg of O_2 (low tide), and in freshly filled burrows 13.7 mm Hg of O_2. O_2 consumption of *Arenicola* was the same in low and high tide water.[43] The hemoglobin in these worms appears to function in O_2 transport, and it may provide an O_2 store during prolonged pauses between periods of respiratory irrigation, but it is not needed as a store between tides.

In the fresh-water snail *Planorbis* also the hemoglobin is well suited for O_2 transport; the P_{50} is 7.4 mm at 20° C, there is a positive CO_2 effect, and *in vivo* the oxyhemoglobin bands disappear when the O_2 in the water outside reaches 25 mm Hg. High concentrations of CO_2 are probably never encountered.[199] At partial pressures down to 54 mm Hg (7.7 per cent oxygen saturation) skin breathing is sufficient; at O_2 between 7.2 per cent and 3 per cent the snails were seen frequently at the surface for lung breathing and the Hb was not completely saturated; below 3 per cent O_2 they were at the surface continually. In the presence of CO the snails appeared normal in high O_2 water but became sluggish in water with 3 per cent O_2. The amount of O_2 held in the blood would supply normal needs for only a few minutes. It appears that there is normally a very steep O_2 gradient from water to tissues, that skin breathing is adequate at high O_2, and that at low oxygen the lungs are used and that hemoglobin is necessary at low O_2 but may be used at higher oxygen concentrations.

In the preceding examples it appears likely that the storage function of Hb is minor except for periods of normally interrupted ventilation, that the cellular enzymes function at extremely low partial pressure of O_2, and that Hb has a transport function; it is probable that debts develop in periods of oxygen lack.

In endoparasites the function of hemoglobin is not clear. In the nematodes *Nippostrongylus, Nematodirus,* and *Haemonchus,* hemoglobin is readily oxygenated and deoxygenated, with P_{50} less than 0.05 mm Hg for dilute solutions (0.7 $\times$ 10^{-4} gm atoms Fe/l).[162] However, *in vivo* the Hb of *Nippostrongylus* is deoxygenated when the worms are in a medium containing 13 mm Hg of O_2 and that of *Nematodirus* and *Haemonchus* is deoxygenated when the worms are in a medium of 9 mm Hg of O_2. The normal oxygen concentration in the intestine where they live (4 to 9 mm Hg for *Nematodirus* in sheep) is below the critical oxygen pressure for their metabolism (about 50 mm Hg). Their oxygen consumption was not reduced by CO in the range 30 down to 5 mm O_2. Hence the worms normally are not exposed to oxygen which would permit maximal metabolism and saturation of their hemoglobin. Their cellular oxygen pressure is probably very low, and the worms appear to metabolize normally with Hb inactivated. Likewise, *Ascaris* Hb has a high affinity for oxygen; the P_{50} is only 0.09 mm at a concentration and temperature at which beef Hb has a P_{50} of 6 mm Hg. *Ascaris* Hb differs from that of *Nippostrongylus* and *Nematodirus* in being very slow to unload its oxygen. The rate of deoxygenation by a reducing agent ($Na_2S_2O_4$) is 150 seconds for perienteric hemoglobin as compared with 0.008 second for sheep Hb under similar conditions. When worms were put into nitrogen the Hb of the body wall, but not of the perienteric fluid, became visibly deoxygenated, and the worms asphyxiated without using the O_2 of their hemoglobin. Similarly for *Strongylus,* the time for half-deoxygenation is 750 seconds as compared with 600 seconds for *Ascaris.* Davenport[32] suggested that the Hb in these nematodes may be a functionless metabolic by-product. The larvae of the botfly *Gastrophilus* lack Hb while they are in the well-oxygenated tissues of the throat of the horse, but acquire Hb when they enter the oxygen-poor stomach, and it is suggested that the Hb in tracheal cells of the fly larvae permits acquisition of more oxygen when it is occasionally available from bubbles.[109]

A few aquatic larvae of chironomids and some Crustacea have hemoglobin. The hemoglobin of *Chironomus* larvae has a very low P_{50} (0.17 to 0.6 mm Hg), but *in vivo* it is deoxygenated when the O_2 in water outside corresponds to 13 mm Hg. The burst of activity and the associated extra O_2 consumption after a period of anaerobiosis are abolished by CO (Chapter 7).[187, 188] Oxygen consumption of *Chironomus* and even more strikingly of *Tantytarsus* is unaffected by CO down to about one-quarter to one-half air saturation. Chironomids alternate respiratory and feeding activities, and the hemoglobin store may provide oxygen during the interruption of respiration for feeding. In low oxygen (7.5 to 9 per cent air saturation), feeding may be suspended and respiratory movements continuous. CO causes no alteration in respiratory movements at air saturation.[189] Normally feeding stops at saturation below 10 per cent of air; after CO no feeding was seen at saturation below 26 per cent of air. The hemoglobin appears to be necessary at low oxygen concentrations but not at high. It may also provide small stores for use between ventilatory irrigation periods and may permit postanaerobic activity. Two pale species continued feeding at low O_2 even in the presence of CO and also in the presence of cyanide; hence they may differ not only in lacking Hb but also in the nature of their cell enzymes. In a red daphnid *Simocephalus*, CO reduced the O_2 consumption in O_2 concentrations below 2.5 cc O_2/l, not above. Pale daphnids are O_2 conformers, pink have definite P_c; hatching time is longer in CO.[88]

Both *Daphnia* and *Artemia* develop hemoglobin when kept in low environmental oxygen.[64] Poisoning by CO appears to have no effect on normal activity of adult *Daphnia* in full aeration, but in low O_2 the pale animals die sooner and have fewer parthenogenetic eggs than do those with hemoglobin.[63] *Artemia*, if they have hemoglobin, not only live longer in low oxygen (1 ml O_2/l), but consume more oxygen at concentrations above 1 ml/l.[73]

In summary: Hemoglobin may function differently in various animals. Observations on deoxygenation *in vivo* show that sometimes the O_2 gradient is very steep and that one cannot infer the limiting environmental pressure from the P_{50} of the pigment. The cellular enzymes of many animals appear to function normally at less than 1 mm Hg of

O_2; the pigments are deoxygenated *in vivo* and metabolism is reduced when the environmental O_2 is much higher. The amount of oxygen held as a store in Hb is small but may be useful for short periods of hypoxia. The function of hemoglobin in nematodes is unknown.

Effects of Environments Low in Oxygen. The Hb content of the blood is normally high in animals which live at high altitudes, and when animals go from sea level to high altitudes the Hb content of their blood increases. The oxygen capacity of the blood is higher at high altitudes than at sea level[30, 82, 92, 112, 153] (Table 34).

When animals are first transported to high altitudes, red cells may be released from body stores; later hematopoiesis is increased, possibly under stimulation of a hormone known as hematopoietin. There is an increase in blood volume, due largely to the increase in cells. The pressure for half-saturation of the hemoglobin does not change significantly when measured at a constant pH, i.e., the nature of the hemoglobin is not altered although there are reports of increased amounts of fetal Hb.[37] In sheep, one form of hemoglobin (Hb II) is in higher proportion at altitude.[89] However, there may be a fall in alkaline reserve or acid-binding capacity so that CO_2 effects are more marked and the effective P_{50} may actually increase.[112]

The red cell count and hematocrit index of acclimated sheep, rabbits, and dogs are elevated, but in the native llama and vicuna, blood counts are not much different at sea level from in the mountains.[82] The oxygen equilibrium curves of llama and vicuna, and also of mountain ostrich and huallata, lie to the left of those of related species at sea level, that is, the hemoglobin of high altitude animals has a high O_2 affinity. Dogs reared at an altitude of 14,890 ft. had 40 per cent more Hb in their blood and some 65.7 per cent more myoglobin in their muscles than did dogs at sea level.[92, 184] However, dogs which were kept at 18,000 ft. for 6 hours each day for several months showed an increase in hemoglobin of 34 per cent but no increase in their myoglobin.[25]

The life span of circulating red blood cells in man is the same (111 to 121 days) at altitude as at sea level;[154] hence the increase in count is due to stimulation of red cell formation. In adult rats subjected to 50 mm Hg of O_2 (30,000 to 40,000 ft.) for 2 hours daily in a decompression chamber there appeared hemoglobin of the fetal (high affinity)

TABLE 34.   OXYGEN CAPACITY OF BLOOD AT HIGH ALTITUDES AND SEA LEVEL

Animal	Altitude	Red cell count (10^6/mm^3)	Hematocrit (% cells)	O₂ capacity (vol %) blood	O₂ capacity (vol %) cells
Man	sea level	5.0	46	21	45.7
	17,600′ residents	7.37	59.9	30	
	transients	5.95		25.1	
	sea level	5.14	46.8 (Hb 16.0 gm %)		
	14,900′ residents	6.15	59.9 (Hb 29.76 gm %)	26	
	transients	5.64	52.1	22	
Sheep	sea level	10.5	35.3	15.9	45.5
	15,420′	12.05	50.2	18.9	38.8
Rabbit	sea level	4.55	35	15.6	44.1
	17,500′	7.00	57	22.1	39.4
Dog	sea level		34.6 (Hb 11 gm/100 ml)		
	14,900′		50.0 (Hb 15.4 gm/100 ml)		
Vicuna	sea level	14.1	29.8	17.0	57.1
	15,420′	16.6	31.9	18.2	58.5
Llama	sea level	11.4	38.6	23.5	61.2
	9,240′	12.3	28.2	17.1	56.7
Ostrich	12,000′	2.18	33.8	13.9	41.2
Huallata	17,500′	3.27	59.1	23.6	40.1

Detailed references are given in Table 57 in first edition of this book.

type.[11] Of two species of the Russian mouse *Apodemus,* one, *sylvaticus,* lives on both mountains and plains, the mountain populations having higher hemoglobin concentrations, while the other species, *agrarius,* is restricted to plains, and its hemoglobin is low.[104] Cytochrome c increases two or three times in the muscles of guinea pigs kept in low O_2.[34]

There are reports of failure of low O_2 to stimulate erythropoiesis in poikilothermic vertebrates. In the box turtle, for example, decompression to 35,000 ft. for 18 hours per day resulted in no rise in red cell count; apparently the respiratory stimulation and the normal blood capacity to transport oxygen were adequate for metabolic needs.[7] However, in goldfish kept for a week at one-third to one-half of air saturation there was an increase in circulating hemoglobin.[145]

In several crustaceans, hemoglobin synthesis is markedly stimulated by low oxygen. *Daphnia* collected or reared in water low in oxygen are red; those from high oxygen are pale.[63, 85] There is no correlation with CO_2 in the water although ferrous salts and vitamin B_{12} appear to stimulate hemoglobin synthesis. *Daphnia pulex* increases its Hb concentration more than *D. obtusa* and *D. magna* when kept together,[28] but races of *D. magna* appear to differ in ability to synthesize Hb.[78] Hemoglobin is transferred from the adult to the parthenogenic eggs before they are laid. In *Artemia* the Hb index rises as the O_2 concentration falls in high salinity.[73] *Daphnia*

gains or loses hemoglobin in about 10 days; in low oxygen its muscle cytochrome increases, as does the hemoglobin in muscle and central nervous system. Mammals conserve and reuse the iron from Hb breakdown; in *Daphnia,* on the contrary, iron is not conserved but is excreted by the maxillary glands.[63]

Blood hemoglobin concentration increases in reduced oxygen not only in several crustaceans (mostly cladocerans and phyllopods) but also in the dipteran larvae *Chironomus* and *Anatopynia,* and in young *Planorbis,* but not in numerous other invertebrates—*Arenicola, Tubifex, Scoloplos, Physa,* and older *Planorbis.*[66] In several groups of invertebrates there is little difference in O_2 consumption between those with Hb and those without it, and a few snails and oligochaetes with Hb consume less O_2 than others without it. Carbon monoxide has irregular effects on metabolism. Some species —*Artemia, Sabella, Physa,* adult *Planorbis,* and *Eupolymnia*—are tolerant of 1 atmosphere of O_2; others even with Hb are injured by high O_2—*Tubifex, Chironomus, Arenicola.* Tolerance of low oxygen is not necessarily correlated with sensitivity to high O_2 or with presence of Hb. It is probable that hemoglobin functions in several ways. One function in animals poisoned even at atmospheric pressures of O_2 may be as an O_2 "buffer" to protect tissues which normally function at very low O_2 pressures, that is,

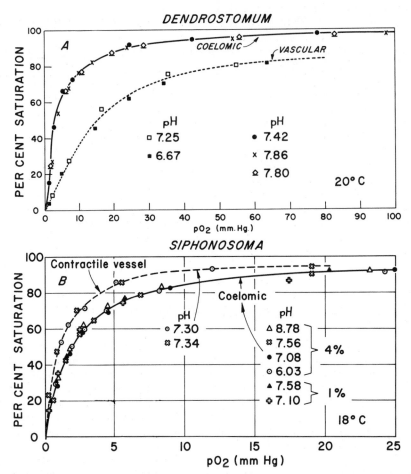

FIGURE 62. Oxygen transfer system for sipunculid hemerythrins. *A, Dendrostomum zostericolum,* a tentacle breather. Oxygen diffuses through tentacles, is conveyed by vascular hemerythrin into blood-filled diverticula, which extend into coelom where O_2 is transferred to coelomic hemerythrin of high O_2 affinity. *B, Siphonosoma ingens,* a skin breather. Oxygen diffuses through body wall to coelom, is transferred from coelomic hemerythrin to the vascular pigment, which has higher affinity for O_2. Each curve includes values determined over a wide pH range, showing lack of Bohr effect in sipunculid hemerythrins. (From Manwell, C.: Comp. Biochem. Physiol., vol. 1.)

to allow O_2 transport without exposing the tissues to high oxygen pressures.[133]

Function of Chlorocruorin (Chl). In a series of papers, Fox[61, 65] has considered the function of chlorocruorin in sabellid and serpulid worms, particularly in *Spirographis* (*Sabella*). The sigmoid dissociation curve of this pigment yields a value of n = 3.4. The oxygen equilibrium curve is shifted to the right with increased acidity and with rise in temperature as in vertebrate hemoglobins. The P_{50} is sufficiently high (27 mm Hg at pH 7.7 and 20°) that the pigment probably is deoxygenated in the tissues and oxygenated at the gills. The oxygen capacity (9.1 ml O_2/100 ml blood) is higher than in most invertebrates. Chlorocruorin has a higher affinity for CO than does any hemoglobin, and

the oxygen consumption of the worms is reduced by CO at all concentrations of oxygen (Fig. 60d).[48, 137] The blood of *Serpula* has both hemoglobin and chlorocruorin; both pigments are deoxygenated together, but if human Hb is added it remains oxygenated when the *Serpula* pigments are deoxygenated; hence the worm's pigments have low O_2 affinity.[67] *Potamilla* has Chl in its blood and hemoglobin in muscles; probably the hemoglobin facilitates diffusion from the low-affinity chlorocruorin. It may be concluded that chlorocruorin is definitely an oxygen carrier functioning normally at high oxygen pressures.

Function of Hemerythrin. In phascolosoma the O_2 equilibrium curve of hemerythrin at 20° shows a P_{50} of 8 mm Hg; a rise in temperature shifts the curve to the right, but changes in pH do not have much effect on it.[116, 123, 134] Similar absence of Bohr effect is found for *Dendrostomum* hemerythrin[127] (Fig. 62). In *Sipunculus* also the P_{50} was 8 mm Hg whether the CO_2 was 0.07 or 80 mm Hg.[56] The oxygen in the coelomic fluid of *Sipunculus* in sea water corresponded to 32 mm Hg, which is above the saturation pressure for hemerythrin. However, tissue pressures are probably lower, and in the mud at low tide the worm is undoubtedly exposed to lower oxygen concentrations. Hemerythrin is not poisoned by CO. In brachiopods the hemerythrin shows a Bohr effect (Fig. 63), in contrast to all known sipunculid hemerythrins.

Hemerythrin from the vascular system (tentacular circulation, main contractile vessel, and "polian" diverticulae) of *Dendrostomum zostericolum* is a different protein from the hemerythrin in the coelom;[127] the vascular hemerythrin has a lower O_2 affinity ($P_{50} = 40$ to 45 for vascular, $P_{50} = 4.5$ mm for coelomic cells). Apparently the vascular hemerythrin transports O_2 from the high oxygen pressure of sea water to the coelom and the coelomic hemerythrin constitutes a transfer system between vascular pigment and tissue (Fig. 62). In a burrowing sipunculid, *Siphonosoma ingens,* which does not use the tentacles in respiration, the vascular pigment has a higher oxygen affinity than the coelomic pigment (as in *Nephthys* Hb); here the transfer is through body wall to coelom and then to the high-affinity vascular pigment.

Function of Hemocyanin. The blood pigment hemocyanin which occurs in many molluscs and arthropods can combine reversibly with oxygen. The higher the hemocyanin content of the blood as measured by the copper concentration, the greater is the oxygen capacity (p. 207). The equilibrium curve gives n = 4 for *Homarus* at pH 8.08 and n = 2 at pH 7.4; similarly in *Busycon* and *Limulus* n approaches 1 at pH 5.79 and is larger at higher pH values.[151] Thus there is interaction between O_2-binding sites as in hemoglobin.

In the cephalopod molluscs, hemocyanin clearly functions as an oxygen carrier. The blood of the squid *Loligo* has an oxygen capacity of 4.2 vol per cent;[151] arterial blood contained on the average 4.27 vol per cent of O_2 and 3.82 vol per cent of CO_2, whereas venous blood had 0.37 vol per cent of O_2 and 8.27 vol per cent of CO_2. Thus approximately 92 per cent of the oxygen was removed in the course of circulation, three times the percentage in man. Such high transfer of oxygen to the tissues fails to provide much reserve against hypoxic stress. The half-saturation value (36 mm Hg of O_2 at 0 mm CO_2 and 23°) is high enough to make the squid sensitive to the oxygen concentration in the medium. Similar data were obtained on *Octopus* where the O_2 capacity of the blood is 4.2 to 5.0 vol per cent.[193, 194] The color of the blood can be seen to change as it passes through the gills of a squid so that the oxygenated blood is distinctly blue. In the cephalopods, CO_2 and increased acidity shift the equilibrium curve to the right as they do in hemoglobin; in *Sepia*, P_{50} is 8 mm Hg

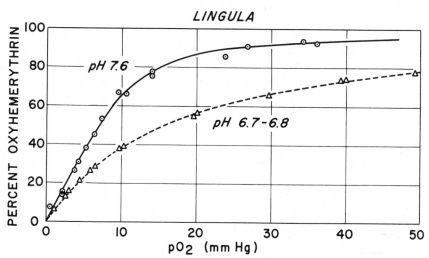

FIGURE 63.   Oxygen equilibrium curves of hemerythrin from the brachiopod *Lingula* at pH 7.6 and 6.7 to 6.8. Positive Bohr effect. (From Manwell, C.: Science, vol. 132.)

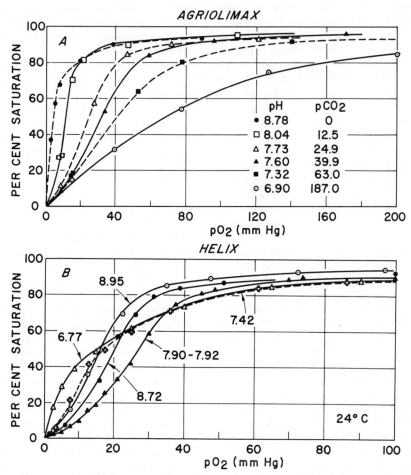

FIGURE 64. Oxygen equilibrium curves for molluscan hemocyanins. A, *Agriolimax* at the indicated pH's and corresponding partial pressures of CO_2; positive Bohr effect. B, *Helix:* change in shape of the equilibrium curve with pH; positive Bohr effect only between pH 8.9 and 7.9. (Courtesy of C. Manwell.)

partial pressure of O_2 at 0.25 mm Hg of CO_2 and 45 mm Hg of O_2 at 5.3 mm Hg of CO_2.[196] The effect of CO_2 upon dissociation of oxyhemocyanin accounts for about one-third of the respiratory exchange in the squid.[151] Also, a rise in temperature raises the pressures of loading and unloading. In *Sepia* and *Octopus* the P_{50}'s are lower than in squid, and these can survive in lower oxygen concentrations, although their hemocyanin is necessary in oxygen transport.

In the gastropod *Helix* the P_{50} is 12 mm Hg at 20° and 0 mm CO_2.[147] A "normal" Bohr effect occurs in Agriolimax but not in *Helix* hemocyanin (Fig. 64). In *Busycon*, P_{50} is lower, the arterial oxygen is at 36 mm Hg and the venous at 6 mm Hg, corresponding to an unloading to the tissues of 1.7 vol per cent. Less than 10 per cent of this oxygen could be carried in solution.[57] Apparently in *Busycon* the tissue oxygen pressure is low

and the hemocyanin transports much of the needed oxygen. Some gastropods, e.g., *Busycon* and *Cryptochiton*, use Hcy for O_2 transport in blood but have myoglobin in certain muscles, particularly the radular muscle;[72] the O_2 affinity of the myoglobin is greater than that of Hcy;[193] hence the muscle pigment appears to facilitate diffusion as in vertebrates[129] (Fig. 65).

The function of hemocyanin as an O_2 carrier in the arthropods has been questioned. The P_{50} lies in a usual physiological range, 11 to 13 mm Hg of O_2 for *Limulus*, and for *Homarus* 6 mm Hg of O_2 at 0.5 mm CO_2, and 25 mm Hg of O_2 at 9.9 mm Hg of CO_2. Also when *Limulus* or some of the crabs are bled the blood is pale, hence deoxygenated, and on exposure to air it becomes blue. Like some hemoglobins, hemocyanins show a maximum P_{50} at some pH, and the pH effect depends much upon the dilution and type of buffer (Fig. 66). In *Loligo, Homarus, Panulirus, Maja,* and *Cancer* the minimum O_2 affinity is on the acid side of neutrality as with hemoglobin, and the P_{50} moves to the right as CO_2 is added. However, in *Limulus, Busycon,* and *Helix* the minimum affinity is in the alkaline range, and lowering the pH in the physiological range shifts the equilibrium curve to the left, i.e., it increases the O_2 affinity, a negative Bohr effect.

The following data show the part played by Hcy in O_2 transport in several crustaceans:[152]

Species	Postbranchial blood			Prebranchial blood		
	mm O_2	vol % O_2	Hcy % sat	mm O_2	vol % O_2	Hcy % sat
Panulirus interruptus	7	0.82	54	3	0.35	22
Loxorhynchus grandis	8	0.41	68	3	0.17	30
Homarus americanus	5	0.44	49	3	0.18	20

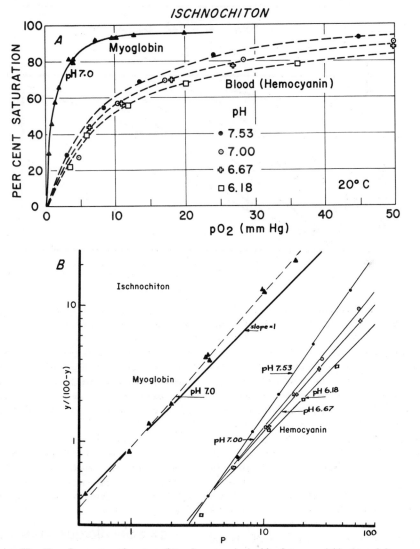

FIGURE 65. Transfer system of oxygen from hemocyanin in blood to myoglobin in radular muscle of the gastropod *Ischnochiton*. *A*, linear plot of O_2 equilibrium curves at different pH's. Hemocyanin shows weak Bohr effect. (From Manwell, C.: Unpublished data.) *B*, double logarithmic plot of same data showing decrease in n of hemocyanin with lower pH. (From Manwell, C.: Arch. Biochem. Biophys., vol. 89.)

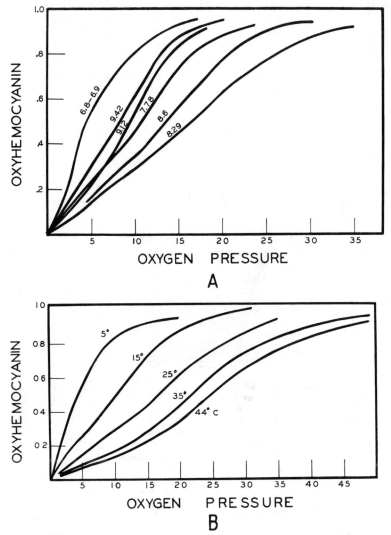

FIGURE 66. *A*, equilibrium curves of *Limulus* hemocyanin at different pH's. *B*, at different temperatures. (From Redfield, A. C., and Ingalls, E. N.: J. Cell. Comp. Physiol., vol. 3.)

These results indicate that in *Panulirus* only about 0.5 ml of O_2 is delivered by 100 ml of blood, but some 90 per cent of that which is exchanged is carried by the hemocyanin (Fig. 67). Similarly in *Maja*, hemocyanin transports some oxygen but is not saturated; in the soft-shelled stage of this crab, hemocyanin in the blood is only 1 per cent of that in hard-shelled adults (p. 71, Chapter 3), yet the oxygen concentration in the blood of soft crabs is only half that in hard ones. Apparently dissolved O_2 is adequate in the soft crabs.[200]

The pH difference between prebranchial and postbranchial blood in *Panulirus* is only 0.02 unit, which corresponds to a shift in the oxygen partial pressure of only 0.7 mm Hg; hence the Bohr effect is negligible. In the lobster the Bohr effect is positive and large. The reverse Bohr effect in *Limulus* and in *Busycon* is small and its action has probably been exaggerated; however; it may have an adaptive value in water low in O_2 and high in CO_2.[195]

In summary: A respiratory function for hemocyanin has been demonstrated in both molluscs and arthropods; in cephalopods the pigment operates near capacity while in arthropods it normally never becomes saturated.

CARBON DIOXIDE TRANSPORT

CO_2 Equilibrium Curve. The amount of carbon dioxide, like the amount of oxygen in body fluids, greatly exceeds the amount in solution. The solubility of CO_2 in human

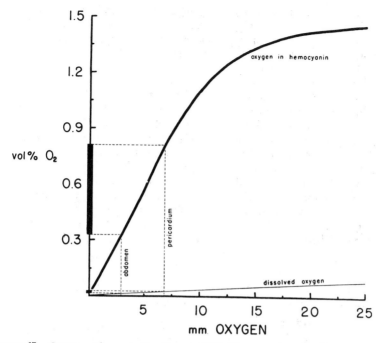

FIGURE 67. Oxygen exchange in *Panulirus* at 15°C. Heavy portion of ordinate, volumes per cent oxygen given up in tissues. (From Redmond, J. R.: J. Cell. Comp. Physiol., vol. 46.)

blood is 48 vol per cent at 760 mm Hg at 37.5°; the CO_2 pressure in alveolar air is 40 mm Hg. Hence the amount of CO_2 which might be dissolved in blood is 2.5 vol per cent. Actually, arterial blood contains 45 to 50 and venous blood 55 to 60 vol per cent. Similarly, sea water has a solubility coefficient at 24° of 0.71 vol per cent CO_2, and in equilibrium with air where the CO_2 partial pressure is 0.23 mm Hg, it would dissolve 0.0215 vol per cent; normally, sea water contains about 4.8 vol per cent of CO_2. The difference between the CO_2 dissolved and CO_2 actually contained is due to combination, largely as bicarbonate, with cations from various buffers. For each fluid containing buffers a CO_2 equilibrium curve can be constructed by equilibrating with a known CO_2 pressure and measuring the volume per cent taken up. Thus in the two examples above, in human blood 40 to 50 vol per cent corresponds to 40 mm Hg of CO_2, whereas in sea water 4.8 vol per cent corresponds to 0.23 mm Hg of CO_2. Typical CO_2 equilibrium curves (Fig. 68) indicate differences in the CO_2-combining ability of different species. Aquatic animals with a very weak buffering supply of cations, such as ascidians, may actually contain less total CO_2 than the surrounding water.[57]

The CO_2 content of circulating blood de-

pends on the total buffering capacity and on the partial pressures of CO_2 in body tissues and outside the respiratory surface. A few selected values for freshly drawn blood are given in Table 35. In terrestrial vertebrates the CO_2 pressure to which blood is exposed

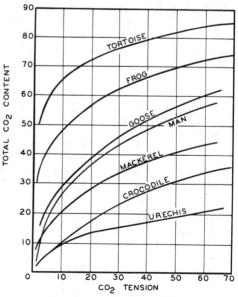

FIGURE 68. Carbon dioxide equilibrium curves, volumes per cent of CO_2 as function of P_{CO_2} in mm Hg. (Data assembled from Redfield, A. C.: Biol. Rev., vol. 9.)

in the lungs is high (40 mm Hg in many mammals), whereas in the water to which the gills of aquatic animals are exposed the CO_2 pressure is low (0.23 mm Hg in equilibrium with air). Actually the partial pressure in the blood of aquatic vertebrates is lower than in terrestrial vertebrates so that in both mammals and fish the CO_2 gradient between blood and medium is about 6 mm Hg. In mammals the difference between arterial and venous CO_2 indicates an unloading of about 10 per cent of the total in the lungs and loading of a similar amount in body tissues. The total CO_2 in the blood is less and the percentage gained in tissues and lost in gills is greater in aquatic vertebrates than in terrestrial vertebrates. The partial pressure

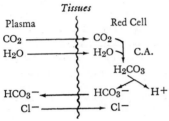

of CO_2 in the blood of hibernating mammals is less than in nonhibernating ones.[124]

Transport of CO_2 in Vertebrates. Carbon dioxide diffuses from tissues into blood according to the pressure gradient and is carried in the plasma as dissolved CO_2. A small portion of it reacts with water to form carbonic acid: $CO_2 + H_2O \rightarrow H_2CO_3$. Carbonic acid in the plasma, like lactic acid, is buffered by bases, largely from proteins. However, the hydration of CO_2 occurs too slowly to provide for the known rate of load-

ing in the tissues; most of the CO_2 diffuses directly into red blood cells where its hydration is catalyzed by the enzyme, carbonic anhydrase:

$$CO_2 + H_2O \underset{}{\overset{\text{carbonic anhydrase}}{\rightleftharpoons}} H_2CO_3$$

The H_2CO_3 formed in the red cells dissociates to HCO_3^- and H^+, and most of the HCO_3^- leaves the red cells in exchange for Cl^- from the plasma. In arterial blood about 67 per cent of the HCO_3^- is in the plasma, and in venous blood about 65.5 per cent. In the plasma, Na^+ balances the HCO_3^-, and Cl^- shifts from plasma to red cells in the tissues and back out of the red cells in the lungs as follows:

In the red cells most of the buffering is provided by the hemoglobin

$$BHb + H^+ \rightleftharpoons HHb + B^+$$

Phosphate contributes only slightly to the buffering. The resulting cation (B^+) from hemoglobin is balanced by the Cl^-. Deoxygenated Hb is a weaker acid (pK = 7.95 in horse) than is oxygenated Hb (pK = 6.68 in horse);[198] hence as O_2 is given off in the tissues more cations (B^+) are freed, and in the lungs as CO_2 is lost the stronger oxyHb attracts more base, thus freeing more CO_2.[139] It has been calculated that for each O_2 taken on there is an increase of negative charge per hemoglobin to about 0.6 equivalent and an equal displacement of HCO_3^-.[198] The reciprocal effect of oxygenation on acid strength of the hemoglobin, the so-called Haldane effect, accounts for the CO_2 exchange. In addition to the CO_2 transported by the above buffers, a small amount, some 5 to 10 per cent of the total in the blood, combines reversibly with hemoglobin as a carbamino compound.

The over-all relation between pH and CO_2 can be expressed by the Henderson-Hasselbach equation:

$$pH = pK + \log \frac{HCO_3^-}{H_2CO_3}$$

where pK is 6.1 for H_2CO_3. In respiratory

TABLE 35. CO_2 CONTENT OF FRESHLY DRAWN BLOOD

Animal	Blood	Vol %	mm Hg
man[23]	arterial	45-50	40-42
	venous	50-53	45-47
alligator[87]		38.6-44	
trout[51]	venous	19.4-22.8	8-10
carp[51]	venous	28.6-36.4	5-10
sucker[51]	venous	36.3-47.8	7- 9
sea robin[163]	arterial	6.5	2
toadfish[163]	venous	13.3	7
Raja ocellata	arterial	7.7	1.3
	venous	10.8	2.6
Urechis[149]		7- 9	9
Limulus[149]		10-20	
Astacus[41]		25-35	
Sepia[41]		11-14	
several echinoderms[41]		5- 6	
sea water		4.8	0.23

acidosis the blood pH falls and HCO_3^- rises, while in respiratory alkalosis blood pH rises and HCO_3^- falls; in metabolic acidosis the HCO_3^- declines and in metabolic alkalosis the HCO_3^- rises.

Pigments as Buffers. A titration curve of blood shows the change in pH with addition of acid or alkali (Fig. 69). In general, animals low in blood protein are less well buffered than those with high serum proteins or with cells containing a pigment. The buffer value of blood for added CO_2 is given by[38, 56, 60]

$$\beta = \frac{\Delta\,(BHCO_3)}{\Delta\quad pH}$$

Some values of β in mEq/l whole blood follow:

man	30.8	skate	4.6-6.5 (plasma)
horse	25.26	Urechis	4.9
alligator	22.6	Sipunculus	3.5
crocodile	18.2		

The greater effectiveness of dexoygenated hemoglobin in buffering acid than of oxygenated Hb is indicated as follows:[147]

$$\frac{-\Delta BHCO_3}{O_2}$$

Urechis	0.0	mackerel	0.70	goose	0.50
toadfish	0.45	crocodile	1.05	man	0.49
		turtle			
		(Chelydra)	0.22		

In the crocodile the change in acid strength of hemoglobin after oxygenation is greater than it is in man.[38] Hemoglobins low in histidine are poorer buffers than those high in histidine. In the tautog and some other fish, oxygenation decreases the CO_2-combining power at low CO_2 values, but above 50 mm of CO_2 the curves for oxygenated and deoxygenated bloods are similar. After hemolysis, however, the deoxygenated blood combines with more CO_2 at all pressures.[164] In general, those animals in which CO_2 increases the oxygen affinity are the ones in which oxygenation decreases the CO_2-binding power. The buffering capacity of trout and mackerel is high, whereas that of carp, toadfish, and skate is low.[56] The buffer value of the serum proteins is greater per gram of protein in the skate and crocodile than in mammals.[147]

In invertebrates most of the buffering appears to reside in blood proteins, and the

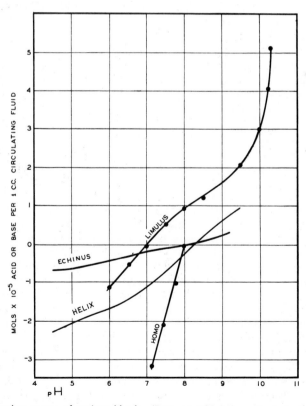

FIGURE 69. Titration curves of various bloods. (Data assembled from Barcroft, J.: Features of the Architecture of Physiological Function, Cambridge University Press; and Redfield, A. C.: Quart. Rev. Biol., vol. 8.)

principal proteins are the respiratory pigments.[41] In *Urechis,* for example, the plasma of the coelomic fluid has practically no buffering capacity, but the corpuscles are capable of buffering to about the same degree as corpuscles of a vertebrate of similar oxygen capacity. The coelomic fluid of the sea urchin, which contains little protein, has very little buffering power.[141] In those bloods which contain hemocyanin, most of the buffering is due to this pigment. In *Limulus,* for example, phosphates are negligible, but purified hemocyanin can bind 1.6×10^{-3} mols of acid per gram and in the presence of salts can bind much more.[151] The titration curve of hemocyanin or of *Limulus* serum, and also of *Helix,* shows the presence of several acid- and base-binding groups. Deoxygenated Hcy of *Maja, Octopus,* and *Loligo* is a weaker acid, hence binds more CO_2 than oxyHcy; in those animals where the Bohr effect is negative in the physiological range either there is no effect of oxygenation on buffering (*Limulus*) or the oxyHcy binds more CO_2 (*Busycon*).[151] In animals with calcium-containing shells— some molluscs and crustaceans—an important source of base for buffering acid is the shell.

In air-breathing insects carbon dioxide is lost directly by the tracheae. However, the blood is buffered, partly at least by the high concentration of amino acids. In the parasitic *Gastrophilus,* serum proteins (10.75 gm/100 ml) account for about 62 per cent of the total buffering: the partial pressure of CO_2 is very high (300 to 500 mm Hg) and the blood pH low (6.64).[122]

Carbonic Anhydrase. Carbonic anhydrase is widely distributed in the animal kingdom.[52, 57, 76, 179] It plays a part in the acidification of urine in the vertebrate kidney (p. 69) and in secretion of acid gastric juice; its role in the pancreas, lens, and retina has not been established. It is present in coelenterates, especially in tentacles of Anthozoa. It occurs in the respiratory trees and gonads of echinoderms. Carbonic anhydrase is found in coelomic fluid of *Sipunculus* and *Arenicola* but not in that of most other invertebrates; however, it is present in blood of earthworm and *Nereis,* which also contains hemoglobin. A rich supply of the enzyme is present in gills of polychaetes; most molluscs show little or none in blood, but there is much carbonic anhydrase in the gills of squid and in gills and mantle of pelecypods, especially in oysters.[106] In arthropods the gills of *Limulus* contain large amounts of the enzyme, those of *Homarus* and *Libinia* less; it also occurs in the stomach of crustaceans. Insects lack carbonic anhydrase in their blood but may have it in various tissues. Carbonic anhydrase appears to facilitate the hydration of respiratory CO_2 in blood cells of terrestrial vertebrates and in gills of aquatic animals; it is important also in other tissues where transfer of CO_2 and formation of bicarbonate have functions other than respiration.

COLLOID OSMOTIC FUNCTION OF PIGMENTS

Besides functioning in oxygen transport, as temporary oxygen reserves and as buffers, blood pigments, when they occur in solution in the plasma, may provide blood colloid. In animals with a heart, particularly those with an exoskeleton, the hemolymph (blood) is under hydrostatic pressure. Such animals would tend to lose fluid, even though at osmotic equilibrium with the sea, were it not for the proteins of their bloods. In them the concentrations of pigment proteins are considerable—often up to 5 per cent in crustacea and cephalopods. Precise correlations between hydrostatic pressure and blood proteins in aquatic animals have not been made.

CONCLUSIONS

Phylogenetically, blood pigments represent a labile set of characters. Hemochromogens, being universally distributed in aerobic cells, serve as blood pigments in several unrelated groups of animals; hemoglobins have evolved numerous times. The heme is the same, but the globins differ greatly—in amino acid composition, molecular size, electrophoretic mobility, immunological properties, and oxygen affinity. In one species, e.g., man, several hemoglobins may occur. Some of these are sequential during fetal development; others are genetic mutants of adults, affecting only one or a few amino acid residues. Physicochemical differences between hemoglobins show species and genera differentiation. The larger hemoglobins are carried in solution in the plasma, the smaller ones in cells. A single hemoglobin unit has a hyperbolic equilibrium curve; a multiple unit hemoglobin molecule may show interaction among the units, hence a sigmoid oxygen equilibrium curve.

Chlorocruorin has a porphyrin which differs from hemoglobin in only one side group of one pyrrol ring; both chlorocruorin and hemoglobin occur in a few serpulids. Only one other iron pigment, hemerythrin, has been used in oxygen transport. Hemocyanin is a very different sort of molecule, larger, a copper-protein, and may occur as several polymers within the same animal.

The coupling of oxygen to the pigments, particularly to hemoglobin, remains a major problem of protein chemistry although present evidence favors configurational changes in the molecule. The explanation of oxygen binding must account for the decrease in O_2 affinity by lowered pH (positive Bohr effect), the increased acid strength of the protein on oxygenation, the interaction between hemes and the sigmoid dissociation curve, the decreased O_2 affinity with increased temperature, and the effects of dilution and salts on oxygen binding. A molecule may react differently when inside a cell or in solution. As the site of proton-binding, sulfhydryl and imidazole groups have each been proposed. A pigment may show a Bohr effect in one species (hemerythrin in Lingula) and no Bohr effect in another animal (hemerythrin in Phascolosoma).

Whether a pigment molecule loads or unloads O_2 depends on the partial pressure of oxygen where it happens to be at a given instant. In some animals—e.g., squid—particularly, all the O_2 is transferred in one circulation cycle; in mammals one-fifth to one-third of the O_2. In some arthropods the hemocyanin never becomes fully oxygenated, yet the tissue oxygen pressures are such that the small amount of O_2 delivered comes from the pigment. In *Ascaris* the hemoglobin appears never to lose its oxygen. In chironomid larvae and some annelids the pigment remains oxygenated except in hypoxic conditions and may provide a store of oxygen for brief periods of respiratory deficiency. In other animals, *Tubifex* for example, the pigment is unloaded when the oxygen in the water outside is well above the P_{50}; hence tissue pressures must be exceedingly low. In some groups of animals—polychaetes, crustaceans, molluscs—the species lacking transport pigments get on well alongside species containing pigments. Several kinds of animal, e.g., *Daphnia,* synthesize hemoglobin only if in an environment low in oxygen. A number of pigments serve to facilitate diffusion of O_2; these are intermediate in O_2 affinity between transport pigments and cell enzymes; examples are myoglobin, fetal Hb, coelomic hemerythrin in Dendrostomum, and muscle hemoglobin in hemocyanin-containing gastropods.

In addition to functions in oxygen transport, the blood pigments constitute the principal buffers and when free in solution provide colloid osmotic pressure to blood. Ecologically, many animals are limited in range by their blood pigments. Correlations between oxygen-combining power and amount of pigment occur, as at high altitude or in oxygen-deficient water. Adaptation with respect to the effects of CO_2 and temperature on oxygen affinity with added CO_2 is considerable in squid and in fish from fast waters; it is less in fish from sluggish and acid water and in terrestrial animals. The CO_2 effect is reversed in some sluggish animals which have hemocyanin.

The hemoglobins and hemocyanins present a pattern of greater functional versatility and consequent ecological significance than any other class of biochemical compounds.

REFERENCES

1. ALBRITTON, E. C., ed., Standard Values in Blood. Handbook of Biological Data. Philadelphia, W. B. Saunders Co., 1952, pp. 199.

2. ALLEN, D. W., GUTHE, K. F., and WYMAN, J., J. Biol. Chem. *187*: 393-410, 1950. O_2 equilibrium of hemoglobin.

3. ALLEN, D. W., and WYMAN, J., J. Cell. Comp. Physiol. *37*: 371-374, 1952. Duck hemoglobin.

4. ALLEN, D. W., and WYMAN, J., J. Cell. Comp. Phys. *39*: 383-390, 1952. O_2 equilibrium of Arenicola hemoglobin.

5. ALLEN, D. W., *et al.,* J. Biol. Chem. *203*: 81-87, 1953. Fetal and adult hemoglobin.

6. ALLISON, A. C., Science *122*: 640, 1953. Genetic control of hemoglobins.

7. ALTLAND, P. D., *et al.,* Am. J. Physiol. *180*: 421-427, 1955; Proc. Soc. Exp. Biol. Med. *99*: 456-459, 1958. Blood formation in turtles.

8. ANSON, M. L., *et al.,* Proc. Roy Soc. London, B, *97*: 61-83, 1924. Absorption spectra of hemoglobins.

9. *BARCROFT, J., Features of the Architecture of Physiological Function. Cambridge University Press, 1934, 368 pp.

10. BARCROFT, J., *et al.,* J. Physiol. *83*: 192-214, 1934. O_2 transport by fetal and maternal blood of goat.

11. BARKER, J. N., Am. J. Physiol. *189*: 281-289, 1957. Role of hemoglobin affinities in tolerance of hypoxia.

12. BARRON, D. H., and MESCHIA, G., Cold Spring Harbor Symp. *19*: 93-101, 1954. Oxygen exchange across placenta.

13. *BARTELS, H., Handbuch Zool. *5*: 1-56, 1959; Pflüg. Arch. ges. Physiol. *268*: 334-365, 1959. Physiological constants of blood, particularly mammals.

14. BEADLE, L. C., J. Exp. Biol. *34*: 1-10, 1957. Respiration in oligochaete Alma.

15. BENESCH, R. E., *et al.,* J. Biol. Chem. *216*: 663-676, 1955. Sulfhydryl groups in different hemoglobins.

16. BENZER, S., and INGRAM, V. M., Nature *182*: 852-853, 1958. Electrophoresis of human hemoglobins.

17. *BERLIN, N. I., *et al.,* Physiol. Rev. *39*: 577-616, 1959. Summary of life span of red blood cells.

18. BLACK, E. C., Biol. Bull. *79*: 215-229, 1940. O_2 transport by fish blood.

19. BLACK, E. C., J. Fish. Res. Bd. Canada *12*: 917-929, 1955; *14*: 117-134, 1957. Blood lactic acid following exercise, fish.

20. BLACK, E. C., and IRVING, L., Tr. Roy. Soc. Canad. Biol. Sci. *31*: 29-32, 1937. O_2 transport by fish blood.

21. BLACK, E. C., *et al.,* Canad. J. Zool. *32*: 408-420, 1954. Effect of CO_2 on O_2 utilization by fish.

22. BOARDMAN, N. K., and ADAIR, G. S., Nature *177*: 1078-1079, 1955. Horse myoglobins.

23. BOCK, H. V., *et al.,* J. Biol. Chem. *59*: 353-378, 1924. CO_2 and O_2 dissociation curves, blood of man.

24. BOERI, A., and GHIRETTI-MAGALDI, A., Biochim. Biophys. Acta *23*: 489-493, 1957. Properties of hemerythrin.

25. BOWEN, W. J., and EADS, H. J., Am. J. Physiol. *159*: 77-82, 1949. Effect of altitude on myoglobin in dogs.

26. BURKE, J. D., Physiol. Zool. *26*: 259-266, 1953. O_2 capacity in mammals.

27. CALIFANO, L., and BOERI, E., J. Exp. Biol. *27*: 253-256, 1950. Properties of hemovanadin from Phallusia.

28. CHANDLER, A., Proc. Zool. Soc. London *124*: 625-630, 1954. Hemoglobin variation in Daphnia.

29. CHANDRASEKHAR, N., Nature *184*: 1652-1653, 1959. Fish hemoglobins.

30. CHIODI, H., J. Appl. Physiol. *10*: 81-87, 1957. Adaptations to high altitudes.

31. DAUSEND, K., Ztschr. vergl. Physiol. *14*: 557-608, 1931. Respiration and hemoglobin function in Tubifex.

32. DAVENPORT, H. E., Proc. Roy. Soc. London, B, *136*: 255-270, 271-280, 1949. Hemoglobins of nematodes.

33. DAWSON, W. R., Physiol. Zool. *33*: 87-103, 1960. Properties of blood of lizard Eumeces at high temperatures.

34. DELACHAUX, A., and TISSIERES, A., Helvet. Med. Acta *13*: 333, 1946. Increase in muscle cytochrome in low O_2.

35. DESSAUER, H. C., *et al.,* Arch. Biochem. Biophys. *71*: 11-16, 1957. Electrophoretic separation of hemoglobins, amphibians and reptiles.

36. DHÉRÉ, C., Rev. Suisse de Zool. *35*: 277-289, 1928. Respiratory pigments, invertebrates.

37. DILL, D. B., Life, Heat and Altitude. Cambridge University Press, 1938, 211 pp.

38. DILL, D. B., and EDWARDS, H. T., J. Biol. Chem. *90*: 515-530, 1931; J. Cell. Comp. Physiol. *6*: 243-254, 1935; Biol. Bull. *62*: 23-26, 1932. Respiratory properties of blood in crocodile, alligator, and skate.

39. *DRASTICH, L., Pflüg. Arch. ges. Physiol. *219*: 227-232, 1928. Comparative hematology.

40. DUNLAP, J. S., JOHNSON, V. L., and FARNER, D. S., Experientia *12*: 352-353, 1956. Multiple hemoglobins in birds.

41. DUVAL, M., and PORTIER, P., C. R. Acad. Sci. *184*: 1594-1596, 1927. CO_2 content of invertebrate bloods.

42. EDWARDS, H. T., and DILL, D. B., J. Cell. Comp. Physiol. *6*: 21-35, 1935. Properties of blood of gila monster (Heloderma).

43. ELIASSEN, E., Arbok Univ. Bergen Natur. *12*: 2-9, 1955. O_2 supply to Arenicola at ebb tide.

44. ELLIS, M. M., MEIRICH, A. D., and ELLIS, M. D., Bull. U. S. Bur. Fish. *46*: 509-546, 1930. Properties of mussel blood.

45. ENDRES, G., Proc. Roy. Soc. London, B, *107*: 241-247, 1930. Blood of marmot.

46. EVANS, J. V., *et al.,* Nature *178*: 849, 1956. Genetics of hemoglobin differences in sheep.

47. EWER, R. F., J. Exp. Biol. *18*: 197-205, 1942. Hemoglobin function in Chironomus.

48. EWER, R. F., and Fox, H. M., Proc. Roy. Soc. London, B, *129*: 137-153, 1940; Publ. Staz. Zool. Napoli *24*: 197-200, 1953. Chlorocruorin function.

49. FÄNGE, R., and AKESSON, B., Arkiv f. Zool. *3*: 25-31, 1951. Hemerythrin in coelomic cells of Priapulids.

50. FELSENFELD, G., J. Cell. Comp. Physiol. *43*: 23-28, 1954. Binding of copper by hemocyanin.

51. FERGUSON, J. K. W., and BLACK, E. C., Biol. Bull. *80*: 139-152, 1941. CO_2 transport in blood of fish.

52. FERGUSON, J. K. W., *et al.,* J. Cell. Comp. Physiol. *10*: 395-400, 1937. Carbonic anhydrase in invertebrates.

53. FISCHER, H., and DEILMAN, K. O., Hoppe-Seylers Ztschr. Physiol. Chem. *280*: 186-216, 1944. Properties of Spirographis chlorocruorin.

54. FISCHER, H., and VON SEEMAN, C., Hoppe-Seylers Ztschr. Physiol. Chem. *242*: 133-157, 1936. Properties of Spirographis chlorocruorin.

55. FISH, G. R., J. Exp. Biol. *33*: 186-195, 1956. Respiration in African fish.

56. *FLORKIN, M., Ann. Physiol. *10*: 599-694, 1934. Review of respiratory functions of body fluids.

57. *FLORKIN, M., L'evolution biochemique. Paris, Masson et Cie, 1944, 210 pp.

58. FLORKIN, M., and REDFIELD, A. C., Biol. Bull. *61*: 421-426, 1931. Respiratory function, blood of sea lion.

59. FORBES, W. H., and ROUGHTON, F. J. W., J. Physiol. *71*: 229-256, 1931. Differences between hemoglobin solution and whole blood.

60. FOREMAN, C. W., J. Cell. Comp. Physiol. *44*: 421-430, 1954. O_2 equilibrium curves of various mammalian hemoglobins.

61. Fox, H. M., Proc. Roy. Soc. London, B, *99*: 199-217, 1926; *111*: 356-373, 1932; *115*: 368-373, 1934; Nature *162*: 20, 1948. Chlorocruorin.

62. Fox, H. M., J. Exp. Biol. *21*: 161-164, 1945. O_2 affinities of invertebrate hemoglobins.

63. Fox, H. M., Proc. Roy. Soc. London, B, *135*: 192-212, 1948; *136*: 388-399, 1949; *138*: 514-528, 1951; *141*: 179-189, 1953; Nature *166*: 609-610, 1950; Bull. Soc. Zool. France *80*: 288-298, 1955. Hemoglobin synthesis and function in Daphnia.

64. Fox, H. M., Nature *164*: 59, 1949; *171*: 162, 1953. Distribution of hemoglobin in crustaceans.

65. Fox, H. M., Proc. Roy. Soc. London, B, *136*: 378-388, 1949. Comparison of chlorocruorin and hemoglobin.

66. Fox, H. M., Proc. Roy. Soc. London, B, *143*: 203-214, 214-225, 1955. Effect of O_2 on hemoglobin synthesis and function, invertebrates.

67. Fox, H. M., Nature *168*: 112, 1951. Blood pigments of Serpula.

68. Gaumer, A. E. H., and Goodnight, C. J., Am. Midl. Nat. *58*: 332-340, 1957. O_2 transport by blood of turtles.

69. Gelineo, A., and Gelineo, S., C. R. Soc. Biol. *149*: 1410-1413, 1955. Hemoglobin concentrations in fish and birds.

70. Gibson, Q. H., Proc. Roy. Soc. London, B, *143*: 334-342, 1955. Reactions of annelid hemoglobins with O_2 and CO.

71. Gibson, Q. H., and Roughton, F. J. W., Proc. Roy. Soc. London, B, *143*: 310-334, 1955; J. Physiol. *136*: 507-526, 1957. Kinetics of hemoglobin combinations.

72. Giese, A. C., Anat. Rec. *113*: 103, 1952. Myoglobin in muscles of chitons.

73. Gilchrist, B. M., Proc. Roy. Soc. London, B, *143*: 136-146, 1954. Hemoglobin in Artemia.

74. Gjönnes, B., and Schmidt-Nielsen, K., J. Cell. Comp. Physiol. *39*: 147-152, 1952. Respiratory characteristics of kangaroo rat blood.

75. *Goodwin, T. W., Biochemistry of pigments, *in* The Physiology of Crustacea, edited by T. H. Waterman. New York, Academic Press, 1960, pp. 101-119.

76. *von Goor, H., Enzymologia *13*: 73-164, 1948. Carbonic anhydrase.

77. Green, A. A., and Redfield, A. C., Biol. Bull. *64*: 44-52, 1933. Blood of porpoise.

78. Green, J., Proc. Roy. Soc. London, B, *145*: 214-232, 1956. Variations in hemoglobin of Daphnia.

79. von Grembergen, G., Nature *174*: 35, 1954. Hemoglobin of a nematode.

80. Halbrecht, I., and Klibanski, C., Nature *178*: 794, 1956. Hemoglobin of human embryos.

81. Hall, F. G., J. Physiol. *83*: 222-228, 1934. Hemoglobin function in chick.

82. Hall, F. G., J. Biol. Chem. *115*: 485-490, 1936; J. Mammal. *18*: 468-472, 1937. Blood of animals living at high altitudes.

83. Hall, F. G., et al., J. Cell. Comp. Physiol. *8*: 301-313, 1936. Blood of animals living at high altitudes.

84. Haughton, T. M., et al., J. Exp. Biol. *35*: 360-368, 1958. O_2 equilibrium curves, alkaline denaturation of earthworm hemoglobins.

85. Hildemann, W. H., and Keighley, G., Am. Natur. *89*: 169-174, 1955. Hemoglobin synthesis, Daphnia.

86. Hill, R., Proc. Roy. Soc. London, B, *120*: 472-483, 1936. Muscle hemoglobin.

87. Hopping, A., Am. J. Physiol. *66*: 145-163, 1923. Alligator blood.

88. Hoshi, T., Scient. Rep. Tohoku Univ. *23*: 35-58, 1957. Hemoglobin in a daphnid.

89. Huisman, T. H., et al., Nature *182*: 171-174, 1958. Sheep hemoglobins.

90. Hunt, J. A., and Ingram, V. M., Nature *183*: 1373-1375, 1956; *184*: 640-641, 1957. Amino acid sequences in hemoglobins.

91. Hunt, J. A., and Lehman, H., Nature *184*: 872-873, 1957. Amino acid sequences in hemoglobins.

92. Hurtado, A., et al., Am. J. Med. Sci. *194*: 708-713, 1937; Arch. Int. Med. *75*: 284-323, 1945. Effects of altitude on hemoglobin and myoglobin.

93. Ingram, V. M., Biochim. Biophys. Acta *28*: 539-545, 1958; *36*: 402-411, 1959. Normal and sickle cell hemoglobins, man.

94. Irving, L., Safford, V., and Scott, W. J., J. Cell. Comp. Physiol. *13*: 297-313, 1939. Properties of fox blood.

95. Irving, L., et al., J. Cell. Comp. Physiol. *6*: 393-403, 1935. Properties of seal blood.

96. Irving, L., et al., Biol. Bull. *80*: 1-17, 1941. Temperature and O_2 affinity of fish blood.

97. Itazawa, W., Bull. Jap. Soc. Sci. Fish. *23*: 71-80, 1957. Gas content of blood of fish.

98. Johnson, M. L., J. Exp. Biol. *18*: 266-277, 1941. Hemoglobin function in Lumbricus.

99. Jones, J. D., J. Exp. Biol. *32*: 110-125, 1955. Hemoglobin function in polychaete Nephthys and Arenicola.

100. Jonxis, J. H. P., *in* Haemoglobin, edited by F. J. W. Roughton and J. C. Kendrew. New York, Interscience Publishers, 1949, pp. 261-267. Properties of fetal hemoglobin.

101. Jope, E. M., *in* Haemoglobin, edited by F. J. W. Roughton and J. C. Kendrew. New York, Interscience Publishers, 1949, pp. 205-219. Ultraviolet spectral absorption of hemoglobin.

102. Joubert, F. J., Biochim. Biophys. Acta *14*: 127-135, 1954. Hemocyanin of crayfish.

103. Jürgens, O., Zool. Jahrb. Abt. allg. Zool. u. Physiol. *55*: 1-46, 1935. Circulation and respiration in polychaetes.

104. Kalabuchov, N. J., J. Anim. Ecol. *6*: 254-272, 1937. Blood adaptations of altitude rodents.

105. Katz, A., and Chernoff, A. I., Science *130*: 1574-1576, 1960. Structure of adult and fetal hemoglobins, man.

106. Kawai, D. K., Mem. Coll. Sci. Univ. Kyoto B, *21*: 39-44, 1954. Carbonic anhydrase in oyster.

107. Keilin, D., Nature *171*: 922-925, 1953. Heme linkage and position of globin.

108. Keilin, D., and Hartree, E. F., Nature *168*: 266-269, 1951. Criticism of "erythrocruorin" concept.

109. Keilin, D., and Wang, Y. L., Biochem. J. *40*: 855-867, 1946. Hemoglobin of Gastrophilus.

110. Kendrew, J. C., and Perutz, M. F., Proc. Roy. Soc. London, A, *194*: 375-398, 1948. X-ray analysis of adult and fetal hemoglobins.

111. Kendrew, J. C., et al., Nature *174*: 946-949, 1954; *181*: 662-666, 1958; *185*: 422-427, 1960. Structure of myoglobin.

112. Keyes, A., et al., Am. J. Physiol. *115*: 292-307, 1936. Blood equilibrium with O_2 at high altitudes.

113. Klotz, I. M., and Klotz, T. A., Science *121*: 477-480, 1955. Comparison of oxygenation reactions in hemocyanin, hemerythrin, and hemoglobin.

114. Klotz, I. M., et al., Biol. Bull. *107*: 315, 1954; Arch. Biochem. Biophys. *68*: 284-299, 1957. Nature of active sites in hemerythrin.

115. Klotz, T. A., and Klotz, I. M., Biol. Bull. *107*: 300, 1954. Oxygenation reaction of hemocyanin.

116. Kubo, M., Bull. Chem. Soc. Japan *26*: 189-192, 1953. O_2 equilibrium of Phascolosoma hemerythrin.

117. Kunkel, H. G., et al., J. Clin. Invest. *36*:

1615-1625, 1957. Types of human hemoglobin, especially A_2.

118. KÜNZER, W., Nature *179*: 477-478, 1957. Human embryo hemoglobin.

119. LAUFFER, M. A., and SWABY, L. G., Biol. Bull. *108*: 290-295, 1955. Molecular constants of hemocyanin.

120. LEIN, A., and PAULING, L., Proc. Nat. Acad. Sci. *42*: 51-54, 1956. Isocyanide affinity of horse myoglobin.

121. LEITCH, I., J. Physiol. *50*: 370-379, 1916. Hemoglobin function in Planorbis and Chironomus larvae.

122. LEVENBOOK, L., J. Exp. Biol. *27*: 158-191, 1950. CO_2 transport in insect blood.

123. LOVE, W. E., Biochim. Biophys. Acta *23*: 465-471, 1957. Properties of hemerythrins.

124. LYMAN, C. P., and HASTINGS, A. B., Am. J. Physiol. *167*: 633-637, 1951. CO_2 transport, hibernating mammals.

125. MALOEUF, N. S. R., Ztschr. vergl. Physiol. *25*: 1-28, 1937. Oxygen capacity, Mytilus, Asterias body fluids.

126. MANWELL, C., Science *126*: 1175, 1957; Physiol. Zool. *31*: 93-100, 1958. Larval and adult hemoglobins in ovoviviparous dogfish and oviparous teleost.

127. MANWELL, C., Science *127*: 592-593, 1958; *132*: 550-551, 1960. O_2 equilibrium of Phascolosoma and Lingula hemerythrins.

128. MANWELL, C., Science *127*: 705-706, 1958. Respiratory properties of hemoglobin of diving birds.

129. MANWELL, C., J. Cell. Comp. Physiol. *52*: 341-352, 1958; Arch. Biochem. Biophys. *89*: 194-201, 1960. O_2 equilibrium of hemocyanin and myoglobin of Cryptochiton.

130. MANWELL, C., Biol. Bull. *115*: 227-238, 1958. Hemoglobin of hagfish.

131. MANWELL, C., J. Cell. Comp. Physiol. *53*: 61-74, 1959. Properties of annelid hemoglobins.

132. MANWELL, C., J. Cell. Comp. Physiol. *53*: 75-84, 1959. Absence of Bohr effect in Cucumaria hemoglobin.

133. *MANWELL, C., Ann. Rev. Physiol. *22*: 191-244, 1960. Respiratory pigments.

133a. MANWELL, C., Comp. Biochem. Physiol. *1*: 267-285, 1960. Histological specificity of respiratory pigments.

134. MARRIAN, G. F., J. Exp. Biol. *4*: 357-364, 1927. Hemerythrin.

135. McCARTHY, E. F., J. Physiol. *102*: 55-61, 1943; Cold Spring Harbor Symp. *19*: 133-140, 1954. Fetal hemoglobin.

136. McCUTCHEON, F. H., J. Cell. Comp. Physiol. *29*: 333-344, 1947. O_2 affinity of hemoglobin of turtles and elasmobranchs.

137. MENDES, E. G., Pub. Staz. Zool. Napoli *22*: 348-366, 1950. Respiratory function of chlorocruorin.

138. DE MARCO, C., and ANTONINI, E., Nature *181*: 1128, 1958. Amino acid composition of fish hemoglobin.

139. MARGARIA, R., and MILLA, E., Boll. Soc. ital. Biol. sper. *31*: 1250-1253, 1955. Effect of CO_2 on oxygen equilibrium of hemoglobin.

140. MILLIKAN, G. A., J. Physiol. *79*: 158-179, 1933. Kinetics of hemocyanin and hemoglobin.

141. PANTIN, C. F. A., J. Linn. Soc. Zool. *37*: 705-711, 1932. Physiological adaptation.

142. PAUL, W., and ROUGHTON, F. J. W., J. Physiol. *113*: 23-35, 1951. O_2 equilibrium curve of sheep hemoglobin.

143. PAULING, L., *in* Haemoglobin, edited by F. J. W. Roughton and J. C. Kendrew. New York, Interscience Publishers, 1949, pp. 57-65. Morphology of hemoglobin molecule.

144. PERUTZ, M. F., Proc. Roy. Soc. London, A, *195*: 474-499, 1949; Nature *185*: 416-422, 1960. X-ray diffraction analysis of methemoglobin.

145. PROSSER, C. L., *et al.,* Physiol. Zool. *30*: 137-141, 1957. Adaptation of goldfish to low oxygen.

146. RAMIREZ, J. R., and DESSAUER, H. C., Proc. Soc. Exp. Biol. Med. *96*: 690-694, 1957. Hemoglobins of turtle Pseudemys scripta.

147. *REDFIELD, A. C., Quart. Rev. Biol. *8*: 31-57, 1933; Biol. Rev. *9*: 175-212, 1934. Reviews of respiratory functions of blood pigments.

148. *REDFIELD, A. C., *in* Copper Metabolism, edited by W. D. McElroy and B. Glass. Johns Hopkins Press, 1950, pp. 174-190. Hemocyanin.

149. REDFIELD, A. C., and FLORKIN, A. M., Biol. Bull. *61*: 185-210, 1931. Respiratory function of blood of Urechis.

150. REDFIELD, A. C., and INGALLS, E. N., J. Cell. Comp. Physiol. *3*: 169-202, 1933. O_2 dissociation curves of bloods containing hemocyanin.

151. REDFIELD, A. C., *et al.,* J. Exp. Biol. *6*: 340-349, 1929; J. Cell. Comp. Physiol. *1*: 253-275, 1932; *3*: 169-202, 1933. O_2 equilibrium curves of hemocyanin-containing bloods.

152. REDMOND, J. R., J. Cell. Comp. Physiol. *46*: 209-247, 1955. Respiratory function of crustacean hemocyanin.

153. REISSMAN, K. R., Am. J. Physiol. *167*: 52-58, 1951. Circulatory changes in dogs at altitude.

154. REYNAFAJE, C., *et al.,* Proc. Soc. Exp. Biol. Med. *87*: 101-102, 1954. Life span of red cells in man at high altitude.

155. RIGGS, A. F., J. Gen. Physiol. *35*: 41-44, 1951. O_2 equilibrium of eel hemoglobin.

156. RIGGS, A. F., J. Gen. Physiol. *35*: 23-40, 1951. Properties of tadpole and frog hemoglobins.

157. RIGGS, A. F., J. Gen. Physiol. *36*: 1-16, 1952; *39*: 585-605, 1956. Sulfhydryl groups and structure of hemoglobin.

158. RIGGS, A. F., Nature *183*: 1037-1038, 1959. Molecular adaptation in hemoglobins.

158a. RIGGS, A. F., J. Gen. Physiol. *43*: 737-752, 1960. Nature of Bohr effect.

159. *ROCHE, J., Ann. Rev. Biochem. *5*: 463-484, 1936. Blood pigments.

160. ROCHE, J., and FONTAINE, M., Ann. Inst. Oceanog. Monaco *20*: 77-87, 1940. Amino acid composition of various blood pigments.

161. RODMAN, G. P., and EBAUGH, F. G., Fed. Proc. *15*: 155-156, 1956; Proc. Soc. Exp. Biol. Med. *95*: 397-401, 1957. Electrophoretic separation of animal hemoglobins.

162. ROGERS, W. P., Austral. J. Sci. Res. B. Biol. Sci. *2*: 287-303, 399-407, 1949. Hemoglobin function in nematode parasites.

163. ROOT, R. W., Biol. Bull. *61*: 426-456, 1931. O_2 transport by blood of marine fish.

164. ROOT, R. W., and IRVING, L., J. Cell. Comp.

Physiol. *16*: 85-96, 1940; Biol. Bull. *81*: 307-323, 1941. O₂ transport by blood of tautog.

165. DE ROSSI-FANELL, C., *et al.*, Biochim. Biophys. Acta *38*: 380-381, 1960. Amino acids in various hemoglobins.

166. ROSTORFER, H. H., and RIGDON, R. H., Biol. Bull. *92*: 23-30, 1947. O₂ transport, resistance to anoxia, chicks and ducklings.

167. RUUD, W., Nature *173*: 848-850, 1954. Fish without hemoglobin.

168. ST. GEORGE, R. C. C., and PAULING, L., Science *114*: 629-634, 1951. Morphology of hemoglobin molecule.

169. SALAMON, K., J. Gen. Physiol. *24*: 367-375, 1941. Kinetics and absorption bands of invertebrate hemoglobins.

170. SCHMIDT-NIELSEN, K., and LARIMER, J. P., Am. J. Physiol. *195*: 424-428, 1958. O₂ affinity of hemoglobin in relation to body size.

171. SCHOLANDER, P. F., Acta physiol. scand. *41*: 340-344, 1957. O₂ equilibrium curves for fish blood.

172. SCHOLANDER, P. F., Science *131*: 585-590, 1960. O₂ transport through hemoglobin solutions.

173. SCHOLANDER, P. F., and VAN DAM, L., Biol. Bull. *107*: 247-249, 1954. Role of hemoglobin in secretion of gases into swim bladders.

174. SCHOLANDER, P. F., and VAN DAM, L., J. Cell. Comp. Physiol. *49*: 1-3, 1957. Concentration of hemoglobin in arctic fishes.

175. SCHROEDER, W. A., *et al.*, J. Biol. Chem. *187*: 221-240, 1940. Amino acid composition of mutant hemoglobins.

176. SCHULMAN, M. P., and WALD, G., Biol. Bull. *101*: 239-240, 1951. Valence of copper in hemocyanin.

177. SCHWEER, M., Ztschr. vergl. Physiol. *42*: 20-42, 1959. Metabolism of leeches with and without hemoglobin.

178. SCOTT, W. J., Biol. Bull. *61*: 211-222, 1931. Respiratory function, Amphiuma blood.

179. SOBOTKA, H., and KANN, S., J. Cell. Comp. Physiol. *17*: 341-348, 1941. Carbonic anhydrase in fish and invertebrates.

180. SOUTHWORTH, F. C., and REDFIELD, A. C., J. Gen. Physiol. *9*: 387-403, 1926. Respiratory function of turtle blood.

181. STEIN, W. H., *et al.*, Biochim. Biophys. Acta *24*: 640-642, 1957. Amino acid composition of human hemoglobins.

182. *SVEDBERG, T., and PEDERSEN, K. O., The Ultracentrifuge. 1940, Oxford University Press, New York, Johnson Reprint Corp., 1959, 478 pp.

183. TRISTRAM, G. R., *in* Haemoglobin, edited by F. J. W. Roughton and J. C. Kendrew. New York, Interscience Publishers, 1949, pp. 109-113. Amino acid composition of hemoglobins.

184. VAUGHAN, B. E., and PACE, N., Am. J. Physiol. *185*: 549-556, 1956. Myoglobin changes at high altitudes.

185. VICKERY, H. B., Ann. New York Acad. Sci. *41*: 87-120, 1941; J. Biol. Chem. *144*: 719-730, 1942. Amino acids of hemoglobins.

186. WALD, G., and RIGGS, A., J. Gen. Physiol. *35*: 45-53, 1951. Hemoglobin of lamprey Petromyzon.

187. WÄLSHE, B. M., J. Exp. Biol. *24*: 343-351, 1947. Function of hemoglobin in chironomid Tantytarsus.

188. WÄLSHE, B. M., J. Exp. Biol. *24*: 329-342, 1947; *27*: 73-95, 1950; *28*: 57-61, 1951. Function of hemoglobin in various chironomids.

189. WÄLSHE-MAETZ, B. M., Physiol. Compar. Oecol. *3*: 135-154, 1953. Metabolism of Chironomus plumosus.

190. WASTL, H., and LEINER, G., Pflüg. Arch. ges. Physiol. *227*: 367-420, 421-459, 1931. Dissociation curves of bird blood.

191. WEBB, D. A., J. Exp. Biol. *16*: 499-523, 1939; Pub. Napoli Staz. Zool. *28*: 273-288, 1956. Vanadium in ascidians.

192. WILLMER, E. N., J. Exp. Biol. *11*: 283-306, 1934. Function of blood of tropical fish.

193. WINTERSTEIN, H., Biochem. Ztschr. *19*: 384-424, 1909. Respiratory function of blood of marine invertebrates.

194. WOLVEKAMP, H. P., Ztschr. vergl. Physiol. *25*: 541-547, 1938. O₂ transport and hemocyanin in Octopus.

195. WOLVEKAMP, H. P., and WATERMAN, T. H., *in* Physiology of Crustacea. 1960, New York, Academic Press, pp. 35-100.

196. WOLVEKAMP, H. P., *et al.*, Arch. Néerl. Physiol. *26*: 203-211, 1942. O₂ and CO₂ transport by blood of cephalopods.

197. WOLVEKAMP, H. P., *et al.*, Arch. Néerl. Physiol. *25*: 265-276, 1941; *28*: 620-629, 1947. Respiratory function in blood of Arenicola, Helix, and Homarus.

198. *WYMAN, J., Adv. Protein Chem. *4*: 407-531, 1948. Heme proteins.

199. ZAAIJER, J. J. P., and WOLVEKAMP, H. P., Acta Phys. Pharm. Néerl. *7*: 56-77, 1958. O₂ equilibrium in blood of snail Planorbis.

200. ZUCKERKANDL, E., C. R. Soc. Biol. *151*: 524-528, 1957. Oxygen capacity and copper content of Maja blood.

Chapter 9

TEMPERATURE

INTRODUCTION

Temperature limits the distribution of animals and at the same time determines their rate of activity. The range of environmental temperatures on earth is much greater than the range permissive of active life. In general, life activities occur only within the range of about 0° to 40°C; most animals live within much narrower limits; some survive but are inactive below 0°; some animals live in warm springs, and a few bacteria and algae are active in springs as hot as 70°C. Since temperature is a measure of molecular agitation, it limits the rate of chemical reactions, and it is one factor in the control of growth and metabolism.

Many animals correspond in body temperature to the environment; these are the "cold-blooded" or poikilothermic (ectothermic) animals. Fewer kinds of animals regulate their body temperature; they are the "warm-blooded" or homeothermic (endothermic) animals. Heterothermic animals are those with limited temperature regulation. The temperature of any metabolizing cell is necessarily higher than the temperature of its medium because oxidation and glycolysis liberate heat. The internal temperature of a large fish may be above that of the water; the increment is 0.012° in trout,[118] 6° in striped marlin.[216] The temperature of an animal depends on the balance of those factors which tend to add heat and those which tend to subtract it. Heat may be gained by metabolic production of heat and by absorption of heat, largely from solar radiation; heat is lost by radiation, convection, conduction, and vaporization of water, and heat loss is favored by the transfer of heat from the interior to the body surface by circulating fluids. Poikilothermic animals, although at the temperature of the environment, are not without some thermal control by behavior,

by entering a state of dormancy, or by metabolic and nervous compensations. Homeotherms maintain relative constancy of body temperature by protective behavior, by altering insulation and heat transfer, and by varying heat production. Some of them hibernate. Sensory mechanisms signal the changes in temperature which evoke the various protective responses.

The measurement of temperature is so easy, by mercury thermometer, thermistor, or thermocouple, that the literature on temperature relations is vast.[23, 36, 41, 234]

THERMAL PROPERTIES OF WATER: SURVIVAL LIMITS OF ANIMALS

The temperature relations of animals to their environment are closely connected with their water balance. The thermal properties of water are important in determining the thermal relations of animals. The heat conductivity of water (0.0014 cal/cm/sec/°C) is low compared with that of materials such as metals, but it is higher than that of many other liquids, e.g., ethyl alcohol, 0.00042, and olive oil, 0.000395. In addition, the specific heat of water is high, 1.0 cal/gm/°C, as compared with 0.09 cal/gm/°C for copper and 0.535 for ethyl alcohol, and animal tissues, except compact bone, require 0.7 to 0.9 cal to raise the temperature of 1 gm of tissue 1 degree.

$$\text{Thermal diffusivity} = \frac{\text{heat conductivity}}{\text{density} \times \text{specific heat}}$$

Low thermal diffusivity results in slow warming or cooling and limited conduction of heat within an animal; fat is a good heat insulator but not as good as air. Animals with much tissue mass are slow to warm or cool, most of their transfer of heat is by circulating body fluids, and a sluggish circulation makes for slow heat transfer.

Natural waters (hot springs excepted), because of their high specific heat and small heat conduction, rarely have a temperature above the limit for most aquatic animals, i.e., 35 to 40°C. At the cold extreme, the freezing point of aquatic animals (except such animals as marine bony fish and brine shrimp) is usually similar to or lower than the freezing point of the medium (Chapter 2). Since ice has a lower specific gravity than water, aquatic animals do not freeze so long as they remain in water beneath ice. Terrestrial animals are subject to much greater fluctuations in temperature than aquatic ones, and their body temperature is closely related to their water balance. Water has a high heat of fusion (79.7 cal/gm); aqueous solutions supercool by several degrees, especially in capillary spaces, and bound water is resistant to freezing. Hence some animals supercool, and partially dehydrated animals (or those with some extracellular water replaced by organic solvents) can withstand temperatures well below the freezing point of water without their tissues becoming frozen. Water loss by vaporization has a marked cooling effect on any moist surface (585 cal lost per gm water evaporated at 20°C), and at high air temperatures animal body temperatures are limited by the heat of vaporization of water.

Causes of death at either low or high temperature are not well understood and are certainly multiple. As the body temperature of homeotherms becomes lowered, cardiac and respiratory activities are slowed and hypoxia may result. Integration by the central nervous system fails, as indicated by the failure of behavior patterns. As the temperature of body cells is lowered, the rate of energy liberation may be insufficient for maintenance. At freezing temperatures ice crystals may disrupt intracellular organization. Increased osmoconcentration may result from extracellular freezing followed by dehydration of cells. When body temperatures are raised the transport of oxygen by pigments tends to be reduced, water loss by evaporation may be increased, and desiccation may occur. As the temperature rises, enzymes pass their optima at the temperature where inactivation exceeds activation and synthesis, lipids change in state, and cell membranes become increasingly permeable. At higher temperatures general protein denaturation occurs, and toxic substances may be released from damaged cells. Within a restricted temperature range, life processes continue and the means by which animals maintain themselves despite environmental heat and cold are multiple.

TEMPERATURE CHARACTERISTICS

Chemical reactions are accelerated as temperature rises. A frog swimming in ice water cannot go faster than energy is made available in its muscles. Several methods have been devised for comparing quantitatively the magnitude of the effect of temperature upon chemical reactions.[163] The most widely used is the Q_{10} approximation. The Q_{10} is the factor by which a reaction velocity is increased for a rise in temperature of 10°C.

$$Q_{10} = \left(\frac{K_1}{K_2}\right)^{\frac{10}{t_1 - t_2}}$$

where K_1 and K_2 are velocity constants corresponding to temperatures t_1 and t_2. Rate (V_1 and V_2) is normally used in place of the rate constant. However, the rate of enzymatic reactions is not a linear function of temperature, and Q_{10} varies over the temperature range. Hence the temperature range for which a Q_{10} is calculated should be stated. A more useful method is to plot log velocity against temperature and read the Q_{10} from the curve. Some functions are linear, most are logarithmic, to temperature. Physical properties of solutions are less sensitive to temperature and Q_{10} is between 1 and 2; chemical reaction rates are usually more than doubled per 10°C; hence Q_{10} is between 2 and 3. A Q_{10} of 2.5 means an increase in rate of 9.6 per cent per degree.

Enzymatic reactions are accelerated by temperature far more than can be accounted for by increased molecular agitation. The critical incremental energy of activation in a reaction is given by the Arrhenius μ:

$$\frac{K_2}{K_1} = -\frac{\mu}{R} \ln\left(\frac{1}{T_2} - \frac{1}{T_1}\right)$$

$$\log(K_2 - K_1) = -\frac{\mu}{4.6}\left(\frac{1}{T_2} - \frac{1}{T_1}\right)$$

where K_1 and K_2 are velocity constants (proportional to measured velocities) at absolute temperatures T_1 and T_2 and R is the gas constant (1.98 calories/mol). When the log (base 10) of a velocity is plotted against the reciprocal of the absolute temperature, most biological reactions (and all simple chemical reactions) give a straight line, the slope of which is $\mu/4.6$. Definite values of μ characterize specific catalysts irrespective of substrate, and it has been postulated that the μ of a complex biological reaction is really that of its limiting or pacemaker step. When μ is calculated for a variety of biological reactions, certain values appear regularly and these values may be those of common enzymes. In the absence of kinetic analyses, however, a given temperature characteristic does not imply a specific enzyme, and a useful quantitative comparison of temperature effects is given by a Q_{10} calculated from a logarithmic plot over a specified temperature range.

FREEZING; WINTER HARDENING

Protoplasm, which is an aqueous solution, freezes at a few degrees below zero. Slow freezing is more deleterious than fast. If the rate of cooling through the temperature range of freezing is rapid, about $100°C/sec$, ice crystals do not form and the organism is "vitrified."[187] When vinegar nematodes (Anguillula), Protozoa, muscle fibers, and many other cells are placed directly into liquid air ($-197°C$), they are solidified in an amorphous state; if they are then rewarmed rapidly by immersion in water or mercury at $30°C$ they revive.[187] If freezing occurs, either by slow cooling or by slow warming from liquid air temperature through the range -40 to $0°C$, the cells are usually killed.

Some organisms—winter-hardened insects and encysted Protozoa—survive long periods at subzero temperatures, and cells such as mammalian sperm can be stored in a frozen state. Dry cysts of the ciliate Colpoda can be revived after 16 hours in liquid air or 1 hour at $100°C$; wet cysts are killed above $45°C$.[287] Larvae of arctic aquatic insects can be repeatedly frozen and thawed without apparent damage.

Why are most tissues readily killed by freezing? One effect of freezing is disruption of protoplasmic organization by ice crystals. This has been demonstrated for amoebae,[45] and in plants,[182] but it seems not important in many animal cells; intertidal animals may revive after cellular distortion by freezing.[166] A second effect is the slowing of metabolism by cold, such that the Q_{10} is very large below $0°C$. Chironomid larvae frozen at $-15°C$ consumed oxygen at the rate of 0.1 mm^3/gm/hr as compared with 500 mm^3 at $20°C$.[257] The diffusion of oxygen and carbon dioxide in ice is much slower than in water (CO_2 diffuses $50,000$ times more slowly). However, metabolic reduction seems not critical because many cells survive vitrification or supercooling at subfreezing temperatures. Third, different enzymes differ in their temperature characteristics and, even above freezing, enzymic balance may be lost.

A more serious effect of freezing is on water distribution. When a salt solution freezes slowly, water crystallizes and concentrated salt is trapped in the interstices of the crystals, the osmotic concentration of the yet unfrozen fraction of the solution rises, and, since initial freezing is usually extracellular, water is drawn out of the cells.[206] As freezing continues, water which was bound to ions or proteins becomes frozen so that with time and lower temperature a greater percentage of the total water is frozen. Many cells can endure brief periods of freezing but not prolonged freezing, particularly at low temperatures. In a frog sartorius muscle, ice forms at $-0.42°$, but the muscle can be kept undamaged when supercooled to $-4°$ for 2 days; it is irritable when thawed after being frozen for a week at $-0.9°C$, for 20 hours at $-2°C$, and for half an hour at $-3.5°C$; hence the principal damage seems due to removal of water from molecular combination.[212] Marine invertebrates, especially molluscs, of the intertidal zone are frequently frozen in the winter. In such animals frozen at $-15°C$ only 55 to 65 per cent of the body water was actually frozen. The percentage of water frozen increases at lower temperatures, and at a given low temperature proportionately less of the water of an animal freezes than of sea water.[166] Even at $-32°C$ frozen chironomid larvae yielded some "blood."[257] The rapid decline in O_2 consumption in the frozen animal may be the result of the increased intercellular salinity rather than of the temperature per se.[166] Probably no animal can survive the freezing of all its water.

Red blood cells or sperm can be stored frozen without damage for many months if they are pretreated with glycerol (or propylene glycol), frozen rapidly, and stored at below $-40°C$.[185, 186] The damage due to freezing can be duplicated by putting the cells into salt concentrations corresponding to those left at different freezing temperatures; hence the protective action of glycerol is by water replacement.

In winter-hardened insects supercooling is important, and some insects (e.g., Cephus) survive supercooling to -23 to $-30°C$ as compared with only -5 to $-8°C$ by less winter-hardy species.[182, 245] An increase in proportion of "bound" to "free" water takes place. In some insects, e.g., Bracon, a parasite on sawflies, supercooling to $-47.2°C$ has been observed, and a Δ hemolymph of $-17.5°C$. In these the glycerol concentration of hemolymph may be 2.7 M. Glycerol, found normally in the hemolymph of such insects as *Bracon* and *Loxostege,* increases the supercooling, lowers the freezing point, and protects tissues if they do freeze.[246]

Vertebrates are limited in their tolerance of freezing. Arctic fish do not survive *total* freezing but may withstand freezing of the body surface.[257] In fish living in deep fjords in Labrador, where the water temperature is $-1.7°C$ winter and summer, the freezing point of the fish is $-0.9°C$, and if the fish are "seeded" (with ice), they freeze at once. Surface fish in water at $5°C$ in summer and $-1.5°$ in winter have a blood Δ of $-0.8°$ in summer and $-1.6°$ in winter, because of some unknown solute in the blood.[258] The deep-water fish, in contrast, live in a state of permanent supercooling.

Hamsters were anesthetized by hypercapnia and chilled to a colon temperature of 15 to $20°C$; they were then immersed in ice water; respiration stopped between 2 and $6°C$ and heartbeat between 0.8 and $2.5°.$[266] Then the animals were put into propylene glycol at -3 to $-14°$ and gradual freezing occurred. If they froze for more than 50 minutes at $-5°$ they were rigid. If they were then rewarmed gradually and artificial respiration was applied, most of the hamsters revived and were entirely normal. Those individuals which were supercooled before freezing and those maintained frozen more than 70 minutes did not recover. All of those recovered in which 15 per cent of the body water had been frozen, and one-third of those recovered in which 45 per cent of total body water had been frozen for 1 hour. Not more than 60 per cent of the brain water could be frozen if recovery was to ensue.[185, 186, 266]

TEMPERATURE RELATIONS OF POIKILOTHERMS

Lethal Temperatures in Poikilotherms (Primarily Aquatic). Death due to cold occurs at temperatures well above freezing in those aquatic animals which show no winter hardening and which cannot endure freezing. Death from heat occurs at temperatures well below those at which proteins are ordinarily denatured. Temperatures which are lethal in a short time are more extreme than those at which death is delayed; hence the only satisfactory definition of a low or high lethal temperature is one above or below which survival is indefinite, that is, death is due to some factor other than temperature. Furthermore, lethal temperatures are alterable according to temperatures previously experienced; hence the acclimation* state should be given. Thus, animals from cold waters have an upper lethal temperature which may be below the low lethal temperature of similar animals from warm waters. For example, *Aurelia* from Halifax had a high lethal of 26.8 to $28°C$ while in those from Tortugas and Florida it was $40°.$[199] Mayfly nymphs from an $11.6°$ stream died at $22.4°$, whereas others of the same species from a $14.5°$ habitat died at $24.7°.$[302] Terebellids in Greenland die when the water temperature rises to 6 to $7°C$, but in the Persian Gulf they live normally at $24°.$[291] Chill coma occurred at $2°$ in cockroaches which had been kept at 14 to $17°$; coma ensued at $9.5°$ when the acclimation had been at $36°$ for 20 hours.[205] A malacostracan from warm brackish water, 37 to $47°C$, was moribund at $35°$, and its low lethal temperature was $30°C.$[9a] The temperature range for development and reproduction differs seasonally and latitudinally, largely conforming with temperature acclimatization. Pelagic larvae are abundant in tropical seas, whereas in the arctic most invertebrates develop viviparously, in broods, or on the bottom, and larval development is relatively faster than in warm waters.[291]

Without consideration of causes of death, the measurement of lethal temperatures *per se* provides a useful description of the zone of tolerance.[30, 102, 103, 106, 203] Many individuals of a given species of aquatic animal can be experimentally acclimated to several temperatures. Then groups from each acclimation temperature are placed directly in a series of baths at high temperatures for heat death determination and others in baths at low temperatures for cold death (Fig. 70). The percentage mortality (probit) is plotted as a function of time at each temperature (Fig. 71), and the time to death of 50 per cent of each group is plotted against exposure temperature (Fig. 72).[29] The median tolerance temperature (LD_{50}) falls at longer times until, after about 48 hours for most animals investigated, no further deaths occur; this lowest temperature causing deaths is the upper incipient lethal temperature. Data for cold death are treated similarly and two lines are plotted, the incipient high and low lethal temperatures against acclimation temperature.

---

* Acclimation, in respect to temperature adaptation, refers to the animal's compensation for persistent change in environmental temperature, usually in the laboratory; acclimatization refers to compensations under field conditions to seasonal and climatic changes, particularly in temperature.

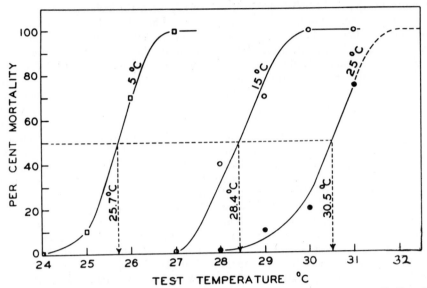

FIGURE 70. Per cent mortality of lobsters at various test temperatures after acclimation to 5, 15, and 25°. (From McLeese, D. W.: J. Fish Res. Bd. Canada, vol. 13.)

The enclosed polygon gives the zone of tolerance (Fig. 73).[106] Acclimation occurs rapidly in the first 12 hours and is virtually complete for most aquatic animals in a few days. For various fish, heat acclimation occurs in about 24 hours, cold acclimation may take 20 days.[30] In goldfish the upper lethal temperature increased 1°C for every 3° rise in acclimation temperature up to 36.5°;[106] the high lethal was then 41°; the low lethal temperature decreased 2 degrees for every 3 degrees fall in acclimation temperature down

to 17°; at this point the low lethal temperature was 0°C. In a roach (*Rutilus*) the high lethal temperature rises 1° per 3° of acclimation, but rate of acclimation is important; rapidly acclimated fish have narrower lethal limits than slowly acclimated ones, and the maximum rate of acclimation is $\frac{1}{20}$° per hour.[52] In earthworms (*Pheretima*), heat tolerance increases 0.3° per 1° rise in conditioning temperature.[114]

The tolerance polygon is fairly characteristic of a species (Fig. 73).[29] Within a tol-

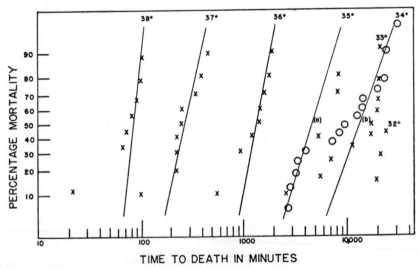

FIGURE 71. Times to death (expressed as probits) at various lethal temperatures of guppies reared at 30°. The circles show results at 34° and suggest that there are two causes of death. (From Gibson, M. B.: Canad. J. Zool., vol. 32.)

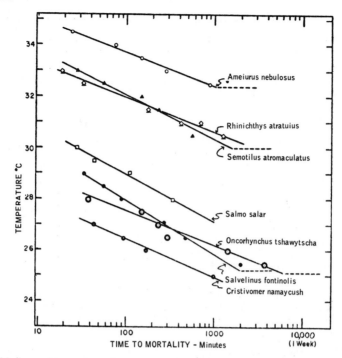

FIGURE 72. Median resistance times for seven species of fish acclimated to 20° and tested at various temperatures. (From Brett, J. R., Rev. Biol., vol. 31.)

erance polygon are smaller polygons for development and motor activity, i.e., these functions are more limited in their temperature limits. Fourteen species of fresh-water fish from different latitudes were examined for racial differences in temperature polygons. Of these, only three (e.g., the common shiner *Notropus cornutus*) gave different polygons

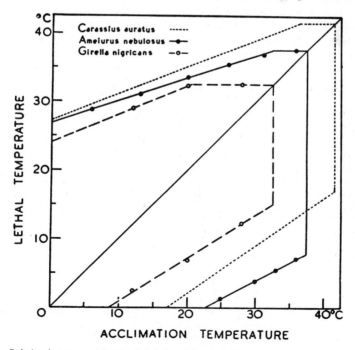

FIGURE 73. Relation between median high lethal and low lethal temperatures as function of acclimation temperatures in three species of fish. Lethal temperature curves connected to provide tolerance polygons. (From Brett, J. R., Univ. Toronto Stud. Biol. ser. 52.)

for populations from Ontario and Tennessee. In others, such as the minnow *Notemigonus crysoleucas,* morphological subspecies have been described, but no temperature differences could be detected.[121] Two geographic races of the brook trout *Salvelinus fontinalis* differ in upper lethal temperatures.[121] Strain W of *Tetrahymena pyriformis* is four times more tolerant of heat than is strain E.[264] A thermal race of *Daphnia atkinsoni* differs from a temperate race by 6°C in its high lethal temperature.[162]

The lethal temperature is influenced not only by acclimation temperature and genetic background, but also by diet, age, size, and environmental factors such as photoperiod, oxygen, and salinity. In lobsters the upper lethal temperature is lowered by decreased salinity and lower O_2 levels.[203] Similarly, *Mytilus* in low salinity are less tolerant of high temperatures,[249] and in *Salmo* the high lethal is raised by increasing calcium and magnesium in the medium.[118] In many animals, especially fish, the critical pressure of O_2 (p. 166) may be raised by high temperature, and the O_2 affinity of hemoglobin decreased; hence heat death may be asphyxial. The leech *Erpobdella* regulates its O_2 consumption down to one-third air saturation in the summer but is a metabolic conformer in winter. Acclimation of sawfly larvae to high temperature increased heat tolerance and raised the osmotic concentration of the blood.[6] Both cold and heat sensitivity of *Tenebrio* larvae were unrelated to water content.[205] Water content *per se* appears to have little relation to lethal temperature.

A variety of effects of dietary lipids on temperature tolerance in poikilotherms has been reported. Heat tolerance of goldfish is said to be increased by high dietary cholesterol; and goldfish had greater heat tolerance when fed lard than when fed fish oil; fats of warm-acclimated fish have lower iodine numbers, hence fewer unsaturated bonds.[153] Blowfly larvae reared at high temperatures were more heat resistant and their fats had lower iodine numbers;[100] a diet of highly saturated fat increased their heat tolerance.[151]

The optimum temperature, that is, the temperature of highest metabolism, can also be altered by acclimation. For example, in goldfish and eels the temperature above which metabolism declines is raised by temperature acclimation.

Heat death is sequential in that different tissues die at different temperatures; at in-creasing temperatures: a frog as a whole; muscle and heart; peripheral nerve.[222] In a skate, with heating, various reflexes disappear in a definite sequence, and muscles can be activated via nerves after spinal reflexes are lost.[20] In the roach, myotomic muscles stop functioning before opercular muscles.[52] In salmon *Oncorhynchus* the curve relating time to death with temperature rise shows a clear break, probably indicating two causes of death.[29] Yet many tissues of animals of different thermosensitivities may be affected in the same sequence. Two species of skate, and also large and small flounders, differ in lethal temperatures; heart and smooth and striated muscles are affected proportionately by heat in the different species.[20] In summary, there are multiple causes of heat and cold death, and acclimation—seasonal, latitudinal, or experimental—as well as other environmental factors, modifies temperature tolerance in poikilothermic animals.

Acclimation. *Time Course and Patterns of Temperature Acclimation.* In addition to changes in lethal temperatures, poikilotherms show alterations in various rate functions, in behavior, and in biochemical activity in accordance with temperature of acclimation. When the temperature is raised or lowered abruptly, most poikilotherms show an initial overshoot or shock reaction, sometimes an undershoot on cooling. In *Artemia* the O_2 consumption overshoots on warming, undershoots on cooling;[113] in goldfish and carp an initial overshoot is found for either warming or cooling. Part of the initial metabolic response is due to increased motor activity resulting from sensory stimulation, but there may be also a general cellular effect since yeast shows a similar overshoot.[113] The initial rate response to temperature change may last for seconds or minutes.

There follows a stabilized rate which may last for many hours; this is the rate which is usually taken for Q_{10} determinations. The stabilized rate depends on the acclimation state, and if the animal is returned to its original temperature during this period the rate returns (sometimes with a brief overshoot) to the initial level.

If an animal is kept at the altered temperature for many days, its rate functions often show some compensation, that is, it becomes acclimated. If it is now returned to the original temperature, the rate function does not return to the original level but rather to a higher or lower value according to the direction of acclimation. For example (Fig.

74), if an animal is moved from one temperature (T_1) to a higher one (T_2) the stabilized rate function is higher (type 4 of Precht), and if there were no acclimation the rate would remain at this level.[233, 234] If compensation is complete, the rate function becomes the same at the acclimation temperature as at the original temperature (type 2). More usually the acclimated rate lies between the first stabilized value and complete acclimation, i.e., there is partial compensation (type 3; Fig. 74). In a few examples there is overcompensation (type 1), and, rarely, undercompensation (type 5).[233, 234]

If, instead of measuring a rate function at the two temperatures of acclimation only, measurements are made of stabilized rates over the entire temperature range, some evidence can be obtained regarding the nature of acclimation (Fig. 75).[235] When there is no acclimation (Fig. 75, pattern I) the rate-temperature curves coincide for animals from either temperature. Frequently there is translation of the curve without change in slope such that the cold-acclimated rate is higher than the warm-acclimated at all temperatures (pattern II A). Or, there may be rotation of the rate-temperature curve about a midpoint (III), i.e., change in slope or Q_{10} only. Commonly, acclimation is a combination of translation with rotation; the two curves may intersect at a high temperature or by extrapolation above the normal range; if the Q_{10} of the cold-acclimated rate is less the change is compensatory (IV A); if the Q_{10} is more, the cold-acclimated curve is to the right (IV B) and the effect is noncompensatory. Conversely, the curves may intersect at a low temperature, in which case a high Q_{10} is compensatory (IV C) and a low one is not (IV D).[235] In all patterns, the inactivation temperature or tolerance limit changes with acclimation.

In comparing rate function, particularly O_2 consumption, it is important that animals of similar body size be compared since often Q_{10} increases with body size, i.e., large individuals of a species may show greater rate change with temperature than do small individuals.[36, 237]

Lack of temperature acclimation (Fig. 75, pattern I) has been reported for O_2 consumption by winter and summer cunner,[126] by various Brazilian insects, winter and summer,[84] and by seaweeds.[166] There is also little or no displacement of Q_{10} curves when metabolism of some tropical and arctic terrestrial insects[257] and firebrat and snow cricket is

compared.[84] A marine nematode, *Enoplus,* has the same Q_{10} of O_2 consumption, winter and summer.[303] *Tribolium* acclimated at 18 to 38° shows little Q_{10} acclimation.[82] *Balanus balanoides,* whether from Maine or Woods Hole, showed the same Q_{10} for rate of development over the temperature range tested.[10]

Translation of the rate-temperature curve without change in slope, that is, shifting to the left or up after cold acclimation (Fig. 75, pattern II A), is shown by O_2 consumption in several beetles[198] (Fig. 76), the crucian carp,[279] *Lumbriculus,*[174] *Planaria gonocephala* in summer and winter,[247, 248] by the salamander *Eurycea,*[294] by heart rate of *Daphnia,*[234] by winter and summer heart rate of *Gammarus,*[179] and by certain aquatic arctic and tropical insects;[257] it is also shown by comparing northern species of frogs with southern;[286] by the lizard *Sceloporus* at 16° and 23°;[66] *Corethra* larvae heart rate;[229] O_2 consumption by the crab *Pachygrapsus,*[241] and by the gills of *Mytilus.*[249]

Reverse translation such that the curve of the cold-acclimated animal lies to the right and below that of warm-acclimated ones (Fig. 75, pattern II B) may occur in situations where other factors such as reduced O_2 or salinity may complicate the response. An example is the O_2 consumption of Alaskan fresh-water gammarids[179] and of fresh-water limpets.[26]

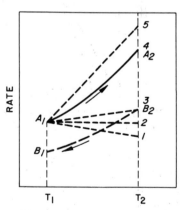

FIGURE 74. Diagram of types of acclimation according to Precht. Animal acclimated at T_1, transferred to T_2; the rate function rises along line A_1A_2. If no acclimation occurs, it remains at A_2 (pattern 4). If acclimation is complete the rate at T_2 becomes same as at T_1 (pattern 2). Commonly, partial acclimation occurs (pattern 3); there may be hypercompensation (pattern 1) or undercompensation (pattern 5). If an animal in pattern 3 (B_2) is returned from T_2 to T_1 its rate falls as at B_1. (Modified from Precht, J., Christophersen, J., and Hensel, H.: Temperatur und Leben. Springer-Verlag.)

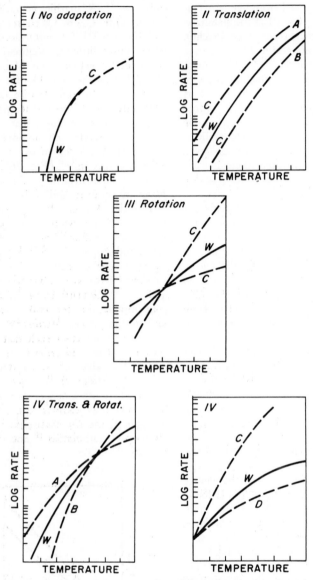

FIGURE 75. Patterns of rate functions measured at different temperatures for animals acclimated to two temperatures. In each diagram (except IV) C = cold acclimation, W = warm acclimation.

Rotation or change in Q_{10} without shift in position of the rate curves (pattern III) is rare. For a salamander, *Plethodon*,[294] clockwise rotation, i.e., reduction in Q_{10} on cold acclimation is reported,[294] and in winter frogs as compared with summer ones, counterclockwise rotation is reported for heart rate.[267]

The most common pattern of acclimation is clockwise rotation combined with translation so that the two rate curves intersect by extrapolation above the normal temperature range and the Q_{10} is reduced by cold acclimation (pattern IV A). The "normal" rate is then higher for cold- than for warm-

acclimated animals. Q_{10} is often lower for animals from higher latitudes. Examples are: pumping of water by *Mytilus* from different latitudes[236] (Fig. 77), heart rate of the newt *Triton*,[235] O_2 consumption by frogs acclimated to temperatures of 5° and 25°.[238] The Q_{10} curves of cold-acclimated *Uca rapax* from Florida intersect the curves of warm-adapted individuals at a high temperature, but the intersection for *U. rapax* from Jamaica is lower.[295]

The Q_{10} of the cold-acclimated animals may be greater, that is, rotation may be counterclockwise, and the two rate curves

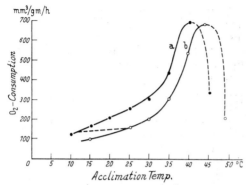

FIGURE 76. Oxygen consumption of potato beetles *Melasoma populi* at different temperatures: *a,* acclimation temperature 12°; *b,* 25°. (From Marzusch, K.: Ztschr. vergl. Physiol., vol. 34.)

intersect at a low temperature, often by extrapolation below the normal biological range (Fig. 75, pattern IV C). Above the intersection, the rate is greater for cold-acclimated than for warm-acclimated animals. This pattern is reported for rate of locomotion of the flagellate *Peranema*,[235] O_2 consumption of cold and warm water planaria,[247, 248] O_2 consumption by crucian carp acclimated to 5° and 16°,[279] and for O_2 consumption of brain tissue of goldfish.[101] Patterns IV B and IV D have rarely been indicated.

Change in position of a rate/temperature curve (translation) implies a change in activity (in the thermodynamic sense) of some enzyme system. Change in slope (rotation) suggests a change in Q_{10} and hence in activation energy. Factors most likely to cause translation are: a change in enzyme concentration, a change in controlling conditions—ionic strength, pH, water activity—or a change in relation among enzymes in series or parallel. Factors most likely to change slope are: alteration of the enzymatic protein, a change in some cofactor, or a shift in control of a reaction to alternate enzymatic pathways.

In general, compensation for cold by acclimatizing reactions is more marked in aquatic than in terrestrial poikilotherms, although it does occur in snails and some insects (e.g., cockroach). Ecological correlations are often evident. Pumping of water by *Mytilus californianus* is at the same rate at 6.5°C in mussels from Friday Harbor (48° 27′ N) as at 12° in animals from Los Angeles (34°N).[236] Animals high in the intertidal zone are subject to greater temperature extremes, particularly to higher temperatures, than those living low inter-

tidally; the heart rates of limpets *Acmaea* from low on the beach were higher at a given temperature than those from the high intertidal, and when the animals were transferred to a higher or lower tidal level, the hearts beat at the rate characteristic of the new level within 2 to 4 weeks.[261] Latitudinal compensations are reported also for O_2 consumption by *Uca* moved between New York and Florida, for heart rate of crabs *Hippolyte* from Plymouth and Tamaris; and for pulsation rate of dorsal vessels of the polychaete *Perinereis* from Plymouth and Tamaris (corrected for size).[97, 98] Extrusion of the body of periwinkles is more easily elicited by sea water at 5° in February than in August, and at 40°C the response is better in August.[221]

Rates of embryonic development show similar seasonal and latitudinal compensations. Time for two cleavages in eggs of a sea urchin, *Paracentrotus*, at Naples follows:[150]

Season	Water temperature (°C)	Test temperature (°C)	Time for 2 cleavages (minutes)
summer	26-27	26	25
		13	91
winter	13	26	30.8
		13	71

Environmentally induced compensation may be superimposed on genetic differences. *Rana pipiens* from the northern United States have a lower temperature range for development than have southern populations. The Q_{10} of development is higher for southern animals.[210] Crosses between the northern and southern races of frogs can be made in the laboratory, but so many abnormalities appear that hybrids could not live in nature. Costa Rican mountain *Rana pipiens* resemble the northern populations in some but not all respects, and the differences in temperature responses are genetic.[210, 297] Similar develop-

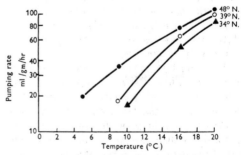

FIGURE 77. Log rate of pumping by *Mytilus californianus* at different temperatures. Animals from three latitudes as indicated. (From Bullóck, T. H.: Biol. Rev., vol. 30.)

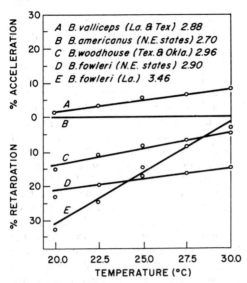

FIGURE 78. Relative rate of development of embryos of Bufo from various localities. Rates expressed relative to rate of development of *Bufo americanus* from northeastern states. Q_{10} values between 20 and 30° are given for each group. (Modified from Volpe, E. P.: Physiol. Zool., vol. 30.)

mental differences as a function of temperature are found in related species of *Bufo* from northern and southern states[296] (Fig. 78), in Australian frogs,[211] and in various cladocerans.[35]

Oysters *Crassostrea virginica* from Virginia, where spawning normally occurs at 25°C, failed to spawn during 2 years in Long Island Sound where the water temperature did not reach 25°C; thus physiological races are indicated.[184] Similarly, the oyster drills *Urosalpinx* from Virginia and Delaware have different temperature thresholds for spawning.[272] Growth rates of Alaskan populations of several marine snails were much faster at a given temperature than for the same species from Southern California; in the middle of the physiological range the Q_{10} values in the northern snails were higher in those which showed no overlap in rates.[70] Whether these differences are genetic or environmentally determined is not known.

Rate functions which do not correspond to the preceding patterns have been described. The heart rate of a carp rises rapidly with temperature in the low range, remains on a plateau for a wide range, and then rises again, probably because several pacemaker reactions are involved.[207] In some insects the Q_{O_2} versus temperature curve is maximum for a given intermediate acclimation (to 30°C) and moves to the right and downward for

both lower and higher acclimation temperatures (e.g., in *Tribolium*).[82] An analysis at the cellular and enzymatic level is necessary for an explanation of the varied effects of temperature.

In summary: Many animals are adapted by genetic selection to their particular environmental temperatures. In addition, many poikilotherms show compensatory responses of various rate functions during temperature acclimation. Others show little or no acclimation. There are instances of lack of compensation of one function but not of others in an animal, of compensation in one state (e.g., dormancy in insects) but not in another (e.g., feeding), and of compensation at one season but not at another. Environmental factors such as oxygen, salinity, nutrition, and photoperiod modify the acclimating responses to temperature. The net effect of acclimation where it occurs is to impart some independence of temperature to poikilotherms.

Cellular Mechanisms of Acclimation. Physical factors in acclimation have already been mentioned. The water content may be less in warm acclimation (frogs,[233] goldfish,[279] insect blood[6]). Also, the iodine number of body fats may be lower (blowfly larvae,[100] goldfish[143]).

Enzymatic changes have been indicated above in terms of either the conditions for enzyme activity or the nature of the enzyme protein. Changes have been observed in excised tissues and even in partially purified enzyme systems removed from acclimated animals. The Q_{O_2} of excised brain, but not of muscle, from goldfish acclimated to 20° is higher, and the rate of opercular movement at a given temperature is higher, than from goldfish acclimated to 27°.[101] Similarly, the metabolic rate of brain and liver from polar cod *Boreogadus* is higher at low temperatures and has a lower Q_{10} than the brain and liver of the temperate-water fish *Idus*.[227] Crabs *Pachygrapsus* from low temperatures had at 16° a higher total metabolism and higher Q_{10} of muscle but not of brain than those from higher acclimation temperatures.[241] Isolated gills from cold-acclimated clams *Venus*[149] and *Mytilus*[249] consume more O_2 than gills from warm-acclimated individuals. Muscle from 5° frogs metabolizes more than that from 25° frogs.[238] An increase in heat resistance with high temperature acclimation was noted for tissue oxidation and dehydrogenase activity in goldfish, but catalase heat resistance was relatively independent.[233, 234] Dehydrogenase activity may be affected differently in different organs of *Helix*.[233]

Nonoxidative enzymes also are altered in response to temperature. The protease (cathepsin) of *Helix* stomach juice shows higher inactivation temperature with warm acclimation of the snail, but the lipase shows no change.[208] Muscle apyrase levels and apyrase Q_{10} (see p. 429) were similar for warm- and cold-water fish of different species.[274] The temperature optimum for acetylcholine acetylase from the brain of a fish, *Labrus*, is 25°; from a rabbit, 42°.[208a] Proteolytic activity is greater and heat inactivation temperature lower for casein bacteria reared at 20° than at 40°.[49, 50] The oxygen dissociation curve of hemoglobin of *Rana* from a 25° environment lies to the left of the curve for pigment from frogs in a 15° environment,[175, 275] that is, the affinity of the pigment for oxygen is greater after warm acclimation, an effect in reverse direction to the direct action of temperature on hemoglobin.

Unicellular organisms also show compensatory adaptations to temperature. In yeast grown at 20°C the Q_{10} measured at a given temperature is higher, methylene blue reduction faster, and the limiting high temperature is lower than in yeast grown at 40°C. The inactivation temperature for catalase is lower, the splitting of casein and leucylglycine faster in the 20° yeast.[49, 50]

There are genetic strains of microorganisms, the thermophiles, adapted enzymatically to higher temperatures than mesophiles. For example, indophenol oxidase of the thermophilic *Bacillus subtilis* is inactivated at 60°, as compared to 41° for *B. myxoides*. Organized protoplasmic proteins of thermophilic bacteria as exemplified in the flagella are more stable with respect to denaturation either by heat or by such agents as urea and detergents. There is evidence for more or stronger hydrogen bonding in the polymerized proteins of the thermophilic species.[176]

The ways in which temperature induces biochemical changes are not known. In higher animals there may be some intermediation of hormones. The response of an isolated frog heart can be changed from the temperature-dependent winter type to the less dependent summer type by injecting the frog with thyroxin.[267] Conflicting results are reported for fish: in *Carassius* interference with thyroid activity by treatment with thiourea eliminated the acclimation of oxygen consumption,[279] whereas in *Leuciscus* the metabolic adapta-

tion was increased as measured both for intact fish and for muscle succinoxidase.[5] Since metabolic compensations occur also in microorganisms, it is probable that direct cellular effects of temperature are widespread.

An explanation in terms of enzyme induction might be based on the fact that energy is made available to cells by multiple enzymatic pathways, several in parallel, some cross-linked, several acting on the same substrate, and more than one using the same coenzyme (p. 186). If the temperature characteristic of one path is greater than that of a parallel but cross-linked one, substrate of the first may accumulate in the cold and serve to induce synthesis of more of the enzymes of the alternate system. The O_2 consumption by gills from cold-acclimated goldfish is greater and shows a greater sensitivity to cyanide and less sensitivity to iodoacetate than the metabolism of gills from warm-acclimated fish.[87] The Q_{O_2} at 20° of liver homogenates from goldfish acclimated to 20° was 43 per cent greater than for those from fish acclimated to 30° and the difference for mitochondrial respiration was 12 per cent; oxidative phosphorylation was reduced in the cold-acclimated mitochondria.[165] In *Streptococcus cremoris* growth at high temperature favors production of more acetoin and less butylene glycol; low-temperature cultures produce more lactic acid even when tested at the same temperature as high-temperature cultures.[148] This suggests a shift in metabolic pathways in the acclimation process. It is possible, therefore, that thermal acclimation at the cellular level may result from a type of enzyme induction. Some compensations in latitudinally separate populations have become genetically fixed.

Sensory and Behavioral Acclimation of Aquatic Poikilotherms. In addition to the changes in lethal temperatures and the metabolic adaptations described above, poikilotherms show adaptive behavior which permits a degree of independence of temperature.[99] The classic experiments of Jennings[160] showed that ciliate Protozoa tend to aggregate in a region of thermal neutrality, avoiding extremes of cold and heat. This is not a direct orientation but rather selection by trial and error from characteristic "shock" reactions of backing and turning at thermal stimulations. Blood-sucking leeches show a positive thermotaxis.

Water temperature is important in determining the distribution of many fish; however, its effect is modified by the presence of

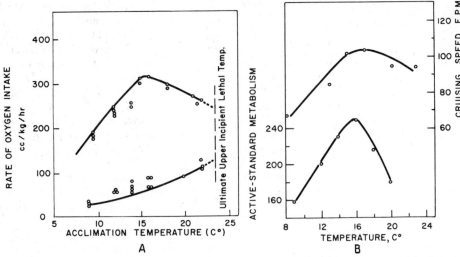

FIGURE 79. *A*, rate of oxygen consumption in maximum sustained activity (*upper curve*) and at rest at standard conditions (*lower curve*) for yearling lake trout measured at temperatures of acclimation. Incipient upper lethal temperature 23.5°.

B, upper curve: relation between steady swimming speed and temperature. *Lower curve*: difference between active and standard metabolism (metabolism available for activity) in relation to temperature. (From Gibson, E. S., and Fry, F. E. J.: Canad. J. Zool., vol. 32.)

O_2 and CO_2. In a gradient tank, fish, by a combination of locomotor characteristics, tend to aggregate at a "selected" temperature. In this range the frequency of movements is least but cruising speed is maximal.[281, 282] Herring are said to show selective aggregation in water temperature gradients of 0.5° and to be able to detect gradients as small as 0.2°.[263] Goldfish and bullheads react to increases or decreases of 0.05° per minute.[7] The temperature selected depends on the acclimation temperature and the rate of transfer from one temperature to another; hence the term "optimal temperature" has little meaning in gradient behavior.

The temperature which an animal selects in a gradient is usually below a high, above a low, and the same as an intermediate acclimation temperature. The temperature selected by the fish *Girella* rose from 18 to 24.3° during acclimation from 10 to 30°.[56] Similar rise in selected temperature with higher acclimation temperature was found in sockeye salmon,[107] and in carp (up to 30° selected after acclimation to 35°).[231] Reverse effects have also been reported in rainbow trout *Salmo gairdneri* and in the lizard *Sceloporus*;[305] the selected temperature is lower when the acclimation temperature is higher. Spontaneous movements of trout show two maxima, one at the temperature of selection, the other just below high lethal temperature.[93, 280]

The maximum cruising speed of sockeye salmon from open lakes is at 15.5°C, while that of coho salmon from warmer streams is at 20°; similarly the scope for activity at low temperature is greater for the sockeye than the coho.[32] The maximum cruising speed of goldfish corresponds to the selected temperature (except in warm acclimation) and rises with acclimation temperature.[105] Also the maximum distance moved by a salmon or trout in response to a shock increases to a peak at the selected temperature, and the "optimal" temperature varies with acclimation.[93]

When the rate of oxygen consumption at rest (standard metabolism) at different acclimation temperatures is subtracted from the O_2 consumption at maximum activity, the difference gives the cost of the activity. For lake trout the difference rises to a peak at the acclimation temperature as does the temperature of maximum steady swimming[111] (Fig. 79). It may be argued that cruising speed is limited by available energy and that acclimation consists in altering the availability and utilization of oxygen. However, with electrical stimulation higher rates of O_2 consumption are obtained than when a fish is swimming in a rotating chamber; hence the O_2 consumption can hardly be limiting in the latter condition. Also some trout show two maxima of cruising speed,[280] and one of these is lost after damage to the cerebel-

lum. Temperature selection is upset by lesions to the forebrain,[93] and various experiments indicate that the critical modification
in acclimation occurs in the central nervous
system rather than in sense organs. It is suggested that the oxygen utilization reflects the
demand created by activity rather than determines the speed and that, while acclimation
can alter oxidative enzymes, it also brings
about changes in the central nervous system
which better permit behavior at one temperature than at another. Temperature acclima-

tion may therefore include both an enzyme
induction process[235] and a kind of "learning."[93]

**Temperature Sense in Aquatic Verte-
brates.** Temperature may affect the activity of the nervous system directly. It may
also alter the "spontaneous" input of impulses
from the neuromasts of the lateral line organ.
When the temperature is rapidly raised to
28° for *Ameiurus,* or to 27° for *Fundulus,*
a sudden flutter-type reaction occurs; this disappears after the lateral line nerves are cut.

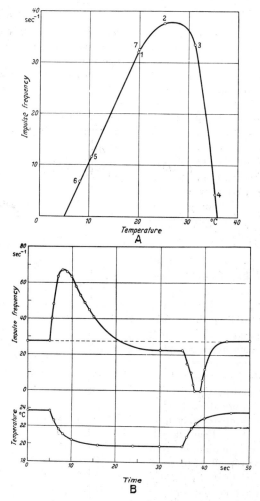

FIGURE 80. *A,* steady frequency of impulses in single nerve fiber from ampulla of Lorenzini of
Mustelus laevis at different temperatures showing optimum temperature.

B, transient change in frequency in single fibers on cooling and then rewarming of ampulla. (From
Hensel, H.: Pflüg. Arch. Physiol., vol. 263.)

The following reactions were not abolished by cutting the lateral line nerve: aggregation in a temperature gradient,[280] turning by the tail fin in response to local application of cold or warm water to the flank,[74] and conditioned feeding responses.[74] It is probable that each of these is mediated by unidentified skin thermoreceptors. Gradient selection is lost when the skin is cocainized. Threshold of stimulation of a small area of skin is much higher than for stimulation of a large area; hence there must be central summation.[7] In the amphibian *Xenopus* the lateral line organ is stimulated transiently by cold and depressed by heat, with a threshold rate of change of 0.3°/sec at the surface.[218]

In elasmobranchs there are large sensory bulbs on the surface of the head, the ampullae of Lorenzini, which are temperature receptors.* The nerve fibers from these ampullae show autonomous rhythmic activity which is maximal in frequency at 20° and declines to cessation at temperatures below 2° and above 34°. Rapid cooling causes a sudden and temporary increase in frequency; warming, a sudden decrease. Responses to as little as 0.05°C change can be detected (Fig. 80).[129] Strong mechanical stimulation inhibits the steady discharge. The response is independent of any temperature gradient across the organ, that is, it depends on the temperature of the endings. Thus response to thermal stimulation represents a frequency modulation of a preexisting rhythm and the ampullae give not only a steady signal of existing temperature but also transient signals of temperature change.

Temperature Relations of Terrestrial Poikilotherms (Except Reptiles). Terrestrial animals are subject to greater temperature fluctuations and have their heat balance more intimately related to their water balance than do aquatic animals. (See Uvarov's review of insects and climate, reference 292.)

In air, loss of heat by conduction is less important than in water, and heat loss by radiation and convection and by vaporization is more important. It is more difficult than is sometimes realized to compare body temperature with air temperature. Few animals have continuous surface evaporation, as from a wet-bulb thermometer, yet all have some evaporation. Hence, where there is no active temperature regulation, the body temperature must be lower than a dry-bulb temperature and may be higher than surface temperatures. Active physiological regulation is demonstrated by measuring body temperature in a saturated atmosphere or by comparing it with a thermometer from which there is vaporization equal to that from the body surface.

Arthropods. Winter-hardening and metabolic acclimation have already been considered. Many temperate zone insects undergo periods of diapause, usually nymphal or pupal, which can be broken only by a period of chilling. The hormonal basis for this will be considered in Chapter 20.

BODY TEMPERATURE; REGULATION. The body temperature of insects and isopods may be different from that of the air because of loss of heat by vaporization, production of heat by metabolism, and absorption of heat by radiation. Several large insects (*Blatta* and *Periplaneta*),[220] the desert locust *Schistocerca*,[28] and the grasshopper *Gastrimargus*[177] showed body temperature 2.6° lower than air, and evaporated 0.06 gm H_2O/hr, while *Armadillidium* was only 0.4° below air temperature and lost 0.002 gm H_2O/hr.[80, 81] The temperature of a live *Ligia* is higher than of a dead one in moist air but lower in dry air

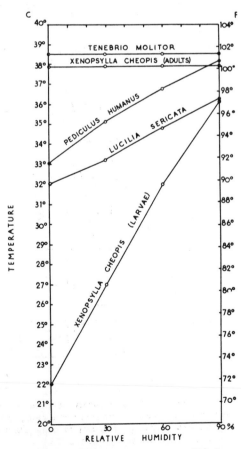

FIGURE 81. Highest temperature at which insects can survive exposure for 24 hours at different humidities. (From Mellanby, K.: J. Exp. Biol., vol. 9.)

* Recent evidence (Loewenstein, W. R., Nature *188*: 1034-1035, 1960) indicates that the ampullae of Lorenzini function primarily as pressure receptors.

in the sun. Heat gain by conduction is very low, but the gain by radiation is about equally balanced by loss by convection and evaporation.[81]

Most water loss by insects is from the spiracles, and death in warm dry air may result from desiccation rather than from heat *per se*. Regulation of water loss from spiracles was considered in Chapter 2, p. 39. The temperature which was lethal within 1 hour for a series of small insects which lack mechanisms for water retention, *Xenopsylla, Pediculus, Lucilia,* and *Tenebrio* under 30 mg, was independent of humidity.[205] However, for death in 24 hours lethal temperatures were much lower in dry air than in moist air (Fig. 81). Apparently the 1-hour death was thermal, the 24-hour death was by desiccation. In chinch bugs survival at temperatures below about 50° is favored by high humidity; at higher temperatures survival is better at low humidity (Fig. 82). Apparently death at temperatures below 48 to 50° is due to desiccation and at higher temperatures to some direct effect of the heat. The water permeability of waxy insect cuticle increases with temperature; hence evaporative loss may be independent of saturation deficit (see p. 39).

Metabolic heat of poikilotherms is considerable and may increase, particularly in flight muscles during activity. Some insects show warming-up movements of the wings before flight; others show muscle action potentials but no visible movement (Fig. 83). Warm-up takes longer at low than at high air temperature; the butterfly *Vanessa* warmed up for more than 6 minutes at 11°, 1½ minutes at 23°, 18 seconds at 34°, and not at all at 37°.[77] Muscle temperature in this butterfly is about 35° at take-off and 37° during active flight. The rise in body temperature in flight may be so much as to restrict flight of desert insects. A locust is unable to dissipate much excess heat by increasing evaporation; in fact, its adaptations are for water conservation, and hence it cannot maintain flight after the body temperature reaches 40°. The hairs on noctuid and hawk moths provide good insulation and permit the temperature in the prothorax to rise 8° to 9° above air temperature during flight.[51]

Metabolic heat is used to varying extents for temperature regulation by colonial Hymenoptera and termites. The temperature optimum for brood development for the ant *Formica rufa* is 23 to 29°; for honeybees it is 34.5 to 35°, and brood survival is limited to 32 to 36°. In the summer when the air temperature rises above the optimum for the brood the bee workers transport and spread water in the hive and aid evaporation by fanning. High CO_2 and low O_2 may also stimulate fanning. When the hive tempera-

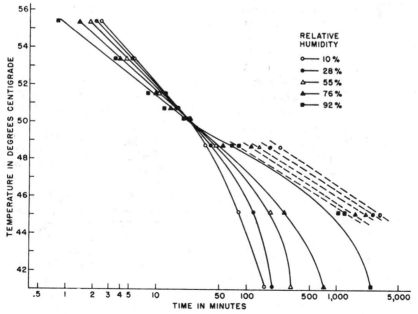

FIGURE 82. Median lethal temperatures for death of chinch bugs at different humidities as function of time of exposure without food. Broken lines show effect of providing water in food. (From Guthrie, F. E., and Decker, G. C., J. Econ. Ent., vol. 47.)

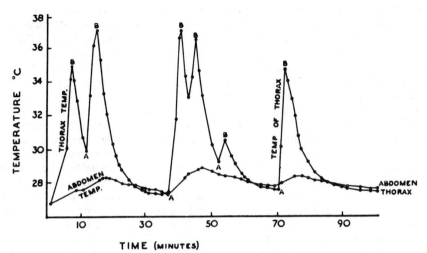

FIGURE 83. Influence of three bursts of muscular activity on body temperature of a female cecropia moth. *A* to *B* represents periods of wing movement. (From Oosthuizen, M. J., J. Ent. Soc. South Africa, vol. 2.)

ture is dangerously high, different functions of water dispersal are divided among the various workers.[183] In winter most colonial Hymenoptera cluster together and the temperature of the cluster may be kept well above the air temperature. If the air temperature falls to 8 to 10°, bees show great uneasiness, the outer bees are more active than those in the interior of the cluster, and outer and inner ones frequently change places. Heat is conserved by the insulation of the nest wall and sometimes by closing nest openings. Ants build special hibernating chambers; body water content also is decreased and metabolism reduced during hibernation. Cold rigor occurs in bees at about 7°, in wasps and ants at about 0°. The temperature of a bivouac of army ants is higher than that of surrounding air. The temperature of an occupied termite mound may be 14 to 18 degrees higher than an unoccupied region.[252] Thus colonial insects utilize physical and chemical means in maintaining relatively constant temperature of the nest.

Absorption of radiant heat from the sun is another means of raising body temperature in insects, and in the sun an insect may have a higher temperature than a mammal.[225] Rucker[244] measured absorption of different wave lengths, particularly in the infrared, and correlated absorption with pigmentation; a light colored snout beetle, *Compus niveus,* absorbs 26 per cent and a dark carrion beetle, *Silpha obscura,* absorbs 95 per cent of the infrared impinging on it. A dark brown grasshopper on sunny desert

sand remained 4 to 5° warmer than a light buff grasshopper.[42, 43] Exposure to sunlight caused an average rise of 8.1° in body temperature of *Melanoplus.*[228] Desert locusts (*Schistocerca*) are very inactive at below 17°C, begin to move at 17 to 20°, and at this temperature in the morning take a position on an eastern slope with their bodies oriented perpendicularly to the sun's rays, thus receiving maximal radiation. At 28° they start to migrate, and at about 40° may rest on a bush, parallel with the sun's rays, thus receiving minimal radiation. In the evening when the temperature falls the locusts again aggregate in a position perpendicular to the sun's rays, this time on a western slope.[98a]

As an insect's temperature rises, a series of states can be recognized—from cold stupor, intermittent activity, through normal activity, excitement, to heat stupor.[28] In a given habitat each species has its threshold temperature for each stage, and the body temperature for normal activity of insects in the sun is often several degrees above air temperature.

TEMPERATURE SENSE. Another means of maintaining some independence of environmental temperature in terrestrial arthropods is selection of a "preferred" temperature when subjected to a gradient.[99] In many, for example, bees, ants, locusts, flour beetles, and ticks, acclimation to a high temperature results in selection of a high temperature. Ants acclimated to 3 to 5° aggregated at 23.5° while others acclimated to 25 to 27° selected 32.0°.[138] For others, e.g., wireworms, acclimation temperature has little effect on selected temperature. The selected temperature may be relatively sharp or cover a broad range. Selected temperature may vary according to diet and stage in the life cycle. For example, dung maggots while actively feeding select a temperature of 30 to 37° which is within the range of their medium; when they are ready to enter the ground for pupation the selected temperature is changed to 15°.[290] A feeding housefly larva has a thermoselection range of 15 to 33°; for a prepupating larva it is 8 to 20°.[116a] Insects with high lethal temperatures tend to have high selected temperatures, diurnal species usually select higher temperatures than nocturnal ones, and geographic races (in *Carabus*) have different temperatures of selection. Blood-sucking insects—mosquitoes,[34] *Rhodnius*—are attracted to their prey partly by odors but also by temperature. *Tribolium castaneum* moves to higher temperatures in a gradient than *T. confusum*; this correlates with their geographic distribution.[112]

Selection in a gradient depends more upon air than on substratum temperature; hence the receptors must not be contact receptors. The selected temperature tends to be higher in moist than in dry air. In crickets[138] and *Lithobius*,[21] however, the antennae perceive air temperature and the tarsi ground temperature. The blood-sucking *Rhodnius*, bedbugs, honeybees, and phasmids have antennal thermoreceptors. In the beetle *Dorcus* the maxillary palpi are most sensitive, the antennae slightly less sensitive; in *Dorcus* and the heteropteran *Pyrrhocoris* heat receptors are identified with thin walled trichoid sensillae.[108] *Locusta migratoria* has paired sensory patches, head antennal crescents, and thoracic and abdominal fenestrae, which are sensitive to heat; if one head (antennal) crescent is destroyed the grasshopper no longer turns toward a heat source on that side.[265] Beetles have heat receptors which are trichoids on the terminal segments of antennae.[108]

Scorpions "stilt"—raise the body above the substratum—at temperatures above 28°, and they show reverse phototaxis, from positive to negative, in the heat; the sting bulb, pedipalps, and legs are thermosensitive.[3]

Isolated ganglia of cockroach, crayfish, or slugs are depressed transiently by a rise and temporarily stimulated by a fall in temperature; the nerve cord of a roach acclimated to 30° is stimulated at 27°. The temperature optimum in terms of minimum number of impulses (after a few minutes) and behavioral aggregation is the same as the acclimation temperature, at least in the midrange.[173] Thus temperature can stimulate either peripheral sense endings or the central ganglion.

In summary: Insects, like other poikilotherms, conform to the environmental temperature. However, they can maintain some independence of extreme temperatures by metabolic compensations in acclimation; by regulating water loss, hence evaporative cooling; by using metabolic heat (in exercise); by clustering, fanning, transporting water, and constructing insulated abodes (colonial species); by orientation and absorption of radiant heat; and by aggregation in regions of "preferred" temperatures.

Terrestrial Poikilotherms with Moist Body Surface. The temperature of a slug, an extended *Helix,* or a frog is below that of surrounding air as measured by a dry-bulb thermometer unless the air is fully saturated. However, the temperature of these animals approaches that of a wet-bulb thermometer. The temperature of an earthworm in dry air soon rises above the wet-bulb temperature because of decreasing surface evaporation, but in water the temperature in the intestine conforms to the environmental temperature. In air the temperature of a moist nonregulating animal is between wet-bulb and dry-bulb temperatures. In still air the body temperature of a frog is closer to that of a dry-bulb temperature, and in moving air it approaches the wet-bulb temperature. In a toad at 27.6° and relative humidity of 82 per cent, the body temperature was 26.5°; at the same temperature with relative humidity of 27 per cent the deep body temperature was 17.5°.[204] The metabolism of an amphibian calculated for 37° is only one-fifth that of a mouse of comparable size. At 20° the metabolism of a frog corresponded to a heat production of 6 cal/hr, but it lost 3.2 gm water per hour, which absorbed 1850 cal;[204] hence in moist animals in air the heat loss by vaporization normally exceeds heat production, and the body temperature is lower than in water of the same environmental temperature.

Animals in moist air may show a selected temperature range for activity. Slugs are most active in response to a falling temperature in the range 4 to 20°; it is not known whether there are specific surface thermoreceptors or whether the responses result from changes in temperature of the nervous system, but environmental changes as small as 0.1° are perceived.[57] An earthworm has heat receptors in its skin, and a frog has both heat and cold receptors. Earthworms *Pheretima* showed greatest burrowing activity at 20° and aggregated at about this temperature in a gradient.[114]

Temperature Relations of Reptiles. Temperature relations of reptiles are of particular interest because homeotherms evolved from primitive reptiles. In a large poikilotherm such as a python changes in body temperature may lag several hours behind air temperature.

Reptiles with horny scales are less permeable to water; hence their temperature is less dependent on humidity, and they lose much less water by vaporization than do amphibians. When the relative humidity was lowered from 100 to 7 per cent at 20°, the body temperatures of horned toad, turtle, and alligator were lowered by only 1° as compared with 8° in salamander and frog.[117]

Metabolic heat production varies greatly among reptiles but is similar to that of amphibia and much less than in mammals. Comparative metabolic rates of poikilothermic vertebrates at 16°C are given in Table 36.[24]

TABLE 36.   METABOLIC RATES OF POIKILO-
THERMIC VERTEBRATES AT 16°C
BODY TEMPERATURE

Animal	Weight	Cal/kg/ 24 hours	Cal/m²/ 24 hours
goldfish	4- 9 gm	8-12	19-22.4
frog	35-50 gm	5.8-12.8	17.5-46.2
tortoise	135 gm	1.0	33
rattlesnake	2- 5 kg	0.77	9.6
alligator	53 kg	0.85	25.4
bat	6 gm	20.7	

Benedict recorded a temperature of 33.5°C between the coils of a python incubating eggs in an air temperature of 31°.[24]

The most important temperature adaptations of reptiles are behavioral. Many snakes and lizards bask in the sun and absorb much radiant heat. They also gain heat by conduction from rocks and sand. Lizards in the sun at air temperature of 13° had a cloacal temperature of 38°.[55] A high-altitude lizard was observed emerging from its burrow when the air was −5°C; after a time in the sun the lizard attained a body temperature of 26°C.[226] Desert animals forage during the periods of the day when the temperature is neither too cold nor too hot. The horned toad *Phrynosoma* burrows at temperatures above 40° or below 20°, and a desert iguana

seeks shade when its body temperature approaches 43°.[300] Temperatures selected are usually in the upper part of the normal activity range and may be only a few degrees below the critical maximum; they vary for different reptiles, for example, copperheads selected 27 to 28°, blue racers 31° and collared lizards 38°.[94]

The desert iguana *Dipsosaurus* continues activity at body temperature up to 47 to 48°C but starts to pant at 43°; body temperature in dry air was within 0.5° of that of the environment.[288] The Q_{10} for its O_2 consumption over the range 19 to 45°C is 2.5°; heart strips of this iguana develop maximum tension at 25° to 33°, but contract at temperatures as low as 1.5° and up to 50°.[66]

A skink, *Eumeces,* is less tolerant of high body temperature than the iguana. The skink does not pant, its electrocardiogram is grossly abnormal at above 41°C body temperature, and injury results after several hours at above 40°. The range for maximal tension of heart muscle is 16 to 26° for skink.[66]

An important factor limiting survival of reptiles at temperatures above 45° is the decreased affinity of the hemoglobin for oxygen (Chapter 8). At 50° the blood of a chuckwalla, *Sauromalus,* could not become more than 50 per cent saturated with oxygen at atmospheric pressure.[85]

In turtles and frogs the arterial pressure is directly related to blood temperature, and after the brain is pithed the blood pressure is no longer responsive to temperature. Local warming or cooling of the base of the brain of a turtle affects the blood pressure; possibly the temperature-regulating center of homeotherms evolved from a region of the hypothalamus responsible for circulatory adjustment. Another hypothesis for the origin of warm-bloodedness (endothermy) is that the skin is respiratory in amphibia, is heat-absorbing in many land reptiles (ectothermy), and becomes heat-dissipating in birds and mammals. In lizards in the sun an artificial fur coat retarded absorption of heat. The increased circulation in warmed skin facilitates heat absorption. Vasomotor control may have been a preadaptation which reversed in function on the transition from ectothermy to endothermy.[56]

Temperature sense is well developed in pit vipers (Crotalidae), which have facial temperature-sense pits, and in some boas with labial pits which are temperature receptors. The membrane at the base of the pit of the viper contains many free nerve endings extending palmate over 1500 μ^2, and behind the membrane is an air space which reduces thermal loss (in Crotalidae).[37] Action potentials in the branches of the trigeminal nerve to the pit show continuous activity. The organ is specialized for radiant heat detection and responds to long infrared, 0.5 to 15 μ, not to near infrared and visible rays. The discharge is increased by emanations from a warm source. Temperature detection is directional, and shadows passing over the pit are readily detected. From the modulation of the steady discharge it is calculated that as small a change as 0.003° in the pit membrane can be detected, or a threshold stimulus of 5 $\times$ 10^{-10}cal/0.1 sec; this means that objects can be distinguished by their radiation where surface temperatures are as little as 0.1°C apart; a 0.4° temperature rise increased the frequency of nerve impulses from 18/sec to 68/sec.[37]

TEMPERATURE RELATIONS OF HOMEOTHERMS

The preceding sections show that poikilothermic animals, by means of various compensatory reactions, may not be wholly at the mercy of the environmental temperature. Homeotherms—birds and mammals—maintain regulated temperature independent of the environment; they conserve heat at low environmental temperatures and dissipate it at high temperatures. Their temperature-regulating center in the hypothalamus makes reflex responses to deviations from a temperature norm and acts as a thermostat. In addition, homeotherms metabolize more intensely than poikilotherms, even at the same body temperature, and homeotherm metabolism is minimal over a thermoneutral range, rising at the stress of low environmental temperature or with high body temperature. Homeotherms have various insulations—fur, feathers, subcutaneous fat, and associated vasomotor reactions of blood flow; heat is dissipated by such means as sweating and panting. The net result of the summed chemical and physical reactions to temperature stress is the maintenance of internal temperature constancy despite varying thermal gradients between body and environment. This may be contrasted with poikilotherms where, aside from behavioral regulation of body temperature, the best regulated response to temperature stress is a tendency to maintain constancy of rates despite varying body temperature.

The difference in metabolism between a poikilotherm, a homeotherm, and a homeotherm capable of hibernation, each 2.5 kg. in weight and at 37°, is shown in the following from Benedict:[24, 25]

	Cal/kg/24 hr	Cal/m²/24 hr
rattlesnake	7.7	91
rabbit	44.8	619
woodchuck	28.7	418

The tissues of cold-blooded and warm-blooded animals show differences: striated muscle of a frog enters heat rigor at 47°, of a rabbit at 53°. The heart rate of a warm-blooded animal accelerates with environmental temperature in the range 20° to 35° at the rate of 14 to 19 beats/min/°C; in turtles and frogs the acceleration is 1/min/°C.[1]

Body Temperatures. Body temperatures tend to be higher in birds than mammals. All homeotherms show diurnal fluctuations; the diurnal maxima come by day or by night according to whether the mammal or bird is diurnal or nocturnal in activity. Birds and mammals which are active in dim light have maximum body temperature at dawn and sunset. Fluctuations in temperature occur also with exercise, feeding, and digestion, with maturity, reproductive cycle, age, and other conditions. There is no regular correlation of temperature with body size.[213] The temperature of man is usually given as 37°, the colon temperature; the skin is several degrees cooler, varying with the region. A temperature of 37° is not reached until about an inch within the body surface.[41] The *average* temperature of mammals as measured by heat transfer is 2 to 4° lower than the colonic temperature.[122]

Some representative "normal" rectal temperatures are given in Table 37.

The more primitive mammals are heterothermic; their body temperature, although well above that of the environment, fluctuates with air temperature, especially in periods of inactivity. During normal activity they have lower body temperature than do higher mammals. Heterothermy is shown in varying degrees among monotremes, marsupials (Fig. 84), and edentates.

Thermal Stimulation. The mechanisms of heat regulation are activated in two ways: by thermal receptors in the skin, and by direct stimulation of the thermoregulator in the brain by changes in blood temperature.

Thermal Sense. Heat and cold receptors are distributed in a definite pattern in the skin, the warmth receptors usually deeper

TABLE 37. NORMAL BODY TEMPERATURE AND LETHAL BODY TEMPERATURE OF HOMEOTHERMS[*]

Animal	Body temperature (°C)	Low lethal (°C)	High Lethal (°C)
shrew[213]	38.8		44.1
raccoon[96]	38.1		
skunk[96]	36.4		
dog	38.5	15-18	41.7
Eskimo dog	38.3		
white fox	37.7		
cat	38.2	18	43.4
rat[1]	38.1	15-18 (10-12 hr)	42.5
guinea pig[2]	38.1	18	42.8
hamster[2] (active)		3.8	42
rabbit	39.1	23	43.4
kangaroo rat[64]	37.2 (in 23° air)		
ground squirrel	37.2 (in 23° air)		
cow	38.6		
man	37.0	24-25	43.4
hen	40.5	23	45.5-47
English sparrow[172]	41.5		46.8
chipping sparrow	40.5		43.5
white-crowned sparrow	41.67 (deep body) 40.0 (cloaca)		
poorwill	40.6-43.1		
pigeon[273]	41 -42		
mourning dove[15]	day 41.8, night 39.5		
brown towhee[63]	day 41.8, night 39.1 in 23° air		
petrel[91]	at rest 37° in exercise 39.7°		
junco	42.8 (deep body) 40.0 (cloaca)		
pigeon	41.8		
house wren[171]	40.6	32	46.8

[*] Values from Precht, Christophersen, and Hensel,[234] and at equable air temperatures in the range of thermoneutrality, usually 18 to 25°C, unless otherwise noted.

than the cold receptors; cold receptors are the more abundant. Some thermoreceptors may be encapsulated, but many are free nerve endings. Much sensory summation occurs in

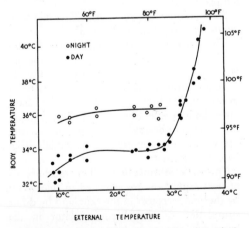

FIGURE 84. Body temperature as function of air temperature in a nocturnally active Central American opossum, Metachirus. (From Morrison, P. B.: J. Cell. Comp. Phys., vol. 27.)

that the sensation threshold for stimulation of large areas is less than that for stimulation of single sensory endings. Sensations can be had for changes in temperature of a few thousandths of a degree in a second. Heat (infrared) stimulation can also elicit pain, and both heat and pain sensations are conducted in small sensory fibers, but different receptors are involved and the threshold for pain is higher. Some cold receptors are sensitive to pressure also.

Impulses have been recorded from nerve bundles and from single sensory fibers from cold and warmth receptors.[75, 76, 128, 130, 131] Both types of receptor show steady ("spontaneous") activity; the fibers from warm receptors are active over the range from 20 to 47° with a maximum frequency between 38 and 43°, while the fibers from cold receptors are active between 10 and 40° with maximal frequency between 20 and 34° (Fig. 85). The maximal steady frequency from cold receptors is about 10/sec, from warmth receptors 3.7/sec, but the warmth fibers discharge more irregularly than the cold fibers.

When the skin temperature is abruptly raised there is a sudden brief increase of discharge from heat receptors which lasts a second or two, then the discharge settles down to the frequency corresponding to the temperature; on removal of the heat stimulus the warmth fiber temporarily reduces its frequency or stops. Similarly, when the temperature is lowered, a cold fiber gives a sudden brief extra discharge (at frequency as high as 140/sec) and then settles at its new frequency, higher than before because the temperature is lower; on removal of the cold stimulus the activity of the cold fiber is temporarily inhibited. Cold fibers are silent between about 35 and 45°, but between 45 and 50° they show increased discharge, a paradoxical response of cold fibers to heat. By measurement of cutaneous temperature and by applying the thermal stimulation beneath the skin as well as from outside, it was determined that stimulation depends on the absolute temperature of the ending rather than on the thermal gradient (Fig. 85). Thus by different optimal temperatures of the stationary discharge and the reversed transient responses in cold and warmth receptors the organism is informed both of constant temperature and of changes in skin temperature.[307]

The Regulating Center. Impulses from temperature receptors ascend via lateral spinothalamic tracts and the thalamus to the hypothalamus, from which various autonomic reflex responses are activated. In the hypothalamus are also centers which are themselves sensitive to temperature. There is lack of agreement regarding the localization of the heat- and cold-regulating centers; there is probably some intermingling of the temperature-sensitive cells, and they may be mutually inhibitory. Dogs with lesions in the posterior hypothalamus lost ability to regulate in the cold,[27] and cats with lesions in the posterolateral hypothalamus became somewhat poikilothermic.[201] Local warming of the anterior hypothalamus of a cat caused peripheral vasodilation and increased breathing.[277] Lowering blood temperature without cooling the skin can induce shivering. Thus the hypothalamus provides both a center for reflex thermoresponses and a second level of detecting mechanism, responding to changes in blood temperature.

Responses to Cooling. When the skin cold receptors are stimulated, reflex responses

tend to conserve heat. Blood vessels in the skin constrict, hairs or feathers may be erected, and an animal may reduce exposure by folding its legs. Vasoconstriction in man may reduce heat loss by one-sixth to one-third. For many animals the layer of superficial tissues may serve as insulation and protect like fur. The fat layer of the seal is cooler than the deeper tissues. Some animals have the "shell" cool and the "core" warm; others do not markedly differentiate a "shell."

As cooling continues, muscle activity can be detected, first as action potentials, then as visible shivering. A rat from a warm room moved to 6°C shows in a few minutes increased oxygen consumption.[125] The increased muscle activity is partly nervous in origin, partly by adrenal medulla. The initial reflexes originate peripherally, and the heat-

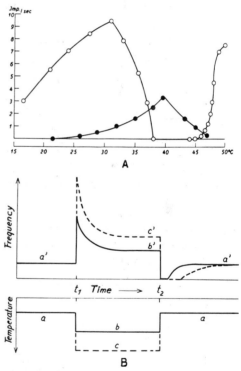

FIGURE 85. Frequency of nerve impulses in fibers from temperature receptors of cat as function of temperature of end organs. *A*, o = steady frequency from cold receptor in response to lowering of temperature as well as to excessive warming of skin. • = activity of warm receptor as skin temperature is raised to 40°; decline at higher temperature. (From Dodt, E., and Zotterman, Y.: Acta physiol. scand., vol. 26.)

B, Time course of response of cold receptor to 2° of cooling as shown in lower half of record. Initial burst of impulses followed by steady increased frequency and inhibition on return to normal temperature. (From Hensel, H., and Zotterman, Y.: Acta physiol. scand., vol. 23.)

regulating center comes into action after the blood temperature is lowered.[44, 60] Shivering begins, however, before the deep temperature is lowered.

Continued exposure to cold activates the adrenal cortex, probably via the pituitary and corticotropic hormone (ACTH), and stress signs such as reduction in eosinophil and lymphocyte counts may result. Tissue ascorbic acid rises, and ascorbic acid administered to rats increases their resistance to cold.[73] In man during the first few hours in the cold there is hemoconcentration and decrease in blood volume.

After the increased heat production resulting from shivering, there may appear increased general metabolism, in part due to liberated noradrenaline. When noradrenaline is injected, it has a rapid calorigenic action which increases with cold acclimation and which can occur after evisceration; thus the effect is not due to shivering or to metabolism of liver and other abdominal tissues.[71, 72] The general metabolic response involves also both the thyroid and the adrenal cortex.

The normal rat regulates body temperature in air down to $-10°C$; the rat lacking either thyroid or adrenal, down to $-2°C$; and if lacking both endocrines, the rat regulates body temperature down to $10°C$.[289] The adrenal cortex shows increased P^{32} turnover during the first few hours in the cold.

Behavioral responses such as huddling, improved nest building,[260] burrowing beneath snow, and reducing body surface by curling, all favor heat conservation in the cold.

When metabolism of homeotherms is measured as a function of environmental temperature, a neutral range of minimum oxygen consumption is found at air temperature slightly below body temperature. As the air or water temperature is lowered, insulating mechanisms (including vasomotor responses) maintain body temperature until the critical temperature (t_c) is reached. Below this temperature heat production must increase. Above the thermoneutral range, cooling mechanisms are ineffective and oxygen consumption rises. The increased heat production along with inadequate heat dissipation intensifies the effect of a hot environment. In small mammals the thermoneutrality range is so narrow as to be a minimum point in the metabolism/temperature curve. In animals where the surface-to-weight ratio is less and where insulation by fur or feathers is more adequate, the t_c is low, and as insulation improves in winter acclimation, the t_c may be lowered. Also the range of thermoneutrality can be changed with acclimation. Thermoneutrality in Abert towhee from the desert

TABLE 38.   CRITICAL TEMPERATURE OF MAMMALS[109, 125, 157, 178]
(°C, in air unless stated)

	Low environmental		High environmental
	summer	winter	
ground squirrel	5		
lemming	20	14	
weasel	15		
hamster	20		
pig	0		
sloth	25-27		
man[90]	27-28	26	
	33 in water		
harbor seal	<-10		
	$+10$ in water		
harp seal	0 in water		
red fox	8	−13	
red squirrel	20	20	
porcupine	7	−12	
mountain goat[178]		−30	20
kangaroo rat (Dipodomys)	31		34
Panama mouse and squirrel	27		
deer mouse	30		
dog	25		27
rabbit	17		
rat	25		

is 25 to 35°; for the brown towhee from cool coastal slopes it is 23 to 33°.[63] The ortolan bunting has a thermoneutral range of 32 to 38°; it breeds farther south than the yellow bunting with thermoneutrality at 25 to 32°.[298]

The critical air temperature for large tropical mammals and man is 25 to 27°, while for the arctic fox it is −30° (perhaps −40° when the fox is curled up). Several recently obtained t_c values are given in Table 38.[155-157, 172, 256, 262] Animals with low t_c tend to have a lower slope of the metabolism/temperature curve and for a number of mammals these curves extrapolate back to body temperature (Fig. 86). The slopes for hibernators tend to be steeper than for non-hibernators.

When the body temperature falls, circulation of oxygenated blood is reduced. When this occurs in the brain, paralysis may ensue. Blood flow may be much reduced as a result of lowered cardiac output and especially of increase in blood viscosity, so that flow may stop in vessels of rat mesocecum at 20° and in hamster cheek pouch at 5 to 10°C.[196] Oxygen consumption is reduced by 65 per cent in a dog at 25°C body temperature and by 90 per cent in a rat at 15°C body temperature. Cardiac arrest precedes respiratory depression. A cat loses consciousness at a body temperature of 25 to 27°C, but some reflexes remain at lower temperatures and death ensues in a cat at about 16°C. In man, mental defect is detected at 35°C body temperature; respiration continues to 25°C. When a dog is cooled to 20 to 25°C, breathing stops; a rat stops breathing at 10 to 14°. The values taken for low lethal temperatures vary considerably with the time of exposure, but some representative figures are given in Table 37. In general, heterothermic animals and mammals capable of hibernating (whether in or out of hibernation) have lower lethal body temperature than true homeotherms.

In summary: Exposure of homeotherms to cold elicits a series of responses, first via skin receptors, second by the thermoregulatory center. Initial insulating reactions are vasomotor response, fur or feather erection, and postural changes, then shivering and increased heat production under influence of the adrenal medulla and thyroid. Later, stress responses involving the adrenal cortex result in generalized metabolic increase. Differences in the critical environmental temperature at which the insulation is inadequate to maintain body temperature are correlated with the season and with the ecologic background of the animal.

Acclimation to Prolonged Exposure to Cold. When birds and mammals are maintained in the cold for several weeks various signs of acclimation appear. First there is an extension of the limiting low temperature when measured as either survival time or as ability to maintain thermal balance.[125] Striking differences in survival time in the cold have been observed for starved rabbits and laboratory rats according to acclimation.[262] However, in mice and rats with access to food the limiting low temperature is more nearly similar for cold-acclimated and warm-acclimated ones.[125] Dogs in cold water normally had a terminal rectal temperature of 18.6°, but if they had been acclimated to cold they survived to chilling of 14.9°.[54]

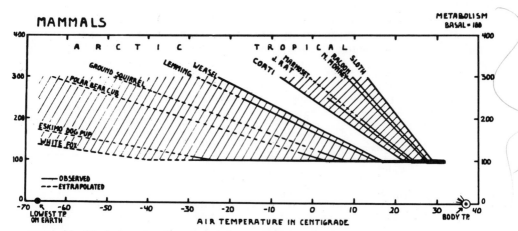

FIGURE 86. Metabolism of arctic and tropical mammals in resting state as function of air temperature. Solid lines represent average measurements; broken lines are extrapolations. Critical temperature at points where metabolism diverges from standard value. (Courtesy of P. F. Scholander.)

Body temperature of active mammals is essentially the same at all seasons and in all climates. Body temperature does not show adaptive changes.

Metabolism in the cold may rise initially and level to a plateau; for example, in a rat at 5°, metabolism rises for 3 days and remains high for 3 weeks. If the metabolism of a rat from the cold is measured at 30° rather than in the cold, the metabolism is not elevated for several days, but, with time, the increased heat production persists when the rat is removed from the cold for measurement. Dogs which had been kept 3 months in the cold showed a metabolic rate 50 per cent higher at 24 to 27° than dogs which had been kept at 24 to 27°.[109, 110] Hemoglobin concentration in the blood was greater in the cold-acclimated dogs.

The maintained high metabolism requires the presence of the thyroids; the initial response does not. The thyroids of a rabbit increase in activity after 1 week in the cold. After metabolism increases, food intake also rises. The high metabolic rate is not entirely from muscular activity, since it occurs in animals which have been curarized[152] or anesthetized, and an acclimated animal continues to show increased metabolism after evisceration.

The increased metabolism of animals acclimated to cold for a few weeks has been observed in dogs (Table 39), rabbits, dormice, spermophiles, pigeons, siskins, and goldfinches[110] (Fig. 87). No increase at the acclimation temperature was seen in deer mice, but those from 10°C were able to continue to increase their metabolism down to a lower lethal temperature than those from 30°.[122, 123]

The time during which an unacclimated rat can maintain body temperature by elevating metabolism is shorter at lower temperatures. Acclimation to cold extends the range and time through which heat production equals maintenance of thermal balance.[71, 72]

When rats whose fur was clipped were placed at 1.5°, those from 30° died in an average of 11.6 hours, while those which had been acclimated at 1.5° before clipping survived on the average 4.2 days, some to 60 days.[262] Survival in the cold is reduced by adrenalectomy and thyroidectomy. The effect of cold acclimation is lost in some 4 days at 30°.[262] The oxygen consumption of acclimated and nonacclimated rats was similar at 2°, but when measured at 30° it was higher for cold-acclimated rats, and the elevated metabolism was maintained longer at 2° in the acclimated group. Mice maintained at −3° bred and maintained the colony; the metabolism remained elevated through six generations in the cold.[11] After acclimation in the cold, oxygen consumption of hamsters and rats at 25° remained high for at least a week.[9]

Tissues from rats acclimated to 5° for 10 days showed elevated Q_{O_2} at 37°; in older rats, only the liver showed the persistent increase.[301] The increase in muscle and liver Q_{O_2} was less if the animals had been thyroidectomized. The Q_{O_2} of skeletal muscle from lemmings acclimated to 1°C was 40 per cent greater than from lemmings kept at 17°.[93] Increase in succinoxidase has been reported for various tissues of cold-acclimated animals, as have an increase in utilization of glucose, increased pyruvate formation, and decrease in use of hexosemonophosphate shunt.[120] Phosphorylation by mitochondria of cold-acclimated rats is reduced,[269] and it is suggested that there may be an enzymatic shunt to a TPNH path which yields more heat and less ATP.[224]

The critical temperature is not changed in cold-acclimated animals; hence insulative change must be negligible. In fact, increased

TABLE 39. METABOLISM OF ANIMALS ACCLIMATED TO COLD

Animal	Acclimation temperature °C	Heat production (Cal/m²/24 hr)	Temperature of measurement (°C)
dog[109]	4-5	1128	25
	25	871	25
rat[262]	1.5	1339	30
	30	1020	30
pigeon[109]	1-3	1084	30
	29-30	850	30
ground squirrel[109]	18-23	702	32.5
	29-32	451	32.5

vascularity of the skin, e.g., in rabbit ears, has frequently been observed in cold acclimation. The vascularization of ear vessels of a white rat kept at 6° increased twelve times and that in leg muscles by 50 per cent.[140] The effective over-all insulation has been calculated from the formula:[125]

$$\frac{t_{core} - t_{critical}}{\text{heat production at neutrality}} = \text{insulation} \times \text{a constant}$$

The insulation of a number of mammals and birds showed a decrease of as much as 53 per cent on cold acclimation in the laboratory.[122] The increased peripheral blood flow increases loss of heat and opposes the effect of metabolic increase. As exposure to cold continues, there may be some increase in fur thickness, which tends to counteract the increased vascularity. The rate of loss of acclimatized state upon return from cold to warmth is faster than the rate of gain of acclimation.

Acclimatization to Cold Climates. In cold climates the compensation by increased heat production, as observed in the laboratory, can be only a temporary solution to lasting cold stress. Animals in winter conditions or in the Arctic or Antarctic show changes which are different from those reported for acclimation for a few weeks in a cold room. The time of natural exposure is longer, the seasonal cold increases gradually, and photoperiod, nutrition, and other undefined environmental factors interact in such a way that cold *per se* may not be the critical factor.

Winter mammals and birds are better able to survive extreme cold than are summer ones. For example, *Peromyscus maniculatus* when supplied food *ad libitum* showed a 200-minute survival limit at −35°C in the winter and at −15°C in the summer.[125] Similar extension of survival limits has been observed for nonmigrant birds. It is probable

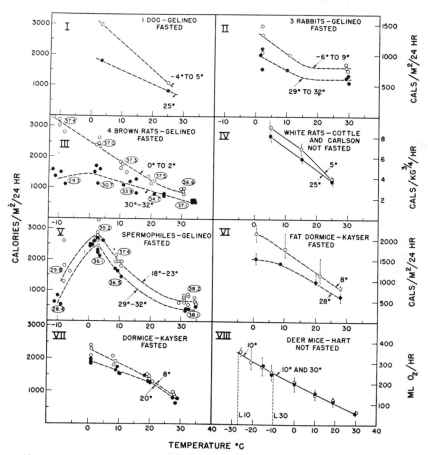

FIGURE 87. Temperature-metabolism curves of mammals acclimated to warm (●) and cold (o) temperatures as indicated. Circled numbers give mean body temperatures; L_{10} and L_{30}, survival limits for 200 minutes. (From Hart, J. S.: Rev. Canad. Biol., vol. 16.)

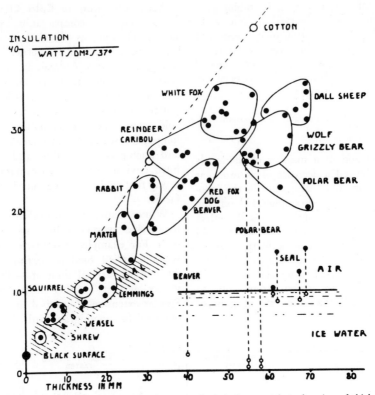

FIGURE 88.   Maximum insulation of fur of arctic and tropical mammals as function of thickness. Values for aquatic animals are given in air (●) and in ice water (o). Insulating value of medium weight cotton is given by broken line. (Courtesy of P. F. Scholander.)

that in addition to changes in heat retention there are central nervous adjustments which favor survival. Decreasing slopes of metabolism-temperature curves in a series *Peromyscus > Zapus > Microtus > Citellus* may correspond to relative insulation.[213]

Measurements of insulative value of fur and feathers show marked increases in the winter over summer values, especially in large birds and mammals in which the surface area is small relative to the heat-producing mass. Thicker and more effective winter coats have been found in fox, porcupines, squirrels, dogs, and rabbits. Plumage in adult English sparrows was 29 per cent heavier in winter than in summer.[172] In white rats kept outdoors in winter at average temperature 10° the fur became thick; that of rats kept indoors at 6° did not; both groups of rats showed increased vascularization. There were fewer cold lesions, e.g., to ears, in the acclimatized rats.[133-137] Fasted pigeons lived 48 to 144 hours at −40°C; metabolism increased four times; plucked pigeons died in 20 to 30 minutes.[276] Evening grosbeaks have a t_c of 16°; gray jays, 0 to 10°C; yet both live in freezing

temperatures. The skin temperature of the grosbeak was 36 to 38° in air from 15.8 to −13.6°; hence at low temperature the bird relies more on heat production than on insulation.[68]

In arctic animals not only is the fur thicker but it is better insulation. Maximal insulation (without going to a vacuum) is given by still air, and this has a value of 4.7 clo/in. The *clo unit* is one developed for clothing and is based on heat loss for a given temperature gradient, area, and time.[41] A plot of insulation against thickness of fur for a series of arctic animals gives a slope of 3.7 clo/in, which approaches the best insulating fabrics[119] (Fig. 88). The smaller arctic mammals (weasels, lemmings) have less insulation than larger ones. On the average, the insulation of arctic mammals is some nine times better than that of tropical ones.[156, 157] Seal blubber is such good insulation that the skin temperature is only slightly above that of the surrounding water, while the visceral temperature is kept constant at 37°; hence heat loss by conduction and convection is negligible.[156, 157] The insulation increase in winter is greater for large mammals (52 per cent for black bear and 41 per cent for wolf) than for small mammals (21 per cent for deer mouse and 16 per cent for hare). Insulation increases in a series from shrew to rabbit.[123]

Vasomotor adaptations may be even more important than fur. Animals with a low critical temperature tend to have thick fur or feathers, yet over a wide range of environmental temperatures and constant metabolism the body temperature remains constant. This implies sensitive vasomotor control. Also animals with differently insulating fur or feathers may live in similar environments, particularly in the tropics; their microclimates may be different but so may their vasomotor controls. Vasomotor adaptations permit cold extremities. The temperature of the foot of a gull on an ice floe, the lower legs of a reindeer, the flippers of a seal, or the flukes of a whale may be below 10°. When the domestic pig is in −12° air, the skin on the dorsal surface is at 10 to 12°, on the nose 17° to 18°, on the lower leg 9°; the body temperature at a depth of 45.7 mm is 38.4°.[154]

In some animals the arteries and veins run parallel to or intertwined with one another in a rete. Where there is close apposition between arterial and venous blood, there is heat transfer by countercurrent exchange. Hence an extremity may remain cool but receive adequate oxygen if heat flow is from artery to vein. In a sloth where a rete occurs in the limbs, a cooled forelimb or leg rewarms slowly; the limb of a coati or monkey, which has no rete, rewarms after cooling five times faster than the sloth's.[254, 255] Whales have a countercurrent arrangement of vessels to tail flukes and flippers, with a large central artery surrounded by spiraling rings of small veins;[293] the flukes and flippers can function at a lower temperature than the body.[254, 255] A rete exists in the axilla of penguins. Where there is a rete, heat dissipation is not proportional to the total body surface.[253] The harp seal in 10° water has a skin surface temperature of 10°; at 22-mm depth below the skin, 22°C; at 35 mm depth, 39°C. In water at 1°C, the web between the phalanges is at 6 to 8°C. A critical temperature was not reached in ice water.[155]

The fact that the temperature of appendages in arctic animals often is below 10° necessitates chemical changes in the tissues. The melting point of the fat declines from the thigh down the leg of a caribou; the melting point of marrow fat of phalanges of arctic animals (fox, caribou, Eskimo dog) may be 10 to 15° and that from near the head of the femur 45°, and in the foot pad the fat may remain soft down to 0°.[158]

Enzymes of cells in the skin and appendages are heterothermic in that they tolerate a temperature range of some 35°, more than many poikilothermic animals; these enzymes should be of great interest for kinetic studies. Different regions of the same cell or of a nerve fiber differ chemically; in the metatarsal portion of the leg nerve of a cold-acclimated herring-gull, conduction stops at 2.8 to 3.9°, whereas the tibial portion of the same nerve is blocked at 11.7 to 14.4°.[47] The tibial nerve of a nonacclimated hamster conducts at temperatures down to 3.4°; a rat's nerve blocks at 9°.[48] The blood phospholipids and fatty acids may be higher in concentration in arctic than in temperate animals.[304] In general, fats are more used metabolically in the arctic.

Further evidence for improved insulation in the winter is the lowering of the critical temperature of metabolism in many mammals (red fox, porcupine, Eskimo dog, lemming; Table 40). In these arctic animals the

TABLE 40. SEASONAL DIFFERENCES IN CRITICAL TEMPERATURE AND BASAL METABOLIC RATE[157]

	Low critical temperature (°C)		BMR (ml O₂/gm/hr)	
	summer	winter	summer	winter
red fox	+8	−13	0.55	0.50
red squirrel	+20	+20	0.70	0.50
porcupine	+7	−12	0.42	0.43
black brant	+6	+6	0.85	0.71
northwest crow	−5	−7	2.3	2.8

winter metabolism is actually less than the summer when measured at a given air temperature (Fig. 89). The lowering of t_c and of metabolism is the reverse of the effect of laboratory acclimation. Also the rate of increase in metabolism per degree of lowering of the air temperature is less for arctic than for temperate species. In small mammals, e.g., deer mice, the t_c may not be lowered and the winter and summer metabolism curves are superimposable except that, in the winter, metabolism continues to rise and body temperature is maintained down to lower air temperature.[123, 125]

Wild white-footed mice, *Peromyscus leucopus*, collected in the winter, have a lower O₂ consumption than do laboratory mice

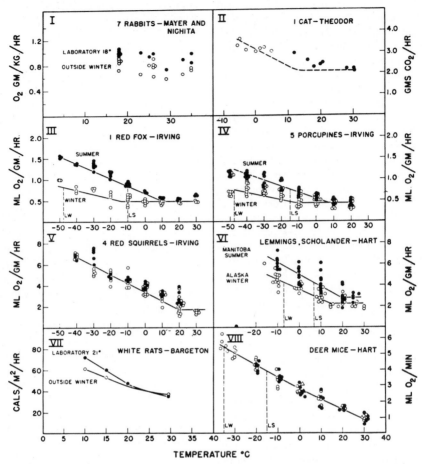

FIGURE 89. Temperature-metabolism curves for fed mammals acclimatized to summer (or laboratory) (●) and winter (○). Broken vertical lines, winter and summer limits (for deer mice for 200 minutes' survival). (Data from Hart, J. S.: Rev. Canad. Biol., vol. 16.)

tested at 1 to 2°. The wild mice have a thicker pelage than laboratory mice:[123]

greater energy expenditure at low temperatures than at high, but thermoneutral or basal

		O₂ consumption (1—2°, ml/mouse/hr)	Pelage insulation (°/cal/hr/m²)
wild	summer	185	0.180
	winter	165	0.228
laboratory	30° acclimated	204	0.146
	10° acclimated	201	0.156

In some birds, e.g., wild turkey, the winter metabolism was less than the summer; in others, e.g., brant, no difference was found. In English sparrows as in deer mice the winter maximum or limiting metabolism was some 30° lower than in the summer (Fig. 89). The English sparrow increased its gross energy linearly with decreasing air temperature at 0.0167 Cal/gm/day/°C; winter birds reached 1.31 Cal/gm/day as a limit at —34°C; the limit for summer birds was 1.02 Cal/gm/day at 0°C.[59] In acclimatized mammals and birds, therefore, there may be

metabolism per se is not adaptive; rather the most striking changes are in insulation and in tolerance limits.

Acclimatization studies in man reveal what may be racial differences. In nonacclimatized men from the temperate zone attempting to sleep in the cold, a decline in temperature of extremities and restlessness occurred, but little increase in metabolism; acclimatized soldiers slept well in the cold, foot temperature was maintained, and metabolic rate elevated. Australian aborigines, accustomed to sleeping with a fire on one side, slept well with cold extremities (foot temperature 12 to 15°C), and showed no elevation in metabolism; evidently their adaptation must be nervous and permits cooling of the periphery, while in temperate zone man the adaptation is metabolic, and keeps the periphery warm[259] (Fig. 90). The microclimate of Eskimos and Lapps under their fur clothing is really tropical, and the low critical temperature is about 27° for them as for temperate zone men.[259] For man on a bicycle ergometer, t_c is 26°. Acclimatized man shows vascular tolerance of skin cooling and maintains skin circulation longer in cold.

In summary: The long-term temperature compensations of homeotherms are multiple, differ very much with species, and natural acclimatization is different from laboratory acclimation to cold. In both laboratory and field compensation there is increased ability to carry out life functions at lower environmental temperatures. Body temperature does not change adaptively. Many laboratory animals, when kept in the cold, show persistent elevation of metabolism resulting from enzyme alterations. They usually show no change in critical temperature and may show increased skin vascularity, thus reduced insulation. In natural acclimatization, metabolism usually does not increase but is either unchanged or decreased. The critical environmental temperature becomes lowered as insulation increases in quantity and quality. The minimum temperature at which metabolism can maintain body temperature is lowered. Vasomotor adaptations are important, probably associated with changes in the autonomic nervous system, and surface tissues function at temperatures much below rectal temperature. Arctic animals tend to seek and remain in relatively warm microclimates even during the winter.

Responses and Acclimation to Heat. When an animal is placed in a hot environment the heat receptors of the skin are stimulated, and reflex responses favoring dissipation of heat result. Cutaneous vessels dilate, there is increased blood flow in the skin, thermal conductance of the peripheral tissues increases five to six times, and there is increased heat loss. There is also increase in insensible water evaporation. If balance is not maintained the skin temperature rises, and reflex sweating occurs in animals with sweat glands or panting in animals in which sweat is not an important avenue of cooling. The threshold skin temperature for sweating by man varies for different body regions but is about 30 to 32°; evaporation increases abruptly in a camel at 35°C,[251] in a donkey at 31°C air. At high humidities evaporation and insensible water loss are less than in dry heat.

The relative loss of water by respiratory tract, by sweat glands, and by evaporation from skin varies according to species. Man under basal conditions loses about 20 per cent

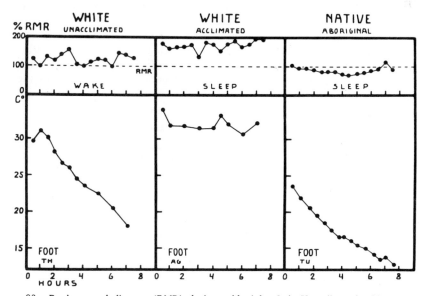

FIGURE 90. Resting metabolic rate (RMR) during cold night. *Left,* Unacclimated white man, unable to sleep—declining skin (foot) temperature. *Center,* White man acclimated to sleeping in cold—elevated metabolism and maintained skin temperature. *Right,* Australian aborigine—asleep with cooled skin. (From Scholander, P. F.: Fed. Proc., vol. 17.)

of his heat by vaporization, in exercise 75 to 80 per cent. Loss of heat by radiation exceeds loss by vaporization at low temperatures, but above about 31° loss by vaporization predominates in man at rest. Loss of heat by radiation, convection, and conduction is reduced by insulation. Heat loss by terrestrial mammals with or without hair is twice as great in water as in air. Man in cool air may lose by evaporation 1 l of water per day; in hard work on the desert he may evaporate 1.5 l per hour. Output of sweat increases 20 gm/hr for each 1°C rise in air temperature. Man loses quantities of salt in sweat; the sweat of a burro contains much less chloride. As water and salt are lost by sweat, the urinary loss is reduced. In man the glands of the palm are emotionally controlled, the others thermally. Animals which pant, e.g., dogs and cattle, lose water from the respiratory tract, and this may result in increased chloride concentration in the blood and, in some, alkalosis as a result of the blowing off of CO_2. Some mammals, particularly the marsupials, such as opossums, salivate profusely and lick their fur when heated. In Australian marsupials the best regulation occurs in the macropods, less in phalangers, and the least in marsupial mice.[242] All higher mammals except rodents and lagomorphs have skin glands, in which the efficiency for producing sweat varies. Most nonprimates have apocrine-type glands which open into or close to hair follicles, while the eccrine-type glands in primates are often separate from hair follicles. Rodents are poor regulators in heat and may wet their fur with external water or saliva; they increase ventilation also. Most mammals have less control than man of evaporative heat loss at high temperatures

and show greater body temperature rise; man's tropical origin is reflected in his temperature relations.

In birds, vaporization which occurs as air passes through the air sacs has a cooling effect. Birds dust themselves and thus increase heat loss by conduction. They also pant when body temperature rises and drink more water. When its body temperature was 42.6°C a mourning dove panted, and at air temperature of 39°C it consumed four times more water than at 23°C.[12, 13, 17] Many birds and mammals reduce heat stress by behavioral responses. They may seek shade, burrow underground, or wallow in shallow water; they extend their appendages, and birds fan their wings and use other means to increase evaporative cooling. In man at high temperatures there may be an increase in plasma volume as fluid shifts from interstitial space to the vascular bed.[19] Later, more red blood cells enter the circulation, and blood volume may increase by 20 to 30 per cent after a week in the heat. If water lost by sweat is not replaced the blood volume decreases.

When cooling mechanisms fail and body temperature rises, the O_2 consumption increases because of the direct cellular effect of heat and also the increased ventilation; possibly the increased metabolism may be part of the regulating mechanism since it is less in thyroidectomized and hypophysectomized rats. The zone of neutrality (minimum metabolism) does not extend to high air temperatures, that is, the upper t_c is usually just below or near body temperature. In some small birds and mammals there is no plateau of neutrality, and the upper and lower t_c are the same.[213] Table 41 gives critical temperature for a number of birds. In the cardinal

TABLE 41.   CRITICAL TEMPERATURE OF BIRDS

	Weight	Low critical temperature (°C)	High critical temperature (°C)
Widow bird	11 gm	37	37
House wren[171]	10	37.8	37.8
English sparrow[59, 172]	29	37	37
		32 summer	
		32 winter	
Yellow bunting[298]	26	25	33
Ortolan bunting[298]	26	32	38
Abert towhee[63]	47	25	35
Cardinal[65, 67]	38-48	24 summer	33
		18 winter	33
Northern crow[157]	30	− 7	
Brant[157]		6	
Pigeon[273]		14	
Vulture[88]		24	
Frigate bird[88]		20	
Gray jay[63]		0 = −10 winter	

Richmondena the lower t_c changes seasonally but not the upper t_c.[65, 67]

Heat shock (hyperpyrexia) results if the thermoregulatory center fails and body temperature rises critically. Heat exhaustion can occur in man without rise in body temperature and is largely due to dehydration and changes in salt balance; exhaustion may occur in ample hydration if excessive amounts of salt are lost. Heat stroke results from brain damage. Heat death is due in large part to cardiovascular failure. The tolerated temperature is less with external than with internal warming; a man loses consciousness when heated externally to a rectal temperature of 38.6°C, yet in fever the temperature may go to 42° and in exercise the body temperature may reach 40° without harm.[299]

The net effect of acclimation to a hot environment is a higher capacity for activity and less discomfort on heat exposure. In man copious sweating occurs; the capacity for moisture production may be doubled; sweating starts at a lower skin temperature; skin temperature is more readily reduced, and sweat contains less salt. Cardiovascular efficiency improves and the pulse remains steady. For example, the rise in heart rate with increased air temperature is less in native Nigerians than in Europeans.[180] Rats acclimated to cold are more sensitive to heat than are warm-acclimated rats, and the latter are more sensitive to cold.[95]

Many tropical mammals are genetically adapted to heat. Indian cattle are more tolerant of heat than are European cattle. At 27°C Indian cattle gained weight as readily as at 10°C, while shorthorn cows decreased food consumption and decreased growth in the heat.[33, 164] European cows show some acclimation during which their blood volume is restored.[58] Buffalo cows in hot air increase ventilation, have lower pulse rate, and show less rise of body temperature than do cattle. Northern fur seal bulls have very limited temperature control and on a warm day at 10°C may die of overheating.[17]

Many tropical mammals are not lacking in insulating fur even though they have high critical temperature (sloth in Table 38). Scholander suggests the need for insulation in rapidly falling night temperature. Fur is also a barrier to heat gain; the body temperature of a camel in the sun rises appreciably after shearing. A camel tolerates wide fluctuations in temperature; the rectal temperature can vary from 34 to 40° if it is without

water, less if water is supplied. If the tolerated body temperature is high, there is less gradient and less heat gain from the environment.[251] The body temperature of a rhinoceros can range from 34.5 to 37.5°C.[4] A high body temperature is an adaptation to a warm climate.

In summary: Acclimatization to heat is by lowered threshold for sweating, dilution of sweat, improved cardiovascular efficiency (in man); one genetic adaptation is tolerance of elevated body temperature (camel).

Development of Homeothermy. Newborn mammals or recently hatched birds show poor temperature regulation. A 2-day mouse, for example, is essentially poikilothermic; at 10 days a mouse regulates in intermediate air temperatures and at 20 days at extreme temperatures. A 6-day rat has a body temperature only 1.3 to 1.8° above the environment in the range of 24 to 37°, and 0.5° or less above the air at 20°; at 12 to 16 days control occurs only during activity, and at 25 days the rat approaches the adult condition. Tundra voles at 11 to 12 days had a temperature of 35.4° in the nest, but outside in air of 0° their body temperature ranged from 2.5 to 16°; at 28 days they reached the adult value of 38.3°.[215] A pig shows fair regulation at 1 day.[217] An opossum is born in an immature state and shows its first regulation at 60 days.[230]

Young naked birds (altricial) like herons require much parental care and show wide temperature fluctuations, less after they acquire down. Precocial birds like gulls have better temperature control when hatched, and the young are given less parental care. Nests are important in temperature maintenance in young birds. A chipping sparrow changes from poikilothermic to homeothermic at 7 days, and at 2 days is only 3° warmer than its environment.[65] House wrens show partial regulation down to 26° air temperature at 9 days, regulation at subnormal body temperature at 12 days, and at 15 days maintain body temperature of 40° down to 10° air temperature (Fig. 91).[171]

The lack of thermal regulation in young birds and mammals is reflected in lower lethal body temperatures in the cold as follows.[1]

Low Lethal Temperatures (°C)

adult hamster	3.8	newborn hamster	1
cat	19	kitten	7-8
guinea pig	17	newborn guinea pig	14-16

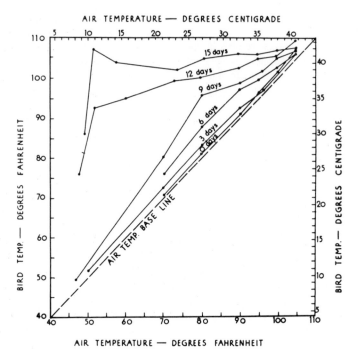

FIGURE 91. Body temperature of wrens at different air temperatures at different ages after hatching. (From Kendeigh, S. C.: J. Exp. Zool., vol. 82.)

In dogs the development of heat conservation lags behind development of heat production.[202]

Development of homeothermy has been correlated with myelination in nerve fibers of the hypothalamus and with increase in metabolic rate. Regulation is accompanied by increased sensitivity of the heat center and increased basal metabolism.

Heterotherms. All temperature regulators show some normal variation in body temperature, especially diurnally. A few birds and mammals regulate well when active but less well at rest, and some primitive mammals show wide fluctuations in correspondence with the environment (Table 42). Monotremes, some marsupials, armadillos, sloths, and anteaters tend normally to have low body temperatures.[88, 306] Body temperature range for activity is wide for heterotherms, as follows (in °C):[86]

hedgehog (*Erinaceus*)	31.1-36.7
ground squirrel (*Citellus*)	30.0-39.0
hamster (*Cricetus*)	32.5-35.5
dormouse (*Muscardinus*)	31.0-38.0
opossum (*Marmosa*)	29.3-37.8

An Australian vespertilionid bat (*Miniopterus*) was homeothermic with rectal temperatures of 39.1° when awake but quiescent and 41° in flight, and it was poikilothermic when asleep; by contrast a fruit bat, *Pteropus*,

like most mammals, did not become poikilothermic at rest.[214] In a series of tropical mammals the mice and squirrels regulated with t_c about 27°, but armadillos, opossums, and three-toed sloths showed a wide range of body temperature and metabolism according to environmental temperature.

Body temperatures of heterotherms tend to be low[86, 88, 306] (Table 42).

Animals which are capable of hibernation can tolerate lower body temperature when awake than can other mammals. For example, the hearts of hedgehog and hamster continue to beat until the temperature drops to 1.5 to 6° as compared with the internal temperature of 16 to 18° tolerated by rat and rabbit.[142] A nonhibernating hamster survives a body temperature of 4°.[1] Ground squirrels in Alaska maintain a constant high temperature in summer, are poikilothermic in hibernation in winter, but fluctuate (are heterothermic) in fall and spring.[147] A kangaroo rat maintains its body temperature in cool air, but in environments above 32° its body temperature rises.[250]

Some animals go into long periods of sleep in the winter but do not truly hibernate. For example, a black bear in its winter den at an outside temperature of —25° had a rectal temperature of 31.3 to 34°.[146] Similar partial hibernation (torpidity) is noted in skunks,

TABLE 42. BODY TEMPERATURE IN RELATION TO AIR TEMPERATURE IN HETEROTHERMS

Animal	Air temperature (°C)	Body temperature (°C) (usually rectal)
Monotremes		
Echidna	15	28
	20	30.4
Ornithorhynchus	20	32.6
	32	33.6
Marsupials		
Didelphis	14	32
Didelphis (opossum)	25	34.5
Metachirus	20	34
Edentates		
Dasypus (armadillo)	24-30	33-35
	5-30	30-35
Bradypus tridactylus (sloth)	19-25.8	30-32.9
Bradypus cuculliger (sloth)	24.5-32.4	27.7-36.8
Chiropterans[86]		
Hipposideros	29	34.4 fasting
		37.7 with food
Eptesicus	27.9	34.0 fasting
		38.0 with food
Rhinolophus	28	36.2
	14	22.2

Detailed references are given in Table 62 in first edition of this book.

pocket gophers, and opossums. Others, such as bats[145] and hummingbirds, poorwills,[159] and swifts, maintain high body temperatures when active but their temperature drops to that of air or nearly so when asleep. Thus they show diurnal torpidity. A birchmouse, *Sicista,* shows much diurnal fluctuation in body temperature. It may be within 1 degree of the air temperature when the animal is asleep by day and 34 to 38° at midnight during activity; at very low air temperatures the birchmouse hibernates.[161]

The tissues near the surface of many homeotherms withstand wide temperature fluctuations and are in this sense heterothermic. *In vitro* experiments with mammalian tissues are normally done at 37°, but a more normal temperature for peripheral blood vessels, skin, and muscles might be 33°.[41]

Heterothermy permits conservation of food reserves, but it does limit the speed with which an animal can change from rest to activity.

Migration and Hibernation. Some birds migrate with the seasons; some fish also make limited seasonal migrations. In birds, migration is a complex response, initiated by changes in energy balance coordinated with seasonal variations in air temperature and photoperiod. With their high body temperature and high metabolic rate, small birds lose weight rapidly during a few hours without food at low air temperature. The length of the daylight period must be sufficient to permit the bird to eat enough for reserves to last overnight. During the winter, survival of English sparrows without food at −14° is 19 hours; at 34° it is 61 hours.[59] During the warmer summer months the resistance of sparrows to hunger is decreased; at −14° starvation survival time is 11 hours. For the house wren, a migratory species, the summer survival time at −14° is less than 5 hours. Differences between species in survival time without food depend on utilization of energy reserves and on the metabolic rate necessary for maintenance of body temperature. Thus, climatic factors influence both migration and distribution. The changes associated with migration are complex and the endocrine responses, particularly to photoperiod, will be discussed in Chapter 20. Caged migratory birds show nocturnal unrest in the spring at the time of rapid fat deposition and weight gain. Thus, while temperature is only one of several initiating factors, it is a critical one.

Hibernation in mammals is an alteration of temperature regulation so that the animal becomes poikilothermic down to temperatures slightly above 0°C. By this definition there is no essential difference between the daily sleep of a bat and the winter sleep of a

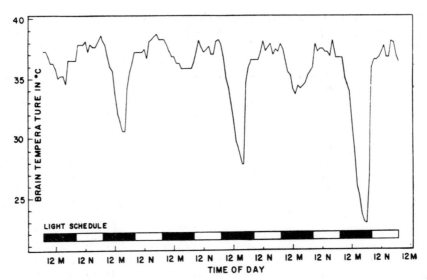

FIGURE 92.   Brain temperature of a ground squirrel in test drops of temperature preparatory to hibernation.
(From Strumwasser, F.: Am. J. Physiol., vol. 196.)

ground squirrel. Actually, hibernation is more than setting the thermoregulator down, it involves changes in most organ systems while homeostasis of the organism as a whole is maintained. Only a few mammals, mostly monotremes, insectivores, rodents, and bats, are capable of hibernation, but some others, such as bears, go without food for long periods but maintain body temperature. A few birds—poorwills, some hummingbirds, and swifts—which can enter a state of torpidity at low temperatures, resemble hibernating animals in that the body temperature can drop only to some limit, for example, a poorwill to 4.8° in air at 3.5° C.[18, 159] It is hoped that knowledge of hibernation may aid in understanding normal temperature regulation. Hibernation has been recently reviewed by many.[139, 167-170, 190, 193]

Preparation for Hibernation. Some hibernators such as the ground squirrel *Citellus* accumulate much fat in the fall; they have a respiratory quotient (p. 186) greater than 1 and synthesize much fat from carbohydrate.[89] Others such as the hamster *Mesocricetus* do not accumulate fat, but when put into the cold they store food and delay entering hibernation much longer than do ground squirrels.[188] In the cold (5°) hamsters desaturate their fat and deposit new fat of high iodine number and lower melting point.[92] Hibernators fail to give the usual endocrine responses of pituitary and adrenal cortex to cold stress. Hedgehogs can be induced to hibernate in the summer by means of insulin injections and then being placed into cold;

the insulin level in their blood is elevated in natural hibernation.[283] The thyroid is involuted at the season of hibernation, and thyroxin injections can retard hibernation. Hypophysectomy can induce a poikilothermic state, and pituitary injections can arouse hibernating hamsters. Adrenalectomized animals do not hibernate but may die of hypothermia.[190]

Citellus, the ground squirrel, with thermocouples implanted in the brain, on entering hibernation shows successive test drops in brain temperature, each a little lower than the previous one (Fig. 92).[278] As hibernation becomes deeper, each plateau persists longer. The temperature drops slowly, 2° to 4° per hour; the drops are associated with vasodilation in the skin and reduction in muscle tone. At 33° to 34° rectal temperature there is an abrupt drop in heart rate. Breathing rate also shows that the entrance into hibernation is stepwise, not all-or-none.[278]

The seasonal variation in tendency to hibernate has an endocrine basis, as if the nervous system is capable of entering the state of hibernation only in a given endocrine state.[170] Yet there appears to be no causal relation between any single endocrine[69] or brown fat (the so-called hibernation gland) and hibernation.

The usual stimulus to hibernation is cold. However, mere chilling is not enough unless the animal as a whole is in a state of readiness. Temperature regulation is poor prior to hibernation and heat production is reduced faster than the body temperature falls.[168, 169] A hamster, which is very slow to enter hibernation, increases its oxygen consumption by two and one half to three times when the air temperature is dropped from 30° to 5°, whereas a ground squirrel goes directly into hibernation. Hibernators are more tolerant of anoxia than are non-hibernators.[140]

The State of Hibernation. The magnesium concentration in blood serum is high in hibernating hedgehogs and marmots, in bats hibernating at 13° but not at 17° to 20°, and in hibernating ground squirrels.[239, 240] Awakening does not require a lowering of serum magnesium. Other blood electrolytes are little changed. Blood sugar is lowered in many species, not in others. Serum proteins increase in hibernating hamsters.[270] The leukocyte count is markedly reduced. In ground squirrels there is a slight decrease in

(pattern III of p. 245), while for both respiration and glycolysis of brain slices the rate-temperature curves are shifted as in pattern II (p. 245).[270]

In hibernation the metabolism is reduced by twenty to a hundred times.[181] For example, a marmot awake at 10° produced 2.8 KCal/kg/hr but in hibernation it produced only 0.09 KCal/kg/hr.[167] The respiratory quotient corresponds to metabolism of fat. Forced breathing of CO_2 causes an increase in breathing rate and subsequent increase in heart rate; hence the respiratory center retains its sensitivity.[188, 192, 194, 195] When stimulated by CO_2 a ground squirrel remained asleep with faster breathing, while a hamster awoke. Despite the low metabolic rate, appreciable weight is lost during hibernation, as indicated by the following data for the brown bat:[22]

	Male weight (gm)	Female weight (gm)	Body fat (%)
before hibernation	21.5	20.5	28
after 180 days hibernation	16.1	13.7	10

plasma volume.[284] Clotting time is prolonged, apparently by decrease in prothrombin, an adaptation which prevents thrombus formation during hibernal sleep.[284] Hibernating ground squirrels and bats are very resistant to x-irradiation; after irradiation there is little apparent effect until arousal some days later, when the usual drop in blood cells occurs.[268]

As body temperature is lowered, the heart slows to a minimal rate, and at slightly below 3° the beat is irregular in most species.[61, 62] The heart of an active ground squirrel beats at 200 to 400/min, that of a dormant one at 7 to 10/min.[284] The electrocardiogram is altered, the P-T interval (p. 399) lengthened, and block of conduction at the auriculo-ventricular junction results in uncoordinated beats.[46, 219] Breathing becomes slowed and very irregular. In hibernating *Cricetus* (hamster), stimulation of the vagus is without effect on the heart. Isolated hearts of hibernators beat down to lower temperatures (below −1°C for *Citellus*) than do the hearts of nonhibernators (13° to 16° for *Sciurus* and 7°C for *Tamias*);[191] hedgehogs and hamster hearts stop at 1.5° to 6.0°; rat and rabbit hearts, at 16° to 18°[142] (Fig. 93). Enzymatic differences exist between tissues of hibernants and nonhibernants. The Q_{O_2} of ventricular muscle of a hamster (hibernating or not) shows a lower Q_{10} and crosses the curve for rat ventricular O_2 consumption

The metabolism of a torpid hummingbird at 20°C is 1.7 ml O_2/gm/hr as compared with 0.39 in the bat *Myotis* and 0.28 in a lizard at the same temperature.[18] Metabolism is similar to normal in hibernation in that specific dynamic action of proteins can be obtained.[170]

The temperature of hibernating mammals is essentially that of the surrounding air, and there may be fluctuations in temperature which roughly follow those of the air. At an ambient temperature of 3 to 5°, rectal temperature of a hibernating hamster is less than 0.5° above the air temperature.[188, 192, 194, 195] Temperature at the esophagus may be 0.2 to 0.8° higher than at the colon.[2] *Citellus* in air of 5.5° has a brain temperature 2.3° to 2.5° above air; in air of 2°C, 4° above; i.e., brain temperature remains at about 6.1° in deep hibernation. Skin temperature fluctuates much more than brain. When the air temperature approaches 0°, some animals (hamster, woodchuck, dormouse) tend to hold the body temperature at about 2°, and their oxygen consumption actually increases.[189] Some animals (hamsters and ground squirrels) awaken when the air drops to 0°, but some do not, and individuals which fail to respond to the 0° temperature die.[89] Thus the thermoregulator is not completely turned off but rather set at a very low point. Hibernating bats often fail to arouse in the cold and die from cold—tropical bats at 8°, temperate

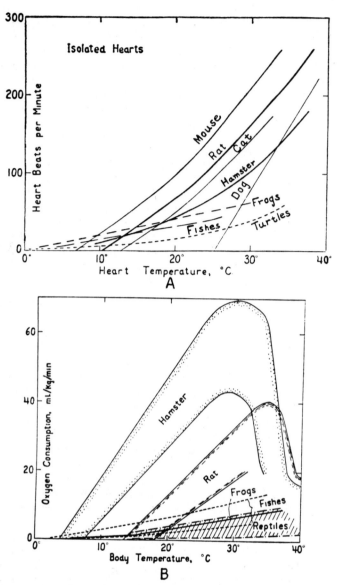

FIGURE 93. *A*, comparison of rate of beat of isolated hearts of various vertebrates at different temperatures. *B*, rates of oxygen consumption in various vertebrates in relation to body temperature. (From Adolph, E. J.: Am. J. Physiol., vol. 166.)

zone ones at —5°.[86] The pocket mouse *Perognathus* without food entered hibernation at 20° and aroused if air temperature reached 2°.[12, 13, 17] Normally some hibernants awaken periodically, some to eat and drink. Tagged bats show much individual variation in their winter movements. Ground squirrels were awake 7 per cent of the time during the winter. A ground squirrel uses during an arousal of a few hours (at an average of once every 11 days) as much body reserves as in 10 days of sleep.[168, 169] Hamsters awaken every 1.6 to 2.7 days.

Activity in the nervous system does not entirely stop when the body cools. Cortical activity (as brain waves) is lost in a hamster at about 19°, although some cortical responses to peripheral nerve stimulation could be elicited at as low as 9.1°.[46] In the ground squirrel, brain waves persisted down to 12°[170] and in the woodchuck to 11°.[188, 192, 194, 195] The bulboreticular system of the brain is least resistant to cold and, on awakening, the limbic system first becomes active. *Citellus* as it enters hibernation shows cortical waves at 10/sec; there is still some cortical activity, low in amplitude, manifest at 5°. *Citellus* can still localize sound, erect pinnae, vocalize, and move about at brain temperature 6.1°.[278]

Arousal. Arousal from hibernation is a rapid awakening, requiring less than an hour in a bat, less than 3 hours in most other hibernators. Bats kept in a refrigerator for 144 days without food were capable of sustained flight after 15 minutes at room temperature.[223] A ground squirrel's temperature may rise from 4° to 35° in 4 hours;[89] a birchmouse may warm by 1° per minute.[161] The arousal in a mammal is a process of self-warming and does not require a warm environment, whereas arousal in a dormant poikilotherm depends on environmental heat. Arousal can be initiated by slight warming, by sound, mechanical disturbance, injection of water. First, breathing becomes regular and, as warming occurs, more frequent. Oxygen consumption may increase faster than the warming.[232] The temperature of the chest rises first and blood distribution permits warming the anterior half before the posterior half of the body.[2] Muscle action potentials indicate activity before visible movements, and the heart and chest muscles must be important sources of heat. Temperature rises slowly at first, then rapidly, finally more slowly (Fig. 94). The heart accelerates rapidly, e.g., in a spermophile[243] asleep at 5° the heart rate was 2 to 3/min; on awakening at 8° it was 7 to 20/min; at 14°, 200/min, and at 20°, 300/min. Blood pressure rises to normal levels before the heart

rate is normal. This fact together with drug experiments indicates that the heart is being driven to its capacity at each temperature by the sympatheticoadrenal system.[46, 193] As the animal emerges from dormancy there is a metabolic overshoot indicated by high O_2 consumption and CO_2 production during the period of final temperature rise. Oxygen consumption by a hamster rose from 0.5 ml/kg/hr to 2258 ml/kg/hr during 1 hour and 40 minutes.[168, 170] Liver glycogen becomes markedly reduced. Electrical activity of the brain shows marked increase at about 20°, varying with species.[46] However, the total phenomenon of arousal is best interpreted as a mass discharge of those parts of the brain concerned with heat production, and of the sympathetic and motor systems.[193]

In summary: Hibernators differ from non-hibernators in many details, for example, in deposition of desaturated fats, in failure of adrenal responses to cold, and in low sensitivity of nerves to cold. Entering hibernation is a process involving many organ systems; the most important change is in the setting of the temperature-regulating center. The nervous system retains its integrative control and can be roused by extreme cold as well as by warm air.

CONCLUSIONS

The crux of temperature relations of animals is the utilization of the temperature acceleration of reaction-rates, the van't Hoff-Arrhenius law, and at the same time maintenance of some independence of the limita-

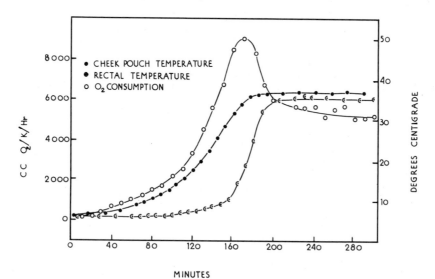

FIGURE 94. Time course of waking of hamsters from hibernation at 4.5°C. (From Lyman, C. P.: J. Exp. Zool., vol. 109.)

tions of this law. If life processes depended on molecular collision rates only, or if enzymes had low activation energies, hence low temperature dependence, metabolic activity would be very slow indeed. A Q_{10} of 2.5, or increase of 9.6 per cent per degree, is a common value for enzymatic acceleration. This means, however, that cold imposes a limiting sluggishness on all energy-yielding reactions. Also life functions cannot proceed if the particular protoplasm concerned is frozen. At the other extreme, at temperatures around 40°, changes occur in proteins and lipids which render them useless for active cells.

The modifications used to survive the temperature strait jacket are many and various. At the low end some animals endure prolonged extreme cold by encysting, by wintering in a diapausal state, by supercooling, by accumulating organic solutes, some by withstanding freezing of part of their body water, and a few warm-blooded animals by tolerating a body temperature drop to nearly 0°. Many animals seek protection from cold by burrowing or migrating. Each of these patterns requires a period of preparation, and the signals which elicit seasonal physiological change are difficult to discern. Compensations for cold less extreme than freezing include a variety of acclimations. Subtle changes in water content, lipid saturation, and especially in enzymes tend to lower lethal temperatures and to permit metabolic activity at a higher rate than would be possible by strict conformity with the van't Hoff-Arrhenius rule. Behavioral adaptations tend to move animals toward "optimal" temperatures and help some of them use radiant heat. Behavioral and central nervous changes permit near-normal activity at low temperatures where, despite some compensations, the absolute metabolic rates are lower than at higher temperatures. Warm-blooded animals compensate for cold by diminishing heat transfer to the skin, by increased insulation, and by producing more heat. A few conserve body heat by lapsing into virtual poikilothermy when asleep. Reflex control is maintained at low body temperatures in hibernation. Striking differences between seasonal or latitudinal adaptations—acclimatization—and long-term responses to laboratory cold—acclimation—have been observed in homeotherms; such differences appear less marked in poikilotherms. Individual enzymes can be adaptive—in their activation energy, in temperature of denaturation, and in total activity—in the same animal according to acclimation, in different tissues at different temperatures, as in skin and liver of some homeotherms, in different animals according to their genotype—whether poikilotherm or homeotherm, thermophile or mesophile, hibernant or nonhibernant.

At high environmental temperatures there is a close relation between thermal and water balance. Some animals conserve water and protect themselves against heat by estivation. Behavior favors the seeking of tolerable temperatures. Biochemical compensations result in metabolism which is not so intense as in low-temperature systems transferred directly to warm media. Protection against desiccation often goes with protection from heat, yet evaporative cooling is effectively used by some animals, particularly some insects and the homeotherms. In general, there are fewer adaptive protections against heat than against cold.

Thus while most animals conform to the environment with respect to their body temperature, they do have some compensatory capacity, and those animals which regulate body temperature show some internal fluctuations. Quite apart from body temperature per se, biochemical systems rely upon the balance between heat gain and loss in animals. Most heat gain is by internal production, some by absorption of solar radiation, some, rarely, by conduction. Most heat loss is by conduction and convection in water, and in air some is by radiation, but much is by vaporization.

All of the temperature compensations in both poikilotherms and homeotherms are complex and each has its limit. Hence the causes of cold and heat death are multiple and sequential for the tissues. However, better understanding of temperature death might reveal temperature compensation mechanisms. An important problem for the near future is to learn how environmental temperature can bring about changes in cellular enzymes, and the nature of nervous compensations.

Many of the adaptive responses to temperature are environmentally induced changes in individual organisms. These may be diurnal, seasonal, and latitudinal and are often associated with phases of a life cycle. In addition, many response patterns are genetically fixed, and adapted races and species occur for each type of ecological niche. Latitudinal races and species are determined by the total environment, not by temperature alone, yet experimentation has convincingly demonstrated the importance of temperature in limiting animal distribution.

Animals have many ways of detecting temperature change. First is the direct effect of temperature on cellular reactions. Nervous systems respond directly to changes in their temperature; some nerves are more sensitive than others. Many animals also have peripheral receptors which are particularly sensitive to temperature. These have not been much studied in invertebrates, but in vertebrates they signal the environmental temperature by a steady discharge, and changes in temperature by a transient modulatory response.

It is noteworthy that the temperatures for maximum growth, activity, and preference are related to environmental temperatures. "Optimal" temperatures tend to be several degrees below lethal values and on the high side of normally experienced temperatures; this may represent a compromise between maximum metabolic activity and inactivation of essential proteins. Animal temperatures are poised as high as is commensurate with a margin of safety. In birds the margin between body temperature and death is narrowest. Burton[41] points out that homeotherms have evolved mainly in regions of the world where the mean annual temperature is between $21°$ and $26°$, that with a Q_{10} of 2.5 and heat loss proportional to the gradient inside to outside, maximum stability of temperature regulation would result from a body temperature a few degrees below lethal levels. From many viewpoints, the temperature relations of poikilotherms as well as homeotherms represent a balance between dependence and regulation.

REFERENCES

1. ADOLPH, E. F., Am. J. Physiol. *166*: 62-74, 75-91, 92-103, 1951. Responses of various mammals to hypothermia.
2. ADOLPH, E. F., and RICHMOND, J., J. Appl. Physiol. *8*: 48-58, 1956. Rewarming after hibernation and artificial cooling.
3. ALEXANDER, A. J., and EWER, D. W., J. Exp. Biol. *35*: 349-359, 1958. Reactions of scorpions to temperature.
4. ALLBROOK, D. B., et al., J. Physiol. *143*: 51-52P, 1958. Temperature relations of rhinoceros.
5. AUERBACH, M., Ztschr. f. Fisch. Hilfswiss. *6*: 605-620, 1957. Role of thyroid in temperature adaptation of fish.
6. BALDWIN, W. F., and HOUSE, H. L., Canad. J. Zool. *32*: 9-15, 1954. Modification of lethal temperatures in insects.
7. BARDACH, J. E., Am. Naturalist *90*: 309-318, 1956. Thermal sensitivity of goldfish.
8. BARDACH, J. E., and BJORKLUND, R. G., Am.

* Reviews

Naturalist *91*: 233-251, 1957. Thermal sensitivity of fishes.
9. BARGETON, D., Arch. Sci. Physiol. *9*: 47-62, 1955. Acclimation of rats to cold.
9a. BARKES, D., Hydrobiol. *13*: 209-235, 1959. Thermal tolerance of warm-water malacostracan.
10. BARNES, H., and BARNES, M., Limnol. Oceanog. *3*: 29-32, 1958. Development of barnacles from different localities.
11. BARNETT, S. A., and MANLY, B. M., Proc. Roy. Soc. London, B, *151*: 87-105, 1959. Effects of low temperature on breeding of mice.
12. BARTHOLOMEW, G. A., Physiol. Zool. *29*: 26-40, 1956. Temperature relations of a macropod marsupial.
13. BARTHOLOMEW, G. A., and CADE, T. J., J. Mammal. *38*: 60-72, 1957. Temperature relations of pocket mouse.
14. BARTHOLOMEW, G. A., and DAWSON, W. R., Condor *52*: 58-60, 1952. Body temperature of nestling gulls.
15. BARTHOLOMEW, G. A., and DAWSON, W. R., Ecology *35*: 181-187, 1954. Temperature relations in mourning dove.
16. BARTHOLOMEW, G. A., and DAWSON, W. R., Ecology *35*: 466-472, 1954. Temperature regulation in young pelicans, herons, and gulls.
17. BARTHOLOMEW, G. A., and WILKE, F., J. Mammal. *37*: 327-337, 1956. Body temperature of fur seal.
18. BARTHOLOMEW, G. A., et al., Condor *59*: 145-155, 1957. Torpidity in swift, hummingbird, and poorwill.
19. BASS, D. E., and HENSCHEL, A., Physiol. Rev. *36*: 128-144, 1956. Responses of body fluid compartments to heat and cold.
20. BATTLE, H. I., Tr. Roy. Soc. Canada Ser. III, *20*: 127-143, 1926; Contr. Canad. Biol. Fish., N. S., *4*: 497-500, 1929. Failure of various tissues in relation to thermal death in fish.
21. BAUER, K., Zool. Jahrb. Abt. Allg. *65*: 267-300, 1955. Temperature receptors in *Lithobius*.
22. BEER, J. R., and RICHARDS, A. G., J. Mammal. *37*: 31-41, 1951. Hibernation, big brown bat.
23. *BELEHRADEK, J., Ann. Rev. Physiol. *19*: 59-82, 1957. Physiological aspects of heat and cold.
24. BENEDICT, F. G., Carnegie Inst. Washington, publ. 425, 539 pp., 1932. Body temperature, reptiles.
25. BENEDICT, F. G., Carnegie Inst. Washington, publ. 503, 1938, 215 pp. Vital energetics in comparative metabolism.
26. BERG, K., Hydrobiologia *5*: 331-350, 1953. Temperature and metabolism, fresh-water limpets.
27. BLAIR, J. R., and KELLER, A. D., J. Neuropath. Exp. Neurol. *5*: 240-256, 1946. Heat-regulating center in dog and cat.
28. BODENHEIMER, F. S., Zool. Jahrb. Abt. Syst. *66*: 113-151, 1934. Temperature relations, grasshoppers, bees, and ants.
29. BRETT, J. R., Publ. Ontario Fish. Res. Lab. *63*: 1-49, 1944; J. Fish. Res. Bd. Canada *9*: 265-323, 1952. Lethal temperatures of fresh-water fish and temperature tolerance of young salmon.
30. *BRETT, J. R., Quart. Rev. Biol. *31*: 75-87, 1956. Principles of thermal requirements of fish.
31. BRETT, J. R., in Investigations of Fish-Power

Problems, edited by P. A. Larkin. University of British Columbia, 1958, pp. 69-83. Implications and assessments of environmental stress.

32. BRETT, J. R., et al., Bull. Fish. Res. Bd. Canada *114*: 1-26, 1959. Effect of temperature on cruising speed of young salmon.

33. BRODY, S., University of Missouri Coll. Agriculture Research Bull. *423*: 1-43, 1948; Nineteenth Internat. Physiol. Congress, p. 234, 1953. Reactions of cattle to temperature and humidity.

34. BROWN, A. W. A., Nature *167*: 202, 1951. Thermotaxis in mosquitoes.

35. BROWN, L. A., Am. Nat. *63*: 248-264, 346-352, 443-454. Temperature relations and growth of northern and southern Cladocera.

36. BULLOCK, T. H., Biol. Rev. *30*: 311-342, 1955. Temperature adaptation in poikilothermic animals.

37. BULLOCK, T. H., Fed. Proc. *12*: 666-672, 1953. Anatomy and physiology of infra-red sense organs in facial pit of pit vipers.

38. BULLOCK, T. H., and COWLES, R. B., Science *115*: 541-543, 1952. Anatomy and physiology of infrared sense organs in facial pit of pit vipers.

39. BULLOCK, T. H., and DIECKE, F. P. J., J. Physiol. *134*: 47-87, 1956. Anatomy and physiology of infrared sense organs in facial pit of pit vipers.

40. BULLOCK, T. H., and Fox, W., Quart. J. Micr. Sci. *98*: 219-234, 1957. Anatomy and physiology of infrared sense organs in facial pit of pit vipers.

41. *BURTON, A. C., and EDHOLM, O. G., Man in a Cold Environment. London, Edward Arnold & Co., 273 pp., 1955.

42. BUXTON, P. A., Proc. Roy. Soc. London, B, *96*: 123-131, 1924. Insect life in deserts.

43. BUXTON, P. A., Animal Life in Deserts. London, Edward Arnold & Co., 1923, 176 pp.

44. CARLSON, L. D., Proc. Soc. Exp. Biol. Med. *85*: 303-305, 1954. Reflex of shivering.

45. CHAMBERS, R., and HALE, H. P., Proc. Roy. Soc. London, B, *110*: 336-352, 1932. Ice formation in amoebae.

46. CHATFIELD, P. O., and LYMAN, C. P., Am. J. Physiol. *163*: 566-574, 1950; Electroencephalog. Clin. Neurophysiol. *6*: 403-408, 1954. Circulatory and nervous changes during arousal in hibernating hamsters.

47. CHATFIELD, P. O., LYMAN, C. P., and IRVING, L., Am. J. Physiol. *172*: 639-644, 1953. Physiological adaptation to cold of leg nerves of gull.

48. CHATFIELD, P. O., et al., Am. J. Physiol. *155*: 179-185, 1948. Resistance of hamster and rat nerves to cold.

49. CHRISTOPHERSEN, J., and PRECHT, H., Biol. Centralbl. *69*: 300-323, 1951; *70*: 261-274, 1951; *71*: 585-601, 1952. Temperature adaptation of enzyme systems in yeast and bacteria.

50. CHRISTOPHERSEN, J., and THIELE, H., Kieler Milchwirtschaft Forschungsberichte *4*: 683-700, 1952. Temperature adaptation of enzyme systems in bacteria.

51. CHURCH, N. S., J. Exp. Biol. *37*: 171-185, 186-212, 1960. Heat loss and body temperatures of flying insects.

52. COCKING, A. W., Nature *180*: 661, 1957; J. Exp.

Biol. *36*: 203-226, 1959. Rate of temperature acclimation and heat death in fish.

53. COTTLE, W., and CARLSON, L. D., Am. J. Physiol. *178*: 305-308, 1954. Cold adaptation in rats.

54. COVINO, B. G., and BEAVERS, W. R., Am. J. Physiol. *191*: 153-156, 1957. Cardiovascular response to hypothermia.

55. COWLES, R. B., Science *105*: 282, 1947. Temperature of desert reptiles.

56. COWLES, R. B., Evolution *12*: 347-357, 1958. Evolution of dermal temperature regulation.

57. DAINTON, B. H., J. Exp. Biol. *31*: 165-187, 187-197, 1954. Behavior responses of slugs to temperature.

58. DALE, H. E., and BRODY, S., University of Missouri Exp. Station Bull. no. 562, 1-27, 1954; no. 608, 1-17, 1956. Environmental temperature and blood changes in cattle.

59. DAVIS, E. A., Auk *72*: 385-411, 1955. Seasonal changes in energy balance of English sparrow.

60. DAVIS, T. R. A., and MAYER, J., Am. J. Physiol. *181*: 669-674, 1955. Physiological stimulus for shivering.

61. DAWE, A. R., Am. Heart J. *59*: 78-89, 1960. Characteristics of hibernating heart.

62. DAWE, A. R., and MORRISON, P. R., Am. Heart J. *49*: 367-384, 1955. Characteristics of hibernating heart.

63. DAWSON, W. R., University of California Publ. Zool. *59*: 81-124, 1954. Temperature regulation and water requirements of towhees.

64. DAWSON, W. R., J. Mammal. *36*: 543-553, 1955. Metabolism in relation to temperature in desert rodents.

65. DAWSON, W. R., Physiol. Zool. *31*: 37-48, 1958. Temperature relations in cardinals.

66. DAWSON, W. R., and BARTHOLOMEW, G. A., Physiol. Zool. *29*: 40-51, 1956; *31*: 100-111, 1958; *33*: 87-103, 1960. Physiological responses of lizards to temperature.

67. DAWSON, W. R., and EVANS, F. C., Physiol. Zool. *31*: 315-327, 1958. Development of homeothermy in sparrows.

68. DAWSON, W. R., and TORDOFF, H. B., Condor *61*: 388-396, 1959. O_2 consumption in relation to temperature, evening grosbeaks.

69. DEANE, H. W., and LYMAN, C. P., Endocrinology, *55*: 300-315, 1954. Hormones in relation to hibernation.

70. DEHNEL, P. A., Physiol. Zool. *28*: 115-144, 1955; Biol. Bull. *110*: 43-53, 1956. Rate of growth of snails and *Mytilus* as function of latitude and intertidal level.

71. DEPOCAS, F., Canad. J. Biochem. Physiol. *36*: 691-699, 1958. Chemical thermogenesis in rats.

72. DEPOCAS, F., HART, J. S., and HEROUX, O., J. Appl. Physiol. *10*: 393-397, 1957. Heat and cold acclimation in rats.

73. DESMARAIS, A., Rev. Canad. Biol. *16*: 189-248, 1957. Ascorbic acid in relation to cold resistance.

74. DIJKGRAAF, S., Ztschr. vergl. Physiol. *27*: 587-605, 1940. Temperature sense in fish.

75. DODT, E., Pflüg. Arch. Physiol. *263*: 188-200, 1956. Mode of stimulation, temperature receptors, mammals.

76. DODT, E., and ZOTTERMAN, Y., Acta physiol. scand. *26*: 345-357, 1952. Mode of stimulation, temperature receptors, mammals.

77. DOTTERWEICH, H., Zool. Jahrb. Abt. allg. *44*: 399-425, 1928. Warming-up of butterflies for flight.

78. DOUDOROFF, P., Biol. Bull. *75*: 494-509, 1934; *88*: 194-206, 1945. Thermotaxis and thermal resistance of fish.

79. EDNEY, E. B., J. Exp. Biol. *28*: 271-280, 1950; *30*: 331-349, 1953; Nature *170*: 586-587, 1952. Temperature relations of wood lice.

80. *EDNEY, E. B., Biol. Rev. *29*: 185-219, 1954. Temperature relations of arthropods.

81. *EDNEY, E. B., Water Relations of Terrestrial Arthropods. Cambridge University Press, 1957, 108 pp.

82. EDWARDS, D. K., Canad. J. Zool. *36*: 363-382, 1958. Acclimation and metabolism at different temperatures in *Tribolium*.

83. EDWARDS, G. A., and GONZALES, M. D., Acta Physiol. Latinoamerica *4*: 121-132, 1954. Seasonal metabolism, tropical insects.

84. EDWARDS, G. A., and NUTTING, W. L., Psyche *57*: 33-44, 1950. Metabolism of firebrat and snow cricket.

85. EDWARDS, H. T., and DILL, D. B., J. Cell. Comp. Physiol. *6*: 21-35, 37-42, 1935. Temperature effect on blood of gila monster and chuckwalla.

86. EISENTRAUT, M., Biol. Zentbl. *60*: 199-209, 1940; Ztschr. Säugetierkunde *21*: 49-52, 1956. Body temperature of lower mammals.

87. EKBERG, D. R., Biol. Bull. *114*: 308-316, 1958. Temperature acclimation and tissue metabolism, goldfish.

88. ENGER, P. S., Acta physiol. scand. *40*: 161-166, 1957. Temperature relations of tropical mammals and birds.

89. ERIKSON, H., Acta physiol. scand. *36*: 75-78, 1956. Body temperature, arctic ground squirrels.

90. ERIKSON, H., et al., Acta physiol. scand. *37*: 35-39, 1956. Critical temperature in naked man.

91. FARNER, D. S., J. Appl. Physiol. *8*: 546-548, 1956. Body temperature of small petrel.

92. FAWCETT, D. W., and LYMAN, C. P., J. Physiol. *126*: 235-237, 1954. Composition of body fat of hibernants in relation to temperature.

93. *FISHER, K. C., in Physiological Adaptation, edited by C. L. Prosser. Washington, American Physiological Society, 1959, pp. 3-49. Adaptation to temperature in fish and small mammals.

94. FITCH, H. S., Publ., University of Kansas Museum *8*: 417-476, 1956. Temperature selection by amphibians and reptiles.

95. FLEISCHNER, J. R., and SARGENT, F., Am. J. Physiol. *14*: 789-797, 1959. Crossed sensitization of rats to heat and cold.

96. FOLK, G. E., Am. Nat. *91*: 153-166, 1957. Body rhythms of mammals in the cold.

97. Fox, H. M., Proc. Zool. Soc. London *A, 106*: 945-955, 1936; *A, 109*: 141-156, 1939. Activity and metabolism of poikilotherms from different latitudes.

98. Fox, H. M., and WINGFIELD, C. A., Proc. Zool. Soc. London, *A, 107*: 275-282, 1937. Activity of Pandalus from different latitudes.

98a. FRAENKEL, G., Biol. Zentbl. *49*: 657-680, 1929. Orientation of desert insects.

99. *FRAENKEL, G., and GUNN, D. L., The Orientation of Animals. Oxford, Clarendon Press, 1940, Chapter 14. Temperature reactions.

100. FRAENKEL, G., and HOPF, H. S., Biochem. J. *34*: 1085-1092, 1940. Temperature adaptation and saturation of phosphatides, blowfly larvae.

101. FREEMAN, J. A., Biol. Bull. *99*: 416-424, 1950. Brain metabolism, temperature adaptation, fish.

102. *FRY, F. E. J., Publ. Ontario Fish. Res. Lab. *68*: 1-62, 1947. Theory of temperature adaptation.

103. *FRY, F. E. J., Annales Biol. *33*: 205-219, 1956. Lethal temperature as a tool in taxonomy.

104. *FRY, F. E. J., Ann. Rev. Physiol. *20*: 207-224, 1958. Temperature compensation.

105. FRY, F. E. J., and HART, J. S., J. Fish. Res. Bd. Canada *7*: 169-175, 1949. Cruising speed of goldfish in relation to temperature.

106. FRY, F. E. J., et al., Rev. Canad. Biol. *1*: 50-56, 1942; Publ. Ontario Fish. Res. Lab. *66*: 1-35, 1946. Lethal temperatures of fish in relation to acclimation.

107. GARSIDE, E. T., and TAIT, J. S., Canad. J. Zool. *36*: 563-567, 1958. Selected temperatures in rainbow trout.

108. GEBBHARDT, H., Experientia *7*: 302-303, 1951; Zool. Jahrb. Abt. allg. *63*: 558-592, 1953. Localization of temperature receptors in insects.

109. GELINEO, S., C. R. Soc. Biol. *116*: 672-674, 1934; *127*: 1357, 1938; *147*: 138-140, Arch. Sci. Biol. Belgrade *6*: 235-248, 1954. Thermogenesis, development of homeothermy, and blood changes in hibernating and nonhibernating mammals at different temperatures in relation to acclimation.

110. GELINEO, S., Arch. Sci. Physiol. *9*: 225-243, 1955. Temperature relations of small birds.

111. GIBSON, E. S., and FRY, F. E. J., Canad. J. Zool. *32*: 252-260, 1954. Cruising speeds of lake trout at different temperatures.

112. GRAHAM, W. M., Animal Behaviour *6*: 231-237, 1958. Thermal preference of *Tribolium*.

113. GRAINGER, J. N. R., Nature *178*: 930, 1956; pp. 79-90 in Physiological Adaptation, edited by C. L. Prosser, 1958, Washington, Amer. Physiological Society. The initial metabolic responses to temperature change in poikilotherms.

114. GRANT, W. C., Anat. Rec. *117*: 561, 1953. Temperature tolerance in earthworms.

115. *GUNN, D. L., Biol. Rev. *17*: 293-314, 1942. Review, body temperature of poikilotherms.

116. GUTHRIE, F. E., and DECKER, G. C., J. Econ. Ent. *47*: 882-887, 1954. Effect of humidity on heat death of chinch bugs.

116a. HAFEZ, M., J. Exp. Zool. *124*: 199-229, 1953. Thermal selection, housefly larvae.

117. HALL, F. G., and ROOT, R. W., Biol. Bull. *58*: 52-58, 1930. Thermal and water balance, amphibians and reptiles.

118. HALSBAND, E., Ztschr. f. Fisch. Hilfsswiss. *2*: 228-270, 1953. Internal temperature, fish.

119. HAMMEL, H. T., Am. J. Physiol. *182*: 369-376, 1955. Thermal properties of fur.

120. HANNON, J. P., and VAUGHAN, D. A., Am. J. Physiol. *198*: 375-380, 1960. Glycolytic enzymes in cold-acclimated rats.

121. HART, J. S., Publ. Ontario Fish. Res. Lab. *72*:

1-79, 1952. Lethal temperatures of fish from different latitudes.

122. HART, J. S., Canad. J. Zool. *31*: 80-98, 112-116, 1953. Relation between thermal history and cold resistance in rodents.

123. HART, J. S., Canad. J. Zool. *34*: 53-57, 1956. Seasonal changes in insulation, mammals.

124. HART, J. S., and HEROUX, O., Canad. J. Biochem. Physiol. *33*: 428-435, 1955; Canad. J. Zool. *31*: 528-534, 1953. Exercise and temperature regulation, lemmings and rabbits; seasonal changes in insulation, mammals.

125. *HART, J. S., Rev. Canad. Biol. *16*: 133-174, 1957. Climatic and temperature-induced changes in energetics of homeotherms.

126. HAUGAARD, N., and IRVING, L., J. Cell. Comp. Physiol. *21*: 19-26, 1943. Winter and summer metabolism in tautogs.

127. HAZELHOFF, E. H., Physiol. Comp. Oecol. *3*: 343-364, 1954. Temperature control in beehives.

128. HENSEL, H., Pflüg. Arch. Physiol. *256*: 195-211, 1952. Electrophysiological studies of heat and cold receptors of mammals.

129. HENSEL, H., Experientia *11*: 325-327, 1955; Ztschr. vergl. Physiol. *37*: 509-526, 1955; Pflüg. Arch. Physiol. *263*: 48-53, 1956. Temperature reception by ampullae of Lorenzini in elasmobranchs.

130. HENSEL, H., STROM, L., and ZOTTERMAN, Y., J. Neurophysiol. *14*: 423-429, 1951. Electrophysiological studies of heat and cold receptors of mammals.

131. HENSEL, H., and ZOTTERMAN, Y., Acta physiol. scand. *22*: 96-105, 106-113, 1950; *23*: 291-319, 1951; J. Physiol. *115*: 16-24, 1951; J. Neurophysiol. *14*: 377-385, 1951. Electrophysiological studies of heat and cold receptors of mammals.

132. HERAN, H., Ztschr. vergl. Physiol. *34*: 179-206, 1952. Temperature sense of honeybees.

133. HEROUX, O., Canad. J. Biochem. Physiol. *37*: 1247-1253, 1254-1270, 1959. Laboratory acclimation and seasonal acclimatization to cold in relation to metabolism, insulation, and skin vascularity in white rats.

134. HEROUX, O., and CAMPBELL, J. S., Canad. J. Biochem. Physiol. *37*: 1263-1269, 1959. Laboratory acclimation and seasonal acclimatization to cold in white rats.

135. HEROUX, O., DEPOCAS, F., and HART, J. S., Canad. J. Biochem. Physiol. *37*: 473-478, 1959. Laboratory acclimation and seasonal acclimatization to cold in relation to metabolism and insulation in white rats.

136. HEROUX, O., HART, J. S., and DEPOCAS, F., J. Appl. Physiol. *9*: 399-403, 1956. Laboratory acclimation to cold in relation to metabolism in white rats.

137. HEROUX, O., and ST. PIERRE, J., Am. J. Physiol. *188*: 163-168, 1957. Laboratory acclimation to cold in relation to skin vascularity in white rats.

138. HERTER, K., Biol. Zentbl. *43*: 282-285, 1923; Ztschr. vergl. Physiol. *1*: 221-288, 1924. Temperature sense, insects.

139. *HERTER, K., Handbuch der Zool. *8*: Heft 4, 1-60, 1956. Review on hiberation.

140. HIESTAND, W. A., *et al.,* Physiol. Zool. *23*: 264-

268, 1950. Resistance to hypoxia in hibernators and nonhibernators.

141. HIGGINBOTHAM, A. C., and KOON, W. E., Am. J. Physiol. *181*: 69-71, 1955. Temperature regulation in opossum.

142. HIRVONEN, L., Acta physiol. scand. *36*: 38-46, 1956. Temperature range for heart of hibernants and nonhibernants.

143. HOAR, W. S., and COTTLE, M. K., Canad. J. Zool. *30*: 41-48, 49-54, 1952. Relation of dietary fat and tissue fat to temperature tolerance, goldfish.

144. HOAR, W. S., and ROBERTSON, G. B., Canad. J. Zool. *37*: 419-428, 1959. Effect of photoperiod on temperature resistance in goldfish.

145. HOCK, R. J., Biol. Bull. *101*: 289-299, 1951. Metabolic rate and body temperature of bats.

146. HOCK, R. J., Proc. Second Alaska Science Conference, A. A. A. S., pp. 310-312, 1951; Fed. Proc. *16*: 440, 1957. Temperature and metabolism of bears.

147. HOCK, R. J., Josiah Macy, Jr., Conference on Cold Injury, 1958, pp. 61-133. Hibernation.

148. HOFFMAN, U., Dissertation, Kiel University, 1952. Temperature adaptation of enzymes of *Streptococcus.*

149. HOPKINS, H. S., J. Exp. Zool. *102*: 143-148, 1946. Temperature adaptation, clam gills.

150. HORSTADIUS, S., Biol. Generalis *1*: 522-536, 1925. Temperature and rate of development, sea urchin eggs.

151. HOUSE, H. L., *et al.,* Canad. J. Zool. *36*: 629-632, 1958. Thermal conditioning and diet, temperature resistance of insects.

152. HSIEH, A. C. L., and CARLSON, L. D., Am. J. Physiol. *188*: 40-44, 1957. Effect of thyroid on metabolic responses to cold, rats.

153. IRVINE, D. G., NEWMAN, K., and HOAR, W. S., Canad. J. Zool. *35*: 691-709, 1957. Effects of diet on temperature resistance of goldfish.

154. IRVING, L., J. Appl. Physiol. *9*: 414-420, 1956. Physiological insulation in bare-skinned swine.

155. IRVING, L., and HART, J. S., Canad. J. Zool. *35*: 497-511, 1957. Metabolism and insulation of seals in water and air.

156. IRVING, L., and KROG, H., J. Appl. Physiol. *7*: 355-364, 1955. Insulation and metabolism of arctic animals in winter and summer.

157. IRVING, L., KROG, H., and MONSON, M., Physiol. Zool. *28*: 173-185, 1955. Insulation and metabolism of arctic mammals in winter and summer.

158. IRVING, L., SCHMIDT-NIELSEN, K., and ABRAHAMSEN, N. S., Physiol. Zool. *30*: 93-105, 1957. Melting points of animal fats in cold climates.

159. JAEGER, E. C., Condor *51*: 105-109, 1949. Hibernation of poorwill.

160. JENNINGS, H. S., Carnegie Inst., Washington, publ. 16, pp. 1-28, 1904. Reactions of ciliates to heat and cold.

161. JOHANSEN, K., and KROG, J., Am. J. Physiol. *196*: 1200-1204, 1959. Body temperature and hibernation, birchmouse, Sicista.

162. JOHNSON, D. S., J. Animal Ecol. *21*: 118-119, 1952. Thermal race, Daphnia.

163. JOHNSON, F. A., EYRING, H., and POLISSAR,

M. J., Kinetic Basis of Molecular Biology. New York, John Wiley & Sons, 1954, 874 pp.

164. JOHNSON, H. D., et al., University of Missouri Coll. of Agriculture Research Bull. 683: 1-31, 1958. Temperature tolerance of breeds of cattle.

165. KANUNGO, M., and PROSSER, C. L., J. Cell. Comp. Physiol. 54: 259-263, 265-274, 1960. Biochemical changes in temperature acclimation, goldfish tissues.

166. KANWISHER, J. W., Biol. Bull. 109: 56-63, 1955; 113: 275-285, 1957; 116: 258-264, 1959. Amount of frozen water, histology, and metabolism of tissues of frozen intertidal animals and plants.

167. *KAYSER, C., Biol. Rev. 25: 255-282, 1950. Review on hibernation.

168. KAYSER, C., Ann. Biol. 57: 109-150, 1953. Metabolism of hibernants.

169. KAYSER, C., Rietsch, M. L., and LUCOT, M. A., Arch. Sci. Physiol. 8: 155-193, 1954. Metabolism of hibernants.

170. *KAYSER, C., Rev. Canad. Biol. 16: 303-389, 1957; Ann. Rev. Physiol. 19: 83-120, 1957. Hibernation, hypothermia.

171. KENDEIGH, S. C., J. Exp. Zool. 82: 419-438, 1939. Development of temperature control, wren.

172. KENDEIGH, S. C., J. Exp. Zool. 96: 1-16, 1944. Effect of temperature on metabolism, English sparrow.

173. KERKUT, G. A., and TAYLOR, B. J. R., Nature 178: 426, 1956; J. Exp. Biol. 34: 486-493, 1957; Behaviour 13: 259-279, 1958. Temperature stimulation of isolated ganglia and tarsal receptors, cockroach; ganglionic responses, slug and crayfish.

174. KIRBERGER, C., Ztschr. vergl. Physiol. 35: 175-198, 1953. Metabolic adaptations to temperature, earthworms.

175. KIRBERGER, C., Ztschr. vergl. Physiol. 35: 153-158, 1953. Temperature changes in O_2-binding by blood, Rana.

176. KOFFLER, H., Proc. Nat. Acad. Sci. 43: 464-477, 1957; Bacteriol. Rev. 21: 227-240, 1957. Enzymes of thermal bacteria.

177. KOIDSUMI, K., Mem. Fac. Sci. Agric. Taihoku 12: 281-380, 1935. Quoted in 115. Temperature relations of grasshopper.

178. KROG, H., and MONSON, M., Am. J. Physiol. 178: 515-516, 1954. Critical temperature of mountain goat.

179. KROG, J., Biol. Bull. 107: 397-410, 1954. Seasonal changes in temperature sensitivity of fresh-water Gammarus.

180. LADELL, U. S., J. Physiol. 135: 52P-53P, 1957. Effect of heat on native Africans.

181. LANDAU, B. R., and DAWE, A. R., Am. J. Physiol. 194: 75-82, 1958. Metabolism of hibernating Citellus.

182. *LEVITT, J., Protoplasmatologia 8: 1-87, 1958. Frost, drought, and heat resistance.

183. LINDAUER, M., Ztschr. vergl. Physiol. 36: 391-432, 1954. Temperature regulation in beehive.

184. LOOSANOFF, V. L., and NOMEJKO, C. A., Biol. Bull. 101: 151-156, 1951; 103: 80-96, 1952. Physiological races of oysters.

185. LOVELOCK, J. E., Biochim. Biophys. Acta 10: 414-426, 1953; 11: 28-36, 1953; Biochem. J.

58: 618-622, 1953; Proc. Roy. Soc. London, B, 147: 427-433, 1957. Mechanism of damage by freezing; protection by glycerol; mammalian tissues, red cells and sperm.

186. LOVELOCK, J. E., and SMITH, A. U., Proc. Roy. Soc. London, B, 145: 427-442, 1956. Mechanism of damage by freezing; protection by glycerol; mammalian tissues, red cells, and sperm.

187. *LUYET, B., and GEHENIO, P. M., Biodynamica Monograph 1: 1-341, 1940; Biodynamica 6: 141-149, 1947. Life and death at low temperature; survival of animals after freezing in liquid air.

188. LYMAN, C. P., J. Exp. Zool. 109: 55-78, 1948; Am. J. Physiol. 167: 638-643, 1951; J. Mammal. 35: 545-552, 1954. Preparation for and arousal from hibernation; changes in blood and tissue chemistry in hibernation, hamsters and ground squirrels.

189. LYMAN, C. P., Am. J. Physiol. 194: 83-91, 1958. Metabolism and heart rate of woodchucks entering hibernation.

190. LYMAN, C. P., and DAWE, A. R., eds., Mammalian hibernation, Bull. Mus. Comp. Zool. Harvard, 124: 1-549, 1960.

191. LYMAN, C. P., and BLINKS, D. C., J. Cell. Comp. Physiol. 54: 53-63, 1959. Effect of temperature on isolated hearts, hibernators and nonhibernators.

192. LYMAN, C. P., and CHATFIELD, P. O., J. Exp. Zool. 114: 491-515, 1950. Arousal in hibernating hamsters.

193. *LYMAN, C. P., and CHATFIELD, P. O., Physiol. Rev. 35: 403-425, 1955. Physiology of hibernation in mammals.

194. LYMAN, C. P., and HASTINGS, A. B., Am. J. Physiol. 157: 633-637, 1951. Blood chemistry in hibernating hamsters and ground squirrels.

195. LYMAN, C. P., and LEDUC, E. H., J. Cell. Comp. Physiol. 41: 471-488, 1953. Preparation for and arousal from hibernation; changes in blood and tissue chemistry in hibernation, hamsters.

196. LYNCH, H. F., and ADOLPH, E. F., J. Appl. Physiol. 11: 192-196, 1957. Blood flow in hypothermia.

197. MARSH, C., and MILITZER, W., Arch. Biochem. Biophys. 36: 269-275, 1952. Malic dehydrogenase from thermophilic bacteria.

198. MARZUSCH, K., Ztschr. vergl. Physiol. 34: 75-92, 1952. Metabolic acclimation to temperature; beetles.

199. MAYER, H. E., Carnegie Inst. Washington. Tortugas Papers 6: 1-24, 1914. Temperature tolerance, tropical marine poikilotherms.

200. McCAULEY, R. W., Canad. J. Zool. 36: 655-662, 1958. Thermal relations of geographic races, Salvelinus.

201. McCRUM, W. R., J. Comp. Neurol. 98: 233-281, 1953. Location of temperature-regulating center in hypothalamus.

202. McINTYRE, D. G., and EDERSTROM, H. E., Am. J. Physiol. 194: 293-296, 1958. Development of homeothermy in dogs.

203. McLEESE, D. W., J. Fish. Res. Bd. Canad. 13: 247-272, 1956. Effect of temperature salinity and oxygen on survival of lobsters.

204. MELLANBY, K., J. Exp. Biol. *18:* 55-61, 1942. Body temperature, frogs.

205. MELLANBY, K., Nature *181:* 1403, 1958. Water content and sensitivity of insects to heat.

206. MERRYMAN, H. T., Science *124:* 515-521, 1956. Mechanics of freezing in living cells and tissues.

207. MEUWIS, A. L., and HEUTS, M. J., Biol. Bull. *112:* 98-107, 1957. Temperature dependence of breathing rate in carp.

208. MEW, H. H., Ztschr, vergl. Physiol. *40:* 345-362, 1957. Protease adaptations in *Helix;* temperature adaptation of proteolytic enzymes of frogs.

208a. MILTON, A. S., J. Physiol. *142:* 25P, 1958. Temperature effects on choline acetylase from fish and mammal.

209. *MITCHELL, H. H., and EDMAN, M., Nutrition and Climatic Stress with Particular Reference to Man. Springfield, Ill., Charles C Thomas, 235 pp., 1951.

210. MOORE, J. A., *in* Patterns of Evolution, edited by G. L. Jepson, E. Mayr, and G. G. Simpson. Princeton University Press, 1949, Chap. 17. Evolution *3:* 1-21, 1949; Am. Naturalist *84:* 247-254, 1950. Geographic differences in *Rana pipiens* with respect to effect of temperature on development.

211. MOORE, J. A., Am. Naturalist *86:* 5-22, 1952. Breeding differences of populations of Australian frogs.

212. MORAN, T., Proc. Roy. Soc. London, B, *105:* 177-197, 1929. Critical temperature of freezing in frog muscle.

213. MORRISON, P. R., and RYSER, F. A., Fed. Proc. *10:* 93, 1951; *12:* 100, 1953; Science *116:* 231-232, 1952. Temperature and metabolism of small mammals.

214. MORRISON, P. R., J. Cell. Comp. Physiol. *27:* 125-137, 1946; Biol. Bull. *116:* 484-497, 1959. Temperature relations of marsupials and bats.

215. MORRISON, P. R., *et al.,* J. Mammal. *35:* 376-386, 1954. Development of homeothermy in tundra vole.

216. MORROW, J. E., and MAURO, A., Copeia, pp. 108-116, 1950. Body temperature, large marine fish.

217. MOUNT, L. E., Nature *182:* 536, 1958. Temperature of newborn pig.

218. MURRAY, R. W., Nature *176:* 698-699, 1955; J. Exp. Biol. *33:* 798-805, 1956. Thermal responses of ampullae of Lorenzini, *Raja,* and of lateralis organ, *Xenopus.*

219. NARDONE, R. M., Am. J. Physiol. *182:* 364-368, 1955. Electrocardiogram of ground squirrel in hibernation.

220. NECHELES, H., Pflüg. Arch. Physiol. *204:* 72-93, 1924. Temperature relations, cockroaches.

221. OHSAWA, W., and TSUKUDA, H., J. Inst. Polytech. Osaka Univ., D, *7:* 173-187, 189-196, 1956. Seasonal variations in responsiveness of snails.

222. ORR, P. R., Physiol. Zool. *28:* 290-302, 1955. Heat death of whole animals and tissues, various animals.

223. ORR, R. T., Proc. California Acad. Sci. *28:* 165-246, 1954. Torpidity in bats.

224. PANAGOS, S., *et al.,* Biochim. Biophys. Acta *29:* 204-205, 1958. Phosphorylation in mitochondria from cold-acclimated rats.

225. PARRY, D. A., J. Exp. Biol. *28:* 445-562, 1951. Temperature of arthropods in sunlight.

226. PEARSON, O. P., Copeia, pp. 111-116, 1954. Habits of a lizard.

227. PIESS, C. N., and FIELD, J., Biol. Bull. *99:* 213-224, 1950. Tissue metabolism of fish from different latitudes.

228. PEPPER, J. H., and HASTINGS, E., Ecology *33:* 96-103, 1952. Effect of solar radiation on temperature of grasshoppers.

229. PERTTUNEN, V., and LAGERSPETZ, K., Arch. Soc. Zool. Bot. Fennicae Vanamo *11:* 65-70, 1956. Temperature acclimation of heart and muscle in Dipteran *Corethra.*

230. PETAJAN, J. H., and MORRISON, P. R., Physiologist *1:* 60, 1958. Development of homeothermy in opossums.

231. PITT, T. K., *et al.,* Canad. J. Zool. *34:* 555-557, 1956. Temperature selection by carp.

232. POPOVIC, V., Arch. Sci. Physiol. *11:* 29-36, 1957. Heat production by hibernating *Citellus.*

233. PRECHT, H., *in* Physiological Adaptation, edited by C. L. Prosser. Washington, American Physiological Society, 1958, pp. 50-78. Patterns of temperature adaptation.

234. PRECHT, H., CHRISTOPHERSEN, J., and HENSEL, H., Temperatur und Leben 1955. Berlin, Springer-Verlag, 514 pp.

235. PROSSER, C. L., *in* Physiological Adaptation, edited by C. L. Prosser. Washington, American Physiological Society, 1958, pp. 167-180.

236. RAO, K. P., Biol. Bull. *106:* 353-359, 1954; *104:* 171-181, 1953. Pumping rates of *Mytilus* from different latitudes.

237. RAO, K. P., and BULLOCK, T. H., Am. Naturalist *88:* 33-44, 1954. Q_{10} as function of body size and habitat temperature.

238. RIECK, A. F., *et al.,* Proc. Soc. Exp. Biol. Med. *103:* 436-439, 1960. O_2 consumption by temperature acclimated amphibians.

239. RIEDESEL, M. L., Tr. Kansas Acad. Sci. *60:* 99-141, 1957. Serum magnesium in hibernants.

240. RIEDESEL, M. L., and FOLK, G. E., Nature *177:* 668, 1956. Serum magnesium in hibernants.

241. ROBERTS, J. L., Physiol. Zool. *30:* 232-255, 1957. Thermal acclimation of metabolism in crab *Pachygrapsus.*

242. ROBINSON, K. W., and MORRISON, P. R., J. Cell. Comp. Physiol. *49:* 455-478, 1957. Reactions of lower mammals to heat.

243. ROHMER, F., HIEBEL, G., and KAYSER, C., C. R. Soc. Biol. *145:* 747-752, 1951. Electroencephalograms and cardiograms of hibernating mammals.

244. RUCKER, F., Ztschr. vergl. Physiol. *21:* 275-280, 1934. Infrared reflection, insects.

245. SALT, R. W., Canad. J. Zool. *34:* 1-5, 283-294, 391-403, 1956. Ice formation and supercooling in insects.

246. SALT, R. W., Proc. 10th Internat. Entomol. Cong. *2:* 73-78, 1956; Canad. J. Zool. *37:* 59-69, 1959. Supercooling; role of glycerol in lowering freezing point of cold-hardy insects.

247. SCHLIEPER, C. R., Verh. Deutsch. Zool. Ges,

267-272, 1952. Temperature-metabolism relations in aquatic animals.

248. SCHLIEPER, C. R., et al., Zool. Anz. *149*: 163-169, 1952; Biol. Zentbl. *71*: 449-461, 1952. Temperature-metabolism relations in planarians.

249. SCHLIEPER, C. R., et al., Kieler Meeresforsch. *14*: 3-10, 1958. Interrelation between temperature and salinity effects on bivalve molluscs.

250. SCHMIDT-NIELSEN, K., in The Biology of Deserts, edited by J. L. Cloudsley-Thompson. London Institute of Biology, 1954, pp. 184-187. Heat regulation in desert mammals.

251. SCHMIDT-NIELSEN, K., et al., Am. J. Physiol. *188*: 103-112, 1957. Temperature and water relations of camels.

252. SCHNEIRLA, T. C., et al., Ecol. Monog. *24*: 269-296, 1954. Temperature of termite bivouacs.

253. SCHOLANDER, P. F., Evolution *9*: 15-26, 1955. Evolution of climatic adaptation in homeotherms.

254. SCHOLANDER, P. F., and KROG, J., J. Appl. Physiol. *10*: 404-411, 1957. Countercurrent and vascular heat exchange; sloths.

255. SCHOLANDER, P. F., and SCHEVILL, W. E., J. Appl. Physiol. *8*: 279-282, 1955. Countercurrent and vascular heat exchange; whales.

256. SCHOLANDER, P. F., et al., Biol. Bull., *99*: 259-321, 1950. Metabolic reactions of arctic homeotherms to temperature stress.

257. SCHOLANDER, P. F., et al., Physiol. Zool. *26*: 67-92, 1953; J. Cell. Comp. Physiol. *42* suppl. 1: 1-56, 1953. Climatic adaptations in arctic and tropical poikilotherms (plants and animals).

258. SCHOLANDER, P. F., et al., J. Cell. Comp. Physiol. *49*: 5-24, 1957. Supercooling and osmoregulation in arctic fish.

259. SCHOLANDER, P. F., et al., J. Appl. Physiol. *10*: 231-234, 1957; *13*: 211-218, 1958; Fed. Proc. *17*: 1054, 1958. Reactions to cold in Lapps, Norwegians, and Australian aborigines.

260. SEALANDER, J., Am. Mid. Nat. *46*: 257-311, 1951; Ecology *33*: 63-71, 1952; Biol. Bull. *104*: 87-99, 1953. Body temperature, behavior, insulation of small mammals in the cold.

261. SEGAL, E., et al., Nature *172*: 1108, 1953; Biol. Bull. *111*: 129-152, 1956. Temperature adaptations of heart rate, intertidal molluscs.

262. SELLERS, E. A., et al., Am. J. Physiol. *163*: 81-91, 1950; *165*: 481-485, 1951; *167*: 644-655, 1951; *177*: 372-376, 1954. Acclimation to cold in rats; effects of various treatments on metabolism and tissue enzymes.

263. SHELFORD, V. E., and POWERS, E. B., Biol. Bull. *28*: 315-334, 1915. Reactions of fish in thermal gradients.

264. SLATER, J. V., Am. Naturalist *88*: 168-171, 1954. Temperature tolerance in *Tetrahymena*.

265. SLIFER, E. H., Proc. Roy. Soc. London, B, *138*: 414-437, 1952. Thermoreceptors in *Locusta*.

266. SMITH, A. U., Proc. Roy. Soc. London, B, *145*: 391-426, 1956; Nature *182*: 911-913, 1958. Cooling of hamsters to below 0° C.; revival.

267. SMITH, C. L., J. Exp. Biol. *28*: 141-164, 1951. Temperature-pulse rate of isolated frog heart.

268. SMITH, D. E., et al., Experientia *10*: 218, 1954; Proc. Soc. Exp. Biol. Med. *86*: 473-475, 1954. Prolonged clotting of blood of dormant bat.

269. SMITH, R. E., and FAIRHURST, A. S., Proc. Nat. Acad. Sci. *44*: 705-711, 1958. Oxidative phosphorylation by mitochondria from cold-acclimated rats.

270. SOUTH, F. E., Physiol. Zool. *31*: 6-15, 1958; Am. J. Physiol. *198*: 463-466, 1960. Enzymatic patterns of tissues from hibernant and non-hibernant mammals.

271. SPARCK, R., K. Danske Vidensk. Selsk. Skr. Biol. Med. *13*: 1-27, 1936. Metabolism of lamellibranchs from different latitudes.

272. STAUBER, L. A., Ecology *31*: 107-118, 1950. Physiological races of oysters and oyster drills.

273. STEEN, J., Acta physiol. scand. *39*: 22-26, 1957. Temperature acclimation and metabolism in pigeons.

274. STEINBACH, H. B., J. Cell. Comp. Physiol. *33*: 123-131, 1949. Temperature characteristics of muscle apyrase.

275. STRAUB, M., Ztschr. vergl. Physiol. *39*: 507-523, 1957. Changes in oxygen dissociation curves of blood with temperature adaptation.

276. STREICHER, E., et al., Am. J. Physiol. *161*: 300-306, 1950. Survival of pigeons and ducks in cold.

277. STRÖM, G., Acta physiol. scand. *21* suppl. 20: 47-76, 1950. Effects of local thermal stimulation of hypothalamus, cat.

278. STRUMWASSER, F., Am. J. Physiol. *196*: 8-30, 1959. Electrical activity of brain and temperature of brain in hibernation, *Citellus*.

279. SUHRMANN, R., Biol. Zentbl. *74*: 432-448, 1955. Thyroid in relation to temperature acclimation in fish.

280. SULLIVAN, C. M., J. Fish. Res. Bd. Canada *11*: 153-170, 1954. Temperature detection and response in fish.

281. SUMNER, F. B., and LANHAM, U. N., Biol. Bull. *82*: 313-327, 1942. Metabolism and tolerance of fish from warm and cold springs.

282. SUMNER, F. B., and SARGENT, M. C., Ecology *21*: 45-54, 1940. Metabolism and tolerance of fish from warm and cold springs.

283. SUOMALAINEN, P., and PETRI, E., Experientia *8*: 435-436, 1952. Effect of pancreas and insulin on hibernation, hedgehog.

284. SVIHLA, A., et al., Science *14*: 298-299, 1951; *15*: 306-307, 1952; Am. J. Physiol. *172*: 681-683, 1953. Clotting delay and other blood changes in hibernation, ground squirrels.

285. TASHIAN, R. E., Zoologica *41*: 39-47, 1956. Geographic variation, tropical and temperate *Uca*.

286. TASHIAN, R. E., and RAY, C., Zoologica *42*: 63-68, 1957. Metabolism of tropical and arctic amphibians.

287. TAYLOR, C. V., et al., Physiol. Zool. *9*: 15-26, 1936. Effects of high temperatures on cysts of *Colpoda*.

288. TEMPLETON, J. R., Physiol. Zool. *33*: 136-145, 1960. Respiration and water loss at high temperatures, desert iguana.

289. THIBAULT, O., Rev. Canad. Biol. *8*: 3-131, 1949. Endocrines and temperature acclimation, rats.

290. THOMSEN, E., and THOMSEN, M., Ztschr. vergl.

Physiol. *24*: 343-380, 1937. Temperature selection by fly larvae.

291. THORSON, G., Verh. Deutsch. Ges. Wilhelmshaven *45*: 276-327, 1951. Distribution of invertebrate larvae in ocean at different latitudes.

292. *UVAROV, B. P., Tr. Entomolog. Soc. London *79*: 1-247, 1931. Insects and climate.

293. VAN UTRECHT, W. L., Zool. Anz. *161*: 77-82, 1958. Heat exchange in peripheral circulation of whale.

294. VERNBERG, F. J., Physiol. Zool. *25*: 243-249, 1952. Seasonal variation in O_2 consumption of salamanders.

295. VERNBERG, F. J., Biol. Bull. *117*: 163-184, 582-593, 1959. Physiological variation between tropical and temperate zone fiddler crabs.

296. VOLPE, E. P., Evolution *6*: 393-406, 1952; Physiol. Zool. *26*: 344-354, 1953; Am. Naturalist *89*: 303-317, 1955; Physiol. Zool. *30*: 164-176, 1957. Temperature tolerance and rates of development of different species and races of *Bufo*.

297. VOLPE, E. P., Am. Naturalist *91*: 303-309, 1957; Tulane Stud. Zool. *1*: 110-123, 1954. Temperature tolerance and development of races and hybrids of *Rana pipiens*.

298. WALLGREN, H., Acta Zool. Fennica *84*: 1-110, 1954. Metabolism of buntings as function of temperature and distribution.

299. WEBB, P., and VEGHTE, J. H., Physiologist *1*: 84, 1958. Upper limits of rectal temperature in man.

300. WEESE, A. O., Biol. Bull. *32*: 98-116, 1917. Thermal reactions, Phrynosoma.

301. WEISS, A. K., Am. J. Physiol. *177*: 201-206, 1954; *188*: 430-434, 1957. Tissue metabolism of rats acclimated to cold.

302. WHITNEY, R. J., J. Exp. Biol. *16*: 374-385, 1939. Thermal resistance of mayfly nymphs from ponds and streams.

303. WIESER, W., and KANWISHER, J., Biol. Bull. *117*: 594-600, 1959. Metabolism of marine nematode at different seasons.

304. WILBER, C. G., Med. Bull. St. Louis Univ. *4*: 112-119, 1952. Fat usage in arctic.

305. WILHOFF, D. C., and ANDERSON, J. D., Science *131*: 610-611, 1960. Selected temperature, lizard.

306. WISLOCKI, G. B., and ENDERS, R. K., J. Mammal. *16*: 328-329, 1935. Body temperature of sloths, anteaters, and armadillos.

307. *ZOTTERMAN, Y., Ann. Rev. Physiol. *15*: 357-372; *in* Josiah Macy, Jr., Conference on Nerve Impulse, 1953, pp. 140-206. Physiology of temperature receptors.

Chapter 10

MECHANORECEPTION, EQUILIBRIUM RECEPTION, AND PHONORECEPTION

A sense organ is susceptible to stimulation in either of two elementary ways—chemical or mechanical. Gustatory and olfactory receptors are sensitive to chemicals, photoreceptors are stimulated by products of a photochemical reaction, and temperature receptors respond by modulation of chemically controlled spontaneity. Mechanical stimulation ranges from *steady pressure,* as in tension receptors of muscles, blood-pressure-sensing elements, and some statoequilibrium receptors, through *low frequency stimulation* as in many tactile and proprioceptive endings and rotation receptors, to *stimulation* by *higher frequency* as in lateral line organs and vibration receptors, to *stimulation* by *very high sound frequencies* as in phonoreceptors. Mechanoreceptors function in reception of stimuli impinging directly from proximal sources and those from a distance; they are important in posture, locomotion, and other coordinated movement. Mechanoreceptors aid not only in reception of sound, and in orientation with respect to gravity and acceleration, but also in perception of substratum and contact surfaces, velocity of water or wind, and depth of water: thus they are of importance in ecology.

MECHANORECEPTION

The General Nature of Mechanical Stimulation. The sensitivity of cells to mechanical deformation of the surface is rather general. Hearts beat more strongly when distended, and some smooth muscles respond actively to stretch. Nerve fibers have been stimulated mechanically with an air jet and a strength-duration curve prepared by varying the air pressure and duration of stimulation.[19] Stretching a striated muscle can, by enhancing membrane excitability, remove a partial block (by drugs) of neuromuscular transmission.[91] An amoeba stops locomotion when stimulated by sudden pressure and is refractory to subsequent mechanical stimulation for a brief time after locomotion resumes. The hair cells of the cochlea of vertebrates are stimulated by movements estimated to be as small as 10^{-9} cm.[14]

Why some cell membranes are very sensitive to deformation and others relatively insensitive is not known. Evidence will be given below that deformation alters the ion permeability of excitable sense cells, allowing current to flow, which may stimulate associated nerve endings.

Histological Types of Mechanoreceptors. In evolution the differentiation of certain epithelial cells into receptors probably occurred before the differentiation of conducting nerve cells. The simplest nervous mechanoreceptors are free nerve endings which lie between or beneath epithelial cells. Many types of specialized terminal bulbs, discs, corpuscles, and spirals have been described. Other kinds of receptor endings are encapsulated, as the pacinian corpuscles of mammalian tendons and mesentery. Sensory hairs are widely distributed in many kinds of animals, and at the base there may be free nerve endings, knobs, or specialized spirals. Frequently, sensory cells are grouped in organs, as in earthworms. Arthropods have many sensory hairs, particularly at joints of appendages, and also short sensory spines and setae with bipolar sense cells.[8, 9] Insects have a variety of specialized sense cells associated with a semiflexible cuticle; these may be sensory spines, campaniform sensilla (Fig. 95), and chordotonal organs. In the campaniform sensilla of insects a terminal filament ends in a rod under a thin cuticular dome which magnifies surface strains. Processes

285

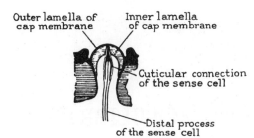

FIGURE 95. Diagram of campaniform sensilla of insect. (From Pringle, J. W. S.: J. Exp. Biol., vol. 15.)

from several sensilla converge on one sensory axon.[153] A chordotonal sensillum has a sensory filament on an elastic strand stretched between two points on the body wall and is primarily a sound receptor. Scorpions and other arachnids have regions where the chitin is thinned along grooves with sensilla beneath.[156] In *Limulus* and crustaceans, sense cells occur in regions of joints where there is no cuticular modification.[158]

Muscles, tendons, and joints contain proprioceptive endings, often associated with specialized muscle fibers. In arthropods proprioceptors often occur at intersegmental folds of cuticle. Many crustaceans have joint receptors which are sensitive to movement in one direction only.[200-202] Vertebrate muscles have sensory spindles and tendon organs. Each muscle spindle consists of a few intrafusal muscle fibers with contractile striated portions at the ends and with sensory endings in the central portion. The spindle sense endings are of two types, the primary nuclear bag or annulospiral ending and the secondary myotube or flower-spray ending (Fig. 96). The primary endings are connected to fast (60 to 120 m/sec) nerve fibers (12 to 20 μ diameter), and the secondary endings connect to slow (30 to 50 m/sec) nerve fibers (4 to 12 μ diameter).[71, 100, 101] Many mammalian spindles have both primary and secondary endings, others only one type. The eye muscles contain spindles in artiodactyls and higher primates, but not in rodents or carnivores.[33] Frog muscles have endings only of the primary type; fish have no muscle spindles but do have proprioceptors in abundance in the fins. Tendon organs are connected with large nerve fibers like those serving the primary spindle endings.

In vertebrates the lateralis-labyrinth system is built on a common plan from fish lateral line through the labyrinths to the cochlea. Hair cells (neuromasts) are mechanically stimulated and, in turn, excite the branched

nerve endings which embrace them. The sensory hairs in the cristae of elasmobranch semicircular canal ampullae have the microfilament pattern characteristic of cilia (Chapter 16).[129]

There is wide variation in the location of

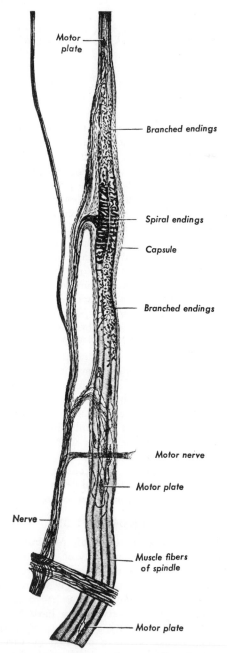

FIGURE 96. Diagram of nerve endings in a mammalian muscle spindle. Motor plates are endings on intrafusal muscle fibers. The motor nerve goes to extrafusal fibers of the same muscle. (From Maximow and Bloom.)

the nuclei of sensory neurons. In the earthworm, epidermal sense cells synapse in a peripheral plexus, and there are many epidermal sense cells per afferent neuron in the segmental nerves. In crustaceans a single nerve fiber enters a sensory hair and the nucleus lies at its base. The cell bodies of most tactile and proprioceptive endings of vertebrates are located in dorsal spinal ganglia or in sensory centers in the lower brainstem. Cell bodies of the nerve fibers innervating neuromasts are in nearby ganglia. Mechanoreceptors differ widely in the kind of deformation which produces stimulation; they also differ in sensitivity and in persistence of response to maintained stimulation (adaptation).

Mechanism of Excitation in Mechanoreceptors. *Generator Potentials in Crustacean Stretch Receptors, Amphibian Muscle Spindles, and Mammalian Pacinian Corpuscles.* Alexandrowicz[6, 7] described large stretch receptors in the dorsal abdomen and thorax of decapod and stomatopod Crustacea, and similar receptors in other crustaceans. Each segment has two pairs of receptors. One of each pair adapts rapidly, the other slowly. Each receptor consists of a thin muscle which is embraced by the basket-like dendrites of a large sensory neuron whose axon passes centrally. In the lobster *Homarus* each of the muscles of a paired receptor receives a large motor fiber; in the crayfish one of the muscles receives several small motor fibers.[57] In *Homarus* the pair of receptors also receives a pair of accessory nerve fibers, and in the crayfish it receives a single accessory fiber which gives off branches to each set of sensory dendrites. The sense cells can be stimulated by passive stretch or by contraction of

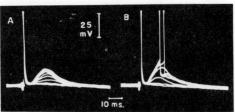

FIGURE 98. Potentials recorded intracellularly from cell body of abdominal stretch receptor of lobster. Electrical stimuli applied to nerve containing both sensory and motor axons. Initial deflections are antidromic impulses in sensory axons. *A*, stimuli at 4 per second elicit transient membrane potential reductions which follow the time course of tension changes. *B*, stimuli at 10 per second, contractions reach threshold for discharge of sensory cell at about 22 mv depolarization, and two impulses are set up. (From Eyzaguirre, C., and Kuffler, S. W.: J. Gen. Physiol., vol. 39.)

the muscle induced by motor impulses[116] (Fig. 97).

Intracellular records from the sense cell show a resting membrane potential of 70 mv. Stretch depolarizes so that the membrane potential can be set at different values. The graded generator potential (the depolarization set up by stretch) spreads electronically from the dendrites over the sense cell soma, and, at a critical depolarization level of 10 mv in the slow-adapting cell and at 20 mv in the fast-adapting cell, an impulse is initiated (Fig. 98), that is, the firing level is 60 or 50 mv membrane potential. The generator potential is maintained, and spike discharge continues for several hours during prolonged stretch in the slowly adapting receptor, but impulses stop in less than a minute in the fast receptor[202] (Fig. 99). Records obtained by external microelectrodes show that, although the generator potential originates in the dendrite, impulses start in the axon and propagate to the soma as well as along the length of the axon. Apparently the current density in the narrow axon is greater than in the soma and the threshold for firing of the axon, serving as an electrical source for the generator sink, is lower than that of the soma.[50, 55, 117]

A single stretch receptor from the abdomen of any one of a variety of insects has a dual function—response both to static displacement and to velocity of stretch.[126]

A large pacinian corpuscle of the mammalian mesentery can be stimulated by as small a movement as 0.5 μ applied during 0.1 msec.[60] Each corpuscle consists of a number of concentric layers surrounding a free

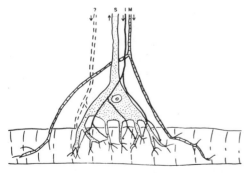

FIGURE 97. Diagram of abdominal stretch receptor in a decapod crustacean. *S*, sensory fiber from stretch receptor; *1* and *7*, inhibitory fibers ending on stretch receptor; *M*, motor fibers to the muscle to which the receptor is attached. (From Kuffler, S. W.: Exp. Cell. Res., suppl. 5, 1958.)

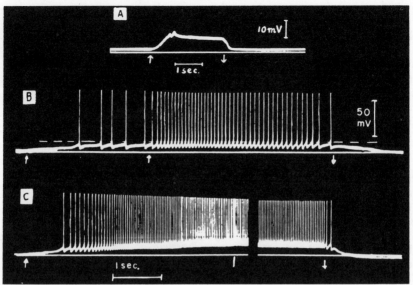

FIGURE 99. Potentials recorded intracellularly from crustacean stretch receptor. *A*, generator potential during subthreshold stretch, graded according to "deformation." Arrows, beginning and end of stretch. *B*, at critical level of depolarization conducted impulses appear. At second arrow, additional stretch increases firing frequency. *C*, stretch gradually increased between first arrow and vertical line. Relaxation followed by transient hyperpolarization. (From Kuffler, S. W.: Exp. Cell. Res., suppl. 5, 1958.)

terminal of nonmyelinated nerve; the myelin sheath begins and one node occurs inside the capsule, another node just outside (Fig. 100*A*). Electrical responses from a corpuscle consist of a generator potential which is graded in amplitude and latency according to strength of mechanical stimulation and which reaches critical amplitude, then is followed by an all-or-none spike.[10] The effective stimulus is not pressure or duration of distortion but rate of mechanical deformation.[75] The generator potential decays to zero in 4 to 8 msec.[131, 132, 134] By the use of nerve blocking agents such as procaine, or a sodium-free medium, or by mechanical damage, it has been shown that the generator potential arises in the free terminal process inside the capsule. By use of polarizing currents[40] and local damage[131, 132, 134] the first spike is shown to arise from the intracapsular node (Fig. 100*B*). When paired mechanical stimuli are delivered the generator potentials can sum but the nodal spike shows absolute refractoriness for 2.5 msec and relative refractoriness for 7 to 10 msec; during such time the generator potentials may reach 85 per cent of the amplitude of a spike. Impulses follow the generator 1:1 at 150/sec at a low strength of tap, and up to 280/sec at four times this strength; the generator potential (but not the nerve impulses) follows stimuli well at 650/sec.[131, 132, 134] A high concentration of acetylcholine esterase occurs in the nerve tip, none in the hull.[133]

A sensory spindle of a frog muscle consists of a spiral of nerve endings around the central part of an intrafusal muscle fiber. Under slight tension a regular train of impulses passes centripetally; when the extrafusal fibers of the muscle contract the stretch on the spindle is decreased and the sensory discharge is momentarily suspended, to resume at increased frequency during relaxation.[137] In isometric contraction there may be enough pull by extrafusal fibers on the spindle to stimulate it. Electrical records from the muscle spindle show graded generator potentials which give rise to all-or-none impulses.[73, 113] Mechanical deformation by stretch causes local potential changes in the sensory endings which at a critical level cause regenerative propagating impulses. The generator potential is analogous to a synaptic potential and is apparently not due to a specific change in sodium permeability as is the nerve impulse.[40] The frog muscle spindle can discriminate a change in load of about 10 per cent.[119]

Generator potentials have been studied in detail also in vertebrate phonoreceptors (see p. 304), where they occur in hair cells and stimulate sensory nerve endings.

Adaptation of Mechanoreceptors. The intensity of any sensory message is determined by the frequency of discharge in single neurons and by the number of active neurons. The frequency increases with increasing tension or pressure on a mechanoreceptor. Adaptation is the decreasing responsiveness of sensory endings during maintained stimulation and is indicated by decreasing frequency of sensory impulses. Sensory discharge is slower than the maximum frequency of nerve impulses; hence it is not limited by the nerve refractory period. Adaptation is also not fatigue in the sense of metabolic failure. Adaptation does not reside in the nerve. This has been shown by firing impulses back toward a sense organ (e.g., cutaneous receptor) antidromically. A mechanoreceptor responds less for a given movement with slow mechanical deformation than for the same movement with rapid deformation. The adaptation of pacinian corpuscles resembles in time course and other properties the rise in threshold of a nerve fiber during stimulation (accommodation).[75] Those mechanoreceptors in a rabbit incisor tooth which adapt fastest activate the highest-velocity nerve fibers.[147]

Mechanoreceptors differ in rate of adaptation—from those which give only one im-pulse per stimulation to those which continue to discharge more or less indefinitely during maintained mechanical deformation. Tactile hairs and touch receptors adapt rapidly. Each sensory hair along the margin of the telson and uropods of a crayfish gives only one impulse when flexed.[159] Hair receptors in the skin of a rabbit give one or two impulses. Tactile endings of frog skin given an initial burst of 4 to 12 impulses lasting 0.1 to 0.2 sec for maintained mechanical stimulation. A pacinian corpuscle gives a short burst of impulses, initially at high frequency, adapting in a few seconds to zero or low frequency[75] (Fig. 100).

The campaniform sensilla of insects are also intermediate in speed of adaptation and respond to strains in the cuticle. The discharge from joint receptors of insect legs starts at a high frequency (100 to 300/sec) and falls after 1 to 2 seconds to low levels.[153]

Stretch receptors in muscles adapt slowly compared with tactile receptors. Impulses from single spindles in a frog toe muscle under load start at 120 to 260 per second and decline to a rate of about 20 per second, which is maintained steadily for many min-

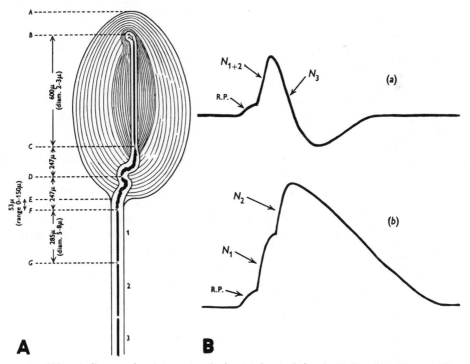

FIGURE 100. A, diagram of pacinian corpuscle showing location of nodes D, F, and G. (From Quilliam, T. A., and Sato, M.: J. Physiol., vol. 129.) B, electrical responses to mechanical stimuli recorded from pacinian corpuscle, (a), without polarizing current, (b), with anodal polarizing current. R.P., receptor potential; N_1, N_2, N_3, and N_{1+2}, phases of response appearing at respective nodes. (From Diamond, J., Gray, J. A. B., and Sato, M.: J. Physiol., vol. 133.)

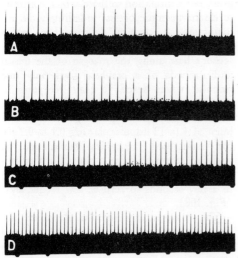

FIGURE 101. Steady discharge in single fiber of carotid sinus nerve at the following perfusion pressures: *A*, 40 mm Hg; *B*, 80 mm Hg; *C*, 140 mm Hg; *D*, 200 mm Hg. Time marked in 0.2 sec. (From Bronk, D. W., and Stella, G.: J. Cell. Comp. Physiol., vol. 40.)

utes.[137] Frequency of afferent discharge depends not only on the amount but also on the rate of development of tension. Stretch receptors in fins of the elasmobranchs *Raja* and *Scyllium* adapt slowly and maintain a steady discharge longer than do muscle receptors of amphibians and mammals and may continue to fire for more than an hour.[124]

Virtually no adaptation occurs in the pressure receptors of the carotid sinus of mammals (Fig. 101). Some of the endings are continually active and increase in frequency of discharge with each pulse wave; others of the sensory endings fire three or four impulses for each pulse. When the carotid artery is at steady pressure in a cat there is little stimulation until the pressure rises above 40 to 50 mm Hg.[118] The frequency of discharge increases continuously up to pressures of 200 mm Hg. There may be a slight decline in frequency after the initial response to pressure, but an equilibrium frequency is maintained more or less indefinitely according to the intrasinus pressure.[24]

A secondary type of adaptation is the falling out of responses when a receptor is stimulated repetitively. Impulses may follow the first few stimuli and then skip more and more. Evidence from pacinian corpuscles indicates that adaptation to repetitive stimulation is failure of the generator potential to initiate impulses. Tactile endings in frog skin follow mechanical stimuli at a rate as high as 250 to 300 per second initially, then drop to 150 per second for 30 to 60 seconds, and finally drop to occasional impulses.[93] Continued repetitive stimulation of the skin keeps the endings adapted, even though there may be no nerve impulses. Increase in potassium content of the saline speeds adaptation, and repeated mechanical beating of the skin by an air jet increases the potassium content of the bathing saline; hence the adaptation may result from accumulated potassium around nerve endings.[93] A stretch receptor of the abdomen of any one of many insects follows stimulation well at 5 stretches per second, less well at higher rates.[126]

Regulation of Sensory Discharge from Mechanoreceptors. The frequencies of sensory impulses from mechanoreceptors are primarily determined by the strength and rate of application of the stimulation. The response of a frog's muscle spindle increases in frequency in proportion to the weight applied to the muscle over a wide range.[119] When a femoral spine on the leg of a cockroach was stimulated by sinusoidal deflections the frequency of impulses on the ascending wave of deflection was higher with steep amplitude of deflection than with more gradual deflection, and peak frequency preceded the maximum tension, that is, the response followed the rate of movement and thus showed a phase advance over the stimulus.[158]

The discharge from stretch receptors within a muscle may be regulated by contraction of the muscle. Mammalian muscle spindles are in parallel with the extrafusal or principal fibers of the muscle, while the tendon organs are in series with these muscle fibers. Both types of receptor can be stimulated by stretch on the muscle, but the threshold of the sensory spindles is lower. The intrafusal muscle fibers are innervated by slow efferent nerve fibers; these thin muscle fibers cause no appreciable tension in the muscle as a whole. They contract only at their ends and thus pull on the noncontractile central portion where the sense endings are located. The extrafusal muscle fibers are innervated by fast efferent nerve fibers, and when they contract the tension on the spindles which are in parallel is relaxed; hence the afferent discharge from a spindle under slight rest tension is briefly interrupted during contraction and resumes at a higher frequency when the muscle as a whole relaxes[73]

(Fig. 102). The secondary (small fiber) spindle endings have a higher threshold to stretch than the primary ones.

Tendon sense organs respond to either passive stretch or to muscle contraction and adapt more slowly to stretch than do the spindles. If both fast and slow motor nerve fibers are stimulated together there may be spindle discharge during muscle contraction. When a muscle is suddenly stretched the spindles are stimulated, and their afferent impulses elicit monosynaptic reflex contraction of the extrafusal fibers. Contraction of the muscle stimulates the tendon receptors and interrupts the discharge of spindles. The sensory impulses from the tendon organs then reflexly inhibit the contraction.

The slow system (intrafusal muscle fibers) is excited by higher centers in the central nervous system (particularly the cerebellum and reticulum); it continues activity after spinal deafferentation.[53] Slow fiber activity keeps the spindles tonically active in advance of a contraction, and less stretch is necessary to excite a sensory spindle during tonic activity of the intrafusal fibers than in its absence.[71, 101]

Responses from the dorsal stretch receptors of crustaceans are modulated not only by the contraction of the attached muscle but also by inhibitory impulses in the accessory nerve fibers which end on the dendrites of the receptor cell. The accessory fiber (or fibers) inhibits by preventing the generator potential from attaining the firing level. If the receptor is under stretch and slightly depolarized the inhibitor hyperpolarizes, whereas in a relaxed receptor the inhibitor depolarizes (Fig. 103). The inhibitor tends to place the membrane at an equilibrium about 6 mv more depolarized than the resting potential, and if the membrane is set at this potential by applied current the inhibitor can prevent impulse generation without itself altering the membrane potential (Fig. 104).[55, 117] The resting potential is 70 mv, inhibitory equi-

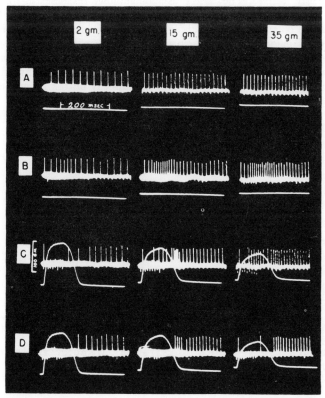

FIGURE 102. Muscle spindle, afferent impulses, during contraction of flexor digitorum longus, cat. External tensions on muscle—2, 15, and 35 gm. A, steady discharge from nonstimulated muscle; B, stimulation of single efferent fiber to the muscle spindle (9 stimuli at 100/sec); C, stimulation of efferent fiber to spindle and of part of motor nerve to the remainder of the muscle; D, stimulation of large motor fibers only. Impulses in the motor fibers to intrafusal muscle fibers increase frequency of sensory discharge from the spindle. Contraction of extrafusal fibers causes cessation of sensory discharge. (From Hunt, C. C.: Cold Spring Harbor Symp., vol. 17.)

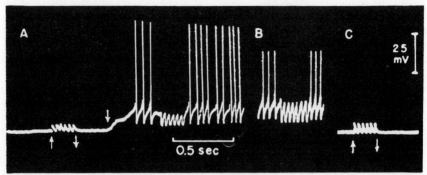

FIGURE 103. Inhibitory potentials recorded intracellularly from crustacean receptor. *A,* receptor partly relaxed; six inhibitory impulses cause depolarization potentials (arrows); at third arrow, stretch causes 20 mv depolarization and three sensory impulses, followed by inhibitory train, setting up repolarization potentials; continued stretch results in afferent impulses. *B,* inhibitory train inhibits sensory impulses and causes repolarization potentials. *C,* during complete relaxation of cell, inhibitory depolarization potentials. (From Kuffler, S. W., and Eyzaguirre, C.: J. Gen. Physiol., vol. 39.)

librium potential is 64 mv, and firing level is 50 mv.

Stimulation of sympathetic nerve supply to frog skin lowers the threshold, slows the adaptation of tactile receptors, and may make them spontaneously active. The effect is greatest if the skin is under tension, and enhancement can be obtained also by bathing the endings with epinephrine-norepinephrine.[130] The frog skin also contains pressure receptors which activate the slow nerve fibers and other endings (pain) with still slower afferent fibers. Injury such as scraping the skin, and also antidromic impulses, sensitizes these slowly adapting endings to pressure stimulation.

Recent evidence indicates some regulation of auditory responses in mammals by motor impulses in the eighth nerve to the cochlea.[69a]

It is concluded that responses of mechanoreceptors can be modulated not only by external stimuli but by motor impulses to attached muscles and by efferent fibers acting directly on the sensory endings.

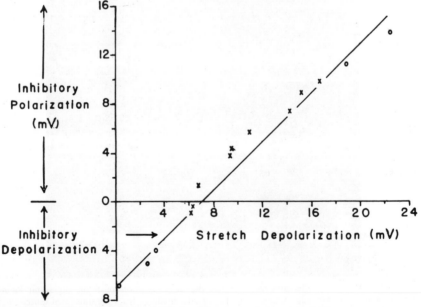

FIGURE 104. Inhibitory potential amplitudes at different membrane potential levels in crustacean stretch receptor. *Abscissa:* depolarization in millivolts produced by stretch without discharge of cell; *ordinate:* inhibitory potential amplitudes. Inhibitory equilibrium level, 6.4 mv. At lower (more negative) membrane potentials, inhibitory impulses depolarize. At higher (nearer zero) membrane potentials, they polarize. (From Kuffler, S. W., and Eyzaguirre, C.: J. Gen. Physiol., vol. 39.)

Pain. In many body regions where there are specialized sensory endings there are also free nerve endings which connect to small afferent fibers. Many of the free nerve endings are pain receptors which differ from other receptors in that they can be stimulated by any of several means—mechanical, chemical, heat, or other stimuli. In cutaneous nerves of the frog, responses to touch are carried at 10 to 12 m/sec and those to high pressure at 1.5 to 4.5 m/sec; in a cat the impulses from sensory hairs travel at 30 to 60 m/sec while "pain" impulses are conducted at less than 5 m/sec.[96, 208] The maximum frequency of discharge in the small fibers from the skin is lower than from tactile receptors; the response gradually builds up and adapts very little. Pain endings are sensitized and possibly stimulated within the body by chemicals such as histamine which are liberated from injured cells nearby. The pain sense areas are relatively large and not so well localized subjectively as the areas for tactile and similar stimulation.

The identification of pain endings in animals is not readily made except in terms of the slow impulses coming from free endings without specialized sensitivity. Pain endings may be associated with specialized corpuscles, for example, in the mammalian intestine; they predominate in the pulp of teeth, the cornea, and tympanic membrane. Whether the free nerve endings associated with small impulses in invertebrates should be considered as pain receptors is not known. In the earthworm the afferent impulses set up by tactile and proprioceptive stimulation are large and fast compared with the impulses initiated by noxious stimuli, particularly chemical.

Locomotor Behavior Initiated by Mechanoreceptors. Postural reflexes involving receptors in muscles and on the body surface are known for virtually all multicellular animals (see Chapter 21). Animals with jointed appendages have position detectors, for example, the chordotonal and other cuticle-connected receptors of insects and the tendon and joint receptors of vertebrates. The joint receptors of crustaceans and insects are very sensitive to vibration of the substratum (e.g., in *Dytiscus*).[99]

Many animals react directly to mechanical stimulation. Most fish, when stimulated on one side near the posterior end, turn the caudal fin toward the side of stimulation. Many sessile animals such as hydroids, sea anemones, holothurians, and ascidians withdraw by a strong body contraction when stimulated mechanically at the anterior end.

Many animals, particularly those which crawl, tend to collect in crevices and along surfaces, displaying thigmotaxis. This reaction provides shelter and may be overcome by another stimulus such as light. When thigmotactic animals crawl along one side of an object they turn toward the stimulating surface when they reach the end of the object, whereas if they crawl in the crack between two symmetrical objects they continue straight ahead at the end. If, after the animal has given the positive response to an edge, the stimulating object is withdrawn, the crawling animal then straightens the anterior end to be in line with the posterior end, the homostrophic reflex. These contact reactions depend on unequal stimulation of the two sides and have been demonstrated for many animals—earthworms, diplopods, insect larvae, and young mammals.[36]

Another type of contact orientation is rheotaxis or orientation to a stream of water. Planaria react positively to a stream, by means of receptors scattered over the body surface; their speed of rheotaxis increases to a maximum as the rate of flow increases.[178] Paramecia are normally positively rheotactic. Blind fish do not orient in a stream unless they touch the bottom, and orientation is controlled by the relation between the bottom and the stream.[45] Chum salmon discriminate water speed more sharply than coho salmon and tend to move into faster water.[95, 135]

Anemotaxis or orientation to air currents is seen in flying animals, insects for example. In flies, antennal sense organs are sensitive to wind and elicit postural changes according to speed of air flow.[97] Flight by a locust can be initiated by blowing on wind-sensitive hairs on the head, and orientation in flight is maintained by wind pressures on the wings with stimulation of sensilla at the wing base.[195] In population cages placed in the wind, vestigial-winged *Drosophila* increase in number more than wild-type flies,[90] i.e., wind is a natural selective agent.

Absence of ventral surface stimulation initiates righting reactions in snails, starfish, and some insects. Lifting the sucker of a leech initiates swimming. In many insects, e.g., flies, flight is initiated by removal of contact stimulation of the tarsi. Rhythmic movements of a spinal dogfish can be inhibited by ventral contact. The position of the head of a honeybee with respect to gravity is maintained by reflexes originating in sensory bristles on the episternum. Thus proprioceptors and tactile receptors are important in gravity orientation.[98]

Surface-swimming water beetles (Gyrinidae) detect water waves by club-shaped sense endings on the second segment of the antennae. By mechanical echolocation they avoid bumping into objects.[51] Water bugs which use plastron respiration (see p. 157) have pressure receptors on the sterna of the second abdominal segment associated with spiracles. By these they detect changes in the size of the air bubble and swim upward if hydrostatic pressure increases.[190]

Many animals select their locality by mechanical cues. In the crayfish genus *Orconectes, O. fodiens* is restricted to mud bottoms and sluggish water and *O. propinquus* to gravel and rock bottom and running water.[21] The cypris larvae of barnacles tend to settle in grooves and concavities; thus they settle more on rough than on smooth surfaces.[35]

Responses to Hydrostatic Pressure. Hydrostatic pressure increases approximately 1 atmosphere with each 10 meters vertical descent below water surface. Pressures of the order of a few hundred atmospheres decrease protoplasmic viscosity, block cell division, and may kill surface animals. Proteins become denatured at a few thousand atmospheres; 100 to 500 atmospheres often inhibit the denaturation of proteins by other agents.[104] Yet some fish and deep-sea invertebrates live at ocean depths of 2 miles where the pressure exceeds 600 atmospheres. Some (barophilic) bacteria from oceanic depths where pressures are as much as 1000 atmospheres do not grow well at 1 atmosphere but do grow at high pressures.[207] The sensitivity to hydrostatic pressure of the enzymes of such organisms must be different from that of corresponding systems of surface organisms.

Many plankton organisms tend to occupy certain levels in the water; some of them migrate diurnally from one pressure to another. Pressure sense is important in the vertical migration of larvae of decapod crustaceans,[85] which swim upward in response to pressure increase. They are, however, less sensitive than fish.[115]

The swim bladder of fish is more important in hydrostatic orientation than in respiration (see p. 189). A decrease in pressure by a fraction of an atmosphere results in an increase in gas content in the swim bladder (guppies); gas must be secreted to maintain the fish at a density which keeps it at a constant level.[102] Gas is lost from the swim bladder when hydrostatic pressure increases. Increases in bladder gas content occur when *Fundulus* is transferred from sea water to the less dense fresh water.[18] Physoclyst fish from which gas had been withdrawn and which were forced to remain near the surface regenerated only about half as much gas in a day as when kept at a depth.[34, 105] For fish of equal densities, the volume of the swim bladder is less (about 5 per cent of body) in marine physoclysts than in freshwater ones, and the marine fish can move over a wider range of depths.[106] Changes in swim bladder pressure in the carp cause responses of fins, heart, and breathing—all of which cease after autonomic nerves to the bladder are cut. Gas secretion into the bladder is facilitated by the splanchnic nerve and gas liberation by the vagus.[61] The swim bladder of *Hippocampus* has anterior and posterior chambers, and release from a resting place is compensated by expansion of the posterior chamber.[150] Pressure changes are in part detected by the inner ear (which is often connected by ossicles to the swim bladder), in part by stretch receptors in the swim bladder. The swim bladder is an effector containing sensory mechanisms which aid in maintaining fish at constant hydrostatic pressure.[43]

Lateral Line Organs. Teleost and elasmobranch fish and a few amphibians have a complex system of sensory canals along the sides of the body and often over the head. Each canal may be an open groove; it may be covered except for occasional exits, or it may be open at the ends. In the wall of the tube are epithelial cells and specialized hair cells called neuromasts. These are often grouped together as sensory hillocks with the hair processes projecting into a gelatinous cupula. The neuromasts are innervated by branched fibers of the lateral line nerve which enters the brain mainly with the tenth nerve, partly with the seventh and ninth nerves. The lateral line is increasingly protected in fish exposed to rougher waters[204] (Fig. 105).

Lateral line nerve fibers show a continuous background of spontaneous activity which originates in the neuromasts. Superimposed on this are responses to mechanical stimulation by water waves on the flank (Fig. 106). In the elasmobranch *Raja,* perfusion of the canal from head toward tail increased the frequency in some nerve units and decreased it in others, while perfusion from tail to head had opposite effects.[169] In a Japanese eel both thick and thin nerve fibers end on a cluster of sense cells. Thin fibers mediate

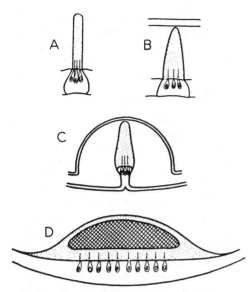

FIGURE 105. Diagrams of sensory epithelium in different organs of acoustic lateralis system. *A,* free cluster of sensory cells; *B,* lateral line canal organ (neuromasts); *C,* ampulla of semicircular canal; *D,* otolith organ. (From Dijkgraaf, S.: Experentia, vol. 8.)

low threshold responses which adapt slowly; thick fibers mediate high threshold response at higher frequency and with rapid adaptation. Single thick fibers show several spikes per cycle of low-frequency wave stimulation (<20/sec), one spike at 20 to 50/sec (sometimes to 100/sec), and irregular responses at still higher frequencies.[108] In *Ameiurus* (now *Ictalurus*) the nerve fibers synchronize with stimuli up to about 100/sec, in *Fundulus* up to 180/sec.[92, 184] Similar modulation by mechanical stimulation of spontaneously active neuromasts has been seen in the amphibian *Xenopus*.[48]

In the ruff (*Acerina*) each cluster of hair cells is surrounded by a jelly cupula. Electrical recording from close to the cupula shows responses which vary in voltage with the amplitude of the mechanical wave and are double the frequency of the water currents.[103] It is postulated that this is a generator (microphonic) response caused by movement of the cupula over the hair cells, and that it stimulates the branched nerve fibers which innervate the hair cells.

The spontaneous discharge in the lateral line nerve varies with temperature but is not important in responses of fish to temperature. The lateral line responds to vibrations in the water of several hundred per second, but conditioning experiments show that fish do not "hear" with their lateral line; also the lateral line is not important in orientation to water currents (rheotaxis). Rather, the lateral line is concerned with "distant touch": in sensing ripples, in localizing moving objects such as other aquatic animals, and in detecting fixed objects by reflected waves. The lateral line is often very prominent in deep sea fishes.

Vibration Sense. Vibration receptors are intermediate between motion receptors and phonoreceptors. Some of these are rapidly adapting mechanoreceptors which respond to closely repeated deformations; others are really phonoreceptors, which respond to low-frequency sound waves. In general, the frequency range between 0.1 and 100/sec is considered to cover vibration.

Lateral line organs are sensitive to vibrations in water and may follow such vibrations at frequencies below about 100/sec. In fish the sacculus-lagena responds to low frequencies and is more sensitive below 200 to 500

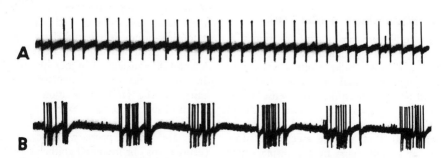

FIGURE 106. Impulses in lateral line nerve from the toad *Xenopus*. *A,* spontaneous activity; *B,* response to water waves corresponding to bursts of impulses. (From Dijkgraaf, S.: Experientia, vol. 12.)

cps (cycles per second) than the ear of mammals. The most important receptors for vibration of substratum in all vertebrates are probably the joint receptors.

Arthropods are extremely sensitive to vibrations of the substratum—solid or liquid. The sensory elements are usually sensilla attached at joints to chitin, which may or may not be modified to amplify movement. Numerous crustacean and insect joint receptors are sensitive to posture but also to movement of the joint. They respond to vibration of the substratum. This type of receptor has been described in crustaceans—*Carcinus*[27] crayfish, and in insects *Dytiscus* and *Locusta*.[159] Many insects have scattered groups of hairs, particularly on abdomen, legs, and cerci, which follow vibrations of substratum and of air. Since they are sensitive to air-borne waves, they may be considered as low-frequency phonoreceptors.

It is advantageous for a spider to be very alert to vibrations in its web. The house spider *Achaearanea* has lyriform organs or sensilla beneath modified thin chitin near the tarsal-metatarsal joints which respond to air-borne or substrate-borne sound.[194] Unlike typical phonoreceptors, the frequency range detected is greater when the tarsus is weighted than when it is free. Hence the receptor is partly tuned by its own resonant frequency and can discriminate well in the range 100 to 1000 cps. The frequency of maximum sensitivity can be altered by stress on the legs as in walking over the web.[194] The spider was responsive to 2000 cps vibrations only 25 Å in amplitude and attacked a source of vibration on the web at 400 to 700 cps. It is probable that excitation is similar in vibration receptors to that in other mechanoreceptors. The similarity of vibration receptors to tactile and proprioceptors at the lower frequency limit and to sound receptors at the higher frequencies illustrates the continuum of mechanoreceptors.

EQUILIBRIUM RECEPTION

The equilibrium position of an animal is arrived at by its orientation with respect to gravity, and this results from a variety of sensory signals—visual, proprioceptive, tactile, and the special equilibrium sense. Many equilibrium receptors give two kinds of signal—static or positional, and dynamic or accelerational. Both require mechanical stimulation of sensory hairs by the displacement of particles (otoliths) or fluid. Orientation with respect to gravity may reverse with

stage in life cycle or with competing stimuli.

Orientation to Gravity; Geotaxis. Many organisms orient to gravity by unknown means. In growing seedlings the shoots show a negative and the roots a positive geotropism. Protozoa such as *Paramecium* show negative geotaxis.

Many organisms (turbellarians, polychaetes, holothurians, brachiopods, dipteran larvae, and branchiate snails) show positive geotaxis. Many of these burrow in mud or sand; the downward direction of burrowing in many polychaetes is mediated by statocysts.[26] A staphylinid beetle which burrows in sand continues to burrow vertically even after the burrow has been turned sidewise by as much as 70°.[25]

Many other animals—pulmonate snails, crabs, some beetles, young rats—show negative geotaxis mediated by several sense modalities. When these animals are placed on an inclined plane in air they choose a direction of ascent which deviates from the horizontal by an angle, θ, which is related to the angle of inclination of the plane, α. For many kinds of animals the angle of orientation up the plane varies as the logarithm of sin α; the pull of gravity on an inclined plane is sin α.[36] Addition of a weight (wax) to the abdomen of a beetle increases the angle of orientation, θ, while adding the weight at the anterior end or removing the abdomen decreases θ. Male fiddler crabs show a greater θ when the larger of the two claws is on the downward side of the animal.[36] A young rat tends to roll when the orientation angle, θ, is low or the inclination, α, is high; an increase of α is compensated by an increase of θ. The geotaxis of these animals is dependent on a series of postural reflexes elicited via statocysts, proprioceptors, and perhaps cutaneous sense organs.

Stimulation of Statocysts by Gravity and Acceleration. *Morphology of Statocysts.* Gravity receptors or statocysts are usually approximately spherical in form, are lined with sensory hair cells, and contain statoliths—either secreted skeletal spheres or grains of sand moving in a liquid medium. A statolith is usually of higher specific gravity than the liquid and is supported on sensory hairs. As the animal's position is changed, the direction of the force exerted by the statolith on the sensory hairs is altered. The hair cells are either primary sensory neurons (crustaceans) or modified epithelial cells with nerve processes around them (vertebrates).

The sensory input to the central nervous

system varies according to the shearing force exerted on different regions of the sensory epithelium. If the freely movable statolith is surrounded by sensory hairs on all sides, a specific group of hairs will be stimulated at each position of the animal in space. Usually the statolith is of greater specific weight than its medium, as it is in the statocysts of certain coelenterates, ctenophores, worms, molluscs, crustaceans, and vertebrates. Scyphomedusan coelenterates have eight statocysts radially arranged around the margin of the mantle. Statoliths inside the statocysts are tiny sacs filled with amorphous bodies, mainly calcium.[205] *Pecten* has two statocysts close to the pedal ganglia; the statoliths on left and right sides differ, as does the length of sensory hairs.[26] Octopus has well-developed statocysts, but their removal causes only slight disorientation.[206]

In some water bugs (*Nepa, Notonecta*)[163] a thin layer of air is held to the body surface by fine hairs. If the body is turned, the air bubble (gaseous statolith) is displaced upward and this stimulates adjacent sensory hairs. Since it has a lower specific weight than its surrounding medium the air bubble "statolith" exerts an *upward* pressure. No true statocysts are known in insects. The only statocysts for which the mode of stimulation is well known are those of vertebrates and crustaceans.

The vestibular labyrinth of the inner ear of all vertebrates consists of two portions; the lower portion comprises the sacculus and lagena or cochlea and the upper portion consists of the utriculus and semicircular canals. There are three semicircular canals in vertebrates except in some cyclostomes (e.g., Petromyzon) which lack the horizontal canal. The sense cells (hair cells) are similar to those of the lateral line organ, and the labyrinth-lateral line constitutes a single complex. In the utriculus, sacculus, and in fish lagena the hair cells occur in a cluster on a plate or macula, often more than one macula per chamber. Each utriculus and sacculus contains one or more otoliths. The hair cells of the semicircular canals are contained in ampullae at the junction with the utriculus; they are grouped in a cupula above which rests (with hair processes embedded) a gelatinous crista which nearly fills the ampulla.[3] The membranous part of the labyrinth is filled with the fluid endolymph. The hair cells are innervated by branched nerve fibers of neurons with their cells in the vestibular (Scarpa's) ganglion.

Crustacean statocysts are spherical sacs at the base of the antennae which contain statoliths replaced at each molt from foreign bodies such as sand grains. When iron particles were substituted for statoliths, a magnet held above a crab caused the animal to turn over on its back. There are at least two types of sensory hair, the free thread hairs and the hook hairs (statolith bearing). These hairs are processes of sensory neurons with cell bodies in the statocyst wall, hence are unlike the hair cells of vertebrates[30] (Fig. 107).

Method of Stimulation of Statocysts. Investigations on fish[98] and Crustacea[176] have shown that the effective stimulating force of the statolith is not the component pulling or pressing on the sensory epithelium but the force component acting parallel to the sensory epithelium, the shearing force. This mode of stimulation appears to hold for other vertebrates as well as for fish.[177]

The vestibular labyrinth of fish has been more amenable than that of other vertebrates to surgery and electrical recording. Lowenstein and his associates have recorded impulses from single sensory nerve fibers while stimulating various regions of the labyrinth of the skate *Raja clavata* (Fig. 108).[123] Spontaneous discharge from unstimulated endings seems to be characteristic of neuromasts in general; however, not all fibers are active at a given time. Records from the nerve from the utriculus show a decrease in spontaneous frequency when the nose of the fish is up, an increase when the side from which records are being taken is up, a decrease with that side down. Fibers from the lagena are maximally active in the normal position and decrease in frequency with either side down. Hence in the ray, all three otolith organs participate in the response to gravity, and the frequency of nerve impulses is proportional to the shearing force[123, 127, 128, 177] (Fig. 109A and B). Responses to sound vibration are registered from utriculus and sacculus. Electrical records from single nerve fibers of the vestibular tract in the medulla of bony fish (*Tinca, Esox, Ameiurus*) show, in response to tilting, nerve impulses similar to those in *Raja*, that is, frequency changes superimposed on the spontaneous background.[174-176] Stimulation occurs when the statolith presses tangentially on the side of the macula.[98]

Each semicircular canal is stimulated by acceleration in the plane of that canal.[52] The discharge recorded from a nerve fiber from the ampulla of the horizontal canal of the

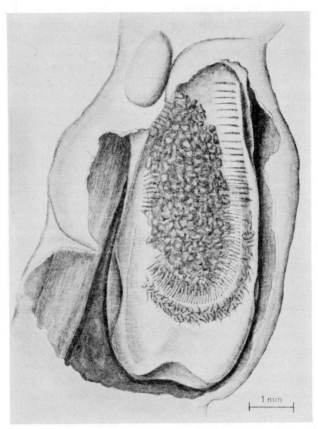

FIGURE 107.   Statocyst of lobster as seen from above. Statolith mass in contact with inner three rows of sensory hairs. Fine medial thread hairs project horizontally from medial wall. Large hairs on antero-lateral wall. (From Cohen, M. J.: J. Physiol., vol. 130.)

ray *Raja* increased upon rotation ipsilaterally at about 3 degrees/sec, while rotation contra-laterally inhibited the spontaneous discharge. Single fiber frequency of discharge increases with rate of linear or rotational acceleration (Fig. 109C). The impulse discharge from the horizontal canal is increased by *ipsilateral* (ampulla trailing) and decreased by *contra-lateral* (ampulla leading) rotary displacement.[123, 127, 128] The vertical canals respond to rotation about all three axes. Postrotatory effects such as after-depression or augmentation of discharge are related to such well-known after-effects as nystagmus.

The cupula-endolymph may be considered as a highly damped torsion pendulum. Visual-ization of the cupula in the pike (*Esox*) showed the period of this pendulum to be some 20 seconds.[3, 181] The frequency of im-pulses in nerves from ampullae of the ray, in response to sinusoidal swing of the fish, lead or lag the points of reversal of direction. The decline in frequency with time, after a change in velocity of rotation, corresponds to

a ratio of damping (moment of friction) over the cupula-restoring couple of about 40 seconds.[81] Similar results have been obtained with frogs.[167] Inertia of the endolymph and cupula is viewed as causing displacement of the cupula on acceleration, and frictional re-sistance of the small canals is viewed as damp-ing the response of the whole system. Ob-servations on a number of mammals, and also on pigeons, show a threshold accelera-tion of 0.1 to 0.5 degree per second of arc per second of time.[54, 196] The latency of compen-satory head or eye movement decreases as the rate of rotation increases up to a limit.[70]

The basic mechanism of excitation appears to be similar in all statocysts. Electrical re-cording with microelectrodes from the labyrinth of a carp, *Cyprinus,* shows a small direct current, the endolymph positive by 5 to 7 mv with respect to perilymph, which is additive with the resting potential of the hair cells. The hair cells of the ampulla of the horizontal canals show graded depolariza-tion on accelerative rotation toward the

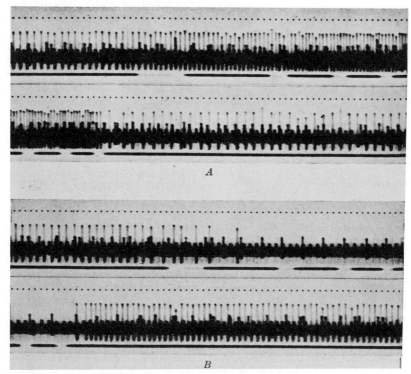

FIGURE 108. Oscillographic record of impulses from nerve branch to horizontal ampulla of skate, showing responses of single fiber to angular acceleration to the left, *A*, and to the right, *B*. Acceleration is 15 degrees per second in *A* and 20 degrees per second in *B*. In *A*, stimulation, and in *B*, inhibition. (From Lowenstein, O., and Sand, A.: Proc. Roy. Soc. London, B, vol. 129.)

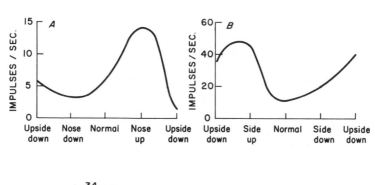

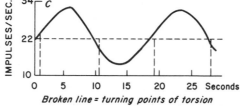

FIGURE 109. Impulses in vestibular nerves of ray (*Raja clavata*) *A*, frequency of impulses coming from utriculus as head was tilted with nose down or nose up. *B*, response from utriculus when side of head was tilted up or down. *C*, frequency of impulses in fiber from semicircular canal during rotation at 18.5 degrees per second in the plane of the canal. (*A* and *B* modified from Lowenstein, G., and Roberts, T. D. M.: J. Physiol., vol. 110. *C* modified from Groen, J. J., Lowenstein, O., and Vendrik, A. J. G.: J. Physiol., vol. 117.)

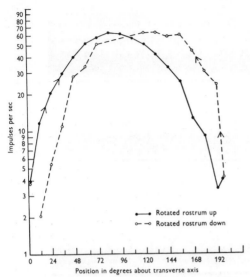

FIGURE 110. Frequency of impulses in nerve from statocyst nerve of lobster. Response to continuous rotation in opposite directions about transverse axis. Each point is average frequency over a 12-degree interval. (From Cohen, M. J.: J. Physiol., vol. 130.)

ampulla, repolarization on deceleration, and hyperpolarization on acceleration in the opposite direction.[111] These graded depolarizations and hyperpolarizations are generator potentials similar to those of other mechanoreceptors; presumably they stimulate the nerve endings. Depolarization of the hair cells appears to correlate with an increase, and hyperpolarization with a decrease, in spontaneous firing of nerve impulses. Similarly in the guinea pig the membranous ampulla and endolymph are positive (by some 40 mv) to the surrounding perilymph and bone. Depolarization results from utriculopetal rotation of the horizontal and from utriculofugal rotation of the vertical ampulla; hyperpolarization results from reverse rotations.[192] Thus the shearing force in one direction decreases the resting potential (depolarization) and leads to an increase in impulse frequency, while in the opposite direction hyperpolarization and decrease in impulse frequency result.

Impulses in single fibers of the statocyst nerve of the lobster *Homarus* show that some receptors are sensitive to absolute position. Frequency of impulses is maximal at an angle of 96 to 120 degrees about the transverse axis. Other receptors are sensitive to direction of movement (Fig. 110). Some fibers show responses to acceleration and some to vibrations. Fibers of all types show some spontaneous activity, and responses to displacement of the hairs consist of increases or decreases

in impulse frequency. The thread hairs respond to accelerations of 6 to 9 degrees/sec. The hook hairs signal position and direction of movement; they are no longer stimulated after the statoliths have been removed.[30-33]

Information Transmitted from Statocysts to Central Nervous System. Many observations have been made on the behavior of animals when one labyrinth or statocyst has been damaged or removed. In general, these animals show a turning orientation around the long axis, that is, they tilt to the side of the damaged statocyst and continue to turn in that direction.

Removal of one utriculus from an elasmobranch or teleost results in lasting deviations of the eyes and fins, although some central compensation takes place.[122, 177] Removal of sacculus and lagena causes much less defect in gravity responses. When the utriculi of frogs were destroyed by cautery, responses to tilting and linear acceleration were abolished, but section of the saccular nerves did not disturb orientation.[16] Impulses in vestibular nerves from frogs[167] and from the vestibular tract of the medulla of cats[2] have been recorded on tilting; there is very slow adaptation. In man the utriculus seems to be involved in motion sickness. In rabbits, stimulation of the sacculus elicits vertical eye movements.[26] In all of the vertebrates the utriculus is important for sensing position and probably for sensing linear rotation to some extent; the sacculus supplements the utriculus and may be important in vibration sense.

Removal of one utricular statolith from a fish causes persistent turning, but if those on both sides of a fish are removed so that no stimulation of the sensory epithelium occurs, the fish shows no turning reaction and behaves approximately normally. Similar results are obtained with crustaceans (*Astacus, Crangon, Palaemonetes, Homarus* and others) by observing the angle of the eyestalk with respect to the body axis. Leg and eyestalk movements result from direct stimulation of the statocyst hairs (Fig. 111). After one statocyst is removed, the reactions are displaced toward the defective side and there is a tendency for the animal to circle toward that side. Crabs may show some central compensation for removal of a statocyst.[176] In shrimps the eyestalk deviation is proportional to the sine of the angle of the dorsoventral axis with respect to gravity. The crabs *Carcinus* and *Maja* normally show compensatory eye movements during rotation, also after-responses (nystagmus) when turning is suddenly stopped. Blinding does not eliminate these reflexes, but removal of the statocysts eliminates the after-responses and disturbs equilibrium. The hook hairs which bear the statoliths seem to be position receptors and the thread hairs appear to respond to angular displacements about all three body axes.[47]

It is concluded for crustaceans that continuous discharge of the sensory epithelium of one statocyst results in asymmetric stimulation and leads to the turning reaction. The shearing force from the midline to the side increases sensory input, from side to midline decreases it. The magnitude of the reaction after extirpation of one statocyst or of one statolith is half that of a normal crab. Thus the excitatory signals of the two statocysts sum in the central nervous system, and the resultant constitutes the information delivered by the statocysts regarding position in space.

Control of Orientation with Respect to Gravity. Experiments with fish[23, 98] and with Crustacea[176] show that these animals maintain position or direction of swimming which deviates from normal posture in such a way as to maintain a certain state of statocyst excitation. Fish assume a position with respect to gravity and lateral light so that the excitation resulting from light and gravity is kept constant. When a fish is rotated sidewise the fins bend in a way to lead to automatic righting, and in response to left and right turning the trunk muscles make compensatory bends.[44] Some fish normally swim at a fixed angle to the horizontal and this angle varies diurnally. The angle of tilt can be changed by varying gravity stimulation or by removing one statolith. If both statoliths are removed, centrifugation is without effect.[23]

Orientation of any animal to gravity can be visualized as a feedback system as follows: The central nervous system, as a result of many impinging sensory signals, initiates motor responses determining a given course of locomotion. Statocyst excitation then reaches the central nervous system where it is compared with the "reference level," and turning movements are initiated which result in correspondence between the statocyst input and the "reference level." Statocyst excitation may result from the animal's own movements or from external forces.

Many insects are able to transpose an angle gained in relation to a light source when on a horizontal plane into a position with respect to gravity when on a vertical plane. By this means bees communicate the direction of a

food source to other workers in the hive.[67] Dung beetles similarly orient on a vertical surface with an angle to gravity equal to that which they previously assumed to light.[17] This behavior indicates retention of a pattern and comparison in time of two different kinds of stimulation.

The oblique downward course of shrimp swimming from the surface was measured under variations in gravity by slow centrifuging. The shrimps changed swimming direction in such a way that the statocyst excitation remained constant.[176] When a jellyfish is tilted the lower portion of the mantle contracts more strongly than the upper and the animal rights itself.[58] Removal of several of the statocysts disorients the jellyfish. Ctenophores likewise have functional statocysts. If a frog, rabbit, or monkey is rotated horizontally around the long axis while suspended, the leading limb flexes while the trailing limb extends. If a quadripedal animal is tilted downward the limbs on the side toward which it is tilted extend while those on the opposite side flex.[16] If the head is raised, extensor tone in the forelegs increases while that of hind limbs decreases; lowering the

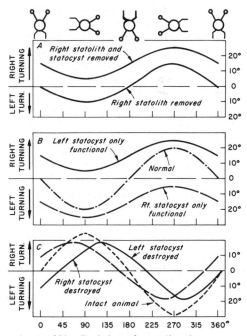

FIGURE 111. Deviation of eyestalks of crustacean (e.g., *Palaemonetes*) during rotation as indicated by diagrams at top of figure and in degrees at bottom.

Ordinate: eyestalk deviation measured as the differences between the dorsoventral axis of the crab and the bisector of the angle between the two eyestalks at each position. *A, B, C* show effects of stated sensory deficiencies. (From Schöne, H.: Unpublished data.)

head decreases tone in forelimbs. A normal cat lands on its feet when it falls, but if bilaterally labyrinthectomized it fails to do so.

Removal of one or both labyrinths often produces abnormal posture initially, but compensation usually occurs, particularly if the eyes are functional. Visual cues are important in righting in dogs, cats, and man, much less so in rabbits and guinea pigs. If a labyrinthectomized rabbit is held in the air by its pelvis the head falls into abnormal positions according to gravity. If the rabbit is placed on its side on a table the head is righted, but if, in addition, a board is placed on the upper side of the animal the head is not righted; asymmetrical stimulation of cutaneous receptors affords a sensory cue for righting. Also if while the head is held the rabbit lies on a table so that it cannot right itself the trunk will right, and forced rotation of the head will increase extensor tonus on the side toward which the nose is turned; these responses of trunk and legs result from stimulation of proprioceptors in the neck.

The sensory input from the labyrinths, eyes, muscle, joint, and skin receptors together initiate a series of reflexes which maintain normal orientation of an animal with respect to gravity and which counteract acceleration in all planes. These responses occur by spinal and lower brain mediation, and there is no well-defined cortical projection from the labyrinths. Postural responses involving stimulation of the labyrinth can be conditioned.[196]

Orientation of Flying Insects. Flight in insects can be initiated by interruption of tarsal contact with substratum, by wind on the head, or by strong nonspecific stimuli; flight is maintained by wind stimulation of sense organs at the wing bases and on the head. Deviation from balance in flight may be analyzed as pitching or rotation anteroposteriorly about the transverse axis, rolling about the longitudinal axis, and yawing about the dorsal-ventral axis. The sensory input for balance is partly visual, partly by wing sense organs (particularly in insects with two pairs of wings), by sensory hairs at the region of head attachment in Odonata,[143] and by the halteres or modified hindwings in Diptera. Each haltere is a dumbbell-shaped organ with one or two muscles and an abundance of campaniform sensilla at its base. The halteres oscillate at some 100 to 200 cps, in a vertical plane during flight in synchrony with the wings. The contractions of the haltere muscle depend on its mechanical properties and are

more frequent than the activating nerve impulses, as are contractions of the indirect flight muscles.[59, 172]

Removal of the halteres seriously interferes with ability to fly and particularly affects ability to maintain orientation in the horizontal plane.[29] A haltere oscillates in the vertical plane with slight backward tilt. Yawing (rotation around the vertical axis) would tend to move the haltere vertically by the torque because of its displaced center of gravity. This gyroscopic torque fluctuates at twice the frequency of the haltere oscillation. Sensory nerve impulses from the halteres show a burst for each half-cycle of oscillation.[154] During yawing the nerve discharge is augmented much more than it is during rolling. Each haltere can indicate rotations about the vertical (yawing) and horizontal (rolling) axes, and since the planes of vibration are different on the two sides, the central nervous system can resolve information about rotation in the transverse axis (pitching).

Removal of one haltere has little effect on flight, but, if the fly is blinded in addition, compensatory wing movements become very erratic.[56] Removal of both halteres results in general lethargy, uneven flight, and inability to maintain normal attitude in flight. The halteres are therefore gyroscopic sense organs of equilibrium.[29]

PHONORECEPTION AND ECHO-ORIENTATION

Sound as a stimulus consists of sinusoidal mechanical waves which, in pure tones, can be described in terms of frequency and amplitude. As sound waves progress through a medium the velocity of particle movement leads particle displacement. Speed of transmission and attenuation with distance varies with the medium. The velocity of sound in air at $20°$ is 1125 feet per second, or 343 meters per second, and in water it is 4.7 times that rate. Sound intensity is usually expressed as sound pressure level in dynes/cm^2. The faintest sound heard by man is about 0.0001 dyne/^{2}; ordinary conversation is approximately 1 dyne/cm^2; and painful sound, as from some airplane motors, about 300 dynes/cm^2. The best human threshold at 1000 cps is about 0.0002 dyne/cm^2, which is equal to 10^{-16} watt/cm^2. Sound intensity can be given in dynes/cm^2 but is usually expressed as decibels which give the logarithm of the ratio of two pressures. The human threshold is usually designated as the reference level for the logarithmic decibel (db) scale of sound intensities. Sound on a busy street at 2 dynes/cm² corresponds to 80 db.

Phonoreceptors are sense organs in which sound waves in air or water are transmitted through fluid and solid structures and excite nerve impulses. In general, phonoreceptors are most sensitive in a particular limited frequency range. At the low frequency end (<50/sec) phonoreception overlaps with the vibration sense. In some animals low frequencies only are detected, and hearing and vibration reception are the same. Usually, however, the receptor organs which serve for low frequencies (vibration) are different from those for high-frequency sound. Vibration receptors usually are specialized nerve endings of joints, muscle, or cuticle, while phonoreceptors usually have specialized receptor cells which activate nerve endings. The properties of a given receptor for frequency discrimination do not necessarily guarantee that the central nervous system will "hear" to a corresponding degree. Analysis of the functional capacity of receptors must, therefore, be combined with behavioral methods and measurements in the nervous system for a complete understanding of phonoreception.

To follow the sequence of events between the incidence of sound waves on a phonoreceptor and impulses in the auditory nerve requires knowledge of the physics of sound transmission in the receptor, of the biological mechanoelectrical transduction in the sensory membrane, and of the stimulation (usually electrical) of nerve endings. The only phonoreceptor for which such an analysis has been made with any completeness is the mammalian ear. (See reviews by Davis,[37] Bekesy,[14, 15] and Tasaki.[185])

Morphology and Stimulation of Vertebrate Ear. The external ear aids localization of sound and tends to concentrate impinging high-frequency sound waves by reflection. The auditory canal is separated from the cavity of the middle ear by the tympanic membrane. The middle ear is filled with air and contains three small bones, the malleus, incus, and stapes. Sound waves in air are transmitted by the tympanic membrane to the malleus, which is attached to the membrane and rocks with the incus about a common axis. The incus in turn rocks the stapes. The foot plate of the stapes fills the oval window, which opens into the inner ear. Small muscles attached to the malleus and stapes limit the amplitude of vibration of these bones. The eustachian tube connects

the middle ear to the pharynx and equalizes the air pressure in the middle ear with that of the environment. Below the oval window is the round window, closed by an elastic membrane which allows the fluid in the inner ear to move with movements of the stapes. The ratio of areas of tympanic membrane and stapes imparts to the middle ear a mechanical advantage of 13 times;[82] lower vertebrates, which have no middle ear, lack this advantage.

The inner ear is a fluid-filled system of cavities, one portion of which constitutes the labyrinth organs of equilibrium, the other the cochlea. The auditory portion of the inner ear appears first as the lagena in fish and amphibians; this lengthens in mammals, where it is coiled in a spiral. In cochleas with a long distance from stapes to the helicotrema at the apex of the spiral (55 mm in elephant) there is more mechanical resolution than in shorter ones (7 mm in a mouse).[14] The spiral cochlear tube is divided longitudinally by Reissner's membrane and the basilar membrane to form three long spiral canals. The two outer canals, scala vestibuli and scala tympani, are filled with perilymph; the tunnel of Corti, between internal and external hair cells, contains similar fluid. The scala media, between Reissner's membrane and the basilar membrane, contains endolymph. This fluid has thirty times more potassium and one-tenth as much sodium as the perilymph. The endolymph is probably secreted by the stria vascularis.[37]

The organ of Corti, located on the basilar membrane in the scala media, contains two sets of sensory cells and three rows of external and a single row of internal "hair cells." The hair processes are capped by the gelatinous but fibrillar acellular tectorial membrane. The latter is probably composed of secreted glycoprotein. The hair cells are innervated by radial fibers with their cell bodies in the cochlear ganglion imbedded in the bony labyrinth and their axons making up much of the eighth cranial nerve; each fiber innervates one or two hair cells. The external hair cells are innervated by spiral fibers with cells in the spiral ganglion. In addition, an intraganglionic spiral bundle contains fibers of cells in the medulla on both the same and opposite side; these fibers appear to be efferent to the hair cells.

The physics of wave propagation in the cochlea has been elucidated by von Bekesy by direct microscopic observations of vibrations in different regions when excited by sinusoidal displacement of the stapes. The maximum amplitude of displacement varies in its position along the cochlea according to the frequency. The maximum of instantaneous displacement travels as a wave crest along the cochlear partition away from the stapes. The shift in maximum displacement for a given frequency *change* $\Delta_{n/n}$ (where n = frequency) is the mechanical resolving power.

The normal human ear is sensitive to frequencies from about 15 or 20 cycles per second to between 16,000 and 20,000. There is much individual variation, and sensitivity to high tones diminishes with age. The threshold is lowest at 1500 to 2000 cycles. At the threshold of hearing the amplitude of vibration of the tympanic membrane is less than 10^{-9} cm at 3000 cycles.

Human frequency discrimination is better at medium and high intensities; at 60 db man can recognize about 1800 differences in tone. This discrimination is due in part to differences in the position of the maximum of displacement. High tones activate only the basal turn of the cochlea, and the apex of the cochlea is most sensitive to the lowest tones. Local lesions in the organ of Corti produced by prolonged exposure to pure tones, by local surgery, or by drugs cause loss of sensitivity in corresponding ranges.

The guinea pig cochlea has been carefully mapped by electrical recording following local lesions. Records from single fibers of the auditory nerve show fairly sharp limits of cut-off toward the higher frequencies. In general, the fibers arising in the basal turn respond to tones of any audible frequency, but those from the upper turn respond only to low frequencies.[187] Both primary and secondary neurons respond to only a narrow band of frequencies at threshold but to a wider band at higher intensities. Long regions of the basilar membrane respond to a given tone of high intensity, and the basal turn can respond to the entire frequency range. However, each point along the membrane shows maximal movement and, hence, stimulation at a particular frequency. In addition, there is reflex inhibition in the cochlear nucleus and in the cochlea itself.[69] Mutual inhibitory action tends to increase contrast where there is a change in the gradient of amplitude of displacement.[14] Neurons connected with different portions of the cochlea are separated spatially in the tracts, the intermediate nuclei and auditory cortex; hence tone discrimination is maintained in the

brain. In the cochlear nucleus of a cat the neurons responding to high-frequency sound lie dorsally; the low frequency ones, ventrally.[166]

Several electrical phenomena in the cochlea can be measured. The endolymph of the scala media is electrically positive by about 80 mv with respect to surrounding tissue and perilymph.[142] This DC potential is called the endocochlear potential (Fig. 112). The cells surrounding the scala media (including the organ of Corti) are electrically negative inside by about 70 mv, as are other tissue cells. Hence 150 mv potential exists between the interiors of the hair cells and the endolymph.[180]

When the ear is stimulated by sound, an alternating microphonic potential (cochlear microphonic, CM) is generated in the cochlea. It can easily be recorded from the round window. The CM varies in amplitude according to sound intensity. It is an alternating current response of the hair cells without measurable latency. It follows the wave form of imposed sound very faithfully up to the level at which distortion begins. The source of CM is the hair cells, particularly the external ones. The microphonic response is apparently caused by shear forces due to the movement of the tectorial membrane over the hair cells.[38]

An additional electrical response to a tone is a direct current response called the summating potential (SP).[39] This arises in the internal hair cells, and probably to a less extent in external hair cells also. Usually, scala media becomes more negative to scala tympani. The summating potential, like CM, is produced by bending or shearing of the hairs of the hair cells. Bending the hairs by means of a microneedle in different directions can produce potentials in either direction much like CM and SP. Symmetrical vibration causes the cochlear microphonic potential; unsymmetrical one-way displacement, the summating potential.

Auditory nerve impulses at the internal auditory meatus have a latency with respect to the CM of close to 1 msec. Single fiber responses are brief all-or-none spikes which are more or less synchronized with sound waves at frequencies much above 2000 cps. They show a refractory period of about 1 msec. A fiber may give one to three impulses to a single low frequency wave and double or triple spikes to a single very brief 8000 cps pip of sound.[187, 188] For longer lasting sounds the frequency of spikes in a given nerve fiber increases up to some optimum frequency and then decreases. At a given sound frequency the spike frequency increases with increasing sound intensity. Spontaneous activity is observed in many auditory fibers in the absence of sound.[187]

The current theory of stimulation of the nerve endings is as follows: The endocochlear and intracellular potentials provide a battery with an EMF of 150 mv across the hair-bearing ends of the hair cells. The magnitude of the measured potential varies with displacement of the basilar membrane and consequent bending or shearing of the hair cells; this change constitutes the CM and SP. The movement of the hairs is assumed to alter their electrical resistance so that current flows. The change of potential is due to the change in IR drop across the membrane. The change in current stimulates the nerve endings directly or indirectly. Slight mechanical deformation of the distal processes of the hair cells has thus a valve action by changing membrane resistance, permitting the generator potentials to appear, and allowing flow of current.

Hearing in Vertebrates. *Fishes.* In fishes the inner ear (Fig. 113*A*) is related to the lateral line organ in its ontogeny, in the hair cell nature of the sensing elements, and in the spontaneous activity in the sensory nerves.

Elasmobranch fish show behavioral response to vibrations in the water, and the response persists after the cutting of cutaneous and lateral line nerves but not after the eighth cranial nerve is cut. In the elasmobranch *Raja* impulses are recorded in response to low-frequency sound (of up to 120 cps) from nerve twigs to two sensory maculae in the sacculus and to one in the utriculus; no such response occurs in the nerve from the lagena. A "cochlear microphonic" up to 750 cps has been observed, and all nerve twigs showed spontaneous impulses.[123, 127, 128]

Bony fish have been extensively studied by conditioned reflex techniques with respect to hearing threshold, range, and pitch discrimination. In general, the Ostariophysi hear better than other fish. They have a set of bones, the weberian ossicles, connecting the swim bladder with the inner ear. The gas of the swim bladder imposes an acoustic discontinuity in the sound path, and the ossicles provide coupling to the sensing elements. The goldfish (*Carassius auratus*) can hear tones up to 3000 to 4000 cps; little loss resulted from injury to the utriculus, but when the sacculus and lagena were also damaged, reactions remained only to low tones (250 to 500 cps).[20] The European minnow *Phoxinus* hears over a wide range up to 6000 cps.[68, 87] *Phoxinus* can distinguish musical thirds in the 400 to 800 cps range, or 3 to 4 per cent

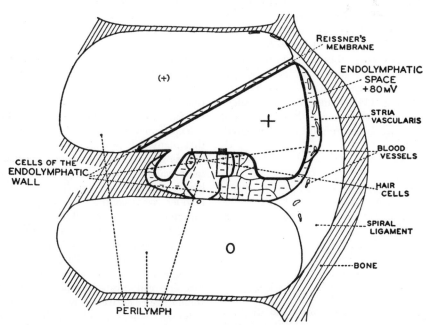

FIGURE 112. Diagram of cross-section of cochlea of a mammal, showing DC potential between scala media and surrounding regions. (From Davis, H.: Physiol. Rev., vol. 37.)

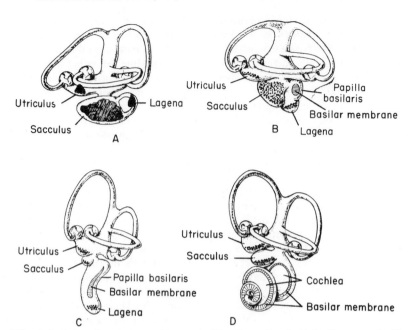

FIGURE 113. Labyrinths of various vertebrates. *A*, fish; *B*, turtle; *C*, bird; *D*, mammal. (From von Frisch, K.: Biol. Rev., vol. 11.)

frequency difference. This discrimination is not lost after removal of the weberian ossicles but is lost when the lagena is removed.[46, 49] Low frequencies (150 cps) are detected by touch as well as by the sacculus-lagena; very low frequencies (16 cps), by tactile sense only.[68] The audiogram of the catfish *Ameiurus* shows a nearly constant threshold from 60 to 1600 cps; above this range the threshold rises sharply, but conditioned responses have been obtained at frequencies as high as 13,100 cps.[12, 152] In the low-frequency range the catfish hears fainter sounds than does man (in air), but its threshold rises more rapidly at higher frequencies (Fig. 114). Removal of the malleus (a weberian ossicle) from both sides reduced the sensitivity by thirtyfold to a hundredfold.

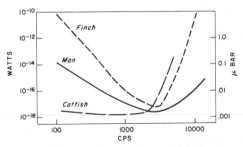

FIGURE 114. Audiograms from a bird (finch), a fish (catfish), and a mammal (man). (From Autrum, H., and Poggendorf, D.: Naturwissenschaften, vol. 181.)

Among nonostariophysids (which lack weberian ossicles) the upper hearing limit for *Corvina* is 1000 and for *Sargus*, 1250 cps;[46, 49] threshold is relatively constant below those frequencies. For *Gobius*, which lacks also a swim bladder, the upper limit of hearing is only 800 cps. Removal of the pars inferior (sacculus-lagena) from *Gobius* raised the threshold for the higher tones markedly, for low tones (100 cps) only slightly. In nonostariophysids the best frequency discrimination that has been demonstrated is about three-fourths of a low tone or 9 per cent frequency difference. If the fish has contact with the ground, low tones (less than 100 cps) can be heard as well without the ears as with them.[46, 49]

Experience with sonar instruments shows that many fish produce sounds. Some of the sounds come from the mouth parts, but the most varied sounds come from the swim bladder. Bands of muscle on the swim bladder wall contract tetanically, and the movement is transmitted to the gas in the swim bladder which acts as a resonator. The male toadfish (*Opsanus*) "calls" principally in the breeding season. The sea robin appears to have a grunt for alarm and a staccato breeding call; imitations played back to sea robins were answered by their own calls, although other sounds inhibited them.[146] Maximum energy of the grunt of a blenny *Chasmodes* is in the 80 to 180 cps range; of the "boat whistle" of a toadfish *Opsanus* it is at 250 cps, and maximum energy of the grunt of a gobiid is at 110 to 150 cps. Duration of the sounds is usually 50 to 350 msec.[189] It is probable that there is some communication or association of fish by means of calls; also the hearing sense leads to escape reactions.

Amphibians. In amphibia the lagena is slightly longer than in fish, and anurans (but not urodeles) have a middle ear. The frog's middle ear consists of the ear drum, an air cavity, and a bony columella which connects the drum with the inner ear. This adaptation transmits vibrations of air to the liquid phase of the inner ear as in mammals. Frogs are reported to have been conditioned to sounds over a range of 50 to 10,000 cps but do not appear to discriminate tones. Microphonic potentials were obtained at from 50 to 3500 cps, with maximum sensitivity between 400 and 1500.[183]

The urodele *Amblystoma* responded to sound up to about 200 cps and *Salamander* to higher frequencies. The upper limit was reduced after removal of the labyrinth, but responses to low frequencies persisted, presumably mediated by cutaneous receptors.

Reptiles. Structures characteristic of a true cochlea first appear in reptiles. In alligators the lagena is attached to two sides of the surrounding cavity, thus forming three ducts, and the floor of the lagena becomes the basilar membrane. Reptiles other than snakes have a middle ear which contains a bony columella. The tympanic membrane may be depressed below the body surface to form an external auditory meatus. Snakes have no middle ear but do have a columella attached to the quadrate bone. This makes snakes relatively insensitive to air-borne sounds but very sensitive to earth-borne vibrations.

The range for the auditory nerve response for a tortoise (box turtle) was narrow, 80 to 130 cps.[1] The cochlear response of several kinds of turtles has a relatively high threshold, low maximum voltage, and shows little response above 5000 cps.[198] An alligator gave good electrical responses well above 1000 cps.

The lizards *Lacerta* and *Tachydromus* respond to sound up to 8000 and 10,000 cycles, but there is no evidence that they are capable of frequency discrimination.

Birds. The ear of birds is similar in structure to that of reptiles yet their range of sensitivity and pitch discrimination is much greater. The cochlear microphonic potential of the pigeon follows sound up to a limit at 25,000 cps with lowest threshold at 3200

cps.[179] The optimum frequency is near that of man but the threshold is higher (Fig. 20).[62] After the cochlea was removed, good microphonic potentials were obtained in the range 100 to 3000 cycles from the ampullae of the semicircular canals.

Conditioning experiments show parrots and crossbills to hear and discriminate well over the range 40 to above 14,000 cycles. Pheasants hear up to 10,500, with their lowest threshold at 6000 cps.[182] A variety of songbirds were conditioned best at about 3200 cps. They responded also to vibrations (100 to 3200 cps), with maximum sensitivity at 800 cps. This low-freqency sense persisted after destruction of the ear and may be mediated by the organ of Herbst, a mechanoreceptor between the tibia and fibula.[179]

Sound production and detection are of considerable social importance in birds. Different species and some local races may be distinguished by their calls. There is evidence that the sound pattern is in part innate and in part learned. Distinctiveness of song for different species is greater where there are many sympatric species than on islands where few related species exist.[136] Different calls serve various purposes among birds. In crows an alarm call is distinct from an assembly call. The distress call of a French crow evoked no response from American crows; three French crow species failed to respond to the alarm of American crows, but they did react to the American crow assembly call as to their own distress call.[66] Herring gull calls differ for food finding, alarm, trumpeting which evokes chorusing, and a restricted "mew."[62]

Recent evidence[77] indicates that the Venezuelan oilbird *Steatornis* and an Asian swift *Collocalia,* each of which lives in deep caves, make use of echo-orientation when flying in the dark. *Steatornis* emits brief clicks, each consisting of sound within the range of 6100 and 8570 cps; the bird uses its eyes in the light but can dodge obstacles well in total darkness so long as its ears are intact. No ultrasonic component of its cry was detected, in contrast to bats. *Collocalia* emits 5 to 10 clicks/sec with a 4000 to 5000 cps component; orientation is visual in the light, acoustic in dark caves.[149]

Mammals. In all mammals the cochlea is coiled, in the duckbilled platypus a quarter turn, a whale 1.5 turns, the horse 2, man 2.75, cat 3, pig and guinea pig nearly 4 turns. The audiogram of man shows maximum sensitivity in the range from 800 to 2500 cps with an upper limit around 16,000. The audiograms for other animals have not always been obtained with sufficiently pure tones, but in general they have form similar to that for man but with somewhat higher thresholds and often indications of hearing at higher frequencies. Some dogs hear up to 35 kc, rats and guinea pigs to 40 kc. Threshold of hearing for a cat is close to man's, from 100 to 3000 cps, but it then remains lower up to 15,000 cps.

By observation of reflexes of pinna and vibrissae it was found that a variety of small mammals—mostly mice—can hear in the range from 6 to 98 kc.[171] A dormouse (*Muscardinus*), for example, had a minimum threshold (about 0.01 dyne/cm^2) at 20 kc. A deer mouse *Peromyscus* could be conditioned over the range 10 to 65 kc.[167] Various mice and shrews produce tones up to 30,000 cps; these may be useful in social contacts, possibly in orientation.[107] Cochlear potentials have been recorded from the ear of a kangaroo rat (*Dipodomys*) over a range from 100 to 20,000 cps, showing maximum sensitivity at 2000 to 4000 cps.[109]

The ear of Cetaceans is well adapted for underwater hearing, especially at high frequencies. Whales, porpoises, and dolphins have long been known to make a variety of noises, whistles, squeals, barks, mews, yelps, clicks, and rasping sounds. The sounds contain many components up to 100 kc. The porpoise *Tursiops* is particularly vocal when excited and may use its sounds in social communication.[203] Another genus, *Stenella*, lives in clearer water than *Tursiops* and is less vocal. *Tursiops* has been conditioned to accept fish on acoustic stimulation of low intensity from 150 to about 100,000 cps.[170] There is evidence that porpoises locate fish by echo ranging. As they approach objects while "searching" for food the intensity and continuity of their sound emission increase, and they avoid transparent partitions, apparently by sound reflection.[114]

It is evident that what is called audible sound for man is not necessarily equivalent to what is audible for other animals. Fish can "hear" at lower frequencies and many mammals at higher frequencies (ultrasonic) than man.

Acoustic Orientation in Bats. Sound production, hearing ability, and echo ranging are better understood in bats than in other animals.[77]

The Microchiroptera feed largely on flying insects. The vespertilionid bat *Myotis* has been most studied, and this bat can avoid small objects such as wires suspended in a totally dark room. When either the ears or mouth is sealed, the bats are reluctant to fly, and in a dark room they hit suspended objects and walls. As *Myotis* flies it continuously emits vocal cries; these consist of periodic clicks, each of which lasts on the average 2.3 msecs, which at its high frequency extends out in air only about 69 cm[86] (Fig. 115). Each sound pulse starts at a high frequency, about 70 to 80 kc, and ends at a lower frequency (30 to 45 kc), with maximum energy at about 50 kc. The pulses are repeated during free flight at about 30/sec, but as an object is approached the repetition rate rises to some 50/sec, and repetition rates as high as 150/sec are reported.[76, 78] These bats also emit sounds at about 7 kc, and clicks audible to man.

The emission of the ultrasonic cries is facilitated by modifications of the vocal cords in the muscular larynx and the presence of membranous laryngeal ventricles which serve as acoustic resonators. The intensity of the sound pulses is several dynes/cm^2 at a distance of 30 cm, and within 5 to 10 cm from the bat's mouth it may be 60 dynes/cm^2 or 109 db.[76, 78, 80]

Records made during flight in nature show that the pulse durations are longer and the frequency more uniform than in a closed room. For example, the big brown bat *Eptesicus* emits pulses averaging 3 msec in the laboratory and 15 msec in the field; the frequency during cruising is low—30 to 35 kc. When the bat dives toward a target the repetition rate rises to as much as 200 per second, frequency rises, and pulse duration drops to about 1 msec. In avoiding small objects such as wires a greater distance is needed, and the bats emit individual pulses of higher frequency than with large objects.[76, 78]

Cochlear microphonics recorded from the ears of various Vespertilionidae show responses at low frequencies (30/sec), one maximum at about 10 kc in all species and a second maximum at 30 to 50 kc in *Eptesicus*. Cochlear microphonic potentials were obtained up to more than 90 kc.[76,78] The basal portion of the cochlea is unusually large, and the brain is built around the central acoustic system.

Other families of Microchiroptera have different patterns of acoustic orientation from the Vespertilionidae. The long-eared bat

Plecotus flies more slowly, emits sounds by either mouth or nostrils, and the pulses are shorter and of lower frequency (35 kc at start, down to 24 kc at end) than in *Myotis*. In another family of insectivorous bats, the horseshoe bats or Rhinolophidae, vocal pulses average 65 msec in duration, are of uniform high frequency (80 or 100 kc in two species), low repetition rate (5 to 7/sec in flight), and high intensity.[144, 145]

One of the American fruit-eating bats (Microchiroptera), *Carollia,* emits pulses averaging 1.4 msec in duration, of variable frequencies, but usually of low sound intensity—3 dynes/cm^2 at a few inches (compared to 100 dynes/cm^2 by *Myotis* at the same distance). Others of the same group of leafnose bats emit similar low intensity whispers.

Attempts to jam the reflected sound by other sounds are unsuccessful unless the background sounds are extremely intense; the bats distinguish an echo of 35 db from an 80 db noise. The time between pulses and the briefness of the pulses is normally sufficient for the echo.[76, 78]

The Megachiroptera (old-world fruit and vampire bats) show much variation in modes of orientation while in flight. Of eight genera which have been examined, seven orient visually, and one (*Rousettus*) orients either visually or acoustically according to the illumination.[148] The sounds of *Rousettus* are 4 msec pulses of decreasing amplitude and 10 to 18 kc frequency; they are not vocalized and appear to be emitted at the sides of the lips.[79] The use of echolocation appears to have evolved independently in the Megachiroptera and Microchiroptera, and among the Microchiroptera a variety of adaptive specializations has appeared in sound production, detection, and use in behavior.

Phonoreception and Sound Production in Arthropods. Insects have receptors which cover a wide sensory range from low-frequency vibrations to medium-frequency sound; the receptors are tactile sensilla and chordotonal organs which may or may not be in tympanic organs. Tympanic organs occur in scattered families of Orthoptera, Hemiptera, and Lepidoptera, sometimes on abdomen or thorax, sometimes on forelegs. A tympanic organ consists of (1) a thin cuticular membrane associated with tracheae or air sacs, often protected by a fold in the exoskeleton, and (2) groups of chordotonal sensilla attached either to the tympanum or to the associated tracheae. Other chordotonal organs (scolopidia) without association with tympanal membranes are located on pliable regions of the cuticle, particularly between segments in many insects.[139] These are sensi-

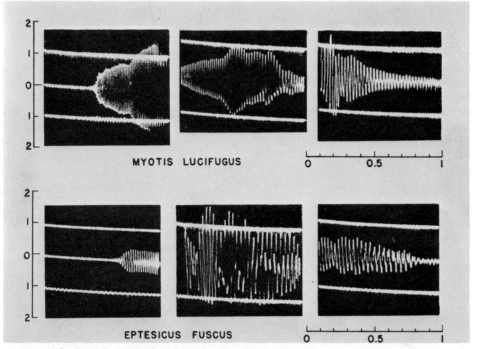

FIGURE 115.   Records of cries from bats. *A,* series of pulsed cries from bat *Myotis lucifugus* in pursuit of small target under natural conditions. *B,* beginning and end of pulses from *Eptesicus fuscus* under laboratory conditions. (From Griffin, D. H.: Listening in the Dark. Yale University Press, 1958.)

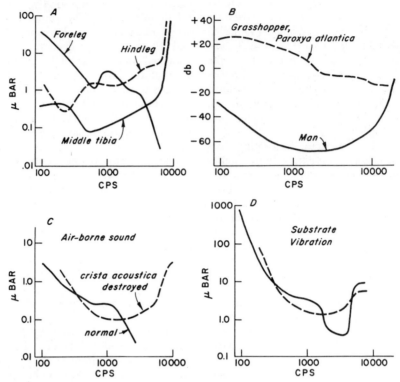

FIGURE 116. Audiograms for locust and grasshopper:
A, relative sensitivity determined by sensory nerve impulses of tympanal organs of locust to air-borne sound of fore, middle, and hind legs. *B,* relative sensitivity of grasshopper tympanal organ compared with ear of man. *C,* response from foreleg of locust before and after injury to sensory cells. *D,* sensitivity of foreleg receptor to substrate vibration. ———— normal, ——————— after destruction of crista acustica. (*A, C,* and *D,* modified from Autrum, H.: Ztschr. vergl. Physiol., vol. 28; *B* from Wever, E. G., and Vernon, J. A.: Proc. Nat. Acad. Sci., vol. 43.)

tive to low-frequency vibrations (beetles, flies) and some to higher frequency sound, as Johnston's organ on the second segment of the antenna of mosquitoes, or subgenual organs in the tibia of Orthoptera. Each chordotonal organ (whether in a tympanic organ or not) contains a number of scolopidia, each with a distal cap cell surrounding a sense rod (scolopale) which is attached to the terminal filament of the sense cell. The terminal filament is surrounded by a sheath cell, and the nucleus of the sense cell is at the base of the scolopidium.

Sensory hairs (sensilla) are widely distributed—on the surface of caterpillars, on cerci of crickets, cockroaches, and grasshoppers—and are sensitive to low-frequency vibrations.

The sensitivity of tympanic organs has been ascertained by recording action potentials in the sensory nerves and by noting behavioral responses to sounds. Tympanic organs are relatively insensitive to low frequencies, but at 10,000 cps and above, the

sensitivity approaches or even exceeds that of the human ear (Fig. 116). A response was present in two katydids at from 800 to above 45,000 cycles, in *Gryllus* from 300 to 800 cps, and in *Locusta* from 300 to above 10,000 cps.[199] A locust turns to face the source of a sound and extends its forelegs, which bear tympani. Electrical responses from the tympanic organ show that sensitivity increases to a peak at 1000 cps, then decreases, and then rises again up to some 90 kc. The high frequency sensitivity is lost if the crista of the tympanic organ is destroyed. The threshold at frequencies above 10 kc may approach 0.04 μ bar or 0.04 dyne/cm² (1 bar; 1 megadyne/cm²), which is lower than that of the human ear at this frequency (Fig. 116). In the grasshopper *Paroxya* the nerve impulses are synchronous with sound frequencies below 200 cps and asynchronous from 450 to 10,000 cps.[199] In a number of other Acridiidae synchronous impulses in tympanal nerves were found up to 90 cps,

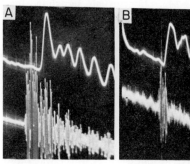

FIGURE 117. *Upper records,* response in tympanic nerve of moth, *Prodenia; lower records,* cries of bat near moth. *a,* bat cry in sonic range, predominant frequencies 10 to 15 kc. *b,* shorter bat cry, frequency >20 kc. Response of moth ear persists after stimulus has ceased. (From Roeder, K. D., and Treat, A. E.: J. Exp. Zool., vol. 134.)

asynchronous above this frequency, and responses fell off sharply above 1200 cps.[87]

Male katydids sing in concert and male and female crickets are attracted to each other by song. Singing by katydids and attraction of crickets and cicadas can be induced by appropriate artificial sounds, and young adult katydids responded over a range of 400 to 28,000 cps.[4, 164] Extirpation of the tympanic organ abolished the normal responses.

The tympanic organs of some moths are sensitive to very high frequencies. In a noctuid moth each sensillum of the tympanic organ contains 2 scolopes (sense cells) which differ in threshold. They respond to sound over the range of 3 to 240 kc but are most sensitive at 15 to 60 kc. The nerve fiber response is asynchronous, i.e., does not correspond to the sound frequency, but single fibers may fire at 1000/sec, and this response

adapts rapidly (Fig. 117). Bats which prey on these moths emit high-frequency sounds, and it is apparent that the moths detect approaching bats by means of tympanic organs.[165] Records from the tympanic nerves show that the moths detect bats at a distance much greater than that at which they show behavioral escape reactions. The scape moth *Ctenucha* responds to sound frequencies of 150 to 15,000 cps and at high intensities to yet higher frequencies so long as the tympanic organs are intact[63] (Fig. 118).

Chordotonal organs which occur without tympanic membranes in the tibiae of Orthoptera, Blattaria, Lepidoptera, and a few Hymenoptera detect substrate vibrations up to 8000 cps.[173] The subgenual organ on the leg of *Locusta* and *Decticus* responds to vibrations of the substrate with maximum sensitivity at 1500 to 2000 cps. Threshold at this frequency is given as 3.6×10^{-9} cm movement.[11, 13] Johnston's organ in the pedicle of the antenna of male *Aedes aegypti* responds to sounds from flying females or tuning forks and initiates mating reactions. In this organ noninnervated hairs set a flagellum in motion which amplifies the sound to stimulate the chordotonal organ. The frequency of sensitivity ranges from 400 to 525 cps in young males to 250 to 700 cps in older ones.[168]

The nerves serving hair sensilla of a variety of Acridiidae give bursts of impulses which synchronize to tones below 300 cps.[87] Hair sensilla of abdominal sternites respond to vibrations of the substratum. The cercal nerve of a cricket gives responses to tones up to 3000 to 4000 cps; below 300 cps the impulses synchronize with stimuli and some double spikes occur; at frequencies higher

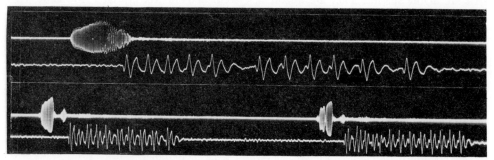

FIGURE 118. Simultaneous recording of the cries made by a flying bat while feeding in the laboratory (*upper traces*), and the tympanic nerve response of a moth (*Agroperina dubitans*) to the same cries (*lower traces*). Both responses were recorded on tape at 120 inches/second and subsequently photographed. The shape of the spikes has been distorted by filtering. (Recorded by Frederic A. Webster and Kenneth D. Roeder.) On the upper trace ┣━━━━━━━━┫ = 10 msec; on the lower two traces, ┣━━━━┫ = 10 msec.

than 400 cps bursts of impulses drop to half or quarter the stimulus frequency.[160, 161] Some Lepidopteran caterpillars respond to sounds up to 500 cps, possibly by sensory hairs.[141]

Insects produce sounds usually by rasping one skeletal structure over another, for example, a scraper on one wing across a file on the other, or a ridge on a leg against the wing, as in many Orthoptera.[64] In cicadas a cuticular diaphragm is vibrated by a group of high-frequency muscles, and pulses of sound at 3700 to 4200 cps are produced (see page 447, Chapter 14). *Locusta migratoria* song may go to 14,000 cps. The sounds may be very complex and compounded of resonance frequencies, sometimes ultrasonic, superposed on the impact frequency of the scraping structures.[151, 193] Males of six species of cicada show distinctive sound patterns which serve to isolate each species by sexual attraction. Sounds differ for congregational chorus, courtship, and alarm.[4]

From the lack of synchronization of nerve impulses with sound and from behavior tests with pure tones it appears that frequency discrimination is poor in insects. Thresholds of insects for moderate frequency sound are high. Apparently, insect ears are not adapted for the frequency discrimination and harmonic analysis which are so important in mammals. The nerve discharge in insects often shows bursts of impulses at the modulation frequency of a modulated sound and relatively independent of the carrier frequency. It appears that insects distinguish sounds by modulation frequency or repeated patterning of pulses—temporal pattern of sound units rather than wave form and phase. Pulsed sounds seem to be detected better than pure tones.[160, 161]

The sounds produced and detected by insects are highly specific. They are important in bringing the two sexes of a species together. Usually the male is the primary sound producer, but females may respond with sound.

For avoidance of predators, phonoreception is also important—low-frequency vibration sense in general, high-frequency reception in some moths. Phonetic analysis of songs of insects of 160 species in fourteen families and six orders showed differences in all, even in species not much different morphologically.[4] In some cicadas a single twitch of the tymbal muscle elicited by one volley of nerve impulses sets up a damped oscillation of the tymbal membrane; in others one nerve impulse elicits several twitches of the muscle[84] (Chapter 14). Intersexual signaling may have evolved from movements made during copulation.[155] The repetition rate of chirps varies with temperature, 260/min at 8° and 780/min at 26° in a grasshopper, *Nesconocephalus*.[65]

The sensory hairs of other arthropods are very sensitive to low-frequency sound. Spiders orient to sound transmitted through the web, and isopods are extremely sensitive to substrate vibrations. Some shrimp and mysids are sensitive to sound waves in the water and become less sensitive after extirpation of the statocyst. The nerve fibers connected to certain hairs in the statocysts of decapod crustaceans show good responses to sound (see p. 300). The statocyst, although primarily an equilibrium receptor, apparently has a dual function as does the sacculus of fish. Crustacea lack chordotonal organs such as are found in insects. Snapping shrimp make sounds of considerable intensity with their claws; this sound is a warning signal and can stun small animals.

CONCLUSIONS

The stimuli which affect mechanoreceptors, equilibrium receptors and phonoreceptors constitute a continuum from steady pressure through rapid deformation, or from low-frequency vibration to ultrasonic vibrations. Mechanoreceptors are mainly tactile or proprioceptive; equilibrium receptors are stimulated by gravity and by acceleration or deceleration; phonoreceptors are stimulated by sinusoidal vibrations of various frequencies and their harmonic and amplitude modulations.

Stimulation by mechanical means is not restricted to specific receptors since most, perhaps all, excitable cells are sensitive to deformation of the surface. In some cells, stretch is sufficient to depolarize the membrane and to stimulate; in other cells, stretch merely enhances the excitability to other agents. The basic problem of the nature of the deformation effect remains unsolved. Apparently some membranes become increasingly ion permeable when deformed, and local currents are set up, but more complete explanation must await better understanding of the ultramicroscopic structure of excitable membranes.

There are two general types of mechanoreceptors: (1) those in which part of the sensory neuron is stimulated by deformation and (2) those in which epithelial cells set up electrical currents which in turn stimulate embracing nerve fibers. In both types the actual stimulation of the sensory axons appears to be electrical. An example of the first type is the stretch receptor of crustaceans; deformation of the dendrites causes a partial gradable depolarization of the cell body, a "generator potential" which at some critical level sets off a sensory impulse. Similar local generator potentials have been recorded from pacinian corpuscles and from the sensory endings of muscle spindles. It is probable that generator potentials occur wherever free or encapsulated nerve endings are stimulated by deformation, for example, in the sense hairs of crustaceans and the sensilla of insects. Examples of the second type of mechanoreceptor, where special sense cells are deformed, are found in the lateral line and in the vestibular and cochlear receptors of vertebrates.

Across the membrane separating the interior of sensory cells of the mammalian cochlea from endolymph there exists a resting DC potential of some 150 mv which diminishes on deformation so that current flows out through the many fine processes of the embracing sensory neurons. The resting potential is less across the corresponding membranes of vestibular ampullae and lateral line neuromasts, but the method of stimulation appears to be similar to that in the cochlea. It is of interest that the hairlike endings of crustacean statocysts are processes of primary sense cells which are stimulated by the shearing of statoliths, while in the ampullae of vertebrate equilibrium organs the stimulation of the nerve endings is indirect, that is, by epithelial sensory cells.

Some mechanoreceptors show "spontaneous" activity; hence from these there is some level of input to the central nervous system. In such sense organs responses are a modulation of a preexisting level of activity, either an increase or a decrease. This is well shown in the responses of fish equilibrium receptors. Other mechanoreceptors are silent when at rest, as in most tactile hairs and encapsulated touch receptors. Whether spontaneously active or not, mechanoreceptors are often under reflex regulation from the central nervous system. The dendrites of the crustacean stretch receptors receive direct innervation by inhibitory fibers, and they are also regulated by tension developed in the attached muscle. Mammalian muscle spindles are regulated by axons controlling tension in intrafusal muscle fibers. Excitability of tactile endings in the skin of a frog can be altered by impulses in sympathetic nerves to the skin, and the auditory nerve contains some efferent fibers. Probably feedback from central nervous systems by efferent fibers in sensory nerves will be found to be a general phenomenon.

The membranes of mechanoreceptors differ greatly in whether they fire once or many times for a given stimulation. Some, like the slowly adapting crustacean stretch receptors and the carotid sinus pressure receptors of mammals, continue to discharge almost indefinitely during maintained deformation. Low-frequency receptors may give several impulses at a declining rate and then stop. High-frequency phonoreceptors and some tactile endings must respond only once per deflection. Whether the falling off of responses on repeated stimulation is by the same mechanism as adaptation to maintained deformation is not known. Position with respect to gravity is detected by plants and unicellular animals, which lack special equilibrium organs. Statocysts have evolved independently several times; most of them contain a particle (or several), foreign or secreted, resting on sensitive hairs. Statocysts are most common in animals which either live in water, free from the substrate, or which are evolved from swimmers. Many animals rely on asymmetrical tactile and proprioceptive stimulation for cues as to equilibrium; others, particularly terrestrial animals, use vision as an important means to orientation in space.

Response to mechanical vibration, whether carried by water, by solid substratum or in air, is a refinement of responses to touch and pressure. Many animals, for example, most orthopterans, have different sense organs for substratum vibration and for air-borne sound, although the two may overlap in frequency. The distinction between water- or air-borne sound and substratum or water vibration is not sharp, particularly in insects, reptiles, and fish. Receptors for air-borne sound have evolved along different lines in insects and vertebrates; repetition of pattern and modulation frequency seem more important for insects; tone (frequency) and intensity, for vertebrates. Other animals, e.g., crustaceans, detect sound frequencies by either their statocysts or tactile receptors, but only insects, birds and mammals detect air-borne sound of high frequencies. Many animals hear a range of sounds inaudible to the human ear. There is evidence that sound is used for species identification by insects; the possible use of it by crustaceans (e.g., snapping shrimp) and by fish is not known. Echolocation of objects at a distance appears to be used in water by a few aquatic insects, to a small extent by fish (by lateral line organs), probably by cetaceans, and in air by many bats and a few birds. The pattern of echolocation is very different in the insectivorous microchiroptera from what it is in the one family of vampire bats which echo-orient.

The vertebrates have modified and built upon the basic neuromast structure of lateral line organs to form the sensing elements of equilibrium and acceleration (labyrinth) and high-frequency vibration (phonoreceptor). Sound is detected in different parts of the labyrinth in fishes (utriculus in some, sacculus-lagena in many), in the lagena of amphibians and reptiles, and in the cochlea of mammals; birds appear to have retained some sound detection by the labyrinth. Auditory acuity is enhanced in some fishes by a bony coupling of gas bladder to labyrinthine ear, and in air-breathing vertebrates by the ossicles of a middle ear. The swim bladder of fish serves not only in transmission of sound, but in regulation of depth level in water (and as a store of oxygen).

Mechanoreceptors occur in wider variety than any other types of sense organ. New structures with a given receptor function have evolved many times. Mechanoreception in its broadest sense is both the most primitive and the most specialized of sensory functions. Mechanoreceptors have in common the graded depolarization of a cell membrane by deformation and the production of a generator potential which initiates nerve impulses.

REFERENCES

1. ADRIAN, E. D., J. Physiol. *92*: 9P-11P, 1938. Effect of sound on reptiles.
2. ADRIAN, E. D., J. Physiol. *101*: 389-407, 1943. Impulses in vestibular nerve.
3. AHRENS, W., Ztschr. vergl. Physiol. *32*: 49-59, 1950. Visualization of otoliths in fish.
4. ALEXANDER, R. D., Ohio J. Sci. *57*: 153-163, 1957. Sound production, crickets, cicadas.
5. ALEXANDER, R. D., and MOORE, T. E., Ohio J. Sci. *58*: 107-127, 1958. Sound production, crickets, cicadas.
6. ALEXANDROWICZ, J. S., Quart. J. Micr. Sci. *92*: 163-199, 1951; *93*: 315-346, 1952; J. Mar. Biol. Assn. U. K. *31*: 277-286, 1952; *35*: 129-144, 1956. Stretch receptors in muscles of Homarus, Leander, Palinurus, and the Paguridae.

* Reviews

7. ALEXANDROWICZ, J. S., Pubbl. Staz. Zool. Napoli *25*: 94-111, 1953; *29*: 213-225, 1957. Sense elements in Stomatopods.
8. ALEXANDROWICZ, J. S., J. Mar. Biol. Assn. U. K. *37*: 379-396, 1958. Proprioceptors in Crustacea.
9. ALEXANDROWICZ, J. S., and WHITEAR, M., J. Mar. Biol. Assn. U. K. *36*: 603-628, 1957. Receptor elements in coxal region of decapod Crustacea.
10. ALVAREZ-BUYLLA, R., and RAMIREZ DE ARELLANO, J., Am. J. Physiol. *172*: 237-244, 1953; Acta physiol. latino-am. *9*: 178-187, 1959. Local responses in pacinian corpuscles.
11. AUTRUM, H., Ztschr. vergl. Physiol. *28*: 326-352, 1940; *28*: 580-637, 1941. Acoustic sense in insects.
12. AUTRUM, H., and POGGENDORF, D., Naturwissenschaften *18*: 434-435, 1951. Auditory sense in catfish Ameiurus.
13. AUTRUM, H., and SCHNEIDER, W., Ztschr. vergl. Physiol. *31*: 77-88, 1948. Vibration sense in insects.
14. VON BEKESY, G., Nature *169*: 241-242, 1952. Mechanics of hearing.
15. VON BEKESY, G., and ROSENBLITH, W. A., *in* Handbook Experimental Psychology, edited by S. Stevens. John Wiley & Sons, 1951, pp. 1075-1115. Mechanical properties of the ear.
16. BIRUKOW, G., Ztschr. vergl. Physiol. *34*: 448-472, 1952. Gravity responses, frog.
17. BIRUKOW, G., Ztschr. vergl. Physiol. *36*: 176-211, 1954. Transfer from phototaxis to geotaxis in dung beetle, Geotrupes.
18. BLACK, V. S., Biol. Bull. *95*: 83-93, 1948. Gas changes in swim bladder of Fundulus in different densities.
19. BLAIR, H. A., Am. J. Physiol. *114*: 586-593, 1936. Mechanical stimulation of nerve.
20. BOIE, H., Ztschr. vergl. Physiol. *30*: 181-193, 1943. Hearing in goldfish.
21. BOVBJERG, R. V., Physiol. Zool. *25*: 34-56, 1952. Substrate selection by crayfish Orconectes.
22. BOYCOTT, B. B., Proc. Roy. Soc. London, B, *152*: 78-87, 1960. Structure and function of statocysts in Octopus.
23. BRAEMER, W., and BRAEMER, H., Ztschr. vergl. Physiol. *40*: 529-542, 1958. Gravity orientation by various fish.
24. BRONK, D. W., and STELLA, G., J. Cell. Comp. Physiol. *1*: 113-130, 1932; Am. J. Physiol. *110*: 708-714, 1935. Responses of carotid sinus to pressure.
25. BUCKMANN, D., Ztschr. vergl. Physiol. *36*: 488-507, 1954. Geotaxis in burrowing beetles (Staphylinidae).
26. VON BUDDENBROCK, W., Zool. Jahrb. abt. allg. *35*: 301-356, 1915; Vergleichende Physiologie I, Sinnesphysiologie, 1952, Basle, Birkhauser, pp. 233-387. Statocysts in Pecten, invertebrates in general; mechano-senses.
27. BURKE, W., J. Exp. Biol. *31*: 127-138, 1954. Proprioception and vibration sense organ in Carcinus.
28. CAUSSE, R., and GONDET, I., J. Physiol. Path. Gen. *42*: 169-185, 1950. Vestibular function in mice.
29. CHADWICK, L. E., Aerodynamics of Flight, *in*

Insect Physiology, edited by K. Roeder. New York, John Wiley & Sons, 1953, pp. 577-655.

30. *COHEN, M. J., J. Physiol. *130*: 9-34, 1955; *in* Physiology of Crustacea, edited by T. Waterman. New York, Academic Press, 1961, vol. 2, pp. 65-108.

31. COHEN, M. J., Proc. Roy. Soc. London, B, *152*: 30-48, 1960. Analysis of function of statocysts of Crustacea.

32. COHEN, M. J., *et al.,* Experientia 9: 434-435, 1953. Analysis of function of statocysts of Crustacea.

33. COOPER, S., *in* Structure and Function of Muscle, edited by G. H. Bourne. New York, Academic Press, 1960. Muscle spindles and muscle receptors.

34. COPELAND, D. E., J. Exp. Zool. *120*: 203-212, 1952. Reflex filling of swim bladder in physoclistous fish.

35. CRISP, D. J., and BARNES, H., J. Animal Ecol. *23*: 142-162, 1954. Distribution of barnacles according to substratum.

36. CROZIER, W. J., *et al.,* J. Gen. Physiol. 6: 531-537, 1934; *10*: 195-203, 257-269, 789-802, 1928. Stereotactic and geotactic responses.

37. *DAVIS, H., Physiol. Rev. *37*: 1-47, 1957; Ann. Otol. Rhin. Laryng. *67*: 789-802, 1958. Fourth Macy Conference on Nerve Impulse, 1953, pp. 58-139. Mechanism of cochlear excitation, pp. 1116-1142 *in* Handbook of Experimental Psychology, edited by S. Stevens. New York, John Wiley & Sons, 1951.

38. DAVIS, H., TASAKI, I., and GOLDSTEIN, R., Cold Spring Harbor Symp. *17*: 143-154, 1952. Sequence of electrical events in excitation of cochlea.

39. DAVIS, H., *et al.,* Am. J. Physiol. *195*: 251-261, 1958. Summating potential of the cochlea.

40. DIAMOND, J., GRAY, J. A. B., and INMAN, D. R., J. Physiol. *141*: 117-131, 1958; *142*: 382-394, 1958. Initiation of impulses; generator potentials in pacinian corpuscles.

41. DIAMOND, J., GRAY, J. A. B., and SATO, M., J. Physiol. *133*: 54-67, 1956. Initiation of impulses in pacinian corpuscles.

42. DICE, L. R., and BARTO, E., Science *116*: 110-111, 1952. High-frequency hearing by Peromyscus.

43. DIJKGRAAF, S., Ztschr. vergl. Physiol. *30*: 39-66, 1942; Experientia 6: 188-190, 1950. Swim bladder reflexes in fish.

44. DIJKGRAAF, S., Physiol. Compar. Oecol. 2: 81-106, 1950. Equilibrium reception in fish.

45. *DIJKGRAAF, S., Experientia 8: 205-206, 1952. Comparison of lateral line system and labyrinth of ear in fish.

46. DIJKGRAAF, S., Ztschr. vergl. Physiol. *34*: 104-122, 1952. Hearing in fish.

47. DIJKGRAAF, S., Experientia *11*: 329-333, 1955; *11*: 407-414, 1955; Pubbl. Staz. Zool. Napoli *28*: 341-358, 1956. Rotation reflexes, role of statocysts in setting eye movements, Crustacea.

48. DIJKGRAAF, S., Experientia *12*: 276-282, 1956. Electrophysiology of lateral line of Xenopus.

49. DIJKGRAAF, S., and VERHEIJEN, F. J., Ztschr. vergl. Physiol. *32*: 248-256, 1950. Hearing in fish.

50. EDWARDS, C., and OTTOSON, D., J. Physiol. *143*: 138-148, 1958. Site of initiation of impulses in crustacean stretch receptor.

51. EGGERS, F., Zool. Anz. *68*: 184-192, 1926. Echolocation and function of Johnston's organ in gyrinid beetles.

52. VON EGMOND, A. A. J., *et al.,* J. Physiol. *110*: 1-17, 1949. Mechanics of the semicircular canal.

53. ELDRED, E., *et al.,* J. Physiol. *122*: 498-523, 1953. Supraspinal control of muscle spindles.

54. VAN EYCK, M., Arch. Int. Physiol. *57*: 102-105, 231-236, 1949. Electrical responses from semicircular canals of pigeons.

55. EYZAGUIRRE, C., and KUFFLER, S. W., J. Gen. Physiol. *39*: 87-119, 121-153, 1955. Excitation of crustacean stretch receptors.

56. FAUST, R., Zool. Jahrb. Allg. Zool. Physiol. *63*: 325-366, 1952. Function of halteres in flies.

57. FLOREY, E., and FLOREY, E., J. Gen. Physiol. *39*: 69-85, 1956. Histology of stretch receptors of Crustacea.

58. FRAENKEL, G., Ztschr. vergl. Physiol. 2: 658-690, 1925. Equilibrium sense in medusae.

59. FRAENKEL, G., Proc. Zool. Soc. London, *109*: 69-78, 1939. Function of dipteran halteres.

60. *FRAENKEL, G., and GUNN, D. L., The Orientation of Animals. Oxford, Clarendon Press, 1940. 352 pp.

61. FRANZ, G., Ztschr. vergl. Physiol. *25*: 193-238, 1937. Swim bladder reflexes in fish.

62. FRINGS, H., and SLOCUM, B., Auk 75: 99-100, 1958. Hearing range of birds.

63. FRINGS, H., and FRINGS, M., Science *126*: 24, 1957. Hearing in moths.

64. FRINGS, H., and FRINGS, M., J. Exp. Zool. *134*: 411-425, 1957. Sound production by male grasshoppers.

65. *FRINGS, H., and FRINGS, M., Ann. Rev. Entomol. 3: 87-106, 1958. Uses of sounds by insects.

66. FRINGS, H., *et al.,* Wilson Bull. *67*: 155-170, 1955; Ecology *39*: 126-131, 1958. The meaning of calls in crows.

67. *VON FRISCH, K., Aus dem Leben der Bienen, Berlin, Julius Springer, 1927.

68. VON FRISCH, K., and DIJKGRAAF, S., Ztschr. vergl. Physiol. *22*: 641-655, 1935; Biol. Rev. *11*: 210-246, 1936. Hearing in Phoxinus.

69. *GALAMBOS, R., Physiol. Rev. *34*: 497-528, 1954. Neural mechanisms in audition.

69a. GALAMBOS, R., J. Neurophysiol. *55*: 424-437, 1956. Suppression of auditory nerve activity by efferent fibers.

70. GERNANDT, B., J. Neurophysiol. *12*: 173-184, 1949; Acta physiol. scand. *21*: 61-72, 1950. Neural responses from stimulation of semicircular canals.

71. *GRANIT, R., Receptors and Sensory Perception. Yale University Press, 1955, 369 pp.

72. GRANIT, R., and HENATSCH, H. D., J. Neurophysiol. *19*: 356-366, 1956. Reflex control of mammalian muscle spindles.

73. GRANIT, R., and KAADA, B. R., Acta physiol. scand. *27*: 130-160, 1953. Reflex control of mammalian muscle spindles.

74. GRAY, J. A. B., and MALCOLM, J. L., J. Physiol. *115*: 1-15, 1951. Excitation of touch receptors in frog skin.

75. GRAY, J. A. B., and MATTHEWS, P. B. C.,

J. Physiol. *113*: 475-482, 1951; *114*: 454-464, 1951; Gray, J. A. B., and Malcolm, J. L., Proc. Roy. Soc. London, B, *137*: 96-114, 1950. Excitation of pacinian corpuscles.

76. GRIFFIN, D. R., Experientia *7*: 448-453, 1951; J. Exp. Zool. *123*: 435-465, 1953. The sounds of bats; obstacle avoidance by acoustic orientation.

77. *GRIFFIN, D. R., Am. Scientist *41*: 209-244, 1953. Listening in the Dark, 1959. Yale University Press, 413 pp.

78. GRIFFIN, D. R., and GALAMBOS, R., J. Exp. Zool. *89*: 475-490, 1942. The sounds of bats; obstacle avoidance by acoustic orientation.

79. GRIFFIN, D. R., et al., Biol. Bull. *115*: 107-113, 1958. Echolocation in fruit bat Rousettus.

80. GRINNELL, A. D., and GRIFFIN, D. R., Biol. Bull. *114*: 10-22, 1958. Sensitivity of echolocation in bats.

81. GROEN, J. J., LOWENSTEIN, O., and VENDRIK, A. J. G., J. Physiol. *117*: 329-346, 1952. Mechanical analysis of responses from end-organs of horizontal semicircular canal in elasmobranch labyrinth.

82. GUELKE, R., and KEEN, J. A., J. Physiol. *116*: 175-188, 1952. Movement of auditory ossicles.

83. HABGOOD, J. S., J. Physiol. *111*: 195-213, 1950. Sensitization of sensory endings of frog's skin.

84. HAGIWARA, S., Physiol. Compar. Oecol. *4*: 142-153, 1956. Mechanism of sound production in cicada.

85. HARDY, A. C., and BAINBRIDGE, R., Nature *167*: 354-355, 1951. Responses of crustaceans to hydrostatic pressure.

86. HARTRIDGE, H., J. Physiol. *54*: 54-57, 1920; Nature *156*: 490-494, 1945. Acoustic control of flight in bats.

87. HASKELL, P. T., J. Exp. Biol. *33*: 756-766, 1956. Hearing in orthoptera.

88. HASKELL, P. T., and BELTON, P., J. Exp. Biol. *33*: 756-766, 1956. Hearing in orthoptera.

89. VON HEEL, W. H. D., Experientia *12*: 75-77, 1956. Pitch discrimination in minnow Phoxinus.

90. HERITIER, P. L., et al., C. R. Acad. Sci. *204*: 907-909, 1937. Wind as selective agent for insects.

91. HISADO, M., J. Fac. Sci. Hokk. Univ. ser. 6, *14*: 74-82, 1958. Effect of stretch on neuromuscular transmission.

92. HOAGLAND, H., J. Gen. Physiol. *16*: 695-714, 1933; *17*: 77-82, 1933. Activity in lateral line nerve of catfish.

93. HOAGLAND, H., J. Gen. Physiol. *19*: 221-228, 1935; *19*: 943-950, 1936. Adaptation of cutaneous receptors in frog.

94. HOAGLAND, H., and RUBIN, M. A., J. Gen. Physiol. *19*: 939-942, 1936. Adaptation of cutaneous receptors in frog.

95. HOAR, W. S., J. Fish. Res. Bd. Canada *81*: 241-263, 1951. Behavior of salmon in relation to stream currents.

96. HOGG, B. M., J. Physiol. *84*: 250-258, 1935. Slow impulses in cutaneous nerves, frogs.

97. HOLLICK, Q. S., Phil. Trans. Roy. Soc. London, B, *230*: 357-390, 1940. Sense organs of flight, flies.

98. VON HOLST, E., Ztschr. vergl. Physiol. *32*: 60-120, 1959; Symp. Soc. Exp. Biol. *4*: 143-172,

1950. Combination of light and gravity in orientation of fish; function of statolith system.

99. HUGHES, G. M., Nature *170*: 531-532, 1952. Abdominal mechanoreceptors in insects.

100. HUNT, C. C., Cold Spring Harbor Symp. *17*: 113-123, 1952; J. Gen. Physiol. *38*: 117-131, 1954. Muscle stretch receptors, their reflex function.

101. HUNT, C. C., and KUFFLER, S. W., J. Physiol. *113*: 298-315, 1951. Muscle stretch receptors, their reflex function.

102. JACOBS, W., Ztschr. vergl. Physiol. *27*: 1-28, 1939. Swim bladder of fish and orientation with respect to depth.

103. JIELOF, R., et al., J. Physiol. *116*: 137-157, 1952. Microphonics of lateral line organ.

104. JOHNSON, F. A., EYRING, H., and POLISSAR, M., Kinetic Basis of Molecular Biology. New York, John Wiley & Sons, 1954, 897 pp.

105. JONES, F. R. H., J. Exp. Biol. *28*: 553-566, 1951; *29*: 94-109, 1952. Swim bladder and vertical movements of fish.

106. *JONES, F. R. H., and MARSHALL, N. B., Biol. Rev. *28*: 16-83, 1953. Structure and functions of teleostean swim bladder.

107. KAHMANN, H., and OSTERMANN, K., Experientia *7*: 268-269, 1951. Production of high-frequency tones by mice and shrews.

108. KATSUKI, Y., Jap. J. Physiol. *1*: 87-99, 264-268, 1951. Electrical responses from lateral line organ of fish.

109. KATSUKI, Y., and DAVIS, H., J. Neurophysiol. *17*: 308-316. 1954. Electrophysiology of ear of kangaroo rat.

110. KATSUKI, Y., et al., Jap. J. Physiol. *1*: 179-195, 1951; *2*: 93-102, 1951. Electrical responses from lateral line organ of fish.

111. KATSUKI, Y., et al., Proc. Japan Acad. Tokyo *30*: 248-255, 1954. Electrical responses from hair-cells of ear of fish.

112. KATSUKI, Y., et al., J. Neurophysiol. *22*: 343-359, 1959. Activity of auditory tract in brain of ca⁺.

113. KATZ, B., J. Physiol. *111*: 248-282, 1950. Initiation of impulses in stretch receptors in muscles of frog.

114. KELLOG, W. N., Science *128*: 250-252, 1952; *128*: 982-988, 1958. Echo ranging in porpoise.

115. KNIGHT-JONES, E. W., and QASIM, S. Z., Nature *175*: 941-942, 1955. Responses of marine plankton animals to hydrostatic pressure changes.

116. KUFFLER, S. W., J. Neurophysiol. *17*: 558-574, 1954; Exp. Cell. Res., suppl. *5*: 495-519, 1958. Stretch receptors of lobster.

117. KUFFLER, S. W., and EYZAGUIRRE, C., J. Gen. Physiol. *39*: 155-184, 1955. Synaptic inhibition of crustacean stretch receptor.

118. LANDGREN, S., Acta physiol. scand. *26*: 1-56, 1952. Excitation of carotid pressure receptors.

119. VON LEEUWEN, S., J. Physiol. *109*: 142-145, 1959. Analysis of response of frog muscle spindle.

120. LINDAUER, M., and NEDEL, J. O., Ztschr. vergl. Physiol. *42*: 334-364, 1959. Gravity sense and orientation of head in honeybee.

121. *LISSMANN, H. W., Symp. Soc. Exp. Biol. *4*: 34-59, 1950. Proprioceptors.

122. *LOWENSTEIN, O., Symp. Soc. Exp. Biol. *4*: 60-

82, 1950; *in* Physiology of Fishes, edited by M. E. Brown. New York, Academic Press, 1957, Chapter 2, part 2, pp. 155-186.

123. LOWENSTEIN, O., Proc. Roy. Soc. Med. *45*: 133-134, 1952. Equilibrium function of otolith organs and semicircular canals of elasmobranch Raja, analyzed by nerve impulse recording.

124. LOWENSTEIN, O., J. Exp. Biol. *33*: 417-421, 1954. Pressure receptors in fin of dogfish.

125. LOWENSTEIN, O., J. Physiol. *127*: 104-117, 1955. Electrical polarization of labyrinth of ray.

126. LOWENSTEIN, O., and FINLAYSON, L. H., Proc. Roy. Soc. London, B, *148*: 433-449, 1958; Comp. Biochem. Phys. *1*: 56-61, 1960. Structure and responses of abdominal stretch receptors of insects.

127. LOWENSTEIN, O., and ROBERTS, T. D. M., J. Physiol. *110*: 392-415, 1950; *114*: 471-489, 1951. Responses to vibration in isolated elasmobranch labyrinth.

128. LOWENSTEIN, O., and SAND, A., Proc. Roy. Soc. London, B, *129*: 256-275, 1940. Equilibrium function of otolith organs and semicircular canals of elasmobranch Raja, analyzed by nerve impulse recording.

129. LOWENSTEIN, O., and WERSALL, J., Nature *184*: 1807-1808, 1959. Electron microscopy of sensory hairs in cristae of Raja.

130. LOWENSTEIN, W. R., J. Physiol. *132*: 40-60, 1956; *133*: 588-602, 1956. Effects of stretch and sympathetic stimulation on activity of touch receptors in frog skin.

131. LOWENSTEIN, W. R., J. Gen. Physiol. *41*: 825-845, 847-856, 1958. Facilitation and refractoriness in pacinian corpuscles.

132. LOWENSTEIN, W. R., and ALTAMIRANO-ORREGO, R., J. Gen. Physiol. *41*: 805-824, 1958. Generator potentials, initiation of impulses, refractoriness in pacinian corpuscles.

133. LOWENSTEIN, W. R., and MOLINS, D., Science *128*: 1284, 1958. Cholinesterase in pacinian corpuscle.

134. LOWENSTEIN, W. R., and RATHKAMP, R., J. Gen. Physiol. *41*: 1245-1265, 1958. Initiation of impulses in pacinian corpuscles.

135. MACKINNON, D., and HOAR, W. S., J. Fish. Res. Bd. Canada *10*: 523-538, 1953. Responses of salmon fry to currents.

136. MALER, P., Nature *176*: 6-8, 1955. Characteristics of animal calls.

137. MATTHEWS, B. H. C., J. Physiol. *71*: 64-110, 1931; *72*: 153-174, 1931; *78*: 1-53, 1933. Receptors in mammalian and frog muscle.

138. MAXIMOW, A. A., and BLOOM, W., Textbook of Histology, 1942. Philadelphia, W. B. Saunders Co., pp. 197-203. Figures of mechanoreceptors.

139. MCINDOO, N. E., J. Comp. Neurol. *34*: 173-199, 1922. Auditory sense of bee.

140. MERTON, P. A., Acta physiol. scand. *29*: 87-88, 1953. Slowly conducting muscle spindle afferents.

141. MINNICH, D. E., J. Exp. Zool. *72*: 439-453, 1936. Responses of caterpillars to sound.

142. MISRAKY, G. A., *et al.*, Am. J. Physiol. *194*: 393-402, 1958. Electrical properties of wall of endolymphatic space of cochlea, guinea pig.

143. MITTELSTAEDT, H., Ztschr. vergl. Physiol. *32*: 422-463, 1950. Optomotor responses and gravity orientation in flying dragonflies.

144. MOHRES, F. P., Ztschr. vergl. Physiol. *34*: 547-588, 1953. Acoustic and other orientation in bats Rhinolophidae, Vespertilionidae.

145. MOHRES, E. P., and KULZER, E., Ztschr. vergl. Physiol. *38*: 1-29, 1956. Acoustic and other orientation in fruit bats.

146. MOULTON, J. M., Biol. Bull. *111*: 393-398, 1956; *114*: 357-374, 1958. Acoustic behavior of sea robins and other fish.

147. NESS, A. R., J. Physiol. *126*: 475-493, 1954. Mechanoreceptors of rabbit incisor.

148. NOVICK, A., J. Exp. Zool. *137*: 443-461, 1958. Orientation in paleotropical bats.

149. NOVICK, A., Biol. Bull. *117*: 497-503, 1959. Acoustic orientation in cave swiftlet.

150. PETERS, H. M., Ztschr. vergl. Physiol. *33*: 207-265, 1951. Role of swim bladder in orientation of sea horse.

151. PIERCE, G. W., Songs of Insects. Harvard University Press, 1948.

152. POGGENDORF, D., Ztschr. vergl. Physiol. *34*: 222-257, 1952. Auditory sense in catfish Ameiurus.

153. PRINGLE, J. W. S., J. Exp. Biol. *15*: 101-131, 1938. Proprioception in insects.

154. *PRINGLE, J. W. S., Phil. Tr. Roy. Soc. London, B, *233*: 347-384, 1948; Insect Flight. Cambridge University Press, 1957, 133 pp. Gyroscopic mechanism of halteres of Diptera.

155. PRINGLE, J. W. S., Proc. Linn. Soc. London *167*: 144-159, 1957; J. Exp. Biol. *31*: 525-560, 1954; Acta Physiol. Pharmacol. Néerl. *5*: 88-97, 1956. Structure and physiology of sound-producing organs in insects, particularly cicadas.

156. PRINGLE, J. W. S., J. Exp. Biol. *32*: 270-278, 1955. Function of lyriform organs in arachnids.

157. PRINGLE, J. W. S., J. Exp. Biol. *33*: 658-667, 1956. Proprioception in Limulus.

158. PRINGLE, J. W. S., and WILSON, V. J., J. Exp. Biol. *29*: 220-234, 1952. Response of cockroach mechanoreceptor to harmonic mechanical stimulus.

159. PROSSER, C. L., J. Cell. Comp. Physiol. *16*: 25-38, 1940. Sensory responses from single hairs of crayfish.

160. *PUMPHREY, R. J., Symp. Soc. Exp. Biol. *4*: 3-18, 1950. Hearing.

161. PUMPHREY, R. J., and RAWDON-SMITH, A. F., Proc. Roy. Soc. London, B, *121*: 18-27, 1936. Hearing, particularly in insects.

162. QUILLIAM, T. A., and SATO, M., J. Physiol. *129*: 167-176, 1955. Histology of pacinian corpuscles.

163. RABE, W., Ztschr. vergl. Physiol. *35*: 300-325, 1953. Orientation of backswimmers and other aquatic insects.

164. REGEN, J., Pflüg. Arch. Physiol. *155*: 193-200, 1913; Sitzungsb. Akad. Wiss. Wien *132*: 81-88, 1923. Orientation of female orthopterans to male songs.

165. ROEDER, K. D., and TREAT, A. E., J. Exp. Zool. *134*: 127-157, 1957. Sound reception by tympanic organ of noctuid moths.

166. ROSE, J. E., GALAMBOS, R., and HUGHES, J. R., Bull. Johns Hopkins Hosp. *104*: 211-251, 1959. Electrical activity of cochlear nuclei, cat.

167. Ross, D. A., J. Physiol. *86*: 117-146, 1936. Responses from frog vestibular nerve.

168. Roth, L. M., Am. Midl. Nat. *40*: 265-352, 1948. Hearing in mosquitoes.

169. Sand, A., J. Physiol. *89*: 47P-49P. 1937. Effect of fluid flow on activity of lateral line of Raja.

170. Schevill, W. E., and Lawrence, B., J. Exp. Zool. *124*: 147-165, 1953. Conditioned responses of porpoise to high-frequency sound.

171. Schleidt, W. M., Experientia *7*: 65-66, 1961; Die Naturwiss. *39*: 69-70, 1952. Reactions of voles and mice to high-frequency sound.

172. Schneider, G., Ztschr. vergl. Physiol. *35*: 416-458, 1953. Halteres and equilibrium in blowflies (Calliphora).

173. Schneider, W., Ztschr. vergl. Physiol. *32*: 287-302, 1950. Sound reception in various insects.

174. Schoen, L., Ztschr. vergl. Physiol. *32*: 121-150, 1950; *39*: 399-417, 1957. Reflexes and electrical responses of vestibular system of fish.

175. Schoen, L., and von Holst, E., Ztschr. vergl. Physiol. *32*: 552-571, 1950. Role of lagena and utriculus in orientation of fish.

176. Schöne, H., Ztschr. vergl. Physiol. *36*: 241-260, 1954; *39*: 235-240, 1957; Anat. Rec. *134*: 635, 1959. Statocyst function and equilibrium orientation in crustaceans.

177. *Schöne, H., Ergeb. d. Biol. *21*: 163-209, 1959. Role of statolith organs and eyes in space orientation.

178. Schwartz, E., C. R. Soc. Biol. *146*: 768-771, 1952. Rheotropisms of Planaria.

179. Schwartzkopff, J., Experientia *5*: 159-161, 1949; Ztschr. vergl. Physiol. *31*: 527-608, 1949; *34*: 46-68, 1952; *41*: 35-48, 1958. Hearing in various birds; cochlear potentials, conditioned responses.

180. Smith, C. A., et al., Am. J. Physiol. *173*: 203-206, 1958. DC potentials of membranous labyrinth, guinea pig.

181. Steinhaus, W., Pflüg. Arch. Physiol. *232*: 500-512, 1933. Observations on cupula in living fish.

182. Stewart, P. A., Ohio J. Sci. *55*: 122-125, 1955. Audiogram of pheasant.

183. Strother, W. F., J. Comp. and Physiol. Psychol. *52*: 157-162, 1959. Electrical responses from auditory mechanism of frog.

184. Suckling, E. E., and Suckling, J. A., J. Gen. Physiol. *34*: 1-8, 1950. Responses of lateral line system of Fundulus.

185. *Tasaki, I., Ann. Rev. Physiol. *19*: 417-438, 1959. Hearing.

186. Tasaki, I., and Davis, H., J. Neurophysiol. *18*: 151-159, 1955. Impulses in individual fibers of cochlear nucleus, guinea pig.

187. Tasaki, I., and Fernandez, C., J. Neurophysiol. *15*: 497-512, 1952. Cochlear microphonics, impulses in cochlear nucleus, guinea pig.

188. Tasaki, I., et al., J. Acoustic. Soc. Am. *26*: 765-773, 1954. Source of cochlear potentials.

189. Tavolga, W. N., Bull. Mar. Sci. Gulf Carib. *8*: 278-284, 1958; Physiol. Zool. *31*: 259-271, 1958. Underwater sound production by fish.

190. Thorpe, W. H., and Crisp, D. J., J. Exp. Biol. *24*: 310-328, 1947. Orientation of aquatic insects in relation to plastron respiration.

191. Treat, A. E., and Roeder, K. D., J. Insect Physiol. *3*: 262-270, 1959. Nerve elements of tympanic organs of moths.

192. Trincker, D., Pflüg. Arch. Physiol. *264*: 351-382, 1957. Electrical responses of cupula system on rotation, guinea pig.

193. Wakabayashi, T., and Hagiwara, S., Jap. J. Physiol. *3*: 249-253, 1953. Mechanical and electrical events in sound production by cicadas.

194. Walcott, C., and Van der Kloot, W. G., J. Exp. Zool. *141*: 191-244, 1959. Physiology of spider vibration receptor.

195. Weis-Fogh, T., Nature *164*: 873-874, 1949; Phil. Tr. Roy. Soc. London, B, *239*: 553-585, 1957. Mechanoreceptors in relation to flight in locusts.

196. *Wendt, G. R., in Handbook of Experimental Psychology, edited by S. Stevens. New York, John Wiley & Sons, 1951, pp. 1191-1223. Vestibular functions.

197. Wever, E. G., J. Comp. Psychol. *10*: 221-223, 1930; J. Exp. Psychol. *126*: 281-286, 1940. Audiogram of man and cat.

198. Wever, E. G., and Vernon, J. A., Proc. Nat. Acad. Sci. *42*: 213-220, 1956. Audiograms of various turtles.

199. Wever, E. G., and Vernon, J. A., Proc. Nat. Acad. Sci. *43*: 346-348, 1957; *45*: 413-419, 1959. Auditory sensitivity of grasshopper, Paroxya, and other Orthoptera.

200. Wiersma, C. A. G., J. Mar. Biol. Assn. U. K. *38*: 143-152, 1959. Proprioceptors in joints of crabs.

201. Wiersma, C. A. G., and Boettiger, E. G., J. Exp. Biol. *36*: 102-112, 1959. Proprioceptors in joints of crabs.

202. Wiersma, C. A. G., et al., J. Exp. Biol. *30*: 136-152, 1953. Physiology of muscle stretch receptors of crayfish.

203. Wood, F. G., Bull. Mar. Sci. Gulf Carib. *3*: 120-133, 1953. Underwater sound production by porpoises Tursiops and Stenella.

204. *Wright, M. R., Quart. Rev. Biol. *26*: 264-280, 1951. Lateral line system.

205. Yamashita, T., Ztschr. Biol. *109*: 111-122, 1956. Statoliths in sense organs of Aurelia; impulses from these sense organs.

206. Young, J. Z., Proc. Roy. Soc. London, B, *152*: 3-29, 1960. Structure and function of statocysts in Octopus.

207. Zobell, C. E., and Morita, R. Y., J. Bacteriol. *73*: 563-568, 1956. Barophilic bacteria in deep sea sediments.

208. Zotterman, Y., J. Physiol. *95*: 1-28, 1939. Electrophysiological investigation of touch, pain, and tickling.

CHEMORECEPTION

Chapter 11

Chemoreception by animals shows a broad spectrum of sensitivities. Analysis of the sense, particularly in man, has led to a classification into three categories—general chemical sense, gustation or taste, and olfaction or smell. Difficulties arise in applying this classification to studies of the sensitivity of aquatic animals to solutions, to distinguishing chemical stimuli for such diverse acts as ingestion and egg laying, and to measuring the distance at which a substance is perceptible. However, it is practical to distinguish those receptors which have high sensitivity and specificity, which in air-breathers respond to volatile materials, and which are "distance chemical receptors" as *olfactory*; the receptors of moderate sensitivity, stimulated by dilute solutions, which are usually associated with feeding as *gustatory* or "contact chemical receptors," and those receptor endings which are relatively insensitive and nondiscriminating and which lead to protective responses, as *general chemical sense*.

Chemoreception is of importance in the location and testing of food, in initiating escape from noxious agents, in finding mates and associates, and in identifying hosts and sites for oviposition. In general, animals respond to "attractants" by positive chemotaxes, to "repellents" by negative taxes or rejection responses.

BEHAVIORAL SIGNIFICANCE AND PHYSIOLOGY OF CHEMORECEPTION

Chemoreception in Invertebrates (Except Insects). Protozoa, like many other cells, show general chemical sensitivity. Local application of weak alkali at one side on an amoeba leads to pseudopodial extension on that side; local application of relatively strong acid or salt solution may cause pseudopods to form on the opposite side. Ciliates and flagellates show avoidance reactions to various chemicals. They may aggregate in a slightly acid region. Ciliary reversal is brought about by a variety of chemicals, particularly by monovalent cations in the series: $K^+ > Li^+ > Na^+ > NH_4^+$. Chemotaxis is observed in the aggregation of myxamoebae, in the approach of leukocytes to organic particles, and in feeding behavior of Protozoa.

Sponges show a general chemical sensitivity to contaminants in the water; they may regulate inflow through ostia and currents in canals, and may close oscula in response to chemicals in the water. It has been suggested that an important form of coordination in sponges may be by the transport of chemicals in the canal system. Coelenterates show remarkable chemical discrimination, particularly for meat juices. Sea anemones actively transport bits of food toward the mouth and inert particles away from it. The tentacles of anemones and the oral arms of medusae show extreme sensitivity to food chemicals.

Planaria have chemoreceptors at the sides of the head which detect food placed at some distance; other chemoreceptors in the central region of the head function during feeding, hence are properly called taste receptors. In the presence of food a planarian increases its random movement, turns more frequently when in regions of lower concentration of the food stimulus so that it approaches the food, and when close (8 cm) the planarian moves toward the food and waves the anterior end from side to side (klinotaxis).[58]

Chemoreception is important also in location of food by molluscs. The flow of water through the mantle cavity of bivalves is regulated in accordance with the dissolved chemicals. Terrestrial snails appear to use chemical sense in locating food. *Pecten* is very sensitive to dissolved organic matter, particularly to fluid from its natural enemy the starfish. Limpets from the lower intertidal zone are repelled by starfish fluid, but limpets from the high intertidal where starfish do not occur fail to show the escape reaction.[12]

Annelids show taste as well as general chemical sense. Darwin found that earthworms could distinguish between green and red cabbage and between carrot and celery and other pairs of leaves. The anterior end of an earthworm is very sensitive to volatile materials such as xylene or ether, and the entire body to acids and salts. The impulses in segmental nerves in response to dilute acid on the skin are in very small fibers.[79]

Crustaceans must be well supplied with chemoreceptors, especially with taste endings on the mouthparts. Responses to dilute sucrose have been recorded from antennule nerves of crabs.[50] Impulses have been set up in gnathobase nerves of *Limulus* by clam extracts, and feeding reflexes initiated.[8]

Often symbiosis, commensalism, and parasitism involve chemoreception. The polychaete *Arctonoe* goes to its commensal host, a starfish *Evasterias*, by chemotaxis. When *Arctonoe* in a Y-tube is presented the choice between plain sea water and starfish-inhabited sea water, the worm selects the latter; the attractant substance appears to be a protein. Solution from an aquarium containing injured starfish repels *Arctonoe*.[17] The miracidia of digenetic trematodes attach only to their host species of snail even in the presence of other kinds of snails, apparently by specific chemical attraction.[7] A sessile rotifer, *Collotheca*, attaches only to the fresh green leaves of the plant *Utricularia* even in the presence of many other plants; the older leaves give off a substance repellent to the rotifer, while young leaves are attractant. Fresh-water mites *Unionicola* live normally as parasites on the gills of a mussel, *Anodonta*; the mites when in water away from the host are photopositive, but after a little water from the mantle cavity of a mussel is added they immediately reverse to negative phototaxis. Water from other mussel species is ineffective. The effect of the chemical control of phototaxis is to keep the mite within the host.[101a]

The clown fish *Amphiprion* commonly associates with a sea anemone *Stoichaetis*, swimming unharmed among the tentacles; similar size fish of other species which come within range receive nematocyst discharges from the anemone. *Amphiprion* after mucus removal becomes a target for the nematocysts. A rod coated with mucus from most fish stimulates nematocyst discharge by the anemone, but mucus from *Amphiprion* in-hibits the anemone's response to mechanical stimulation by the rod.[18]

Behavioral Aspects of Chemoreception in Insects. Insects have attained a high degree of specialization in chemoreceptors. Some of their receptors are particularly sensitive to volatile material, hence are called distance or olfactory organs; these are often on antennae, sometimes on labial palps, and they may be pore plates (sensilla placodea), thin cones and pegs (sensilla basiconica), or pegs or cones in pits (sensilla coeloconica).[23, 25] Hygroreceptors are a type of distance chemoreceptors. In *Tenebrio* these are antennal pegs and pits; in a louse they are antennal tuft organs which sense the degree of humidity of the air. Grasshoppers have on antennal flagellae humidity detectors which are not the chemosensitive basiconic pegs[89] (see Chapter 2, p. 39). The mosquito *Aedes* has CO_2 detectors on the first flagellar segment of the antennae; by antennal receptors it can perceive also at a distance odors, moisture, and warmth; labial palps may detect blood.[80] Other chemoreceptors are contact or taste organs and may be located on antennae (bees, ants), mouthparts and tarsi (Diptera, Lepidoptera, Trichoptera, Hymenoptera), or on ovipositors (Ichneumonids, Gryllidae). Many contact chemoreceptors are thin hairs which contain the endings of two chemoreceptor nerve fibers. In addition, insects show general chemical sensitivity which persists after specific receptors have been amputated. All of the described chemoreceptors are covered by a cuticle which is thinner than that on the rest of the body and is presumably permeable.[44]

In the grasshopper, contact chemoreceptors are long pegs, the basiconic sense organs (Fig. 119). Each of these has about five sensory neurons with processes projecting inside the cuticular sheath toward the tip, which has an opening less than 2 μ in diameter.[90] The distance chemoreceptors (olfactory) are short, thin walled pegs, coeloconic sense organs. These have at their base a cluster of neurons (average, 37), and the dendritic processes branch extensively to terminate in several 0.1 μ pores on the sides of the peg. At the base is a 1 μ spot which does not receive nerve processes but is the opening through which the old peg sheath is withdrawn at the molt (Figs. 120, 121).[89]

Some insects are sensitive to natural organic compounds which are not smelled by man. Male moths (e.g., gypsy moths) are attracted from a distance of a mile or two by an odor from the scent gland of the female. Males deprived of their antennae do not orient toward the female; males will attempt copulation with blotting paper previously touched to the female scent gland.[55] The sex attractant has been identified as dextrorotatory 10-acetoxy-1-hydroxy-cis-7-hexadecene. Methyl eugenol is used to collect male oriental fruit flies from at least a quater-mile radius. Parasitic insects (e.g., Hymenoptera) are attracted by specific odors to their host, even when tunneled in wood. Bait once visited by flies becomes more attractive to other flies than fresh bait.

Social insects live in a world of odors; they distinguish not only food odors but caste odor, hive odor, sting and wax odor.[65] Ants recognize and admit nest mates, but after these have been washed with water or smeared with body juices of ants from other nests, they are attacked as intruders. Honeybee scouts associate certain aromas, particularly those from flowers, with food; others do not.

Food selection by insects is almost exclusively by chemo-orientation, mostly by taste.[34]

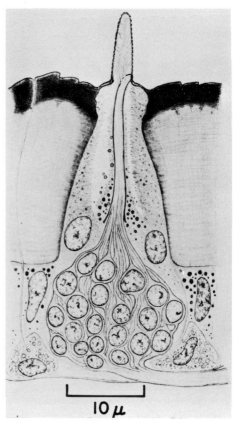

FIGURE 120. Distance chemoreceptor, short coeloconic sense organ of grasshopper. (From Slifer, E.: J. Morphol., vol. 105.)

Most phytophagous insects feed on only a few kinds of plant. Some insects formerly thought to be monophagous, or feeding only on one species of plant, feed on several closely related plants, often of one genus. Other insects (oligophagous) feed on more species, either many or all of one family of plants. Polyphagous insects, e.g., locusts, feed on a wide variety of plants, but no phytophagous insect feeds indiscriminately on all plants.

The degrees of specificity of plants as insect food are explained by the occurrence in plants of secondary organic compounds which either make given plants highly acceptable to certain insects or make them unacceptable (repellent) for all but certain species. Potato beetles and tobacco hornworms are restricted to Solanaceae; the beetles feed on potato, but nicotine makes tobacco unacceptable and the glycoside tomatin makes tomato unacceptable to them. Potato treated with nicotine or tomatin becomes unacceptable. Hornworms feed on tomato or tobacco but not normally on potato. Mexican bean beetles feed on plants of the

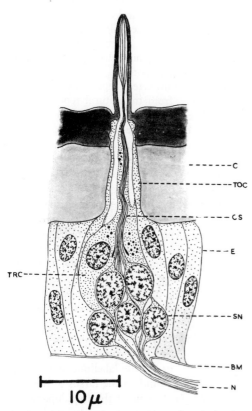

FIGURE 119. Contact chemoreceptor, long basiconic peg organ of grasshopper. (From Slifer, E., Prestage, J. J., and Beams, H. W.: J. Morphol., vol. 101.)

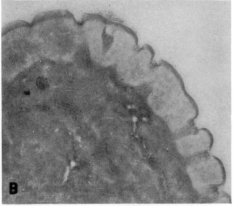

FIGURE 121. Electron micrographs of tip of distance chemoreceptor of grasshopper. *A*, tangential section showing pores; *B*, higher magnification of pores with fine nerve endings. (From Slifer, E.: Unpublished data.)

genus *Phaseolus* and on some soybeans but not on most other Leguminosae.[34]

The evolution of flowering plants during the Cretaceous was accompanied by a reciprocal development of insects. Attractants in flowers for certain insects make for cross-pollination. Repellents in plants protect them against being eaten by insects in general, but the same substances may be neutral or attractant for certain insects.[34]

The sensory basis for preference for specific compounds may have a genetic origin or may be habituation passed on in behavior. Of two groups of the butterfly genus *Papilio*, one feeds on plants of the family Rutaceae, the other on Umbelliferae and sometimes also on Rutaceae; apparently the former group evolved first and those living on Umbelliferae later.[20] *Papilio* will feed on non-Umbelliferae if the leaves contain methyl chavicol (anise). Caterpillars of *Papilio* from carrots are attracted to methyl chavicol; those from rue, to methylnonyl ketone.[20] The active agents attracting cabbage butterflies *Pieris* to

cruciferous plants are the mustard glucosides sinigran and sinalbin.[98] The caterpillars will feed on other plants painted with mustard oil glucosides. Silkworms are attracted to mulberry and closely related plants by a hexenal plus some unknown substance; the selectivity is lost after the maxillae are removed. Some aphids have different host plants in winter and summer. *Aphis fabae* on sugar beet in summer grows faster on virus-infected than on uninfected plants.[56]

An apple bug, *Rhogoletis pomella*, occurs in two races, one on apple, the other on blueberry; the bug does not live if transferred directly to the other kind of plant.[95] Two morphologically similar races of *Psyllia mali* are separated by living on hawthorn and apple; no cross-mating attempts and no transfer to the other kind of tree were successful.

Larval conditioning can alter within limits the chemobehavior of the adult. *Drosophila* larvae were fed on a medium containing peppermint; on emergence the flies showed positive chemotaxis for peppermint.[96] A hymenopteran (*Nemeritis*) is normally parasitic on the moth *Ephestia*, but if larvae of the moth *Meliphora* are smeared with extract of *Ephestia* the adult *Nemeritis* will lay some eggs and the larvae will grow on the *Meliphora*. As adults these *Nemeritis* prefer *Ephestia* but are somewhat attracted to *Meliphora*, which normal *Nemeritis* avoid.[97] *Dixippus* transferred repeatedly for several generations from the natural food, privet, to ivy came to accept the ivy which had previously been rejected.[87] In general, adult insects lay their eggs on the same kind of plant (or host animal) on which they fed as larvae. The nervous mechanism for the larval conditioning merits study.

Physiology of Chemoreceptors in Insects. The reactions of an insect to a chemical depend both on stimulation of the sense organ and on central nervous responses. Certain substances are acceptable, and stimulation of taste receptors by them causes extension of the proboscis, especially in flies and lepidopterans. Other substances are unacceptable, and stimulation by these causes withdrawal of the proboscis. These reactions have been used to localize receptors by stimulation of single hairs on the labellum of the horsefly *Tabanus*,[38] and on the tarsus of the blowfly *Phormia*.[44] Some of the Lepidoptera have contact chemoreceptors on tarsi and on the terminal part of the proboscis.[37] Trichoptera (caddis flies) are chemosensitive on tarsi, and on tips of maxillary and labial palpi and haustellum.

In bees acceptability of solutions has been tested by measurements of amount drunk (crop load), duration of feeding, and by various conditioning methods. Von Frisch found that certain sugars are additive in their stimulating effect; hence by comparing the concentration of a second sugar which must be added to a solution of sucrose which is just below threshold concentration, the effectiveness of various sugars can be ascertained.[39]

The threshold varies with physiological state. Previous feeding is important. In general, hungry insects have lower taste thresholds than satiated ones. By stimulating simultaneously via two sets of chemoreceptors, e.g., two tarsi, central summation and inhibition can be demonstrated. When one tarsus is stimulated by sugar (acceptable) and another by alcohol (unacceptable) the proboscis is retracted.[21] Rejection is greater when the two opposing stimuli are applied to one than to two legs.[23] Many compounds (e.g., salt solution) are accepted when dilute but are rejected when concentrated. Tarsal threshold for sucrose is lowest at 22 to 26° in blowfly, and sensitivity decreases at lower and higher

temperatures; labellar receptors are not so affected by temperature.[27]

Chemoreceptors are usually connected with very small nerve fibers, and many attempts to record impulses in single fibers from chemoreceptors, especially olfactory ones, have failed.[15] Mass recording from antennal and other nerves of the roach has succeeded.[82] A useful technique employs a glass capillary placed over a chemoreceptor hair; the capillary contains the compound to be tested and serves for both the stimulus and recording electrode.[51, 53] A single labellar hair of *Phormia* contains three neurons, processes from two of which penetrate the hair. Sugars which provoke proboscis extension set up small spikes (S), whereas salts, acids, and alcohols which are rejected evoke larger spikes (L) (Fig. 122). Latency of response to salt may be as little as 10 msecs. It is concluded that one receptor ending is stimulated by acceptable substances and the other by unacceptable ones.

The frequency of impulses varies with the concentration of the solution presented, and sensory adaptation occurs in from 1 to 13 seconds. Adaptation can occur in one hair without an effect on neighboring ones.[24]

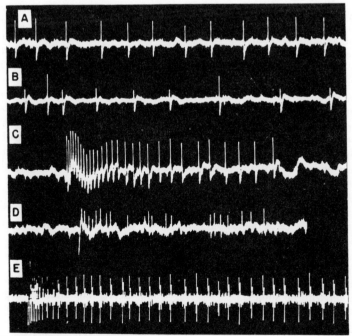

FIGURE 122. Electrical responses from contact chemoreceptor of Phormia. *A*, maintained stimulation of large fiber only by 0.5 M NaCl. *B*, maintained stimulation of small fiber, two large spikes seen; 0.25 M sucrose in 0.1 M NaCl. *C* and *D*, mechanical stimulation of large and small fibers. *E*, initial stimulation of both large and small by 0.5 M NaCl. (From Hodgson, E. S., and Roeder, K. D.: J. Cell. Comp. Physiol., vol. 48.)

Acceptability is related to high frequency of S impulses. The frequency for sucrose and fructose is 50 to 57/sec, for xylose and raffinose 10/sec.[51, 53]

The third neuron of a hair responds to mechanical stimulation,[104] and the L- and S-receptors can be stimulated mechanically when not adapted to chemical stimulation. Both large and small spikes are obtained in response to salt and sugar stimuli respectively after the tip of the hair has been removed; hence the entire distal process is sensitive. On contact with the open distal tip a resting membrane potential of 50 to 70 mv was measured.[104] Anodal polarization by current applied externally at the base of the hairs, and probably affecting the nerve cells, decreases the response and can cause rejection of sugar; cathodal polarization increases the response and can elicit acceptance of salt.[6] Intracellular polarization of the receptor hairs is effective, in the opposite polarity, anodal polarization increasing the responses and cathodal blocking them.[104] Large and small receptors are not entirely independent, since a chemical which stimulates one receptor cell tends to inhibit the other; thus contrast is enhanced.[51, 53] Absence of a behavioral response may result from stimulation of the L-receptor and lack of stimulation of the S-receptor (e.g., by dulcitol), or from lack of stimulation of either (as with ribose).

In the beetle *Leptinotarsa,* unlike *Phormia,* each chemoreceptor hair contains processes of five sense cells, and both large and small nerve spikes are observed in response to stimulation by salt. Simultaneous stimulation by sugar reduces the response to salt solution. Nerve responses to active plant glycosides (e.g., tomatin) are pH-dependent.[93] The corresponding receptors (basiconic pegs) of grasshoppers and of a butterfly have five or more neurons.[70]

Potential differences have been recorded between the tip and base of the antenna of a silk moth in the presence of odors.[83] When the wall of a labellar hair of *Calliphora* was pierced by a microelectrode, sugar and salt caused maintained depolarization with superimposed spikes; quinine and $CaCl_2$ caused hyperpolarization with no spikes.[70]

The initiation of feeding, its rate and termination in insects such as the blowfly *Phormia* are controlled by reflexes initiated by chemoreceptors. Proboscis extension can be initiated by olfactory stimulation of antennae, by taste and possibly touch on tarsi, and by internal factors.[30] When the proboscis is extended, chemosensory hairs on the labellar lobes are stimulated to regulate extension of the proboscis and to initiate sucking. Then as the mouthparts open, chemoreceptors on interpseudotracheal papillae between the labellae must be stimulated for feeding to continue. Thus, four sets of chemoreceptors monitor feeding in a hierarchical control. The duration and rate of sucking depend partly on sensory adaptation, and a fly may take more of a sugar of low-acceptance threshold and show slower adaptation, e.g., it may take more sucrose than fucose or sorbose. During sucking of sugar solution, sensory adaptation raises the threshold; at a certain level of sensitivity sucking stops, and by disadaptation the threshold falls and sucking resumes. Thus, satiety is monitored by sensory adaptation and by central inhibition. Termination of a feeding reaction is independent of blood sugar level or crop or midgut content, but rather is controlled by sensory impulses from the foregut via unidentified receptors to the brain, where they inhibit activity initiated by the oral chemoreceptors. After the recurrent nerve from the foregut has been cut, feeding may continue intermittently until the fly bursts.[30]

Chemoreception in Vertebrates. The distinction between olfaction and taste in vertebrates is based on (1) location and innervation of the receptors, (2) greater sensitivity of olfactory endings, and (3) taste stimulation by dissolved matter and stimulation of smell by volatile substances in terrestrial animals.

Taste organs of vertebrates are normally located in the mouth. In fish, however, taste buds occur not only in the mouth (pharynx), but also on gills, skin, and barbels; they are innervated by the seventh, ninth, and tenth cranial nerves.[46] In mammals the taste buds are grouped in ampullae on the tongue; each taste bud consists of sense cells innervated by a cluster of nerve endings coming respectively from fibers of the seventh, ninth, and tenth nerves from front to back of the tongue. Sensory connections are within the face area of the cerebral cortex.

Olfactory organs are innervated by the first cranial nerve. The olfactory organ consists of epithelial cells (often pigmented) between which protrude the hairs or processes of primary neurons. Man has 10 to 20 $\times$ 10^6 receptors in a 5 cm^2 area, and each receptor cell has 6 to 8 hairs. The axons from these neurons synapse in the olfactory bulb which (in mammals) contains several cell types, among them the prominent mitral and tufted cells. Axons from these neurons go to the frontal lobe, particularly to the pyriform cortex. Albino mammals lack pigment in the olfactory epithelium and are said to have lower olfactory acuity.[4]

The olfactory epithelium is usually stimulated by agents carried over it in ventilation. In some mammals the main stream of respired air does not pass over the secluded olfactory epithelium, but sniffing increases the volume passing through the smelling region. Fish have various arrangements of olfactory sacs. In elasmobranchs the olfactory pits are usually on the ventral side of the snout, sometimes open to the mouth, and water enters during swimming or respiratory movements. In most teleosts the pit is high on the head and water from the respiratory current does not enter it, but rather water is moved in and out during swimming and respiratory movements of the mouth or by ciliary action. In lungfishes the nasal sac opens into the mouth as in higher vertebrates.[4]

Physiology of Taste. That the taste organs over the body of fish are important is shown by feeding responses toward meat juice applied on the flanks or barbels (catfish and others).[76] Even the fin rays are sensitive to sardine oil and acid, and the skin of a catfish shows general chemical sense as well as specific tastes—acid, alkaline solution, salt. Minnows deprived of olfactory organs have been conditioned to taste sucrose at 2×10^{-5} M, NaCl at 4×10^{-5} M, and quinine at 0.0025 per cent.[59]

Amphibia have taste buds on the tongue, and impulses have been recorded from the glossopharyngeal nerve of a frog. Large fibers respond to stimulation by pure water, and the response of the water receptors is abolished by isotonic saline but not by sugar. Other fibers respond to hypertonic salt, and smaller fibers are activated by acid on the tongue.[105]

Conditioned responses and general behavior indicate that rodents and other common laboratory mammals resemble man in taste for sweet, bitter, salt, and acid. The extent to which taste distinctions are sensory or central is debated, but much evidence indicates several kinds of taste receptor. In man the lowest threshold for sweet is at the front of the tongue, for bitter at the back, and for salt and sour at the sides in overlapping areas of the tongue. Cocaine abolishes the four taste modalities in the sequences: bitter, sweet, salt, and sour; gymnemic acid abolishes sweet and bitter, but not salt or acid taste. Adaptation is faster for salt than for sweet or bitter. A given sensation, e.g., sweet, can result from stimulation by unlike compounds. Some persons are unable to taste bitter substances (such as p-ethoxyphenyl thiourea, $p\text{-HOC}_6\text{H}_4\text{NHCSNH}$) to which other persons are quite sensitive. Some kinds of taste sensitivities are inherited.[92] Taste is one factor in regulating feeding and drinking. Rats made salt deficient by adrenalectomy have a greater preference for salt solution over water than nondeficient rats; however, the taste thresholds are similar, and the greater salt hunger appears to have a central nervous locus.[78] Insulin-induced hypoglycemia seems to lower the taste threshold for sugar in man. Dryness of the throat can initiate thirst although the general sensation is more closely related to total body water. Hunger pains may be initiated by contractions of the stomach. Both thirst and hunger seem to depend on stimulation of specific regions of the brain (see Chapter 21).

Impulses in single gustatory nerve fibers of the cat show mixed specificities. Some fibers respond to acids at pH below 2.5, others to NaCl and also to choline chloride.[77] Still others are "water" taste fibers, probably responding to the washing away of salts.[16] Water taste endings are stimulated by solutions more dilute than 0.03 M NaCl, whereas the salt taste endings require NaCl more concentrated than 0.05 M. Some acid taste fibers of the cat respond also to quinine, others also to salt, others simply to acid.[77] Only rare fibers in the cat respond to sugar. In the rabbit, sugar is more effective than quinine.[78] A hamster or guinea pig is more sensitive to sugar than is a cat. A fiber may respond to two or more of the taste stimuli but at different thresholds. In the rat one fiber responds more to NaCl, less to sugar; another fiber, in reverse order. Similar mixed fiber responses have been recorded from dogs; saccharin elicits either no response or impulses in smaller fibers than does sugar; gymnemic acid fails to abolish the response to saccharin but does abolish that to sugar, whereas in man it abolishes all sweet taste; hence saccharin may taste bitter to a dog.[5] Some fibers of the chorda tympani nerve of cat, dog, and pig respond when the tongue is bathed with distilled water; apparently some receptors respond to an increase in ions, others to a decrease.[62] Water response is greater in rabbit and cat than in guinea pig, hamster, and dog.[9] Rat and man lack a water taste; calf, cat, and lamb lack sweet taste. Fibers of the chorda tympani of a monkey give responses to NaCl, acid, quinine, sugar, and water placed on the tongue; sucrose endings respond to saccharin also.[41] Chickens respond to salt, glycerin, ethylene glycol, quinine, acid, and water but not to sucrose and saccharin. Pigeons lack response to quinine. Evidently there are several kinds of taste receptors, and some of these respond with different thresholds to compounds giving two sensations. Behavioral tests of taste discrimination often give lower thresholds than does nerve recording. Hence much of the sensory discrimination of taste must be central.

Physiology of Smell. Olfactory endings show greater sensitivity and much more selectivity and variety than gustatory ones. Fish differ in apparent dependence on olfaction, and the differences are correlated with their anatomy and ecology.[94] Both eyes and nasal sacs are important in schooling and nonpredatory fish (*Phoxinus, Gobio*); the eyes are more important in daylight predators (*Esox, Gasterosteus*). Organs of olfaction are better developed than those of vision in nonschooling predators (*Anguilla, Lota*). When the olfactory sac in *Ameiurus* was irrigated with fluid containing odorous material such as decaying meat,[3] impulses were recorded in the long stalk connecting the olfactory bulb with the brain.

Dogfish with one olfactory sac plugged turn toward the intact side when feeding. Minnows (*Phoxinus*) have been shown by conditioned reflex tests to be able to distinguish by olfaction different species of fish; this is important in discriminating their own species from other harmless ones and from predator species.[46] Conditioning techniques have demonstrated remarkable olfactory sensitivity of minnows for food plants and for water from different streams bordered by different vegetation. Washes from closely related plants could be distinguished from each other after dilution tens of thousands of times. There is evidence that migrating fish, particularly salmon, locate their home waters by characteristic odors.[45] Stream selection appears to be random, after the olfactory sacs have been plugged. The sensitivity of minnows to chlorophenols is much greater than that of man, and *Phoxinus* can detect eugenol at 6×10^{-14} parts and phenylethyl alcohol at 4.3×10^{-14}.[73]

In conditioning experiments eels detected β-phenylethyl alcohol down to 2.8×10^{-18}, trout to 9.9×10^{-9}.[94]

Olfaction in amphibians, reptiles, and birds is poorly understood and is probably a less used sense. Monophasic electrical responses have been recorded from the nasal epithelium of a frog during stimulation by various odors.[75]

Many mammals depend on olfaction for much of the discrimination of food quality and for location of prey and predators. Olfaction is some 10,000 times more sensitive than taste. Rodents learn with difficulty by olfactory cues and probably have a lower olfactory acuity than man, but rats can be trained to locate buried objects by odor. Carnivores are more sensitive then rodents, and the ability of dogs to follow trails and to locate underground objects (e.g., truffles) is well known. Tactile signals probably add to olfactory ones in trailing. In most mammals a large portion of the forebrain is olfactory and the olfactory organs are highly developed; most mammals are macrosmatic, i.e., have well-developed sense of smell; primates and whalebone whales are microsmatic (with slight sense of smell), and toothed whales anosmatic or lacking in sense of smell. A rabbit has a total of 50 to 100×10^6 olfactory receptor cells.[4]

Nerve impulses have been recorded from secondary neurons—axons of mitral and tufted cells in the olfactory bulb, especially in rabbits.[2] When odorous air is breathed, a burst of impulses accompanies each inhalation in accordance with the presence or absence of specific volatile substances. In the anterior part of the bulb, responses to fruity odors, e.g., amyl acetate, predominate; the posterior bulb responds to oily volatiles, e.g., benzene; hence there seems to be some spatial localization in the olfactory bulb. Adrian finds that some one odor is more effective than others in stimulating single mitral units, although related substances may also stimulate, especially in higher concentrations. The latency for volatile esters is shorter than that for heavier oils.[2] The olfactory bulb shows high-frequency (70 to 100/sec) spontaneous activity which is replaced by lower frequency rhythms (50 to 70/sec) during olfactory stimulation. Some cells in the olfactory bulb discharge continuously and others whenever air passes through the nose, while a third group responds specifically to odors.[101] Impulses recorded from the primary olfactory nerve fibers in the nasal septum of the opossum show considerable specificity of the sensory endings.[9, 11]

Continued stimulation by an odor results in adaptation, both in olfactory sensation and in electrical responses from the bulb. Adaptation is proportional to the molecular concentration within the nasal passages, and there is some cross-adaptation between odors and some masking by similar compounds. Self-adaptation is much greater than heterogeneous adaptation. The olfactory acuity varies with the physiological state, e.g., hunger. Threshold concentration varies with temperature and humidity, which alter the volatility of stimulating compounds.

By measuring the masking or cross-adaptation, coefficients of likeness are obtained for olfaction by man; if complete likeness gives a coefficient of 1, amyl and butyl acetates give a coefficient of 0.89, benzaldehyde and nitrobenzene 0.40. The small amount of chemical likeness between odorous compounds makes probable a very large number of classes of odors distinguished by man.[68, 69] Classical psychological theory recognizes nine classes of odors, each with several subdivisions. Evidence from subjective reports of odors, masking, gradual recovery of olfactory abilities after anesthesia, and fatigue (adaptation), all indicate that there are several classes of odors. For example, camphor, eucalyptol, and eugenol are in one class, and citrol and safrol in another.

Further evidence for multiple types of receptors comes from the marked differences for man in threshold concentrations of different substances in inhaled air—ethyl mercaptan 7×10^{-13} M, amyl thioether 5.8×10^{-8} M, amyl acetate 3×10^{-7} M, ethyl ether 7.8×10^{-5} M.[78] The least concentration difference, ΔS, which can be distinguished from another concentration, S, is given by $\Delta S/S$, the Weber coefficient. This differential sensitivity is greatest at low concentrations and may approach 0.1 at moderate concentrations;[78] for taste, $\Delta S/S$ is usually 0.2 in man, 0.25 in the honeybee.[23]

CELLULAR MECHANISMS OF CHEMOSTIMULATION: CONCLUSIONS

Attempts to formulate a unified theory of chemical stimulation have not been successful. In the series from general chemical sense through taste to olfaction there are a few common principles, but variations in specificity indicate that there are probably many types of sensitive membranes. In part, chemoreception is related to the permeability of cell surfaces, to adsorption and to chemical reactions at surfaces. There is evidence that chemostimulation may set up generator potentials. Many chemoreceptors show no spontaneous activity. A few olfactory receptors are spontaneously active.

General Chemical Sense. General chemical sense and taste (contact chemoreception) overlap with respect to acids and salts. Strong acids, particularly inorganic acids, stimulate according to the hydrogen ion concentration. Weak acids, usually organic, appear to enter cells mainly as undissociated molecules and then stimulate; hence they are effective in proportion to the concentration of undissociated molecules. Organic acids are more effective than inorganic acids at the same pH. In the mouth, acids interact with salivary buffers, and the anions may modify the stimulation. Organic acids are increasingly effective with increased length of carbon chain, and side chains may alter stimulation. Electrical polarization of the human tongue causes a sour sensation at the anode, probably because of intracellular ion movements rather than any change in pH of the saliva.

General chemical stimulation of many cells by salts is most effective when the salts are univalent, and the cation effect greatly predominates. The cation series roughly follows mobilities: $NH_4^+ > K^+ > Rb > Na^+ > Li^+$. Anions which form complexes with free calcium, e.g., citrate and oxalate, may stimulate by calcium withdrawal. In contrast to general chemical stimulation by cations, taste buds of vertebrates are stimulated more by the anions; $NaCl$ and Na_2SO_4 taste salty; $NaHCO_3$ and $NaNO_3$ do not. The chlorides vary in effectiveness, however, roughly according to the cationic mobility series. Various sodium salts differ in stimulating effect.[10]

Salts and acids elicit rejection reactions in insects—in *Cecropia* larvae, in the water beetle *Laccophilus,* on the legs of *Tabanus,* and on the ovipositors of hymenopterans.[48] In general, the series of cations is $H_3O^+ > NH_4^+ > K^+ > Na^+ > Li^+$. In a few insects, calcium and magnesium are said to be more effective than sodium;[35, 36] in others they are not.[48] The anion series for rejection is $OH^- > I^- > Br^- > SO_4^= > Cl^- > $ acetate $> PO_4^=$.[48] Two stimulating actions are indicated in flies, where dilute salt solutions are accepted and strong solutions are not.

Taste. The sensation of sweetness is given in man by many sugars which contain fructose or glucose. The sweet taste is also given by the very different molecule saccharin and by salts such as lead acetate and some beryllium salts. Dextrorotatory asparagin tastes sweet; the levo- form is tasteless.

Glycols form a series from sweet (ethylene) to bitter (hexamethylene).

Taste sensitivities of a number of animals to the same substances are compared in Table 43. Von Frisch tested thirty-four sugars and related compounds on bees; of these thirty are sweet to man and nine acceptable (sweet?) to the honeybee. For example, substances not accepted by the bee but sweet to man are mannitol, sorbitol, xylose, galactose, and melibiose.[39]

In adult blowflies the intake of a sugar need not be related to nutritive value but is related to taste preference and varies with concentration; for example, 0.1 M fucose (non-nutritional) is accepted over 0.1 M mannose (nutritional), and 0.1 M fucose over 0.1 M sorbose (both non-nutritional).[30, 47] Other insects show sensitivities similar to the bee as follows:[23]

bee mouthparts: sucrose = maltose, trehalose, fructose = glucose > fucose > galactose.
Calliphora leg: sucrose = maltose > trehalose = cellobiose > lactose and fructose > fucose > glucose = galactose.
Calliphora mouthparts: sucrose = maltose > trehalose = cellobiose > lactose; fructose > fucose > glucose > xylose = mannose.
Phormia legs: sucrose = maltose > trehalose > cellobiose > lactose; fructose > fucose = glucose > sorbose > mannose.

Nerve impulses from labellar chemoreceptors of *Phormia* show that D- and L-arabinose are additive.[51, 53] However, L-arabinose is acceptable in terms of tarsal and labellar stimulation but is repellent to interpseudotracheal papillae; hence the papillae receptors must differ from the others.[23] It appears that in all

these insects, α-glucosides are the most stimulating of disaccharides, and fructose, glucose, and fucose the most effective monosaccharides.

Fish have been trained to discriminate among several sugars. The threshold of minnows for sucrose is some 500 times lower than the human threshold.[46]

The subjective taste of bitter is given by very dissimilar substances such as quinine, strychnine, and some Mg^{++} and NH_4^+ salts. Bitter and sweet tastes tend to go together in homologous series in that a small difference in a molecule may change the taste from sweet to bitter; initial sweet may leave a bitter aftertaste, and the antagonist, gymnemic acid, depresses both sweet and bitter taste.[78]

Whether there is anything in insects comparable to the bitter taste may be questioned. According to Dethier, tests of some 300 compounds on insects show some thirty sugars or sugar derivatives as acceptable, and virtually all the others, including some inorganic compounds, as unacceptable. Acceptable compounds stimulate the S-receptors; unacceptable compounds stimulate the L-receptors. An unacceptable sugar (ribose) elicits no S response and decreases the frequency of L impulses initiated by dilute salt.[51, 53] The stimulating effectiveness of rejected compounds for homologous series of aldehydes, ketones, alcohols, and glycols increases, i.e., the threshold concentration falls, as the carbon chain is increased. Often in a series a break occurs at some critical C length (Fig. 123).

The threshold molar concentrations for taste of alcohols by blowflies are: methyl 11.3, ethyl 3.2, n-butyl 0.66, n-amyl 0.1,

TABLE 43.   TASTE AND GENERAL CHEMICAL SENSE THRESHOLD

	NaCl	HCl	Quinine	Sucrose	Saccharin
Vertebrates					
Man[78, 86]	1-3.5×10^{-2} M	102×10^{-3} M	1.5-4×10^{-7} M	1-2×10^{-2} M	2×10^{-5} M
	1×10^{-2} M		1.1×10^{-7} M		1.1×10^{-4} M
	7.36×10^{-3} M				
Rat[54b]					
(discrimination)			7.6×10^{-7} M	9.3×10^{-3} M	
Frog[105]	0.1-0.17 M				
Minnows[59]	4×10^{-5} M		0.0025%	2×10^{-5} M	
Insects[21, 23, 39, 93]					
Calliphora				1×10^{-2} M	
Apis	0.24 M in sucrose	1×10^{-3} M	8×10^{-4} M (in sucrose)	0.8-7×10^{-2} M	
Pyrameis				1×10^{-2} M (fed)	
				8×10^{-5} M (starved)	
Danaus				9.8×10^{-6} M	
Tabanus				0.5-11×10^{-2} M	
Aquatic beetles			1.25×10^{-6} M		
Leptinotarsa	10^{-2} M to 5×10^{-3} M				

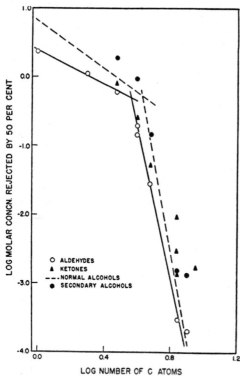

FIGURE 123. Threshold concentrations for rejection (proboscis withdrawal) of various aldehydes, ketones, and alcohols applied to tarsi of blowfly as a function of number of carbon atoms in stimulating compounds. (From Chadwick, L., and Dethier, V. G.: J. Gen. Physiol., vol. 32.)

n-hexyl 0.012, secondary n-octyl 0.0021.[29] Effectiveness is altered when functional groups are changed—OH groups raise the threshold especially when terminal; branching of a chain tends to raise the threshold concentration; a second OH decreases the stimulating effect, as does a second halogen;[29] n-ketones are more effective than isoketones. Stimulating efficiency increases with lipid solubility, with higher boiling points, or thermodynamic activity. The best correlation seems to be as the inverse of water solubility. Homologous series often increase in effectiveness very slightly up to about five carbons; then they increase in effectiveness much more; perhaps the lower compounds enter in an aqueous phase, higher ones in lipid.[29] When applied in oil the effective threshold concentrations from methanol to octanol cover less than one log unit and show no break; when applied in water the range covers more than four log units and breaks as two curves.

Contact or taste chemostimulation appears to occur in relatively few types of receptor.

The stimulation by sugars seems to be by a different mechanism from that by other organic substances. One kinetic analysis[20] assumes the formation of a complex of sugar-receptor molecule which then causes depolarization.

Olfaction. Olfaction or distance chemoreception is mediated by the chemoreceptors which are most sensitive and most varied in specificity. In contrast to contact stimulation by both electrolytes and nonelectrolytes, where a few correlations with physical properties are possible, the sensitivity to volatile or to highly dilute materials shows very little correlation with obvious chemical properties. Subjective measures of odor sensitivity in man and masking and cross-adaptation of odors have led psychologists to several classifications, all of them in nonchemical terms, e.g., fruity, ethereal, resinous, spicy, foul, burnt. An attempt at a chemical classification is that of Adrian,[2] based on electrical responses in the olfactory bulb; four classes are recognized: aromatic hydrocarbons, paraffin hydrocarbons, terpenes and related substances, and ethereal esters and ketones.

The most complete review of the enormous literature on chemical senses is that of Moncrieff who arrived at sixty-two general principles relating chemical structure to odor. There is some similarity in odors of substances of similar chemical structure, e.g., homologous series, yet frequently isomers and stereoisomers have dissimilar odors and, conversely, dissimilar substances may have similar odors. In some series the odor increases with chain length up to an optimum. In man the threshold for alcohols and paraffins is minimal at four to five aliphatic carbons.[71] Very large molecules may be less odorous because they are less volatile. Fish olfactory organs detect specific organic compounds in even lower concentrations in water than those in air detected by mammals (Table 44).

The threshold concentration for detection by bees or man of a series of ethyl esters fell with increasing length of carbon chain to a minimum at C_{12} (ethyl caproate) and then rose for longer molecules. For a series of fatty acids the lowest olfactory threshold for the bee was C_4 (butyric acid)[84] (Fig. 124). Similarly, the permeability of red blood cells for esters is maximum at an intermediate number of carbons; apparently lipoid solubility limits on the side of smaller molecules and molecular size limits on the high side.

TABLE 44. OLFACTORY THRESHOLDS

	Man[86]	Dog[72]	Bee[84]	Other insects[84]	Fish[45, 64, 94]
ammonia	1.75×10^{-6}			Musca 2.0×10^{-6}	
amylalcohol	1.1×10^{-8}				
benzaldehyde	4×10^{-9}				
benzol	6.8×10^{-8}			Habrobracon 6.4×10^{-6} to 3.8×10^{-5}	
butyric acid	1.13×10^{-11}	1.5×10^{-17}	1.7×10^{-9}		
caproic acid	3.3×10^{-10}	6×10^{-18}	3.6×10^{-10}		
citral	6.6×10^{-10}		1×10^{-10}		
diacetal					
ethanol	5.4×10^{-6}	1.7×10^{-18}		Musca 7.2×10^{-3} Habrobracon 1.6×10^{-4}	
ethyl ether	1.34×10^{-8}				
ethyl mercaptan	7×10^{-13}				
eugenol	1.4×10^{-9}		3.3×10^{-11}		eel 4.9×10^{-12} minnow 3.8×10^{-10}
ionon	5×10^{-13}	5.1×10^{-17}	2.5×10^{-11}		eel 9.7×10^{-16}
isovalerenic		1.8×10^{-7}			
phenol p-chlorophenol	1×10^{-7} to 4.3×10^{-8}				bluntnose minnow 4×10^{-9}
β-phenyl propylalcohol	1.1×10^{-11}		3.8×10^{-12}		eel summer 2.9×10^{-18} eel winter 3.7×10^{-18} minnow 1.2×10^{-7} trout 3.6×10^{-10}
propionic acid	6.7×10^{-10}		7×10^{-10}		
pyridine	5×10^{-10}				
resorcinol					roach 5.4×10^{-7}
skatol	3×10^{-12}			Geotrupes 2.3×10^{-8}	
trinitrobenzene					roach 1.4×10^{-6}

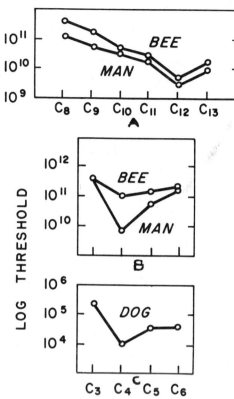

FIGURE 124. Threshold concentrations in log of number of molecules per cm^3 for olfactory stimulation as function of number of carbon atoms. *A*, esters on bee and man. *B* and *C*, volatile fatty acids on bee, man, and dog. (From Schwarz, R.: Ztschr. vergl. Physiol., vol. 37.)

Figures 123 and 124 indicate a real difference between taste and olfaction.

Bees have been trained to distinguish the odors of forty-seven essential oils and their constituents. In general, bee sensitivities are less than those of man and discriminations similar. For example, p-cresol methyl ether is distinguished from m-cresol methyl ether. Bees show remarkable ability to distinguish one scent in a mixture.[81] Volatile attractants to flies are of increasing effectiveness for higher boiling point and longer chain length, and effectiveness varies inversely with water solubility. This suggests that similar rules may apply for both contact and distance chemoreception in insects. Certainly, in both, the stimulating substances must go into solution before they can act on a cell membrane.

Hypotheses of Chemical Stimulation. Several of the many hypotheses of chemical stimulation may be mentioned. Frings postulated a "taste spectrum," the lowest threshold cells producing the sensation sweet, the maximum number of active cells producing sour; this agrees with the changes in modality according to concentration but can hardly explain the same sensation produced by very dissimilar substances.[35] A dual hypothesis based on insect contact reception[10] is that some substances such as sugars react chemically before stimulating, while other substances such as salts, acids, and alcohols are nonspecific and are bound loosely to some polyelectrolyte at the receptor cell surface. The high temperature dependence of insect chemoreception is not compatible with an adsorption mechanism.[51, 53]

A hypothesis of smell is that many odorous substances absorb in the infrared and show a Raman shift, that is, light waves are scattered by these substances as longer wave lengths. One idea is that the sense cells are stimulated by scattered light; another theory is that absorption of heat from epithelial cells by the odorous agent would cool the epithelium. However, certain optical isomers with similar Raman spectra have different odors, some isotopic molecules such as n-butyl alcohol and its deuterated form have similar odors but different Raman spectra, and other substances like glycerol show a Raman shift but are odorless.[66, 78] Also, electrical responses from the olfactory epithelium of a frog are abolished by covering the epithelium with a plastic membrane which transmits infrared.[75] One wonders why the olfactory epithelium of mammals is so highly pigmented.

Another hypothesis is that chemical stimulation causes liberation of a nerve excitant. Acetylcholine can stimulate the respiratory chemoreceptors of the cat carotid sinus. Acetylcholine enhances responses of taste fibers of a frog.[105] Anticholinesterases have no effect on responses of labellar chemoreceptors of flies.[51] Whatever the mechanism, ion permeability must be increased for excitation to occur.

Stimulating effectiveness may be related to thermodynamic activity, particularly when considered in terms of cohesive energy densities of both stimulant and receptor membrane, that is, the internal attractive forces holding molecules together. Thermodynamic activity is indicated by the ratio of the vapor pressure at threshold to the vapor pressure of pure stimulating substance.[71] In addition, molecular shape influences effectiveness, presumably in relation to configurations in the membrane; rigid molecules are more effective than flexible ones and stimulation may require disruption of a molecular lattice.[71]

Molecular configuration correlates well with stimulation for a series of butanes of similar cohesive energy densities. Of two geometrical isomers of butane, the *cis* form is some hundred times more effective in human olfaction than the *trans* form.[71] Effectiveness of several benzenes for fish is not correlated with lipid solubility but is affected by substituent groups and their position on the ring.[64]

According to a recent hypothesis,[19] olfactory threshold is related to a critical number of odorous molecules adsorbed within a given area of cell membrane and the adsorption constant for passing from air to the oil-water interface. The decrease in adsorption constant with rising temperature can account for the rise in olfactory threshold as temperature is raised. Contact chemoreception is less influenced than olfaction by molecular morphology.[19]

A multiple hypothesis seems necessary. Taste and olfaction appear to be different in mechanism. All stimulating substances must pass through or act at cell surfaces. This means that they must first go into solution and must be distributed between aqueous and lipid components. Next, it is probable that membrane depolarization results; this will be better understood when it becomes possible to record from inside chemoreceptor cells. Depolarization could be caused by various ions, as is probable in general chemical sensitivity; a parallel is the chemical depolarization of nerve fibers or the stimulation of nerve cells. In the cockroach the sensitivity of central nerve cells to a variety of chemicals parallels and is greater than that of peripheral chemoreceptors.[82] However, taste receptors of a rat tongue are a thousand times more sensitive to salt than is the taste nerve.[9, 11] Membrane depolarization could also be brought about by specific substances, either by the chemical stimuli or by the products of their reactions at the cell surface.

It is probable that there are many kinds of cell membrane with respect to chemical sensitivity. It is known that synaptic membranes are very different from conducting membranes; some membranes are depolarized by acetylcholine, some by epinephrine; others are hyperpolarized by acetylcholine (Chapters 14, 21). There is indirect evidence for numerous chemical transmitters of nerve impulses, each presumably combining with specific receptors. Chemoreceptor cells certainly differ in sensitivity to organic compounds; examples are: vertebrate taste cells, the two cells of fly chemoreceptor hairs, and the ap-

parent mosaic of sensitivities in mammalian olfactory epithelium. Furthermore, the same cell may be stimulated by several different substances but at different thresholds. It is not unreasonable to assume different active sites on the same receptor cell, some more specific than others. The understanding of chemoreception requires analysis at the molecular level of membrane structure.

REFERENCES

1. ABEL, E., Oster. Zool. Ztschr. *3*: 83-125, 1951. Sense of smell, lizards.
2. ADRIAN, E. D., J. Physiol. *115*: 42P, 1951; Nineteenth International Physiological Congress, pp. 151-152, 1953; Acta physiol. scand. *29*: 5-14, 1953; Brit. M. J. *1*: 287-290, 1954; J. Physiol. *128*: 21P-22P, 1955. Electrical responses from different parts of olfactory tract, mammals.
3. ADRIAN, E. D., and LUDWIG, C., J. Physiol. *94*: 441-460, 1938. Nervous discharges from olfactory organs of fish.
4. ALLISON, A. C., Biol. Rev. *28*: 195-244, 1953. Morphology of olfactory system in vertebrates.
5. ANDERSSON, B., *et al.*, Acta physiol. scand. *21*: 105-119, 1950. Responses from taste fibers of dog.
6. ARAB, Y. M., J. Insect Physiol. *2*: 324-329, 1958. Behavioral responses to electrical stimulation of blowfly chemoreceptors.
7. BAER, J. G., Ecology of Animal Parasites, University of Illinois Press, 1951, 224 pp.
8. BARBER, S. B., Anat. Rec. *111*: 561-562, 1951; J. Exp. Zool. *131*: 51-69, 1956. Chemoreception in Limulus.
9. BEIDLER, L. M., J. Neurophysiol. *16*: 595-607, 1953. Analysis of taste responses, mammals.
10. BEIDLER, L. M., J. Gen. Physiol. *38*: 133-139, 1954; The Physiologist *3*: 5-12, 1960. Theory of taste and olfaction.
11. BEIDLER, L. M., *et al.*, Am. J. Physiol. *181*: 235-240, 1955. Analysis of taste responses, mammals.
12. BULLOCK, T. H., Behaviour *5*: 130-140, 1953. Predator recognition by intertidal gastropods.
13. BUTLER, C. G., Proc. Roy. Soc. London, B, *138*: 403-413, 1951. Olfaction in discovery of food by honeybee.
14. CHADWICK, L., and DETHIER, V. G., J. Gen. Physiol. *32*: 445-452, 1949. Stimulation of blowfly by aliphatic aldehydes and ketones.
15. CHAPMAN, J. A., and CRAIG, R., Canad. Entomol. *85*: 182-189, 1953. Electrical analysis of chemoreception in insects.
16. COHEN, M. J., *et al.*, Acta physiol. scand. *33*: 316-332, 1955. Response of spectrum of taste fibers in cat.
17. DAVENPORT, D., and HICKOK, J. F., Biol. Bull. *100*: 71-83, 1951. Commensalism between starfish and polychaete *Arctonoë.*
18. DAVENPORT, D., and NORRIS, K. S., Biol. Bull. *115*: 397-410, 1958. Symbiosis of sea anemone and pomacentrid fish.

* Reviews

19. Davies, A. T., and Taylor, F. H., Biol. Bull. *117*: 222-238, 1959. Role of adsorption and molecular morphology in olfaction.

20. Dethier, V. G., Biol. Bull. *72*: 7-23, 1937; *76*: 325-329, 1939; Am. Naturalist *75*: 61-73, 1941. Chemoreception in relation to choice of food plants by lepidopteran larvae.

21. Dethier, V. G., Am. J. Physiol. *165*: 247-250, 1951; J. Gen. Physiol. *35*: 55-65, 1951; Biol. Bull. *102*: 111-117, 1952; *103*: 178-189, 1952. Stimulation of tarsal chemoreceptors in flies by various organic molecules.

22. Dethier, V. G., Biol. Bull. *105*: 257-268, 1953. Summation and inhibition of responses to tarsal chemostimulation.

23. *Dethier, V. G., *in* Insect Physiology, edited by K. D. Roeder. New York, John Wiley & Sons, 1953, pp. 544-576. Chemoreception.

24. *Dethier, V. G., Quart. Rev. Biol. *30*: 348-371, 1955. Physiology and histology of contact chemoreceptors of blowfly.

25. *Dethier, V. G., *in* Molecular Structure and Functional Activity of Nerve Cells, edited by R. G. Grenell and L. J. Mullins, American Institute of Biological Sciences Publ. *1*: 1-30, 1956. Chemoreceptor mechanisms.

26. Dethier, V. G., Exp. Parasitol. *6*: 68-122, 1957. Sensory physiology of blood-sucking arthropods.

27. Dethier, V. G., and Arab, Y. M., J. Insect. Physiol. *2*: 153-161, 1958. Effect of temperature on contact chemoreception in blowfly.

28. Dethier, V. G., and Bodenstein, D., Ztschr. Tierpsychol. *15*: 129-140, 1958. Hunger in the blowfly.

29. Dethier, V. G., and Chadwick, L. E., J. Gen. Physiol. *33*: 589-599, 1950. Relation between solubility and stimulating effect of inorganic and organic compounds.

30. Dethier, V. G., *et al.,* Biol. Bull. *111*: 204-222, 1956. Relation between taste and ingestion of carbohydrates, blowfly.

31. Dethier, V. G., and Yost, M. T., J. Gen. Physiol. *35*: 823-839, 1952. Olfactory stimulation by homologous alcohols.

32. Fishman, I. Y., J. Cell. Comp. Physiol. *49*: 319-334, 1957. Single fiber gustatory impulses in rat and hamster.

33. Forrester, A. T., and Parkins, W. E., Science *114*: 5-6, 1951. Test of infrared absorption theory of olfaction.

34. *Fraenkel, G., Science *129*: 1466-1470, 1959. The Raison d'être of Secondary Plant Substances. Copenhagen, Proceedings of the International Zoological Congress, 1953, 1956, pp. 383.

35. Frings, H., Experientia *7*: 424-426, 1951. The taste spectrum.

36. Frings, H., and Frings, M., Biol. Bull. *111*: 92-100, 1956. Contact chemoreceptors in adult Trichopera (caddis flies).

37. Frings, H., and Frings, M., Biol. Bull. *110*: 291-299, 1956. Location of contact chemoreceptors in Lepidoptera.

38. Frings, H., and O'Neal, B. R., J. Exp. Zool. *103*: 61-79, 1946. Contact chemoreceptors in females of horsefly Tabanus.

39. *von Frisch, K., Ztschr vergl. Physiol. *21*: 1-156, 1934. Comparative physiology of taste, particularly in honeybees.

40. *Gerebtzoff, M., J. Physiol. Paris *45*: 247-283, 1953. Olfaction.

41. Gordon, G., *et al.,* Acta physiol scand. *46*: 119-132, 1959. Responses of taste fibers in chorda tympani of monkey.

42. Gotz, B., Experientia *7*: 406-418, 1951. Chemical sex attractants in Lepidoptera.

43. Göz, H., Ztschr. vergl. Physiol. *29*: 1-45, 1941. Olfactory discrimination by fish.

44. Grabowski, C. T., and Dethier, V. G., J. Morphol. *94*: 1-19, 1954. Structure of tarsal chemoreceptors of blowfly, Phormia.

45. Hasler, A. D., and Wisby, W. J., Tr. Am. Fish Soc. *79*: 64-70, 1950; Hasler, A. D., Am. Naturalist *85*: 223-238, 1951. Quart. Rev. Biol. *31*: 200-209, 1956. Discrimination of stream odors and of pollutants by fish.

46. *Hasler, A. D., *in* Physiology of Fishes, edited by M. E. Brown. New York, Academic Press, 1957, vol. 2, part 3, chap. 2. Olfactory and gustatory sense in fishes.

47. Hassett, C. C., *et al.,* Biol. Bull. *99*: 446-453, 1950. Comparison of nutritive value and taste thresholds of carbohydrates, blowfly.

48. Hodgson, E. S., Physiol. Zool. *24*: 131-440, 1951. Reaction thresholds of an aquatic beetle to salts and alcohols.

49. Hodgson, E. S., Biol. Bull. *105*: 115-127, 1953. Chemoreception in aqueous and gas phases by a beetle.

50. *Hodgson, E. S., Quart. Rev. Biol. *30*: 331-347, 1955. Chemoreception in invertebrates.

51. Hodgson, E. S., J. Insect Physiol. *1*: 240-247, 1957; Biol. Bull. *115*: 114-125, 1958. Electrophysiological analysis of responses of single chemoreceptor hairs of Diptera; chemoreceptors of terrestrial and fresh-water arthropods.

52. Hodgson, E. S., and Barton-Browne, L., Anat. Rec. *137*: 365, 1960. (Abstr.). Mechanical stimulation of chemoreceptors.

53. Hodgson, E. S., and Roeder, K. D., J. Cell. Comp. Physiol. *48*: 51-76, 1956. Electrophysiological analysis of responses of single chemoreceptor hairs of Diptera.

54. Hudson, B. N. A., J. Exp. Biol. *33*: 478-492, 1956. Chemical factors in oviposition site selection by mosquitoes.

54a. Jacobson, M., *et al.,* Science *132*: 1011-10112, 1960. Sex attractant of female gypsy moths.

54b. Kappauf, U. E., Personal communication. Taste discrimination in rats.

55. Kellog, V. L., Biol. Bull. *12*: 152-154, 1906-1907. Chemical attraction between silk moths.

56. Kennedy, J. S., and Booth, C. O., Ann. Appl. Biol. *38*: 25-64, 1951. Food selection by aphids.

57. Kleerekoper, H., and Mogensen, J. A., Ztschr. vergl. Physiol. *42*: 492-500, 1959. Scent of trout.

58. Koehler, O., Ztschr. vergl. Physiol. *16*: 606-756, 1932. Sense physiology of fresh-water planaria.

59. Kriner, M., Ztschr. vergl. Physiol. *21*: 317-342, 1934. Chemical discrimination by minnows.

60. Kuhn, R., and Gauche, A., Naturforsch. *2*: 407-409, 1947. Alkaloid glycosides of Solanaceae in relation to feeding by potato beetles.

61. Lal, K. B., Nature *132*: 934, 1933; Ann. Appl. Biol. *21*: 641-648, 1934. Biological races of Psyllia on different food trees.

62. Liljestrand, G., and Zotterman, Y., Acta physiol. scand. *32*: 291-303, 1954. Water taste in mammals.

63. Mangold, O., Zool. Jahrb. Abt. allg. Zoo. Physiol. *62*: 441-512, 1951. Chemical discrimination by earthworms.

64. Marcström, A., Ark. Zool. *12*: 335-338, 1959. Thresholds for aromatic substances in fish *Leuciscus.*

65. McIndoo, N. E., J. Exp. Zool. *16*: 265-346, 1914; Biol. Bull. *28*: 407-461, 1915; J. Comp. Neurol. *31*: 405-427, 1920. Olfactory sense of honeybee, Coleoptera, Orthoptera.

66. Miles, W. R., and Beck, L. H., Proc. Nat. Acad. Sci. *35*: 292-310, 1949. Infrared absorption hypothesis of olfaction.

67. Minnich, D. E., J. Exp. Zool. *36*: 445-457, 1922. Tarsal sensitivity to sugar, butterfly Pyrameis.

68. Moncrieff, R. W., J. Physiol. *113*: 301-316, 1956. Olfactory adaptation and odor likeness.

69. *Moncrieff, R. W., The Chemical Senses, New York, John Wiley & Sons, 1946, 424 pp.

70. Morita, H., and Yamashita, S., Science *130*: 922, 1959. Generator potential of insect chemoreceptor.

71. *Mullins, L. J., Ann. New York Acad. Sci. *62*: 247-276, 1955. Theory of olfaction.

72. Neuhaus, W., Ztschr. vergl. Physiol. *38*: 238-258, 1956. Olfactory thresholds in dog.

73. Neurath, H., Ztschr. vergl. Physiol. *31*: 609-626, 1949. Olfactory sense in minnows.

74. Ohsawa, W., and Tsukuda, H., J. Inst. Polytech. Osaka Univ. D, *6*: 71-96, 1955. Chemical stimulation and extruding response of periwinkle.

75. Ottoson, D., Acta physiol. scand. *35*, suppl. 122: 1-83, 1956. Electrical activity of olfactory epithelium.

76. Parker, G. H., Smell, Taste and Allied Senses in Vertebrates. Philadelphia, J. B. Lippincott, 1922.

77. Pfaffman, C., J. Cell. Comp. Physiol. *17*: 243-258, 1941; J. Neurophysiol. *18*: 429-440, 1955. Gustatory nerve impulses, rat, cat, rabbit.

78. *Pfaffman, C., in Experimental Psychology, edited by S. Stevens. New York, John Wiley & Sons, 1951, pp. 1143-1171. Chemical sense.

79. Prosser, C. L., J. Exp. Biol. *12*: 95-104, 1935. Impulses in segmental nerve of earthworm.

80. Rahm, N., Rev. Suisse Zool. *65*: 779-792, 1958. Localization of chemoreceptors in mosquitoes.

81. Ribbands, C. R., Proc. Roy. Soc. London, B, *143*: 367-379, 1955. Scent perception of honeybee.

82. Roys, C. C., Ann. New York Acad. Sci. *58*: 250-255, 1953; Biol. Bull. *115*: 490-507, 1958. Responses of taste receptors and other nerve tissues of cockroach to chemicals.

83. Schneider, D., Experientia *13*: 89-91, 1957. Electrical responses from moth antennal receptors during chemostimulation.

84. Schwarz, R., Ztschr. vergl. Physiol. *37*: 180-210, 1955. Olfactory thresholds of honeybee.

85. Schwinck, I., Ztschr. vergl. Physiol. *37*: 439-458, 1955. Localization and morphology of chemoreceptors in silk moth.

86. von Skramlik, E., Pflüg. Arch. Physiol. *249*: 702-716, 1948; Handbuch der Physiologie der niederen Sinne, Bd 1, Leipzig, Georg Thieme, 1926, 532 pp. Smell and taste in man.

87. Sladden, D. E., Proc. Roy. Soc. London, B, *114*: 441-449, 1934; *119*: 31-46, 1935. Transference of induced food habit from parent to offspring.

88. Slifer, E. H., J. Exp. Zool. *130*: 301-317, 1955. Proc. Roy. Entomolog. Soc. London *31*: 95-98, 1956. Detection of odors and location of receptors in grasshoppers.

89. Slifer, E., J. Morphol. *105*: 145-191, 1959. Ultrastructure of chemoreceptors and other sense organs on antennal flagellum of grasshopper.

90. Slifer, E., Prestage, J. J., and Beams, H. W., J. Morph. *101*: 359-381, 1957. Structure of long basiconic sensory pegs of grasshopper.

91. Smyth, T., and Roys, C. C., Biol. Bull. *108*: 66-76, 1955. Chemoreception in insects and the action of DDT.

92. Snyder, L. H., Ohio J. Sci. *32*: 436-440, 1932. Inheritance of taste differences in man.

93. Stürckow, B., Ztschr. vergl. Physiol. *42*: 255-302, 1959. Behavior and electrophysiological studies on chemoreception in potato beetle Leptinotarsa.

94. Teichman, H., Ztschr. Morphol. Okol. Tiere *43*: 171-212, 1954; Ztschr. vergl. Physiol. *42*: 206-254, 1959. Olfaction in fish, particularly Anguilla.

95. *Thorpe, W. H., Biol. Rev. *5*: 177-212, 1930. Biological races identified by food plant selection.

96. Thorpe, W. H., Proc. Roy. Soc. London, B, *127*: 424-433, 1939. Preimaginal olfactory conditioning in insects.

97. Thorpe, W. H., and Jones, F. G. W., Proc. Roy. Soc. London, B, *124*: 56-81, 1937. Olfactory conditioning in a parasitic insect.

98. Thorsteinson, A. J., Canad. J. Zool. *31*: 52-72, 1953. Chemotactic responses in relation to food plants, Lepidoptera.

99. Valentine, J. M., J. Exp. Zool. *58*: 165-227, 1931. Olfactory sense of flour beetle Tenebrio.

100. Verschaeffelt, E., Proc. Acad. Sci. Amsterdam *14*: 536-542, 1910. Food selection by herbivorous insects.

101. Walsh, R. R., Am. J. Physiol. *186*: 255-257, 1956. Single cell activity in olfactory bulb, rabbit.

101a. Welsh, J. H., Biol. Bull. *61*: 497-499, 1931. Host effect on light responses of parasitic water mites.

102. Willis, E. R., and Roth, L. M., J. Exp. Zool. *121*: 149-179, 1952; *127*: 117-152, 1954. Reactions of Aedes and of Tribolium to carbon dioxide.

103. Wolbarsht, M. L., Science *125*: 1248, 1957. Water taste in Phormia.

104. Wolbarsht, M. L., J. Gen. Physiol. *42*: 393-428, 1958. Electrical activity in chemoreceptors of blowfly; effects of polarization.

105. Zotterman, Y., Experientia *6*: 57-58, 1950; Acta physiol. scand. *37*: 60-70, 1956; Ann. N. Y. Acad. Sci. *81*: 358-366, 1959. Species differences in water, sweet and salt taste.

Chapter 12

PHOTORECEPTION

Responsiveness to light is a universal capacity of living things.[146] Defined as light is that portion of the electromagnetic spectrum ranging in wave lengths from about 2000 to 100,000 Å or 200 to 10,000 mμ. Within this range the radiation can be detected and studied by optical means. For the human eye the sensitivity range is from about 4000 to about 7500 Å (visible light), while light of shorter and longer wave lengths is referred to as ultraviolet and infrared, respectively. The sensitivity of radiation receptors of some organisms extends beyond the "visible" and into the ultraviolet, and of some others into the infrared.

The physical properties and actions of light render responsiveness to it a very useful capacity. For plants, energy, especially of the longer wave lengths of visible light, is essential to photosynthesis, and illumination from other ranges of the spectrum, both longer and shorter wave lengths, participates in adaptive phototropic responses of the plants and, through adaptive response to the annual change in daily light periods, in gearing germination and flowering to the most favorable times of year.

For animals, whose nutrition depends upon plants, and thus upon photosynthesis indirectly, light plays the role of a very effective token stimulus. The reflective and absorptive characteristics of light apprise the animal of changes in its physical environment. Intensity changes associated with shadows of moving objects inform the animal of the presence of enemy or prey. And since in aerial conditions the longer wave length infrared is usually associated with visible light, brighter illumination signals to the animal a warmer, dryer environment, and lower illumination signals a cooler, damper one. Also, as for the plants, response to photoperiod is for numerous animals critically involved in the regulation of their annual reproductive cycles.

Finally, in the more highly differentiated species of animals there are well-defined special organs, or eyes, for photoreception, which display a number of specialized light-receptive capacities ranging from the ability to localize accurately the direction from which light comes (direction eyes), to the ability to differentiate the detailed patterns of light reflection from the composite of objects in direct line of vision (image-forming eyes). The culmination of evolution in this direction occurs in eyes which differentiate even the qualitative and quantitative color and hue differences of light.

Light in nature is always to a greater or lesser degree polarized as a consequence of the Tyndall-Rayleigh effect of light scattering in gaseous or liquid media and the Fresnel effect of reflection and refraction at interfaces. The plane of polarization is related, consequently, to the direction with respect to the sun or other light source. The photoreceptive systems of many animals, particularly arthropods, are capable of resolving the plane of the polarized light. Such visual polarization analyzers appear to be used in the orientational movements and migrations of a wide variety of animals.

Though photoreception involves a wide diversity of gross structural organization and correlated physiological properties, reflecting great differences in light-analyzing capacities of organisms, the fundamental mechanism underlying the photochemical activation of a light-receptive pigment, and the primary excitation-initiating process, seems to be far more similar among animals.

PHOTORECEPTORS AND ORIENTATION

Animals, and plants as well, are typically oriented in space and time. There is some normal position of the body with respect to gravity or to surface of contact. The fish in water, the fly in air, the mosquito on wall or ceiling, or the growing plant, each has its characteristic orientation. This basic bodily orientation is termed *primary*. In addition, organisms tend to orient their bodies, and commonly move, in response to various stimuli in their immediate environment. *Secondary orientations* are chiefly responsible for the observed distributions of species among the various specific niches of the environment. The line between primary and secondary orientations, however, often becomes difficult to define; both obviously depend upon a functional receptor-adjustor-effector mechanism of the organism.

To respond to any given stimulus modality requires first some receptor mechanism sensitive to it. Light plays an important part in orientation of organisms. Utilization of the directional properties of light resides in the optics of the photoreceptor and in the organization of the central nervous system. The mere presence of a photoreceptor does not indicate the nature of the orientation. Fraenkel and Gunn[78] have reviewed the general problem of types of animal orientation, with emphasis upon light responses, and have advanced a useful classification of them. The term *tropism* is restricted to orientation of sessile animals and plants. The term *taxis* is applied to the directed orientation of animals which move in their environment, and *kinesis* to non-directed, velocity changes of the organism in response to changes in intensity of environmental stimulating factors. Distribution of animals in space may depend on either taxes, kineses, or both.

The classification of Fraenkel and Gunn subdivides both kineses and taxes on the basis of fundamental differences in mechanism. Kineses are subdivided into *orthokinesis,* in which the rate of linear movement is involved, and *klinokinesis,* involving the rate of change of direction, or turning. Both types of kineses are dependent upon a receptive system capable of distinguishing intensity differences. It can be demonstrated that with a simple direct relationship between intensity of the environmental factor and the kinetic response, the organisms will come to aggregate at the low end of an environmental gradient, and with a simple inverse relationship, at the high end of a gradient, even though only nondirected movements with respect to the gradient have occurred.

Taxes have also been subdivided. In *klinotaxis,* the directed movements toward or away from a stimulus source depend upon frequent bending movements of the head to permit *successive comparisons* of stimulus strength on the two sides. This kind of orientation, a photoklinotaxis, is found in such organisms as fly maggots and *Euglena,* which have good intensity discrimination but poor direction receptors. *Tropotaxis* is a smooth straight orientation toward or away from a stimulus source by *simultaneous bilateral equating* of stimulation. This kind of orientation, exhibited for example in phototropotaxis of many planarians and sow bugs, depends upon a bilateral arrangement of receptors possessing some good degree of direction localization. That a continuous equating occurs in this type of orientation is seen from the compromising path displayed in response to two simultaneous light sources and to circling (circus) movements when one eye is blinded. With the left eye blinded the circus movements are counterclockwise in a negatively tactic organism and clockwise in a positively tactic one.

Telotaxis is smooth straight orientation toward or away from stimulus source, without a bilateral balance of right and left stimulation. That telotaxis requires no bilateral equating of stimulus is evident from the selection of one of two light sources offered and to the absence of circus movements after unilateral blinding. Telotaxis requires an eye capable of good directional localization, and a mechanism inhibiting response to other stimulating sources simultaneously present. Phototelotaxis occurs in the crustacean *Hemimysis* and under some conditions in bees, crabs, and flies.

Another kind of orientational response with special regard to light is the *dorsal light reaction* which contributes to primary orientation. This last is dependent upon light, to a greater or lesser degree in different animals. The brine shrimp *Artemia* may be readily induced to swim upside down by illumination from below. The shrimp *Leander* and the fish *Crenilabrus* respond to illumination from the side by inclining the body toward the light source, a response greatly increased in strength following destruction of the static organs.

Many animals orient with respect to a light source, but assume a path at some particular angle with respect to the source other than directly toward or away from it. This *light-compass orientation* requires the possession of an image-forming eye, upon which the light source may be fixated by any region of the eye. This reaction is illustrated by the (marine gastropod) nudibranch *Elysia,* which appears to wander aimlessly in diffuse light, but to take a straight path in the presence of a horizontal light beam. Even though the animal's direction may bear any angular relationship to the light source, and the direction may change from time to time, there is a true orientation to the source since the direction of orientation can be shifted in a predictable manner by changing the position of the light source. The nudibranch tends to keep its same angle. Such a light-compass reaction forms the basis of sun-, moon- and star-compass orientation reported for such animals as homing birds, fishes, insects, and crustaceans; in these the angular orientation changes at rates which just compensate for the earth's rotation relative to sun, moon, and stars, changes regulated by the so-called living clock-system.

LIGHT SENSITIVITY WITHOUT EYES

It has long been known that plants utilize light not only for photosynthesis but also for phototropism. Many plants bend toward the source of illumination. Phototropism is particularly marked in blue light, which results in relatively little photosynthesis, and appears associated with yellow pigments (carotenoids) present in plants, though the specific pigment has yet to be identified.

Sensitivity of the general body surface to light exists in species of several phyla of animals, including even some fishes and amphibians.[162] Protozoa such as *Amoeba, Stentor,* and *Peranema* respond to changing intensity of illumination of any part of the body by a cessation of movement resulting from gelation in the illuminated region (Fig. 125). If the whole body is illuminated, locomotion is greatly retarded or stopped, because of gelation at the tips of the pseudopods (Fig. 125). However, if illumination is continued, locomotion gradually increases and becomes normal in 6 to 30 minutes, depending on light intensity.[153] In the absence of light-sensitive organelles and in view of the periodically fluid condition of amoeba protoplasm, there is probably a direct effect of light on sol-gel reversibility.

Diffuse sensitivity to light also exists among the echinoderms.[160] Iridophores, glistening reflectors in the skin, appear to serve as reflectors for the dermal photoreceptive elements.[160] The distribution of dermal sensitivity corresponds strikingly with that of neural elements, suggesting sensitivity of nerves themselves to light. Experiments have given direct evidence that this is true.[254] Pigment movement in dermal chromatophores, which disperse their pigment in light and concentrate it in darkness, provides a screen for the sensitive elements. Dermal chromatophores play a role analogous to that played by the retinal pigments of specialized eyes. Protection of photoreceptors from bright

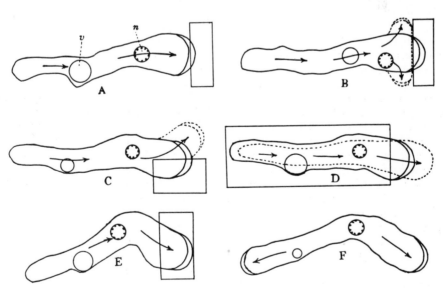

FIGURE 125. Responses of *Amoeba* to localized illumination (rectangular areas). Arrows show the direction of protoplasmic streaming. Broken lines in *B, C,* and *D* indicate position of animal shortly after illumination. *F* shows the position and direction of streaming assumed by *E* after illumination. *v*, Contractile vacuole; *n*, nucleus. (From Mast, S.: *in* Protozoa in Biological Research, edited by G. Calkins and F. M. Summers. Columbia University Press.)

light is accomplished by some sea urchins by covering their bodies with foreign objects picked from the environment.[161] The entire surface of *Holothuria* is photosensitive, and two pigments are present, one of which is a fluorescent greenish yellow.[50] The reactions of three species of *Holothuria* vary with the amount of this pigment present, and young specimens of *H. captiva* which have little pigment are less reactive than the heavily pigmented adults. Therefore, the greenish yellow fluorescent pigment is postulated to be either the photosensitive pigment or a sensitizer. Starfishes, though normally possessing functional eyespots,[101] continue to respond to light after removal of the eyes, indicating dermal light sensitivity.[190]

Jennings,[127] in his monograph on the behavior of the starfish, described reactions to light. In general, if the direction of illumination is such that one part of the animal is more intensely illuminated than another, the animal will move in the direction of the less intensely illuminated side. Under uniform but sudden illumination the animal exhibits increased locomotor activity, a kinesis which gradually subsides.

Many annelids (e.g., *Lumbricus*) possess no macroscopic photoreceptors, yet the entire body is sensitive to light. Sensitivity is greatest on the prostomium, next greatest on the dorsal region of the next few anterior segments and on a few of the most posterior segments, and least on the middle of the body. The regions of greatest sensitivity coincide with the highest concentration of the so-called epithelial light cells of Hess, which are single-cell photoreceptors each with an apparent refractile body connected to neurofibrillae. The relative frequency of occurrence of these receptors in certain segments is as follows:[108] prostomium, 57; segment 1, 26; segment 2, 10; segment 3, 7; segment 11, 1; last segment, 14; penultimate, 4; antepenultimate, 2. The distribution of light sensitivity thus parallels the distribution of the light-sensitive cells. In some oligochaetes the photoreceptors are found directly on the nerves of the cerebral ganglia. Earthworms are positively phototactic at very low intensities of illumination and negatively phototactic at higher intensities.[182] The type of orientation which these worms exhibit most often is klinotaxis.

The molluscs display great diversity in the mechanism of photoreception, ranging from a diffuse light sensitivity to a photoreceptor as complex as the human eye. The diffuse sensitivity to light in the clam *Mya arenaria*

is confined largely to the siphon. Under conditions of constant illumination the siphon is extended; when illumination increases the siphon is withdrawn. Photoreceptors similar to those in the earthworm have been reported.[148]

In the clam *Mactra,* mantle nerves, including branches to the siphon, have been found directly sensitive to light. In nerves discharging spontaneously at 5 impulses/sec in darkness, illumination causes reduction in frequency; there is a large off-discharge upon cessation of light stimulation.[132] Some nerve fibers of *Mya* and *Venus* also show comparable light response. The genital ganglion of the gastropod *Aplysia* also exhibits the capacity to respond to light.[4, 5]

The sixth abdominal ganglion in the crayfish is photosensitive,[181] and the discharge patterns in the afferent photoreceptor fibers from the ganglion have been investigated in both excised nerve cords and single fibers in the intact organism.[133, 134] It is postulated that the receptive elements are only slightly modified neural ones.

Certain neural elements in the brain of lamprey eels, minnows, and ducks are sensitive to illumination.

EYES AS SPECIAL PHOTORECEPTORS

Localized photoreceptors are present in a great variety of organisms and exhibit great diversity of structure. The photoreceptors may be classified on the basis of their gross function. Thus certain eyes function only as intensity receptors while others function in varying degrees in form perception and pattern vision. The latter group, furthermore, forms a large group of extreme morphological diversity.

Morphology. The simplest types of eyes appear in the flagellate Protozoa. Stigmas and ocelli occur only in flagellates. The stigma of *Euglena* (Fig. 126) is a mass of orange-red granules shading on one side a swelling on the flagellum which is the actual light-sensitive element. Electron micrographic study reveals the eyespot area to comprise forty to fifty tightly packed rods imbedded in a matrix.[249, 250] The eyespot and flagellum base appear to form an intimate functional association. In phototaxis the organism gradually alters its orientation through changes in direction of the beat of the flagellum in response to the periodic shading, until the organism becomes oriented (see Fig. 128). In the Phytomonadida the stigma consists of a refractile structure which serves as a lens and

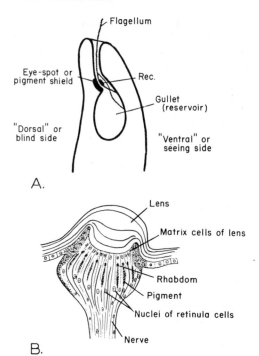

A.

B.

FIGURE 126.   *A*, side view of *Euglena viridis*, showing the eyespot or pigmented shield and the enlargement at the base of the flagellum (*Rec.*), believed to be the photoreceptor. (From Fraenkel, G. S., and Gunn, D. L.: The Orientation of Animals. Oxford University Press.)

B, ocellus of *Aphrophora spumaria* (after Imms and Link). (From Wigglesworth, V. B.: The Principles of Insect Physiology. Methuen & Co.)

neurons, the axons of which extend into the brain. The light receptive, or retinal, neurons possess a lamellar structure as revealed by the electron microscope. The individual plates are double-membraned and stacked at right angles to the long axis of the cells. There are about 8 to 10 of the plates per micron.[250]

Some annelida (e.g., *Nereis*) have ocelli. In the Mollusca there exist several types of photoreceptors which transcend in complexity the simple ocelli heretofore discussed. The complex structure of the eye of *Nautilus*, consisting of an open pit, without a lens; the eye of *Helix*, consisting of a completely enclosed receptor containing a lens-like material; and the eye of *Pecten* (Fig. 129), consisting of a lens and a double layer of retinal cells, backed by a tapetum, suggest that these permit pattern vision as well as intensity perception. One of the most complicated of molluscan eyes is that of *Sepia* (Figs. 127, 129).

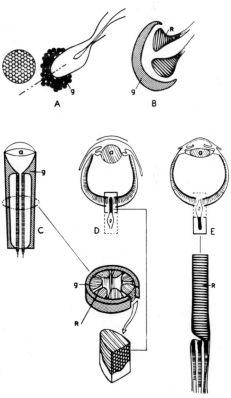

FIGURE 127.   Schematic representation of eye structures: *A*, stigma (eyespot); *B*, Planaria eye; *C*, insect ommatidium; *D*, mollusc eye (Octopus and Sepia), and *E*, vertebrate eye. Location of photoreceptor elements and their microstructure is indicated: *a*, lens; *g*, pigment (sheath) granules; *R*, retinal structures. In *A*, *C* and *D* the retinal structures *R* are packed rods or tubes and in *B* and *E* they are packed plates or discs. (From Wolken, J. J.: Ann. New York Acad. Sci., vol. 74.)

covers the opening of a cup-shaped mass of pigment. The light-sensitive material is between the lens and the inner surface of the cup. The function of the pigment in both the preceding instances is to render the receptive organelle a directional detector useful in phototaxis. The stigmas of fresh-water Dinoflagellida are similar to those of Phytomonadida. Those of certain marine dinoflagellates are much larger. In general appearance they resemble the ocelli of flatworms and are called ocelli.

The ocelli of coelenterates vary considerably in structure, ranging from a simple layer of sensory cells mingled with pigment cells, as in *Turris*, to cup-shaped ocelli in *Sarsia* (Fig. 129) and *Tiaropsis*.

The ocelli of flatworms, similar in general appearance and in principle to the stigmas of the Phytomonadida and Dinoflagellida, possess a pigmented cup and a light-sensitive layer within the cup (Fig. 129). There is often also a lens. The pigment cup may consist of a single cell. However, the sensitive layer is cellular and is composed of primary

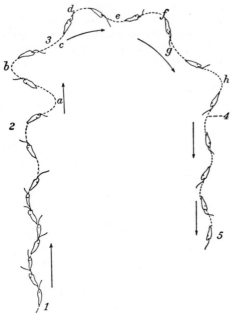

FIGURE 128. Orientation of swimming *Euglena* to light. From *1* to *2*, light from direction of top of page; *2*, direction of light reversed. The animal swerves to the dorsal side each time the receptor is shielded from the light by the eye spot. (From Jennings, H. S.: Behavior of Lower Organisms. Columbia University Press.)

In structure and development it is comparable to the eyes of vertebrates. There is a corneal surface which may be covered by lids; an iris and a lens separate two eye chambers, an anterior and a posterior; the lens is suspended and can be moved by a ciliary muscle; the retina lines the back of the eye; and the eyeball is surrounded by cartilage. During development the eye originates as an ectodermal pit, the lining of which forms the retina. The lens is formed in two parts: the inner part at the point of closure of the pit, and the outer part from a circular fold which forms the iris. Secondary and tertiary neurons are located in an optic ganglion immediately behind the retina rather than on the front of the retina as in vertebrates. Functionally as well as structurally, the eye of *Sepia* is similar to that of vertebrates, except that the retinal elements are not inverted.

The retinal elements of both *Octopus* and *Sepia* have their distal portions differentiated into a structure displaying a remarkable resemblance to the rhabdomeres of the arthropod eye. These are tightly packed rods, evident by electron microscopy, in which the rods are stacked at right angles to the long axis of the retinal cells.[250]

Photoreceptors and Direction. The photoreceptor of *Euglena* and related forms is a directional receptor by virtue of the associated and pigmented stigma. This orange-red pigment mass serves to shield the sensitive swelling in the flagellum base when illumination strikes the ventral side. When exposed to a single light source *Euglena* moves directly toward or away from it, depending on the intensity. When the direction of illumination is changed suddenly, the animal reorients, as shown in Figure 128. This directional orientation, klinotaxis, is made possible by means of regular deviations in movement (pendular or spiral), and involves comparison of intensities at successive points in time. The coelenterate *Hydra* behaves in this way, as does the post-trochophore larva of *Arenicola* and the tadpole larva of the ascidian *Amaroucium*. Earthworms and maggot larvae of several species of flies[78] may also exhibit exploratory pendular movements leading to orientation.

With the advent of bilaterally arranged paired receptors, a peripheral mechanism exists which may permit direct orientation to light. In *Planaria maculata,* which possesses two cup-eyes, the animal orients so that the two eyes are equally stimulated. This type of orientation, tropotaxis, involves the continuous comparison of intensities on two receptors simultaneously. In contrast, photokinesis is shown by *Planaria* deprived of their eyes and illuminated. They show increased random activity in light and ultimately aggregate in the darkest region of the environment.[208]

A similar type of behavior occurs in another planarian, *Dendrocoelum.*[213] Under uniform illumination directly from above, the animal lacks a directional response. The perception of light merely increases its random angular motion. This is photoklinokinesis.[78]

PHOTORECEPTORS AND PATTERN VISION

Light-sensitive organs capable of pattern vision have evolved several times. The eyes of *Pecten, Nautilus,* and *Helix* probably function in pattern vision; the complex eye of cephalopods, e.g., *Sepia* (Fig. 129), which resembles in structural complexity the eye of vertebrates, seems capable of pattern vision and of form perception. In the arthropods the compound eye serves in pattern vision, and in the vertebrates a distinctly different photoreceptor eye has evolved.

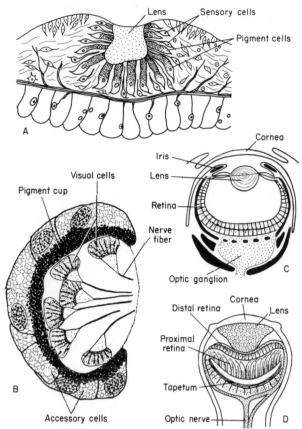

FIGURE 129. Diagrammatic representation of photosensitive organs. *A*, section through the ocellus of *Sarsia*. *B*, transverse section of the eye of *Planaria maculata*. *C*, section through eye of *Sepia*. *D*, section through eye of *Pecten*. (Redrawn from Hyman,[122] Taliaferro,[208] and Borradaile and Potts.[23])

The Compound Eyes of Arthropods.

The eyes of arthropods are of two general types: compound eyes and ocelli. All compound eyes are constructed so that an image is formed; some ocelli (e.g., the lateral ocelli or stemmata of insect larvae and pupae) are also capable of forming images, but others (e.g., ocelli of adult insects) are primarily simple organs of intensity response.

The compound eye is an effective organ of vision which has developed along quite different morphological and optical lines from the eye of vertebrates.[252] The focusing mechanism works on a different optical principle, and the focus is always fixed. In many compound eyes at least, the light-gathering power is far inferior to that of the vertebrate eye. However, the compound eye also has advantages, especially in that the field of view is very great and may encompass well over 200 degrees, as in the stalked eyes of the crayfish and many other decapod crustaceans.

Structure of the Compound Eye.

The compound eye comprises, superficially, a number of transparent facets in the cuticle of the head or eyestalk.[62] Beneath each facet lies the dioptric apparatus and elongated light-sensitive retinula cells, with associated nerve fibers extending into the central nervous system. Each facet together with its underlying elements is called an ommatidium. The retinula cells of all the ommatidia, collectively, make up the retina. The facets, together, form the cornea, which, along with the underlying dioptric crystalline cones, serve as lenses. Each ommatidium usually has seven or eight retinula cells, arranged around a central refractile rod, the rhabdom, including the inner differentiated edges, rhabdomeres, of the retinula cells and a central matrix. Each retinula cell is a primary neuron and is continuous with a postretinal axon. The rhabdom is assumed to be the light-receptive portion of the retinula cells. The ommatidium appears to function as a unit, with only the axon of one of the retinula cells, the eccentric one, conveying optic impulses. Some compound eyes (*Limulus*; the moth *Erebus*) have large eccentric cells; others (insects such as *Lucilia* and *Musca*) have a circle of uniform retinula cells.

The fine structure of the retinula cells and their rhabdomeres has been carefully examined by electron microscopy in insects[70, 85, 251] and *Limulus*.[159] Each rhabdomere in *Limulus* consists of what appears to be densely packed microvilli, outgrowths of opposing central faces of adjoining retinula surfaces. Each rhabdomere thus comprises a contribution from two cells, each cell contributing a wedge, whose edge impinges on a longitudinal axial canal of the rhabdom. The axial canal contains the dendritic process of the eccentric cell.

In the insect eye, molecular morphology of the retinula system is fundamentally similar to that of *Limulus*. Again, retinula microvilli, tightly packed, give rhabdomeres comprising a rod system with rods all oriented at right angles to the long axis of the ommatidium, and with the various rhabdomeres of the seven to eight retinula cells oriented each in a different axis (Fig. 130). All the ommatidia are oriented similarly in terms of the eccentric cell, suggesting that the orientation may play some important role, as for example in resolution of the plane of polarized light.

In many nocturnal insects (e.g., noctuid moths) tracheae are grouped around the retinula cells, especially at the basal end of the rhabdom. The tracheae reflect light distally through the ommatidium and appear to play a role analogous to that of the tapetum lucidum of vertebrates.

In insects the whole ommatidium is encased in a sheath of dark pigmented cells made up of two sections: the *primary iris cells* around the crystalline cone, and *secondary iris cells* which may enclose both the primary iris cells and the retinula cells. The proximal ends of the ommatidia rest on a fenestrated membrane through which the axons and tracheae pass. In primitive Crustacea (e.g., *Gammarus*), the retinula cells contain all of the black pigment and extend distally to surround the crystalline cone. In higher Crustacea (e.g., shrimp, crayfish), black proximal pigment is contained within the retinula cells, but the black distal pigment occupies separate cells. A light-reflecting pigment is located in other cells surrounding the retinula cells.

A comparison of the orientation capacities of a series of flies of several mutant types of eye-color has suggested the importance and role of the retinal pigment for vision.[71]

Diurnal Movements of Eye Pigments. In compound eyes there is movement of pigments which mechanically adapt the eye to the illumination level.[176] On the left in Figure 246 (Chapter 20) is shown the position of the pigments in *Palaemonetes* adapted to bright light, and, in the center, pigment position in animals adapted to extremely dim light or to darkness. In shrimp and crayfishes the distal pigments show a graded degree of placement over a wide intensity range.[72, 196] In *Palaemonetes* the dark pigment ensheaths the ommatidium by day and leaves it predominantly naked by night.[138, 243] The reflecting pigment moves outward to surround the retinula cells by night. This makes the eye glow when suddenly exposed to light at night.

A comparable proximodistal movement of pigment occurs in eyes of many insects in response to illumination change.[57] In *Limulus*, dark pigment in response to light and darkness moves transversely among and away from the rhabdomeres.[159]

Retinal pigments of many arthropods may persist in day-night changes even when kept under unchanging illumination in the laboratory. Such a diurnal rhythm of pigment migration was first discovered in the noctuid moth *Plusia* and later has been observed in the coddling moth *Carpocapsa*[40] and in numerous crustaceans including *Macrobrachium*,[243, 244] *Cambarus*,[18] two macrurans and four brachyurans,[245] and *Anchistioides, Cambarus, Homarus, Orconectes,* and *Palaemonetes*.[31, 138]

A persistent rhythm is readily observed in crayfish, which, if kept in constant darkness, will exhibit an orange eyeshine at night but not during the day. The diurnal rhythm of eyeshine may persist for months under conditions of constant darkness and temperature.[18, 244] These rhythmic changes are presumed to be timed by the same basic daily rhythmic mechanism which regulates numerous other phenomena. The role of the endocrine system in controlling crustacean pigment migration is discussed in Chapter 20. In insects the retinal pigments are presumed to be neurally controlled.[57]

Image Formation. The crystalline cone is the principal refractive element of the compound eye, and it is not adjustable. Each ommatidium, therefore, has a fixed focus. The crystalline cone is made up of concentric lamellae, the more central layers of which have a higher refractive index than the more peripheral ones. The cone is therefore a virtual lens cylinder. Figure 131 shows light passing through such a lens. If the length of the cylinder is equal to its focal length (A), a beam of parallel light (mpn) which enters perpendicular to one end of the cylinder (edge ab) is focused on the other end (edge

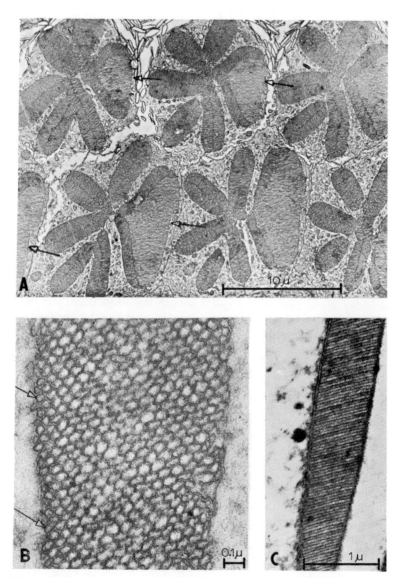

FIGURE 130. A, electron micrograph of cross-section through a group of retinulae of *Erebus*. Each retinula consists of radially arranged retinula cells, and the rhabdomere segments of each abut the rhabdomere segments of the adjacent retinula cells. Arrows give the orientation of the eccentric rhabdomeres; the eccentric cell cytoplasm lies peripheral to the large eccentric cell rhabdomere.

B, Greatly magnified electron micrograph of longitudinal section through a rhabdomere of *Musca*, oriented to show the fine tubular compartments in cross-section.

C, Electron micrograph of longitudinal section through a rhabdomere of *Musca*, oriented in the long axis of the tubular compartments.

(From Fernandez-Moran, H.: Exp. Cell Res., vol. 5.)

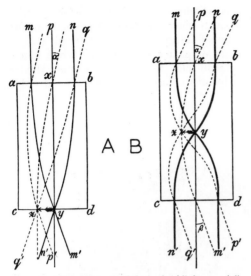

cd), and emerges as a divergent beam (*n'p'm'*). Other beams of light (*p*) entering at an angle to the axis of the cylinder emerge at an angle (*p'*). This permits, theoretically, inverted image formation, but since this image is limited to only seven or eight retinula elements which probably function as a unit, it is probably useful merely as a spot of light rather than as an image. If the lens cylinder is twice as long as its focal length (*B*), the beam emerges as a parallel beam whose angle of emergence (*B*) is equal and opposite to the angle of incidence (*a*).

In an arthropod eye there is one of two mechanisms for image formation, *superpositional,* using the double-focal-length cylinder, or *appositional,* utilizing the single focal-length one.

In the apposition eye, Figure 132 I*A*, the iris pigment completely sheaths the ommatidium, and the light which strikes the rhabdom and associated retinula cells is chiefly that which enters nearly parallel to the axis of the particular ommatidium. In Figure 132 I*B*, a superposition eye, the pigment cells do not completely sheath the ommatidium, and light entering through a number of crystalline cones may be brought to bear on any given retinula bundle. Figure 132 II illustrates the two mechanisms of image formation. In *A* is shown the so-called apposition image, in which each rhabdom receives chiefly the light which enters the ommatidium parallel to its axis. In this type the length of the crys-

talline cone may be equal to its focal length. In Figure 132 II*B* is shown an image formed by *superposition,* in which light from point *e* may pass through any of a number of crystalline cones and be bent (as in Figure 131), so as to be focused on a single rhabdom. In this type the length of the crystalline cone is optimally twice the focal length. If the secondary iris pigment should migrate as shown in Figure 132 II*A,* then the superposition eye might function as an apposition eye.

In general, most diurnal insects have apposition eyes, and nocturnal ones have superposition eyes. Undoubtedly there are many intermediate types. The apposition eye is adapted to function at high light intensity and is relatively inefficient as a light-gathering device. The superposition eye is adapted to low light intensities and is much more efficient for gathering light than the apposition eye, but is less efficient than most vertebrate eyes.

Since the image formed by the apposition eye is made up only of spots of light of different intensities, each of which has entered through a single ommatidium, the image is often referred to as a mosaic one. In the superposition eye, light which is focused on a single rhabdom (Fig. 132 II*B*) may enter through a number of ommatidia so that, though the image is still a mosaic, it is so in a sense more like that for the vertebrate eye. In a vertebrate eye, the image registered at individual cones or at small groups of rods and/or cones may also be considered as a mosaic but of much finer grain. In *Limulus* the evidence points to the conclusion that the retinula complex of each ommatidium behaves as a unit and can in fact be excited by light from a rather wide visual angle, exceeding by far the morphological ommatidial angle.[235, 238]

Ocelli of Arthropods. A simple type of arthropod eye, found in the larvae of Lepidoptera, Trichoptera, Collembola, and other insects, consists of a structure somewhat comparable to a single ommatidium of a compound eye. These simple eyes are known as stemmata, or lateral ocelli, and may occur singly or in small groups scattered on the sides of the animal. In the larvae of Tenthredinidae and many Coleoptera there is only one ocellus on each side, which contains many retinulae, each with several sense cells and a rhabdom, perhaps with pigment cells, all beneath a single lens. This more complicated type of lateral ocellus is capable of distinguishing form (Fig. 126B) and perhaps color. In the larvae of *Cicindela* there are six stemmata on each side: two large, two small, and two vestigial. The large ones have 6350 visual cells each and are apparently capable of detecting form and, when all of the stemmata are functioning together, of determining distance.[79]

Dorsal ocelli of insects are the simple eyes which usually occur in the frontal region of the head between the compound eyes. In general, the structure is similar to that of the complex stemmata described above. The dorsal ocelli of agrionids and libellids have a tapetum and, when the animal is brought from darkness to bright light, there is a rapid movement of brown pigment across the white fundus within a few seconds. The ocelli have a high light-gathering power, with apertures estimated at *f* (i.e., focal length divided by diameter) 1.8 for *Eristalis* and 1.5 for *Formica* females, whereas the facets of appositional compound eyes have apertures of *f* 2.5 to 4.5 and, therefore, a much lower light-gathering power. In sphingids and noctuids the superpositional compound eyes have a high light-gathering power, and ocelli are absent. The ocelli are poorly adapted for image formation for at least two reasons: the angular separation of the rhabdoms is great (3 to 10 degrees), and the image is usually focused far behind the retina (e.g., in *Eristalis* the retina is 0.11 mm behind the lens and the focal plane is 0.29 mm).[111, 112]

Most spiders have eight ocelli distributed over the dorsal portion of the cephalothorax. Two of these are known as principal or direct eyes, and the others as lateral or indirect eyes. In the direct eyes the sensory portion of each sense cell is in front of the cell body, and in the indirect ocelli the sensory portion is behind the cell body. The direct eyes are movable by means of radially distributed muscles and permit the animal to fixate its prey without shifting its body.

Other arthropods have various arrangements of ocelli. Many species have ocelli with several retinulae; others (myriapods) have groups of such ocelli placed contiguously so that they may tend to simulate a compound eye.

One of the probable functions of dorsal ocelli of insects is to influence the level of central nervous activity. There is evidence that on reduction in illumination, impulses in the ocellar nerve increase brain activity and consequent facilitation of reflexes in lower centers. Shadows would result in accelerated responses. It is also possible that there would be increased hormone production by neurosecretory elements of the central nervous system.

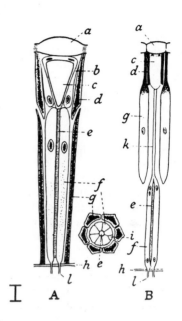

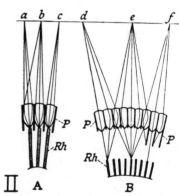

FIGURE 132. I. Diagram of the two types of ommatidium. *A*, from eye forming apposition image (after Snodgrass); *B*, from eye forming superposition image (after Weber). *a*, corneal lens; *b*, matrix cells of cornea; *c*, crystalline cone; *d*, iris pigment cells; *e*, rhabdom; *f*, retinal cells; *g*, retinal pigment cells; *h*, fenestrated basement membrane; *i*, eccentric retinal cell; *k*, translucent filament connecting crystalline cone with rhabdom; *l*, nerve fibers.

II. Diagram to show image formation, by (*A*) an apposition eye and (*B*) a superposition eye. *a-f*, luminous points with the rays emitted by them; *P*, pigment; *Rh*, rhabdom (after Kühn).

(From Wigglesworth, V. B.: The Principles of Insect Physiology. Methuen & Co.)

VISUAL ACUITY, INTENSITY DISCRIMINATION, AND PERCEPTION OF PATTERN

Visual acuity is a measure of the capacity of the eye to distinguish between separate contours as being discrete. This is expressed in terms of visual angle which is subtended. By definition, one minute of arc represents unit visual acuity. Visual acuity is thus a measure of the pattern-resolving power of the photoreceptor, which, in turn, depends upon the dioptric apparatus and retina. Indissociably, acuity depends upon the differentiation of two contours as distinct upon the basis of intensity discrimination (see also color discrimination), and hence acuity and intensity discrimination go hand in hand in the resolution of visual pattern.

Optomotor responses have been utilized very profitably in the study of form and intensity resolution by the eye.[105, 106] The majority of animals possessing eyes perform directed movements when subjected to movement of their visual field. Typically, animals such as crabs, aquatic insects, hovering insects, and fishes, which normally tend to hold stationary positions, will move along with motion of the visual field. This is probably a consequence of a reflex locomotor maintenance of a portion of the environment fixated upon the visual field in the face of water or wind currents. On the other hand, rapidly moving animals such as bees and flies tend to move against a moving visual field. Experimentally, a moving visual field is usually obtained by placing an animal in a narrow glass cell or a cylindrical jar and subjecting the animal's visual field to a vertically dark striped plate or outer cylinder which occupies the organism's total visual field, and is capable of being moved or rotated in either direction at any desired speed. Means may also be provided for altering the intensity differences between the alternating dark and light stripes. The stripe widths may also be varied.

Visual acuity is a function of light intensity. It is very poor at low illuminations and increases to maximum at high illuminations. The relationship of acuity to the logarithm of illumination describes a sigmoid curve. This is to be explained in terms of a general statistical distribution of thresholds in the retinal population, and hence by the density in the retina of the functioning elements. When two types of receptive elements with different sensitivity ranges are present, as in the case of the rods and cones of the vertebrate eye, this curve may have two segments. At their maxima when all elements are operative, visual acuity of the human eye is 2.0 to 2.5, of *Drosophila* about 1/1000 of man (0.0018), of the honeybee about 1/100 of man (0.017).

Similarly, intensity discrimination is much lower at lower illuminations than at higher ones. In *Drosophila* at low illumination the brighter light must be of the order of a hundred times that of the dimmer one to be distinguished, or in other terms: $\Delta I/I$ approximates 100, but as illumination increases $\Delta I/I$ falls to about 1.5 in this fly. Comparable values for the honeybee and man are 0.25 and 0.006, respectively.

In many arthropods the ommatidial angle increases toward the periphery of the eye, and it has been demonstrated that acuity becomes correspondingly reduced.[106]

While the arthropod compound eye does not fare well in comparison with the vertebrate eye in intensity discrimination and acuity, it does seem to be highly adapted for rapid temporal resolution of the visual field in rapidly flying insects. Whereas flicker fusion frequency for man approximates 45 to 55/second, the corresponding values for rapid fliers like the bee and blowfly are of the order of 200 to 300/second,[7] while slower moving insects show flicker fusion at much lower frequencies. Such "fast" and "slow" eyes have correlated quite different electroretinograms (ERG), reflecting a self-quenching visual system in the fast type. The flying insect is adapted, therefore, to resolve the pattern of a rapidly changing visual field. In fact, there is evidence that the recognition and discrimination of visual patterns by the compound eye involve such temporal resolution.[248]

In the compound apposition eye the light-resolving power is theoretically limited by ommatidial diameter according to the equation:

$$\theta = 1.22 \frac{\lambda}{\delta}$$

where θ is resolving power in radians, λ the wave length of the light, and δ the diameter of the visual aperture. Visual acuity is clearly limited also by the ommatidial angle, with an angle of two times the ommatidial one permitting one unstimulated ommatidium to lie between two stimulated ones. Optimum optical conditions involve the best compromise, therefore, between ommatidial angle and size. A study of a wide range of insect species has suggested that the acuity of the compound eye, at least in those areas where the ommatidial angles are smallest, approaches the theoretical limit set by the wave length of the light.[14] In many insects the ratio $\frac{\phi}{\theta}$ approaches unity, where ϕ equals the ommatidial angle and θ the resolving power. In the bee $\theta = \frac{\phi}{0.61}$.

Insects with small eyes, however, tend to have ommatidia slightly larger than the theoretical optimum, presumably because resolution becomes limiting. In adaptation to dim light, acuity is sacrificed for resolution by increase in ommatidial size, or the arthropod shows many of the advantages of the simple eye by a shift to the superposition eye. In a simple eye, like that of the vertebrate, both sensitivity to light and acuity increase with eye size; they increase in proportion to the square of the pupil diameter, or pupil area.

In the vertebrate camera eye also, acuity is usually very close to the theoretical limit set by the wave length of light and pupil size. For the human eye the maximum possible acuity can be calculated at about 47 seconds, while empirically it lies only a few seconds less.

THE VERTEBRATE CAMERA EYE

Morphology. The eye of man is rather generalized in structure and may be taken as representative of the vertebrate group.

The eye is comparable to a camera in many respects. There is a photosensitive screen (retina) on which the cornea and lens form an inverted image in accordance with principles of geometric optics. The aperture of the lens is varied by the iris, and the eyelids are used as a lens cover to exclude light and lessen the possibility of mechanical injury to the corneal surface. The photosensitive screen is backed by a layer of black pigment which reduces internal reflection and thereby enhances the clarity of the image. Part of the focusing mechanism (i.e., the lens), is also variable (by contraction of the ciliary muscle), so that objects at very different distances may be seen with equal sharpness if they are not viewed simultaneously.

Focusing of light on the retina is brought about partly by the curvature of the cornea, which has a refractive index (1.376) much higher than that of air (1.00), and partly by the lens, which has a refractive index (1.42) slightly higher than that of the aqueous and

vitreous humors (each 1.33). Since the greatest difference in refractive index, and also the greatest curvature, is found at the air-corneal interface, this is really the most important refracting surface in the formation of the image. The lens serves in a capacity comparable to that of a fine adjustment on a microscope, giving a delicate and accurate control over a short range. The range over which the lens can change the focus of the eye is known as the accommodation range, and the phenomenon as accommodation.

The accommodation range is as much as 15 to 20 diopters (a diopter is the reciprocal of the focal length in meters) in young children and only about 4 diopters after the age of about 42 years. This means that young children can focus objects as close as 2 inches from the eye as well as those at infinity. The decrease in accommodation permits adjustment after age 42 only from about 8 inches to infinity. The relaxed normal eye is focused for infinity, and accommodation is accomplished by the elasticity of the lens when the ciliary muscles are contracted. The decrease in focusing power with age is caused by the hardening of the lens and its consequent failure to become slightly rounder and thicker when contraction of the ciliary muscle would normally permit it to do so. This is the normal condition of presbyopia (meaning "old" sight), which is an almost inevitable concomitant of old age, and precludes clear close vision. It can readily be corrected by means of spectacles, and when the power of accommodation is very low, and the rigid lens not naturally adjusted to infinity, two pairs of spectacles, or a bifocal pair, are employed, with one lens for near and one for distant objects.

Abnormalities of vision occur in man, consequences of defective eye development. These, which may also be corrected by spectacles, are: (1) elongated eyeball, resulting in nearsightedness, or myopia, in which the image is focused in front of the retina, (2) short eyeball, resulting in farsightedness or hypermetropia, in which the image tends to be formed behind the retina, and (3) nonuniform curvature of the lens or cornea, resulting in astigmatism, the occurrence of different focal points of beams of light in different planes, e.g., vertical lines may appear blurred when horizontal lines at the same distance are not blurred.

Structure of the Retina. The structure of the retina is shown in Figure 133. In this figure the light enters at the bottom, which

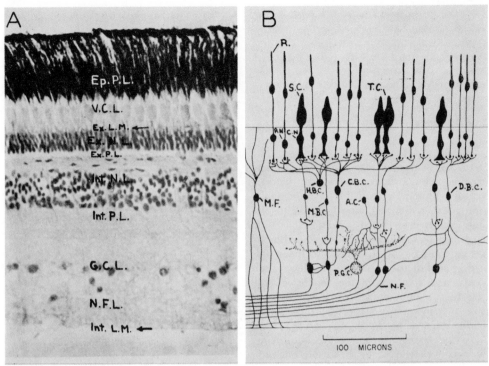

FIGURE 133.   Photomicrograph of the retina of the salmon Oncorhynchus with a diagram of the neurological arrangement therein. *A.C.*, amacrine cell; *C.B.C.*, "centrifugal" bipolar cell; *C.N.*, cone nucleus; *D.B.C.*, "diffuse" bipolar cell; *Ep.P.L.*, epithelial pigment layer; *Ex.L.M.*, external limiting membrane; *Ex.N.L.*, external nuclear layer; *Ex.P.L.*, external plexiform layer; *G.C.L.*, ganglion cell layer; *H.B.C.*, "horizontal" bipolar cell; *Int.L.M.*, internal limiting membrane; *Int.N.L.*, internal nuclear layer; *Int.P.L.*, internal plexiform layer; *M.B.C.*, "midget" bipolar cell; *M.F.*, mullerian fiber; *N.F.*, nerve fiber; *N.F.L.*, nerve fiber layer; *P.G.C.*, "parasol" ganglion cell; *R.*, rod; *R.N.*, rod nucleus; *S.C.*, single cone; *T.C.*, twin cone; *V.C.L.*, visual cell layer. (From Ali, M. A.: Canad. J. Zool., vol. 37.)

is the front of the retina, passes through the layer of nerve fibers, a layer of tertiary or large ganglionic neuron cell bodies, a layer of synapses, a layer of secondary neuron cell bodies including the bipolar cells (the inner nuclear layer), another synaptic layer, and then through the cell bodies (outer nuclear layer) of the rods and cones, which are the primary neurons or sense cells. The portion of the rod or cone corresponding to the dendrite of the primary neuron contains the photosensitive material. The light which passes the photosensitive elements is absorbed by the darkly pigmented choroid.

The neuronal connections of the retina are complex. They have been worked out in great detail,[179] and some of the types of connections are shown diagrammatically in Figure 133. Some cones synapse with a nerve fiber which receives no impulses from other rods or cones. Such a cone has an "exclusive line" to the brain. Other cones are connected to nerve fibers which receive also impulses originating in other cones or in rods. Certain cones which are connected to an "exclusive" fiber are also

connected through secondary neurons (inner nuclear layer) to nerve fibers which receive impulses from several or many rods and cones. The nerve fibers of the retina pass across the inner surface of the retina and enter the optic nerve. The region of exit of the nerve contains no rods and cones; it is insensitive to light, and is termed the "blind spot."

In one region of the retina close to the optical axis of the eye the rods are fewer in number and the cones are much more numerous. This is the area centralis. In birds, a few mammals, and reptiles and fishes the area centralis is thinner than the surrounding retina, because of a decreased thickness of the layer of secondary and tertiary neurons, and is referred to as the fovea centralis. In the fovea of certain birds (e.g., hawks, swallows, terns) these neuronal layers are not merely thinner, but their thickness varies in such a way as to spread the image over a larger surface, thereby permitting a higher degree of visual acuity. This spreading lens effect is caused by the fact that the refractive index of the retinal tissue is greater than that of the vitreous body. The fovea of man is a broad area with very little if any such spreading power.

The two types of sense cells, rods and cones, provide a duplex system adapted to function effectively over two different intensity ranges. The rods are much more sensitive to light than the cones and thereby are adapted to function at very low intensities of light, ranging from moderately clear moonlight downward to the lower limit of visibility.

The ultrastructure of the rods and cones has been extensively investigated by electron micrography[69, 187, 189, 200, 201] (Fig. 134). The outer segment of the rod cell, attached to the inner segment by a thin stalk, appears to be a highly differentiated cilium. It possesses an axial structure resembling the organization of the typical cilium (even to the detail of having nine pairs of peripheral filaments) which is rooted in the inner segment by an enlargement suggestive of a basal body. To one side of the cilia-like axis is a stack of double-membraned discs oriented at right angles to the long axis of the segment. It has been postulated that the discs are highly flattened protein sacs enveloping a double layer of lipids.[201, 202] This plated structure contains the rhodopsin molecules held in specific orientation. The inner segment is richly provided with large mitochondria. This arrangement suggests that the primary photochemical event occurs in the outer segment, thus setting off chemical changes in the mitochondria of the inner segment. Energy transformations in the latter probably mediate not only events leading to cell excitation, but recovery phenomena as well.

At higher light intensities the photosensitive substance (rhodopsin) of the rods is almost completely bleached, and the rods are relatively ineffective; in fact they reach maximal sensitivity only after a half hour or more in the dark. The cones contain a photosensitive material (iodopsin) which is not so readily affected by light, and therefore they are able to function efficiently at a higher intensity range. The existence of these two types

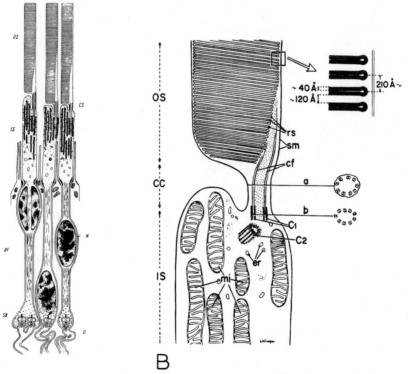

FIGURE 134.   *A*, diagrammatic representation of electron microscopic observations of mammalian rod cells. (From Sjöstrand, F. S.: Ergebn. Biol., vol. 21.) *B*, enlarged diagram of distal region of rod cell. (From de Robertis, E.: J. Gen. Physiol., vol. 43.)

OS, outer segment; *IS*, inner segment; *CC, CS*, connecting cilium; *mi*, mitochondria; *rs*, rod sacs; *cf*, ciliary filaments; *sm*, surface membrane; C_1, C_2, centrioles; *er*, endoplasmic reticulum; *N*, nucleus; *SB*, synaptic body; *RF*, rod fiber; *D*, dendrite of bipolar neuron.

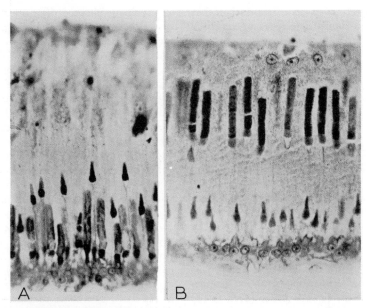

FIGURE 135. *A,* photomicrograph of depigmented retina of the catfish, *Ameiurus,* killed during the dark-adapted, or nighttime, state of rods and cones, showing contraction of cones and elongation of rods.

B, comparable depigmented retina in the light-adapted, or daytime, state of the retinal elements. (From Welsh, J. H., and Osborn, C. M.: J. Comp. Neurol., vol. 66.)

of sense cells gives a combination of sensitivity ranges which accounts for the extremely efficient functioning of the human eye over an intensity range of at least eight logarithmic units. Other vertebrates and invertebrates detect flickering light over most of this range, despite the lack of such duality of structure, but their ability in terms of other visual functions is probably not as good.

Apart from the fact that the rods and cones in duplex retinas function in different intensity ranges, they differ in another very fundamental manner. The cones are of several types which are differentially sensitive to light of various wave lengths, and this differential sensitivity is essential for color discrimination. Certain fishes, especially ones inhabiting the brighter surface waters, possess twin cones as well as the more typical single ones. All of the rods of any given animal seem to have the same spectral sensitivity and probably serve only to detect differences in intensity.

VISUAL ADAPTATIONS OF VERTEBRATES

The structure and function of the eyes of vertebrates show an astounding range of adaptation to the conditions under which the animal lives. Consequently, rather closely related species which live under different conditions may have quite different vision. This range of adaptation has been described in considerable detail by Walls.[231]

Adaptations to Illumination Level. Animals which are equally active by day and night have mechanisms which permit adjustments of the visual system over a wide range of light intensities. Both rods and cones are present. Movements of the dark pigment reversibly into the layer of sense cells occur which screen intense light from some of the rods and cones, especially the rods (e.g., numerous fishes).[1, 246] Movements of rods and cones into the pigment layer in intense light may occur (*Ameiurus,* a catfish; Fig. 135). There is high mobility of the pupil, especially in higher vertebrates where positional changes of both pigment and visual cells are minimal.

Animals which are predominantly diurnal, i.e., active chiefly by day, have a high visual acuity, brought about in several ways. There is a relatively large eye with long lens-retinal distance. Birds, chameleons, and all habitually diurnal animals have a greater lens-retinal distance than animals active both day and night such as cougars, dogs, and dromedaries, and very much greater lens-retinal distances than nocturnal animals such as opossums, house mice, lynxes, and frogs. There is an increase in the relative number of cones and a decrease in the absolute number of cones which contribute to any one tertiary neuron.

This presumably results in greater resolving power of the retina. Special cone-rich areas are present, the so-called central areas or foveas, e.g., the flat central area of frogs, the cup-shaped fovea of man, and the acutely depressed fovea of birds. Foveal specialization is carried to its extreme in certain birds, where the shape of the fovea, together with the difference in refractive index of vitreous body and retina, spreads the image over a larger number of cones, thereby acting as a localized negative lens. Intraocular color filters develop which absorb in the blue end of the spectrum and thereby reduce chromatic aberration at the retinal surface and consequently increase acuity. Red or yellow oil droplets occur in the cones of turtles and most lizards and birds; lampreys, some lizards, snakes, insectivores, man, and most Sciuridae possess a yellowish lens, and in ground squirrels and prairie dogs it is almost orange; a yellowish cornea occurs in *Amia, Esox, Cyprinus,* and a few other fishes; man has a yellow fovea.

Adaptations of nocturnal animals tend to increase the sensitivity of the eye. There is an increase in number of rods and also in number of rods associated with each tertiary neuron. An increase in sensitivity by this method simultaneously sacrifices visual acuity somewhat. There is commonly a slit pupil instead of a round one, permitting a much greater range of aperture size. A reflecting layer on the choroid, or tapetum lucidum, is well developed. This causes light penetrating the retina to be reflected back. While this increases sensitivity, it simultaneously decreases acuity. Light reflected out through the pupil is responsible for the "eyeshine" commonly noted (e.g., cats) in nocturnal vertebrates of all classes.

Adaptations to Space and Motion. Any object in visual space may have a number of perceptible characteristics, such as size, shape, pattern, brightness, color, position, motion, and distance. We are aware of these qualities by virtue of the retinal image which is translated on the basis of experience into what we consider to be the actual size, shape, and position of the object. The special adaptations which permit enhancement of the perception of some of the above characteristics are as follows:

Accommodation and Its Substitutes. Accommodation, i.e., focusing of the image, may be brought about in various ways. In lampreys, teleosts, and probably holosteans, the active process of accommodation moves the lens backward to permit focusing on distant objects. In elasmobranchs, amphibians, and snakes the lens is actively moved forward to adjust for near objects, and in mammals, birds, and reptiles other than snakes the curvature of the lens is increased in order to focus on near objects.

Visual Angles and Fields. The angle of vision of a single vertebrate eye is generally about 170 degrees; it is lower, 110 degrees or less, for certain air-living animals (owls) and deep-sea fishes, and higher, 200 degrees or more, for the cat eye. For the human eye it is 150 degrees.

The position of the eyes in the head determines the presence and extent of the binocular field. A few vertebrates (lampreys, hammerhead sharks, a few large-headed teleosts, the amphibian *Cryptobranchus,* penguins of the genus *Spheniscus,* and the larger whales) have no binocular field of vision, i.e., both eyes can never focus on the same object at the same time. In most fishes, however, there is a binocular field horizontally directly ahead involving usually from 4 to 40 degrees. Most birds have binocular fields; these are known to vary from 6 to 10 degrees in parrots to 60 to 70 degrees in owls. Some birds even have a binocular field of view *below* the bill, e.g., a bittern can assume a "freezing" posture with its bill almost vertical and still have a binocular field ventral to the raised head, i.e., horizontally. In simians and man the binocular field is about 140 degrees, i.e., the visual field is almost entirely binocular. Hares have monocular fields of 190 degrees which overlap to form small binocular fields both anteriorly and posteriorly.

Eye Movements and the Fovea. Movement of the eyes of man may be involuntary or voluntary. Involuntary movements are those which form automatic reflexes for the purpose of maintaining the visual field constant during locomotion and during passive movements of the head and body. During voluntary movements the two eyes may be moved independently, but ordinarily they are coordinated in such a manner that the same point of an object is always focused simultaneously on the two foveas.

In most lizards and in birds the movement of the two eyes is normally independent; in some fishes and in chameleons it is generally independent, but becomes coordinated when objects are observed in the binocular field. In birds, moving objects are usually followed by movement of the entire head, and fixation may be either monocular or binocular. Many birds (accipitrines, swallows, etc., which are mostly flight feeders) have two foveas in each eye, one of which is used monocularly and one binocularly. Since the eyes are directed at an angle of as much as 45 degrees or more from each other, the usual central foveas are useful only monocularly, but the second foveas are placed on the temporal surfaces of the retinas so that they may be used simultaneously in a binocular manner.

Depth Perception. Perception of depth and distance may be obtained either binocularly or monocularly. Such perception depends on retinal image size, perspective, overlap and shadow, vertical nearness to the horizon, aerial perspective (objects with dim or bluish outlines normally appear more distant) and parallax. Parallax is the most important of all clues. Side-to-side movements of the head are used by some animals as a means of improving parallax, whether they possess monocular or binocular vision. Many shore birds use vertical bobbing of the head in a similar manner.

Movement Perception. The perception of movement and the factors which influence it are decidedly complex. Under most conditions a small object moving on an otherwise motionless field can be detected more easily than the same object if not moving. The movement of an image on the retina causes a change in the stimulation pattern which is more easily detected than the details of the same pattern if it is unchanging. There is, however, obviously an optimum rate of change. The change must be neither too fast nor too slow. This is one reason flicker fusion curves offer a valuable index of vision.

One specialized mechanism for the improvement of motion perception, by the production of discontinuous images for localized areas of the retina of birds, is the pecten. Of the thirty or more theories concerning the function of the pecten, the one most probably correct is that of Menner,[157] who pointed out that the pecten serves as a grating which casts a shadow on the retina. An object which is moving across the field of vision forms an image behind the pecten which is discontinuous for localized areas of the retina. The fusion frequency is higher for light of a given flickering intensity for birds with a pecten than for animals lacking a pecten, particularly when the light is on for a high proportion of a cycle.[51]

Adaptations to Media and Substrate.
Aquatic Vision. One of the most striking differences between aerial and aquatic vision is in the field of view. The aquatic field of view, diagrammatically illustrated in Figure 136, depends upon the refraction and reflection of light at a water-air interface. There is total reflection when the angle is less than 48.8 degrees (fresh water). Since the cornea has almost the same refractive index as the water, its curvature is nearly useless as a focusing device. Therefore, the eye surface may be molded into the streamlining of the animal. The lens and its movements become of greater importance in focusing images on the retina.

In deep-sea fishes a variety of devices tend to increase visibility at low intensities. Some of these are larger eyes, larger lenses and pupils, greater concentration of rods, tubular eyes which sacrifice peripheral vision for a more effective central vision, and various patterns of bioluminescence to illuminate the objects to be seen.

Aerial Vision. The dioptric differences between eyes adapted to vision in air and in water are pronounced and have already been mentioned. Another group of differences includes those pertaining to protection of the cornea, especially from drying. In man and many other animals this is accomplished by blinking. In birds and some mammals, however, there is an additional structure, the nictitating membrane, which probably covers the cornea most of the time during flight and prevents drying by the rapid air stream to which the eye is exposed.

Air-and-Water Vision. Animals which live in both air and water must have an exceptional range of accommodation in order to see well in both media. A fish in air is myopic (nearsighted), and any air-living vertebrate when under water is hypermetropic (farsighted). *Anableps* has two pupils for each eye and two retinas, one for use in air and one for water, each with appropriately adapted lens and corneal surface.

Spectacles. Whenever an eye is free to rotate under a fixed transparent covering through which the light passes, the covering is referred to as a spectacle or goggle. A spectacle may be simply the corneal surface which does not rotate with the eye (lampreys, lungfishes, eels, etc.) or it may be a window in a movable lower lid (some turtles and lizards) or a window in a structure formed by the permanent fusion of both lids (snakes, certain fish, and many lizards). The last type of spectacle forms a permanent secondary protective covering which is separated from the cornea by a liquid. This type is one commonly seen in snakes and spectacled lizards.

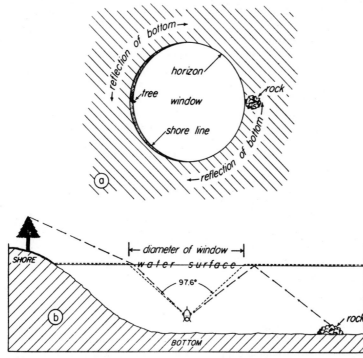

FIGURE 136. Diagram showing the upward visual field of a fish. *a*, the aerial window as seen from below; *b*, explanation of the aerial window, assuming calm water. Light rays striking the water surface within the window are refracted, while those striking outside the window are reflected. (From Walls, G. L.: The Vertebrate Eye and Its Adaptive Radiation. Cranbook Institute of Science, Bulletin 19.)

In these the outer surface is periodically replaced when the animal molts.

COLOR PERCEPTION

Color vision serves a very distinct purpose, in that it increases the visibility of objects and provides an additional kind of light-borne information concerning objects of the environment. By these characteristics it enhances the ability of the animal to obtain food or to escape enemies. Numerous behavioral experiments have indicated that color vision occurs sporadically among crustaceans, insects, cephalopods, and vertebrates from fishes through mammals.[215] The demonstrated distribution suggests that it has arisen independently a number of times, at least once in each of these major systematic groups. It has also been demonstrated with electrical methods that the neurons of the optic nerve are so connected that at least certain fish, turtles, anurans (frogs), and higher placentals have a physiological basis for color vision.[87]

PHOTIC BEHAVIOR WITH IMAGE-FORMING EYES

Taxes. The presence of a compound eye, consisting of many ommatidia, supplemented by additional ocelli, provides an organism with a great number of individual photoreceptors pointing in different directions. The camera eye provides the fully equivalent functional situation.

It has already been stated that bilaterally paired intensity receptors permit a type of orientation called *tropotaxis*, based upon simultaneous comparison of two intensities incident on the right and left end-organs, and image formation permits a more advanced type of orientation termed *telotaxis*, in which orientation to an illuminated source occurs without bilateral comparison.[78]

The latter implies that, out of a variety of stimuli present, one may dominate the response and control the resultant orientation. Response to other sources of stimulation is inhibited. One means of distinguishing tropotactic and telotactic types of orientation is to remove one of the eyes. The behavior is essentially unaltered for a telotactic response, but circling (circus) movements either toward or away from the blinded eye occur typically for tropotactic mechanisms.

Orientation by Polarized Light. The polarization pattern of plane-polarized light from blue sky is determined by the specific relationship of the direction of the patch of blue sky relative to the position of the sun. Experiments with many animals, bees,[80, 81] beetles,[20, 171] flies, lepidopterans,[204, 241, 242] *Daphnia*,[17, 203] ants,[216] mysids,[13] spiders,[171] amphipods,[175] and plankton, have shown them capable of distinguishing the plane of polarized light, and in a number of instances also able to substitute polarized sky light for direct view of the sun in a light-compass orientation.

The optical mechanism for analysis of the polarization pattern by the eye has not been definitely established. Various mechanisms are theoretically possible, and probably the actually operating mechanisms differ from species to species.[236] One such mechanism is that the receptive elements of the eyes possess a birefringent system selectively passing one, and absorbing or eliminating the other (dichroic), of the two light vectors. Physiological evidence has been advanced favoring this hypothesis of mechanism.[11, 205] The complex laminated and fenestrated structure of the arthropod rhabdom revealed by electron micrography also gives circumstantial support to the view.[70, 85, 159, 251]

Evidence has been presented to indicate that the insect ommatidium when observed as fixed preparations does, in fact, possess in its variously oriented rhabdomeral organization a dichroic system which could provide the initial step in resolution of the plane of polarized light.[203] However, a careful reexamination of fresh preparations has failed to confirm the existence of such dichroism.[217] This question is still unresolved.

A second optical mechanism which apparently contributes at least in some measure is differential refraction and reflection from the eye-external-medium interface in accordance with Fresnel's law. This has been postulated to be the chief means of orientation of *Drosophila* and *Daphnia* to polarized light.[17, 204] The ultimate resolution of the plane of light by this mechanism would be reduced to an intensity discrimination.

Submarine illumination is characterized by patterns of polarized light in some large measure arising directly from sky light polarization, but to some degree also due to scattering in the water itself.[236] In submarine situations still another means exists for response to polarized light descending from above. There is differential light scattering by particulate matter suspended in the water. Mysids, which oriented strongly to the plane of polarized light in a medium made turbid

with microorganisms, ceased to display a significant orientation in clear, carefully filtered water.[13] However, in some aquatic arthropods orientation to polarized light is independent of general phototaxis, and separate mechanisms of detection of intensity and of plane of polarization are postulated.[125a]

It has been postulated that polarized light patterns may play important roles in the regulation of the migrations of plankton and other marine and fresh-water animals.[237]

Light-Compass Reaction. The light-compass reaction also depends upon image-forming eyes. This reaction is of considerable importance in the foraging expeditions of such insects as ants and bees, of such crustaceans as *Talitrus* and *Tylos,* of birds, fishes, and doubtless numerous other creatures. It constitutes the dominant sensory means which guides the animal to and from the nest, hive, or home. The structural basis for the light-compass reaction is an eye in which a small source of light can be highly localized upon the retina. Once a certain angular orientation relative to the sun, moon, or stars is assumed, the arthropod has merely to retain the light image in the same region of the retina in order to remain oriented.

The use of celestial bodies for light-compass orientation and navigation in specific compass directions on the earth, or between one specific point and another, obviously demands that the light-compass angle change continuously to correct for the rotation of the earth relative to these bodies. For appropriate correction, the rate of angle change for solar orientation should average 360 degrees in 24 hours, for lunar orientation 360 degrees in about 24.8 hours and for star orientation, 360 degrees in about 23.94 hours. It has, in fact, been established that the organism, by means of a biological clock system,[30, 240] does alter its orientation angle at these proper rates to compensate for the earth's rotation. This has been established for solar navigation for many animals including bees and other insects,[20, 21, 129, 149, 173, 174, 186] amphipods and isopods,[172, 174] birds,[109, 140, 154] turtles,[86] and fishes.[102, 199] It has been possible to alter experimentally and in a predictable manner the direction of flight of bees trained to feed in a particular direction from their hives,[149, 186] the direction of migration of amphipods and isopods on their beaches,[172] and of homing of pigeons,[110, 198] by experimentally resetting the organisms' timing system by artificial cycles of light and darkness. Bees trained to fly toward a feeding station at a particular sun angle at a particular time of day at one longitude were found to retain the same sun angle 24 hours later after a rapid displacement in longitude, and to forage now in a different compass direction.[186] The new compass direction was quite predictable in terms of the difference between the two local sun times.

Evidence suggests that the amphipod *Talitrus* and the isopod *Tylos* orient by the moon,[172] and a number of birds orient and navigate by the stars, in clock-regulated manners.[197] Warblers have been reported, from observations made in a planetarium where artificial celestial changes could be made rapidly to indicate different longitudes and latitudes, able to reorient themselves to their apparent geographical location.

PERCEPTION OF WEAK MAGNETIC FIELDS

Studies on the orientation of mud snails, *Nassarius,* in weak experimental magnetic fields have indicated that these animals not only perceive small changes in strength of the horizontal component of the field, but possess a mechanism for distinguishing the direction of this component. Differences in orientational behavior of snails, initially set upon paths in different compass directions in the earth's field, alone indicate the snails also able to distinguish compass directions in the absence of any obvious cues. The character of the snails' response to weak fields of bar magnets exhibits periodisms of solar day, lunar day, and semimonthly frequencies. South-bound snails tend to turn clockwise when the field is increased near the times of sunrise in the solar day, moonrise in the lunar day, and new and full moons in the monthly cycles, and to turn counterclockwise at all other times. For each of the two kinds of day an experimental field at right angles to the body axis exerts the greater effect when sun or moon is above the horizon and a parallel field exerts greater effect when sun or moon is below the horizon. The two magnetic orientations are equivalent near sunrise and moonrise and sunset and moonset. In other words, the snails appear to possess a "clock"-regulated orientational response to magnetic fields. Fluctuations in strength of the magnetic response of the snails are correlated significantly with fluctuations in strength of the phototactic response.[32]

The planarian *Dugesia* also displays orientational responses to weak magnetic fields.

It has been postulated that magnetic response is widespread, if not of universal occurrence, among organisms and has adaptive significance for biological clocks, orientations, and migrations of various kinds of organisms in nature, although such significance has yet to be established.[32]

VISUAL PIGMENTS

Photochemical reactions in eyes lead to electrical events (generator potentials) which initiate nerve impulses. Light incident upon a receptor must be absorbed before it can initiate a chemical reaction, and the ratio of absorbed to incident light may be taken as a measure of the density of pigment. In a few cases of general protoplasmic sensitivity to bright light, the sensitive substance is unknown, for example in amoebae, and in the direct responses of chromatophores to illumination (Chapter 19). In all specific photoreceptor cells studied thus far, absorption of light is by one class of compounds, the carotenoids, which are conjugated with some specific protein. Receptor carotenoids are yellow-to-red pigments, fat soluble when unconjugated, highly unsaturated, and identifiable by their absorption spectra. Absorption spectra differ according to whether or not the pigments are bound to protein. The wave lengths of light which are most effective in stimulation are those absorbed most by the photosensitive carotenoid-proteins. Many photoreceptors have, in addition, filtering and reflecting pigments which vary the amount of light impinging on the photosensitive cells; examples are the melanin-containing iris pigment cells of arthropods, the oil droplets in the retina of birds, and the pecten in the eye of some birds.

Action Spectra

Relative sensitivity as a function of wave length gives the action spectrum of a photosensitive system. For example, the phototropic bending of the oat shoot *Avena* is most effectively stimulated by blue light (440 mμ). Other wave lengths adjusted to the same intensity as the blue are less effective for a given phototropic bending response. An extracted carotenoid yields an absorption curve which corresponds closely to the action spectrum.[223] Photoperiodic responses of certain green plants are elicited by long wave lengths —about 660 mμ.

There are many living cells which can be made photosensitive by dyes. In giant nerve cells of *Aplysia* both the heme-proteins and carotene-proteins which are present impart photosensitivity. Stimulation of the heme-protein is best at 579 mμ; oxygen is required for the response.[4, 5] These cells are not photo-receptors in the strict sense but illustrate the widespread occurrence of photochemical sensitivity.

Visual Purples (Scotopsins)

The best-known visual pigments are the visual purples which occur in the rods of vertebrate retinas and in eyes of many invertebrates. A visual purple consists of a carotenoid chromophore, retinene, similar in many kinds of animal, and a protein, opsin, which may be different. The general term for the retinene-opsin of the rods of many vertebrates is *rhodopsin,* so called because it gives fresh dark-adapted retinas a red color. Rod pigments also are called scotopsins because they function in dim light, and cone pigments are called photopsins because they function in bright light. The absorption spectrum of rhodopsin has been measured in dark-adapted fresh retinas; contamination by other absorbing substances cannot be completely excluded. A preferred method is to extract in darkness the rhodopsin from rods by means of an aqueous solution of a dispersing agent such as digitonin. This was first done by Kühne in 1880 and has been extensively repeated on retinas of many kinds of animals. Another method is to bleach the retina (or the extract) by illumination and then to measure the loss in absorption at different wave lengths, i.e., to observe the difference spectrum between bleached and unbleached rhodopsin. Conversely, the bleaching efficiency of different wave lengths can be ascertained. The identity of rhodopsin with the true visual pigment is established by comparing its absorption curve with the curve for visual sensitivity as determined by behavior or by electrical responses from the eye. The optimum wave length for rhodopsin absorption and rod stimulation is about 500 mμ (yellow-green); slight differences have been reported for various eyes, but to only a few have all the preceding criteria been applied (Table 45).[41, 55, 141, 220]

TABLE 45. WAVE LENGTHS IN mμ OF MAXIMUM ABSORPTION (λ MAX) (ABSORPTION SPECTRA EXCEPT WHERE OTHERWISE GIVEN)

	Scotopsins		Photopsins	
	Rhodopsin (retinene$_1$ pigments)	Porphyropsin (retinene$_2$ pigments)	Iodopsin (retinene$_1$)	Cyanopsin (retinene$_2$)
Mammals				
man (solution)[47]	497			
man (in vivo)[194, 195]	501		540, 590	
monkey[115a]	500			
cattle[115a]	504			
sheep[115a]	500			
rat[43]	498			
cat[55, 89]	497		560 (photopic dominator)	
guinea pig[25]	498			
hamster[25]	502			
sloth[46]	493			
gray squirrel[2]			535 (ERG)	
Birds				
chicken[220, 224]	502		562	
chicken[3, 209]	510		562 (ERG)	
great horned owl[46]	504			
Reptiles				
alligator[228]	500			
turtle[58]			528 (behavior)	620-645 (ERG)
tortoise[91, 137]				620 (photopic dominator)
gecko[45]	523 (524 reflex)			
synthetic cyanopsin[225]				620
Amphibians				
frog adult[222]	502			
frog tadpole[131]		512		600 (ERG)
Xenopus A$_1$/A$_2$ = 68/32[54, 228]	503	523	550 (behavior)	
Triturus[222]	502 (terrestrial eft)	512 (aquatic adult)		

TABLE 45—(*Continued*)

	Scotopsins		Photopsins	
	Rhodopsin (retinene₁ pigments)	Porphyropsin (retinene₂ pigments)	Iodopsin (retinene₁)	Cyanopsin (retinene₂)
Marine fish				
flounder[220]	503			
scup, barracuda[220]	498			
cod[220]	496			
cusk[220]	494			
dogfish[220]	505			
lancet, rosefish[57]	480			
series of deep-sea fishes[60]	485			
Scombresox[60]	508			
Euryhaline fish				
Gillichthys[166]	512			
eel[39]	487 (marine silver)	520 (fresh-water yellow)		
Fresh-water fish				
pickerel[46]		522		
carp, sunfish[48, 220]		522-525		
tench[52, 88]	467 (25%)	533 (75%)		620 (photopic dominator)
rainbow trout[26]	507	533		
pike[55]		533		
bleak[26, 53]	510	533, 550	600	
carp[55, 165]		523, 550	600 (ganglion)	650 (ganglion response)
Cyclostomes				
Petromyzon[46]	497			
lamprey[44, 222]	500 (downstream)	518 (upstream)		
Molluscs				
squid[118]	500			
octopus[118]	483			
Arthropods				
lobster[227]	515			
Euphausius[130]	462			
Limulus[120]	520			
*Calliphora[11, 232]	540, 630 (ERG)		341 (ERG)	
*Musca[24]	437			
*Drosophila[222a]	436			
*Apis[84]	440			
	490 (ERG)		335-340 (ERG)	
*Periplaneta[232]	507 (ERG)		355 (ERG)	

* Pigments not based on retinene.

Photochemistry of Rhodopsin. When rhodopsin is exposed to light it bleaches to a yellow mixture which consists of *retinene* and the protein *opsin*. After longer exposure to light the rod pigment is converted to another carotenoid, *vitamin A*. After return to darkness the visual purple becomes partially regenerated. When the photodecomposition of rhodopsin is conducted at low temperatures and the extract is in glycerin, the reaction is seen to be more complex than the direct conversion of visual purple to retinene (Fig. 137). Light isomerizes the 11-cis form to the all-trans configuration (Fig. 138). The first product is lumi-rhodopsin, a reddish purple compound which is stable only at temperatures colder than −40°C; this reaction is a photoisomerization.[118] At higher temperatures lumi-rhodopsin goes entropically (thermally) to meta-rhodopsin or visual orange, which is stable at below −15° to −20°C, and consists of all-trans retinene with rearranged opsin.[220, 223] At temperatures above −15° metarhodopsin goes by hydrolysis to all-trans retinene and the protein opsin; the retinene absorbs maximally at 385 mμ. Retinene can be conjugated with protein as in metarhodopsin, and the complex can change color according to pH. The action of light is therefore photochemical isomeriza-

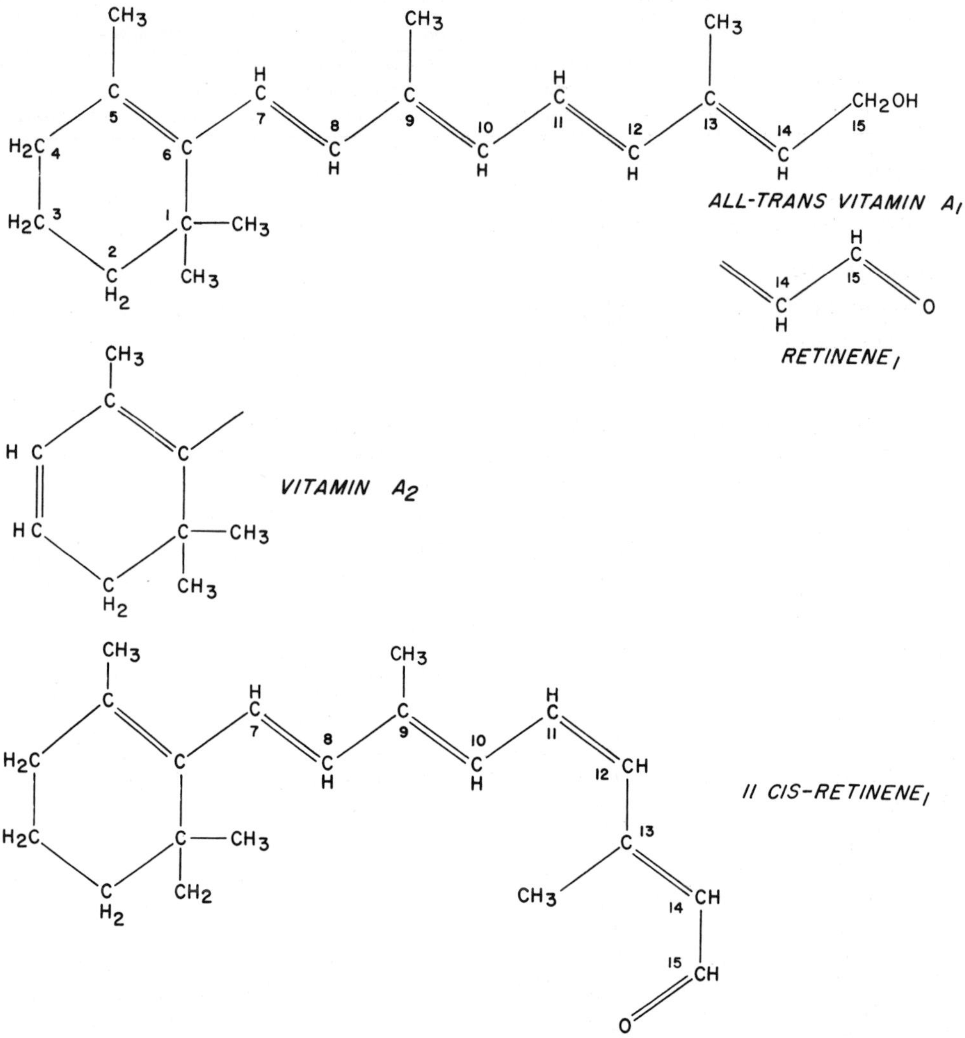

FIGURE 137. Structural formula of all-trans vitamin A_1, the terminal portions of the molecules of retinene$_1$ and of vitamin A_2, and formula of 11-cis retinene$_1$. (Modified from Wald, G., et al.: Proc. Nat. Acad. Sci., vol. 41, and Wald, G.: in Handbook of Physiology. American Physiological Society.)

tion; the subsequent rearrangement and hydrolysis are thermal. Retinene is vitamin A aldehyde[229] (Fig. 137). All-trans retinene is reduced by alcohol dehydrogenase plus DPN to all-trans vitamin A, which is retinene alcohol.[119, 223]

Before rhodopsin can be regenerated the all-trans retinene or all-trans vitamin A must be isomerized to the 11-cis configuration. Much of the regeneration uses the vitamin A from the blood; liver stores all-trans vitamin A, and 11-cis (neo-b) vitamin A is not found outside the retina. In vitamin A deficiency, liver vitamin A declines first, and then the electroretinogram diminishes as rhodopsin decreases in amount in the retina.[67] An isomerase is present in the retina which converts

some of the all-trans retinene to the 11-cis form.[114] 11-cis Retinene may be formed in three ways: In the light, particularly upon short wave-length illumination, there is some photoisomerization resulting in an equilibrium of about 15 per cent 11-cis retinene. In the dark the enzyme retinene isomerase yields 5 per cent 11-cis retinene from all-trans retinene. Light plus isomerase increases isomerization by five times and results in an equilibrium at 32 per cent neo-b retinene. In addition, 11-cis retinene is formed from the cis vitamin A in the retina, which results from isomerization by some unknown means (Fig. 138). A small amount of 11-cis retinene is stored in the retina unattached to opsin. Measurements of bleaching and of regeneration of rhodopsin in intact human eyes indicate that the photoisomerization is negligible.[194]

Rhodopsin has a molecular weight of 40,000 and contains one retinene per molecule. It is estimated that there are 4.2×10^6 molecules of rhodopsin per limb of each rod in cattle. Retinene is bound by an amino group of the opsin, and illumination frees one titratable acid group and exposes one SH (sulfhydryl).[115]

Distribution of Rhodopsins. A number of isomers other than the all-trans and 11-cis of retinene$_1$ and vitamin A$_1$ are known, but 11-cis (neo-b) retinene is found in rhodopsin of mammals, birds, adult amphibians, most reptiles, and marine fish (Table 45). Many rhodopsins exist, based on retinene combined with slightly different protein. The differences are shown by different wave lengths of maximum absorption (λ_{max}) e.g., monkey 500, cattle 498, chicken 512, bullfrog 508, cusk 500, dogfish 497, squid 493, octopus 475 mμ.

The rod pigment in fresh-water fish and some aquatic amphibians has its maximum absorption 20 mμ farther toward the red than the rhodopsin of terrestrial vertebrates and marine fish[221] (Fig. 139A). The retinene and vitamin A in eyes of these fresh-water animals have one more conjugated double bond and are called retinene$_2$ and vitamin A$_2$ as in Figure 137. Retinene$_2$ combined with opsin proteins gives visual violet or porphyropsin with maximal absorption at 522 mμ (bluegill or white perch). The porphyropsin cycle is similar to that of rhodopsin. Porphyropsins vary slightly in absorption peaks because of the protein, but all are based on retinene$_2$.

Fish which spawn in fresh water but spend most of their adult life in the ocean (anadromous fish such as salmon) have more porphyropsin than rhodopsin. The eel, which spawns in the ocean but matures in fresh water (catadromous fish), has both pigments, more rhodopsin than porphyropsin. An immature European eel in fresh water has a purple retina, but on preparation for migration to the ocean the absorption peak of the retinal pigment shifts some 33 mμ toward the shorter wave lengths of deep-sea rhodopsin.[39] The retina of brackish-water *Fundulus* is intermediate in rhodopsin/porphyropsin ratio. The lamprey *Petromyzon marinus* spawns in fresh water streams, and on its way down to the ocean or to the Great Lakes its retina contains rhodopsin and vitamin A$_1$; on its way upstream as a young adult it has porphyropsin and vitamin A$_2$.[222] The change to porphyropsin occurs at a second metamorphosis before reproduction. Frog tadpoles which are just entering metamorphosis have both rhodopsin and porphyropsin with the latter predominating; later in metamorphosis they show equal amounts of vitamins A$_1$ and A$_2$; newly emerged frogs show a preponderance of rhodopsin. Similarly, the salamander *Triturus* as a fresh-water larva has porphyropsin; as a terrestrial adult it has rhodopsin.[42, 222]

A number of variants in the opsins yield different pigments which have been designated by their absorption maxima rather than by special names. The euryhaline fish *Gillichthys* of Pacific Coast mud flats has a peak at 512 mμ, intermediate between frog and carp, yet the retina contains vitamin A$_1$.[166] Some fresh-water fish (e.g., pike) have a porphyropsin with maximum absorption at 533 mμ, and the tench has, besides this pigment, 25 per cent of its pigment absorbing at 467

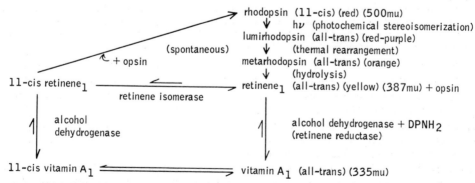

FIGURE 138. Diagram of cycle of photoactivation and synthesis of rhodopsin. (Modified from Wald, G.: *in* Handbook of Physiology. American Physiological Society.)

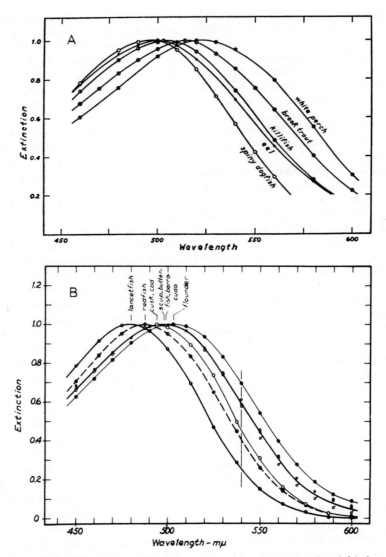

FIGURE 139. Absorption spectra of retinal extracts from various fishes. *A*, series of fish from different salinities showing transition from an exclusively rhodopsin to an exclusively porphyropsin system. The permanently marine dogfish has rhodopsin alone (λ_{max} 497 mμ); the catadromous eel and brackish-water killifish have predominantly rhodopsin; the anadromous brook trout possesses predominantly porphyropsin, and the fresh-water white perch has wholly porphyropsin (λ_{max} 522 mμ). (From Wald, G., *et al.*: Science, vol. 128.)

B, the rhodopsin of fish taken at various depths in the sea. Lancet fish normally found below 200 fathoms has λ_{max} of 480 mμ; surface forms (scup, butterfish, barracuda, flounder) have λ_{max} 498 to 503 mμ. Cusk and cod (from summer depths of 40 to 50 fathoms have λ_{max} 494 to 496 mμ, and redfish (from 100 fathoms) has λ_{max} of 488 mμ). (From Wald, G., *et al.*: Nature, vol. 180.)

mμ.[55] The retina of deep-sea fish has a high density of pigment, and the absorption peak is some 20 mμ to the left of that of surface marine fish. For this reason, the golden pigment of the conger eel has been called chrysopsin or deep-sea rhodopsin.[60] At ocean depths the shorter wave lengths penetrate best, and a series of fish is found with pigments of optimum absorption toward the blue as they occur in deeper water[230] (Fig. 139B).

Fish	Depth (fathoms)	λ_{max} (mμ)
flounder	2- 10	503
cod	5- 75	496
rosefish	40-195	488
lancet fish	200	480

The distal segments of rods of deep-sea fish are very long, the density of visual pigment is high, and more than 90 per cent of blue-green light striking the retina is absorbed.[61] Also, luminous crustaceans used by fish as food emit blue light.[46]

The rod pigment of the alligator and rattle-snake is rhodopsin. A gecko has a pigment absorbing maximally at 524 mμ, yet it has vitamin A$_1$.[45] It has been suggested that the gecko is descended from diurnal reptiles with pure cone retinas, that it has become nocturnal and its receptors have become rodlike. *Xenopus* retina contains both vitamins A$_1$ and A$_2$,[54, 228] 92 per cent porphyropsin (λ_{max}, 523 mμ), and 8 per cent rhodopsin (λ_{max} 502 mμ). Behavioral and chromatophore responses show minimum visual sensitivity at 510 mμ where the difference between the two pigments is minimal; hence, the intermediate absorption depends on a mixture, not on a new pigment.[54] Various euryhaline fish also have mixtures of pigments.

Cone Pigments (Photopsins)

The pigments of the cones are less well known than those of the rods, but there is behavioral and electrical evidence for several

is obtained (Fig. 141). Cyanopsin resembles in its spectral absorption the photopic sensitivity of the turtle *Testudo* and the tench *Tinca* as recorded electrically.[88, 225] Extraction of the pure cone retina of a tortoise (*Geoclemys*) yielded a pigment with difference maximum at 650 mμ.[137]

Cones of an adult frog contain iodopsin only; those of a tadpole probably contain cyanopsin; the ERG of dark-adapted frogs shows a peak corresponding to rhodopsin, and of light-adapted frogs, to iodopsin; while the dark-adapted tadpole eye is most sensitive at 600 mμ (which is close to cyanopsin).[131] In fresh-water fish two retinene$_1$ pigments (λ_{max} 467 and 508 mμ) have been found in different proportions in various species. Which of these are in rods (rhodopsin or porphyropsin) and which in cones (iodopsin or cyanopsin) is unknown.[52, 55]

The relations among the various pigments may be summarized as follows (absorption maxima vary somewhat according to specific opsin):

$$\begin{array}{l} \text{DPN} \\ \text{Vitamin A}_1 \rightleftharpoons \text{retinene}_1 \quad \left\{ \begin{array}{l} + \text{ rod opsin} = \text{rhodopsin } (\lambda_{max}\,500) \\ + \text{ cone opsin} = \text{iodopsin } (\lambda_{max}\,562) \end{array} \right. \\ \quad 335\text{ m}\mu \qquad\quad 380\text{ m}\mu \\[2mm] \text{Vitamin A}_2 \rightleftharpoons \text{retinene}_2 \quad \left\{ \begin{array}{l} + \text{ rod opsin} = \text{porphyropsin } (\lambda_{max}\,522) \\ + \text{ cone opsin} = \text{cyanopsin } (\lambda_{max}\,620) \end{array} \right. \\ \qquad\qquad\qquad\quad 400\text{ m}\mu \end{array}$$

types of cones (p. 369). Measurements of photosensitivity of predominantly cone eyes, and in foveas and other regions where cones are most abundant (photopic vision), indicate a pigment with maximum absorption some 60 mμ toward the red from rhodopsin. The retina of the pigeon and chicken consists mainly of cones. In the pigeon a photopic maximum sensitivity is at 580 mμ,[90] and in the pure cone retina of the gray squirrel *Sciurus* maximum sensitivity is at 530 mμ;[2] in a snake, *Tropidonotus*, it is at 560 mμ.[91]

Extraction of the cone retina of the chicken yields a pigment with principal absorption at 562 mμ and a secondary peak at 370 mμ.[224] This cone pigment is named iodopsin (Fig. 140). Bleaching of iodopsin yields all-trans retinene$_1$ plus a protein photopsin which differs from scotopsin; reduction by alcohol dehydrogenase yields all-trans vitamin A$_1$. The synthesis of iodopsin requires the 11-cis isomer or neo-b retinene. This cone pigment consists, therefore, of the same retinene as rhodopsin, but a different protein (Table 45).

When retinene$_2$ from fresh-water fish is combined with cone opsin a pigment cyanopsin with absorption maximum at 620 mμ

Pigments of Invertebrates

The visual pigments which have been extracted from invertebrates are similar to vertebrate retinal pigments. Rhodopsin (11-cis retinene$_1$-opsin) has been obtained from eyes of the cephalopods *Loligo*, *Sepia*, and *Octopus*, and also from the crustacean *Homarus*. Maximum absorption of rhodopsin of the squid is at 495 mμ and of octopus at 475 mμ.[118] Rhodopsin from the squid differs from that of vertebrates in the stability of meta-rhodopsin at room temperature. Squid meta-rhodopsin is red in weak acid ($\lambda_{max} = 500$ mμ) and yellow in alkaline solution ($\lambda_{max} = 385$ mμ). Not only is squid metarhodopsin stable at room temperature, but rhodopsin can be regenerated from it in the light, that is, pigment regeneration in the squid does not need a dark reaction.[118] Also, light can isomerize the 11-cis retinene (neo-b) of the squid to the trans isomer. Heat irreversibly bleaches squid rhodopsin. The reversibility of the bleaching in light is efficient in that there need be less of a store of vitamin A$_1$ than in animals requiring a period of dark regeneration. The uniqueness of squid rhodopsin re-

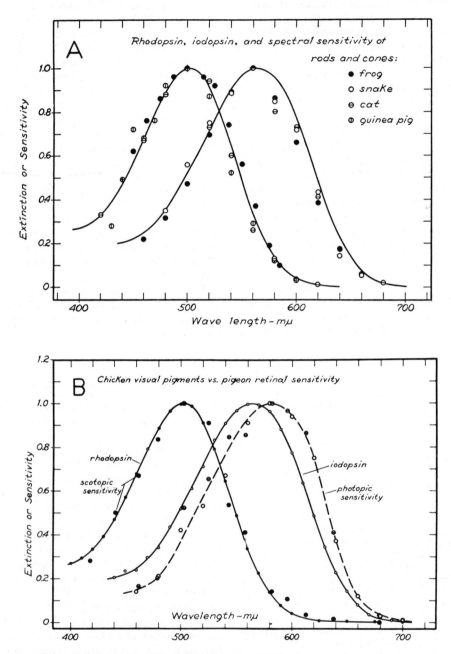

FIGURE 140. *A,* absorption curves of chicken rhodopsin and iodopsin compared with scotopic and photopic sensitivities of various animals. Lines show absorption spectra; points indicate electrophysiological measurements of sensitivity. Scotopic data for frog, cat, and guinea pig; photopic data for frog, snake, and cat. (From Wald, G., Brown, P. K., and Smith, P. H.: J. Gen. Physiol., vol. 38.)

B, absorption curves of chicken rhodopsin and iodopsin compared with spectral sensitivities of light- and dark-adapted pigeons as measured electrophysiologically. Photopic sensitivity is displaced about 20 mμ toward red from iodopsin curve because of filtering action of colored oil globules in pigeon cones. (From Wald, G.: *in* Handbook of Physiology I).[220]

sides in the protein opsin rather than in the prosthetic group.

Vitamin A occurs in many molluscs and crustaceans. In molluscs it is abundant as the all-trans isomer in gonads (*Patella*) or in liver (cephalopods).[74, 75] In crustaceans some 90 per cent of the vitamin A of the entire body is found in the eyes. Vitamin A of the lobster eye is a cis isomer with λ_{max} of 318 mμ.[226, 227] In euphausiid crustaceans 90 per

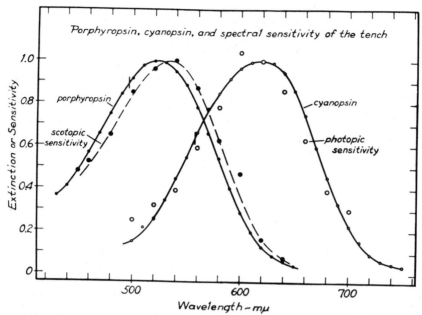

FIGURE 141. Absorption spectra of porphyropsin and cyanopsin compared with the spectral sensitivity of rod and cone vision in fresh-water tench, as measured electrophysiologically. Photopic sensitivity agrees with absorption spectrum of cyanopsin; scotopic sensitivity 10 mμ to red from porphyropsin, probably due to yellow pigmentation. (From Wald, G.: in Handbook of Physiology.)

cent of the vitamin A is neo-b (11-cis). Rhodopsin of a euphausiid shrimp is stable at 20°C and it absorbs at 462 mμ.[130] Lobster rhodopsin absorbs maximally at 515 mμ; lobster retinene, at 370 mμ. Chromatographic separation of pigments from the deepwater prawn *Pandalus* reveals four forms of vitamin A_1:11, 13 di-cis, 11 mono-cis, 13 mono-cis, and all-trans vitamin A_1.[16] Vitamin A_1 occurs also in the eyes of green crab, fiddler crab, and crayfish. *Limulus* eye contains a small amount of a rhodopsin which has a λ_{max} of 520 mμ.[120]

Water extracts of the eyes of *Drosophila* yield some five red and brown pigments, ommochromes, which vary according to genetically determined eye color and are not photosensitive. Housefly heads yield a light-sensitive yellow pigment which absorbs maximally at 437 mμ.[24] Electroretinograms from flies *Calliphora* show peak sensitivity at 540 and at 630 mμ and in the ultraviolet.[12]

Eyes of bees have a photosensitive pigment which absorbs maximally at 440 mμ; this corresponds to a peak of maximum sensitivity of drones at 440 mμ, but worker bees showed sensitivity peaks at 345 mμ and at 535 mμ.[84] Insects appear to have other pigments besides one based on vitamin A_1.

It has been reported that extracted eyes of the annelid *Nereis* yield a photosensitive pigment with maximum absorption at 500 mμ and similar extracts from starfish show a λ_{max} (difference spectrum) at 580 mμ.[177] The maximum sensitivity of a number of molluscs and coelenterates is in the green, in the region of rhodopsin-like pigments. It is concluded that rhodopsin or related pigments are functional in many invertebrates, particularly molluscs and crustaceans.

Absorption of Light by Filter Structures

The spectral sensitivity of an eye is determined not only by the absorption curve of the photopigment but also by any filtering or reflecting materials which influence the light absorbed by the sensitive cells. The retinas of birds contain many droplets of oils of different colors which filter the incident light; these shift the peak of photopic vision to longer wave lengths than the maximum absorption by the cone pigment (Fig. 140). Virtually all eyes have pigments between the photosensitive cells. Frequently these pigments migrate according to the state of dark or light adaptation. The eyes of many vertebrates have at the back of the retina a tapetum or back reflector which permits some light to pass twice through the photosensitive layer. In carnivores the reflecting crystals contain zinc and cysteine; in fish and reptiles they contain guanine.[178]

The lenses of eyes of various animals differ in their transmission. In man, light of wave lengths shorter than 310 mμ is absorbed by the cornea and of wave lengths shorter than 400 mμ, by the lens; a normal person cannot see in the ultraviolet, but a person without a lens can see at wave lengths as short as 360 mμ.[220] The lens of a frog absorbs below 400 mμ like that of man and monkey. Difference in lens absorption in fish is correlated with habitat. The lenses of surface fish such as perch and scup fail to transmit much below 400 mμ; those of butterfish transmit somewhat lower, while the lenses of bottom fish like the dogfish absorb very little down to 300 mμ.[59, 136] A deep-sea eel lens transmits well to 313 mμ.[59] Penetration of longer wave lengths into deep water (below 1150 meters in the sea) is negligible. Hence, it is important that the eyes of deep-water fish function at wave lengths below 475 mμ.[60]

The steps by which the photochemical reaction leads to nerve excitation are poorly known. Conversion of rhodopsin to retinene is accompanied by changes in the opsin such as exposure of sulfhydryl groups, and of an acid-binding group, and a change in isoelectric point.[116] It is suggested that excitation occurs at the change from lumi-rhodopsin to meta-rhodopsin.[117, 223] Electrical evidence (Fig. 142) is that, at least in *Limulus,* some chemical agent reduces resistance of the receptor cells and this leads to a generator potential.

RETINAL POTENTIALS AND OPTIC NERVE IMPULSES

A resting asymmetry potential of 10 to 39 mv between the front and back of the vertebrate eye was discovered by DuBois Reymond in 1859, and the increase in this potential during illumination was discovered by Holmgren in 1865. The resting retinal potential is so oriented that the apical ends of the receptor cells are negative to the basal ends (anterior in the inverted vertebrate eye). Numerous cell layers in addition to receptor cells may contribute to the resting potential.

Electroretinograms

The response during illumination, or electroretinogram (ERG), is primarily an increase in positivity of the basal end of the receptors. In the compound eye of arthropods the sign of the ERG is the reverse of that in the vertebrates, that is, the cornea becomes increasingly negative to the back of the eye. Similarly the cornea of the eye of a cephalo-pod or of the eyespot of a starfish becomes negative to the back of the eye.

Electroretinograms vary in complexity in different animals, and the contributions of receptor cells and of nervous elements in the retina are difficult to resolve. However, there is ample evidence that the photoreceptor cells do show some electrical responses. In the cephalopod *Eledone* the corneal negativity persists at a constant level throughout illumination. In the compound eye of *Limulus* a brief flash is followed by a monophasic ERG, and a longer illumination is succeeded by an initial, then a persistent, negative wave (Figs. 142, 143C). When microelectrodes are inserted into single eccentric retinular cells of *Limulus* a resting potential of some 50 mv is recorded, and on illumination the cell is depolarized in a graded manner (Fig. 142A). Only the one (or two) eccentric cell shows large generator potentials, which may give rise to spikes which propagate centrally in their axonic processes. In those insect eyes which lack eccentric cells, each retinula cell shows both fast and slow electrical waves.

The frequency of impulses is proportional to the amplitude of the generator potential, and depolarization of an eccentric cell increases spike frequency on illumination while hyperpolarization decreases it. Similarly, cathodal polarization of the cornea can initiate optic nerve impulses[82, 99] (Fig. 142C). The photosensitive pigment appears to occur along the folded rhabdom,[159] and the products of its photoreaction may stimulate the eccentric cell. On illumination the membrane resistance is reduced, and on darkening the resistance may increase; during electrical polarization no such resistance change occurs[82] (Fig. 142B). Hence it is postulated that the graded electrical response results from chemical stimulation. The ERG spreads electrotonically from receptor cell to axon, and ommatidial current is outward proximally.[210] The small retinular cells may show small responses to light, but their function is unknown.

Vertebrate Electroretinograms. The electroretinogram of a vertebrate eye typically consists of a small initial negative a-wave, followed by a large positive b-wave, then a maintained c-wave which is less positive than the b-wave or even slightly negative; finally, there is usually a positive d-wave or off-wave on cessation of illumination (Fig. 143). The ERG can be analyzed by a variety of methods. The sequence described above is found in a retina like that of the frog, with five to ten times as many rods as cones. When the

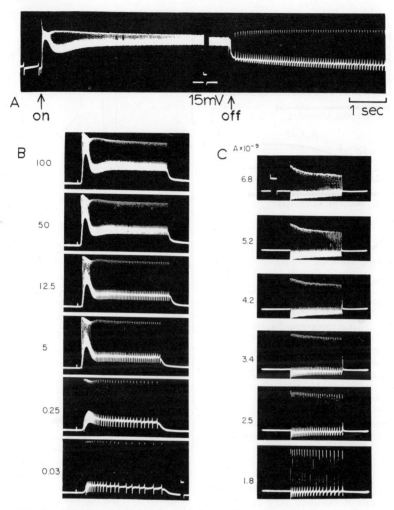

FIGURE 142. Intracellular responses from eccentric retinula cell of *Limulus*.

A, slow frequency at rest: *on*, transient response and sustained depolarization and high frequency during illumination; also an after-discharge or *off* response with gradual recovery of spike size. (Courtesy of M. G. F. Fuortes.)

B, responses to light of different intensities; relative intensities given by figures at left. Small initial deflection on each record shows beginning of illumination. Calibration of 20 mv. Latency decreases with increasing intensity. (From Fuortes, M. G. F.: Am. J. Ophth., vol. 46.)

C, response to depolarizing currents. Numbers at left give depolarizing current in A × 10^{-9}. Bridge input arranged so small current is indicated downward during pulse. Calibration 20 mv in top record. (From Fuortes, M. G. F.: Am. J. Ophth., vol. 46.)

retina is light adapted so that rod responses are reduced the positive c-wave may disappear, and the off-effect is reduced. A dark-adapted frog eye is excited by low intensities of light, and its ERG shows large positive components, while in a light-adapted eye the negative phases are more prominent[87] (Fig. 143*A*). A fish (perch) ERG is shown in Figure 144, together with an analysis of rod and cone responses.[207] Pure cone eyes (e.g., some reptiles) give all the components except a positive c-wave, that is, cone eyes tend to have more exaggerated negative components,

large on- and off-waves.[76, 88] The positive c-wave is large in mammalian eyes, in which rods are dominant,[168] and also in the cone-free gecko.[63]

When a frog eye is treated with ether or by asphyxia a stepwise loss of components of the ERG occurs, indicating that the ERG consists of three components: P_I, a slow positive deflection; P_{II}, an initial and maintained positive wave, and P_{III}, a resistant negative wave. The d-wave or "off-effect" results from a persistent P_{II} after P_{III} vanishes when illumination is stopped.[87] A normal ERG re-

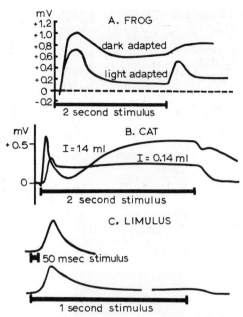

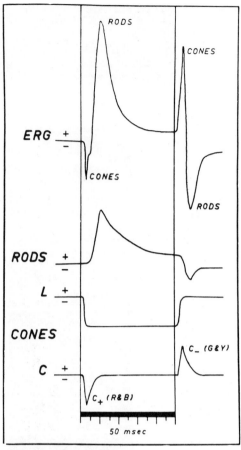

FIGURE 143. Electroretinograms. Square deflection below records indicates duration of light stimulus.

A, light-adapted and dark-adapted frog showing large off response when light adapted.

B, response of cat eye to low intensity (0.14 milli-lambert) and high intensity (14 millilamberts).

C, electroretinograms to short and long exposure, *Limulus*.

(*A* and *B* modified from Granit, R.: Sensory Mechanisms of the Retina. Oxford University Press.)

FIGURE 144. Suggested component analysis of electroretinograms from a fish retina which contains both rods and cones. Response of luminosity cones is designated by *L* and response of chromoreceptor (red-blue, green-yellow) cones by *C*. (From Svaetichin, G.: Acta physiol. scand., vol. 29.)

mains in a frog eye after cocainization.[170] The b-wave is eliminated by treatment with iodoacetate, and it declines very rapidly in asphyxia in cat and monkey, but slowly in frog and turtle. Treatment with azide causes visible damage to the pigment epithelium in rabbits, and with this a marked reduction in the c-wave.[168] When young mice are treated with glutamate, the retinal ganglion cells are destroyed and the b-wave is lost; hence the a-wave appears due to retinal receptor elements.[180]

The frog ERG varies in amplitude with the area illuminated. No ERG is detected 300 μ from an illuminated spot and none to test lights on a bright background.[27] A normal ERG is recorded by small electrodes penetrating the retina from the anterior surface until the receptor layer is reached; behind this is a membrane (the R membrane) of electrical resistance many times greater than that of the rest of the retina.[28, 29, 212]

Arthropod Electroretinograms. Arthropods are of two types according to properties of their ERG's.[6, 7, 252] One type (exemplified by *Limulus*, *Cambarus*, *Eriocheir*,[139] *Dytis-*

cus, cockroaches, *Vanessa*, *Dixippus*, *Tachycines*, and other nocturnal and/or slow-moving insects) has a "slow" type eye[124] (Fig. 145*A*). The ERG is usually monophasic, cornea negative, much affected by light and dark adaptation; the amplitude varies with light intensity; sensitivity to light is high; and flicker fusion occurs at a low rate—for example, at high intensities, ERG fusion is at 40 to 50 per second. The crayfish ERG shows a 20 to 30 msec latency followed by a rapidly rising negative wave, then a slow rise, negative plateau, and decline. The fast phase is more sensitive to ether and to temperature than is the slow phase. The waves reverse in polarity across the basement membrane (Fig. 147). In the grasshopper the initial response at low intensities may be positive, and the shape changes with dark adaptation. These "slow" eyed arthropods cease

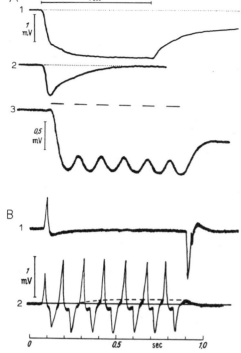

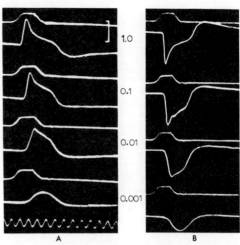

FIGURE 146. *A*, electroretinogram with electrode at retinal layer of *Lucilia*. Light intensities increasing from bottom to top records 0.001, 0.01, 0.1, and 1.0 in relative units. Upper line of each record is stimulus signal.

B, electrical responses from medulla externa (optic ganglion) of *Lucilia*. Intensities as in *A*.

(From Naka, K., and Kumbara, M.: J. Insect Physiol., vol. 3.)

FIGURE 145. *A*, illumination potential of light-adapted eye of *Tachycines*. Stimulus duration in (*1*), 1 sec; in (*2*) 0.01 sec negative downward. (*3*) Response of *Tachycines* to flicker at 6/sec for 1 sec.

B, illumination potential of *Calliphora* in (*1*), constant illumination for 0.8 sec; in (*2*), flicker at 8.7 flashes per sec.

(From Autrum, H.: Ztschr. vergl. Physiol., vol. 32.)

optomotor responses at 5 to 10 per second repetition of a pattern of stripes.[8]

Other arthropods such as flies (*Calliphora, Eristalis, Lucilia*),[6, 167] hymenopterans (*Apis, Vespa, Bombus*), and other fast-flying diurnal insects have eyes of the "fast" type. The ERG is diphasic with large on- and off-waves; the eyes are less sensitive to light adaptation and dark adaptation and are less sensitive to light than are the slow eyes (Figs. 145*B* and 146). The ERG amplitude increases with increasing intensity; responses follow flicker to frequencies as high as 200 to 300 per second, and the animals give optomotor reactions to high frequencies of stripe movement. Fusion of ERG's in the bee occurs at 255/sec as compared to 45/sec in *Periplaneta*.[10] There are marked species differences in relative sizes of positive and negative components of the ERG,

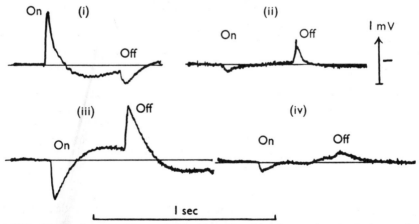

FIGURE 147. Illumination potentials recorded by intraocular electrode at various depths from surface of eye. Locusta compound eye, electrode tip at depths: (*i*) 0.5 mm, (*ii*) 1.0 mm, (*iii*) 1.5 mm, (*iv*) 2.0 mm. Electrode diameter 180 μ. (From Burtt, E. T., and Catton, W. T.: J. Physiol., vol. 133.)

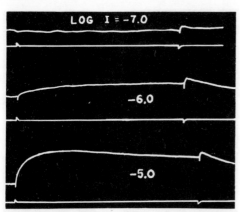

FIGURE 148. Electroretinogram from ocellus of Periplaneta. Stimulus duration 0.5 sec, intensities in log units. On and off of light signaled below each response. (From Ruck, P.: J. Insect Physiol., vol. 1.)

and there may be persistent negativity after the "on" response (Apis).

The isopod *Ligia* is intermediate in showing a fast negative on response and a small positive off effect; its ERG is moderately sensitive to dark adaptation and fuses at flicker below 120/sec at high intensities.[193] In general, it appears that the distinction between "fast" and "slow" eyes of arthropods is relative, and that under different conditions the same eye can show more or less of positive and negative waves.

The ERG of *Limulus* may originate entirely in the receptors, but in insects it is virtually impossible to eliminate contributions from the optic ganglia. When a microelectrode is moved inward from the cornea of a crayfish or of various insects, such as *Locusta*[36] and *Lucilia*,[167] the ERG reverses in polarity at the basement membrane or region just distal to the first ganglion layer (Figs. 146 and 147). In the region of the second and third synaptic layers, nerve spikes are recorded. In *Eristalis* the initial positive on-wave is followed by a negative plateau and this by a negative off-wave, and after some 2 hours only the negative plateau remains.[103] It has been argued that initial + and − waves originate in receptors;[167] it has also been maintained that the entire ERG comes from ganglion cells,[36] and also that the + wave is ganglionic and the − wave, retinular in origin.[9]

Removal of nervous layers of the optic lobe of *Calliphora* makes the ERG more negative and ultimately it resembles the ERG of a slow eye, i.e., is purely negative.[6] In developing *Aeschna* nymphs the optic ganglion is distant from the retina and a simple negative ERG

is recorded; with development the ganglion approaches nearer to the retina and the ERG is of the fast type.[8] In *Ligia,* however, there is no change in the ERG when the ganglion is removed.[193] The form also changes with intensity; in *Lucilia* at low intensity of light the initial response is negative, then positive; at high intensities the response is first positive, then negative.[167] Diurnal changes occur in form and flicker fusion frequency.[125] The ERG of *Dytiscus* and some other beetles changed from monophasic at night to diphasic by day even when the beetles were kept in constant darkness.[49] Cocainization eliminated the "on" and "off" components, leaving only a monophasic ERG in *Dytiscus*.[19] In *Calliphora,* nicotine eliminates the positive component and hypoxia reduces the negative one.[9] In honeybees, on and off effects are lost in CO_2 anesthesia, leaving a sustained component attributed to receptor cells.[84] It appears certain that the receptor cells are responsible for most of the ERG, but the ganglion may also contribute.

The electrical responses from arthropod ocelli resemble those from the compound eyes (Fig. 148). Graded negative ERG's are recorded from ocelli of *Limulus*.[252] The ocelli of *Locusta*,[113] a grasshopper *Oedaleonotus,* and *Apis* show fast positive and slower negative waves. In addition the cockroach has a rapid positive off-wave. Fusion of ocellar ERG is at 200/sec in *Phormia,* 175/sec in a dragonfly, 45 to 60 in *Periplaneta,* and 60/sec in the bee (compared with 265/sec in bee compound eye).[192] In the roach, polarities are reversed when recorded from the back of the ocellus and there is little change on nerve degeneration; hence the ERG is attributed to receptors.

Activity in Optic Ganglia and Retinal Bipolar Neurons

The optic ganglia of many insects show remarkable synchronized rhythms on illumination: slow eyes at 20 to 30/sec, fast at 120 to 160/sec.[191] These rhythms vary in frequency with the intensity of the light and may persist after the light is turned off. The rhythmic illumination potential seems to come from the first synaptic layer.[36] At depths of the second and third synaptic layers, spike maxima are observed. In *Calliphora* the rhythm is at 100 to 250/sec and originates in peripheral optic ganglia.[35]

When a microelectrode is inserted into the retina of a frog or fish from the posterior side, there is sudden appearance of 30 mv resting potentials as the layer of bipolar neurons is entered. When the eye is illuminated, either depolarization or hyperpolarization is observed.[38, 151, 206, 207, 211, 233] This has latency of approximately 15 msec. It was first thought that these maintained responses were recorded from cones, but evidence accumulated that they were from bipolar or second order cells which in carp are 80 to 90 micra from the vitreous side and 160 to 170 micra from the distal tip of rods. Some cells give an L (light) response which consists of hyperpolarization with a peak response at wave lengths between 500 and 700 mμ; the L response of fish from deep water ($>$30 meters) was maximum at shorter wave lengths ($<$530 mμ) than the response of fish from shallow water (maximum at $>$560 mμ).[151] Hyperpolarization in a goldfish bipolar cell is maximum at 615 mμ.[218] Other cells give hyperpolarization (negative intracellular response) with short wave lengths and depolarization (positive response) at long wave lengths (Fig. 149).[151] Two kinds of these chromatic responses were found: Y-B (yellow-blue), which reverse polarity of response at 530 mμ, and R-G (red-green), which have null response at 580 mμ. The chromaticity responses (Y-B and R-G) are more easily fatigued than the luminosity (L) responses.[206] Fish from the family Lutianidae

show only L responses; Servanidae, both L and Y-B; Centropomidae, L and R-G; and Mugilidae, L, Y-B, and R-G responses. The fish from which these double responses were recorded have twin cones, and it is probable that the chromaticity response is the algebraic sum of two responses, one hyperpolarizing and the other depolarizing from the two cones. It is postulated that L is a psp (postsynaptic potential) from bipolar cells with excitatory endings only, and that R-G and Y-B are both excitatory and inhibitory psp's. The amplitude of the L response from one bipolar cell when one cone is illuminated is graded with intensity, and the response increases as nearby cones are stimulated.

Impulses in Ganglion Cells and Optic Nerve Fibers

Arthropod Optic Nerves. Responses in the processes of the primary sense cells are in most eyes relayed directly to interneurons and thence to optic pathways. In *Limulus*, processes of the primary sense cells are believed to constitute the optic nerve, and up until recently no interaction was believed to occur in the retina. Records from single fibers of the *Limulus* optic nerve show trains of impulses (Figs. 150 and 152).[98] During illumination at high intensity there is, after a short

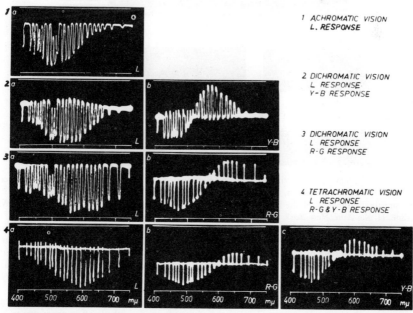

FIGURE 149. Intracellular responses from bipolar cells of retina of fishes from different families to successive flashes of different wavelengths. *1*, Lutianidae living deeper than 30 meters, only *L* (luminosity) response with peak at 490 mμ. *2*, Seranidae with cells showing *L* and *Y-B* (yellow-blue) responses. *3*, Centropomidae with cells showing *L* and *R-G* (red-green) responses. *4*, Mugilidae showing cells of three types of response. Records *2*, *3*, and *4* from shallow-water fish. (From MacNicol, E. F., and Svaetichin, G.: Am. J. Ophth., vol. 46.)

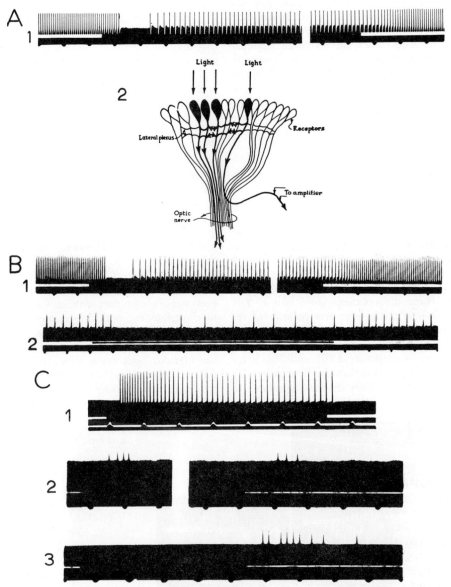

FIGURE 150.   *A*, inhibition of activity of a steadily illuminated ommatidium in Limulus eye produced by illumination of a nearby ommatidia. Experimental arrangement shown in *2*; record in *1*. Blackening of white line signals illumination of the inhibitory ommatidia. Time ⅕ sec. (From Ratliffe, F., Miller, W. H., and Hartline, H. K.: Ann. New York Acad. Sci., vol. 74.)

B, oscillogram of activity of single receptor unit in lateral eye of Limulus showing reduction in frequency when regions of eye near the unit are illuminated. Spot of light on facet from which spikes originate was illuminated first; during time marked by blackening of white line nearby region was illuminated. *1*, inhibitory illumination of annulus around active facet (inner annulus diameter 2 mm, outer annulus diameter 4 mm); *2*, inhibitory illuminated spot, 2 mm diameter and 2 mm from facet from which activity was recorded. (From Hartline, H. K., Wagner, W. H., and Ratliff, F.: J. Gen. Physiol., vol. 39.)

C, impulse patterns in single optic nerve fibers of Limulus. *1*, typical sustained discharge in steady illumination; *2*, synthetic on-off response (1 sec of record removed); *3*, synthetic off response due to appropriate combinations of excitatory and inhibitory effects. (From Wagner, H. G., and Wolbarsht, M. L.: Am. J. Ophth., vol. 46.)

latent period, a series of nerve impulses of high frequency for about a fifth of a second and then impulses continuing at lower but rather constant frequency.[100] At lower intensity the latent period is longer, the graded ERG smaller, and the impulse frequency lower. Impulses stop upon cessation of illumination. Impulses have been recorded in single fibers during periods of illumination as long as 30 minutes. When the intensity needed to produce a constant response in the nerve is ascertained for different wave lengths, a curve results with an optimum at about 520 mμ, the peak for *Limulus* rhodopsin.[98] A given frequency of response in single fibers can be obtained by varying either duration or intensity of illumination, that is, intensity times duration equals a constant over several log units of intensity[99] (Fig. 153). When a single ommatidium is illuminated, usually one nerve fiber is activated, sometimes two.[238] It is possible to inhibit the activity of a single unit by illumination of adjacent elements (Fig. 150). Mutual inhibition between two areas can be removed (disinhibition) by illuminating still another area, and the threshold of inhibition increases with increasing distance. Disinhibition can occur on illumination of a third spot and, by appropriate timing of inhibition, a steady response can be converted to an on-off response.[184, 185] Illumination of a small area reduces frequency of response and raises threshold of elements as much as 5 mm away. Peripheral inhibition may enhance visual contrast.[219]

In *Locusta* the latency of the retinal potential at low illumination is 15.5 msec; latency to the onset of spikes in the optic lobe is 34 msec, and to spikes in the thoracic cord is 53 msec. At higher intensities the retinal potential latency is less; hence the greatest delay for a visual response is synaptic.[36] The on and off responses in *Locusta* nerve fibers correspond to movement of light; an annular movement of 0.2 degree can be detected in the optic ganglion, but for nerve cord detection 0.8 degree movement is required.[36]

Simple Photoreceptors of Invertebrates. Other photosensitive preparations which permit recording from processes of primary sense cells, or at least from secondary neurons, occur in earthworms, molluscs, and the caudal ganglion of the crayfish. The earthworm epithelial photoreceptors are connected, probably via a subepidermal plexus relay, to small axons in segmental nerves; on illumination a discharge builds up gradually.[181] Similarly the sixth abdominal ganglion of a crayfish contains photosensitive neurons which discharge at increasing frequency up to a maximum rate in prolonged illumination.[181] At threshold a primary sensitive neuron may have a latency of 8 to 12 seconds and may show summation with two flashes out to 12 seconds; after stimulation at high intensity one unit may continue to discharge for 60 to 120 seconds.[133, 134]

Along the mantle edge of *Pecten* there is a series of eyes; nerve fibers from the proximal sense cells show a discharge pattern similar to that of *Limulus,* while fibers from the distal part of the retina respond only when the light is turned off. These distal neurons are not active during illumination, and their off discharge can be stopped by illumination.[97] Nerves from the siphon of the clams *Mya* and *Venus* give on-off responses; those from *Spisula* show inhibition of spontaneity and also show off responses; hence they respond to shadows.[132, 134, 135] Inhibitory and excitatory (off) responses have different wave length dependence and may represent different processes. The photosensitive cells lie along distal nerves.

Arthropod Central Paths. When impulses are recorded from the posterior part of the optic lobe of the "brain" of *Limulus,* some fibers show off responses, although none of the primary optic nerve axons show them. Similarly, the circumpharyngeal connectives of crayfish show on, maintained, and off responses.[181] It is postulated by Granit[93] that off responses in general require inhibition during illumination and subsequent release; hence, at least two sets of nerve cells seem needed for off responses.

Vertebrate Optic Nerve Fibers. Impulses in single third order neurons can be recorded in vertebrates from the fibers which pass over the front of the retina before entering the optic nerve, and by microelectrodes from multipolar ganglion cells of the retina. Intraocular fibers of the frog and cat are of several types in response to uniform field. Some respond with an on volley shortly after illumination begins; impulse frequency is initially fast; then, after a pause, impulses continue at low frequency, and there may be an off burst. Other fibers show on and off bursts of impulses but do not respond during continued illumination. Still other fibers give only an off burst of impulses.[66, 97] Goldfish ganglion cells give on, off, and on-off discharges like those of the frog. Each cell serves a receptive field of which the center gives on and the periphery off responses. The center and periphery are differently sensitive to intensity and wave lengths.[218]

The optic nerve of a frog contains some myelinated fibers, and many small nonmyelinated fibers arranged in bundles. Single small fibers receive from a field of less than 3 to 7 degrees when the visual stimulus is a small moving object (e.g., fly), rather than from a uniform field.[155]

Records from optic nerve fibers or from their terminals in the optic tectum show five types of response:[155] (1) detection of a sharp illuminated straight edge, moving or stationary (not of general illumination); (2) convex edge detection, response to a small dark curved object or shadow, moving centripetally or fixed; (3) detection of a contrast change, on and off responses varying with speed of change in illumination; (4) dimming detection, or off response of few spikes; (5) dark detection, ganglion cells spontaneously active at low frequency in light and at increased frequency in reduced light. Responses (1) and (2) give cues of directional movement and occur only in small optic fibers. Each ganglion cell gives only one kind of response.

Single optic nerve fibers of the cat show patterns similar to those of the frog and goldfish. More interaction between neurons within the cat retina is shown by the summation between two spots of illumination, and it is enhanced by strychnine. Individual ganglion cells have shown a variable pattern—on, off, on-off, according to conditions. In a given field an "on" center has an "off" periphery and, vice versa, a mutual inhibition.[143] Individual ganglion cells may show maintained depolarization during stimulation by light for as long as 0.8 sec.[33] Some ganglion cells are spontaneously active in darkness and inhibited by illumination.[142] Each cell receives signals from a visual field 1 to 2 mm in diameter. The pattern and latency of response depend on background illumination, state of adaptation, intensity, and area of illumination.[143] An off area may suppress the discharge from an adjacent on region; impulse frequency may rise to 200 to 500/sec. During dark adaptation, the inhibitory effect of the periphery of a visual field on the center is removed and there may be reversal of on and off responses.[15] Many on-off elements vary in response according to color; the same element fires at different frequencies at different wave lengths of stimulus. The cat retina shows much more variability and integration of response than the frog retina. Fibers in the optic tract (distal to the geniculate body)

showed 24 per cent on, 17 per cent on-off, and 59 per cent off responses.[33]

Projection to Optic Tectum, Geniculate and Optic Cortex. In fish[37] and frogs[83, 92, 155] the retina projects to the optic tectum. The nasoinferior quadrant of the retina is represented along the posterior midline of the tectum; the temporal half of the retina is anterior on the tectum. Similar responses at the terminals of third order neurons (optic nerve fibers) are found in the lateral geniculate of mammals. The optic tectum of the frog has four layers, and near the surface, responses occur to directional movement of an edge or to a dark object on a light field (types 1 and 2). In deeper layers there is detection of contrast and dimming (types 3 and 4, p. 372). Thus each retinal field projects to a given region of the tectum, and the different types of response form an envelope which increases in diameter with depth.

The cells of the lateral geniculate of a cat (fourth order) respond much as do the retinal ganglion cells. Most of them respond when the retina is stimulated by diffuse light. "On" and "off" concentric fields are found, and moving spots on the visual field evoke responses independent of direction. The lateral geniculate nucleus of a monkey consists of six layers: the dorsal ones show mostly on responses; ventral layers give off responses, and each region of the retina projects to each layer in its particular region of the geniculate.[214] The cortex lacks such localization.

In the cat striate cortex the single units show little response on diffuse illumination of the retina, good responses to on and off, directional responses to object movement, and unequal responses for movement in two directions.[121] For a retinal ganglion cell a field may show an on center and off periphery, while in the cortex excitatory and inhibitory areas, on and off with respect to spontaneous activity are found side by side on the retina. Some units show responses from both eyes; others from only one. Evidently in the frog there is more integrating of visual patterns in the retina; in the cat integration of a higher order occurs in the visual cortex.[128]

Not only is there interaction between retinal nervous elements, but there is increasing evidence for regulation of visual input by the central nervous system. Stimulation of the *Limulus* optic nerve decreases the frequency of sensory impulses. In *Calliphora*, centrifugal fibers contact proximal processes of sense cells, and impulses in these fibers may reduce the reaction of the sense cells to light.[7] In the cat, stimulation of a contralateral optic nerve or of the geniculate body in the brain influences the ERG; hence there must be efferent fibers to the retina.

COLOR VISION AND SPECTRAL SENSITIVITY

Three important parameters of light stimuli are spectral quality, intensity, and duration of exposure. Spectral quality can influence response in two ways—by differential sensitivity of receptors to different wave lengths, or by initiation of nervous signals which are interpreted centrally as differences in hue or color. Thus the differences in spectral sensitivity which are shown by every photoreceptor must be distinguished from color vision, which is possible in only a few animals.

Spectral sensitivity curves are obtained by measuring the intensity of different wave lengths necessary for eliciting given responses —growth, behavioral, nervous, retinal. The optimum wave length corresponds to the maximum absorption by the photosensitive pigment, with such shifts as may be caused by filter pigments. A few examples of optimum wave length for taxic responses are: *Mya*, 490 mμ; *Pholas*, 555 mμ;[104] *Diadema* spines, 470 mμ;[163, 253] *Metridium*, 490 to 520 mμ;[169] colonial coelenterates, 474 mμ;[220] *Avena* coleoptiles, at 440 and 470 mμ.[220]

Evidence for Color Vision

Color vision has too often been interpreted in anthropomorphic terms. Actually it may occur at different levels and in different animals may be determined by several means. A single primary sensory fiber, as in *Limulus*, may respond at different frequencies to similar intensities of different wave lengths of light,[98] but color vision based in this way on frequency would be confused with intensity vision. In mammals a given fiber of the optic nerve may also respond with different frequencies, not only to different wave lengths but also at different times after the beginning of illumination by a given wave length. Each nerve fiber is activated by many converging sense cells, yet some color quality is probably transmitted to the brain by the frequency-time pattern of certain spatially located nerve fibers. In general, vertebrate rods are sensitive to low intensity light and are believed to be concerned with brightness discrimination rather than color. The cones have a higher threshold, function only in bright light, and are the color receptors. Rods are more sensitive in the blue; cone sensitivity extends into the red. Cones dark adapt rapidly; rods, slowly. The critical (fusion) flicker frequency rises more steeply in the higher intensity range for cones than for rods.[51] It is postulated that three or more kinds of cone provide for color vision in vertebrates. In those invertebrates where color vision has been demonstrated by several criteria (e.g., diurnal insects) the ommatidia are alike histologically, and nothing like differentiation into rods and cones has been found.

Several kinds of evidence are used for color vision. The most certain are behavioral criteria—color discrimination by man and conditioned reflexes in animals. The behavioral evidence indicates whether the nervous system can use the information supplied by the eye to discriminate colors. When subjective or conditioning evidence is lacking, taxic responses, such as optomotor reflexes (see p. 346), and chromatophore responses can be used as evidence for receptors of different sensitivity maxima. Flicker fusion frequency increases with increasing light intensity; a sudden shift of the resulting curve in some brightness range may correlate with a shift from rods to cones or the equivalent. When the curve of relative spectral sensitivity is measured for different intensity ranges there may be a shift of optimum wave length toward longer values in bright light; this so-called Purkinje shift suggests different receptors for different parts of the color range. This shift has been obtained not only in animals with rods and cones but also in insects such as *Drosophila*.[73]

Since there can be no photochemical response without absorption, the identification of several pigments is further evidence for color vision, although a single pigment can permit detection of different wave lengths. Absorption curves of spectral sensitivity correlate well with curves obtained by electrical and behavioral responses. Modifications may be introduced by filter pigments. A few of the postulated color-receptor pigments have been isolated, iodopsin (λ_{max} = 562 mμ) and cyanopsin (λ_{max} = 620 mμ). One way of explaining color vision is in terms of multiple receptor cells or of multiple pigments within one receptor cell.

The potentialities of an eye for color vision are revealed by electroretinograms and electrical responses of retinal neurons and optic nerve fibers. The retina of the ground squirrel *Citellus* gives a pure photopic ERG—large diphasic waves which fuse at greater than

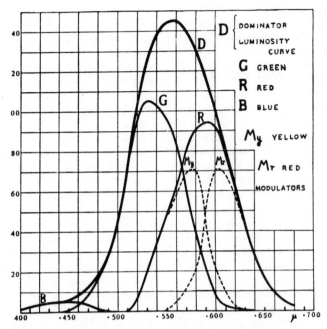

FIGURE 151. Synthesis of the human photopic luminosity curve, *D* (dominator). *B, G,* and *R* represent blue, green, and red fundamental sensation curves. The *R* curve is composed of two modulator curves, *My* and *Mr*. (From Granit, R.: Sensory Mechanisms of the Retina. Oxford University Press.)

100/sec at high intensity—whereas in the ERG of the guinea pig, with a mixed retina, the flicker fusion intensity wave shows two steps.[22] Recent observations on a turtle eye[77] show that it is possible to shift from one white light to another without ERG response, but that on shifting from one color to another (of equal energies) the ERG always shows a response. In a fresh-water turtle three types of cone respond—red, orange, and yellow-green. Intracellular responses from retinal bipolar cells of fish clearly show depolarization in one color range and hyperpolarization at the opposite end of the spectrum[206] (p. 369). Isolated cones from a carp fall into five groups by absorption peaks: 490 to 500, 520 to 540, 560 to 580, 620 to 640 and 670 to 680 mμ; a few cones seem to have two pigments.[96] Behavioral evidence indicates red, green, and blue-violet receptors in carp.

Dominator-Modulator Theory

Granit and his associates recorded impulses from single optic ganglion cells.[87, 92] The threshold illumination needed to activate some of these neurons, plotted as a function of wave length, may give a broad curve with a peak at 500 mμ, corresponding to visual purple. This is the peak for low intensity light and is obtained from fibers of numerous mammals and frog; it corresponds to rod or scotopic vision. At higher intensities the maximum sensitivity of some nerve elements may shift to 560 mμ, the peak for cone or photopic vision. The same nerve fiber may give both response curves; hence rods and cones may converge on the same neuron. In cats, whose behavior indicates color blindness, some 36 per cent of the spikes followed photopic curves, but no photopic curves were found in guinea pigs and rats, which have predominantly rod retinas.[89] Measurements on other eyes show two types of photopic curve, some with a maximum at 560 mμ (cat, frog, snake), corresponding to the pigment based on vitamin A_1 aldehyde, and others (tortoise, tench) with a peak at 620 mμ, the peak based on the A_2 aldehyde.[64] These scotopic or photopic curves are broad and are called dominators. It is possible also to obtain narrow curves called modulators; these may best be shown by measuring the selective bleaching due to different wave lengths. From cat, pigeon, frog, snake (*Trepidonotus*), and tench, red, green, and blue modulators have been obtained; and in a few fibers from the cat and in more from the pigeon, the "red" splits to red and yellow modulator curves. For the cat the peaks are: blue 460 to 470, green 540 to 550, red 600, and yellow 580 mμ[89] (Fig. 151). The dominator peak for the snake *Trepidonotus* is at 560 mμ; modulators are at 600 and 520 mμ.[91] In pigeons the dominator peak is shifted toward the red by 20 mμ beyond the iodopsin peak by filter oil droplets.[65, 90] The same nerve fiber may give more than one modulator curve. The modulator curves of optic nerve fibers are narrower than absorption curves of purified pigments and may represent the difference between two spectral curves. This is also indicated by the cone sensitivity in the periphery and the rodlike sensitivity of the center of the field of one ganglion cell in the goldfish retina.[218] Some neurons of the lateral geniculate (monkey) give on responses to two narrow wave bands; some give on to one color and off to another. This may provide a basis for color contrast.[214] Thus the presence of modulator responses is not sufficient evidence *per se* for color vision.

Human Color Vision

Theories of human color vision have postulated many cell types (polychromatic receptors), or a few. The widely accepted Young-Helmholtz theory postulates three kinds of color receptor because, by appropriate mixing of red, green, and blue light, white is seen. The *spectral sensitivities* of human color vision receptors have been measured by several ingenious methods; maxima are at 440 to 450 mμ, 540 to 550 mμ, and 590 mμ.[128] In recent experiments by Land a colored pattern is photographed twice, using two different wave lengths, and the negatives (black-white) are projected through separate filters whose wave lengths are long and short; the original colors are seen and it is concluded that color vision depends partly on the comparison (centrally) of long- and short-wave length illuminations of a colored object. White light can be used as a long-wave length filter above and as a short-wave length below the comparison color.[145]

Color blindness in humans has provided evidence for theories of color vision. Some partly color-blind individuals are weakly trichromatic in that they can match a given color by amounts of the primary colors different from those required by normal eyes; other individuals are dichromatic, and a few others are completely color blind. Of the dichromats, one type, the deuteranopes, can distinguish yellow from blue but not green from red, and when the condition is extreme, they see both red and green as shades of gray. Another type, the protanope, can distinguish blue from yellow but not red from green and has low sensitivity to red. According to

Granit's modulator theory, color blindness results from reduced sensitivity or even absence of the receptors for particular modulator responses.

By direct measurements of absorption in the foveal retina of man two peaks have been found, 540 and 590 mμ; a dichromat shows only the 540 and deuteranope a greater absorption at 590 than at 540.[195] It is postulated that these correspond to the green and red pigments of the cones; a blue has not yet been detected by direct absorption measurements.

Occurrence of Capacity for Color Vision

The number of kinds of animal in which true color vision (in contrast to differences in spectral sensitivity) has been demonstrated by the above methods is limited. Evidence for discrimination of color by some crustaceans, particularly certain crabs and shrimps, has been obtained from chromatophore responses on different backgrounds and from optomotor responses to colored stripes. Similarly, in *Sepia* on yellow and red background, the yellow and orange chromatophores expand, while on green, the orange are contracted and the yellow expand.[34]

In insects, color vision has been clearly established by taxic behavior and by conditioning for Hymenoptera, probably for some Lepidoptera, Diptera, and Coleoptera. Older experiments show that bees can distinguish four colors: 650 to 530 mμ (red-yellow green), 510 to 480 mμ (blue-green), 470 to 400 mμ (blue-violet), and 400 to 300 mμ (ultraviolet), but bees confuse colors within any one of these categories.[81] For a bee the ultraviolet is the most saturated color, then in decreasing order the blue-violet, yellow, and blue-green. Bees distinguish orange (616 mμ), yellow (588 mμ), green (530 mμ), blue (674 mμ), and ultraviolet (360 mμ).[56] In dark-adapted bees the ERG shows maximum sensitivity at 535 mμ, while after adaptation to yellow the maximum is at 345 mμ. No evidence for a blue receptor was found.[84] In *Calliphora* the electroretinograms show maximum sensitivity in the green (500 mμ) and also in the ultraviolet (341 mμ), and a lower peak at 615 mμ; by behavior tests, color vision appears better in the blue-violet than in the red.[12] Some nocturnal insects (*Dixippus*) are said to lack color vision. Both *Drosophila* and *Apis* show two peaks of maximum phototaxis—*Drosophila* at 487 and 365 mμ, *Apis* at 553 and 365—the ultraviolet being some five times more effective as a stimulating source. Retinograms of dragon-flies indicate that the upper half of the eye has one type of receptor, and is most sensitive at 420 mμ, while the lower half has dichromatic color sensitivity with maxima at 515 and 610 mμ; in their larvae all the receptor elements are maximally sensitive at 515 mμ.[156]

In fish, a number of observations by conditioned reflexes and by chromatophore responses show that many teleosts have good color discrimination. Teleost retinas have cones (often double), and electrical responses from optic neurons show different responses at different wave lengths. On the basis of retinal structure, Walls[231] suggested that color vision is present in the teleosts, is probably present in holosteans, but is absent from chondrosteans, dipnoans, elasmobranchs, and from cyclostomes.

There is no evidence from conditioning for color vision in amphibians, although some cones are present in the frog retina. Reptiles have an abundance of cones, and the ERG responses to color shift in turtles[77] (see p. 374), good photopic modulator responses in snakes (*Trepidonotus*), and chromatophore responses to colored backgrounds in lizards, all establish color vision as fairly certain in these reptiles. Behavioral tests show the tortoise *Testudo* to discriminate blue, green, and red.[183] The retinas of birds are rich in cones; iodopsin has been extracted from chicken retinas, and good photopic-modulator responses were observed in pigeons. Birds make extensive use of color vision in recognition of mates, species, food, and in other aspects of their behavior.

Among mammals, color vision is clearly established only for primates. However, cones are present in retinas of many other mammals, and photopic modulators have been found in cats. Conditioning experiments indicate that if color vision is present in the cat and dog it is very poor.[158] However, in the visual cortex of the cat, two points may differ in response to spectral patterns.[123] There is no behavioral evidence for color vision in laboratory rats, although one wonders whether color may not play a part in substrate and mate recognition by some wild rodents. It is difficult to understand the presence of peripheral components for color vision if they are not utilized by the brain.

Color vision is similar to olfaction in that many degrees of quality of a stimulus appear to be distinguished by few kinds of receptor. Despite intensive study since Thomas Young proposed the trichromatic hypothesis in 1807 and Helmholtz expanded it in 1852, the mechanisms of color vision are still virtually unknown. Several visual pigments are probably present, particularly in cone retinas, but not many. In insects with color vision, histologically different receptor cells and different photosensitive pigments have not been found, although there are many filter pigments. It is not known whether a single receptor (cone or retinula cell) may contain several pigments, whether filter pigments can determine spectral range, or whether different receptor cells are concerned with each modulator response or its equivalent in a neuron. Examples of opposing responses and central antagonisms of responses to complementary colors indicate the importance of contrast in color vision. In any case, several color receptors can converge on one retinal neuron, and a single neuron may give different frequencies of impulses according to the color receptor activating it. Color vision has been studied primarily as a retinal phenomenon; the central nervous analysis of color vision deserves more attention.

DETECTION OF POLARIZED LIGHT

Some animals, particularly arthropods and to a less extent snails, can orient with respect to the plane of polarization of light (p. 353). Part of this orientation may result from intensity differences due to differential reflection from external surfaces and from internal structures in the compound eye. In addition, the alignment of the photosensitive pigment molecules may permit greater stimulation in one plane than in another. The generator potential from retinular cells of *Lucilia*[144] and the frequency of impulses in *Limulus* single optic fibers vary according to plane of polarization; these effects could be due to internal reflection.[234] However, a folded retina of a fish absorbs polarized light differently according to its plane, and apparently the pigment molecules are normally oriented on the outer segments and parallel to the rod axis.[61] Each rhabdom of a compound eye consists of many (20 to 30 $\times$ 10^4) tubular rhabdomeres (Fig. 130). These rhabdomeres are perpendicular to the ommatidial axis, and the pigment molecules could distinguish plane of polarization of incident light.[70]

VISUAL STIMULATION

The initial event in photic excitation is a photochemical reaction. A light-absorbing pigment decomposes to products and, in some unknown way (possibly by altering membrane conductance), causes local graded electrical changes which can be recorded from the photosensitive cells. During light adaptation the concentration of pigment declines, and during dark adaptation the pigment is restored as sensitivity rises. In moderate illumination an equilibrium between decomposition and synthesis of the pigment is achieved. Some receptors, e.g., cones, are adapted for bright light; others, e.g., rods, for vision in dim light.

A variety of quantitative relations between photic stimulation and the magnitude of response (chemical, electrical, behavioral) have been interpreted in terms of the photochemical reactions. One of these is the reciprocity (Bunsen-Roscoe) law, which states that the photochemical effect is equal to the product of light intensity times duration ($E = IT$) (Fig. 152). This has been demonstrated to hold in many organisms for threshold and near-threshold but not for bright light. One of the most thorough tests of this and other quantitative relations in photoreception was the siphon withdrawal response of the clam *Mya* as done by Hecht.[104]

Another quantitative relation describes the reversible reactions of light and dark adaptation. The light reaction as measured by decreasing sensitivity during illumination or by visual purple bleaching is a first order reaction (at least in summer frogs). The dark re-

action, however, goes at first rapidly, then slowly, and is described by second order kinetics. The constants differ for clam, *Limulus,* frog, man, but all of them follow similar curves. From his observations on *Mya,* Hecht postulated a photosensitive substance S as going reversibly to products P and A

$$(S \underset{\text{dark}}{\overset{\text{light}}{\rightleftharpoons}} P + A).$$

As a crude approximation S may be considered as rhodopsin and P and A as retinene and opsin. The light reaction is virtually independent of temperature ($Q_{10} = 1.05$) over the physiological range. The recovery curve or dark reaction is highly dependent on temperature ($Q_{10} = 2.5$ to 3); this was interpreted by Hecht as indicating an enzymatic reaction. Where two or more kinds of receptor cells are functional in different intensities, the dark-adaptation curve has a break, as for the human eye (at least for white light); where there is only one kind of receptor cell as in *Limulus* the dark-adaptation curve is single. In man the half-time for regeneration of cone pigments is 90 seconds, for visual purple it is 30 minutes.[194]

The absolute sensitivity of photoreceptors is high. Calculations of the amount of incident light that is absorbed by photosensitive pigment give percentages for human rods ranging from 2.5 to 20.[47, 239] Hecht estimated that when well dark adapted he could see 5 to 14 quanta of light absorbed by retinal rods.[107]

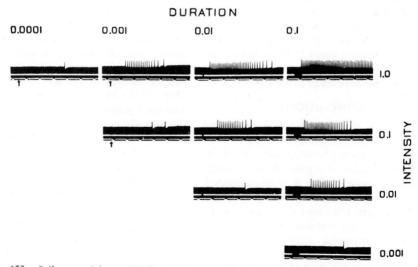

FIGURE 152. Spike potentials recorded from single nerve fibers in response to illumination of the *Limulus* eye with different intensities for various periods. Duration of exposure to light is indicated at the top of each column in seconds; intensity in relative units is indicated at the right (unit intensity 3,000,000 meter candles). The absence of the white line indicates exposure of the eye. For very short exposures the arrows mark the position of the signal. Time in ⅕ sec. (From Hartline, H. K.: J. Cell. Comp. Physiol., vol. 5.)

Absorption by deep-sea fish is much greater. Sensitivity differs in different parts of the retina, and there are diurnal variations. Intracellular records from *Limulus* eccentric retinula cells show graded slow responses which are composed of quantized humps, each of which may represent a response to very few quanta of light.[150] The intensity of light which can be detected above background illumination, that is, the least discriminable difference, varies with the intensity. This is the Weber-Fechner law ($\Delta I/I = k$), which applies to most photoreceptors in low and medium intensity ranges.

Other quantitative relations are obtained by measuring the effect of flickering light. A reduction in the time the light is on is equivalent to a reduction in intensity of continuous light (Talbot's law). The critical or fusion frequency increases with increasing intensity; that is, resolution of separate flashes improves with brightness ($F_c \sim \log I$) (Ferry-Porter law). Fusion frequency has been measured not only subjectively in man but by ERG fusion and by optomotor responses of animals to a field of moving stripes. In general, there is agreement by different methods; hence the limiting processes appear to be in the receptor rather than in the central nervous system. In the fly *Calliphora*, for example, fusion frequency is high (100 to 265/sec); it is relatively independent of state of adaptation but very dependent on temperature.[35] The maximum fusion frequency for vertebrates, e.g., man (45 to 53), is lower than that for insects with "fast" eyes adapted for daylight vision (see p. 367). In sunfish the flicker fusion frequency shifts from 10-15 to 45-50 as intensity increases, and vision goes from rods to cones.[94] High fusion frequency is related to high sensitivity to shadows and to fine movements in patterns.

CONCLUSIONS

Some cells, e.g., amoebae and pigmented neurons of snails, show general light sensitivity, but in most photoreceptors the photosensitive pigment is organized in an intracellular organelle, which is often laminated. Simple photoreceptors are intensity detectors; compound eyes and camera eyes permit pattern vision. Direct responses to light include changes in locomotor activity with general illumination, and tropism or taxis toward or away from light. Geometric optics of photoreceptors provide the basis for most direct responses; coordination in optic ganglia permits some complex photic behavior, and cen-

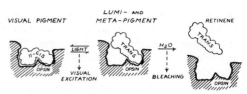

FIGURE 153. Diagrammatic representation of possible fit of retinene on protein opsin and effect of steric changes resulting from illumination. During bleaching the retinene is released from opsin. (From Hubbard, R., and Kropf, A.: Ann. New York Acad. Sci., vol. 81.)

tral nervous localization of photic input further increases the complexity. Photosensitive pigments have different spectral sensitivities, but color vision *per se* requires both peripheral and central components.

The only visual pigments which are known chemically are those containing the aldehyde (retinene) of one or the other form of vitamin A. Variation occurs as differences in the protein with which the retinene is conjugated. The kind of vitamin A may be related to whether the vertebrate lives in fresh water, sea water, or on land; the kind of protein may be related to whether the pigment occurs in rods or cones (vision in bright or dim light; habitat, deep or shallow sea). There are genetic species differences in the proteins (opsins). In invertebrates the occurrence of other types of pigments is indicated by the absorption peaks, e.g., insects with λ_{max} in the ultraviolet.

The means by which the generator potential is produced as a result of the photochemical breakdown of pigment remains unknown.[115] Configurational changes in retinene on illumination may disturb its fit in the opsin molecule and thus expose charged groups which initiate reactions causing resistance change in receptor cell membranes (Fig. 153). Much evidence (especially for *Limulus*) indicates that the generator potential spreads electrotonically and serves as a link to the nerve impulses. In the *Limulus* compound eye only one out of eight to ten retinula cells has an axonic process, and this one may be the only functional receptor.[82]

In no retina, not even in that of *Limulus*, is interaction in the retina lacking. The proximity of ganglion cells to the receptors in most eyes makes analysis of ERG's difficult, and the probability of successfully penetrating a rod or cone with a microelectrode is very remote. There are always many more receptor cells than there are optic nerve fibers, that is, convergence is general. In both compound and camera-type eyes several synaptic relays are interposed between receptor and final afferent neuron, and one field influences an adjacent one. Single optic nerve fibers of vertebrates are activated indirectly by many receptor cells, sometimes by receptors with different spectral properties. Bipolar cells in fish retinas (probably other vertebrates also) give persistent depolarization or hyperpolarizations which appear to be graded synaptic potentials; the retinal ganglion cells show on, on-off, and off impulses and (in some animals) patterned responses to movement of objects in the visual field. In frog optic nerve and tectum, and cat cortex and geniculate, some units respond to direction and rate of movement of an object in the visual field. A considerable amount of integration occurs in ganglionic layers of most eyes.

Projection to the central nervous system is shown by topographic representation of the retina.

In vertebrates the retina is projected over the surface of integrative lobes. In fish and amphibians a point-for-point representation occurs on the contralateral optic tectum, and similar representation is found in the mammalian superior colliculus. In frogs and monkeys several different kinds of response from one visual field are recorded at different depths. In higher mammals the crossed optic tract passes through the geniculate body and projects on the striate cortex of the occipital lobe, with the retina taking a diagonal pattern. Cortical responses show more integration than do the responses from the neurons which enter the cortex from the geniculate.

Since single optic nerve fibers may carry different kinds of signals, for example, from color receptors, and since different fibers give different patterns of response to white illumination—on, on-off, off—and to moving visual field, these signals must be effective both by spatial termination and by the temporal pattern of impulses (frequency in different parts of the response signal). The ultimate interpretation of a visual stimulus must be in the central nervous system, and limitations in vision may be imposed either peripherally or centrally. It is necessary that sense cells, peripheral ganglion cells, and nerve centers be matched. Vision can be only partly understood by a knowledge of visual pigments.

REFERENCES—VISION

1. ALI, M. A., Canad. J. Zool. 37: 965-996, 1959. Retinomotor responses in fishes.

* Reviews

2. ARDEN, G. B., and TANSLEY, K., J. Physiol. 127: 592-602, 1955. Spectral sensitivity of pure cone retina, Sciurus.

3. ARMINGTON, J. C., and THIEDE, F. C., Am. J. Physiol. 186: 258-262, 1956. Purkinje shift in ERG of chicken eye.

4. ARVANITAKI, A., and CHALAZONITIS, N., Arch. Scient. Physiol. 3: 27-44, 1949; 12: 73-106, 1958. Nerve response to light.

5. ARVANITAKI, A., and CHALAZONITIS, N., Bull. Inst. Oceanog. Monaco 87: 1-83, 1960. Photochemical excitation and inhibition of Aplysia neurons.

6. AUTRUM, H., Ztschr. vergl. Physiol. 32: 176-227, 1950; Zool. Gesellsch. 133-143, 1951. Properties of retinal potentials of fast and slow eyes of insect, especially Calliphora and Dixippus.

7. *AUTRUM, H., Experientia 5: 271-277, 1949; Klin. Wchnschr. 31: 241-245, 1953. Reviews of electrophysiology of insect eyes.

8. AUTRUM, H., and GALLOVITZ, U., Ztschr. vergl. Physiol. 33: 407-435, 1951. Electroretinograms of Calliphora and Aeschna.

9. AUTRUM, H., and HOFFMANN, C., J. Ins. Physiol. 3: 122-127, 1960. Origin of diphasic and monophasic responses in compound eye of Calliphora.

10. AUTRUM, H., and STOECKER, M., Ztschr. Naturforsch. 5b: 38-43, 1950. Optomotor reactions and flicker fusion frequency, insect eyes.

11. AUTRUM, H., and STUMPF, H., Ztschr. Naturforsch. 5b: 116-122, 1950. Polarization analysis by insect eye.

12. AUTRUM, H., and STUMPF, H., Ztschr. vergl. Physiol. 35: 71-104, 1953; in Mechanisms of Colour Discrimination, London, Pergamon Press, 1960, pp. 32-39. Spectral sensitivity of Calliphora and Periplaneta eyes.

13. BAINBRIDGE, R., and WATERMAN, T. H., J. Exp. Biol. 35: 487-493, 1958. Turbidity and polarized light orientation in mysid.

14. BARLOW, H. B., J. Exp. Biol. 29: 667-674, 1952. Ommatidial size in apposition eyes.

15. BARLOW, H. B., FITZHUGH, R. and KUFFLER, S. W., J. Physiol. 137: 327-337, 338-354, 1957. Dark adaptation, visual field effects, and Purkinje shift as measured by responses of ganglion cells of cat retina.

16. BARNHOLDT, B., and HJARDE, W., Acta physiol. scand. 41: 49-67, 1957. Chromatographic separation of vitamin A_1 from eyes of Pandalus.

17. BAYLOR, E. R., and SMITH, F. E., Am. Nat. 87: 97-101, 1953. Daphnia orientation in polarized light.

18. BENNITT, R., Physiol. Zool. 5: 65-69, 1932. Rhythmic visual pigment migration, Crustacea.

19. BERNHARD, C. G., J. Neurophysiol. 5: 32-48, 1942. Changes in Dytiscus ERG after cocainization.

20. BIRUKOW, G., Ztschr. vergl. Physiol. 36: 176-211, 1954. Beetle orientation in polarized light.

21. BIRUKOW, G., Cold Spring Harb. Symp. Quant. Biol. 25: 403-412, 1961. Clock-timed orientation to light in insects.

22. BORNSCHEIN, H., and SZEGVARI, G., Ztschr.

Biol. *110*: 285-290, 1958. Flicker fusion of ERG of ground squirrel and guinea pig.

23. BORRADAILE, L. A., and POTTS, F. A., The Invertebrata, New York, Macmillan Co., 1935, 725 pp.

24. BOWNESS, J. M., and WOLKEN, J. J., J. Gen. Physiol. *42*: 779-792, 1959. Photosensitive pigment from housefly.

25. BRIDGES, C. D. B., Nature *184*: 1727, 1959. Visual pigments of laboratory mammals.

26. BRIDGES, C. D. B., J. Physiol. *134*: 620-629, 1956. Visual pigments of fish.

27. BRINDLEY, G. S., J. Physiol. *134*: 339-352, 353-359, 360-384, 1956. Electrical properties and responses to illumination recorded by microelectrodes from frog's retina.

28. BRINDLEY, G. S., J. Physiol. *140*: 247-261, 1958. Source of slow electrical activity in frog's retina.

29. *BRINDLEY, G. S., Ann. Rev. Physiol. *20*: 559-582, 1958. Recent advances in the physiology of vision.

30. BROWN, F. A., Cold Spring Harb. Symp. Quant. Biol. *25*: 57-71, 1961. On the nature of the biological clock.

31. BROWN, F. A., in The physiology of Crustacea, edited by T. H. Waterman. New York, Academic Press, vol. 2, pp. 401-430, 1961. Retinal pigment rhythms in Crustacea.

32. BROWN, F. A., JR., BRETT, W. J., BENNETT, M. F., and BARNWELL, F. H., Biol. Bull. *118*: 367-381; BROWN, F. A., JR., WEBB, H. M., and BRETT, W. J., Biol. Bull. *118*: 382-392; BROWN, F. A., JR., BENNETT, M. F., and WEBB, H. M., Biol. Bull. *119*: 65-74; BROWN, F. A., JR., and BARNWELL, F. H., Biol. Bull. *119*: 306; BROWN, F. A., JR., and HUTTRER, A., Biol. Bull. *119*: 306-307; BROWN, F. A., JR., and WEBB, H. M., Biol. Bull. *119*: 307. Responses to weak magnetic fields.

33. BROWN, K. T., and WIESEL, T. N., J. Physiol. *149*: 537-562, 1959. Intraretinal recording from intact cat eye.

34. von BUDDENBROOK, W., Vergleichende Physiologie, Basel, Birkhäuser, 1952, 504 pp. Vol. I, Sinnesphysiologie.

35. BURKHARDT, D., Ztschr. vergl. Physiol. *36*: 595-630, 1954. Rhythmicity in optic ganglia of Calliphora.

36. BURTT, E. T., and CATTON, W. T., J. Physiol. *133*: 68-88, 1956; *146*: 492-515, 1959. Responses to illumination in optic lobe and nervous system of locust and other insects.

37. BUSER, P., and DUSSARDIER, M., J. d. Physiol. Paris *45*: 57-60, 1953. Projection of retina to optic tectum of fish.

38. BYZOV, A. L., Biophysics *4*: 46-59, 1959. Electrical activity of retina, particularly as recorded from ganglion cells.

39. CARLISLE, D. B., and DENTON, E. J., J. Mar. Biol. Assn. U. K. *38*: 97-102, 1959. Metamorphosis of visual pigments of Anguilla.

40. COLLINS, D. L., J. Exp. Zool. *69*: 165-197, 1934. Retinal pigment migration in moth.

41. *COLLINS, F. D., Biol. Rev. *29*: 453-477, 1954. The chemistry of vision.

42. COLLINS, F. D., LOVE, R. M., and MORTON, R. A., Biochem. J. *53*: 626-636, 1952. Studies on vitamin A in amphibians.

43. COLLINS, F. D., and MORTON, R. A., Biochem. J. *47*: 3-10, 1950. Studies on rhodopsin.

44. CRESCITELLI, F., J. Gen. Physiol. *39*: 423-435, 1956. Nature of lamprey visual pigment.

45. CRESCITELLI, F., J. Gen. Physiol. *40*: 217-231, 1956. Nature of gecko visual pigments.

46. *CRESCITELLI, F., Ann. New York Acad. Sci. *74*: 230-255, 1958; Ann. Rev. Physiol. *22*: 525-578, 1960. Reviews on distribution of visual pigments and their role in vision.

47. CRESCITELLI, F., and DARTNALL, H. J. A., Nature *172*: 195-200, 1953. Human visual purple.

48. CRESCITELLI, F., and DARTNALL, H. J. A., J. Physiol. *125*: 607-627, 1954. Photosensitive pigment of the carp.

49. CRESCITELLI, F., and JAHN, T. L., J. Cell. Comp. Physiol. *13*: 105-112, 1939; *19*: 47-66, 1942. Electrical responses of eyes, insects.

50. CROZIER, W. J., Am. J. Physiol. *36*: 8-20, 1914; Zool. Jahrb., Abt. Allg. *35*: 233-297, 1915. Sensory reactions, Holothuria.

51. CROZIER, W. J., and WOLF, E., J. Gen. Physiol. *27*: 287-313, 1943. Influence of pecten on flicker intensity discrimination.

52. DARTNALL, H. J. A., J. Physiol. *116*: 257-289, 1952. Visual pigment of tench.

53. DARTNALL, H. J. A., J. Physiol. *128*: 131-156, 1955. Visual pigments of bleak, Alburnus.

54. DARTNALL, H. J. A., J. Physiol. *134*: 327-338, 1956. Visual pigments of toad Xenopus.

55. *DARTNALL, H. J. A., The Visual Pigments. New York, John Wiley & Sons, 1957, 216 pp.

56. DAUMER, K., Ztschr. vergl. Physiol. *38*: 413-478, 1956. Color vision in bee.

57. DAY, M. F., Biol. Bull. *80*: 275-291, 1941. Retinal pigment migration in insects.

58. DEANE, H. W., et al., J. Neurophysiol. *21*: 45-61, 1959. Electroretinogram of turtle; form and spectral sensitivity.

59. DENTON, E. J., Bull. Inst. Oceanog. Monaco, 1-10, 1956. J. Physiol. *133*: 56P-57P, 1956. Light transmission by lens of fish; vision of conger eel.

60. DENTON, E. J., and WARREN, F. J., J. Mar. Biol. Assn. U. K. *36*: 651-662, 1957; Nature *178*: 1059, 1956. Visual pigments of deep-sea fish.

61. DENTON, E. J., Proc. Roy. Soc. London, B, *150*: 78-94, 1959. Contributions of oriented photosensitive molecules to absorption by retina.

62. *DETHIER, V. G., Ch. 19, in Insect Physiology, edited by K. D. Roeder. New York, John Wiley & Sons, 1953, pp. 488-522. Application of laws of vision to insects.

63. DODT, E., and HECK, J., Pflüg. Arch. *259*: 226-230, 1954. Retinal potential of gecko Sphaerodactylus.

64. DONNER, K. O., Acta physiol. scand. *21* (suppl. 72): 1-57, 1950. Responses from retinal ganglion cells; frequency patterns, spectral sensitivity.

65. DONNER, K. O., J. Physiol. *122*: 524-537, 1953. Spectral sensitivity of pigeon's retinal elements.

66. DONNER, K. O., and WILLMER, E. N., J. Physiol.

111: 160-173, 1950. Responses from ganglion cells connected to rods of cat.

67. DOWLING, J. E., and WALD, G., Proc. Nat. Acad. Sci. *44*: 648-661, 1958. Vitamin A deficiency and night blindness.

68. EXNER, S., Die Physiologie der facettierten Augen von Krebsen und Insekten, Leipzig, F. Deutsche, 1891, 206 pp.

69. FERNANDEZ-MORAN, H., Prog. Biophys. *4*: 112-147, 1954. Electron microscopy of vertebrate retina.

70. FERNANDEZ-MORAN, H., Nature *177*: 742-743, 1956; Exp. Cell. Res. *5*: 586-644, 1958. Laminated and fenestrated structure of insect rhabdom.

71. FINGERMAN, M., J. Exp. Zool. *120*: 131-164, 1952. Retinal pigments and vision.

72. FINGERMAN, M., J. Cell. Comp. Physiol. *50*: 357-370, 1957. Retinal pigment response to illumination in Cambarellus.

73. FINGERMAN, M., and BROWN, F. A., Physiol. Zool. *26*: 59-67, 1953. Evidence for a Purkinje shift in Drosophila.

74. *FISHER, L. R., and KON, S. K., Biol. Rev. *34*: 1-36, 1959. Vitamin A carotenoids.

75. *FISHER, L. R., et al., J. Mar. Biol. Assn. U. K. *35*: 41-62, 63-80, 1956. Vitamin A carotenoids in invertebrates.

76. FORBES, A., Am. J. Ophth. *46*: 40-42, 1958. Electroretinogram of lizard Sceloporus.

77. FORBES, A., et al., J. Neurophysiol. *18*: 517-535, 1955; *22*: 704-713, 1959. Changes in electroretinograms of turtle and frog with shift in color.

78. FRAENKEL, G. S., and GUNN, D. L., The Orientation of Animals, Oxford University Press, 1940.

79. FRIEDERICHS, H. F., Ztschr. Morphol. Okol. Tiere *21*: 1-172, 1931. Vision in Cicindelidae, Collembola larva and adult.

80. VON FRISCH, K., Die Naturwiss. *35*: 38-43, 1948; Proc. Am. Philosoph. Soc. *100*: 515-519, 1956. Orientation, polarized light, bees.

81. VON FRISCH, K., in Mechanisms of Colour Discrimination, London, Pergamon Press, 1960, pp. 11-28. Color sense of insects.

82. FUORTES, M. G. F., Am. J. Ophth. *46*: 210-223, 1958; Symposium on Dendrites, Electroencephalog. Clin. Neurophysiol. suppl. *10*: 70-73, 1958. Electrical activity of single cells in eye of Limulus.

83. GAZE, R. M., Quart. J. Exp. Physiol. *43*: 209-214, 1958. Retinal projection to optic lobe of frog.

84. GOLDSMITH, T. H., Proc. Nat. Acad. Sci. *44*: 123-126, 1958; Ann. New York Acad. Sci. *74*: 223-229, 1958; J. Gen. Physiol. *43*: 775-799, 1960. Visual pigments and spectral sensitivity of eye of bees.

85. GOLDSMITH, T. H., and PHILPOTT, D. E., J. Biophys. Biochem. Cytol. *3*: 429-440, 1958. The microstructure of the compound eyes of insects.

86. GOULD, E., Biol. Bull. *112*: 336-348, 1957. Sun orientation in turtles.

87. GRANIT, R., Sensory Mechanisms of the Retina. Oxford University Press, 1947, 412 pp.

88. GRANIT, R., Acta physiol. scand. *2*: 334-346, 1941. Relation between rod and cone photosensitive substances.

89. GRANIT, R., Acta physiol. scand. *2*: 93-109, 1941; *5*: 219-229, 1943; *18*: 281-294, 1949; J. Neurophysiol. *8*: 195-210, 1945. Spectral properties of visual receptors in mammals, especially cats.

90. GRANIT, R., Acta physiol. scand. *4*: 118-124, 1942. Photopic spectral sense of pigeon.

91. GRANIT, R., Acta physiol. scand. *5*: 108-113, 1943. Red and green receptors in snake Trepidonotus.

92. GRANIT, R., Receptors and Sensory Perception. Yale University Press, 1955, 369 pp.

93. *GRANIT, R., and THERMAN, P. O., J. Physiol. *91*: 127-139, 1937. Theory of on-off responses in the retina.

94. GRUNDFEST, H., J. Gen. Physiol. *15*: 307-328, 507-524, 1932. Spectral sensitivity of sunfish Lepomis.

95. GUNTER, R., J. Physiol. *118*: 395-404, 1952; *123*: 409-415, 1954. Spectral sensitivity of dark- and light-adapted cats.

96. HANAOKA, T., and FUJIMOTO, K., Jap. J. Physiol. *7*: 276-285, 1957. Absorption spectrum of single cone in carp retina.

97. HARTLINE, H. K., J. Cell. Comp. Physiol. *11*: 465-478, 1938; Am. J. Physiol. *121*: 400-415, 1938. Responses from optic nerve of mollusc Pecten and of frog.

98. HARTLINE, H. K., J. Cell. Comp. Physiol. *5*: 229-247, 1934. Electrical responses from single optic nerve fibers, Limulus.

99. HARTLINE, H. K., and GRAHAM, C. H., J. Cell. Comp. Physiol. *1*: 277-295, 1932. Visual response in Limulus.

100. HARTLINE, H. K., and McDONALD, P. R., J. Cell. Comp. Physiol. *39*: 225-254, 1947. Adaptation of single visual elements, Limulus.

101. HARTLINE, H. K., WAGNER, H. G., and RATLIFF, F., Cold Spr. Hbr. Symp. *17*: 125-141, 1952; J. Gen. Physiol. *39*: 651-673, 1956; *40*: 357-376, 1957. Inhibitory interaction among ommatidia of the eye of Limulus.

102. HASLER, A. D., Science *132*: 785-792, 1960; HASLER, A. D. with H. O. SCHWASSMANN, Cold Spring Harb. Symp. Quant. Biol. *25*: 429-441, 1961. Sun orientation in fishes.

103. HASSENSTEIN, B., J. Ins. Physiol. *1*: 124-130, 1957. ERG of Sarcophaga and Eristalis.

104. HECHT, S., J. Gen. Physiol. *2*: 229-246, 337-348, 1920. Intensity effect and kinetics of photoreception, Mya.

105. HECHT, S., and WALD, E., J. Gen. Physiol. *17*: 517-547, 1934. The visual acuity and intensity discrimination of Drosophila.

106. HECHT, S., and WOLF, E., J. Gen. Physiol. *7*: 727-760, 1929. The visual acuity of the honeybee.

107. HECHT, S., et al., J. Gen. Physiol. *25*: 819-840, 1942. Energy quanta and vision.

108. HESS, W. N., J. Morphol. *41*: 63-93, 1925. Photoreceptors of Lumbricus.

109. HOFFMANN, K., Ztschr. Tierpsychol. *11*: 453-475, 1954. Clock-timed sun orientation in birds.

110. HOFFMANN, K., Cold Spring Harb. Symp. Quant. Biol. *25*: 379-387, 1961. The orientational clock of birds.

111. HOMANN, H., Ztschr. vergl. Physiol. *1*: 541-578, 1924. Function of ocelli of insects.

112. HOMANN, H., Ztschr. vergl. Physiol. *20*: 420-429, 1934. Physiology of spider's eye.

113. HOYLE, G., J. Exp. Biol. *32*: 397-407, 1955. Functioning of insect ocellar nerve.

114. HUBBARD, R., J. Gen. Physiol. *39*: 935-962, 1956. Retinene isomerase.

115. HUBBARD, R., J. Gen. Physiol. *37*: 381-399, 1954; HUBBARD, R., *et al.*, J. Gen. Physiol. *36*: 415-430, 1953; Proc. Nat. Acad. Sci. *42*: 578-580, 1956. Molecular size, geometrical isomers of vitamin A and retinene; visual excitation.

115a. HUBBARD, R., BROWN, P. K., and KROPF, A., Nature *183*: 442-446, 1959. Action of light on visual pigments.

116. HUBBARD, R., and KROPF, A., Nature *183*: 448-450, 1959. Chicken lumi-iodopsin and meta-iodopsin.

117. *HUBBARD, R., and KROPF, A., Ann. New York Acad. Sci. *81*: 388-398, 1959. Molecular configuration and visual excitation.

118. HUBBARD, R., and ST. GEORGE, R. C. C., J. Gen. Physiol. *41*: 501-528, 1958; HUBBARD, R., *et al.*, Nature *183*: 446-448, 1959. Rhodopsin system of the squid and octopus.

119. HUBBARD, R., and WALD, G., Science *115*: 60-63, 1952; J. Gen. Physiol. *36*: 269-315, 1952. Cis-trans isomers of vitamin A and retinene in the rhodopsin system.

120. HUBBARD, R., and WALD, G., Nature *186*: 212-215, 1960. Visual pigment of Limulus.

121. HUBEL, D. H., J. Physiol. *147*: 226-238, 1959; *148*: 574-591, 1959; *150*: 91-104, 1960. Single unit responses in geniculate and cortex of cat to visual stimulation.

122. HYMAN, L. H., The Invertebrates: Protozoa through Ctenophora, McGraw-Hill Book Co., 1940, 726 pp.

123. INGVAR, D. H., Acta physiol. scand. *46* (suppl. 159): 1-105, 1959. Spectral sensitivity of cat as measured in cerebral visual centers.

124. JAHN, T. L., and CRESCITELLI, F., J. Cell. Comp. Physiol. *12*: 39-55, 1938; *13*: 113-119, 1939. Electrical responses of eyes of grasshopper and moth.

125. JAHN, T. L., and WULFF, V. J., Physiol. Zool. *16*: 101-109, 1943. Visual diurnal rhythm, Dytiscus.

125a. JANDER, R., and WATERMAN, T. H., J. Cell. Comp. Physiol. *65*: 137-160, 1960. Sensory discrimination between polarized light and light intensity by arthropods.

126. JENNINGS, H. S., Behavior of Lower Organisms. Columbia University Press, 1906, 366 pp.

127. JENNINGS, H. S., Univ. Calif. Publ. Zool. *4*: 53-185, 1907. Behavior of starfish Asterias.

128. JUDD, D. B., Ch. 22, p. 811-867 *in* Handbook of Experimental Psychology, edited by S. Stevens, New York, John Wiley & Sons, 1951. Basic correlates of the visual stimulus.

129. KALMUS, H., Nature *184*: 228, 1959. Orientation to polarized light.

130. KAMPA, E. M., Nature *175*: 996-998, 1955. Photosensitive pigment from eyes of euphausiids.

131. KENNEDY, D., J. Cell. Comp. Physiol. *50*: 155-166, 1957. Spectral sensitivity of tadpoles and adult frogs.

132. KENNEDY, D., Biol. Bull. *115*: 338, 1958. Nerve response to light in molluscs.

133. KENNEDY, D., Ann. New York Acad. Sci. *74*: 329-336, 1958-1959. Electrical activity of a "primitive" photoreceptor.

134. KENNEDY, D., Am. J. Ophth. *46*: 19-24, 1958; J. Gen. Physiol. *43*: 655-670, 1960. Responses from crayfish caudal photoreceptor.

135. KENNEDY, D., Personal communication. Neural photoreception in bivalve mollusc Spisula.

136. KENNEDY, D., and MILKMAN, R. D., Biol. Bull. *111*: 375-386, 1956. Selective light absorption by lenses of lower vertebrates.

137. KIMURA, E., and HOSOYA, Y. Jap. J. Physiol. *6*: 1-11, 1956. Properties of pigment from cones of tortoise.

138. KLEINHOLZ, L. H., Biol. Rev. *17*: 91-119, 1942. Rhythmic retinal pigment movements.

139. KONISHI, J., Rep. Fac. Fish., Pref. Univ. Mie. *2*: 138-144, 145-150, 1955. Electrical responses from eyes of Panulirus and Eriocheir.

140. *KRAMER, G., Ibis *101*: 399-416, 1959. Review of bird orientation in homing.

141. *KRAUSE, A. C., Tab. Biol. *22*: 200-270, 1951. Visual purple.

142. KUFFLER, S. W., Cold Spring Hbr. Symp. Quant. Biol. *17*: 281-292, 1952; J. Neurophysiol. *16*: 37-68, 1953. Discharge patterns and functional organization of mammalian retina.

143. KUFFLER, S. W., *et al.*, J. Gen. Physiol. *40*: 683-702, 1957. Activity in cat retina in light and darkness.

144. KUWABARA, M., and NAKA, K., Nature *184*: 255, 1959. Response of Lucilia retinula cell to polarized light.

145. LAND, E. H., Proc. Nat. Acad. Sci. *45*: 115-129, 636-644, 1959. Scient. Am. *200*: 84-99, 1959. A contrast hypothesis of color vision.

146. *LE GRAND, Y., Light, Colour and Vision. New York, John Wiley & Sons, 1957, 512 pp.

147. LENNOX, M. A., J. Neurophysiol. *21*: 70-84, 1958. "On" response in optic tract fibers of cat.

148. LIGHT, V. E., J. Morph. Physiol. *49*: 1-42, 1930. Photoreceptors of Mya.

149. LINDAUER, M., Cold Spring Harb. Symp. Quant. Biol. *25*: 1961. Sun orientation in bees.

150. MACNICHOL, E. F., Exp. Cell. Res. *5*: 411-425, 1958. Subthreshold excitatory processes in the eye of Limulus.

151. MACNICHOL, E. F., and SVAETICHIN, G., Am. J. Ophth. *46*: 26-40, 1958. Electric responses from isolated retinas of fishes.

152. MAST, S. O., *in* Protozoa in Biological Research, edited by G. Calkins and F. M. Summers. Columbia University Press, 1941, pp. 271-351.

153. MAST, S. O., and STABLER, N., Biol. Bull. *73*: 126-133, 1937. Light and activity of amoeba.

154. MATTHEWS, G. V. T., J. Exp. Biol. *24*: 508-536, 1951. Sun navigation by homing pigeons.

155. MATURANA, H. R., LETTVIN, J. Y., McCULLOCH, W. S., and PITTS, W. H., J. Gen. Physiol. *43* (suppl.): 129-175, 1960. Anatomy and physiology of vision in frog.

156. Mazokin-Prshniakov, G. A., Biophysics *4*: 46-57, 1959. Color vision in dragonfly and bee.

157. Menner, E., Zool. Jahrb., Abt. Allg. *58*: 481-538, 1938. Function of the avian pecten.

158. Meyer, D. R., *et al.*, J. Neurophysiol. *17*: 289-294, 1954. Absence of color vision in cat.

159. Miller, W. H., J. Biophys. Biochem. Cytol. *3*: 421-428, 1958. Morphology, ommatidia, compound eye Limulus.

160. Millott, N., Nature *171*: 973-974, 1953; Philosoph. Tr. Roy. Soc. London, B, *238*: 187-220, 1954. Light responses, echinoderm Diadema.

161. Millott, N., J. Exp. Biol. *33*: 508-523, 1956. Covering reaction of sea urchins.

162. Millott, N., Endeavour *16*: 19-28, 1957. Photoreception in eyeless animals.

163. Millott, N., and Yoshida, M., J. Exp. Biol. *34*: 394-401, 1957. Spectral sensitivity of echinoid Diadema.

164. *Milne, L. J., and Milne, M., part 1, Handbook of physiology. American Physiological Society, 1959, vol. 1, pt. 1, pp. 621-645.

165. Motokawa, K., *et al.*, J. Neurophysiol. *20*: 186-199, 1957. Receptor potential of vertebrate retina.

166. Munz, F. W., J. Gen. Physiol. *40*: 233-249, 1956. Photosensitive pigment of euryhaline fish Gillichthys.

167. Naka, K., and Kuwabara, M., J. Ins. Physiol. *3*: 41-49, 1959; J. Exp. Biol. *36*: 51-61, 1959. Electrical response from compound eye of Lucilia and of crayfish.

168. Noel, E. K., Am. J. Ophth. *48*: 347-369, 1959. Effects of enzyme poisons on ERG.

169. North, W. J., and Pantin, C. F. A., Proc. Roy. Soc. London, B, *148*: 385-396, 1958. Sensitivity to light in sea anemone Metridium.

170. Ottoson, D., and Svaetichin, G., Cold Spring Hbr. Symp. *17*: 165-173, 1952; Acta physiol. scand. *29*: 31-39, 1953. Electrical activity of frog retina.

171. Papi, F., Ztschr. vergl. Physiol. *37*: 230-233, 1955. Orientation to polarized light; beetles, spiders.

172. Pardi, L., Ztschr. Tierpsychol. *11*: 175-181, 1954. Isopod, amphipod orientation by sun, moon.

173. Pardi, L., Boll. Inst. Mus. Zool. Univ. Torino *5*, No. 1, 1-39, 1955-1956. Solar orientation of Tenebrionid Phaleria.

174. Pardi, L., Ztschr. Tierpsychol. *14*: 261-275, 1958. Phaleria light-compass response.

175. Pardi, L., and Papi, F., Ztschr. vergl. Physiol. *35*: 459-489, 490-518, 1953. Celestial orientation in arthropods.

176. *Parker, G. H., Ergebn. Biol. *9*: 239-291, 1932. Review of retinal pigment movements.

177. Peskin, J. C., Science *114*: 120-121, 1951. Photolabile pigments of invertebrates.

178. Pirie, A., Endeavour *17*: 181-189, 1959. Reflecting materials in eyes.

179. Polyak, S. L., The Vertebrate Visual System. University of Chicago Press, 1957, 1390 pp.

180. Potts, A. M., and Modrell, A. W., Fed. Proc., *19*: 303, 1960 (abstr.). Selective destruction of retinal ganglion cells and effect on ERG.

181. Prosser, C. L., J. Cell. Comp. Physiol. *4*: 363-377, 1934; J. Exp. Biol. *12*: 95-104, 1935. Photoreceptor physiology in crayfish and earthworm.

182. Prosser, C. L., J. Comp. Neurol. *59*: 61-91, 1934. Light orientation in earthworm, Eisenia.

183. Quaranta, J. V., Zoologica *37*: 295-311, 1952. Color vision of giant tortoise Testudo.

184. Ratliff, F., and Hartline, H. K., J. Gen. Physiol. *42*: 1241-1255, 1959. Responses of Limulus optic nerve to patterns of illumination.

185. Ratliff, F., Miller, W. H., and Hartline, H. K., Ann. New York Acad. Sci. *74*: 210-222, 1958; Science *126*: 840-841, 1957. Neural interaction and change of response pattern in Limulus eye.

186. Renner, M., Cold Spring Hbr. Symp. Quant. Biol. *25*, 1961. Sun navigation in bees.

187. de Robertis, E., J. Biophys. Biochem. Cytol. *2*: 319-330, 1956. Electron microscope observations on the submicroscopic organization of the retinal rods.

188. de Robertis, E., J. Gen. Physiol. *43* (suppl.): 1-6, 1960. Some observations on the ultrastructure and morphogenesis of photoreceptors.

189. de Robertis, E., J. Gen. Physiol. *43* (suppl. 2): 1-13, 1960. Ultrastructure of retinal rods.

190. Rockstein, M., Nature *177*: 341-342, 1956. Both eyespots and skin photosensitive in Asterias.

191. Roeder, K. D., J. Cell. Comp. Physiol. *14*: 299-307, 1939. Synchronized activity in optic ganglia of grasshopper.

192. Ruck, P., J. Cell. Comp. Physiol. *44*: 527-533, 1954; J. Ins. Physiol. *1*: 109-123, 1957; *2*: 261-274, 1958. Electrical responses from ocelli of insects; grasshopper, Apis, and others.

193. Ruck, P., and Jahn, T. L., J. Gen. Physiol. *37*: 825-849, 1954. Responses from ocellus of isopod Ligia.

194. Rushton, W. A. H., J. Physiol. *134*: 11-29, 1956; J. Gen. Physiol. *41*: 419-428, 1957. Absorption difference spectrum and regeneration of rhodopsin in living human eye.

195. Rushton, W. A. H., Nature *179*: 571-573, 1957; Ann. New York Acad. Sci. *74*: 291-304, 1958. Cone pigments of man.

196. Sandeen, M. I., and Brown, F. A., Physiol. Zool. *25*: 222-230, 1952. Retinal pigment response to illumination in Palaemonetes.

197. Sauer, F., Cold Spring Hbr. Symp. Quant. Biol. *25*: 463-473, 1961; *with* E. Sauer, Die Vogelwarte *20*: 4-31, 1959. Orientation of birds by stars.

198. Schmidt-Koenig, K., Ztschr. Tierpsychol. *15*: 301-331, 1958. Twenty-four-hour periodicity and pigeon orientation; effects of rephasing cycles.

199. Schwassmann, H. O., Cold Spring Hbr. Symp. Quant. Biol. *25*: 443-450, 1961. Sun orientation of fishes.

200. Sjöstrand, F., J. Cell. Comp. Physiol. *33*: 383-403, 1949. Electron micrography of vertebrate retina.

201. Sjöstrand, F. S., J. Cell. Comp. Physiol. *42*: 15-44, 45-70, 1953. Ultrastructure of rods and cones of mammals.

202. *Sjöstrand, F. S., Ergebn. Biol. *21*: 128-160, 1959. Ultrastructure of retinal receptors.

203. Smith, F. E., and Baylor, E. R., Ecology *41*: 360-363, 1960. Bees, Daphnia, and polarized light.

204. Stephens, G. C., Fingerman, M., and Brown, F. A., Ann. Entomol. Soc. America *46*: 75-83, 1953. Polarized light orientation in Drosophila.

205. Stockhammer, K., Ztschr. vergl. Physiol. *38*: 30-83, 1956; Ergebn. Biol. *21*: 23-56, 1959. Detection, analysis, polarized light, insect eye.

206. Svaetichin, G., Acta physiol. scand. *29* (suppl. 106): 565-600, 1953; *39* (suppl.) 19-54, 55-66, 1957; Svaetichin, G., *et al.,* J. Gen. Physiol. *43*: 101-114, 1960. Spectral response curves from single retinal units, fishes.

207. Svaetichin, G., *et al.,* J. Gen. Physiol. *43* (suppl.): 101-114, 1960. Cone vision in fishes.

208. Taliaferro, W. H., J. Exp. Zool. *31*: 59-116, 1920. Photic orientation, Planaria.

209. Tanabe, I., Jap. J. Physiol. *3*: 95-101, 1952. Photosensitive pigment from chicken retina.

210. Tomita, T., Jap. J. Physiol. *6*: 327-340, 1956; J. Neurophysiol. *20*: 245-254, 1957. Potentials from eye of Limulus.

211. Tomita, T., Jap. J. Physiol. *7*: 80-85, 1957; J. Neurophysiol. *15*: 75-84, 1952. Complex intraretinal potentials from cyprinid fish and frogs.

212. Tomita, T., and Torihama, Y., Jap. J. Physiol. *6*: 118-136, 1956. Ganglionic origin of intraretinal potentials.

213. Ullyott, P., J. Exp. Biol. *13*: 253-278, 1936. Photic orientation of a planarian.

214. de Valois, R. L., J. Gen. Physiol. *43* (suppl. 2): 115-128, 1960. Color vision in monkeys.

215. *Viaud, G., *in* Mechanisms of Colour Discrimination, London, Pergamon Press, 1960, pp. 41-57. Survey of occurrence of color vision in animals.

216. Vowles, D. M., J. Anim. Behav. *3*: 1-13, 1955. Orientation of ants to polarized light.

217. de Vries, H., and Kuiper, J. W., Ann. New York Acad. Sci. *74*: 196-203, 1958. Optics of the insect eye.

218. Wagner, H. G., *et al.,* J. Gen. Physiol. *43*: 45-62, 1960. Responses of retinal ganglion cells in goldfish.

219. Wagner, H. G., and Wolbarsht, M. L., Am. J. Ophth. *46*: 46-59, 1958. Impulse patterns in single optic nerve fibers of Limulus.

220. *Wald, G., Harvey Lect. *41*: 117-160, 1946-47; J. Opt. Soc. America *41*: 949-956, 1951; *in* Comparative Biochemistry, edited by M. Florkin and H. S. Mason. New York, Academic Press, 1960, vol. 1, pp. 311-345; *in* Enzymes, edited by O. H. Gaebler. New York, Academic Press, 1956, pp. 355-367; *in* Handbook of Physiology. 1959, vol. 1, pt. 1, pp. 671-692. Reviews on distribution, chemical properties, and evolution of visual pigments.

221. Wald, G., J. Gen. Physiol. *22*: 391-775, 1938-39; *30*: 41-46, 1946. Evolution of visual pigments.

222. Wald, G., pp. 337-376 *in* Trends in Physiology and Biochemistry, edited by E. S. G. Barron. New York, Academic Press, 1952.

J. Gen. Physiol. *40*: 901-904, 1957. Metamorphosis of visual system in amphibians and sea lampreys.

222a. Wald, G., and Allen, G., J. Gen. Physiol. *30*: 41-46, 1946. Fractionation of eye pigments of Drosophila.

223. Wald, G., and Brown, P. K., J. Gen. Physiol. *35*: 797-821, 1952. Role of sulfhydryl groups in bleaching and synthesis of rhodopsin.

224. Wald, G., Brown, P. K., and Smith, P. H., J. Gen. Physiol. *38*: 623-681, 1955. Iodopsin.

225. Wald, G., Brown, P. K., and Smith, P. H., Science *118*: 505-508, 1953. Cyanopsin.

226. Wald, G., and Burg, S. P., J. Gen. Physiol. *40*: 609-626, 1957. Vitamin A of lobster.

227. Wald, G., and Hubbard, R., Nature *180*: 278-280, 1957; Wald, G., and Burg, S. P., J. Gen. Physiol. *40*: 609-626, 1957. Visual pigments of lobster.

228. Wald, G., Nature *175*: 390-391, 1955; Wald, G., *et al.,* J. Gen. Physiol. *40*: 703-714, 1957. Visual pigments of Xenopus and of alligator.

229. Wald, G., *et al.,* Proc. Nat. Acad. Sci. *41*: 438-451, 1935. Structure of vitamin A and retinene.

230. Wald, G., *et al.,* Nature *180*: 969-971, 1957; Science *128*: 1481-1490, 1958. Visual pigments and depths of habitat of marine fishes.

231. *Walls, G. L., The Vertebrate Eye and Its Adaptive Radiation. Cranbrook Inst. Sci. Bull. *19*: 1942, 785 pp.

232. Walther, J. B., and Dodt, E., Ztschr. Naturforsch. *14*: 273-278, 1959. Spectral sensitivity and ERG's of insect eye.

233. Watanabe, K., and Tosake, T., Jap. J. Physiol. *9*: 84-93, 1958. Functional organization of cyprinid fish retina.

234. Waterman, T. H., Tr. New York Acad. Sci. *14*: 11-14, 1951; Ztschr. vergl. Physiol. *43*: 149-172, 1960; Waterman, T. H., and Bainbridge, R., J. Exp. Biol. *35*: 487-493, 1958. Visual mechanisms of orientation of crustaceans to polarized light; response of Limulus eye to polarized light.

235. Waterman, T. H., Proc. Nat. Acad. Sci. *40*: 252-257, 1954. Directional sensitivity of single ommatidia, Limulus.

236. Waterman, T. H., Proc. Nat. Acad. Sci. *40*: 258-262, 1954; Science *120*: 927-932, 1954. Responses to polarized light, Limulus and submarine animals.

237. Waterman, T. H., *in* Perspectives in Marine Biology, edited by A. A. Buzzati-Traverso. University of California Press, 1958, pp. 429-450. Polarized light navigation by plankton.

238. Waterman, T. H., and Wiersma, C. A. G., J. Exp. Zool. *126*: 59-86, 1954. Only one optic fiber active per ommatidium stimulated in Limulus.

239. *Weale, R. A., Physiol. Rev. *35*: 233-246, 1955. The absolute threshold of vision.

240. *Webb, H. M., and Brown, F. A., Physiol. Rev. *39*: 127-161, 1959. Timing mechanism for persistent rhythms.

241. Wellington, W. G., Ann. Entomol. Soc. America *48*: 67-76, 1955. Orientation to polarized light in Diptera, Hymenoptera, and Lepidoptera.

242. WELLINGTON, W. G., SULLIVAN, C. R., and GREEN, G. W., Canad. J. Zool. *29*: 339-351, 1951. Orientation of insects to polarized light.

243. WELSH, J. H., J. Exp. Zool. *56*: 459-494, 1930. Visual pigment migration in Palaemonetes.

244. WELSH, J. H., Proc. Nat. Acad. Sci. *16*: 386-395, 1930; Biol. Bull. *70*: 217-227, 1936; J. Exp. Zool. *86*: 35-49, 1941. Crustaceans, retinal pigment migration.

245. *WELSH, J. H., Quart. Rev. Biol. *13*: 123-139, 1938. Diurnal rhythms; Arthropods.

246. WELSH, J. H., and OSBORN, C. M., J. Comp. Neurol. *66*: 349-359, 1937. Diurnal rhythm in fish retina.

247. WIGGLESWORTH, V. B., The Principles of Insect Physiology. London, Methuen & Co., 1939, 434 pp.

248. WOLF, E., and ZERRAHN-WOLF, G., J. Gen. Physiol. *20*: 511-518, 1937. Flicker and the reactions of bees to flowers.

249. WOLKEN, J. J., J. Protozool. *3*: 211-221, 1956. Molecular morphology of eyespot of Euglena.

250. WOLKEN, J. J., Ann. New York Acad. Sci. *74*: 164-181, 1958. Studies of photoreceptor structures.

251. WOLKEN, J. J., CAPENOS, J., and TURANO, A., J. Biophys. Biochem. Cytol. *3*: 441-448, 1957. Photoreceptor structures in Drosophila melanogaster.

252. *WULFF, V. J., Physiol. Rev. *36*: 145-163, 1956. Physiology of compound eye.

253. YOSHIDA, M., J. Exp. Biol. *34*: 222-225, 1957. Light-sensitivity in echinoid Diadema.

254. YOSHIDA, M., and MILLOTT, N., Experientia *15*: 13-15, 1959. Photosensitive nerves in echinoid.

Chapter 13

CIRCULATION OF BODY FLUIDS

In the preceding chapters physiological and biochemical adaptations to specific environmental factors have been described. We now pass to a series of functions serving in reactions of the organism to its total environment, and integrating the organism as a whole. We shall consider first the circulation of body fluids from one part of an animal to another and the hydrostatic properties of various fluid compartments.

TYPES OF TRANSPORT MECHANISMS

A definitive and mutually exclusive morphological classification of transport mechanisms is impossible; various animals have dissimilar structures serving the same function, and many degrees of intergradation exist. The following is a functional classification:

Intracellular Transport. In protozoans there is usually much protoplasmic movement, which supplements diffusion. Protoplasmic streaming may follow a definite course, as in the circulation of food vacuoles in ciliates. In metazoans some protoplasmic streaming occurs in most, if not all, cells; it is most evident in amoeboid cells, but lapsed-time motion pictures show some streaming even in neurons.

Movement of External Medium. In some animals, particularly sponges and coelenterates, the water in which they live provides the medium for transport. The medium passes through definite channels and may be propelled by ciliary, flagellar, or muscular activity (Fig. 154*A*).

Movement of Body Fluids by Somatic Muscles. Body fluid is circulated in a pseudocoelom in nematodes (Fig. 154*B*), entoprocts, and rotifers. Some transport occurs in the mesodermally lined coelom of echinoderms, annelids, sipunculids, ectoprocts, and chordates. In some polychaetes and holothurians the coelomic fluid contains corpuscles with respiratory pigments. The coelom is reduced, in those molluscs with hemocoelic circulation, to the pericardial cavity and the lumen of gonads and kidneys, and, in crustaceans, to the cavities of gonads and kidneys. In vertebrates the coelom persists as peritoneal, pericardial, and pleural cavities.

Movement of Hemolymph in an Open Vascular System. Most arthropods and many molluscs and ascidians have an "open" circulatory system in which a heart pumps hemolymph (often called blood) (Fig. 154*E*). The hemocoel is derived from the primary body cavity (blastocoel), and hemolymph moves slowly back from intercellular spaces and hemocoelic sinuses to the heart, from which it leaves in arteries for the tissue spaces.[157] Aquatic isopods have well-developed vessels and indistinct lacunae; in terrestrial isopods the vessels are reduced and lacunae well differentiated.[186] In various echinoderms the coelomic fluid, haemal fluid, and intercellular space are in communication in different degrees; ambulacral fluid is separate.

Movement of Blood in a Closed Vascular System. A closed system of tubes, often with one or more pumps, is found in oligochaetes, many polychaetes, leeches, phoronids, nemerteans, cephalopod molluscs, holothurian echinoderms, and vertebrates. The blood comes into intimate association with the tissues, by capillaries, with or without sinuses.

Lymph Channels. In vertebrates the intercellular space (primary body cavity) is connected with the blood vascular system through lymph channels. These converge on veins and form a lined network which may be as extensive as the capillary bed. In some animals (amphibians and a few teleosts) there may be lymph hearts.

A circulatory system may be considered as

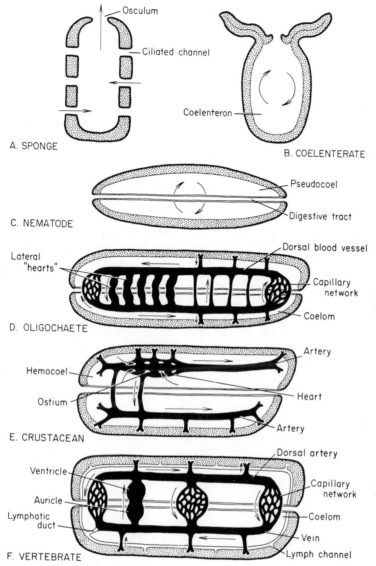

FIGURE 154. Diagrams of systems of internal transport. *A*, "sponge" type, with flagellated channels; *B*, "coelenterate" type; *C*, "nematode" type, with pseudocoel primary body cavity; *D*, "oligochaete" type, with coelom and closed blood system; *E*, "crustacean-molluscan" type, with blood system open to hemocoel which is derived from primary cavity or blastocoel; *F*, "vertebrate" type, with coelom, closed vascular system, and lymphatic channels.

consisting of two parts: the peripheral circulation and the pump, or heart. The peripheral portion will be considered first.

FLUID COMPARTMENTS

Fluid compartments of several typical kinds of animal may be compared as follows:

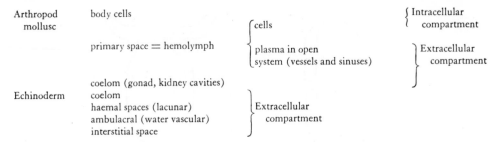

Blood Volume. The extracellular fluid compartment may be estimated by measuring the dilution of some substance which fails to penetrate tissue cells and which is not rapidly excreted or phagocytized. No single material is useful for all animals, but those which have been widely useful are thiocyanate ion, inulin, and radiosodium. Blood volume may be measured by (1) bleeding and then estimating residual blood, (2) tagging the red cells (in vertebrates) by carbon monoxide or by injecting cells containing radioactive iron, chromium, or phosphorus from a donor animal, or (3) labeling the plasma with a dye (Evans blue), which combines with plasma albumin, or injecting protein iodinated with I[131]. By each of the methods of tagging, the dilution is measured, and also the hematocrit value (per cent of cells), and total blood volume is estimated. Mixing time varies according to activity and kind of animal and ranges from 30 seconds to 30 minutes. In exercise, areas of circulation may open up and larger volumes may be obtained than in rest.

The various methods give values of blood volume which differ slightly; the bleeding method tends to give low values, and determinations by tagged cells are usually 12 to 15 per cent less than by plasma labeling.[3, 135] Some of the published values of blood volume have been summarized (Table 66 in the first edition of this book and references 28 and 120). Representative older data and re-

TABLE 46.   BLOOD VOLUME OR EXTRACELLULAR SPACE

Animal	Blood vol (per cent body weight) (method)	Animal	Blood vol (per cent body weight) (method)
Man[23]	6.2-7.0 (tagged cells)	Squalus[26, 200]	6.6 (dye)
	17.5 (ECS, antipyrine)		6.8 (dye), 21.7 sucrose,
Man at sea level[23]	7.0 (Hct 32)		12.7 (inulin)
at 14,900'	8.3 (Hct 47.5)	Raja[128]	4.6 (dye)
Dog[109]	9.5 (CO), 10.5 (dye), 9.4 (I protein)	Petromyzon[200]	8.5 (dye), 18.47 (sucrose)
		Periplaneta adult[143]	19.5 (dye)
Dog[135]	8.0 (dye), 6.2 (bleeding)	Japanese beetle larva[14]	40.8 (MnCl₂)
Goat[108]	7.3 (dye), 6.1 (Cr[151])	Cambarus[166]	25.1 (dye), 25.6 (SCN)
Cow[23]	7.5 (tagged cells)	Eriocheir[115]	33 (SCN)
Laboratory rat[92]	5.7 (dye + tagged cells)	Homarus[27]	17 (by wt), 20 (by vol)
Rabbit[3]	6.5 (dye + tagged cells)		(dye)
Cow[172]	5.2-5.7(dye)	Maja (hard shelled)[219]	8 (bleeding), 15 (protein)
Pig[28]	8.2 (dye), 8.0 (P[32] cells)	(freshly molted)	29 (bleeding), 70 (protein)
Opossum[28]	5.8 (dye), 5.5 (P[32] cells) Hct 35	Octopus	5.8 (dye), 28 (inulin)
Guinea pig[127]	7.5 (I[131])	Cryptochiton	43.8 (inulin)
Rabbit[135]	5.7 (dye), 4.3 (bleeding)	Aplysia	79 (inulin)
Pigeon[169]	7.8 (bleeding)	Archidoris	65 (inulin)
Chicken[196]	9 (♂), 7 (♀) (dye)	Achatina	40.3 (inulin)
Rana pipiens[166]	8.0 (dye)	Arion	36.6 (inulin)
Turtle[183]	7.4 (dye)	Mytilus	50.8 (inulin)
Alligator[39]	4.2 (dye)	Mazaritana[94]	49 (inulin + dye)
Several teleosts[128, 200]	2.8 (dye), 14 to 20 (ECS sucrose)	(fresh-water bivalve)	
Ameiurus[166]	1.8 (dye)	Sipunculid[53]	
Anguilla[37]	2.9	(Dendrostomum	47
Squalus[128]	8.7 (dye)	Sipunculus)	50

(ECS—extracellular space; Hct—hematocrit or per cent cells in blood)

cent measurements are presented in Table 46.

Blood volume is usually expressed as percentage of body weight on assumption of a specific gravity of 1.0; in some animals with heavy skeletons the deviation from unit specific gravity is sufficient that blood volume must be expressed as per cent of body volume rather than of weight.

The blood volume in mammals comprises normally 7 to 10 per cent of the body weight; extracellular fluid space corresponds to 18 to 25 per cent of the body weight. Relative blood volume decreases with increasing body size in mammals and is higher in infants than in adults.[75] Birds and amphibians have blood volume similar to that of mammals.[108] In elasmobranchs the blood volume is less (about 5 per cent of body weight); teleosts have the least blood (1.5 to 3 per cent).[128] The octopus has a blood volume of 5.8 per cent and extracellular space of 28 per cent.[129]

In animals with open circulation the blood volume is essentially the same as total extracellular volume in animals with a closed circulation. In *Cambarus* both the Evans blue and thiocyanate spaces are 25 per cent of body weight.[166] Blood volume of the crab *Maja* decreases from 29 per cent immediately after molt to 8 per cent after hardening of the shell.[219] Blood volume of many adult insects is less (5 to 25 per cent) than that of larval insects (25 to 40 per cent).[217] In pelecypods and gastropods the total blood volume is probably very large; in *Chiton* the hemolymph volume may be 90 per cent of body volume.[129]

A small circulating blood volume is more efficient than a large blood volume in that the same blood is reused more frequently in transport; on this basis the circulation of bony fish is much more efficient than of crustaceans. However, a large volume may be useful when the blood serves, in addition to the function of transport of oxygen, CO_2, food and wastes, as a source of antibodies, a store of phagocytic cells, and to provide a hydrostatic skeleton.

Blood volume may vary under certain conditions. At high altitudes the plasma volume of mammals decreases, the red cell volume increases, and blood volume may increase slightly.[23] The blood volume helps to maintain normal blood pressure, and after severe hemorrhage, cells and fluid are poured into the circulation from body stores. Mammalian blood volume is partly regulated by reflexes originating in volume receptors in the cardiac auricles. Loss of more than 30 per cent of

blood volume by rapid hemorrhage is fatal to man. In contrast, a Japanese beetle can survive loss of 50 per cent of its blood.[14]

FLUID PRESSURE AND FLOW

Pressure in Closed Circulatory Systems.

In any closed tubular system containing a pump, a head of hydrostatic pressure is developed at the pump and the pressure declines with frictional loss in the tubes, particularly if the tubes are distensible. The principles of blood flow hemodynamics have been extensively studied and are discussed in detail in textbooks of mammalian physiology. Representative values of blood pressure are given in Table 67 of the first edition of this book and in reference 120, and some selected values in Table 47. In young adult men the pressure in a large artery at the time of heart contraction (systole) is about 120 mm Hg, and at the time of heart relaxation (diastole) it is about 80 mm Hg, often written 120/80. The difference, or pulse pressure, decreases as the blood passes through smaller vessels. Pressure in the pulmonary artery is about 25/10 mm Hg. Velocity of flow is slow in the vast capillary bed; then in the veins velocity increases slightly although pressure continues to decrease. In mammals the cross-section of total capillaries is some 800 times that of the aorta, and the velocity is proportionately slowed. Pressure in the hepatic artery may be 120 mm Hg while that in the hepatic portal vein is only 5 mm Hg.

In birds and mammals the arterial blood pressure rises with age, and it is higher in males than in females as shown by the following data for chickens:[196]

	male	*female*
10-14 month chicken	164 mm Hg	131 mm Hg
42-54 month chicken	188 mm Hg	163 mm Hg

Blood pressure is normally determined by the peripheral resistance, the head of pressure built up by the heart, and the volume of blood. Peripheral resistance is varied by constriction and dilatation of arterioles and capillaries, constriction of arterioles being by action of smooth muscle and constriction of capillaries largely by endothelial contraction. Pulmonary capillaries are especially distensible. The vessel responses may be local, as by direct irritation of capillaries, by axon reflexes (i.e., reflexes via efferent branches of sensory neurons), or the peripheral response may be truly reflex, or hormonal.

Pressure receptors of mammals are located in the carotid sinus, in the aortic bodies of

TABLE 47. BLOOD PRESSURES

Animal	Site of measurement	Systolic/diastolic pressure or systolic only (mm Hg)
Man	radial artery	120/80
Rhesus monkey[190]		159/127
Horse[120]	carotid artery	183
Dog	femoral artery	110
Rabbit	femoral artery	90-100
Rat[93]	carotid artery	77
Guinea pig[126]	carotid artery	77/47
Hamster[17]	cheek pouch	76
Bat[93]	wing vein	16-26
Ornithorhynchus[61]	carotid artery	14
White leghorn fowl[196]	10-14 mo.	♀ 131 ♂ 164
	30-38 mo.	♀ 155 ♂ 188
Pseudemys elegans[64]	aorta	42/32
Rana[185]	aorta	22/11
Rana[20]	aorta	27
Anguilla[142]	ventral aorta	35-40
Anguilla[142]	pneumogastric artery	16-22
Anguilla[37]	ventral aorta	25-60
Lophius[24]	branchial artery	29-33
Large-mouth bass[82]	aorta	44
Chinook salmon[74]	ventral aorta	75
	dorsal aorta	53
Channel catfish[81]		39.6/30.1
Channel catfish[82]		30/23
Squalus[26]	ventral aorta	32/16
	dorsal aorta	16/10
Scyllium[151]	ventral aorta	25/20
Raja[179, 180]	ventral aorta	16/7.4
Homarus[27]	ventricle	
	at rest	13/1
	in activity	27/13
Cancer[27]	ventricle	8
Carcinus[158]	sternal sinus	9.6
Maja[49]	heart	4/3.3
	thoracic sinus	1.8/2.5
Cambarus[95]	cheliped sinus	7.4
Dragonfly nymph[177]	abdominal hemocoel	33
Teredo[117]	intramantle	0.4-1.2 (in burrow)
Anodonta[158]	heart	4.4
Octopus[67]	aorta	40-60
	gill veins	5-6
Helix[182]	heart	1.1
	gill veins	0.4
Limnaea[158]	hemocoel	2.2-8.1
Arenicola[33]	body cavity	
	quiet	9.0
	active	26.4
Neanthes[218]	body cavity	
	quiet	0.73
	active	11
	dorsal vessel	
	quiet	1.1-7.2
	active	17.6
Lumbricus[148]	body cavity	
	quiet	1.5
	active	10
Golfingia[218]	body cavity	
	quiet	2.2-2.9
	active	14-79

TABLE 47—(*Continued*)

Animal	Site of measurement	Systolic/diastolic pressure or systolic only (mm Hg)
Sipunculus[218]	body cavity	
	quiet	1.5
	active	15.8
		70.5 (burrowing)
Ascaris[79]	pseudocoel	70
Holothuria[155]	body cavity	
	quiet	0.11
	active	1.1
Caudina[215]	body cavity	
	quiet	11
	active	29.4
Thyone[218]	body cavity	
	quiet	0-1.8
	active	to 27.1

the aortic arch, in the heart, particularly the auricles, and in pain endings. A frog has cardiac receptors comparable to those in mammals.[147] Sensory impulses go to the vasomotor center in the medulla of the brain, from which vasomotor messages leave via autonomic nerves. In mammals the sympathetic supply to blood vessels is vasoconstrictor, and pressure varies according to the level of sympathetic discharge. There are parasympathetic vasodilators in the head, some sympathetic vasodilators elsewhere, and spinal sensory neurons elicit vasodilation axon reflexes.[64] Sympathetic vasoconstriction is associated with liberation of adrenaline-noradrenaline* (sympathin), and epinephrine (adrenaline) from the adrenal medulla causes general vasoconstriction; sympathetic vasodilators liberate acetylcholine as a transmitter. The vasomotor center also receives impulses from a variety of sensory paths, and a delicate balance exists between vasoconstriction and vasodilation.

Acetylcholine causes a fall in pressure, as does histamine. Serotonin (5-hydroxytryptamine) raises blood pressure in the dog, lowers it in the cat. Posterior pituitary extracts raise blood pressure in mammals by the action of vasopressin; oxytocin has little or no effect on blood pressure in mammals. In birds, however, the depressor action of oxytocin is dominant so that injections of posterior pituitary extracts lower blood pressure. The duckbilled

* Adrenaline (adr) and noradrenaline (noradr) (equivalent to epinephrine and norepinephrine) are natural compounds occurring in the body. Adrenalin and Noradrenalin are synthetic commercial products identical with the natural substances. Sympathin is the mixture of adrenaline and noradrenaline liberated at adrenergic nerve endings.

platypus is unique among mammals in showing a fall in blood pressure with pituitary injection.[61] There is much variability among different vertebrates as to relative sensitivity to posterior pituitary fractions, probably because the neurohypophyseal polypeptides differ for different animals (p. 546).[214]

In general, the resting blood pressure is higher in large mammals than in small ones; carotid pressure in the horse ranges up to 190 mm Hg. Arterial pressure at birth in the rabbit is 21 mm Hg, in the cat 25 to 30 mm Hg, and in the sheep, an animal more mature at birth, 73 mm Hg.[10] During the first 3 weeks after birth the arterial pressure of a rat rises from 20 to 75 mm Hg.[121] Blood pressure rises also with exercise. Animals which are normally horizontal, as rabbit and snake, are more sensitive to pressure increases associated with a vertical position, in which they lose consciousness sooner than primates, which normally assume a vertical posture.

High body (brain) temperature results in elevated blood pressure in homeotherms, and also in frog, alligator, and turtles. Local warming in the midcerebrum at the level of the third ventricle of *Pseudemys* causes a rise in blood pressure; local cooling, a fall. Peripheral circulation regulates warming of lizards exothermally, vasodilation favoring heat absorption and vasoconstriction reducing it.[174]

The circulation is somewhat more sluggish, and pressures are lower in cold-blooded than in warm-blooded vertebrates. The systolic arterial pressure in the frog is 30 mm Hg. The blood pressure is higher in bony fishes than in elasmobranchs; in both there is a drop in pressure in the gills and a second drop in the tissues. The ratio of pressure in the branchial (ventral) arteries to pressure in the dorsal artery is about 3 to 2 (Table 47). In the dogfish[26] and eel[37] blood pressure varies directly with body size; pressure in fish is also closely correlated with heart rate.[82]

Regulation of blood pressure in fishes contrasts with that in tetrapods. The heart of fishes receives only what may be called parasympathetic (vagus) innervation, and the peripheral vessels, sympathetic innervation.[6] If water flow over the gills of a skate or shark is stopped, the heart stops and blood pressure falls; if the fish is injected with a little atropine, which blocks cardiac inhibition by the vagus, cessation of water flow does not affect heart rate and blood pressure.[179] Increase in pressure in perfused branchial arteries sets up sensory impulses in branchial nerves, and the sensory discharge occurs when the arteries fill at each heart beat.[97] The branchial vessels of elasmobranch (*Squalus*), teleost (eel),[104] and salamander (*Necturus*) are homologous with the carotid sinus and carotid bodies of mammal and bird. Gill receptors in the eel can be stimulated by brief touch or maintained pressure.[142] Injection of adrenaline causes a prolonged pressor effect (rise in blood pressure) in dogfish.[97] The branchial vessels dilate to adrenaline, as do mammalian coronaries, in contrast to visceral vessels, which constrict in response to adrenaline.[104] Injection of acetylcholine inhibits the heart of fish (skate) but causes a rise in blood pressure as a result of general vasoconstriction, an effect not antagonized like the cardiac action, by atropine.[134] In the eel, acetylcholine constricts branchial vessels, causing an initial fall in blood pressure; then the pressure rises; adrenaline dilates the branchial vessels, constricts systemic ones.[37, 142] In tetrapods acetylcholine constricts some vessels (e.g., in the lungs), but causes dilatation of most vessels, and the dilatation is antagonized by atropine.

In summary: The blood pressure of fish falls when the heart is stopped by the vagus, and branchial receptors resemble those of the mammalian carotid sinus. In fish, acetylcholine constricts most arteries and raises blood pressure, whereas in mammals it is a vasodilator and lowers pressure. Adrenaline constricts systemic vessels in both mammals and fish and dilates coronaries in mammals and branchials in fish. It appears that the receptor molecules of the fish vessels must differ from those of mammals.

Cephalopod molluscs which have a closed circulatory system show pressures in the cephalic artery of 48 to 60 mm Hg and in gill vessels of 5.4 to 6.1 mm Hg.[67, 69] In earthworms, adrenaline (in high concentrations) dilates and acetylcholine constricts small vessels.[137]

Pressure in Open Circulatory Systems. One of the most striking differences between open and closed circulations is the low and variable pressure in the open systems. In large crustaceans, such as the lobster, the systolic pressure at rest may be some 12 to 17 cm H_2O and at diastole less than 1 cm H_2O.[27] Thus percentage change with the pulse is often much greater than in animals with closed circulations. During motor activity the ventricular pressure in a lobster may increase to 37 cm H_2O at systole and 17 cm H_2O at diastole.[27] The pressure in open circulatory systems may vary by several times according to motor activity. Simultaneous measurements in several regions of a crayfish show that the pressure increases are not equal throughout the system and may be greater in an active appendage than in an inactive one; the pressure at the distal end of a leg may be temporarily higher (8 to 10 cm H_2O) than at the proximal end (6 to 8 cm H_2O), and pressure in a leg may briefly exceed the pressure at the heart.[95] Pressure regulation and direction of blood flow in open vascular systems are poorly understood. The flow in sinuses may be controlled more by the activity of somatic muscles than by the heart and vessel size. Septa separate afferent and efferent channels in the gills of crayfish and lobster[85] and in the legs of dragonfly nymphs.[131]

In some insects negative pressures have been recorded, and it is suggested that the heart may have an aspirator action. However, in dragonfly nymphs and crayfish, negative pressures were recorded only when the animals were lethargic or anesthetized, and in measurements on lobsters no negative pressures were observed, although diastolic values approached zero. In dragonfly nymphs the pressure in the abdomen rises and falls with breathing movements.[131] In fresh-water mussels the pressure in the heart and pericardial sinus is low (about 10 mm H_2O), but when the body contracts this pressure may double.[95]

In molluscs (except cephalopods) and crustaceans the blood volume is comparable to the volume of total extracellular fluid of a vertebrate, yet the blood pressure of a 20-gm crayfish is only about 30 per cent of that of a 20-gm mouse. The velocity of circulation in the crayfish is therefore very low; a lobster circulates its blood volume in 3 to 8 minutes[27] as compared with 21 seconds in a man. The sluggishness of blood flow may be a limiting factor in the size of animals with an open circulation. The control of the pressure in the open systems is closely correlated with motor activity.

Hydrostatic Skeletons. In many animals with pressure in either hemocoel or coelom related to motor activity, the fluid-filled system provides rigidity which has skeletal function.[34] In spiders, for example, the legs are flexed by muscles, but leg extension appears due to pressure on fluid in the legs; if the blood volume is reduced the legs are flexed; if fluid volume is increased the legs remain extended.[54] *Teredo* in its burrow is turgid and has an intramantle pressure of 5 to 17 mm H_2O; when outside the burrow its pressure is only 2 to 5 mm H_2O.[117] The siphons of bivalve molluscs become extended when fluid from the mantle cavity is forced into them.[35]

Hydraulic mechanisms are important for locomotion in echinoderms which move by means of tube feet. Extension of tube feet of starfish results from contraction of the ampulla with flow of fluid into the tube feet; withdrawal results from contraction of the longitudinal muscles of the tube foot.[191] The tube feet of a starfish can develop a suction pressure of 3000 gm and by periodic pull can open a bivalve mollusc.[119]

In holothurians the anterior ambulacral system consists of two portions separated by a valve: the tentacular ducts which feed fluid into the tentacles, and the Polian complex of radial ducts, ambulacral ring, and Polian vesicles, which is a fluid reservoir for the tentacular system. In *Thyone,* pressure is normally higher in the tentacular duct (10 to 25 cm H_2O) than in the Polian complex (3 to 3.5 cm H_2O); in the body cavity of *Thyone* pressure is low (0 to 2.5 cm H_2O) when the animal is relaxed, but may rise to as much as 35 cm H_2O when it is contracted.[218] In Holothuria the coelomic pressure at rest is 16 mm H_2O; it rose periodically with contraction, and when acetylcholine was injected the pressure reached 19 cm H_2O.[155]

Burrowing worms, particularly sipunculids and some annelids, depend on changes in pressure in coelomic fluid to provide turgidity for burrowing. In *Arenicola,* pressure in the anterior body cavity averaged 12.2 cm H_2O when the animal was at rest, 36 cm H_2O when active, and 27 cm H_2O when burrowing; removal of some coelomic fluid delayed burrowing.[33, 34] In *Glycera* and *Neanthes* the pressure increased from 1 to 2 cm H_2O at rest to 15 to 18 cm H_2O in activity.[218] The coelomic pressure in the anterior segment of an earthworm is 2 cm H_2O when relaxed and 13.5 cm H_2O when active; for a body diameter of 0.6 cm a thrust of 8.5 gm is provided.[148] In burrowing, the anterior end is inserted into a crevice and inflated; the longitudinal muscles are much stronger than the circular muscles. The pressure in the tail may be less than in the anterior end, and the septa prevent flow of fluid but transmit some of the pressure change throughout the system; segmentation may provide some local independence and pressure control.[35]

In sipunculids high turgidity is essential for burrowing, and eversion of the proboscis is accompanied by elevated internal pressure. In the body cavity of large *Sipunculus,* pressures as high as 600 cm H_2O have been recorded, and in small *Golfingia* (phascolosoma) pressures range from 2.8 cm of body fluid in the relaxed state to 108 cm when contracted.[218] *Sipunculus* is unable to burrow if the posterior part of the body wall is paralyzed by deganglionation, but if a ligature is placed ahead of the paralyzed portion, the anterior part can disappear rapidly into the sand.[203] The magnitude and speed of change of pressure are probably greater in sipunculids than in any other animal group.

The pressure in the coelenteron of a sea anemone is small (1 to 2 mm H_2O) but positive, and on contraction of the body may rise to 10 to 15 mm H_2O.[12] Local contraction raises internal pressure, and this causes other body muscles to do more work; pressure falls when the coelenteron is emptied, and pressure rises as sea water is taken in. Hydrostatic skeletons which provide rigidity under body wall contraction furnish less independence of parts than a segmented exoskeleton or endoskeleton, and they can be maintained only by muscular work. However, the hydrostatic skeleton may be caused to appear to diminish by variations in internal pressure according to an animal's need. In many animals, then, the fluid system functions not only for circulation but to provide body rigidity when needed.[34]

TYPES OF HEARTS: PATTERNS OF BLOOD FLOW

Any system for circulating a mass of fluid requires a repeating pump. To assure that fluid goes in a constant direction the pump either must be equipped with suitable valves to prevent back flow or must compress its contained fluid in a continuous progressive

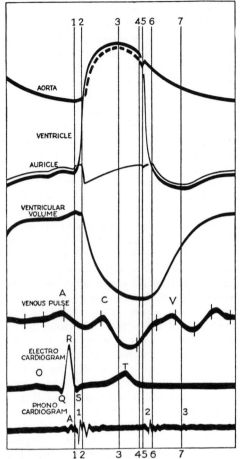

FIGURE 155. Correlated events of the cardiac cycle. Venous pulse, electrocardiogram, and heart sounds in man; aortic pressure, auricular pressure, ventricular pressure, and ventricular volume adapted from the dog. *1,* closure of the AV valves and beginning of ventricular contraction; *2,* opening of aortic valves; *2-3,* maximal ejection phase; *3-4,* reduced ejection phase; *4-5,* protodiastolic phase with closure of aortic valves at *5; 5-6,* isometric relaxation, opening of AV valves at *6; 6-7* rapid filling; *7* to auricular systole is phase of diastasis. Time marks at 0.1 sec on venous pulse curve apply to lower three curves. (From Hoff, H. E., *in* Howell's Textbook of Physiology, 1946.)

wave; some hearts do both. Morphologically, hearts may be classified as (1) chambered hearts, (2) tubular hearts, (3) pulsating vessels, or (4) ampullar accessory hearts.

Chambered Hearts. Chambered hearts are well known in vertebrates and molluscs. In vertebrate hearts the sequence of contraction is essentially similar whether the heart is two-sided (four- or three-chambered) or one-sided (two-chambered). During ventricular contraction while the aortal (semilunar) valves are open, the aorta fills and the heart

empties; ventricular systole (contraction) stops when ventricular pressure falls below that of the aorta, and the aortal valves close (Fig. 155). During ventricular contraction the auricular pressure is below that in the ventricle and the auriculoventricular (AV) valves remain closed; as the auricles fill, their pressure gradually rises while the ventricular pressure is falling, the AV valves then open, blood enters the ventricle, and the auricles contract until the high pressure in the ventricles closes the AV valves. In man the ventricles first contract with the AV valves closed (isometric contraction) for 0.05 sec, then during ejection of blood (isotonic) for 0.22 sec; ventricular relaxation lasts 0.53 sec, the auricles contract for 0.11 sec and are in diastole 0.69 sec.[86]

In fishes, with their single auricle and ventricle, the blood passes through the gill vessels before entering the aorta; hence the heart must provide pressure for traversing two capillary beds. The evolution of the two-sided heart began with air-breathing fish. In modern dipnoans the return of blood from the air bladder is separate from the return from the rest of the fish; Devonian lungfish appear to have had considerable separation of aerated and deaerated blood in the heart.[65] Amphibians, with much skin breathing, have less separation of the two sides of the heart; they lack a ventricular septum although they have ventricular folds and have complete or partial separation within the auricle. Some reptiles (crocodiles) have a complete ventricular septum; in lizards and snakes the septum is incomplete.[65] By radiography, use of dyes, and oxygen determinations it has been shown that in the ventricles of lizard,[66] caiman,[209] and turtle[194] there is relatively complete separation of streams of aerated and deaerated blood. A two-channel heart not only separates oxygenated from oxygen-depleted blood but also permits higher pressures in systemic arteries than are possible when the blood has first passed through gill capillaries. The establishment of a low pressure respiratory blood shunt and consequent higher systemic pressure aided reptiles and homeotherms to withstand the rigors of terrestrial life.

The chambered hearts of molluscs consist of one or two auricles (four in tetrabranch cephalopods) and one ventricle. In cephalopod molluscs, blood returns from the body by veins to the branchial hearts at the base of the gills and passes from the gills by veins to the auricles of the systemic heart. This arrangement of "booster" hearts proximal to the gills is more efficient than is the plan in fishes in which the heart has to overcome the resistance of vessels in both gills and body tissues.

Tubular Hearts. The systemic hearts of most arthropods consist of contractile tubes. There may be a thin receiving chamber (atrium) surrounding part of the heart, as in *Limulus,* or the heart may be free in a large pericardial sinus. It is usually anchored at several corners and receives blood through paired valved ostia. In crustaceans, blood leaves the heart by arteries, passes from small arterioles into tissue sinuses which ultimately carry it to the gills, and branchial veins return the blood to the pericardium. In many insects the heart is suspended by variously arranged alary muscles which maintain tension on the heart and by their contraction may expand the heart and cause a negative pressure. Blood leaves by one or several arteries, always at the anterior end, sometimes also laterally and posteriorly. The entire tubular heart may contract nearly simultaneously or it may show a wave of contraction.

The heart of tunicates is a delicate nonvalved tube lying in the pericardium. Blood does not flow in a definite circuit, but the heart pumps for a time in one direction and then reverses its beat.

Pulsating Vessels. Blood vessels which contract with peristaltic waves are widely distributed. In annelids many blood vessels show rhythmic peristaltic waves. In the earthworm the contraction waves in the dorsal vessel pass from the posterior to the anterior end at a speed of about 20 mm sec, and waves are repeated at about 15 to 20/min.[36] The lateral vessels of the earthworm, usually referred to as hearts, contract at rates differing from the dorsal vessel and each heart beats at its own rate although the two hearts of a segment tend to contract together. Leeches have two lateral vessels which contract alternately. In *Arenicola* the blood flows forward in the dorsal vessel, passing on each side by the gastric plexus to the lateral gastric vessel, thence to the lateral heart, which pumps to the ventral vessel. The area connecting the lateral gastric vessel to the heart beats before the heart and sometimes beats several times during a single contraction of the heart. The dorsal vessel, the lateral, esophageal, and some nephridial vessels are contractile; the ventral vessel and posterior gastric vessels are not.[71, 167] In some holothurians pulsating vessels of the haemal system contract peristaltically; in others, contraction is local and fluid circulation must be slight.

The distinction between tubular hearts and contractile vessels is not sharp in many insects, for example, dipteran larvae. In *Amphioxus* many vessels are contractile, and the heart is little more than "sinus venosus" and "conus arteriosus."[189]

Ampullar Hearts. Accessory hearts are boosters which propel blood through peripheral channels. The branchial hearts of cephalopods consist of a spongy endothelial tissue surrounding many small vessels.[125] Accessory hearts are common in insects, particularly at the base of antennae, at the attachment of wings, and in legs.

Fishes, amphibians, and reptiles have lymph hearts which are contractile enlargements of lymph vessels and which tend to force lymph into the veins. Lymph enters veins at many points and not through thoracic ducts as in birds and mammals. The lymph hearts are composed of striated anastomosing fibers and may have valves which prevent backflow of lymph.

HEART RATE AND OUTPUT

In many published tabulations of heart rates the states of activity, excitement, or anesthesia are not given.[120, 175] In most animals where there is nervous regulation of the heart, the rate of beat increases during exercise. For example the heart rate of a *Sphinx* moth is 40 to 45/min when at rest, 110 to 140 when active.[211] In general, heart rate is lower in sluggish animals than in related active ones. In clams the heart rate ranges from 0.2 to 22/min; in squid and octopus it is 40 to 80/min. Heart rate in fast fish exceeds the rate in sluggish fish.

Rate of heartbeat increases with internal pressure in many animals, particularly in invertebrates, where a plateau may be reached at "optimal" pressure.

In general, heart rate is faster in small animals than in large animals of similar kinds. The heart of *Daphnia* beats at 250 to 450 per minute (20°C), of *Asellus* 180 to 200/min, and of a crayfish 30 to 60/min. In a series of crabs the heart rate declined exponentially with increasing body size but with a slope slightly less than the decline in metabolic rate with increasing body size.[181] The heart rate in an elephant or horse is 25 to 40/min, in a dog 80/min, in a cat 125/min, in rabbit 200/min, and in mice 300 to 500/

min. In small birds the heart may beat several hundred times per minute as compared to 150 to 300 in domestic fowl.

Heart rate is very sensitive to body temperature. In poikilotherms the rate rises two to three times per $10°$ rise in temperature over a normal biological range. Similar increases with temperature occur in homeotherms; the basal rate at a given temperature, however, is higher than in poikilotherms. Diving mammals, birds, and turtles show bradycardia (slowing of heart rate) during a dive (p. 177). Fish (trout) show a similar slowing of heart rate on removal from water, bradycardia which is not due to reduced O_2 per se.[184] In *Mytilus* the heart rate is lower in water which is low in O_2 or high in CO_2 than in well-aerated water.[178]

Cardiac output is often given as minute volume or volume of blood as fraction of body weight driven by the heart per minute. A few representative data in ml/100 gm body wt/min follow:[181, 182]

man	6-10	sucker	0.4
dog	13.9	carp	0.76
cat	69	Helix	5
catfish	1.1		

The total work in gm cm/min/gm/heart weight done by the heart has been calculated from the cardiac output and arterial pressure as follows:[181, 182]

man	4,000	mouse	50,000
rabbit	21,000	frog	12,000
		Helix	3,600

Thus the work done by the heart tends to be highest in animals with high heart rates and high blood pressure. Total work rises to a maximum at some "optimal" pressure, e.g., in *Helix* at 30 cm H_2O.

The time for a complete circulatory circuit is obtained by injecting a dye or other tagged material into a vein and timing its appearance in an artery of the corresponding region. In mammals the circulation time is a few seconds (rabbit 7.5, dog 16, man 23 seconds). In a series of crabs, circulation times are slightly longer (37 to 65 seconds);[181] in a cockroach, 5 to 6 min.[38] In several insects (Hemiptera) times of 20 to 35 minutes have been obtained.[40]

A heartbeat can be analyzed in terms of (1) the origin of the excitation, the pacemaker; (2) conduction of the excitatory signal, the electrocardiogram; (3) contraction, and (4) reflex regulation.

PACEMAKERS

Cardiac rhythms, unlike respiratory rhythms, usually originate within the active organ itself rather than in extrinsic nerve centers. A heartbeat may be neurogenic (originating in ganglion cells) or myogenic (originating in muscle or modified muscle). The cellular basis for rhythmic activity may be essentially similar in all those tissues where a continuous energy source (e.g., oxidation) results in repetitive activity—a relaxation oscillator. The following criteria are useful in distinguishing the myogenic or neurogenic nature of pacemakers: (1) presence or absence of ganglion cells; if present, their removal stops a heartbeat; (2) detection of pacemaker region by localized warming, or by excision of different regions; (3) determination of the point of origin of the electrical wave of excitation, the electrocardiogram; (4) effects of drugs, particularly ether, which in low concentrations inhibits ganglion cells, and acetylcholine, which stimulates ganglion cells, inhibits innervated myogenic hearts, and is without effect on noninnervated myogenic hearts, and (5) the electrocardiogram, which is oscillatory in neurogenic hearts and consists of large slow waves in myogenic hearts. Pacemakers of molluscan, arthropod, and tunicate hearts have been discussed by Krijgsman.[110-114]

Myogenic Hearts. The hearts of vertebrates and of molluscs are myogenic. In an adult frog or fish the beat normally originates in the sinus venosus and in the adult bird or mammal in the sinoauricular node. The fibers of embryonic heart muscle in tissue culture develop rhythmic contractions. In a chick embryo, coordinated contractions start in the aortal end of the ventricle after only 29 hours of incubation and, with development, the pacemaker moves toward the sinus where recovery between beats is fastest.[156] If the sinus venosus is removed from an adult amphibian heart the normal rhythm stops, and other regions may take over initiation of regular but slower contractions. Fragments of embryonic rat hearts prior to innervation beat independently; the rate in sinoatrial fragments is twice as fast as in ventriculobulbar fragments, and a gradient exists along the embryonic heart tube.[77] In adult mammalian hearts, local cooling or warming is most effective in altering rate when applied in the sinoauricular region; electrical stimulation elicits normal electrocardiograms only when applied at the S-A node, and the first trace of action potential in the heart appears in this region. Upon local warming of fish hearts, the sinus, the auricular floor, or the AV junction could become the pacemaker.[189] The muscle of the sinus region differs from other regions in its rapid recovery of excitability; other regions are, however, capable of spontaneous rhythmicity.

Cells of the sinus pacemaker region of a frog heart show graded, slowly rising potentials which, at a critical height of some 15 mv depolarization, give rise to spikes which exceed 70 mv and are conducted. Auricular fibers show none of the slow prepotentials preceding the conducted spike.[94]

The wave of excitation which originates in the sinus is conducted over the atrial myocardium (in mammals at 1 m/sec) and then, after an AV delay, spreads over ventricular muscle (poikilotherms) or in birds and mammals over the specialized conducting Purkinje tissue (at 5 to 6 m/sec) (Fig. 155). The vertebrate heart contains nerve cells, particularly in the region of the pacemaker, but these are secondary neurons of the vagus system.

Acetylcholine (ACh) inhibits adult vertebrate hearts in both amplitude and rate (see Fig. 162). Embryonic hearts prior to vagal innervation are either insensitive to ACh, as in *Fundulus*,[4] or are inhibited by relatively high concentrations as in the chick[42, 160] or rat.[77] Acetylcholine esterase in vertebrate hearts increases during development and is maximal at the time of innervation.[187] The hearts of vertebrates are much less sensitive to ether than are the nervous systems.

Molluscan hearts also are myogenic. Nerve cells occur in or near the heart in cephalopods, but these are secondary neurons of regulating nerves.[168] In the heart of the clam or mussel the beat can originate at any point and the contraction can be local or complete.[18] In snails (e.g., *Achatina*) the pacemaker is diffuse; but injury at the aortal end is particularly effective in interrupting normal beats.[46]

The hearts of molluscs are very sensitive to pressure; they fail to give maximum beats unless distended, and when internal pressure increases, the beats are stronger and more frequent. In *Octopus vulgaris* no beat was recorded at pressures below 2 cm H_2O, and the frequency was higher at an internal pressure of 8.5 cm H_2O (69/min) than at a pressure of 4.5 cm H_2O (52/min).[67] Isolated strips of *Anodonta* and *Mytilus* hearts beat under tension.[159] The vertebrate heart also adapts to a given load so that as the blood volume in the heart is increased the strength of the beat increases (Starling's law).

Acetylcholine inhibits the hearts of molluscs (Gastropoda, Pelecypoda, Cephalopoda). Hearts of some, like *Venus,* are inhibited by very low concentrations (10^{-12}); others, like *Mytilus,* are scarcely affected by ACh (Table 48; Fig. 162).

The hearts of tunicates are fragile tubes without valves; they beat for a time in one direction, then in the reverse direction, and there is a pacemaker at each end. The periodic reversal in *Ascidiella* has been ascribed to build-up of back pressure.[83] However, isolated hearts of *Ciona* show the same alternation of direction;[138] also when the center at one end is destroyed the remaining center elicits a series of normal beats, then abnormal ones; when a heart is driven electrically the threshold rises at the end of a pulsation series. It is concluded that the excitability of each pacemaker rises and falls during each series of beats. Histological reports disagree, but it is unlikely that pacemaker ganglion cells occur in tunicate hearts.[51, 111, 114] Most tunicate hearts are insensitive to acetylcholine although it is claimed that the visceral, but not the abvisceral, pacemaker is sensitive in *Polucitor*.[51] In *Ciona intestinalis* the hypobranchial pacemaker has a higher frequency than the visceral one; acetylcholine is ineffective at 10^{-6}, weakly stimulates at higher concentrations, and slightly inhibits at 10^{-3}.[111, 114] Tunicate hearts are very little affected by removal of the central ganglion, and reflex effects are reported as lacking in most tunicates[111, 114] (but not in *Ciona*). It seems probable that tunicate hearts, like those of early vertebrate embryos, are noninnervated and myogenic.

In the lower crustaceans *Artemia* and *Eubranchipus,* acetylcholine is without effect on the heart; there seems to be no reflex inhibition; hence these hearts are probably noninnervated myogenic. The heart of *Daphnia* is inhibited by ACh, as is the scorpion heart; ganglion cells appear to be absent. Many insects, especially larvae, have myogenic hearts.

Neurogenic Hearts. The hearts of most crustaceans and of *Limulus* have nerve ganglion cells on the dorsal surface which originate the excitation wave for the heartbeat (Fig. 156). The heart ganglion of *Ligia* has six neurons, *Astacus* 15, and *Aquilla* 14; hearts of other Macrura, Anomura, and

TABLE 48. TYPICAL ACTIONS OF DRUGS ON HEARTS
(Data for lowest effective concentrations)

Drug	Vertebrate (e.g., frog)	Mollusc (e.g., Venus)	Arthropods Adult (e.g., crayfish or cockroach)	Anopheles larva (also Artemia for many drugs)
Acetylcholine (or mecholyl)	— rate and — amplitude (may stimulate in very low conc.)	— amplitude (very sensitive)	+ rate	0
Eserine (physostigmine)	potentiates ACh inhib. potentiates vagal inhib.	potentiates ACh inhib. potentiates nervous inhib.	potentiates ACh action	0 potentiation of ACh
Curare	no ACh antag.	no antag.	some antag. of ACh	0
Atropine	antagonizes ACh (muscarinic) antag. vagal inhib.	no ACh antag.	antagonizes ACh accel.	0
Mytolon		blocks ACh and nervous inhib.		
Bu4, Et4		antag. ACh inhib.		
Nicotine	high conc. blocks vagal synapses	— in low conc.	+ low conc. high conc. stops	0
5-Hydroxytrypt-amine	increases heart output in dog, slight + on rate	+ amplitude low conc.; slight + rate		
Bromo lysergic diethylamide		antag. 5HT accel.		
Adrenaline	+ rate	slight + amplitude; slight + rate not very active		0
Ergotamine	antag. adrenaline accel			

+ stimulation
— inhibition
0 no effect

inhib = inhibition
antag = antagonism
accel = acceleration
conc = concentration

Detailed references are given in Table 68 in first edition of this book.

Brachyura have nine neurons, of amphipods and of a mysid *Praunus*, six.[1] There are both large (usually unipolar) and small multipolar neurons. *Panulirus* has five large and four small neurons in its cardiac ganglion. Removal of the ganglion stops the heart.[132] The hearts of higher crustaceans are stopped by low concentrations of ether (one half to one quarter water saturation) and are accelerated by acetylcholine.[146, 162] The inter-action among the heart ganglion cells is discussed on page 401.

The role of the dorsal ganglion is well shown in *Limulus*. The *Limulus* heart has eight pairs of ostia which divide it into nine segments (Fig. 156); the anterior half has five pairs of arteries plus one anteromedian artery. Lateral nerves run along each side of the heart and are connected by thin nerve bundles to the median ganglion. Small multi-

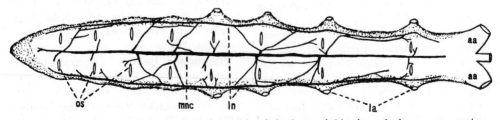

FIGURE 156. Diagram of dorsal view of ventricle of the heart of *Limulus polyphemus*. *aa*, anterior aortae; *la*, lateral aortae; *os*, ostia; *mnc*, median nerve cord (pacemaker ganglion); *ln*, lateral nerves. (From Carlson, A. J.: Am. J. Physiol., vol. 12.)

polar neurons are scattered throughout the ganglion and large unipolar neurons are located mostly in segments 4 and 5. Local warming alters the heart rate most when applied to the fourth and fifth segments. The heart stops beating when the ganglion is removed, but if tension is then applied by inflation or if the heart is stimulated by NaCl, there may be some local and peristaltic contractions which are unlike the normal synchronized beat. In *Limulus* embryos a myogenic peristaltic beat begins at 22 days, but no nerves are present until the twenty-eighth day.[32] The adult heart is accelerated by acetylcholine, but the embryonic heart prior to innervation is unaffected by the drug.[162, 164] Conduction of excitation is by the median and lateral nerves.

The hearts of some insects—honeybee, cockroach, and others—particularly adults—contain nerve cells which are probably pacemakers. The hearts of the cockroach *Periplaneta*,[110, 113] the grasshopper *Melanoplus*,[78] the cricket *Stenopelmatus*,[43] and the honeybee are accelerated by acetylcholine. In a Japanese cicada ganglionic pacemakers appear to be located in segments 2 and 7 of the heart.[96] The hearts of insects are normally kept under tension by the dorsal suspensory ligaments and alary muscles, and transection of these suspensions often stops the heart. The hearts of many insects show periodic reversal of direction of beat.[73] Absence of nerve cells has been reported for hearts of various larvae; hearts of larval *Anax* and adult *Belostoma* lack nerve cells, and they beat so long as dorsal suspensory ligaments are intact. Nerve cells were not found in hearts of some larvae, e.g., army worms. The hearts of larval wax moths *Galleria* are not affected by acetylcholine;[139] in *Anopheles* larvae drugs such as ACh, mecholyl, curare, and ether have little or no effect, and reflex slowing and acceleration do not occur.[98] In larvae of the dipteran *Chaoborus* ligation and cautery show that the beat can originate anywhere on the heart, and central nervous effects are lacking.[45] Evidently the hearts of many adult insects are neurogenic; the hearts of many larvae and probably of some adults are noninnervated myogenic, and the hearts of all insects are very sensitive to applied tension.

Among annelids, nerve cells have been described in the hearts of *Arenicola*[30] and *Lumbricus*[195] but not in *Nereis*.[171] The *Arenicola* and *Lumbricus* hearts are accelerated by acetylcholine[164] (Fig. 162). Disten-

tion by blood is important in establishment of contraction.

Lymph hearts of amphibians (frogs and toads) and fish (eel) are normally under control of the spinal cord.[161, 170] When the connections of the anuran lymph heart to the spinal cord are cut, the heart stops; later it may show spasmodic beats. Anterior and posterior homolateral hearts are normally synchronized, but each heart is driven by a localized region of the spinal cord. Local cooling or warming of the spinal cord slows or speeds the lymph hearts.[55] Lymph hearts transplanted to the lymph sac of the tongue may beat strongly although spasmodically. Nerve cells have not been found among the branched striated muscle fibers. In intact animals, acetylcholine (10^{-4} to 10^{-6}) may raise the tone and even stop the heart in systole, but denervated transplanted lymph hearts are accelerated by acetylcholine.[161, 170] The responses of lymph heart muscle to electrical stimulation change after denervation. Lymph hearts are more similar to striated muscle, which is excited by ACh, than to systemic hearts; normally lymph hearts are controlled by the spinal cord, but they can revert to irregular myogenic beats.

ELECTROCARDIOGRAMS

The conduction of the excitatory signal from the pacemaker to and within the muscle of the heart is manifest by an action potential wave. Because of the synchronization of many discharging units, the recorded potentials are large, even at some distance from the heart. At the same time the geometrical relations in chambered hearts are such that a complex wave is recorded. The electrocardiogram (ECG) is different in myogenic hearts with muscular conduction from the ECG in neurogenic hearts with nervous conduction.

The complex electrocardiogram of vertebrates represents a wave front spreading over the heart.[22, 88] The ECG is similar whether ventricular conduction is in Purkinje tissue (mammals and birds) or in muscle (poikilotherms) and whether there is a ventricular septum. Typically the ECG consists of a series of slow waves, upward (negative) deflections called P, R, and T, and downward (positive) deflections, Q and S (Fig. 157). The P wave corresponds to conduction in the auricles, the PQ interval represents delay at the auriculoventricular junction, and the QRS complex corresponds to conduction in the ventricles. The T wave represents re-

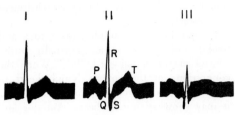

FIGURE 157. Electrocardiograms from man, leads I, II, and III. (From Katz, L. N.: Electrocardiography. Lea & Febiger.)

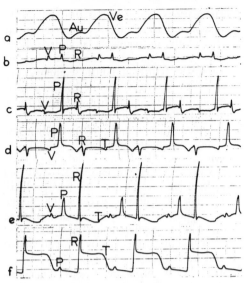

polarization of the ventricular surface, an upright T indicating earlier repolarization of the left side and an inverted T indicating earlier repolarization of the right side of the heart.[87]

The per cent of time occupied by the different phases of the ECG is similar in mammals with very different heart rates as follows:[44, 212]

	P-R interval (%)	Q-T interval (%)	rate/min
man	30	70	72
crocodile	30	70	36
mouse	57	42	635
rabbit	40	60	250
horse	35	65	38

In a hibernating hedgehog the heart is slowed, the P-R interval more than other components.[176]

In amphibians and fishes a wave arising in the sinus venosus precedes the P; this sinus wave is seen in an isolated sinus venosus[9] or after removing the ventricle[152] (Fig. 158).

Records obtained with intracellular microelectrodes show that each muscle fiber in the heart remains depolarized for 0.1 to 1.5 sec (see Fig. 163). The T wave of the ECG represents the end of the plateau and repolarization of ventricular fibers.[84]

The electrocardiogram of the myogenic heart of a mollusc also consists of waves lasting for tenths of a second. These slow waves may be complex and may include waves of several rates (Octopus;[123] Aplysia;[89] Helix[58]). The electrocardiograms of oyster[198] and of fresh-water mussel consist normally of a diphasic faster component at the beginning of contraction and a slow wave during contraction (Fig. 159). The electrocardiogram of the ascidian Perophora consists of a series of slow waves.[51]

Neurogenic hearts of arthropods show electrocardiograms of oscillatory fast waves, each lasting only tenths of msecs; they also show slow waves, the nature of which is not well understood. Oscillatory ECG's have been re-

FIGURE 158. Electrocardiograms recorded from different regions of the heart of a frog. V, activity in sinus venosus. P, Q, R, S, T same as in Figures 155 and 157. a, mechanical record showing contractions of auricles and ventricle; active electrode in b on sinus venosus; c, left auricle; d, junction of auricle and ventricle; e, midventricle; f, tip of ventricle. Voltage calibration b, c, d, e 4 mv/cm; f 20 mv/cm.

corded from many arthropods—Astacus,[89] Panulirus,[130] Melanoplus,[41] Galleria,[139] and Dytiscus[50] (Fig. 159). The pattern of ECG in arthropods varies according to electrode position, temperature, and other factors. In Melanoplus, treatment with cold saline tends to suppress the oscillations and to emphasize the large fast waves[41] (Fig. 159). In the cicada Cryptotympana the ECG is markedly simplified but still oscillatory after alary muscles are cut.[96] The oscillations correspond to the discharge from the pacemaker ganglion cells, and the presence or absence of an oscillatory ECG under physiological conditions

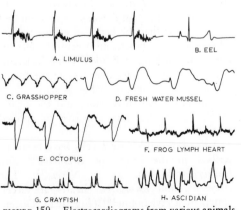

A. LIMULUS   B. EEL

C. GRASSHOPPER   D. FRESH WATER MUSSEL

E. OCTOPUS   F. FROG LYMPH HEART

G. CRAYFISH   H. ASCIDIAN

FIGURE 159. Electrocardiograms from various animals.

may be an indication of whether a heart is neurogenic or myogenic. The ECG of the polchaete *Arenicola* consists of oscillations as well as slow waves.[164]

When potentials are recorded from isolated pacemaker ganglia, repetitive spikes are superimposed on slow potentials. In *Limulus* a single neuron discharges several (two to fifteen) times during a burst, lasting approximately a half second for each heartbeat (Fig. 161,IIIb).[164] Each neuron usually discharges initially at a high rate and later at decreasing frequency. Records from the midsegments where the large unipolar pacemaker cells are located show slow waves lasting more than 0.1 sec with axon spikes superimposed. Similar spikes and slow waves are seen even with single ganglion cells in *Panulirus*.[130]

Crustacean Heart Ganglia. The small number of nerve cells in the cardiac ganglion of crustaceans constitutes an integrated rhythmic system.[25, 76, 132, 210] In lobster *Homarus* and in *Palinurus,* there are five large anterior and four smaller posterior cells; in crabs (*Cancer*) the posterior cells are larger (Fig. 160). External recording shows that each cell discharges many impulses (twenty to ninety) in each cardiac burst, that there may be slow waves on which spikes are superimposed, and that there may be some interburst impulses. The four smaller neurons are normally pacemaker or driver cells; the larger ones are motor neurons or followers, although when separated from the posterior cells they may show spontaneity, often not in bursts.

Pacemaker cells show slow pacemaker potentials which may spread over the cell body and which give rise to spikes; spikes appear to originate in the axon, to spread over the cell body, and they may arise at different phases of the pacemaker potential (Fig. 161, II). The pacemaker potential appears to arise in dendritic or soma regions.[25]

The follower neurons may show (1) slow maintained depolarizations on which are superimposed (2) small synaptic potentials due to impulses from driver neurons, and (3) occasional spikes (Fig. 161,I). Another pattern lacks the sustained depolarization, another includes interburst spontaneous impulses, and another contains only bursts of spikes without synaptic potentials. One large follower neuron can affect another electrotonically, as shown by intracellular recording from adjacent cells, and two impulses can coexist in different parts of the same neuron. Followers do not influence drivers by spikes but may influence them electrotonically.

The crustacean heart ganglion is inner-

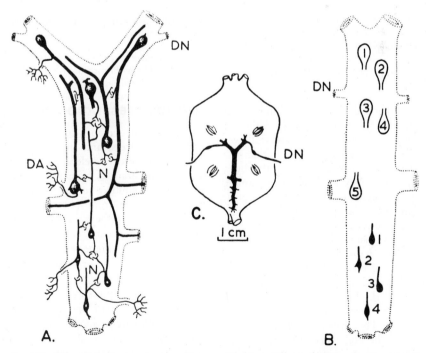

FIGURE 160. Diagrams of crustacean cardiac ganglia. *A,* ganglion of *Homarus*: *N,* neuropile; *DA,* dendritic arborizations; *DN,* dorsal nerve; *B,* heart of *Palinurus*: nerve cells and direction of major axons, large cells anterior, small cells posterior; *C, Homarus* heart: anterior and posterior arteries, four ostia, cardiac ganglion, and dorsal nerves. (From Maynard, D. M.: Biol. Bull., vol. 109.)

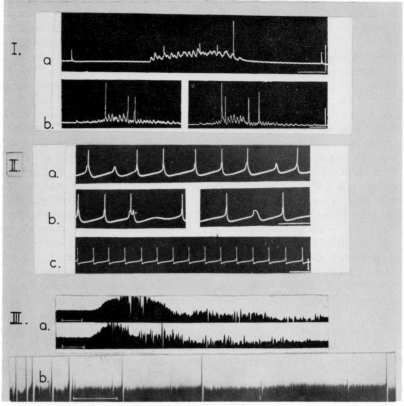

FIGURE 161. Potentials recorded from cardiac ganglion cells.

I, records from follower cells of crab, slow depolarization (in *a*), small synaptic potentials and spikes of varying sizes.

II, records from spontaneously active cells of lobster; pacemaker potentials (*a* and *b*) in different relations to spike and not necessarily giving rise to spike. (From Bullock, T. H., and Terzuolo, C. A.: J. Physiol., vol. 138.)

III, Potentials from isolated cardiac ganglion of limulus; *a,* multifiber preparation with slow waves and spikes; *b,* single fiber spikes discharging at declining frequency. (From Prosser, C. L.: J. Cell. Comp. Physiol., vol. 21.)

vated by both accelerator and inhibitor nerves from the central nervous system. Inhibition may be equal on both driver and follower neurons, or it may affect one more than the other; acceleration can be interrupted by a brief inhibitory volley but may then resume, indicating persistence of an accelerating agent. The control of ostia appears to be separate from that of the pacemaker ganglion. Stretching the heart increases frequency of beat, possibly by mechanical stimulation of processes on some of the ganglionic neurons.

In summary: Some cardiac neurons are independently rhythmic, yet there are interactions between them suggestive of reverberating circuits. The driver neurons are normally small; the followers are large motor neurons activated by driver impulses, influencing each other and activating the muscle. In addition, there is control by extrinsic nerves and by stretch.

NERVOUS REGULATION OF HEARTS

The vascular demands for blood vary with activity and stress, and in efficient vascular systems the heart accelerates or decelerates reflexly. The brain of higher vertebrates contains in the medulla a vasomotor center which receives impulses from (1) specific vascular receptors such as those in the carotid sinus and heart, (2) general somatic and visceral receptors, and (3) higher centers in the brain. The heart rate rises in compensation for a fall in blood pressure, and the heart slows when the blood pressure rises. The vagus nerves slow the heart and reduce its amplitude of contraction; the primary vagal fibers terminate in ganglia located in the heart, and secondary vagal neurons end in the heart musculature and nodal tissue. Secondary sympathetic fibers elicit cardioacceleration. Adrenaline added directly to the heart accelerates it, but in intact animals reflex control usually prevents marked acceleration on injection of adrenaline. The embryonic heart beats for some days before innervation; during this early period reflex regulation of heart rate cannot occur.

Activity in the sympathetic fibers to the heart is associated with liberation of sympathin, a mixture of epinephrine (adrenaline) and norepinephrine (noradrenaline). Acetylcholine (ACh) is released at vagal synapses. Atropine blocks the inhibiting action of the vagus and of ACh by combining with an ACh receptor, and physostigmine (eserine) enhances both effects by inhibiting acetylcholine esterase. In a turtle, atropine blocks inhibition due to *postganglionic* vagus stimulation; nicotine blocks *preganglionic* inhibition, i.e., at synapses; hence the ACh action at synapses and at muscle is different.[68]

Cardioregulation is essentially similar in mammals, birds, reptiles, and amphibians. The two vagi are not always equivalent, e.g., in a lizard *Chromastyx* the right vagus is a more effective inhibitor than the left.[105] Sympathetic innervation of the heart is lacking in elasmobranchs and teleosts. However, fish hearts are readily slowed; in the ganoid *Acipenser,* for example, stimulation of the skin, especially on the head, or the fins or barbels, results in reflex standstill of the heart, an effect antagonized by atropine.[106] In various bony fish (conger eel, pike) the vagus nerves slow the heart, an effect antagonized by atropine; perfused ACh has no negative tonotropic effect (reduction of muscle tone); hence the chronotropic fibers, but not the tonotropic ones, appear to be cholinergic.[100] Afferent fibers in the vagus from the heart of a catfish regulate cardiac reflexes.[118] Vagal inhibition of the heart of the elasmobranch *Scyllium* can be elicited reflexly by afferents in the vagus, hypobranchial, and lateral line nerves.[124]

In cyclostomes the hearts of myxinoids, e.g., *Myxine,* have no regulating nerves and are relatively insensitive to acetylcholine, even after eserinization.[60] By contrast, the lampreys (*Lampetra*) show vagal inhibition although acetylcholine accelerates, an effect not antagonized by atropine or potentiated by eserine. The *Lampetra* heart contains many ganglion cells.[5, 60, 149, 153]

Vagal impulses and applied acetylcholine shorten the duration of the cardiac action potential, i.e., hasten repolarization (Fig. 165C). The pacemaker potential of the sinus region becomes reduced and conduction may be blocked.[88, 94] Sympathetic nerve impulses increase the rate of depolarization of the pacemaker region; hence the frequency of beats is increased.

Most molluscan hearts appear to receive both inhibitory and accelerator innervation. In numerous pelecypods and gastropods, stimulation of the visceral ganglia can result in either cardiac inhibition or acceleration. In some, e.g., *Mya, Anodonta, Venus,* inhibition is predominant; in others, e.g., chitons, *Aplysia, Haliotis, Archidoris, Ariolimax,* acceleration is more evident.[31] In *Helix, Limax,* and the nudibranch *Triopha,* both inhibitor and augmentor fibers arise in the pleural ganglion. In *Venus,* nervous inhibition is often followed by acceleration, and when inhibitory nerve endings are blocked by the drug Mytolon (benzoquinonium), acceleration results from nerve stimulation.[207, 208] In the gastropod *Dolabella* the posterior part of the visceral ganglion inhibits and the anterior part accelerates the heart.[52] Visceral nerves of cephalopods (*Octopus*) slow the heart, and one nerve volley may delay one heartbeat.[8] The visceral nerves also contain accelerator fibers of higher threshold than the inhibitory fibers;[157] amplitude of beat may build up during repetitive stimulation.[67, 69] The beat of the branchial vessels is regulated from the visceral ganglion.[140]

Acetylcholine inhibits the heart of all classes of molluscs (Fig. 162). Eserine enhances inhibition by visceral ganglion stimulation in *Venus* and *Dolabella*;[52] it fails to potentiate nervous inhibition in cephalopods. Mytolon, a curarimimetic drug, strongly antagonizes both ACh and nervous inhibition in *Venus*[207, 208] but not in *Helix*.[70] Evidence for chemical mediation of inhibition has been obtained by perfusion experiments in *Venus* and *Dolabella*; it is probable that the mediator is acetylcholine. However, perfusates from heart of *Octopus* and *Eledone* during visceral nerve stimulation did not contain ACh.[67, 69] In *Helix* visceral nerve stimulation liberates an agent active in inhibiting other snail hearts; also an isolated heart of *Helix* liberates into the bathing medium a stimulating agent; neither of these is ACh.[101]

The heart of *Venus* and of some other molluscs is accelerated by low concentrations of 5-hydroxytryptamine (serotonin or 5HT); this substance is present in various ganglia of bivalves and gastropods and also in large amounts in the salivary glands of cephalopods. Bromo lysergic diethylamide antagonizes the acceleration by 5HT but LSD (lysergic acid

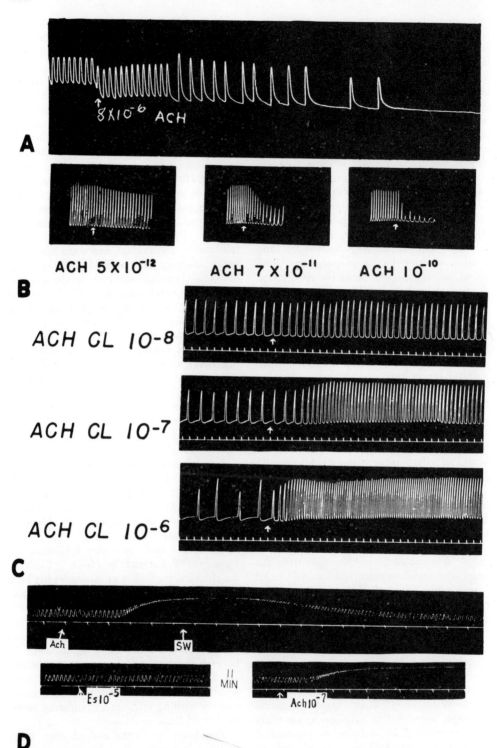

FIGURE 162. Effects of drugs on various hearts.

A, effect of acetylcholine (8 parts in 10^6) on turtle heart.

B, effect of acetylcholine in three concentrations on heart of *Venus mercenaria*. (From Wait, R. B.: Biol. Bull., vol. 85.)

C, effect of three concentrations of acetylcholine on heart of the lobster. (From Welsh, J. H.: J. Cell. Comp. Physiol., vol. 19.)

D, effect of acetylcholine (1 in 10^7) before and after eserinization of heart of *Arenicola*. (From Prosser, C. L., and Zimmerman, G. L.: Physiol. Zool., vol. 16.)

diethylamide) mimics 5HT.[207, 208] It seems reasonably well established that nervous inhibition is mediated by acetylcholine and that acceleration is by 5-hydroxytryptamine in most molluscs; in cephalopods other mediators are indicated.

The hearts of Crustacea and *Limulus* receive from the central nervous system several regulating nerves which are distributed to the pacemaker ganglion and to the muscle. The heart of *Callinectes* receives two pairs of accelerator and one pair of inhibitory nerves. Cerebral ganglion stimulation results in inhibition of the heart in crayfish, crabs, and *Limulus*.[31, 192] In *Limulus* the inhibitory nerves arise in the posterior part of the brain; in Crustacea both inhibitor and accelerator nerves arise from the subesophageal ganglion; the inhibitors always arise anterior to the accelerators. The stomatogastric nerves have no effect on the heart. In *Panulirus* both inhibition and acceleration build up on repetitive stimulation; inhibition requires a frequency greater than 15 per sec, and acceleration is maximal at about 60 impulses per sec.[132] Amphipods[1] have two pairs of cardiac nerves, stomatopods have three pairs, and a mysid one pair.

The acceleration of crustacean hearts by acetylcholine qualitatively resembles acceleration by cardioaccelerators (Fig. 162). Eserine may enhance nervous acceleration in *Astacus*[210] but not in *Cancer*;[192] atropine antagonizes ACh acceleration but has no effect on nervous stimulation. The identity of possible chemical mediators of cardioregulation in arthropods is uncertain. In insects the alary muscle innervation may be independent of heart innervation.

Crustacea of several groups have a pericardial organ which may be an endocrine gland. In *Cancer, Homarus,* and *Squilla* an extract of this organ increases both amplitude and frequency of heartbeat; in *Maia,* it increases amplitude and decreases frequency.[2] It is suggested that one active agent in the extract may be dihydroxytryptamine.

EFFECTS OF DRUGS ON HEARTS

The preceding evidence regarding pacemakers indicates that, in general, acetylcholine inhibits innervated myogenic hearts, accelerates neurogenic hearts, and is without effect on noninnervated myogenic hearts; pacemakers of neurogenic hearts are readily inhibited by ether which has little or no effect on myogenic hearts (Fig. 162). Preceding evidence regarding nervous regulation of hearts indicates that inhibitory nerves liberate acetylcholine in vertebrates (vagus nerves) and in some pelecypods and gastropods, that excitatory nerves liberate adrenaline-noradrenaline in vertebrates (sympathetic nerves) and 5-hydroxytryptamine in some molluscs.

When various potentiating and inhibiting drugs are compared, when drug concentrations over a wide range are tested, and when many species of animal are used, numerous unexplained exceptions to the preceding generalizations appear. Analysis of the action of drugs requires measurements other than rate and amplitude of heartbeat.

Eserine (physostigmine) or prostigmine prevents hydrolysis of acetylcholine by acetylcholine esterase. Potentiation of the inhibitory effect of ACh has been reported for various vertebrates, snails, and bivalves; potentiation of ACh acceleration occurs in *Limulus,* crustaceans (*Astacus, Panulirus, Homarus, Cancer*), insects (*Stenopelmatus, Periplaneta*), and annelids (*Lumbricus, Arenicola*). Acetylcholine esterase is present in all hearts tested, more in *Limulus* heart ganglion than muscle, very little in the *Venus* heart. No measurements of acetylcholine esterase are available for hearts which are unaffected by the drug except for *Myxine* in which there is less of the enzyme than in the more sensitive *Lampetra*.[5]

Atropine antagonizes both ACh and vagal inhibition in the hearts of vertebrates; it antagonizes ACh acceleration in *Astacus, Homarus, Panulirus, Cancer, Melanoplus,* and *Periplaneta.* No antagonism of ACh has been found in a variety of molluscs. The receptor cells in which ACh is blocked by atropine are nerve cells in vertebrate hearts (vagus secondary neurons) and in arthropods (pacemaker ganglia), whereas in molluscs in which atropine does not block, the site of ACh action is muscular.

Nicotine may initially slow the vertebrate heart; later and in high concentrations it may block the vagus and accelerate; nicotine is not an antagonist of acetylcholine on the vertebrate heart. In molluscs, nicotine inhibits in a manner resembling acetylcholine (*Anodonta, Sepia, Anomia, Venus, Ostrea*).[101, 102] In neurogenic arthropod hearts nicotine initially accelerates in low concentrations (*Homarus, Cancer, Astacus, Periplaneta, Melanoplus, Limulus*). In *Limulus* after initial stimulation nicotine paralyzes by blocking the pacemaker ganglion,[164] and in *Periplaneta* nicotine may antagonize the stimulating action of high but not of low concentrations of ACh.[110]

While acetylcholine is said to inhibit the hearts of vertebrates, under certain conditions isolated mammalian and toad hearts are stimulated, particularly in amplitude, by lower concentrations of ACh than are inhibitory.[133, 193] In a heart-lung preparation (dog) small amounts of ACh maintain a fibrillation started by electrical stimulation.[29] This stimulation may be partly due to adrenaline release and partly a direct stimulation of the heart, especially when antagonized by atropine. A heart stopped by lack of K is then stimulated by ACh. Some ACh is normally liberated from the beating, isolated rabbit heart.[29]

Intact lymph hearts of frogs show increased tone with ACh. Innervated hearts of certain cyclostomes (*Lampetra*) are said to be accelerated by ACh. Lymph hearts stop in systole when ACh is administered, presumably by stimulation of the spinal cord pacemaker.[55]

Many molluscan hearts are inhibited by very low concentrations of acetylcholine (10^{-7} in *Loligo*, 10^{-10} to 10^{-12} in *Venus*) (Fig. 162). In *Venus* the action appears to be on the pacemaker reactions; the electrocardiogram is reduced more than is the mechanogram, and the ACh effect is blocked by tetraethylammonium but not by atropine.[207, 208] Some other lamellibranch hearts such as *Anodonta*,[190] *Amphidesma*,[159] *Cyprina*, *Mya*, and the snail *Buccinium*[207, 208] and *Dolabella*[52] are inhibited by very low concentrations. Other bivalves such as *Mytilus*, *Ostrea*, *Gryphaea*, and *Modiolus* are relatively insensitive, and at ACh 10^{-5} to 10^{-3} the heart may even show an increase in amplitude and frequency.[159] The reason for the striking difference in ACh effect on two groups of molluscs is unknown. Molluscan hearts, like vertebrate hearts, are relatively insensitive to ether.

The neurogenic hearts of many arthropods are accelerated by acetylcholine, at slightly higher concentrations than are needed to inhibit the very sensitive molluscan and vertebrate hearts (Fig. 162). Hearts of these arthropods—crabs, crayfish, *Asellus*, *Gammarus*, some adult insects—are inhibited by low concentrations of ether. In other arthropods—*Daphnia*, *Artemia*, *Simocephala*, nymphs of *Cleon*, *Anopheles* larvae—the hearts are resistant to ether. Of these, the hearts of *Daphnia*[13, 15] and of a scorpion,[103] apparently myogenic, are inhibited by ACh. Hearts of others—*Artemia*, *Eubranchippus*, larvae of *Limulus*,[164] *Galleria*, *Anopheles*, and of two hemipterans *Belostoma* and *Lethoceros*[136]—are insensitive to acetylcholine. In several of this latter group no reflex effect on the heart

of general body stimulation has been found and in some, e.g., the larvae of the dipteran *Chaoborus*, destruction of the nervous system does not alter heartbeat. Probably these arthropods have noninnervated myogenic hearts.

In *Periplaneta* the accelerating action of dilute ACh (10^{-5} to 10^{-8}) is not blocked by nicotine or hexamethonium but is blocked by atropine. Eserine lowers the threshold for this action. High concentrations of ACh (10^{-3} to 10^{-5}) also stimulate the heart, and this action, in contrast to that at low concentration, is blocked by nicotine but not by atropine.[144] Apparently there are two sites of action of ACh on the *Periplaneta* heart. This heart (and that of the crab *Maja* is also accelerated by adrenaline (10^{-7} to 10^{-6}) and slowed by the adrenaline antagonist, ergotamine.[110, 113] One hypothesis is that there are primary cholinergic pacemaker cells and secondary adrenergic ones; another is that ACh acts in low concentrations on the pacemaker ganglion cells and in high concentrations on muscle.[213]

The action of acetylcholine has been classified as muscarinic or nicotinic. On vertebrate hearts the action is muscarine-like and antagonized by atropine; on sympathetic ganglia it is nicotine-like, blocked by curare and tetraethylammonium. In the *Venus* heart ACh is not antagonized by atropine; it is antagonized by tetraethylammonium and Mytolon, but not by curare or sparteine, which antagonize ACh on sympathetic ganglia.[122] Mytolon does not antagonize ACh in *Helix* heart, but it does in *Spisula*. In *Periplaneta*, acceleration by ACh is blocked by both atropine and curare.[144] It appears, therefore, that the classification of ACh action as muscarinic or nicotinic is inadequate.

The preceding pharmacological data indicate marked differences in the receptor molecules of hearts of different kinds of animals, even of related genera. Sensitivity to ether may be a simpler criterion of myogenicity or neurogenicity than the effect of ACh. There are multiple effects of agents like acetylcholine. Much of the confusion in interpretation might be resolved if more kinds of measurement were made—on activity of pacemaker cells, conducting systems, activation of myocardium, and contraction. For example, microelectrode records show that one inhibiting effect of ACh on vertebrate hearts is to shorten the duration of depolarization of conducting muscle; this may be responsible for the negative inotropic action. Records from single pacemaker neurons of the *Limulus* heart show that ACh makes a rhythmic discharge continuous, and the heart may be stopped in systole because of the continuous asynchronous pacemaker discharge.

Epinephrine (adrenaline) is a normal stimulating agent for vertebrate hearts, and 5-hydroxytryptamine (serotonin) for some mollusc hearts. In the cyclostome *Myxine* adrenaline accelerates only after treatment with dihydroergotamine; however, extracts of the *Myxine* heart yield adrenaline, noradrenaline, and some other catechols.[153] Applied adrenaline stimulates most hearts in either rate or amplitude: molluscs *Aplysia, Loligo*,[67, 69] fresh-water mussel,[141] *Ostrea*,[101] *Pecten*,[90] *Anomia*,[145] and *Venus*,[162, 165] and arthropods *Limulus*,[32] *Astacus*,[43] *Carcinus, Maja*,[206] *Panulirus*,[206] and *Homarus*,[206] and annelids *Lumbricus* and a leech.[72] Other hearts are said to be unaffected by adrenaline (*Ciona*,[7] *Nereis*,[62] *Artemia*,[162, 165] *Anopheles* larvae).[98] In some invertebrates where there is an effect, the sensitivity is relatively low and it is improbable that adrenaline is the normal neural accelerator. In the squid, sensitivity to norepinephrine is greater than in frog heart. Related catechols have been isolated from a number of molluscs.[153]

Serotonin (5-hydroxytryptamine) has variable circulatory effects in mammals according to species and state of the nervous system; it is primarily pressor in dogs and depressor in cats, and effects on the heart parallel those on blood pressure.[154] Molluscan hearts are much more sensitive to 5HT than are other hearts, and the threshold for *Venus* is 10^{-10}, *Spisula* 10^{-10}, *Anodonta cygnea* 10^{-9}.[56, 57, 59, 202] Snail hearts (*Buccinium*) also show increased beat in 5HT. In a crab, *Cancer,* 5HT accelerates like ACh, but at fairly high concentration. Lysergic acid diethylamide stimulates the *Venus* heart, but the brominated compound antagonizes 5HT. Gamma aminobutyric acid decreases the burst frequency and duration in lobster heart ganglia; however, it appears not to be the inhibitory transmitter in crustacean hearts in general.

EFFECTS OF SALTS ON HEARTS

Hearts continue to beat for many hours outside the animal body in a solution of properly balanced salts. The anions make little difference unless they are toxic, and most hearts beat actively in a neutral mixture of the chlorides of sodium, potassium, and calcium (see Chapter 3); a few hearts, especially those of marine molluscs, require magnesium in addition. The effects of any single cation are multiple and depend on the condition and

previous history of the heart. The effects of an ion also vary with the concentration of other ions, e.g., calcium antagonizes some effects of sodium, and potassium antagonizes some other sodium actions. Ionic ratios such as $(Na + K)/Ca$ may be more significant than absolute concentrations of each ion. The effects of excess or deficiency of an ion *in vivo* may differ from the effects of similar variations on isolated hearts. Specific ions may act differently on pacemaker, conduction, and contraction mechanisms. Ionic effects are not correlated with neurogenicity or myogenicity of a pacemaker or with cardiac innervation.

Sodium chloride comprises the bulk of the solute in all body fluids and in physiological salt solutions. Effects of a deficit in Na^+ can be ascertained only by maintaining the osmotic concentration of a solution by adding a substance such as sucrose or choline chloride; effects of excess Na^+ are difficult to separate from osmotic effects, and in pure NaCl solution there is a deficiency of K^+ and Ca^{++}. In general, high sodium concentration stimulates rate and increases amplitude and tone; low sodium reduces rate and amplitude of beat (Table 49). In pure NaCl solution the beat is often fast but irregular. The pacemaker neurons of crustacean hearts are stimulated by excess Na^+, which is antagonized in order by $Ca^{++} > K^+ > Mg^{++}$.[25]

In perfused vertebrate hearts, excess potassium may have a very slight initial stimulating effect on rate but a marked depressant action on the conducting and contracting systems so that the heart may stop in diastole. Molluscan hearts are not very sensitive to changes in potassium but may be slightly accelerated by high K^+, and great excesses (six to seven times) may stop the heart in systole; there is no such effect on contraction and conduction as in vertebrates. Arthropod hearts, with nervous pacemakers and conduction systems, are more sensitive to potassium than molluscan hearts. High potassium stimulates the pacemaker and the low-potassium effect in *Limulus* is continuous high-frequency discharge of the ganglion and interruption of the normal rhythm.[164] Rhythmic bursts of nerve impulses are converted to continuous trains by high K^+ in lobster heart. Similarly in the noninnervated myogenic heart of *Anopheles* larvae high potassium causes fast shallow beats and leads later to asynchrony.[98] A grasshopper heart is relatively insensitive to ion balance; the heart beats at a ratio Na:K over the range 3 to 30.[11]

TABLE 49.   TYPICAL EFFECTS OF IONS IN HIGH (SUPRAOPTIMAL) AND REDUCED (SUBOPTIMAL)
CONCENTRATIONS ON HEARTS WITH RESPECT TO RATE, AMPLITUDE, TONE, AND
STATE WHEN ARRESTED

Animal	Rate	Amplitude	Tone	Arrest
High Sodium				
Frog	+	sl +	+	tends to systole
Oyster	+			systole
Crayfish	+	+		systole (pure NaCl)
Limulus	+	—		
Anopheles larva	+			
Low Sodium				
Frog	—	conduction	impaired	systole
Crayfish	—	—		diastole
High Potassium				
Frog	+, then — or 0		0 or sl —	diastole
Oyster	+			6 × diastole
Venus	irregular		—	systole
Maja	+	+	+	systole
Limulus	+	fast weak beat		systole, then relaxes
Anopheles larva	+	fast weak beat		
Gryllus	+		+	
Galleria larva				systole
Low Potassium				
Frog	sl —	0, sl —	—	systole
Oyster	sl +			systole
Venus	0, sl +	—		
Homarus	+			diastole
Limulus	+	—		diastole
High Calcium				
Frog	sl +	+	+	systole
Oyster	—	+	+	diastole
Venus	—	+ then —		6 × diastole
Helix	sl —	—	—	diastole
Crayfish	—			diastole
Anopheles larva	+			
Low Calcium				
Frog	sl +, — in zero Ca	—	—	diastole
Oyster	+	—	+	diastole
Venus	+	sl —		semisystole in zero Ca
Helix	0		sl +	
Crayfish	+			systole in zero Ca
Limulus	+			systole
Galleria larva	+			

+ increase
— decrease
0 no effect

Detailed references are given in Table 69 in first edition of this book.

Calcium antagonizes the stimulating effects of potassium and sodium on pacemakers and slows heartbeats. In the perfused vertebrate heart excess calcium enhances contraction or the heart may stop in systole; in absence of calcium the vertebrate heart relaxes and stops in diastole. A heart stopped in zero calcium continues rhythmic action potentials; hence calcium is necessary for contraction. In mammalian cardiac muscle low calcium prolongs the duration of the action potential and high calcium shortens it;[88] reduced Ca initiates spontaneity in an auricle; high calcium also raises the critical potential for spike discharge from the pacemaker, hence slows the heart rate.

In molluscs the inhibiting effect of calcium on the pacemaker is predominant, and in excess Ca^{++} the heart stops in diastole by pacemaker inhibition. In the absence of calcium some molluscan hearts stop in diastole (*Pecten, Ostrea, Anomia*); in others (*Helix, Octopus*) pacemaker stimulation predominates, and in zero calcium the heart stops in systole.

In the lobster heart ganglia, high Ca^{++} prolongs the slow waves, and low calcium converts bursts to trains of impulses.

In arthropods high calcium slows the heart and stops it in diastole, whereas low Ca^{++} accelerates and zero calcium stops the heart in systole. In *Limulus* the systolic action of low calcium results from an increase in gross frequency and in number of active neurons; in zero calcium there is a tendency to asynchronization.[164] In pure $CaCl_2$ the *Anopheles* larva heart is stimulated.[98]

In summary: the pacemaker stimulation of low calcium predominates over the muscle-relaxing effect in arthropods, *Helix, Aplysia,* and *Octopus* but not in vertebrates or in *Pecten* or *Ostrea.*

Magnesium has little effect on vertebrate hearts unless external calcium is reduced; then Mg^{++} prolongs the action potential.[88] Magnesium appears essential for rhythmic beating of the hearts of marine pelecypods and gastropods. In molluscan hearts which require Mg^{++}, its omission results in acceleration and arrest in systole; in excess it inhibits the pacemaker reaction and causes diastolic arrest. Mg^{++} is toxic to several insect hearts and is not needed in a perfusion saline.

Many of the above effects are not referable to single ions but to ionic ratios. For example, in the cricket *Gryllus* optimal beat occurs at a ratio Na/K = 16:1, and at an Na/K ratio of 8, systolic arrest occurs.[16] In the grasshopper *Chortophaga* the optimal Na/K ratio is 3:1, but the heart still beats in a medium where the ratio is 34:1; it beats well over a K/Ca ratio from 1:1 to 3:1.[11, 63]

Vertebrate hearts stimulated electrically at frequencies slightly greater than the normal heart rate show "staircase" or rising tension. A high tension without any "staircase" is shown after reducing the K or increasing the Ca in the saline or after digitalis.[150, 197] Staircase is interpreted as facilitation of the excitation of the contractile proteins. Ions also affect conduction; low calcium protects against the depolarization by low K, and high Ca decreases the reduction of resting potential by high K.[88]

The mere characterization of an ion or drug as stimulating or depressing in a heart is of little value in comparing hearts or in understanding cardiac mechanisms. There is need for more detailed analysis of the cellular action of ions on pacemaker, conducting and contractile systems.

PROPERTIES OF HEART MUSCLE

The muscle tissue of various hearts differs in responses to electrical stimuli, in unit action potentials, and in histology.

A vertebrate heart is absolutely refractory to electrical stimulation during most of systole; it can be excited (is relatively refractory) at the end of systole and during diastole, but an extra contraction elicited during this time is of submaximal height. Recovery is complete by the end of diastole. Any extra contraction superimposed in a series of normal beats is followed by a compensatory pause longer than the normal diastolic pause. Any contraction, rhythmic or in response to an electrical stimulus, is maximal for the state of the heart, although a distended heart is capable of enhanced contractions, an empty mammalian heart shows some summation, and quiescent strips show staircase responses to repeated shocks. The vertebrate heart, therefore, contracts in an all-or-none fashion. When tetanized, the heart shows spasmodic uncoordinated contractions, the condition of "delirium cordis." Anodal polarization results in relaxation of the heart.

Histologically, a vertebrate heart consists of branched striated fibers. The histology, together with the all-or-none contractions, led to the view that the heart is a syncytium. However, there is some grouping of ventricular muscle in bundles,[173] and electron microscopy indicates that the intercalated discs may be complete double membranes which represent cell boundaries. In some areas these double membranes are bounded by patches of dense granules forming platelike structures.[188] Conduction through the vertebrate heart muscle may follow certain "preferred" paths and may not always be alike (turtle). Electrical resistance of strips is sensitive to interspace ion depletion.[91] Hence cardiac muscle is not a true syncytium, but the intercalated discs do not impose any resistance to conduction between fiber segments.

Intracellular electrical records from vertebrate heart muscles, either during normal beats or when stimulated electrically, show much slower repolarization after a spike than in striated muscle (Fig. 163). Purkinje fibers of a dog heart have a resting potential of 90 mv and an action potential of 121 mv which lasts 300 to 500 msecs and conducts at 2 m/sec.[205] The potential overshoot is reduced when the sodium in the medium is lowered, and conduction stops when 70 per cent of the Na^+ is replaced; hence the rising phase of the spike, like that of nerve and striated muscle, depends on a reduced membrane resistance and an influx of Na^{+}[48] (Fig. 164). Comparable results were obtained with frog ventricle; here absolute potentials are lower,[213] and duration of depolarization

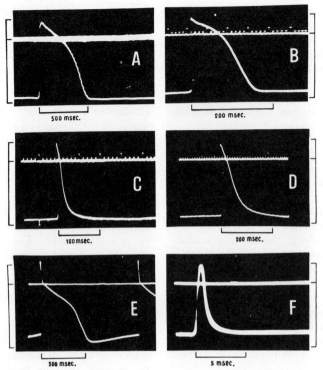

FIGURE 163. Intracellular records of action potentials from various hearts. *A*, frog heart; *B*, dog ventricle; *C*, cat ventricle; *D*, dog auricle; *E*, sheep Purkinje tissue; *F*, rat skeletal muscle. Calibration 100 mv inside negative. (From Weidman, S.: Ann. New York Acad. Sci., vol. 65.)

plateau is longer for ventricular fibers. Different heart muscles differ in duration of the action potential (Figs. 163, 165).[107] In dog, cat, and ungulates the ventricle fibers show a plateau; auricular fibers do not. Rat and mouse hearts show no plateaus. In only those hearts with long plateaus is there a T wave in the ECG. The plateau is prolonged by barium; it is shortened and the membrane

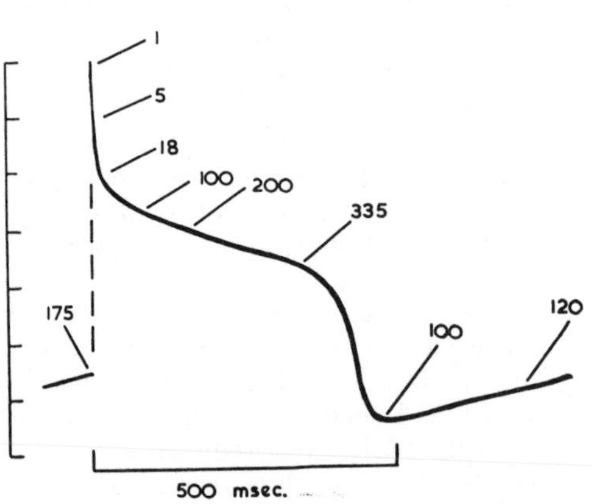

FIGURE 164. Changes in membrane resistance during a single action potential of a Purkinje fiber. Figures give membrane resistance in relative units. (From Weidman, S.: Ann. New York Acad. Sci., vol. 65.)

resistance increased by increased external potassium and by acetylcholine.[201] It appears that the falling phase of the action potential represents K^+ outflux and that the plateau results from decreased K^+ permeability.

Amphibian lymph hearts normally can be tetanized and do not give all-or-none contractions; after denervation and transplantation they resemble a myocardium in all-or-none responses and inability to be tetanized.[55]

Molluscan and arthropod hearts differ strikingly from vertebrate hearts in their responses to electrical stimulation. The muscle of these hearts is excitable at all phases of the cycle, but the threshold is high in systole. An extra contraction is not followed by a corresponding compensatory pause. On repeated stimulation the amplitude of contraction increases and most molluscan and arthropod hearts can be tetanized. These hearts do not contract in an all-or-none fashion; a normal contraction is never maximal. The graded contractions of molluscan and arthropod hearts are not related to the nature of the pacemakers. Anodal polarization slows or stops the heart in diastole as in vertebrates. This graded behavior has been observed in hearts of *Mytilus, Cardium, Ariolimax, Panu-*

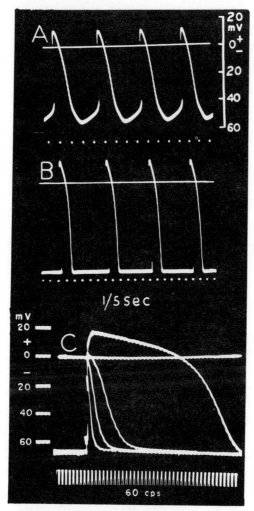

FIGURE 165. Intracellular potentials from heart muscle. *A*, frog sinus venosus, spontaneous pacemaker potentials preceding spikes. *B*, frog auricle, conducted spikes only. *C*, tortoise sinus venosus, electrically driven; *upper record*, before, and *lower records*, during vagal inhibition. (From Hutter, O. F., and Trautwein, W.: J. Gen. Physiol., vol. 39.)

lirus, Limulus, Homarus, Astacus, Periplaneta, Anodonta, and *Octopus*.

Histologically the muscle of molluscan and arthropod hearts is usually striated, sometimes transversely and sharply, sometimes spirally and weakly. This muscle has not been studied by the electron microscope.

Intracellular records from the cicada heart show simple monophasic spikes.[96]

The differences between mollusc-arthropod hearts and vertebrate hearts in response to electrical stimulation, in all-or-none properties, and in action potential duration may eventually be correlated with differences in their histology.

CONCLUSIONS

To be of adaptive value a circulatory system must respond to stress; blood must be available where it is needed—in adequate amounts when required. Open systems—coelom, pseudocoel, or hemocoel—without hearts are adequate where respiratory and nutritional demands are not great. With increase in body size and activity, hearts came into use in some open systems as in crustaceans and molluscs. These hearts are incapable of developing high pressures, however, and circulatory flow is accomplished in part by contraction of somatic muscles. The blood volume is large and transport of oxygen from gills to muscles is relatively slow. Annelids have closed blood vessels, particularly for oxygen transfer, but the coelom remains the main circulatory mechanism for excretion and nutrition. The open system is used in insects, in which the hemocoel performs minor functions only, and transport of air is in tubes direct to the muscles. In some crustaceans the arterial vessels branch extensively before opening to tissue spaces. In cephalopods and vertebrates most of the circulatory system is in closed vessels with the result that systemic pressure is high, velocity of blood flow is high, and blood volume is low. In lower vertebrates the open lymph system with accessory lymph hearts is more important than in higher vertebrates. Among vertebrates there are complex reflex and hormonal systems for maintenance of blood pressure; the extent of pressure-regulating systems among invertebrates is unknown. Frequently the fluid-filled cavities may be less important for circulation than to provide hydrostatic skeleton; such skeletons become rigid or flaccid on demand, are particularly useful for burrowing, but lack the local control and protection afforded by segmented and external skeletons.

Heart muscle in all animal groups has some of the properties of visceral and some of somatic muscle. The vertebrate heart tends to contract in an all-or-none fashion, molluscan and arthropod hearts less so. The property of rhythmic activity is inherent in many nerve cells and visceral muscles, and it is possible that the chemical basis for rhythmicity is similar in all pacemakers. Myogenicity, which is more primitive, is retained in adult vertebrates and molluscs but is replaced by neurogenicity in many adult arthropods. The small number of neurons in crustacean pacemaker ganglia constitutes a complicated integration system. Active heart muscle of vertebrates shows very prolonged action potentials; muscle potentials of invertebrate hearts are more like those of striated muscle.

Nervous regulation of heartbeat has evolved numerous times, often with inhibitory fibers, sometimes with both inhibitory and augmenting fibers. Most embryonic hearts beat before they are innervated, and in some animals—*Artemia,* many insects such as *Anopheles* larvae, and in myxinoid fish—the hearts remain myogenic and noninnervated. Activity in cardiac nerves is associated with liberation of chemical mediators. The inhibitory mediator is acetylcholine in vertebrates and in some molluscs; the accelerator is epinephrine-norepinephrine in vertebrates, and serotonin in some molluscs. The action of various drugs and salts on hearts depends on what effect is measured and whether the heart is myogenic or neurogenic, and, if myogenic, whether it is innervated or noninnervated.

The evolution of circulatory mechanisms shows many parallel developments, each tending to make a given volume of fluid serve more efficiently the transport needs of the animal. Recognition of varied patterns of peripheral circulation, hemodynamics, and cardiac physiology and pharmacology is more fruitful than attempts to fit many patterns into single schemes.

REFERENCES

1. ALEXANDROWICZ, J. S., J. Mar. Biol. Assn. U. K. *31*: 85-96, 1952; *33*: 709-710, 1954; *34*: 47-53, 1955. Quart. J. Micr. Sci. *75*: 291-309, 1932. Innervation of crustacean hearts.
2. ALEXANDROWICZ, J. S., and Carlisle, D. B., J. Mar. Biol. Assn. U. K. *32*: 175-192, 1953. Function of pericardial organ, crustaceans.
3. ARMIN, J., *et al.,* J. Physiol. *116*: 59-73, 1952. Blood volume, rabbits.
4. ARMSTRONG, P. B., J. Physiol. *84*: 20-32, 1935. Acetylcholine action and development of vagus, fish hearts.
5. AUGUSTINSSON, K. B., *et al.,* J. Physiol. *131*: 257-276, 1956. Histology, biochemistry, and physiology of cyclostome hearts, Myxine and Lampetra.
6. BABKIN, B. P., BOWIE, D. J., and NICHOLLS, J. V., Contr. Canad. Biol. Fish. N. S. *8*: 209-219, 1933. Circulatory reactions of skate, Raja, to drugs.
7. BACQ, Z. M., Bull. Acad. Roy. Med. Belg. Cl. Sci. *20*: 1042-1061, 1934. Physiology of heart of ascidian, Ciona.
8. BACQ, Z. M., *et al.,* Arch. Int. Physiol. *60*: 165-171, 1952. Effect of 5HT on cephalopod hearts.

9. BAKKER, N. C., Ztschr. Biol. *59*: 335-365, 1912. Electrocardiogram, eel.
10. BARCROFT, J., and BARRON, D. H., J. Exp. Biol. *22*: 63-74, 1945. Blood pressure in fetal sheep.
11. BARSA, M. C., J. Gen. Physiol. *38*: 79-92, 1954. Ion effects on heart of grasshopper Chortophaga.
12. BATHAM, E. J., and PANTIN, C. F. A., J. Exp. Biol. *27*: 264-288, 1950. Hydrostatic skeleton of sea anemone Metridium.
13. BAYLOR, E. R., Biol. Bull. *83*: 165-172, 1942. Effect of acetylcholine on Daphnia heart.
14. BEARD, R. L., J. New York Entomol. Soc. *57*: 79-91, 1949. Blood volume, larva of Japanese beetle.
15. BEKKER, J. M., and KRIJGSMAN, B. J., J. Physiol. *115*: 249-257, 1951. Drugs on Daphnia heart.
16. BERGERARD, J., *et al.,* C. R. Soc. Biol. Paris *141*: 1079-1083, 1947; Arch. Sci. Physiol. *4*: 225-240, 1950. Ions on cricket heart.
17. BERMAN, H. J., *et al.,* Fed. Proc. *15*: 17, 1956. Blood pressure, hamster.
18. BERTHE, J., and PETITFRERE, C., Arch. Internat. Physiol. *39*: 98-111, 1934. Automaticity of heart of Anodonta.
19. BIORCK, G., and JOHANSSON, B., Acta physiol. scand. *34*: 257-272, 1955. Vertebrate electrocardiograms.
20. BOYD, I. A., and MACKAY, A. M., J. Physiol. *139*: 11P-12P, 1957. Blood pressure of frog.
21. BRAND, E. D., BRITTON, S. W., and FRENCH, C. R., Am. J. Physiol. *165*: 539-547, 1951. Effect of gravity on circulation, various vertebrates.
22. *BROOKS, C. M., HOFFMAN, B. F., and SUCKLING, E. E., Excitability of the Heart. New York, Grune & Stratton, 1955, 373 pp.
23. *BROWN, E., HOFFER, J., and WENNESLAND, R., Ann. Rev. Physiol. *19*: 231-254, 1957. Blood volume and its regulation.
24. BRULL, L., and CUYPERS, Y., Arch. Int. Physiol. *62*: 70-78, 1954. Blood pressure of Lophius.
25. BULLOCK, T. H., and TERZUOLA, C. A., J. Physiol. *138*: 341-364, 1957. Activity of neurons in crustacean heart ganglion.
26. BURGER, J. W., and BRADLEY, S. E., J. Cell. Comp. Physiol. *37*: 389-402, 1951. Circulation of dogfish, Squalus.
27. BURGER, J. W., and SMYTHE, C. M., J. Cell. Comp. Physiol. *42*: 369-383, 1953. Circulation of lobster, Homarus.
28. BURKE, J. D., Physiol. Zool. *27*: 1-21, 1954. Blood volume in mammals.
29. BURN, J. H., *et al.,* J. Physiol. *128*: 277-283, 1955. Excitatory action of acetylcholine on mammalian heart.
30. CARLSON, A. J., Am. J. Physiol. *22*: 353-356, 1908. Nerve cells in hearts of Nereis and Arenicola.
31. *CARLSON, A. J., Ergebn. Physiol. *8*: 371-462, 1909; Am. J. Physiol. *14*: 16-53, 1905. Invertebrate hearts.
32. CARLSON, A. J., Am. J. Physiol. *12*: 67-74, 1904; *15*: 207-234, 1906; *17*: 177-210, 1906; *21*: 1-10, 1908. Limulus heart physiology.
33. CHAPMAN, G., J. Exp. Biol. *27*: 29-39, 1950. Hydrostatics of worms.

* Reviews

34. *CHAPMAN, G., Biol. Rev. 33: 338-371, 1958. Hydrostatic skeletons.

35. CHAPMAN, G., and NEWELL, G. E., Proc. Roy. Soc. London, B, 145: 564-580, 1956. Hydrostatics of siphon extension in clams.

36. *CLARK, A. J., Comparative Physiology of the Heart. Cambridge University Press, 1927, 157 pp.

37. CLOSE, R. I., M.S. Thesis, Victoria Univ. Coll., New Zealand, pp. 1-44, 1955. Resistance to blood flow in gills of Anguilla.

38. COON, R. F., J. Econ. Entomol. 37: 785-789, 1944. Circulation in cockroach.

39. COULSON, R. A., et al., Proc. Soc. Exp. Biol. Med. 73: 203-206, 1950. Blood volume in alligator.

40. CRAIG, R., and OLSON, N. A., Science 113: 648-650, 1951. Circulation rate, insect.

41. CRESCITELLI, F., and JAHN, T. L., J. Cell. Comp. Physiol. 11: 359-376, 1938. Electrocardiogram, grasshopper.

42. CULLIS, W. C., and LUCAS, C. L. T., J. Physiol. 86: 53P-55P, 1936. Action of ACh on aneural chick heart.

43. DAVENPORT, D., Physiol. Zool. 14: 178-185, 1941; 22: 35-44, 1949; Biol. Bull. 79: 498-507, 1940. Pharmacology of invertebrate hearts.

44. DAVIES, F., et al., Nature 167: 146, 1951. Electrocardiogram, crocodile.

45. DAVIS, C. C., J. Cell. Comp. Physiol. 47: 449-468, 1956. Experiments on heart of larvae of dipteran, Chaoborus.

46. DIVARIS, G. A., and KRIJGSMAN, B. J., Arch. Int. Physiol. 62: 211-233, 1954. Heart function in snail Achatina.

47. DRAPER, M. H., and MYA-TU, M., Quart. J. Exp. Physiol. 44: 71-109, 1959. Conduction velocity in cardiac tissues.

48. DRAPER, M. H., and WEIDMANN, S., J. Physiol. 115: 74-94, 1951. Intracellular records of cardiac action potentials.

49. DUBUISSON, M., Arch. Biol. 38: 9-21, 1928. Pressure in Maja circulation.

50. DUWEZ, Y., C. R. Soc. Biol. 122: 84-87, 1936. Electrocardiogram, Dytiscus.

51. EBARA, A., Sci. Rep. Tokyo Bunrika Daig. B, 7: 199-209, 1954. Reversal of heartbeat in ascidians.

52. EBARA, A., Sci. Rep. Tokyo Kyoiku Daig. 7: 127-138, 1955. Nervous control of molluscan heart.

53. EDMONDS, S. J., Austral. J. Mar. Freshwater Res. 8: 55-63, 1957. Blood volume of Dendrostomum.

54. ELLIS, C. H., Biol. Bull. 86: 41-50, 1944. Mechanics of leg extension, spiders.

55. ENDERLE, J., Arch. Int. Physiol. 58: 361-385, 1951. Automatism of amphibian lymph hearts.

56. ERSPAMER, V., and GHIRETTI, F., J. Physiol. 115: 470-481, 1951. Action of 5HT on mollusc hearts.

57. ERSPAMER, V., and ASERO, B., Nature 169: 800-801, 1952. Identification of enteramine as 5HT.

58. EVANS, C. L., Ztschr. Biol. 59: 397-414, 1912. Electrocardiogram, Helix.

59. FÄNGE, R., Experientia 11: 156, 1955. Effect of 5HT on mussel heart.

60. FÄNGE, R., and OSTLUND, E., Acta Zool. 35: 289-305, 1954. Drug effects on teleost, elasmobranch, and cephalopod hearts.

61. FEAKES, M. J., et al., J. Exp. Biol. 27: 50-58, 1950. Effect of pituitary hormones on blood pressure of Ornithorhynchus.

62. FEDERIGHI, H., J. Exp. Zool. 60: 257-294, 1928. Contraction of Rouget type cells in annelid vessels.

63. FISZER, J., C. R. Soc. Biol. Paris 144: 812-814, 1956. Drug action on heart of cricket.

64. *FOLKOW, B., Physiol. Rev. 35: 629-663, 1955. Nervous control of blood vessels.

65. *FOXON, G. E. H., Biol. Rev. 30: 196-228, 1955. Problems of the double circulation in vertebrates.

66. FOXON, G. E. H., et al., Proc. Zool. Soc. London 126: 145-157, 1956. Blood flow in lizard heart.

67. FREDERICQ, H., Bull. Acad. Roy. Med. Belg. 25: 611-623, 1939. Effects of drugs and nerves on cephalopod hearts.

68. FREDERICQ, H., Publ. Staz. Zool. Napoli 27: 114-120, 1955. Postganglionic vagus fiber stimulation in heart of turtle.

69. FREDERICQ, H., and BACQ, Z. M., Arch. Internat. Physiol. 49: 490-496, 1939; 50: 169-184, 1940. Effects of drugs and nerves on cephalopod hearts.

70. GADDUM, J. H., and PAASONEN, M. K., Brit. J. Pharmacol. 10: 474-483, 1955. Use of molluscan hearts for assay of 5HT.

71. GAMBLE, F. W., and ASHWORTH, J. H., Quart. J. Micr. Sci. 41: 1-42, 1898. Anatomy of Arenicola.

72. GASKELL, J. F., Phil. Tr. Roy. Soc. London, B, 205: 153-210, 1914. Pharmacology of blood vessels of leech.

73. GEROULD, J. H., Biol. Bull. 64: 424-431, 1933; Acta Zool. Stockholm 19: 297-352, 1938. Reversal of direction of beat in insect hearts.

74. GREENE, C. W., Bull. U. S. Bur. Fish. 24: 429-456, 1904. Blood pressure of salmon.

75. *GREGERSEN, M. I., and RAWSON, R. A., Physiol. Rev. 39: 307-342, 1959. Blood volume.

76. HAGIWARA, S., and BULLOCK, T. H., J. Cell. Comp. Physiol. 50: 25-47, 1957. Intracellular potentials in lobster cardiac ganglion neurons.

77. HALL, E. K., Anat. Rec. 111: 381-400, 1951; 118: 175-184, 1954; J. Cell. Comp. Physiol. 49: 187-200, 1957; 53: 31-40, 1959. Intrinsic contractility and drug effects in heart of rat embryo.

78. HAMILTON, H. L., J. Cell. Comp. Physiol. 13: 91-104, 1939. Effect of drugs on grasshopper heart (Melanoplus).

79. HARRIS, J. E., and CROFTON, H. O., J. Exp. Biol. 34: 116-130, 1957. Internal pressure in nematodes.

80. HART, J. S., Canad. J. Res. D, 21: 77-84, 1943. Cardiac output, fresh-water fish.

81. HART, J. S., Proc. Florida Acad. Sci. 7: 221-246, 1944. Blood pressure and cardiac output, fish.

82. HART, J. S., Canad. J. Zool. 35: 195-200, 1957. Circulation in fish.

83. HAYWOOD, C. A., and MOON, H. P., J. Exp. Biol. 27: 14-28, 1950. Mechanics of vascular system of tunicate Ascidiella.

84. HECHT, H. H., Ann. New York Acad. Sci. *65*: 700-733, 1957. Transmembrane potentials of frog heart.

85. HERRICK, F. H., Bull. U. S. Bur. Fish. *29*: 149-408, 1909. Morphology of circulatory system, lobster.

86. HOFF, H. E., *in* Howell's Textbook of Physiology, edited by J. F. Fulton. Philadelphia, W. B. Saunders Co., 1946, pp. 717-780. Cardiac cycle.

87. HOFF, E. C., *et al.,* Am. Heart J. *17*: 470-488, 1939. Development of electrocardiogram.

88. HOFFMAN, B. F., and SUCKLING, E. E., Am. J. Physiol. *170*: 357-362, 1952; *173*: 312-320, 1953; *186*: 317-324, 1956. Transmembrane potentials, mammalian heart fibers; effects of drugs, ions, and vagus nerve.

89. HOFFMAN, P., Arch. f. Anat. Physiol. pp. 135-174, 1911; Ztschr. Biol. *59*: 297-313, 1912. Electrocardiograms of invertebrates.

90. HOGBEN, L. T., and HOBSON, A. D., J. Exp. Biol. *1*: 487-500, 1924. Effect of drugs on hearts of Maja and Pecten.

91. HOSHIKO, T., *et al.,* Proc. Soc. Exp. Biol. Med. *101*: 602-604, 1959. Impedance measurements on cardiac muscle.

92. HUANG, K., and BOUDURANT, J. H., Am. J. Physiol. *185*: 441-445, 1956. Blood volume, extracellular space in rats.

93. HUGGEL, H. J., Rev. Suisse Zool. *66*: 315-321, 1959. Blood pressure, bat.

94. HUTTER, O. F., and TRAUTWEIN, W., J. Gen. Physiol. *39*: 715-733, 1956. Vagal and sympathetic effects on pacemaker potentials in heart, frog.

95. INADA, C., Master's thesis, University of Illinois, 1947. Blood pressure in animals with open circulatory systems.

96. IRISAWA, H., *et al.,* Jap. J. Physiol. *6*: 150-161, 1956. Electrograms of heart of cicada.

97. IRVING, L., *et al.,* J. Physiol. *84*: 187-190, 1935. Branchial pressure receptors in dogfish.

98. JONES, J. C., J. Morphol. *94*: 71-123, 1954; J. Exp. Zool. *133*: 125-144, 573-589, 1956. Heart of Anopheles, histology and effects of salts and drugs.

99. JULLIEN, A., Des réactions comparées des coeurs de vertébrés et d'invertébrés vis-à-vis des electrolytes et des drogues. 1936. Paris, Baillière, Tindale & Cox, 210 pp.

100. JULLIEN, A., and RIPPLINGER, J., C. R. Soc. Biol. Paris *140*: 1186-1189, 1951; *145*: 1560-1563, 1951; *146*: 1326-1329, 1952. Effects of vagus nerve and of acetylcholine on fish hearts.

101. JULLIEN, A., and RIPPLINGER, J., C. R. Soc. Biol. Paris *144*: 544-545, 1950; *146*: 1943-1946, 1952; *149*: 722-723, 1955; *150*: 190-196, 1956; J. Physiol., Paris *421*: 613-615, 1950; *47*: 200-205, 1955. Effects of acetylcholine, liberation of ACh-like substance, Helix heart.

102. JULLIEN, A., *et al.,* C. R. Soc. Biol. Paris *127*: 621-623, 1938; *129*: 667-670, 1938. Drugs on molluscan hearts.

103. KANUNGO, M. S., Biol. Bull. *113*: 135-140, 1957. Effects of drugs on scorpion heart.

104. KEYS, A., and BATEMAN, B., Biol. Bull. *63*: 327-336, 1932. Branchial responses to adrenaline in eel.

105. KHALIL, F., and MALEK, S. R. A., Physiol. Comp. Oecol. *2*: 386-390, 1952. Nervous control of lizard heart.

106. KISCH, B., Am. J. Physiol. *160*: 552-555, 1950. Reflex control of heart of ganoid fish Acipenser.

107. KLEINFELD, M., *et al.,* Circulation Res. *2*: 488-493, 1954. Barium effects on ventricular fibers of frog.

108. KLEMENT, A. W., *et al.,* Am. J. Physiol. *181*: 15-18, 1955. Blood volume, goat.

109. KRIEGER, H., *et al.,* Proc. Soc. Exp. Biol. Med. *68*: 511-515, 1948. Blood volume, several methods, dog.

110. *KRIJGSMAN, B. J., Biol. Rev. *27*: 320-346, 1952. Physiology of arthropod hearts, especially Periplaneta.

111. *KRIJGSMAN, B. J., Biol. Rev. *31*: 288-312, 1956. Pacemaker function in hearts of tunicates.

112. *KRIJGSMAN, B. J., and DIVARIS, G. A., Biol. Rev. *30*: 1-39, 1955. Contractile and pacemaker mechanisms in hearts of molluscs.

113. KRIJGSMAN, B. J., and KRIJGSMAN, N. E., Nature *165*: 936-937, 1950; Bull. Entomol. Res. *42*: 143-155, 1951. Physiology of heart of Periplaneta.

114. KRIJGSMAN, B. J., and KRIJGSMAN, N. E., Arch. Internat. Physiol. *67*: 567-585, 1959. Pacemaker function in heart of Ciona.

115. KROGH, A., Osmotic Regulation in Aquatic Animals. Cambridge University Press, 1939, pp. 65-98. Water distribution crustacea, thiocyanate space in Eriocheir.

116. KRUTA, V., C. R. Soc. Biol. Paris *122*: 583-585, 1936. Cardiac effects of visceral nerves in cephalopods.

117. LANE, C. E., and TIERNEY, J. Q., Bull. Mar. Sci. Gulf Carib. *1*: 104-110, 1951. Hydrodynamics and respiration in Teredo.

118. LAURENT, P., J. Physiol. Paris *49*: 254-259, 1957. Afferent impulses in cardiac nerve of teleosts.

119. LAVOIE, M. E., Biol. Bull. *111*: 114-122, 1956. How sea stars open bivalves.

120. *LEHMAN, G., Tabul. Biol. *1*: 107-150, 1925. Circulatory constants.

121. LITCHFIELD, J. B., Physiol. Zool. *31*: 1-6, 1958. Blood pressure, infant rats.

122. LUDUENA, F. P., and BROWN, T. G., J. Pharmacol. Exper. Therap. *105*: 232-239, 1952. Mytolon and related antagonists of ACh on Venus heart.

123. LUISADA, A., J. Physiol. Path. Gén. *30*: 593-603, 1932. Electrocardiograms from Octopus.

124. LUTZ, B. R., Biol. Bull. *59*: 170-186, 211-221, 1930. Innervation of heart and cardiac reflexes in elasmobranch Scyllium.

125. MARCEAU, F., C. R. Acad. Sci. Paris *138*: 1177-1179, 1904; *139*: 150-152, 1904. Histology of molluscan hearts.

126. MARSHALL, L. H., and HANNA, C. H., Proc. Soc. Exp. Biol. Med. *92*: 31-32, 1956. Blood pressure in guinea pig.

127. MASOUREDI, S. P., and MELDER, L. R., Proc. Soc. Exp. Biol. Med. *78*: 264-266, 1951. Blood volume in guinea pig.

128. MARTIN, A. W., *in* Studies Honoring T. Kin-

caid. University of Washington Press, 1950, pp. 125-140. Blood volume of fish.

129. MARTIN, A. W., *et al.,* Fed. Proc. *15*: 125, 1956; J. Exp. Biol. *35*: 260-279, 1958. Blood volumes of various molluscs.

130. MATSUI, K., Sci. Rep. Tokyo Kyoika Daig. B, *7*: 231-256, 257-268; *8*: 148-177, 1957; Jap. J. Zool. *12*: 189-201, 1958. Electrocardiogram of lobster, extracellular and intracellular.

131. MAYER, E., Ztschr. Morph. Ökol. Tiere. *22*: 1-52, 1931. Circulation, pressure, dragonfly nymphs.

132. MAYNARD, D. M., Biol. Bull. *104*: 156-170, 1953; *109*: 420-436, 1955. Activity patterns and extrinsic control of cardiac ganglion, lobster.

133. McDOWALL, R. J. S., J. Physiol. *104*: 392-402, 1946. Stimulation of heart by ACh.

134. McKAY, M. E., Contr. Canad. Biol. Fish. N. S. *7*: 17-29, 1931. Effect of drugs on circulation of skate.

135. McLAIN, P. L., *et al.,* Am. J. Physiol. *164*: 611-617, 1951. Comparison of methods for blood volume.

136. MENDES, E. G., Zoologica *21*: 55-68, 1957. Pharmacology, hearts of Hemiptera.

137. MENDES, E. G., and NANATO, E. F., Zoologia *21*: 153-166, 1957. Cutaneous circulation in earthworms.

138. MILLAR, R. H., Nature *170*: 851-852, 1952. Reversal of heart beat in tunicates.

139. MILLMAN, N., Master's thesis, Brown University, 1938. Heart physiology of Galleria.

140. MISLIN, H., Experientia *6*: 46-468, 1950. Regulation of circulation in Octopus.

141. MOTLEY, H. L., Physiol. Zool. 7: 62-84, 1934. Physiology and pharmacology of heart of fresh-water mussels.

142. MOTT, J. C., J. Physiol. *114*: 387-398, 1951. Control of circulation in eel.

143. MUNSON, S. C., and YEAGER, J. F., Ann. Entomol. Soc. America *42*: 165-173, 1949. Blood volume, Periplaneta.

144. NAIDU, M. B., Bull. Entomol. Res. *46*: 205-220, 1955. Effect of ions and drugs on heart of cockroach.

145. NAVEZ, A. E., Mem. Mus. Nat. Hist. Belg. *3*: 701-737, 1936. Cardiac rhythm in mollusc, Anomia.

146. NEEDHAM, A. E., Nature *166*: 9-11, 1950. Effect of ether on cardiac pacemakers.

147. NEIL, E., and ZOTTERMAN, Y., Acta physiol. scand. *20*: 160-165, 1950. Vagal afferent fibers in cat and frog.

148. NEWELL, G. E., J. Exp. Biol. *27*: 110-121, 1950. Hydrostatic pressure in movements of earthworms.

149. *NICOL, J. A. C., Biol. Rev. *27*: 1-49, 1952. Autonomic nervous system of lower chordates.

150. NIEDERGERKE, R., J. Physiol. *134*: 569-583, 1956. Action of Ca^{++} on heart.

151. NIZET, E., and DOHRN, A., C. R. Soc. Biol. Paris *146*: 1831-1833, 1952. Blood pressure in Scyllium.

152. OETS, J., Physiol. Comp. Oecol. *2*: 181-186, 1950. Electrocardiogram, fish.

153. ÖSTLUND, E., Acta physiol. scand. *31,* sup.

112: 1-67, 1954. Distribution of catechol amines in lower animals.

154. PAGE, I. H., J. Pharm. Exp. Therap. *105*: 58-73, 1952. Vascular action of serotonin.

155. PANTIN, C. F. A., and SAWAYA, P., Zoologia *18*: 51-60, 1953. Coelomic pressure in Holothuria.

156. PATTEN, B. M., Am. Scientist *39*: 225-243, 1951; Am. J. Anat. *53*: 349-375, 1933. Initiation of beats in chick heart.

157. PEARSON, J., Liverpool Mar. Biol. Comm. Mem. *16*: 1-209, 1908. Cancer.

158. PICKEN, L. E. R., J. Exp. Biol. *13*: 309-328, 1936. Blood pressure in crustaceans and *Peripatopsis.*

159. PILGRIM, R. L. C., J. Physiol. *25*: 208-214, 1954. Action of drugs on hearts of bivalve molluscs.

160. PLATTNER, F., and HOU, C. L., Pflüg. Arch. Physiol. *228*: 281-294, 1931. ACh on chick heart.

161. PRATT, F. H., and REID, M. A., Proc. Soc. Exp. Biol. Med. *29*: 1019-1021, 1932. Activity of transplanted lymph hearts.

162. PROSSER, C. L., Biol. Bull. *83*: 92-102, 1940; *83*: 145-164, 1942. Effects of drugs on hearts of *Venus, Limulus* embryos, various arthropods.

163. PROSSER, C. L., Biol. Bull. *78*: 92-102, 1940. Acetylcholine and nervous inhibition, Venus heart.

164. PROSSER, C. L., J. Cell. Comp. Physiol. *21*: 295-305, 1943; Biol. Bull. *98*: 254-257, 1950. Pacemaker discharge, Limulus heart; ECG of Arenicola.

165. PROSSER, C. L., and JUDSON, C., Biol. Bull. *102*: 249-251, 1952. Effects of drugs on heart of *Stichopus.*

166. PROSSER, C. L., and WEINSTEIN, S. J. F., Physiol. Zool. *23*: 113-124, 1950. Blood volume, catfish, crayfish.

167. PROSSER, C. L., and ZIMMERMAN, G. L., Physiol. Zool. *16*: 77-83, 1943. Effects of drugs on hearts of annelids, Arenicola, Lumbricus.

168. RANSOM, W. B., J. Physiol. *5*: 261-341, 1883. Cardiac rhythm of invertebrates, particularly molluscs and tunicates.

169. REICHERT, E. T., and BROWN, A. P., Carnegie Inst. Washington Publ. no. 116, 1909. Blood volume data.

170. REID, M. A., J. Exp. Zool. *76*: 47-65, 1937. Activity of transplanted lymph hearts.

171. RETZIUS, G., Biol. Unters. *12*: 75-78, 1905. Nerve cells on blood vessels of polychaetes.

172. REYNOLDS, M., Am. J. Physiol. *173*: 420-427, 1953. Blood volume of cow.

173. ROBB, J. S., Am. J. Physiol. *172*: 7-13, 1953. Specialized conducting tissue in turtle heart.

174. RODBARD, S., *et al.,* Am. J. Physiol. *160*: 402-408, 1950. Temperature on vasomotor control in turtle.

175. ROGERS, C. G., Textbook of Comparative Physiology. New York, McGraw-Hill Book Co., 1938, 715 pp.

176. SARAJAS, S., Acta physiol. scand. *32*: 28-38, 1954. Electrocardiogram of hedgehog.

177. SCHAFER, G. D., Stanford University Publ. Sci. *3*: 307-337, 1923. Pressure in hemocoel of insects.

178. Schlieper, C., Kieler Meeresforsch. *11*: 139-148, 1955. Effects of O_2 and CO_2 on heart rate of Mytilus.

179. Schoenlein, C., Ztschr. Biol. *32*: 511-547, 1895. Circulatory pressure, elasmobranchs.

180. Schoenlein, C., and Willem, V., Bull. Scient. France Belg. *26*: 442-468, 1894. Circulatory pressure, elasmobranchs.

181. Schwartzkopff, J., Naturwissenschaften *40*: 585-586, 1953; Experientia *11*: 323-325, 1955; Biol. Zentbl. *74*: 480-497, 1955. Comparative study of cardiac efficiency, especially in crustaceans.

182. Schwartzkopff, J., Ztschr. vergl. Physiol. *36*: 543-594, 1954. Cardiac efficiency, Helix.

183. Semple, R. E., Fed. Proc. *19*: 79, 1960. Blood volume in turtle.

184. Serfaty, A., and Reynaud, P., J. Physiol. Paris *49*: 378-381, 1957; Bull. Soc. Zool. Fr. *82*: 49-56, 1957. Control of heart rate, electrocardiogram, fish hearts.

185. Shannon, E. W., and Wiggers, C. J., Am. J. Physiol. *128*: 709-715, 1939. Dynamics of frog and turtle heart.

186. Silen, L., Acta Zool. *35*: 11-70, 1954. Circulatory system of isopods.

187. Sippel, T. O., J. Exp. Zool. *128*: 165-184, 1955. Development of cholinesterase in hearts.

188. Sjöstrand, F. S., et al., J. Ultrastr. Res. *1*: 271-287, 1958. Ultrastructure of intercalated disks of cardiac muscle.

189. *von Skramlik, E., Ergebn. Biol. *11*: 1-130, 1935; *18*: 88-286, 1941. Circulation in fishes, molluscs, and ascidians.

190. Smith, C. C., and Ansevin, A., Proc. Soc. Biol. Med. *96*: 428-432, 1957. Blood pressure of rhesus monkey.

191. Smith, J. E., Phil. Tr. Roy. Soc. London, B, *232*: 279-310, 1946. Mechanics of starfish tube foot-ampulla system.

192. Smith, R., Biol. Bull. *93*: 72-88, 1947. Action of nerves and drugs on heart of Cancer.

193. Spadolini, I., J. Physiol. *109*: 308-313, 1949. Dual action of ACh on toad heart.

194. Steggerda, F. R., and Essex, H. E., Am. J. Physiol. *190*: 320-326, 1957. Circulation in turtle.

195. Stubl, H., Pflüg. Arch. Physiol. *129*: 1-34, 1909. Rhythm of earthworm pulsating vessels.

196. Sturkie, P. D., et al., Fed. Proc. *12*: 140, 1953; Am. J. Physiol. *174*: 405-409, 1953. Blood pressure, chickens.

197. Szent-Györgyi, A., in Chemical Physiology of Contraction in Body and Heart Muscle. New York, Academic Press, 1953, Chap. 12.

198. Taylor, I. R., and Walzl, E. M., J. Cell. Comp. Physiol. *18*: 278-280, 1941. Electrocardiogram of oyster.

199. TenCate, J., and Resinck, M. J., Physiol. Comp. Oecol. *3*: 337-342, 1954. Effect of drugs on heart of Anodonta.

200. Thorson, T. B., Physiol. Zool. *31*: 16-23, 1958; Science *130*: 99, 1959. Fluid compartments in sea lamprey and in various fish.

201. Trautwein, W., and Dudel, J., Pflüg. Arch. Physiol. *266*: 324-334, 653-664, 1958. Action of acetylcholine on membrane of heart muscle.

202. Twarog, B., and Page, I. H., Am. J. Physiol. *175*: 157-161, 1953. Sensitivity of molluscan hearts to 5-hydroxytryptamine.

203. von Uexkull, J., Ztschr. Biol. *44*: 269-344, 1903. Hydrostatic pressures in Sipunculus.

204. *Visscher, M. B., and Stephens, G. J., Ann. Rev. Physiol. *19*: 359-385, 1957. Heart.

205. Weidmann, S., Ann. New York Acad. Sci. *65*: 663-678, 1957. Resting and action potentials of cardiac muscle.

206. Welsh, J. H., J. Exp. Biol. *16*: 198-219, 1939; Physiol. Zool. *12*: 231-237, 1939; J. Cell. Comp. Physiol. *19*: 271-279, 1942. Effect of acetylcholine on crustacean hearts.

207. Welsh, J. H., Nature *173*: 955, 1954; Biol. Bull. *102*: 48-57, 1952; J. Mar. Biol. Assn. U. K. *35*: 193-201, 1956; Ann. New York Acad. Sci. *66*: 618-630, 1957. Use of molluscan hearts for assay of ACh and 5HT; chemical transmitters in regulation of molluscan hearts.

208. Welsh, J. H., and McCoy, A. C., Science *125*: 348, 1957. Chemical transmitters in regulation of molluscan hearts.

209. White, F. N., Anat. Rec. *125*: 417-432, 1956. Blood flow in reptilian heart.

210. Wiersma, C. A. G., and Novitski, E., J. Exp. Biol. *19*: 255-265, 1942. Nervous regulation of crayfish heart.

211. *Wigglesworth, V., Principles of Insect Physiology. London, Methuen & Co., 1939, Chap. 10.

212. Wilber, C. G., J. Mammal. *36*: 283-286, 1955. Electrocardiogram of raccoon.

213. Woodbury, L. A., et al., Am. J. Physiol. *164*: 307-318, 1951. Membrane potentials of single cardiac muscle fibers, frog.

214. Wooley, P., J. Exp. Biol. *36*: 453-458, 1959. Effect of posterior pituitary extracts on blood pressure of various vertebrates.

215. Yazaki, M., Sci. Rep. Tohoku Univ., Ser. IV, *5*: 403-414, 1930. Circulation and pressure in holothurian, Caudina.

216. Yeager, J. F., and Munson, S. C., Arthropoda *1*: 255-265, 1950. Blood volume, insects.

217. Yeager, J. F., and Tauber, O. E., Ann. Entomol. Soc. America *25*: 315-327, 1932. Blood volume, insects.

218. Zuckerkandl, E., Biol. Bull. *98*: 161-173, 1950. Pressure in holothurians and sipunculids.

219. Zuckerkandl, E., Cahiers de Biol. Mar. *1*: 25-36, 1960. Blood volume of Maja.

Chapter 14

MUSCLE AND ELECTRIC ORGANS

The speed of locomotion of an animal, and hence its ability to get food and to escape from predators, is limited by the reaction times of its muscles. Muscles perform, in addition to locomotion, functions associated with digestion, excretion, and reproduction, and most animals have muscles of several characteristic reaction times.

Contractile fibers occur in Protozoa, for example in the myonemes of *Vorticella* and *Stentor*. In sponges, contractile epithelial cells and myocytes can close the oscula, while animals of all the higher phyla have cells specialized for contraction. The cellular mechanism of contraction and relaxation resides in certain proteins which can develop tension reversibly, and these contractile proteins are similar in motile cells so varied as muscles, embryonic fibroblasts, and flagellated sperm. Similar contractile machinery can give, at one extreme, the high speed of a mammalian eye movement or the beat of a mosquito's wing and, at the other extreme, the sluggish motion of a vertebrate intestine or of a sea anemone.

A comparative study of muscles reveals striking differences, particularly in the following properties: (1) time relations of movement—contraction and relaxation rates, time constants of excitation, frequency of stimulation for fused responses; (2) mode of neuromuscular excitation and its dependence on facilitation; (3) mechanical (viscoelastic) properties, as manifest by maintenance of tension, tonus, and effects of quick stretch and release; (4) spontaneous rhythmicity and its nervous control; (5) the coupling of membrane to activation and provision of energy for contractile elements; and (6) the nature of the contractile proteins.

GROSS FUNCTIONS OF MUSCLE

Muscles have been classified in many ways and no single classification is entirely satis-factory. We shall first put muscles into two groups according to their arrangement and gross function:

1. Muscles with origins and insertions on skeletal structures, either endoskeletal or exoskeletal, or on skin. These muscles are generally phasic, or of brief rapid movement. Examples are the muscles which move such appendages as legs, wings, and mouth parts, muscles which protrude or retract proboscis or tentacles, muscles which close the valves of a mollusc. Such muscles often occur in antagonistic pairs—contraction of one reflexly inhibiting contraction of the other, one causing movement in one direction, the other in the opposite direction; other muscles are opposed by an elastic ligament, as clam adductors. Usually phasic muscles form part of a lever system and function by shortening (isotonic contraction) or by developing tension while at a constant length (isometric contraction). No muscle functions purely isotonically or isometrically, but a particular muscle can approach one or the other of these conditions.

2. Muscles arranged around hollow structures, lacking strict origins and insertions, one portion of the muscle inserting into and hence pulling on another portion of itself. These are predominantly "holding" or tonic muscles. Examples are the muscles of the bladder, the walls of ureter, uterus, and gastrointestinal tract, some hearts, also the body wall muscles of annelids, holothurians, and other "hohlorganartige Tiere," as Jordan called them. In general, muscles of hollow structures are slower than phasic inserted muscles; they also occur in pairs, e.g., the circular and longitudinal muscles of the body wall of annelids, producing reciprocal movements. They contract against sacs of fluid rather than against skeletal or cuticular structures. Tonic muscles are generally nonstriated, but some are striated.

417

Both the phasic and tonic types of muscles are under reflex control, but many of the tonic hollow-organ type are capable of spontaneous rhythmicity. In some tonic muscles conduction is entirely by nerves (tubular invertebrates); in others, conduction is from muscle fiber to fiber (vertebrate visceral muscle). Phasic muscles are often organized into motor units, a few or many fibers or, occasionally, a whole muscle receiving innervation from one nerve fiber. Many muscles receive several overlapping polyneuronal innervations—different nerve fibers for fast contractions, for slow contractions, and sometimes for inhibition.

Gradation of rate and strength of contraction may be by one or more of the following mechanisms: (1) Gradation of movement in a muscle organized in many motor units is regulated from the central nervous system, which activates few or more units. (2) Activity in many muscles can be graded by variation in frequency of motor stimulation of individual units, high frequencies eliciting strong contractions. (3) Wherever multiple innervation occurs, different excitatory nerve fibers cause contractions of different rates, and inhibitory axons may diminish the effect of the excitatory. (4) Mechanical properties may determine the duration and magnitude of contractile response to a given stimulus.

TIME RELATIONS OF MUSCLE

The most striking differences among muscles are in their time relations, yet it is impossible to use any single criterion of speed of movement for all muscles, and different measures of speed often have different cellular bases. Differences in speed may be correlated with the histology of the muscle—the presence or absence of striations, the fiber length, and amount of connective tissue—and speed may correlate with differences in the muscle proteins and may be determined by the type of neuromuscular excitation.

Table 50 (see also references 36 and 103) gives some representative data for contraction and relaxation times and fusion frequencies. The measurements for different muscles are not really comparable. Contraction and relaxation times for fast muscles are usually given for twitches in response to single shocks, yet some muscles give little or no contraction to a single stimulus, and rate measurements are possible only for tetanus. A muscle with multiple innervation may show fast or slow contraction according to which motor nerve fiber excites it.

Contraction rates and tensions are very sensitive to temperature, and the magnitude and direction of temperature effect may be different for different muscles. In a frog sartorius as the temperature is lowered the rate of tension development is slowed and the twitch tension is considerably increased, while the tetanic tension is slightly decreased; twitch tension passes through a minimum at 20 to 25°C.[62] Wing-beat frequency of locusts is relatively constant over the temperature range of flight, and unlike frog striated muscle the twitch force of locust flight muscle increases with rising temperature.[38] The myogenic spontaneous contractions of a fish intestine increase logarithmically in rate with rising temperature, but the activity which is under nervous control can be abolished by a 6° rise in temperature.[47]

Some holding muscles contract rapidly yet may remain contracted for long periods, showing a virtually infinite relaxation time; some of these muscles (e.g., in molluscs) give quite different relaxation rates according to how they are stimulated (by direct or pulsed current or by chemicals) so that the same muscle shows several time constants.

Under experimental conditions, stimulation of a muscle is usually by way of intrinsic nerve fibers, and the measured excitation constants may be those of nerve rather than of muscle. Classical notions of muscle physiology have come from a study of those muscles in which individual fibers give all-or-none contractions. Actually the majority of muscles which have been studied give graded contractions, and in these the contraction and relaxation times are different according to the number and time relations of stimuli delivered. In general, high fusion frequency with repetitive stimulation is correlated with short contraction and relaxation times. However, in some, e.g., insect indirect flight muscles, there may be several twitches for one action potential, and the wing-beat frequency may actually exceed the fusion frequency obtained by electrical stimulations of the motor nerve. Measured fusion frequency of muscles is strongly influenced also by the moment of inertia of the lever and by the means used to couple the muscle to the lever.

For the above reasons, time constants of muscles have little meaning except for specific conditions of stimulation, and only general comparisons can be made among muscles (Table 50). In general, the fastest muscles which twitch to every stimulus are the extrinsic eye muscles of mammals at body

TABLE 50. TIME RELATIONS OF MUSCLES

Muscle	Contraction time, sec	Time for 1/2 relaxation, sec	Fusion frequency (per sec)
Mammals			
Cat, internal rectus[290]	0.0075 to 0.010		35.0
Cat, inferior oblique[290]	0.0187		69.0
Cat, crureus[105, 106]	0.0609		
Cat, gastrocnemius[290]	0.039	0.040	100
Cat, sartorius[290]	0.0287		23
Cat, soleus[290]	0.077	0.079	32
Man, gastrocnemius	0.110		
Rat, gastrocnemius	0.034	0.112	
Lower vertebrates			
Frog sartorius at 11.6°C	0.110	0.230	12.6
Frog sartorius at 16.4°C	0.075	0.110	16.4
(winter frogs) at 21.9°C	0.040	0.050	25.1
(winter frogs) at 25.2°C	0.023	0.033	31.3
Turtle retractor penis[101]	0.400	1.000	
Opsanus bladder muscle[255]	0.005 to 0.008	0.075	
Arthropods			
Schistocerca, wing muscle[38]	0.025	0.250 to 0.340	
Decticus leg muscle[256]	0.200	0.200	36-50
Astacus, abdomen flexor[187]	0.040		
Limulus, abdominal muscle	0.197	0.435	
Molluscs			
Pinna, adductor[2]	0.200	2.0	
Mytilus, byssus retractor[2]	1.000	4.0 to 6.0	
Mytilus, byssus retractor	3.990	17.7	
Pecten, striated	0.046	0.04	
Pecten, nonstriated	2.28	5.14	
Helix, tentacle retractor[265]	2.5	25.000	0.3 to 1/sec
Cephalopod chromatophore[31]	0.110	0.200 to 0.500	
Squid mantle	0.068	0.106	35/sec
Helix, pharynx retractor[2]	0.200 to 0.250	1.300 to 1.500	5 to 8/sec
Worms			
Phascolosoma			
fast } proboscis retractor	0.087	.095	
slow } proboscis retractor	0.54	2.7	
spindle[229]	1.5-2	3-4	
Echinoderms			
Thyone lantern retractor	3.9	5.7	
Thyone longitudinal retractor	3.1		
Stichopus longitudinal retractor[217]	1.0		
Coelenterates			
Medusae	.4-.8		
Metridium retractor[109]	.2-.3		
Sea anemone sphincter[206, 245]	5.0		
Sea anemone (slow circular)	120.		
Mammalian smooth			
Cat uterus[34]	1.8		
Cat intestine	3.0	3-4	
Cat stomach[198]	2.2		
Cat nictitating membrane	1.5	2-3	
Lower vertebrate smooth			
Turtle intestine[101]	30.0	36.0	
Dogfish mesenteric[229]	15-20	20-30	

temperature. The internal rectus of the eye of a cat contracts in less than 10 msec, and mechanical fusion does not occur at a frequency below 350 per sec. A hummingbird "standing still" in air shows a wing beat 55 times a sec. Wing frequencies of some Diptera and Hymenoptera are often several hundred per second, and midge wings have been measured at 2200 per sec.[257] This means that the indirect flight muscles must contract and relax within about 1 msec. Evidence will be presented below that these speeds of wing muscles are due to oscillatory mechanical properties and that they do not receive motor impulses from the nervous system at these high rates.

A large number of striated muscles—vertebrate limb muscles and insect leg muscles—have isometric contraction times of 25 to 80 msec and half-relaxation times only a little longer. The white muscles of vertebrates are a little faster but fatigue more readily than the vertebrate red muscles. Muscles of vertebrate embryos have longer time constants of contraction and excitation than do corresponding adult muscles and show graded responses. The muscle on the swim bladder of the toadfish *Opsanus* contracts in response to a motor nerve volley in 5 to 8 msec, and relaxes in 5 to 7 msec, and sound is produced during 2.5 msec.[255] The slow visceral muscles of most arthropods are striated. Many muscles of invertebrates, some of them nonstriated, contract at about the same rates as do vertebrate leg muscles (approximately 100 msec contraction time—Table 50). However, the invertebrate muscles differ more in relaxation times. The adductor muscles of bivalve molluscs are usually composed of a striated portion, which contracts and relaxes rapidly, and a nonstriated portion, which may contract fairly rapidly and which remains contracted for many seconds without further stimulation. The ratio of contraction time to time for half relaxation for many striated muscles is 1:2; for holding muscles of bivalve molluscs it is 1:8 to 1:20.[122]

Visceral smooth muscles of vertebrates contract slowly, often requiring several seconds, although they may not remain contracted as long as some molluscan holding muscles. The slowest contractions are the bending reactions of sessile sea anemones where one rhythmic movement may extend over many minutes. Tonic or maintained contraction can be distinguished from slow relaxation. In many postural muscles, tone is maintained by continuous low level nervous activation. In others, such as vertebrate smooth muscles, tension is related to stretch and there is no true "rest length."

Speed of conduction correlates with contraction rates. A frog semitendinosus fiber 126 μ in diameter conducts at 2.4 m/sec in Ringer solution, and a 100 μ fiber conducts in Ringer solution at 1.3 m/sec.[116] Vertebrate smooth muscle usually conducts at 3 to 5 cm/sec.

Meaningful quantitative measures of time relations among muscles are difficult to obtain,

but the preceding data indicate that muscles occur in a spectrum of time relations covering a range of some ten thousandfold. The elucidation of the numerous bases for this tremendous range in speeds of movement is one of the most challenging problems in comparative physiology.

HISTOLOGICAL TYPES OF MUSCLES

A cursory histological look at various muscles in different animals reveals the incompleteness of the classification of muscle as striated, cardiac, or smooth. There are many kinds of both striated and nonstriated muscle. Vertebrate cardiac muscle is of branched striated fibers, yet the intercalated discs are double membranes which interrupt the fibrils,[254] and the muscle can no longer be considered a histological syncytium (see p. 409, Chapter 13). The nonstriated muscles of molluscs may have fibers several centimeters long and both the long- and short-fibered nonstriated muscles of various invertebrates are very different physiologically from the short-fibered, nonstriated visceral muscles of vertebrates. Myofilaments are more apparent in invertebrate nonstriated than in ver-

FIGURE 166. *A*, Light micrograph of circular muscle fiber of coelenterate Aurelia showing striations. (From Horridge, A.: Quart. J. Micr. Sci., vol. 95.)

B, light micrograph of contracted fiber from longitudinal muscle of body wall of earthworm *Lumbricus terrestris* showing double-oblique apparent striation. (From Hanson, J.: J. Biophys. Biochem. Cytol., vol. 3.)

tebrate smooth fibers. It is desirable that the term "smooth muscle" be restricted to vertebrate visceral muscle.

In general, muscles are divided into fibers, sometimes multinucleate, sometimes uninucleate. The amount of connective tissue in which muscle fibers are embedded differs greatly in different kinds of muscles. The outer layer of the fiber membrane (outer sarcolemma) appears to be in common with connective tissue and may contain fine filaments; the inner layer is probably the physiological plasma membrane. The total thickness of the sarcolemma is about 75 to 100 Å, the plasma membrane 25 Å.[20] Many muscle fibers contain fibrils; others lack them. The contractile proteins are always organized into myofilaments irrespective of whether these are built into fibrils or are free in the sarcoplasm of the fiber. The organization of contractile proteins in myofilaments is known best for a few mammalian striated muscles.

Striated Muscles. Striations must have originated early in the evolution of muscles and many coelenterate fibers are cross-striated[143] (Fig. 166A). Cross-striated fibers

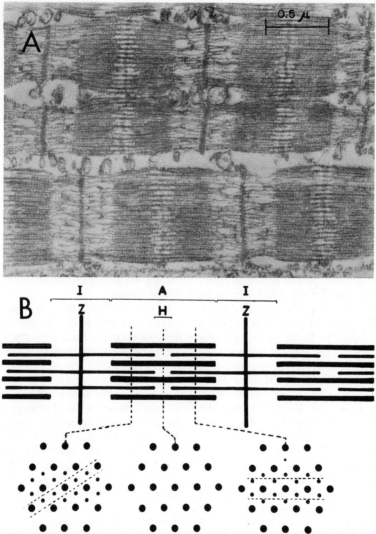

FIGURE 167. A, electron micrograph of longitudinal section through several fibrils of a glycerol-extracted fixed rabbit psoas muscle. The light I bands are crossed by the Z lines and contain thin myofilaments; the dense A bands contain thick filaments in the center of the band and thin ones which enter from the I bands. B, diagram of arrangement of thick and thin protein filaments in a myofibril. Upper portion of figure shows sarcomeres in longitudinal section aligned opposite corresponding bands of A; below are transverse sections through three zones of the A band as indicated. (From Huxley, H., and Hanson, J.: in Structure and Function of Muscle, edited by G. Bourne. Academic Press.)

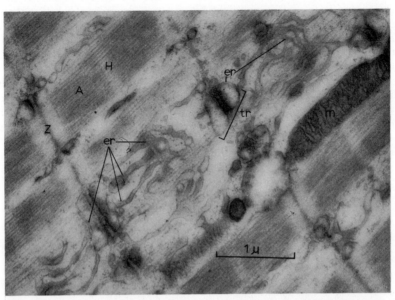

FIGURE 168. Electron micrograph of longitudinal section of a muscle fiber from a caudal myotome of an Amblystoma larva. Sarcoplasm between myofibrils contains endoplasmic reticulum (*er*) which appears as canaliculi and vesicles. At level of Z bands the vesicles of opposed sarcomeres are dilated, and between them are smaller vesicles, forming a vesicular triad (*tr*). (From Porter, R. K., and Palade, G. E.: J. Biophys. Biochem. Cytol., vol. 3.)

occur in nearly every phylum. Cross striations consist of alternating strongly birefringent and weakly birefringent regions, the anisotropic (A) and the isotropic (I) bands. The I bands (light in transmitted, dark in polarized light) are divided by the Z lines which are transverse boundaries between the structural units, the sarcomeres; one sarcomere consists of two light areas (halves of two I bands) and the included A band (Fig. 167). In the middle of an A band is a lighter H region which may have in its center an M line. Many fibrils are aligned with respect to the striations and between the fibrils is a granular sarcoplasm which may contain many mitochondria. In the sarcoplasm is a vesicular network corresponding to an endoplasmic reticulum[214, 215] and connected in some species with the Z lines. The reticular system consists of vesicles which form a bracelet around a sarcomere and connect by interfibrillar vesicles to the reticulum of adjacent sarcomeres. In the region of the Z line in some muscles and at the A-I junction in others, two adjacent sets of reticular bulbs separated by small intermediary vesicles form transverse "triads" (Fig. 168).[214, 215] In these regions there may be also an indentation of

the sarcolemma. The reticulum of vertebrate "slow" fibers is more diffuse and does not form regular rings of vesicles[211] (Fig. 169*A*). In crustacean muscle there is extensive infolding of the cell membrane between the A and I bands.

It was formerly thought that sarcomere length is shorter in the fastest striated muscles, but so many exceptions are known that the statement is not valid. In the psoas muscle of the rabbit the distance from Z to Z is 2.3 μ, the length of an A band is 1.5 μ.[120] The fibers of the high-frequency insect flight muscles are of wide diameter, have large fibrils (sarcostyles) widely separated, short striations, and many mitochondria and tracheoles penetrating inside the fibers. In the slower leg muscles of insects, fiber diameter is less, fibrils are narrow and closer together, sometimes branched, and with wider striations.[73, 269] In more primitive insects (e.g., *Periplaneta*) all muscles are of the non-sarcostyle type.[74] Fibrils of both vertebrate and insect striated muscles contain two sorts of filaments—thick, 110 to 140 Å, and thin, 40 Å in the A band, the thin filaments grouped in a hexagon around a thick one.[160, 161] The thin filaments run from a

Z line to the H zone of the A band, thus extending through an I band and part way through an A band. The thick filaments consist of the protein myosin and extend through the A band only.[120, 138, 160, 231] The myofilaments in rabbit psoas show a periodicity of about 400 Å or less, and bridges connect thick to thin filaments every 400 Å in frog muscle so that each thick filament has six bridges per 400 Å.[160]

There are several suggested interpretations of the cross-striations of muscle. One suggestion relates the striations to contraction. There is much disagreement in histological descriptions of the changes with contraction, partly because electron microscopists have often not used sections thin enough to see discrete filaments. Birefringence falls during isotonic contraction, an indication of increased randomness of the proteins. In isometric contraction, or shortening by not more than 10 per cent of fiber length, there is no change in sarcomere (band) length although the H bands become denser. At extensions beyond 140 per cent of rest length in frog muscle, the two halves of the I band become thinner

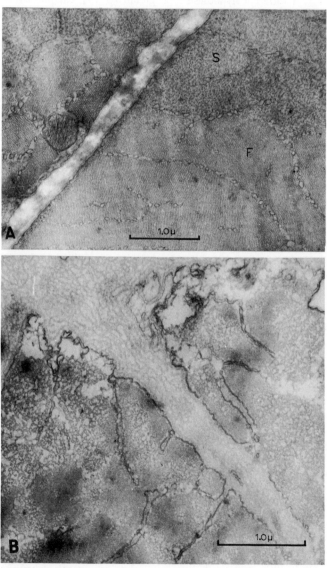

FIGURE 169. *A*, Electron micrograph of cross-section of tonus bundle from iliofibularis of frog *Rana temporaria* showing "fast" fibers (*F*) with sharp filaments in fibrils separated by regular vesicles of endoplasmic reticulum, and "slow" fibers (*S*) with irregular reticulum and filaments not in distinct myofibrils. *B*, Electron micrograph of cross-section of muscle from crab *Carcinus maenas*. Section through I band. Invaginations are more common at level of Z line than in A bands. (Courtesy of L. D. Peachey.)

laterally; at contractions below 90 per cent rest length the I is shortened and the A band widened laterally. With more shortening, the ends of an A band approach the Z line, and at lengths of less than 65 per cent, dense contraction bands appear.[157, 158, 160] In some insect muscles the contraction bands are seen with less shortening of the I.[10] Material passes from I into A during contraction, even without a change in A band length, and since all myosin is in A, it has been suggested that actin slides along myosin molecules.[161] At extreme shortening when contraction bands appear, there may be a folding or crumpling of the protein in A. A different hypothesis[260] postulates a folding of the associated myosin and actin at all degrees of contraction. In certain insect muscles where striations appear to spiral, a contraction wave may follow the spiral striations.[167]

A second meaning of striations relates to speed of movement. In general, fast phasic muscles are striated and slow tonic muscles nonstriated. Yet there are many exceptions to this generalization. Some vertebrate striated muscles (e.g., frog rectus abdominis) are slower than many invertebrate nonstriated ones (e.g., phascolosoma [*Golfingia*] proboscis retractor). Vertebrate visceral muscles are nonstriated, yet those of the slow insect intestine are striated.

A third interpretation of striations relates to the spread of excitation from the surface of a fiber inward to the contractile elements. When frog and lizard striated fibers were stimulated with microelectrodes, the threshold was lowest when the electrode was opposite the Z line,[156, 159] where rows of vesicles converge on the fiber membrane. Crab and lizard fibers were most excitable at the boundary between the A and I bands (where the cell membrane is infolded).[34, 156] Conduction of the excitation inward may be by these lines, and there may be internal conduction along the sarcoplasmic reticulum.[74] Frog "slow" fibers respond to stimuli applied over either A or I bands, and in these the vesicular reticulum is not so oriented to the Z line as in "fast" fibers (Fig. 169B). In nonstriated fibers of trematode cercariae, rows of reticular vesicles extend in only as far as myofilaments occur. Most striated fibers are large in diameter, 50 to 100 μ, whereas most nonstriated fibers whether they are long (1 to 2 cm) or short (less than 0.1 mm) are of small diameter, 3 to 5 μ, and lack a symmetrical vesicular reticulum. The reason nonstriated fibers are narrow may be that in them the contractile

material must be excited directly from the membrane while in striated muscles excitation may be conducted inward along some of the intrafiber vesicles. Evidence is strong, therefore, that the vesicular reticulum conducts excitation from the fiber membrane inward to the contractile filaments.

In amniotes and some fish, striated muscle may be white or red; there are also red muscles in invertebrates, e.g., the nonstriated radular muscles of snails. In vertebrate white muscle the fibrils are close together and abundant; in red muscle the fibrils are less densely packed and the sarcoplasm is rich in myoglobin (p. 198, Chapter 8). Muscle nuclei are peripheral in white fibers; some nuclei are central in red fibers. White muscle is faster and fatigues more rapidly than red muscle. In birds the white muscle contains more glycogen, the red more fat.[97] The myoglobin content is associated with oxygen stores, as in red muscles of many diving mammals. In the slow-moving sloth all skeletal muscles are of the sarcoplasm-rich red type.[134]

Nonstriated Muscles. Nonstriated muscles may be long fibered, as in molluscan adductors, where fibers may be 2 cm long.[29] They may be short, 0.05 to 0.5 mm, as in sea anemones[103] or in the phascolosoma proboscis retractor or vertebrate smooth muscle. They may be surrounded by much connective tissue, as in holothurian long body-wall retractors or *Mytilus* byssus retractor, or there may be little connective tissue, as in the phascolosoma retractor or oyster adductors.[12] In short-fibered nonstriated muscle fibers no true fibrils are usually seen, but there are filaments of various size and abundance. The myonemes of the stalk of the ciliate *Vorticella* contain filaments resembling those of muscle. In mammalian uterine muscle the filaments vary with the stage in the reproductive cycle and seem controlled by hormones. Uterine muscle filaments are 100 to 200 Å thick and may contain ovoids which give an appearance of periodicity.[195] Between the myofilaments of some smooth muscles (e.g., mammalian intestine) are dark bodies which consist of noncontractile protein of unknown function.[50] The short-fibered nonstriated muscles have mitochondria, particularly at the ends of nuclei, and the fibers are closely packed in the more rapidly conducting muscles but widely separated in nonconducting smooth muscle.[50]

The nonstriated fibers of molluscan adductor and other tonic muscles are distinguished by small (50 Å) filaments containing actomyosin, and large ones (150 to 1500 Å diameter) containing paramyosin (Fig. 170). The paramyosin filaments show in the electron microscope 140 Å periods which result in a unit cell of 725 Å, as can be demonstrated by x-ray diffraction (Fig. 172). The two kinds of filaments are interconnected by many bridges. Needlelike fibrils removed from *Venus* muscle and presumably identical with

the large paramyosin filaments show a periodicity of 140 Å in the electron microscope. Paramyosin filaments reconstituted from extracted protein show a 1400 Å period.[137]

Other nonstriated muscles have a helical or spiral arrangement of fibrils which may in the light microscope give the impression of fine diagonal striations. Most of the muscles of cephalopods are helical; both striated and

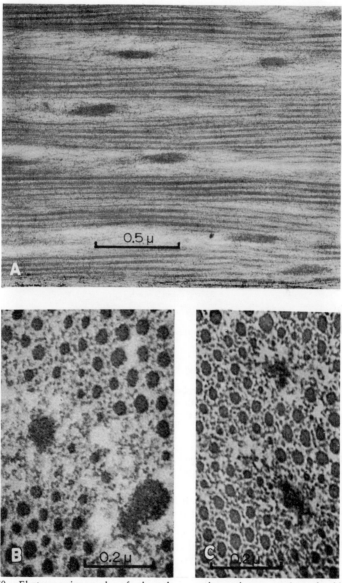

FIGURE 170. Electron micrographs of glycerol-extracted translucent portion of adductor of oyster *Gryphaea angulata*. *A*, Longitudinal section of one fiber; thick and thin filaments are oblique to fiber axis and are grouped in arrays which partly overlap. The branching and anastomosing bands of filaments are oblique to fiber axis, hence give a double-oblique striation in the light microscope. Dense bodies lie in the regions of thin filaments. Thick filaments are paramyosin. *B*, transverse section of extended fiber showing separate regions of thick and thin filaments. *C*, transverse section of fiber shortened just below minimal length in body. Small filaments closely interspersed among thick (paramyosin) filaments. (*A* and *B* from Hanson, J., and Lowy, J.; *C* from Hanson, J., and Lowy, J.: J. Physiol., vol. 149.)

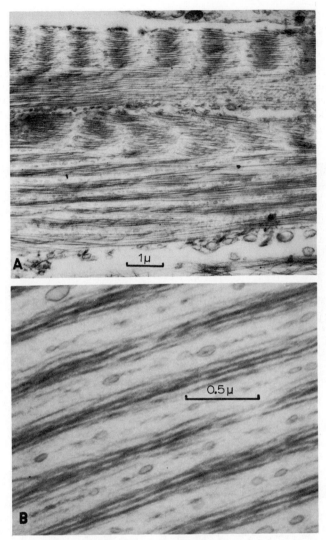

FIGURE 171. Electron micrographs of glycerol-extracted earthworm muscles. *A*, longitudinal sections of portions of two fibers. Unstriated fibrils with sarcoplasmic reticulum between them. *B*, longitudinal section at higher magnification of fibrils with extensive reticulum between them. (Courtesy of J. Hanson and J. Lowy.)

classical nonstriated are also found. Helical fibers occur also in some echinoderms and ascidians.

Many annelids have helical muscles, e.g., in the earthworm where individual fibers are flat ribbons (Figs. 166B, 171) 20 μ wide, 2.5 μ thick, and 2 to 3 mm long. Each fiber contains peripheral fibrils which pass diagonally in a right-hand spiral at a 10-degree angle to the fiber axis when the fiber is extended, and at a 30-degree angle to the fiber axis when the fiber is shortened by 50 per cent. The overlap of the spiralling fibrils on the two surfaces of the fiber gives the appearance of oblique striations. Each fibril is composed of some 100 filaments in cross-section, and the

fibrils may show a periodicity of 300 to 500 Å.[119]

In squid muscle there is a left-hand spiral of peripheral fibrils, a core of mitochondria; the fibrils contain thick (100 to 140 Å) filaments about 350 Å apart and thin (50 Å) ones distributed irregularly among the thick ones. The *Helix* pharynx retractor has two sizes of filaments.[121]

The translucent fast portions of adductor muscles of bivalve molluscs have an apparent striation, sometimes spiral; the opaque slow portions do not. Recent evidence[171] is that the striations are due to bands of granules, each "sarcomere" being 1 to 5 μ long. Similarly, in earthworm fibers, thick and thin fila-

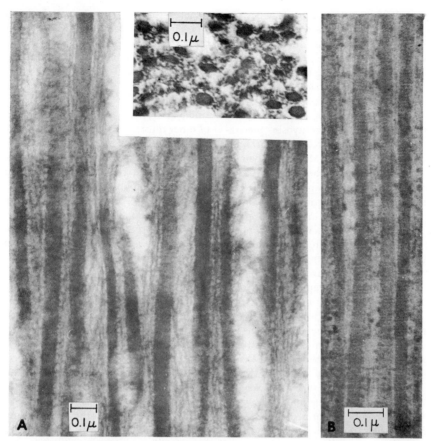

FIGURE 172. Electron micrographs of anterior byssus retractor of *Mytilus edulis*. Longitudinal section of muscle: *A*, fixed when relaxed; *B*, fixed when contracted; *inset*, cross-section of glycerinated muscle. Periodicity shown in contracted filaments, *B*. Thick (paramyosin) filaments, each surrounded by thin (actomyosin) filaments. (Courtesy of W. H. Johnson.)

ments are reported which spiral when contracted; in the middle of the thin filaments are J granules. *Nereis* shows a similar arrangement except that the J particles are tubular; some fifteen oblique thin filaments connect to one J tube.

It must be concluded that the wide spectrum of muscles with respect to time relations is matched by (but not necessarily related to) a wide variety of histological types, from cross-striated, spiral-striated, to long-fibered and short-fibered nonstriated. Certainly it is time for histologists to discard the fiction that there are only three kinds of muscle fiber.

CHEMICAL BASIS OF CONTRACTION

Contractile Proteins. All muscles contain large amounts of protein, formerly called myosin, now known to consist of several proteins. The differences between extracted proteins may depend partly on how the large molecules are broken. The best known of the proteins are actin and myosin, which combine as the contractile protein complex actomyosin. Properties of the muscle proteins have been reviewed frequently. Myosin (or actomyosin) is extracted in alkaline KCl solution of high ionic strength (0.6 N); actin and myosin differ in solubilities in dilute KCl and in resistance to organic solvents, and relative amounts of actin and myosin are assayed by viscosity measurements. The proteins of a rabbit psoas muscle consist of about 44 per cent myosin, 15 per cent actin, 3 per cent tropomyosin, and 32 to 37 per cent stroma and sarcoplasmic globular proteins.

Actin has a molecular weight (as a monomer) of about 60,000, and does not show streaming birefringence. It can transform, in the presence of salts, from a globular (G) to a fibrous (F) protein. The polymerized F actin consists of linear aggregates of ovoids of G actin.

Myosin has a molecular weight (M.W.) of about 420,000.[186, 200, 201] It is a long molecule, some 100 times longer than wide. On partial digestion with trypsin it breaks into heavy (H) meromyosin of M.W. 329,000 (550 Å long) and light (L) meromyosin of M.W. 126,000 (400 Å long); there are two light and one heavy meromyosins in a single myosin molecule.[260] Reconstituted L-meromyosin filaments have a 400-Å period in the electron microscope. L-meromyosin precipitates at a slightly higher KCl concentration than does H-meromyosin. Myosin enzymatically splits adenosine triphosphate (ATP), liberating the terminal phosphate and releasing energy. This ATPase action resides in the H-meromyosin. When F-actin and myosin are mixed in dilute KCl in a combining proportion of 1:2.5, the gel actomyosin is formed. This has high flow birefringence and high viscosity. According to Huxley's interpretation of electron micrographs of striated muscle, myosin is restricted to the thick filaments of the A bands while actin threads run from the Z line to the edge of the H region at each end of a sarcomere (Fig. 167). By fluorescent antibody methods the L-meromyosin is found on lateral parts of the A bands, H-meromyosin in the narrower M zone.[89, 142] In embryonic myoblasts myosin can be demonstrated by fluorescent antibodies in A regions before striations are apparent microscopically.

It is possible that the properties and abundance of the various contractile proteins may differ in various muscles and may be correlated with their time relations and tension development. Because optimal conditions for extraction appear different for different muscles, detailed comparisons have not been possible. Actin and myosin are less readily separated in frog, fish, and limulus muscle than in mammals. Also, insect actomyosin is not readily dissociated to myosin and actin. Fish myosin can be separated from actin, but the tendency to molecular aggregation is greater than in rabbit muscle. Crayfish tail muscle yields myosin similar to that of vertebrate muscle. In the muscle of haddock and torpedo, myosin constitutes 70 per cent of the total protein, while in mammals it is only 40 per cent. Embryonic muscle has relatively more of sarcoplasmic than contractile proteins. In a chick embryo before the twelfth day of incubation the actomyosin (AM) is less than 1 mg/gm; thereafter it increases rapidly to the adult level of 50 mg/gm.[65] In denervated muscle the myosin content decreases with time. In uterine smooth muscle the actomyosin content increases by several times

under action of estrogen and in pregnancy.

Tropomyosin constitutes 3 to 8 per cent of the protein in mammalian striated muscle fibrils. It has a molecular weight of 68,000 to 150,000, is some twenty-six times longer than it is thick, and shows slight positive flow birefringence.[186, 212] The amino acid composition of tropomyosins is better known than of other muscle proteins because tropomyosins are readily crystallized and they resist denaturation by ethanol ether. Tropomyosins are unusual in containing very little proline and no tryptophan. One group of tropomyosins (class A) can be salted out in more dilute ammonium sulfate, and there are fewer negative charges than in another group (class B) which is more water soluble. Tropomyosins B have higher ratios of lysine to arginine than tropomyosins A. Vertebrate smooth muscle has relatively more of the water-soluble tropomyosin than does striated muscle.[186] Various molluscs and crustacea have small amounts of tropomyosin B with lower lysine-arginine ratio than do vertebrates, but molluscs have larger amounts of tropomyosin A.[178, 251] The annelids *Lumbricus* and *Arenicola* have tropomyosin A but not B. The function of tropomyosins is unknown.

Bivalve molluscs have in their holding muscles a protein, paramyosin, which was first identified by its long periodicities (p. 425). Paramyosin has many of the chemical properties of tropomyosin A and the two may be identical in molluscs. *Pinna* paramyosin contains no tryptophan or proline, small amounts of glycine, phenylalanine, histidine, and cysteine, and much glutamic acid and lysine.[13] Paramyosin probably does not participate in contraction directly. Paramyosin from *Venus* or *Mytilus* precipitates sharply at pH just below neutrality, where actomyosin at proper ionic strength remains in solution.[166]

Theories of Contraction.   Three types of simplified contractile system are being used in attempts to understand the basis of contraction. Actomyosin, extracted in alkaline 0.6 N KCl, forms gel threads when extruded into dilute KCl. The monolayers of surface spread actomyosin can be compressed into fibers. Extraction of muscle by 50 per cent glycerol removes salts, small organic molecules, and soluble proteins, and leaves bundles of fibers which contain the contractile proteins. Each of these three models contracts and develops tension under the influence of 2 to 3 mM ATP in the presence of Mg^{++}. Extraction with glycerol has been applied to many kinds of muscle, and the observed contractions are very similar. The tension developed by the glycerol model is similar to that developed by living muscles.

Actomyosin in 0.6 M KCl can be dissociated to actin and myosin by ATP, and when the ATP is dephosphorylated AM can re-form. Also ATP decreases the viscosity of AM solution and plasticizes threads of AM, and after dephosphorylation of ATP the viscosity increases and threads are inextensible. If the ATPase of M is poisoned the thread remains extensible although contraction is inhibited.

According to the Szent-Györgyi's view of contraction, excitation in the presence of Ca^{++} causes actin and myosin to combine to form a more rigid molecule, actomyosin. Then the H-meromyosin by its ATPase action splits ATP, and the resulting energy is transferred to L-meromyosin which, because of loss of electrical charge, folds to give a contraction. An alternative hypothesis is that the actin molecules slide along the myosin (p. 424). The cyclic opening and closing of the cross-links between actin and myosin are thought to correspond to the binding and dephosphorylation of ATP. By this means the actin of the I bands moves into the A band.

There are also two views regarding the role of ATP. One is that its energy is transferred directly and that no contraction can occur without ATPase action.[277, 278] This is supported by the fact that contractions cease when ATPase is inhibited, e.g., by salygran.[277, 278] Another view is that ATP provides a polyvalent anion which neutralizes charges on myosin and thus causes contraction; hence splitting of ATP is not essential for contraction.[203] This opinion is supported by observation of contraction without breakdown of ATP,[90, 199-201] and by the fact that contractions (of an abnormal sort) can be caused by unsplittable polyvalent anions.[203] There is no doubt, however, that in normal contraction phosphate energy is utilized from ATP-phosphagen stores.

Relaxation can be brought about by high concentrations of ATP. Adenosine triphosphate at 0.0001 M contracts and at 0.01 M plasticizes actomyosin filaments.[277, 278] Relaxation can be caused also by mixtures of agents which rephosphorylate ADP to ATP, for example, phosphocreatine and creatine kinase or myokinase.[202] Actomyosin threads are made plastic (relaxed) by ATP when ATPase is poisoned. The relaxing factor, which inhibits myosin ATPase, is found in small particulates, possibly in the microsomes

of muscle.[20] It requires Mg^{++},[86] can be inhibited by Ca^{++} or by carnosine,[98] and may be α-glycerophosphate.[195a] According to Weber, if ATP is not broken down or if an excess of ATP is added, the muscle model becomes plastic; ATP causes contraction and is split with the result that the contracted muscle is rigid. Relaxation could, then, be the result of resynthesis of ATP with its resulting plasticizing effect.

The universality of actomyosin shortening under the influence of ATP, Mg^{++}, and K^+ is corroborated by measurements on various glycerol-extracted muscles from many kinds of animals. Extracted fibroblasts and embryonic cells in early telophase show equatorial constriction when ATP is added. Flagella of sperm and trypanosomes become independently rhythmic in ATP and Mg^{++}.[140] The glycerol-extracted myonemes of *Vorticella* react like glycerol-extracted muscle and contract rhythmically in ATP-Ca.[277, 278] Glycerinated preparations of spermatozoa show rhythmic contractions in ATP.[23] An actomyosin-like protein has been extracted from myxomycetes (see p. 471). Evidently the contractile protein gels of all animals are similar.

Adenosine Triphosphatase. ATPase activity has been examined in extracts of many muscles. The ATPase of vertebrate striated muscle myosin is activated by Ca^{++} and inhibited by Mg^{++} at the optimum pH of 9.0. Another ATP-splitting enzyme in muscle is activated by Mg^{++} and has an optimum pH of 7.0.[118] Uterine muscle has a much lower ATPase activity (3 to 10 per cent) than skeletal muscle (on a total protein basis). The calcium-activated ATPase of *Pecten* and *Anodonta* adductors is greater per gram in the fast (translucent) portion than in the slow (opaque) portion.[270] The paramyosin in these muscles has no ATPase activity.[246] Activity is two to three times greater in flight than in leg muscles of *Locusta migratoria*.[99, 100] In giant water bugs *Lethocerus,* the leg muscle has more apyrase (ATP-splitting enzyme) than has wing muscle.[174, 233] The fly *Musca* has an Mg^{++}-activated, but no Ca^{++}-activated ATPase in the myosin, but does have a Ca^{++}-activated ATPase in muscle mitochondria.[274] Squid mantle contains only Ca^{++}-activated ATPase, and this is inactivated at temperatures above 31°.[274] Limulus, crayfish, and *Echiurus* muscles have Ca^{++}-activated ATPase which is inhibited by Mg^{++} at a critical concentration and has a pH optimum of 9.0.[197] ATPase

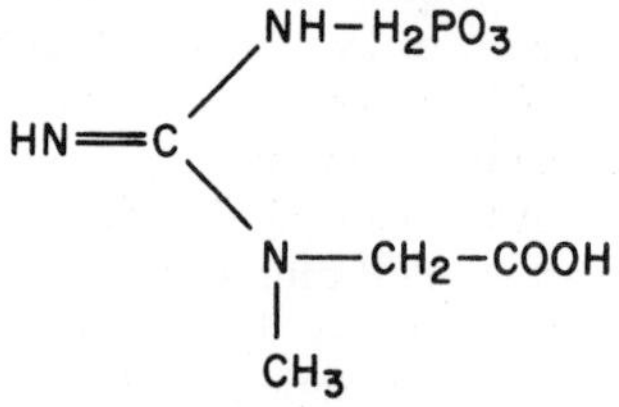

phosphorylcreatine

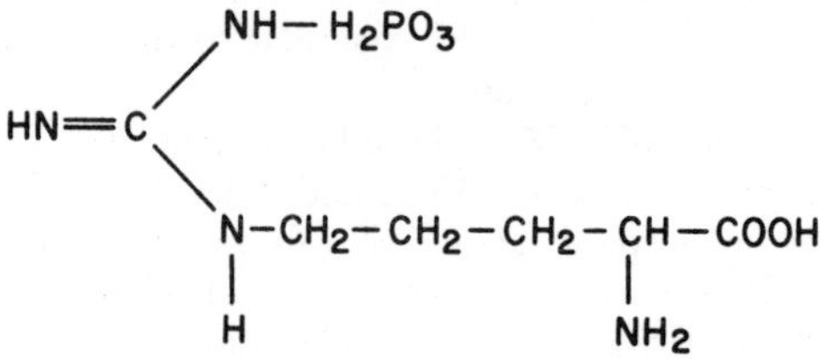

phosphorylarginine

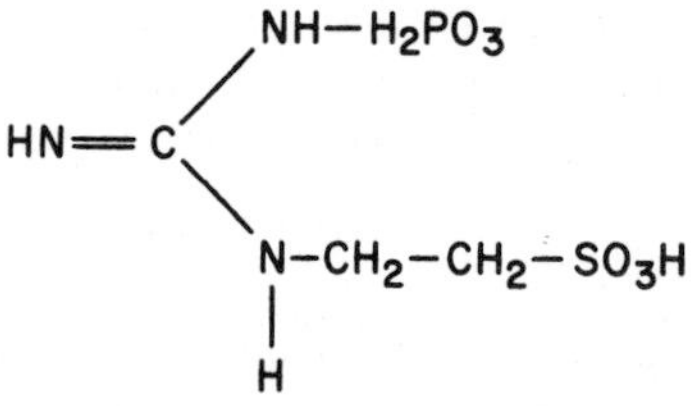

phosphoryltaurocyamine

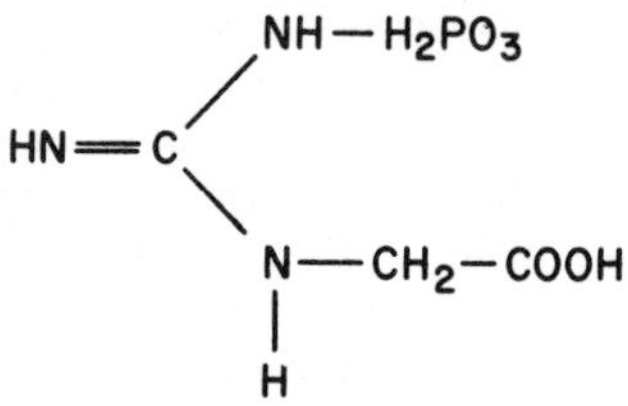

phosphorylglycocyamine

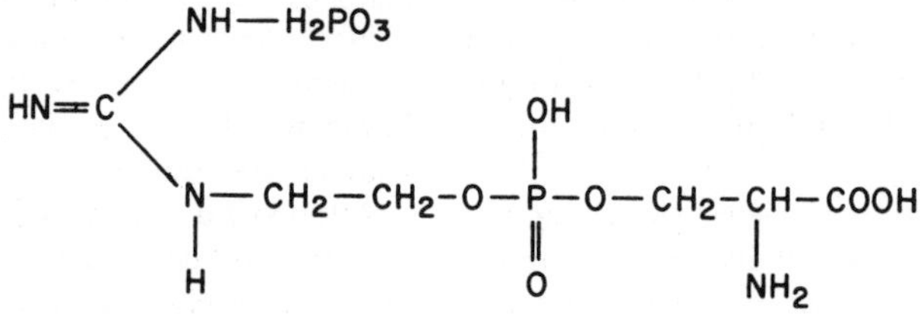

phosphoryllombricine

FIGURE 173. Chemical formulas of phosphagens.

action of AM from a sea anemone (*Anthopleura*) is enhanced more by Mg^{++} than by Ca^{++}; the pH optimum is 7.0. *Echiurus* ATPase is activated by Ca^{++} and inhibited by Mg^{++}.[197] Relative ATPase activity measured in amount of inorganic phosphorus liberated per unit nitrogen under similar conditions (not necessarily physiological) follows: rabbit 1050, frog 210, *Maja* 60, *Scyllium* 21, *Pleuronectes* 20, *Mya* 9.[153]

In summary: Some muscle ATPase is activated by Ca^{++}, some by Mg^{++}; the myosin ATPase may be different from that in mitochondria. Reports which fail to agree on the composition of the same muscle may result partly from the presence of actomyosin in some and of myosin in other extracts, and in differences in the percentage of the total protein which is myosin. In general, striated muscles and muscles capable of high speeds seem to have more ATPase activity than slow muscles. Whether the ATPase activity truly limits the speed of contraction can only be learned when measurements are made under optimal physiological conditions, which are not the same for different muscles.

Distribution of Phosphagens. Irrespective of whether breakdown of ATP is essential for contraction *per se,* there is little doubt that, under the ATPase action, energy is at some stage transferred from ATP to the contractile system. The classical view is that, during contraction, oxidation cannot keep up the supply of ATP; hence immediate phosphorylation of ADP is normally from a phosphagen, usually either phosphorylcreatine (PC) or phosphorylarginine (PA) (Fig. 173). An alternative is that energy is liberated by direct dephosphorylation of PC or some other compound. The phosphagen is reloaded with active phosphate by mitochondrial ATP, formed either oxidatively or in the glycolytic cycle in which lactic acid is produced. Part of the lactic acid is oxidized and a larger part is reconverted to glycogen, usually in the liver. Smooth and cardiac muscles of

TABLE 51. DISTRIBUTION OF PHOSPHORYLARGI-
NINE AND PHOSPHORYLCREATINE IN MUSCLE
OF VARIOUS ANIMALS[14, 15, 75, 239, 240, 266]

Animal group	phosphoryl-arginine	phosphoryl-creatine
Coelenterates	+	−
Nemerteans	+	−
Sipunculids	+	−
Molluscs	+	−
Arthropods	+	−
Annelids (see text)		
Echinoderms		
Asteroids	+	−
Holothurians	+	−
Echinoids		
adults 3 species	+	−
4 species	+	+
Ophiuroids		+
Prochordates		
Hemichordates	+	+
Ascidians Ascidia	+	−
Pyura	−	+
Styela	−	+
Cephalochordates	−	+
Vertebrates	−	+

mammals have about one tenth the PC concentration of striated muscle.

The phosphagens of different animals differ according to the nitrogen base (type of guanidine)—(Table 51). The muscles of all chordates contain PC; muscles of all arthropods, molluscs, flatworms, sipunculids, and coelenterates contain PA. However, creatine is found in sperm of *Sipunculus* and in the anemone *Calliactis,* and both creatine and arginine are found in sponges.[239, 240] The protozoan *Tetrahymena* appears to have a different phosphorylated guanidine.[249]

The annelids are unique in having a variety of phosphagens. Many polychaetes, particularly the free-swimming, have PC, but *Nereis diversicolor* has a unique phosphorylglycocyamine (PG). Two species of *Arenicola* have phosphoryltaurocyamine (PT). *Glycera gigantea* muscles contain both phosphagens, PT and PC; *G. convoluta* contains PC only.[135] *Spirographis* is the only polychaete thus far known to contain PA.[239, 240] In the earthworm *Lumbricus* a different phosphagen, phosphoryllombricine (PL) is found, and still another in the leech *Hirudo*.[18] In echinoderms, only arginine phosphagen is found in holothurians and starfish and only creatine in ophiuroids; some genera of echinoids have both PC and PA; other genera have only PA.[14, 15, 108, 301] The hemichordates have both PC and PA; the cephalochordates, like vertebrates, PC only. The

presence of creatine in muscles of many polychaetes and of all chordates is an example of convergent evolution.

MECHANICAL PROPERTIES AND THE "ACTIVE STATE"

Muscles have mechanical properties which affect their contractions and which can be represented by a model consisting of a contractile element (CE) in series with a series elastic element (SE), and both of these in parallel with another elastic element (PE) (Fig. 174). The components of this model differ in different muscles.[117, 252]

Series Elastic Element. This resides in tendon or other connective tissue at the end of a muscle and perhaps in the contractile material itself. It can be observed in an active muscle when the parallel elasticity is taken up, and series elasticity is measured as change in length (extension) when an isotonically contracting muscle is released against different loads.[165] Series elasticity or compliance can be increased by attaching springs at the ends of a striated muscle; the rate of tension development is then reduced, the height of a twitch lowered, and the tetanus-twitch ratio raised.[125]

Parallel Elastic Element. When an unstimulated muscle is stretched, it develops elastic tension in a nonlinear fashion, little tension with initial stretch, and increasingly more tension as stretch approaches the breaking point (Fig. 175). Tension is set up in the parallel elastic element only when a muscle is at a length greater than the rest length or

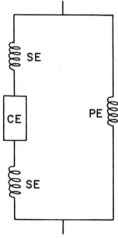

FIGURE 174. Schema of mechanical arrangement of striated muscle. *CE,* contractile element; *SE,* series elastic, and *PE,* parallel elastic elements.

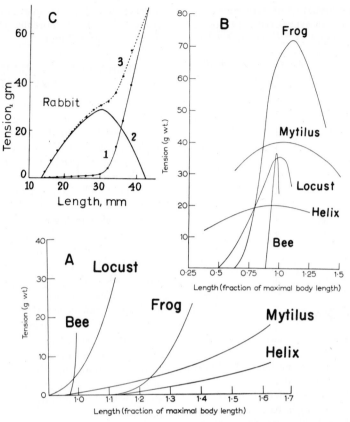

FIGURE 175. *A*, Tension-length curves of muscles at rest. Bumblebee (*Bombus*) flight muscle; locust (*Schistocerca*) flight muscle, 11°C; Frog sartorius, 0°C; *Mytilus* anterior byssal retractor 14°; *Helix* pharynx retractor 14°C. (From Hanson, J., and Lowy, J., *in* Structure and Function of Muscle, edited by G. Bourne. Academic Press.) *B*, tension-length curves for active muscles in relative units. Bumblebee flight muscle; locust; frog sartorius; *Helix* pharynx retractor; *Mytilus* anterior byssal retractor. (From Hanson, J., and Lowy, J., *in* Structure and Function of Muscle, edited by G. Bourne. Academic Press.) *C*, tension-length curves of rabbit uterus: (1) rest tension as function of length; (2) active tension; (3) combined tensions. (Modified from Csapo, A; *in* Structure and Function of Muscle, edited by G. Bourne. Academic Press.)

the normal length in the animal; at less than rest length the mechanical system consists of only SE and CE. Observations on intact and on emptied striated muscle fibers (frog and insect) show the resistance to stretch to be partly in connective tissue, partly in sarcolemma,[230a] and partly in the sarcoplasm.[38, 253] Flight muscles of insects, which have little connective tissue, are less extensible (develop more elastic tension) than vertebrate muscle, and their sarcoplasmic resistance to stretch is relatively higher.[38] Many short-fibered nonstriated muscles are more extensible than striated muscles, and extension during passive stretch may be initially fast, then slow. The phascolosoma proboscis retractor is readily stretched to more than ten times its "rest" length. For nonstriated muscles it may be difficult to know the "rest" or *in vivo* length, although this may be taken as the length at

which a passively extended muscle begins to develop elastic tension.[64]

Contractile Element. The contractile element is plastic in the inactive state and relatively stiff when activated; decrease in its extensibility is a measure of the active state. Properties of the contractile element are obtained from isotonic, relatively isometric, and true isometric contractions.

Isotonic contractions are those in which shortening occurs at a constant load, and this kind of contraction provides evidence concerning the kinetics of the shortening process. The velocity of shortening as a function of load (force-velocity relation) is given by the equation:

$$V = (P_o - P)b/(P + a)$$

where V is velocity of shortening, P_o is the maximum tension the muscle can develop,

P a given load, a is a constant with dimensions of a force, and b a constant with dimensions of velocity. Thus the velocity of shortening depends on the difference between the force on the muscle and the maximal force it can develop.[128] Force-velocity curves for a variety of muscles have similar shapes but different constants (Fig. 176). The maximum velocity occurs at zero load, and different muscles show a considerable range of speed of shortening. That point on the force velocity curve where velocity is zero is the point of tetanic tension. In frog muscle this value is much less dependent on temperature than is the point of maximum velocity.

Isometric contractions occur at a constant length, with both ends of the muscle fixed so that no shortening can occur. This kind of response can be obtained over a wide range of lengths and is not a "true isometric" response of the contractile element since internal shortening is allowed by the series elastic component. When a given muscle is stimulated at different lengths the isometric tension decreases when the muscle extension is longer than its normal length in the body; tension is also less at shorter than rest length (Fig. 175B). The maximal tension at near rest length is seen in nonstriated as well as in striated muscles and in single isolated striated fibers. The maximum tension developed by frog skeletal muscle is 3 kg/cm²; by the flexor of the human elbow, 4 kg/cm²; and by the smooth adductors of bivalve molluscs, 8 kg/cm².[5]

Most muscles develop more tension on repetitive stimulation than in single twitches. Stimulation is usually through intrinsic nerves, and the higher tetanic tension may be partly the result of the requirement for neuromuscular facilitation and the bringing of more fibers into action with repetitive stimuli. Muscles which give little response to single stimuli and require repetitive activation are called iterative; those which give near-maximal responses to single shocks are

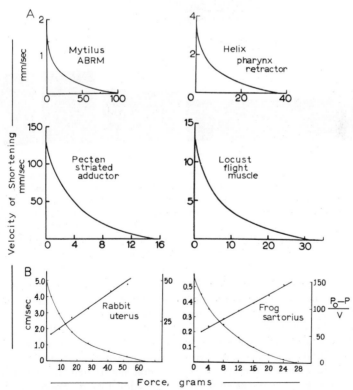

FIGURE 176. Force-velocity curves of different muscles. A, *Mytilus* anterior byssus retractor; *Helix* pharynx retractor; *Pecten*, striated portion of adductor; and Locust flight muscle. (From Hanson, J., and Lowy, J.: *in* Structure and Function of Muscle, edited by G. Bourne. Academic Press.) B, velocity of shortening of frog sartorius and rabbit uterus at different loads; hyperbolic curve gives velocity in cm/sec, straight line the quantity $\dfrac{P_o - P}{V}$ against load. (From Csapo, A.: *in* Structure and Function of Muscle, edited by G. Bourne. Academic Press.)

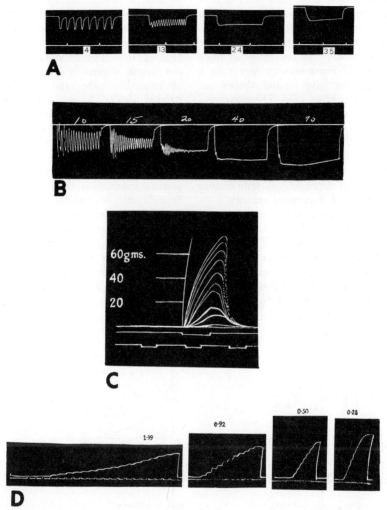

FIGURE 177. Isometric contractions of noniterative and iterative muscles. *A*, contractions of mantle of squid to stimulation of giant fiber at frequencies indicated. (From Prosser, C. L., and Young, J. Z.: Biol. Bull., vol. 73.) *B*, contractions of frog sartorius at given frequencies. *C*, responses of flexor of leg dactylo-podite of *Carcinus* to stimulation at frequencies corresponding to intervals (from highest to lowest tension) of 4, 5.4, 7.3, 9.7, 10.6, 12.6, 15.0, 19.7, 22.5, and 30 msec. (From Pantin, C. F. A.: J. Exp. Biol., vol. 13.) *D*, responses of sphincter of sea anemone to repetitive stimuli at intervals indicated. (From Pantin, C. F. A.: J. Exp. Biol., vol. 12.)

called noniterative (Fig. 177). However, when stimulation is maximal or when stimulation of the muscle fibers is direct, tetanic tension is usually higher. This is interpreted as due to the taking up of series elastic compliance in the single contraction, and once the series elastic elements are extended the energy of further contractions can go into tension maintenance. Fusion frequency is a measure of the maximum speed with which some relaxation can occur.

The events occurring during the latent period between the stimulus and the onset of contractions are associated with activation. Before an isometric contraction there may be

initial extension (latency relaxation); this is attributed to a lengthening of the parallel elastic elements while the initial contraction takes up slack in the series elastic elements.[124, 168] Latency relaxation is apparent only at lengths greater than rest length. Several nonstriated muscles of invertebrates, e.g., adductors of *Pinna*, fail to show any latency relaxation.[2] Heat production also precedes tension development. The initial heat is already being liberated by frog striated muscle at a maximal rate half way through the latent period, and the maximum of heat production is already past before the contraction peak is reached.[130, 131]

The relaxation after a passive stretch occurs in two phases, an initial fast and a subsequent slow phase. A correlation between the half-time of decay of this stress relaxation and the speed of contraction is indicated by the following:[3]

Muscle	Half-time of passive relaxation (seconds) fast	slow	Maximum speed of shortening in contraction (lengths/ second)
Mytilus			
byssus retractor	5.8	65.0	0.09
Helix			
pharynx retractor	0.3	7.7	0.17
Pinna adductor	0.27	6.0	0.3
Tortoise			
iliofibularis	0.23	6.2	0.33
Pecten striated		3.0	0.6
Toad sartorius	0.02	1.5	1.5

Active State. The decrease of extensibility, i.e., stiffening, which begins before tension is developed is one measure of the activation of the contractile element.[96, 126] The true isometric response of the contractile elements, or active state curve, is obtained by a combination of mechanical methods.[287, 288] If a stretch is applied during the latent period of a twitch, the tension which develops may be as great as in tetanus, because the extension of the elastic elements is done by the stretch. No extra tension is developed when a muscle is stretched at the peak of the twitch. The time of zero velocity, i.e., at the peak of the twitch, lies on the active state curve. If the muscle is suddenly released during the contraction, tension drops briefly to zero and then redevelops to a level slightly less than the corresponding phase of the twitch. A series of quick releases with subsequent tension redevelopment shows the decay of some active process capable of initiating further shortening. The tension curve resulting from quick stretches before the peak of the twitch and quick releases afterward gives the time course of the active state of the contractile element. The beginning of rise of tension in response to a second of paired stimuli, and the time at which tension begins to decline after tetanus, may be used to check the rising and falling phases.[58, 235, 236] In general, the active state rises rapidly, 40 msec for frog sartorius at 0°C.[127, 287, 288] It declines to zero at about half the twitch duration (frog sartorius, locust flight muscle) (Fig. 178). In some nonstriated muscles there is little redevelopment of tension upon release after the peak of tension; hence the active state decays rapidly relative to the tension (Pinna adductor,[2] Mytilus byssus retractor,[1] phascolosoma proboscis retractor[229]) (Fig. 178).

When a frog striated muscle is cooled, the twitch tension increases and action potential is prolonged,[276] whereas the tetanus tension is unaffected or slightly reduced. Application of quick stretches and releases shows that the decay of the active state has a larger temperature coefficient than does the speed of shortening. The temperature for peak twitch tension is higher for summer frogs than for winter ones, and seasonal effects have been seen in a number of mechanical properties of frog muscle. The tension developed by an actomyosin thread increases with temperature, less steeply in frog than in rabbit actomyosin; hence a frog muscle can work at

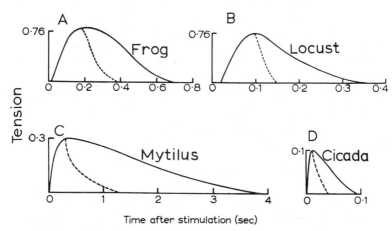

FIGURE 178. Isometric twitches (solid) and decay of active state curves (broken): *A*, frog sartorius at 0°C; *B*, locust flight muscle; *C*, *Mytilus* pedal retractor at 14°; *D*, cicada tymbal muscle at 30°. (From Hanson, J., and Lowy, J.: *in* Structure and Function of Muscle, edited by G. Bourne. Academic Press.)

lower temperatures.[259] Replacement of chloride in the saline by nitrate, iodide, or thiocyanate prolongs the active state and increases twitch tension,[168] while iodoacetate shortens the active state.[3] In nitrate Ringer solution the twitch tension does not decline so much with rise in temperature as in Cl^- Ringer solution.[132, 235, 236] Nitrate slows the rise and markedly prolongs the active state.[58] Dilute adrenaline increases twitch tension in mammal (but not in frog), probably by prolonging the active state.[103, 104] Hydrostatic pressure also prolongs the active state.[34a]

Treatment of a frog sartorius with hypertonic solution, saline or sucrose, reduces twitch tension by marked retardation of the velocity of shortening; initial heat production and action potentials are virtually unaffected, and the muscle becomes resistant to stretch; hence the time course of active state is not much changed.[144]

The active state curve gives the time course of the net processes responsible for tension development. Activation of the contractile proteins may be controlled by events at the cell membrane and in the coupling between membrane and protein. Chemical analyses indicate that the anions act on the active state before they could penetrate appreciably to the fiber interior, and the effect is quickly washed away by chloride Ringer solution. Thiocyanate and iodide (but not nitrate)[81] prolong the negative afterpotential in single striated muscle fibers.[192] A kinetic analysis of the rise in active state in NO_3 and Cl^- indicates that the rising phase is limited more by the inward excitatory coupling than by the membrane conduction.[58] When striated muscle fibers are activated the influx of sodium increases as does outflow of potassium; these ionic movements are presumably associated with conduction of impulses as in nerve.[7, 139] Muscle differs from nerve in showing a marked increase in influx of calcium; this Ca^{++} influx is 60 per cent greater during twitches in NO_3^- than in Cl^-; it increases in K^+ contracture and much of the exchangeable Ca^{++} is in the A bands.[21] Possibly the coupling between plasma membrane and contractile protein includes entry of Ca^{++} and release of bound Ca^{++} along the endoplasmic reticular vesicles.

Most of the preceding data concerning the active state have been obtained with frog sartorius at $0°C$. Such information as is available for other muscles (Fig. 178) indicates quantitative differences. The methods used with sartorius are not necessarily applicable to nonstriated and cardiac muscles, but extension to other muscles of the theory developed with sartorius may help explain the most elusive problem in muscle physiology, the coupling between membrane and contractile protein.

ACTIVATION OF MUSCLES

Relatively few important qualitative differences among muscles have been described with respect to contractile proteins, enzymes, and mechanical properties. Greater differences are known for the modes of natural stimulation. Nervous control of muscles has been reviewed by Katz and by Hoyle.[52, 149, 169]

Postural muscles of all animals, whether striated or not, are normally activated via motor nerve impulses. Two general patterns by which nerve impulses stimulate muscles follow:

nerve impulse → chemical → end-plate → muscle → activation of contractile elements
transmitter / potential / impulse

nerve impulse → chemical → end-plate potential → activation of contractile elements
transmitter / (junction potential)

Two steps are all-or-none—the self-propagating nerve, and muscle impulses. Fast striated muscles of vertebrates conform to the first pattern.[84, 85]

Vertebrate Fast Postural Muscles. A vertebrate motor end-plate is diagramed in Figure 179. The motor axon lacks myelin sheath in the vicinity of the end-plate, then it branches into a number of end-feet. At the region of the end-feet the triple-layered sarcolemma folds into many troughs (Fig. 179A and B). Section of a trough of a reptilian motor end-plate shows from the sarcoplasm outward (1) a 100 Å line which is the inner sarcolemma, (2) a light zone, (3) a dense 200 Å zone which is common to sarcolemma and axon, (4) a 100 to 200 Å light zone and (5) a dense layer next to the axoplasm[22, 63, 238] (Fig. 179). At the edges of a trough the Schwann cytoplasm separates terminal axoplasm from extracellular space. Layer (5) is probably the plasma membrane of the axon. The net effect of the folding is to increase greatly the surface area, particularly of the muscle membrane. When stained for cholinesterase (ChE), the stain is densest in the subneural (muscular) lamellae; furthermore, this enzyme persists after denervation; hence

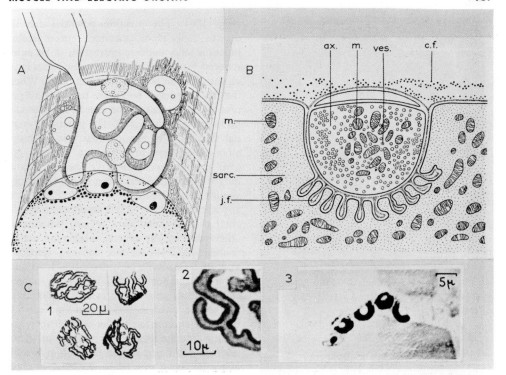

FIGURE 179. *A*, diagram of motor end-plate on mammalian striated muscle fiber. Myelin sheath of nerve axon lost before ending; nuclei of glial cells outside nerve ending. Rows of "gutters" or invaginations are regions of closest contact between nerve and muscle membranes. *B*, detailed cross-section of one branch of end-plate. *ax.*, axoplasm; *m.*, mitochondria; *ves.*, vesicle; *sarc.*, sarcoplasm; *j.f.*, junctional folds. *C*, enlargements of portions of end-plates of intercostal muscles of mouse, stained for cholinesterase; *1* and *2*, surface views at low and high magnifications, and *3*, transverse cut through end-plate leaflets. (*A* and *C* from Couteaux, R.: *in* Problèmes de structure, d'Ultrastructure et de fonctions cellulaires, edited by J. A. Thomas. Masson et Cie., *B* from Couteaux, R.: *in* Structure and Function of Muscle, edited by G. Bourne. Academic Press.)

the ChE is most concentrated in the muscular sole-plate and relatively dilute in teloglia and axon (Fig. 179*C*). Mitochondria are abundant in both terminal axoplasm and sarcoplasm. The motor endings of fish tend to be compact rings; those of reptiles and birds are

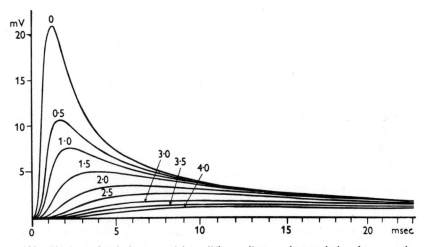

FIGURE 180. Tracings of end-plate potentials at different distances from end-plate focus; numbers give distances in mm × 0.97 from end-plate center. Curarized muscle. (From Fatt, P., and Katz, B.: J. Physiol., vol. 115.)

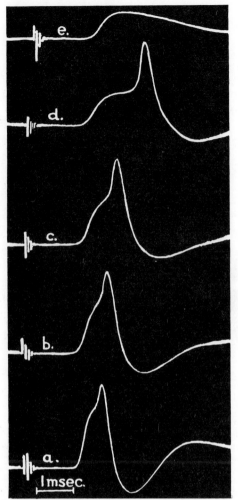

FIGURE 181. Action potentials from region of end-plate in frog sartorius: *a*, before curarization; *b* to *d*, increasing degrees of curarization; *e*, curarization complete. Propagated spike arises from junction potential in *a-d*. (From Kuffler, S. W.: J. Neurophysiol., vol. 5.)

more diffuse "en grappe" endings;[268] in mammals many endings are "en plaque" or platelike.[59] The en plaque terminations of mammals are common in phasic muscles such as the rectus oculi. En grappe endings occur in tonic muscles such as some facial muscles and the sphincter ani. The en grappe endings stain more for butyryl (nonspecific) cholinesterase than for acetylcholinesterase.[111]

When a motor impulse arrives at a vertebrate motor end-plate, acetylcholine is released during about 0.5 msec and results after about 1 msec in an end-plate (junction) potential (j.p.). This potential is local, is graded in size, and spreads electronically for a few millimeters around the end-plate where it initiates the muscle action potential[205, 261]

(Fig. 180). The junction potential can be detected only at or near the neuromuscular junction, and under curarization it becomes reduced,[83] and the muscle impulse arises later on the junction potential[180] (Fig. 181). When the j.p. is reduced by curare to about 30 per cent of its maximum, the muscle impulse can no longer be initiated.[180] The junction potential persists long enough that two or more all-or-none nerve impulses can summate to give an enhanced potential. The j.p. is prolonged as much as ten times by eserinization; similar potentials can be elicited by local applications of very small amounts of acetylcholine at the end-plate region, whereas at other parts of the muscle membrane acetylcholine (ACh) does not cause a response, and ACh is ineffective intracellularly. Tubocurarine antagonizes the action of applied ACh without an effect on resting potential.[175] If a nerve impulse is followed immediately by direct stimulation to the muscle fiber, the muscle impulse passes over the end-plate but leaves a residuum of the junction potential; hence the same membrane does not produce both.[180] The postsynaptic membrane is electrically "inexcitable," i.e., it is normally stimulated chemically.[109a] An internal electrode beneath an end-plate does not detect appreciable current from the nerve impulse; hence the transmitter is not the nerve current. Acetylcholinesterase (AChE) in the end-plate declines with time elapsed after degeneration of motor nerves.[204]

Denervation increases sensitivity of muscle to intravenously injected ACh.[232] Acetylcholine can be recovered from perfused muscle during nerve stimulation.

By intracellular recording, and varying the ionic composition of the bathing medium, Katz and his colleagues have shown that the end-plate potential in frog muscle results from a general increase in ion permeability, i.e., a short-circuiting quite unlike the specific increase in sodium permeability of the propagated impulse of nerve or muscle (see p. 590). If the resting potential (R.P.) is varied by polarization via a second internal electrode the j.p., unlike an action potential, is proportional to the resting potential. The end-plate potential, unlike the muscle spike, is relatively insensitive to external sodium, and the j.p. can be produced by the membrane in response to acetylcholine even in the absence of Na and after depolarization by K_2SO_4. Resistance of the end-plate drops to 1 per cent of the resting value during activity. Differences between the end-plate potential

TABLE 52. COMPARISON OF JUNCTION POTENTIAL AND SPIKE FOR FROG SARTORIUS
AT 15 TO 20°C[52, 85, 177, 205]

Properties	Junction potential	Muscle spike
initiated by	acetylcholine	outward local currents
conduction	local; electrotonic spread	propagates at 1 m/sec
size	graded, up to 30-40 mv	all-or-none, 20-30 mv overshoot on R.P. of 90 mv
rate of rise	220 v/sec	650 v/sec
rise time (20 to 100% peak)	1.5-2.1 msec	0.45 msec
fall time (peak to 50%)	3.8 msec	2 msec
conductance		
rise phase	general increased permeability to ions	increased Na^+ permeability
fall phase		increased K^+ permeability
sensitivity to Na replacement	relatively insensitive	blocked in low Na^+
sensitivity to membrane potential	increased by hyperpolarization and decreased by depolarization	may be blocked by hyperpolarization; goes toward Na equilibrium
space constant of membrane	2.5 mm	1.9 mm
time constant of membrane	21 to 27.msec	17 msec
resting membrane resistance	4000 ohms cm^2 throughout fiber	
membrane capacitance	6 $\mu f/cm^2$	5 $\mu f/cm^2$

and the muscle impulse are summarized for the frog sartorius in Table 52.[85, 207, 262]

From unstimulated muscles, internal microelectrodes record at regions of end-plates random miniature junction potentials (less than 1 mv each) which are increased by Prostigmin, reduced by tubocurarine, and lost on denervation. These miniature junction potentials are interpreted as spontaneous activity resulting from the liberation of constant small amounts of acetylcholine.[45, 53, 84] Increase in osmotic concentration of the bathing saline causes a much greater increase in frequency of small junction potentials.[94] An end-plate potential results from the summation of many miniature potentials; calcium is necessary for the liberation of the acetylcholine which results in these potentials.[189]

The preceding description of neuromuscular transmission is most complete for the frog sartorius. However, the essential features have also been observed in lizards[79] and mammals.[80, 154] No electrical measurements have been reported on neuromuscular junctions in fish. The end-plate potentials in mammalian muscle are more attenuated than they are in amphibian fast fibers;[30] velocity of conduction of action potentials is 3.4 to 5 m/sec in the rat anterior gracilis,[162] which is several times faster than in frog muscle. Species differences in the end-plate membranes are indicated by differences in sensitivity to the blocking agents tubocurarine and decamethonium; the junctions in the hen, cat, and man are more sensitive to decamethonium than to tubocurarine; in dog and rabbit, they are equally sensitive to each.[302] Decamethonium is more effective in blocking red than white muscles of a cat; tubocurarine is the reverse.[210] Tubocurarine blocks by competition with the ACh receptor in the muscle, decamethonium blocks by depolarizing, botulinum toxin poisons the liberation of ACh.

Vertebrate Slow Postural Muscles. The motor nerve fibers which elicit fast twitches in frog muscles are 10 to 12 μ in diameter and conduct at 10 to 40 m/sec. In addition, smaller (5 to 8 μ) axons, conducting at 2 to 8 m/sec, innervate many frog muscles.[263, 264] When conduction in the large nerve fibers is blocked or when the small fibers are dissected out and stimulated separately, the muscles give little contraction to single impulses but increasing response on repetitive stimulation and much slower contractions than when stimulated by the large axons[181-183, 185] (Fig. 182). When the small nerve fibers are stimulated, the muscle shows no all-or-none propagated impulses but only junction-type potentials which are smaller (7 to 15 mv) than the end-plate potentials of the fast system. Externally recorded potentials of the slow fibers are three to five times longer than of fast fibers; these do not propagate. On repetition the small junction potentials summate greatly and plateau at 20 to 50 mv depolarization of the end-plate region. They are followed by hyperpolarization or

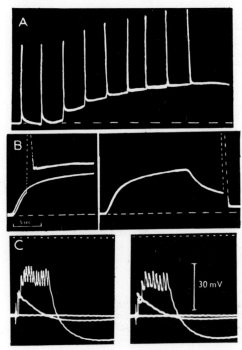

FIGURE 182. Tension records from frog iliofibularis, which contains fast and slow fibers. *A*, "fast" nerve fibers stimulated at 1/sec and, after two twitches, "slow" nerve fiber stimulation started. Twitch sums with tension in slow muscle fibers. *B*, two tension records superimposed: small-nerve stimulation at 30/sec causes smooth tension rise; in second exposure a burst of twitches is added and afterward the slow fibers maintain enhanced tension. During relaxation of slow fibers tetanus in fast fibers causes collapse of residual tension. *C*, intracellular potentials from one slow muscle fiber. Separate traces of a single junction potential and of tetanus, at 160/sec (*left*) and 150/sec (*right*). Note facilitation of potential. (*A* and *B* from Kuffler, S. W., and Vaughan Williams, E. M.: J. Physiol., vol. 121.) (*C* from Kuffler, S. W., and Vaughan Williams, E. M.: J. Physiol., vol. 121.)

undershoot of potential.[45] The membranes of slow motor system muscles show good rectification.[46] Exploration of many fibers with microelectrodes, in muscles such as iliofibularis, semitendinosus, and gastrocnemius, shows that different fibers receive the two kinds of innervation and the resting potential of the slow muscle fibers is lower (about 60 mv) than that of the fast fibers (about 90 mv). Slow fibers give small junction potentials which are increased by Ca^{++} and decreased by Mg^{++}. Only the fast type response occurs in sartorius or adductor longus; predominantly the slow type takes place in rectus abdominis and iliofibularis (Fig. 182). The slow type muscle fibers have many motor nerve endings; hence conduction in their

nerves is sufficient and muscle impulses are not needed. The slow fibers are some one hundred times less fatigable than the fast fibers, and slow fiber motor units develop less tension than fast. Acetylcholine or direct current stimulation causes a prolonged contraction in the slow fibers, and such muscles as the rectus abdominis are used to assay acetylcholine.[184] Tubocurarine is less effective on slow than on fast endings; the slow fibers are stimulated reflexly by specific low-frequency afferent fibers, and in intact amphibians some continuous discharge of the slow system is observed. Thus the slow system maintains tone; the fast one gives quick phasic contractions.

In mammals, all fibers of postural muscles are innervated by motor fibers of the fast or twitch type (8 to 18 μ diameter and 50 to 104 m/sec velocity).[183] However, there are some small (3 to 8 μ diameter and 15 to 50 m/sec velocity) motor fibers which do not increase muscle tension but do influence the afferent discharge from muscle sensory spindles. Inside these spindles are intrafusal muscle fibers, contraction of which increases or modulates the sensory discharge from a stretched spindle (p. 290).[155, 156] Large axons may innervate a muscle fiber at two or more points while slow fibers have more extensive innervation.[161] These intrafusal fibers may receive "slow" innervation.[154] However, intrafusal fibers of the tenuissimus of the cat show propagation, block in curare, and lack of eserine potentiation; hence they are of the "fast" type.[80] In newborn kittens all skeletal muscles are of the "slow" type, and change to the "fast" pattern occurs at 6 to 7 weeks.[43] In the biventer cervicis of a chicken (a red muscle), some fibers are "slow," and some are twitch fibers as indicated by differences in rise time of their potentials.[102]

Frog and toad muscle spindles also have intrafusal fibers, some of which give fast spikes with an overshoot;[79] others show some slow properties. A single intrafusal fiber may receive both fast and slow innervation by branches of nerve fibers to extrafusal muscle fibers.[107]

In summary: Vertebrate skeletal muscles are organized in units, and each unit consists of those muscle fibers (often several hundred) innervated by one motoneuron. Most muscles consist of many "fast" motor units, and each muscle fiber is activated by a graded end-plate potential to give an all-or-none propagated muscle impulse. Some muscle fibers receive "slow" motor nerve fibers; they give only the graded junctional electrical responses. Gradation of movement in the fast postural muscles is mainly by variation in the number of motor units activated in the spinal cord; gradation by variation in frequency of nerve impulses is slight in the fast muscle fibers but is very important in the slow tonic fibers.

Crustacean Muscles. Crustacean postural muscles resemble the slow motor system of the frog in depending on nerve rather than on muscle conduction but show also polyneuronal innervation of muscle fibers. Early histological studies showed that whole muscles in many crustaceans and insects are innervated by only two (or a few) axons and that each muscle fiber has polyneuronal innervation, i.e., each fiber receives branches from two or more axons (Fig. 183). Many crustacean leg muscles have triple innervation, and quintuple innervation has been observed in the flexor muscle of the carpopodite in *Panulirus*.[123] Nerve endings occur profusely over the surface of a muscle fiber, and the whole muscle may be considered as one motor unit. Usually one innervating axon is inhibitory, the others are excitatory and elicit contractions of different speeds and facilitation requirements.[95]

Not all the fibers within a muscle are innervated by all axons. Sampling many fibers by microelectrodes in the main flexor of the claw of *Panulirus* showed that 7 per cent of the fibers received four motor (excitor) axons each, 27 per cent received three, 26 per cent received two, and 38 per cent received one excitor fiber.[283] There is great variation in innervation pattern from muscle to muscle and for corresponding muscles in different species of crustaceans. In some, e.g., *Eupagurus,* and in the Astacura the opener of the dactylopodite and extensor of the propodite usually has a single motor axon; the closer, bender, and extensor may have three, and extensor of carpopodite has four.[286] Frequently one axon serves several muscles. Wiersma postulates that the primitive pattern was of one fast and one slow motor axon; this is usually retained for closer, bender, and extensor of the claw, but opener and stretcher have one (often the same axon) and flexor four.

Stimulation of a large motor axon going to a muscle causes a contraction of short latency, rapid shortening, high tension, and twitch nearly as great as tetanus; this response includes the action potential which, while it may not be complete depolarization

of the muscle, shows little facilitation. Stimulation of the second or intermediate size axon causes a contraction which builds up slowly so that there is an apparent long latency, marked facilitation, and low tension; muscle action potentials are initially small (incomplete depolarization), and on repetition facilitate greatly. When a whole nerve is stimulated, a transition from slow to fast contraction occurs as the frequency increases.[70] Fatigue of the slow system does not at the same time fatigue the fast one. Stimulation of the third, usually smallest, axon inhibits the response to the motor fibers and is more effective against the slow than the fast contraction. During inhibition the contraction may be suppressed, but facilitation may continue as shown on release from inhibition. When a moderate level of contraction is being maintained by repeated low-frequency stimulation of a fast fiber, and an extra impulse is interpolated in the series, a larger contractile response is triggered, and this level of contraction is then maintained.[284]

The distinction between fast and slow responses is quantitative. The stimulation frequency for maximum contraction elicited by slow fibers is less than that for fast fibers. At low frequencies (40 to 50/sec) the difference in response between the two fibers is slight, but at high frequencies (over 100/sec) the fast contraction is greater.[285] The amount of facilitation required to elicit a contraction varies with the species, and there are differ-

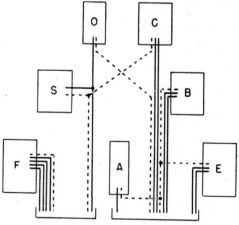

FIGURE 183. Scheme of innervation of distal muscles in legs of Astacura (crayfishes). Solid lines, motor axons; broken lines, inhibitory axons. Nerve bundles indicated by square brackets at bottom. *O,* opener; *C,* closer; *S,* stretcher; *B,* bender; *F,* main flexor; *A,* accessory flexor; *E,* extensor. (From Wiersma, C. A. G., and Ripley, S. H.: Physiol. Comp. Oecol., vol. 6.)

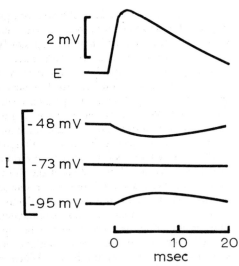

FIGURE 184. Intrafiber responses of opener of claw of hermit crab. *E*, response due to stimulation of motor axon. *I*, responses due to stimulation of inhibitor axon with membrane potential lowered from level of 73 mv to 48 mv and raised to 95 mv. (From Fatt, P., and Katz, B.: J. Physiol., vol. 121.)

ences in the ratio of numbers of inhibitor to excitor impulses required for suppression of contraction. The claw opener of *Eupagurus* has a single motor axon and stimulation at low frequency gives a slow facilitating contraction, yet intercalated shocks give quick strong contractions; hence one axon can elicit either slow or fast responses according to how it is stimulated.[282] In some species one axon, either excitor or inhibitor, serves two muscles, and innervation is not necessarily reciprocal. Some excitor axons discharge repetitively to single stimuli; these have long accommodation and short excitation constants (p. 596). For example, the fast closer of the crayfish claw is not repetitive and has a high threshold and an accommodation constant (λ) of 7.7 msec; the single opener gives repetitive discharges and has a λ of 48.2 msec, and a shorter excitation time-constant.[294, 295]

Intracellular recordings from crustacean muscle fibers show that each type of motor axon causes a junctional type of potential. The electrical response resulting from stimulation of a fast axon is relatively large, but it can be graded and rarely shows any overshoot of depolarization and little summation; it fatigues rapidly. Stimulation of slow fibers elicits small junction potentials which facilitate greatly (Fig. 184). Repetitive stimulation of some slow fibers results in contraction without more than a few (or 1 to 2) millivolts depolarization of a 70 mv resting poten-

tial.[152] It is postulated that in these muscle fibers the nerve transmitter may act directly on the contractile system without membrane participation. Normally no propagated impulses occur, although transmembrane stimulation demonstrates that some crustacean muscle fibers are capable of propagation.[87] Such all-or-none propagation is not necessary, since the nerve fibers conduct much more rapidly than the muscle, and there are many nerve terminations along a muscle fiber, and the junction potential type of electrical responses are adequate to elicit contractions.

Stimulation of crustacean inhibitor fibers alone may give no detectable electrical response. However, if the resting membrane potential has been previously displaced by a polarizing current, an inhibitory impulse tends to shift the membrane potential toward the normal resting level.[87] If the resting potential is less than normal the inhibitor increases it, that is, hyperpolarizes; if the membrane potential is high, the inhibitor depolarizes. The resting potential is some 6 mv more negative than the reversal potential for inhibition (Fig. 184).

An inhibitor may attenuate the junction potential of a subsequent excitor impulse arriving as much as 20 msec later; this reduced electrical response is accompanied by reduced contraction. In addition, an inhibitor may reduce contraction without reduction in the electrical response, the so-called direct inhibition or uncoupling of excitation. Hyperpolarization or increasing the resting membrane potential is therefore not necessary for inhibition of contraction, although it often occurs, and the time course of electrical inhibition is longer than that of direct inhibition. Inhibition is less effective on fast than on slow excitation in some preparations. It has been suggested that, as in vertebrate endplate potentials, an excitor short-circuits the membrane potential, while an inhibitor reduces the resistance in series with the membrane battery.[87] The action potentials of a *Carcinus* muscle increase in amplitude and duration when external sodium is replaced by choline; hence the potentials are not solely sodium spikes (Fig. 185). Stimulation of a slow axon normally increases the electrical conductance of the muscle, but in a medium high in calcium, conductance decreases; hence stimulation may have a dual effect on ion movement.[69]

Whether, in crustaceans, each excitor and inhibitor axon acts by liberating a different chemical transmitter is unknown. Drugs which block or potentiate transmission in vertebrate muscles (tubocurarine and the like) are without effect at reasonable concentrations, and it seems certain that acetylcholine, adrenaline, and 5-hydroxytryptamine are not concerned in crustacean neuromuscular transmission. Gamma amino butyric acid (GABA) mimics the effects of the inhibitory transmitter in increasing the membrane potential, increasing the Cl^- permeability, and in being antagonized by picrotoxin; it inhibits contraction of crayfish muscle at low (10^{-7}) concentrations. Picrotoxin can also block inhibitory endings. However, GABA has not been isolated from perfused legs during inhibition, and the inhibitory transmitter is probably not GABA, but it may be a related chemical.[110, 176, 237]

Motor control in Crustacea is graded very differently from that in vertebrates. Very few motor axons serve a whole muscle, one axon may even serve two or more muscles, yet each fiber receives several motor axons, and each muscle fiber can give quick strong contractions or slow graded ones according to which motor axon activates it. There is marked frequency dependence of the muscle responses, especially for slow axon stimulation, and extra impulses interpolated in a train of the fast type can "set" a contraction at a new level. In addition, peripheral inhibition may reduce a contraction. Conduction in the muscle fibers is normally lacking, and activation is by junction-type potentials; apparently some slow motor axons and inhibitory axons can act on the contractile system with little or no electrical manifestation at the fiber membrane. Such a complex peripheral system of gradation is efficient in minimizing the required motoneurons and central control; the integration which is accomplished in the spinal cord of vertebrates is carried out in the claws and legs of crustaceans. In *Limulus* the closer of the claw of the walking

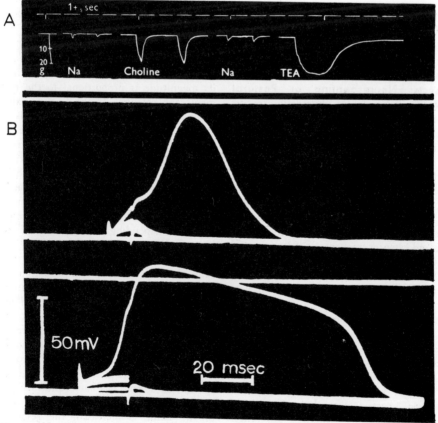

FIGURE 185. Effects of sodium replacement on responses of flexor of dactylopodite of crab *Portunus*. *A*, twitches (contractions downward) in leg perfused with saline containing Na, choline, Na, and tetraethylammonium (TEA). *B*, intracellular electrical responses of muscle bathed with Na-free saline containing 4.4 mM of TEA (above) and 22 mM TEA (below). (From Fatt, P., and Katz, B.: J. Physiol., vol. 120.)

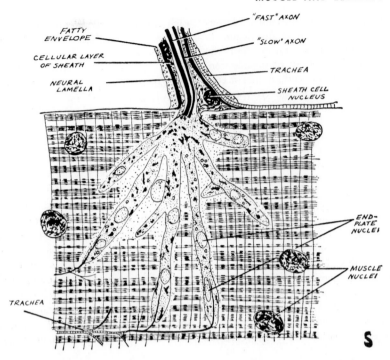

FIGURE 186. Drawing of motor end-plate on locust leg muscle showing fast and slow motor axons serving same end-plate. (From Hoyle, G.: *in* Recent Advances in Invertebrate Physiology, edited by B. T. Scheer. University of Oregon Press.)

legs receives slow and fast excitor but no inhibitor nerve fibers.[148]

Insects: Nonresonating or Postural Muscles. Polyneuronal innervation occurs in insects in a simpler form than in crustaceans. This has been studied mainly in leg and abdominal muscles of locusts, roaches, and the walking stick *Dixippus*. Double, sometimes triple, innervation, is found and an entire muscle may receive only two axons (e.g., levator and depressor tibiae of *Locusta*), or a muscle may be divided into several motor units each receiving two axons (flexor tibiae and extensor trochanteris of *Locusta*).[145] Many motor end-plates are distributed at 40 to 80 μ intervals along single muscle fibers, and two axons may enter a single end-plate (Fig. 186).[147]

One motor axon is normally fast; the other, slow. Stimulation of a slow (6 μ) axon elicits in *Locusta* leg muscles little or no contraction at below 10/sec, but elicits increasing contraction at up to a maximum of 150 or more per sec.[145, 147, 234] Only some 30 to 50 per cent of muscle fibers receive slow innervation. Intrafiber records show marked differences from fiber to fiber; in some, a large junction potential with an overshoot beyond the 60 mv resting potential is recorded, and there is little summation on repetition (Fig. 187A).

In other fibers the electrical response is initially small but facilitates very much, and its magnitude is proportional to the resting membrane potential. In the *Locusta* extensor tibiae, typical slow junction potentials were found in only about 10 per cent of the fibers. In about 20 per cent of the fibers a third type of response occurs, a small depolarization which may last 800 msec and which summates on repetition but does not facilitate (Fig. 187C). The slow depolarization is accompanied by a tetanic mechanical response at a level depending on frequency of stimulation.[51, 147]

The basalar muscle of lamellicorn beetles causes both downstroke and pronation of the wing. The fibers have single innervation by slow fibers, and muscle potentials facilitate.[67]

Stimulation of the fast axon to an insect leg muscle elicits a large electrical response which may be graded and may have the spike-like property of overshooting past zero membrane potential (Fig. 187A). The fast response does not facilitate, and when the preparation is cooled or magnesium content of the saline is increased, the response is reduced so that a true junction potential is clearly separable from the spike. The response is the same at all points along the muscle fiber, the spike is not propagated, and conduction is in nerve elements.[146] Transmembrane stimulation elicits graded spikes which do not propagate; hence they may be called "local spikes." The lack of propagation is surprising since fast axons can elicit both junctional and spike responses locally. Both fast and slow junction potentials have been distinguished from the nonpropagating spikes; the junction potentials are augmented by hyperpolarization and decreased by depolarization of the muscle membrane. Spikes are blocked by hyperpolarization and made repetitive by depolarization.[54] A prothoracic muscle of *Carausius* shows (in response to its fast nerve fiber) junction potentials which sum and spikes which have a refractory period, and (in response to its slow nerve fiber) shows junction-type potentials which facilitate on repetition. The same fiber can show both fast and slow responses.[293]

There is similar dual innervation in the closer muscle of a locust spiracle. Carbon dioxide opens the spiracle by reducing the muscle response; the mechanical response is affected more than the electrical.[150]

Not all leg muscles have dual innervation. The extensor tibialis of the metathoracic leg of *Locusta* receives a single fast axon.[147]

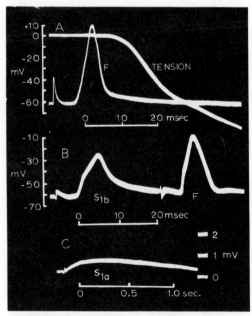

FIGURE 187. Intracellular electrical responses of muscle fibers of locust to stimulation of different motor nerve fibers. *A*, action potential and tension (downward) in response to "fast" impulses; *B*, electrical response of same fiber to one slow (S_{1b}) and one fast (*F*) fiber impulse; *C*, Electrical response to a second type of slow (S_{1a}) nerve impulse. (Modified from Hoyle, G.: Proc. Roy. Soc. London, B, vol. 143.)

Responses of trochanter muscles of *Periplaneta* are likewise of the junction-potential type.[241, 242]

No inhibitory axons have been found in insect motor nerves. However, in the *Locusta* metathoracic leg there is a third axon which can hyperpolarize when the resting potential is low; possibly it functions to set the membrane potential. Hoyle[145] recorded from freely moving locusts and found most of the normal activity to be of the slow type, reinforced by occasional fast bursts. Gradation of movement is mainly by selection in the central nervous system of fast or slow axon and by frequency of firing of slow impulses.

In summary: Insect muscles have junction-type and spike-type membranes. How the two slow depolarizing responses function and why the fast spikes do not propagate remain to be learned.

Insects: Resonant Flight and Tymbal Muscles.

The muscles of flight in Hymenoptera and Diptera and the muscles of sound production in Homoptera contract at higher frequencies than any other known muscles. In the Odonata, Lepidoptera, and Orthoptera, flight muscles are direct, i.e., are attached to wing articulations; they have many small fibrils and are only a little faster than leg muscles. The flight muscles of the insects of higher orders, however, are indirect, i.e., connect with the wings through a complex skeletal lever system in the thorax; they have a few very large fibrils (sarcostyles) in which the myofilaments are also large (90 to 100 Å).[57, 219]

Wing frequencies measured stroboscopically and by sound frequency in free flight have been correlated with muscle contractions and action potentials recorded under some restraint. In *Drosophila* one cycle of wing motion corresponds to one cycle of flight sound. The frequency increases if the wings are clipped, and with rise in temperature.[55, 56] Wing frequency is inversely proportional to approximately the cube root of the moment of inertia of the wings. The frequency is also inversely proportional to atmospheric pressure.[55, 56, 257] The maximum wing frequency that has been recorded is 2218 beats/sec in a midge, *Forcips*, maintained at a high temperature and with wings clipped.[257] The flight tone of *Chironomus* is 600 to 650/sec; thoracic movements are at a slightly lower frequency when restrained. The midge indirect muscle must be capable of contracting and relaxing within 0.45 msec.[257] In the larger insects with direct flight muscles, e.g., *Locusta*,

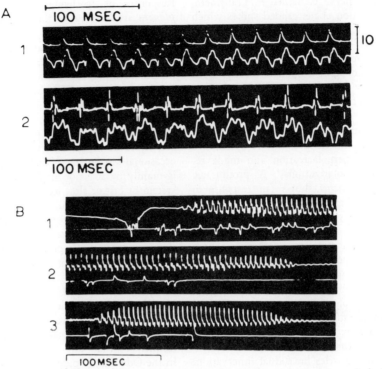

FIGURE 188. *A*, movements of thorax (upper traces) and spike potentials (lower traces) during flight showing synchronization of spikes with movements: *1*, moth *Agrotis*; *2*, *Periplaneta*. *B*, action potentials (lower traces) and thoracic movements (upper traces) during flight in insects where movements and potentials are not synchronized: *1*, onset of flight, *Calliphora*; *2*, termination of flight, *Calliphora*; *3*, short midair flight, *Eristalis*. (From Roeder, K. D.: Biol. Bull., vol. 100.)

wing frequency is relatively independent of temperature although thoracic temperature must rise to some critical value (about 25°) for flight, and frequency is not affected by cutting or loading, i.e., is independent of inertia.

Numerous analyses of the aerodynamics of insect flight deal with energy requirements and air currents.[136] The most intensive study is that of Weis-Fogh on *Locusta*.[163, 279] The power output is high—some 5 Cal/kg/hr—and flight speed is influenced by wing frequency, wing loading, body shape, and numerous other factors. Flight speed records reach 150 to 375 cm/sec in some flies.[136] Regulation of flight has been described in terms of the aerodynamics of wind forces on a wing[55, 56] and the acceleration and inertia of a wing.[257] Lift and thrust are somewhat independent, and lift is not much influenced by body angle but more by wing tilt. In *Locusta*, flight can be initiated by removal of tarsal contact with a substrate, by general nonspecific stimulation, and by wind on sense endings on the head; maintenance of flight requires wind against the wings although

wind on the head can maintain flight for some time.[163, 279] Flight velocity in the locust is less affected by environmental temperature than in *Drosophila* because in the locust thoracic temperature rises because of muscle contraction.[55, 56]

In insects with direct flight muscles, wing frequencies may reach 20 to 40 per second; there is synchrony between muscle contractions and action potentials, and wing amputation has little effect on frequency. In a roach and a moth, *Agrotis*, for example, muscle potentials can repeat at intervals of 20 msec with no facilitation[241, 242] (Fig. 188*A*). In flies and hymenopterans where wing muscles are indirect, however, there is no synchrony between muscle contractions and action potentials; there may be in intact insects one muscle spike per 5 to 20 wing beats (Fig. 188*B*). Amputation of the wings nearly doubles the beat rate without a change in spike frequency.[26, 241, 242] The indirect muscles cannot be driven by nerve stimulation as fast as the normal beat; bumblebee flight muscle tetanizes at 40/sec,[241, 242] and haltere contractions in flies are independent of shock frequencies above about 40/sec.[216] The muscles cannot be stimulated directly, yet the myogenic rhythm exceeds the frequency of nerve stimulation. In the Dipteran flight muscles there may be an overshoot (100 mv action potential with 70 mv resting potential), but there is no propagation in the muscle fibers.[24]

Similarly, in some species of cicadas, e.g., *Platypleura,* sound is produced at 200 c/sec (maximum 5400 to 7000 c/sec) by a tymbal organ in which the muscle action potentials are 50/sec and one nerve impulse corresponds to one muscle action potential. One axon supplies the entire muscle. After destruction of the tymbal membrane a 1:1 relation between muscle potential and contraction is found; if the tymbal membrane is loaded the frequency of beat is reduced.[217] In many other species of cicadas, e.g., *Meimura,* the tymbal muscle contractions, as in locust wing muscles, follow the nerve impulses, and electrical fusion occurs at about 120/sec.[113] Intracellular records from these muscles show potential responses with no overshoot, although in the cicada *Platypleura,* which has a frequency in excess of the impulses, an overshoot is found.[112, 114] As in flight muscles, when tymbal frequency is 1:1 with action potentials there is little effect of amputation of the tymbal membrane, whereas those tymbae in which sound frequency exceeds impulse frequency show an increase of beat on amputation.

Explanation of the several contractions per nerve impulse and of wing beat speed higher than fusion frequency is based on mechanical properties of the muscles. In Diptera the indirect flight muscles (of wing or haltere) are connected to skeletal elements which comprise a scutellar lever which has two stable positions, up and down. When muscle contraction moves one arm of this lever beyond its midpoint the skeletal elements spring in, shorten the muscle slightly, and release tension on it; then the elasticity of the skeletal elements (tymba) or contraction of an antagonistic muscle (paired indirect flight muscles) restores the lever to the up position and stretches the muscle. Redevelopment of tension follows this quick stretch, and contraction again pulls the lever down.[24, 66, 218] Similarly in the tymbum the muscle pulls the tymbal membrane beyond a point of instability; it snaps inward, releasing tension, then the membrane is restored by its own elasticity and stretches the muscle to give another contraction.[217] This cycle can be repeated so long as the "active state" of the muscle remains, and only

enough nerve impulses need be supplied to maintain this active state.[219]

The regulation of wing-beat frequency is different in bumblebees[25, 27] and lamellicorn beetles.[194] If the contractions are recorded under isometric conditions or isotonically when the muscle is loaded above a critical damping, the tension which is developed rises with length of the muscle along a curve parallel to the resting tension-length curve. However, under conditions where shortening can occur under relatively low inertial loads, the stimulated muscle oscillates at a frequency which is relatively independent of stimulation frequency but which varies with the mass and stiffness, e.g., in the beetle under a given load at 35/sec over a stimulation range of 10 to 60/sec. The curve described by the oscillation lies between the resting and active tension-length curves in *Bombus* and on the active one in the beetle *Oryctes* (Fig. 189).

In summary: the flight muscles of the more primitive and larger insects resemble their leg muscles in responding with a contraction for each nerve impulse. The flight muscles of the small fast Diptera and the tymbal muscles of some Homoptera show myogenic rhythms dependent on release, and they stretch and contract several times per nerve impulse. The flight muscles of some Hymenoptera and Coleoptera oscillate according to their mechanical properties.

Fast Short-Fibered Muscles of Invertebrates. A number of invertebrates have postural muscles intermediate between the fast striated fibers of vertebrates and arthropods and the slow smooth fibers of vertebrates. These muscles are nonstriated (or spiral); they vary in fiber length although they are usually longer than smooth muscle fibers, and in all of them conduction appears to be by nerve rather than from muscle fiber to fiber.

The proboscis retractor of the sipunculid worm *Golfingia* (phascolosoma) consists of small (0.5 mm $\times$ 5 μ) nonstriated fibers with very little connective tissue. The retractor is richly innervated from the cerebral ganglion by axons of two sizes (2 μ and 1 μ); all the muscle fibers are similar in size. The muscle gives fast phasic contractions much like those of some striated muscles (87 msec contraction time and 950 msec for half-relaxation) and tonic contractions of 540 msec contraction time and 2700 msec half-relaxation time.[223, 226] External recording reveals two types of action potential, spikes which are conducted at 1.3 m/sec which

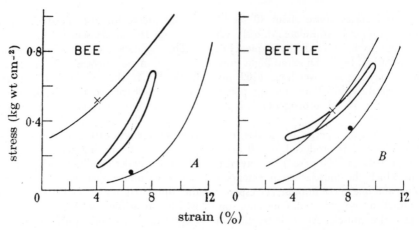

FIGURE 189.   Comparison of nonoscillatory and oscillatory tension-length curves of (*A*) *Bombus* (bee) and (*B*) *Oryctes* (beetle) fibrillar muscle. Tension (stress in kg/cm²) as function of stretch in per cent increase in length. Nonoscillatory stress-strain curve for each muscle in active and resting states; loop shows oscillation which appears during appropriate damping; • and x give unstimulated and stimulated nonoscillatory working points. (From Machin, K. E., and Pringle, J. W. S.: Proc. Roy. Soc. London, B, vol. 151.)

fatigue on repetition, and slow waves conducted at 0.3 m/sec which facilitate on repetition (Fig. 190). The fast potentials are correlated with the phasic twitch; the slow potentials, with maintained tonic contraction. The muscle is sensitive to acetylcholine. The slow waves are enhanced by eserine; tubocurarine blocks both types of response at the point of application but permits conduction through this region. After degeneration of the nerves, conduction is absent but local contractions persist. At high recording rate, nerve impulses corresponding to both the fast and slow velocities are seen preceding the muscle potentials. The nerve impulses are blocked by tetracaine but not by tubocurarine. Intracellular recording is difficult because of the small diameter of the fibers. However, contact by microelectrodes with cell interiors clearly shows that some fibers give only fast or only slow, and many fibers give both fast and slow potentials.[225] Dual innervation by fast and slow nerve fibers resembles that in arthropod striated muscle.

The pharyngeal retractors of holothurians are similar to the phascolosoma proboscis retractors. The retractors of *Cucumaria* are innervated from the circumoral ring, and when

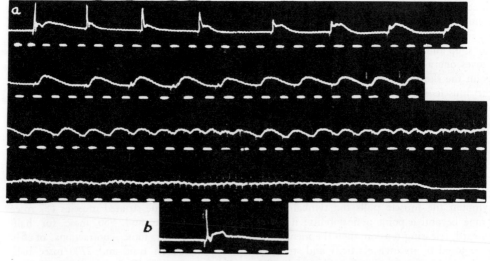

FIGURE 190.   Electrical responses from proboscis retractor of phascolosoma (*Golfingia*): *a*, action potential series at gradually increasing frequency showing decline of spikes and increase in slow wave; *b*, response to single stimulus. (From Prosser, C. L., et al.: J. Cell. Comp. Physiol., vol. 38.)

they are stimulated via the nerve, both phasic and tonic contractions can be seen. Fusion is at 2.5/sec and maximum tension at 5/sec. Facilitation of the response is markedly enhanced by eserine,[213] and neuromuscular block occurs with tubocurarine. The action potentials show two components, fast and slow, much like those in phascolosoma. The muscle is very sensitive to acetylcholine; *Stichopus* retractor has been used for bioassay of ACh.[8]

The long body-wall retractors of *Thyone* increase in tension with increasing frequency of stimulation up to about 1/sec, and they maintain contraction as long as 10 seconds after a stimulus. They have much more connective tissue than the pharyngeal retractors or the phascolosoma muscle. The sea cucumber body-wall retractors show electrical responses only out to 8 to 10 mm from a stimulating cathode; these potentials are conducted at 17 cm/sec and are enhanced by eserine. The muscle is innervated at intervals closer than 1 mm by branches from the radial nerves, and conduction appears to be entirely by these nerves.[220]

It seems probable that both the holothurian and phascolosoma muscles are innervated by cholinergic nerves and that they depend on nervous conduction.

The dorsal muscles of *Peripatopsis* are nonstriated, are sensitive to acetylcholine, and their responses are potentiated by eserine; in this they are unlike the muscles of chilopods, diplopods, and insects. In its muscles, *Peripatopsis* is more like an annelid than like an arthropod.[78] Strips of the longitudinal muscles of the body wall of an earthworm show a smooth tetanus when stimulated at 0.4/sec; enhanced excitability persists for half a second after a single shock and for some 30 seconds after tetanus. This facilitation is increased and its decay delayed for as long as 3 minutes by eserinization.[28] The response of the body wall of the sabellid *Branchioma* to giant nerve fiber stimulation shows no facilitation on repetition.[208] The dorsal body wall of leeches is so sensitive to ACh (1 part in 10^{-9}) that this muscle is useful as a bioassay. Muscles of the nereid *Neanthes* show fast and slow responses to nerve stimulation; hence dual innervation is likely.[291] A leech muscle shows only the facilitating slow response.

It is difficult to know to what extent the varied time relations of response of coelenterates are properties of the muscles or of the nerve nets, and details will be considered under nerve nets (Chapter 21). Sea anemones and medusae can give both fast and slow contractile responses.[44, 206, 245] For example, the sphincter ring alone of *Calliactis* can give both[206, 245] (Fig. 191). Both responses of anemones require facilitation, the fast more than the slow, and the typical fast response occurs at stimulation intervals of less than 2 seconds. The latency of the fast response may be 0.1 sec, of the slow one 30 to 120 sec.[206, 245] The maximum tension that can be developed in a slow contraction is less than the maximum facilitated fast response although it may exceed a brief fast response. Redevelopment of tension after quick release is similar in the two kinds of response and similar to the tension redevelopment by vertebrate striated muscle. Chemical agents which are active on muscles of other phyla show little effect in coelenterates, but tryptamine and, to a less degree, 5-hydroxytryptamine enhance both fast and slow responses of sea anemones.[206, 245] It is probable that coelenterate muscles have double innervation; certainly they are not more primitive than muscles of other phyla. In all the somatic short-fibered nonstriated muscles of invertebrates conduction appears to be by intrinsic nerves.

Conduction by mechanical pull is indicated for the nonstriated spindle muscle of phascolosoma. This muscle, around which the intestine coils, is stimulated to contract by a slight stretch, and conduction in the muscle requires successive pull from one region to the next. Thus the spindle muscle is unlike the proboscis retractor, in which conduction is by nerves, and unlike vertebrate smooth muscle where there may be electrical conduction from fiber to fiber.[229]

Molluscan Muscles. Molluscs have varied and different means of gradation of speed and strength of contraction. The entire mantle of a squid must contract rapidly and synchronously to provide the jet stream for either escape from large fish or attack on small ones. In *Loligo* the mantle is innervated from the stellate or mantle ganglion by a set of ten giant axons on each side, the one to the posterior region being exceptionally large (up to 0.5 mm diameter). A single impulse in each giant axon elicits an all-or-none contraction of the thousands of muscle fibers in the mantle, and repetitive stimulation does not increase the response (Fig. 177A).[299, 300]

Contraction time is about 60 msec and relaxation takes 200 msec. The mantle also re-

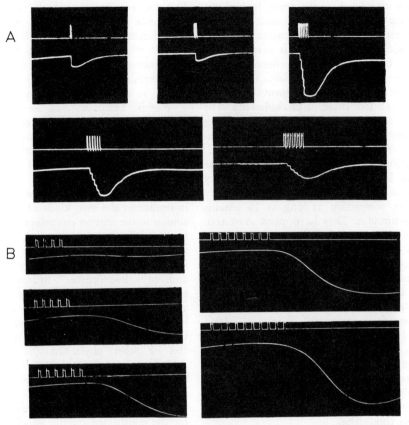

FIGURE 191. Fast and slow responses of sphincter muscle of sea anemone *Calliactis*. *A*, facilitated quick response to two stimuli at separations of 0.5 and 1.0 sec, and to six stimuli at 1.0, 1.5, and 2.0 sec intervals. *B*, slow responses to four, five, six, eight, and ten stimuli at frequency of 1/sec. Contraction recorded downward. (From Ross, D. M.: J. Exp. Biol., vol. 34.)

ceives many small fibers alongside the giant axons, which elicit a slow-type facilitating response.[291]

The retractor of the pharynx of *Helix* shows two components in its action potential, fast and slow waves; both decline on repetitive stimulation at 10/sec. The contraction increases on repetition and shows maximum summation at 20 msec intervals.[230, 247] Double innervation is indicated. The columellar muscle of *Helix* is fairly sensitive to both ACh and Adr; its sensitivity to ACh is increased by eserine and antagonized by atropine but not by tubocurarine. The red radular muscle of *Buccinium* contracts in acetylcholine, is relaxed by 5-hydroxytryptamine, and becomes rhythmic when both compounds are applied simultaneously.[83, 133]

Bivalve molluscs can close their shells very rapidly (100 msec, *Pecten*), and they can also hold their shells closed against tensions of 1 to 4 kg/cm² for many hours or days. In most bivalves the adductor contains a trans-

lucent soft portion which may be striated and which contracts and relaxes rapidly and fatigues after brief contraction. In *Pecten* the valve hinge is elastic and, by repeated brief contractions and water ejection at the sides, the scallop swims through the water. A smaller portion of the adductor consists of opaque, tough fibers which may extend the length of the muscle; this muscle can remain contracted for hours or days with little or no fatigue. Electrical recordings from the intact adductors of *Pecten* show fast synchronized response of the striated fibers when reflex closing occurs. During maintained closing there is irregular electrical activity of low amplitude and frequency in the nonstriated fibers. A stimulus delivered over the nerve to the muscle every few seconds keeps *Pecten* contracted. Stimulation of some afferent fibers to the visceral ganglion causes contraction; stimulation of others causes relaxation, presumably via inhibitory efferent axons.[17, 190, 191] Maintenance of contraction is, according to this evidence, a tetanic response to low-frequency stimulation.

There is also evidence for a holding or catch mechanism within the muscle itself. If the visceral nerve of *Pecten* is cut while the muscle is contracted, or if the scallop contracts against a block of wood which is then withdrawn, the muscle remains contracted, even when forcibly stretched. The byssus retractors of *Mytilus* consist of long (often 2 cm) nonstriated fibers. When stimulated with a direct current (DC) pulse of 1 sec or longer the muscle contracts and may not relax for many minutes (Fig. 192*A*). When stimulated with alternating current or a train of pulsed DC (pulse widths 60 msec) delivered at 10 to 60/sec for a few seconds, the muscle gives a quick twitchlike contraction which relaxes rapidly (Fig. 192*B*). By lengthening the repetitive pulses, intermediate contractions can be obtained. If, while in tonic contraction following DC stimulation, a brief series of pulses is delivered, relaxation occurs promptly.[166]

The tension of the phasic contractions increases with increasing frequency of pulses up to several per second. Successive action potentials increase in amplitude at 0.5/sec and fuse at 5 to 7/sec.[91, 226] Action potentials may sum at up to 3 second intervals.[248] No propagated impulses are observed in mus-

cles in which the innervation is blocked by drugs. One explanation of these properties of the isolated *Mytilus* muscle is based on the observation of small random electrical activity during tonic contraction of isolated muscles; such activity is attributed to ganglion cells which are excited by the direct current.[151, 190, 191] Other investigators have not seen the spontaneity when preparations were in good condition[271] and have failed to find ganglion cells.[6] Acetylcholine causes contraction which persists long after an initial depolarization and repolarization.[271] Relaxation may be due to inhibitory impulses. Serotonin (5-hydroxytryptamine, 5 HT) abolishes the tonic contraction, and this relaxation is unaccompanied by electrical change; after 5 HT no DC contractions can be elicited.[271]

Strong DC stimulation (especially anodally) of the pedal ganglion elicits a tonic contraction which can be terminated, as can that due to DC stimulation of the muscle, by weak AC stimulation or cathodal pulses to the ganglion.[209, 260a, 292] There is evidence for both excitatory and inhibitory innervation of the muscle.

Mechanical properties suggest a nontetanic explanation of the tonic contractions. If during an isometric *phasic* contraction the *Mytilus* retractor is allowed to shorten slightly, its tension falls to zero and redevelops as in

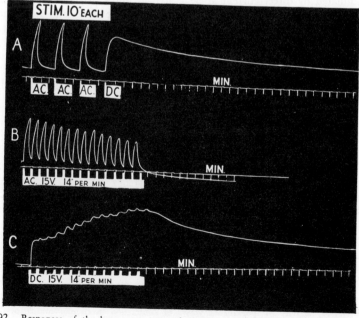

FIGURE 192. Responses of the byssus retractor of *Mytilus* to stimulation with pulsed and direct currents. *A*, three contractions in response to stimulation by alternating current for 10 sec each and response to stimulation by DC for 10 sec. *B*, response to AC for 14 sec of each minute. *C*, response to DC 14 sec per minute. Delayed relaxation and summation with DC; fast relaxation and fatigue with AC stimulation. (From Winton, F. R., J. Physiol., vol. 88.)

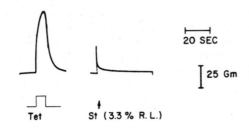

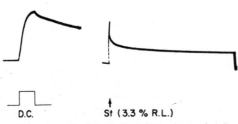

20 SEC

25 Gm

Tet   St (3.3 % R.L.)

D.C.   St (3.3 % R.L.)

FIGURE 193. Effects of stretch (*St*) of 3.3 per cent of rest length following tetanic stimulation (*Tet*) of *Mytilus* byssus retractor; and effect of similar stretch following direct current stimulation (*D.C.*). (Courtesy of W. H. Johnson.)

striated muscle. On the contrary, if a byssus retractor in *tonic* contraction is released, there is no redevelopment of tension at the shorter length; if it is stretched after such a release, tension returns to the tonic level which it would have had if the release had not occurred. If stimulated by direct current at 80 per cent of "rest" length there may be stiffening or resistance to stretch without development of tension. After DC stimulation the muscle is stiff, and after AC stimulation it is plastic, as indicated by effects of stretch (Fig. 193). Evidently some sort of stiffening or "catch" mechanism rather than tetanus is the

basis for tonic contraction to direct current stimulation. The holding function may depend on the paramyosin so characteristic of molluscan muscles. Evidence from glycerinated *Mytilus* muscle suggests that the shortening is due to the actomyosin and the tension maintenance or stiffening to the paramyosin, perhaps by crystallization. In the adductor of the large clam *Pinna*[2] and in *Mytilus* anterior byssus retractor,[190, 191] relaxation is delayed relatively longer after decay of the active state than in frog striated muscle. In intact clams it is probable that tension is maintained both by occasional impulses from the central nervous system and by the "catch" properties.

Vertebrate Multiunit Nonstriated Muscles. The nonstriated muscles of vertebrate iris, ciliary muscle, nictitating membrane, pilomotors, and many arteries and arterioles resemble the fast nonstriated muscles of invertebrates more than visceral smooth muscle. They do not show intrinsic spontaneity, but depend on nervous or hormonal stimulation; they are relatively fast, and they appear to be activated in motor units resembling those of striated muscle.[32, 93] Action potentials from the nictitating membrane of a cat increase in size and in complexity (Fig. 194*C*), and sometimes become oscillatory as more sympathetic axons to the muscle are stimulated.[72] The postganglionic sympathetic fibers which activate most of these muscles liberate sympathin (adrenaline and noradrenaline); the fibers to the iris, however, are cholinergic (p. 403, Chapter 13).

Tension developed by such muscles as the nictitating membrane increases as the number of excitatory impulses is increased up to some limit. It has been postulated[243, 244, 267] that

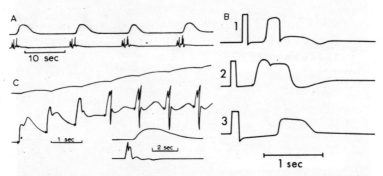

10 sec

1 sec

2 sec

1 sec

FIGURE 194. Different types of electrical response in various smooth muscles. *A*, mechanical (*upper*) and electrical (*lower*) activity in spontaneous waves of contraction in circular muscle of cat intestine: spikelike action potential. (From Prosser, C. L., and Sperelakis, N.: Am. J. Physiol., vol. 187.) *B*, diphasic (*1*), partly monophasic (*2*), and wholly monophasic (*3*) records in response to shock in rat ureter. (From Prosser, C. L., et al.: Am. J. Physiol., vol. 181.) *C*, electrical (*lower*) and mechanical (*upper*) responses of nictitating membrane of cat in response to series of stimuli applied to cervical sympathetic nerve; inset shows response to single volley of nerve impulses. (Courtesy of R. A. Nystrom.)

some of this facilitation in mechanical response results from diffusion of the transmitter through the muscle because the maximum tension when only a few nerve fibers are stimulated repetitively approaches the maximum which obtains when the whole trunk is stimulated. In skeletal muscle, on the contrary, the maximum tension depends on the number of motor units stimulated. Similar gradation of response occurs in the nonstriated muscle with injections of varying amounts of adrenaline.[243, 244]

An alternative hypothesis states that autonomic effector cells occur in complexes, each of which is innervated by several axons, that transmitter is liberated along the terminal branches of these axons, and that it need not diffuse beyond a restricted complex of cells. With such multiple innervation the response elicited by a fraction of the axons could approach that produced by the total number.[133a]

Smooth Muscle. Nonstriated muscles with properties which class them as smooth muscles are known only among visceral muscles of vertebrates. Vertebrate smooth muscles are short fibered (less than 0.5 mm long) and slow of action; they are often capable of spontaneous rhythmicity and of easy stimulation mechanically. Their activity is regulated by but is not dependent on the autonomic nervous system. Complex movements such as intestinal peristalsis are mediated by local reflexes. Conduction in smooth muscle, unlike that in invertebrate short-fibered nonstriated muscles, is slower than in any known nerve fibers (3 to 5 cm/sec) and is from smooth muscle fiber to fiber. Conduction occurs in nerve-free smooth muscle, as in the chick amnion,[228] in chick tissue cultures, in deganglionated mammalian intestinal muscle,[77] and in visceral muscles where ganglion cells have been blocked by nicotine, hexamethonium, or other drugs. Conduction can occur in the absence of any gross mechanical movement, and both mechanical and electrical responses may be graded. Drugs such as acetylcholine and adrenaline, which affect spontaneity and contraction, do not in physiological concentrations influence conduction in the muscle; ACh may cause prolonged depolarization, and Adr may polarize.[40]

In ganglion-free rings of circular muscle from the cat intestine, conduction spirals around the ring and signals can cross a narrow bridge of tissue. After the bridge is cut, leaving two separate rings, conduction goes from one to the other if they are shoved into close physical contact and if excitability at the region of contact is high.[224, 258] There is decrementing electrical spread sidewise from fiber to fiber at one-tenth the velocity in the direction of the long axis of the fibers. Electron micrographs give no evidence for protoplasmic continuity such as one would expect in a syncytium. There are bridges crossed by cell membranes, and extracellular space is low. Velocity is highest (15 cm/sec in pig esophagus) where the fibers are closest together and intercellular space is least. Appropriate electrode placement gives wave forms corresponding to a core conductor. It is postulated that conduction is by current flow from cell to cell in the long regions of overlap where effective resistance is relatively low.

The muscle of the uterus varies with estrogen level in excitability, spontaneity, and ability to conduct. The activity of intact visceral muscle is strongly influenced by intrinsic ganglionic plexuses and by extrinsic autonomic nerves. In mammals the complex peristaltic and pendular movements of the intestine require the ganglion cells of the myenteric plexuses.[179] The vagus increases and sympathetics decrease activity, although the sympathetic can either excite or inhibit according to the state of the muscle. Acetylcholine stimulates and adrenaline inhibits activity even of ganglion-free muscle; atropine antagonizes the action of acetylcholine. In fish (trout) nervous activity in the gut is abolished by warming, and coordinated peristalsis is lost.[47]

Just prior to a spontaneous action potential, prepotentials have been seen by external recording from a pacemaker region of the ureter[33] and by intracellular recording from intestinal muscle and uterus.[41] The slow prepotential waves may be virtually simultaneous in many near-by cells.

Many smooth muscles are excited by appropriate mechanical stimulation even in the absence of intrinsic reflexes. Increased tension on guinea pig taenia coli lowers the membrane potential and increases spontaneous activity.[39] Dogfish mesenteric and various mammalian visceral muscles are stimulated by quick stretch to depolarization and active contraction.[50] However, conduction passes a region of mechanical immobilization; hence it does not depend on successive pull from cell to cell.

Some smooth muscles (ureter, stomach) show prolonged depolarization lasting as much as a second, as does heart muscle (Fig. 194B). Others—intestine and uterus—show both slow graded waves and spikelike action potentials (Fig. 194A). Contractions

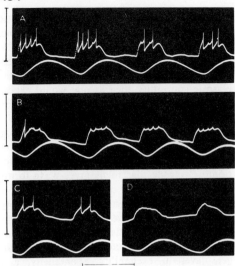

are associated with the spikes. Intracellular recording shows resting potentials lower (40 to 50 mv) than in striated muscles; action potentials may be graded, but overshoots have been observed for the spikes[141] (Fig. 195). The duration of depolarization can be shortened by adrenaline (stomach[34] and ureter[227]) or by reduced calcium; depolarization time is lengthened by atropine (ureter) and by quaternary ammonium compounds. When smooth muscle is stimulated electrically, there may be summation of mechanical responses on repetition, and refractoriness of conducted responses lasts for many seconds (10 to 20 seconds in uterus,[281] 1 to 3 seconds in intestinal circular muscle[224, 258]). Spontaneous activity in single cells sometimes shows double spikes only 10 msec apart;[42, 224, 258] hence the long refractoriness is in the intercellular conduction, not in single fibers.

Various smooth muscles in the same animal and in different animals differ much more than do striated muscles; a wide range exists for shape and duration of action potentials, electrical excitability, effects of stretch and tension, and especially for action of chemical mediators and drugs. A few examples from the extensive literature on comparative pharmacology may be cited. Adrenaline usually relaxes the entire intestine, but in guinea pigs it relaxes the duodenum and contracts the lower ileum,[273] and in fetal guinea pigs both regions are contracted by adrenaline;

hence the response of the duodenum reverses with development.[76]

The muscularis mucosae is depolarized and contracted by adrenaline or by acetylcholine. In cats and guinea pigs, but not in rabbits, atropine blocks the stimulation by nicotine of parasympathetic secondary neurons.[273] The uterine region of the oviduct of a hen is relaxed by adrenaline, while the albumen-secreting and infundibular regions are contracted by it. Oxytocin is a specific stimulant for pregnant uterus, yet other smooth muscles are not affected by it.[196]

Estrogen treatment increases membrane potentials (from 35 to 58 mv) in the uterus and causes much spontaneous activity; progesterone causes higher potentials (64 mv) and reduced activity. Adrenaline relaxes the uterus of a rat and contracts the uterus of rabbit or human in all hormonal stages; in cats, however, adrenaline relaxes the nonpregnant and contracts the pregnant uterus. Similarly, blood vessels in different body regions are affected in reverse ways by acetylcholine and adrenaline.[221]

In mammals, the vagus is normally excitatory and the sympathetic (splanchnic) inhibitory to stomach and upper intestine. Yet there is evidence for some excitant fibers in the sympathetics[220] and inhibitory fibers in the vagus.[297] In some teleost fish (trout) the vagus innervates stomach only, and both nerves are excitant to the stomach; adrenaline antagonizes acetylcholine in the intestine but is synergistic with it in the stomach. It is postulated that the usual pattern in mammals is of cholinergic excitatory primary and secondary vagal neurons and of cholinergic primary but adrenergic inhibitory secondary sympathetic neurons. In the trout, however, both vagal and splanchnic endings on stomach muscle appear to be cholinergic and excitatory; the splanchnic to the stomach is likewise cholinergic.[49] Sympathetic and parasympathetic controls of smooth muscle are not antagonistic in fish. In elasmobranchs both sympathetic and vagus nerves stimulate the stomach; adrenaline inhibits the intestine and stomach; however, the splanchnic stimulates these regions.[193] In a cyclostome, *Myxine,* where there are no sympathetic nerves, the vagus has no visible effect on intestinal movement, but acetylcholine stimulates and atropine, nicotine, and adrenaline inhibit muscular activity.[82]

In summary: Conduction in visceral smooth muscle appears to be by current flow from fiber to fiber, and the excitability is determined by the membrane potential, which can vary with tension, with the presence of ACh or Adr, with autonomic nerve impulses and, in uterus, with hormones.

Invertebrate Visceral Muscles. Whether any invertebrate visceral muscles are similar to vertebrate smooth muscle is not known. The gut muscles of many arthropods are striated, even though afibrillar;[73] many other invertebrates have nonstriated visceral muscles. Visceral activity may depend on the central nervous system (cockroach crop and gizzard), or spontaneous contractions may continue in isolation (*Dytiscus* foregut and intestine). Some invertebrate digestive tracts are stimulated by both acetylcholine and adrenaline (earthworm crop, *Arenicola* esophagus, crayfish stomach[92]); others are inhibited by ACh and stimulated by Adr (*Sepia* rectum and stomach); still others are stimulated by ACh and inhibited by Adr (earthworm gut). Probably these drug effects depend more on intrinsic nerve plexuses than on differences in the muscles. Activity of the inner stomach of the crayfish is increased by acetylcholine at concentration of 10^{-11}.

In the tube-dwelling polychaete *Arenicola* the proboscis consists of buccal mass, pharynx, and esophagus; the stomatogastric nerve plexus extends over the pharynx and esophagus and connects to the circumesophageal ring of the central nervous system. The esophagus is a pacemaker region for rhythmic activity not only of the esophagus but of the buccal mass and a portion of the body wall.[280] The esophageal activity is stimulated by adrenaline or by acetylcholine. The buccal mass is capable of small asynchronous activity when separated from the esophagus, and buccal activity is inhibited by adrenaline. In the polychaete *Glycera* also, waves of activity originate in the stomatogastric system of pharynx and esophagus. Impulses from the central nervous system can elicit a different rhythm.[280]

With respect to conduction, activation, speed, and other properties, there are many kinds of nonstriated muscles. Even the visceral smooth muscle of vertebrates varies from organ to organ, from species to species, and with physiological state.

ELECTRIC ORGANS

The first bioelectric potentials observed by man were the discharges from electric fish; today the large flat cells of electric organs are providing valuable evidence regarding the nature of biopotentials. Several interesting historical accounts of electric organs are available.[10, 14] The electric catfish *Malopterus* was known to the ancient Egyptians, and the Romans named the "torpedo," which is an elasmobranch or ray. "Electric therapy" with electric fish was recommended by Galen; it was used by Indians of Guiana and by eighteenth century Europeans. The large electric fresh-water "eel" *Electrophorus* (formerly *Gymnotus*) was brought to Europe by South American explorers, and the nature of the shock it delivered was the cause of much speculation in scientific journals. Toward the end of the eighteenth century several observers suggested that the shock was similar to lightning or to the electrostatic discharge from a Leyden jar. In 1773 John Walsh related that the shock from a *Torpedo* is conducted through metals but not through glass or air. The Cambridge physicist Cavendish built a model of a *Torpedo*, from which he deduced the distinction between potential difference and quantity of electricity. Faraday made crucial tests on *Electrophorus* by means of a galvanometer and spark gap. He prophetically remarked that if the nature of the electric discharge were understood, one might "reconvert the electric into the nervous force."

An electric organ consists of columns of plates, electroplaxes, which run dorsoventrally in the electric rays and longitudinally in the electric eel. In *Torpedo marmorata* each organ has about forty-five columns of 400 plates per column; the main organ of *Electrophorus* has some seventy columns of more than 6000 plates each. The electroplates in each column are in series electrically, the columns in parallel. The electroplaxes are derived embryologically from electroblasts similar to the sarcoblast precursors of muscle fibers. The elongate multinucleate cell enlarges laterally, and nuclei increase around the cell periphery. One surface, usually the electronegative, becomes innervated; the other is frequently papilliform. Some electroplaxes are modified muscle fibers; others are modified motor end-plates. In *Narcine* each plate receives four motor axons.[18]

When an electric fish discharges, each organ fires a train of spikes—usually three to five, sometimes twenty to thirty. In *Electrophorus* the spikes are of constant height, each about 2.5 msec in duration and 4 to 8 msec apart. In *Torpedo* each spike in a series may last 3 to 5 msec.

The individual pulses in *Electrophorus* can attain in open circuit as much as 600 volts

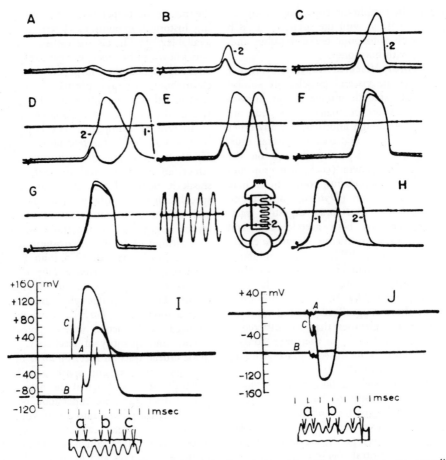

FIGURE 196. *A-H*, neurally evoked responses in the eel electroplax. The responses at two recording sites (1 and 2 of inset) are shown simultaneously. A weak stimulus to one of the nerve trunks supplying the cell produced simultaneously at both sites of the latter a small depolarizing potential (*A*), which increased (*B*) with a stronger stimulus to the nerve. Progressively stronger stimulation of the nerve caused a spikelike response (*C*) at site 2, where the initial depolarization is largest. A spike developed subsequently (*D*) and propagated to recording site 1, arising there after a local response. Still stronger stimuli caused this region to become active earlier (*E*) and synchronously with region 2 (*F,G*). The early neurally evoked depolarization does not appear when the cell is excited directly (*H*). The zero potential is shown as the third trace. The resting potential of the cell is the deflection between traces 1 and 3. Time calibration, 1000/sec. (From Grundfest, H.: Ann. New York Acad. Sci., vol. 66.)

I and *J*, membrane potentials in an electroplax from organ of Sachs of *Electrophorus*. *I* recorded by approaching through innervated face as indicated in diagram. *a*, both electrodes outside surface of plate; *b*, one electrode inside (resting potential and response with overshock); *c*, response across plate. *J* recorded by penetrating noninnervated face. No action potential until electrodes are across innervated as well as noninnervated face. (From Keynes, R. D., and Martins-Ferreira, H.: J. Physiol., vol. 119.)

and can in short circuit deliver an ampere of current. The maximum power may exceed 100 watts. The discharge from *Torpedo* is usually 20 to 30, sometimes 50 volts, which in sea water amounts to several amperes of current. *Torpedo occidentalis* has been reported as delivering over 1000 watts (one large specimen developed 6 kw!). The higher voltage depends on the longer column of plates in *Electrophorus* and is correlated with its fresh-water habitat, while the marine torpedoes can deliver more power at lower volt-

age with shorter columns since they discharge in sea water.

When a microelectrode is inserted into an electroplax of *Electrophorus*, a resting potential of 90 mv (the inside negative) is measured across both innervated and noninnervated surfaces. When the electroplate discharges, the innervated (posterior) surface reverses its polarity by some 60 mv, but the noninnervated surface potential remains unchanged. Hence the two surfaces in series give a total cell potential of 150 mv[15] (Figs.

196, 197). Direct electrical stimulation of innervated surface gives a local prepotential out of which rises a full-fledged propagating action potential; stimulation via the nerve gives a graded junction (postsynaptic) potential followed by an action potential with overshoot.[13] The junction potential is analogous to an end-plate potential in that it can be elicited during refractoriness resulting from direct stimulation, it is fatigued on repetition, and reduced by tubocurarine and decamethonium; it shows facilitation (maximum 10 to 40 msec and lasting to 200 to 2000 msec),[3] and facilitation is increased by anticholinesterases.[12] The innervated face of the electroplate of *Electrophorus* is electrically excitable after nerve degeneration. The electric tissue is very rich in acetylcholine, acetylcholinesterase, and the phosphagen phosphorylcreatine;[6] ChE is maximum in concentration at the anterior end where there are most electroplates per centimeter.[20] Thus an *Electrophorus* electroplax is similar to a striated muscle fiber; the innervated surface contains junction regions like motor end-plates, intermingled with spike-producing membrane.[13] In *Malapterus,* the electric catfish of Africa, both innervated and noninnervated faces of the electroplax are excitable, but the amplitudes differ and, on excitation, the noninnervated face becomes negative to the innervated. In the elasmobranch *Torpedo* the resting

potential is 40 to 50 mv, action potential 55 to 60 mv, that is, there is little overshoot across the innervated surface. The duration of the spike is 3.5 to 4 msec at 8°; the electric organ can be excited only by the nerve, not by direct stimulation, and the total response is reduced by tubocurarine or atropine.[5, 8] When denervated the *Torpedo* electroplax can be stimulated by acetylcholine, but under no condition is the electroplax membrane electrically excitable.

The electroplate of *Torpedo* is therefore similar to a motor end-plate while that of *Electrophorus* resembles a muscle fiber. The electroplax of marine fish *Raja,*[8] *Astrocopus,* and *Narcine* resembles that of *Torpedo* in electrical inexcitability, while those of freshwater fish—several species of *Electrophorus* and the African *Malapterus*—have electrically excitable spike-generating membranes.[13]

In the knife fish *Gymnotus carapo* the electroplaxes are in four tubes, innervated rostrally in one and caudally in three. Both surfaces of each plate give spikes, and each can be excited electrically. Normally the innervated side is activated first so that it is negative, then positive. The noninnervated surface is active in reverse sequence. Each electroplax receives several nerve fibers whose effect can sum.[7]

The synchrony of electric discharge is remarkable and is essential for maximum power

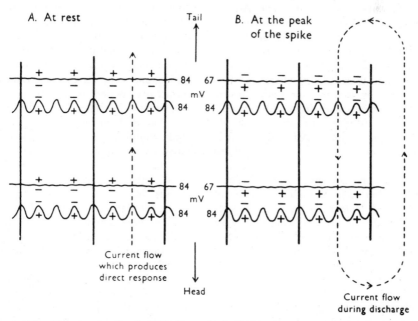

FIGURE 197. Diagram of pairs of electroplaxes of *Electrophorus* at rest and in activity showing how voltages of successive plates add in series. (From Keynes, R. D., and Martins-Ferreira, H.: J. Physiol., vol. 119.)

output. Regions 5 cm apart synchronize within less than 0.5 msec.[3] The two organs of a torpedo are said to discharge within 0.1 msec of each other, and all the electroplates of a 6-foot *Electrophorus* are activated within about 1.5 msec, which corresponds to an apparent velocity of conduction of 1600 m/sec contrasted to its spinal cord velocity of 30 m/sec. This near-synchrony indicates precise timing in the central nervous system; motor impulses going to distant electroplaxes leave earlier or travel faster than those to nearer parts of the organ; differences in peripheral facilitation may increase the synchrony.[3] The reflex discharge in *Torpedo marmorata* can result from tactile or proprioceptive stimulation, but not from lateral line or labyrinth. The electric organ can follow stimuli to the electric lobe of the brain at up to 150/sec.

One function of the electric discharge in *Electrophorus* and *Torpedo* is to stun small prey fish. Another function is electro-echolocation. *Electrophorus* has in addition to the main electric organ two smaller ones on each side, the posterior organ of Sachs and a ventral organ of Hunter. The smaller organs, especially those of Sachs, give off low amplitude periodic discharges while the fish is quietly swimming, and apparently the fish senses changes in the electric field which surrounds it. Similarly the *Gymnotidae* (knife fishes) give off a low-voltage discharge at 65 to 300 pips per second.[9] The African *Gymnarchus* discharges continuously at 200 to 300/sec, low amplitude, 0.2 msec wide pulses. This fish differentiates between conductors and nonconductors in the surrounding water and is sensitive to alteration of its electric field by magnetic or static disturbances; it normally lives in muddy water.[16] What sensory receptors are used for the direction finding is not known; possibly they are lateral line organs. Lissman calculated that differences as small as 1 mv in the field between head and tail can be detected. There seems to be no direction-finding function in torpedoes and *Malapterus*. A third possible function of electric organ discharge may be the maintenance of territoriality by individual fish.[19] Eight species of mormyrids show continuous discharge which increases in frequency when another fish of the same species approaches.[19]

Small electric fields have been detected in water around some fish, e.g., eel, produced not by electric organs but by somatic muscles.[16] A lamprey, *Petromyzon*, sets up spikes recorded as several hundred microvolts in a field extending several centimeters ahead of the fish and posterior to the gills; these spikes are associated with breathing movements. There is no evidence, however, that electrical activity from muscles is used in direction finding.

Electric organs have evolved independently in several groups of unrelated fish in both fresh and salt water. Some electric organs are modified muscles, others are modified motor end-plates. High voltage results from reversal of polarization of one side of a plate, and not of the other, so that the two surfaces add in series. The discharge may be emitted periodically for stunning prey, or continuously for locating objects in surrounding water or establishing domination over territory.

CONCLUSIONS

Animals are distinguished from plants by their ability to make rapid movements, and speed of animal movement is frequently limited by muscles. The speeds of muscles cover a ten thousandfold range from the fastest to the slowest. The most rapid contractions are in dipteran indirect flight muscles, but here the frequency of contraction is determined by mechanical resonant properties, and there is not a complete activation for each beat. The fastest muscles for complete excitation and contraction are mammalian extraocular muscles (10 msec). Postural muscles of vertebrates and many invertebrates show intermediate speeds (40 to 100 msec). Molluscan holding muscles can contract quickly but are very slow in relaxation. Vertebrate visceral muscles take seconds for contraction and relaxation, and some sea anemone muscles may contract over periods of minutes.

Numerous histological correlations with speed have been noted—striations, fiber length, abundance of myofibrils, lack of connective tissue. However, so many exceptions exist that few generalizations are possible. Minor differences occur in the relative amounts of various contractile proteins—myosin, actin, tropomyosin—in different muscles, but these cannot explain the range of speeds. Paramyosin seems to be restricted to molluscan holding muscles. The enzymes associated with hydrolysis of ATP and the compounds which ultimately provide energy for muscle contraction show qualitative and quantitative differences, and these may be one factor contributing to the spectrum of time relations. Most critical is the activation process—neuromuscular transmission, conduction, and activation of the contractile mechanism.

The contractile protein actomyosin is composed of actin and myosin, and the myosin can be split into smaller units. Some of these have enzymatic capacity. Contraction requires some sort of interaction between myosin and actin. The means of energy transfer remains unknown. Of the several theories of activation and contraction, it may well be that some apply to one type of muscle, e.g., striated. Other theories may apply to other types of muscle.

The variety of patterns of stimulation of muscles is as great as the range of speeds of contraction. Most fast muscles are activated by a single nerve impulse to give one or several contractions. Slower muscles require facilitation of many impulses before full tension can be developed. Some fast muscles (vertebrate) show graded junction potentials and all-or-none muscle impulses. Slow striated muscles (vertebrate slow and many arthropod limb muscles) use the junction potentials to activate contractile elements, and conduction is entirely by way of nerves on the muscle. Some insect muscles show fast and slow junction potentials and graded spikes which propagate. Nonstriated muscles may be long-fibered (mollusc adductors) or very short (vertebrate smooth). In the invertebrate nonstriated postural muscles, whether long- or short-fibered, conduction appears always to be by nerves. Multiple motor innervation of muscle, both striated and nonstriated, occurs widely. In vertebrate nonstriated muscles, some (e.g., nictitating membrane) require nerve conduction; in others (true smooth muscle of the viscera), conduction is from muscle fiber to fiber. Little is known about invertebrate visceral muscles, but in one (spindle muscle of phascolosoma) conduction is by mechanical pull from fiber to fiber. Vertebrate smooth muscle conducts as a core conductor with relatively low resistance between the fibers.

Gradation of movement in vertebrates is largely by varying in the spinal cord the number of motor units activated. Where slow systems occur, gradation is by frequency of impulses and by shifting between fast and slow fibers. In crustaceans further gradation is possible by inhibitory axons.

One of the major unknowns in muscle physiology is the coupling between the action potential at the muscle fiber surface and the contraction of the actomyosin. One clue is the presence of well-organized vesicles of endoplasmic reticulum or deep infoldings of the membrane in fast muscles, irregular vesicles in slower ones, and the absence of such a system in very thin nonstriated fibers. Calcium appears to be released from sites on the vesicular membranes.

Transmission at neuromuscular junctions is by chemical mediators, which are unidentified except for acetylcholine, noradrenaline, and probably 5-hydroxytryptamine. The junction membranes usually differ electrically from conducting membranes, even of the same muscle cell. Electric organs have evolved several times and some of these are modified junctional membranes while others resemble muscle fibers. The high voltages developed by some electric organs depend on the asymmetrical depolarization of the individual cells so that they add in series by rows.

REFERENCES
Muscle

For references to electric organs, see page 466.

1. ABBOTT, B. C., and LOWY, J., J. Physiol. *120*: 50P, 1953. Mechanical properties of Mytilus muscle.
2. ABBOTT, B. C., and LOWY, J., J. Mar. biol. Assn. U. K. *35*: 521-530, 1956. Mechanical properties of Pinna adductor muscle.
3. ABBOTT, B. C., and LOWY, J., Proc. Roy. Soc. London B, *146*: 281-288, 1957. Stress relaxation in various muscles.
4. ABBOTT, B. C., and LOWY, J., Nature *178*: 147-148, 1956; J. Physiol. *141*: 398-407, 1958. Mechanical properties of snail and Mytilus muscles.
5. ABBOTT, B. C., and LOWY, J., J. Physiol. *141*: 385-397, 1958. Contraction of Mytilus muscles.
6. ABRAHAM, A., and MINKER, E., Nature *180*: 925-926, 1957. Innervation of molluscan muscles.
7. ADRIAN, R. H., J. Physiol. *133*: 631-658, 1956. Ionic gradients and membrane potentials in frog muscle.
8. AMBACHE, N., and SAWAYA, P., Physiol. Comp. Oecol. *3*: 53-56, 1953. Use of holothurian muscle for acetylcholine assays.
9. AMBACHE, N., et al., J. Exp. Biol. *21*: 46-57, 1945. Pharmacology of earthworm crop and gizzard.
10. ASHLEY, C. A., et al., J. Exp. Med. *94*: 9-20, 1951. Electron microscopy of contracted skeletal muscle, vertebrates.
11. *AUBERT, X., J. Physiol. Paris *48*: 105-153, 1956. Mechanical and chemical properties of muscle.
12. BAILEY, K., Symp. Soc. Exp. Biol. *9*: 183-202, 1955. Proteins of the myofibril.
13. BAILEY, K., Biochim. Biophys. Acta *24*: 612-619, 1957. Invertebrate tropomyosin.
14. *BALDWIN, E., Comparative Biochemistry, Cambridge University Press, 1937, Chap. 5;

* Review

Dynamic Aspects of Biochemistry, Cambridge University Press, 1947, Chap. 11.

15. BALDWIN, E., and YUDKIN, W. H., Proc. Roy. Soc. London, B, *136*: 614-631, 1950. Distribution of phosphagens in various invertebrates.

16. BATHAM, E. J., and PANTIN, C. F. A., Quart. J. Micr. Sci. *92*: 27-54, 1951; J. Exp. Biol. *31*: 84-103, 1954. Muscular system and spontaneous activity in Metridium.

17. BAYLISS, L. E., *et al.,* Proc. Roy. Soc. London, B, *106*: 363-376, 1930. Adductor mechanism of Pecten.

18. BEATTY, I. M., *et al.,* Nature *183*: 591, 1959. Structure of lombricine.

19. BENDALL, J. R., Nature *181*: 1188-1190, 1958. Muscle-relaxing factors.

20. *BENNETT, H. S., *in* Frontiers in Cytology, edited by S. L. Palay, Yale University Press, 1958, pp. 343-380; *in* Structure and Function of Muscle, edited by G. Bourne, New York, Academic Press, 1960, pp. 137-181. Structure of striated muscle.

21. BIANCHI, C. P., and SHANES, A. M., J. Gen. Physiol. *42*: 803-815, 1959. Calcium influx in skeletal muscle in rest and activity.

22. BIRKS, R., *et al.,* J. Physiol. *150*: 134-144, 1960. Fine structure of neuromuscular junction of frog.

23. BISHOP, D. W., Nature *182*: 1638-1640, 1958. Motility of sperm flagellum.

24. BOETTIGER, E. G., *in* Invertebrate Physiology, edited by B. Scheer. University of Oregon Press, 1957, pp. 117-142. Interpretation of insect flight muscle.

25. BOETTIGER, E. G., Ann. Rev. Entomol. *5*: 1-16, 1960. Insect flight muscles and their basic physiology.

26. BOETTIGER, E. G., and FURSHPAN, E., Biol. Bull. *102*: 200-211, 1952. Mechanics of flight movements in Diptera.

27. BOETTIGER, E. G., and FURSHPAN, E., Biol. Bull. *107*: 305, 1954; J. Cell. Comp. Physiol. *44*: 340, 1954. Mechanical properties of insect flight muscles.

28. BOTSFORD, E. F., Biol. Bull. *80*: 299-313, 1941. Drug effects on earthworm body wall.

29. BOWDEN, J., Internat. Rev. Cytol. *7*: 295-335, 1958. Structure and innervation of lamellibranch muscle.

30. BOYD, J. A., and MARTIN, A. R., J. Physiol. *132*: 74-91, 1956. End-plate potentials in mammalian muscles.

31. BOZLER, E., Ztschr. vergl. Physiol. *12*: 579-602, 1930; *13*: 762-772, 1931; *14*: 429-449, 1931. Contraction, conduction, and mechanical properties of molluscan muscles.

32. BOZLER, E., Biol. Symp. *3*: 95-110, 1941. Motor organization of smooth muscle.

33. BOZLER, E., Am. J. Physiol. *136*: 543-552, 1942. Pacemaker activity in mammalian ureter.

34. *BOZLER, E., Experientia *4*: 213-218, 1948. Conduction, automaticity, and tonus of mammalian visceral muscles.

34a. BROWN, D. E., Cold Spring Harbor Symp. *4*: 242-251, 1936. Effect of hydrostatic pressure on isometric twitches.

35. BROWN, G. L., and HARVEY, A. M., J. Physiol.

93: 285-300, 1938. Neuromuscular conduction in the fowl.

36. *BRÜCKE, E. T., Ergebn. Biol. *6*: 327-425, 1930. Muscle time constants.

37. *BUCHTAL, O., *et al.,* Physiol. Rev. *36*: 503-538, 1956. Mechanical and chemical events in muscle contraction.

38. BUCHTHAL, F., and WEIS-FOGH, T., Acta physiol. scand. *35*: 345-364, 1955; *39*: 246-276, 1957. Contractions and mechanical properties of muscles of insects, particularly locusts.

39. BÜLBRING, E., J. Physiol. *128*: 200-221, 1955. Relation between membrane potential, spike discharge, and tension in taenia coli.

40. *BÜLBRING, E., Gastroenterologia *85*: 130-140, 1956. Conduction in visceral muscle.

41. BÜLBRING, E., J. Physiol. *135*: 412-425, 1957. Effects of electric currents and of drugs on spontaneous potentials in taenia coli.

42. BÜLBRING, E., *et al.,* J. Physiol. *142*: 420-437, 1958. Excitation and conduction in taenia coli of guinea pig.

43. BULLER, A. I., ECCLES, J. C., and ECCLES, R. M., J. Physiol. *143*: 23P-24P, 1958; *148*: 78P, 1959. Transition from slow to fast contraction pattern in kitten muscles.

44. BULLOCK, T. H., J. Cell. Comp. Physiol. *22*: 251-272, 1943. Neuromuscular facilitation in scyphomedusae.

45. BURKE, W., J. Physiol. *135*: 511-521, 1957. Spontaneous potentials in slow muscle fibers of frog.

46. BURKE, W., and GINSBORG, B. L., J. Physiol. *132*: 586-598, 1956. Electrical properties of slow muscle fiber membranes.

47. BURNSTOCK, G., J. Physiol. *141*: 35-45, 1958. Quart. J. Micr. Sci. Effects of nerves, drugs, temperature on smooth muscle of fish gut.

48. BURNSTOCK, G., Quart J. Micr. Sci. *100*: 183-198, 1959. The morphology of the gut of the brown trout (*Salmo trutta*).

49. BURNSTOCK, G., Quart. J. Micr. Sci. *100*: 199-219, 1959. The innervation of the gut of the brown trout.

50. BURNSTOCK, G., and PROSSER, C. L., Am. J. Physiol. *198*: 921-925; *199*: 553-559, 1960. Effects of stretch on conduction; comparative electrical measurements on smooth muscles.

51. DEL CASTILLO, J., *et al.,* J. Physiol. *121*: 539-547, 1953. Neuromuscular transmission in a locust.

52. DEL CASTILLO, J., and KATZ, B., Prog. Biophys. Biophysic. Chem. *6*: 121-170, 1956. Neuromuscular transmission.

53. DEL CASTILLO, J., and KATZ, B., Proc. Roy. Soc. London, B, *146*: 339-381, 1957. Effects on end-plate potentials of local application of drugs; miniature junction potentials.

54. CERF, J. A., GRUNDFEST, H., HOYLE, G., and McCANN, F. V., J. Gen. Physiol. *43*: 377-395, 1960. The mechanism of dual responsiveness in muscle fibers of the grasshopper *Romalea microptera*.

55. CHADWICK, L. E., Biol. Bull. *100*: 15-27, 1951; *in* Insect Physiology, edited by K. D. Roeder, New York, John Wiley and Sons, 1953, pp. 577-614.

56. CHADWICK, L. E., and WILLIAMS, C. M., Biol.

Bull. *97*: 115-137, 1949. Insect flight, especially in Drosophila.

57. CHAPMAN, G. B., J. Morphol. *95*: 237-261, 1954. Electron microscopy of insect flight muscle.

58. CLOSE, R. I., to be published. Time course of the active state in frog sartorius.

59. COLE, W. V., J. Comp. Neurol. *102*: 671-715, 1955. Motor endings in striated muscles of vertebrates.

60. CONNELL, J. J., Biochem. J. *70*: 81-91, 1958. Proteins of fish muscle.

61. COOPER, S., and ECCLES, J. C., J. Physiol. *69*: 377-385, 1930. Time relations of mammalian muscles.

62. CORVALLO, J. and WEISS, G., J. Physiol. Path. Gen. *2*: 225-236, 1900. Effect of temperature on contraction of frog muscle.

63. *COUTEAUX, R., Rev. Canad. Biol. *6*: 563-711, 1947; Internat. Rev. Cytol., *4*: 335-375, 1955; *in* Problèmes de structure, d'ultrastructure et de fonctions cellulaires, edited by J. A. Thomas. Paris, Masson et Cie, 1955, pp. 167-230; *in* Structure and Function of Muscle, edited by G. Bourne. New York, Academic Press, 1960, pp. 337-380. Structure of motor end-plates and distribution of cholinesterase in them.

64. CSAPO, A., Modern Trends in Obstetrics and Gynecology, 2nd Series, edited by K. Bowes. London, Butterworth & Co., Ch. 2, pp. 20-48; *in* Structure and Function of Muscle, edited by G. Bourne. New York, Academic Press, 1960, pp. 229-264. Mechanical and chemical properties of uterine smooth muscle, particularly as influenced by hormones.

65. CSAPO, A., and HERRMANN, H., Am. J. Physiol. *165*: 701-710, 1951. Changes in contractile proteins of chick during embryonic development.

66. DANZER, A., Ztschr. vergl. Physiol. *38*: 259-283, 1956. Flight apparatus of Diptera as resonance system.

67. DARWIN, F. W., and PRINGLE, J. W. S., Proc. Roy. Soc. London, B, *151*: 194-203, 1959. Morphology and potentials of basalar muscle of lamellicorn beetles.

68. DUBUISSON, M., Muscular Contraction. Springfield, Ill., Charles C Thomas, 1954, 234 pp.

69. DUDEL, J., and KUFFLER, S. W., Nature *187*: 246-248, 1960. Excitation, inhibition, and conductance changes in crayfish muscle.

70. EASTON, D. M., Physiol. Comp. Oecol. *4*: 415-428, 1957. Facilitation and inhibition in crustacean neuromuscular systems.

71. ECCLES, J. C., KATZ, B., and KUFFLER, S. W., J. Neurophysiol. *4*: 362-387, 1941. Time relations of end-plate potentials; effects of drugs.

72. ECCLES, J. C., and MAGLADERY, J. W., J. Physiol. *90*: 31-67, 1937. Action potentials of nictitating membrane.

73. EDWARDS, C., *et al.,* J. Physiol. *133*: 412-469, 1956. Effects of cations on active state of muscle.

74. EDWARDS, G. A., *et al.,* Quart. J. Micr. Sci. *96*: 151-159, 1955; J. Biophys. Biochem. Cytol. *2*: 143-156, 1956; *4*: 107-114, 251-256, 1958; Ann. Entomol. Soc. America *42*: 459-467, 1954. Electron microscopy of striated muscle, especially of insects; cytology of endoplasmic reticulum.

75. *ENNOR, A. H., and MORRISON, J. F., Physiol. Rev. *38*: 631-674, 1958. Biochemistry of phosphagens.

76. *VON EULER, U. S., Ergebn. Physiol. *46*: 261-307, 1950; Pharmacol. Rev. *3*: 247-277, 1951; Noradrenaline. Springfield, Ill., Charles C Thomas, 1956, 383 pp. Physiology and pharmacology of adrenal medullary hormone and of transmitters at adrenergic nerves.

77. EVANS, D. H. L., and SCHILD, H. O., J. Physiol. *119*: 376-399, 1953. Reactions of plexus-free circular muscle of cat jejunum.

78. EWER, D. W., and VON BERG, R., J. Exp. Biol. *31*: 497-500, 1954. Pharmacology of dorsal muscles of Peripatopsis.

79. EYZAGUIRRE, C., J. Neurophysiol. *20*: 523-542, 1957. Functional organization of neuromuscular spindle in toad.

80. EYZAGUIRRE, C., J. Physiol. *150*: 169-185, 1960. Electrical activity of mammalian intrafusal fibers.

81. FALK, G., and LANDA, J. F., Am. J. Physiol. *198*: 289-299, 1960. Prolonged electrical responses of skeletal muscle.

82. FÄNGE, R., Arkiv Zool. *40*: 1-9, 1948. Pharmacology of Myxine gut.

83. FÄNGE, R., and MATTISSON, A., Acta Zool. *39*: 53-64, 1958. Physiology of radular muscle of Buccinium.

84. *FATT, P., 199-213 *in* Handbook of Physiology, sect 1, Neurophysiology, vol. 1, Chap. VI. Washington, American Physiological Society, 1959. Skeletal neuromuscular transmission.

85. FATT, P., and KATZ, B., J. Physiol. *115*: 320-370, 1951. Intrafiber analysis of end-plate potentials.

86. FATT, P., and KATZ, B., J. Physiol. *117*: 109-128, 1952. Spontaneous subthreshold activity at motor nerve endings.

87. FATT, P., and KATZ, B., J. Physiol. *120*: 171-204, 1953; *121*: 374-389, 1953. Electrical properties of crustacean muscle, effects of inhibitory nerve impulses.

88. *FEIGEN, G. A., Ann. Rev. Physiol. *18*: 89-120, 1956. Relaxation of muscle.

89. FINCK, H., HOLTZER, H., and MARSHALL, J. M., J. Biophys. Biochem. Cytol. *2* (suppl.): 175-178, 1956. Distribution and development of myosin in glycerol-extracted muscle as revealed by fluorescent antimyosin.

90. FLECKENSTEIN, A., *et al.,* Nature *174*: 1081-1083, 1954. Contraction of muscle without breakdown of ATP.

91. FLETCHER, C. M., J. Physiol. *90*: 233-253, 415-428, 1937. Excitation and electrical responses from Mytilus anterior byssus retractor.

92. FLOREY, E., Ztschr. vergl. Physiol. *36*: 1-8, 1954. Pharmacology of crayfish gut muscle.

93. *FURCHGOTT, R. F., Pharmacol. Rev. *7*: 185-265, 1955. Pharmacology of vascular smooth muscle.

94. FURSHPAN, E. J., J. Physiol. *134*: 689-697, 1956. Osmotic effects on spontaneous activity at motor nerve endings.

95. *FURSHPAN, E. J., *in* Handbook of Physiology. Washington, American Physiological Society,

1959, Sect. 1, vol. 1, pp. 239-254. Invertebrate neuromuscular transmission.

96. GASSER, H. S., and HILL, A. V., Proc. Roy. Soc. London, B, 96: 398-437, 1924. Dynamics of muscular contraction.

97. GEORGE, J. C., et al., J. Anim. Morphol. Physiol. 4: 96-100, 119-123, 1957. Chemistry of flight and heart muscles of birds.

98. GERGELY, J., Ann. New York Acad. Sci. 81: 490-504, 1959. Relaxing factor of muscle.

99. GILMOUR, D., J. Biol. Chem. 175: 477-478, 1948. ATPase action of insect muscle.

100. GILMOUR, D., and CALABY, J. H., Enzymologia 16: 23-40, 1953. Myokinase and pyrophosphatase of insect muscle.

101. GILSON, A. S., et al., Ann. New York Acad. Sci. 47: 697-714, 1947. Time relations of various muscles.

102. GINSBORG, B. L., J. Physiol. 48: 50P-51P, 1959. Fast and slow fibers in chick muscle.

103. GOFFART, M., Arch. Internat. Physiol. 60: 318-418, 1952. Time constants of muscles.

104. GOFFART, M., and RITCHIE, J. M., J. Physiol. 116: 357-371, 1952. Effects of adrenaline on mammalian muscle.

105. GORDON, G., and HOLBOURN, A. H. S., J. Physiol. 110: 26-35, 1949. Mechanical activity of single motor units.

106. GORDON, G., and PHILLIPS, C. G., J. Physiol. 110: 6P-7P, 1949. Slow and fast units in cat tibialis anterior.

107. GRAY, E. G., Proc. Roy. Soc. London, B, 146: 416-430, 1957. Spindle and extrafusal innervation of frog muscle.

108. GRIFFITHS, D. E., et al., Biochem. J. 65: 612-617, 1957. Phosphagens in echinoids.

109. GRIMSTONE, A. V., et al., Quart. J. Micr. Sci. 99: 523-540, 1958. Fine structure of mesenteric muscles in Metridium.

109a. *GRUNDFEST, H., Ann. New York Acad. Sci. 66: 537-591, 1957. Types of excitable membranes.

110. GRUNDFEST, H., et al., J. Gen. Physiol. 42: 1301-1323, 1959. Pharmacology of lobster neuromuscular transmission.

111. HAGGQUIST, G., Acta physiol. scand. 48: 63-70, 1960. Cholinesterase in motor nerve endings, skeletal muscle.

112. HAGIWARA, S., Jap. J. Physiol. 3: 284-296, 1953. Neuromuscular transmission in insects.

113. HAGIWARA, S., Bull. Tokyo Med. Dent. Univ. 1: 113-124, 1959. Myogenic rhythm of sound-producing muscles in cicadas.

114. HAGIWARA, S., and WATANABE, A., Jap. J. Physiol. 4: 65-78, 1954. Action potentials in muscles of insects.

115. HAGIWARA, S., and WATANABE, A., J. Physiol. 129: 513-527, 1955. The effect of tetraethyl-ammonium chloride on the insect muscle membrane examined with an intracellular electrode.

116. HAKANSSON, C. H., Acta physiol. scand. 41: 199-216, 1957. Responses of frog muscle fibers at different degrees of stretch.

117. HAMOIR, G., Adv. Protein Chem. 10: 227-288, 1955. Proteins of fish muscle.

118. *HAMOIR, G., J. de Physiol. Paris 48: 155-205, 1956. Structure and biochemistry of striated muscles.

119. HANSON, J., J. Biophys. Biochem. Cytol. 3: 111-122, 1957. Structure of muscle fibers of earthworm body wall.

120. HANSON, J., and HUXLEY, H. E., Symp. Soc. Exp. Biol. 9: 228-264, 1955; in Structure and Function of Muscle, edited by G. Bourne. New York, Academic Press, pp. 188-227, 1960. Morphological evidence for sliding molecule hypothesis of muscle contraction.

121. HANSON, J., and LOWY, J., Nature 180: 906-909, 1957; 184: 286-287, 1959. J. Physiol. 149: 31P-32P, 1959. Structure of nonstriated muscles of various invertebrates.

122. *HANSON, J., and LOWY, J., in Structure and Function of Muscle, edited by G. Bourne. New York, Academic Press, 1960, pp. 265-335. Structure and function of contractile apparatus of muscles of invertebrate animals.

123. van HARREVELD, H., and WIERSMA, C. A. G., J. Exp. Biol. 16: 122-133, 1939. Quintuple innervation of Panulirus muscle.

124. HILL, A. V., Proc. Roy. Soc. London, B, 136: 211-219, 242-254, 399-435, 1949. The onset of contraction, energetics of relaxation in striated muscle.

125. HILL, A. V., Proc. Roy. Soc. London, B, 138: 325-329, 1951. Effect of series compliance on tension development in muscle twitch.

126. HILL, A. V., Proc. Roy. Soc. London, B, 138: 329-348, 1951. Transition from rest to activity in striated muscle.

127. HILL, A. V., Proc. Roy. Soc. London, B, 138: 349-354, 1951. Effect of temperature on tension development by muscle.

128. HILL, A. V., Proc. Roy. Soc. London, B, 141: 104-117, 1953. Mechanical properties of active muscle.

129. *HILL, A. V., Science 131: 897-903, 1960. Production and absorption of heat by muscle.

130. HILL, A. V., Proc. Roy. Soc. London, B, 148: 397-402, 1958. Time course of heat production, relation between heat and total work in contracting muscle.

131. HILL, A. V., and HOWARTH, J. V., Proc. Roy. Soc. London, B, 151: 169-193, 1959. Time course of heat production; relation between heat and total work in contracting muscle.

132. HILL, A. V., and MACPHERSON, L., Proc. Roy. Soc. London, B, 143: 81-102, 1954. Effect of nitrate, iodide and bromide on active state duration.

133. HILL, R. B., Biol. Bull. 115: 471-482, 1958. Effects of drugs on Busycon muscles.

133a. HILLARP, N.-Å., in Handbook of Physiology, sect 1, Neurophysiology, part 2, Chap. 38, pp. 979-1006. Washington, American Physiological Society; Acta physiol. scandinav. 46 (suppl. 157): 1-38, 1959. Peripheral autonomic mechanisms.

134. *HINES, M., Quart. Rev. Biol. 2: 149-180, 1927. Red and white muscle.

135. HOBSON, G. E., and REES, K. R., Biochem. J. 61: 549-552, 1955. Annelid phosphagens.

136. HOCKING, B., Tr. Roy. Entomol. Soc. London 104: 223-345, 1953. Intrinsic range and speed of flight of insects.

137. HODGE, A. J., Proc. Nat. Acad. Sci. 38: 850-

855, 1952. Periodism in reconstituted paramyosin from Venus adductors.

138. HODGE, A. J., J. Biophys. Biochem. Cytol. 2: 131-142, 1956. Fine structure of striated muscle.

139. HODGKIN, A. L., and HOROWICZ, P., J. Physiol. 145: 405-432, 1959. Movements of sodium and potassium in single muscle fibers.

140. HOFFMANN-BERLING, H., Biochim. Biophys. Acta 27: 247-255, 1958. Properties of glycerinated stalk of Vorticella.

141. HOLMAN, M. E., J. Physiol. 136: 569-584, 1956; 137: 77P-78P, 1957; J. Physiol. 141: 1464-1488, 1958. Effects of sodium chloride and potassium chloride concentrations on potentials and tension in guinea pig taenia coli.

142. HOLTZER, H., MARSHALL, J. M., and FINCK, H., J. Biophys. Biochem. Cytol. 3: 705-724, 1957. Distribution and development of myosin in glycerol-extracted muscle as revealed by fluorescent antimyosin.

143. HORRIDGE, A., Quart. J. Micr. Sci. 95: 85-92, 1954. Histology of Aurelia.

144. HOWARTH, J. V., J. Physiol. 144: 167-175, 1958. Effects of hypertonic solutions on active state of frog muscle.

145. HOYLE, G., J. Physiol. 121: 32P-33P, 1953; Proc. Roy. Soc. London, B, 143: 281-291, 343-367, 1955. Functional morphology of neuromuscular transmission in locust muscles.

146. HOYLE, G., J. Physiol. 127: 90-103, 1955. Effects of cations on neuromuscular transmission in insects.

147. HOYLE, G., in Recent Advances in Invertebrate Physiology, edited by B. Scheer. University of Oregon Press, 1957, pp. 73-98. Nervous control of insect muscles.

148. HOYLE, G., Biol. Bull. 115: 210-218, 1958. Neuromuscular transmission in Limulus.

149. *HOYLE, G., Comparative Physiology of Nervous Control of Muscular Contraction. Cambridge University Press, 1957, 147 pp.

150. HOYLE, G., J. Ins. Physiol. 3: 378-394, 1959; 4: 63-79, 1960. Neuromuscular control of insect spiracles.

151. HOYLE, G., and LOWY, J., J. Exp. Biol. 33: 295-310, 1956. Tetanic hypothesis of holding by Mytilus muscle.

152. HOYLE, G., and WIERSMA, C. A. G., J. Physiol. 143: 403-453, 1958. Analysis of fast and slow contractions, inhibition in crustacean muscle by intracellular recording.

153. HUMPHREY, G. F., Physiol. Comp. Oecol. 1: 89-94, 1948. ATPase of myosin from marine animals.

154. HUNT, C. C., and KUFFLER, S. W., J. Physiol. 113: 283-297, 1951. Activation of mammalian muscle spindles by small-nerve fibers.

155. HUNT, C. C., and KUFFLER, S. W., J. Physiol. 126: 292-303, 1954. Multiple innervation of cat and frog muscle fibers.

156. HUXLEY, A. F., Prog. Biophys. 7: 257-318, 1957. Muscle structure and theories of contraction.

157. *HUXLEY, A. F., Ann. New York Acad. Sci. 81: 446-452, 1959. Theories of muscular contraction.

158. HUXLEY, A. F., and NIEDERGERKE, R., J. Physiol. 144: 403-425, 1958. Dimensions of striations in rest, contraction and stretch.

159. HUXLEY, A. F., and TAYLOR, R. E., J. Physiol. 144: 426-441, 1958. Local activation of frog and crab striated muscle.

160. HUXLEY, H. E., J. Biophys. Biochem. Cytol. 3: 631-647, 1957. Ultrastructure of striated muscle.

161. HUXLEY, H. E., and HANSON, J., in Structure and Function of Muscle, edited by G. Bourne. New York, Academic Press, 1960, pp. 183-227. Molecular basis of contraction in striated muscles.

162. JARCHO, L. W., et al., Am. J. Physiol. 168: 446-487, 1952. Conduction in mammalian skeletal muscle, action of neuromuscular blocking agents.

163. JENSEN, M., Phil. Tr. Roy. Soc. London, B, 239: 511-552, 1956. Biology and physics (aerodynamics) of locust flight.

164. JEWELL, B. R., J. Physiol. 149: 154-177, 1959. Phasic and tonic responses of Mytilus byssus retractor.

165. JEWELL, B. R., and WILKIE, D. R., J. Physiol. 143: 515-540, 1958. Analysis of mechanical components of frog striated muscle.

166. JOHNSON, W. H., and TWAROG, B. M., J. Gen. Physiol. 43: 941-960, 1960; with Kahn, J. S., Science 130: 160-161, 1959. Mechanism of prolonged contractions in molluscan muscles.

167. JORDAN, H. E., J. Morphol. 96: 513-536, 1955. Histology of insect muscle.

168. KAHN, A. J., and SANDOW, A., Ann. New York Acad. Sci. 62: 137-175, 1955. Effects of anions on skeletal muscle.

169. *KATZ, B., Biol. Rev. 24: 1-20, 1949. Neuromuscular transmission in invertebrates.

170. KATZ, B., and KUFFLER, S. W., Proc. Roy. Soc. London, B, 133: 374-389, 1946. Excitation of neuromuscular system in Crustacea.

171. KAWAGUTI, S., and IKEMOTO, N., Biol. J. Okayama Univ. 4: 207-216, 1958; 5: 57-87, 1959. Electron microscopy of muscles of nereid worm, oyster, and earthworm.

172. KAY, C. M., Biochim. Biophys. Acta 27: 469-477, 1958. Physicochemical properties of Pinna tropomyosin.

173. KAY, C. M., and BAILEY, K., Biochim. Biophys. Acta 31: 20-25, 1959. Chemistry of Pinna tropomyosin.

174. KENNEY, J. W., and RICHARDS, A. G., Entomol. News 66: 29-36, 1955. Enzymatic properties of leg and flight muscle proteins, giant water bug.

175. KIRSCHNER, L. B., and STONE, W. E., J. Gen. Physiol. 34: 821-834, 1951. Action of neuromuscular blocking agents.

176. VAN DER KLOOT, W. G., and ROBBINS, J., Experientia 15: 35-36, 1959. Effects of GABA and picrotoxin on crayfish muscle.

177. KOKETSU, K., and NISHI, S., J. Physiol. 139: 15-26, 1957. Electrical properties of intrafusal muscle fibers in frog.

178. KOMINZ, D. R., SAAD, F., and LAKI, K., in Conference on Chemistry of Muscular Contraction. Tokyo, Committee of Muscle Chemistry of Japan, 1957, pp. 66-75. Chemical characteristics of annelid, mollusc, and arthropod tropomyosins.

179. Kosterlitz, H. W., *et al.*, J. Physiol. *133*: 681-694, 1956. Mechanism of peristaltic reflex in guinea pig ileum.

180. Kuffler, S. W., J. Neurophysiol. *5*: 18-26, 1942. End-plate potentials.

181. Kuffler, S. W., Am. J. Phys. Med. *34*: 161-171, 1955. Properties of slow motor system in frog.

182. Kuffler, S. W., and Gerard, R. W., J. Neurophysiol. *10*: 383-394, 1947. The slow motor system in frogs.

183. Kuffler, S. W., and Hunt, C. C., Assn. Res. Nerv. Ment. Dis. Proc. *30*: 24-47, 1950. Patterns of innervation of intrafusal and extrafusal muscle fibers in mammals.

184. Kuffler, S. W., and Vaughan Williams, E. M., J. Physiol. *121*: 289-340, 1953. Properties of slow skeletal fibers and their neuromuscular junctions, frog.

185. Kuffler, S. W., *et al.*, J. Neurophysiol. *10*: 395-408, 1947. Properties of slow motor system in frog.

186. Laki, K., J. Cell. Comp. Physiol. *49* (suppl. 1): 249-265, 1957. The composition of contractile muscle proteins.

187. Lapicque, L., C. R. Soc. Biol. *128*: 688-692, 1938. Time constants of excitation of various muscles.

188. Lawrie, R. A., Nature *170*: 122-123, 1952. Biochemical differences between red and white muscles.

189. Lilly, A. W., J. Physiol. *133*: 571-587, 1956; *136*: 595-605, 1957. Quantal release of transmitter at mammalian neuromuscular junctions.

190. Lowy, J., J. Physiol. *120*: 129-140, 1953; *124*: 100-105, 1954; Nature *176*: 345-347, 1955. Contraction and relaxation systems in molluscan muscles.

191. Lowy, J., and Millman, B. M., Nature *183*: 1730-1731, 1959. Contraction and relaxation in muscles of Mytilus and Pecten.

192. Lubin, M., J. Gen. Physiol. *49*: 335-349, 1957. Effect of iodide and thiocyanate on mechanical and electrical properties of frog muscle.

193. Lutz, B. R., Biol. Bull. *61*: 93-100, 1931. Regulation of visceral muscle, elasmobranchs.

194. Machin, K. E., and Pringle, J. W. S., Proc. Roy. Soc. London, B, *151*: 204-225, 1959. Mechanical properties of a beetle flight muscle.

195. Mark, J. S. T., Anat. Rec. *125*: 473-493, 1956. Electron microscopy of uterine smooth muscle.

195a. Marsh, B. B., Bioch. Biophys. Res. Comm. *3*: 233-238, 1960. Muscle relaxing factor.

196. Marshall, J. M., Am. J. Physiol. *197*: 935-942, 1959. Effects of estrogen and progesterone on potentials in uterine muscle fibers.

197. Maruyama, K., Enzymologia *17*: 90-94, 1954; Biochim. Biophys. Acta *16*: 589-590, 1955; Biol. Bull. *114*: 95-105, 1958. ATPase in contractile protein from echiuroid, sea anemone, and crayfish.

198. McSweney, M. A., and Robeson, J. M., J. Physiol. *68*: 124-131, 1929. Contraction rate of mammalian stomach.

199. Mommaerts, W. F. H. M., Nature *174*: 1083-1084, 1954. Contraction of muscle without breakdown of ATP.

200. Mommaerts, W. F. H. M., *in* Enzymes, Units of Biological Structure and Function, edited by O. H. Gaebler. New York, Academic Press, 1956, pp. 317-324; Science *126*: 1294, 1957. Enzymatic properties, actomyosin.

201. Mommaerts, W. F. H. M., and Aldrich, B. B., Biochim. Biophys. Acta *28*: 627-636, 1958. Molecular size of actomyosin.

202. Moos, C., and Lorand, L., Biochim. Biophys. Acta *24*: 461-479, 1957. Contraction and relaxation of glycerinated muscle.

203. Morales, M. F., *in* Enzymes, Units of Biological Structure and Function, edited by O. H. Gaebler. New York, Academic Press, 1956, pp. 325-336. Role of ATP in muscle contraction.

204. Nachmansohn, D., J. Physiol. *95*: 29-35, 1939. Cholinesterase of muscle.

205. Nastuck, W. L., J. Cell. Comp. Physiol. *42*: 249-272, 1953. Electrical activity at neuromuscular junctions.

206. Needler, M., and Ross, D. M., J. Mar. Biol. Assn. U. K. *37*: 789-805, 1958. Fast and slow contractions in sea anemone Calliactes.

207. Nicholls, J. G., J. Physiol. *131*: 1-12, 1955. Electrical properties of denervated skeletal muscle.

208. Nicol, J. A. C., J. Exp. Biol. *28*: 22-31, 1951; Physiol. Compar. Oecol. *2*: 339-345, 1952. Excitation stimulation of muscle by giant nerve fibers in sabellid Branchioma.

209. Nieuwenhoven, L. M., Investigation of structure and function of anterior byssal retractor muscle of Mytilus edulis. Thesis, University of Utrecht, 1947, 120 pp.

210. Paton, W. D. M., and Zaimis, E. J., J. Physiol. *112*: 311-331, 1951. Effects of neuromuscular blocking agents in mammals.

211. Peachey, L. D., Personal communication.

212. *Perry, S. V., Symp. Soc. Exp. Biol. *9*: 203-226, 1955; Physiol. Rev. *36*: 1-76, 1956. Relation between structure, chemical composition, and contraction of muscle proteins.

213. Pople, W., and Ewer, D. W., J. Exp. Biol. *31*: 114-126, 1954; *32*: 59-69, 1955. Properties of myoneural junction in holothurian pharyngeal retractor.

214. Porter, K. R., J. Biophys. Biochem. Cytol. *2* (supp): 163-170, 1956. Sarcoplasmic reticulum in striated muscle fibers.

215. Porter, K. R., and Palade, G. E., J. Biophys. Biochem. Cytol. *3*: 269-299, 1957. Sarcoplasmic reticulum in striated muscle fibers.

216. Pringle, J. W. S., J. Physiol. *108*: 226-232, 1949. Excitation and contraction of insect flight muscles.

217. Pringle, J. W. S., J. Exp. Biol. *31*: 525-560, 1954. Physiological analysis of sound production in cicadas.

218. Pringle, J. W. S., J. Physiol. *124*: 269-291, 1954; *in* Recent Advances in Invertebrate Physiology, edited by B. Scheer. University of Oregon Press, 1957, pp. 99-115. Myogenic rhythms in certain insect muscles.

219. *Pringle, J. W. S., Insect Flight, Cambridge University Press, 1957, 133 pp.

220. Prosser, C. L., J. Cell. Comp. Physiol. *44*: 247-254, 1954. Conduction in longitudinal muscles of holothurian Thyone.

221. *Prosser, C. L., *in* Structure and Function of Muscle, edited by G. Bourne. New York, Academic Press, 1960, vol. 2, pp. 387-434.

222. Prosser, C. L., Burnstock, G., and Kahn, J., Am. J. Physiol. *199*: 545-552, 1960. Electron microscopy of smooth muscle.

223. Prosser, C. L., and Melton, C. E., J. Cell. Comp. Physiol. *44*: 255-275, 1954. Conduction by nerves in proboscis retractor of sipunculid Golfingia.

224. Prosser, C. L., and Sperelakis, N., Am. J. Physiol. *187*: 536-545, 1956. Conduction in ganglion-free rings of intestinal muscle of cat.

225. Prosser, C. L., and Sperelakis, N., *54*: 129-133, 1959. Double innervation of fibers in proboscis retractor of sipunculid Golfingia.

226. Prosser, C. L., *et al.,* J. Cell. Comp. Physiol. *38*: 299-319, 1951. Conduction by nerves in proboscis retractor of sipunculid Golfingia.

227. Prosser, C. L., *et al.,* Am. J. Physiol. *181*: 651-660, 1955. Action potentials of rat ureter.

228. Prosser, C. L., *et al.,* Am. J. Physiol. *187*: 546-548, 1956. Electrical activity in chick amnion.

229. Prosser, C. L., *et al.,* J. Cell. Comp. Physiol. *54*: 135-146, 1959. Conduction by stretch in spindle muscle of Golfingia and conduction in mesenteric muscle of dogfish.

230. Ramsay, J. A., J. Exp. Biol. *17*: 96-115, 1940. Properties of buccal retractor of Helix.

230a. *Ramsey, R. W., *in* Medical Physics, edited by O. Glaser. Chicago, Year Book Publishers, 1944, pp. 788-798.

231. Randall, J. T., J. Cell. Comp. Physiol. *49* (suppl.): 199-220, 1957. Distribution of proteins in bands of striated muscle.

232. Reid, G., and Vaughan Williams, E. M., J. Physiol. *109*: 25-31, 1949. Development of sensitivity to acetylcholine in denervated muscle.

233. Richards, A. G., and Kenney, J. W., Entomol. News *66*: 29-36, 1955. Chemical differences between leg and flight muscle of giant water bug.

234. Ripley, S. H., and Ewer, D. W., S. African J. Sci. *49*: 320-322, 1953. Neuromuscular facilitation in locust.

235. Ritchie, J. M., J. Physiol. *124*: 605-612, 1954; *126*: 155-168, 1954. Analysis of active state of frog muscle; effects of anions.

236. Ritchie, J. M., and Wilkie, D. R., J. Physiol. *130*: 488-496, 1955. Effect of prior stimulation on active state of frog muscle.

237. Robbins, J., and van der Kloot, W. G., J. Physiol. *143*: 541-552, 1958. Effects of picrotoxin on crayfish muscle.

238. Robertson, J. D., J. Biophys. Biochem. Cytol. *2*: 381-394, 1956. Ultrastructure of reptilian myoneural junction.

239. Roche, J., Biochim. Biophys. Acta *24*: 514-519, 1957. Distribution of various phosphagens in invertebrates.

240. Roche, J., *et al.,* Comp. Biochem. Physiol. *1*: 44-55, 1960. Distribution of various phosphagens in invertebrates.

241. Roeder, K. D., Biol. Bull. *100*: 95-106, 1951. Potentials of thoracic muscles in relation to flight in insects.

242. Roeder, K. D., and Weiant, E. A., J. Exp. Biol. *27*: 1-13, 1950. Neuromuscular transmission in cockroach.

243. Rosenblueth, A., Biol. Symp. *3*: 111-120, 1941; Transmission of Nerve Impulses at Neuroeffector Junctions and Peripheral Synapses. New York, John Wiley & Sons, 1950.

244. Rosenblueth, A., and Rioch, D. M., Am. J. Physiol. *106*: 365-380, 1933. Mediators and conduction in smooth muscles.

245. Ross, D. M., Experientia *13*: 192-194, 1957; J. Exp. Biol. *34*: 11-28, 1957. Fast and slow contractions in sea anemone Calliactis.

246. Ruegg, J. C., Helvet. Physiol. Pharmacol. Acta *15*: 33-35, 1957. ATPase action of myosin from Pecten muscle.

247. Sato, M., Tamasige, M., and Ozeki, M., Jap. J. Physiol. *10*: 85-98, 1960. Electrical activity of the retractor pharynx muscle of the snail.

248. Schmandt, W., and Sleator, W., J. Cell. Comp. Physiol. *46*: 439-473, 1955. Action potentials in Mytilus byssus retractor.

249. Seaman, G. R., Biochim. Biophys. Acta *9*: 693-696, 1952. Phosphagens of protozoa.

250. Semba, T., and Hiraoka, T., Jap. J. Physiol. *7*: 64-71, 1957. Responses of stomach and intestine to autonomic nerve impulses.

251. Sheng, P., and Tsao, T., Scientia Sinica *4*: 157-176, 1955. Comparative properties of tropomyosins.

252. Shtrankfeld, I. G., Biophysics *2*: 167-175, 1957. Viscous-elastic properties of different types of muscles.

253. Sichel, F. J. M., Am. J. Physiol. *133*: 446-667, 1941. Elasticity of sarcolemma and of entire skeletal muscle fiber.

254. Sjöstrand, F. S., and Anderssen-Cedergren, E., J. Ultrast. Res. *1*: 74-108, 1957, 271-287, 1958. Ultrastructure of skeletal muscle filaments at different degrees of shortening.

255. Skoglund, C. R., Biol. Bull. *117*: 438, 1959. Neuromuscular mechanisms of sound production in Opsanus tau.

256. Solf, V., Zool. Jahrb. Abt. Allg. Zool. Physiol. *50*: 174-264, 1931. Contraction rates of Orthopteran muscles.

257. Sotavalta, O., Nature *170*: 1057-1058, 1952; Biol. Bull. *104*: 439-444, 1953. Flight tone and thoracic vibration frequency in midges.

258. Sperelakis, N., and Prosser, C. L., Am. J. Physiol. *196*: 850-856, 1959. Conduction in ganglion-free rings of intestinal muscle of cat.

259. *Szent-Györgyi, A., Chemistry of Muscular Contraction. New York, Academic Press, 1951, 162 pp. Chemical Physiology of Contraction in Body and Heart Muscle, New York, Academic Press, 1953, 135 pp.

260. *Szent-Györgyi, A. G., Adv. Enzymol. *16*: 313-360, 1956. Structural and functional aspects of myosin.

260a. Takahashi, K., Annot. Zool. Jap. *33*: 67-84, 1960. Nervous control of *Mytilus* byssal retractor.

261. Takeuchi, N., and Takeuchi, A., Nature *181*: 779, 1958. Time course of end-plate potential.

262. Tasaki, I., and Hagiwara, S., Am. J. Physiol. *88*: 423-429, 1957. Capacitance of muscle fiber membrane.

263. Tasaki, I., and Kano, H., Jap. J. Med. Sci. III, 9: 1942. Isolation of the slow motor fiber system.

264. Tasaki, I., and Mizutani, K., Jap. J. Med. Sci. III, 9: 1942. Isolation of the slow motor fiber system.

265. TenCate, J., and Verleur, J. D., Physiol. Compar. Oecol. 2: 346-354, 1952. Time relations and mechanical properties of Helix muscles.

266. Thoai, N. V., et al., Biochim. Biophys. Acta 11: 593, 1953; 14: 76-79, 1954. Annelid phosphagens.

267. Thompson, J. W., J. Physiol. 141: 46-72, 1958. Responses of isolated nictitating membrane of cat.

268. *Tiegs, O. W., Physiol. Rev. 33: 90-144, 1953. Innervation of voluntary muscle.

269. Tiegs, O. W., Phil. Tr. Roy. Soc. London, B, 238: 221-359, 1955. Histology of insect flight muscle.

270. Tonomura, Y., et al., Arch. Biochem. Biophys. 59: 76-89, 1955. Contractile proteins of Pecten.

271. Twarog, B. M., J. Cell. Comp. Physiol. 46: 141-163, 1953; 44: 141-164, 1954; J. Physiol. 152: 220-246, 1960. Responses of molluscan muscle to acetylcholine and 5-hydroxytryptamine; tension maintenance, electrical responses.

272. Ulbrecht, G. M., Naturforsch. 7B: 434-443, 1952. ATPase of various nonstriated muscles.

273. *Vaughn Williams, G. M., Pharmacol. Rev. 6: 159-190, 1954. Mode of action of drugs on intestinal motility.

274. de Villafranca, G. W., Biol. Bull. 108: 113-119, 1955. ATPase in invertebrate muscles.

275. de Villafranca, G. W., et al., Biochim. Biophys. Acta 34: 147-157, 1959. Localization of contractile proteins in Limulus muscle.

276. Walker, S. M., Am. J. Physiol. 157: 429-435, 1949. Effects of temperature on rat and frog muscle.

277. *Weber, H. H., Harvey Lect. 49: 37-56, 1953-54; Ann. Rev. Biochem. 26: 667-698, 1957; The Motility of Muscle and Cells. Harvard University Press, 1958, 69 pp.

278. *Weber, H. H., and Portzell, H., Ergebn. Physiol. 47: 369-468, 1952. Review of function of contractile proteins.

279. Weis-Fogh, T., J. Exp. Biol. 33: 668-684, 1956; Phil. Tr. Roy. Soc. London, B, 239: 415-510, 553-584, 1956. Biology and physics (aerodynamics) of locust flight.

280. Wells, G. P., J. Exp. Biol. 14: 117-157, 290-301, 1937. Movements of esophagus of Arenicola and proboscis of Glycera.

281. West, T. C., and Landa, J., Am. J. Physiol. 187: 333-337, 1956. Transmembrane potentials and contractility in rat uterus.

282. Wiersma, C. A. G., J. Comp. Neurol. 74: 63-79, 1941; J. Exp. Biol. 28: 13-21, 1951; Arch. Néerl. Zool. 11: 1-13, 1955. Functional analyses of distribution of nerves to muscles of various crustaceans.

283. *Wiersma, C. A. G., in Recent Advances in Invertebrate Physiology, edited by B. Scheer. University of Oregon Press, 1957, pp. 143-159. Neuromuscular transmission in crustaceans.

284. Wiersma, C. A. G., and Adams, R. T., Physiol.

Comp. Oecol. 2: 20-33, 1949. Influence of nerve impulse sequence on contractions of different crustacean muscles.

285. Wiersma, C. A. G., and van Harreveld, A., J. Exp. Biol. 15: 18-31, 1938. Optimal frequencies of fast and slow systems in crustacean muscles.

286. Wiersma, C. A. G., and Ripley, S. H., Physiol. Comp. Oecol. 2: 327-336, 391-405, 1952. Innervation patterns of crustacean limbs.

287. *Wilkie, D. R., Progr. Biophys. 4: 288-324, 1954; J. Physiol. 134: 527-530, 1956. Measurements of mechanical properties of frog muscle.

288. Wilkie, D. R., and Macpherson, L., J. Physiol. 124: 292-299, 1954. Duration of active state in frog muscle.

289. Williams, C. M., and Galambos, R., Biol. Bull. 99: 300-307, 1950. Analysis of flight sound in Drosophila.

290. Wills, J. H., Am. J. Physiol. 136: 623-628, 1942. Speed of cat muscles.

291. Wilson, D. M., J. Exp. Biol. 37: 46-72, 1960. Transmission in muscles of annelids and cephalopods.

292. Winton, F. R., J. Physiol. 88: 492-511, 1937. Responses of Mytilus muscle to alternating and direct current.

293. Wood, D. W., J. Exp. Biol. 35: 850-861, 1958. Electrical and mechanical responses of tibial flexor of stick insect, Carausius.

294. Wright, E. B., and Adelman, W. J., J. Cell. Comp. Physiol. 43: 119-132, 1954. Accommodation constants of single motor axons of crayfish.

295. Wright, E. B., and Coleman, P. D., J. Cell. Comp. Physiol. 43: 133-164, 1954. Excitation and conduction in single motor axons of crayfish.

296. Wu, K. S., J. Exp. Biol. 16: 184-197, 1939. Physiology and pharmacology of earthworm gut.

297. Youmans, W. B., Am. J. Med. 13: 209-226, 1952. Neural regulation of gastric and intestinal motility.

298. Young, J. Z., Proc. Roy. Soc. London, B, 120: 303-318, 1936. Innervation and reactions to drugs of viscera of teleosts.

299. Young, J. Z., J. Exp. Biol. 15: 170-185, 1938. Giant fiber control of squid mantle.

300. Young, J. Z., and Prosser, C. L., Biol. Bull. 73: 237-241, 1937. Responses to repetitive stimulation of squid giant fiber.

301. Yudkin, W. H., J. Cell. Comp. Physiol. 44: 507-518, 1954. Transphosphorylation in echinoderms.

302. Zaimis, E. J., J. Physiol. 122: 238-251, 1953. Species differences in action of neuromuscular blocking agents.

REFERENCES

Electric Organs

For references to muscle, see page 459.

1. Albe-Fessard, D., and Chargas, C., J. Physiol. Paris 46: 823-840, 1954. Summation of electroplax responses.

2. Albe-Fessard, D., and Martins-Ferreira, H.,

J. Physiol. Pathol. Gen. *45*: 533-546, 1953. The nervous basis for synchronization of discharge in electric organs of Electrophorus.

3. ALBE-FESSARD, D., *et al.,* J. Neurophysiol. *14*: 243-252, 1951. The nervous basis for synchronization of discharge in electric organs of Electrophorus.

4. ALTAMIRANO, M., *et al.,* J. Gen. Physiol. *38*: 319-360, 1955. Electrical properties of membranes of Electrophorus electroplaxes.

5. AUGER, D., and FESSARD, A., C. R. Soc. Biol. *135*: 76-78, 1941. Effects of drugs on discharge of electric organ.

6. BALDWIN, E., J. Exp. Biol. *10*: 212-221, 1933. Phosphorylcreatine in electric tissue.

7. BENNETT, M. V. L., and GRUNDFEST, H., J. Gen. Physiol. *42*: 1067-1104, 1959. Electrophysiology of electric organ of Gymnotus.

8. BROCK, L. G., and ECCLES, R. M., J. Physiol. *142*: 251-274, 1958. Properties of torpedo electric organ.

9. COATES, C. W., *et al.,* Science *120*: 845-846, 1954. Electrogenesis in knifefishes.

10. COX, R. T., Am. J. Physics *11*: 13-22, 1943. Characteristics of electric fish discharge.

11. COX, R. T., *et al.,* Ann. New York Acad. Sci. *47*: 487-500, 1943. Characteristics of electric fish discharge.

12. FESSARD, A., Arch. Internat. Physiol. *55*: 1-26, 1947; Proc. Roy. Soc. London, B, *140*: 186-189, 1952. Effects of nerves on electric organs.

13. *GRUNDFEST, H., Progr. Biophys. *7*: 1-85, 1957. Review of electrogenesis.

14. *KEYNES, R. D., Endeavour *15*: 215-222, 1956; *in* Physiology of Fishes, edited by M. E. Brown. New York, Academic Press, 1957, vol. 2, pp. 323-343. Historical accounts of physiology of electric fishes.

15. KEYNES, R. D., and MARTINS-FERREIRA, H., J. Physiol. *119*: 315-351, 1953. Intracellular analysis of potentials in Electrophorus electroplaxes.

16. LISSMAN, H. W., Nature *167*: 201-202, 1951; J. Exp. Biol. *35*: 156-191, 1958. Behavioral interpretation of discharge from African electric fishes.

17. LISSMAN, H. W., and MACHIN, K. E., J. Exp. Biol. *35*: 451-486, 1958. Behavioral interpretation of discharge from African electric fishes.

18. MATHEWSON, R., *et al.,* Biol. Bull. *115*: 126-135, 1958. Morphology of electric organ of Narcine.

19. MOHRES, F. P., Naturwissenschaften *44*: 431-432, 1957. Interpretation of electric discharge in terms of territoriality.

20. NACHMANSOHN, D., *et al.,* J. Gen. Physiol. *25*: 75-88, 1951; J. Neurophysiol. *4*: 348-361, 1941; *5*: 499-516, 1941. Acetylcholinesterase in electric organ of Electrophorus.

Chapter 15

AMOEBOID MOVEMENT

Protoplasmic streaming occurs in many living cells, possibly in all. Diffusion is too slow a process for the transport of solutes from one part of a cell to another, and active cytoplasmic movement provides a rapid transport mechanism. Streaming may proceed in a fixed path and may be fast enough for direct microscopic observation, as the cyclosis around the vacuole of some plant cells, or the transport of food vacuoles and granules about the body of a ciliate protozoan. In other cells, streaming may be slow and may be more of a churning than a fixed current; such cytoplasmic activity is best seen by accelerated motion pictures, as of tissue cultures of fibroblasts or of tips of growing nerve fibers. The effects on streaming of a variety of environmental factors have been examined,[8, 30] but the molecular mechanisms remain unknown.

TYPES OF AMOEBOID CELLS AND PSEUDOPODS

Amoeboid movement has much in common with protoplasmic streaming, and an elucidation of the transformation of chemical energy to mechanical work in one will facilitate an understanding of the other. Amoeboid movement is accompanied by changes in cell shape, by the extension of pseudopods, and often by progressive motion. Amoeboid movement may be directed locomotion as in rhizopod Protozoa, in the plasmodium of myxomycetes, in amoeboid leukocytes, and in amoebocytes or wandering cells of many kinds of animals; or amoeboid movement may consist in the extension, flexion, and retraction of processes (pseudopods) concerned primarily in feeding, as in most Foraminifera, Heliozoa, Radiolaria, vertebrate macrophages, and reticuloendothelial cells. Locomotory amoeboid movement requires attachment to some substrate; nonpolarized amoeboid movement occurs in free pseudopods.

In free-living amoeboid animals the manner of locomotion differs slightly according to cell form and type of pseudopod.[22] Pseudopods may be lobopods, broad to cylindrical and round at the tip (Fig. 198); they may be filopods, slender with pointed tips; they may be reticulopods, threadlike, branching, and anastomosing as in Foraminifera, or they may be axopods with a central axial rod as in Heliozoa and Radiolaria (Fig. 198). Locomotion by lobopods has been much studied; filopods, reticulopods, and axopods may show streaming without accompanying change in length, and axopods may be very contractile.

Amoebae differ greatly in cell form. *Amoeba limax* has a single lobose pseudopod; the stellate form of amoebae has many free pseudopods. *A. proteus* and *A. dubia* are multipodal with several attached pseudopods with streaming in varying amounts in each. Amoebae may have surface ridges, as in *A. verrucosa,* or they may have an irregular "tail" or uroid, as in *Pelomyxa palustris* (Fig. 198). Lymphocytes likewise vary, sometimes having a broad advancing pseudopod and a smaller tail or they may be wormlike. A given amoeboid cell may take on different forms under various conditions. For example, *Amoeba proteus* in distilled water becomes stellate or radiate, but in dilute saline is monopodal; it is also stellate prior to fission. Amoebae have a central fluid plasmasol (endoplasm) and an outer viscous plasmagel (ectoplasm). The gel is thick in *A. proteus,* *A. verrucosa, Pelomyxa carolinensis,* and *P. palustris,* but it is thin in *A. dubia* and in the parasitic *A. blattae.*

GENERALIZED PICTURE OF AMOEBOID MOVEMENT

A "typical" amoeba consists of a thin outer layer, the plasmalemma, which has adhesive properties, is not wet by water, and slides freely over the next inner layer. Electron micrographs show the plasmalemma to consist of two darkly staining layers separated by a clear layer.[37] Beneath the plasmalemma is a hyaline layer which is fluid, as judged by brownian activity when particles enter it. This layer is very thin in a region of attachment to substrate; it often thickens as an extensive hyaline cap at the front of an advancing pseudopod. Next is the ectoplasm or cylinder of plasmagel, which is relatively viscous. In a monopodal amoeba the gel thickens gradually from anterior to posterior end. In many species it extends as a thin plasmagel sheet beneath the anterior hyaline cap, a sheet which frequently ruptures, allowing granules to enter the hyaline cap. The frequency of rupture into the hyaline cap may be different in each of several advancing pseudopods. The endoplasmic core of the amoeba is the plasmasol in which granules flow freely forward. The nucleus is normally in the plasmasol; the Golgi apparatus and contractile vacuole are in the plasmagel. Both regions contain various granules, food vacuoles, and crystals. The protoplasm is hyperosmotic in freshwater amoebae, nearly isosmotic in marine and parasitic amoebae, and the plasmagel imparts a turgidity which results in the nonspherical cell forms.

Local viscosity has been estimated from movements of granules in amoebae in the microscope-centrifuge.[3] The lowest viscosity is in the "shear" zone between the gel and sol, and the axial sol can move forward as a relatively uniform core.[1] Also low viscosity is found in the posterior recruitment zone where gel is converted to sol. Neither gel nor sol shows homogeneous viscosity, but both are structured.[3] The viscosity of both gel and sol is greater anteriorly than posteriorly and local viscous regions are indicated in the sol.

Locomotion, as observed microscopically, depends on three basic factors. (1) Attachment to the substrate. This is facilitated by traces of salts, particularly by calcium in the medium; Ca^{++}, Mg^{++}, and K^+ are additive for attachment but not for locomotion. The firmest attachment is at the tips, and new pseudopods are more firmly attached than old ones. (2) Plasmagel is continuously being converted to plasmasol at the posterior

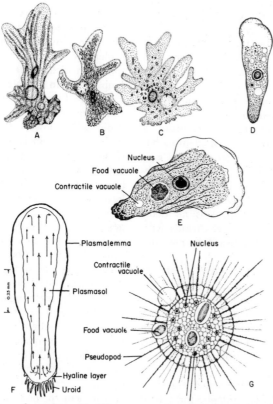

FIGURE 198. Drawings of amoebae with different types of pseudopods. *A, Amoeba proteus*; *B, Amoeba discoides*; *C, Amoeba dubia*; *D, Amoeba limax*; *E, Amoeba verrucosa*; *F, Pelomyxa palustris*; *G*, heliozoan *Actinosphaerium eichhorni*. (From Schaeffer, A. A.: Amoeboid Movement. Princeton University Press; Kuhn, A. R.: Morphologie der Tiere in Bildern. Borntraeger; Mast, S. O.: Physiol. Zool., vol. 7.)

end or at some fixed region, and plasmasol is converted to plasmagel anteriorly or in any extending pseudopod. As plasmasol flows forward, granules either are deflected laterally to become plasmagel or break into the hyaline cap and then gelate as a new cap is formed. (3) The force that causes forward flow of the plasmasol. Both elastic and contractile forces are indicated. Elasticity is shown when ectoplasm is stretched on a microneedle. Considerable force can be developed by the pseudopods of a food cup. Slime molds show protoplasmic flow in one direction, then reversal of direction. A slime mold can be kept in an hourglass form in a chamber of two compartments connected by a channel. Hydrostatic pressure applied on one side can stop the flow in that direction, and the pressure necessary to prevent flow fluctuates periodically, i.e., the balancing pressure is $\pm$ 5 to 10 cm H_2O.[19]

There are several theories for the locomotor force of amoebae, but most of them postulate contractile proteins and either a "squeezing" or "pulling." Lateral examination of granules in an amoeba or lymphocyte and of particles adhering to the plasmalemma has shown that in an advancing cell the granules in the gel remain fixed until the posterior end reaches them, when they enter the sol. Particles on the ventral attached plasmalemma are also fixed, but particles elsewhere on the plasmalemma, both dorsal and ventral, move forward. The plasmalemma is continuously reconstituted at the posterior end and in freely extending pseudopods. In *A. verrucosa,* a "rolling" movement of the plasmalemma has been described.[18, 26] In other species, e.g., *Difflugia,* there may be a "walking" movement, the advancing tip attaching and the remainder being pulled forward. In the reticulopods of Foraminifera there is no outer tube of gel but rather two gel threads with movement of granules outward in one and back in the other.[16]

Freely crawling amoebae move at rates of 0.5 to 4.5 μ per second, most of them at the rate of about 1 μ per second. Monopodal individuals travel faster (4.6 μ/sec) than multipodal ones (2.1 μ/sec).[34] Lymphocytes in tissue culture moved an average of 0.55 μ/sec, whereas nonpolarized macrophages averaged 0.004 μ or less per second.[9]

In feeding, those amoebae which travel by small pseudopods, as *A. proteus,* form food cups consisting of lateral and dorsal pseudopods flowing around a food mass which may itself be motile. The pseudopods of the cup meet distally, and the food mass is incorporated into a food vacuole. In amoebae with a single broad pseudopod, as *A. limax,* but not in others, there appears to be some adhesion of food to the plasmalemma. Furthermore, the surface of reticulopods and axopods is sticky, and food adheres to their surface.

The sol flows in channels, and islands of gel may often be seen in a broad region of sol. Individual granules only a few microns apart in a slime mold may move in opposite directions, and flow direction at a given point reverses with irregular periodicity.[38]

THEORIES OF AMOEBOID MOVEMENT

In the effort to account for the different interrelated features of amoeboid movement many theories have been proposed. They are not mutually exclusive, and several of them are simultaneously applicable.

1. The first of these theories was popular from 1835 until 1875 and has recently been revived in modified form by Allen. It is postulated that contractile strands of gel occur in various regions, particularly in advancing pseudopods which pull the protoplasmic mass ahead.

2. A second theory invoked surface tension forces and was based on the analogy of amoeboid movement with the movement of a mercury drop toward some salt such as potassium dichromate, or with currents in a drop of oil in contact with a soap. It was favored by Bütschli (1892), Rhumbler (1898), and Tiegs (1928). It postulates that an organic solute lowers the surface tension at some point on an amoeba, and a pseudopod is there extended. A drop of paraffin oil can form a cap on an amoeba, a pseudopod forms beneath it, and fountain streaming without locomotion can continue beneath the cap for hours. There is, however, abundant evidence against surface tension as the factor normally responsible for amoeboid movement. The forces which can be developed are much greater than the measured "surface tension." The tension at the cell periphery, as measured by the centrifugal force to pull an oil droplet through the surface, is 1 to 3 dynes/cm or lower—slightly more than the peripheral tension in marine eggs but lower than the tension of 20 dynes/cm at the interface of olive oil and water.[14, 24] Calculations indicate that tensions of 1 to 3 dynes/cm would be sufficient to force the sol forward, but an amoeba can develop much greater tensions in its periphery, as when it pinches a Paramecium in two.[26] The currents in the plasma-

lemma are forward, not backward as on the surface of a drop of mercury or oil moving by means of a "pseudopod." Further, there is no reasonable suggestion regarding the nature and method of secretion of a solute which might lower surface tension locally.

3. Related to the surface tension concept is that of elasticity of the ectoplasm. Measurements of the extensibility of strands of myxomycete plasmodia gave a value of Young's modulus of 9×10^4 dynes/cm^2, which is about one-thirtieth as elastic as muscle.[31] The elastic tension of the gel presumably resides in the protein molecules, which are also contractile. Elasticity *per se* is insufficient to account for locomotion in the absence of some means of stretching the cells.

4. The solute drag theory of Rashevsky[35] states that if a solute diffuses down a concentration gradient, it carries with it by momentum other molecules. Diffusion drag is explained in terms of gradients of metabolic products and local variations in them. This theory has been revived by Stewart[38] to explain the reversible and periodic flow, different directions of movement of particles close to one another, and other special features of locomotion in slime molds.

5. Another "chemical" theory is that water is removed by some sort of "syneresis" from protein at the posterior end and that the forward tide of syneretic fluid is important in locomotion.[32, 33] The tail of some amoeboid cells (*A. limax, P. palustris*, mammalian lymphocytes) wrinkles during locomotion as if water were removed. The hyaline layer is 0.5 μ thick at the rear end and 20 μ at the advancing tip of an amoeba. Recent measurements of the refractive index of *Amoeba proteus* and *A. dubia* show that in sustained locomotion the refractive index rises toward the tail, this region having 6 to 40 per cent more organic matter (protein) than the advancing tip, and this gradient of refractive index disappears on cessation of movement.[2] It is possible that this change in distribution of water may be associated with the contraction of protein filaments and that locomotion does not result from syneretic flow.

6. A great deal of evidence indicates contractility of the gel. This could "pull," as in (1) above, or could "squeeze" the sol forward. The gel or ectoplasmic layer increases in thickness posteriorly.[28] Electron microscopy reveals filaments resembling myofilaments in the gel.[37] *Amoeba proteus* and amoebocytic tissue culture cells show some birefringence, none in the axial regions of a pseudopod, but this birefringence does not change with movement.[29] The axopods of Heliozoa and Radiolaria are very contractile and are birefringent.[36] A protein has been extracted from slime molds[23, 40] which has many of the properties of actomyosin; it is soluble in 1 mol KCl at pH 8.2, it forms a viscous solution and shows decreased viscosity when ATP is added; it also appears to dephosphorylate ATP to AMP, which increases its viscosity.[19, 23, 40] Injection of ATP into the tail of an amoeba caused initial contraction followed by liquefaction of the gel.[10, 12]

The mode of contraction of the protein is as uncertain as the mode of contraction of actomyosin in muscle. One hypothesis is that the protein molecules fold at the posterior end (under the action of ATP) and then liquefaction occurs. The reverse process of gelation occurs at the anterior end. The protein in the sol is thought to consist of folded molecules while those in the gel are extended. This concept is supported by the observation that neutral red is accumulated most in the tail where the unfolded protein molecules present more available regions of adsorption, although other explanations of this phenomenon are possible.[12]

Elasticity, combined with the contractility, may explain two-way flow away from a constricted region or into an inflated region.[17] When gel becomes thin it no longer contracts and flow reverses (myxomycetes).[17] Contractile strands in the sol can move adjacent granules in different directions and against bulk flow.

Another suggestion, similar to the sliding molecule hypothesis of muscle contraction (see p. 429), is that a shearing occurs between sliding filaments of gel.[30] This was supported for the fine reticulate pseudopods of a foraminiferan *Allogromia*.[16] These 5 μ thick reticulopods lack a central core of sol and lack an outer hyaline layer but appear to consist of two semicircular threads of gel, one of which moves forward, the other backward. It is postulated that one gel filament shears on the other much like two millipeds traveling in opposite directions, the legs of one pushing back and of the other forward.

7. A slightly different characterization of the gel is based on its colloidal properties. Amoeba gel decreases in viscosity under high hydrostatic pressures and at decreasing temperature. Actomyosin behaves similarly and gels of this kind undergo volume increase ($+ \Delta V$) and absorption of heat (endothermic) on gelation.[20, 25] Similarly, when living

amoebae are subjected to high hydrostatic pressure; the "viscosity" falls, the gel solates, and locomotion stops. At 2000 lb/in² the pseudopods are long and cylindrical; at above 6000 lb/in² no new pseudopods are formed; at about 6500 lb/in² terminal spheres appear on pseudopods and the cells become balls of fluid. A series of functions—amoeboid movement, chromatophore expansion, cyclosis in *Elodea*, cleavage in *Arbacia* eggs—are similarly stopped as the protoplasmic rigidity decreases under high pressures. These are in contrast to bioluminescence, ciliary movement, muscle contraction, and nerve conduction which may be enhanced by pressure, probably because of membrane effects.[14, 24] The critical pressure to cause collapse of pseudopods and to give spherical cell form is less at low than at high temperatures, and the gel strength as measured by centrifugation decreases more with high pressure at 15° than at 25°C.[25] When ATP is added to the medium, the pressure required to make the amoebae spherical is greater; this agrees with the initial increase in viscosity of the gel protein on treatment with ATP and the initial apparent contraction of live amoebae on ATP injection.

8. A recent hypothesis combines several features of others and adds new ones. This is the "fountain" hypothesis of Allen.[1a] When a large *Pelomyxa* is broken in a small quartz tube under oil the isolated fragment shows streaming, first with the axial sol flowing forward and the gel backward, then with several channels making U-bends at one end. The velocity of flow toward the bend or fountain is faster and the width of the channel less than the flow away from the bend in the gel. In a normally advancing pseudopod the cylinder of sol shortens and thickens in the "fountain" zone. It is postulated that gel strands, attached to the rim of the advancing tube, contract and pull the anterior sol forward; water is removed to the hyaline cap by syneresis and passes back under the plasmalemma to be returned to the protein at the posterior zone of recruitment of sol. Flow is chiefly at the boundary or shear zone between sol and gel. It is argued that contraction at a U-bend between sol and gel can equally well explain amoeboid movement and cyclosis.

MODIFIERS OF AMOEBOID MOVEMENT

Despite the requirement of gel-sol transformation for locomotion and the evidence for contractility of the gel proteins, the rate of amoeboid locomotion is not directly related to the gel-sol ratio. For example, the gel layer of *Amoeba proteus* is thinner at high than at low temperatures,[28] yet the mean viscosity is greater at higher temperatures[21] and the rate of locomotion shows a maximum at 22 to 24°C.[28] Similarly, the gel thickness increases with increasing external acidity, yet *A. proteus* shows maximum rates of locomotion at pH 6.2 and 7.5 when in a salt mixture, but in the presence of single cations Na^+, K^+, or Ca^{++} only one pH optimum.[34] An amoeba which is largely sol, *A. dubia*, shows different dependence of viscosity on ions, as measured by centrifugation, from *A. proteus*, which has relatively more gel.[15] The gel-sol ratios, mean viscosities, and rates of locomotion are each affected somewhat differently by different pH and salt combinations. Some of the salt effects may be on the plasmalemma. The frequency of rupture of the plasmagel sheet and entry of endoplasmic granules into the hyaline cap is, however, related to the gel-sol ratio, and those conditions which decrease the amount of gel also increase the frequency of rupture of the gel sheet.

Amoeboid cells respond to an electrical field and show biopotentials. From over the veins of a slime mold, *Physarum*, which reverses its flow every 60 to 90 seconds, action potentials some 30 mv in amplitude and lasting some 70 sec were recorded.[7] In addition, mechanical stimuli elicit graded electrical responses a few seconds in duration.[7, 39] In an electrical field *Amoeba proteus* shows solation on the side toward the cathode and pseudopodia advance in that direction.[13] Migration of plasmodium of *Physarum* toward the cathode results from inhibition of migration on the anodal side. The galvanotaxis is due to current flow, not to electrolytic products in the substrate, and orientation is perpendicular to an AC field or to a DC field which is reversed each minute.[4] Intense illumination or mechanical stimulation of a pseudopod tip induces gelation and streaming reversal in that pseudopod.[27] Volatile fat-soluble anesthetics cause the plasmalemma to rise above the ectoplasm and prevent responses to mechanical stimuli.[11] It is probable, therefore, that the plasmalemma has electrical properties similar to those of other cell membranes and that in some manner it reacts with the gel to activate contraction.

CONCLUSIONS

The preceding evidence gives some indication of the complexity of amoeboid movement. Some environmental factors act principally on the cell surface; others, on gel-sol transformation; and still others, on viscosity and contractility of the gel proteins. There may be more than one method of contraction, and changes in hydration of proteins may occur. Certainly the two-way flow of gel in reticulopods which lack a fluid core, and progression in parasitic gregarines which appear to use an outer layer of contractile fibrils for their gliding movement, must be very different from the forward locomotion of a free amoeba or leukocyte with its contractile gel shell, and from that of a myxomycete which reverses direction of flow periodically. There is little doubt that the gel is contractile and elastic and that gel and sol are not homogeneous in viscosity but are structured. Sharp disagreement persists as to whether the gel is a contractile tube or whether the sol is pulled forward by contractile strands of gel. Perhaps each view is correct. An understanding of muscle contraction and of amoeboid movement may well be mutually helpful.

REFERENCES

1. ALLEN, R. D., J. Biophys. Biochem. Cytol. *8*: 379-397, 1960. Streaming and viscosity in amoeboid cells.

1a. ALLEN, R. D., COOLEDGE, J. W., and HALL, P. J., Nature *187*: 896-899, 1960. Fountain theory.

2. ALLEN, R. D., and ROSLANSKY, J. D., J. Biophys. Biochem. Cytol. *4*: 517-521, 1958. Anterior-posterior water concentration gradient in *Amoeba proteus* and *A. dubia*.

3. ALLEN, R. D., and ROSLANSKY, J. D., J. Biophys. Biochem. Cytol. *6*: 437-446, 1959. Consistency of amoeba cytoplasm.

4. ANDERSON, J. D., J. Gen. Physiol. *35*: 1-16, 1951. Galvanotaxis of slime molds.

5. BROWN, D. E. S., J. Cell. Comp. Physiol. *8*: 141-157, 1936. Effects of hydrostatic pressure on muscle tension.

6. BROWN, D. E. S., and MARSLAND, D. A., J. Cell. Comp. Physiol. *8*: 159-165, 167-178, 1936. Effects of hydrostatic pressure on viscosity of amoebae.

7. BURR, H. S., J. Exp. Zool. *129*: 327-341, 1955. Electrical properties of slime mold Physarum.

8. *DEBRUYN, P. P. H., Anat. Rec. *89*: 43-63, 1940; *93*: 295-307, 1944; *95*: 177-187, 1946. Movement of lymphocytes, leukocytes, and macrophages.

9. *DEBRUYN, P. P. H., Quart. Rev. Biol. *22*: 1-24, 1947. Review, history of theories of amoeboid movement.

10. GOLDACRE, R. J., Internat. Rev. Cytol. *1*: 135-164, 1951. Evidence for folding and unfolding of protein molecules in amoeboid movement.

11. GOLDACRE, R. J., Symp. Soc. Exp. Biol. *6*: 128-144, 1952. Action of anesthetics and responses to touch in amoebae.

12. GOLDACRE, R. J., and LORCH, J. J., Nature *166*: 497-500, 1950. Effects of injection of ATP, accumulation of neutral red in amoebae.

* Review

13. HAHNERT, W., Physiol. Zool. *5*: 491-526, 1932. Reactions of amoebae to electricity.

14. HARVEY, E. N., and MARSLAND, D. A., J. Cell. Comp. Physiol. *2*: 75-97, 1936. Streaming in relation to gel structure; tension at surface of amoeba.

15. HEILBRUNN, L. V., and DAUGHERTY, K., Physiol. Zool. *4*: 635-651, 1931; *5*: 254-274, 1932. Action of cations on viscosity of amoebae.

16. JAHN, T. L., and RINALDI, R. A., Biol. Bull. *117*: 100-118, 1959. Movement in foraminiferan Allogromia.

17. JAHN, T. L., to be published. Adequacy of gel contraction hypothesis of amoeboid movement.

18. JENNINGS, H. S., Carnegie Inst. Wash. Publ. no. 16, 129-234, 1904. Movements and reactions of amoebae.

19. KAMIYAN, N., MAKAJIMA, H., and ABE, S., Protoplasma *48*: 94-112, 1957. Effects of various agents on pressure required to stop flow in Physarum.

20. LANDAU, J. V., Ann. New York Acad. Sci. *78*: 487-500, 1959. Gel-sol transformations in amoebae.

21. LANDAU, J., ZIMMERMAN, A., and MARSLAND, D., J. Cell. Comp. Physiol. *44*: 211-232, 1954. Temperature-pressure effects on *Amoeba proteus*.

22. LEIDY, J., Fresh-Water Rhizopods of North America. Washington, D. C., Government Printing Office, 1879, 324 pp.

23. LOEWY, A. G., J. Cell. Comp. Physiol. *40*: 127-156, 1952. Actomyosin-like protein from plasmodium of myxomycete.

24. MARSLAND, D. A., *in* Structure of Protoplasm, edited by W. Seifriz, 1942, Ames, Iowa, Iowa State College Press, pp. 127-161. Streaming in relation to gel structure; tension at surface of amoeba.

25. MARSLAND, D., Internat. Rev. Cytol. *5*: 199-227, 1956. Protoplasmic contractility in relation to gel structure.

26. *MAST, S. O., J. Morphol. *41*: 347-425, 1926. Structure, movement, locomotion, and stimulation in Amoeba.

27. MAST, S. O., Ztschr. vergl. Physiol. *15*: 139-147, 309-328, 1931. Action of light and electricity on *Amoeba proteus*.

28. MAST, S. O., and PROSSER, C. L., J. Cell. Comp. Physiol. *1*: 333-354, 1932. Effects of temperature, salts, pH on locomotion and gel-sol ratio in amoeba.

29. MITCHISON, J. M., Nature *166*: 313-314, 1950. Birefringence of amoebae.

30. *NOLAND, L. E., J. Protozool. *4*: 1-6, 1957. Protoplasmic streaming.

31. NORRIS, C. H., J. Cell. Comp. Physiol. *16*: 313-322, 1940. Elasticity of myxomycetes.

32. PANTIN, C. F. A., J. Mar. Biol. Assn. U. K. *13*: 24-69, 1923. Locomotion in a marine amoeba.

33. PANTIN, C. F. A., J. Exp. Biol. *1*: 519-538, 1924; *3*: 275-295, 297-312, 1926. Ion effects on amoebae.

34. PITTS, R. F., and MAST, S. O., J. Cell. Comp. Physiol. *3*: 449-462, 1933; *4*: 237-256, 435-455, 1934. Effects of pH and salts on *Amoeba proteus*.

35. RASHEVSKY, N., *in* Advances and Applications

of Mathematical Biology, University of Chicago Press, 1940, pp. 93-100.

36. SCHMIDT, W. J., *in* Die Doppelbrechung von Karyoplasma, Zytoplasma und Metaplasma, Berlin, Borntraeger. 1937, pp. 124-128. Birefringence in axopods of heliozoans.

37. SCHNEIDER, L., and WOHLFARTH-BOTTERMAN, K. E., Protoplasma *51*: 377-388, 1959. Electron microscopy of amoebae.

38. STEWART, P. A., and STEWART, M. T., Exp. Cell. Res. *17*: 44-58, 1959. Protoplasmic movement in slime mold plasmodia; the diffusion drag force hypothesis.

39. TASAKI, I., and KAMIYA, N., Protoplasma *39*: 333-343, 1950. Electrical response of a slime mold to mechanical and electrical stimuli.

40. Ts'o, P. O., EGGMAN, L., and VINOGRAD, J., J. Gen. Physiol. *39*: 325-347, 801-812, 1956. Actomyosin-like protein from plasmodium of myxomycete.

Chapter 16

CILIA

Cilia are motor organelles differentiated at the cell surface. They are capable of performing work by rapid and usually rhythmical movement. They are often classified into two types: (1) flagella, which are relatively larger organelles occurring usually singly or in small numbers upon cells, and (2) cilia proper, which are relatively much smaller and occur characteristically in large numbers upon each cell. Typical flagella characterize the Mastigophora of the phylum Protozoa. Also possessing flagella are the choanocytes of the Porifera, the gastroderm of many coelenterates, the flame end-bulbs of certain rotifers, the solenocytes of annelids, and the sperm cells of most groups throughout the animal kingdom. Cilia proper characterize the ciliated protozoans and are found commonly over the body surface of coelenterates, Turbellaria, and Nemertea. In all other phyla of animals except the Nematoda and the Arthropoda cilia are usually found at specific locations in or on the body.

Ciliary activity is restricted to an aqueous medium, and hence is found only on surfaces which are submerged, or at least covered by an aqueous film. Typical ciliary movement produces either, or both, of two results, depending on the inertia of the ciliated surface. If the inertia is small, then a movement of the ciliated surface through the medium, or locomotion, is effected; if, on the other hand, it is large, or the ciliated structure is not free to move, the external medium is moved over the ciliated surface. It is therefore obvious that ciliated surfaces can become most effective for rapid locomotion only in such small organisms as protozoa, and ciliated larvae. In these forms acceleration to maximum speed is very rapid, and the organisms stop very quickly on cessation of their ciliary activity.

Larger organisms may be moved only sluggishly by cilia. Acceleration is generally slow, and the animals fail to come rapidly to a halt on cessation of ciliary beat. Furthermore, unless such larger free-swimming organisms as, for example, ctenophores, possess a density very close to that of the surrounding medium, cilia are powerless to serve effectively as locomotory organelles. It is interesting, therefore, that the comb-jelly, *Pleurobrachia,* has a water content of 94.73 per cent and density of 1.02741, very close indeed to that of the surrounding sea water.[23, 24]

Cilia are locomotor organelles of many small worms, of numerous rotifers, and even of some snails, e.g., *Nassarius.*

It is perhaps significant that, whereas activity of most ciliated surfaces is continuous throughout the lifetime of the animal, cilia whose primary function is locomotion are commonly under the control of the coordinative mechanism of the organism. This enables the animal adaptively to orient its movement or alter its rate of movement in response to stimuli. This control of locomotor ciliation appears, however, to be superimposed upon a fundamental ciliary automaticity.[15]

In those instances in which the surrounding medium, rather than the ciliated cells, is caused to move, cilia are concerned in one or more of numerous functions, such as feeding, circulation, cleansing, respiration, and the movements of materials within ducts. The action of cilia establishes feeding currents for many ciliate protozoans and for sessile or sluggish species in a wide variety of animal groups. The feeding currents of rotifers are easily observed. The ciliary activity of the tentacles and oral regions of numerous sea anemones and corals is cleansing; it sweeps non-nutritious particles away from the mouth and off the tips of the tentacles.[70] However, in response to food, the tentacles are tipped toward the oral cavity and thereby pass these materials into the gastrovascular cavity. In *Metridium marginatum,* among other species, it has been reported that the direction of the effective beat of the cilia in the stomodeum is reversed under the stimulus of food.[42, 43] The unstimulated cilia normally beat outward, but in the presence of food, e.g., crab flesh, they beat inward. KCl produces an action similar to that produced by food. In *Actinoloba* there are longitudinal grooves in the stomodeum, the cilia on the ridges beating outward and those in the grooves beating inward. The degree of muscular contraction and folding of this organ would therefore be expected to influence strongly the direction of the dominant currents.

Probably nowhere in the animal kingdom are ciliary mechanisms more intricately developed than in the ciliary filter-feeders, principally the lamellibranchs, certain gastropods, and protochordates. Here the systems are organized to set up feeding currents, filter out suspended particles, collect them into specific ciliary tracts, and convey them to the oral opening of the digestive tract. Along the route, special ciliary mechanisms for sorting out the particles on the basis of size, discarding the larger ones, are not uncommon.

Materials are transported within the digestive systems of numerous invertebrates by ciliary action. Definite courses of circulation are present in the coelenteron canal systems of *Aurelia* and *Pleurobrachia*. Ciliary movement contributes importantly to the transport of food in the digestive system of some echinoderms, numerous molluscs,[6] and many other organisms.

A cleansing role of cilia is common for sessile or sluggish animals. The normal direction of the effective beat in sea anemones favors this role, as previously mentioned. In many starfish, cilia beat from mouth toward anus over the entire surface, sweeping away debris. The action of the cilia of the epithelium of the frog's mouth and that of the cilia of the respiratory epithelium of mammals appears also to play this role.

It is self-evident that ciliary movement either on the general body surface of aquatic skin breathers or on specially differentiated respiratory surfaces would facilitate respiratory gaseous exchange by circulation of the ambient medium. Such a respiratory role of cilia is commonplace.

Cilia are essential to the normal circulation of the body fluids in some annelids such as the pelagic polychaete, *Tomopteris*, and the sipunculoids and echiuroids,[35, 36] where a true blood-vascular system is vestigial or absent. In these worms a special system of ciliary tracts causes the coelomic fluids to circulate in a very effective manner. The coelomic fluids of starfishes are circulated in a similar fashion, the action of cilia providing effective circulation even within the dermal papillae. The cerebrospinal fluid of the frog has been reported to be circulated by ciliated epithelia lining the ventricles.[8]

Very commonly among animals, cilia are responsible for facilitating the passage of the materials normally conducted within tubules, particularly those of nephridia and kidneys and the ducts of the genital system.

The foregoing account of cilia suggests the abundant and widespread occurrence and varied functional roles played by these organelles. Although they are by no means able to produce movements of the power and conspicuousness of those effected by muscle contraction, there are numerous instances where cilia normally are indispensable functional constituents of the organism. And in numerous of these instances they perform their assigned functions far more efficiently than would be the case for any conceivable typical muscular mechanism.

The Structure of Cilia. Cilia in living cells show a great uniformity of structure and organization. The cilium appears, optically, quite homogeneous. In appropriately treated ciliated cells the cilium appears to comprise a sheath containing an axial filament. The sheath may be circular or ovoid in cross-section. The axial filament may pursue a straight course through the sheath or may follow a spiral one. The axial filament, not uncommonly, extends distally beyond the limits of the sheath.

The flagellum of some flagellates, e.g., *Euglena*, has attached to the sheath a series of diagonally oriented rodlets or mastigonemes which give the flagellum a feathery appearance.[3, 13, 44, 61] Such flagella are variously called "feather-type," "ciliary," or "stichonematic," in contrast with the simpler type. The proximal end of the axial filament is invariably associated with a basal granule, which is believed to be derived from the cell centrosome. Many cytologists have described systems of fibrils proceeding from the basal granules to the vicinity of the cell nucleus.

The ultrastructure has been disclosed with the aid of electron micrographs for the cilia of such protozoans as *Paramecium, Frontonia, Colpidium, Euplotes,* for the gill cilia of bivalve molluscs (Mytilus, Hyridella), for cilia of the rat epididymis, and numerous other cases (Fig. 199).[2, 11, 12, 17, 46, 47, 49, 52, 54, 63, 68, 69]

There appears to be a remarkable similarity in organization of cilia from a wide variety of sources ranging from Protozoa to mammals. This typically involves a cylindrical array of nine parallel fibrils surrounding a pair of axial fibrils. The outer fibrils, with a diameter of 250 to 500 Å, are about twice as thick as the axial ones.

All these observations, together with the fact that cilia show positive form and intrinsic birefringence,[50, 51] indicate that longitudinally oriented submicroscopic micelles compose the cilium. In this characteristic, therefore, cilia have much in common with the contractile fibrils of muscle tissue.

Cilia often unite to form compound organelles. The cirri of *Euplotes* and the large cilia of *Nephthys* gills may be regarded as composite bodies comprising numerous cilia arising from a number of basal granules in a circular or oval field. The ciliary elements adhere closely to one another in a viscous matrix. The cilia of such a cirrus beat in unison. Membranelles of the adoral region of many peritrichs are small platelets of fused cilia beating synchronously. The undulating membranes of ciliates such as *Blepharisma* are long rows of cilia, each adhering to its neighbors. The compound character of the membrane may often be demonstrated by its fragmentation by appropriate manipulation with a microdissecting needle. The component cilia, when separated from one another, beat quite independently; when they have reunited, the characteristic coordinated activity giving rise to the undulatory movement is

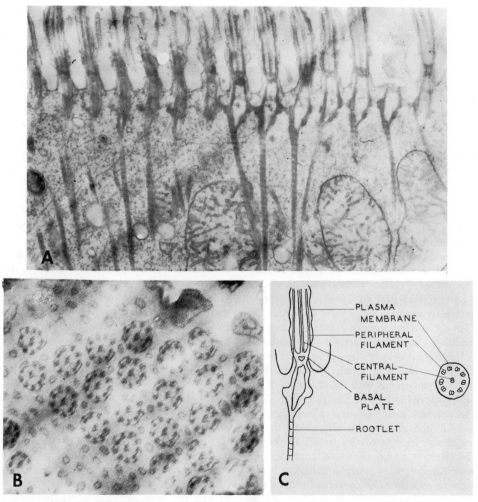

PLASMA MEMBRANE
PERIPHERAL FILAMENT
CENTRAL FILAMENT
BASAL PLATE
ROOTLET

FIGURE 199. Electron micrograph of cilia of the veliger larva of the oyster. *A*, longitudinal section (× 51,500). *B*, transverse section (× 74,500). *C*, Outline sketch identifying major features of *A* and *B*. (Courtesy of D. E. Philpott, and P. S. Galtsoff.)

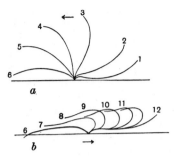

FIGURE 200. Movement of a frontal cilium of *Mytilus*: *a*, effective and, *b*, recovery stroke. (From Gray, J.: Ciliary Movement. Cambridge University Press.)

restored. Such an activity is the result of the metachronic wave of ciliary activity proceeding at right angles to the effective and recovery strokes.

Characteristics of Ciliary Movement. The activity of any cilium may be resolved into one or another, or some combination, of four fundamentally different types of movement.[16] The simplest of these is pendular movement in which the cilium bends back and forth, flexing only at its base.[19] This type is seen for frog pharynx or hypotrich cirri. No difference in the form of the cilium is observed between the effective and the recovery phases of its stroke, the former simply occurring more rapidly than the latter. A second basic type of movement is a flexural one. Bending begins first at the tip of the cilium and passes toward its base; in recovery, the cilium progressively straightens from base to tip. Such hooklike bending is observed in the laterofrontal cilia of lamellibranch gills. The third fundamental type of ciliary activity is undulatory movement. This type is characteristic of flagella. Waves pass along the flagellum from base to tip of the organelle, apparently never in the reverse direction.

Ciliary activity involving a combination of pendular and flexural activities is common. In the frontal cilia of the gill of *Mytilus* the effective stroke is a rapid, stiffly sweeping, pendular movement with the concavity of the mildly curved cilium in advance (Fig. 200). The recovery stroke involves a bending back again of the base of the cilium and then a progressive passage of this flexion to the tip. The effective stroke, therefore, appears to involve movement of a rigid cilium, whereas recovery appears to be concerned with a progressive stiffening from base to tip of an initially limp structure.

The fourth basic type of ciliary movement

is "funnel"-form, or three-dimensional movement.[40, 41] It is seen for the locomotory cilia of protozoans like *Paramecium* and *Colpoda*. This is more complex, involving not only pendular and flexural activities, but also movements out of one plane. In *Paramecium,* the times for effective and recovery stroke of peristomial cilia were found to be, respectively, 0.0046 and 0.35 sec. Isolated from coordinatory stimuli these cilia trace out the form of a funnel or inverted cone, by a counterclockwise motion. Complex movements involving, in addition, the third type of movement, undulatory, are seen for the vibratile organs of the mammalian epididymis and in a number of flagellates as, for example, in *Trypanosoma*. In such organisms as the latter the undulatory and pendular movements need not occur in a single plane, nor need the two occur simultaneously in the same plane. Thus the tip of the flagellum in the course of its beat may trace out an elliptical orbit, a figure 8, or a more complicated figure.

The single vibratile element of the flagellate, *Monas,* has been described as possessing the capacity to carry out numerous complex activities.[21] Forward movement is accomplished by a rapid pendular movement of the flagellum from a position directed forward to one about right angles to the direction of progression. The recovery stroke is typical flexural recovery. The effective stroke may, instead, be initiated near the base and rapidly pass toward the tip. In slower forward movement, the total sweep of the flagellum may be reduced to about half the amplitude, but with the typical form of beat seen in rapid progression. Backward progression is brought about by undulatory activity with waves passing from base to tip of the organ (Fig. 201*C*). Lateral movements result from undulatory movements with the flagellum flexed at about 90 degrees (Fig. 201*D*), and forward movement by directing the flagellum backward. The undulatory activity may involve only the tip of the flagellum, or practically its whole length.

The activity of the flagellum has been investigated with the aid of high-speed cinema photomicrography.[22, 27] Undulatory activity of the flagellum exerts only a pushing action on the medium. Forward locomotion in such common species as *Peranema* and *Euglena,* in which the flagellum was formerly believed to pull the organism and hence function as a tractellum, appears to result from a bending of the whole flagellum, or at least of its active tip, backward. The undulatory activity typically passes from base to tip around the flagellum, as well as along it. Such movement imparts rotational and gyrational components, along with a usual backward thrust. The resulting rotation and gyration of the body of the flagellate around an axis which constitutes the direction of locomotion is considered to provide an important, if not the chief, force propelling the organism forward. The body proper acts under these circumstances as a screw propeller.[25, 26]

From the preceding paragraphs we see that ciliary activity varies greatly in its complexity and variability even in a single cilium; activity seems to be under the control of the general response mechanism of the body.

Cilia are able to propel an organism through the water or propel the surrounding medium past a stationary ciliated cell as a result of a directed thrust upon the medium. More work must be done upon the medium during the effective phase of a stroke than during recovery. In those cases where the effective stroke is pendular and recovery flexural, the mechanism is obvious. Simple pendular ciliary activity would be expected to be quite an inefficient type for directed movement. In undulatory activity the thrust upon the medium is dependent on the progression of a wave along the vibratile organ. A standing wave would obviously exhibit an equalization of all pulls and thrusts. A wave passing from base to tip would exert a thrust away from the cell upon the medium.

Although cilia appear, on observation, to move through the medium at a very high rate, they are actually moving very slowly, as a simple calculation will show. The angular velocity of cilia is high, as is seen from the fact that a cilium may show 10 or 12 cycles per second, but the tip of a cilium is actually moving through the medium at a maximum rate of only a few feet per hour, a rate quite slow in terms of propulsive instruments of the type of which we ordinarily think. The rate of the effective stroke is usually two to ten times that of the recovery.

The reversal of the direction of effective beat of cilia has often been reported. Among the ciliated protozoans, small turbellarians such as *Stenostomum*, and ciliated larvae, reversal of direction of locomotion reflects this reversal of activity. Some early reported cases of ciliary reversal among certain metazoans appear, however, to have an alternative explanation. The apparent reversal on the labial palps of *Ostrea*, and probably also in the gullet of the coelenterate, *Actinoloba*, appears to be explicable in terms of opposite directions of beat of cilia in longitudinal grooves and on ridges, together with muscular movements emphasizing action of one or the other of the two tracts.

The cilia of the lips and gullet of the sea anemone, *Metridium*, and also of other species of anthozoans, whose tentacles are too short for successful transport of food to the mouth, appear capable of reversal of beat in response to direct stimulation by chemical agents. In the normal unstimulated anemone the cilia beat outward. When, however, a piece of crab flesh is brought into contact with the ciliated epithelium, those cilia in the immediate region of the food reverse their beat, now carrying the food into the gullet. Immediately following passage of the particle the cilia resume their outward beat.

The effect of crab flesh in inducing ciliary reversal in the *Metridium* can be imitated through the application of 2½ per cent KCl in sea water or the addition of glycogen.[42] After such treatment the direction of both the effective stroke and metachronic wave is reversed. Such treatment does not reverse the direction of beat of the cilia of the tentacles or siphonoglyphs.

In *Paramecium* ciliary reversal is effected by treatment with KCl and salts of other monovalent cations.[38, 39] When the animal is

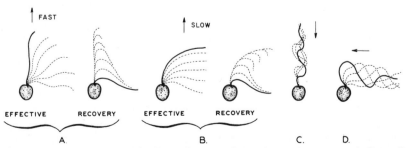

FIGURE 201. Some activities of the flagellum of *Monas* during locomotion. Arrows indicate direction of movement of the organism. (Redrawn from Krijgsman, B. J.: Arch. Protist., vol. 52.)

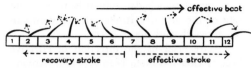

FIGURE 202. Diagrammatic representation of the metachronal rhythm. Cilia 1 to 12 are beating in sequence. (From Gray, J.: Ciliary Movement. Cambridge University Press.)

subjected to a field of electric current flow, there is a reversal of beat of cilia on the end of the animal nearer the cathode.

Ciliary reversal occurs for the ectodermal cilia of amphibian larvae;[60] local ciliary reversal is observed in response to mechanical stimulation. In higher metazoans in general, it appears impossible to effect ciliary reversal.

Ciliary Control and Coordination. Cilia appear to show a well-developed automaticity. The cilia of bits of isolated epithelial tissue continue to beat after removal from the organism. In protozoans the cilia of small enucleated fragments of an individual continue to beat for some time. Sperm cells with the head removed continue to show active locomotion. The automaticity of ciliary action therefore resides entirely in the cilium and an immediately adjacent region of the cell. An organic connection with the basal granule is essential to the beat. Separating the middle piece from a sperm tail or stripping away the surface of a ciliated epithelium in such manner as to break the connections between the cilia and the underlying layer of basal granules results in immediate cessation of ciliary beat.[16] It is not yet fully established whether the basal granules themselves, or some other functional elements in the same general area, are the essential elements for normal rhythmic activity.

Ciliated surfaces typically exhibit metachronism indicating presence of a general coordinating mechanism. Metachronism is a term applied to the orderly succession of initiation of beat of cilia located in a spatial sequence in a ciliated surface (Fig. 202). Each cilium along one axis is, in consequence, very slightly out of phase with its neighbor in front of and behind it in the direction of the metachronic wave propagation. At right angles to this wave, cilia beat isochronically, or in phase with one another, giving an optical picture of waves passing over the epithelium. The crests of the waves include cilia at the peak of their effective stroke; the troughs include those cilia at the ends of their effective strokes and about to commence their recovery.

The direction of the metachronic wave of a ciliated surface often appears to be as fundamental a property of a surface as is the direction of ciliary beat itself. Even a small isolated portion of a ciliated surface may continue to show its own inherent direction of metachronism. This is not disturbed by removing and then replacing, after rotating through 180 degrees, a portion of the ciliated epithelium of the roof of a frog's mouth. In these circumstances the transplanted portion has its metachronic wave proceeding in a direction opposite that of the surrounding tissue.

Among ciliated tissues from various sources, the direction of the metachronic wave bears various relationships to the direction of the effective stroke.[56, 57] In the frog's mouth, the metachronic wave and ciliary effective strokes are in the same direction. In the rows of ciliated combs of ctenophores the two are in opposite directions.[9] In the cilia of the gills of the annelid *Nephthys*[10] and in the lateral ciliated epithelium of *Mytilus* gills[16] the metachronic wave is always at right angles to the effective stroke. In the ciliates *Paramecium* and *Colpoda* in which rapid metachronic waves pass from posterior to anterior tips, the effective stroke may be oblique.[40, 41] In *Opalina,* the direction of the metachronal wave changes freely with the direction of swimming, passing backward, to right or to left[58] (Fig. 203). It has been suggested that the wave as a whole is the propulsive agent, in contrast with the effects of the individual cilia.

The mechanisms of the coordination and control of cilia are largely unknown. There is reason to believe that it is more complex among protozoans, in which a number of complex locomotory patterns are exhibited by a single individual, than in the ciliated epithelia of the larger metazoan invertebrates and vertebrates. In these higher animals the pattern of coordination seems for the most part to be invariable. Among many protozoans there appear to be definite species differences in the pathways of the metachronic wave. This is not interfered with by a transverse cut deep into the animal in *Spirostomum* and *Stentor,* but coordination on the two sides of such an incision is lost in *Paramecium*.[65] Transmission of the metachronic wave would appear to involve an ectoplasmic network in the former species and only ectoplasmic, longitudinal pathways in the latter. Since the silver-line systems of fibrils in the first two species form a network connecting the basal granules, and in the latter species possess only longitudinal fibrils, it has been suggested that this is the conductile system for the metachronic wave in protozoans.

Studies on the progressive anesthetization of the ciliary mechanism has shown that in protozoans the first thing to be lost is the power of ciliary reversal. At a later stage metachronic coordination is lost, leaving the cilia beating independently. Last of all, the cilia entirely cease their activity. This observation has led to the hypothesis that ciliary beat, metachronism, and reversal are controlled by three separate mechanisms. Reversal must be governed by a mechanism of relatively rapid transmission affecting all cilia of the organism nearly simultaneously and passing in all directions over the animal. Transverse cuts passing deeply into those protozoans investigated in this regard do not measurably interfere with the transmission of excitation in response to stimuli which induce ciliary reversal.

Support for the concept of the transmission of excitation in intracellular ciliary coordination by a fibrillar system has come from microdissection studies of the ciliated epithelial cells of clam gills[64, 66, 67] (Fig. 204). Cuts through the distal third of the cell containing the ciliary cone of intracellular fibrils destroy ciliary coordination; cuts through any level of the proximal two-thirds have no such effect. Only when transverse cuts are in the immediate region of the basal granules them-

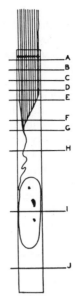

FIGURE 204. Diagram of a ciliated epithelial cell of *Anodonta* showing regions where cuts were made. Cut at *A* always resulted in cessation of ciliary beat. Cuts at *B* through *F* permitted continuation of beat but resulted in more or less loss of normal coordination. Cuts at *G* through *J* resulted in no apparent disturbance of normal ciliary activity. (From Worley, L. G.: J. Cell. Comp. Physiol., vol. 18.)

selves does even the uncoordinated ciliary beat cease. Waves of ciliary metachronism

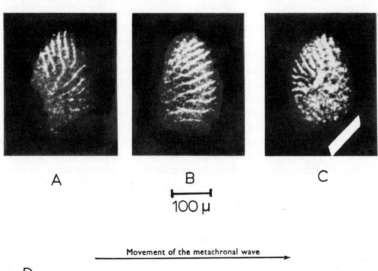

A   B   C

100 μ

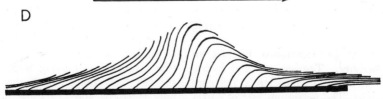

Movement of the metachronal wave ⟶

D

FIGURE 203. The metachronal waves (*D*) of ciliary beat of *Opalina*. Waves pass backward (*B*) in normal swimming; to the right (*A*) when the animal turns left; and to the left (*C*) when the animal turns right. (From Sleigh, M. A.: J. Exp. Biol., vol. 37.)

pass smoothly over large sheets of ciliated epithelial cells; the mechanism for intercellular transmission is unknown.

Although ciliary beat appears in general to be the result of an automaticity of the ciliary mechanism, the cilia in many cases are controlled in their activities by more basic response mechanisms within the organism. The hypotrichs *Uronychia* and *Euplotes* show several types of locomotory patterns. A role of the neuromotor system in control of locomotion in *Euplotes* is suggested from experimental destruction of parts of this system (Chapter 21). In a number of metazoans, both direct and indirect evidence has been advanced pointing to nervous modification of ciliary activity.[15, 28-30]

The rows of ciliary combs of ctenophores are controlled by impulses passing out over the paddle rows from the aboral sense organs.[9] The ciliary systems of the turbellarian *Stenostomum* and of the ciliated larvae of many molluscs and annelids are known to be nerve controlled. The cilia may be active or motionless or, in the case of *Stenostomum,* reversed. A freshly isolated piece of ciliated lip of the snail *Physa* shows no ciliary activity unless a nerve fiber innervating this region is stimulated. On the other hand, pedal ciliary activity in *Alectrion* appears inhibited by nervous action. If the foot is excised, there is temporary cessation of ciliary beat, followed by a resumption, after which the beat continues unabated for the remainder of the life of the ciliated epithelium.

The pharyngeal cilia of the frog are accelerated greatly and the amplitude of the beat increased by electrical stimulation of certain cranial nerves.[31, 55] This response, which has a latent period of about a second, persists for as long as 10 minutes following stimulus cessation. It is not known whether the fibers are sympathetic or parasympathetic, though the bulk of the evidence suggests their belonging to the facialis group. Acetylcholine has been reported to increase ciliary activity.[4, 5, 34, 53] In further support of normal nervous control of the pharyngeal cilia of the frog is the observation that these cilia are normally quiescent;[32, 33] they commence to beat in response to stimuli such as the addition of foreign particles and cease beating after these particles are swept away.

Influence of Environmental Factors on Ciliary Activity. Temperature and hydrogen ion concentration importantly influence ciliary activity. The maximum rate of ciliary activity occurs at about 34°C for *Mytilus* gill

and 35°C for frog epithelium.[16, 31, 43] The Q_{10} varies with the temperature range. For *Mytilus* gill cilia it ranges from near 3 at the lower temperatures to slightly less than 2 at the upper end of the physiological range. Above a critical temperature there is a rapid drop in rate; this critical temperature would be expected to vary with mean habitat temperature.

Hydrogen ion concentration, which varies considerably in nature, has a greater influence on the rate of ciliary activity than does concentration of any other ion.[7, 37, 59] Acids, like carbonic, which penetrate cells more rapidly have a greater effect than those which penetrate less rapidly. High hydrogen ion concentration can completely inactivate cilia. A biological significance of this response of cilia to increased acidity is evident for the bivalve mollusc. After 2 or 3 hours of valve closure there is adequate concentration of CO_2 to inhibit ciliary activity. Inasmuch as O_2 consumption of ciliated tissue is a direct function of the rate of ciliary activity, this inhibitory influence of CO_2 is obviously adaptive. The minimum hydrogen ion concentration effecting inhibition of gill cilia varies with species. For example, it is lower in *Mya,* which customarily dwells in well-aerated water, than in *Ostrea* or *Mytilus.*

A very striking instance of adaptive variation in the minimal hydrogen ion concentration essential for ciliary inhibition has been reported for the cilia of the different portions of the digestive tract of *Mya.* There is a definite correlation between the normal pH of each region of the digestive tract and the pH at which the cilia of that region are brought to rest.

Other cations, and also anions, influence ciliary activity.[16] Potassium produces a transient augmentation of ciliary beat in *Mytilus.*[18] In general, these ions are relatively constant in concentration in any given natural environment. The effects of altering their concentrations and ratios appear to be basic ones, quite comparable to their action on all cells. As with certain other cellular phenomena, cations of the medium have more influence on ciliary beat than have anions.

Theories of Ciliary Movement. Little or nothing is known of the actual mechanism of ciliary motion. Historically, theories have fallen into two general categories: (1) those that assumed the moving force to occur in the cell body proper, with the cilia acting only passively, and (2) those that assumed that the moving force occurred in the cilium itself, the cilia therefore moving as a result of intrinsic contractile capacity. Schafer in 1891 proposed that cilia were passive bodies comparable to hollow elastic structures with differences in the degree of elasticity of various portions of their walls. Ciliary beat was held to be a result of rhythmic surging and ebbing of fluid into and out of these cellular processes.

Much more compatible with our modern theories of the mechanism of action of contractile elements in general is the second type of theory, namely, that the cilium itself contains actively contractile elements responsible for the movements. This view was first proposed by Heidenhain in 1911. Supporting this view are numerous observations. The waves passing out along a flagellum often show no reduction in amplitude as they pass from base to tip; a reduction would be expected were kinetic energy generated only in the cell body proper at the flagellar base. Indeed, in species such as *Peranema,* the undulatory activity may be restricted to the tip region of the flagellum, the rest of the flagellum remaining relatively rigid. Investigations of the fine structure of cilia with the aid of polarized light, x-ray diffraction, and electron micrography reveal a molecular organization resembling strikingly that of muscle which unquestionably possesses intrinsic contractility. Both exhibit a fibrillar structure in consequence of an orientation of elongated molecules or micelles. It has been postulated that the nine fibrils constituting the typical cylindrical array comprise the principal contractile portion, with the paired axial filament determining the direction of the contraction.[49] However, the undulation of the terminal region of the flagellum of *Peranema,* which appears to possess principally the axial fiber, suggests this, too, to be contractile.

The force of ciliary beat in *Paramecium* appears to remain constant; the velocity of the ciliary effective stroke is inversely proportional to the viscosity of the medium in solutions of gum arabic.[45]

Ciliary activity normally involves a utilization of oxygen, the rate of consumption varying with ciliary rate.[16] O_2 consumption increases and beat ceases upon treatment with 2,4-dinitrophenol, probably by uncoupling energy-using steps.[62] However, like muscle, cilia appear capable of acting for a time anaerobically. After administration of 0.1 per cent NaCN to a fragment of *Mytilus* gill, O_2 consumption drops off abruptly, but ciliary activity diminishes much more slowly. Fragments of *Mytilus* gill placed in weak hemoglobin solutions in chambers perfused with damp hydrogen show ciliary beat continuing for some time after dexoygenation of the hemoglobin. After ciliary beat has become very slow under the anaerobic conditions, rapid beat is restored quickly on readmission of oxygen and reoxygenation of the hemoglobin. The cilia of the gill of *Pecten,* on the other hand, are reported to cease beating immediately on removal of oxygen as indicated by the reduction of dyestuffs such as janus green and neutral red, but before nile blue is reduced. The cilia of *Paramecium* cease activity within a few seconds in an O_2-free medium.[14] It is known, nevertheless, that some ciliates are able to carry on normal ciliary movement in natural environments which are practically oxygen free. One cannot yet conclude whether the need for O_2 differs qualitatively or only quantitatively among different species of animals.

REFERENCES

1. ATKINS, D., Quart. J. Micro. Sci. *80*: 321-435, 1938. Ciliary mechanisms, Lamellibranchs.
2. BRADFIELD, J. R., Symp. Soc. Exp. Biol. *9*: 306-334, 1955. Electron micrographs of cilia.
3. BROWN, H. P., Ohio J. Sci. *45*: 247-301, 1945. Structure of protozoan flagellum.
4. BÜLBRING, E., BURN, J. H., and SHELLEY, H. J., Proc. Roy. Soc. London, B, *141*: 445-466, 1953. Acetylcholine and ciliary movement.
5. BURN, J. H., Pharmacol. Rev. *6*: 107-112, 1954. Acetylcholine and ciliary movement.
6. CARRIKER, M. R., Biol. Bull. *91*: 88-111, 1946. Ciliation in gut of Lymnaea.
7. CHASE, A. M., and GLASER, O., J. Gen. Physiol. *13*: 627-636, 1930. H⁺ ion concentration and ciliary activity.
8. CHU, HSIANG-YAO, Am. J. Physiol. *136*: 223-228, 1942. Ciliary circulation of anuran cerebrospinal fluid.
9. COONFIELD, B. R., Biol. Bull. *66*: 10-21, 1934. Coordination of swimming combs of ctenophores.
10. COONFIELD, B. R., Biol. Bull. *67*: 399-409, 1934. Ciliary movement on Nephthys gills.
11. FAWCETT, D. W., and PORTER, K. R., J. Morphol. *94*: 221-281, 1954. Fine structure of cilia.
12. FISCHBEIN, E., and WORLEY, L. G., Anat. Rec. *123*: 582-583, 1952. Electron micrographs of cilia.
13. FOSTER, E., BAYLOR, M. B., MEINKOTH, N. A., and CLARK, G. I., Biol. Bull. *93*: 114-121, 1947. Structure of protozoan flagellum.
14. GERSCH, M., Protoplasma *27*: 412-441, 1937. O_2 and ciliary activity in Paramecium.
15. GOTHLIN, G. L., Skand. Arch. Physiol. *58*: 11-32, 1930. Influence of nerves on ciliary activity.
16. GRAY, J., Ciliary Movement. Cambridge University Press, 1928.
17. JAKUS, M. A., and HALL, C. E., Biol. Bull. *91*: 141-144, 1946. Fibrillar structure of flagella.

18. KINOSITA, H., Annot. Zool. Japan. *25*: 8-14, 1952. Effect of KCl on cilia.

19. KINOSITA, H., and KAMADA, T., Jap. J. Zool. *8*: 291-310, 1939. Ciliary movement in Mytilus.

20. KNIGHT-JONES, E. W., Quart. J. Micr. Sci. *95*: 503-521, 1954. Ciliary metachronism.

21. KRIJGSMAN, B. J., Arch. Protist. *52*: 478-488, 1925. Flagellar movement in Monas.

22. LOWNDES, A. G., Proc. Zool. Soc. London Sec A *111*: 111-134, 1941. Flagellar movement.

23. LOWNDES, A. G., Nature *150*: 579-580, 1942. Ciliary movement and density, Pleurobrachia.

24. LOWNDES, A. G., Proc. Zool. Soc. London, B, *113*: 28-43, 1943. Density of the Ctenophore, Pleurobrachia.

25. LOWNDES, A. G., Proc. Zool. Soc. London *113*: 99-107, 1943. Activity of protozoan flagellum.

26. LOWNDES, A. G., Proc. Zool. Soc. London *114*: 325-338, 1944. Flagellar activity, Monas and Peranema.

27. LOWNDES, A. G., School Sci. Rev. *100*: 319-332, 1945. Locomotion in Euglena.

28. LUCAS, A. M., J. Morph. Physiol. *51*: 147-193, 1931. Influence of nerves on ciliary activity.

29. LUCAS, A. M., J. Morphol. Physiol. *51*: 195-205, 1931. Influence of nerves on ciliary activity.

30. LUCAS, A. M., J. Morphol. *53*: 243-263, 1932. Influence of nerves in ciliary activity.

31. LUCAS, A. M., J. Morphol. *53*: 265-276, 1932. Influence of temperature on ciliary beat.

32. LUCAS, A. M., Proc. Soc. Exp. Biol. Med. *30*: 501-506, 1933. Control of cilia of frog mouth.

33. LUCAS, A. M., Am. J. Physiol. *112*: 468-476, 1935. Control of cilia of frog mouth.

34. MARONEY, S. P. J., and RONKIN, R. R., Biol. Bull. *105*: 378, 1953. Cholinesterase and ciliary movement.

35. MEYER, A., Ztschr. wiss. Zool. *135*: 495-538, 1929. Coelomic ciliation of annelids.

36. MEYER, A., Zool. Jahrb. Abt. Anat. und Ont. Tiere *64*: 371-436, 1938. Ciliated coelom in Tomopteris.

37. NOMURA, S., Protoplasma *20*: 85-89, 1933. H$^+$ ions and ciliary movement; O$_2$ consumption of cilia.

38. OLIPHANT, J. F., Physiol. Zool. *11*: 19-30, 1938. Influence of chemicals in ciliary beat in Paramecium.

39. OLIPHANT, J. F., Physiol. Zool. *15*: 443-452, 1942. Influence of chemicals on ciliary beat in Paramecium.

40. PARDUCZ, B., Acta Biol. Acad. Sci. Hungaricae *4*: 177-220, 1953. Ciliary activity in infusoria.

41. PARDUCZ, B., Acta Biol. Acad. Sci. Hungaricae *5*: 169-212, 1954. Ciliary activity in infusoria.

42. PARKER, G. H., Proc. Nat. Acad. Sci. *14*: 713-714, 1928. Ciliary reversal by glycogen.

43. PARKER, G. H., and MARKS, A. P., J. Exp. Zool. *52*: 1-7, 1928. Ciliary reversal, Metridium.

44. PETERSON, J. B., Bot. Tidskr. *40*: 373-389, 1929. Structure of feathered flagella.

45. PIGON, A., and SZARSKI, H., Bull. Acad. Polonaise Sci. *3*: 99-102, 1955. Velocity and force of ciliary beat.

46. PORTER, K. R., Harvey Lect. 1955-56, pp. 175-228, 1957. Electron micrographs of cilia.

47. POTTS, B. P., and TOMLIN, S. G., Biochem. Biophys. Acta. *16*: 66-74, 1955. Fine structure of cilia.

48. PURCHON, R. D., Proc. Zool. Soc. London *124*: 859-911, 1955. Ciliation of Pholadidae.

49. ROTH, L. E., J. Biophys. Biochem. Cytol. *2*: 235-240, 1956. Fine structure of cilia.

50. SCHMIDT, W. J., Protoplasma *28*: 18-22, 1937. Birefringence of cilia.

51. SCHMITT, F. O., Physiol. Rev. *19*: 270-302, 1939. Birefringence of cilia.

52. SCHMITT, F. O., HALL, C. E., and JAKUS, M. A., Biol. Symp. *10*: 261-276, 1943. Fibrillar structure of flagella.

53. SEAMAN, J. R., Biol. Bull. *99*: 347, 1950. Acetylcholine and ciliary movement.

54. SEDAR, A. W., BEAMS, H. W., and JANNEY, C. D., Proc. Soc. Exp. Biol. Med. *79*: 303-305, 1952. Fine structure of cilia.

55. SEO, A., Jap. J. Med. Sci., III Biophysics 2: 47-75, 1931. Nervous control of cilia of frog mouth.

56. SLEIGH, M. A., J. Exp. Biol. *33*: 15-28, 1956. Ciliary metachronism and beat, Stentor.

57. SLEIGH, M. A., J. Exp. Biol. *34*: 106-115, 1957. Ciliary metachronism and beat, Stentor.

58. SLEIGH, M. A., J. Exp. Biol. *37*: 1-10, 1960. Ciliary beat, Opalina and Stentor.

59. TOMITA, G., J. Shanghai Scient. Inst. *1*: Sec. IV, 69-76, 77-84, 1934. H ions and ciliary movement.

60. TWITTY, V. E., J. Exp. Zool. *50*: 319-344, 1928. Ciliary reversal in Amphibia.

61. VLK, W., Arch. Protist. *90*: 448-488, 1936. Structure of flagella.

62. WELLER, H., and RONKIN, R. R., Proc. Soc. Exp. Biol. Med. *81*: 65-66, 1952. 2,4-Dinitrophenol on cilia.

63. WOHLFARTH-BOTTERMANN, K., and PFEFFERKORN, G., Protoplasma *42*: 227-238, 1953. Structure of cilia.

64. WORLEY, L. G., Proc. Nat. Acad. Sci. *19*: 320-322, 1933. Metachronism in ciliated epithelium.

65. WORLEY, L. G., J. Cell. Comp. Physiol. *5*: 53-72, 1934. Ciliary coordination in protozoa.

66. WORLEY, L. G., J. Exp. Zool. *69*: 105-121, 1934. Metachronism in ciliated epithelium.

67. WORLEY, L. G., J. Cell. Comp. Physiol. *18*: 187-197, 1941. Ciliary coordination in gill epithelium cells of clams.

68. WORLEY, L. G., FISCHBEIN, E., and SHAPIRO, J. E., J. Morphol. *92*: 545-578, 1953. Ciliary structure.

69. YASUZUMI, G., and WAKISAKA, I., Cytologia *21*: 157-164, 1956. Electron microscopy of cilia.

70. YONGE, C. M., Great Barrier Reef Expedition Sci. Rep. *1*: 13-58, 1930. Ciliary feeding in corals.

Chapter 17

TRICHOCYSTS AND NEMATOCYSTS

TRICHOCYSTS

The ectoplasm of numerous species of ciliates contains explosive bodies known as trichocysts.[5] These are fusiform bodies oriented obliquely or at right angles to the surface. Among various protozoans, they may be uniformly distributed over the surface, as in *Paramecium,* or restricted to certain regions, as in the proboscis of *Dileptus.* They may be projected outward on the ends of long tentacles in feeding specimens of *Actinobolina.*

The trichocysts appear to have their origin within or close to the macronucleus in *Frontonia.* From here they make their way to their definitive position in the ectoplasm, completing their differentiation as they migrate. In *Frorodon* the fully formed trichocyst has the form of a cylindrical sac containing an elongated, coiled filament. In *Paramecium* the undischarged trichocysts possess an ovoid body proper, about 2 to 3 μ long by $\frac{2}{3}$ μ in diameter, and a cap-covered tip of slightly smaller diameter. On discharge, the tip with its covering cap is separated from the body proper through the elongation of a shaft[6] (Fig. 205).

The trichocysts can readily be induced to discharge their filaments through chemical (acid or base), mechanical (pressure), or electrical (condenser discharge or induction shock) stimulation. With electrical stimulation there is an increase in the number discharged as the strength of the stimulus is increased.[20] The total discharge is very rapid, occurring in a matter of a few milliseconds. The discharged trichocyst is needle-like in general form, being ten or more times as long as the undischarged body. The discharged trichocysts of *Paramecium* may be as much as 40 μ long. The trichocysts of *Paramecium* show birefringence, indicating an orientation of elongated submicroscopic particulates in the long axis of the organelle. A study of the extended threads of discharged trichocysts of *Paramecium* with the electron microscope reveals them to be without bounding membrane and to display a periodic transverse banding at intervals of 600 to 650 Å (Fig. 205). The characteristics of the shaft indicate it to be composed of elongated cross-striated protein fibrils showing a periodic structure somewhat resembling collagen fibers. The over-all striation of the organelle appears to be a consequence of the alignment of these fibers in phase with one another. At the tip of the shaft there is a relatively opaque, thornlike body indicative of the presence of a dense proteinaceous structure or of elements of high atomic mass.[6, 7, 17]

Little or nothing is known of the mechanism of trichocyst discharge or to what extent trichocysts are activated other than in direct response to environmental stimuli. The trichocysts appear connected with the silver-line system, which some consider to have a nerve-net type of conductile function. The mechanism of discharge probably involves either a hydration of some protein within the trichocyst or a rapid osmotic inflow of water on excitation of these organelles.

FIGURE 205. Electron micrograph of discharged *Paramecium* trichocysts, shadow-cast with chromium. (From Jakus, M. A., and Hall, C. E.: Biol. Bull., vol. 91.)

The role of trichocysts in protozoans is still not definitely established. They have been considered by many to possess a protective function. This appears doubtful in such species as *Paramecium,* which are readily ingested by *Didinium* even after the *Paramecium* has exploded many of its trichocysts. More probably the trichocysts function here as organs of attachment.[19] In ciliates such as *Dileptus* and *Actinobolina,* prey coming in contact with a region of the body bearing trichocysts appears to be paralyzed instantly, as if a toxin were associated with the discharged trichocysts. Among the dinoflagellates, *Polykrikos* and *Nematodinium,* there are trichocysts that bear a very close resemblance structurally to the nematocysts of coelenterates and which are frequently called nematocysts. Trichocysts in various stages of differentiation have been found within these dinoflagellates.

Another type of effector organelle very closely resembling the coelenterate nematocyst is the polar capsule of sporozoans of the groups Myxosporidia and Actinomyxidia. Within the digestive tract of host organisms, the action of the digestive juices induces these capsules to discharge their spirally coiled hollow thread after the fashion of a nematocyst. The discharged filament serves as a means of temporary anchorage of the parasite to the host tissues.

NEMATOCYSTS

The nematocysts of coelenterates are extremely small intracellular structures of spherical, ovoid, or spindle form. They consist of a capsule within which a hollow thread, continuous with one end, is introverted and coiled.[5, 18, 21] Albuminoid protein and various phenols have been found inside the capsules; the capsule itself is probably collagen-like.[2, 3, 4, 8, 11, 14] The discharge of the nematocyst involves a rapid expulsion of the thread-like process by eversion (Fig. 206). There is usually a cap or operculum covering that region of the undischarged nematocyst through which the thread is ejected. The nematocysts are produced within interstitial cells either at their final site or at some distance from this site, to which they move by ameboid activity or passive transportation. A cell containing a nematocyst is known as a cnidoblast or nematocyte. The portion of the cnidoblast containing the nematocyst eventually comes to occupy a superficial position and usually develops at its outer end a bristle-like projection, the cnidocil. The latter is imbedded in a small crater-like elevation on the

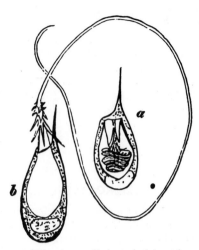

FIGURE 206. An undischarged (*a*) and a discharged (*b*) nematocyst located in its cnidoblast. The spine-like projection of the cnidoblast is the cnidocil. (Redrawn from Sedgwick.)

cell. The cnidoblast also often differentiates trichite-like supporting rods in its peripheral regions and often, too, a fibrillar network associated with the capsule of the nematocyst and extending proximally in the cell from it. In *Diadumene,* it is held that the fully developed nematocyst is extracellular.[24, 27]

The nematocysts of coelenterates are divisible into two major groups, the spirocysts of the Zoantharia, which are acid-staining bodies possessing peculiar adhesive threads, and the basic-staining nematocysts proper. The latter are widely distributed through the whole phylum. They are of many types in terms of character of their discharged threads. In some, e.g., the volvents, the thread is closed at its tip and forms a tightly coiled filament on discharge, wrapping itself about bristles or fibers of organisms in whose presence they are discharged. Most other types have open tips and are believed to penetrate prey, injecting into them a toxic substance. The threads of these latter types commonly possess an armature in the form of three spiralling rows of spines which serve effectively to anchor the thread into tissues which have been penetrated. The penetrating capacity of at least some types is so great that even the chitinous cuticles of small organisms can be punctured.

The sting of numerous species gives rise to severe itching and other skin disorders in man. The toxicity is very great in a few coelenterates such as *Physalia,* and some larger scyphozoan jellyfish such as *Dactylometra,* even enough to render them highly dangerous to man. Their sting may in some cases produce serious illness or even death. The nature of the toxin associated with nematocysts is unknown.[15]

The cnidoblasts respond as independent effectors in the discharge of their nematocysts. They are discharged by many chemical agents, including both strong acids and bases.[26] There is no evidence of control of these by any coordinatory mechanism within the organism. In their normal responses, and in response to highly localized electrical stimuli, there is complete restriction of the discharge to the specific region excited.[12, 13] Intense mechanical stimulation by inert objects will induce only a weak discharge, whereas mild mechanical stimulation by natural foods is sufficient to evoke a strong response (Fig. 207). Submersion of cnidoblasts in a weak extract of a normal food which will typically not itself induce discharge will greatly lower the threshold of these effectors in *Anemonia* to purely mechanical stimuli.[12] The specific food factors that are involved in this sensitization are lipoidal substances adsorbed upon proteins. The adsorptive forces are so strong that the factors cannot be removed by ether extraction, but they can be with alcohol. The active chemical substances appear to have properties resembling sterols and phospholipins and to be highly surface-active. In view of the rapid and thorough discharge of nematocysts even to dried foods,

it would appear that the normal reaction must be "contact-chemical" in character, chemical sensitization to mechanical stimulation occurring almost instantaneously.

These highly specialized characteristics of excitation of nematocysts in *Anemonia* are peculiarly adapted to the normal functional roles of these effectors. The value of having the nematocysts withhold their discharge until the instant of mechanical contact is readily seen in comparing the results of stimulating discharge by a piece of cotton soaked in bile salts with that by a similar piece soaked in an extract of normal food material. In the former case the nematocysts are induced to discharge before contact by the diffusion outward of the bile salts, which are highly potent cnidoblast excitors, and therefore before the discharge can result in any attachment of the discharging filaments to the cotton fibers, as occurs in the case of normal food substances.

The cnidocils, when present, are probably concerned with the excitation process. That they are nonessential, however, is indicated by the fact that they are absent in many of the anthozoans. It would appear that in their absence the cnidoblast surface comprises the natural receptive area for the response.[27] Nematocysts may be extruded, unexploded, in response to K^+, NH_4^+, and in absence of ions, in an active process capable of sup-

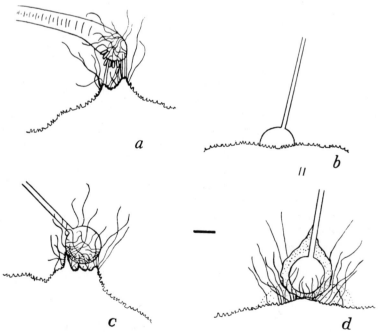

FIGURE 207. Discharge of nematocysts of *Anemonia* to various stimuli. *a*, Touch by a human hair. *b*, Touch by a clear, blunt glass rod fails to cause discharge. *c*, Response to clean glass rod after sensitization of the cnidoblasts with dilute saliva extract. *d*, Response to glass rod smeared with alcohol extract of *Pecten* gill. (From Pantin, C. F. A.: J. Exp. Biol., vol. 19.)

pression by Mg^{++}, Cl^-, Br^-, and anesthetics.[16, 24] Isolated nematocysts may retain for a time their capacity to discharge, longest in M1 glycerol solution, shorter in isotonic $CaCl_2$, $NaCl$, KCl, or sea water.[22, 25] Discharge has been postulated to result from weakening of an operculum or plug.[23]

The mechanism of discharge of nematocysts is not well understood. Two types of theories in particular have found favor among students in this field; both types have in common the postulation that an increased pressure within the capsule forces out the filament. One theory considers the pressure increase following stimulation to be the result of a passage of water into the capsule. Some have believed the nematocyst operates as a simple osmometer. Others think the water inflow associated with hydration and swelling of colloids within the nematocyst in response to change in pH, and a consequent swelling of colloidal material contained therein. A second type of theory attributes the increase in pressure to a contraction of the capsule, either of itself or by a fibrillar network associated with the capsule. It is possible that mechanisms fitting both theories are to be found among the numerous nematocyst types of the various coelenterate species. The nematocysts of *Metridium* appear to discharge as a result of inflow of water; those of *Physalia* appear to require the activity of contractile fibrils of the nematoblast.

Functional nematocysts have been found in the flatworm, *Microstomum,* and in the sea slug, *Aeolis*.[9, 10] It has been conclusively demonstrated that these nematocysts have been derived from the coelenterates on which these animals feed. It is interesting that, in the appropriation of coelenterate nematocysts, these flatworms and molluscs selectively utilize only certain types. For example, *Microstomum* digests the volvents and utilizes the penetrants. The sea slugs, feeding on *Pennaria,* utilize only the highly effective type known as the microbasic mastigophores, to the exclusion of other types. The appropriate nematocysts are quite concentrated in the bodies of their new carriers and would appear to serve as effective defensive weapons. This phenomenon involves, obviously, loss of responsiveness to their new host. A comparable loss is seen between the commensally related hermit crab and sea anemone.[1]

REFERENCES

1. BERNER, L., Bull. Soc. Zool. France 78: 221-226, 1953. Nematocyst response in commensal relationship.
2. BOISSEAU, J. P., Bull. Soc. Zool. France 77: 151-169, 1952. Chemical contents of nematocysts.
3. HAMON, M., Nature 176: 357, 1955. Chemical nature of nematocysts.
4. HAMON, M., Bull. Soc. d'Hist. Nat. l'Afrique du Nord 46: 169-179, 1955. Chemistry of nematocysts.
5. HYMAN, L. H., The Invertebrates, New York, McGraw-Hill Book Co., 1940. Trichocysts and nematocysts.
6. JAKUS, M. A., J. Exp. Zool. 100: 457-485, 1945. Trichocysts; structure and properties.
7. JAKUS, M. A., and HALL, C. E., Biol. Bull. 91: 141-144, 1946. Electron micrographs of trichocysts.
8. JOHNSON, F. B., and LENHOFF, H. M., J. Histochem. Cytochem. 6: 394, 1958. Nature of Hydra nematocyst capsule.
9. KEPNER, W. A., J. Morphol. 73: 297-311, 1943. Nematocysts in nudibranchs.
10. KEPNER, W. A., GREGORY, W. C., and PORTER, R. J., Zool. Anz. 121: 114-124, 1938. Nematocysts of Microstomum.
11. LENHOFF, H. M., KLINE, E. S., and HURLEY, R., Biochem. Biophys. Acta 26: 204-205, 1957. Chemistry of Hydra nematocyst.
12. PANTIN, C. F. A., J. Exp. Biol. 19: 294-310, 1942. Control of nematocyst discharge.
13. PARKER, G. H., and VAN ALSTYNE, M. A., J. Exp. Zool. 63: 329-344, 1932. Control and mechanism of nematocyst discharge.
14. PHILLIPS, J. H., Nature 178: 932, 1956. Chemical nature of Metridium nematocysts.
15. PHILLIPS, J. H., and ABBOTT, D. P., Biol. Bull. 113: 296-301, 1957. Toxin of Metridium nematocyst.
16. PICKEN, L. E. R., Quart. J. Micr. Sci. 94: 203-227, 1953. Corynactis nematocysts.
17. POTTS, B., Biochem. Biophys. Acta 16: 464-470, 1955. Electron microscopic study of trichocysts.
18. ROBSON, E. A., Quart. J. Micr. Sci. 94: 229-235, 1953. Electron microscopic study of nematocysts.
19. SAUNDERS, J. T., Proc. Cambridge Phil. Soc. (Biol. Sci.) 1: 249-269, 1925. Function of trichocysts of Paramecium.
20. SCHMITT, F. O., HALL, C. E., and JAKUS, M. A., Biol. Symp. 10: 261-276, 1943. Trichocysts.
21. YANAGITA, T. M., J. Facul. Sci. Tokyo Univ. 6: 97-108, 1943. Nematocyst discharge.
22. YANAGITA, T. M., Nat. Sci. Report: Ochanomizu Univ. 2: 117-123, 1951. Physiology of isolated nematocysts.
23. YANAGITA, T. M., Jap. J. Zool. 12: 363-375, 1959. Responses of isolated nematocysts.
24. YANAGITA, T. M., J. Exp. Biol. 36: 478-494, 1959. Extrusion of nematocysts.
25. YANAGITA, T. M., J. Fac. Sci. Tokyo Univ. 8: 381-400, 1959. Response of isolated nematocysts.
26. YANAGITA, T. M., and WADA, T., Nat. Sci. Report, Ochanomizu Univ. 4: 112-118, 1953. Nematocyst discharge by acids and bases.
27. YANAGITA, T. M., and WADA, T., Cytologia 24: 81-97, 1959. Physiology of acontia and nematocysts.

Chapter 18

BIOLUMINESCENCE

The ability to produce light is very widely distributed among bacteria, fungi, and animals.[21, 23-25] It seems to have arisen independently numerous times during evolutionary history. Among animals, luminous representatives have been described for all the major phyla from Protozoa through Chordata. Minor phyla for which reports of luminous species are lacking are the Mesozoa, Entoprocta, Phoronidea, Echiuroidea, Sipunculoidea, Brachiopoda, Onychophora, Lingualtula, and Tardigrada. There appears to be little or no general pattern in the distribution of the capacity among or within the animal groups; its occurrence is quite sporadic. It may occur in one species of a genus and be absent in another. Practically all of the known luminous species are marine or terrestrial. Luminescent marine species are found among the abyssal, littoral, and planktonic faunas. The only reported luminescent animals from fresh water are a glowworm and a snail. The only described luminescent cavernicolous animal is a dipteran larva.

Luminescence in animals is the result of chemiluminescent reactions in which a substrate is oxidized. The chemiluminescent reaction is sometimes associated with the presence of special granules in the cytoplasm of the luminous tissue. In many organisms the light-producing reactants are expelled to the exterior where the actual reactions in production of light occur. This type of light production is known as *extracellular* luminescence, in contrast with *intracellular* luminescence, in which the light-yielding reaction proceeds within cells. In animals with extracellular luminescence the light-producing organs take the form of unicellular or multicellular glands which secrete to the exterior. Sometimes a differentiation of two types of secretory cells is observed in luminous glands, e.g., *Cypridina*. Both contribute to light production.

In higher animals with intracellular luminescence there is a general tendency toward an evolution of specialized photogenic organs. In the protozoans the luminescing granules are dispersed uniformly throughout the surface layer of the cytoplasm. In other animals the light cells typically show characteristic patterns of distribution. In many higher animals such as cephalopods, crustaceans, insects, and fishes, the light-producing cells may form only a portion of organs which possess, in addition to these cells, light-absorbing and light-reflecting layers, light filters, refractive bodies, and nerve supply. Such organs superficially resemble photoreceptors.

It is by no means always an easy matter to determine whether any particular luminescent animal possesses of itself the ability to generate light. Such luminescence may result from the presence of luminescent bacteria in or on the organism in question. One criterion for distinguishing between bacterial luminescence and that originating within animal cells is that in the former case the light is continuous, whereas in the latter it is usually produced intermittently, and commonly only in response to external stimuli. There are a number of exceptions to this, however. Many truly photogenic cells of animal origin exhibit a continuous glow. On the other hand, luminescence of bacterial origin can be made to give the semblance of intermittency as, for example, in the fish *Photoblepharon,* where the symbiotic luminous bacteria are in a light-producing organ with a movable lid capable of screening the light.

Occurrence of Bioluminescence Among Animals. Among the Protozoa there are numerous luminescent species. These are marine radiolarians and dinoflagellates. The best-known examples of the latter group are *Noctiluca* and *Gonyaulax*.[38] The light-producing granules are located throughout the organism but particularly in the periph-

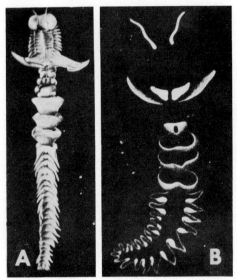

FIGURE 208. *Chaetopterus.* *A*, dorsal view (after Trojan). *B*, a luminescent individual in darkness (after Panceri). From Harvey, E. N.: Living Light. Princeton University Press.)

eral regions. *Noctiluca* glows briefly in response to mechanical stimulation; the glow originates in the region of the oral groove and spreads as a wave over the body.

Numerous coelenterates are known to be luminous. These include a number of hydroid polyps, jellyfishes,[11] siphonophores, sea pens, and sea pansies.[12, 64, 65, 71] Luminescence occurs only in response to stimuli. The natural stimulus is probably mechanical. The region immediately stimulated is first to respond, followed by a wave of luminescence proceeding out from that point. In the jellyfish, *Pelagia,* the extent of spread of the luminescence is a direct function of the strength of the stimulus. Light production in coelenterates appears in part to be extracellular, since luminous mucus can usually be readily rubbed from the surface of the organisms, but is also intracellular in both sea pens and hydromedusae. Light cells occur on the marginal canal of hydromedusae.

Numerous Ctenophora are luminous.[7, 27] Here the light-producing cells are located along the meridional gastrovascular canals in the vicinity of the germ cells. These organisms luminesce in response to stimuli, but the response is inhibited by light.[41] After subjection to daylight, the organisms regain full responsiveness after a short time in darkness.

Only a single luminous nemertean, *Emplectonema kandai,* has been described. Photo-

genic cells, producing light intracellularly, are distributed over the whole worm. A local response to localized tactile stimulation is seen. A generalized response follows stretching of the animal.

Among the Annelida, luminescence is restricted to species of terrestrial oligochaetes and marine polychaetes. Many earthworms, e.g., *Eisenia submontana,* on irritation, eject a luminous slime. This may come from the oral or anal opening or from the dorsal pores. The polychaete *Chaetopterus*[58-60, 62] exhibits a striking luminosity, much of the surface becoming luminous whenever the worm is disturbed (Fig. 208). The photogenic cells are located in the hypodermis along with mucus cells, both of which secrete their products to the exterior (Fig. 209*C*). There is nerve control of light production; stimulation of the anterior end of the worm results in a wave of light production passing posteriorly. In the transparent pelagic *Tomopteris* the photogenic organs are specialized nephridial funnels. In luminous scale worms the light originates in certain cells in the dorsal overlapping scales.[61, 63] Stimulation of any portion of the body results in a wave of light production passing up and down the body from the point of excitation, moving posteriorly with more facility than anteriorly and thus indicating a role of a partially polarized nervous system.

Luminous species of arthropods are numerous. They are largely crustaceans[14] and insects, rarely myriapods[13] and arachnids. In fact, it is from a luminous ostracod, *Cypridina,* and the firefly that we have learned much of the fundamental characteristics of the basic photogenic process. The light-producing organ of *Cypridina* is a large gland located near the mouth. Two kinds of cells can be seen in the living gland, one containing large yellow granules (luciferin) and the other, small colorless granules (luciferase). The granules are ejected by muscle contraction, and the luminescence is extracellular.

In those copepods showing photogenic capacity the source of the active agents which are expelled into the sea water is small groups of greenish secretory cells on various parts of the body.

Many euphausids and shrimp possess rather highly differentiated organs having a reflecting layer and lens associated with the light-producing cells (Fig. 209*A*). These organs are distributed widely over the surface of the body. The numerous organs appear coordinated through the nervous system inasmuch as the sequence of their activity may, as in *Sergestes,* for example, follow an anteroposterior progression. The deep-sea shrimp, *Acanthephyra purpurea,* has, in addition to typical photophores (luminous organs) of the general type just described, glands near the mouth from which luminescent substances may be forcefully ejected so as to permit the shrimp to escape from predators in a luminous cloud.

Among the insects, luminescence is restricted to members of very few orders. A few species of Collembola have been described as glowing continuously, although varying in intensity with the state of excitation of the individual. The larvae of the fungus gnat, *Ceratoplanus,* and of the tipulid fly, *Bolitophila,* have been described as luminescent, and in the latter species the adults are also. The light appears to arise in the malpighian tubules.

Perhaps the most familiar and striking examples of light production in organisms are to be found among the Coleoptera, specifically the lampyrids and elaterids.[5] In these "fireflies" or "lightning bugs" the photogenic organ is typically located ventrally in the posterior abdominal region. The organ is composed of two cellular layers, a ventral layer of light-producing cells and a dorsal

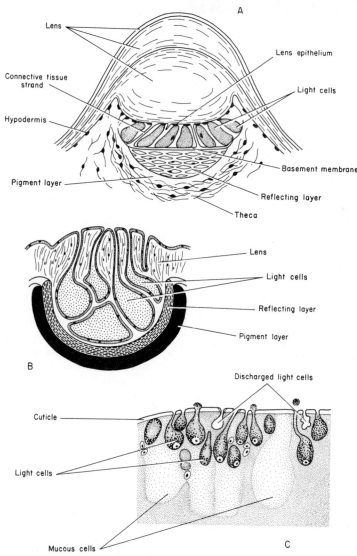

FIGURE 209. *A,* section through a light organ of the deep-sea shrimp *Sergestes. B,* section through light organ of the cephalopod, *Rondeletia. C,* section of a luminous area of *Chaetopterus* epidermis (after Dahlgren). (*A* and *C* from Harvey, E. N.: The Nature of Animal Light. J. B. Lippincott Co.)

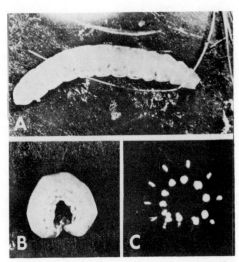

FIGURE 210. Female larva of the beetle *Phengodes*. *A*, dorsal view. *B*, lateral view. *C*, luminous specimen in darkness. (From Harvey, E. N.: Living Light. Princeton University Press.)

or internal layer of "reflecting" cells. The reflecting cells contain minute particles of a purine base, probably urates. This layer is said to serve as a diffusing reflector for the photogenic cells, while simultaneously being a dorsal shield. The photogenic organ is richly provided with tracheal vessels which terminate in numerous tracheal end-cells. Nerves pass into the organ.

Flashing of the firefly is controlled by the nervous system. One remarkable aspect of the activity of these organs, which indicates this, is the synchronous flashing of some tropical fireflies.[3] The fireflies appear normally to flash at random, but may, when large numbers of individuals are assembled together, flash synchronously, or exhibit some coordination of activity in the assemblage as seen in waves of flashing which proceed out rapidly from some individual of the group.

The elaterid "cucujo" beetle, *Pyrophorus*, of the West Indies has a pair of greenish luminescent organs dorsolaterally on the prothorax and an orange-yellow organ on the ventral surface of the first abdominal segment. The South American "railway worm," *Phrixothrix*, possesses a reddish luminescence on the head and greenish luminous spots segmentally arranged along the body. A North American species of the related genus, *Phengodes* (Fig. 210), in its photogenic organs resembles somewhat the South American species, except that it lacks the red head organ. The North American species has been

reported to glow continuously, unlike most luminescent animals.

Several species of myriapods secrete a luminous slime in much the same manner as the luminous earthworms. A luminous pycnogonid has been described.

The rock-boring clam *Pholas* has a number of photogenic glands which secrete into the siphon.[70] Some nudibranchs have distributed over the body luminescent cells which flash when the animal is appropriately stimulated. Of the molluscs, however, the cephalopods as a group show the highest development of this capacity. A large number show luminescence. In many, as for example, *Loligo*, the luminous organs are open structures and contain luminous bacteria. In others, probably the majority, light is produced by cells of the animal itself (Fig. 209). In one squid, *Heteroteuthis*, there is an unpaired luminous organ which opens into the mantle cavity and expels a luminous cloud through the siphon when the animal is disturbed. Some species of squids, such as the firefly squid *Watasenia*, have complex patterns of luminous organs of the intracellular type over the body. A still higher state of differentiation is observed in such deep-sea forms as *Lycoteuthis diadema*. In the latter as many as four different colors are produced by the various luminescent organs.

Only the Ophiuroidea among the echinoderms contain luminous species. A number of these have unicellular photogenic organs scattered over the body, and luminesce in response to any disturbance of the animal.

Light production among the chordates is restricted to the protochordates and fishes. A luminous slime is produced by some species of *Balanoglossus*. Among the tunicates, the luminescence of *Pyrosoma*, a colonial species, is the best known. This organism luminesces on stimulation, and a wave of photogenic activity spreads out over the whole colonial organism. Since activity may be induced in such a colony by using a light flash as a stimulating agent, light perhaps operates as a stimulus for the natural spread of activity in the colony from one luminescing individual to adjacent ones.

The elasmobranch and especially the teleost fishes have numerous luminescent representatives, particularly among those inhabiting the depths of the seas. In some, like *Photoblepharon*, *Anomalops*, *Physiculus*, *Leiognathus*, and *Monocentris*, the light is due to the presence of symbiotic bacteria in special organs found in the cheeks or lower jaw.

In another, *Malacocephalus,* luminescent bacteria are expelled from ventral sacs onto the ventral surface of the body when the fish is excited. Still others, as *Astronesthes* and *Stomias,* possess well-differentiated eyelike organs with lenses and pigmented cups. In some fishes the appearance of light on stimulation is slow. In *Porichthys* a latent period of 8 to 10 seconds is observed upon sympathetic neural stimulation; then the light lasts for about 20 seconds. Injection of adrenaline will activate the photogenic organs in this fish, but with a latent period so long that it is doubtfully a normal means of control of the flashes of these organs.[20]

Physical Characteristics of Animal Light. The intensity of light produced by photogenic organs is relatively low.[69] The light of a firefly, *Photinus,* is the equivalent of 0.0025 to 0.02 candles; that of the "cucujo" beetle, 0.0006 to 0.006 candles. Such values in candles do not give a good measure of the brightness of the actual luminescing surfaces, since these values vary with the areas of the surfaces. Furthermore, since the surfaces are relatively small, the values are likely to suggest smaller values of surface brightness than are actually present. Since organisms vary considerably from one species to another, the order of brightness of luminescing surfaces is expressed in lamberts or millilamberts. Measurements of the surface brightness of a number of luminescing organs have given, in general, values ranging from 0.3 to 45 millilamberts.

The color of the light produced by various photogenic organs of animals varies all the way from blue through red. There is occasionally a difference in the colors of light emitted from different organs of the same animal. It is possible that in some cases these color differences are due to the presence of colored membranes covering the luminous areas, but in most cases they appear definitely due to differences in the chemiluminescent system. There is very little design evident in the distribution among animals of the colors of emitted light. However, blue and yellow luminescence tends to predominate somewhat among the lower phyla. Greenish and reddish tints and white, and instances of the simultaneous emission by an animal of lights of more than one color, tend to predominate among arthropods and members of the echinoderm-chordate line.

Study of a number of species gives reason to believe that the light emitted by any single organ shows a continuous spectrum spreading over a restricted region of the visible range of wavelengths.[4, 25, 67, 68, 70] The spectral range for a few animals is found in the following list.

Species	Wavelengths (mμ)
Chaetopterus insignis	550-440
Photinus pyralis	670-510
Pyrophorus noctilucus	640-468
Photuris pennsylvanica	590-510
Cypridina hilgendorfii	610-415
Phengodes laticollis	650-520
Aequorea forskalea	600-460
Pholas dactylus	650-450
Photoblepharon (bacterial)	640-450

When one recalls that the range of wavelengths visible to the human eye extends approximately from 725 to 400 mμ it is evident from the foregoing table that, in all of the common luminescent species whose spectra have been examined, the light produced is entirely within the visible range. Ultraviolet radiation has never been recorded for any photogenic organ. Furthermore, no significant infrared or heat radiation is produced; hence animal light is said to be a cold light. This fact has led to the popular notion that animal light is nearly 100 per cent efficient. To determine the actual luminous efficiency of any light source, however, it is necessary to take into consideration the spectral energy curve for visibility of the particular organism for which the luminous efficiency is being calculated. If the light were 100 per cent efficient for the human eye, all the radiation would be at the wavelength of maximum sensitivity of the eye. For an eye with the spectral sensitivity characteristics of the human, the light of the firefly *Photuris* is about 92 per cent efficient, that of *Photinus,* about 87 per cent. For the bluish light of *Cypridina* and *Chaetopterus,* the maximum emissions of which lie still further from the region of maximum sensitivity for the human eye, the luminous efficiencies are of the order of 20 per cent or less. However, all of these exhibit strikingly higher luminous efficiencies, of course, than do modern incandescent and fluorescent lamps which approximate 12 and 3 per cent, respectively. We must always bear in mind that the luminous efficiencies would have more real comparative biological significance if they were calculated in terms of the spectral energy curves of sensitivity of the photoreceptive mechanisms of those species reacting in nature to these light sources.

The Mechanism of Light Production. The actual light-yielding reactions of animals have received considerable study. The solution of the problem of their general nature has been somewhat simplified through the discovery that these reactions will proceed *in vitro* in a manner qualitatively indistinguishable from those proceeding *in vivo*.[15-17] It has been known for many years that the luminescent cells or tissues of certain animals, or their products, can be dried with a resultant cessation of light emission. When water is added the materials will again luminesce. Hence the final reactions are obviously not dependent on the vital organization of cells, although the production of the specific materials which participate in these reactions does have such dependence.

In addition to an aqueous medium, photogenic reactions of most animals require also the presence of free oxygen.[33, 34, 37] This appears equally true, whether the reactions occur within the living organism or in extracts of dried preparations of luminous organs. It is true, however, that in some instances the necessary partial pressure of oxygen is extremely small. The only critical experiments which have indicated that luminescence can occur in the complete absence of oxygen have been performed on certain radiolarians, the jellyfish, *Pelagia* and *Aequorea*, and certain ctenophores. One must conclude that in these animals either the reactions are basically different from those in most other animals or a source of oxygen is available in the material of the extracts. The latter alternative appears the more probable.

It was clearly demonstrated many years ago that the photogenic reaction in the beetle, *Pyrophorus*, and in the mollusc, *Pholas*, involved two organic substances. These were separated from one another by utilizing the characteristics (1) that one substance was less heat stable than the other, and (2) that when the luminescent reaction had run its course one of the substances, the relatively heat-unstable one, remained. The one that was relatively heat stable was named luciferin, the other, luciferase. Luciferin solutions could be obtained free from luciferase by extracting the luminous organs in hot water; luciferase could be obtained free from luciferin by extracting the organs in cold water and then permitting the extract to luminesce to exhaustion.

Luciferin and luciferase have also been differentiated in the polychaete worm *Odontosyllis*, in a snail *Latia*, in the ostracods *Cypridina* and *Pyrocypris*, in deep-sea shrimp *Heterocarpus* and *Systellaspis*, in the fish *Parapriacanthus*,[20] and in several species of beetles. However, careful search has failed to reveal their presence as such in most other common luminous groups. It is reasonable to assume that the functional counterparts of these substances are nonetheless present in these latter groups, since there is conspicuous similarity in the general properties of bioluminescence, wherever it occurs.

The photogenic materials show a certain degree of group specificity. Luminescence will result only when the luciferin and luciferase from the same or from two rather closely related species are mixed, as for example with two genera of fireflies or two genera of ostracods. No light usually results on the mixing of these substances obtained from two widely separated genera in the same subphylum, as for example, the ostracod *Cypridina*, and a decapod, shrimp. Similarly no light ordinarily results when the two materials come from different phyla. However, the luciferin and luciferase of the teleost fish *Apogon* and the crustacean *Cypridina* are mutually substitutable.[42]

Relatively little is known as to the chemical nature of the various luciferins and luciferases, but even from that small amount of knowledge it is evident that these differ very widely, at least from one group of animals to another. In three species, the bacterium *Achromobacter*, the ostracod *Cypridina*, and the firefly *Photinus*, in which the chemical basis of light production has been extensively investigated, not only do the luciferins and luciferases differ from one to the other, but the nature of other agents participating in the light reactions also differs. Therefore, we are clearly dealing with a multiplicity of processes in which the only common denominator appears to be the emission of light through a chemiluminescent reaction, involving an enzyme-catalyzed generation of the excited state of an organic emitter, or photogen. It is a reaction which is quite different from ordinary metabolic ones, in that the emission of light quanta requires liberation of energy in units of 40 to 60 Kcal, depending upon the wavelength of the light, instead of in units about one-quarter this size.

All studies indicate luciferases to be nondialyzable and to show a number of properties characteristic of a protein.[19, 36, 37] Such properties include heat lability; precipitation by alcohols, saturated ammonium sulfate, and alkaloidal reagents; destruction by proteinase; and induction of an antiluciferase on injection into a rabbit. Furthermore, careful study of the reaction kinetics of *Cypridina* luciferase shows it to have characteristics of a typical enzyme, although it will not oxidize an unlimited quantity of luciferin. The enzyme gradually becomes denatured. Luciferase of the firefly, *Photinus,* has been purified and crystallized. It is a water-insoluble protein, a euglobin, with a molecular weight of about 100,000, and with an isoelectric point between 6.2 and 6.3. Ultracentrifugation studies of bacterial luciferase suggest a molecular weight of about 85,000. Luciferins[9, 43, 44, 51, 53, 54, 72-77, 79, 80] appear definitely to be nonprotein. They are dialyzable, indicating relatively small molecular weight. They are all fluorescent. Only for bacteria does the nature of the luciferin appear well established and to be riboflavin phosphate (FMN). For the firefly *Photinus,* the luciferin, though not identical with that of the bacteria, appears to resemble it to a good degree in molecular size and basic structure. Evidence suggests *Cypridina* luciferin, on the other hand, to be a cyclic chromopolypeptide.

Just as the luciferins and luciferases differ from group to group, so do other substances found essential for the luminescent reaction.[28, 45, 46, 48-50, 52, 55] For the bacterium *Achromobacter,* in addition to the "luciferin," water, O_2, and luciferase, a long-chain (6 to 14 carbons) aldehyde, e.g., dodecyl, is necessary:

$$FMNH_2 + RCHO + O_2 + enzyme \longrightarrow light + products$$

For this reaction, TPNH or DPNH (reduced triphosphopyridine or diphosphopyridine nucleotide) appears normally to reduce FMN to produce active "luciferin."

For animals, the two most studied luminescent systems, those of *Cypridina* and the firefly *Photinus,* show quite substantial differences from one another, and from the bacterial one just described. The luminescent reaction system of *Cypridina* appears outwardly the simpler of the two, the simplicity probably correlated with the normal occurrence of the luminescent reaction outside the body in the sea water. The light gland possesses two types of cells, one discharging the luciferin, and the other, the luciferase. The dissolved products of these two kinds of granules, with free O_2, react to give light:

$$LH + enzyme + O_2 \longrightarrow light + enzyme + inactive products$$

Cypridina luciferin is readily oxidized by numerous oxidizing agents, but yields light only when oxidized in the presence of luciferase (see exception below).

Just as no oxidizing agent has been discovered which will, in the presence of *Cypridina* luciferin, produce light, so also has no substrate except the luciferin yet been found which, on oxidation in the presence of luciferase, yields light.

The kinetics of the *Cypridina* luciferin-luciferase reaction have been carefully investigated. The reaction appears monomolecular. There is also a rather high temperature coefficient (Q_{10}) having an average value, in the functional range, of 2.74, lower at the lower end of the temperature range and higher at the higher end. The velocity constant of the reaction is proportional to the luciferase concentration. The total light emitted is proportional to the quantity of luciferin, other conditions being equal. However, the total amount of light is also influenced by the amount and type of salt content of the extract, the pH, and the temperature of the medium. The efficiency of light production in terms of units of luciferin decreases as the temperature rises from 18 to 28°C.

When luciferin and luciferase are first mixed in an oxygenated medium, the time required for the intensity of the flash to reach a maximum is longer (0.03 sec) than when oxygen is added to an oxygen-free and hence nonluminescing mixed solution of the two photogenic substances (0.008 sec). This suggests that the reaction between luciferin and luciferase is slow, compared with the rate of the reaction which involves the oxygen.

Cypridina luciferin is apparently oxidized in two ways: (1) through action of luciferase, with light emission, and (2) through other than luciferase activity, without light production. The latter reaction, but not the former, seems to be reversible in the presence of reducing agents. This freshly reduced luciferin is able to emit light when oxidized in the presence of luciferase. Luciferin oxidized in the presence of luciferase, on the other hand, is not capable of being reduced again by reducing agents; hence the oxidation in the presence of luciferase must be substantially different from oxidation by other oxidizing agents.

Detailed studies of the spectrographic changes in *Cypridina* luciferin during its oxidation both in the absence and in the presence of luciferase have indicated that the steps are the same in the two instances. Reduced *Cypridina* luciferin, with a maximum absorption at 435 mμ, becomes oxidized to a form with a maximum absorption at 465 mμ, and then this latter substance is destroyed. The total amount of light produced is proportional to the initial amount of absorption at 435 mμ. The rate of these oxidative changes is about 100 times as rapid in the presence of luciferase as in its absence.

Such observations as the foregoing, and further detailed studies of the kinetics of the bioluminescent reaction, together with an observation that luciferin in 95 per cent ethyl

emits a quantum of light upon decomposition. Under normal circumstances the intermediate gives rise to an inactive complex immobilizing the enzyme. This is presumed true since repeated additions of fresh enzyme to the system are accompanied by brief light flashes. And since additions of inorganic pyrophosphate similarly result in light flashes, it is presumed that the latter operates to reconvert some of the inactive complex into a photogenically active intermediate.

The firefly *Photinus* reaction scheme may be depicted as follows:

$$\text{L*. Enz. Mg. AMP} \longrightarrow \text{light} + O_2$$
$$\uparrow$$
$$LH_2 + \text{Enz} + \text{Mg} + \text{ATP} \rightleftharpoons LH_2.\ \text{Enz. Mg. AMP} + \text{pyrophosphate}$$
$$\text{(active intermediate)}$$
$$\text{pyrophosphate} \longrightarrow \text{↓↑} \text{Mg}^{++} + \text{pyrophosphatase}$$
$$LH_2.\ \text{Enz. Mg. AMP. Mg. Pyrophosphatase}$$
$$\text{(inactive complex)}$$

alcohol at 70°C will luminesce, have given strong support to the view that the actual light-emitting molecule is the luciferin.[29]

All our present knowledge of the properties of the bioluminescent process in *Cypridina* appears capable of fitting into the following scheme of reactions:

$$LH_2 + \text{enzyme} + \tfrac{1}{2}O_2 \longrightarrow L* + L'\text{ase} + H_2O$$
$$L* + \text{enzyme} \longrightarrow L + \text{light}$$

In the firefly *Photinus,* the system involving intracellular light production appears to be more complicated. There is no comparable, readily oxidizable luciferin extractable. Rather, there is a precursor, or a proluciferin, which, before light production, must undergo certain dark-reactions. Here, in addition to O_2, ATP and Mg^{++} are necessary.[56] The overall reaction may be written:

$$LH_2 + Mg^{++} + \text{ATP} + \text{enzyme} \longrightarrow \text{light} + \text{enzyme} + \text{inactive products}$$

In experiments using purified firefly luciferase the initial light intensity varies with both the ATP and the Mg^{++} concentrations. Since the optimum ratio for these two is 1, a role of a Mg^{++}-ATP complex is indicated. The reaction appears highly specific for ATP since other phosphorylated compounds are ineffective. When ATP and Mg^{++} are present in excess the light intensity varies with the luciferin concentration and, other factors equal, the initial light intensity is a direct function of the luciferase concentration up to a certain limiting value.

There is evidence to suggest that an active intermediate, luciferin-Mg^{++}-luciferase-ATP, is formed and that this complex in the presence of O_2 generates an excited state and

Although many other luminescent species have been investigated briefly for a possible role of ATP in the luminescent reaction, only for species of *Renilla* (Anthozoa),[8] and for certain other Coleoptera, have positive results been obtained.

Variations in electrical potential in light organs have been described as accompanying light production in some fireflies.[30-32] In adults, which show a flickering light, a rhythmical variation in electrical potential was reported, and in larvae, lacking a flickering character of light, a single, long-duration, potential variation. Tracheal end-cells occur in adults and are absent in larvae. Confirmation of these suggestive observations is desirable.

The Control of Bioluminescence. Among animals the production of light is typically not a continuous process. Light is usually produced intermittently in response to external stimuli.[6, 66] This fact is of such generality that, when an animal appears to have continuous luminescence, it can usually be assumed that this is the result of the presence of symbiotic, pathogenic, or transient luminescent bacteria within or upon that animal.

The means of control of light production in animals are fundamentally of three types. The first two are observed in extracellular luminescence. In those instances where luminescent materials are expelled from a photogenic sac into the surrounding sea water on stimulation (e.g., the cephalopod *Hetero-*

teuthis, the ostracod *Cypridina,* and the shrimp *Acanthephyra)* the control is indirect and operates by means of typical neuromuscular mechanisms. On the other hand, a slightly different situation obtains in those organisms which can secrete a luminescent slime over the surface of the body. Such animals include the luminescent earthworms, *Chaetopterus,* myriapods, some coelenterates, and the clam *Pholas.* In these there is a control of a secretory process by direct nervous or, possibly also in some cases, endocrine excitation. The third general type of control applies to those numerous animals where the luminescence is an intracellular phenomenon. This is obviously the situation in such well-known animals as *Noctiluca,* jellyfishes, ctenophores, insects, and certain fishes. Here we have to do with some mechanism whereby excitation of the luminescent cell results in the contained photogenic substances reacting to produce light. This may come about (a) through rapidly making small quantities of one of the essential organic photogenic agents available for reaction within the cell, (b) through temporarily rendering the intracellular medium favorable for the luminescent reactions such as through control of oxygen, water, or hydrogen ions, or (c) through altering the direction of paths of chemical change to favor chemiluminescent ones.

We can at present do little more than speculate on the means by which the animal can, in response to stimuli, give very brief and intense flashes of light which vie in rate of development and decline of intensity with the best of incandescent lamps. In multicellular organisms the flashing is typically associated reflexly with tactile or photic receptors. The reflex pathways may involve the nervous system alone, or both nerves and endocrines. In the coelenterate *Renilla,* the spread of luminescence over a stimulated animal proceeds in all directions at a rate characteristic of nerve-net transmission. Excessive stimulation can give rise to a state of excitation causing luminescence to persist for some time. In the ctenophore *Mnemiopsis,* the tactile receptors involved in reflex light production lie along the conducting pathways underlying the rows of ciliated combs. In the response the neuro-effector mechanism displays the phenomenon of facilitation quite like that seen in neuromuscular junctions.

Most studies of the control of luminescence have concerned fireflies. Among other stimuli, visual cues normally excite a responsive flash in these insects. The photogenic organ is in-

nervated, but it is not definitely established whether the nerve supply goes to the photogenic cells proper or to the tracheal endings within the light organ. In the latter case, the nerves might be supposed to innervate some mechanism located in the tracheal end-cell.

Two general types of theories for the control of flashing in the firefly have been advanced. The first type presumes that the flash depends on a rapid admission of oxygen to anoxic photogenic cells. This is considered to be brought about either by direct nervous control of admission of O_2 in the tracheal end-cells or by means of a stimulated increase in metabolites in the photogenic tissue and a consequent osmotic withdrawal of water from the terminal portion of the tracheal tubules with the result that oxygen would be brought directly to the glandular elements. The presence of oxygen would then permit an oxidation of the metabolites, again reducing the osmotic pressure of the cell contents, and permit restoration of water to the tubules and re-exclusion of the oxygen. In support of an oxygen-control mechanism is the fact that microscopic observations of a luminescing gland show the brightest light to come from the immediate vicinity of the ends of the tracheal tubules. An end-cell valve mechanism is not essential, however, since some insects, especially larvae of fireflies, which show at least some degree of intermittency in light production, even though not true flashing, do not have differentiated tracheal end-cells. And, of course, rapid flashing can occur in many organisms having no tracheal system.

The second general type of postulated mechanism is a direct nervous excitation of the light-producing cells through photogenic nerves (Fig. 211). A means of nervous regulation of rapid flashing in response to nerve excitation in the firefly is suggested in the role of pyrophosphate in rapidly converting inactive complex into active intermediate. The pyrophosphate arising from nerve excitation:

$$(ACH \rightarrow Choline + Ac \xrightarrow[CoA]{ATP}$$

$Ac \cdot CoA + Ad + POP)$ has been postulated to play this role naturally. Favoring such a hypothesis over an O_2-control one is the observation that "pseudoflash" in fireflies (effected by O_2-deprivation followed by rapid O_2 readmission), or a comparably induced *in vitro* flash, has time constants so much longer than the normal fly flash as to make unlikely a normal regulatory role by O_2 control.[35] Furthermore, a comparable control to

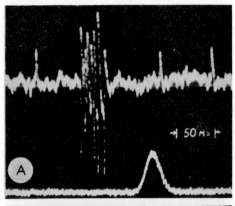

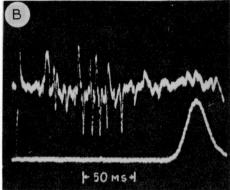

FIGURE 211. Spontaneous and electrically driven flashes in the light organ of *Photuris pennsylvanica* together with associated neural action potentials recorded from the ventral surface of the light organ. *A*, spontaneous. *B*, electrical stimulus to brain (stimulus artifact at extreme left) followed by neural volley and flash. (Courtesy of Case, J., and Buck, J. B.: Unpublished data.)

that of this postulated direct nervous one has potentially a much wider application including control in animals without tracheal systems.

In the fishes *Poricthys* and *Echiostoma,* there is evidence that the normal reflex pathways of control of flashing in the system of photogenic organs include sympathetic nervous innervation. A slow response is also seen in response to adrenin injection.

There have been a number of observations indicating that bright light inhibits the production of light by animals, although in most cases we know little or nothing of the mechanism of this inhibition, whether directly upon the photogenic reaction system or on mechanisms concerned normally with reflex excitation. It may result, as some evidence indicates for ctenophores, from a direct destruction of photogenic material within the light-producing cells. In these animals, extracts

made from specimens exposed to sunlight show practically no capacity to luminesce. Furthermore, after exposure to bright light animals such as ctenophores and the cnidarian *Renilla* have to be kept in darkness often for several minutes before they will again luminesce.

There have been a number of reported observations of a persistent daily rhythmicity in the capacity of certain species of animals to luminesce. Such a rhythm has been described as persisting for several days in constant darkness in the firefly *Photinus,*[1] in the balanoglossid *Ptychodera,*[10] in the dinoflagellate *Gonyaulax,*[39, 78] and probably also in the jellyfish, *Pelagia.*[40, 57]

The luminescent responses of ctenophores and hydromedusae have been shown to be readily fatigable and to exhibit recovery in much the same fashion as other typical sensory-neuroeffector mechanisms.

Functional Significance of Bioluminescence. The significance of light production in the lives of many of the organisms possessing this capacity is far from obvious. That some survival value is commonly associated with this function is, however, likely, inasmuch as most higher organisms which luminesce have evolved specialized light cells or organs for the purpose. Moreover, the flashing itself may become incorporated into the general response mechanism of the organism.

Three general types of functions have been ascribed to animal luminescence. One of these is the luring of food, but as yet there has been no conclusive evidence for this. A second function ascribed to the organs is that they serve as protective devices. They may operate through warning or frightening predators; by concealing the light-emitting animals, as in the ejection of a luminous cloud by the deep-sea shrimp *Acanthephyra* and the squid *Heteroteuthis*; or through distracting predators. The pattern of nervous control of luminescence in such an annelid as the scale worm *Acholoe* appears to suggest this last role. When the worm is transected, as by an attacking predator, the posterior portion alone luminesces brightly, while luminescence is inhibited in the anterior portion. This behavior conceivably results in a greater chance for the more viable anterior part to escape. Autotomized scales of this worm also flash rhythmically. Suggestive also of such an emergency protective role of luminescence is the fact that adrenin supplements the nervous system in inducing bright and extensive luminescence in certain fishes. An interesting variation of the protective function of bio-luminescence in organisms has been advanced, namely, that stimulation to luminescence of one individual in a group might serve as a warning to its fellows and permit their escape.

The function of luminescent organs having best observational and experimental support up to the present is that of serving as signals for bringing together the two sexes in mating. The fireworm of Bermuda, *Odontosyllis*, provides a well-established illustration of this role.[18] The females, which exhibit a marked lunar periodicity, appear during mating periods at the surface of the sea where they swim in small circles, luminescing brilliantly. Males from deeper water swim directly toward the luminescing females and join in the mating "dance"; both sexes then liberate their gametes into the water together. If, perchance, no male joins a luminescing female in a short time, her light gradually fades, but after a brief period of rest her photogenic organs again become active and the luminescent "dance" is repeated. Males moving directly toward a luminescing female but failing to reach her before the end of a luminous period have been observed to cease their directed movement and wander aimlessly until the female again luminesces.

Other well-established cases of the use of light production as mating signals have been described for various species of fireflies.[2] In many species the females, which may even be wingless, remain in the grass while the males fly about. The males fly toward females which signal in response to their flashes. The various species differ in characteristics of their flashing, such as in the frequency, total number of flashes, color, intensity, and duration of each flash. The female responds in a characteristic manner to flashing of the male of the same species. The female of *Photinus,* for example, always flashes about 2 seconds after the flash of the male. The male continues to respond to the female until the two sexes have met. The attracting light response of the female can be imitated by use of a flashlight which is operated to flash with the temporal characteristics of a typical responding female for a species. Numerous other suggestive examples of a role of luminescence in the mating reactions of animals have been described, but most of them require more convincing descriptions, or experimental study, before they can be accepted as such.

However, inasmuch as it is difficult to imagine any functional significance of bio-luminescence in bacteria or fungi, we prob-ably can assume that bioluminescence has arisen as a fortuitous correlate of the cellular oxidative mechanism, persisting in many animals, especially lower ones, despite no obvious survival value.[26] Secondarily, the phenomenon became utilized in special manners in higher animals, as potentially useful roles of bio-luminescence came into existence.

REFERENCES

1. Buck, J. B., Physiol. Zool. *10:* 45-58, 1937. Diurnal rhythm in Photinus luminescent mechanism.
2. Buck, J. B., Physiol. Zool. *10:* 412-419, 1937. Luminescence in firefly mating.
3. Buck, J. B., Quart. Rev. Biol. *13:* 301-314, 1938. Synchronous flashing of fireflies.
4. Buck, J. B., Proc. Rochester Acad. Sci. *8:* 14-21, 1941. Spectrometric studies of firefly lights.
5. Buck, J. B., Ann. New York Acad. Sci. *49:* 397-482, 1947. Luminescence in fireflies.
6. Buck, J. B., *in* The Luminescence of Biological Systems, edited by F. H. Johnson. Washington, A.A.A.S., 1955, pp. 323-332. Control of bio-luminescence.
7. Chang, J. J., J. Cell. Comp. Physiol. *44:* 365-394, 1954. Luminescence of Mnemiopsis.
8. Cormier, M. J., J. Am. Chem. Soc. *81:* 2592, 1959. ATP for *Renilla reniformis* luminescence.
9. Cormier, M. J., and Strehler, B. L., J. Am. Chem. Soc. *75:* 4864-4865, 1953. Bacterial luciferin.
10. Crozier, W. J., Anat. Rec. *20:* 186-187, 1920. Diurnal rhythm in Ptychodera luminescence.
11. Davenport, D., and Nicol, J. A. C., Proc. Roy. Soc. London, B, *144:* 399-411, 1955. Hydro-medusoid luminescence.
12. Davenport, D., and Nicol, J. A. C., Proc. Roy. Soc. London, B, *144:* 480-496, 1955. Luminescence of sea pens.
13. Davenport, D., Wootton, O. M., and Cushing, J. E., Biol. Bull. *102:* 100-110, 1952. Luminous millepede.
14. Dennell, R., J. Linn. Soc. *42:* 393-406, 1955. Luminescence in Crustacea, Decapoda.
15. Dubois, R., C. R. Soc. Biol. *37:* 559-562, 1885. Luciferin and luciferase in Pyrophorus.
16. Dubois, R., C. R. Soc. Biol. *39:* 564-566, 1887. Luciferin and luciferase in Pholas.
17. Dubois, R., C. R. Soc. Biol. *48:* 995-996, 1896. Luminous glands of Pholas.
18. Galloway, T. W., and Welch, P. S., Tr. Am. Micr. Soc. *30:* 13-39, 1911. Luminescence of Odontosyllis during mating.
19. Green, A. A., and McElroy, W. D., Biochem. Biophys. Acta *20:* 170-176, 1956. Crystal luciferase.
20. Greene, C. W., and Greene, H. H., Am. J. Physiol. *70:* 500-507, 1924. Luminescence in Porichthys; action of adrenaline.
21. Haneda, Y., *in* The Luminescence of Biological Systems, edited by F. H. Johnson. Washington, A.A.A.S., 1955, pp. 335-385. Luminous organisms of Far East.
22. Haneda, Y., and Johnson, F. H., Proc. Nat.

Acad. Sci. *44*: 127-129, 1958. Luciferin-luciferase of a fish.

23. HARVEY, E. N., The Nature of Animal Light. Philadelphia, J. B. Lippincott, 1920, 182 pp.

24. HARVEY, E. N., Living Light. Princeton University Press, 1940, 328 pp.

25. HARVEY, E. N., Bioluminescence. New York, Academic Press, 1952, 649 pp.

26. HARVEY, E. N., Fed. Proc. *12*: 597-606, 1953. Evolution of bioluminescence.

27. HARVEY, E. N., and CHANG, J. J., Science *119*: 581, 1954. Luminous response of Mnemiopsis.

28. HARVEY, E. N., and HANEDA, Y., Arch. Biochem. Biophys. *35*: 470-471, 1952. ATP in luminescence.

29. HARVEY, E. N., and TSUJI, F. T., J. Cell. Comp. Physiol. *44*: 63-76, 1954. Luciferin luminescence with luciferase.

30. HASAMA, B. Cytologia *12*: 366-377, 1942. Electrical potential variations in photogenic organs.

31. HASAMA, B., Cytologia *12*: 378-388, 1942. Electrical potential variations in photogenic organs.

32. HASAMA, B., Cytologia *13*: 155-161, 1944. Electrical potential variations in photogenic organs.

33. HASTINGS, J. W., J. Cell. Comp. Physiol. *39*: 1-30, 1952. O_2 and bacterial and fungal luminescence.

34. HASTINGS, J. W., J. Cell. Comp. Physiol. *40*: 1-9, 1952. O_2 and Cypridina luminescence.

35. HASTINGS, J. W., and BUCK, J. B., Biol. Bull. *111*: 101-113, 1956. Control of firefly flash.

36. HASTINGS, J. W., and McELROY, W. D., The Luminescence of Biological Systems, edited by F. H. Johnson. Washington, A.A.A.S., 1955, pp. 257-264. Bacterial luciferase.

37. HASTINGS, J. W., McELROY, W. D., and COULOMBRE, J., J. Cell. Comp. Physiol. *42*: 137-150, 1953. O_2 and firefly luminescence.

38. HASTINGS, J. W., and SWEENEY, B. M., J. Cell. Comp. Physiol. *49*: 209-226, 1957. Diurnal rhythm in light reactants.

39. HASTINGS, J. W., and SWEENEY, B. M., Biol. Bull. *115*: 440-458, 1958. Diurnal rhythm of Gonyaulax light.

40. HEYMANS, C., and MOORE, A. R., J. Gen. Physiol. *6*: 273-280, 1923. Diurnal rhythm in Pelagia luminescence.

41. HEYMANS, C., and MOORE, A. R., J. Gen. Physiol. *7*: 345-348, 1925. Inhibition of ctenophore luminescence by light.

42. JOHNSON, F. H., HANEDA, Y., and SIE, Ed. H.-C., Science *132*: 422-423, 1960. Cypridina and Apogon, Luciferin-Luciferase mutually interchangeable.

43. MASON, H. S., J. Am. Chem. Soc. *74*: 4727, 1952. Purification of Cypridina luciferin.

44. MASON, H. S., and DAVIS, E. F., J. Biol. Chem. *197*: 41-45, 1952. Purification of Cypridina luciferin.

45. McELROY, W. D., J. Biol. Chem. *191*: 547-557, 1951. Firefly luminous system.

46. McELROY, W. D., Harvey Lect. 240-266, 1957. Chemistry and physiology of bioluminescence.

47. McELROY, W. D., and CHASE, A. M., J. Cell. Comp. Physiol. *38*: 401-408, 1951. Purification of Cypridina luciferase.

48. McELROY, W. D., and COULOMBRE, J., Fed. Proc. *10*: 219, 1951. ATP and light production.

49. McELROY, W. D., and COULOMBRE, J., J. Cell. Comp. Physiol. *39*: 475-485, 1952. ATP and light production.

50. McELROY, W. D., COULOMBRE, J., and HAYS, R., Arch. Biochem. Biophys. *32*: 207-215, 1951. Properties of firefly pyrophosphatase.

51. McELROY, W. D., and GREEN, A. A., Arch. Biochem. Biophys. *56*: 240-255, 1955. Bacterial luminous system.

52. McELROY, W. D., and HASTINGS, J. W., The Luminescence of Biological Systems, edited by F. H. Johnson. Washington, A.A.A.S., 1955, pp. 161-198. Firefly luminous system.

53. McELROY, W. D., HASTINGS, J. W., SONNENFELD, V., and COULOMBRE, J., Science *118*: 385-386, 1953. Bacterial luminous system.

54. McELROY, W. D., HASTINGS, J. W., SONNENFELD, V., and COULOMBRE, J., J. Bacteriol. *67*: 402-408, 1954. Bacterial luminous system.

55. McELROY, W. D., and HARVEY, E. N., J. Cell. Comp. Physiol. *37*: 1-7, 1951. Firefly luminous system.

56. McELROY, W. D., and STREHLER, B. L., Arch. Biochem. Biophys. *22*: 420-433, 1949. ATP and Photinus luminescence.

57. MOORE, A. R., J. Gen. Physiol. *9*: 375-381, 1926. Diurnal rhythm in Pelagia luminescence.

58. NICOL, J. A. C., J. Mar. Biol. Assn. U. K. *30*: 417-431, 1952. Chaetopterus light glands.

59. NICOL, J. A. C., J. Mar. Biol. Assn. U. K. *30*: 433-452, 1952. Nerve control of light production in Chaetopterus.

60. NICOL, J. A. C., J. Mar. Biol. Assn. U. K. *31*: 113-144, 1952. Nerve control of light production in Chaetopterus.

61. NICOL, J. A. C., J. Mar. Biol. Assn. U. K. *32*: 65-84, 1953. Luminescence in polynoid worms.

62. NICOL, J. A. C., J. Mar. Biol. Assn. U. K. *33*: 173-175, 1954. Chaetopterus luminescence.

63. NICOL, J. A. C., J. Mar. Biol. Assn. U. K. *33*: 225-255, 1954. Light control in polynoid worms.

64. NICOL, J. A. C., J. Exp. Biol. *32*: 299-320, 1955. Luminescence in Renilla.

65. NICOL, J. A. C., J. Exp. Biol. *32*: 619-635, 1955. Nerve control of luminescence in Renilla.

66. NICOL, J. A. C., The Luminescence of Biological Systems, edited by F. H. Johnson. Washington, A.A.A.S., 1955, pp. 299-319. Control of luminescence.

67. NICOL, J. A. C., J. Mar. Biol. Assn. U. K. *36*: 529-538, 1957. Character of polynoid light.

68. NICOL, J. A. C., J. Mar. Biol. Assn. U. K. *36*: 629-642, 1957. Character of Chaetopterus light.

69. NICOL, J. A. C., J. Mar. Biol. Assn. U. K. *37*: 33-41, 1958. Polynoid light intensity.

70. NICOL, J. A. C., J. Mar. Biol. Assn. U. K. *37*: 43-47, 1958. Character of Pholas light.

71. PARKER, G. H., J. Exp. Zool. *31*: 475-513, 1920. Spread of luminescence in Renilla.

72. STREHLER, B. L., Arch. Biochem. Biophys. *32*: 397-406, 1951. Firefly luminous system.

73. STREHLER, B. L., J. Am. Chem. Soc. *75*: 1264, 1953. Bacterial luminous system.

74. STREHLER, B. L., The Luminescence of Biological Systems, edited by F. H. Johnson. Washington, A.A.A.S., 1955, pp. 209-240. Bacterial luminous system.

75. STREHLER, B. L., and CORMIER, M. J., Arch. Biochem. Biophys. *47*: 16-33, 1953. Bacterial luminous system.

76. STREHLER, B. L., HARVEY, E. N., CHANG, J. J., and CORMIER, M. J., Proc. Nat. Acad. Sci. *40*: 10-12, 1954. Bacterial luminous system.

77. STREHLER, B. L., and McELROY, W. D., J. Cell. Comp. Physiol. *34*: 457-466, 1949. Firefly luciferin.

78. SWEENEY, B. M., and HASTINGS, J. W., J. Cell. Comp. Physiol. *49*: 115-128, 1957. Diurnal rhythm in Gonyaulax light.

79. TOTTER, J. R., and CORMIER, M. J., J. Biol. Chem. *216*: 801-811, 1955. Bacterial luciferin.

80. TSUJI, F. I., CHASE, A. M., and HARVEY, E. N., The Luminescence of Biological Systems, edited by F. H. Johnson. Washington, A.A.A.S., 1955, pp. 127-156. Cypridina luciferin.

Chapter 19

CHROMATOPHORES AND COLOR CHANGE

INTRODUCTION

The ability to change color through movements of pigments within certain integumentary cells or organs is widely distributed among animals. It has been observed for numerous cyclostomes, fishes, amphibians, and reptiles among the vertebrates; among the invertebrates it is exhibited by many higher crustaceans, cephalopods, and leeches and a few insects, echinoderms, and polychaetes. A comparable activity has been described for a euglenoid protozoan. The spectacular color changes of the chameleon between black and green and the rapid color changes of the octopus were described as early as the fourth century B.C. by Aristotle, and those of fishes were described somewhat later by Pliny, who observed the changes of the dying mullet. The first changes recorded in amphibians were in the frog, and those in crustaceans were in the prawn, *Hippolyte*.[165] The relatively rapid color changes in the cephalopods were early demonstrated to be due principally to the activity of special organs in the skin, to which the name cromofora was given. Later, the movements of pigments in special integumentary organs were shown clearly to account for color changes in the chameleon,[187] the frog,[8] and crustaceans.[239] These special organs have come to be known as chromatophores.

Brücke[50] made studies on the physiology of color change in the chameleon; Pouchet,[227, 228] in crustaceans and fishes; and Gamble and Keeble,[109, 145, 146, 147, 148] in crustaceans. All these early investigators concluded that the chromatophore systems were under the control of the nervous system or the chromatophores responded directly to the action of environmental stimuli. The possibility of a role of hormones in color changes

was suggested first by the discovery that frogs are blanched by injection of adrenaline.[173] The early work on chromatophores has been thoroughly reviewed in the extensive accounts of van Rynberk[236] and Fuchs.[106] Later general summaries include those of Hogben,[127] Parker,[198, 214] and of Fingerman,[88] and ones covering separate groups, the vertebrates,[223, 288] insects,[240] and crustaceans.[32, 55, 158] The pigments of animals have been described in other summaries.[98, 115]

CHROMATOPHORES: STRUCTURE AND METHODS OF ACTION

Chromatophores are special pigment cells located in the skin or often even in certain deeper tissues of the body of an animal. Chromatophores possess the ability to bring about redistributions of their pigment in such a manner as to influence the general coloration of the animal. A pigment that is concentrated into a small ball (punctate) contributes little or nothing to the gross coloration of the individual, whereas its dispersion to cover a larger surface (reticulate) results in its imparting its tint to the animal. The foregoing mechanism of action (concentration and dispersion of pigment) is referred to as physiological color change. The chromatophores may also influence the coloration of an animal through their accumulation or production of pigment or their loss or destruction of it. This latter mode of action is termed morphological color change.

Physiological Color Changes. Chromatophores are of two major types. One type is seen among the cephalopod molluscs. It is a complex organ with a pigment-containing cell with numerous radially arranged smooth muscle fibers associated with it (Fig. 212). The second, more common, type is found in most color-changing species. It comprises a single cell or small syncytium, usually of highly branched outline, and within which pigment distribution is altered by streaming movements.

The chromatophore of cephalopods comprises a central uninucleate cell filled with pigment and possessing a highly elastic cell membrane.[17] Radiating out from the central cell in the plane of the skin are from 6 to 20 or more uninucleate smooth-muscle fibers. All the fibers of a chromatophore usually contract simultaneously, stretching out the small, spherical, central, pigmented cell into a disc having a diameter fifteen to twenty times that of the original sphere. The spherical form is restored by the elasticity of the membrane of the central pigmented cell after relaxation of the radiating fibers. A single nerve fiber is said to supply each muscle fiber;[126] its terminal arborizations disperse broadly over the surface of the muscle. No motor end-plates are present, and curare is reported to be ineffective in blocking nervous activation. The muscle fibers show a rapidity of contraction to electrical stimuli approaching that of striated muscle fibers (Chapter 14).

Little or nothing is known about the chemical nature of the pigments of cephalopods. Octopus possesses two kinds of chromatophores, one containing a reddish-brown pigment, and the other a yellow. The squid, *Loligo,* has three types: brown, red, and yellow. Underlying these chromatophores is an immobile layer of light-reflecting pigment. By means of their special type of chromatophores the cephalopods are able to show more rapid color changes than other animals.

In animals other than the cephalopods, the chromatophores are single cells (e.g., in most vertebrates) or closely associated groups of cells or syncytia (e.g., in crustaceans). These were once thought to be ameboid cells, contraction of whose processes resulted in a concentration of the pigment mass into a small sphere, and whose extensive pseudopodial production resulted in a broad dispersal of the pigments. Now it is generally believed that the chromatophore has a permanent arborized form, and that the pigment granules either become concentrated into the chromatophore center to form a punctate mass or become dispersed to varying degrees through the intricately branching structure[179] to impart color to the macroscopic appearance of the animal. Matthews and others have reported observing branches of chromatophores whose pigment was in the punctate condition. Also supporting this view has been the demonstration of the striking similarity, even to the minute terminals of a chromatophore, after pigment dispersal on two different occasions[25, 221, 265] (Fig. 213). An electron micrographic study of *Lebistes* chromatophore suggests the pigment to occupy a sac in the cell cytosome. The chromatophore membrane appears to possess contractile fibrils.[76]

In typical details of form, pigments, and reactions, however, each animal, species, or group has its own chromatophoral peculiarities. Chromatophores are known as monochromatic, dichromatic, or polychromatic, depending on whether they possess one, two, or more kinds of pigment. The crustaceans commonly possess dichromatic or polychromatic chromatophores, with each pigment typically dispersing out into its own proc-

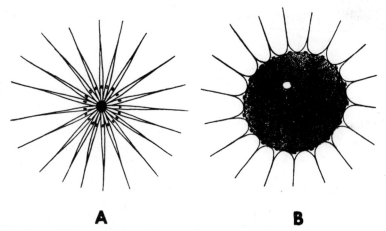

A **B**

FIGURE 212. The cephalopod chromatophore. *A,* pigment concentrated; *B,* pigment dispersed. (From Bozler, E.: Ztschr. vergl. Physiol., vol. 8.)

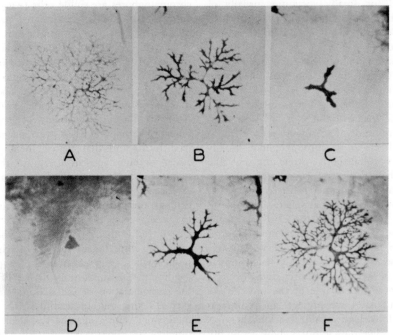

FIGURE 213.   A series of photographs of a single white chromatophore of *Palaemonetes* as its pigment fully concentrates in response to a black background, and then redisperses on return of the animal to a white background. (From Brown, F. A., Jr.: J. Exp. Zool., vol. 71.)

esses and, when concentrated into the chromatophore center, possessing its own distinct individuality. In fact, in the responses of the crustacean chromatophore system to colored backgrounds the several pigments within a

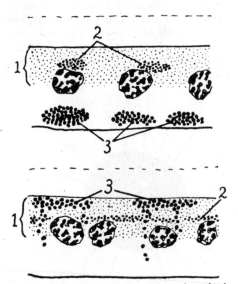

FIGURE 214.   Diagrammatic sections through the epidermis of light-(*upper*) and dark-(*lower*) adapted *Carausius*. The coarsest stippling (3) indicates brown-black pigment; the intermediate stippling (2), red pigment; and the finest (1), yellow-green pigment. (From Giersberg, H.: Ztschr. vergl. Physiol., vol. 7.)

single chromatophore may show a considerable degree of independence of one another.[26, 145, 162]

In insects the epidermal cells themselves serve as functional chromatophores. During darkening of the skin the dark brown-black pigment within these cells migrates from small concentrated masses below an evenly dispersed yellow and green pigmented layer to a more superficial position, where it disperses (Fig. 214). The red pigment during skin darkening disperses from small spherical masses to form a continuous sheet of pigment. Thus the forces which operate in pigment concentration and dispersal in chromatophores in general are apparently of such a nature as can operate within the limits of conventionally shaped cells.

Migration of a red hematochrome pigment in *Euglena*, from a deeper position in the body internal to the chloroplasts to a dispersed, superficial position, results in a green to red color change in response to elevated light intensity.[141, 142]

In and associated with the chromatophores of crustaceans are a number of different colors of pigments. The kinds which are present vary with the species and even occasionally among individuals within the same species having different histories. Yellow and red pigments appear to be of quite general occurrence within the group. These are carotenoids of various kinds, some often conjugated with proteins.[75, 169] Also of quite general presence is a reflecting white pigment. The majority of the macruran decapods possess a transparent blue pigment, which is a carotenoid conjugated with a protein.[285] The application of heat or alcohol to integument containing the blue pigment results in its rapid transformation from a water-soluble blue to a fat-soluble red pigment. In some crustaceans a black or brownish-black pigment is present. Such black pigment, found in the natantian *Crago* and in isopods such as *Ligia,* appears to be an ommochrome; in some of the true crabs the pigment may be melanin.[118]

The chromatophores of the vertebrates resemble those of crustaceans. Unlike in the latter, however, they usually comprise single cells and are for the most part monochromatic. The predominant pigment is melanin, and it is the activity of the melanophores which is principally responsible for the conspicuous color changes in this group. In many vertebrates, reflecting white chromatophores, termed iridoleucophores or antaugophores, are also found.[104] Chromatophores known as lipophores, containing fat-soluble red pigment (erythrophores) or yellow pigment (xanthophores), are often present. These pigments are carotenoids.[97] In addition to these more conventional types of pigment cells, there are sometimes glistening bluish-green bodies, the iridophores, whose color and color changes are structural ones dependent on the form, arrangement, and movements of fine, plate-like crystals.

Supplementing the contribution of the chromatophores themselves to the coloration of the vertebrates there is often, as in the cephalopods, an immobile layer of whitish or yellowish pigment. This pigment is responsible entirely for the tint of the animal when the active chromatophores contribute little or nothing, or it cooperates with the chromatophores in producing the normal coloration. In species such as the lizard, *Anolis,* the central bodies of the melanophores lie beneath such a passive layer of pigment. As the animal darkens in response to appropriate stimulation the melanin streams within melanophore processes to a position superficial to the inert light-colored layer, thereby concealing the latter[110, 152] (Fig. 215).

The rate of physiological color change is limited by the rates of mechanical response of the effector organ and of its controlling mechanism. There is, however, great variation in such rates among animals. The squid is able to carry out maximum color change in a matter of seconds, as is also the squirrel fish, *Holocentrus.* A few minutes suffice for maximum color change in the minnows,

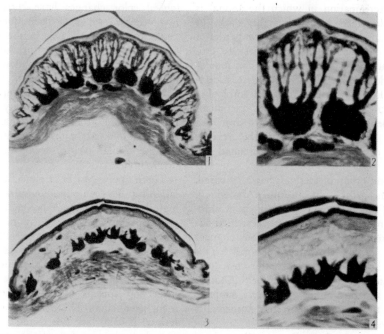

FIGURE 215. Sections through scales of *Anolis* showing the condition of the chromatophores, 1,2, in the brown state and 3,4, in the green state. From Kleinholz.[152]

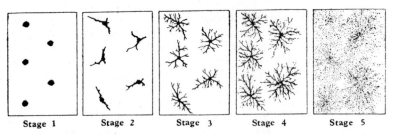

| Stage 1 | Stage 2 | Stage 3 | Stage 4 | Stage 5 |

FIGURE 216. Melanophores showing various degrees of pigment dispersion. *1*, punctate; *2*, punctostellate; *3*, stellate; *4*, reticulostellate; *5*, reticulate. (From Matsumoto, K.: Biol. J. Okayama Univ., vol. 1.)

Fundulus and *Lebistes.* From one to several hours are needed by many crustaceans, insects, and the catfish *Ameiurus,* and days are required for comparable maximum changes in flatfishes, the eel, *Anguillula,* elasmobranchs, and amphibians.

A number of methods have been utilized in the measurements of physiological color changes. These have been critically reviewed by Parker.[213] None of the methods permits complete differentiation between influences which are in part the result of morphological color changes and those which are purely physiological. Instead, the measurements are generally based on time intervals of sufficient brevity to assure that morphological changes would not have influenced the results significantly. One group of methods employs simply the gross changes in color of the animal as an index of the extent of dispersion of the dark pigments. This may involve a visual determination in which the animal is merely described as being light, dark, or intermediate, or in which subjective grades of variation between known extremes are estimated and expressed numerically[30] in four or five grades. Some of the subjective aspects have been removed by a method employing photometric determination of the fraction of the incident light reflected from a unit area of skin surface[124, 192, 291] or the relative amounts of light transmitted by isolated fish scales.[260]

A second group of methods has been based, not on the gross light absorptive changes in the skin, but rather on the changes in chromatophores themselves. One of these methods is measurement of the actual diameter changes in the individual chromatophores. This method has been employed for fish and crustacean chromatophores.[25, 27, 266] Another method, and one rather extensively adopted, describes the chromatophore state numerically as follows[177, 257] (Fig. 216):

1 = Punctate; 2 = Punctostellate; 3 = Stellate; 4 = Reticulostellate; 5 = Reticulate.

This system has the advantage that quick inspection can, after a little practice, yield numerical values adequate for many comparative purposes.

The preceding methods have sometimes been supplemented with photomicrography[201] or the rapid (often heat) fixation of the animal to provide temporary or permanent skin preparations.[27, 292]

Morphological Color Changes. Morphological color changes involve actual changes in quantity of pigment within the animal or its integument. In the normal adaptive color changes of animals, physiological and morphological color changes proceed simultaneously. The morphological changes may result in both an increase in the amount of pigment within each pigment cell and an increase in the number of functional chromatophores per unit area of skin.[24, 193] Quantitative studies of morphological color changes have correspondingly involved two types of techniques: (1) the determination of changes in the number of functional chromatophores per unit area of surface, and (2) the determination of changes in the total pigment content of the animals by chemical extraction and colorimetric determinations of pigment quantity in the extracts (Fig. 217). This subject has been ably reviewed for vertebrates by Sumner,[273] and a quite similar picture seems to obtain for invertebrates.

There appears to be a close functional relationship between physiological and morphological color changes. A correlation between the two has been noted by many investigators.[12, 148] Maintained concentration of a pigment within a chromatophore seems usually to be correlated with a reduction in quantity of that pigment, and, conversely, pigment dispersion appears associated with the pigment production. This relationship has been termed Bábàk's law.[12] It would appear either (1) that pigment formation or destruction results from the state of dispersion of the

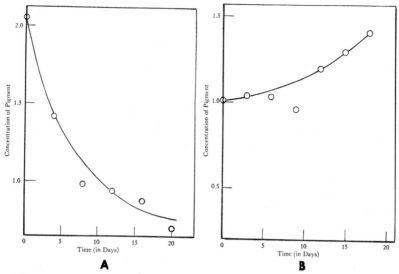

FIGURE 217. *A*, graph showing rate of loss of red pigment from the bodies of *Palaemonetes* kept on a white background. *B*, graph showing increase in quantity of red pigment in the bodies of animals kept on a black background. (From Brown, F. A., Jr.: Biol. Bull., vol. 57.)

pigment, or (2) that both physiological and morphological color changes are effected in a parallel manner by the same controlling mechanisms. The latter view seems to prevail, supported especially by the fact that the process may even involve the production of new chromatophores.

COLOR CHANGES IN ANIMALS

The chromatophore system of animals is influenced by a number of factors.

Temperature. Temperature appears to influence importantly the coloration of many animals. Low temperatures usually induce darkening in *Hyla*[67] and *Phrynosoma*.[208] Elevation of temperature results in concentration of the dark pigment with consequent lightening of the animal.[208] Among the invertebrates, on the other hand, the situation is not as uniform. Both *Callinectes* and *Palaemonetes* lighten with increasing temperature.[80] The shrimp *Macrobrachium* darkens at both high and low temperatures,[258] as does also the isopod *Idothea*.[82, 183] *Hippolyte* and *Uca*, on the other hand, tend to blanch at both high and low temperatures.[40, 109] The walking stick, *Carausius*, is black at 15°C and green at 25°C.

Humidity. *Carausius* is influenced by a change in humidity. High humidity induces darkening.[111] *Rana* darkens in a damp environment and lightens in a dry one.[234, 235]

Tactile Stimulation. In general, tactile stimulation seems to have only little influence on the chromatophore system. It was once

believed that the color changes of the tree frog were to a great extent response to the texture of the background to which it was attached, the frog becoming dark on a rough background and green on a smooth one, but it is now generally agreed that this is not the case. Tactile stimulation of the suctorial discs of certain cephalopods has been reported to influence the chromatophores reflexly.[268] Schlieper[245] has reported that *Hyperia galba*, a crustacean parasite on jellyfishes, becomes pale when normally attached to its host but darkens when swimming freely. Attachment to any surface, whether black or white, is said to induce in this parasite the paling response which is obviously adaptive, since it usually becomes attached only to its highly transparent normal host.

Psychical Stimuli. The chromatophores of some animals appear to be influenced by psychic states. An excited squid or cuttlefish shows extraordinary plays of color. Such color plays may be caused by the presence of a predator, such as a large crab. The changes often take the form of waves of change passing smoothly and rapidly over the surface of the body. Color plays also frequently appear to contribute in some manner to mating behavior in these animals.

Reptiles and some fishes show also characteristic color changes when excited. The horned toad *Phrynosoma* on strong excitement exhibits a blanching known as "excitement pallor." The frog *Xenopus* darkens during excitement; adrenin administration

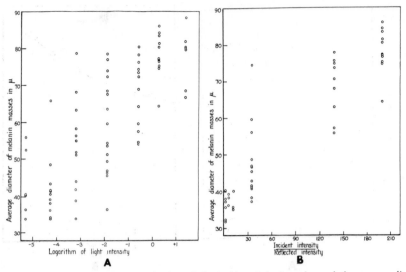

FIGURE 218. *A*, relationship between the log of the incident light intensity and the average diameter of the melanophores of the minnow, *Ericymba*. *B*, relationship between the ratio of *incident intensity* to *reflected intensity* striking the eye and the average melanophore diameter. (From Brown, F. A., Jr.: Biol. Bull., vol. 70.)

produces the same response.[53, 137, 149] *Anolis* when going into combat with another or when manipulated roughly shows a peculiar change of coloration to a mottled condition.[152]

Light. The most important single environmental factor influencing the state of the chromatophore system of animals is light, and in the great majority of animals the method of action of the light involves principally the eyes, central nervous system, and various types of efferent pathways, nervous, hormonal, or both. The importance of the eyes is clearly manifested in the immediate cessation, or great change in character, of color changes on the blinding of an animal. Color changes which are controlled by way of the eyes are known as secondary responses, in contrast with primary responses, which are those proceeding under the influence of light through routes other than the eyes. The latter may involve either a direct action of light on the chromatophores or an influence of light operating reflexly on the chromatophores through extraocular receptor mechanisms.

Secondary color changes dominate the situation in most adult animals. Through a wide range of light intensities these changes are determined by the values of the ratios of the amount of light directly striking the eye from above to the amount of light reflected from the background on which the organism resides. On an illuminated black background where the ratio is large, the animal becomes

dark, and on an illuminated white background where the ratio is small, the animal becomes pale, irrespective of the total illumination. There is often a good direct correlation between the value of the ratio of incident light to reflected light, the albedo, reaching the eye of the animal and the degree of black pigment dispersion[27, 278] (Fig. 218*B*), or the amount of melanin formed in melanophores.[273, 276] Furthermore, either of these melanophore responses varies significantly with variation in intensity within a wide range of total illumination.

Adaptive morphological color changes in response to background have been reported for the chromatophores of crustaceans[15, 24] and for melanophores,[274] lipophores,[1] and iridoleucophores[275] of a number of fishes. Functional melanophores have been induced to form on the normally unpigmented ventral surface of flounders either by placing normal fish in black tanks illuminated from below, or by blinding the animals and illuminating them from below.[196]

The influence of a black background may be simulated in many animals by opaquing the lower half of the eye. This has been demonstrated for the walking-stick *Carausius*,[10, 230] the shrimps *Palaemonetes*[119] and *Leander*,[120] and teleost fishes.[54]

The character of the influence of light in the secondary color responses of animals is obviously one especially adapted to provide the animal with a certain degree of protective or obliterative coloration with respect to its background. As might be anticipated, the function appears in general better developed in animals which are bottom dwellers, or which spend much of their time quietly attached to objects, than in forms which are more freely mobile.

The adaptation to color of background is, in many instances, not restricted to simple blanching and darkening of the skin on white and black backgrounds, respectively. Adaptations of the prawn *Hippolyte* to many colors and tints of background were described many years ago.[145, 188] More recently it has been shown that *Crago* will change its coloration to match red and yellow backgrounds, in addition to black and white.[162] Palaemonetes has been shown to change its color within a few days to accord with black, white, red, yellow, blue, or green backgrounds.[25] The crab *Portunus ordwayi*,[2] adapts to black, white, red, and yellow, as does also *Planes*.[125] The cephalopods *Sepia* and *Octopus* possessing black, orange, and yellow chromatophores, in addition to iridophores, show striking color responses to background.[167, 168]

Some of the most striking examples of color adaptation in vertebrates are seen in flatfishes. The changes in the flounder *Paralichtys albiguttus* on red, green, yellow, and blue backgrounds have been described.[170, 176] This fish, moreover, is able to simulate rather strikingly the color pattern of the background, thus rendering its protective coloration even more effective. Many other teleosts and amphibians are able to show yellow tints in response to yellowish backgrounds.

These adaptations to color of background are the result of appropriate differential movements of the various pigments within the chromatophores, supplemented by morphological color changes to reinforce these physiological ones and by immobile integumentary pigments. In these activities the animal may show the capacity to induce changes in the distributions or amounts of its various pigment types more or less independently of one another, thus indicating complex mechanisms of chromatophore control. Species may be limited in the colors of background to which they can adapt themselves, through lack of suitably colored pigments. For example, *Crago* lacks blue pigment and hence is unable to adapt to either blue or green. *Palaemonetes,* possessing red, yellow, and blue pigments, can, by appropriate pigment manipulation, become almost any color, including black. On the other hand, some species possess pigments of particular colors yet appear to show no ability to adapt to backgrounds of those colors. An example of this is seen in *Carausius,* which is apparently unable to become reddish, despite the possession of a red pigment in its integument.

For the color-adaptive ability, the eyes function not only in their capacity to differentiate incident and reflected light but also in their capacity to distinguish lights of different wavelengths by that portion of the retina stimulated by the reflected light.

The primary chromatophore responses of most adult higher animals are subordinated to the secondary. In the typical adult organism they are best made evident through blinding the animal. Many animals are able to show considerable dispersion and concentration of their pigments in light and darkness respectively, after blinding, but usually there is no longer any response to the background. Examples of chromatophore response in blinded animals have been described for all the major animal groups which exhibit color changes.

A striking exception to the rule of loss of background-color matching is reported for a number of orthopterans.[71-73] The color is also apparently independent of food. It is believed to involve the epidermal cells acting as independent effectors.[150] The chromatophores of Zooea larvae of *Crago* appear to exhibit only primary responses to illumination.[219] The degree of influence of the primary responses, relative to the secondary responses, appears to vary from species to species or even among the various pigment types within a single species.

The most general mechanism of primary response is one of a direct influence of light on the chromatophores. In this response the chromatophore acts as an independent effector. Primary responses of this character have been observed in (1) vertebrate chromatophores after complete denervation of the pigment cells by nerve transection and degeneration, (2) localized light responses in species whose chromatophores are normally not innervated, and (3) in young specimens whose chromatophores have not yet come under the control of a typical secondary mechanism.

Color changes in response to light may be reflexly induced in the absence of eyes. It has been shown for *Phoxinus* that the midbrain is a receptive mechanism for this response.[241] The pineal body has been reported to be a receptor organ in the pigmentary response of

FIGURE 219. The fiddler crab *Uca pugnax* in dark, daytime, and pale nighttime phases.

Lampetra larvae,[296] with the eyes dominating this response in the adult.

The majority of adult animals showing color changes have their coloration correlated within wide ranges of illumination with background color rather than with general intensity of illumination. In the total absence of light there is typically a blanching of the animal, but often not to the extent observed in response to an illuminated white background. Some species, such as *Crago* and *Xenopus,* become intermediate in shade through partial dispersion of their melanin. It has been shown for the minnow, *Ericymba,* that upon a black background there is no influence of amount of illumination on the coloration as long as the illumination is higher than 1.75 foot candles; at illuminations below this value the average diameter of the melanophores is a linear function of the logarithm of the incident light, down to 0.00053 foot candles, which has the same influence as complete darkness[27] (Fig. 218*A*).

Diurnal Rhythms. Another important factor operating in the control of chromatophores in many animals is a persisting daily rhythm.[270] Many species of animals continue to show their characteristic night-day color changes even when kept under constant conditions as regards temperature and illumination, especially in constant darkness. Such rhythms may persist for a considerable time. The rhythm in *Idothea* kept in total darkness persists at least 8 or 9 weeks.[183] In *Uca,* the diurnal rhythm whereby the animals pale by night and darken by day[7, 44] (Fig. 219) is so strong that only slight color change can be induced by variation in background or illumination.[40] Some interesting characteristics of the rhythmical mechanism controlling *Uca* chromatophores have been reported.

The times of darkening and lightening in

the daily cycles persisting in constant conditions in the laboratory may be reset by a few daily cycles of appropriately timed light or temperature changes[45, 269, 289] to occur at any arbitrarily desired time of day, and then these new temporal relations to solar-day and night will persist in the 24-hour rhytnm until they are again reset. Furthermore, even detailed changes in the character of the daily patterns of color change, and ranges of daily change, may be altered experimentally, to persist later under constant laboratory conditions.[37, 42] The timing mechanism responsible for measuring the recurring 24-hour cycles is independent of temperature over at least a 20°C range,[44] and its accuracy during the measurement of one cycle is not affected even when crabs are concurrently being flown by airplane west through 50° of longitude,[46] yielding about a 27½-hour artificial day of all local-time related geophysical fluctuations.

The discovery that, under some conditions, a rhythm of color change, with events reset to occur at a different time of day, would gradually drift back to its initial times, required the postulation that a serial dependence of at least two timing centers was present.[45] To effect a permanent rhythm shift, both centers needed to be reset.

Evidence has been obtained that the resetting of the phases of the color change by light and temperature depend upon a diurnal rhythm of responsiveness of the crabs,[35, 269, 289] the crabs responding to increased illumination or temperature only during the nighttime phase of their normal rhythm by a resetting of the color-change time. This has been postulated to be the mechanism by which the crabs attune their color-change rhythm in nature adaptively to the day-night cycles.[33]

Superimposed upon the persistent diurnal rhythm of color change is a lower amplitude tidal rhythm, paralleling the 12.4-hour ocean tides,[36, 78, 79, 85] which modulates the daily one to yield persistent semimonthly patterns of fluctuation in the day by day color-change cycles. The tidal rhythms of color change, with period related to the earth's rotation relative to the moon, also appear to persist indefinitely in constant conditions in the laboratory and to display the same kind of extraordinary properties as those mentioned earlier for the diurnal ones.[47] There is every evidence that the tidal rhythms of color change are adjusted to tidal times of local beaches by the time of uncovering of the crab burrows by the receding water.[79, 84, 93]

To the extent they have been analyzed, the properties of the persistent rhythms of color change in other animals appear similar to those described for the crabs. Persistent rhythms have been found for color changes not only for many other crustaceans but also for vertebrates such as *Lampetra*,[296] *Phoxinus,* salamander larvae, frogs, *Phrynosoma*,[233] and the chameleon,[298] and in the phasmid, *Carausius,* and the echinoderm, *Diadema*.[185]

In some instances where the diurnally rhythmic changes are normally masked by secondary responses to illuminated backgrounds, an underlying influence of the rhythm may be evident in an increased rapidity of those responses which tend to support, and the sluggishness of those which tend to antagonize, the particular phase of the underlying persistent rhythm at that moment. Thus many animals more readily adapt to an illuminated white background during the night phase and to an illuminated black one during the day phase, or show corresponding differing susceptibilities to injection of color-change hormones between the night and day phases.

FUNCTIONAL ORGANIZATION OF CHROMATOPHORE SYSTEMS

Annelids. Certain annelids become pale in darkness and dark when illuminated. This has been observed for the polychaete *Nereis dumerilii*,[122] and leeches *Piscicola geometra*,[139, 140] *Protoclepsis tessellata*,[271] *Hemiclepsis marginata*,[139, 140] *Glossiphonia complanata*,[139, 140, 290] and *Placobdella parasitica* and *P. rugosa*.[264] In no case has any response to color of the background been demonstrated.

The rhynchobdellid leech *Placobdella parasitica,* a common parasite on turtles of the central United States, possesses three types of pigment cells. These pigments contribute to the mottled brownish and white coloration shown by these animals. The amount of white varies considerably from specimen to specimen, ranging from the greater part of the dorsal surface to a few minute lateral papillae and a short median line, both restricted to the anterior half of the animal. One type of cell containing a pale yellowish, granular pigment occupies the characteristic longitudinal mid-dorsal stripe, the numerous light papillae, and segmental blocks along the margin. These cells show no physiological reponses. Distributed over all the darker areas of the body are relatively large chromatophores containing dark greenish pigment. This latter pigment

participates in physiological color changes. Another pigment, reddish brown, is also located within functional chromatophores. These last chromatophores are much smaller than the greenish ones and are located more superficially. The green pigment is alcohol soluble; the reddish-brown pigment is alcohol insoluble. The European leech *Protoclepsis tessellata* possesses three pigments: brown, green, and yellow. The Mediterranean polychaete *Nereis dumerilii* possesses yellow and violet chromatophores.

The leech *Placobdella parasitica,* like other annelids showing physiological color changes, blanches in darkness and darkens when illuminated. The time required for the greenish pigments, which are predominant in these changes, to complete their concentration in darkness or dispersion in light is approximately 1 hour.

There are several types of evidence all pointing to nervous control of the green chromatophores. Decapitation or any other transection or injury to the nervous system results in a darkening of pale animals kept in darkness. This darkening may persist for many hours. If a uniformly pale leech in darkness is stimulated faradically at either the anterior or posterior end the whole animal darkens. If, however, the experiment is repeated with a specimen whose nerve cord has been transected in the middle, only that half of the animal receiving the stimulus darkens, the body beyond the point of transection remaining light. There is little evidence for direct action of light on the chromatophores.

The two eyespots at the anterior end appear to play an active but by no means an exclusive role in the responses. Decapitated specimens show the characteristic changes even though responding more sluggishly. When specimens are brought from darkness into light and one-half of the body is immediately covered with opaque paper, the covered portion remains largely in the dark-adapted phase while the uncovered portion becomes completely light adapted. The results are more striking when the posterior end is covered than when the anterior end is. These experiments suggest a role of generally distributed photoreceptors operating through segmental reflexes.

The reddish-brown pigment of *Placobdella parasitica* responds independently of the green and shows no predictable responses to background or to light intensity. Its condition is more or less variable in normal specimens.

When dispersed it can usually be made to concentrate by intense stimulation of the animal. In animals with transected cords, the response to electrical stimulation, when it occurs, passes as for the green cells, only to the point of transection. Thus it would appear that the nervous system controls the reddish-brown chromatophores directly, but that excitation induces concentration rather than dispersion as for the green.

Echinoderms. The sea urchins, *Arbacia pustulosa, Centrostephanus longispinus, Diadema antillarum* and *Diadema setosum,* become lighter in color on transfer from light to darkness.[153, 184, 185, 283, 294] Illuminated *Arbacia pustulosa* are blackish in color whether on a white or on a black background, but in darkness become brown in color. *Centrostephanus longispinus,* which are dark purple in light, change in darkness to gray. The physiological color changes require about 1 or 2 hours for their completion. Microscopic examination of tube feet removed from light-adapted and dark-adapted individuals shows numerous reddish-brown chromatophores with their pigment dispersed in the light-adapted and concentrated in the darkness-adapted individuals. The color changes in these urchins are due to the movements of pigments within definite chromatophores, but morphological color change also occurs. The chromatophores of isolated tube feet which have been mounted on a microscope slide respond to illumination and darkness in the same manner as when they are present in the intact animal, indicating that the chromatophores are responding to the light either directly or by way of local reflex pathways comparable to those known to function in the locomotor movements of the tube feet. Studies with highly restricted points of illumination suggest the chromatophores to respond directly to light.

The American species of *Arbacia, Arbacia punctulata,* appears to show no color changes comparable to those just described.[199]

Cephalopods. Many cephalopods show remarkably rapid color changes as a result of the activity of their peculiar type of chromatophores. These changes may result from many different types of stimuli, but light is one of the most important.

The chromatophores are primarily controlled by the nervous system. Cutting a nerve innervating a particular region of the body results in an immediate cessation of all color changes in that region. It was shown long ago that after a mantle connective is cut[99] there is a paralysis of the chromatophores of the corresponding half of the body and a persisting blanched coloration. Since the connectives between mantle ganglion and the chromatophores are still intact it is evident that the ganglion contributes little to the control by itself and that the normal control over the responses resides in higher centers of the nervous system. The cerebral ganglion of the brain appears to possess an inhibitory center for the chromatophore system;[225, 226, 248] after its destruction or inactivation there is tonic expansion of the chromatophores. The inhibitory center is believed to operate through control of the color center[249] located in the central ganglia, which in turn operates through motor centers found in the subesophageal ganglia. The motor centers each control the chromatophores of the corresponding halves of the body.

The eyes are the chief sense organs influencing the central nervous centers. Bilateral blinding does not eliminate changes of color, but the changes which then occur are in no sense adaptive ones. If only one eye is blinded, the responses of the chromatophores on the corresponding side of the body are diminished.

Another significant source of influence on the color-control centers is the suckers on the arms. If these are all extirpated there is a considerable loss of tone in the chromatophores and, hence, skin lightening occurs.[268] Removal of both eyes and suckers, however, does not entirely eliminate the chromatophore responses. After such an operation vigorous stimuli will still result in color changes, probably as a result of stimulation of organs such as tactile ones and organs of equilibrium.

The chromatophores on the side of the animal that is lowermost when the animal is in contact with the substrate always are more contracted than those of the remainder of the body.[249] This is not a direct influence of illumination as one might first suspect, for it cannot be reversed by illumination from below instead of above. Rather, it appears to be part of a postural response involving stimulation of tactile receptors reflexly through the central nervous system, resulting in the localized chromatophore contraction.

The substances tyramine and betaine are known to be present in the blood of cephalopods. The former, like adrenin, increases the tonus of the motor centers, resulting in a darker coloration.[250] Betaine, on the other hand, like pilocarpine or acetylcholine, appears to decrease the chromatophore tone by stimulation of the inhibitory center. If one transfuses blood from a characteristically darker species, such as *Eledone* or *Octopus macropus,* into a lighter species, such as *O. vulgaris,* the latter darkens.[251] Interconnection of the circulatory system of the two will yield comparable results. Tyramine is known to be more concentrated in the blood of these darker species than in that of the lighter ones. Surgical removal of the posterior salivary gland, known to be the important source of tyramine in the blood of these animals, results in an increase in paleness and a complete loss of tone of the chromatophores.[251] Darkening may be induced again by injection of tyramine solutions. The results suggest that tyramine, and probably betaine as well, function as humoral agents operating to modify through the central nervous centers the general tone of the chromatophores. Furthermore, studies of denervated chromatophores[252, 253] suggest that both tyramine and betaine also exert a tone-increasing action on the chromatophores themselves, thus functioning directly as well as indirectly on the chromatophores.

Superimposed upon the slower humoral influence is the more conspicuous nervous mechanism responsible for the rapid color changes. Certain observations have led to the hypothesis that the chromatophores have a double innervation. If an isolated piece of the integument of *Loligo* containing chromatophores is allowed to stand for some time, the chromatophores first contract and later reach a condition of maintained partial expansion. Chromatophore contraction results from electrical stimulation of these latter. Here, therefore, electrical stimulation appears to act to inhibit the tonus of the chromatophore musculature.[17, 18] On the other hand, single electrical shocks to the chromatophore nerve, or to the chromatophores themselves, give single twitches of the chromatophore muscle. Repeated shocks give tetanus and, consequently, chromatophore expansion. It has therefore been concluded that *Loligo* chromatophore muscles receive double innervation, both an excitatory and an inhibitory element.

Insects. A number of insects can change their coloration in response to external stimuli, usually as the result of morphological color changes only. Among factors effecting the changes are temperature, humidity, general activity, and illumination. In only a few species are there the relatively rapid physiological color changes.

Many butterfly pupae are darker or lighter in coloration, depending on whether they are reared at lower or higher temperatures, respectively. The effect of temperature operates in *Vanessa* through the head, the pupa taking on a coloration which is determined by the temperature of that portion of the body when the head and body are maintained at different temperatures.[112] The prepupal color changes of caterpillars have been found by ligation experiments to depend normally on hormones. Clearly involved are ecdysone from the prothoracic glands and probably also the juvenile hormone.[52, 123] A similar influence of temperature on the degree of development of the dark pigments has been observed for the wasp, *Habrobracon,*[143, 246, 247] and the bug, *Perillus.*[154]

The colors of *Pieris brassicae* are due to melanin in the cuticle, white pigment in the hypodermal cells, and green pigment in the deeper tissues. The coloration of these pupae is also influenced by the backgrounds. On black or red background the pupae are grayish white, whereas on green or orange backgrounds they are clear green, the latter background suppressing formation of the black and white pigments.[63, 64] Exposing the pupae to colored lights gives the same results as the colored backgrounds. The eyes or some other head structure is essential for the response, for it ceases and the animals behave as in darkness when the eyes are extirpated or the animal is decapitated.[19, 20-22]

The migratory locust, *Locusta migratoria,* shows a limited ability to adapt its coloration to backgrounds.[77] Through variations in the quantities of yellowish and black pigments the locusts may become yellowish white, brown, or black. The quantity of black pigment formed seems to depend on the ratio of incident to reflected light striking the eyes; the amount of the yellowish pigment appears to depend on the predominant wavelengths present, being formed more rapidly at longer wavelengths (550 to 660 mμ) and less rapidly at shorter ones (450 to 500 mμ). When this species enters its swarming, migratory phase a skin coloration darker than in the solitary phase is produced. There is some evidence that the darker coloration is a result of the more intense metabolic activity. When migrating locusts are returned to solitary conditions they will regain their lighter color phase, but this color change is delayed if the isolated locust is kept in a constantly excited state.[77]

A few insects show color change which can be traced to redistribution of pigments within

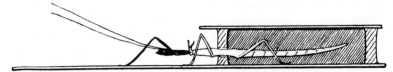

FIGURE 220. Diagram illustrating the use of a moist chamber as a stimulus for producing darkening in *Carausius*. The darkening in this instance is in response to abdominal stimulation and commences at the head and passes posteriorly only as far as an anterior thoracic ligature. (From Giersberg, H.: Ztschr. vergl. Physiol., vol. 9.)

pigment cells or chromatophores. *Corethra* shows a rapid physiological color change of its air sacs.[60, 175] This last is due to the presence of special pigment cells. On a black background the pigment becomes dispersed, and the pigment cells are scattered uniformly over the sacs. On a white background the pigment concentrates, and the cells appear to wander to one side of the sacs. The eyes are involved in these reactions, as is also the brain. A hormonal factor present in the brain, and to a lesser extent in the corpora allata, disperses the dark pigment.[60, 62]

The color changes of the Phasmid *Carausius morosus* have been investigated rather extensively. The hypodermal cells of this species contain four pigments, brown (melanin), orange-red and yellow (lipochromes), and green.[111, 243, 244] The brown and orange-red pigments show active concentration and dispersion within the cells in response to external stimuli. The green and yellow pigments show no such activity. Therefore the green varieties found in nature show no physiological color changes while the brown ones do. Brown specimens are usually dark by night and pale by day, as a result of dispersion and concentration, respectively, of the brown and orange-red pigments. A partial independence of a direct influence of light in these changes is indicated by the persistence of typical day-night cycles of color change in animals kept in constant darkness.[144, 243, 244] It is possible to reverse the rhythm by keeping the animal in illumination by night and in darkness by day, whereupon the newly established rhythm will continue in constant darkness.

Utilizing the fact that high humidity also produces body-darkening, Giersberg[111] ingeniously proved that the effect of this stimulus on the chromatophores is indirect, operating by way of afferent nervous pathways, the brain, an endocrine source, and finally a blood-borne agent. When the posterior half of a pale *Carausius* is inserted into a small moist chamber the whole animal darkens in 30 to 60 minutes (Fig. 220). The darkening commences at the anterior end, which lies outside of the chamber in dry air, and gradually spreads backward over the whole body. Returned to dry air, the animal lightens again in 1 to 2 hours. If a ligature is then drawn tightly around the anterior thoracic region and the experiment repeated, the darkening spreads back only as far as the constricted region. If the ventral nerve cord is carefully transected between the subesophageal and the first thoracic ganglia, or between the subesophageal and the supraesophageal ganglia of an otherwise normal pale animal and the experiment repeated, there is no darkening whatsoever, but if the animal is turned about and the head inserted into the moist chamber, the head darkens first and the darkening then spreads out over the body in just the same fashion as seen in unoperated specimens. In the ligatured animal the nerve pathways are apparently still able to conduct anteriorly the nerve impulses arriving from the nerve endings of the abdominal region which are stimulated by the moisture. A blood-borne hormone, liberated at the anterior end, is unable to diffuse posteriorly past the ligature. After nerve-cord transection the nerve impulses are prevented from reaching the brain and stimulating the liberation of a hormonal substance. Hormone production can still be effected by stimulation of nerve endings anterior to the operated region, and then the active principle is free to pass posteriorly in the body fluids.

Further evidence that the physiological color changes in *Carausius* are predominantly controlled by hormonal material has come from transplantation of portions of the skin of one animal to another.[138] The transplanted tissue begins to show color changes entirely paralleling those of the host in 2 or 3 days. It is unlikely that the transplant tissue would have received any innervation from the host nervous system in such a short period. In fact, normal hypodermal tissue shows no indications of innervation.

The eyes of *Carausius* are essential to the normal responses to light.[10] Section of the optic tracts or blackening of the eye surface stops the responses.

Carausius also shows responses to background when humidity and illumination are kept constant. It turns dark colored on black and red surfaces and light colored on white and yellowish ones. The background responses are determined by the ratio of light striking the dorsal and the ventral halves of the eyes. Painting the lower half of the eyes black brings about darkening as on a black background.

The brain appears to be the chief source of a color-change hormone. After brain extirpation the animals become pale gray. Injection of brain extract darkens the insects.[61, 62] An active factor, termed the C-substance, has been isolated electrophoretically.[159]

Morphological color changes in response to illumination, background, and humidity also occur in *Carausius* and appear to involve the same mechanism of control as does the physiological change. Such change, however, requires stimulation over a much longer period.[10, 112] It has been suggested that the substances normally influencing physiological changes so modify the general nutrition and metabolism of the insects as to result in further changes in color through pigment formation or destruction.

Certain mantids also exhibit diurnal color changes[105] which correspond very closely with the diurnal movements of the retinal pigments in the lateral regions of the compound eye.

Crustaceans. The crustaceans exhibit some of the most remarkable instances of color adaptation to be found in the animal kingdom. Most crustaceans possess within their chromatophores white, red, yellow, and often also black, brown, and blue pigments. By appropriate rearrangements of the individual pigments within the chromatophores many crustaceans are able to approximate rather closely the colors of the backgrounds upon which they come to lie.

Although it was believed by all the early investigators that the chromatophores were controlled by nerves, there was never any satisfactory demonstration of nerve terminations at the chromatophores, nor did nerve transection ever appear to interfere directly with the responses of the chromatophores within the animal. Koller,[161, 162] working with *Crago vulgaris*, provided the first clear evidence that a blood-borne agent was active in controlling the chromatophores. He found that transfusion of blood from a specimen darkened on a black background into a light animal kept on a white background would cause darkening of the light animal. No evidence for a lightening factor was obtained, however, by the reciprocal transfusion. He also observed that blood from a yellow-adapted specimen would render yellow a white-adapted specimen.

Perkins[221] discovered that, although denervation of an area of the body of *Palaemonetes* in no way interfered with the responses of the region when the animal was placed on a black or white background, occlusion of the blood supply to any region resulted in an immediate cessation in the responses of that region. Upon readmission of blood to the region, that region changed its color at once to harmonize with the color of the remainder of the body. These results were interpreted to indicate that factors for dark-pigment dispersion and concentration were conveyed to the individual chromatophore by way of the blood. Extraction and injection of various parts of the body showed that the eyestalks contain a potent factor for concentrating the predominant red pigment and dispersing the white[222] in *Palaemonetes* and hence for blanching the animal. Removal of the eyestalks results in a permanently darkened condition of the animal. These results were quickly confirmed by Koller,[163] working with *Crago, Leander,* and *Processa.* The hormonal substance involved was shown by reciprocal injection experiments to be neither species nor genus specific. Since these pioneering efforts, numerous investigators have shown that either the eyestalks or, in a few species, the anterior thoracic region contains the source of a material influencing the state of the chromatophores.

Decapod crustaceans which have been investigated extensively with respect to their eyestalk hormonal activities in color changes appear to fall, with a rare exception, into three groups with respect to roles of eyestalks in their chromatics (Fig. 221). Group I contains such genera as *Palaemonetes, Peneus, Hippolyte, Leander, Orconectes,* and *Cambarellus,* and the single brachyuran genus, *Sesarma.* Their chromatophore systems usually contain red, yellow, blue, and white pigments. Group II includes only the genus *Crago,* which has a complex pigmentary system with no less than eight differently responding chromatophore types, enabling the shrimp to show not only general shade and tint changes, but also a certain degree of change in color pattern. The chromatophores

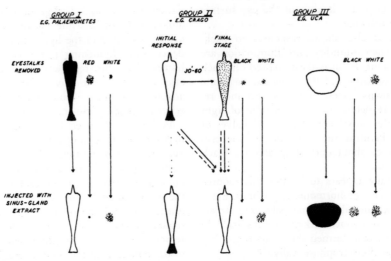

FIGURE 221. Schematic representation of the coloration of eyestalkless crustaceans and state of the dominant chromatophores for each of the three differently responding groups, and of the responses of these to injection of eyestalk or sinus gland extract. Solid arrows indicate extract of total water-soluble material, dashed arrows indicate an alcohol-insoluble fraction, and dotted arrows indicate an alcohol-soluble fraction. (From Brown, F. A., Jr.: Action of Hormones in Plants and Invertebrates. Academic Press.)

contain black, brown, red, yellow, and white pigments. Group III includes most true crabs (brachyurans) which have been investigated except *Sesarma*.[69] These include *Eriocheir, Hemigrapsus, Callinectes,* and *Uca.* The best known of these is the fiddler crab *Uca,* which commonly contains black, red, yellow, and white pigments in the chromatophore system.

After removal of the eyestalks from a member of any one of the three groups, the characteristic type of response for that particular group is observed. In Group I the animals darken rapidly through complete dispersion of their red and yellow pigment and become quite dark (although usually not as dark as in normal response to a black background) in an hour or two. They remain in this condition indefinitely. The white pigment usually undergoes a transitory concentration and thereafter exhibits a variable state. *Crago,* of Group II, most commonly shows a more complex change after eyestalk removal. First there is a transitory darkening of the telson and uropods and a blanching of the remainder of the body, which lasts from ½ to 1 hour. This is followed by a complete blanching of the telson and uropods and darkening of the body to an intermediate and mottled coloration. The white pigment on the body initially concentrates but then assumes an intermediate condition. The crab *Uca,* of Group III, blanches rather quickly after removal of its eyestalks, its black chromatophores becoming

for the most part punctate, and its white ones commonly broadly reticulate. This condition is maintained without significant change indefinitely. Thus, we see eyestalk removal from various crustaceans resulting in three types of conditions: body darkening, adoption of an intermediate coloration, and body blanching. In all three, the animals lose practically all of their responses to changes in background or illumination.

Injection of eyestalk extract into Group I animals results in rapid blanching.[83, 86, 94, 242] In Group II there is complete blanching of both the body and telson and uropods. In Group III, on the other hand, there is a blackening of the whole body.[16, 68, 177] These strikingly different results observed for the animals of Groups I, II, and III are explained chiefly in terms of differences in the responses of the chromatophore systems to the eyestalk hormones, since reciprocal injections demonstrate that extracts of eyestalks from specimens of other groups produce in the specimens of any given group a response qualitatively the same as that produced by the specimen's own eyestalks. For example, eyestalk extracts prepared from animals of Group I darken eyestalkless specimens of Group II.

The place of normal liberation of the chromatophorotropins from the eyestalk is the sinus gland (Fig. 241). This was postulated and strongly supported by Hanstrom.[118, 119] This gland had been described earlier,[117, 256] and at that time was called the "blood gland," since it was first believed to be homologous with a blood-forming gland in the eyestalks of *Crago,* which had erroneously been considered to be the source of the active material.[164] This gland occurs in practically all of numerous crustaceans in which it has been sought. Hanstrom, using eyestalkless specimens of *Uca, Palaemonetes,* or *Penaeus* as animals for bioassay in his numerous experiments, found that eyestalks of animals whose sinus glands were located in the head near the brain (*Gebia* and *Hippa* [*Emerita*]) showed no chromatophorotropic activity. When the eyestalks of other species were sectioned in various ways, the sections possessing the sinus gland always showed activity; other parts were relatively inactive. By utilizing the species differences in the anatomical arrangement of eyestalk organs, Hanstrom was able to get, one by one, all the remaining organs of the eyestalk into portions of the stalk showing activity. Furthermore, no other structure in the stalk gave histological evidence of having secretory activity except a glandular organ called the X-organ. Sections containing the X-organ, but not the sinus gland, were inactive; and removal of the X-organ from eyestalks did not diminish their chromatophorotropic activity. It was thus concluded that the sinus gland was the only eyestalk source of hormones influencing the red or black pigments in the test animals employed.

Hanstrom's conclusions were confirmed by Brown,[29] who found that the sinus glands could be removed and extracted by themselves, and that such extracts possessed essentially all the activity of total stalks despite the fact that their volume was only about 1 per cent of that of the stalk tissue. Such extracts elicited about 80 per cent of the response from whole stalks for both *Palaemonetes* red and *Uca* black chromatophores. Thus, for these two widely different chromatophore types, the sinus glands are the chief eyestalk reservoir of hormonal material. Furthermore, implantation of a sinus gland into the ventral abdominal sinus results in a blanching of the animal which lasts about 100 times as long as the effects of an injection of extract that is the equivalent of approximately one gland.

It is generally conceded that the sinus glands are not the site of synthesis of the chromatophorotropins. Rather, these are believed produced within neurosecretory cell bodies, clustered into groups termed X-organs.

(See chapter on Endocrines.) The sinus gland, a composite of enlarged terminations of these neurosecretory cells, is only the organ of storage and liberation of the active hormones. This functional relationship between X-organs and sinus glands, initially established from studies on hormonal control of molt, from morphological interrelationships, and observations of the actual passage of secretory granules to the sinus gland within the X-organ–cell axons, was given direct experimental support by the finding that X-organ extirpation in *Leander* terminates color changes, the prawns remaining with dispersed dark pigment.[218]

The X-organ–sinus gland complex of the eyestalk provides more than one chromatophorotropin. This was demonstrated first by means of a comparative study of the relative influences of extracts of the eyestalks of seven genera of crustaceans in concentrating *Palaemonetes* red pigment and dispersing *Uca* black pigment.[41] The ratio of the effect of extracts on two chromatophore types, *Uca* black and *Palaemonetes* red, was called the U/P ratio. The U/P ratios obtained for eyestalks or sinus glands from different sources varied from one genus to another. For example, *Crago* sinus glands showed a relatively high value, whereas those of *Palaemonetes* showed a relatively low value. *Uca* yielded an intermediate value. The order for the seven species investigated showed no correlation with either the sizes of the animals or the relative potencies as assayed on *Uca.* The hypothesis proposed to explain these data—namely, that sinus glands differed from one another in the proportions of two principles, (1) a factor predominantly darkening *Uca* (UDH), and (2) a factor predominantly lightening *Palaemonetes* (PLH)—was given strong support by the discovery that the sinus glands of each species yielded two active fractions, one alcohol soluble, and the other alcohol insoluble. The former gave a very low U/P ratio, as if possessing a larger proportion of PLH, and the latter gave a high U/P ratio, suggesting a larger proportion of UDH. It was possible to restore the initial U/P ratio for the glands of a species simply by recombining the two fractions. These results indicate species representing Groups I, II, and III possess two eyestalk chromatophorotropins but in differing proportions.

The sinus glands of the crustaceans from Group III which have been so far examined lack an activity shown by glands of species

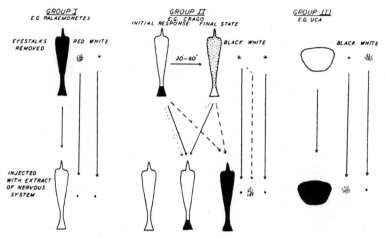

FIGURE 222. Schematic representation of the coloration of eyestalkless crustaceans and state of their dominant chromatophores for each of the three differently responding groups, and of the responses of these to injection of extracts of the nervous system. Solid arrows indicate extract of total water-soluble material, dashed arrows indicate an alcohol-insoluble fraction, and dotted arrows indicate an alcohol-soluble fraction. (From Brown, F. A., Jr.: Action of Hormones in Plants and Invertebrates. Academic Press.)

of Groups I and II. This has been established through the discovery that, whereas extracts of the eyestalks or sinus glands of species of Group I or II will lighten the telson and uropods of *Crago* within 3 or 4 minutes after injection, sinus glands of species of Group III fail to do so.[34, 49] This is so despite the fact that Group III eyestalks are apparently as effective in lightening the bodies of *Crago* as are eyestalks from other groups. This principle, which is present in Groups I and II but absent in Group III, has been called *Crago*-"tail"-lightening hormone (CTLH). Though at least three chromatophorotropins occur, therefore, in crustacean sinus glands, two possibilities exist: (1) species in Groups I and II possess three principles and those of Group III possess two principles, or (2) all possess only two principles, with one of the two differing in physiological properties between Groups I and II and Group III.

The eyestalks are not the sole sites of production of chromatophorotropins in crustaceans. It is well known that undisturbed eyestalkless specimens of *Crago* not uncommonly exhibit random color changes. Eyestalkless crustaceans may be induced to undergo color changes through the action of blood-borne factors by electrical or other stimulation of the cut ends of the optic nerves. Crustaceans of Group I are induced to blanch, but whereas blanching under the influence of sinus gland principles includes white-pigment dispersion, by this means the white usually concentrates. Members of Group III darken,

but here, too, the white concentrates as the black disperses, unlike under sinus gland influence. The responses of *Crago* of Group II appear more complex, and its reactions to electrical stimulation of its optic nerve stubs provided a clue which led to the discovery of an additional source of the chromatophorotropins in crustaceans. If stimulation is mild, the whole animal blackens; if stimulation is intense only the telson and uropods darken, the remainder of the body blanching. Some chromatophorotropins arising outside of the eyestalks could obviously antagonize the activity of sinus gland factors in some responses and supplement them in others.

Extracts of the central nervous organs of certain species of Group I, on injection, lighten eyestalkless specimens and concentrate white pigment[23, 48, 83, 87, 136, 155] (Fig. 222). Similarly, extracts of the *Uca* nervous system disperse red and simultaneously concentrate white pigment. Extracts of the nervous system of *Crago,* of Group II, lighten the body and darken the telson and uropods while concentrating white pigment. Therefore, in all three groups, injection of extracts of central nervous system organs produces the same major results as strong stimulation of the eyestalks of eyestalkless animals.

The major portion of the telson- and uropod-darkening action, as well as body-lightening activity of *Crago,* resides in an organ of the head region which has been termed the postcommissural organ.[30, 156] (See chapter on Endocrines.) The remainder of

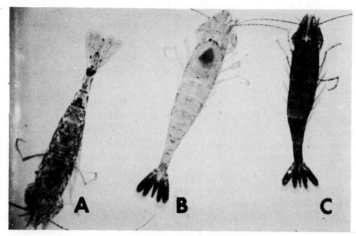

FIGURE 223. Appearance of three *Crago*, closely matched in coloration initially, in response to injection of various solutions: *A*, Sea water (control, exhibiting no change); *B*, total water-soluble fraction of tritocerebral commissures; *C*, an alcohol-insoluble residue of the commissures. (From Brown, F. A., Jr., and Klotz, I. M.: Proc. Soc. Exp. Biol. Med., vol. 64.)

the central nervous system, however, possesses substantial body-lightening activity. This latter fact, together with the discovery that an alcohol-soluble fraction of the tritocerebral commissures possesses very strong body-lightening and no "tail"-darkening activity, while the alcohol-insoluble fraction causes strong "tail"-darkening and simultaneously strong body-darkening,[38] establishes the presence of two chromatophorotropins in *Crago* nervous systems (Fig. 223). One lightens the body but not the "tail" of *Crago*, and hence has been called *Crago*-body-lightening hormone (CBLH); the other, in the presence of CBLH darkens only the "tail," but in the absence of CBLH darkens the whole body and is hence called *Crago*-darkening hormone (CDH). The striking difference between strong and weak stimulation of the eyestubs in this species appears a consequence of the liberation of both principles with strong stimulation, and exclusively CDH with weak stimulation.

A survey of the influence on *Crago* of extracts of the nervous systems of various species of Group I led to the conclusion that all possess both CDH and CBLH, although in none of these other species is it as localized as in *Crago*.[39] These hormones are usually widely distributed along the nervous system (*Palaemonetes, Cambarus, Homarus*) or restricted to regions other than the tritocerebral commissures (e.g., to the posterior portion of the thoracic cord in *Pagurus* and other Anomurans). In some nervous systems, and more especially in some portions of the

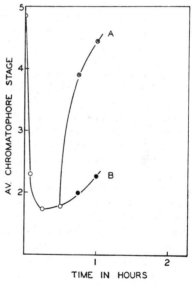

FIGURE 224. Demonstration of dual control of red chromatophores of *Palaemonetes*. Response of red chromatophore to injection into eyestalkless animals of an extract of postcommissural extract, followed, at the end of 30 minutes, by injection of extract of abdominal nerve cord in half the animals (*A*) and of sea water, as control, into the remaining half (*B*). (From Brown, F. A., Jr., Webb, H. M., and Sandeen, M. I.: J. Exp. Zool., vol. 120.)

nervous systems, the ratio of CDH activity to CBLH activity is so large that the extracts blacken eyestalkless *Crago* at least as effectively as the alcohol-insoluble fraction of the *Crago* tritocerebral commissures (e.g., lobster or crayfish abdominal cords). The high CDH activity of lobster abdominal cords appears to be associated chiefly with the sheath rather than in ganglionic cells and nerve fibers. In contrast to crustaceans of Group I, those of Group III appear to possess no CDH anywhere within their central nervous systems or, for that matter, anywhere in their bodies. CBLH is present in the nervous systems of all crustaceans examined.

It has been established that *Uca* of Group III, though possessing no CDH, does actually possess at least two chromatophorotropins in its nervous system,[238] a black dispersing and a white concentrating factor. This evidence comes from comparison of the relative influences of extracts of the brain, circumesophageal connectives, and thoracic cord on eyestalkless *Uca*. Extracts of the brain and thoracic cord show strong activity in black-pigment dispersal and simultaneously leave white pigment dispersed or induce its dispersal. Extracts of connectives, on the other hand, produce only a weak black-dispersing action but cause concentration of the white pigment. The differing results cannot be duplicated simply by varying the concentration of nervous system extract. Although these observations establish the presence of two chromatophorotropins, they do not permit one to decide between two possibilities: (1) all portions have a black-dispersing and white-concentrating action, with the brain and thoracic cord having in addition an antagonistic white-dispersing agent; and (2) all portions have a white-dispersing and a black-dispersing action, but the connectives alone contain a white-concentrating principle. The presence of a black-concentrating factor has been demonstrated for *Uca*; this pigment, therefore, is under dual control by two antagonistic hormones. The red-pigment cells respond differently from the black.[31]

Numerous reciprocal-injection experiments among *Crago, Uca,* and *Palaemonetes,* in which the comparative distributions of *Crago*-darkening, *Crago* body-lightening, *Uca* black-dispersing, and *Uca* white-concentrating activities within the various nervous systems are compared, show rather clearly that CDH and UDH cannot be the same, or like CBLH or UWCH. However, there is still a possibility that CBLH and UWCH are identical since there is a qualitative parallel in their distributions within the three nervous systems studied. Certain quantitative differences of activity, however, cast doubt on this identity.

Until the active principles are available fully free of one another, great difficulty will be experienced in determining their individual roles. Paper electrophoresis has begun to serve as a highly effective means for these separations.[87, 89, 159, 160] It is interesting that the dispersing and concentrating hormones for crayfish red pigment are of opposite signs, — and +, respectively.[87, 89]

The dark-pigment–regulating hormone is inactivated by an enzyme present in integument and liver extracts.[56] It is also inactivated by chymotrypsin, suggesting peptide bonds to be present.[220]

In extended periods of adaptation to background there appears to be an accumulation in crayfishes of that color-change hormone, darkening or lightening, which is not being used under the particular conditions. Upon change of background, an excess of hormone is first liberated, the rate of secretion declining to a lower stable level later.[90, 91, 92]

In summary: Decapod crustacean nervous systems possess at least three or four chromatophorotropins. Their roles in the total chromatic responses of the whole organism have not been worked out for any one species. It seems likely, however, that the nervous-system chromatophorotropins, together with those from the sinus glands, will be shown to go far toward accounting for the intricate control of the crustacean pigmentary systems.

A study of the time relations of melanophore changes in the isopod *Ligia oceanica,* during light to dark, and background changes led to the hypothesis of a dual endocrine control of these pigment cells, with operation of both a darkening or B-substance, and a lightening, or W-substance.[262] The chromatophore systems of isopods show considerable variability in their capacity to respond to background or illumination changes. It has been established that extracts of their heads concentrate the dark pigment in a variety of species of isopods including *Sphaeroma, Idothea,* and *Ligia.*[57, 190, 195] In some other species of *Ligia,* extract of heads disperses the dark pigment.[82] In *Trachelipus* there is evidence suggesting the presence of both concentrating and dispersing hormones.[181] In brief, the evidences from assay of head extracts appears to support the hypothesis that isopod dark chromatophores, like most other crustacean chromatophores, are regulated by a pair of antagonistic hormones. Since the pigment remains fully dispersed after extirpation of the organ of Bellonci, an organ closely associated with the optic lobes and sinus glands of *Sphaeroma* and believed to be homologous with the decapod X-organs, it has been suggested that this is a source of a pigment-concentrating factor.[224]

In the stomatopod *Squilla*,[157] extracts of the postcommissural organs and of the central nervous organs disperse dark pigment.

Vertebrates. All the vertebrates possessing chromatophores show, in general, a fundamental similarity in their functional organization of this system. It seems profitable to develop the evolutionary trends separately within each of the major divisions of the vertebrates in which functional chromatophores are found.

Amphibians. The amphibians may show in their early development a period in which only primary color responses occur, the animals darkening in light and becoming pale in darkness. This was originally described for very young Axolotl by Bábàk[11] and has since been observed in very young *Rana pipiens*[135] and *Amblystoma*.[171] These changes do not involve the eyes. It has been suggested that this is a period during which the eyes are still nonfunctional.[287] Other amphibians appear to show the secondary types of response involving stimulation through the eye immediately on hatching. Such species are *Bombinator* and *Hyla*,[11] and *Xenopus*.[287] In the secondary phase, primary responses are still operating but are dominated by the secondary ones.

Investigation of the physiology of color changes in amphibians has provided no evidence of any direct nervous control of the integumentary melanophores. The striking discovery was made very early that hypophysectomized tadpoles remain pale indefinitely.[263] This strongly suggested that the pituitary might be the normal source of a melanin-dispersing hormone in amphibians. The relation of the hypophysis to color

changes in *Rana* was carefully investigated by Hogben and Winton.[132, 133, 134] Upon hypophysectomy the animals were rendered pale and refractory to further color changes. Removal of the anterior lobe by itself, however, showed no significant interference with the background responses. Extracts of the posterior lobe showed a tremendous capacity to darken pale frogs. All attempts to produce specific chromatophore responses through nerve stimulation or nerve transection failed. Therefore, these workers concluded that the color changes in *Rana* were accountable in terms of the activity of a single hormone arising in the posterior lobe of the pituitary, whose concentration in the blood was controlled by environmental stimuli operating through the eyes. This conclusion has been confirmed through transfusion of blood from a dark to a light *Rana*.[217]

More recently much work has been done on *Xenopus*,[130, 131] in which, also, direct innervation of the melanophores seems to be lacking. *Xenopus*, too, lightens after hypophysectomy and darkens on injection of extracts of posterior lobe of the pituitary. A critical and detailed examination of the characteristics of change of the melanophores of *Xenopus* after transfer from a white to a black background and the reverse, from black to darkness and reverse, and from white to darkness and reverse (Fig. 225) failed to permit an adequate explanation in terms of a single principle and led to the postulation that the hypophysis produces two principles, one with melanin-dispersing action, referred to as the B-substance (MSH), and the other with melanin-concentrating action, called the W-substance (MCH). All the data obtained appeared readily interpretable in terms of an excitation of secretion of the W-substance by

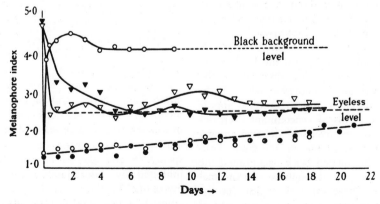

FIGURE 225. Changes in melanophore state in *Xenopus* after transfer from white to black backgrounds and vice versa, and from black background to darkness. (From Hogben, L., and Slome, D.: Proc. Roy. Soc. London, B, vol. 120.)

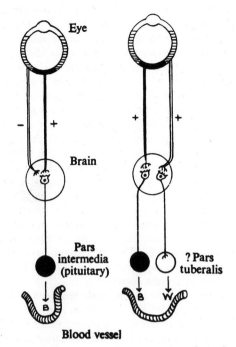

FIGURE 226. Schematic representation of two hypotheses of hormonal control of melanophores in *Xenopus,* one involving a single hormone, and the other, two. (From Hogben, L., and Slome, D.: Proc. Roy. Soc. London, B, vol. 120.)

stimulation of peripheral retinal elements and excitation of secretion of the B-substance by stimulation of basal retinal elements (Fig. 226). Furthermore, the data require the additional assumption that the W-substance is added to the blood more slowly than the B-substance and also disappears from the blood more slowly. The B-substance and the W-substance are antagonistic. Thus, according to this hypothesis, in an illuminated environment B-substance is always secreted, but its secretion is reduced in low illumination and in darkness. The responses to black and white illuminated backgrounds involve changes in the amount of the W-substance and consequently changes in the B/W ratio. The very slow responses observed in the change from an illuminated white background to darkness and the reverse appear explicable in terms of concomitant decreases or increases, respectively, of the two antagonistic substances. In the change from darkness to an illuminated black background the melanophores pass through a supernormal phase (more dispersed than typical for the background), a fact explainable in terms of a more rapid secretion of B-substance than of W-substance. As the latter increases to its

full quantity, the melanin reaches its slightly less dispersed final state. Similarly, in passing from an illuminated black background to darkness the melanophore passes through a transitory stage of greater concentration than the ultimate state, apparently due to a more rapid reduction in B-substance than in W-substance.

Direct evidence for the existence of the W-substance in *Xenopus* has come from observations on the responses of the animals to environmental stimuli after various types of operative procedures.[131] When the anterior lobe of the hypophysis is removed the animal responds quite as it does normally. When the anterior lobe and the pars tuberalis are extirpated, the melanophores become maximally dispersed and show no background response. When the posterior lobe is removed, the animals are maximally pale. The source of the darkening hormone appears definitely to reside in the intermediate lobe.[9, 131] Removal of the whole gland leaves the pigment slightly dispersed and nonresponsive. All these facts fit the hypothesis of the existence of two factors, with perhaps the pars tuberalis responsible for the W-substance and the posterior or the intermediate lobe for the B-substance. Support for the presence of two factors also comes from the relative effects of injection of B-substance into completely hypophysectomized *Xenopus*[131] as compared with its effects in normal animals or animals with only the posterior lobes removed (Fig. 227). As would be expected, a larger dose is required in the last two types of recipients to bring about a given response, while in those with complete hypophysectomy a smaller dose has an equivalent action. The latter observation finds a most logical explanation in terms of the resulting absence of an antagonist to MSH. A melanocyte-concentrating factor has been separated from MSH-containing extracts by differential solubility in alcohol;[66] the MCH was believed to be from the hypothalamus.

MSH darkens *Rana pipiens,* and *R. clamitans* and *Hyla,* and adrenin blanches them,[189, 291] these reactions even proceeding in isolated frog skin *in vitro.*[291] Sodium ions are specifically essential to the MSH response,[172] and the MSH response is also inhibited by iodoacetate, which suppresses glycolysis.[291] Thyroxin darkens *Xenopus,* apparently by indirect stimulation of MSH secretion.[58] ACTH disperses the melanin in *Hyla.*[66] There is suggestive evidence that

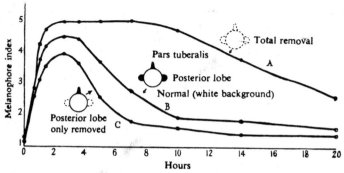

FIGURE 227. Responses of the melanophores of *Xenopus* on a white background to injection of equivalent doses of pituitary extracts into totally hypophysectomized specimens, specimens with only posterior lobe removed, and normal specimens. (From Hogben, L., and Slome, D.: Proc. Roy. Soc. London, B, vol. 120.)

frog skin itself possesses a melanocyte-concentrating factor.[255]

Fishes. The fishes, which have probably been more intensively investigated than any other group, with respect to their chromatophore system and color changes, have several types of chromatophores. The most common and conspicuous type is the melanophore. Other common types contain yellow pigment (xanthophores), red pigment (erythrophores), and white pigment (iridoleucophores). In addition, many fishes possess chromatophores containing small clusters of glistening platelike crystals that impart a bluish green structural coloration (iridosomes).

The activities of the melanophores are the principal ones involved in the conspicuous responses to light and darkness and to black and white backgrounds in fishes. The mechanism of response in fishes, as with amphibians, commonly shows a change from primary to secondary color responses during their early development. Young *Perca* and *Salmo*[65, 191] *Macropodus*,[280] and *Hoplias*[182] show a transition in response mechanism. On the other hand, a number of other species appear not to pass through a phase of primary responses but to have initially the secondary type. The latter species include *Fundulus*,[114, 293] *Lebistes, Xiphophorus, Gambusia*,[280] *Scyllium*,[287] and *Mustelus*.[203] A number of fishes normally showing secondary color responses will revert to primary responses after blinding.[280]

The secondary color responses of fishes are dependent typically upon the eyes. They involve nervous pathways to the central nervous system, thence either to endocrine glands affecting the chromatophores through blood-borne hormones, or by way of efferent nerv-ous pathways directly to the chromatophores where chemical mediators are liberated by the nerve terminations. Both hormonal and nervous mechanisms may cooperate in many cases. There is considerable variation among fishes as to the normal mechanism of control. Parker,[212] the leading investigator in the field of animal color changes, divided the fishes into three groups on the basis of the degree to which direct innervation of the melanophores is found. Dineuronic chromatophores possess double innervation with separate dispersing and concentrating fibers. Mononeuronic chromatophores possess single innervation in which the activity is always pigment concentrating. Aneuronic chromatophores possess no innervation, their secondary responses being regulated solely by activity of blood- and lymph-borne chemical factors.

The great majority of the teleost fishes thus far carefully investigated appear to possess dineuronic melanophores. One type of innervating nerve fiber, a pigment-concentrating one, is readily demonstrated by electrical stimulation of appropriate loci in the central nervous system, of central nerve tracts, or of peripheral nerves. The extent of the area of the skin blanching under this stimulation parallels the area of the skin innervated by these nervous elements. Furthermore, after denervation of any area of the skin the denervated area no longer exhibits blanching responses to stimulation of the nerves central to the point of denervation, even though responses may continue in the adjacent areas. Therefore the blanching produced by nerve stimulation in the animals is a result of localized responses at the region of the nerve terminations and is not due to freely diffusible substances in the blood. The action of the concentrating fibers is believed[209] to be medi-

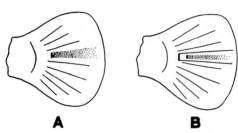

A   **B**

FIGURE 228.   *A*, dark band in caudal fin of white-adapted *Fundulus* produced by severance of radial nerves. *B*, Redarkening of a faded band following a second, more distal, cut. (From Parker, G. H.: Proc. Nat. Acad. Sci., vol. 20.)

ated through adrenin-like material which diffuses away from the nerve terminations.

The presence of a second set of fibers, pigment-dispersing ones, has been demonstrated for many teleosts through experimentation with melanophores of the tail fins. If, in a teleost such as *Fundulus,* kept on an illuminated white background, a group of the radiating caudal nerves is cut by a transverse incision, the band of fin innervated by these fibers darkens quickly and then over the course of a few days fades again[200] (Fig. 228). If now a second cut is made parallel to the first cut, and somewhat distal to it, the faded band will repeat its transient darkening. This latter behavior has led to the hypothesis that the melanophore response observed is due to a restimulation of the dispersing nerve fibers that have been transected and stimulated by the first incision. It cannot be explained simply in terms of transection of the concentrating fibers, as possibly the response to the first cut could be. Interpolation of a cold block between the point of nerve transection and the melanophores abolishes the response.[205] Such redarkening of faded bands after a second incision has been observed by a number of investigators for a number of species of teleost fishes. These include *Holocentrus,*[206] *Parasilurus,*[178] *Pterophyllum,*[281, 282] *Ameiurus,*[210] and *Gobius.*[102] An activation of melanin-dispersing fibers in the catfish tail has also been produced by electrical stimulation.[216]

Other lines of evidence, both morphological and physiological, have given further support to the hypothesis of a dual innervation of teleost melanophores. Ballowitz[13] many years ago clearly demonstrated that the melanophores of the perch receive nerve terminations from more than one fiber, thus providing an anatomical basis for the conclusions reached by more recent physiological experimentation.

Furthermore, a critical examination has been made of the responses of chromatophores at the edges of denervated caudal bands of *Fundulus,*[186] and of those near the regenerating front of nerve fibers in the course of reinnervation of denervated bands,[4] as the animals darken on black backgrounds and lighten on white ones. These observations provide suggestive evidence that many of the melanophores located in these regenerating fronts possess only one type of fiber, either concentrating or dispersing, but not both as under normal circumstances. Some of these melanophores show rapid pigment concentration and very slow dispersion; others show the reverse. Studies of the influence of drugs on chromatophores of *Phoxinus*[113] and *Fundulus*[259] also support the concept of a dual innervation.

The dispersing fibers appear to exert their action on the melanophores through the mediation of acetylcholine. Acetylcholine is known to cause dispersion of the melanin of fishes when the latter are eserinized to prevent rapid destruction of the material. In fact, a bioassay of the acetylcholine content of the skin of a dark-adapted catfish *Ameiurus*[209] or snakefish *Ophiocephalus* showed its presence in a concentration of about 0.078 gamma per gram of skin. This is approximately the concentration of acetylcholine which, when injected into the body fluids of eserinized fish, was in general nontoxic and at the same time quite effective upon melanophores.

Of the fishes thus far investigated the dogfishes *Mustelus* and *Squalus* appear to possess mononeuronic melanophores. If a transverse cut is made in the pectoral fin of a dogfish of intermediate tint a light band is produced distal to the point of the cut. Such light bands may be revived after they have redarkened[204] or may be produced by electrical excitation[202] of the integumentary nerves. These bands follow the distribution of the cut nerves and not necessarily of the blood vessels. Furthermore, light bands may be produced by a similar transverse cut in a fin from which the blood supply has been cut off. All these facts point to a nerve supply to the melanophore whose function it is to induce pigment concentration. There is no indication whatsoever that pigment-dispersing nerve fibers are present in this animal.

Parker[211] postulated that the concentrating fibers influence the melanophores through the production of a chemical mediator which he called selachine. If skin from a pale animal is extracted with ether or olive oil, but not water, the material may be extracted. Injections of an olive-oil extract of this substance into a dark-adapted animal will produce temporary lightening, which spreads very slowly from the point of injection. Olive oil by itself produces no such effect.

The other elasmobranch fishes which have been investigated, the skate *Raja*,[207] the dogfish *Scyllium*,[295] and the lamprey *Lampetra*,[296] show no evidence of direct innervation of their melanophores, and hence their melanophores are believed to be aneuronic.

Blood-borne agents typically supplement the nervous system in the secondary responses of the melanophores of fishes to light stimuli. In the more primitive fishes, such as the cyclostomes and the elasmobranchs which possess aneuronic color cells, hormones alone are the agents involved. Among these hormones an important substance is a pigment-dispersing principle from the pituitary, the B-substance of Hogben, or MSH.[297] This substance is secreted from the posterior lobe of the pituitary. Lundstrom and Bard[174] observed that hypophysectomized *Mustelus* become and remain pale. The fish may be darkened again by injection of extract of the posterior lobe. A similar role of a posterior-lobe principle has since been demonstrated for other elasmobranchs, *Raja* and *Scyllium*,[128] and the cyclostome *Lampetra*.[296]

There is some evidence that in *Scyllium* and *Raja* a second neurohumor from the pituitary acts as a pigment-concentrating agent.[128] Evidence for a role of such a body-blanching principle has been derived from studies of the characteristics of the melanophore responses to background and light-intensity changes and to the influence of hypophysectomy on the state of the pigments, and of pigmentary responses to injections of posterior-lobe extract. The general methods of experimentation and logic involved in these experiments are the same as those developed in the studies of amphibian melanophore control. According to the bihumoral concept of Hogben and his associates the state of the melanophores in these fishes is determined by the ratio of MSH to MCH present in the blood at any given instant, and this ratio is in turn controlled by visual stimuli. The visual stimuli, through differential, dorsoventral, retinal stimulation, result in different rates of secretion of the two principles by their respective sources.

The chromatic pituitary hormone involved in melanin dispersion seems also to be present and active in normal color change to a greater or lesser degree in most teleost fishes. The eel *Anguilla* shows sluggish color changes requiring days for completion.[191] In this fish, despite the apparent presence of both concentrating and dispersing nerve fibers, color changes seem predominantly determined by hormones. In its activity in the eel, MSH is believed to be assisted by an MCH.[286] That direct innervation does play some role in color changes in this fish is seen in the limited background response after hypophysectomy.

An MSH is found to be slightly less important in normal color changes in the catfish *Ameiurus*. Hypophysectomized catfishes continue to show color changes in response to black and white backgrounds but show only an intermediate degree of darkening on black.[3] Injection of posterior lobe extract will, however, completely blacken these fish. Here we must assume that blood-borne MSH supplements the action of dispersing nerve fibers in the normal responses to black backgrounds; there is as yet no evidence for the operation of an MCH in this species.

The killifish *Fundulus*, on which a vast amount of research has been done, is a species in which the dominant mechanism of melanophore control is nervous. Color changes are very rapid, only a minute or two being required for nearly maximal color change. These changes continue to occur in hypophysectomized specimens.[180] Furthermore, injection of extracts of posterior lobe into pale fish on a white background does not produce significant darkening. Since such extracts will induce darkening in denervated areas of the skin, we must conclude that the chromatophores are normally influenced to some extent by MSH which is shown to be present in their pituitaries.[6, 151] However, its normal influence is probably seen only in the production of extreme conditions of dark adaptation maintained over relatively long periods. In *Macropodus*, studies of hypophyseal influences after interference with nerve supply to the melanophores indicated that a pituitary MSH was not significantly involved.[284]

All teleost fishes thus far investigated appear to fall into a series in the relative influences of direct innervation and blood-borne hormones. A reasonable hypothesis has been advanced that the humoral control is phylogenetically the older, and that direct nervous control has been superimposed upon it in those fishes of more recent evolutionary origin.[287] Direct nerve control is associated with

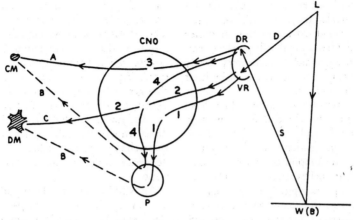

FIGURE 229. Diagram of the controlling mechanism of melanophores in the eel *Anguilla*. *L*, incident light; *W(B)*, white or black background; *DR*, dorsal retina; *VR*, ventral retina; *CNO*, central nervous system; *P*, pituitary; *A*, adrenergic fibers; *C*, cholinergic fibers; *B*, blood and lymph; *DM*, dispersed melanin; *CM*, concentrated melanin. (From Parker, G. H.: Quart. Rev. Biol., vol. 18.)

more rapid response to background, which has become possible through a simultaneous increase in the speed of the melanophore change itself. The typical teleost controlling mechanism for melanophores is diagramed in Figure 229.

A survey of the characteristics of the response of melanophores of fishes to war gases suggests the presence of two differently responding types, with catfishes possessing one type and scaly fishes the other.[231] Sodium ions appear to be peculiarly effective in inducing melanin dispersion in *Fundulus*,[107] recalling its role in contributing to MSH action in frogs.

Very much less is known about the control of the erythrophores, xanthophores, iridoleucophores, and iridosomes than about the control of the melanophores. The erythrophores of the squirrelfish *Holocentrus* are rapidly responding effector organs.[206] Through their activity the fish can change from red to white in about 5 seconds, and make the reverse change in about 20 seconds. These responses may be induced by change from black to white background and vice versa. Transection of nerve tracts in a fish on a white background results in dispersion of red pigment. The areas blanch again in a short while and may be darkened again by a second more distal cut, indicating the presence of dispersing nerve fibers. The presence of concentrating nerve fibers can be demonstrated by electrical stimulation of the medulla, resulting in rapid concentration of pigment of all innervated erythrophores. Experimentally denervated cells fail to give this response.

Adrenin concentrates the pigment. Pituitary extracts from other squirrelfish produce no effect when injected into normal light-adapted or dark-adapted specimens. It thus appears that the erythrophores of *Holocentrus* normally are exclusively under nervous control.[261] The erythrophores of *Phoxinus*, on the other hand, have been shown to be influenced by a principle from the hypophysis.[113, 121]

The xanthophores of *Fundulus* appear to possess double innervation, comprising concentrating and dispersing fibers.[101] A concentrating hormone, probably adrenin, also appears to be responsible for the concentration of the pigment which results from handling of the fish. This latter concentration occurs as rapidly in denervated xanthophores as in innervated ones. On the other hand, intraperitoneal implantation of *Fundulus* pituitaries into hypophysectomized specimens induces pigment dispersion in denervated xanthophores, regardless of color of background. Such implants also impede the typical pigment concentration in innervated cells in response to blue or white backgrounds.[103] It therefore appears that several factors normally influence the state of the xanthophores in this species. Melanophores and xanthophores of *Fundulus* react independently in background responses.[5]

A number of fishes, including *Fundulus*, possess reflecting-white chromatophores known as guanophores or iridoleucophores.[100] These may show physiological changes in the adaptive responses of the fish to background. They continue to respond to background after hypophysectomy and after sufficient dosage of the fish with ergotamine to prevent any response of the accompanying melanophores. They disperse their pigment under the influence of adrenin.[194] In *Bathygobius,* experiments involving nerve transections and hypophysectomy led to the conclusion that the iridoleucophores are regulated importantly by local innervation, though they are also hormonally influenced.[104]

Iridosomes play only a passive role in adaptive color changes, becoming more or less obscured through activity of the other chromatophore types. Normally these bodies are green or blue. They are highly responsive to certain environmental stimuli, changing reversibly through the spectral colors to red on excitation and in the opposite direction on recovery. This response is direct and does not involve coordinating mechanisms within the animal, either nervous or humoral.[96]

Reptiles. The regulatory system of the melanophores of reptiles shows, as in the fishes, a great diversity. It appears to involve, to differing degrees in different reptiles, the activities of hormones and nerves.

The melanophore responses of the iguanid *Anolis* have been investigated extensively by Kleinholz.[152] These lizards show a color change ranging from bright green to dark brown. They typically assume the former color in an illuminated white container and the latter in an illuminated black one. The response to change from a white to black background is usually completed in 5 to 10 minutes. The reverse change normally requires 20 to 30 minutes. These background-induced responses depend on the eyes; they cease after bilateral blinding. However, such blinded specimens still are capable of color change; they darken in light and become pale in darkness, through primary responses.

For many years after Brücke's[50] classic studies of color change in the chameleon, in which he demonstrated nervous control of the melanophores by the sympathetic system, it was considered that reptilian chromatophores generally were thus controlled. Studies on *Phrynosoma,*[233] however, provided basis for a strong suspicion that nerves were not the sole method of control. The lizard *Hemidactylus* becomes pale in color after hypophysectomy. Hypophysectomized *Anolis* remain permanently bright green[152] (Fig. 230). They no longer darken in response to a black background or bright light. They can be darkened readily by injection of extracts of whole pituitary of fishes or the intermediate

lobes of frogs or reptiles. The melanophores of the rattlesnake appear also to be normally dispersed by a principle from the pituitary.[232]

Transection of nerves, such as section of the spinal cord at various levels, or cutting the sciatic nerve in *Anolis,* in no way interferes with the normal color responses. In fact, attempts at histologic demonstration of nerve terminations at the melanophores have been uniformly unsuccessful. Skin grafts very soon show color changes which are synchronous with those of the host. Exclusion of the blood supply from any region, on the other hand, results in a paling of the region in about 15 minutes.

The roles of the animal's own hypophysis and adrenals can be shown by electrical stimulation with one electrode placed in the cloaca and the other in the mouth. Stimulated pale animals kept in darkness become uniformly dark brown. Denervated areas respond just as do the innervated ones. Similar stimulation of hypophysectomized specimens gives, on the other hand, a characteristic mottling of the body. This last is not obtained after both adrenalectomy and hypophysectomy. Furthermore, injection of adrenin or of extracts of the animal's own adrenals in Ringer solution produces the typical mottling. Adrenalectomized animals lighten in response to a white background. All of these observations, and others, point strongly to the conclusion that the melanin in *Anolis* normally disperses in response to MSH from the intermediate lobe, and that its gradual disappearance from the circulation suffices to account for lightening. Rapid blanching which normally follows electrical stimulation or excitement may perhaps be accounted for by integumentary vasoconstrictor activity, and under some circumstances by the production of adrenin.

Light appears to have no significant influence on the melanophore state in intact *Anolis,* other than through the eyes.

The available evidence indicates roles of both nerves and hormones in the melanophore responses of the iguanid, *Phrynosoma.* The early work of Redfield[233] on this form has been largely confirmed and considerably extended by Parker.[208] These animals are normally gray with characteristic black patches. The latter patches show no color changes, whereas the intervening area varies with appropriate stimulation from dark gray to pale grayish white. These changes are due primarily to melanophore activities. Darkening of the animal occurs in about 15 minutes,

FIGURE 230. A normal dark and a hypophysectomized light *Anolis.* (From Kleinholz, L. H.: J. Exp. Biol., vol. 15.)

and lightening in approximately twice that time.

Phrynosoma darkens on an illuminated black background, at low temperatures, and in response to very strong illumination. It lightens on an illuminated white background, at high temperatures, and in darkness.

The melanophores are normally under the influence of pigment-concentrating nerve fibers. Stimulation of a sciatic nerve will induce lightening in the corresponding hind leg. Electrical stimulation of the roof of the mouth or of the cloaca results in a paling of the whole animal, which is quickly reversible. Following denervation of a region of the body, leg, or lateral trunk, similar stimulation results in a lightening of all regions except the denervated one, despite the fact that the melanophores in the denervated area still show pigment concentration in response to an injection of adrenin. No indication of pigment-dispersing fibers has been uncovered in this species.

Phrynosoma, like *Anolis,* after hypophysectomy becomes pale and remains so indefinitely. Injection of extract of *Phrynosoma*

pituitary induces strong darkening either in normal pale or in hypophysectomized individuals. Furthermore, injection of defibrinated blood from a dark specimen into the leg of a pale one produces darkening in the latter. These results provide strong evidence that a pituitary MSH is normally concerned in body darkening. An action of a pigment-concentrating hormone is also seen in that adrenalin or extract of *Phrynosoma* adrenals strongly blanches dark specimens. The presence of a similarly acting agent in the blood of white-adapted animals is seen in that their defibrinated blood will, on injection into a leg of a dark specimen, lighten the latter. It has been known for a long time that animals held on their back or otherwise stimulated to struggle vigorously will lighten rapidly. By comparison of the influences of denervation and occlusion of blood supply on the production of this type of lightening it can be clearly demonstrated that a blood-borne agent is involved. These observations lead to the obvious conclusion that the paling is brought about by two methods, nervous and hormonal, either one alone capable of producing the response.

Both the dispersing hormone from the pituitary and the concentrating hormone from the adrenals operate directly on the melanophores; each is capable of exhibiting its complete action after nerve transection and degeneration of the nerve fibers.

The influence of temperature and of light and darkness on the melanophores of *Phrynosoma* is a direct one, in which the melanophores act as independent effectors. The responses may be obtained locally by application of the stimulus to the specific region in completely denervated portions of the body. Since even degeneration of the innervating fibers does not result in termination of the response, axon reflexes cannot be responsible.

The coordination of the melanophores of chameleons *Chamaeleo* or *Lophosaura,* unlike that in the iguanids, appears to be exclusively nervous.[129] Nerve transection is followed by a darkening of the area normally innervated. These nerves are of the autonomic nervous system. The melanophores are readily caused to concentrate their pigment by electrical stimulation of the nerves. The results of nerve transection have been interpreted to be the result of the absence of tonic impulses reaching the pigment cells.[237, 298] There is no clear evidence as yet that the pigment is actively dispersed by a second set of nerve fibers, as appears to be true of many teleosts.

There is little or nothing known for the most part as to possible roles of hormones in the color changes in the chameleon, but the fact that color patterns can be produced on the body by alternate light and shadow[50] argues against any substantial importance of such factors.

The melanophores of intact animals respond to light and darkness by pigment dispersion and concentration, respectively. Dark regions produced by denervation show no such responses. These results were interpreted by Zoond and Eyre[298] to prove that the responses of the melanophores can occur only by way of reflexes involving the central nervous system. But Parker[208] has pointed out the possibility of an alternative interpretation, that the pigment cells in these forms may show direct response when their state is not determined by a dominating mechanism.

In summary: We appear to find among the reptiles, as with fishes, a spectrum of mechanisms of coordination of the chromatophores, ranging from systems involving probably primitive hormonal control, through those in which both nerves and hormones cooperate, to those largely dominated by direct innervation.

FUNCTIONAL SIGNIFICANCE OF CHROMATOPHORES AND COLOR CHANGE

Since the responses of the chromatophores are predominantly responses to color or shade of background, one is led to the hypothesis that the color changes contribute significantly to the obliterative coloration of the animal for protection or aggression and hence increase its chances for survival. Among the few experimental demonstrations that animal color changes do actually increase chances for survival, a view often questioned, is that of Sumner,[272] in which he found that fishes given time to change their coloration were seized in smaller percentages by a predatory bird than were unadapted ones. Similarly, in insects, *Acrida* and *Oedipoda* larvae were found captured to smaller extent by birds when the insects were on backgrounds of their adaptation coloration.[74] It has also been clearly demonstrated that fishes which are black adapted tend to select black backgrounds when given choice of black or white, more commonly than do white-adapted individuals[43, 176] (Fig. 231), and that the rate

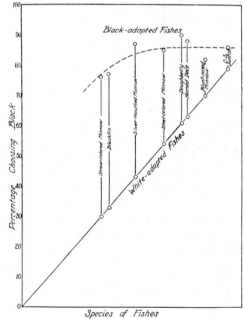

FIGURE 231. Percentage choice of a black over a white background for each of eight species of fishes adapted to black and white backgrounds. (From Brown, F. A., Jr., and Thompson, D. H.: Copeia, vol. 3.)

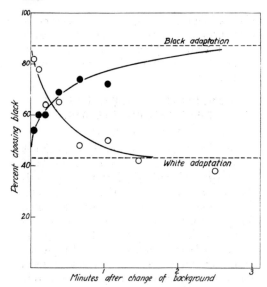

FIGURE 232. The rate of change in percentage choice of a black background following transfer of *Ericymba* from a black to a white background and vice versa. (From Brown, F. A., Jr., and Thompson, D. H.: Copeia, vol. 3.)

of change of choice with change of background in *Ericymba* is approximately the same as the change in skin coloration (Fig. 232). Fishes with more rapid and striking color changes seem to have their choice more strongly modified along with background adaptation than do ones with less effective changes. The crayfish *Cambarus* also appears to possess an adaptive background selection.[28]

Chromatophores appear also to serve in the protection of animals from bright illumination which may be deleterious. In some animals, e.g., certain leeches and sea urchins, the chromatophore pigment disperses only in response to bright illumination and with no regard to a possible protective coloration in relation to the background. The black and white pigments in the crab *Uca* are normally dispersed in light during the daytime and concentrated in darkness at night. This is due partly to an inherent rhythm and partly to a response to total illumination. It is also noteworthy in this regard that the white chromatophores of such brilliant-light–inhabiting Sargasso-weed crustaceans as *Latreutes fucorum*, *Leander tenuicornis*, and *Hippolyte acuminata* are very abundant and richly charged with reflecting white pigment. In bright illumination this pigment disperses broadly, providing a continuous layer of a very effective diffusing reflector. Since the primary color responses of animals are those of pigment dispersal in light and pigment con-

centration in darkness, it appears reasonable to postulate that this light-protective function of chromatophores is a primitive one, with a role in obliterative coloration appearing later in evolution of chromatophore systems. The formation of melanin in human skin in response to bright sunlight, is, in effect, a morphological color change of this same character.

Another function which has been attributed to chromatophores is thermoregulation.[14, 197] The desert lizard *Phrynosoma*, is light at night and during midday and dark during the early morning and late afternoon.[166] These and similar observations have led to the hypothesis that the chromatophores function in thermoregulation in this species. The animal apparently is adaptively controlling heat absorption and radiation at the various times of day by chromatophore activities. Strongly supporting this view are the observations of numerous investigators of reptilian color change that elevation of the body temperature to approximately 40°C leads to melanin concentration and that lowering of the temperature to about 5°C leads to dispersion.[208] The black pigment of the crab *Uca* also tends to concentrate as the body temperature is elevated to about 25 to 30°C.[40] These conditions obviously result in control of the amount of light absorbed by the black pigment in a manner beneficial to the animal. The differential reflection of light from frog skin, favoring reflection of the longer, heating wavelengths, together with reflectance changes correlated with the color changes also supports a thermoregulatory role.[59]

One additional role of color changes in animals is suggested by the color displays that sometimes accompany mating behavior in such species as *Anolis*.[116] During pairing the males show a striking change from green to brown. Color displays are also associated with the breeding season in certain teleosts and cephalopods. The importance of these mating color displays is unknown. Special nuptial morphological color changes are not infrequently associated with the breeding season.[215]

SUMMARY

Color changes involving movements of pigments, and increases or decreases of pigments, within special bodies in the integument, the chromatophores, have been observed among reptiles, amphibians, teleosts, elasmobranchs, cyclostomes, crustaceans, insects, cephalopods, annelids, and echinoderms. These color changes are most characteristically ones involving adaptive adjustment of the animal to the color of its background through a functional relationship between the eyes and the chromatophores, although total illumination, temperature, humidity, tactile stimuli, endogenous rhythms, and numerous other factors may also influence the color changes.

The reflex pathways, initiated at the eyes, which are responsible for the control of the color changes in all crustaceans, insects, amphibians, and many fishes and reptiles, involve hormones. Both blood-borne hormones and direct innervation operate importantly in most other species, with the possible exception of the chameleon among the reptiles and such fishes as *Fundulus* and *Macropodus* among the teleosts, and possibly also in leeches where nervous reflexes possess dominant or exclusive control. Responses of the chromatophore system to light continue in most animals in the absence of the eyes, either through the responses of the chromatophores acting as independent effectors or reflexly through other light receptors, e.g., the pineal complex. These latter are responses only to intensity of illumination and bear no relation to color of background, and typically operate to render the animal darker in higher illumination and lighter in lower.

Several functions have been ascribed to the chromatophore system, among them being: (1) protective and aggressive coloration; (2) thermoregulation; (3) protection of the body tissues from intense illumination; and (4) mating color displays.

REFERENCES

1. ABRAMOWITZ, A. A., Proc. Nat. Acad. Sci. *21*: 132-137, 1935. Morphological color change, *Fundulus* xanthophores.
2. ABRAMOWITZ, A. A., Proc. Nat. Acad. Sci. *21*: 677-681, 1935. Adaptation to colored backgrounds, Crustacea.
3. ABRAMOWITZ, A. A., Biol. Bull. *71*: 259-281, 1936. Hypophysis and color change in Ameiurus.
4. ABRAMOWITZ, A. A., Proc. Nat. Acad. Sci. *22*: 233-238, 1936. Dual innervation of teleost melanophores.
5. ABRAMOWITZ, A. A., Am. Naturalist *70*: 372-378, 1936. Independence of action of melanophores and xanthophores, Fundulus.
6. ABRAMOWITZ, A. A., Biol. Bull. *73*: 134-142, 1937. Role of hypophysis in Fundulus color change.
7. ABRAMOWITZ, A. A., and ABRAMOWITZ, R. K., Biol. Bull. *74*: 278-296, 1938. Diurnal rhythm and chromatophore state, Crustacea.
8. ASCHERSON, Arch. Anat. Physiol. wiss. Med. *7*: 15-23, 1840. Color change, frog.
9. ATWELL, W. J., and HOLLEY, E., J. Exp. Zool. *73*: 23-42, 1936. Pituitary in amphibian color change.
10. ATZLER, M., Ztschr. vergl. Physiol. *13*: 505-533, 1930. Relation of eyes to *Carausius* color change.
11. BÁBÀK, E., Arch. ges. Physiol. *131*: 78-118, 1910. Color change in young Amphibia.
12. BÁBÀK, E., Arch. ges. Physiol. *149*: 462-470, 1913. Relationship of morphological to physiological color change, vertebrates.
13. BALLOWITZ, E., Ztschr. wiss. Zool. *56*: 673-706. 1893. Innervation of melanophores of teleosts.
14. BAUER, V., Ztschr. allg. Physiol. *16*: 191-212, 1914. Melanophores in heat regulation.
15. BOWMAN, T. E., Am. Naturalist *76*: 332-336, 1942. Morphological color change, Cambarus.
16. BOWMAN, T. E., Biol. Bull. *96*: 238-245, 1949. Chromatophore hormones in Hemigrapsus.
17. BOZLER, E., Ztschr. vergl. Physiol. *7*: 379-406, 1928. Cephalopod chromatophores and their innervation.
18. BOZLER, E., Ztschr. vergl. Physiol. *8*: 371-390, 1929. Cephalopod chromatophores and their innervation.
19. BRECHER, L., Arch. Entw.-Mech. *45*: 273-322, 1919. Color change in insect pupae.
20. BRECHER, L., Arch. Entw.-Mech. *50*: 40-78, 1922. Color change in insect pupae.
21. BRECHER, L., Arch. Entw.-Mech. *50*: 209-308, 1922. Color change in insect pupae.
22. BRECHER, L., Arch. Mikr. Anat. *102*: 501-548, 1924. Color change in insect pupae.
23. BROWN, F. A., JR., Proc. Nat. Acad. Sci. *19*: 327-329, 1933. Chromatophorotropins from the crustacean central nervous system.
24. BROWN, F. A., JR., Biol. Bull. *57*: 365-380, 1934. Morphological color change; Palaemonetes.
25. BROWN, F. A., JR., J. Morphol. *57*: 317-333, 1935. Adaptation to colored backgrounds, Crustacea. Behavior of chromatophores in color change in Palaemonetes.
26. BROWN, F. A., JR., J. Exp. Zool. *71*: 1-15, 1935. Functional independence of pigments, crustaceans.
27. BROWN, F. A., JR., Biol. Bull. *70*: 8-15, 1936. Total illumination and chromatophore state, fishes; ratio of incident to reflected light and color change; measurement of chromatophore activity.
28. BROWN, F. A., JR., Ecology *20*: 507-516, 1939. Adaptive background selection by crayfishes.
29. BROWN, F. A., JR., Physiol. Zool. *13*: 343-355, 1940. Crustacean sinus gland and color change.
30. BROWN, F. A., JR., Physiol. Zool. *19*: 215-223, 1946. Central nervous sources of crustacean chromatophorotopins; measurement of chromatophore activity.
31. BROWN, F. A., JR., Biol. Bull. *98*: 218-226, 1950. Responses of Uca red chromatophores.
32. BROWN, F. A., JR., Action of Hormones in Plants and Invertebrates. New York, Academic Press, 1952. Review of crustacean color change.
33. BROWN, F. A., JR., Science *130*: 1535-1544, 1959. Timing of biological rhythms.
34. BROWN, F. A., JR., and EDERSTROM, H. E., J. Exp. Zool. *85*: 53-69, 1940. Chromatophoro-

tropins from the crustacean central nervous system.

35. BROWN, F. A., JR., Fingerman, M., and HINES, M. N., Biol. Bull. *106*: 308-317, 1954. Shifting phases of color change rhythm.

36. BROWN, F. A., JR., FINGERMAN, M., SANDEEN, M. I., and WEBB, H. M., J. Exp. Zool. *123*: 29-60, 1953. Tidal and monthly rhythms of color change in Uca.

37. BROWN, F. A., JR., and HINES, M. N., Physiol. Zool. *25*: 56-70, 1952. Persistent modifications of daily color change cycles.

38. BROWN, F. A., JR., and KLOTZ, I. M., Proc. Soc. Exp. Biol. Med. *64*: 310-313, 1947. Chemical separation of chromatophorotropins from Crustacean central nervous system.

39. BROWN, F. A., JR., and SAIGH, L. M., Biol. Bull. *91*: 170-180, 1946. Central nervous sources of chromatophorotropins, Crustacea.

40. BROWN, F. A., JR., and SANDEEN, M. I., Physiol. Zool. *21*: 361-371, 1948. Uca color response to light and temperature; light intensity and Uca color change.

41. BROWN, F. A., JR., and SCUDAMORE, H. H., J. Cell. Comp. Physiol. *15*: 103-119, 1940. Two chromatophorotropins from crustacean sinus glands.

42. BROWN, F. A., JR., and STEPHENS, G. C., Biol. Bull. *101*: 71-83, 1951. Persistent modification of daily color-change cycles by photoperiod.

43. BROWN, F. A., JR., and THOMPSON, D. H., Copeia 3: 172-181, 1937. Adaptive background selection by fishes.

44. BROWN, F. A., JR., and WEBB, H. M., Physiol. Zool. *21*: 371-381, 1948. Diurnal rhythm in Uca color change.

45. BROWN, F. A., JR., and WEBB, H. M., Physiol. Zool. *22*: 136-148, 1949. Shifting by light of phases of color-change rhythm.

46. BROWN, F. A., JR., WEBB, H. M., and BENNETT, M. F., Proc. Nat. Acad. Sci. *41*: 93-100, 1955. Color change rhythms during change of longitude.

47. BROWN, F. A., JR., WEBB, H. M., BENNETT, M. F., and SANDEEN, M. I., Physiol. Zool. *27*: 345-349, 1954. Temperature independence, tidal rhythm of color change.

48. BROWN, F. A., JR., WEBB, H. M., and SANDEEN, M. I., J. Exp. Zool. *120*: 391-420, 1952. Dual control of Palaemonetes red chromatophores.

49. BROWN, F. A., JR., and WULFF, V. J., J. Cell. Comp. Physiol. *18*: 339-353, 1941. Chromatophorotropins from the crustacean central nervous system.

50. BRÜCKE, E., Denkschr. Akad. Wiss. Wien. *4*: 179-210, 1852. Color changes in the Chameleon.

51. BUCHHOLZ, R., Arch. Anat. Physiol. wiss. Med. pp. 71-81, 1863. Color changes, fishes.

52. BÜCKMANN, D., J. Insect Physiol. *3*: 159-189, 1959. Control of prepupal color change in Cerura caterpillars.

53. BUERGERS, A. C. J., BOSCHMAN, T., and VAN DER KAMER, J. C., Acta Endocrinol. *14*: 72-82, 1953. Xenopus darkening by adrenin and in excitement.

54. BUTCHER, E. O., J. Exp. Zool. *79*: 275-297, 1938. Relation of portions of eyes to color changes, fishes.

55. CARLISLE, D. B., and KNOWLES, F. G. W., Endocrine Control in Crustaceans. Cambridge University Press, 1959, 120 pp.

56. CARSTAM, S. P., Nature *167*: 321-322, 1951. Enzyme inactivating red-pigment—concentrating factor.

57. CARSTAM, S. P., and SUNESON, S., Kungl. Fysiogr. Sällskap. Lund. Förhandl. *19*: 1-5, 1949. Isopod chromatophorotropins.

58. CHANG, C. Y., Science *126*: 121-122, 1957. Thyroxine and Xenopus melanophores.

59. DEANIN, G. G., and STEGGERDA, F. R., Proc. Soc. Exp. Biol. Med. *67*: 101-104, 1948. Light reflection from frog skin.

60. DUPONT-RAABE, M., Arch. Zool. Exp. Gèn. *86*: 32-39, 1949. Regulation of color change in Corethra.

61. DUPONT-RAABE, M., C. R. Acad. Sci. *228*: 130-132, 1949. Chromatophorotropins of insects.

62. DUPONT-RAABE, M., Ann. Biol. *32*: 247-282, 1956. Mechanism of color change in insects.

63. DÜRKEN, B., Ztschr. wiss. Zool. *116*: 587-626, 1916. Color change in insect pupae.

64. DÜRKEN, B., Arch. Mikr. Anat. *99*: 222-389, 1923. Color change in insect pupae.

65. DUSPIVA, F., S.-B. Acad. Wiss. Wien. Math.-Nat. Kl. *140*: 553-596, 1931. Color change in young fishes.

66. EDGREN, R. A., Proc. Soc. Exp. Biol. Med. *85*: 229-230, 1954. Hyla darkening by ACTH.

67. EDGREN, R. A., Proc. Soc. Exp. Biol. Med. *87*: 20-23, 1954. Hyla color change and temperature.

68. ENAMI, M., Biol. Bull. *100*: 28-43, 1951. Neurosecretion and color change in Eriocheir.

69. ENAMI, M., Biol. Bull. *101*: 241-258, 1951. Neurosecretion and color change in Sesarma.

70. ENAMI, M., Science *121*: 36-37, 1955. A melanocyte-concentrating factor.

71. ERGENE, S., Ztschr. vergl. Physiol. *32*: 530-551, 1950; *34*: 69-74, 159-165, 1952; *35*: 36-41, 1953; *37*: 221-229, 1955; *38*: 311-316, 1956. Adaptation to colored backgrounds in Orthoptera.

72. ERGENE, S., Zool. Jahrb. *81*: 604-609, 1953. Color adaptation in Orthopterans without molting.

73. ERGENE, S., Zool. Anzeiger. *153*: 110-113, 1954. Color change in adult Oedaleus without molting.

74. ERGENE, S., Mitt. Zool. Mus. Berlin *29*: 127-133, 1953. Selective value of background color adaptation.

75. FABRE, R., and LEDERER, E., Bull. Soc. Chim. Biol. *16*: 105-118, 1934. Chemical nature pigments, Crustaceans.

76. FALK, S., and RHODIN, J., Proc. Stockholm Conf. Electron Microsc. Stockholm, Almquist and Wiksells, 1957. Electron micrographic study of teleost chromatophore.

77. FAURE, J. C., Bull. Ent. Res. *23*: 293-405, 1932. Color change in Locusts.

78. FINGERMAN, M., Biol. Bull. *109*: 255-264, 1955. Tidal rhythms of color change in Callinectes.

79. FINGERMAN, M., Biol. Bull. *110*: 274-290, 1956. Tidal rhythms of color change in Uca; phasing of color-change tidal rhythm by tides.

80. FINGERMAN, M., J. Exp. Zool. *133*: 87-106, 1956. Response of Callinectes melanophores to background, light and temperature.

81. FINGERMAN, M., Science *123*: 585-586, 1956. Uca pigment-concentrating factor.

82. FINGERMAN, M., Tulane Stud. Zool. *3*: 139-148, 1956. Hormones and Ligia chromatophores.

83. FINGERMAN, M., Tulane Stud. Zool. *5*: 137-148, 1957. Dual control of Cambarellus red chromatophores; background responses in Cambarellus.

84. FINGERMAN, M., Biol. Bull. *112*: 7-20, 1957. Phasing of tidal rhythm of color change in nature.

85. FINGERMAN, M., Am. Naturalist *91*: 167-178, 1957. Review of crustacean tidal rhythms of color change.

86. FINGERMAN, M., Am. Midl. Nat. *60*: 71-83, 1958. Chromatophore system of Orconectes.

87. FINGERMAN, M., Tulane Stud. Zool. *7*: 21-30, 1959. Electrophoretic separation of crayfish chromatophorotropins.

88. FINGERMAN, M., Internat. Rev. Cytol. *8*: 175-210, 1959. Review: physiology of chromatophores.

89. FINGERMAN, M., and AOTO, T., J. Exp. Zool. *138*: 25-50, 1958. Electrophoretic separation of color-change hormones of crayfish.

90. FINGERMAN, M., and AOTO, T., Physiol. Zool. *31*: 193-208, 1958. Crayfish hormones and long-term color adaptation.

91. FINGERMAN, M., and LOWE, M. E., Physiol. Zool. *30*: 216-231, 1957. Crayfish color-change ability facilitated by use, sluggish with disuse.

92. FINGERMAN, M., and LOWE, M. E., Tulane Stud. Zool. *5*: 149-171, 1957. Rate of hormone secretion following background change in Cambarellus.

93. FINGERMAN, M., LOWE, M. E., and MOBBERLY, W. C., Limnol. Oceanog. *3*: 271-282, 1958. Phasing of tidal rhythm of color change.

94. FINGERMAN, M., SANDEEN, M. I., and LOWE, M. E., Physiol. Zool. *32*: 128-149, 1959. Color-change hormones of Palaemonetes.

95. FINGERMAN, M., and TINKLE, D. W., Biol. Bull. *110*: 144-152, 1956. Response of white chromatophores of Palaemonetes to light, temperature, and background.

96. FOSTER, K. W., Proc. Nat. Acad. Sci. *19*: 535-540, 1933. Control of iridosome changes in Fundulus.

97. FOX, D. L., Ann. Rev. Biochem. *16*: 443-470, 1947. Chemical nature of pigments, review.

98. FOX, D. L., Animal Biochromes and Structural Colors. Cambridge University Press, 1953.

99. FREDERICQ, L., Arch. Zool. expér. gén. *7*: 535-583, 1878. Control color change, Cephalopods.

100. FRIES, E. F. B., Proc. Nat. Acad. Sci. *28*: 396-401, 1942. Control of Fundulus leucophores.

101. FRIES, E. F. B., Biol. Bull. *82*: 261-272, 1942. Control of Fundulus xanthophores.

102. FRIES, E. F. B., Biol. Bull. *82*: 273-283, 1942. Dual innervation of teleost melanophores.

103. FRIES, E. F. B., Physiol Zool. *16*: 199-212, 1943. Control of Fundulus xanthophores.

104. FRIES, E. F. B., J. Morphol. *103*: 203-254, 1958. Physiology of Fundulus reflecting chromatophores.

105. FRIZA, F., Ztschr. vergl. Physiol. *8*: 289-336, 1928. Diurnal color changes in Mantids.

106. FUCHS, R. F., Winterstein, Handb. vergl. Physiol. *3*, pt. 1: 1189-1656, 1914. Color change, review.

107. FUGII, R., J. Fac. Sci., Tokyo, Sec. IV, *8*: 371-380, 1959. Melanin dispersion in Fundulus by sodium ions.

108. GABRITSCHEVSKY, E., J. Exp. Zool. *47*: 251-267, 1927. Color changes in spider, Misumena.

109. GAMBLE, F. W., and KEEBLE, F. W., Quart. J. Micr. Sci. *43*: 589-698, 1900. Color changes, crustaceans; influence of temperature.

110. VON GELDERN, C. E., Proc. California Acad. Sci. Sec. IV *10*: 77-117, 1921. Chromatophore activity, Reptilia.

111. GIERSBERG, H., Ztschr. vergl. Physiol. *7*: 657-695, 1928. Color change in *Carausius;* influence of humidity.

112. GIERSBERG, H., Ztschr. vergl. Physiol. *9*: 523-552, 1929. Temperature and morphological color changes, insects.

113. GIERSBERG, H., Ztschr. vergl. Physiol. *13*: 258-279, 1930. Control of erythrophores of Phoxinus; influence of drugs.

114. GILSON, A. S., JR., J. Exp. Zool. *45*: 415-455, 1926. Color change in young fishes.

115. GOODWIN, T. W., *in* The Physiology of the Crustacea, edited by T. H. Waterman. New York, Academic Press, 1960, vol. 1, pp. 101-140.

116. HADLEY, C. E., Bull. Mus. Comp. Zool. *69*: 108-114, 1929. Color changes during mating of lizards.

117. HANSTRÖM, B., Zool. Jahrb. Abt. Anat. Ontog. Tiere. *56*: 387-520, 1933. The crustacean sinus gland.

118. HANSTRÖM, B., Proc. Nat. Acad. Sci. *21*: 584-585, 1935. Sinus gland and color change, Crustacea.

119. HANSTRÖM, B., Kungl. Svenska Vetenskap. Handl. *16*: 1-99, 1937. Relation of portions of eyes to color changes, Crustacea. Crustacean sinus gland and color change.

120. HANSTRÖM, B., Kungl. Fysiogr. Sällsk. Handl. N. F. *49*: 1-10, 1938. Relation of portions of eyes to color changes, Crustacea.

121. HEALEY, E. G., J. Exp. Biol. *31*: 473-490, 1954. Color change control in Phoxinus.

122. HEMPELMANN, F., Ztschr. wiss. Zool. *152*: 353-383, 1939. Color change, Polychaetes.

123. HIDAKA, T., Annot. Zool. Japan. *29*: 69-74, 1956. Control of pupal color in Lepidoptera.

124. HILL, A. V., PARKINSON, J. L., and SOLANDT, D. Y., J. Exp. Biol. *12*: 397-399, 1935. Measurement of chromatophore activity.

125. HITCHCOCK, H. B., Biol. Bull. *80*: 26-30, 1941. Adaptation to colored backgrounds, Crustacea.

126. HOFMANN, F. G., Arch. Mikr. Anat. *70*: 361-413, 1907. Innervation, cephalopod chromatophore.

127. HOGBEN, L. T., The Pigmentary Effector System. Edinburgh, Oliver and Boyd, 1924. 152 pp.

128. HOGBEN, L. T., Proc. Roy. Soc. London B, *120*: 142-158, 1936. Hypophysis in elasmobranch melanophore control.

129. HOGBEN, L. T., and MIRVISH, L., Brit. J. Exp.

Biol. *5*: 295-308, 1928. Control of color changes in Chameleons.

130. HOGBEN, L., and SLOME, D., Proc. Roy. Soc. London, B, *108*: 10-53, 1931. Mechanism of chromatophore control, *Xenopus*.

131. HOGBEN, L., and SLOME, D., Proc. Roy. Soc. London, B, *120*: 158-173, 1936. Mechanism of chromatophore control, *Xenopus*.

132. HOGBEN, L., and WINTON, F. R., Proc. Roy. Soc. London, B, *93*: 318-329, 1922. Hypophysis and amphibian color change.

133. HOGBEN, L., and WINTON, F. R., Proc. Roy. Soc. London, B, *94*: 151-162, 1922. Hypophysis and amphibian color change.

134. HOGBEN, L., and WINTON, F. R., Proc. Roy. Soc. London, B, *95*: 15-30, 1923. Hypophysis and amphibian color change.

135. HOOKER, D., Am. J. Anat. *16*: 237-250, 1914. Color change in young Rana.

136. HOSOI, T., J. Fac. Sci. Imp. Univ. Tokyo *3*: 265-270, 1934. Chromatophorotropins from the crustacean central nervous system.

137. HUDSON, B., and BENTLEY, G. A., Lancet *1*: 775, 1955. Adrenin darkening in Xenopus.

138. JANDA, V., Zool. Anz. *115*: 177-185, 1936. Color change in skin transplants in *Dixippus*.

139. JANZEN, R., Ztschr. Morph. Okol. Tiere *24*: 327-341, 1932. Color change, leeches.

140. JANZEN, R., Zool. Anz. *101*: 35-40, 1932. Color changes, leeches; Hemiclepsis and Glossiphonia.

141. JOHNSON, L. P., Tr. Am. Micr. Soc. *56*: 42-48, 1939. Color changes, Euglena.

142. JOHNSON, L. P., and JAHN, T., Physiol. Zool. *15*: 89-94, 1942. Color changes, Euglena.

143. KAESTNER, H., Arch. Entw.-Mech. Org. *124*: 1-16, 1931. Temperature and morphological color change, insects.

144. KALMUS, H., Ztschr. vergl. Physiol. *25*: 494-508, 1938. Diurnal rhythm in *Carausius* color change.

145. KEEBLE, F. W., and GAMBLE, F. W., Proc. Roy. Soc. London, B, *65*: 461-468, 1900. Functional independence of pigments, crustaceans.

146. KEEBLE, F. W., and GAMBLE, F. W., Proc. Roy. Soc. London, B, *71*: 69-71, 1903. Color changes, crustaceans.

147. KEEBLE, F. W., and GAMBLE, F. W., Philosoph. Tr. Roy. Soc. London, B, *196*: 295-388, 1904. Relationship of morphological to physiological color change, crustaceans.

148. KEEBLE, F. W., and GAMBLE, F. W., Phil. Tr. Roy. Soc. London, B, *198*: 1-16, 1905. Color changes, crustaceans.

149. KETTERER, B., and REMILTON, E., J. Endocrinol. *11*: 7-18, 1954. Xenopus darkening by adrenin and in excitement.

150. KEY, K. H. L., and DAY, M. F., Australian J. Zool. *2*: 309-363, 1954. Primary color change in grasshopper, Kosciuscola.

151. KLEINHOLZ, L. H., Biol. Bull. *69*: 379-390, 1935. Role of hypophysis in Fundulus color changes.

152. KLEINHOLZ, L. H., J. Exp. Biol. *15*: 474-499, 1938. Control of color changes in Anolis.

153. KLEINHOLZ, L. H., Pubbl. Staz. Zool. Napoli *17*: 53-57, 1938. Color change, echinoderm.

154. KNIGHT, H. H., Ann. Ent. Soc. America *17*: 258-272, 1924. Temperature and morphological color change, insects.

155. KNOWLES, F. G. W., Physiol. Comp. Oecol. *2*: 284-296, 1952. Color changes after sinus gland removal.

156. KNOWLES, F. G. W., Proc. Roy. Soc., London, B, *141*: 248-267, 1953. Postcommissural organs and color change.

157. KNOWLES, F. G. W., Pubbl. Staz. Zool. Napoli *24* (suppl.): 74-78, 1954. Color change control in Squilla.

158. KNOWLES, F. G. W., and CARLISLE, D. B., Biol. Rev. *31*: 396-473, 1956. Review of crustacean color change.

159. KNOWLES, F. G. W., CARLISLE, D. B., and DUPONT-RAABE, M., J. Mar. Biol. Assn. U. K. *34*: 611-635, 1955. Chemical properties of Carausius chromatophorotropin.

160. KNOWLES, F. G. W., CARLISLE, D. B., and DUPONT-RAABE, M., C. R. Acad. Sci. *242*: 825, 1956. Chemical properties of crustacean chromatophorotropin.

161. KOLLER, G., Verh. deutsch. zool. Gesell. *30*: 128-132, 1925. Mechanism of chromatophore control, Crustacea.

162. KOLLER, G., Ztschr. vergl. Physiol. *5*: 191-246, 1927. Functional independence of pigments, crustaceans; color adaptations; mechanism of chromatophore control.

163. KOLLER, G., Ztschr. vergl. Physiol. *8*: 601-612, 1928. Mechanism of chromatophore control, Crustacea.

164. KOLLER, G., Ztschr. vergl. Physiol. *12*: 632-667, 1930. Hormones in Crustacean color change.

165. KRÖYER, H., Kong. Dansk. Videnskap. Selskabet *9*: 209-361, 1842. Color changes, Hippolyte.

166. KRÜGER, P., and KERN, H., Arch. ges. Physiol. *202*: 119-138, 1924. Melanophores and heat regulation.

167. KÜHN, A., Ztschr. vergl. Physiol. *32*: 572-598, 1950. Background adaptation in Sepia and Octopus.

168. KÜHN, A., and HEBERDEY, R. F., Zool. Anz. *231*: suppl. 4, 1929. Adaptation to colored backgrounds, Cephalopoda.

169. KÜHN, A., and LEDERER, E., Ber. deutsch. chem. Ges. *66*: 488-495, 1953. Chemical nature pigments, crustaceans.

170. KUNTZ, A., Bull. U. S. Bur. Fish. *35*: 1-29, 1916. Adaptation to colored backgrounds, fishes.

171. LAURENS, H., J. Exp. Zool. *16*: 195-210, 1914. Color change in young Amblystoma.

172. LAURENS, H., J. Exp. Zool. *18*: 577-638, 1915. Color change in young Amblystoma.

173. LIEBEN, S., Centralbl. Physiol. *20*: 108-117, 1906. Adrenaline and color change, frog.

174. LUNDSTROM, H. M., and BARD, P., Biol. Bull. *62*: 1-9, 1932. Hypophysis in elasmobranch melanophore control.

175. MARTINI, E., and ACHUNDOW, I., Zool. Anz. *81*: 25-44, 1929. Color changes in Corethra.

176. MAST, S. O., Bull. U. S. Bur. Fish. *34*: 173-238, 1916. Adaptation to colored backgrounds, fishes; adaptive background selection.

177. MATSUMOTO, K., Biol. J. Okayama Univ. *1*: 234-248, 1954. Neurosecretion and color change in crustaceans; color-change hormones of Eriocheir.

178. MATSUSHITA, K., Sci. Rys. Imp. Univ. Sendai, 4, Biol. *13*: 171-200, 1938. Dual innervation of teleost melanophores.

179. MATTHEWS, S. A., J. Exp. Zool. *58*: 471-486, 1931. Mechanism of pigment migration in chromatophores, fish.

180. MATTHEWS, S. A., Biol. Bull. *64*: 315-320, 1933. Color changes in hypophysectomized Fundulus.

181. McWHINNIE, M. A., and SWEENEY, H. M., Biol. Bull. *108*: 160-174, 1955. Color change in Trachelipus.

182. MENDES, E. G., Bol. Fac. Filos. Ciên. Letr. Univers. São Paulo, 15, Zool. *6*: 285-299, 1942. Color change in young fishes.

183. MENKE, E., Arch. ges. Physiol. *140*: 37-91, 1911. Diurnal rhythm and chromatophore state, Crustacea; influence of temperature on chromatophores.

184. MILLOTT, N., Nature *170*: 325-326, 1952. Color change daily rhythm in Diadema.

185. MILLOTT, N., Experientia *9*: 98-99, 1953. Color changes in Diadema in response to illumination.

186. MILLS, S. M., J. Exp. Zool. *64*: 231-244, 1932. Dual innervation of teleost melanophores.

187. MILNE-EDWARDS, H., Ann. Sci. Nat., Sec. 2, Zool. *1*: 46-54, 1834. Color change, Chameleon.

188. MINKIEWICZ, R., Bull. Acad. Sci. Cracovie. 918-929 (November), 1908. Adaptation to colored backgrounds, Crustacea.

189. MUSSBICHLER, H., and UMRATH, K., Ztschr. vergl. Physiol. *32*: 311-318, 1950. MSH and adrenin on Hyla melanophores.

190. NAGANO, T., Sci. Rep. Tohoku Univ. ser. 4 *18*: 167-175, 1949. Color changes in isopods.

191. NEILL, R. M., J. Exp. Biol. *17*: 74-94, 1940. Color change in young fishes; color change in Anguilla.

192. NOVALES, R., Physiol. Zool. *32*: 15-28, 1959. MSH action on isolated frog skin.

193. ODIORNE, J. M., Proc. Nat. Acad. Sci. *19*: 329-332, 1933. Morphological color change, fishes.

194. ODIORNE, J. M., Proc. Nat. Acad. Sci. *19*: 750-754, 1933. Adrenaline and teleost leucophores.

195. OKAY, S., C. R. Ann. Arch. Soc. Turq. Sci. Phys. Nat. *12*: 101, 1946. Color change hormones in isopods.

196. OSBORN, C. M., Proc. Nat. Acad. Sci. *26*: 155-161, 1940. Induced pigmentation on ventral surface of flounder.

197. PARKER, G. H., J. Exp. Zool. *3*: 401-414, 1906. Melanophores and heat regulation.

198. PARKER, G. H., Biol. Rev. *5*: 59-90, 1930. Chromatophores, review.

199. PARKER, G. H., Proc. Nat. Acad. Sci. *17*: 594-596, 1931. Color change, Echinoderm.

200. PARKER, G. H., Proc. Nat. Acad. Sci. *20*: 306-310, 1934. Dual innervation of Fundulus melanophores.

201. PARKER, G. H., Proc. Am. Philosoph. Soc. *75*: 1-10, 1935. Measurement of chromatophore activity.

202. PARKER, G. H., Biol. Bull. *68*: 1-3, 1935. Innervation of Mustelus melanophores.

203. PARKER, G. H., Biol. Bull. *70*: 1-7, 1936. Color change in young elasmobranchs.

204. PARKER, G. H., Biol. Bull. *71*: 255-258, 1936. Single innervation of Mustelus melanophores.

205. PARKER, G. H., Cold Spring Harbor Symp. Quant. Biol. *4*: 358-370, 1936. Cold-block of chromatophore nerves.

206. PARKER, G. H., Proc. Nat. Acad. Sci. *23*: 206-211, 1937. Control of erythrophores of Holocentrus; dual innervation of melanophores.

207. PARKER, G. H., Proc. Amer. Philosoph. Soc. *77*: 223-247, 1937. Control of elasmobranch melanophores.

208. PARKER, G. H., J. Exp. Biol. *15*: 48-73, 1938. Control of color changes in Phrynosoma; influence of temperature.

209. PARKER, G. H., Proc. Am. Philosoph. Soc. *83*: 379-409, 1940. ACH and fish color change.

210. PARKER, G. H., Proc. Am. Philosoph. Soc. *85*: 18-24, 1941. Dual innervation of teleost melanophores.

211. PARKER, G. H., J. Exp. Zool. *89*: 451-473, 1942. Chemical mediator in Mustelus melanophore control.

212. PARKER, G. H., Quart. Rev. Biol. *18*: 205-227, 1943. Vertebrate color changes, review.

213. PARKER, G. H., Biol. Bull. *84*: 273-284, 1943. Methods of measurement of color changes.

214. PARKER, G. H., Animal Colour Changes and Their Neurohumors. Cambridge University Press, 1948, 377 pp.

215. PARKER, G. H., and BROWER, H. P., Biol. Bull. *68*: 4-6, 1935. Seasonal development of nuptial secondary sex coloration, Fundulus.

216. PARKER, G. H., and ROSENBLUETH, A., Proc. Nat. Acad. Sci. *27*: 198-204, 1941. Electrical stimulation of melanophore nerves.

217. PARKER, G. H., and SCATTERTY, L. E., J. Cell. Comp. Physiol. *9*: 297-314, 1937. Hormonal control Rana color change.

218. PASTEUR, C., C. R. Acad. Sci. *246*: 320-322, 1958. Effect of X-organ extirpation on Leander color change.

219. PAUTSCH, F., Bull. Internat. Acad. Polon. Sci. Classe. Sci. Math. Nat. ser. B. *7*: 511-523, 1951. Primary response in Crangon Zoea.

220. PEREZ-GONZÁLEZ, M. D., Biol. Bull. *113*: 426-441, 1957. Crustacean chromactivator destroyed by chymotrypsin.

221. PERKINS, E. B., J. Exp. Zool. *50*: 71-105, 1928. Pigment migration in chromatophores, Crustacean. Mechanism of chromatophore control.

222. PERKINS, E. B., and SNOOK, T., J. Exp. Zool. *61*: 115-128, 1932. Mechanism of chromatophore control, Crustacea.

223. PICKFORD, G. E., and ATZ, J. W., The Physiology of the Pituitary Gland of Fishes. New York Zoological Society, 1957.

224. PIGEAULT, N., C. R. Acad. Sci. *246*: 487-489, 1958. Organ of Bellonci and isopod color change.

225. PHISALIX, C., Arch. Physiol. Norm. Path., ser. 5 *4*: 209-224, 1892. Control color change, cephalopods.

226. PHISALIX, C., Arch. Physiol. Norm. Path., ser. 5 *6*: 92-100, 1894. Control color change, cephalopods.

227. POUCHET, G., J. Anat. Physiol. *8*: 401-407, 1872. Color changes, crustaceans, fishes.

228. POUCHET, G., J. Anat. Physiol. *12*: 1-90, 113-165, 1876. Color changes, crustaceans, fishes.

229. POULTON, E. B., The Colors of Animals. (1890). New York, D. Appleton and Co., 360 pp.

230. PRIEBATSCH, I., Ztschr. vergl. Physiol. *19*: 453-485, 1933. Relations of portions of eyes to color changes, insects.

231. PROSSER, C. L., VON LIMBACH, B., and BENNETT, G. W., Physiol. Zool. *20*: 349-354, 1947. Reactions of fish chromatophore to war gases.

232. RAHN, H., Biol. Bull. *80*: 228-237, 1941. Hypophysis and color change in rattlesnake.

233. REDFIELD, A. C., J. Exp. Zool. *26*: 275-333, 1918. Control of color change in *Phrynosoma*; diurnal rhythm of color change.

234. ROWLANDS, A., J. Exp. Biol. *27*: 446-460, 1950. Humidity and Rana color change.

235. ROWLANDS, A., J. Exp. Biol. *29*: 127-136, 1952. Humidity and Rana color change.

236. VAN RYNBERK, G., Ergebn. Physiol. *5*: 347-571, 1906. Color change, review.

237. SAND, A., Biol. Rev. *10*: 361-382, 1935. Control of color changes in Chameleons.

238. SANDEEN, M. I., Physiol. Zool. *23*: 337-352, 1950. Chromatophorotropins of Uca.

239. SARS, G., Histoire naturelle des Crustacés d'eau douce de Norvège. Christiania, 1867, 145 pp. Color changes, Crustaceans.

240. SCHARRER, B., Action of Hormones in Plants and Invertebrates. New York, Academic Press, 1952. Review of insect color change.

241. SCHARRER, E., Ztschr. vergl. Physiol. *7*: 1-38, 1928. Pineal body and color changes, fishes.

242. SCHEER, B. T., and SCHEER, M. A. R., Pubbl. Staz. Zool. Napoli *25*: 397-418, 1954. Color changes in Leander.

243. SCHLIEP, W., Zool. Jahrb. Physiol. *30*: 45-132, 1910. Color change in *Carausius*; diurnal rhythm in *Carausius* color change.

244. SCHLIEP, W., Zool. Jahrb. Physiol. *35*: 225-232, 1915. Color change in *Carausius*; diurnal rhythm in *Carausius* color change.

245. SCHLIEPER, C., Ztschr. vergl. Physiol. *3*: 547-557, 1926. Color change in *Hyperia galba*.

246. SCHLOTTKE, E., Ztschr. vergl. Physiol. *3*: 692-736, 1926. Temperature and morphological color change, insects.

247. SCHLOTTKE, E., Ztschr. vergl. Physiol. *20*: 370-379, 1934. Temperature and morphological color change, insects.

248. SERENI, E., Boll. Soc. Ital. Biol. Sper. *2*: 377-381, 1927. Control color change, Cephalopods.

249. SERENI, E., Ztschr. vergl. Physiol. *8*: 488-600, 1928. Inhibitory color-change center, cephalopods. Postural chromatophore reflexes, Cephalopods.

250. SERENI, E., Boll. Soc. Ital. Biol. Sper. *3*: 707-711, 1928. Betaine and tyramine in cephalopod color change.

251. SERENI, E., Boll. Soc. Ital. Biol. Sper. *4*: 749-753, 1929. Salivary gland (tyramine) and cephalopod color change.

252. SERENI, E., Ztschr. vergl. Physiol. *12*: 329-503, 1930. Color change mechanism, Cephalopods.

253. SERENI, E., Biol. Bull. *59*: 247-268, 1930. Direct action of betaine and tyramine on cephalopod chromatophores.

254. VON SIEBOLD, K. T. E., Die Susswasserfische von Mittleuropa. Leipzig, 1863, 431 pp. Color change, fishes.

255. SIEGLITZ, G., Ztschr. vergl. Physiol. *33*: 99-124, 1951. Melanin-concentrating factor in frog skin.

256. SJÖGREN, S., Zool. Jahrb. Abt. Anat. Ontog. Tiere *58*: 145-170, 1934. The crustacean sinus gland.

257. SLOME, D., and HOGBEN, L. T., South African J. Sci. *25*: 329-335, 1928. Measurement of chromatophore activity.

258. SMITH, D. C., Biol. Bull. *58*: 193-202, 1930. Temperature and color change, Crustacea.

259. SMITH, D. C., J. Exp. Zool. *58*: 423-453, 1931. Autonomic drugs and teleost color change.

260. SMITH, D. C., J. Cell. Comp. Physiol. *8*: 83-87, 1936. Measurement of chromatophore activity.

261. SMITH, D. C., and SMITH, M. T., Biol. Bull. *67*: 45-58, 1934. Control of erythrophores of *Holocentrus*.

262. SMITH, H. G., Proc. Roy. Soc. London, B, *125*: 250-263, 1938. Dual control of isopod melanophores.

263. SMITH, P. E., Anat. Rec. *11*: 57-64, 1916. Hypophysis and amphibian color change.

264. SMITH, R. I., Physiol. Zool. *15*: 410-417, 1942. Mechanism of color change, leeches.

265. SPAETH, R. A., Anat. Anz. *44*: 520-524, 1913. Pigment migration in chromatophore, fish.

266. SPAETH, R. A., Am. J. Physiol. *41*: 597-602, 1916. Measurement of chromatophore activity.

267. STEGGERDA, F. R., and SODERWALL, A. L., J. Cell. Comp. Physiol. *13*: 31-37, 1939. Dual humoral control of melanophores, *Rana pipiens*.

268. STEINACH, E., Pflügers Arch. Physiol. *87*: 1-37, 1901. Tactile stimuli and color change, Cephalopods.

269. STEPHENS, G. C., Physiol. Zool. *30*: 55-59, 1957. Phase shifting of color-change rhythm by temperature cycles; sensitivity rhythm.

270. STEPHENS, G. C., Am. Naturalist *91*: 135-152, 1957. Review of crustacean daily rhythms of color change.

271. STSCHEGOLEW, G. G., Rev. Zool. Russe *7*: 149-166, 1927. Color change, leeches.

272. SUMNER, F. B., Am. Naturalist *69*: 245-266, 1935. Protective value of fish color change.

273. SUMNER, F. B., Biol. Rev. *15*: 351-375, 1940. Morphological color change in fishes and amphibians, review.

274. SUMNER, F. B., Biol. Bull. *84*: 195-205, 1943. Morphological color changes, Girella, Fundulus.

275. SUMNER, F. B., Proc. Nat. Acad. Sci. *30*: 285-294, 1944. Morphological color change, Guanin.

276. SUMNER, F. B., and DOUDOROFF, P., Proc. Nat. Acad. Sci. *23*: 211-219, 1937. Ratio of incident to reflected light and morphological color change.

277. SUMNER, F. B., and DOUDOROFF, P., Biol. Bull. *84*: 187-194, 1943. Assay of melanin in fishes.

278. SUMNER, F. B., and KEYS, A. B., Physiol. Zool. *2*: 495-504, 1929. Ratio of incident to reflected light and color change.

279. SUNESON, S., Kungl. Fysiogr. Sällsk. Handl. N.F. *58*: 5, 1947. Color change system of *Idothea*.

280. Tomita, G., J. Shanghai Sci. Inst. IV 2: 237-264, 1936. Color change in young fishes; color change in blinded teleosts.

281. Tomita, G., J. Shanghai Sci. Inst. IV 4: 1-8, 1938. Dual innervation of teleost melanophores.

282. Tomita, G., J. Shanghai Sci. Inst. IV 5: 151-178, 1940. Dual innervation of teleost melanophores.

283. von Uexküll, J., Ztschr. Biol. 34: 319-339, 1896. Color change, Echinoderm.

284. Umrath, K., and Walcher, H., Ztschr. vergl. Physiol. 33: 129-141, 1951. Control of Macropodus melanophores.

285. Verne, J., Arch. Morph. Gén. Exp. 1923, 168 pp. Chemical nature pigments, Crustaceans.

286. Waring, H., Proc. Roy. Soc. London, B, 128: 343-353, 1940. Dual hormonal control of Anguilla melanophores.

287. Waring, H., Biol. Rev. 17: 120-150, 1942. Vertebrate color changes, review.

288. Waring, H., and Landgrebe, F. W., The Hormones, edited by G. Pincus and K. V. Thimann. New York, Academic Press, 1950. Vertebrate color change, review.

289. Webb, H. M., Physiol. Zool. 23: 316-336, 1950. Shifting by light, phases of color-change rhythm.

290. Wells, G. P., Nature 129: 686-687, 1932. Color change, leeches.

291. Wright, P. A., Physiol. Zool. 28: 204-218, 1955. Isolated Rana (pipiens and clamitans) melanophore response to MSH and adrenin.

292. Wykes, U., J. Exp. Biol. 14: 79-86, 1937. Measurement of chromatophore activity.

293. Wyman, L. C., J. Exp. Zool. 40: 161-180, 1924. Color change in young fishes.

294. Yoshida, M., J. Exp. Biol. 33: 119-123, 1956. Color change in Diadema, a direct chromatophore response.

295. Young, J. Z., Quart. J. Micr. Sci. 75: 571-624, 1933. Control of elasmobranch melanophores.

296. Young, J. Z., J. Exp. Biol. 12: 254-270, 1935. Pineal body in color change, Lampetra; control of Lampetra melanophores.

297. Zondek, B., and Krohn, H., Klin. Wchnschr. 11: 405-408, 1932. Intermedin in melanophore responses.

298. Zoond, A., and Eyre, J., Phil. Trans. Roy. Soc. London, B, 223: 27-55, 1934. Control of color change in Chameleons; diurnal rhythm of color changes.

Chapter 20

ENDOCRINE MECHANISMS

The production and dispersal within the organism of chemical substances which subserve definite integrating and coordinating roles, and thereby supplement the activity of the nervous elements, are characteristic of all living things. Such substances may be referred to descriptively as chemical coordinators. In the broadest sense, every substance which enters the body fluids from the external environment or from the constituent cells of a higher organism and thus contributes to the normal composition of the internal medium is a chemical coordinator. O_2 and CO_2, for example, operate importantly in the coordination of organismic activities. Other coordinatory substances, such as the D vitamins, may enter the body or may under certain circumstances be synthesized within certain cells of the organism and thence be liberated into the blood. Chemical substances may be more restricted in their region of origin within the body and adaptively participate in a specialized activity within the organism, e.g., secretion of the duodenal mucosa which stimulates the liberation of pancreatic juice in response to the presence of food in the duodenum. Many groups of higher organisms have specialized glandular cells, tissues, or organs which elaborate coordinatory substances for the organism as a whole. This latter development seems to have paralleled the specialization and restriction within the organism of numerous other organs and organ systems; these developments could come about only as soon as an effective mechanism for internal transport, or a circulatory system, was provided. It is therefore not surprising to find specialized endocrine organs chiefly among the annelids, molluscs, arthropods,[70, 210, 274, 289, 398, 476] and vertebrates.

The terms hormones or endocrines are applied to special chemical coordinators which are produced at some more or less restricted region or regions within the organism and which possess specific physiological action usually elsewhere in the body. They are usually, but not always, produced in well-defined glandular organs. Endocrinologists disagree on how broadly one should interpret the definition of a hormone. Obviously, in view of the complete intergradation of all types of chemical coordinators with one another it is impossible to draw a sharp line between the hormones, on the one hand, and other chemical coordinators, on the other. Ascorbic acid may fulfill the definition of a hormone for the rat, for example, and yet appear as a vitamin for man.

Our knowledge of the modes of action of most chemical coordinators is still too scanty to permit any classification of them in terms of how a substance exerts its influence, e.g., whether it actively participates in chemical reactions, acts only as a biocatalyst, or operates only at the cell surface. In view of the inherent impossibility of arriving at a clear and restricted definition of a hormone, it is proposed in this chapter to deal only with chemical coordinators which have come to be widely accepted as endocrines.

The important point to emphasize for comparative physiological purposes is that in a number of phyla and classes of animals special chemical substances are produced which are essential to normal development and functional integration of the body. The points of origin within the organism, the specific chemical nature of the hormones, and the methods of transport are secondary in importance. The nature of the effects which are produced depends as much on the nature of the reacting tissues as on the chemical properties of the circulating hormone. Hormones spreading randomly through the body in the body fluids are obviously powerless to produce tissue and organ differentiation, or induce any directed or organized activities, in the absence of an underlying gene-determined differentiation. The activities of hormones are in a sense, therefore, super-imposed on the basic pattern of the organism, and serve to bring into full functional development and activity the numerous and complex latent differentiations. In a study of endocrine mechanisms the phylogenetic and ontogenetic development of ability to respond to an endocrine is therefore as important as the appearance of the endocrine itself.

The two major integrative systems of the body, the nervous and endocrine systems, are intimately interrelated functionally.[402, 403, 474] Nerve cells generally play the dual role of conduction of excitation and the secretion of such neuroendocrine substances as the neurohumors, acetylcholine,[45, 165, 230] noradrenine,[159] and 5-hydroxytryptamine,[312, 356, 473] which have important roles at interneuronal and neuromotor junctions. In addition, special groups of nerve cells have become specialized as important sources of neurosecretory substances which, transported by the blood, function in manners quite comparable to the true hormones produced by gland cells unrelated to nerves (Fig. 233). Examples of such neurohormones are oxytocin and vasopressin produced in cells of the vertebrate hypothalamus, an active principle liberated by a cell cluster in the caudal region of the spinal cord of fishes, the urohypophysis, and numerous crustacean and insect hormones produced in nervous elements in the brain and nerve cord. The adrenal medulla itself is embryologically of neural origin, arising from centrifugally migrating cells which are homologues of the sympathetic postganglionic nerve cells.

The relationship between the nervous system and the endocrine system extends even further. There is substantial evidence that the secretion of tropic hormones of the anterior lobe of the pituitary, the adrenocorticotropic, gonadotropic, and thyrotropic ones, is very importantly regulated by action of neurosecretory substances originating in the hypothalamus and transported to the anterior lobe by way of a highly specialized vascularization known as the hypophyseal portal system. The excitation of the adrenal medulla is directly nervous, and all the remaining glands are indirectly subjected to nervous modification through regulation of their vasomotor elements. In brief, it is apparent that the endocrine system is predominantly subservient to and in part evolved from the nervous system. This intimate, hierarchical organization of the two systems leads to a highly efficient coordinatory biological mechanism.

The three animal groups in which the endocrine system has been most extensively investigated, the vertebrates, crustaceans, and insects, while displaying among them numerous kinds of remarkable similarities of functions and superficial organizational plans, show no recognizable true homologies. The hormones, which are more or less similar in chemical nature among the animals of any one of these main groups, appear usually quite different from those in the other groups. Consequently, it has seemed the wisest procedure to deal in this chapter with comparative aspects within each group separately.

VERTEBRATES

Endocrine Glands

Thyroid. This gland, phylogenetically related to the protochordate endostyle,[308, 309, 418] arises in the mammal as an unpaired endodermal evagination of the pharyngeal floor. It loses its connection with the gut, separating as a bilobed gland. The gland becomes organized in the form of numerous follicles bounded by secretory epithelium and contain-

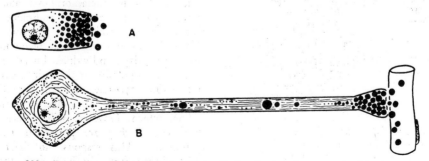

FIGURE 233. Comparison of a typical glandular cell of endocrine character, *A*, with a neurosecretory cell, *B*. In the latter the elaborated hormone is transmitted by the axon to be liberated into the blood at some distance from the cell body proper. (From Scharrer, E., and Scharrer, B.: Rec. Progr. Horm. Res., vol. 10.)

ing an iodine-rich colloid. The height of the epithelial cells varies directly with the glandular activity. Secretion may be either into the follicle lumen or directly into the blood. The colloid includes a protein of high molecular weight (700,000), iodothyroglobulin.

The thyroid absorbs food-derived inorganic iodides and oxidizes them to free iodine which is then incorporated into protein, usually within the follicles. Iodinated tyrosin units combine to provide a series of thyronines—diiodothyronine; triiodothyronine, and tetraiodothyronine or thyroxin.

Thyroxin (Tetraiodothyronine)

$$HO \underset{I}{\overset{I}{\diamondsuit}} - O - \underset{I}{\overset{I}{\diamondsuit}} - CH_2 - CH \overset{NH_2}{\underset{COOH}{<}}$$

The thyronines, especially thyroxin, are liberated from the gland following their dissociation from the follicular globulin, or may under some circumstances be secreted directly into the blood. In either case, in the blood, the hormonal molecules are adsorbed to carriers, plasma globulins or albumins, during their transport.

The roles of thyroid hormone in mammals are numerous. It accelerates oxidative metabolism in cells at large, normally being responsible for 30 to 49 per cent of resting metabolic rate. The mechanism of the metabolic action of thyroxin is a much debated issue. The various hypotheses which have been advanced have included the uncoupling of oxidative phosphorylations in the energy conversion system of the cells, altering the enzyme-catalyzed oxidative pathways from more to less biologically efficient ones, producing changes in quantities of certain respiratory

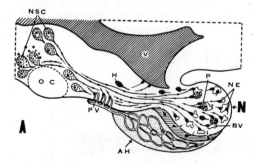

FIGURE 234. The relationship between the hypothalamic neurosecretory cells (*NSC*) and the neurohypophysis (*N*) and adenohypophysis (*AH*). *BV*: blood vessels; *H*: Herring bodies; *NE*: nerve endings; *OC*: optic chiasma; *P*: pituicytes; *PV*: hypophyseal portal vessels; *V*: ventricle. (From Enami, N.: *in* Comparative Endocrinology. John Wiley & Sons.)

enzymes, and influencing the permeability of the mitochondrial boundaries.

Thyroid hormone is essential to normal growth and differentiation, particularly of the hard or cornified derivatives such as bone or hair, and exerts a regulatory action on amounts of intercellular substances of tissues. It facilitates utilization of carbohydrate. Thyroid hormones maintain normal excitability of such elements as central nervous centers and cardiac muscle.

The thyroid appears also to exercise influence upon other endocrine glands. It stimulates the adrenal cortex. Normal gonadal activity depends upon thyroid function. Thyroxin seems in some manner to cooperate with antidiuretic hormone (ADH) in regulation of water. And participating in its own regulation, thyroid hormone depresses the secretion of thyrotropic hormone by the anterior lobe and, possibly also, directly, its own production of hormone.

Control of the thyroid is predominantly by way of thyroid-stimulating hormone (TSH). All phases of synthesis and release of thyroid hormone are facilitated by TSH.

Secretion of TSH is, in turn, regulated by the hypothalamus, presumably by a neuroendocrine transmitted through the hypophyseal portal system.[121, 197, 198, 220, 331] The anteriormost region of the median eminence appears to be especially concerned.[181, 219] The chief environmental factor responsible for altering thyroid activity is temperature,[62, 64, 80, 81, 125, 508] which is believed to exert its action through hypothalamic mediation.

It was discovered many years ago[203] that the feeding of thyroid gland material to amphibians hastens metamorphosis and, conversely, that removal of the rudiment of the thyroid from larval forms prevents metamorphosis. Metamorphosis can be obtained in thyroidectomized individuals by administration of thyroglobulin or thyroxin. Less effective is diiodotyrosine, and still less effective are inorganic salts of iodine or elemental iodine, which, however, will induce metamorphosis if they are present in sufficient quantities.[12] This response to thyroxin is quite distinct from the increase in the general rate of metabolism. Dinitrophenol, a powerful stimulant of metabolism, has no influence on metamorphosis. Acetylated thyroxin, on the other hand, retains its normal capacity to induce metamorphosis although it has lost entirely its metabolism-stimulating action.

Various amphibian species differ greatly among themselves in their responsiveness to thyroxin. During their early development, none of them shows ability to respond to this hormone, but most acquire the capacity at some particular stage in their development. Some species, like the Mexican axolotl, never develop any considerable degree of reactivity to this metamorphosis-inducing factor, and hence normally do not metamorphose. Axolotls can be made to metamorphose by large doses of thyroxin; other species, such as *Necturus*, appear never to develop the reactivity and never metamorphose. That the failure of metamorphosis in *Necturus* is the result of failure of tissue response rather than of the absence of an appropriate thyroid principle is shown by the fact that *Necturus* thyroid will accelerate metamorphosis in *Rana clamitans*.[436]

In amphibian development, including metamorphosis, there is an orderly sequence of changes. This sequence appears due, at least in part, to gradually increasing thyroid activity and developing responsiveness of the various tissues of the organism to the hormone.[11, 35, 51, 156, 157, 290-293, 319, 366, 468]

The capacity of amphibians to metamorphose is lost after hypophysectomy.[4, 8, 427] This activity has been traced to the anterior lobe;[10] the principle involved is ineffective in inducing metamorphosis after complete thyroidectomy.[9] The thyroids are also known not to accumulate any colloid in the absence of the hypophysis. This demonstrates that, in amphibians, the production and liberation of the thyroid hormone, and hence metamorphosis, are under the control of the hypophysis.

Among teleost fishes it is known that the thyroid gland is concerned in metamorphosis in eels and in certain flatfishes,[207, 345] and that changes in the amount of thyroxin available will, in other species, result in alterations in growth rates and in body form.[19, 200, 214, 242, 246, 269, 302, 315, 352, 461] Furthermore, as in higher vertebrates, the pituitary of lower vertebrates yields a thyrotropic principle (TSH) on whose activity the development and secretion of the thyroid depends.[5, 191, 279, 354]

It is interesting that, despite the influences of the thyroid on teleost growth and devel-opment, there is still no decisive demonstration that in fishes the thyroid influences the general metabolic rate.[158, 243, 327, 328, 424] In fact, in poikilotherms in general, reports from work with various species indicate a variety of kinds of results.

Experiments involving thyroid administration to fishes appear to indicate that this hormone has no influence on O_2 consumption in guppies and goldfish.[158, 424] Treatment with thiourea does not significantly alter O_2 consumption in Fundulus.[327] Injection of extracts of thyroid glands of Bermuda parrot fish increased O_2 consumption in white grunts, but only when the latter fish weighed more than about 15 gm.[425] As in most fish, administration of thyroid to *Rana pipiens* tadpoles prior to changes of metamorphosis resulted in no alteration in O_2 consumption.[231] In adult *Rana pipiens*, on the other hand, administration of thyroid increased O_2 consumption substantially,[465] and if the animals were kept at temperatures higher than about 13°C caused reduction in body weight. Among the reptiles and birds the effect of thyroid administration on the basal metabolic rate appears quite similar to that observed in mammals. Pigeons show a marked reduction in basal heat production after complete thyroidectomy.[322] Young pythons, during long-continued thyroid feeding, show greatly increased excitability and weight reduction.[295]

Other thyroid roles have been reported for fishes. It is concerned in the regulation of liver glycogen[173] and with osmoregulation.[172, 426] In euryhaline fishes greater thyroid activity is associated with more saline media.[237] In the stickleback *Gasterosteus* it is increase in thyroid activity which is responsible for the migration from salt to fresh water, a selection related to its breeding habit. This change is subject to photoperiodic regulation.[25]

Thyroid •response in acclimatization to temperature differs among fishes. Whereas most fishes show higher thyroid activity at higher temperatures, the trout *Salmo* and the minnow *Umbra* show higher activity at lower temperatures as does the homoiotherm.[193, 353]

The thyroid gland is an organ highly specialized organically for binding iodine. This capacity is not only widespread among the endostyles of amphioxus[31, 304, 441] and Urochordates such as *Ciona*,[30] but is observed in the dermal glands of hemichordates. Iodine binding appears to occur not uncommonly with the exoskeletal scleroproteins of many invertebrates.[44, 192, 194]

Adrenal Cortex. This endocrine organ is always closely associated anatomically in the vertebrate with the adrenal medulla of quite different genesis. It is derived from mesoderm to right and left near the base of the dorsal mesentery at the level of the primary urogenital differentiation. In the mammal the adrenal cortex, as the term indicates, wholly encompasses the medullary elements. The cortex is relatively thick, yellow in color, and appears stratified as three regions, a thin outermost zona glomerulosa, a deeper, middle zona fasciculata, and an innermost zona reticularis.

All the adrenal cortical hormones are steroids. Extracts of the gland have revealed more than twenty-five different steroids, though relatively few of these have ever been demonstrated to reach the blood stream. Presumably most of the twenty-five are precursors in hormone synthesis.

The cortical hormones fall into three categories: sex hormones, glucocorticoids, and mineralocorticoids. The locus of their production in the cortex is still an open question with two principal views being entertained. One view is that of the three cortical zones, the sex hormones are produced by the reticularis, the glucocorticoids by the reticularis and fasciculata, and the mineralocorticoids by the glomerulosa. The alternative hypothesis is that the three zones reflect a cycle of secretion, the secreting cells for all the hormones originating in the glomerulosa and gradually moving into the reticularis as their synthetic and secretory phases become completed.

The sex hormones from the cortex include estrogens, androgens, and progesterone. Androgens appear to be the chief ones in the mammal. In both genetic males and females, these androgens appear to contribute to regulation of normal muscular and skeletal development, differentiation of external genitalia and hair-growth patterns, and to sexual behavior and drive.

Glucocorticoids effect profound regulatory actions upon metabolic transformations in the body, which in turn underlie behavioral changes. This group of steroids is therefore the most critical of the cortical steroids for maintained viability of the adult mammal. Glucocorticoids by themselves will permit survival following adrenalectomy. The best known of these steroids are:

Cortisone
(Compound E)

Hydrocortisone
(Compound F)

The glucocorticoids and mineralocorticoids are characterized by having ketones at positions 3 and 20, and a hydroxyl group at 21. Glucocorticoids bear an oxygen at position 11, while mineralocorticoids are usually without it. There is not, however, sharp differentiation of physiological action between the two groups of compounds.

The actions of glucocorticoids on carbohydrate and protein metabolism are extensive and large. They direct activities toward increasing carbohydrate by increasing glucogenic processes and at the same time depressing glucolytic ones. Liver glycogen increases. Glycosuria results from action of the hormone to reduce tubular resorption of glucose in the kidneys. On the other hand, glucocorticoid-influenced metabolism favors protein catabolism, and consequent increased nitrogen excretion. This is superficially evident in such histological changes as a reduction in connective and lymphatic tissues, muscle, alterations in bone structure, and inhibition of various phenomena involved normally in the body's reaction to irritants, injury, and allergenic agents. Glucocorticoids exert other actions, too. They participate in the distribution and regulation of water and electrolytes, in a manner qualitatively similar to that of mineralocorticoids, and encourage rapid regulation by the body in response to excess water.

They also maintain the normal state of low permeability of the membranes, including the synovial ones. They stimulate gastric secretion and hence are ulcer producing. And as would be expected from their basic metabolic functions, derangements of mental function are related to abnormal amounts of these hormones.

The best-known mineralocorticoids are

11-Desoxycorticosterone and Aldosterone

As would be expected perhaps from its hydroxyl group at position 11, aldosterone also possesses glucocorticoid properties.

Mineralocorticoid action is chiefly upon regulation of body electrolytes and water. 11-Desoxycorticosterone, which lacks entirely glucocorticoid properties, effects increased urinary excretion of potassium and phosphate and reduced excretion of sodium, chloride, and water. It is believed to exert its action chiefly upon the renal tubules, regulating in the ascending limb of Henle's loop and the distal tubule the resorption of sodium in exchange for hydrogen and potassium ions which are excreted.[343]

The adrenal cortex exhibits altering rates in its secretion of hormones in response to physiological demands as a consequence of extrinsic controls. Most prominent by far is the hormone corticotropin (ACTH) from the adenohypophysis, which seems to stimulate to some extent the production of all three cortical hormone types, but especially the glucocorticoids.

The response of the body to any stress involves secretion of ACTH by the adenohypophysis. The consequent production of adrenocortical hormones assists the body to meet the increased demands upon it. There are three theories as to the means by which stress effects ACTH secretion. One view is that depletion of the cortical hormones through use constitutes the chief stimulus. A second theory is that adrenin liberated in response to stress stimulates the hypophysis. A third theory proposes that a resting level of ACTH production is maintained under hypothalamic direction and that stress elevates this level. There is some evidence that level of blood potassium itself regulates directly the cortical production of mineralocorticoids. Adrenocortical secretion appears mediated by the hypothalamus since interruption of blood and nerve connections between the hypothalamus and the pituitary abolishes the response to stress.

There are adequate reasons to postulate that there is a common pattern of regulation of water and electrolyte and of carbohydrate metabolism in all vertebrates. Hydrocortisone and corticosterone have been demonstrated in all the major vertebrate classes, and though aldosterone has not been adequately sought, there is reason to believe that this, too, is widespread.[265, 268] In frogs, an interesting seasonal difference in response to total adrenalectomy has been noted. The frogs tolerate this condition in winter but not in summer. In summer, unless they are kept in isotonic saline, the operated frogs accumulate H_2O and K^+, lose Na^+, and succumb in a day or two.[266, 267]

Corticosteroids appear to facilitate ovulation in both mammals[437, 438] and amphibians,[100, 101, 416, 499, 501] even *in vitro*.[510, 513]

Pancreas. In the pancreas, of endodermal origin by budding from the acini, are the islets of Langerhans. These contain three or four kinds of cells. Alpha cells with acidophilic granules, more abundant in the peripheral than central regions of the islets, are believed to be the source of glucagon.[251] Beta cells, comprising the majority, are the source of insulin. In addition, a third cell type is the gamma, without granular contents and of unknown function.

Both insulin and glucagon are proteins. Insulin (M.W. 12,000; isoelectric point, pH 5.4) contains fifty-one amino acids whose arrangement has been fully worked out. In structure the hormone comprises two peptide chains, one acidic and the other basic; the two chains are connected by two disulfide linkages. Species difference has been found in the sequence of three amino acids at a specific locus in the acidic chain.[224] While there is a general immunological similarity among insulins from different species, this is not total, as is evident from antibody production.[15, 340, 341] Glucagon is a straight polypeptide chain of twenty-nine amino acids.[38, 144, 170]

Insulin plays an important role in regulation of carbohydrate metabolism. It acts to increase the conversion of glucose into glycogen in both muscle and liver. It facilitates the production of fat from carbohydrate and stimulates protein synthesis. It also acts to accelerate the oxidation of glucose in muscle and elsewhere. The modes of action of insulin are not yet known with surety. Two hypotheses are prevalent. The first one, and that one for which most evidence has been amassed, is that insulin facilitates the movement of glucose through cell membranes. The second hypothesis is that insulin accelerates within the cell the hexokinase-catalyzed reaction:

$$\text{glucose} + \text{ATP} \longrightarrow \text{glucose} - \text{6-phosphate} + \text{ADP}$$

When insulin level falls below minimally adequate levels, blood glucose increases because of depression of the mechanisms for its removal and use, and it may be lost in the urine. Fat becomes oxidized in far larger than normal proportions and acidic ketone bodies such as acetone, acetoacetic acid, and hydroxybutyric acid accumulate. These are excreted as sodium and potassium salts, reducing in the body the alkali reserve and lowering blood pH. Protein is catabolized and the nitrogen excreted.

The second islet hormone, glucagon, antagonizes insulin in that it stimulates glyco-

appears chiefly regulated directly by the blood sugar level, a rise stimulating insulin liberation, and a fall, glucagon. Glucagon in effect stimulates insulin secretion and vice versa. Somatotropic hormone from the adenohypophysis stimulates insulin, and probably also glucagon, liberation. Androgens also stimulate the islets.

There is considerable variability in relative importance among vertebrates of the two pancreatic hormones. Among mammals there is high sensitivity to insulin lack in dogs, cats, and rats, and generally less sensitivity among herbivores. Reptiles and birds are generally less sensitive to insulin;[335, 434] the effect of insulin lack is transitory in birds.[332, 333] Tortoises exhibit hyperglycemia following pancreatectomy.[171] On the other hand, reptiles and birds are highly responsive to glucagon, with reptiles being especially well provided with α-cells. Amphibians contrast with the sauropsidans in being generally very sensitive to insulin, or its lack, and parallelly often having an absence of α-cells.[229, 336, 337, 423, 429, 509]

Adrenal Medulla. The medullary tissue is of ectodermal origin arising from the same embryonic tissue, the neural crests, that generates the sympathetic ganglia. The secretory cells are, in effect, postganglionic elements of the sympathetic system and remain synaptically associated with preganglionic fibers. The gland is especially richly vascularized. The mammalian adrenal medulla is known to secrete two closely related hormones, one the primary amine, adrenin, and the other the secondary amine, noradrenin.[159] The levorotary isomers are the natural, active ones. In structure, these hormones are related as follows:

Transmethylation (from methionine)

Noradrenin   Adrenin

genolysis in the liver. Glucagon appears to effect an increase in the phosphorylase content of the liver; the phosphorylase catalyzes the production of glucose-1-phosphate from glycogen. Glucagon, on the other hand, facilitates the oxidation of glucose in the tissues; its action here is like that of insulin. Glucagon also acts to raise kidney thresholds for sodium, potassium, and phosphate.

The secretion of the two islet hormones

Glands differ in the relative amounts of these two hormones which they contain. The proportion of the two which is liberated varies with the origin of nervous stimulation. Although not fully established, evidence suggests that the two hormones are secreted by two types of medullary cells. Within the medullary cells the hormones are contained inside vesicles.[53, 240, 422]

Adrenin and noradrenin effect in general

a qualitatively similar action on heart, blood vessels, and smooth muscle and also upon carbohydrate metabolism. However, there are important quantitative differences. Upon the vascular system both increase the excitability and contractility of heart muscle with a consequent rise in blood pressure. While both hormones constrict visceral vessels and those of skin and mucous membranes, and both elevate pulmonary blood pressure, adrenin effects increased blood flow through the muscles, heart, liver and brain, causing thereby an over-all drop in peripheral resistance, while noradrenin constricts to varying degrees all peripheral vessels except those of somatic muscle and liver, yielding a slight rise in peripheral resistance. Following noradrenin administration, heart output is reflexly held reduced by way of pressure receptors.

Adrenin produces a rapid increase in blood sugar; noradrenin is only about 25 per cent as effective in this role. Sugar is released from glycogen in the liver. Simultaneously, the hormone facilitates oxidation of glucose in other tissues to lactic acid which, carried to the liver, replenishes the glycogen supply. The hormone also reduces the use of glucose by the tissues.

Adrenin has a much stronger action than noradrenin in relaxing the pulmonary bronchial muscles. This difference, together with the substantially different cardiovascular action of the two hormones, probably accounts in large measure for the apprehensive and other nervous responses to increased adrenin, but not to noradrenin.

Numerous other responses to adrenin occur. These include pupillary dilatation, pilomotor response, sweat-gland inhibition, relaxation of gut and bladder muscles (except for the sphincters which are stimulated), contraction of spleen capsule, secretion of saliva, and facilitated blood coagulation.

Adrenin increases ACTH and decreases TSH production by the adenohypophysis and depresses ADH liberation from the neurohypophysis.

The adrenal medulla is controlled exclusively by the sympathetic nervous system. The degree of its tonic activity is believed related to total afferent nervous activity and perhaps to fluctuate with it. The gland appears dispensable, its absence capable of being fully compensated by the noradrenin production by adrenergic fibers and by actions of cortical hormones. However, normally, any rapid drop in blood sugar, or stress, stimulates production of adrenin, this hormone con-

tributing to a rapid compensatory response. The normal stimuli for specific liberation of noradrenin are less clear.

Parathyroid. The parathyroid glands of the mammal are four in number, and of endodermal origin from the third and fourth pharyngeal pouches. They contain two types of cells, the chief cells and oxyphilic cells. The latter are filled with acidophilic granules. The evidence suggests the parathyroid hormone to be a protein of high molecular weight, probably about 650,000.

The hormone appears concerned almost wholly with the regulation of calcium and phosphate metabolism. The hormone effects a fall in blood phosphate and its elimination by the kidneys together with a rise in blood calcium and its loss by a similar route. The hormone regulates only the ionized calcium and phosphate, not that which is bound to protein or in the body fluids in un-ionized form.

Control of secretion is effected by the serum level of calcium. Drop in calcium stimulates the gland. A rise in serum phosphate exerts a similar action but only indirectly through the correlated change in calcium.

The mechanism of action of parathyroid hormone is still not known with certainty. There is support for each of two hypotheses. The first, the renal theory, is that the chief site of action is in regulating the renal excretion of the two ions. The second, the osseous theory, is that the primary site of action of the hormone is upon the osteoblasts and osteoclasts regulating the secretion and resorption of the osseous elements. The hormone favors movement of calcium and phosphate from bone to blood.

However, in view of the numerous essential roles of calcium, including nerve and muscle excitability, muscle contractility, and membrane permeability, and the roles of phosphate in buffering, carbohydrate metabolism, and structural elements such as nucleoproteins and phospholipins, the regulation of these two materials is a problem of prime importance to the organism.

Neurohypophysis. This organ is not an endocrine gland in the same sense as the previous vertebrate ones we have discussed. Not only does it arise as an outpocketing of the floor of the brain, but it retains its connection throughout life with the latter organ. Its hormones now are clearly established to be formed in the supraoptic and paraventricular nuclei of the hypothalamus and later transported within nerve fibers to the neurohypophysis, there to be liberated into capillaries upon appropriate stimulation. Electron microscopy has shown the secretory material within the cells to be contained within vesicles.[29, 135, 176] The organ liberates two hormones, the antidiuretic hormone (ADH), or vasopressin, and oxytocin, each polypeptide comprising eight amino acids, of which six are common to the two.[458-460]

Antidiuretic Hormone. The chief action of this in the mammal is to increase the absorption of water in the kidney tubules. Correlations have been found between nerve cell content of ADH and water retention.[199, 405, 497] ADH acts directly upon the tubules, particularly the loop of Henle, the distal convoluted tubule, and the collecting tubule. A second, less important action is upon the vascular system in which it causes principally constriction of the arteriovenous capillaries.

Oxytocin. This hormone induces contraction of smooth muscle, especially that of the uterine wall, and to a lesser extent of the

Oxytocin (Pitocin)

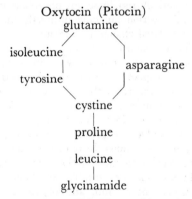

urinary bladder, gallbladder, and intestine. Its uterine effect is counteracted by progesterone. Oxytocin plays a special role in lactation, contracting smooth muscle in the mammary glands, including the myoepithelial cells, to eject the milk. It influences the permeability to water of the bullfrog bladder.[394]

The neurohypophysis is dually controlled through the stalk upon which it depends for inflow of its hormones[97, 239, 362] and for the stimulus for release of its hormones into the blood.[380] The means for differential control of liberation of the two hormones is still not known. The secretion of ADH is continuous, but its rate is regulated by osmotic pressure of the blood, lowered osmotic pressure inhibiting hormone release.[357] The receptor for osmotic pressure is thought to be the cells of the supraoptic nucleus itself. Many other factors also influence ADH secretion. Increased

secretion is effected by stress, reduction in blood fluid volume, and drugs such as morphine and nicotine. Reduced secretion is brought about by increased blood fluid volume and by cold exposure.

Oxytocin is secreted at the time of mammary gland activity in response to stimulation of the nipple. Afferent nervous impulses pass to, and activate, the hypothalamic center. Other stimuli believed to initiate oxytocin liberation by afferent nervous activity are uterine distention late in pregnancy and, in some species, also mating. Adrenin, on the other hand, inhibits secretion.

Among mammals there are two vasopressins which differ by a single amino acid. Lysine vasopressin is found in the pig and

Vasopressin (Pitressin)

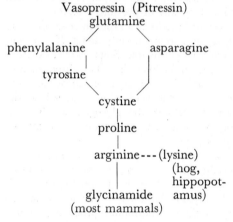

hippopotamus and arginine vasopressin in all other mammals investigated. The actions of the two may differ substantially. On the dog, for example, the arginine form possesses about six times the potency of the lysine form in antidiuretic action.[396, 452, 453] Birds and poikilothermous vertebrates possess neurohypophyseal water-regulatory hormones

Arginine Vasotocin

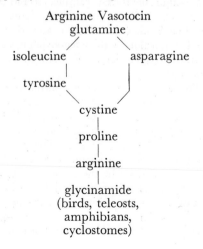

which are different from those of the mammal.[162, 232, 393-397] It appears probable that this principle is a related substance, arginine vasotocin. Oxytocin has been identified in fishes, amphibians, and birds.[372] The spawning reaction is induced in the minnow *Fundulus* by administration of posterior lobe extracts of mammals or by synthetic oxytocin.[487]

Adenohypophysis. This gland, of ectodermal origin, arises as an outpocketing of the roof of the pharynx. This outpocketing, Rathke's pouch, comes into close association with a comparable outpocketing of the infundibulum which will become the neurohypophysis. Rathke's pouch gives rise to the three major divisions of the adenohypophysis as follows: The posterior wall remains thin, becoming the pars intermedia, the anterior wall becomes greatly thickened to form the pars distalis, and a dorsal portion of the pouch extends toward the infundibulum forming the pars tuberalis. Seven hormones have been demonstrated to arise in the adenohypophysis. Since at least five of these exert important regulatory actions on other endocrine glands, this gland is in large measure a master gland of the endocrine system.

Growth or Somatotropic Hormones. These are proteins with a molecular weight in the range 25,000 to 50,000, comprising either large branched or small unbranched amino acid chains.[36, 280, 313, 338, 485] Each is most active for its normal host, but there is a suggestion that they all possess a common core structure. Evidence suggests their source to be the orange acidophils of the pars distalis.

Growth hormone (STH) normally stimulates growth in young animals, acting to accelerate protein synthesis and depress catabolism of amino acids. This results in nitrogen retention, and an increase in water and salts as in normal growth, and a reduction in fats. The hormone also promotes increased bone growth, both periosteal ossification and normal cartilage proliferation and bone synthesis at the diaphyso-epiphyseal region to produce bone lengthening.

In adult carnivores the growth hormone is diabetogenic, neutralizing the action of insulin. The islet beta-cells are first stimulated by growth hormone and later atrophy, resulting in permanent diabetes.

Growth hormone is essential for lactation in the mammal, probably in terms of its role in protein synthesis.

In fishes, STH possesses a molecular size comparable to the smaller mammalian ones[486] and is essential to growth in length.[373, 374, 435]

Little is known about regulation of secretion of growth hormone. There is no evidence for hormonal regulation, but some reason to believe that hypothalamic control exists.

Thyroid-Stimulating Hormone. This is believed to be a glycoprotein, with a molecular weight of about 10,000, produced by the blue basophils. The specific chemical structure of the hormone is unknown though it seems clear that there are differences among species.[174] The principal role of TSH is to stimulate thyroid activity in all its aspects. It increases the quantity of intracellular colloid and induces hormone liberation. It increases the height of the follicle cells, their rate of iodine uptake, and hormone synthesis.

There are also other effects of TSH on the body, most notable of which is a swelling of the orbital content of the eye, including the muscles, by water uptake and fat accumulation. An exophthalmic condition is the consequence. Comparable water and fat accumulations occur elsewhere in the body—in the blood and skeletal muscles—but less conspicuously.

There is a reciprocal regulating action of thyroid hormone and TSH. The former, probably by influence upon the hypothalamus, depresses TSH secretion. Though this relationship is the primary regulating mechanism for TSH production, adrenin and the corticosteroids also reduce TSH production, thereby accounting for reduced thyroid activity in initial response to stress other than cold stress which has the opposite action. Stress, therefore, normally stimulates ACTH liberation while inhibiting TSH, except for cold stress which stimulates production of both.

Adrenocorticotropic Hormones (ACTH). These hormones are polypeptides; their site of origin in the gland is still unknown, though some reasons exist for presuming it to be the chromophobe cells. There appear to be three corticotropic hormones. Their molecular weight is about 4500. They possess up to thirty-nine amino acids of which a certain sequence of twenty-four is essential. Of these a series of thirteen is in common with the melanocyte-stimulating hormone, α-MSH.[252, 313, 314, 421] ACTH is, correspondingly, reported to melanize goldfish.[112]

ACTH stimulates the adrenal cortex, inducing hypertrophy particularly of the zona fasciculata, and causing secretion of glucocorticoids. Mineralocorticoid secretion appears unaffected.

Hypophyseal secretion of ACTH is normally regulated by the hypothalamus which, in turn, is probably influenced by blood titer of the corticosteroid. In stress, accelerated ACTH secretion is in part neurally effected by way of the hypothalamus, in part by an exciting action of adrenin on the hypothalamic center as well as the gland itself. The midregion of the median eminence appears normally involved in the regulation,[182, 183, 201, 254-256] though a basal level of secretion is maintained without such regulation.

Follicle-Stimulating Hormone (FSH). This is a glycoprotein believed to be produced by the pale basophils of the pars distalis. Its role is to stimulate growth of ovarian follicles in the female and promote spermatogenesis in the male.

Luteinizing Hormone (LH) or Interstitial Cell–Stimulating Hormone (ICSH). This hormone is a glycoprotein with both interspecific and intraspecific differences in molecular weight ranging from 30,000 to 100,000.[233, 376, 429, 430] It is probably produced by the pale basophils of the pars distalis.

Luteinizing hormone stimulates in the female the ovarian secretion of both estrogen and progesterone, and in the male, the testicular secretion of androgens. The secretion of the gonadotropins is regulated by the hypothalamus.[20-22, 130, 131, 383] The posterior portion of the median eminence appears involved. The hypothalamus is, in turn, regulated by the level of circulating gonadal hormones as well as by numerous other factors such as light and temperature, presence of mates, and genital stimulation.

Prolactin or Luteotropic Hormone (LTH). This is a protein generally considered produced by the red acidophils of the pars distalis. It has a molecular weight of about 25,000 but may show species differences, as for example between ox and sheep.[184, 313]

The roles of this hormone are known in the mammal for the female in which it is responsible for maintenance of the corpus luteum and its continued production of progesterone. It supplements the actions of the gonadal hormones in effecting mammary gland development, thereafter being essential for normal lactation, in collaboration with thyroid hormone and adrenocorticoids.[347] A third conspicuous action of prolactin is to encourage maternal instincts and behavior. There is also evidence indicating prolactin to influence prostate development in the male,[111] synergizing with sex hormones and gonadotropins.

The secretion of prolactin is hypothalamically regulated, even though a basal level of production seems maintained without regulation.[344, 348] During lactation its continued production depends upon nipple stimulation and activation of afferent pathways to the brain which, in turn, stimulates the adenohypophyseal activity as well as oxytocin liberation from the neurohypophysis for milk ejection.

Among vertebrates other than mammals, in addition to its well-known action on the crop gland of pigeons in stimulating "milk" secretion, prolactin cooperates with melanocyte-stimulating hormone in increasing integumentary pigmentation in fishes[375] and is responsible for the water-drive of the red eft stage of the newt *Triturus*.[195]

Melanocyte-Stimulating Hormone (MSH).[301] This hormone formerly termed intermedin is polypeptide in nature.[185-189, 222, 223, 305, 309] Two kinds have been isolated: α-MSH with thirteen amino acid residues and β-MSH with eighteen. A seven-amino acid sequence is common to both these and also to ACTH, probably accounting for the commonly observed melanophore-stimulating action of ACTH. In the human, β-MSH contains twenty-one amino acids. MSH is believed to be produced in the pars intermedia.

While MSH effects pigment dispersion in the melanophores of lower vertebrates, its roles in birds and mammals have been uncertain. There is evidence that it stimulates melanin synthesis in mammalian skin by activating tyrosinase.

MSH clearly stimulates production of new pigment,[350, 377, 449] especially in fishes and amphibians, though appearing specifically to suppress guanine deposition in the skin.[26] There is some evidence,[147] based upon differential alcohol solubilities, that vertebrates also possess a melanin-concentrating hormone, MCH, probably of hypothalamic origin.

MSH secretion is depressed by glucocorticoids, this perhaps accounting for the melanization of the skin in cases of adrenocortical insufficiency.

The subneural gland of ascidians has often been considered on the basis of its superficial structure to be the forerunner of the pituitary gland of the vertebrate. However, assays of the subneural gland have revealed no MSH, gonadotropins, or vasopressin, though an oxytocin-like principle has been found.[128]

Urohypophysis. An endocrine organ bearing a striking morphological resemblance to the hypothalamus-neurohypophysis complex is located in the caudal region of the spinal cord of fishes.[146, 148-152] As with the neurohypophysis, neurosecretion appears to pass from cell bodies in the cord to their terminations in the urohypophysis. Electron microscopy reveals the typical intracellular spherules and ellipsoids of neuroendocrine elements. A conspicuous element of the gland is zinc. Evidence suggests the gland to possess a salt-regulatory role.

Ovary. This gland secretes two kinds of hormones, both steroids. The first type is the estrogens. These are secreted before ovulation by the theca interna of the developing follicle and later, after ovulation, by the granulosa and theca-lutein cells. Estrogens are also secreted by the placenta. Although still others are reported, two of the more common estrogens are:

Estradiol   Estrone

These are transported in the blood largely bound to protein. Estradiol is the more potent in action. These hormones are essential to the normal sexual development of the accessory and secondary characters of the female mammal. They stimulate growth of the uterine endometrium, its glands and vascularization, and increase activity of the myometrium. They induce cornification of the vaginal epithelium and complete the development of the oviducts. In low titers, estrogens normally contribute to follicle differentiation, but in higher titers, depress this by reducing FSH secretion. They contribute to the normal growth and differentiation of the mammary glands.

Estrogens contribute to the feminine form and stature by influence on bone growth. They depress growth of long bones and stimulate closure of epiphyses. They cause increased protein synthesis and retention of sodium, calcium, phosphate, and water. They reduce activity of the sebaceous glands.

A second hormone of the ovary is progesterone:

Progesterone

This is thought produced by the granulosa and theca-lutein cells of the corpus luteum. Progesterone is also secreted by the placenta and the adrenal cortex. This hormone is responsible for the activation of the secretory phase of the uterine endometrium, thereby supplementing the estrogenic activity. Contrary to the action of estrogens, progesterone inhibits the myometrium. It effects mucification of the vaginal mucosa. In cooperation with estrogen, low titers of progesterone stimulate LH production; higher titers inhibit it. Progesterone supplements estrogen in inducing mammary gland development. Progesterone, unlike androgens and estrogens, promotes protein destruction.

Ovarian secretion is controlled by three hormones of adenohypophyseal origin. FSH stimulates follicle development and estrogen secretion. In this it is assisted by LH, which also produces ovulation and corpus luteum development. A third hormone, prolactin, stimulates secretion of progesterone by the corpus luteum.

Estrogens depress FSH secretion and induce LH and prolactin production. Progesterone inhibits LH secretion and encourages FSH production by the adenohypophysis. The actions and interactions of the ovary and hypophysis and these five hormones are responsible for the regulation of the menstrual and estrus cycles of the mammal.

During pregnancy the placenta assumes the role of an endocrine organ, producing hor-

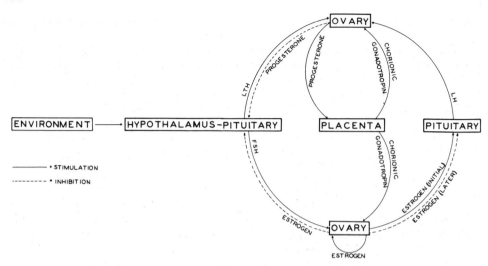

FIGURE 235. Diagram representing the major endocrine influences operating during the normal reproductive cycle of the adult female mammal.

mones assuring more or less its own maintenance until parturition. The inner cytotrophoblast of the placenta secretes chorionic gonadotropin, a hormone resembling LH in its physiological action and replacing hypophyseal secretion. The outer syncytial trophoblast secretes estrogens and progesterone, both essentially the same hormones which are of normal ovarian origin.

Although the mammary glands are initiated in their development by estrogens, and this action supplemented by action of progesterone, the relative roles of the two hormones vary from species to species. Prolactin contributes in its role in stimulating progesterone secretion, but also contributes directly to the mammary glandular development and its final secretion of milk. Also essential to milk production are STH, corticosteroids from the adrenal, and thyroid hormone. Oxytocin, from the neurohypophysis, causes milk ejection by stimulating the contractile elements of the glandular ducts.

Testis. Androgens are produced by the testis. Most important and potent of them is testosterone, though others may be secreted.

Testosterone

They are produced in the cells of Leydig, and possibly elsewhere. The roles of androgens are numerous. One important group of actions is on the male accessory and secondary sexual characters and sexual behavior, being essential to normal development of these. In general metabolic action, androgens supplement STH in accelerating tissue growth, including protein synthesis. It simulates the adrenocortical mineralocorticoids in retaining action of sodium, potassium, chloride, and phosphate. It promotes bone growth and final closure of the epiphyses. It stimulates red cell production and blood flow through the tissues. It stimulates the glands of the skin and the production of melanin.

Control of the testis is exercised primarily by the adenohypophysis, though its activity is modified by both the thyroid and the adrenal cortex (Fig. 236). FSH and ICSH (= LH) from the hypophysis are principally involved. The former stimulates the germinal epithelium and initiates spermatogenesis, and the latter stimulates testosterone production and thereby controls development of the sex characters. The testis in turn influences the adenohypophysis. After castration the beta-cells of the latter organ become enlarged and FSH production is increased. This appears due to the absence of testosterone, and possibly estrogens which normally act to depress FSH secretion. To account for a regulatory action of the germinal epithelium on FSH production, two kinds of hypotheses have been advanced. One is that the germinal epithelium, Sertoli cells, or even the developing sperm cells secrete a hormone, possibly an

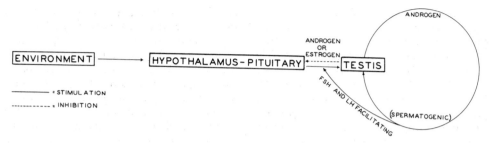

FIGURE 236. Diagram representing the major endocrine influences operating during the normal reproductive cycle of the adult male animal.

estrogen. Estrogen may even be produced in the Leydig cells under stimulation of FSH. The second is that FSH is used up by the germinal epithelium and that FSH itself in the blood normally suppresses further secretion.

Low titers of androgens appear essential for spermatogenesis, though higher titers have deleterious action by suppressing FSH production or even by direct action on the germinal epithelium.

Hormones and Reproduction

The gonadotropins, FSH, LH, and LTH, occur in all classes of vertebrates.[241] In the absence of gonadotropins, such as normally accompanies hypophysectomy, the ovary shows an arrest of development in young mammals and a reduction in size in adults. In the latter instances existing follicles become atretic. FSH in excess, on the other hand, will stimulate the simultaneous maturation of an excessive number of follicles. In some mammals, such as the rabbit and ferret, ovulation from mature follicles occurs only after mating or after some other effective stimulus. Such stimulation is known to induce the liberation of LH, which causes the ovulation.[160, 161] In other mammals, including the human, no special stimulation of the accessory complex is essential to induce ovulation. In all mammals LH is normally responsible for the formation of corpora lutea in the ruptured follicles.

Estrus cycles cease upon removal of the hypophysis. These may be restored, however, by hypophyseal implants, but only when the implants are made under the median eminence of the hypothalamus.[221, 349] The gonadotropins are not sex specific. They regulate the activity of the testis as well as of the ovary. Removal of the pituitary in the male results in an arrest of testicular function and reduction in size of the testes. Activity of the testes can be maintained in hy-

pophysectomized individuals by pituitary implants or extract injection. Many mammals which breed only at certain sharply delimited periods of the year may have their testes rendered unseasonably active by treatment with gonadotropins. This has been demonstrated for such species as the ground squirrel *Citellus* and the alpine marmot *Marmota*. After the mating season in such species the testes normally recede into the abdomen and spermatogenesis ceases. Administration of pituitary gonadotropin, or even chorionic gonadotropin, found normally only in pregnant females, will reverse these processes at any season.

An enlargement of the ovaries of the horned lizard *Phrynosoma* has been obtained by FSH and LH from hog pituitary and by serum from pregnant mares.[330] Hypophysectomy in the turtle *Emys* has shown the gonad and secondary sex characters dependent on the pituitary.[114]

Female frogs and toads may be induced to ovulate at any time of the year, except immediately after an egg-laying period, by injection of macerated anterior lobe of the pituitary.[389-391] Preparations of pituitaries from females are about twice as effective as those from males. The ovulation, which will occur between the second and fourth days, includes rupture of the follicles and expulsion of the eggs by contraction of smooth muscle fibers in the follicle wall. Injection of pituitary extract into male frogs induces amplexus. These sex reactions in amphibians may also be induced by pituitary extracts from other amphibians, from fishes,[496] mammals,[511] or may even occur in response to chorionic gonadotropin from pregnancy urine. Reciprocal injection experiments have indicated substantial differences in the active factor, LH, among various vertebrates.[501]

Premature spawning has been induced in several species of fishes after injection of fresh pituitary glands from other fishes. The ovoviviparous fish *Cnasterodon* was caused to spawn more than 2 weeks before the normal time after treatment with pituitaries from *Micropagon* and *Luciopimelodus*.[249] The Brazilian species, *Pimelodus*[91] and *Prochilodus*,[365] which normally spawn after the heavy rains that in Brazil follow a long period of drought, were induced to produce eggs and sperm during the period of drought within 1 to 3 days after an intramuscular injection of pituitaries from these same species. Rainbow and brown trout, *Salmo gairdnerii* and *S. fario,* in Wisconsin, were caused to produce mature eggs and sperm 6 to 7 weeks before the normal spawning season by intraperitoneal injections of fresh or acetone-dried pituitary glands from the carp.[227] FSH from sheep and serum from pregnant mares were without such effect. Increase in size of the ovocytes and ovaries of the lamprey *Petromyzon* and precocious sexual maturity were observed after treatment with human pregnancy urine.[90, 119] Hypophysectomy in the killifish *Fundulus* is followed by regressive changes in the ovaries and testes, compared with controls.[325] When the gland is removed in the autumn the gonads fail to undergo their normal spring enlargement. Furthermore, implantation of adult pituitaries at 3-day intervals into immature *Fundulus* induces within 4 weeks a considerable degree of gonadal activation in both sexes, together with production of secondary sexual pigmentary changes in the males characteristic of the breeding season.[326] Spawning in *Fundulus* appears to be under direct pituitary control.[373]

Androgens are found in all vertebrates. The primary function of androgens is to stimulate the development and activity of the male accessory reproductive organs. They are also responsible in part for differences in the conformation of the male body, the lower pitch of the human male voice, the characteristic distribution of hair, male pugnacious assertiveness, and many special male secondary sex characteristics such as the swollen clasping digits of the male frog, the comb of the cock, the crest of the newt, and the nuptial coloration and gonapodal appendages of certain viviparous fishes. Many of these are characters whose presence is largely restricted to the breeding season.

The various androgens differ from one another in their over-all potency and their relative effects on the numerous individual characters within the body, and these differences in turn may vary from species to species. This complicates greatly the problem of the roles of androgens within the body.

The testis comprises the principal source of androgens. This organ, furthermore, shows the capacity to extract less potent androgens from the circulating blood and convert them to substances of increased potency. Numerous observations have indicated the interstitial glandular cells to be the specific source. Reduction or disappearance of the seminal epithelium following x-radiation or ligation of the vasa efferentia or in cryptorchidism has been reported to cause no atrophy of the interstitial glandular tissue and no loss of androgenic potency. In the newt *Triton cristatus* there is no interstitial glandular tissue in the testes until the approach of the breeding season. At this time certain portions of the seminiferous epithelial tissue become transformed to produce a glandular body, and this transformation is temporally associated with the differentiation of the characteristic seasonal secondary sexual adornments in the male. Destruction of this glandular tissue is the equivalent of total castration in preventing development of these characters. In the stickleback *Gasterosteus* there is very close correlation between the annual cycle of differentiation of interstitial glandular cells and the cycle of secondary sex characters and behavior, such as skin coloration, secretion of nest-building mucus, and mating behavior. The latter characteristics in this species, on the other hand, show no relationship to amount of spermatogenic activity. That the seminiferous epithelium is not a significant source of androgen has also been demonstrated by removal of the greater part of the testes of cocks and assay of these organs after regeneration. The regenerated organs are principally seminiferous epithelial tissue with a great paucity of interstitial tissue, and correspondingly, there is evidence of only little androgen production by such organs.

These and numerous other experiments suggest that the interstitial glandular cells are the points of origin of testicular androgens.

Androgens are also produced by organs other than the testes. Male accessory reproductive structures have been maintained in full functional activity in castrated specimens by grafted ovarian tissue. Among fowl, the combs of both the cock and the hen are stimulated by androgens. The ovaries of the hen normally produce enough androgen to maintain a certain degree of development of the comb; after ovariectomy there is atrophy of the comb. The seasonal yellowing of the bills of both male and female starlings and blackening of the bills of male and female English sparrows are responses to androgens, estrogens being ineffective in this respect. Black-crowned night herons show, during the breeding season, certain changes in plumage coloration common to both sexes. Many observations such as the foregoing establish decisively the ovaries as a site of androgen production.

Another source of androgens is the adrenal gland. Implantation of adrenal tissue in young cocks results in precocious development of male sex characters and behavior. Castration of young rats does not result in atrophy of accessory genital structures for many days unless there is simultaneously complete adrenalectomy. Androgens are still excreted in the urine of animals after castration. Extracts of adrenal tissues have been found to yield the androgenic substance, adrenosterone, and the mineralocorticoid, desoxycorticosterone, the latter having an activity about the equivalent of that of androsterone, and the former having activity of about one-fifth of this value.

There is little evidence of any significant storage of androgens in the body. They are usually rapidly destroyed and therefore must be constantly produced if their influence is to be maintained. Certain poeciliid fishes can, however, be treated with androgens for only a few hours, but the activity of the androgens continues for many days. This observation appears to indicate either an actual or an effective storage within the body. The pigmented fat-body of the hibernating woodchuck, the so-called hibernating gland, has a remarkably high androgen content. The androgens are inactivated principally in the liver. The androgenic activity of blood leaving the liver is much less than that of blood entering this organ. Products of the inactivation are both inactive substances and androgens of somewhat lower activity, such as androsterone. Estrogens are also commonly produced in the process. These products of metabolic conversion are excreted by the kidney.

The relation of androgens to the development of the characteristic male suspensor organs, gonapodia, and to the smaller body size in male poeciliid fishes has been carefully analyzed.[447] Castration of males during the metamorphosis of the anal fin into a gonapodium results in immediate cessation of the process. Application of androgenic hormones to castrated males or to normal females can induce full development of the male characters which are typical of the species. It has

been shown that progressively larger concentrations of hormones are required for consecutive steps in the development of the gonapodium, with a concentration of one part of hormone in 4.2×10^{10} parts of water being sufficient to induce the first step. The gonapodium normally develops under the influence of a gradually increasing concentration in the blood of androgen from the fish's own testes. A certain optimum concentration is required for normal development of each step, higher concentrations inhibiting growth and inducing precocious differentiation. In toads the clasp reflex is lost following castration.[86, 250]

Estrogen is a term applied to any substance which will produce the characteristics of normal estrus, including cornification in the vagina, in an adult mouse. Estrogens are produced in ovaries of all vertebrates.

The placenta, both the maternal and the embryonic portion, contains abundant estrogen of much the same character as ovarian estrogen. Furthermore, oophorectomy in certain pregnant mammals does not result in significant change in the term of pregnancy or in any permanent reduction in the amount of estrogen excreted in the urine. In such cases the pubic symphyses also become separated normally, a change ordinarily conditioned by joint action of estrogen and progesterone.

Estrogens are also produced by the testes of males. In fact, the tissue with the highest-known estrogen yield is the stallion testis, in which estrone is the substance present. The testicular source appears to be, as for the androgens, the interstitial glandular cells. Estrogens have also been extracted from the adrenals.

Estrogens are very rapidly inactivated in the living body. Studies on the relation between site of transplantation of ovarian tissue and the physiological actions of the implants indicate the liver to be the principal site of destruction. Estrogen-containing blood passing through the liver reappears largely free of active concentrations of the hormone. Destruction of hepatic cells by carbon tetrachloride permits the hormone titer in the blood to rise with expected effects on estrus of the animal. Liver slices inactivate estradiol *in vitro* through the action of some CN-sensitive mechanism. Progesterone, on the other hand, diminishes the rate of estrogen inactivation and thus permits a higher titer to be maintained in the blood, from which much is then able to escape into the urine.

The kidneys and liver are the principal organs of estrogen excretion, although the relative importance of the two organs is not yet known.

The organ and tissue changes induced by estrogens are characterized by large variations in degree of responsiveness of the different cells and tissues to the hormone, thereby giving rise to gradients of response. Also characterizing the responses is a very high degree of reversibility of the changes when the concentration of the hormone declines. Such reversibility of the changes is most evident in many of the secondary and accessory sex character changes paralleling the reproductive cycles in many species.

As with the androgens, the specific threshold and character of the responses are determined by the inherent cellular characters, as can be seen in the unchanged character of the response as the individual tissues are transplanted to novel sites within the body. The relation of the response to the genetic constitution of the species is seen in reciprocal transplantations of feather-bearing skin between the sexes in fowl, resulting in the characteristic feather types for the host sex.

Progesterone. This substance is concerned primarily with those changes in the mammal associated with pregnancy and parturition. The chief sources of progesterone are the corpora lutea of the ovary.

Progesterone is also produced in the adrenals. Not only has progesterone been demonstrated in this organ, but desoxycorticosterone also in part simulates the action of progesterone. Extracts of adrenals can produce typical progestational alterations in the uterus in rabbits if, as a preliminary, they are treated with estrogen.

The placenta is also an important natural source of progesterone. In the mammal the placenta is believed normally to take over after a time the major share of production of the normal progesterone of pregnancy. Even after the total removal of the ovaries of pregnant rats sufficient progesterone is liberated from the placenta to carry the animals to normal terms. In man this change-over of control from corpora lutea to placenta is considered to occur between the seventy-ninth and the ninetieth day of pregnancy.

Progesterone is not stored in the body; it disappears very rapidly from the blood. Injection of progesterone, or the normal production of this hormone, is followed by the appearance of corresponding amounts of rela-tively inert alcohol, pregnanediol, in the urine. The preponderance of evidence points to the progestational endometrium of the uterus as the principal organ concerned in this conversion, which is principally in evidence in the progestational phases of the sexual cycle and usually ceases on hysterectomy. Furthermore, it is greatly reduced by injections of estradiol, which is known to suppress the progestational condition. That the progestational endometrium is not the sole site of the conversion is seen in the excretion of pregnanediol in males, and occasionally in females after hysterectomy.

The corpora lutea which are formed from the follicles, either without ovulation, as in the case of atretic follicles, or after ovulation, vary considerably in the extent of their development. Their greatest development accompanies gestation; lesser development is associated with lactation and pseudopregnancy, and the typical corpora lutea of ovulation are still smaller. The corpora lutea are dependent for their development on a supply of LH from the pituitary. Mammals appear to vary considerably in their need for external stimuli to encourage the necessary production of LH. An adequate stimulus has been shown to be copulation in the case of the rabbit. Suckling and lactation have been shown to stimulate its production in the rat, and psychic stimuli, such as the mere presence of a second individual, have been found effective in such animals as the pigeon and the rabbit. That the last stimulus is visual, at least for the pigeon, is demonstrated by the fact that a mirror image is often sufficient to produce the effect.

While all investigators are agreed that LH is essential for the initial development of the corpora lutea, and LTH to activate their secretion, there is much controversy as to other endocrine factors participating in the maintenance of these bodies. There appears to be good evidence from a number of types of experiments that the absence of FSH contributes significantly to their maintenance and that LH is nonessential. Gonadal hormones assist in their maintenance, probably through a suppression of FSH liberation by the pituitary. Comparison of experiments in which the embryos have been removed, leaving the placentae in situ, with those in which the placentae as well are excised, clearly demonstrates that the latter organs yield hormonal material which can operate to maintain the corpora lutea. These results also appear capable of interpretation in terms of suppression of FSH production by placentally derived gonadal hormones. That still other factors may contribute to the total explanation is seen in the observation that the corpora lutea may be maintained even after complete removal of the fetuses and placentae, provided the uteri are kept distended by such inert bodies as pellets of paraffin wax.

Corpora lutea have been described even for the poikilothermic vertebrates, but their highest development appears to be associated with viviparity in the mammal. They are said to be absent in birds and oviparous reptiles, but present in certain pregnant viviparous snakes,[14, 67, 324] such as *Crotolus* and *Bothrops,* the viviparous lizard *Zootoca,*[358] and viviparous anuran, *Nectophrynoides.*[297-300] Outside of the mammal there is no clear evidence that they are essential to the maintenance of pregnancy.

It has been postulated that corpora lutea arose evolutionarily as a clean-up process following ovulation, with progesterone being one simple end-product.[241] In the primitive mammals, the progesterone came to function in holding eggs to time of laying. In fact, in marsupials the period of gestation is only the length of the luteal phase of the estrous cycle. In rats and mice where gestation is still longer, a chorionic LTH arose to maintain the corpora lutea. In horses and primates where gestation is still longer the luteal phase was extended first by chorionic LTH and later a placental autonomy developed, with the placenta providing not only progesterone but also many additional essential factors as estrogens and prolactins.

Relaxin. Relaxin, a nonsteroidal substance, insoluble in fat solvents, is found within the corpora lutea and can be isolated from the blood of pregnant rabbits. It is probably a protein or polypeptide. It is capable of relaxing markedly the pelvic girdle of a guinea pig in 6 to 12 hours after a single injection. Progesterone and estradiol induce the secretion of relaxin in female rabbits unless they are castrated and hysterectomized. The latter observations indicate the ovaries and uterus to be essential to this response to the gonadal hormones.

Luteotropic Hormone (LTH or prolactin). The production of milk is an adaptation of all mammals, and such birds as the pigeon, for postpartum nutrition of their young. Hence it is not surprising to find that there is a considerable influence of gonadal hormones on milk-producing glands of the organism. The mammary glands of the mammalian fetus become enlarged under the influence of the hormonal complex of the maternal blood supply, but regress on parturition and typically remain so until sexual maturity, when the animal's own hormonal supply becomes adjusted for their development. The mammae of some mammals, such as the monkey *Macacus,* develop fully under the administration of estrogens alone. Other species, such as the rabbit, require administration of both estrogens and progesterone for similar development. Since mammary growth cannot be induced by the foregoing hormones after hypophysectomy, additional substances from the pituitary are also essential to normal mammary development and function. These include LTH, STH, and oxytocin. Normal adrenal functioning is also essential to continued lactation.

Control of Reproductive Cycles and Behavior. The pituitary gland through the production of gonadotropins is the principal endocrine organ through which reproductive activities are governed. We, therefore, with reason, look to a study of factors controlling this organ to supply us with fundamental information as to the mechanism of control of reproductive rhythms and adaptive reproductive responses of the organism to its external environment.

The pituitaries of young mammals are bipotential organs which normally develop into either a male or female type, under the influence of the particular gonad present. The gland is typically a larger organ in the adult female than in the male. Both female and male pituitaries normally produce FSH and LH in relatively large amounts. The primary difference between male and female pituitaries is one of cycle differences. Ovarian implants, but not testis implants, suppress FSH production by the adult pituitary in castrated females; in castrated males only testis implants will suppress FSH production. Thus, the adult pituitary has developed into differently responding male and female types, in contrast with its sexually indifferent condition in newborn mammals.

During the growth of a young mammal there is a gradual increase in the production of gonadotropins up to the time of sexual maturity, when the gonads are consequently brought to their complete functional state and their estrogens and androgens contribute to the full differentiation of the secondary and accessory sexual characteristics. The animal is now capable of normal reproductive activity. This is, in the vertebrates, typically a cyclical phenomenon with the periodicity often correlated with the annual solar cycle in such an adaptive fashion as to assure the young of a favorable time of year for birth and early postnatal development. In some species the reproductive periodicity bears much less or no relationship to external environmental stimuli and appears to result from a wholly inherent rhythmical mechanism, as in the cases of the rat, mouse, and man.

A vast amount of research has been done on the contributions of the interactions of endocrine sources to the maintenance of the normal cycles of mammals. The endocrine actions and interactions of the major organs participating in the normal reproductive cycles are indicated for the female mammal in Figure 235, and for the male in Figure 236.

In the female the pituitary, through FSH production, stimulates the development of the ovarian follicles and interstitial tissues, with a consequent increase in estrogen production. The rising concentration of estrogen in the blood mimics FSH and furthers the ovarian development. At the same time the estrogen gradually suppresses FSH production by the pituitary while at first strongly encouraging LH liberation by the pituitary. Over a longer period estrogen suppresses LH liberation. LH liberated from the pituitary stimulates ovulation in many mammals, and in all it stimulates the differentiation of corpora lutea with the subsequent production by them of progesterone. Although LH induces differentiation of the corpora lutea, an additional pituitary principle, Luteotrophin, is needed for stimulating the actual secretion of progesterone. Luteotrophin is believed to be identical with the lactogenic principle. Progesterone cooperates with estrogen in the further suppression of the production of FSH by the pituitary. In case of pregnancy, the placentae of the developing embryos are activated in the presence of progesterone and proceed to liberate substantial amounts of chorionic gonadotropin, the activity of which very closely resembles that of pituitary LH. This gonadotropin contributes to the suppression of production of both pituitary gonadotropins through its stimulation of greater gonadal hormone production.

The corresponding endocrine interactions participating in the male reproductive cycle are simpler. Gonadotropin from the pituitary activates the interstitial and spermatogenic tissues of the testes, with the resultant increase in testosterone production in the former. This androgen simultaneously stimu-lates further development of the spermatogenic epithelium and facilitates the influences of both FSH and LH. As the blood titer of androgen gradually rises this hormone suppresses pituitary gonadotropin production. The decline of androgen production after pituitary suppression eventually leaves the latter free to initiate a new cycle of reproductive activity.

In a few species there tends to be an annual reproductive period at a particular season of the year, without any regard to any particular factor of the external environment. Such an operation of an inherent rhythm has been clearly demonstrated for certain organisms which continue to breed indefinitely during the same calendar months after transfer from the northern to the southern hemisphere, or vice versa. Other species on similar transfer more or less rapidly undergo a readjustment of their breeding period to the corresponding season for their new locality.[321] The readiness with which the organism makes such an adjustment appears to be a function of the relative degree to which the breeding cycle depends on external factors.

Of all the external stimuli known to exert an influence on reproductive cycles, one of the most effective so far demonstrated is light and photoperiodism.[32, 163, 164, 262, 388, 506] Among certain north temperate zone birds it has been shown that the testis of the male normally reaches a peak of its annual cyclical activity in the late spring. Experiments on male juncos, sparrows, and starlings have clearly shown that gradual increase in length of the daily period of illumination through supplementary artificial lighting will bring the activity of the testis to a maximum at a time not typical for the species. Properly controlled experiments have shown that it is the light itself rather than the resulting longer daily periods of activity or feeding which is the actual determining factor. Immediately following one period of breeding activity the bird is refractory to response to photoperiod again.[334] A similar subjection to increased periods of illumination over a period of about 2 months has been found to bring female ferrets into estrus in winter, a time at which in their normal reproduction cycle they are in anestrus.[46] Similar observations have been made on mice (*Peromyscus*).[477] Such reptiles as *Anolis, Xantusia,* and *Lacerta* respond to photoperiod.[34] Among the fishes the reproductive cycle of trout, sunfishes, and several species of minnows has also been shown to be importantly influenced by photoperiodism.[82, 216-218, 228, 245, 448, 457]

In the field mouse, *Microtus,* the gonads have been shown to diminish in size during treatment of the animal with gradually decreasing periods of illumination.[27]

Such experiments as these appear to indicate that the gradual changes in day length in the annual solar cycle constitute a very effective stimulus in determining the normal annual reproductive cycles of many species of vertebrates.[505]

In the immature duck whose gonads are normally stimulated by increased illumination, it has been shown that pituitaries from illuminated specimens show increased gonadotropic activity over those of untreated controls when implanted into immature mice. Red and orange lights are more effective than other colors in inducing the effect. The eyes are not essential to the reaction; direct illumination of the pituitary resulting from illumination of the orbit after enucleation effectively activates the gland. When light is conducted directly to the pituitary through a quartz rod, blue light, which otherwise shows only small influence, becomes quite as effective as red and orange. Reproductive cycles continue in the duck in either constant light or dark, but the period ceases to be annual.[43]

A similar effect of light on the reproductive cycle through other routes than the eyes has been shown for sparrows. In the ferret, on the other hand, division of the optic nerves completely inhibits the action of light, indicating the retina of the eyes to be the effective receptor in this species.

Nervous connection of the hypothalamus with other parts of the nervous system is usually essential to normal sexual functioning. Nervous connection between the hypothalamus and the pituitary is essential for certain aspects of control of the reproductive cycle,[41, 320] as for example ovulation in the rabbit, but appears nonessential in numerous other instances, the conduction in these latter cases apparently being humoral. Secretory granules accumulate in nerve loops of the median eminence in white-crowned sparrows; held on an 8-hour light regimen they disappear, and the testes recrudesce when the light periods are increased to 20 hours.[351]

The temperature of the external environment has been shown to play an important role in determining the time of gonadal development and appearance of secondary sex characters in the stickleback (*Gasterosteus*), a sufficient rise in temperature rapidly in-ducing these changes. Low temperature and darkness such as normally obtain during its annual period of hibernation will activate the gonads in the ground squirrel *Citellus* at any season. Both light and temperature influence the reptilian sexual cycle.[33]

Factors other than light and temperature are often important. Periods of rainfall with the correlated increase in green vegetation serve as the stimulus to reproduction in the equatorial weaver finch *Quelea.*[127]

Hormones and Gastrointestinal Coordination

In the mammal the integration of the activities of various parts of the digestive system in dealing with ingested food is in part endocrine in character.[196, 202, 259, 260] The major hormones and their general sites of formation and regions of actions are shown diagrammatically in Figure 237.

The pyloric mucosa on appropriate stimulation secretes into the blood a hormone, gastrin. Noninnervated, transplanted gastric pouches are caused to secrete in response to the presence of food in the stomach of the animal. For a long time gastrin was believed to be identical with histamine, but it is now known that histamine-free extracts of the pyloric mucosa will stimulate secretion of a highly acid gastric juice with very little peptic activity and simultaneously stimulate pancreatic secretion. However, there is some reason to believe that histamine also plays here the role of a hormone.[407] By fractional precipitation the gastric stimulant, gastrin, has been separated from the activator of the pancreas; the latter resembles very closely the secretin obtained from the duodenal mucosa.

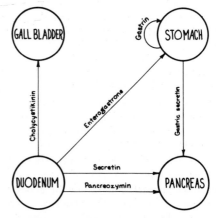

FIGURE 237. Diagrammatic representation of the sources and points of action of the principal hormones operating in gastrointestinal coordination.

Gastrin and gastric secretin appear to have protein-like properties.

The duodenal mucosa quantitatively stimulates the pancreas to liberate its digestive juice through action of a polypeptide hormone, secretin.[202] It was formerly thought that secretin stimulated mainly the secretion of water and bicarbonate by the pancreas and that the production of enzymes was nervously controlled, but no consistent data were obtained to support this hypothesis. The variable concentrations of enzyme in pancreatic juice that have been reported to be produced in response to secretin injections appear to find their explanation in terms of the presence of a second hormone in the crude extract. One fraction stimulates the secretion chiefly of water and inorganic salts from a denervated pancreas. A second fraction stimulates pancreatic enzyme secretion. The active factor of this latter fraction has been termed pancreozymin.

Another active principle from the duodenum, and one which has been separated from crude secretin extracts, is cholecystokinin, a powerful agent in producing gallbladder contraction.

A fourth factor, enterogastrone, has been isolated from the duodenal mucosa. This factor inhibits gastric secretion of HCl and gastric motility. The activity of enterogastrone appears to be principally antisecretory, and since in the presence of enterogastrone the gastric juice produced under the influence of gastric stimulants such as histamine is low in acid content and rich in pepsin it would appear that enterogastrone preferentially inhibits the acid-secreting parietal cells of the stomach.

Other gastrointestinal chemical coordinators have been proposed on the basis of brief experiments, but these appear to have a more questionable existence than the aforementioned ones.

Coloration and Seasonal Color Changes of Birds and Mammals

Among the numerous species of birds which show differentiation of hen and cock plumages a wide variety of mechanisms is involved.[120, 129] In the English sparrow the control of plumage type is exclusively genetic. Among pheasants, the plumage type is determined by simultaneous action of genes and hormones. In perhaps the majority of birds, however, the plumage typical of one sex is neutral; that of the other sex is determined by blood-borne hormones. In the common domestic fowl the neutral type appears to be the cock plumage, with the hen type the result of action of estrogens. In African weaver finches, the neutral type is the hen plumage; the cock plumage is the result of action of hypophyseal hormones.[122, 417, 500] Only in the herring gull, among the birds thus far studied, does the cock type of plumage depend on action of androgens.[63]

In the majority of common birds the adults undergo a rather complete postnuptial molt immediately after the breeding period; the new regenerating plumage becomes the winter or eclipse plumage. A second, usually much less extensive molt, the prenuptial, occurs in the spring. The regenerating plumage constitutes the breeding or nuptial plumage. This latter molt is most extensive in those species which exhibit conspicuous breeding coloration. The times at which birds assume the nuptial and winter plumages are governed by a number of factors. In some species, such as the African weaver finch *Pyromelanox* and the starling, the changes appear due to an inherent cyclically rhythmic hypophyseal activity,[498] although the occurrence of the rhythm may depend in part on length of daily light periods.[78, 85, 311] Some other species, such as mallard ducks, the white-throated sparrow, and the bobwhite, can be induced to molt and undergo a plumage-type change at a time other than their regular season by subjection to artificially increasing or decreasing light periods. Therefore, the annual plumage changes of most birds, like migrating and breeding activity, appear to be controlled in good measure by the annual cycle of day lengths.

Certain northern birds and mammals show a seasonal color change from brown in summer to white in winter. The times of these changes in such forms as the ptarmigan *Lagopus*,[248] the ermine *Mustela*,[50] and the varying hare *Lepus*[318] have been shown to be determined by the seasonal changes in day lengths; the animals could be caused to whiten out of season by appropriate experimental alteration of the daily lighting. Experiments involving masking of the varying hare[318] indicate that the eyes are the normal receptors. Both in the natural cycle of color change and in color changes induced artificially by modification of illumination, the varying hare is physiologically brown when large amounts of gonadotropic hormones are present in the blood and is physiologically white when these hormones are low in concentration. Molting in a physiologically brown animal is followed by production of brown hair; in a physiologically white one, by production of white hair. Extracts of whole pituitary containing gonadotropic hormones will convert physiologically white animals into physiologically brown ones and simultaneously induce shedding of the white hair. Hypophysectomy in ferrets abolishes the cyclic molting.[47, 49] No endocrine gland other than the pituitary appears to be involved in these color changes. Castrated and thyroidectomized hares undergo the normal seasonal color changes.[318]

Hormones and Bird Migration

Some years ago it was postulated that the migrational behavior of birds was under the control of hormones from the gonads.[385-387] Northward migration of birds in the northern hemisphere was considered a result of the recrudescence of the gonads in the spring; regression of the gonads after the breeding season was correlated with southward migration. In the junco, the northward migration appeared correlated with periods of great interstitial cell activity of the gonads. In the crow, southward migration appeared independent of gonadal regression. In the European starling, northward migration appeared correlated with gonadal secretion and southward migration with absence of secretion.[83, 84]

Other evidence seems to indicate with moderate clarity that changes in gonadal activity are not causally related to migrational behavior.[163, 208, 501] Removal of gonads does not appear to abolish migrational behavior. Furthermore, many birds migrate while they are still sexually immature.[507] Migrant juncos retained as long as 2 months after their normal time of migration would still move northward on release, although their gonads were already in breeding condition.[503] Birds retained in their wintering grounds during the summer, and thus prevented from spring migrating and breeding, nonetheless underwent the typical gonadal regression and fat deposition observed in birds preparing for the annual fall migration.[504] Examination of the pituitaries of juncos showing increase in testis size, and of birds later during breeding, revealed cytological evidence of much more active secretion of this gland than during the winter when testis size was minimal. Furthermore, injections of antuitrin-G containing several anterior lobe principles will induce a condition of increased gonad size and heavy fat deposition which resembles closely those characteristics in a bird ready to migrate. These observations strongly suggest that the pituitary is an important conditioning agent for migration.

Within many species of birds, including juncos, it is possible to differentiate two types of individuals. Some individuals are normal migrants, and others are nonmigrants or residents. These two types can sometimes be clearly differentiated into morphologically different subspecies or varieties, whereas again they may comprise quite similar individuals. An individual bird may belong to both types at different times during its life. There appears to be good evidence that similar treatment of "residents" and "migrants" with increased light periods will result in gonadal recrudescence in both instances, yet only the migrants will exhibit fat deposition and subsequent migration.

Such observations as these lead to the concept that an inherent potentiality to migrate exists in certain birds, but that the behavior patterns which initiate and carry out the migratory flight are activated or influenced by seasonally varying external factors, principally temperature,[52, 271] and changing day lengths. These factors appear to operate initially by way of the anterior lobe of the pituitary.[48] Hormones from this organ then gradually alter the physiological state of the bird, one or more of these latter alterations probably serving as the immediate stimulus to migration. It has been suggested that the fundamental alteration in physiological state involved here is the deposition of fat which would provide the energy for the migrational flight.

HORMONES AND PIGMENT-CELL ACTIVITIES

Integumentary Chromatophores. The roles of hormones in the control of the integumentary color changes in cephalopods, crustaceans, insects, fishes, amphibians, and reptiles have been dealt with at some length in Chapter 19 and will not be reviewed here.

INSECTS

The insects possess an endocrine system organized, in its functional plan, remarkably like that of the vertebrate. Dominating the system are the central nervous organs, themselves in part neuroendocrine. Clusters of neurosecretory cells in the brain, comprising the pars intercerebralis, secrete hormonal material liberated into the blood by way of organs posterior to the brain known as the corpora cardiaca. Such a secretory complex is highly comparable to the hypothalamic-neurohypophyseal system. This complex regulates the activity of an endocrine gland of the anterior thoracic region of the body, the prothoracic gland. Closely associated with the corpora cardiaca in most insects are other glands, the corpora allata, which also have their activity regulated by the brain. Other parts of the central nervous system, particularly the subesophageal ganglia, are also sites of neuroendocrine cells. Hence, again, as in the vertebrates, the neural and endocrine systems are very intimately interrelated in a unitary coordinatory system.

Molt, Pupation, and Metamorphosis in Insects. The postembryonic development of insects comprises an orderly series of stages in the course of which the insect becomes transformed from a larva to an adult or imago. The process involves growth by means of a series of molts and a metamorphosis in which the larval characters are lost and imaginal ones differentiated. In the hemimetabolous insects, such as Orthoptera (e.g., grasshoppers, cockroaches, and walking sticks), the Hemip-

tera (e.g., bedbugs and *Rhodnius*) and Odonata, the transition from larval to adult condition is characteristically a gradual one in which the developing young, typically known as nymphs, in succeeding molts come gradually to resemble more and more nearly the adult. In such hemimetabolous insects, however, the last nymphal molt is usually associated with by far the most striking transformation and hence one which is commonly considered the metamorphic molt.

In holometabolous insects, as the Lepidoptera (e.g., moths and butterflies) Diptera (e.g., *Drosophila* and blowflies), and Coleoptera (beetles), very little change of form in the direction of the adult occurs during the larval series of molts, these being primarily growth changes. These rapidly growing larvae are usually given such terms as maggots and caterpillars. The last larval molt is associated with the formation of a pupa. The pupal stage, whose length often depends upon external factors such as temperature and light,[306, 363] often includes an extended period of quiescence or diapause. During the pupal stage the larval organism becomes completely transformed into an adult, a spectacular metamorphosis. There is no fundamental difference between the two foregoing types of development, the observed dissimilarities being primarily ones in the times at which the processes of imaginal differentiation occur. The latter are extended to a considerable extent over the whole of the larval period in the Hemimetabola and largely confined to the pupal stage in the Holometabola.

The number of larval or nymphal stages in development differs from species to species, but is usually a constant for each species. The bug *Rhodnius,* for example, has five nymphal stages or instars, the orthopteran *Carausius* has six, and the dipteran *Drosophila* has three. It is now well established that the sequence of events in the growth and differentiation in the postembryonic insect is in good measure under the integrating action of hormones derived from the animal's endocrine system[59, 412, 483] (Fig. 238).

A common plan of the endocrine mechanism regulating growth and differentiation appears to extend throughout the insects.[113, 257, 264, 378, 382, 412, 482, 483, 493, 494] Its essence is as follows: The molt-initiating stimulus, which varies from species to species, induces secretion of a brain hormone which is liberated into the blood from the corpora cardiaca after being transported within nerve axons to that point.[16, 238, 401, 406, 445, 446] The

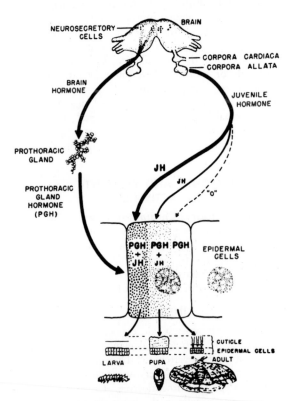

FIGURE 238. Diagrammatic representation of the insect endocrine system involved in growth and differentiation. (From Schneiderman, H. A., and Gilbert, L. I.: *in* Cell, Organism and Milieu. Ronald Press Co.)

brain hormone activates the prothoracic glands which produce the growth and differentiation, or molting, hormone. An active principle of the prothoracic glands has been crystallized and found to have a molecular weight of about 300, an empirical formula of $C_{18}H_{30}O_4$, and to be a 2-β-unsaturated ketone.[88, 270] It has been given the name ecdysone. Two ecdysones are now known, and called α- and β-ecdysone. Ecdysone stimulates the molting processes, effecting immediately such transformations in the epidermis as increase in protein and ribonucleic acid, and increase in mitochondria and the endoplasmic reticulum,[420] irrespective of whether the molt leads to another larval stage, a pupal stage, or the imago.

For larval or nymphal molts a second hormone, whose secretion is also regulated through the brain,[153, 155, 263, 317, 401] is liberated. This one, termed the juvenile hormone, arising from the corpora allata, suppresses pupal and imaginal differentiation. It is secreted in progressively smaller amounts at successive molts. This factor has been found in especially high concentration in the abdomen of male *Cecropia*. Potent extracts have been prepared which display a deep yellow, oily character.[495] Juvenile hormone activity has been found in a wide variety of animals, both vertebrate and invertebrate.

One additional hormone participating in insect development is a diapause hormone secreted by the subesophageal ganglion.[178, 225] Active extracts of this hormone have been prepared.[226]

Underlying the action of endocrine-regulating factors in insect growth and differentiation is a gradually changing pattern of responsiveness of the target tissues to the hormones. These changing competencies contribute quite as importantly as the hormones themselves to the orderly character of insect differentiation.[58-61]

Experiments on the tropical bug *Rhodnius prolixus* were the first to provide a clear demonstration of the action of two of the developmental hormones,[479-481] the one initiating molt accompanied by metamorphosis, and the other inhibiting metamorphosis. The former is now known as the brain hormone,[88] and the latter as the inhibitory, or juvenile, hormone. Roles of these hormones were readily demonstrated in developing *Rhodnius*. This insect, at each nymphal instar, molts a definite number of days after a meal of blood. The distention of the abdomen serves as the adequate stimulus. Following decapitation these insects will survive for 6 to 10 months. It was shown by decapitation at different intervals after feeding that there was a "critical period" occurring a few days after the feeding. Nymphs decapitated before this period never underwent molt; those decapitated afterward did. That the critical period constituted a time when a blood-borne molt-initiating hormone was being liberated from an organ in the head was proved by experimental telobiosis (Fig. 239A) of two decapitated individuals. Under such conditions, for example, molting in a fourth stage nymph decapitated before the critical period was induced by a fourth stage nymph decapitated after the critical period. Both thereby became fifth stage nymphs.

The fifth nymphal stage, upon molt, typi-

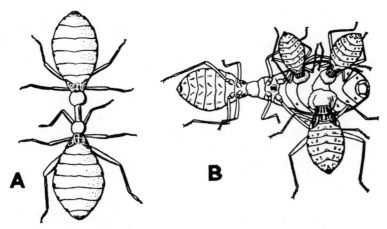

FIGURE 239. Experimental telobiosis and parabiosis in the bug, *Rhodnius*. *A*, telobiosis involving only nymphal instars. *B*, fourth and fifth instar nymphs united telobiotically and parabiotically with an imago. (From Wigglesworth, V. B.: Quart. J. Micr. Sci., vol. 77.)

cally metamorphosed at that time into an adult. When a fifth stage nymph was decapitated after its critical period it was shown by telobiotic union with a first or second stage nymph, decapitated before the critical period, that the fifth stage nymph possessed within its blood a hormonal factor complex which determined molt with metamorphosis. The attached first or second stage nymph became in this instance a diminutive adult. When a fourth stage nymph which would normally molt to become a fifth stage nymph was decapitated after the critical period and united with a fifth stage nymph decapitated before the critical period, the latter molted and became a giant, supernumerary sixth stage nymph instead of an imago. Furthermore, although the adult normally does not molt again, it was made to do so by telobiotic and parabiotic union to two or three fifth stage nymphs decapitated after the critical period. When fourth stage instead of fifth stage nymphs were used, the adult or molt showed a partial return to the nymphal condition (Fig. 239B).

From such experiments it was readily seen that the blood of a nymph after the critical period contains factors that determine molting either without, or with, an accompanying extensive metamorphosis. A careful study of the results of decapitation of third and fourth instar nymphs at different times during the critical period itself showed that, of those molting after decapitation, those decapitated early in the period showed a significant tendency toward premature metamorphosis, while those decapitated later did not do so. This observation indicated that during the critical period of the first four instars a molting and metamorphosis hormone was first liberated and that quickly thereafter a metamorphosis-inhibiting principle was also secreted. The fifth instar alone in *Rhodnius* fails to produce the latter principle.

The source of the metamorphosis-inhibiting or juvenile hormone was found to be the corpus allatum, a median unpaired gland in *Rhodnius* located in the posterior region of the head. The source of the hormone responsible for initiating molting and differentiation is the neurosecretory elements of the pars-intercerebralis of the dorsal midregion of the brain. The elongated form of the head of *Rhodnius* rendered it very simple to cut the head transversely in such a manner as to retain the corpus allatum while the brain was removed. Utilizing this technique in conjunction with telobiotic experiments, as well as by

implanting corpora allata and pars intercerebralis regions of brains into nymphs decapitated before the critical period, one could obtain at will either a nymphal molt or a metamorphic one in *Rhodnius*.

Studies on lepidopterans first demonstrated the role of the prothoracic glands and clarified the relationship of these to the brain hormone. From the time of the original experiments of Kopec[294] on lepidopteran pupation and metamorphosis it was known that at a certain "critical period" prior to pupation a hormone was liberated from the anterior portion of the larva and that this was essential for pupation and metamorphosis. In the silkworm moth *Bombyx* this hormone is produced in the prothoracic gland located in the prothoracic segment.[177] If the prothoracic segment was cut off by ligation from the more posterior regions of the body immediately after pupation the posterior portion failed to develop further. If the constriction were made 12 to 18 hours after pupation the posterior portion metamorphosed normally. If a prothoracic gland was implanted into the posterior portion of a pupa ligated before the 12- to 18-hour "critical period," metamorphosis of this part also proceeded normally; or an abdomen cut off by constriction was induced to metamorphose by connection of its hemolymph cavity with that of a normal metamorphosing specimen, even when the connection was made by way of a glass capillary tube.

In the giant silkworm moth *Platysamia*, after pupation, a dormant period of diapause exists for some 5 to 6 months in pupae maintained at 25°C. When the brain was removed from such a diapausing pupa the insect never metamorphosed although the animal usually survived for about a year.[488] If a pupa was chilled by exposure to a temperature of 3 to 5°C. for 1½ months, metamorphosis then occurred in a little over 1 month after the pupa was restored to the higher temperature. When a chilled pupa was united parabiotically with an unchilled one, both metamorphosed synchronously in about 1½ months (Fig. 240A and B). Implants of brain from a chilled pupa induced metamorphosis in an unchilled pupa.

A reconciliation of the observed influences on metamorphosis of the prothoracic gland, on the one hand, and of the brain, on the other, was effected.[450, 451, 489, 492] In *Platysamia cecropia* the active fraction from the brain arises in the inner mass of each cerebral lobe of the brain, within which are found two groups of neurosecretory cells, a median and a lateral group. The median group of cells corresponds with the pars intercerebralis cells of the hemipterans.[491] To induce metamorphosis of a brainless pupa a portion of a brain containing both groups of neurosecretory cells had to be implanted, suggesting that these two groups collaborate in the production of the material involved. Killed brain, or crude brain extract, was ineffective as a substitute for living brain tissue in inducing metamorphosis. An active extract of silkworm brain has, however, been prepared.[287]

When pupae of *Platysamia* were transected just anterior to the sixth abdominal segment and then a plastex coverslip sealed over the cut end of each portion, preparations were obtained which were viable for 8 months or more and development could be readily observed in them. Chilled anterior portions, or brainless anterior portions which had received an implant of a chilled brain, underwent normal metamorphosis. The posterior portion did not undergo metamorphosis even when a number of chilled brains were implanted into a single abdomen. Such abdomens metamorphosed, however, when they were grafted to metamorphosing anterior portions. An endocrine factor in addition to that from the brain was obviously essential. That the source of the second factor was the prothoracic gland was shown by the induction of pupation of isolated abdomens by the implantation of both chilled brains and prothoracic glands (Fig. 240C and D). The latter could come from either chilled or unchilled pupae. Prothoracic glands by themselves were not adequate. It was clear therefore that metamorphosis normally depends on the production of at least two factors. The first, produced from the brain, activated the prothoracic glands.

Other experiments[490] suggest that the prothoracic gland principle effects termination of pupal diapause and consequent metamorphosis through action on the cytochrome system of the larval tissue.

The brain and the juvenile hormones are not species specific, and the hormones of *Rhodnius* will induce similar changes in other hemipterans, such as *Triatoma* and *Cimex*.

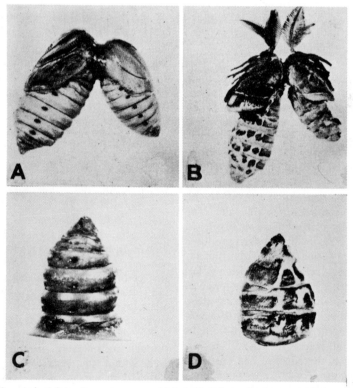

FIGURE 240. *A*, brainless, diapausing pupa (right) of *Telea polyphemus*, grafted to a chilled pupa of *Platysamia cecropia* (left). *B*, same animals after metamorphosis. (From Williams, C. M.: Biol. Bull., vol. 90.) *C*, posterior portion of a diapausing pupa. *D*, metamorphosis of the portion illustrated in *C* occurring after implantation of both chilled brain and prothoracic glands from a diapausing pupa. (From Williams, C. M.: Biol. Bull., vol. 93.)

Among the orthopterans, *Carausius*,[369, 371] *Leucophaea*,[154, 399, 401] and *Melanoplus*,[367] which have been investigated at some length and which show hemimetabolous development, the site of origin of the molt-initiating hormone is the brain, and the brain hormone activates the prothoracic glands. The corpora allata, in all, in addition, produce a juvenile hormone. In *Carausius,* which normally has six nymphal stages, removal of the corpora allata in the third nymphal stage results in a premature metamorphosis, although two nymphal molts usually intervene between the operation and the metamorphosis. This latter is interpreted to mean that the hormone from the gland is stored somewhere in the body over this period. Transplantation of corpora allata from third or fourth instar nymphs into sixth instar nymphs of *Carausius* may produce giant imagos which have undergone as many as three or four additional nymphal molts. In *Leucophaea* which normally possess eight nymphal instars allatectomy of a seventh instar before the critical period results in an adult-like stage following the molt. Such an individual has been termed an "adultoid" and differs from adults in having a smaller size and shorter wings. Allatectomy in fifth or sixth instars results in molt in "preadultoids" which require one additional molt to produce "adultoids."

In the holometabolous dipterans the ring gland of the larva, located dorsal to the brain and between the brain lobes, is the source of a hormone inducing pupation.[205, 206] This gland is a composite including the functional corpora allata, corpora cardiaca, and prothoracic glands. The role of this gland is readily demonstrated by ligating the larva to constrict it into two portions, one containing the brain, and the other without it.[175] If this operation is performed before a certain "critical period," only that portion containing the ring gland pupates; if constriction is produced after the critical period, both portions pupate. Transplantation of a ring gland from a last larval instar into a first larval instar produces premature pupation in the latter. Ring-gland implants will also induce pupation in a portion of a larva cut off by ligation from its own ring gland before the critical period. This hormone is the effective one operating in metamorphosis as well as in pupation.[37] Imaginal discs implanted into the hemocoele of adult flies will not differentiate unless ring glands of late larvae are also implanted.[206] Furthermore, the metamorphosis hormone of Lepidoptera will induce pupation in dipterans.[37]

The corpora allata of the Lepidoptera, like those of the hemipterans and orthopterans, are the source of a juvenile hormone. Allatectomy in caterpillars of younger instars is followed by a premature pupation, and, conversely, implantation of corpora allata from early instars into caterpillars ready to pupate will significantly delay the pupation.[65]

Reproduction. In insects, despite extensive observations on the effects of parasitic castration, surgical castration, and gonad implantation, there is no reliable suggestion as yet that gonadal or other blood-borne hormones significantly influence the differentiation of secondary sex characters. In fact, strong evidence to the contrary is seen in the frequently observed occurrence of gynandromorphism.

The majority of species of insects so far investigated show a hormonal relationship between the corpora allata and the ovaries. Allatectomy in late larval stages or young adults is accompanied by a failure of the eggs in the ovary to undergo their normal growth and development. This has been demonstrated for the hemipteran, *Rhodnius*;[480] the dipterans *Calliphora*,[443, 444] *Lucilia*,[124, 443] and *Sarcophaga*;[124] and the orthopteran *Leucophaea*.[400] Implantation of corpora allata into allatectomized individuals restores the ability to produce normal eggs. On the other hand, no such relationship appears to exist in the orthopteran *Carausius*[369-371] or in lepidoptera.[66] In these instances a brain or corpus cardiacum hormone is presumed to substitute. That a brain secretion plays a role in reproductive regulation is suggested by the correlation between observed increased neurosecretion in the adult and reproductive activity.[16, 136, 137, 346] Evidence for the humoral nature of this relationship was clearly demonstrated by telobiotic experiments in *Rhodnius,* in which the factor concerned was shown to be blood borne, and by transplantation of the corpora allata into allatectomized individuals, which indicated that the corpora allata exert their typical action irrespective of their new location.[480] The influence of the active allatum principle appears to operate through its influence on the deposition of yolk within the eggs rather than on the earlier development of the oocytes. The corpora allata are apparently essential only throughout the period of oocyte growth and yolk deposition of each successive reproductive cycle. It has been shown that allatectomy is followed by profound alterations in the general metabolism of *Melanoplus*.[368] This has led some investigators to support the view that the reproductive functions of the principle from the corpora allata are secondary to more basic metabolic ones.

Allatectomy also depresses the growth and activity of certain female accessory organs in *Calliphora*, *Melanoplus*, and *Leucophaea*, this influence being independent of the presence of the gonads and hence not operating through them.

There is considerable evidence that the ovary also exerts an action on the corpora allata in female insects. Ovariectomy in *Melanoplus*, *Calliphora*, and *Lucilia* leads to hypertrophy of the allata, and perhaps leads to a functional alteration in still other insects, such as *Sarcophaga* and *Leucophaea*.

Allatectomy leads to less distinct results in male insects than in females. The operation in no manner interferes with the production of sperm cells; in fact, allatectomized males of *Leucophaea* show ability to mate with, and effectively fertilize the eggs of, normal females. There are reports, however, that the male accessory glands of *Rhodnius* and of *Calliphora* fail to show normal development after allatectomy. Castration of male *Leucophaea* and *Lucilia* has led to no observable modifications in the corpora allata.

There is some evidence that the roaches *Blatta* and *Blattella* produce within their ovaries a functional counterpart of the mammalian corpus luteum, which contributes to normal egg-producing rhythms of these species.[261] In this rhythm the mature ova are laid in cocoons which are carried about at the genital opening of the female. The ovaries are inhibited while these cocoons are being borne, but are released to further activity after deposition of the cocoons. The ovary is believed to stimulate humorally the brain which in turn inhibits nervously the corpora allata.[153] Implantation of actively growing ovaries into the body of cocoon-bearing females is followed by a rapid change of certain characteristics of the implanted oocytes to resemble those seen in immature ovaries. Extracts of ovaries from animals in the inhibited stage of the normal reproductive cycle yield the same results. Histological examination of ovaries in their normally inhibited stage showed the presence of yellowish granules in the follicle formerly occupied by the developing ova.

CRUSTACEANS

Like that of the vertebrate and the insects, the crustacean endocrine system, a complex one, is functionally very closely related to the central nervous system. Neurosecretory cells in ganglia of the nervous system form hormones which are transported within their axons to places of their liberation into the blood. Conspicuous elements of this system are the X-organs associated with ganglia in the eyestalks of most stalk-eyed crustaceans and in the heads of others. Best known of these are the medulla terminalis X-organ (MTGX) and the sensory papilla X-organ (SPX)[286] (Fig. 241). The sinus gland of the eyestalk (or head) is generally believed to be simply an organ comprising chiefly the hormone-charged terminations of the X-organ neurosecretory cells.[54-56, 138, 145, 209, 323, 339, 364] The secretory materials in the cells appear to be contained in membrane-bounded vesicles.[244, 283, 284, 379]

It has been postulated that the hormones, like the vertebrate hypothalamic ones, are polypeptides.

A second important crustacean endocrine complex comprises secretory nervous cells in the brain, and perhaps also esophageal connective ganglia, with hormone-conducting axons terminating in an organ called the postcommissural gland (Fig. 242) where the substances are released into the blood.[71, 281, 282] Following the same organizational pattern are cells in the ventral ganglionic chain liberating their hormone some distance away in the pericardial organs at the openings of the large veins into the pericardial cavity.[6]

But not all the crustacean endocrine glands are based directly upon nervous secretions. Quite distinct is a pair of glands in the anterior thoracic region in the antennary or maxillary segment. These glands are the Y-organs[139, 179] and are apparently without any direct innervation. They are regulated by secretions from the eyestalk-gland complex. In addition, the ovary serves in an endocrine capacity.[103, 104, 285, 439] There is also an important organ, the androgenic gland, morphologically associated with the sperm duct near its external orifice.[104, 107]

Molting in Crustaceans. The decapod crustaceans in their development typically undergo a number of molts, passing through a series of characteristic larval stages, and after having achieved the body form of the adult they continue to grow through periodic molting of the exoskeleton. Little or nothing

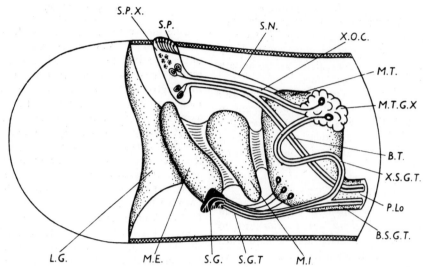

FIGURE 241. Diagram of the eyestalk neuroendocrine complex of the natantian, *Lysmata*. *B.S.*, brain-sinus gland tract; *B.T.*, brain-X-organ tract; *L.G.*, lamina ganglionaris; *M.E.*, medulla externa; *M.I.*, medulla interna; *M.T.* medulla terminalis; *M.T.G.X.*, medulla terminalis ganglionic X-organ; *P.Lo.*, peduncle of optic lobe; *S.G.*, sinus gland; *S.G.T.*, combined sinus gland tract; *S.N.*, sensory nerve; *S.P.*, sensory pore; *S.P.X.*, sensory papilla X-organ; *X.O.C.*, X-organ connective; *X.S.G.T.*, X-organ sinus gland tract. (From Carlisle, D. B., and Knowles, F. G. W.: Endocrine Control in Crustaceans. Cambridge University Press.)

is known regarding the integrating factors concerned in the larval development, although it seems probable that the endocrine factors operating here differ little from those known to be operating in later molting and growth.

The molting process is a complex one. The crustacean is, in fact, at all times during its growing lifetime either preparing for the next molt, or completing the past one. The molting cycle may be divided into four periods: (1) premolt, or proecdysis, a period of active preparation for molt, including gradual thinning of the cuticle, storage in the gastroliths or hepatopancreas of inorganic constituents

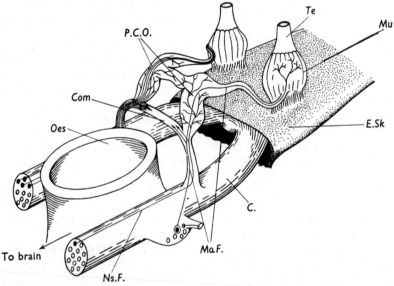

FIGURE 242. Diagram of neurosecretory-postcommissural organ complex of the prawn, *Leander*. *C.*, circumenteric connective; *Com.*, commissure; *E.Sk.*, endophragmal skeleton; *Mo.F.*, motor fiber; *Mu.*, muscle; *Ns.F.*, neurosecretory fiber; *Oes.*, Esophagus; *P.C.O.*, postcommissural organ. *Te.*, tendon. (From Carlisle, D. B., and Knowles, F. G. W.: Endocrine Control in Crustaceans. Cambridge University Press.)

for a new exoskeleton; acceleration of any regenerating tissues, glycogen deposition in epidermal tissues, and numerous other changes; (2) molt, or ecdysis, the splitting and shedding of the old, partially resorbed cuticle, and an abrupt size increase due immediately to absorption of water; (3) postmolt, or postecdysis, a period of rapid redeposition of chitin, inorganic salts to produce a new cuticle, and of tissue growth; and (4) intermolt, or "interecdysis," a period of relative quiescence during which physiological processes normally associated with the active molting process are largely absent, but there is, however, a storing of reserves in the hepatopancreas and elsewhere in anticipation of the next molt. Some crustaceans such as *Maja* and *Carcinus* have terminal growth, passing into a permanent intermolt termed anecdysis.

The molting cycle has been accorded precise means of staging.[107, 110, 132, 133, 204, 406, 410] In the fresh-water crayfish *Cambarus* there is no true larval stage; the individual hatches as a diminutive adult. During its first year of life it molts at intervals of about 12 to 13 days, probably without intervention of any significant intermolt period. After the first growth season there are usually two molts a year, one occurring in the spring, in late April or May, and the other in the summer, in July or August. In these older, mature crayfishes the premolt period is 3 to 5 weeks. During this time there is gradual resorption of the exoskeleton and a deposition of calcium salts in the form of gastroliths in the anterolateral walls of the cardiac stomach. There is also a gradual increase in the rate of oxygen consumption and of water content for a week or so prior to molt, reaching a peak at the time of molt. The period of postmolt is one in which these changes proceed in the opposite direction and require approximately the same time as the corresponding processes of premolt. Postmolt is followed by intermolt, which is of longer duration after the summer than after the spring postmolt.

Observations on changes associated with the molting cycle in other crustaceans show that the hepatopancreas is a site of storage of calcium, phosphates, glycogen, and lipid. The stored salts are not sufficient to account for the total hardening of the exoskeleton, thus making it necessary that the postmolt period be one of rapid absorption of calcium, both directly from the external medium and from ingested food. Gastroliths appear to be an adaptation of such forms as crayfish and *Geocarcinus* to relative inaccessibility of calcium; these are typically absent in marine crustaceans. A study of apparent respiratory quotients shows that although animals in intermolt have a quotient of about 0.8, freshly molted crayfishes show values as low as 0.1 to 0.2 during the first few postmolt hours because of CO_2 fixation during carapace hardening; this value gradually increases to 0.7 to 0.8 during the first postmolt week. This indicates that calcium is avidly taken up from the surrounding medium immediately after molt, and that the rate declines rapidly during the first few days.

It is known that removal of the eyestalks from *Astacus*,[329] *Uca*,[1, 277] *Eriocheir*,[210] *Palaemonetes*,[69] or *Cambarus*[73, 428] results in a more rapid onset of the following and succeeding molts. In young *Cambarus*, in their first year of life, removal of the eyestalks results in a shortening of the period between molts at 20 to 22°C from about 12 days to about 8 days.[428] That this influence is not the result of general operative injury is seen in that other operative injuries, such as destruction of the retinas, which are at least as severe, do not result in such acceleration; if any influence is seen there is a retardation. The remaining two possibilities, that the results are due to (1) the destruction of important nerve centers, or (2) the removal of endocrine organs important in molt regulation, have been resolved in favor of the latter. If both eyestalks are removed from mature crayfishes molt will occur a significant time in advance of that of unoperated controls. If, however, sinus glands from other crayfishes are implanted into the abdomen of such eyestalkless specimens, molting will be delayed beyond the time of that of the controls.[69, 73]

A molt-inhibiting role of the crustacean X-organ–sinus gland complex has received confirmation in studies of the control of gastrolith formation in crayfishes (Fig. 243). These concretions, normally produced only during preecdysis, may be caused to form at other times by excision of both eyestalks or by surgical extirpation of the eyestalk-gland complex.[296, 414] After eyestalk removal during a nonmolting period, such as between September and March, gastroliths of crayfishes commence to form in less than 24 hours at about 20°C and then increase in size slowly during 8 to 10 days, thereafter accelerating rapidly to the time of molt which usually occurs between the fifteenth and twentieth days. Those individuals which survive the molt immediately proceed to form

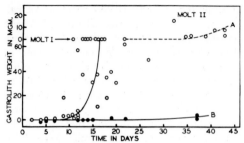

FIGURE 243. *A,* increase in gastrolith size and molting in crayfishes after removal of the eyestalks with their included sinus glands. Note that an animal once molted proceeds almost immediately to prepare for another molt. *B,* eyestalkless crayfishes into which sinus glands are implanted at 3- or 4-day intervals show no gastrolith production. (From Scudamore, H. H.: Tr. Illinois Acad. Sci., vol. 34.)

a new set of gastroliths. If, however, one implants a sinus gland into the abdominal region of eyestalkless animals at 3- or 4-day intervals gastrolith formation is suppressed. If the sinus gland implantations are discontinued, gastroliths begin to form about a week after the last implant, indicating that the implanted glands are no longer effective.

Histological changes in the sinus glands of crustaceans have been shown to be correlated with the molt cycle.[381] Just prior to molt, acidophilic secretory granules appear to be the predominant ones; after molt completion, basophilic ones are more prevalent.

The molting process which is set into operation by eyestalk removal resembles that observed in normal molting animals,[414] and all of the molt-correlated changes ensuing upon eyestalk removal are prevented by implantation of sinus glands. It appears probable, therefore, that all are under the influence, directly or indirectly, of a single molt-inhibiting hormone from the sinus gland. Molting in the crustacean is prevented if the Y-organs are extirpated, and the capacity is restored when Y-organs are reimplanted.[96, 140-142, 180] The Y-organs also exhibit histological cycles correlated with the molting cycle and become greatly reduced in size in crabs which are in anecdysis. The relationship in the regulation of molting between the X-organ–sinus gland complex and the Y-organ has been extensively elucidated. The MTGX-organ produces a hormone which inhibits the Y-organ. This inhibitory hormone is continuously produced during postmolt and intermolts. Cessation of its secretion liberates the Y-organ to secrete molting hormone. Soon after this has occurred, the eyestalk inhibitory factor is ineffective in

stalling the molting sequence. Similarly, removal of the Y-organs, once proecdysis is under way, is powerless to terminate the normal molting sequence of events. These endocrine glands, therefore, are essential primarily for triggering the initiation of molt.

The control of this molt-triggering mechanism is clearly complex and variable in crustaceans, since numerous factors influence the initiation of molt. These include nutrition,[117, 118, 384] temperature, light, and photoperiod,[54, 432] parasitism, injury and state of reproductive activity. The molt-inhibiting hormone from the sinus glands appears to be responsible for the failure of egg-bearing female *Crangon* to molt until the young have hatched,[234] and for the fact that at the annual spring molt of *Cambarus* the egg-bearing females molt several weeks later than the males and only after the young have left the maternal pleopods. Sinus gland removal is just as effective in inducing molt in egg-bearing female crayfishes as is a similar operation in males.[414]

There is evidence suggesting further hormonal regulation of crustacean molting. A molt-accelerating factor has been reported from the MTGX- and SPX-organs of the eyestalk.[92, 99] There is also reason to suspect that at least one additional factor, arising in some region of the body other than the eyestalks, cooperates in the control of molt.[93, 414] A careful study of the deposition of calcium salts in the gastroliths shows that this process is rhythmical, with rapid deposition during the night and little deposition during the day. Suggestive in this regard, is the observation that injection of extract of the brain tissue or strong electrical stimulation of the cut ends of the optic nerves of eyestalkless animals will cause a transitory acceleration in rate of oxygen consumption.

Reproduction. Experiments have indicated that oogenesis, particularly vitellogenesis, in female shrimp of the genus *Leander,* is under the control of a hormone liberated in the sinus glands.[359-361, 440, 512] This hormone appears to be formed in the MTGX-organ[95, 456] and to be a steroid-protein complex.[98] *Leander* reaches the end of its breeding season late in the summer, and its ovaries become tremendously reduced in size and activity and normally remain so during the fall, winter, and early spring. Removal of the eyestalks or only the sinus glands from the eyestalks in such a nonbreeding season as September or October results in a very rapid increase in weight of the ovaries, these organs increasing about seventyfold in 45 days (Fig. 244). Normal eggs may be laid at the end of this period. Unoperated controls show almost no increase during the same period. Implantation of sinus glands into the abdomens of eyestalkless animals will inhibit ovarian development, depressing it even more than is observed in unoperated controls. A similar sort of hormonal relationship between the sinus gland and the ovary, with the sinus gland acting as inhibitor for ovarian maturation, has been demonstrated for the fiddler crab *Uca*.[77] A similar situation appears to obtain for the crayfish.[76] It is presumed to be through this route that light may affect the reproductive cycle.[433]

A further reproductive function of the crustacean sinus gland is observed in the fact that female crayfishes bearing eggs on their pleopods normally postpone their spring molt beyond the time of molting of males and until the young have become free. This adaptive response is apparently the result of activity of a sinus gland hormone, inasmuch as egg-bearing females after sinus gland extirpation molt as readily as do males. The molt-inhibiting and ovary-inhibiting factors are not identical.[94, 115, 126, 134]

An additional endocrine dependence of the ovary has been shown for *Carcinus*. The gonads fail to develop in the absence of the Y-organ. This organ, however, is not essential to the continued maintenance and function of these organs.[17, 18]

There have been numerous observations of the influence of parasitic castration of male decapod crustaceans upon such secondary sex characters as forms of the pleopods, chelipeds, and abdomen. The partial to complete castration which normally results from parasitization by rhizocephalans (parasitic Cirripedia) or bopyrids (parasitic isopods) is commonly accompanied by the failure of these portions of the body to assume their typical masculine form, the specimens approaching the female form in their secondary sexual differentiation.

The interpretations of these results of parasitic castration of male crustaceans in general fall into either one of two categories: (1) those which assume that the presence of the parasite has influenced the expression of the genetic mechanism of sex determination, and (2) those which assume that the testes or some other endogenic endocrine source has been destroyed. In support of the first of these two types of explanations is the observation that certain decapod crustaceans normally possess hermaphroditic gonads or are readily induced to develop them under the influence of parasitization. Some species, such as *Leander*, which show no secondary sexual character changes on castration are thought to possess a relatively stable mechanism of sex determination, not easily influenced by the parasite, whereas others like *Upogebia* are considered to possess very labile mechanisms and consequently show considerable feminization. A number of investigators have noticed that the higher fat content of the blood and liver characteristic of normal females is also often observed in parasitized males. It is postulated by these investigators that the parasite imposes much the same metabolic demands on the host as are normally made by the developing eggs of the ovary, and that associated with the increased fat metabolism is the production of a "sexual formative" stuff which parallelly influences the development of both the gonads and the secondary sex characters.

The second type of explanation of the observed influences of parasitic castration in males assumes the operation of a masculinizing hormone. According to this hypothesis the animal after parasitization does not become feminized but assumes a neutral form, which chances to resemble more clearly the female than the male. Suggestive support for this view is the influences of three species of

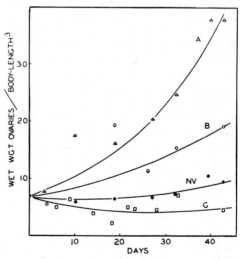

FIGURE 244. Rate of increase in ovarian weight in the shrimp, *Leander*, after: *A*, eyestalk amputation; *B*, sinus gland extirpation; *G*, eyestalk amputation followed by sinus gland implantation. *NV*, normal control. (Redrawn from Panouse, J.: C. R. Acad. Sci., vol. 218.)

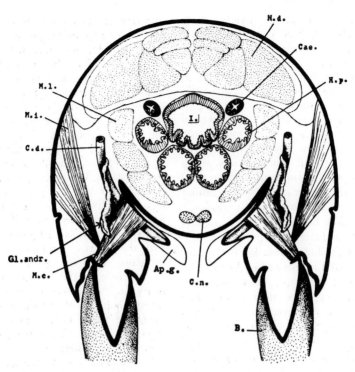

FIGURE 245. Cross-section of the amphipod, *Orchestia*, indicating the location of the androgenic glands
(*Gl. andr.*). *Ap.g.*, genital papilla; *B*, seventh periopod; *Cae.*, intestinal caecum; *C.d.*, vas deferens; *C.n.*,
nerve cord; *H.p.*, hepatopancreas; *M.d.*, *M.l.*, *M.i.*, *M.c.*, muscles. (From Charniaux-Cotton, H.: Bull. Soc.
Zool. France, vol. 83.)

parasites on the crab *Munida sarsi*. Two
smaller parasitic crustaceans, *Triangulus
munidae* and *Lernaeodiscus ingolfi*, totally
or partially castrate the crab and produce
striking modifications in the male secondary
sex characters; a much larger parasite, *Triangulus boschmai*, leaves the gonads functional and does not modify the sex characters.
Such observations appear to exclude in these
instances a direct influence of the metabolic
demands of the parasite in inducing the observed changes. Other investigators, however,
have failed to find a correlation between the
degree of gonadal atrophy and the extent of
suppression of the male characters and have
suggested that a tissue other than the testis
produces the hormone in question.

It seems probable that the answer lies in
the presence of androgenic glands first discovered in *Orchestia* (Fig. 245) but since
found in virtually all crustaceans in which
they have been sought.[105-109] These glands
appear to be absent only in isopods in which
a fully comparable role seems played by the
testes. Extirpation of these glands results in
feminization, an effect reversed by implantation of the glands. Immature females implanted with androgenic glands become mas-

culinized in nearly all sex characters, primary,
accessory, and secondary. The ovaries become
transformed into testes. Even mating behavior
of the masculinized females is male-like. In
the protandrous crustacean *Lysmata* the male
to female transition is correlated with degeneration of the androgenic glands.[109]

There is a seasonal cycle of changes in the
copulatory appendages of the crayfish. These
appendages assume a sexually functional form
(form I) at the time of the late summer molt.
This is a time when the testes are large and
active. At the time of the spring molt, correlated with a period of low gonadal activity,
they revert to a nonfunctional condition
(form II). Experimental induction of molt
during the winter months when testis activity
is similarly low always produces form II.
These changes are endocrine regulated in all
probability by the same endocrine complex
regulating male reproductive activity.

Parasitic castration of female crustaceans is
in general accompanied by little or no change
in the general form of the body and appendages. It has been observed, however, that the
brood pouch of *Asellus* and that of *Daphnia*
fail to develop after injury to the ovaries by
irradiation. In the amphipod *Gammarus*

pulex suppression of the ovaries by a parasitic worm, *Polymorphus minutus,* or by irradiation, has been observed to be associated with failure of the typical marginal bristles of the oostegites to develop. The ability to develop the marginal bristles was restored parallelly with oogenesis after cessation of the irradiation treatments. Female shrimp, *Leander,* castrated by bopyrids or by x-ray irradiation, showed absence of development of the abdominal incubatory chamber and the special guanophores associated with the corresponding abdominal segments.[89, 285] These observations and others strongly support the hypothesis that in these crustaceans the ovaries produce a gynecogenic hormone normally determining certain feminine modifications concerned with provision for the developing young.[102-104, 285, 439] There is suggestive evidence that still other hormones are concerned in the regulating normal sexual development,[28, 116, 431] including one from the eyestalk.

Retinal Pigment Migration. The movements of pigments within the eyes of many animals such as vertebrates, insects and crustaceans contribute importantly to the mechanical adaptation of these organs to changes in light intensity. Only among the crustaceans, however, has clear evidence been presented that hormones are involved in the control of these movements.

The compound eye of crustaceans is made up of a number of units, the ommatidia (Fig. 246). Each ommatidium possesses three functionally distinct groups of pigments. The distal retinal pigment, either ommochrome or melanin, is located in cells which surround the distally placed dioptric apparatus of the ommatidium. In the dark-adapted eye this pigment occupies only a distal position; the pigment disperses proximally in daylight to envelop the whole of the ommatidium as far as the retinula elements. The proximal pigment, chemically like the distal, is located in the retinula cells and migrates to a position proximal to the basement membrane in darkness, and distally to meet the distal retinal pigment in light. In the light-adapted state the whole ommatidium is therefore enclosed in a light-absorbing sleeve of pigment. A third pigment, the reflecting white, comprises probably purines or pteridines.[276] In darkness this pigment occupies a position surrounding the retinula elements, thus constituting a functional tapetum. It migrates to a position proximal to the basement membrane in light.

The distal pigment, also commonly termed

the iris pigment, like the vertebrate iris, exhibits a graded response to light over a wide intensity range.[166, 392] Investigations to determine the extent to which the pigment cells of the right and left eyes of an individual are capable of independent responses to illumination have led to various results. The more recent experiments of this type have led to the conclusion that there is at least a partial interdependence between the two eyes, a darkened eye becoming more or less light-adapted when the contralateral eye is subjected to illumination.[39] Numerous observations have also indicated that one or more of the retinal pigments of numerous species of crustaceans may undergo diurnally rhythmic alterations in their position in animals kept in constant conditions in respect to illumination, especially in constant darkness.[40, 74, 167, 466, 469] *Leander* kept on an illuminated black background has been observed to show a dorsoventral differentiation in position of retinal pigment, apparently the result of the considerably lesser illumination of the ventral than of the dorsal elements of the eyes.[278] These various responses of the retinal pigments suggest that the control of the retinal pigments is not a simple one, but probably involves a direct reaction of the retinal pig-

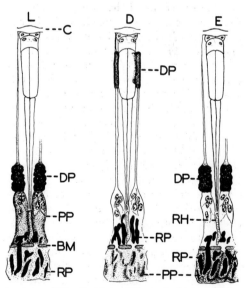

FIGURE 246. Position of the retinal pigments in the ommatidium of the eye of the shrimp, *Palaemonetes, L,* in the light-adapted state; *D,* in the dark-adapted state, and *E,* after injection of eyestalk extract into a dark-adapted specimen kept in darkness. *C,* cornea; *DP,* distal retinal pigment; *PP,* proximal retinal pigment; *RP,* reflecting pigment; *RH,* rhabdome; and *BM,* basement membrane. (From Kleinholz, L. H.: Biol. Bull., vol. 99.)

ment cells to illumination and, in addition, endocrine and possibly also nervous activities.

The eyestalk-gland complex possesses a hormone which influences the position of the retinal pigment,[272, 471, 472] as does also the subesophageal ganglion in *Palaemonetes* and *Cambarellus*.[74, 166] This has been called retinal pigment hormone or RPH. Injection of extracts of the eyestalks of light-adapted *Palaemonetes* into dark-adapted specimens kept in darkness induces a movement of the distal and reflecting pigments to the position characteristic of the light-adapted state. The eyestalks of all crustaceans which have been examined show the presence of RPH in larger or smaller quantities. That this principle is normally concerned with the retinal pigment movements is indicated by the fact that extracts of eyestalks taken from light-adapted individuals show a much greater RPH content than do eyestalks taken from dark-adapted ones.[272] However, it has been reported that the diurnal variation in retinal pigments of certain grapsoid crabs persists even following removal of the sinus glands. A hormone from the eyestalks contributes at least in part to the control of the distal retinal pigment of *Leander*.[278]

The retinal pigments of crayfish show different thresholds of response to RPH.[471] In low concentrations of the hormone only the distal pigment is influenced; with higher concentration both distal and proximal retinal pigments move to the light-adapted state.[273]

The origin of RPH is the MTGX-sinus gland complex of the eyestalk. The sinus gland when extracted alone is able to induce a strong retinal pigment response.

The retinal pigment hormone of the sinus gland will withstand boiling as in the case of the eyestalk chromatophorotropins, but its chemical nature remains unknown. There is ample reason to believe that it is not identical with any of the principal chromatophorotropins, inasmuch as the pigmentary system of the integument ordinarily undergoes its complete gamut of activities in color changes in response to illuminated backgrounds while the eye remains continuously light-adapted. This latter is true despite the fact that the threshold of response of the retinal pigments to eyestalk extract is substantially higher than the threshold of response of the body chromatophores. Such a situation obviously could not obtain were RPH identical with one of the major chromatophorotropins.

A search for a possible comparable endocrine influence on the state of the retinal pigments of the insect *Ephestia* disclosed no evidence of such an endocrine activity. Injection of extracts of the heads of light-adapted moths into either dark- or light-adapted specimens produced no modification in the state of the pigments. Extracts of crustacean sinus glands also showed no activity on the retinal pigments of the moth.

An additional hormone of neurosecretory source exercises a dark-adapting influence on the distal retinal pigment.[75, 166] It was shown possible to induce differential secretion of the two by light stimuli of regulated duration and intensity.[79] There is also evidence that the two hormones are differentially secreted as a daily rhythmic phenomenon.[74, 79, 466] The two retinal-pigment hormones have been separated by electrophoretic means.[168, 169]

Other Phenomena. Heart rate in crustaceans is influenced by endocrine factors. An eyestalk-arising principle accelerates the beat,[470] and in *Palaemonetes* its secretion is correlated with that of certain color-change hormones.[413] There are reasons to believe that the heart and chromatophore activators are not identical.[212, 213, 286] A more specific heart regulatory principle is secreted by a neurosecretory system with secreting areas in the pericardial cavity. These have been termed pericardial organs (Fig. 247). Extracts of these organs increase amplitude of heart beat and exercise other influences apparently in manners differing from species to species. Removal of the eyestalks or of the sinus glands of these stalks of *Cambarus* is promptly followed by an elevation in basal metabolism, as evidenced by the observed increase in O_2 consumption.[54, 414] This can be reduced by injection of aqueous extracts of the glands. Injection of extracts of eyestalks of *Uca*, the fiddler crab, into *Callinectes*, the blue crab, results in a rapid rise in the blood sugar from about 20 mg/100 cc to more than 80.[2, 275] The maximum is reached in 1 hour, and then there is a slow decline to normal. This latter action has been attributed to the presence of a diabetogenic factor in the crustacean sinus gland, and recent work has confirmed this conclusion for the spider crab *Libinia*.

Miscellaneous. Many other invertebrates also show annual or other reproductive rhythms, with periods of sexual activity alternating with periods of inactivity. In most instances there is as yet no knowledge of the pathways through which the gonads are activated or inhibited.

Many species of invertebrate organisms representing many phyla possess a sexual

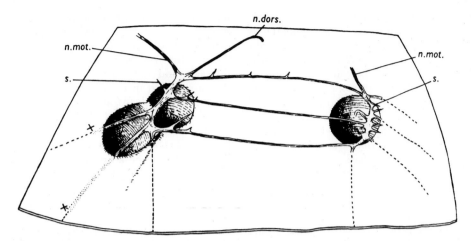

FIGURE 247. The pericardial organs of the crab *Maia* and their relationship to openings into the pericardial cavity of the branchiocardiac veins. Broken lines depict nerves from the central nervous organs. *n.mot.*, nerves innervating muscles; *n.dors.*, dorsal cardiac nerve; *S.*, strands suspending the trunks. (From Alexandrowicz, J. S.: J. Mar. Biol. Assn. U. K., vol. 31.)

dimorphism which has long been suspected to owe its origin, in some measure at least, to hormones comparable to the gonadal hormones of vertebrates.[210, 289] Even to the present, however, no incontrovertible evidence has been advanced to prove this is so except for crustaceans. Nevertheless, there are numerous reports in the literature suggesting hormones to be playing roles in this regard. These come from observations on (1) parallel effects of parasites on gonads and sexual differentiation; (2) parallel cyclical changes in the degree of gonadal activity and certain secondary sexual characters; (3) results of irradiation of the gonads or of the whole organism with x-rays or radium rays; and (4) results of surgical extirpation of gonads.

It has been observed after operative destruction that the normal regeneration of the copulatory apparatus of planarians requires the presence of the gonads, particularly the testes.[454, 455] In earthworms which lack the normal secondary sex character, the clitellum, it has been observed that their testes, but not their ovaries, had been destroyed by the sporozoan *Monocystis*. Surgical extirpation of the segments containing the testes, but not the ovaries, was reported by one investigator to be followed by production of a reduced clitellum or none at all,[215] whereas surgical castration was reported by another investigator to be without any influence on either development of the clitellum or the mating behavior.[23, 24] Since differentiation of the clitellum normally commences simultaneously with the beginning of spermatogenesis, it has been suggested[236] that both of these phenom-

ena are parallelly influenced by an extragonadal hormonal factor, although completion of development of the clitellum may be hormonally determined by a chemical factor liberated by the ripe sperm cells. This latter hypothesis finds support in the observation that removal from mature *Eisenia* of the anterior twelve segments containing the seminal vesicles results in the rapid disappearance of the clitellum and its subsequent failure to redifferentiate.[235]

The periwinkle, *Littorina*, exhibits an annual cycle of development of gonads and accessory characters. Observations on specimens whose gonads were considerably damaged by trematode larval stages revealed incomplete differentiation of their accessory characters. The copulatory arm, or hectocotylus, of cephalopods has been reported as failing to show its characteristic differentiation after surgical castration.[342, 419]

GENERAL CONSIDERATIONS

In any comparative survey of endocrine mechanisms one is impressed by the fact that, in all those animal groups in which endocrine systems have differentiated, the same general types of functions are being subserved by them. In the two very widely separated animal groups, the Arthropoda and the Vertebrata, which are considered by most zoologists to possess no common ancestry short of relatively primitive forms of life, we see the same general distribution of integrative functions between nervous and endocrine systems and coordinated activity of the two. In both the vertebrate and invertebrate, growth, differentiation, reproduction, metabolism, and pigment cells are importantly regulated by hormones. In brief, the endocrine system seems to dominate primarily (a) those functions for which the time required to induce a response is long (as in those activities involving growth and cell differentiation), (b) those processes for which the controlling influence needs to be maintained over long periods (as in the control of various aspects of basic maintenance and metabolism), and (c) situations in which effector organs are to be maintained in one or another condition for extended periods (as with chromatophores).

Within even relatively large natural groups of animals there is commonly a lack of specificity of the hormonal substances. Among the vertebrates the same general functional types of hormones seem rather widely distributed, typically producing within any species a type of response characteristic for that species. It is chiefly the proteinaceous ones which show evidences of differences in detailed chemical character from species to species. Similarly, among the insects, the juvenile hormone, brain hormone, and ecdysone appear interchangeable among the various species and often even among orders. The same appears to hold true for the chromatophorotropins, retinal pigment hormones, and molt-inhibiting hormone among various species of the Crustacea.

Little is known as to chemical or physiological similarities of the active principles among the three major groups with endocrine systems. The corpora cardiaca of insects yield a principle highly active on the chromatophores of crustaceans. A rather extensive literature has developed regarding the influence of invertebrate hormones on vertebrates and especially of vertebrate hormones on invertebrates.[210, 476] Much of the work is confusing and contradictory and gives us little reason for believing that the results have anything other than interesting pharmacological value. The vertebrate chromatophorotropin, melanocyte-stimulating hormone (MSH), and the crustacean hormone, UDH (see p. 517), appear qualitatively to resemble one another in their chromatophorotropic action and in a number of their physicochemical properties.[1] A critical examination, however, gives us strong reason for believing they are not identical.[70]

The nervous systems of a wide variety of animals show histological and, in many cases, excellent physiological evidence for the differentiation of endocrine elements or neurosecretory cells.[211, 404, 406] Such cells have been described particularly for certain portions of the nervous systems of worms, molluscs, arthropods, and vertebrates. In the last group, they are located in the nucleus preopticus of fishes and amphibians, and in the homologous nuclei supraopticus and paraventricularis of reptiles and mammals. These form part of the intimate hypothalamic-hypophyseal complex demonstrated to be a key portion in coordinating neurons and endocrine activities.

In a fully comparable manner, in the insect the pars intercerebralis–corpora cardiaca complex interrelates the nervous and endocrine systems. In the crustaceans, X-organ–sinus gland complexes and brain-secretory cell-postcommissural organ associations form the fully analogous systems. Suggestion that still another large group, the Arachnoidea, possesses the same kind of organization is seen in the fact that there has been found in the nervous system of *Limulus* a quantitative distribution of chromactivating factors for crustaceans closely paralleling the frequency of neurosecretory cells known to occur there.[73, 398] The existence of histological evidence for neurosecretion in annelids and molluscs argues for high probability that a neuroendocrine complex will be found to be a general metazoan characteristic.

Certain large ganglion cells in annelids give a chromaffin-staining reaction characteristic of adrenalin-producing tissues, and extraction and assay of such nervous tissue gives positive physiological tests for adrenaline. Among the vertebrates the medulla of the adrenal gland is derived embryologically from nervous tissue.

In brief, there appears to have been an evolution of certain essential endocrine sources from tissues possessing a simple nervous or conductile function and located within the central nervous system, through an intermediate stage where the cells exhibited their secretory function while still retaining the special conductile ability of nerve cells, to a condition in which the cells have become specialized for endocrine activity alone and form glandular tissues or organs apart from the nervous system. And in those instances where the secreting cell bodies are still retained within nervous organs, special intracellular conductile means are utilized to convey the secreted product beyond the bounds of the highly specialized "brain-blood barriers" and into proximity to their own vascular beds. Secondarily, other endocrine organs appear to have developed morphologically, but never physiologically, independent of either direct or indirect regulation by the nervous system.

It is interesting to note that, in the vertebrates, those hormones from sources of ectodermal or endodermal origin are proteins or polypeptides (e.g., STH, LH, ADH, ACTH, MSH, TSH) or at least contain nitrogen (adrenin); hormones arising from tissues of mesodermal origin are characteristically steroids (sex hormones, cortical principles).

There has been some speculation in the literature as to which is probably the more primitive integrating mechanism within animals—nervous or endocrine. Obviously both mechanisms, when broadly interpreted, extend to all forms of living organisms, both unicellular and multicellular. The phenomena of excitation and conduction and chemical intercellular transmission of information, the basic underlying activities in the physiology of the nervous system, are common to all cells. As was pointed out in the introduction to this chapter, some organizing and differentiating forces obviously had to precede both of these coordinating mechanisms in both phylogeny and ontogeny. In development, gene-induced differentiation must precede organizer activity. There is no good reason to postulate, therefore, that either the excitatory or the chemical coordination factor is phylogenetically the more primitive. Both types of coordinatory mechanisms probably evolved simultaneously and entirely parallelly, and, in response to the functional needs of larger size, multicellular character, and division of labor within organisms, highly specialized, cooperating nervous and endocrine systems became differentiated.

REFERENCES

1. ABRAMOWITZ, A. A., Physiol. Zool. *11*: 299-311, 1938. Similarity of crustacean sinus gland hormone to intermedin.
2. ABRAMOWITZ, A. A., HISAW, F. L., BOETTIGER, E., and PAPANDREA, D. N., Biol. Bull. *78*: 189-201, 1940. Hypophysis and pancreatic diabetes in the dogfish.
3. ABRAMOWITZ, A. A., HISAW, F. L., and PAPANDREA, D. N., Biol. Bull. *86*: 1-5, 1944. Diabetogenic factor in crustacean sinus glands.
4. ADLER, L., Arch. Entwick-Mech. *39*: 21-45, 1914. Hypophysis in amphibian metamorphosis.
5. ALBERT, A., Endocrinology *37*: 389-406, 1945. Thyrotropic principle in fish pituitary.
6. ALEXANDROWICZ, J. S., J. Mar. Biol. Assn. U. K. *31*: 563-580, 1953. Pericardial organs of crustaceans.
7. ALEXANDROWICZ, J. S., and CARLISLE, D. B.,

J. Mar. Biol. Assn. U. K. *32*: 175-192, 1953. Pericardial organs and heart rate.
8. ALLEN, B. M., Science *44*: 755-757, 1916. Thyroid and amphibian metamorphosis.
9. ALLEN, B. M., Science *52*: 274-276, 1920. Pituitary and thyroid in amphibian metamorphosis.
10. ALLEN, B. M., Univ. Calif. Publ. Zool. *31*: 53-78, 1927. Anterior lobe and amphibian metamorphosis.
11. ALLEN, B. M., Anat. Rec. *54*: 45-81, 1932. Hormones and amphibian metamorphosis.
12. ALLEN, B. M., Biol. Rev. *13*: 1-19, 1938. Hormones and amphibian metamorphosis, review.
13. ALLEN, E., Sex and Internal Secretions. Baltimore, Williams & Wilkins Co., 1939, 1346 pp.
14. AMOROSO, E. C., Ann. Endocrinol. *16*: 435-447, 1955. Reptile corpus luteum.
15. ARQUILLA, E. R., and STAVITSKY, A. B., J. Clin. Invest. *35*: 467-474, 1956. Immunological similarity of insulins.
16. ARVY, L., BOUNHIOL, J. J., and GABE, M., C. R. Acad. Sci. *236*: 627-629, 1953. Neurosecretion by corpora cardiaca; increased brain secretion in adult Bombyx.
17. ARVY, L., ECHALIER, G., and GABE, M., C. R. Acad. Sci. *239*: 1853-1855, 1954. Y-organ and gonad development in crabs.
18. ARVY, L., ECHALIER, G., and GABE, M., Ann. Sci. Nat. Zool. Biol. Animale *18*: 263-268, 1956. Gonad regulation by Y-organ in Carcinus.
19. ARVY, L., FONTAINE, M., and GABE, M., J. Physiol. *49*: 685-697, 1957. Hypothalamic control of ACTH and TSH.
20. ASSENMACHER, I., C. R. Acad. Sci. *245*: 210-213, 1957. Hypothalamic control of adenohypophyseal gonadotropins.
21. ASSENMACHER, I., C. R. Acad. Sci. *245*: 2388-2390, 1957. Hypothalamic control of adenohypophyseal gonadotropins.
22. ASSENMACHER, I., Presse Med. *65*: 1612-1614, 1670-1671, 1957. Hypothalamic control of adenohypophyseal gonadotropins.
23. AVEL, M., Bull. Soc. Zool. France *53*: 322-323, 1928. Testes and clitellum formation in earthworms.
24. AVEL, M., C. R. Soc. Biol. Paris *99*: 616-618, 1929. Testes and clitellum formation in earthworms.
25. BAGGERMAN, B., Arch. Néerl. Zool. *12*: 105-318, 1957. Photoperiod and sticklebacks; thyroid increase induction of F.W. selection.
26. BAGNARA, J. T., and NEEDLEMAN, S., Proc. Soc. Exp. Biol. Med. *97*: 671-673, 1958. MSH inhibition of guanine formation.
27. BAKER, J. R., and RANSON, R. M., Proc. Roy. Soc., London, B, *110*: 313-322, 1932. Light and breeding in Microtus.
28. BALESDENT-MARQUET, M. L., C. R. Acad. Sci. *236*: 1086-1088, 1953. Hormone other than ovarian on female sex characters.
29. BARGMANN, W., and KNOOP, A., Ztschr. Zellforsch. *46*: 242-251, 1957. Vesicles in nerve fibers.
30. BARRINGTON, E. J. W., J. Mar. Biol. Assn. U. K. *36*: 1-15, 1957. Protein binding of I in Ciona endostyle.
31. BARRINGTON, E. J. W., J. Mar. Biol. Assn. U. K.

37: 117-125, 1958. Amphioxus endostyle cells binding of I.

32. BARTHOLOMEW, G. A., Bull. Mus. Comp. Zool. Harvard *101*: 433-476, 1949. Photoperiodism and English sparrow.

33. BARTHOLOMEW, G. A., Anat. Rec. *106*: 49-60, 1950. Light, temperature, and reptile sex cycles.

34. BARTHOLOMEW, G. A., *in* Photoperiodism and Related Phenomena in Plants and Animals, edited by R. B. Withrow. A.A.A.S., 1959, pp. 669-676. Photoperiodism and reptiles.

35. BEAUDOIN, A. R., Anat. Rec. *125*: 247-259, 1956. Differential CNS growth with thyroid.

36. BECK, J. C., McGARRY, E. E., DYRENFURTH, I., and VENNING, E. H., Science *125*: 884-885, 1957. Growth hormones differ.

37. BECKER, E., and PLAGGE, E., Biol. Zentbl. *59*: 326-341, 1939. Hormonal control of Dipteran metamorphosis.

38. BEHRENS, D. K., STAUB, A., ROOT, M. A., and BROMER, W. W., Ciba Colloq. Endocrinol. *9*: 167, 1956. Glucagon a polypeptide, crystallized.

39. BENNITT, R., Physiol. Zool. *5*: 49-64, 1932. Interrelation of eyes of crustacean in light adaptation.

40. BENNITT, R., Physiol. Zool. *5*: 65-69, 1932. Diurnal rhythm in crustacean retinal pigment movements.

41. BENOIT, J., and ASSENMACHER, I., J. Physiol., Paris *47*: 427-567, 1955. Hypothalamic control of pituitary in bird.

42. BENOIT, J., ASSENMACHER, I., and BRARD, E., J. Physiol. Paris *48*: 388-391, 1956. Cycles in constant light or dark.

43. BENOIT, J., ASSENMACHER, I., and BRARD, E., C. R. Acad. Sci. *242*: 3113-3115, 1956. Cycles in constant light or dark.

44. BERG, O., GORBMAN, A., and KOBAYASHI, H., *in* Comparative Physiology, edited by A. Gorbman. New York, John Wiley & Sons, 1959, pp. 302-319. Variability in thyroid activity and hormones.

45. BIRKS, R. I., and MacINTOSH, F. C., Brit. Med. Bull. *13*: 157-161, 1957. Acetylcholine as a neurohumor.

46. BISSONNETTE, T. H., Proc. Roy. Soc., London, B, *110*: 322-336, 1932. Photoperiodism and sexual cycle of ferret.

47. BISSONNETTE, T. H., Anat. Rec. *63*: 159-168, 1935. Hypophysis and molting in ferrets.

48. BISSONNETTE, T. H., Wilson Bull. *49*: 241-270, 1937. Hormones in bird migration.

49. BISSONNETTE, T. H., Endocrinology *22*: 92-103, 1938. Influence of the hypophysis upon molting in the ferret.

50. BISSONNETTE, T. H., and BAILEY, E. E., Ann. New York Acad. Sci. *45*: 221-260, 1944. Control of seasonal changes in coat color of the ermine, Mustela.

51. BLACHER, L. J., Trav. Lab. Zool. Exp. Morph. Animals *3*: 172-173, 1928. Hormones and amphibian metamorphosis.

52. BLANCHARD, B. D., Univ. Calif. Publ. Zool. *46*: 1-178, 1941. Temperature change and bird migration.

53. BLASCHKO, H., HAGEN, P., and WELCH, A. D.,

J. Physiol. *129*: 27-49, 1955. Membranes of vesicles.

54. BLISS, D. E., Biol. Bull. *104*: 275-296, 1953. X-organ source of sinus gland hormones; hormonal regulation of crustacean metabolism; inhibition of growth and regeneration of crab by light.

55. BLISS, D. E., DURAND, J. B., and WELSH, J. H., Ztschr. Zellforsch. *39*: 520-536, 1954. X-organ-sinus-gland complex.

56. BLISS, D. E., and WELSH, J. H., Biol. Bull. *103*: 157-169, 1952. X-organ-sinus–gland in brachyurans.

57. BODENSTEIN, D., Cold Spring Harbor Symp. *10*: 17-26, 1942. Hormones in insect development, review.

58. BODENSTEIN, D., J. Exp. Zool. *123*: 189-232, 1953. Hormones in development of Periplaneta.

59. BODENSTEIN, D., J. Exp. Zool. *123*: 413-434, 1953. Molting in cockroaches.

60. BODENSTEIN, D., J. Exp. Zool. *124*: 105-116, 1953. Molting in cockroaches.

61. BODENSTEIN, D., *in* Recent Advances in Invertebrate Physiology, edited by B. T. Scheer. University of Oregon Publications, 1957, pp. 197-211. Importance of development of competence to respond to hormones.

62. BONDY, P. K., Proc. Soc. Exp. Biol. Med. *77*: 638-640, 1951. Normal response of transplanted thyroid to TSH.

63. BOSS, W. R., J. Exp. Zool. *94*: 181-209, 1943. Hormones and plumage type in gulls.

64. BOTTARI, P. M., Ciba Foundation Colloq. Endocrinol. *11*: 52-69, 1957. TSH increase in response to cold.

65. BOUNHIOL, J. J., C. R. Soc. Biol. *126*: 1189-1191, 1937. Corpora allata and Lepidopteran development.

66. BOUNHIOL, J. J., Arch. Zool. Expér. Gén. *81*: 54-64, 1939. Hormones in Lepidopteran reproduction.

67. BRAGDON, D. E., LAZO-WASEM, E. A., ZARROW, M. X., and HISAW, F. L., Proc. Soc. Exp. Biol. Med. *86*: 477-480, 1954. Progesterone in blood of pregnant snakes.

68. BRAUN-MENENDEZ, E., Ann. Rev. Physiol. *6*: 265-294, 1944. Action of renin, review.

69. BROWN, F. A., JR., Anat. Rec. (suppl.) *75*: 129, 1939. Sinus gland and molting in Palaemonetes.

70. BROWN, F. A., JR., Quart. Rev. Biol. *19*: 32-46, 118-143, 1944. Endocrines in crustaceans, review.

71. BROWN, F. A., JR., Physiol. Zool. *19*: 215-223, 1946. Postcommissural gland.

72. BROWN, F. A., JR., Chemistry and Physiology of the Hormones, New York, Academic Press, 1948, vol. I, chap. 5. Crustacean hormones, review.

73. BROWN, F. A., JR., and CUNNINGHAM, O., Biol. Bull. *77*: 104-114, 1939; *81*: 80-95, 1941. Sinus gland hormone and molting in crustacea; Limulus neurosecretion.

74. BROWN, F. A., JR., FINGERMAN, M., and HINES, M. N., Physiol. Zool. *25*: 230-239, 1952. Rhythms in retinal pigment physiology.

75. BROWN, F. A., JR., HINES, M. N., and FINGERMAN, M., Biol. Bull. *102*: 212-225, 1952. Hormonal control of Palaemonetes retinal pigment.

76. Brown, F. A., Jr., and Jones, G. M., Anat. Rec. *99*: 657, 1947. Eyestalks and ovarian growth in crayfishes.

77. Brown, F. A., Jr., and Jones, G. M., Biol. Bull. *91*: 228-232, 1949. Eyestalk-hormone inhibition of ovaries in Uca.

78. Brown, F. A., Jr., and Rollo, M., Auk *57*: 485-498, 1940. Influence of light periods upon plumage type in birds.

79. Brown, F. A., Jr., Webb, H. M., and Sandeen, M. I., J. Cell. Comp. Physiol. *41*: 123-144, 1953. Control of secretion of two retinal hormones.

80. Brown-Grant, K., von Euler, C., Harris, G. W., and Reichlin, S., J. Physiol. *126*: 1-28, 1954. Thyroid response to cold.

81. Brown-Grant, K., Harris, G. W., and Reichlin, S., J. Physiol. *126*: 29-40, 1954. Thyroid response to stress.

82. Bullough, W. S., Proc. Zool. Soc. London, A, *110*: 149-157, 1940. Photoperiod and cyprinids.

83. Bullough, W. S., Phil. Tr. Roy. Soc. London, B, *231*: 165-246, 1942. Gonadal hormones in bird migration.

84. Bullough, W. S., Biol. Rev. *20*: 89-99, 1945. Hormones and bird migration.

85. Burger, J. W., Bird Banding *12*: 27-29, 1941. Influence of light periods upon plumage type in birds.

86. Burgos, M. H., Rev. Soc. Argent. Biol. *26*: 359-371, 1950. Loss of clasp reflex of toads on castration.

87. Burrows, H., Biological Actions of Sex Hormones. Cambridge University Press, 1945, 615 pp.

88. Butenandt, A., and Karlson, P., Ztschr. Naturforsch. *9B*: 389-391, 1954. Crystallization of insect molting hormone.

89. Callan, H. G., J. Exp. Biol. *17*: 168-179, 1940. Parasitic castration and secondary sex characters in crustacea.

90. Calvet, J., C. R. Soc. Biol. *109*: 595-597, 1932. Influence of gonadotropins on cyclostomes.

91. Cardoso, D. M., Arch. Inst. Biol. São Paulo *5*: 133-136, 1934. Hypophyseal gonadotropins in fishes.

92. Carlisle, D. B., Pubbl. staz Zool. Napoli *24*: 279-285, 1953. Molt accelerating principle in MTGX-organ.

93. Carlisle, D. B., Pubbl. staz Zool. Napoli. *24*: 285-292, 1953. Thoracic ganglia accelerate molt in crustacea.

94. Carlisle, D. B., Pubbl. staz Zool. Napoli. *24*: 355-372, 1953. Separation of ovary and molt-influencing hormones.

95. Carlisle, D. B., Pubbl. staz Zool. Napoli *24*: 79-80, 1954. Intra-axonal transport.

96. Carlisle, D. B., J. Mar. Biol. Assn. U. K. *36*: 291-307, 1957. Y-organ activity induces molt.

97. Carlisle, D. B., 2. Internat. Symp. Neurosekr. Springer-Verlag, Berlin-Göttingen-Heidelberg, pp. 18-19, 1958. Intra-axonal transport.

98. Carlisle, D. B., and Butler, C. G., Nature *177*: 276-277, 1956. Ovary-inhibiting hormone a steroid-protein complex.

99. Carlisle, D. B., and Dohrn, P. F. R., Pubbl. staz Zool. Napoli. *24*: 69-83, 1953. Molt acceleration by MTGX-factor.

100. Chang, C. Y., and Witschi, E., Endocrinol. *56*: 597-605, 1955. Estrogens yielding adrenal hyperplasia.

101. Chang, C. Y., and Witschi, E., Endocrinol. *61*: 514-519, 1957. Facilitation of ovulation by cortisone.

102. Charniaux, H., C. R. Acad. Sci. *236*: 141-142, 1953. Ovarian secretion in Orchestia.

103. Charniaux-Cotton, H., C. R. Acad. Sci. *238*: 953-955, 1954. Endocrine action of crustacean ovary.

104. Charniaux-Cotton, H., C. R. Acad. Sci. *239*: 780-782, 1954. Ovarian hormone in crustacean; androgenic gland of Crustacea.

105. Charniaux-Cotton, H., Ann. Biol. *32*: 371-398, 1956. Androgenic gland.

106. Charniaux-Cotton, H., C. R. Acad. Sci. *243*: 1168-1169, 1956. Androgenic gland.

107. Charniaux-Cotton, H., Ann. Sci. Nat. Zool. Biol. Animale *19*: 411-559, 1957. Molting in Orchestia; androgenic gland of crustacea.

108. Charniaux-Cotton, H., Bull. Soc. Zool. France *83*: 314-336, 1958. Crustacean sex differentiation.

109. Charniaux-Cotton, H., C. R. Acad. Sci. *246*: 2817-2819, 1958. Androgenic gland of crustaceans.

110. Charniaux-Legrand, H., Arch. Zool. expér. gén. *88*: 178-204, 1952. Molting in Orchestia.

111. Chase, M. D., Geschwind, I. I., and Bern, H. A., Proc. Soc. Exp. Biol. Med. *94*: 680-683, 1957. Prolactin synergism with sex hormones and gonadotropins. Direct influence of LTH on prostate.

112. Chavin, W., J. Exp. Zool. *133*: 1-46, 1956. Goldfish melanization by ACTH.

113. Church, N. S., Canad. J. Zool. *33*: 339-369, 1955. Hormones and insect molt.

114. Combescot, C., Bull. Soc. Hist. Nat. Afrique Nord. *45*: 366-377, 1955. Hypophysectomy and gonad and secondary sex character dependence in reptiles.

115. Cornubert, G., C. R. Acad. Sci. *238*: 952-953, 1954. Distinction between ovary-inhibiting hormone and molting one.

116. Cornubert, G., Demeusy, N., and Veillet, A., C. R. Acad. Sci. *234*: 1405-1407, 1952. Acceleration of sexual development by eyestalk removal.

117. Costlow, J. D., Jr., and Bookhout, C. G., Biol. Bull. *105*: 420-433, 1953. Nutrition and molting in Barnacles.

118. Costlow, J. D., Jr., and Bookhout, C. G., Biol. Bull. *113*: 224-232, 1957. Nutrition and molting in Barnacles.

119. Damas, H., Bull. Soc. Roy. Sci. Liege *2*: 94-98, 1933. Influence of gonadotropins on cyclostomes.

120. Danforth, C. H., Biol. Symp. *9*: 67-80, 1942. Hormones and plumage changes in birds.

121. D'Angelo, S. A., and Traum, R. E., Endocrinology *59*: 593-596, 1956. Hypothalamic damage disturbs TSH secretion.

122. Davis, D. E., Science *126*: 253, 1957. Effects of castration of starling male singing and aggressiveness.

123. Day, M. F., Biol. Bull. *80*: 275-291, 1941. Control of retinal pigment migration in insects.

124. Day, M. F., Biol. Bull. *84*: 127-140, 1943. Corpus allatum hormone and dipteran reproduction.

125. Del Conte, E., and Stux, M., Nature *173*: 783, 1954. Thyroid response to cold.

126. Demeusy, N., and Lenel, R., C. R. Soc. Biol. *148*: 156-158, 1954. Ovary-inhibiting factor and molting hormone.

127. Disney, H. J. de S., and Marshall, A. J., Proc. Zool. Soc. London *127*: 379-387, 1956. Cycles in equatorial birds.

128. Dodd, J. M., Mem. Soc. Endocrinol. *4*: 166, 1955. Subneural gland of tunicates.

129. Domm, L. V., Sex and Internal Secretions. Baltimore, Williams & Wilkins Co., 1939, pp. 227-327. Hormones and plumage changes in birds.

130. Donovan, B. T., and van der Werff ten Bosch, J. J., J. Physiol. *132*: 57P-58P, 1956. Gonadal control via hypothalamus.

131. Donovan, B. T., and van der Werff ten Bosch, J. J., Nature *178*: 745, 1956. Gonadal control via hypothalamus.

132. Drach, P., Ann. Inst. Oceanog. Paris N.S. *19*: 103-391, 1939. Crustacean molt-cycle stages, Brachyura.

133. Drach, P., Bull. Biol. France Belg. *78*: 40-62, 1944. Crustacean molt-cycle stages, Natantia.

134. Drach, P., C. R. Soc. Biol. *149*: 2079-2083, 1955. Ovary inhibiting factor and molting one.

135. Duncan, D., Anat. Rec. *121*: 430, 1955. Vesicles in nerve fibers.

136. Dupont-Raabe, M., Arch. Zool. Exp. Gén. *89*: 128-138, 1951. Increased brain secretion in adult phasmids.

137. Dupont-Raabe, M., Bull. Soc. Zool. France *76*: 386-397, 1952. Increased brain secretion in adult phasmids.

138. Durand, J. B., Biol. Bull. *111*: 62-76, 1956. X-organ in brachyuran.

139. Echalier, G., C. R. Acad. Sci. *238*: 523-525, 1954. Y-organ and crustacean molt.

140. Echalier, G., C. R. Acad. Sci. *240*: 1581-1583, 1955. Y-organ and crustacean molt.

141. Echalier, G., Ann. Sci. Nat. Zool. Biol. Animale *18*: 153-154, 1956. Y-organ and crustacean molt.

142. Echalier, G., C. R. Acad. Sci. *242*: 2179-2180, 1956. Y-organ and crustacean molt.

143. Edman, P., Fänge, R., and Ostlund, E., 2. Internat. Symp. Neurosekr. Springer-Verlag, Berlin-Göttingen-Heidelberg, pp. 119-123, 1958. Polypeptide nature of neurosecretion.

144. Elrick, H., Staub, A., and Maske, H., New England J. Med. *256*: 742-747, 1957. Properties and role of glucagon.

145. Enami, M., Biol. Bull. *101*: 241-258, 1951. Secretory droplets in X-organ–sinus gland complex; cyclic changes.

146. Enami, M., Gunma J. M. Sci. *4*: 23-36, 1955. Urohypophysis.

147. Enami, M., Science *121*: 36-37, 1955. Separation of an MCH from MSH by differential alcohol solubility.

148. Enami, M., Proc. Jap. Acad. *34*: 44-49, 1958. Zinc in urohypophysis.

149. Enami, M., Proc. Jap. Acad. *34*: 50-55, 1958. Activity of an extract from the caudal neurosecretory system of the eel.

150. Enami, M., Comparative Endocrinology, edited by A. Gorbman. New York, John Wiley & Sons, 1959. Urohypophysis.

151. Enami, M., and Imai, K., Proc. Jap. Acad. *34*: 164-168, 1958. Electron micrography of urohypophyseal secretory system.

152. Enami, M., Miyashita, S., and Imai, K., Endocrin. Jap. *3:* 280-290, 1958. Suggestive function of urohypophysis is salt regulation.

153. Engelmann, F., J. Insect. Physiol. *1*: 257-278, 1957. Ovarian stimulation of brain; inhibition of corpus allatum by brain.

154. Engelmann, F., Ztschr. vergl. Physiol. *41*: 456-470, 1959. Prothoracic glands in adult Leucophaea.

155. Engelmann, F., and Luscher, M., Verhandl. Deutsch. Zool. Ges., Hamburg 215-220, 1956. Nerve inhibition of corpora allata.

156. Etkin, W. N., J. Exp. Zool. *71*: 317-340, 1935. Hormones and amphibian metamorphosis.

157. Etkin, W. N., Analysis of Development, edited by B. H. Willier, P. A. Weiss, and V. Hamburger. Philadelphia, W. B. Saunders Co., 1955. Review of thyroid and amphibian development.

158. Etkin, W. N., Root, R. W., and Mofskin, B. P., Physiol. Zool. *13*: 415-429, 1940. Thyroid and O$_2$ consumption in fishes.

159. von Euler, U. S., Noradrenaline. Springfield, Ill., Charles C Thomas, 1956. Noradrenaline at nerve endings; catachol amines.

160. Everett, J. W., Endocrinology *58*: 786-796, 1956. LH stimulation of ovulation.

161. Everett, J. W., and Sawyer, C. H., Endocrinology *47*: 198-218, 1950. LH stimulation for ovulation.

162. Ewer, R. F., J. Exp. Biol. *29*: 429-439, 1952. Aquatic Xenopus, neurohypophysis, increased water uptake, and urine outflow.

163. Farner, D. S., Recent Studies in Avian Biology, edited by A. Wolfson. University of Illinois Press, 1955, pp. 198-237. Annual stimulus for bird migration; stimulus to bird migration independent of gonads—or perhaps all hormones.

164. Farner, D. S., Photoperiodism and Related Phenomena in Plants and Animals, edited by R. B. Withrow. Washington, A.A.A.S., 1959, pp. 717-750. Photoperiodic control of annual gonadal cycles in birds.

165. Feldberg, W., Physiol. Rev. *25*: 596-642, 1945. Acetylcholine as a neurohumor.

166. Fingerman, M., J. Cell. Comp. Physiol. *50*: 357-370, 1957. Evidence for light- and dark-adapting hormones for retinal pigments of crayfish.

167. Fingerman, M., and Lowe, M. E., J. Cell. Comp. Physiol. *50*: 371-380, 1957. Daily rhythm of crayfish retinal pigment.

168. Fingerman, M., Lowe, M., and Sundararaj, B. I., Am. Midl. Nat. *62*: 167-173, 1959. Electrophoretic separation of dark- and light-adapting retinal pigment hormones.

169. Fingerman, M., Lowe, M. E., and Sundararaj, B. I., Biol. Bull. *116*: 30-36, 1959. Dark-

and light-adapting hormones of Palaemonetes retinal pigment.

170. FOA, P. P., GALANSINO, G., and POZZA, G., Recent Prog. Hormone Res. *13*: 473-510, 1957. Properties and role of glucagon.

171. FOGLIA, V. G., WAGNER, E. M., DE BARROS, M., and MARQUES, M., C. R. Soc. Biol. *149*: 1660-1661, 1955. Pancreatectomy and hyperglycemia and glycosuria in tortoises.

172. FONTAINE, M., Mem. Soc. Endocrin. *5*: 69-81, 1956. Thyroxin in osmoregulation in poikilotherms.

173. FONTAINE, M., BARADUC, M. M., and HATEY, J., C. R. Soc. Biol. *147*: 214-216, 1953. Thyroid in liver glycogen control in poikilotherms.

174. FONTAINE, M., and FONTAINE, Y. A., J. Physiol. Paris *49*: 169-173, 1957. Species differences in TSH.

175. FRAENKEL, G., Proc. Roy. Soc. London, B, *118*: 1-12, 1935. Hormonal control of Dipteran development.

176. FUGITA, H., Arch. Hist. Jap. *12*: 165-172, 1957. Secretory granules.

177. FUKUDA, S., Annot. Zool. Japan 20: 9-13, 1941. Prothoracic glands and Lepidopteran metamorphosis.

178. FUKUDA, S., Proc. Jap. Acad. *27*: 272-677, 1951. Diapause hormone from subesophageal ganglion.

179. GABE, M., C. R. Acad. Sci. *237*: 1111-1113, 1953. Y-organ and molt in crustaceans.

180. GABE, M., Ann. Sci. Nat. Zool. Biol. Animale *18*: 145-152, 1956. Y-organ and molt in crustaceans.

181. GANONG, W. F., FREDRICKSON, D. S., and HUME, D. M., Endocrinology 57: 355-362, 1955. Anteriormost median eminence TSH, next ACTH, and posterior, gonadotropic.

182. GANONG, W. F., GOLD, N. I., and HUME, D. M., Fed. Proc. *14*: 54, 1955. Absence of corticoids in stress after lesions in median eminence.

183. GANONG, W. F., and HUME, D. M., Endocrinology 55: 474-483, 1954. Basal level of ACTH secretion without hypothalamus.

184. GESCHWIND, I. I., Comparative Endocrinology, edited by A. Gorbman. New York, John Wiley & Sons, 1959, pp. 421-443. Prolactin differences between ox and sheep.

185. GESCHWIND, I. I., LI, C. H., and BARNAFI, L., J. Am. Chem. Soc. *78*: 4494-4495, 1956. Structure of β-MSH. Chemistry of MSH.

186. GESCHWIND, I. I., LI, C. H., and BARNAFI, L., Fed. Proc. *16*: 185, 1957. α- and β-MSH; amino acid sequence differences in pig and beef.

187. GESCHWIND, I. I., LI, C. H., and BARNAFI, L., J. Am. Chem. Soc. *79*: 620, 1957. Structure of β-MSH.

188. GESCHWIND, I. I., LI, C. H., and BARNAFI, L., J. Am. Chem. Soc. *79*: 1003-1004, 1957. Structure of β-MSH: 18 amino acids in pig.

189. GESCHWIND, I. I., LI, C. H., and BARNAFI, L., J. Am. Chem. Soc. *79*: 6394-6400, 1957. Structure of β-MSH.

190. GILBERT, L. J., and SCHNEIDERMAN, H. A., Science *128*: 844, 1958. Juvenile hormone in adrenal cortex.

191. GORBMAN, A., Proc. Soc. Exp. Biol. Med. *45*: 772-773, 1940. Thyrotropic principle in fish pituitary.

192. GORBMAN, A., Physiol. Rev. *35*: 336-346, 1955. Bound I in dermal glands of Hemichorda; bound I with exoskeletal scleroproteins.

193. GORBMAN, A., Comparative Endocrinology, edited by A. Gorbman. New York, John Wiley & Sons, 1959, pp. 266-282. Problems in the comparative morphology and physiology of the vertebrate thyroid gland.

194. GORBMAN, A., CLEMENTS, M., and O'BRIEN, R., J. Exp. Zool. *127*: 75-89, 1954. Protein binding of I in stolonic canals, Botryllus.

195. GRANT, W. C., and GRANT, J. A., Biol. Bull. *114*: 1-9, 1958. Prolactin in amphibians; responsibility for water drive in red eft stage of newt, Triturus.

196. GREENGARD, H., The Chemistry and Physiology of Hormones. Washington, A.A.A.S., 1944, pp. 174-178. Hormones and digestion, review.

197. GREER, M. A., J. Clin. Endocrinol. *12*: 1259-1268, 1952. Blocking of TSH secretion by hypothalamic lesions.

198. GREER, M. A., and ERWIN, H. L., J. Clin. Invest. *33*: 938-939, 1954. Blocking of goitrogenic action of thiourea by hypothalamic lesions.

199. GRIGNON, G., Developpement de complexe hypothalamo-hypophysaire chez l'embryon de poulet. Nancy, 1956, pp. 1-286. Low neurosecretory content, ADH, and water retention in spring.

200. GROBSTEIN, C., and BELLAMY, A. W., Proc. Soc. Exp. Biol. Med. *41*: 363-365, 1939. Thyroid and growth in fishes.

201. DE GROOT, J., and HARRIS, G. W., J. Physiol. *111*: 335-346, 1950. Neuroendocrine regulation of ACTH release.

202. GROSSMAN, M. I., Vitam. Horm. *16*: 179-263, 1958. Secretin.

203. GUDERNATSCH, J. F., Arch. Entwick-Mech. *35*: 457-483, 1912. Thyroid and amphibian metamorphosis.

204. GUYSELMAN, J. B., Biol. Bull. *104*: 115-137, 1953. Molting in Uca.

205. HADORN, E., Proc. Nat. Acad. Sci. *23*: 478-484, 1937. Larval ring gland and Dipteran development.

206. HADORN, E., and NEEL, J., Arch. Entw.-Mech. *138*: 281-304, 1938. Larval ring gland and dipteran development.

207. VON HAGEN, F., Zool. Jahrb., Abt. Anat. *61*: 467-538, 1936. Thyroid and metamorphosis in fishes.

208. HANN, H. W., Bird Banding *10*: 122-124, 1939. Castration and bird migration.

209. HÄNSTROM, B., Kungl. svensk. Vetensk. Handl. *16*: 1-99, 1937. X-organs and sinus glands.

210. HÄNSTROM, B., Hormones in Invertebrates. Oxford University Press, 1939, 198 pp.

211. HÄNSTROM, B., Colston Papers, Butterworths Sci. Publ., London *8*: 23-37, 1956. Comparative neurosecretion.

212. HARA, J., Annot. Zool. Jap. *25*: 162-171, 1952. Hormonal regulation of Paratya heart.

213. HARA, J., Annot. Zool. Jap. *25*: 411-414, 1952. Hormonal regulation of crustacean heart.

214. HARMS, J. W., Ztschr. wiss. Zool. *146*: 417-462, 1935. Thyroid and growth in fishes.

215. HARMS, W., Arch. Entw.-Mech. *34*: 90-131, 1912. Testes and clitellum production in earthworms.

216. HARRINGTON, R. W., J. Exp. Zool. *131*: 203-223, 1956. Photoperiod and centrarchids.

217. HARRINGTON, R. W., J. Exp. Zool. *135*: 529-556, 1957. Photoperiod and cyprinids.

218. HARRINGTON, R. W., Photoperiodism, edited by R. B. Withrow. Washington, A.A.A.S., 1959, pp. 651-667. Photoperiodism and fishes.

219. HARRIS, G. W., Bull. Johns Hopkins Hosp. *97*: 358-375, 1955. Anteriormost median eminence TSH, next ACTH, and posteriorly gonadotropic.

220. HARRIS, G. W., *in* Comparative Endocrinology, edited by A. Gorbman. New York, John Wiley & Sons, 1959, pp. 202-222. Hypothalamic control of ACTH and TSH.

221. HARRIS, G. W., and JACOBSON, D., Proc. Roy. Soc. London, B, *139*: 263-276, 1952. Pituitary implants—cyclic nature when under median eminence.

222. HARRIS, J. I., and LERNER, A. B., Nature *179*: 1346-1347, 1957. Amino acid sequence in pig α-MSH.

223. HARRIS, J. I., and ROOS, P., Nature *178*: 90, 1956. Amino acid sequence in pig β-MSH. Chemistry and structure of MSH.

224. HARRIS, J. I., SANGER, F., and NAUGHTON, M. A., Arch. Biochem. *65*: 427-438, 1956. Structure of insulin.

225. HASEGAWA K., Proc. Jap. Acad. *27*: 667-671, 1951. Diapause hormone from subesophageal ganglion.

226. HASEGAWA, K., Nature *179*: 1300-1301, 1957. Extract of diapause hormone.

227. HASLER, A. D., MEYER, R. K., and FIELD, H. M., Endocrinology *25*: 978-983, 1939. Hypophyseal gonadotropins in fishes.

228. HAZARD, T. P., and EDDY, R. E., Tr. Amer. Fish. Soc. *80*: 158-162, 1951. Photoperiod and salmonids.

229. HAZELWOOD, R. L., and LORENZ, F. W., Endocrinology *61*: 520-528, 1957. Sensitivity of birds to glucagon.

230. HEBB, C. O., Physiol. Rev. *37*: 196-220, 1957. Acetylcholine as a neurohumor.

231. HELFF, O. M., J. Exp. Zool. *45*: 69-93, 1926. Influence of thyroxin on O_2 consumption of frog tadpoles.

232. HELLER, H., J. Physiol. *101*: 317-326, 1942. Lower vertebrates; different water-regulatory hormone.

233. HENRY, S., and VAN DYKE, H. B., J. Endocrinol. *16*: 310-325, 1958. Immunological differences in ICSH.

234. HESS, W. N., Biol. Bull. *81*: 215-220, 1941. Inhibition of molting in egg-bearing female crustaceans.

235. HESS, W. N., and BACON, R. L., Anat. Rec. *78*(suppl. 150): 1940. Relation of testes and seminal vesicles to clitellum production in earthworms.

236. HEUMANN, A., Ztschr. wiss. Zool. *138*: 515-554, 1931. Testes and clitellum production in earthworms.

237. HICKMAN, C. P., JR., Canad. J. Zool. *37*: 997-1060, 1959. Greater thyroid activity in euryhaline fish in more saline medium.

238. HIGHMAN, K. C., Quart. J. Micr. Sci. *99*: 73-88, 1958. Neurosecretion by corpora cardiaca.

239. HILD, W., Virchows Arch. *319*: 526-546, 1951. Intra-axonal transport.

240. HILLARP, N. A., and NILSON, B., Acta physiol. scandinav. *31*(suppl. 113): 1954. Vesicles in adrenal medulla cells.

241. HISAW, F. L., *in* Comparative Endocrinology, edited by A. Gorbman. New York, John Wiley & Sons, 1959. Endocrine adaptation of the mammalian estrous cycle and gestation.

242. HOAR, W. S., Endocrine Organs, *in* The Physiology of Fishes, edited by M. Brown. New York, Academic Press, 1957. Thyroid and fish development.

243. HOAR, W. S., Canad. J. Zool. *36*: 113-121, 1958. Absence of thyroid effect on metabolic rate in poikilotherms.

244. HODGE, M. G., and CHAPMAN, G. B., J. Biophys. Biochem. Cytol. *4*: 571-574, 1958. Vesicles in sinus gland.

245. HOOVER, E. E., and HUBBARD, H. E., Copeia 206-210, 1937. Photoperiodism and sexual cycle of trout.

246. HOPPER, A. F., J. Exp. Zool. *119*: 105-109, 1952. Low thyroid prolongation of sex immaturity; thyroxin treatment and early sex development—Lebistes.

247. HOSKINS, E. R., and MORRIS, M., Anat. Rec. *11*: 363, 1917. Thyroid and amphibian metamorphosis.

248. HÖST, P., Auk *59*: 388-403, 1942. Light periods and seasonal plumage changes in the ptarmigan.

249. HOUSSAY, B. A., C. R. Soc. Biol. *106*: 377-378, 1931. Hypophyseal gonadotropins in fishes.

250. HOUSSAY, B. A., Acta Physiol. Latino-Am. *4*: 2-41, 1954. Loss of clasp reflex of toads on castration.

251. HOUSSAY, B. A., *in* Comparative Endocrinology, edited by A. Gorbman. New York, John Wiley & Sons, 1959. Comparative physiology of the endocrine pancreas.

252. HOWARD, K. S., SHEPHERD, R. G., EIGNER, E. A., DAVIES, D. S., and BELL, P. H., J. Am. Chem. Soc. *77*: 3419, 1955. Three corticotropins.

253. HUGHES, T. E., J. Exp. Biol. *17*: 331-336, 1940. Influence of parasitic castration in crustaceans.

254. HUME, D. M., and NELSON, D. H., J. Clin. Endocrinol. *15*: 839-840, 1955. Importance of anterior median eminence, rather than posterior, for ACTH.

255. HUME, D. M., and NELSON, D. H., Surg. Forum. *5*: 568-575, 1955. Importance of anterior median eminence, rather than posterior, for ACTH.

256. HUME, D. M., and WITTENSTEIN, G. J., *in* Proceedings of First Clinical ACTH Conference, edited by J. R. Mote. Philadelphia, Blakiston Co., 1950, pp. 134-146. Neuroendocrine regulation of ACTH release.

257. ICHIKAWA, M., and NISHUTSUTSUJI, J., Annot. Zool. Jap. *24*: 205-211, 1951. Brain, and imaginal development in Lepidoptera.

258. Irving, G. W., Jr., *in* The Chemistry and Physiology of Hormones, edited by F. R. Moulton. Washington, A.A.A.S., 1944, pp. 28-46. Functions of posterior lobe of pituitary, review.

259. Ivy, A. C., Physiol. Rev. *10*: 282-335, 1930. Hormones in digestion, review.

260. Ivy, A. C., Glandular Physiology and Therapy. Chicago, American Medical Association, 1942, Chap. 30. Hormones in digestion, review.

261. Iwanoff, P. P., and Mestscherskoja, K. A., Zool. Jahrb. Abt. allg. Zool. Physiol. *55*: 281-348, 1935. Gonadal hormone in insect reproduction.

262. Jenner, C. E., and Engels, W. L., Biol. Bull. *103*: 345-355, 1952. Photoperiodism, Juncos and white-throated sparrows.

263. Johannsen, A. S., Nature *181*: 198-199, 1958. Inhibition of corpus allatum by brain.

264. Jones, B. M., J. Exp. Biol. *33*: 174-185, 1956. Brain and prothoracic gland in embryonic molts.

265. Jones, I. C., Mem. Soc. Endocrinol. *5*: 102-124, 1956. Corticosteroids in lower vertebrates.

266. Jones, I. C., The Adrenal Cortex. Cambridge University Press, 1957. Role of adrenal cortex; annual rhythm.

267. Jones, I. C., *in* The Neurohypophysis, edited by H. Heller. London, Butterworth & Co. Adrenalectomy in winter and summer frogs.

268. Jones, I. C., Phillips, J. G., and Holmes, W. N., Comparative Endocrinology, edited by A. Gorbman. New York, John Wiley & Sons, 1959. Role of adrenal cortex.

269. Jost, A., Tr. 3rd Conf. Gestation, edited by C. A. Villee. New York, Josiah Macy, Jr., Foundation, 1957. Absence of developmental role of thyroid in homoiotherms.

270. Karlson, P., Ann. Sci. Nat. Zool. Biol. Animale *18*: 125-138, 1956. Chemistry of ecdysone.

271. Kendeigh, S. C., Ecol. Monogr. *4*: 299-417, 1934. Environmental factors and bird migration.

272. Kleinholz, L. H., Biol. Bull. *70*: 159-184, 1936. Eyestalk hormone and retinal pigment migration in crustaceans.

273. Kleinholz, L. H., Biol. Bull. *75*: 510-532, 1938. Hormonal control of crustacean retinal-pigment movements.

274. Kleinholz, L. H., Biol. Rev. *17*: 91-119, 1942. Endocrines in crustaceans, review.

275. Kleinholz, L. H., Biol. Bull. *99*: 454-468, 1950. Hormonal regulation of blood sugar in crustaceans.

276. Kleinholz, L. H., Biol. Bull. *109*: 362, 1955. Reflecting pigment of crustacean eye.

277. Kleinholz, L. H., and Bourquin, E., Proc. Nat. Acad. Sci. *27*: 145-149, 1941. Eyestalks and molting in crabs.

278. Kleinholz, L. H., and Knowles, F. G. W., Biol. Bull. *75*: 266-273, 1938. Movements of retinal pigments of Crustacea in response to backgrounds.

279. Klenner, J. J., Proc. Indiana Acad. Sci. *62*: 318, 1952. Pituitary control of thyroid in larva.

280. Knobil, E., Ganong, W. F., and Greep, R. D., J. Clin. Endocrinol. *14*: 787, 1954. Differences in growth hormones.

281. Knowles, F. G. W., Proc. Roy. Soc. London, B, *141*: 248-267, 1953. Postcommissural organ.

282. Knowles, F. G. W., Pubbl. Staz Zool. Napoli. *24*: 74-78, 1954. Postcommissural organ.

283. Knowles, F. G. W., 2. Internat. Symp. Neurosekr. Springer-Verlag, Berlin-Göttingen-Heidelberg, 1958, pp. 105-109. Secretory granules.

284. Knowles, F. G. W., *in* Comparative Endocrinology, edited by A. Gorbman. New York, John Wiley & Sons, 1959. Secretory granules.

285. Knowles, F. G. W., and Callan, H. G., J. Exp. Biol. *17*: 262-266, 1940. Endocrine action of crustacean ovary. Castration in female crustaceans and secondary sex characters.

286. Knowles, F. G. W., and Carlisle, D. B., Biol. Rev. *31*: 396-473, 1956. Terms MTGX-, SPX-organ. Crustacean chromatophorotropin polypeptides. Crustacean endocrinology, review.

287. Kobayashi, M., and Kirimura, J., Nature *181*: 217, 1958. Extract of brain hormone of silkworm.

288. Koller, G., Ztschr. vergl. Physiol. *12*: 632-667, 1930. Calcium exchange in crustacean molt.

289. Koller, G., Hormone bei wirbellosen Tieren Leipzig, Akademische Verlagsgessellschaft, 1938. 143 pp.

290. Kollros, J. J., Anat. Rec. *125*: 624, 1956. Definite tissue thresholds for thyroid targets.

291. Kollros, J. J., Anat. Rec. *130*: 327, 1958. Thyroid and anuran development.

292. Kollros, J. J., *in* Comparative Endocrinology, edited by A. Gorbman. New York, John Wiley & Sons, 1959, pp. 340-350. Complex reacting system of amphibian development to thyroid activity.

293. Kollros, J. J., and McMurry, V. M., J. Exp. Zool. *131*: 1-26, 1956. Differential CNS growth with thyroid.

294. Kopec, S., Biol. Bull. *42*: 324-342, 1922. Endocrine control of insect development.

295. Krockert, G., Vitam. u. Horm. *1*: 24-31, 1941. Thyroxin and metabolism in Python.

296. Kyer, D. L., Biol. Bull. *82*: 68-78, 1942. Hormonal control of gastrolith formation in crayfishes.

297. Lamotte, M., and Prum, P., C. R. Soc. Biol. *151*: 1187-1191, 1957. Endocrine physiology of a viviparous amphibian.

298. Lamotte, M., and Rey, P., C. R. Acad. Sci. *238*: 393-395, 1954. Corpora lutea in amphibian.

299. Lamotte, M., and Rey, P., C. R. Soc. Biol. *151*: 1191-1194, 1957. Corpora lutea in amphibia.

300. Lamotte, M., Rey, P., and Vilter, V., C. R. Soc. Biol. *150*: 393-396, 1956. Endocrine physiology of viviparous amphibian.

301. Landgrebe, F. W., Ketterer, B., and Waring, H., *in* The Hormones, edited by G. Pincus and K. V. Thimann. New York, Academic Press, 1955, vol. 3. Hormones of the posterior pituitary.

302. La Roche, G., and Leblond, C. P., Endocrinol. *51*: 524-545, 1952. Inhibition of fish development by inhibition of thyroid.

303. Lattin, G. de, and Gross, F., Experientia

9: 338-339, 1953. Testis as an endocrine gland in isopods.

304. LEBLOND, C. P., GLEGG, R. E., and EIDINGER, D., J. Histochem. 5: 445-456, 1957. Proteins of endostyle.

305. LEE, T. H., and LERNER, A. B., J. Biol. Chem. 221: 943-959, 1956. α- and β-MSH.

306. LEES, A. D., in Photoperiodism and Related Phenomena in Plants and Animals, edited by R. B. Withrow. Washington, A.A.A.S., 1953, pp. 585-600. Photoperiodism and insects.

307. LEGRAND, J. J., C. R. Acad. Sci. 239: 108-110, 1954. Testis hormone in isopods.

308. LELOUP, J., J. Physiol. 47: 671-677, 1955. Part of ammocoete endostyle becoming thyroid.

309. LELOUP, J., and BERG, O., C. R. Acad. Sci. 238: 1069-1071, 1954. Part of ammocoete larval endostyle becoming thyroid.

310. LERNER, A. B., and LEE, T. H., J. Am. Chem. Soc. 77: 1066-1067, 1955. Structure of MSH.

311. LESHER, S. W., and KENDEIGH, S. C., Wilson Bull. 53: 169-180, 1941. Influence of light periods on plumage types in birds.

312. LEWIS, G. P., ed., 5-Hydroxytryptamine. London, Pergamon Press, 1958. Serotonin(5-hydroxytryptamine) as a neurohumoral agent.

313. LI, C. H., Symposium on Protein Structure, edited by A. Neuberger. New York, John Wiley & Sons, 1958. Three classes of growth hormone; differences in growth hormones and in sheep and ox prolactin.

314. LI, C. H., et al.: Nature 176: 687-689, 1955. Three corticotropins.

315. LIEBER, A., Ztschr. wiss. Zool. 148: 364-400, 1936. Thyroid and growth in fishes.

316. LONG, C. N. H., Cold Spring Harbor Symp. 10: 91-103, 1942. Hypophysis and growth in mammals.

317. LÜSCHER, M., and ENGELMANN, F., Rev. Suisse Zool. 62: 649-657, 1955. Corpora allatum function in Leucophaea.

318. LYMAN, C. P., Bull. Mus. Comp. Zool. 93: 391-461, 1943. Control of seasonal changes in coat color of the varying hare, Lepus.

319. LYNN, W. G., and WACHOWSKI, H. E., Quart. Rev. Biol. 26: 123-168, 1951. Growth and differentiation effects, Thyroid.

320. MARSHALL, A. J., Mem. Soc. Endocrinol. 4: 75-93, 1955. Hypothalamic control of pituitary in bird.

321. MARSHALL, F. H. A., Biol. Rev. 17: 68-90, 1942. Factors in sexual periodicity.

322. MARVIN, H. N., and SMITH, G. C., Endocrinol. 32: 87-91, 1943. Thyroid and heat production in pigeons.

323. MATSUMOTO, K., Biol. J. Okayama Univ. 4: 103-176, 1958. X-organ in crabs.

324. MATTHEWS, L. H., Mem. Soc. Endocrinol. 4: 129-148, 1955. Reptile corpus luteum.

325. MATTHEWS, S. A., Biol. Bull. 76: 241-250, 1939. Role of gonadotropins in teleosts.

326. MATTHEWS, S. A., Biol. Bull. 79: 207-214, 1940. Role of gonadotropins in teleosts.

327. MATTHEWS, S. A., and SMITH, D. C., Physiol. Zool. 20: 161-164, 1947. Thyroid and fish metabolism.

328. MATTY, A. J., J. Endocrinol. 15: 1-8, 1957. Absence of thyroid effect on metabolic rate in poikilotherms.

329. MEGUŠAR, F., Arch. Entwick-Mech. 33: 462-665, 1912. Eyestalks and molting in Crustacea.

330. MELLISH, C. H., and MEYER, R. K., Anat. Rec. 69: 179-189, 1937. Gonadotropic activity in reptiles.

331. MESS, B., Endokrinol. 35: 296-301, 1958. Hypothalamic control of ACTH and TSH.

332. MIALHE, P., C. R. Acad. Sci. 241: 1621-1624, 1955. Transient diabetes in ducks.

333. MIALHE, P., J. Physiol. Paris 47: 248-250, 1955. Ducks and pancreas.

334. MILLER, A. H., Condor 56: 13-20, 1954. Refractory period in birds.

335. MILLER, M. R., and WURSTER, D. H., Endocrinol. 58: 114-120, 1956. Insulin-resistant reptiles and birds.

336. MILLER, M. R., and WURSTER, D. H., in Comparative Endocrinology, edited by A. Gorbman. New York, John Wiley & Sons, 1959. Sensitivity of amphibians to insulin; insensitivity to glucagon; absence of α-cells.

337. MILLER, M. R., and WURSTER, D. H., Endocrinol. 63: 191-200, 1958. Sensitivity of reptiles to glucagon and abundance of α-cells.

338. MITCHELL, M., GUILLEMIN, R., and SELYE, H., Endocrinol. 54: 111-114, 1954. Differences in growth hormones.

339. MIYAWAKI, M., J. Fac. Sci. Hokkaido Univ. ser. 6, Zool. 12: 516-520, 1956. Secretion by sinus gland.

340. MOLONY, P. J., and COVAL, M., Biochem. J. 59: 179-185, 1955. Immunological similarity of various insulins.

341. MOLONY, P. J., and GOLDSMITH, L., Canad. J. Biochem. Physiol. 35: 79-92, 1957. Antibodies to administered insulin.

342. MONTALENTI, G., and VITAGLIANO, G., Pubbl. Staz. Zool. Napoli 20: 1-18, 1946. Spermatogenesis and hectocotylus development in cephalopods.

343. MOREL, F., Aldosterone. London, J. and A. Churchill Ltd., 1958. Aldosterone.

344. MÜHLBACH, O., and BOOT, L. M., Ann. Endocrinol. 17: 338-343, 1956. Series of pseudopregnancies in mice with extra pituitary subcutaneous-LTH production.

345. MURR, E., and SKLOWER, A., Ztschr. vergl. Physiol. 7: 279-288, 1928. Thyroid and metamorphosis in fishes.

346. NAYAR, K. K., Curr. Sci. 22: 149, 1953. Correlation of insect brain secretion with oviposition.

347. NELSON, W. O., Mécanisme Physiologique de la Secretion Lactée Paris, Publ. de CNRS, 1951. LTH affects mammary tissue.

348. NIKITOWITCH-WINER, M., and EVERETT, J. W., Endocrinol. 62: 513-521, 1958. Luteotropin secreted by implanted pituitary at any site.

349. NIKITOVITCH-WINER, M., and EVERETT, J. W., Endocrinol. 63: 916-930, 1958. Cycles in rats only when pituitary implants under median eminence.

350. ODIORNE, J. M., in Physiology of Fishes, edited by M. Brown. New York, Academic Press, 1957, vol. I. Pigment regulation in fishes, amphibians.

351. OKSCHE, A., LAWS, D., KAMEMOTO, F. I., and FARNER, D. S., Ztschr. Zellforsch. *51*: 1-42, 1959. Secretory granules in nerve loops of median eminence of white-crowned sparrows under 8 hours' light.

352. OLIVEREAU, M., Ann. Inst. Oceanog. *29*: 92-296, 1954. Inhibition of fish development by thyroid inhibition.

353. OLIVEREAU, M., Arch. Anat. Micro. Morph. Exp. *44*: 236-264, 1955. Higher thyroid activity in trout at lower temperatures.

354. OLIVEREAU, M., C. R. Assn. Anat. *43*: 636-657, 1956. Pituitary control of thyroid in larva.

355. PAGE, I. H., Bull. New York Acad. Med. *19*: 461-477, 1943. The physiological action of renin.

356. PAGE, I. H., Physiol. Rev. *38*: 277-335, 1958. Serotonin as a neurohumoral agent.

357. PALAY, S. L., Anat. Rec. *121*: 348, 1955. Vesicles in nerve fibers—the secretion.

358. PANIGEL, M., Ann. Sci. Nat. Zool. *18*: 569-668, 1956. Reptile corpus luteum; presence in all reptiles whether oviparous or viviparous.

359. PANOUSE, J., C. R. Acad. Sci. *217*: 553-555, 1943. Eyestalks and ovarian growth in crustaceans.

360. PANOUSE, J., C. R. Acad. Sci. *218*: 293-294, 1944. Sinus glands and ovarian growth in crustaceans.

361. PANOUSE, J., Ann. Inst. Oceanog. *23*: 65-147, 1946. Sinus glands and ovarian growth in crustaceans.

362. PARDOE, A. Y., and WEATHERALL, M., J. Physiol. *127*: 201-212, 1955. Vasopressin and oxytocin from granules of neurohypophysis.

363. PARIS, O. H., JR., and JENNER, C. E., *in* Photoperiodism and Related Phenomena in Plants and Animals, edited by R. B. Withrow. Washington, A.A.A.S., 1959, pp. 601-624. Photoperiodic control of diapause in insects.

364. PASSANO, L. M., Physiol. Comp. Oecol. *3*: 155-189, 1953. X-organ—sinus gland complex.

365. PERIERA, J., JR., and CARDOSO, D. M., C. R. Soc. Biol. *116*: 1133-1134, 1934. Hypophyseal gonadotropins in fishes.

366. PESELSKY, I., and KOLLROS, J. J., Exp. Cell. Res. *11*: 477-482, 1956. Differential CNS growth with thyroid.

367. PFEIFFER, I. W., J. Exp. Zool. *82*: 439-461, 1939. Corpora allata and reproduction in Orthoptera. Hormonal control of development.

368. PFEIFFER, I. W., J. Exp. Zool. *99*: 183-233, 1945. Corpus allatum and general metabolism in insects.

369. PFLUGFELDER, O., Ztschr. wiss. Zool. *149*: 477-512, 1937. Hormonal control of orthopteran development and reproduction.

370. PFLUGFELDER, O., Ztschr, wiss. Zool. *152*: 384-408, 1939. Hormones in Dixippus reproduction.

371. PFLUGFELDER, O., Ztschr. wiss. Zool. *153*: 108-135, 1940. Hormones in Dixippus development and reproduction.

372. PICKERING, B. T., and HELLER, H., Nature *184*: 1463-1465, 1959. Oxytocin in birds, frogs, and fishes.

373. PICKFORD, G. E., Bull. Bingham Oceanog. Coll. *14*: 46-68, 1953. Control of spawning in Fundulus; fish response to beef growth hormone.

374. PICKFORD, G. E., Endocrinol. *55*: 274-287, 1954. Fish growth to fish growth hormone.

375. PICKFORD, G. E., *in* Comparative Endocrinology, edited by A. Gorbman. New York, John Wiley & Sons, 1959, pp. 404-420. Prolactin cooperation with MSH in fish pigmentation.

376. PICKFORD, G. E., and ATZ, J. W., The Physiology of the Pituitary Gland of Fishes. New York Zoological Society, 1957.

377. PICKFORD, G. E., and KOSTO, B., Endocrinol. *61*: 177-196, 1957. New melanocytes in Fundulus by MSH and prolactin.

378. POSSOMPÈS, B., Arch. Zool. Exp. Gen. *89*: 203-364, 1953. Hormones and Calliphora metamorphosis.

379. POTTER, D. D., 2. Internat. Sympos. Neurosekr. Springer-Verlag, Berlin-Göttingen-Heidelberg, 1958, pp. 113-118. Secretory granules.

380. POTTER, D. D., and LOWENSTEIN, W. R., Am. J. Physiol. *183*: 652, 1955. Conduction of impulses by axons of pituitary stalk.

381. PYLE, R. W., Biol. Bull. *85*: 87-102, 1943. Cycles in histological picture in sinus glands and molting in crustaceans.

382. RAHM, U. H., Rev. Suisse. Zool. *59*: 173-237, 1952. Hormones and Sialis development.

383. RALPH, C. L., and FRAPPS, R. M., Anat. Rec. *130*: 360-361, 1958. Gonadal control via hypothalamus.

384. ROBERTS, J. L., Physiol. Zool. *30*: 232-242, 1957. Nutrition and crab molting.

385. ROWAN, W., Proc. Boston Soc. Nat. Hist. *39*: 151-208, 1929. Factors controlling bird migration.

386. ROWAN, W., The Riddle of Migration. Baltimore, Williams & Wilkins, 1931, 151 pp.

387. ROWAN, W., Proc. Nat. Acad. Sci. *18*: 639-654, 1932. Factors determining bird migration.

388. ROWAN, W., Biol. Rev. *13*: 374-402, 1938. Light and reproductive cycles.

389. RUGH, R., Biol. Bull. *66*: 22-29, 1934. Gonadotropic activity of hypophysis in amphibia.

390. RUGH, R., J. Exp. Zool. *71*: 149-162, 1935. Gonadotropic activity of hypophysis in amphibia.

391. RUGH, R., J. Exp. Zool. *71*: 163-193, 1935. Gonadotropic activity of hypophysis in amphibia.

392. SANDEEN, M. I., and BROWN, F. A., JR., Physiol. Zool. *25*: 223-230, 1952. Retinal pigment response of Palaemonetes to illumination.

393. SAWYER, W. H., Fed. Proc. *14*: 130, 1955. Vasopressin and oxytocic activities in fish pituitary.

394. SAWYER, W. H., Endocrinol. *66*: 112-120, 1960. Neurohypophyseal hormones and water regulation in Rana; neurohypophyseal hormones and frog bladder permeability.

395. SAWYER, W. H., MUNSICK, R. A., and VAN DYKE, H. B., Nature *184*: 1463-1465, 1959. Neurohypophyseal principles in cold-blooded vertebrates.

396. SAWYER, W. H., MUNSICK, R. A.. and VAN DYKE, H. B., Circulation *21*: 1027-1037, 1960. Distribution of posterior lobe hormones.

397. SAWYER, W. H., and SCHISGALL, R. M., Am.

J. Physiol. *187*: 312-314, 1956. Neurohypophysis in terrestrial amphibians; increase in skin uptake of water and renal antidiuresis.

398. SCHARRER, B., Physiol. Rev. *21*: 383-409, 1941. Endocrines in invertebrates, review.

399. SCHARRER, B., Endocrinol. *38*: 35-45, 1946. Hormonal control of orthopteran development.

400. SCHARRER, B., Endocrinol. *38*: 46-55, 1946. Corpus allatum hormone and ovarian growth in Orthoptera.

401. SCHARRER, B., Biol. Bull. *102*: 261-272, 1952. Intra-axonal transport in insects; role of corpus cardiacum; Nerve inhibition of corpora allata.

402. SCHARRER, B., *in* Comparative Endocrinology, edited by A. Gorbman. New York, John Wiley & Sons, 1959, pp. 134-148. Neuroendocrines.

403. SCHARRER, E., *in* Comparative Endocrinology, edited by A. Gorbman. New York, John Wiley & Sons, pp. 233-249. Neuroendocrines.

404. SCHARRER, E., and SCHARRER, B., Physiol. Rev. *25*: 171-181, 1945. Neurosecretion, review.

405. SCHARRER, E., and SCHARRER, B., Handl. Mikr. Anat. Mensch. *6*: 953-1066, 1954. Low neurosecretory content, ADH, and water retention in young.

406. SCHARRER, E., and SCHARRER, B., Rec. Progr. Horm. Res. *10*: 183-240, 1954. Neurosecretion; neuroendocrinology.

407. SCHAYER, R. W., and IVY, A. C., Am. J. Physiol. *189*: 369-372, 1957. Histamine as a hormone.

408. SCHEER, B. T., Recent Advances in Invertebrate Physiology. University of Oregon Publications, 1957, pp. 213-227.

409. SCHEER, B. T., and SCHEER, M. A. R., Pubbl. Staz. Zool. Napoli *25*: 397-418, 1954. Hormones and molting in Leander.

410. SCHEER, B. T., and SCHEER, M. A. R., Pubbl. Staz. Zool. Napoli *25*: 419-426, 1954. Crustacean molt-cycle stages, Natantia.

411. SCHNEIDERMAN, H. A., and GILBERT, L. I., Biol. Bull. *115*: 530-535, 1958. Widespread distribution among animals of juvenile hormone activity.

412. SCHNEIDERMAN, H. A., and GILBERT, L. I., *in* Cell, Organism and Milieu, edited by D. Rudnick. New York, Ronald Press Co., 1959, pp. 157-187. Substances with juvenile hormone activity among animals.

413. SCUDAMORE, H. H., Tr. Illinois Acad. Sci. *34*: 238-240, 1941. Hormonal regulation of crustacean heart rate.

414. SCUDAMORE, H. H., Physiol. Zool. *20*: 187-208, 1947. Sinus gland and O_2 consumption in crayfishes; hormonal control of gastrolith formation in crayfishes.

415. SCUDAMORE, H. H., Biol. Bull. *95*: 229-237, 1948. Molting and seasonal sex cycle in Cambarus.

416. SEGAL, S. J., Anat. Rec. *115*: 205-230, 1953. Estrogens yield adrenal hyperplasia.

417. SEGAL, S. J., Science *126*: 1242-1243, 1957. Gonadotropic control of nuptial plumage in African finches.

418. SEMBRAT, K., Zool. Polon. *6*: 3, 1953. Amphioxis endostyles causing axolotl metamorphosis.

419. SERENI, Am. Jour. Physiol. *90*: 512-513, 1929.

Relation of testes to hectocotylus development in cephalopods.

420. SHAPPIRIO, D. G., and WILLIAMS, C. M., Proc. Roy. Soc. London, B, *147*: 233-246, 1957. Ecdysone induction of increase in mitochondria and endoplasmic reticulum of epithelial cells.

421. SHEPHERD, R. G., *et al.*, J. Am. Chem. Soc. *78*: 5067-5076, 1956. Three corticosteroids.

422. SJOSTRAND, F. S., and WATZSTEIN, R., Experientia *12*: 196-199, 1956. Vesicles in adrenal medulla cells.

423. SMITH, C. L., Nature *171*: 311-312, 1953. Sensitivity of amphibians to insulin (Rana).

424. SMITH, D. C., and EVERETT, G. M., J. Exp. Zool. *94*: 229-240, 1943. Thyroxin and O_2 consumption in fishes.

425. SMITH, D. C., and MATTHEWS, S. A., Am. J. Physiol. *153*: 215-221, 1948. Thyroid and O_2 consumption in fishes.

426. SMITH, D. C. W., Mem. Soc. Endocrinol. *5*: 83-98, 1956. Thyroid in poikilotherm osmoregulation.

427. SMITH, P. E., Anat. Rec. *11*: 57-64, 1916. Hypophysis in amphibian metamorphosis.

428. SMITH, R. I., Biol. Bull. *79*: 145-152, 1940. Eyestalks and molting in young crayfishes.

429. SNEDECOR, J. G., MATTHEWS, H., and MACGRATH, W. B., JR., Poultry Sci. *35*: 355, 1956. Sensitivity of birds to glucagon.

430. SQUIRE, P. G., and LI, C. H., Science *127*: 32, 1958. Interspecific and intraspecific differences in ICSH.

431. STEPHENS, G. C., Biol. Bull. *103*: 242-258, 1952. Eyestalk hormone and cement glands.

432. STEPHENS, G. C., Biol. Bull. *108*: 235-241, 1955. Molt induction in crayfish by photoperiod.

433. STEPHENS, G. J., Physiol. Zool. *25*: 70-84, 1952. Light influence upon cyclic ovarian activity in crayfishes.

434. STURKIE, P. D., Avian Physiology. Ithaca, N. Y., Comstock Publishing Associates, 1954. Insulin-resistant reptiles and birds.

435. SWIFT, D. R., Nature *173*: 1096, 1954. Fish response to beef growth hormone.

436. SWINGLE, W. W., J. Exp. Zool. *36*: 397-421, 1922. Thyroid and amphibian metamorphosis.

437. TAKASUGI, N., J. Fac. Sci. Univ. Tokyo. sec IV *7*: 605-623, 1956. Rat ovulation by stress.

438. TAKEWAKI, K., Annot. Zool. Jap. *29*: 1-6, 1956. Rat ovulation by progesterone and corticosteroid.

439. TAKEWAKI, K., and NAKAMURA, N., J. Fac. Sci. Tokyo Univ. sec. IV *6*: 369-382, 1944. Endocrine action of crustacean ovary.

440. TAKEWAKI, K., and YAMAMOTO, Y., Annot. Zool. Jap. *23*: 187-190, 1950. Hormonal control Paratya ovary.

441. THOMAS, I. M., J. Mar. Biol. Assn. U. K. *35*: 203-210, 1956. Amphioxus endostyle binding of I.

442. THOMSEN, D. L., and COLLIP, J. B., Physiol. Rev. *12*: 309-383, 1932. Action of parathyroid hormone, review.

443. THOMSEN, E., Nature *145*: 28-29, 1940. Corpus allatum hormone and insect reproduction.

444. THOMSEN, E., Vidensk. Meddel. Dansk. Natur-

hist. Foren. *106*: 320-405, 1942. Corpus allatum hormone and dipteran reproduction.

445. THOMSEN, E., J. Exp. Biol. *29*: 137-172, 1952. Neurosecretory brain cells and corpus cardiacum in Calliphora.

446. THOMSEN, E., J. Exp. Biol. *31*: 322-330, 1954. Intra-axonal transport in Calliphora.

447. TURNER, C. L., Physiol. Zool. *15*: 263-280, 1942. Gonadal hormones and secondary sex characters of fishes.

448. TURNER, C. L., Copeia 195-203, 1957. Photoperiod and poeciliids.

449. UMRATH, K., Ztschr. vergl. Physiol. *40*: 321-328, 1957. MSH stimulation of new pigment formation.

450. VAN DER KLOOT, W. G., Biol. Bull. *109*: 276-294, 1955. Controls of diapause in Cecropia.

451. VAN DER KLOOT, W. G., and WILLIAMS, C. M., Behavior *5*: 157-174, 1953. Hormonal control of cocoon formation.

452. VAN DYKE, H. B., ADAMSONS, K., and ENGEL, S. L., *in* The Neurohypophysis, edited by H. Heller. New York, Academic Press, 1957. Differing activities of various vasopressins.

453. VAN DYKE, H. B., ENGEL, S. L., and ADAMSONS, K., Proc. Soc. Exp. Biol. Med. *91*: 484-486, 1956. Differing activities of vasopressins.

454. VANDEL, A., C. R. Acad. Sci. *170*: 249-251, 1920. Gonads and development of planarian copulatory apparatus.

455. VANDEL, A., Bull. Biol. France Belg. *55*: 343-518, 1921. Gonads and development of planarian copulatory apparatus.

456. VEILLET, A., CORNUBERT, G., and DEMEUSY, N., C. R. Soc. Biol. *147*: 1264-1265, 1953. MTGX hormone inhibiting ovaries.

457. VERHOEVEN, B., and VAN OORDT, G. J., Konikl. Ned. Akad. Wetenschap. Proc. C *58*: 628-634, 1955. Photoperiod and Cyprinids.

458. DU VIGNEAUD, V., Science *123*: 967-974, 1956. Differences in pig and beef vasopressin.

459. DU VIGNEAUD, V., LAWLER, H. C., and POPENOE, E. A., J. Am. Chem. Soc. *75*: 4880-4881, 1953. Octapeptides oxytocin and vasopressin.

460. DU VIGNEAUD, V., LAWLER, H. C., POPENOE, E. A., and TRIPPETT, S., J. Biol. Chem. *205*: 949-957, 1953. Octapeptides oxytocin and vasopressin.

461. VIVIEN, J., *in* Traite de Zoologie edited by P. P. Grasse. Paris, Masson et Cie, 1958. 13: fac. II. Thyroid and development of fishes.

462. VOGT, M., Biol. Zentbl. *60*: 479-484, 1940. Corpora allata and reproduction in Drosophila.

463. VOGT, M., Biol. Zentbl. *61*: 242-252, 1941. Corpora allata and reproduction in Drosophila.

464. VOGT, M., Arch. Entwick-Mech. *141*: 424-454, 1942. Corpora allata and reproduction in Drosophila.

465. WARREN, M. R., J. Exp. Zool. *83*: 127-156, 1940. Thyroxin and O_2 consumption in frogs.

466. WEBB, H. M., and BROWN, F. A., JR., J. Cell. Comp. Physiol. *41*: 103-122, 1953. Daily rhythm in Palaemonetes retinal pigment.

467. WEED, I. G., Proc. Soc. Exp. Biol. and Med. *34*: 883-885, 1936. Corpora allata and reproduction in Orthopterans.

468. WEISS, P., and ROSSETTI, F., Proc. Nat. Acad.

Sci. *37*: 540-556, 1951. Differential CNS growth under thyroid.

469. WELSH, J. H., Proc. Nat. Acad. Sci. *16*: 386-395, 1930. Diurnal rhythm in crustacean retinal pigment movements.

470. WELSH, J. H., Proc. Nat. Acad. Sci. *23*: 458-460, 1937. Hormonal influence on crustacean heartbeat.

471. WELSH, J. H., Biol. Bull. *77*: 119-125, 1939. Eyestalk hormone and retinal-pigment migration in crayfish.

472. WELSH, J. H., J. Exp. Zool. *86*: 35-49, 1941. Sinus glands and retinal-pigment migration in crayfishes.

473. WELSH, J. H., Ann. New York Acad. Sci. *66*: 618-630, 1957. Serotonin as a neurohumoral agent.

474. WELSH, J. H., *in* Comparative Endocrinology, edited by A. Gorbman. New York, John Wiley & Sons, 1959, pp. 121-133. Neuroendocrines.

475. WELSH, J. H., and OSBORN, C. M., J. Comp. Neurol. *66*: 349-359, 1937. Diurnal rhythm in activity of elements in catfish retina.

476. VON DER WENSE, T. F., Wirkungen und Vorkommen von Hormonen bei wirbellosen Tieren. Leipzig, J. A. Barth, 1938. 80 pp.

477. WHITAKER, W. L., Proc. Soc. Exp. Biol. and Med. *34*: 329-330, 1936. Photoperiodism and breeding in Peromyscus.

478. WHITE, W. F., and LANDMANN, W. A., J. Am. Chem. Soc. *77*: 1711-1712, 1955. Three corticosteroids.

479. WIGGLESWORTH, V. B., Quart. J. Micr. Sci. *77*: 191-222, 1934. Hormones in insect molt and metamorphosis: Hemiptera.

480. WIGGLESWORTH, V. B., Quart. J. Micr. Sci. *79*: 91-121, 1936. Hormones in molt and metamorphosis and reproduction: Hemiptera.

481. WIGGLESWORTH, V. B., J. Exp. Biol. *17*: 201-222, 1940. Hormones in insect molt and metamorphosis: Hemiptera.

482. WIGGLESWORTH, V. B., J. Exp. Biol. *29*: 561-570, 1952. Hormones and insect molt.

483. WIGGLESWORTH, V. B., The Physiology of Insect Metamorphosis. Cambridge University Press, 1954.

484. WIGGLESWORTH, V. B., Sym. Soc. Exp. Biol. *11*: 204-227, 1957. Corpora allata hormone and larval synthesis.

485. WILHELMI, A., *in* The Hypophyseal Growth Hormone, Nature and Actions, edited by R. W. Smith, Jr., O. H. Gaebler, and C. N. H. Long. New York, Blakiston Co., 1955.

486. WILHELMI, A., *in* The Hypophyseal Growth Hormone, edited by R. W. Smith, Jr., O. H. Gaebler, and C. N. H. Long. New York, Blakiston Co., 1955, p. 59. Crystalline fish growth hormone.

487. WILHELMI, A., PICKFORD, G. E., and SAWYER, W. H., Endocrinol. *57*: 243-252, 1955. Spawning in Fundulus by neurohypophysis. Oxytocin and vasopressin as sex controllers; Mammalian posterior lobe hormones give spawning in Fundulus.

488. WILLIAMS, C. M., Biol. Bull. *90*: 234-243, 1946. Brain hormones in Lepidopteran metamorphosis.

489. WILLIAMS, C. M., Biol. Bull. *93*: 89-98, 1947.

Roles of brain and prothoracic gland principles in Lepidopteran metamorphosis.

490. WILLIAMS, C. M., Anat. Rec. *99*: 591, 1947. Cytochrome system in diapause and development in Cecropia silkworm.

491. WILLIAMS, C. M., Anat. Rec. *99*: 671, 1947. Brain and termination of pupal diapause.

492. WILLIAMS, C. M., Biol. Bull. *94*: 60-65, 1948. Prothoracic glands and insect development.

493. WILLIAMS, C. M., Biol. Bull. *103*: 120-138, 1952. Brain and prothoracic gland in insect metamorphosis.

494. WILLIAMS, C. M., Harvey Lect. *47*: 126-155, 1952. Brain and prothoracic gland in larval-pupal molt.

495. WILLIAMS, C. M., Nature *178*: 212-213, 1956. Storage of juvenile hormone in abdomen of male Cecropia.

496. WILLS, I. A., RILEY, G. M., and STUBBS, E. M., Proc. Soc. Exp. Biol. Med. *30*: 411-412, 784-786, 1933. Hypophysis and sex behavior in Amphibia.

497. WINGSTRAND, K. G., Arkiv. Zool. Soc. *26*: 41-67, 1953. Low neurosecretory material, ADH, and water retention in fetuses and young.

498. WITSCHI, E., Wilson Bull. *47*: 177-188, 1935. Hypophyseal control of plumage in weaver finches.

499. WITSCHI, E., J. Clin. Endocrinol. *13*: 316-329, 1953. Estrogens give adrenal hyperplasia.

500. WITSCHI, E., Mem. Soc. Endocrinol. *4*: 149, 1955. Control of nuptial plumage in African finches.

501. WITSCHI, E., *in* Comparative Endocrinology, edited by A. Gorbman. New York, John Wiley & Sons, 1959. Taxonomic specificity of LH; endocrine basis of reproductive adaptations in birds.

502. WITSCHI, E., and CHANG, C. Y., *in* Comparative Endocrinology, edited by A. Gorbman. New York, John Wiley & Sons, 1959, pp. 149-160. Amphibian ovulation and spermiation.

503. WOLFSON, A., Condor *44*: 237-263, 1942. Factors controlling bird migration.

504. WOLFSON, A., Condor *47*: 95-127, 1945. Controlling factors in bird migration.

505. WOLFSON, A., *in* Comparative Endocrinology, edited by A. Gorbman. New York, John Wiley & Sons, 1959, pp. 38-70. Photoperiodism and bird physiology.

506. WOLFSON, A., Photoperiodism and Related Phenomena in Plants and Animals, edited by R. B. Withrow. Washington, A.A.A.S., 1959. Photoperiodism and annual cycles in birds.

507. WOODBURY, A. M., Auk *58*: 463-505, 1941. Temperature change and bird migration.

508. WOODS, R., and CARLSON, L. D., Endocrinology *59*: 323-330, 1956. Temperature and rat thyroid.

509. WRIGHT, P. A., Endocrin. *64*: 551-558, 1959. Blood sugar studies in the bullfrog.

510. WRIGHT, P. A., Biol. Bull. *119*: 351, 1960. Rana ovulation in vitro by steroids.

511. WRIGHT, P. A., and HISAW, F. L., Endocrinology *39*: 247-255, 1946. Ovulation in frogs with mammalian FSH and LH.

512. YAMAMOTO, Y., Annot. Zool. Jap. *28*: 92-99, 1955. Ovariectomy influence on sinus gland.

513. ZWARENSTEIN, H., Nature *139*: 112-113, 1937. Progesterone and Xenopus ovulation.

Chapter 21

NERVOUS SYSTEMS

Nervous conducting tissue imparts to an animal a high degree of freedom from the environment, and well-developed nervous systems are associated with motility and large body size. Animals with no nervous system or a poorly developed one may be very small and motile (Protozoa and some embryos) or they may be large and sessile (sponges, some coelenterates), but all animals which are both large and motile have rapidly conducting nervous systems. A nervous system permits a range of behavior roughly proportional to its structural complexity.

NON-NERVOUS CONDUCTION

All cells appear to be bounded by a surface layer, sometimes called the plasma membrane, which lies beneath the limiting membrane, and is electrically polarized, normally electrically negative on the protoplasmic interior. Excitation consists of reduction or reversal of the normal polarization. The depolarization may be local or propagated. Excitation, and also conduction, have been described in many plant cells, marine eggs, and in some non-nervous and nonmuscular cells of higher animals; conduction is a wave of depolarization passing along the plasma membrane. Signals may go from cell to cell, as in the petiole of a *Mimosa* plant or in a sheet of ciliated epithelium.

Conduction by intracellular fibrils has been said to occur in a few Protozoa. In ciliates the basal granules (kinetosomes, see Chapter 16) are connected to fibrils (kinetodesmata) which extend in rows and overlap one another in definite patterns.[291, 379] Kinetodesmal fibrils may be connected via a fibrillar network to a central body (motorium) which gives off fibrils to cirri and to other motile membranelles besides the cilia, e.g., in *Euplotes*.[369] The polygonal sculpturing of the pellicle takes silver stain and is not part of either fibrillar system.[316] A lesion between the motorium and cirri in *Euplotes* disrupted coordination between posterior cirri and oral membranelles.[409] A cut through kinetodesmata (and pellicle) interrupted synchronized ciliary waves (metachronism) in *Paramecium*, where the fibrillar system is regular, but not in *Spirostomum*, where it is random.[462] Destruction of the motorium disrupted coordination of oral membranelles in *Chlamydodon*, and ciliary coordination in *Ichthyophthicus*, but not in *Paramecium*.[409] Microelectrodes in *Opalina* record a resting potential and oscillatory action potentials 7 to 35 msec in duration.[252] It is well established that conduction in nerves is a membrane phenomenon; hence, if the ciliate fibrillae are conductile, they cannot be regarded as precursors of nerves. There is no evidence for a molecular mechanism by which intracellular fibrils might conduct signals.

In sponges, spindle-shaped cells around the oscula are contractile. Recent measurements on marine sponges reveal only local contractions in response to mechanical stimuli and no true propagation.[339] Cells with long processes and staining properties similar to those of neurons have been claimed.[87] However, sponges contain so many amoebocytic cells with processes that rigorous functional tests must be made before the existence of neurons in sponges can be accepted. Parker[317] referred to the contractile cells of the osculum as "independent effectors." He suggested also sense cell–muscle cell arcs in coelenterates; the occurrence of these has not been substantiated, and beginning with coelenterates, coordination between sense cells and effectors is primarily nervous.

NERVE IMPULSES

A nerve fiber is bounded by a plasma membrane some 50 to 100 Å thick, outside which there may be various investing sheaths and glial cells. Several nonmyelinated axons (ver-

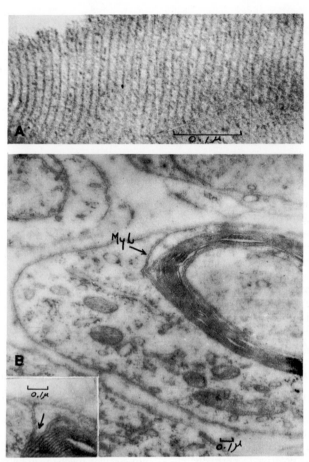

FIGURE 248. Electron micrographs of myelin sheath of sciatic nerve fibers of young mouse: *A*, transverse section through compact myelin; *B*, cross-section of axon surrounded by sheath cell, outer layer of myelin continuous with myelin lamella (*Myl*), formed by sheath cell surface. Inset shows detail of this layer of two dense membranes with intervening less dense region. (From Uzman, B. G., and Nogueira-Graf, S.: J. Biophys. Biochem. Cytol., vol. 3.)

tebrate, squid, lobster) may lie within the cytoplasm of one multinucleate sheath cell. A myelinated fiber lies within a sheath which is a spiral of myelin (Fig. 248). In myelinated fibers of prawns the nucleus of the sheath (Schwann cell) lies inside the single loose layer of myelin; in vertebrates the nucleus lies outside and the myelin is in a tight spiral.[138, 154, 428] Myelinated fibers are unaccompanied by the sheath as they approach their axonal terminals or nerve cell bodies. In vertebrate myelinated fibers the sheath is interrupted by nodes.

Resting Potential; Electrical Parameters of Nerve Membranes. Across the plasma membrane there exists a resting potential (R. P.), which is usually about 60 to 70 mv. True resting potentials of nerves have been measured only in those giant axons and central nervous cell bodies which can accom-

modate a microelectrode (0.5 μ diameter), but measurements from nodes and depolarized ends indicate similar resting potentials in smaller myelinated and nonmyelinated fibers also. The ionic basis for the resting potential is only partly understood. The axoplasm contains much more potassium, less chloride, less sodium, and much less calcium than does extracellular fluid (Chapter 3).

The resting potential can be formally described by the Goldman equation in which the concentration of each ion is multiplied by a permeability constant P which takes into account the apparent mobilities in the membrane.[382]

$$E = \frac{RT}{nF} \ln \left(\frac{P_K[K_i] + P_{Na}[Na_i] + P_{Cl}[Cl_o]}{P_K[K_o] + P_{Na}[Na_o] + P_{Cl}[Cl_i]} \right)$$

where E = equilibrium potential and $\frac{RT}{nF} =$

conversion factor consisting of gas constant, absolute temperature, valence, and Faraday units; o and i refer to outside and inside the fiber. Cl^- refers to ions for which there is no active transport (principally Cl^-). For squid giant axons $P_{Na} = 0.01 P_K$ at rest, and $P_{Na} = 30 P_K$ in activity; both at rest and in activity $P_{Cl} = 0.45 P_K$. P_{Cl} is higher for crab nerve than for vertebrate and squid nerve.

The observed resting potential is close to that calculated for Cl^- and only 10 to 20 mv lower than the potassium equilibrium potential. The membrane potential declines at high concentrations of potassium with a slope approaching that given by the Nernst equation, but it is little affected by potassium in the physiological range. The nodes of isolated myelinated fibers show a small reversible decrease in resting potential as the potassium outside is raised until a critical depolarization occurs; older preparations show a steeper potassium dependence, and there is evidence for several effects of K^+ on membrane potential[221, 393] (Fig. 249).

The resting potential is relatively insensitive to external sodium concentration; the sodium gradient is in reverse for the potential, the permeability to sodium is low, and that which diffuses into nerve fibers is actively extruded. The chloride and potassium gradients approach the Donnan equilibrium, but there may be some active uptake of K^+ and active extrusion of Na^+ is established. The axoplasm has a deficit of inorganic anions; this is made up by organic anions, to which the membrane is not permeable, isethionate,[249]

and amino acids in squid giant axons,[105] (see p. 58, Chapter 2), aspartate and other amino acids in crustacean fibers. When active metabolic transport is stopped by cold, anoxia, or by inhibitors like dinitrophenol, there is passive accumulation of sodium and leakage of potassium.

In prolonged anoxia both the resting potential and the excitability decline. Excitability can be restored by cathodal repolarization by an external battery;[273] hence normal excitability requires the presence of a membrane potential.

In summary: The resting potential is such that the membrane behaves like a potassium electrode, but active processes regulate the distribution of some ions and others follow passively. The membrane potential is the net result of the total distribution of ions.

Chemical differences between different kinds of nerves are known. Crab nerves, for example, are richer in glycogen than are rabbit nerves and can survive anoxia for 540 minutes compared with 24 minutes for rabbit nerves.[381]

The functional cell membrane consists of lipid and protein and has measurable resistance and capacitance. The core-conductor properties of an axon provide the basis for the time constant τ and space constant λ, which express the time of decline and the spatial spread of a transient electric pulse to $1/e$ (approximately 37 per cent) of the applied potential. The time constant in seconds is given by $\tau = C_m R_m$ where C_m is membrane capacity in farad/cm^2 and R_m is membrane specific resistance in ohm cm^2.* The space constant in mm is given by $\lambda = \sqrt{\dfrac{R_m}{R_i - R_o}}$

Some representative values for axons, nerve cells and muscle fibers are given in Table 53. The resistance of the cell membrane exists only across 100 Å; hence the resistivity of the membrane is high, some 10^9 ohms cm. The

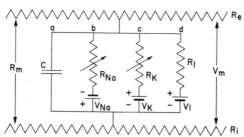

FIGURE 249. Diagram of an element of an excitable membrane of a nerve fiber. C constant membrane capacity; R_{Na} variable permeability channel for Na^+; R_K variable permeability channel for K^+; R_i channel for other ions, especially Cl^-; V_m = membrane potential; R_e external resistance; R_i internal resistance.

Average values for squid giant axon: $R_m = 400$ to 1100 ohms cm^2; $R_e = 20$ ohms cm; $R_i = 30$ ohms cm; $C_m = 1.1$ $\mu F/cm^2$; $V_K = -85$ to -90 mv; $V_m = -60$ to -70 mv; $V_i = -55$ to -60 mv; $V_{Na} = +45$ to $+50$ mv. (Modified from Hodgkin, A. L.: Proc. Roy. Soc. London, B, vol. 148.)

* Specific resistance (r) refers to resistance of a cubic centimeter of material and has units of ohm cm^2/cm = ohm cm. For resistance across a cell membrane the thickness (length) is unknown; hence specific membrane resistance R_m is the resistance of 1 cm^2 of surface irrespective of thickness, l, or $R_m = rl$. Measured resistance is $R = \dfrac{rl}{A}$; hence $R_m = rl = RA$ or ohms cm^2. Capacitance is proportional to dielectric constant D and area A for a given thickness l, $C = \dfrac{DA}{l}$; hence specific membrane capacity $C_m = \dfrac{D}{l} = C/A$ or farads/cm^2.

TABLE 53.   ELECTRICAL CONSTANTS OF NERVE FIBERS, CELL BODIES, AND MUSCLE FIBERS

Nerve or muscle	Diameter or area	C_m $\mu F/cm^2$	R_m ohm cm^2	λ mm	τ msec
Sepia giant axon[440]	200 μ	1.2	9200	2-5	6.2
Loligo giant axon[169, 199, 403, 405]	500 μ	1.1	1500 (rest)	2.5	0.7-1.6
			25 (active)		
Carcinus leg nerve[196]		1.1	3000-7000	2.0	6.2
Carcinus leg nerve fibers[238]		0.72-1.75	2940-3700	1.6-1.8	2.1-5.5
Homarus leg nerve[197, 202, 370]	75 μ	1.3	2290	1.6	2.3
Frog A fibers[401]	node	3-7	8-20		0.06
	internode	0.005	100,000		
Aplysia ganglion cells[407, 408]	600 μ	23	2200		50
Puffer supramedullary cells[39]	250 μ		500-1000	4-6	
Puffer supramedullary cells[174]		5-15	400-1000		
Toad motoneuron[16]	6×10^{-5} cm^2	17.5	270		4.3
Cat motoneurons[99, 114]	5×10^{-4} cm^2	6	400-600		2.5
Mytilus retractor[83]		3.3	61,400	2.4	92.0
Crustacean muscle[131, 132]		20	1000		
Portunas muscle[131, 132]		40	100		
Frog sartorius[238]		5-8	1180-2080	0.55-0.8	10.3
Frog adductor magnus[238]	75 μ	5	1500	0.65	9
Frog extensor digitorum[238]	45 μ	5	4300	1.1	18.5
Cat muscle[53]		2-5	1200-1600		

conductance of the axoplasm, in contrast to that of the membrane, is high, approaching plasma or sea water (R_i = 200 ohms cm).

A nerve impulse is the sum total of physical and chemical events associated with transmission of a signal along an axon. An axon formally resembles a cable with core and external medium of low resistance and membrane of high resistance. An all-or-none nerve impulse is unlike current in a passive electrical conductor in that the impulse is self-propagating, shows no decrement with distance from the source, and is followed by a refractory period. Gradation of all-or-none nerve signals is not by amplitude but by pulse frequency. However, graded "local potentials" can be conducted decrementally. The electrical parameters of an axon membrane can best be considered as due to organic molecules which impede ionic movement. The essence of a self-propagating impulse is the current flowing in the local circuit from depolarized to nondepolarized regions and back externally. The necessity for external current is shown by the higher velocity in an axon immersed in saline (low resistance) than in oil or air.[197, 202, 370] The total current is carried by ions, largely sodium and potassium, moving across the membrane according to their concentration gradients and limited by the permeability of the membrane. Excitation is essentially an increase in ion permeability. During the rising phase of a nerve impulse the membrane resistance drops by some forty times, while the capacity is unchanged.[95, 104]

By means of two electrodes inserted into a squid giant axon, one for current, the other for voltage, the current required to clamp the membrane potential at various voltage levels (depolarization or hyperpolarization) was measured.[199] The current measurements, together with action potential measurements in media in which the Na^+ and K^+ were varied, led to the conclusion that during the rising phase of an action potential (depolarization) the membrane permeability to Na^+ is increased and Na^+ moves into the fiber, and the membrane approaches the sodium equilibrium potential[198, 200, 221] (Fig. 250). The amplitude of the action potential is reduced when sodium in the medium is replaced by some cation such as choline; Li^+ (and in some nerves quaternary cations) can substitute for Na^+. During the descending phase of the action potential sodium inactivation occurs, i.e., Na^+ conductance falls, and the membrane becomes permeable to potassium, which moves out, and the membrane is thus repolarized. In an all-or-none spike an axon is not only completely depolarized, but the potential overshoots so that the inside becomes positive by some 40 mv to the outside; the overshoot varies with the logarithm of the ratio of Na^+ inside to Na^+ outside. Just as the resting potential approaches (but does not reach) a potassium equilibrium potential, the action potential approaches a sodium equilibrium potential. Measurements with radio-active sodium and potassium indicate the inward movement of a few $\mu\mu M$ of $Na^+/$ $cm^2/$impulse (10×10^{-12}mol/cm^2/impulse) and an equal outward movement of potassium. Impulses are also accompanied by increased influx of Ca^{++}, 6×10^{-15}mol/cm^2 or 38 ions/μ^2/impulse in squid giant axons, and calcium is essential to maintenance of normal sodium-potassium permeabilities.[201] The actual potential change results from resistance drop rather than change in ion concentration. An alternate hypothesis to the above of specific increase in Na and K permeability is that there are patches of membrane in either of two stable states of conductance and that activity consists of the shift of more patches to the active state.[404] Cell membranes of the alga *Chara* behave as chlo-ride rather than sodium electrodes during activity.[149]

In many insects the relative concentration of potassium to sodium in hemolymph is much higher than in other animals (Chapter 3), and the hemolymph Mg^{++} is high. The question has been raised how insect nerves could remain polarized. Some insects are very tolerant of potassium and in them nerves and central nervous system are surrounded by a sheath which is virtually impermeable to ions, and after this is slit, high potassium reduces potentials much as in other nerves.[214]

Action Potential Sequence. An action potential consists of a series of electrical phases which can be described in terms of the above electrochemical functions.

1. When a subthreshold current is passed through a nerve, there is current spread ac-

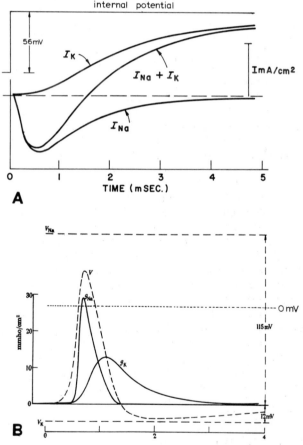

FIGURE 250. *A*, current due to movement of sodium and potassium in squid giant axon when membrane voltage is displaced (depolarized) by 56 mv by "clamping" electrode. $I_{Na} + I_K =$ current in balanced ionic medium. $I_K =$ potassium current when Na replaced by choline, $I_{Na} =$ obtained by difference. Inward current downward, outward current upward.

B, spike (*V*) in squid giant axon; Na^+ conductance (g_{Na}) and K^+ conductance (g_K) calculated from current during depolarization and repolarization. V_{Na} and V_K are Na^+ and K^+ equilibrium potentials. (From Hodgkin, A. L.: Proc. Roy. Soc. London, B, vol. 148.)

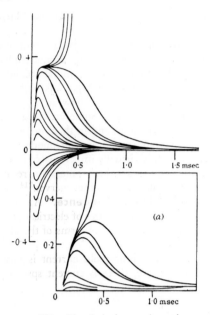

FIGURE 251. Electrical changes in crab nerve at the stimulating electrodes to shocks of increasing intensity. Electrotonic potential at anode (below zero) and in first five records at cathode (above zero); local response in upper records 6 to 9 and beginning of spike in upper three responses. Inset *a*, another series at cathode. (From Hodgkin, A. L.: Proc. Roy. Soc. London, B, vol. 126.)

cording to the time and space constants. The electrotonic or polarization potential is symmetrical in form, but in reverse polarities at cathode (catelectrotonus) and anode (anelectrotonus) (Fig. 251). (The amplitudes in the two directions may differ in axons which show rectification.) An electrotonic wave extends ahead of a propagated impulse and can be detected beyond a region in which conduction has been blocked by cold.

2. As the stimulus strength increases to about half rheobase (threshold for long pulse), a local response or prepotential appears at the cathode (Fig. 251). The prepotential is nonpropagated and graded, but increases out of proportion to the stimulus strength, hence represents active change in resistance. Rhythmic local potentials occur spontaneously in nerve fibers treated with low calcium saline or with citrate.[19] These prepotentials are graded, as are sensory generator potentials (Chapter 10), pacemaker potentials, and end-plate or synaptic potentials (Chapter 14). Some regions of neurons, e.g., dendrites, and soma of many central neurons show only graded potentials or have a high threshold as compared with their axons. Decrementing graded conduction can occur in short neurons by means of local

potentials only. It has been suggested[44] that graded local potentials are the primitive membrane responses, and all-or-none impulses a more recent development. Local potentials have been most studied in nonmyelinated fibers of crab and squid, and have been observed at the nodes of frog and cat myelinated axons.

3. When the stimulus is of threshold size, the local graded potential reaches a critical height and a propagated nerve impulse (spike) arises out of it (Fig. 251). The critical height of the local potential is about 20 per cent of spike height in crustacean fibers.[195] The ratio of total spike height to threshold depolarization is called the safety factor. In fibers showing oscillatory prepotentials, spikes appear when the local or prepotential reaches a critical amplitude.[19] Some crustacean fibers respond repetitively to single shocks; these appear when the local or prepotential reaches rise during stimulation).[463, 464] Spike duration varies with fiber size and speed of conduction (see below), but is usually 0.5 to 1.5 msec. Spike height increases more in some nerves than does velocity with increase in fiber diameter, and spike height may be significant when electrical interaction between neurons occurs. The spike is all-or-none, overshoots zero potential, rises rapidly to its crest and then declines at a decreasing rate.

4. Many axons, e.g., squid giant fibers, show an undershoot or brief hyperpolarization immediately following the spike (Fig. 252). This results in part from continued high potassium permeability.

5. Following the spike and delaying its downward deflection is a negative afterpotential (Fig. 253). This may not be apparent (squid giant axons); it may last 4 to 6 msec (frog A fibers), or it may last many seconds (some crab fibers). The negative after-potential is enhanced by veratrine or by tetanization. Increased amounts of potassium accumulate outside axons in which afternegativity has been enhanced by veratrine.[382] In vertebrate fibers, additional unknown factors are indicated by correlation of afternegativity with oxidative metabolism. Delayed repolarization may also result from other changes in the membrane; for example, squid nerves treated with tetraethylammonium ions give flat-topped impulses resembling[404] the action potentials of heart muscle[404] (Chapter 13). The excitability of frog axons is enhanced during the afternegativity much as in catelectrotonus.

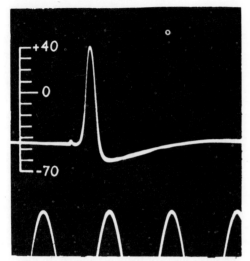

FIGURE 252. Action potential spike recorded between inside and outside of giant axon of squid showing resting potential level, overshoot of spike, and positive undershoot; time calibration 1000/sec. (From Hodgkin, A. L., and Huxley, A. F.: J. Physiol., vol. 104.)

6. A positive after-potential or after-hyperpolarization may follow the return of the membrane potential to rest level. Positive after-potentials are distinct from the undershoot immediately after a spike. After-hyperpolarization is seen particularly well in vertebrate nonmyelinated fibers, and it may persist for a few milliseconds or several seconds. After-hyperpolarization is enhanced by yohimbine, cocaine, low calcium, or tetanus.[382] Tracer and other experiments show that the hyperpolarization results from enhanced net outflow of potassium, that is, continued high potassium conductance long after sodium permeability has returned to its resting low value. Reduction of potassium inside motoneurons abolishes their after-hyperpolarization and may even cause after-depolarization.[114] Excitability may be decreased during the after-positivity (anelectrotonus). In squid and crab nerve, as in frog muscle, membrane stabilizers such as cocaine and local anesthetics do not alter the resting potential, but vertebrate nerves are depolarized by high concentrations and hyperpolarized by low concentrations of these agents.

Adaptations Favoring Speed of Excitation and Conduction. Speed of conduction in nerve fibers and nerve tracts is variable from animal to animal and in different parts of the same animal. Increase in speed of conduction gives an advantage in escape from predators and in other behavior under stress. Time constants of excitation generally parallel speed of conduction. Several commonly used excitation constants are derived from strength-duration or voltage-time curves. A familiar empirical constant is the chronaxie, which is the duration of a stimulus of twice rheobasic strength. The accommodation constant is a measure of the rate of rise in threshold depolarization during passage of a stimulus; this is less than the apparent accommodation or rise in requisite applied voltage. Histological correlates with speed are largely explicable in terms of electrical constants of membranes and axoplasm. The velocity is given by the following:[197, 202, 237, 370]

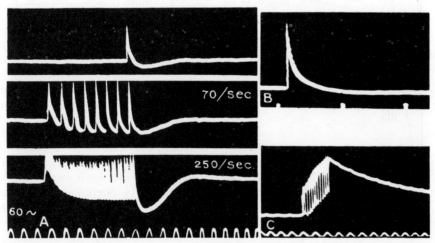

FIGURE 253. A, negative and positive after-potentials of a phrenic nerve (A fibers); enhanced positive potential with increasing frequency of tetanus. B and C, negative after-potentials in response to single and tetanic stimulation in veratrinized nerve. (From Gasser, H. S., and Grundfest, H.: Am. J. Physiol., vol. 117.)

$$V = \frac{S}{\sqrt{2R_m}} \times \frac{\sqrt{a}}{C_m \sqrt{R_i}}$$

where S   is the safety factor,
         a   is radius of fiber,
         R_m is membrane resistance in ohms cm^2,
         C_m is membrane capacitance μF/cm^2,
and R_i is internal resistance in ohms cm.

1. *Length of Nerve Processes.* Animals can react with increased speed when their conducting processes are long and few synapses are interposed. In many coelenterates the nerve net consists of short ($<$ 1 mm) neurons or has junctions at intervals of 100 μ.[315] In these nets conduction is slow—0.78 m/sec in *Renilla,* 0.121 m/sec in *Physalia* filaments, and 0.12 to 0.15 m/sec in *Metridium.*[318] In some anemones there are through tracts of longer neurons where conduction is faster; in *Calliactis,* conduction in the net is 0.04 to 0.15 m/sec and the through conduction 1.2 m/sec.[313] In the ganglionic cords of annelids, conduction in the neuropile where there are segmental synapses is at less than 0.5 m/sec, while in the through-conducting giant fibers it is 10 to 25 m/sec.

2. *Fiber Diameter.* For a given fiber type, e.g., myelinated with nodes or nonmyelinated, velocity is proportional to some constant times fiber diameter, and the constant depends on other fiber characteristics. In large myelinated fibers of mammals, the velocity in meters per second numerically equals the diameter in micra times 6 to 8. Vertebrate nonmyeli-

nated fibers or C fibers are small (usually $\sim$ 1 μ) and of several types. In sympathetic fibers (mammal and turtle) velocity is proportional to the diameter;[150] olfactory fibers of fish (pike) resemble sympathetic fibers, with enhanced excitability during a negative after-potential, and after-positivity is small. In dorsal root C fibers velocity is given by 1.7 times diameter and positive after-potentials mask after-negativity.[150] In giant axons of squid the velocity increase with increasing size is small, exponentially ($V \sim D^{0.61}$ or $V \sim \sqrt{D}$),[341] or linearly (6.5 m/sec for 100 μ increase in diameter).[194] A giant fiber of a crustacean, cephalopod or annelid may have a diameter of tens or several hundreds of micra and conduct many times faster than the small fibers of the same animal. In insects it is rare to find axons more than 1 to 2 micra in diameter; here compactness seems more important than speed of conduction. Large fast fibers have shorter excitation time constants than small slow ones. Developing nerves react with increased velocity with increasing fiber size; for example, a leg nerve of a young rat at 60 days has 2.5 μ fibers conducting at 31 m/sec and at 350 days 4.5 μ fibers at 59 m/sec; the speed for chick sciatic nerve is less than 1 m/sec in an embryo and increases to 50 m/sec by 12 days after hatching.[43] In a kitten, leg fibers increase in size and speed as the leg lengthens so that conduction time to a toe remains relatively constant.[433] A few examples of the relation between fiber size and velocity of conduction are given in Table 54. The increase in velocity with greater diameter results in part from the lower longitudinal resistance internally.

3. *Nerve Fiber Sheath.* The presence of a lipid sheath around an axon is correlated with high velocity of conduction. A myelin sheath stains with osmic acid and when viewed in polarized light shows a positive birefringence with respect to the radially directed optic axis (negative birefringence with respect to the long axis). The birefringence in frog fibers is nearly constant in fibers 9 μ or more in diameter, but diminishes in smaller fibers until it is zero in fibers of 2 μ diameter, and in fibers below that size it reverses sign[376, 410] (Fig. 254). The birefringence of nonmyelinated fibers is normally negative with respect to the radial axis, is due to proteins, and can be counterbalanced by immersion in glycerin of the same refractive index, whereupon a slight positive myelin (lipid) birefringence appears. Many invertebrate fibers show no

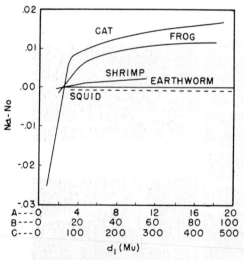

FIGURE 254. Birefringence of sheath as $N_a - N_o$ (birefringence retardation) as function of fiber diameter. Diameters in micra: *A,* cat and frog; *B,* shrimp and earthworm; *C,* squid giant axons. (From Taylor, G. W.: J. Cell. Comp. Physiol., vol. 20.)

TABLE 54.   VELOCITY OF CONDUCTION IN NERVES OF DIFFERENT TYPES

Nerve	Velocity meter/sec	Diameter micra	Temperature (°C)
Aurelia net[207]	0.5	6-12	
Metridium net[367]	0.13		27
Renilla net[303]	0.078		27
Lumbricus ganglionic cord	0.025		
Myxicola giant fibers[304]	3.2-21	90-996	20
Lumbricus median giant[67]	30.0	50-90	22
Lumbricus lateral giant[67]	11.3	40-60	
Megascolex giant[4]	20	20	
Neanthes giant[212]	5	30-37	
Harmothoe giant[212]	4-4.5 lateral 2-2.5 median		
Sepia giant[440]	7	200	17
Loligo giant[95, 104, 168, 194]	20 (18-35)	400 (260-543)	23
Cambarus median giant[451]	18-20	90-180	
Cambarus lateral giant[451]	10-15	70-150	
Lobster giants[414, 416]	11.7 (8-18.4)	121 (102-163)	
Ariolimax nerve[423, 424]	5.5	30-35	
Carcinus leg nerve[196]	3-4	30	21
Lobster leg nerve[20, 196]	14-18	60-80	
Cambarus claw fast closer[463, 464]	20	58	
Cambarus claw slow closer[463, 464]	10	41	
Cambarus claw opener[463, 464]	8	36	
Ameiurus Mauthner fiber[157]	50-60	22-43	10-15
Protopterus Mauthner fiber[457]	18.5	45	
Cyprinus Mauthner fiber[40]	55-63	55-65	
Carp lateral line[258]	47	20	
Trout lateral line[101]	50	22	
	79	27	
Frog A fibers[237, 401, 402]	30	15	
Toad A fibers[283]	20-25	8-15	
Frog B fibers[401]	3-4.5		
Cat spinal tracts[257]	50	5.5	37
Cat A fibers[220]	78-102	13-17	37
Cat B fibers[220]	24-48	4-8	37
Cat skin nerves[150]	0.7-2.3	0.43-1.17	37
Pike olfactory C fibers[150]	0.2		
Frog, turtle C fibers[45, 402]	0.4-0.5	2.5	
Cat dorsal root C fibers[150]	0.6-2	0.5-1.0	
Cat sympathetic C fibers[44, 150]	1-2		

dense myelin when stained with osmic acid, but polarized light and electron microscopy reveal positive birefringence and a loosely myelinated sheath. Treatment with fat solvents eliminates the positive birefringence. A thick myelin layer surrounds the giant fibers of the prawn *Leander*.[203, 204] Electron microscopy shows that the sheath lamellae of vertebrates contain units 60 to 80 Å thick (Fig. 248), and that during embryonic development the sheath layers are deposited by rotation of the sheath cells around the axon.[154, 428] Differences exist in the number of windings of the sheath membranes and in their compactness.

The fastest vertebrate fibers are of medium size (4 to 15 μ) but have thick sheaths (30 to 50 per cent of total fiber diameter), whereas the fastest fibers of invertebrates are large (50 to several hundred micra) but have sheaths which are thin (less than 1 per cent of diameter). The relation between diameter, sheath, and velocity may be summarized by the following: a 4 μ fiber of a cat saphenous nerve at 38° conducts at about the same rate (25 m/sec) as a 650 μ squid giant axon at 20°. Assuming a Q_{10} of 1.5, a cat saphenous fiber of 8 μ would conduct at 20° at the same rate as the squid fiber of 650 μ.[410]

4. *Nodes.* By electrical polarization experiments and by recording at nodes and internodes of vertebrate myelinated axons it has been demonstrated that conduction is saltatory, that is, it jumps from node to node,

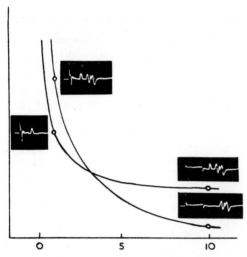

FIGURE 255. Strength-duration curves of large and small fibers of leg nerve of Cancer. *Ordinate,* intensity to elicit response shown. *Abscissa,* duration in msec. With short pulse the fast fiber responds at low intensity, and slow fiber response comes in at higher intensity; with long pulse the threshold for the slow fiber is lower than for the fast fiber. (From Easton, D. M.: J. Cell. Comp. Physiol., vol. 40.)

consuming virtually no time in passing through the internodes.[392] A local circuit for conduction involves outflowing and inflowing current only at the nodes; an internode has high resistance and low capacitance. External current flows outside the myelin.[370] This is a vertebrate adaptation which gives a small increase in velocity so long as the internodes are of appropriate length. At diameters below 1 μ, vertebrate myelinated fibers conduct at about the same speed as nonmyelinated ones. The optimum length of internodes is usually about 1 mm.[258]

5. *Membrane Time Constants.* The differences in velocity of conduction and in excitation time constants depend largely on the capacitance and resistance of the fibers; the histological correlates with speed depend also on these electrical constants. In general, slow conduction is correlated with large membrane time constants (resistance and capacitance). Yet, fast conduction is favored by long space constants or electrotonic spread. The faster nerves have shorter chronaxies (excitation time constants) (Fig. 255). Repetitive response to single shocks is related to lack of accommodation. One portion of a neuron may differ in membrane constants from another region, e.g., soma-dendrite and axon. Some axons tolerate little stretch, e.g., squid fibers fail to conduct at 120 per cent rest length, while others, e.g., in annelids and

other worms, conduct at a constant speed when pulled to a 300 per cent increase in length, or when the diameter is reduced by one half; hence there must be membrane reconstitution.[67, 422]

In addition to the preceding membrane correlations with speed of conduction there are what Bullock has called "intrinsic factors," possibly related to the excitability safety factor or to the rate of rise of local potential.

6. *Giant Fibers.* There are two types of giant fiber systems, each of which has evolved independently several times (see p. 615). The first type consists of a single large nerve cell which gives rise to a large axon. The second type is a functionally continuous system in which processes from a number of nerve cells fuse to form a single large axon. Unicellular giant fibers are found in nemerteans, cestodes, numerous polychaetes, balanoglossids, and lower vertebrates. In polychaetes, e.g., *Halla,* axons arising in large anterior unipolar cells run the length of the nerve cord. In balanoglossids large cells in the collar nerve cord give rise to 3 to 6 μ fibers which are distinct from the ordinary 1 μ fibers. In the base of the medulla of bony fishes, urodeles, and anuran tadpoles occur the large Mauthner and Müller cells of the vestibular reflex system; their fibers (22 to 43 μ in diameter) conduct at 50 to 60 m/sec at 10 to 15°.[406] Müller fibers of lampreys lack myelin sheath and conduct at one-tenth the velocity of fish Mauthner fibers.[40] In some animals the distinction between giant and ordinary neurons is not sharp, and the term giant neuron applies to a large nerve cell and fiber.

The multicellular or functional-syncytium type of giant fiber system has been described in annelids, crustaceans, and cephalopod molluscs. In the ventral nerve cord of the earthworm three giant fibers run the length of the ventral nerve cord, and in each segment they receive processes from large nerve cells. The lateral giant fibers are connected also with each other and give a single action potential spike. Evidence from cutting the giant fibers, from regeneration, blocking by drugs, and from embryonic development shows that the giant fibers of the earthworm mediate quick end-to-end startle contractions.[335] Conduction in the smaller fibers of the cord (including synapses) is about 0.025 m/sec; in the lateral giant fibers it goes at 7 to 17 m/sec, and in the median fiber 17 to 45 m/sec. Some polychaete worms have no giant nerve fibers (*Aphrodite, Chaetopterus*), others have only one (*Arenicola, Pista*), and still others have several, as shown by action potentials in the nerve cords and by histological examination (*Neanthes, Glycera*).[66, 301] In the polychaete *Myxicola* the velocity is proportional to the square root of the fiber diameter.[304]

Decapod crustaceans have median, lateral, and motor giant fibers. In crayfish the paired median giant fibers arise in the brain, decussate there, and pass to the ventral nerve cord. Lateral fibers occur in thorax and abdomen and consist of segmental units which overlap in long side-by-side contacts.[229] The two lateral fibers are connected with one another in each segment; connections with cell bodies are made in each ganglion. The motor giant fibers have cell bodies in one segment, decussate, and pass out in the posterior nerve of that segment. The median and lateral systems independently activate the same motor fibers. In crustaceans the giant fiber system controls quick flipping of the abdomen and may give rise to antennal movements. The segmental connections with cell bodies are shown by the

lack of degeneration when median or lateral giant fibers are transected, as in the prawn *Leander*.[203, 204]

Cephalopod molluscs have a giant fiber system which is intermediate between the unicellular type and the segmentally fused type. In the decapods (squids) a pair of giant cells occur in the posterior palliovisceral ganglion of the brain; their processes fuse and cross, then synapse in the visceral part of the brain with secondary giant neurons which run out in mantle nerves.[466] These synapse with a third set of giant fibers in the stellate or mantle ganglion (Fig. 256). From this ganglion some dozen nerves pass to the muscles of the mantle; each nerve contains one giant fiber, which may be as much as 800 μ in diameter, plus many 1 μ fibers and some intermediate (up to 35 μ) fibers. Each third order giant axon arises by the fusion of processes from 300 to 1500 cells in the stellate ganglion. Each giant axon serves a large area of the mantle, and the largest fibers pass to

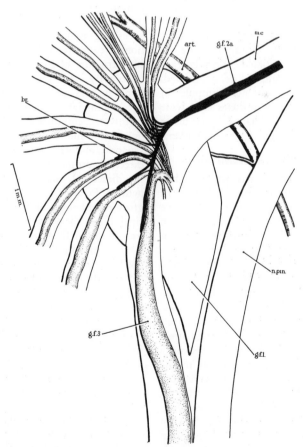

FIGURE 256. Synapse between second order giant fiber (*g.f.2a*) and third order giant fiber (*g.f.3*) in stellate ganglion of squid. Cell bodies of g.f.3 in giant fiber lobe (*g.f.1*). *m.c.*, mantle nerve or connective from "brain." (From Young, J. Z.: Phil. Tr. Roy. Soc. London, B, vol. 229.)

the posterior region so that impulses arrive nearly simultaneously in the entire mantle. Velocities range from 3 to 25 m/sec. Stimulation of a giant fiber elicits maximal contraction of the mantle muscle; hence one syncytial fiber with a large area of circular muscle constitutes a motor unit (Chapter 14). The contraction forces water out of the mantle cavity through the funnel, sending the animal forward or back according to the funnel angle; this escape or feeding reaction is, according to Young, twice as fast by virtue of the giant fiber system as it would be without it.[466] In the decapod *Sepia* the cells contributing to the large giant fibers are scattered through the stellate ganglion. In *Loligo* these cells are confined to a posterior lobe. In octopods *Eledone* and *Octopus* the lobe is present and contains cells which resemble neurons but lack processes; the posterior lobe (epistellar body) receives secondary giant fibers, and its possible neurosecretory function is indicated by atonia of the mantle after removal of the epistellar body.[466]

Giant nerve fibers have evolved many times and may be absent from animals closely related to those which have them. Giant fiber systems function chiefly in rapid startle reactions which are initiated abruptly, are elicited by various stimuli, and are not graded. They are efficient since one nerve impulse in a giant fiber can activate muscles of a wide body area. Conduction in giant fibers is faster than in the synaptic system of small fibers.

INTERNEURONIC TRANSMISSION

Synaptic Structure. There are many histological types of interneuronic junction. In some there is fusion of neurons as in the squid giant fibers; in others, e.g., earthworm giant fibers, there is fusion with retention of intercellular membranes. In some, as in crustacean cardiac ganglia, there is electrical evidence for narrow bridges between neurons. In most interneuronic junctions there is no evidence for protoplasmic continuity, but electron microscopy resolves presynaptic and postsynaptic membranes. In monosynaptic junctions the postneuron makes contact over a large surface with the preneuron, as in the overlapping fibers of coelenterate nerve nets, the septa-like junctions of crayfish lateral giant fibers, and the large' end-bulbs enveloping some cells in the tegmentum of fish.[49] Most junctions have many end-feet, or boutons, from branches of a preaxon and from converging axons, which end on dendrites and on the cell body of the postneuron or on dendrites only. For example, anterior horn cells of the mammalian spinal cord are covered by terminal boutons, and premembranes and postmembranes about 50 Å thick are separated by a cleft of about 200 Å. In the synapses between median and motor giant neurons of crayfish both presynaptic and postsynaptic processes are invested by sheath (Schwann) cells, and a process of the postfiber projects through the sheath into and indents the process of the preneuron.[356] Close apposition of the two membranes is seen also in synapses of frog sympathetic ganglia.[354] At local regions of some synapses the two components of each membrane fuse so that a double membrane rather than a quadruple one is resolved.[274] The term synapse has different meanings according to the level of morphological resolution. Postsynaptic membranes often show a dense aggregation of granules (Fig. 257). A dendrite can best be defined as a receptive membrane. At synaptic membranes there is usually an aggregation of granules, mitochondria, and vesicles, usually behind the presynaptic membrane, sometimes on the postsynaptic side. Evidently the differences in gross histology of interneuronic junctions are greater than the differences in the ultrastructure of the synapses.

Polarity. In some monosynaptic junctions, such as coelenterate nerve nets and the overlapping lateral giant fibers of crayfish and earthworm, impulses can pass in either direction. Most interneuronic junctions are polysynaptic, and transmission goes only in one direction, orthodromically; antidromic (opposite direction) impulses stop at the receiving neuron. Polarity may result partly from the gross morphology of the synapse. The principal cause of polarity is that the chemical transmitter is liberated only at preganglionic axon terminations by orthodromic impulses, not by antidromic impulses.

Synaptic Transmitters. A nerve impulse consists of a series of electrical events based upon ionic currents across a membrane of variable permeability or resistance. The action potential wave might be an adequate stimulus for a postsynaptic membrane. Electrical polarization of a receiving cell can alter its excitability for presynaptic impulses. When two nonmyelinated nerves in proper condition are placed side by side, an impulse can be transmitted from one to the other, and some interaction between fibers is indicated by the speeding of neighboring fibers in a trunk. Transmission in such an artificial synapse, or ephapse, occurs if the impulse in the pre-ephaptic fiber stops at the junction so that the final phase of its potential change is negative or catelectrotonic.[20] There may be an ephaptic delay of 2 to 5 msec between overlapping squid axons. Similarly, electrical transmission across points of contact occurs between two separated lobes of the brain of frogs. Nonsynaptic interaction may be important when the safety factor of adjacent fibers is low.

In crustacean cardiac ganglia,[173] in cells of the visceral ganglion of Aplysia,[20] and in lateral giant fibers of some annelids and crustaceans, a pulse in one cell or fiber is detected with attenuation and slight delay in near-by cells.[72] It is probable that frequently one neuron influences another by its electrical field in the absence of transmission between them.

In the synapse between lateral giant fibers and motor giant neurons of a crayfish the action potential of the prefiber is an adequate

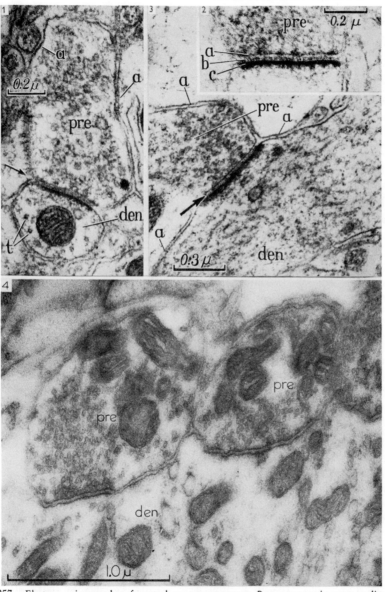

FIGURE 257. Electron micrographs of central nervous synapses. *Pre*: presynaptic axon endings. *den*: dendrite of postsynaptic neuron. Note dense synaptic membranes. *1, 2, 3* axodendritic synapses of the cerebral cortex. (From E. G. Gray, J. Anat., vol. 93.) *4*, axodendritic synapse from abducens nucleus of rat. Note presynaptic vesicles, also mitochondria. (From Palay, S. L.: Exper. Cell. Res. suppl. 5, 1959.)

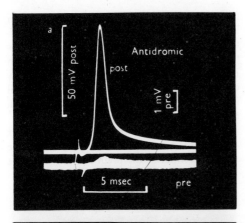

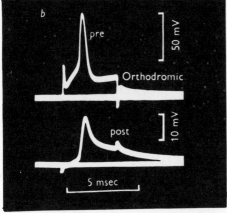

FIGURE 258. Responses at electrical synapse of crayfish. Responses in prefiber and postfiber in response to (*a*) antidromic and (*b*) orthodromic impulses. Note evidence for rectification in that transmembrane current passes orthodromically but not antidromically. (From Furshpan, E. J., and Potter, D.: J. Physiol., vol. 145.)

stimulus to the motor postneuron. Intracellular records show large trans-synaptic currents in the postneuron, but not in the preneuron when impulses are sent in reverse direction (antidromically). The synaptic membrane is a rectifier in that it permits current to flow orthodromically (in normal direction) with low resistance, but not antidromically (Fig. 258). Hence this crayfish synapse is a true polarized synapse with electrical transmission and with virtually no delay to the synaptic potential.[148]

In most interneuronic junctions, certainly in the polysynaptic, just as at neuromuscular junctions, there is ample evidence against the adequacy of the presynaptic action potential as the transmitter, and in favor of chemical transmitters. Intracellular recording from a postsynaptic neuron in the squid stellate ganglion shows that little or no current from the

presynaptic impulse crosses the cell membrane,[73, 175] certainly not enough to serve as a stimulus. Also, postsynaptic polarization which shifts the membrane potential up or down can alter the synaptic potential (analogous to an end-plate potential, p. 438) and can reverse its polarity. The hyperpolarization produced by inhibitory impulses at some synapses cannot easily be explained by the electrical hypothesis. The current required for generation of a synaptic potential is fifty times greater than that available at the node of a presynaptic fiber.[114] These facts, together with other evidence, conclusively rule out electrical transmission at most polysynaptic junctions.

Evidence for chemical synaptic transmitters comes from perfusion experiments, from the effects of potentiating and blocking agents, and from the identification of enzyme systems in nerve centers. The most complete evidence is for acetylcholine as a transmitter at some synapses. Other agents have been suggested and will be discussed (p. 607).

Synaptic Potentials. At interneuronic junctions, graded potentials, analogous to motor end-plate potentials (Chapter 14), precede the initiation of impulses. These junction potentials are either EPSP's (excitatory postsynaptic potentials) or IPSP's (inhibitory postsynaptic potentials).[114, 169, 170] Postsynaptic potentials have been recorded externally in the absence of spikes after impulse initiation has been prevented by a blocking agent (such as curare on sympathetic ganglia,[122] or by fatigue on squid stellate ganglion)[68] (Fig. 259). The EPSP is graded and represents a general increase in ion permeability of the postsynaptic membrane (see Fig. 261).

In motoneurons of the cat spinal cord an EPSP can be prevented by an antidromic impulse for 1.2 msec; therefore the duration of generator depolarizing activity is less than this period.[113, 114] Converging presynaptic impulses cause summation of an EPSP; a motor spike appears earlier as the EPSP increases with facilitation (motoneuron) or later as the EPSP is reduced by fatigue (squid giant synapse). When the EPSP is prolonged there may be several efferent spikes or afterdischarge in response to a single presynaptic impulse. This is especially evident in short inhibitory interneurons (Renshaw cells) where the EPSP normally lasts 50 msec, and after eserinization for 300 msec, during which the cells discharge at high frequency.[114]

In the two-neuron reflex arc of the cat spinal cord the EPSP recorded intracellularly from a motoneuron appears within 0.5 msec after the entry into the cord of a sensory volley; the peak is reached in 1 to 1.5 msec, and the potential declines with a time constant of 4.7 msec, which is longer than the time constant of the membrane as given by resistance and capacity.[99] The current rises steeply and reaches a peak before the voltage. At 10 mv depolarization of a membrane with resting potential of 70 mv, a postsynaptic spike is generated in the initial segment of the neuron. The threshold of the soma-dendrite portion of the neuron is about 30 mv; the EPSP elicited in the soma-dendrite membrane by the synaptic transmitter provides the current which initiates a spike first in the initial segment of the axon; this spike may later invade the soma-dendrite.[114, 115] In cat cervical sympathetic ganglia the rise time of the EPSP is 4 to 9 msec, and the decay time 6 to 12 msec.[116, 120, 121] In the stellate ganglion of a squid at 22°C the EPSP of the third order giant neuron begins after a delay of 0.5 msec, reaches a peak in 0.5 msec, and has a decay constant of 1.2 msec (Fig. 259).[68] Hyperpolarization of either presynaptic or postsynaptic membrane does not alter the PSP.[175] In large ganglion cells of the sea slug *Aplysia* the rise time of an EPSP may be 100 msec and the decay time 500 msec.[407, 408] Subliminal oscillations on the cell surface may give occasional spikes. At electrical synapses the delay is less than 0.1 msec.[148]

In many postsynaptic neurons the synaptic potential spreads electrotonically over the dendrites and soma (vertebrate spinal motoneurons) or over the dendritic branches (crustacean unipolar neurons). The postsynaptic spike usually originates at the axon neck and may or may not invade the soma; in the latter case it is detected in the soma only electrotonically. The postsynaptic membranes of chemical synapses differ from electrically excitable membranes as follows:[170]

Junctional membranes	*Conducting membranes*
excited by chemical transmitters, inexcitable electrically	excited by local electric currents
nonpropagated, graded, transducer potentials, decremental conduction	all-or-none spikes
often no refractory period, potentials sum	refractory period
junction potentials augmented by hyperpolarization and diminished by depolarization	blocked by hyperpolarization, often made repetitive by depolarization.

Synaptic areas and those capable of propagated spikes may be intermingled or in different regions of a neuron.

Facilitation. Most synaptic transmission requires facilitation, that is, more than one incoming impulse is needed to excite a postsynaptic neuron. In a few giant fiber systems (see p. 615) there is one-to-one transmission, but these are specialized systems, and it is probable that primitive interneuronic junctions required facilitation for transmission. The requirement for facilitation gives a safety factor against discharge of efferent neurons upon very slight sensory input. Facilitation differs from summation in that each increment of additional response is greater than the preceding one, that is, responses are not merely additive.

Early Facilitation (Spatially Determined). One afferent impulse alone may not be able to elicit a postsynaptic response, but two converging by different axons onto one motoneuron may be effective. In a crayfish, for example, flexion of one sensory hair on a uropod sends one impulse into the sixth abdominal ganglion. Similar facilitation of response of a single interneuron occurs as increased numbers of sensory fibers are activated[330] (Fig. 260). Stimulation of several adjacent hairs, usually four, is necessary to elicit one postsynaptic impulse.[337] Intracellular records from spinal motoneurons show summation of EPSP's to the threshold depolarization for spike initiation. Maximum summation is at synchrony, and reflex facili-

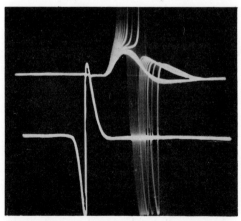

FIGURE 259. Synaptic potentials and action potential spikes from stellate ganglion of squid. *Lower record*: impulse in preganglionic fiber. *Upper record*: postganglionic spike developing later and later out of synaptic potential as fatigue occurs, finally leaving only synaptic potential. (From Bullock, T. H.: Nature, vol. 158.)

R   L

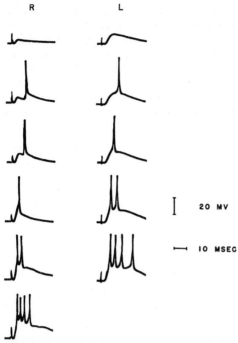

20 MV

⊢——⊣ 10 MSEC

FIGURE 260. Responses of a single interneuron of crayfish abdominal ganglion to stimulation of right (R) and left (L) ventromedial roots. Intensity of stimulation increases from top record downward. Synaptic potential (EPSP) at lowest stimulus intensity and spikes in increasing number with increased synaptic potentials. Note the difference in EPSP level for spiking in the two roots. (From Preston, J. B., and Kennedy, D.: J. Gen. Physiol., vol. 43.)

tation decreases with a time constant of 4 msec, which is close to that for decay of the EPSP.[271] In sympathetic ganglia the EPSP rises during several milliseconds, and successive synaptic potentials can sum. Delayed depolarization can last for seconds. In the oculomotor nucleus of the rabbit, spatial summation is maximum at synchrony and a minimum is reached at a separation of only 0.5 msec.

Delayed Facilitation. Frequently a second period of facilitation can be detected by test volleys in either the same or different incoming fibers, particularly in complex pathways. In flexor reflexes of the cat, for example, a maximum response to a second afferent volley occurs 12 to 20 msec after an initial volley.[102] In some nerve centers the delayed facilitation has been correlated with slow negative after-potentials. Delayed facilitation may result also from by-pass conduction in interneurons. In the rabbit oculomotor nucleus, for example, there are direct connections of ascending axons to the motoneurons and indirect connections via many parallel interneurons. The time course of the late facilitation is such that by-pass impulses from the first afferent volley are arriving at the motoneuron at the same time as the second direct impulses.[272] Prolonged facilitation can occur if there is a chain of successive interneurons. Delayed temporal facilitation is in this sense spatial facilitation.

Inhibition. One important method of grading activity in nerve centers is by reciprocal excitation and inhibition. One afferent pathway may be excitatory for one group of motoneurons and inhibitory for the motoneurons of antagonistic action. Inhibitory neurons appear to act by liberating a chemical transmitter and the same transmitter may be inhibitory on one neuron and excitatory on another. The nature of central inhibition has been elucidated more in the mammalian spinal cord than elsewhere.

Intracellular records from motoneurons show inhibitory postsynaptic potentials (IPSP's) when inhibitory afferents are stimulated. The central delay in a cat cord is about 1.25 msec, or 0.8 msec longer than for the EPSP, and it is probable that all inhibitory paths involve at least one interneuron.[117] The peak of an IPSP is reached in 1.5 to 2 msec, and the time constant of decay is 3 msec. The IPSP is normally a hyperpolarization, for example, from a resting potential of 70 mv to 80 mv. The IPSP is increased if the membrane is partly depolarized on arrival of the inhibitory volley, and the IPSP is decreased or even reversed by electrical hyperpolarization of the membrane (Fig. 262B). Hence the inhibitory equilibrium potential is greater than the normal membrane potential. There is evidence that the IPSP results from an increased permeability to K^+ and Cl^-, in contrast to the general increase in ion permeability of the EPSP and the selective increase in permeability to Na^+ and K^+ in the spike[99] (Fig. 261). When motor reflexes are measured at different intervals between excitatory and inhibitory volleys, inhibition is maximal at the peak of the current generating the IPSP.

Another type of inhibition in the spinal cord is given by the collateral Renshaw cells, which under experimental conditions can be activated antidromically by motor axons (or orthodromically). The impulses in the Renshaw cells converge on the same or near-by motoneurons[56, 117] (Fig. 263). An IPSP appears in the motoneuron after a delay of 1.2 msec, a central time divided equally between the two synapses. By these collateral inhibitory interneurons a negative feedback control is exercised on motoneurons.

The inhibitory synapses, both those of interneurons activated by afferent fibers and those of Renshaw cells activated antidromically, are blocked by strychnine. The nature of the inhibitory mediator is, however, unknown. Tetanus toxin prolongs polysynaptic reflexes but has no effect on monosynaptic reflexes.[57] The synapse at which antidromic impulses activate Renshaw cells is blocked by β-erythroidine (a curarizing agent), and its EPSP is greatly prolonged by eserine; hence the transmitter is probably acetylcholine.[57]

That inhibition is expressed by a hyperpolarization, that is, a setting of the membrane potential toward a lower value or a suppression of excitatory depolarization, seems

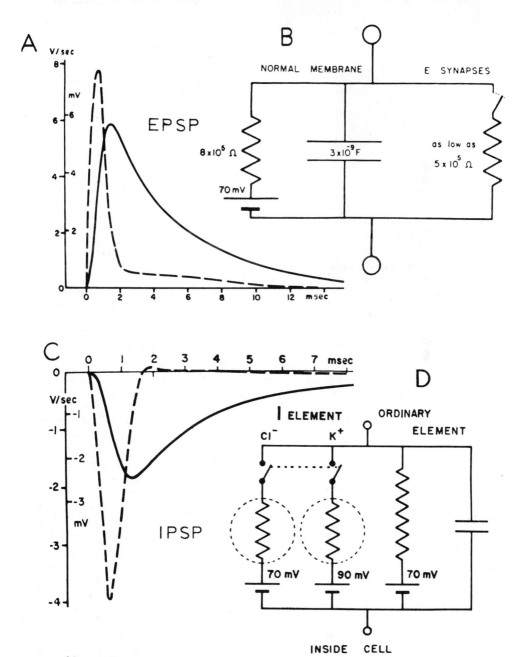

FIGURE 261. *A*, diagram of excitatory postsynaptic potential (solid line) and accompanying current (broken line) together with equivalent circuit, *B*. *C*, Diagram of inhibitory postsynaptic potential and current; *D*, equivalent circuit. *A* and *C* based on data for cat spinal motoneurons. (From Eccles, J. C.: Handbook of Physiology. American Physiological Society.)

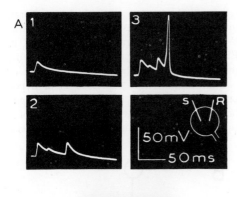

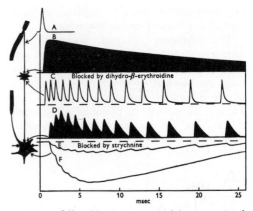

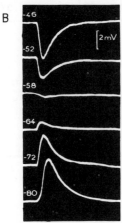

FIGURE 262. *A*, responses of a large nerve cell of *Helix* ganglion, recorded at electrode *R*, stimulated by a second intracellular tip *S*. (*1*) electrotonic potential only; (*2*) two local potentials on electrotonic curve; (*3*) spike appears after series of local potentials. (From Tauc, B.: J. Physiol. Paris, vol. 48.)

B, intracellular responses from soma of large neuron of *Aplysia* ganglion; postsynaptic potentials in response to stimulating a single presynaptic fiber when soma membrane was polarized by a second electrode to voltages given. (From Tauc, L., and Fessard, A.: J. Physiol. Paris, vol. 49.)

FIGURE 263. Diagram summarizing postulated sequence of events from an antidromic impulse to a motoneuron via a Renshaw cell. Motoneuron indicated by large cell body at lower left, myelinated axon interrupted and giving off collateral which synapses on Renshaw cell body (middle left) from which the axon ends on motoneuron. *A*, impulse in motor axon collateral; *B*, postulated concentration of ACh liberated at synaptic terminal; *C*, electrical response in Renshaw cell showing impulses on background of depolarization; *D*, postulated concentration of inhibitory transmitter at terminals of Renshaw axon; *E*, inhibitory postsynaptic potential (IPSP) at motoneuron, and *F*, aggregate IPSP resulting from converging Renshaw axons. (From Eccles, J. C., Fatt, P., and Koketsu, K.: J. Physiol., vol. 126.)

to be general. Hyperpolarizing IPSP's have been observed in sympathetic ganglia, crustacean cardiac ganglia, crustacean muscle (see p. 442 for another type of inhibition in this muscle), stretch receptors (p. 291).

A delayed sort of inhibition with much longer latency occurs in complex reflex pathways. Flexor reflexes in the cat are maximally inhibited if the inhibitory volley precedes the excitatory volley by 30 to 80 msec.[102] Such delayed inhibition may be related to prolonged after-positivity which depresses excitability as in anodal or hyperpolarization. Another mechanism to account for delayed inhibition may be neuron circuits properly timed so that there is cancellation from one

pathway over which impulses arrive at such a time as to hold interneurons refractory.

CENTRAL NERVOUS RHYTHMS
Spontaneous Activity; After-Discharge.
Repetitive activity in nerve centers is well known. When the EPSP is prolonged, a nerve cell may discharge repeatedly, often at high frequency, in response to a single afferent volley. This has been well shown in the Renshaw cells which can discharge at 1000/sec,[117] and in sympathetic ganglion cells after eserinization. Presumably after-discharge during a prolonged EPSP results from persistence of the transmitter.

Repetitive response and spontaneous firing may also result from delay paths and circus conduction. A signal may pass around a ring of neurons, returning periodically to excite the same motoneuron over a side branch. Such circling pathways have been demonstrated in the rabbit oculomotor nucleus.[272] A gross example is given by a doughnut-shaped ring cut from a jellyfish. If a contraction wave is started in both directions, then blocked on one side by pressure, a circusing self-perpetuating wave can continue for many hours; the same units in the nerve net are re-excited repeatedly. "Spontaneous" ac-

tivity commonly results from similar reverberating circuits. The ten-cycle "brain-waves"
recorded from the mammalian cerebral cortex
disappear when radiating connections to
underlying thalamic nuclei are cut, but some
irregular spontaneity persists in isolated
cortex.[78]

Some neurons under conditions of high
excitability, e.g., in low calcium, discharge
without stimulation. *Aplysia* ganglion cells,
for example, show subthreshold oscillations
which frequently reach threshold for spike
discharge.[21] Many kinds of muscle cells, especially heart and smooth muscle, are spontaneously active, even in tissue culture. Isolated
ganglia from invertebrate nervous systems
show spontaneous activity which can be increased or decreased according to the ionic
medium and metabolic conditions. In a
medusa a single marginal ganglion sends
rhythmic impulses to the motor nerve net.
The spontaneous rhythm of the medusa is
modified by input from the net, by gravity

stimulation of the marginal bodies, and (in
some species) by light.[208]

The tendency for discharge independent of
sensory input, whether by reverberating circuits or by independent spontaneity, is greater
in integrative centers than in distributive or
relay centers. In some nerve centers the spontaneous discharge of each neuron is independent of that of other neurons. A given cell may
discharge more or less rhythmically, but different neurons have different frequencies.
Such asynchronous activity is found in ganglionic nervous systems of annelids and
arthropods[339] (Fig. 264C,E,F). The spontaneous impulses originate in the soma of
the neurons and can be enhanced or inhibited
by input from other ganglia or from sense
endings.

Spontaneity in deafferented abdominal ganglia of mantis and cockroach increases when
the connection to the subesophageal ganglion
is cut.[363] In other nerve centers there is some
synchrony among the different neurons. A
synchronized rhythm may be a coordinated

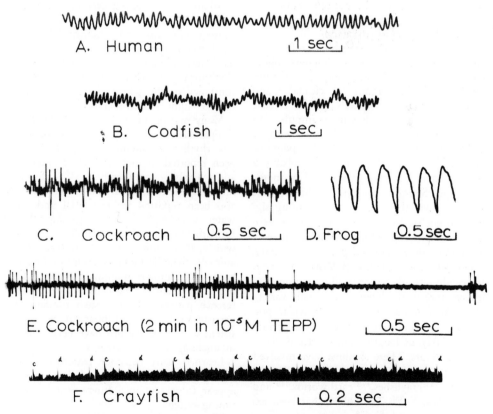

FIGURE 264. Types of "spontaneous" activity in central nervous systems. *A*, human alpha waves;
B, codfish brain waves; *C*, normal cockroach ganglionic activity; *D*, frog forebrain; *E*, bursts in cockroach
after treatment with tetraethylpyrophosphate; *F*, crayfish ganglion, individual units lettered. (*A*, *D*, and
F, from Prosser, C. L.: J. Cell. Comp. Physiol., voi. 22; *B* from Enger, P. S.: Acta physiol. scand.,
vol. 39; *C* and *E*, original records, courtesy of J. Sternburg.)

periodic depolarization of many units, as the vertebrate "brain waves" (Fig. 264*A,B,D*). Or the rhythm may be slower, each unit discharging several times for each wave, as in the ganglionic pacemakers of arthropod hearts (Chapter 13) or in respiratory centers (Chapter 7). In heart ganglia of *Limulus* and crustaceans it is possible to convert the synchronous rhythm into continuous asynchronous activity by ionic and other alterations.

Two mechanisms of synchronization have been suggested: (1) Neurons can be caused to fire together by slow electrical waves, catelectrotonically. Potential gradients exist between the soma and axon regions, at least between ganglia and connectives, between soma and axon of pyramidal cells. Electrical polarization of pacemaker neurons (e.g., *Limulus* heart ganglion) increases the synchronization and frequency of discharge.

2. Circus conduction in a closed circuit with side-branching neurons can maintain a synchronized rhythm. Interruption of corticothalamic radiations in mammals stops synchronized brain waves from the cortex. Interconnections between the various regions of the respiratory center are needed for synchronized respiratory discharge.

Several examples of rhythmic reflex discharges in response to single afferent volleys have been described, for example, motor impulses to tymbal organs for cicada[176] and repetitive discharge of cells of the electric lobe of torpedo to single sensory impulses. In both these the rhythm is set by interneurons.

The widespread occurrence of "spontaneous" activity in nerve centers is probably a sign of "tone." It may be reflected in motor discharge. Sensory input finds the nervous system active; this means that incoming signals do not start central responses from zero activity but may modulate either to increase or to decrease a preexisting level of activity.

Long-Cycle Rhythms of Motor Activity. In conditions of constant illumination and temperature in the laboratory, a wide variety of kinds of animals have been shown to possess rhythms of motor activity with periods about a day in length, ranging from about 19 to 29 hours. These rhythms have involved running activity in mice,[22, 230] rats,[59] salamanders,[345] crayfishes,[172] earthworms,[345] and cockroaches.[181, 355] The subject has been extensively reviewed.[181, 439]

These rhythms, involving coordinated activity of the whole animal, clearly reflect parallel rhythmic activities of the central nervous system. The daily rhythmic behavior patterns of the organisms are adaptively adjusted to the daily rhythms of such factors as light and temperature of the physical environment and normally come to bear species-specific phase relationships in direct response to the environmental cycles of these factors. The animals possess daily cycles of responsiveness to light[438] and temperature[396] changes, becoming rephased when appropriately stimulated during some parts of the cycles, and remaining resistant to rephasing during other parts. Animals are phase adjusted to the physical daily cycles when the times of increased responsiveness to light and temperature fall during the hours of darkness.

The daily patterns of motor activity recurring in constant conditions in the laboratory may commonly be caused to occur, regularly, slightly earlier or later each day as a function of the deviation of the level of constant illumination or temperature away from some optimum values for these.[230, 325] Light and temperature differences within the normal range appear to exercise quite comparable action in advancing or retarding the phase relations of the behavior cycles relative to the 24-hour day. It has been postulated that the consequently observed lengthened or shortened cycles represent a daily autophasing of its behavior pattern in a reaction of the rhythmically responsive animal to physical constancy of the powerful, natural, phasing factors—light and temperature.[60]

Many marine animals appear to have fully comparable, persistent lunar tidal or lunar-day rhythms of motor activity. These have been reported in most detail for crabs[37, 299] and bivalve molluscs.[37, 58, 346] However, lunar-day periodisms in motor activity have also been reported for terrestrial and freshwater animals,[59, 172, 345] suggesting that a fundamental lunar-day periodicity is also widely, if not universally, distributed among animals. Synodic monthly cycles of breeding behavior of numerous animals in nature have been postulated to be a consequence of interference patterns between such fundamental, persistent solar-day and lunar-day cycles. Persistent annual cycles also have been reported in unchanging environments.

Learned daily behavior patterns, such as observed in training of bees, fishes, or birds, appear to rely upon a fundamental 24-hour timing system.

The mechanism responsible for timing the periods of these physiological rhythms of geophysical periods is a remarkable one. Much evidence suggests that the periods of the basic timer for the organism are fully temperature-independent and resistant to drugs. Two fundamentally different views prevail as to the nature of this primary timer. One postulates[22, 326, 355] a fully independent cyclic biochemical timing system within the organism; the other postulates that the organism depends upon information derived from a continuing responsiveness to subtle geophysical factors from which, it has been proved, the animals are not shielded.[60]

CHEMICAL TRANSMITTERS

In previous chapters (13 and 14) it was shown that neuromuscular transmission and cardiac regulation are mediated by chemical transmitters, particularly acetylcholine, epinephrine plus norepinephrine (adrenaline-noradrenaline), and possibly 5-hydroxytryptamine. It is certain that chemical transmission also occurs at many interneuronic synapses, but identification of the active agents has been less definite than at neuromuscular and neurocardiac junctions.

Acetylcholine. Acetylcholine functions at some synapses. This substance has at the choline end of the molecule a quaternary nitrogen atom which bears a positive charge; at the other end (acetyl) is a carbonyl which can be hydrogen bonded. Much of the specificity of blocking and potentiating drugs depends on the charges and dimensions of the acetylcholine molecule, and of receptor molecules (Fig. 265).[298, 447] Two kinds of block may occur—competition with a receptor, and prevention of liberation of free ACh.[76] Receptors differ; hence a drug which blocks at one site is not necessarily effective at another; atropine blocks on the heart and tubocurarine at neuromuscular junctions. Similarly, mimicking drugs differ for different receptors, e.g., muscarine in the heart, nicotine in sympathetic ganglia. Potentiating compounds usually interfere with the enzymatic destruction of liberated acetylcholine.

Enzymes of Cholinergic Systems. Acetylcholine is synthesized in two steps from acetate and choline: (1) acetate + CoA (coenzyme A) → acetyl CoA in the presence of ATP as an energy source and in the presence of Ca^{++}; (2) acetyl CoA + choline → acetylcholine + CoA by the action of choline acetylase. Acetylcholine is believed to be bound normally to cellular protein and to be released on appropriate activation. At the site of release it has a chemical electrogenic action and is then rapidly hydrolyzed according to the reaction:

(3) ACh + H_2O → acetate + choline under the action of acetylcholinesterase (AChEs).

Two classes of cholinesterases are recognized, as follows:

ChE I, acetylcholinesterase, specific cholinesterase
active on acetyl β-methylcholine
inactive on benzoylcholine
most active on acetylcholine
bell-shaped activity-substrate concentration curve, i.e., inhibited by high concentrations of substrate
inhibited more by nitrogen mustards

ChE II, pseudocholinesterase, nonspecific cholinesterase, serum cholinesterase
inactive on acetyl β-methylcholine
splits benzoylcholine
most active on butyryl choline
sigmoid activity-substrate concentration curve, i.e., rises to maximum
inhibited more by diisopropyl fluorophosphate (DFP)

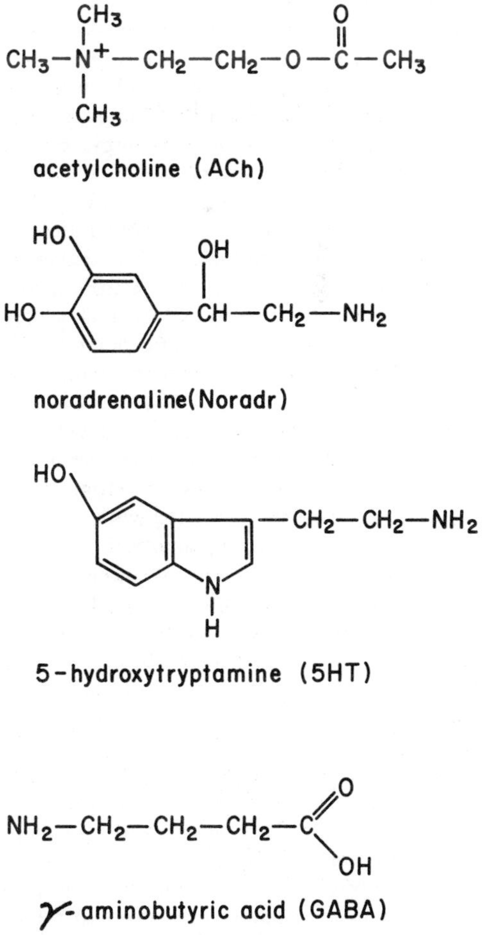

acetylcholine (ACh)

noradrenaline (Noradr)

5-hydroxytryptamine (5HT)

γ-aminobutyric acid (GABA)

FIGURE 265. Chemical formulae of acetylcholine, noradrenaline, 5-hydroxytryptamine, and gamma aminobutyric acid.

Both enzymes are inhibited by Prostigmin and physostigmine (eserine), by tetraethyl pyrophosphate (TEPP), and hexaethyl tetraphosphate (HETP). ChE II is inhibited by mipafox (bis [isopropylamino] fluorophosphine) at 8×10^{-7}M, ChE I at 6×10^{-6}M.[156] The turnover number of acetylcholinesterase is 300,000 molecules acetylcholine per second at 25° for electric organ enzyme. One molecule of the enzyme hydrolyzes one molecule of acetylcholine in 3 to 4 μsec.[298]

Evidence regarding cholinergic transmission is provided by assays for acetylcholine, choline acetylase, and acetylcholinesterase (Table 55), and also by the action of applied ACh, and inhibitors and potentiators. Failure of applied ACh to stimulate a biological preparation or failure of block by eserine does not necessarily contraindicate a cholinergic (ACh-mediated) system, but may mean failure of the applied substance to penetrate a protecting sheath. AChEs is even more widely distributed than ACh and may have functions in addition to the splitting of ACh. Acetylcholinesterase (ChE I) occurs in such non-nervous tissues as red blood cells, submaxillary gland, glial cells, placenta, and in snake venom and *Helix* blood.[24, 25] It is present in sensory nerves and in adrenergic nerves, but is more highly concentrated in motoneurons, more in gray than in white matter (Table 55). It is high in concentration in spinal cord, sympathetic ganglia, thalamus, caudate nucleus, and the like. AChEs occurs in ganglion cells of retina and in chick retina, but not in bipolar or in optic nerve.[136, 137] Ventral roots of the mammalian spinal cord contain some 50 to 300 times more ACh than dorsal roots. Acetylcholine is found not only in excitable tissues but in some inexcitable ones—spleen, placenta—and in ergot. ACh may have functions associated with permeability as well as with excitability.

Choline acetylase is low in most sensory nerves—dorsal roots, optic nerve; it is high in second order sensory neurons (spinocerebellar tract, trapezoid, and the like), and very high in caudate nucleus; it is intermediate in concentration in motor cortex, low in pyramidal tract, and high in ventral roots (Table 55). From this distribution Feldberg suggested that the central nervous system may have alternating cholinergic and noncholinergic neurons.[133, 137] The concentration of ACh in cortex of various mammals is proportional to the number of neurons per unit volume.[417] Some agents block certain central synapses by depolarizing (acetylcholine, deca-methonium); others block without depolarizing (tubocurarine); others inactivate only depolarizing synapses (lower ω-amino acids) and still others hyperpolarizing synapses (strychnine, higher ω-amino acids).[171] It is assumed that the concentration of acetylcholine and of enzymes associated with it in a nerve is related to transmission at the nerve endings.

Cholinesterase II (pseudocholinesterase) is found in liver, serum, gastric mucosa, and capillary walls. In the nervous system it is found in glial cells, in the nuclei of some ganglion cells (histochemical localization), more in white than in gray matter.[250]

Cholinesterase inhibitors such as difluoropyrophosphate (DFP) have been shown to block conduction in axons of lobster, squid, and frog.[298] The possible role of cholinesterase in nerve conduction is obscure.

Function in Vertebrate Nervous Systems. Liberation of acetylcholine during transmission in sympathetic ganglia has been definitely demonstrated. The superior cervical ganglion of a cat can be perfused by a branch of the carotid artery and the perfusate collected from the internal jugular vein. When the preganglionic nerve trunk is stimulated and the ganglion eserinized, ACh is liberated into the perfusate in amounts proportional to the number of impulses entering the ganglion.[135] Injected acetylcholine stimulates ganglion cells to discharge. Acetylcholine is not liberated in appreciable amounts by antidromic impulses, but is still liberated on preganglionic stimulation after block of transmission by nicotine or tubocurarine. Physostigmine protects liberated ACh against destruction by cholinesterase and sensitizes the ganglion cells to ACh. When small amounts of ACh are injected and at the same time a few preganglionic fibers are stimulated, the two stimuli add. Injected ACh depolarizes ganglion cells. Cat superior cervical and stellate ganglia synthesize 3 mg ACh/gm dry weight/hour (or 8 mg/ganglion/hr); after preganglionic fiber degeneration this ACh synthesis declines by 80 per cent in 90 hours.[30] Synthesis of available ACh goes at a relatively constant rate, about 4 mμg/min.[324] Autonomic ganglion cells in the mammalian intestine which are stimulated by nicotine are paralyzed by D-tubocurarine, tetraethylammonium and hexamethonium. Parasympathetic ganglia also are cholinergic; the ciliary ganglion, for example, is blocked by hexamethonium.[324] ACh is released at parasympathetic synapses from

TABLE 55. ACETYLCHOLINE, CHOLINE ACETYLASE, AND ACETYLCHOLINESTERASE CONTENT OF NERVOUS TISSUE

Preparation	ACh content $\mu g/gm$ wet (w) or dry (d)	Choline acetylase μg ACh synthesized per unit of tissue per hour, dry (d) or powdered (p)	ACh esterase amount ACh (except when stated) hydrolyzed per unit of tissue per hour, dry (d) or wet (w)
Tetrahymena[378]			0.08 $\mu g/mg_a/hr$
Trypanosoma[64]	2.8- 8.6 w	71.5 $\mu g/gm_a/75$ min	
Asterias radial nerve			
Squid brain[41, 297]		40-80 $\mu g/mg_p/hr$	0.4 $mg/100\ mg_w/hr$
Squid mantle nerve[298]			200-400 $mg/100\ mg_w/hr$
			0.66 $mg/100\ mg_w/hr$
Octopus ganglion[28]	77 w		
Aplysia ganglion[28]	2 - 3 w		
Octopus salivary gland[28]	1.3 w		
Cancer, Callinectes nerve cord[434, 435]	3.1- 6.6 w		brain 4 $mg/100\ mg_w/hr$
Homarus nerve cord[374a]	15.9 w		22.7 $mg/100\ mg_w/hr$
Limulus nerve cord[385a]	15.2 w		heart ganglia 14.27 $mg/100\ mg_w/hr$
Calliphora head[262, 263, 281, 282]	32.7 w	20. $\mu g/mg_a/hr$	
Musca head[262]	26 w		
Tenebrio head[262]	7.8 w		
Periplaneta head[262]	9.8 w		
Periplaneta			
nerve cord[85, 262]	36.7 w	11-20 $\mu g/mg_a/hr$	54 $\mu M/mg_w/hr$
brain[97]	135.2 w	50.6 $\mu g/mg_a/hr$	
thoracic ganglia[97]	95.4 w		
leg nerve[97]		2 $\mu g/mg_a/hr$	
Electric organ[298]	60-100 w		200-400 $mg/100\ mg_w/hr$
Gadus (whole brain)[25]			3.1 $mg/100\ mg_w/hr$
Raja (whole brain)[25]			0.88 $mg/100\ mg_w/hr$
Squalus (whole brain)[25]			0.23 $mg/100\ mg_w/hr$
Myxine (whole brain)[25]			0.32 $mg/100\ mg_w/hr$
frog brain[133, 434, 435]	5- 10 d		4.7 $mg/100\ mg_w/hr$
pigeon brain[133, 298]	1.5- 3 d		25 $mg/100\ mg_w/hr$
pigeon			
spinal cord[133]		140 $\mu g/gm_a/hr$	
cerebellum[133]		45 $\mu g/gm_a/hr$	
caudate nucleus[133]		180 $\mu g/gm_a/hr$	
cerebral cortex[133]		70 $\mu g/gm_a/hr$	

TABLE 55—(Continued)

Preparation	ACh content μg/gm wet (w) or dry (d)	Choline acetylase μg ACh synthesized per unit of tissue per hour, dry (d) or powdered (p)	ACh esterase amount ACh (except when stated) hydrolyzed per unit of tissue per hour, dry (d) or wet (w)	
rat				
whole brain[133]	1.5- 2 d			0.17 mg Mecholyl/gm$_w$/hr
spinal cord[133]		261 μg/gm$_d$/hr		
medulla[133, 446]	0.6 d		*2.4 mg/100 mg$_w$/hr	
cerebellum[133, 446]	0.1 d	108 μg/gm$_d$/hr	*3.87 mg/100 mg$_w$/hr *1.31 mg/100 mg$_w$/hr	
thalamus[133]		319 μg/gm$_d$/hr	*4.32 mg/100 mg$_w$/hr	
caudate nucleus[133]		505 μg/gm$_d$/hr	*17.9 mg/100 mg$_w$/hr	
cerebral cortex[133, 446]	2.0 d	318 μg/gm$_d$/hr	*2.9 mg/100 mg$_w$/hr	
dog				
dorsal roots[75, 187, 298]		0-25 μg/gm$_d$/hr	1.1- 1.5 mg/100 mg$_w$/hr	
ventral roots[298]			4- 6 mg/100 mg$_w$/hr	
spinal gray[344]	2.6 d			
cerebellum[75, 187, 298, 344]	0.18 d	88 μg/gm$_d$/hr	12- 15 mg/100 mg$_w$/hr	5.6 mg Mecholyl/gm$_w$/hr
thalamus[75, 187, 298, 344]	3.0 d	3100 μg/gm$_d$/hr	6 mg/100 mg$_w$/hr	2.1 mg Mecholyl/gm$_w$/hr
basal ganglia (caudate)[75, 187, 298, 344]	7.0 d	13,000 μg/gm$_d$/hr	50- 60 mg/100 mg$_w$/hr	20.6 mg Mecholyl/gm$_w$/hr
cerebral cortex[75, 187, 298, 344]	4.5 d	3000 μg/gm$_d$/hr	2- 5 mg/100 mg$_w$/hr	0.9 mg Mecholyl/gm$_w$/hr
sympathetic ganglia[298, 344]	25. d		15- 20 mg/100 mg$_w$/hr	
preganglionic sympathetics[298]			4- 6 mg/100 mg$_w$/hr	
dorsal root ganglia[298]			3- 5 mg/100 mg$_w$/hr	
retina[298]			15 mg/100 mg$_w$/hr	
optic nerve[75, 187, 298, 344]	0.3 d	0 μg/gm$_d$/hr	2- 3 mg/100 mg$_w$/hr	0.78 mg Mecholyl/gm$_w$/hr

* Calculated values

the chorda tympani nerve in the submaxillary ganglion.

Some spinal reflexes are depressed (e.g., knee jerk); others are enhanced (e.g., flexors), by eserine.[63] The spinal cord is stimulated to motor discharge when perfused with ACh, particularly after adrenaline, and when afferent fibers in the sciatic nerve are stimulated, a perfusate from the spinal cord contains ACh.[63] ACh injected into the spinal circulation reduces the latency and increases the amplitude of polysynaptic reflexes, and eserine prolongs the spinal effects of ACh. Small amounts of adrenaline potentiate responses to ACh.[77] Observations on monosynaptic spinal reflexes indicate that these are not mediated by acetylcholine. Motoneuron excitation is by some unknown chemical transmitter.

The only spinal cord synapse which is proved to be cholinergic is that on the Renshaw cells (Fig. 263) activated by motor axon collaterals. Antidromic impulses in motoneurons excite these synapses; response measured from a Renshaw cell is potentiated by eserine and blocked by D-tubocurarine; the cell is stimulated by ACh and by nicotine.[103] The motoneuron axons are also cholinergic at their endings on muscle; this is an example of Dale's rule that a neuron liberates the same agent at all its terminals.

The cerebral cortex of mammals is excited by acetylcholine, especially after eserine. High-amplitude, spikelike brain waves are set up and these may be associated with clonic motor activity. The level of ACh in an anesthetized cortex is three times that in cortex taken during a convulsion.[352] Fluid exuding from active cortex (but not from anesthetized) contains considerable acetylcholine. Dendritic postsynaptic potentials in the cortex elicited by thalamic or cortical stimulation are eliminated by D-tubocurarine, but the cortical cell bodies are still excitable.[171] Responses of optic cortex to impulses coming in transcallosal fibers from the opposite cortex are enhanced by ACh or by DFP but blocked by tubocurarine.[281, 282] It is probable that some cortical synapses are cholinergic. Cholinesterase begins to increase in the guinea pig embryo motor cortex before the muscles respond to cortical stimulation, and spontaneous cortical activity appears later.

Distribution in Invertebrates. In protozoans, ACh is present in ciliates and trypanosomes but absent from the nonmotile sporozoan plasmodia. *Tetrahymena geleii* has a specific AChEs which splits ACh at 0.08 μg/hr/mg dry weight.[378] *Trypanosoma rho-*

desiense synthesizes up to 71.5 μg ACh/gm dry weight/75 minutes at 37°C.[64]

Movements of the liver fluke *Fasciola hepatica* were inhibited by ACh whether the ganglion was present or not. These flatworms contain ACh at 0.19 to 1.7 μg/gm wet weight; they also have AChEs and ChAcet.[89] Nemerteans contain much cholinesterase (*Cerebratulus*). A fresh-water nemertean *Prostoma* has much of both ChE I and ChE II; its ChE I is indicated by splitting some 700 mg mecholylcholine/hr/100 mg wet weight.[234] Most of this is probably in muscle. From the stimulating effects of various drugs it is suggested that the sensory nerves of annelids contain acetylcholine.[426, 427] Nerves to some muscles of annelids and sipunculids and to luminous organs of annelids are probably cholinergic (Chapter 14). Ciliated cells of molluscs have ACh and cholinesterase.[64]

Cholinergic inhibitory nerves to the hearts of some pelecypods and gastropods have been mentioned (Chapter 13). Acetylcholine is released on stimulation of nerves to the perfused salivary glands of *Octopus vulgaris*.[29] The brain ganglia of cephalopods contain much ACh; an octopus brain has 77 μg ACh/gm;[28] the brain of a squid hydrolyzes 200 to 400 mg ACh/100 mg/hr. Choline acetylase from the head ganglion of a squid forms 40 to 80 μM ACh/mg protein/hr, a very high rate of activity[41] (Table 55). Synaptic transmission through the stellate ganglion of the squid is not altered by a variety of drugs—tubocurarine, nicotine, acetylcholine, eserine, and the like; hence although transmission is chemical[73] the transmitter is not acetylcholine.[61]

Acetylcholine is ineffective on synapses of crayfish ganglia in concentrations up to 10^{-3},[337] and injections of ACh into crabs have no apparent effect, although eserine facilitates autotomy. Acetylcholine in crayfish perfusion saline does, however, maintain abdominal ganglia in a normal state of excitability for potassium.[337] Transmission across the junctions from lateral giant fibers to motor fibers in the crayfish is electrical (p. 600).[148] Similarly, on synapses of *Callianassa* ACh had no effect, even after eserine, although DFP blocked at 10^{-2}M.[421] It is possible that the lack of effect of ACh on crustacean ganglia is due to failure to penetrate; however, this is unlikely because other agents like nicotine and strychnine are effective, and ACh is effective on cardiac ganglia and stretch receptors in the same animals. The central nervous systems of crayfish, lobster, and various crabs contain significant amounts of ACh (Table 55) and of AChEs. Abdominal ganglia of *Carcinus* contain some five times more ChEI than frog brain.[434, 435] Choline acetylase is present in ganglia of *Carcinides,* but stimulation of a ganglion liberates no detectable ACh.[434, 435]

The acetylcholine system in insects has been much studied because many insecticides are anticholinesterases. The head of a honeybee is rich in ACh and also contains one, possibly two, other choline esters.[26, 290] It is estimated that if all the ACh in the head of a blowfly *Calliphora* (32.7 μg/gm) were in the brain, the concentration would be 500 μg/gm; in *Musca* it would be 170 μg/gm. The nervous system of *Periplaneta* has between 36.7[245] and 79 μg/gm;[97] the brain, 135 μg/gm (wet), and thoracic ganglia, 95 μg/gm.[97] After DDT prostration there is an increase in free ACh in the nerve cord of cockroaches, and a substance appears in the blood which stimulates other nerve cords in low concentrations but blocks in high concentrations.[397] This stimulating substance resembles but is not ACh, it is not epinephrine or histamine, but appears to be an aromatic amine.[383, 397] Topical treatment with tetramethyl pyrophosphate also greatly increases ACh in the central nervous system.[97] Electrical stimulation of the nerve cord increases the free ACh content by 25 to 40 per cent.[97] Choline acetylase is present in blowfly brain at the high activity of synthesis of 0.6 μM ACh/100 μg dry wt/hr.[385]

Acetylcholinesterase is present in high concentrations in insect nervous systems. In its kinetics, high pH optimum, and substrate specificities, insect AChE resembles that from vertebrates.[23, 88, 460] Bee and roach AChEs may differ in activity toward other esters than ACh.[290] The AChEs quantity in the brain of a worker honeybee remains constant as the number of brain cells decreases with age; hence the AChEs/cell increases.[358] AChEs is most concentrated in highly active insects such as flies, less in ants and bees, and least in the more sluggish hemipterans, coelopterans, and lepidopterans.[290] AChEs is present in both supernatant and particulates of fly head.[385] The enzyme is more concentrated in synaptic neuropile than in other regions of *Rhodnius* ganglia.[455]

Applied acetylcholine is normally ineffective on insect nerve cords, for example, on a roach ganglion even at 10^{-2}M.[330] However, after removal of the protective sheath around the nerve cord, applied acetylcholine gives initial stimulation followed by block at the high ACh concentration of 3 to 5 $\times$ 10^{-3}M without eserine, and at 10^{-3} to 10^{-4}M with eserine.[425] Conduction may be blocked by DFP, but not by eserine, and DFP block is reversible.[425] Synaptic potentials in the caudal ganglion are enhanced by eserine.[465] The cholinesterase of the brain of a *Cecropia* declines to zero at the onset of pupation and then rises abruptly just prior to the onset of adult development; electrical activity in the brain and responses to electric stimuli parallel the ChE I. Choline acetylase, on the contrary, remains steadily high throughout pupation, and cholinergic substance (possibly ACh) in the brain rises to a peak late in pupation, declines with the rise in AChEs, and then rises again in the adult. Thus brain activity is correlated more with AChEs than with ACh or choline acetylase.[247] The role of the acetylcholine system in insect nervous systems remains in doubt; possibly ACh is a transmitter which acts very locally at high concentrations.[361] The primary action of DDT is stimulation of sensory nerve endings; in higher concentrations it depolarizes ganglion cells. The release of an ACh-like substance is probably secondary to prolonged sensory bombardment of the nervous system.

The lower vertebrates resemble the mammals insofar as they have been examined. Relative amounts of AChEs are indicated as follows in mm^3 CO_2/100 mg wet weight brain/30 min from ACh hydrolysis.[24, 93]

Dog	Elephant	Rat	Tench	Carp	Trout
59	137	67	127	110	193

Frog brain contains ChE I only, and has very high concentrations in the neuropile of the mesencephalon and isthmus, and in the tectum and basal optic ganglia.[384]

It may be concluded that ACh has been demonstrated as a synaptic transmitter in mammalian sympathetic and parasympathetic ganglia, and in the synapses of collaterals of motoneurons to Renshaw cells in the spinal cord. The probability of cholinergic synapses in other parts of the nervous system of vertebrates is high. There is good evidence that a system using ACh or some related substance is functional in insects. ACh is contraindicated as a transmitter at the squid giant synapse of the mantle ganglion, yet there appears to be an active cholinergic system of some sort in the squid brain. It is probable that many variants of ACh transmission exist, and ACh and ChE may have other functions in nervous systems than synaptic transmission. There is evidence from ChE blocking that ACh may be involved in the alteration of ion permeability during passage of nerve impulses.[298]

The search for other central nervous transmitters continues. The inhibitory transmitter in the spinal cord causes an inhibitory postsynaptic potential which is often a hyperpolarization (p. 602). Inhibitory synapses are blocked by tetanus toxin and by strychnine, and the latter drug has been called the curare of inhibitory transmission.[57, 114] Local application of strychnine reveals many inhibitory synapses in the cerebral cortex but not in the cerebellum.[342] The probability that a similar inhibitory transmitter is present in the animals of many phyla is indicated by the release of excitation by strychnine in earthworms and in some other invertebrates.

Adrenaline-Noradrenaline. A second class of substances elaborated by some nerves is the catechol amines. The best known of these are noradrenaline (NorAdr) and its methylated derivative, adrenaline (Adr), which together constitute sympathin (Chapter 13). Noradrenaline is formed from phenylalanine and hydroxytyramine via dihydroxyphenylalanine;[128] it is decomposed by amine oxidases.

Postganglionic sympathetic neurons are adrenergic and liberate varying proportions of adrenaline and noradrenaline in vertebrate smooth muscle and heart. The adrenal medulla contains enterochromaffin cells which stain for adrenaline and are derived from nervous tissue. The proportion of the total catechol which is noradrenaline in the adrenal medulla varies from 83 per cent in a whale, 73 per cent in dogfish, 25 per cent in mouse, to 2 per cent in rabbit and guinea pig.[449] The sympathetic chain of a cat has 30 to 100 μg noradrenaline-adrenaline (sympathin)/gm; the fibers have four times the concentration of the ganglia. Sympathetic chains contain noradrenaline in μg/gm as follows: dog 7.3, cattle 4, dog vagus 0.1, dog optic nerve 0.1 to 0.15.[128] Spinal cord has less adrenaline-noradrenaline than peripheral nerves, brain still less. In the brain the highest concentration of noradrenaline is in the hypothalamus (1 to 1.4 μg/gm). The sympathin synthesized by the brain of the dog is 10 per cent adrenaline and 90 per cent noradrenaline.[14] High concentrations of sympathin are found in the diencephalon, mesencephalon, and the bulbar regions, and also in the area postrema (which is devoid of nerve cells); the lowest concentrations are in the cerebrum, cerebellum, and

the dorsal and ventral roots.[429] Brain sympathin is 14 per cent adrenaline in dog, 9 per cent in rabbit, 7 per cent in cat, 14.9 per cent in cattle. In fish brains there is less noradrenaline in proportion to adrenaline than in mammals; dogfish sympathetic ganglia have 6.8 μg NorAdr/mg, and 2.8 μg Adr/gm.[127]

Chromaffin cells in the brain of the earthworm stain for adrenaline, and the nervous system has 1.4 μg Adr and 0.32 μg NorAdr/gm wet weight. The salivary glands of *Octopus* have 1 to 10 μg NorAdr/gm wet weight, and no adrenaline.[127] The nervous system of the butterfly *Vanessa* has 0.19 μg noradrenaline, and less than 0.01 μg adrenaline/gm; that of *Tenebrio* larva has 1.3 to 2 μg NorAdr and 0.02 to 0.06 μg Adr/gm.[310]

When injected intra-arterially into a cat, adrenaline enhances spinal reflexes in small doses and depresses them in large doses; similar effects are noted on sympathetic ganglion responses. The latency of these effects is long; hence they are probably vasomotor rather than directly on the synapses.[114] In the cat cortex the negative phase of the response to transcallosal impulses is depressed by adrenaline; hence adrenaline has been suggested as an inhibitory agent.[281, 282] Adrenaline has no marked effect on the invertebrate ganglia to which it has been applied. Sympathin appears to be a transmitter in certain sympathetic neurons. It may have other functions in non-nervous tissues. In invertebrates there is no evidence for the function of the catechol amines, but many animals have chromaffin cells which stain for adrenaline.

5-Hydroxytryptamine. An indolealkylamine of unexplained importance in the nervous system is 5-hydroxytryptamine (5HT). This is the same as serotonin (serum vasoconstrictor) and enteramine (from enterochromaffin cells of salivary glands of cephalopods).[311] 5HT is formed from 5-hydroxytryptophan by tryptophan decarboxylase. It is formed in large amounts in gastrointestinal mucosa and pancreas of higher vertebrates and elasmobranchs, but not in mucosa of cyclostomes and teleosts, where there are no enterochromaffin cells.[117] However, 5HT is a very effective stimulant for fish intestines.[129] 5HT is found in ascidians, prosobranch molluscs, in skin glands of poisonous amphibians, tentacles of coelenterates, and even in trichomes from some plants.[125] It is a potent stimulant for coelenterate nerve nets.[368] Except for certain toad skins more 5HT occurs in the salivary glands of *Octopus vulgaris* and *Eledone moschata* than anywhere else.[125] *O. macropus* has octopamine instead of 5HT and tryamine. 5HT may be the cardioaccelerating transmitter in some pelecypods (Chapter 13). Other quaternary amines are commonly toxins in coelenterates.[448]

In the vertebrate nervous system 5HT more or less parallels sympathin in distribution;[429] there is more in gray than in white matter, most in autonomic centers and the area postrema.[14] This amine is highest in concentration in the rhinencephalon and neostriatum. Concentrations decrease in the following order: hypothalamus > midbrain > spinal cord > cortex; none is found in optic nerve or cerebellum.[14] 5HT makes a cat lethargic and hesitant and suppresses strychnine convulsions.

The Rauwolfia alkaloid reserpine is a sedative (tranquilizer) which is of interest in psychiatric therapy. Drugs of this group appear to act by liberating 5HT in the brain; this is then destroyed and its products excreted.[327] Twenty-four hours after an injection of reserpine 90 per cent of the 5HT had disappeared from a rabbit brain.[189] Stimulation of the central end of the vagus also liberates 5HT in the brain. Reserpine sedation is antagonized by lysergic acid diethylamide (LSD), and injections of LSD decrease the quiescent periods following serotonin (5HT) liberation, and also induce hallucinations and schizophrenic behavior in man. LSD disrupts the spider's spinning of the web in the usual symmetrical pattern.[458] In cats LSD causes sham rage; in guppies and snails it induces maintained locomotor activity. Serotonin made Siamese fighting fish quiescent, and LSD decreased quiescence induced by serotonin.[3, 418]

Amine oxidase is a widespread enzyme or class of enzymes which act on 5HT, adrenaline, and the like. The distribution of amine oxidase in brain parallels the distribution of sympathin and 5HT. Monamine oxidase, measured in number of μg 5HT destroyed/ gm tissue/hr, is in dog brain as follows: medulla 1250, pons 882, hypothalamus 3154, cortex 880.[48] Amine oxidase is found in the digestive tract of earthworms, sea urchins, and starfish.[48] The enzyme is absent from *Amphioxus,* which lacks also chromaffin and enterochromaffin cells. Cephalopods have much of the enzyme in liver. Probably amine oxidases normally keep the concentration of free catechol amines and indoleamines low.

The functions of adrenaline-noradrenaline and of 5-hydroxytryptamine in nervous systems in general remain to be determined. Irrespective of whether they act as synaptic transmitters, they are natural substances which must play some role in the nervous mechanism of behavior.

Other Active Agents. Substance P, first isolated from intestinal smooth muscle and mammalian brain, is a polypeptide. It is most abundant in dorsal roots and columns of the spinal cord, and in some sensory nuclei. It is low in cerebral and cerebellar cortex. It has been suggested as a sensory transmitter although it has no apparent effect when applied to the brain.[134]

Other substances have been extracted from nervous systems (not perfusates) and labeled as excitatory (E) and inhibitory (I) substances, without chemical identification.[140, 141] Both substances are inactivated on standing in a tissue extract. A substance (E) from sensory nerves of vertebrates and from mixed nerves of numerous invertebrates stimulates a bee to circle and stimulates crayfish stretch receptors.[141] A similar extract causes contraction of various annelid muscles.[426, 427] Vertebrate central nervous systems yield a factor which depresses several nervous functions in crayfish and mice.[140] The inhibitory nerves to crayfish heart and stretch receptors contain factor I, which is similar to but much more active than gamma-aminobutyric acid.[141]

Gamma-aminobutyric acid (GABA) is present in nervous tissue of many animals, more in gray than in white matter, much more in cortex than in peripheral nerve. It is concentrated in lobster ganglia. It inhibits crayfish stretch receptors and muscles, but it does not appear in perfusates during nervous inhibition.[123]

GABA inhibits the crayfish heart, and this inhibition as well as that due to nerves is blocked by picrotoxin.[141] It is possible to block depolarizing (excitatory) synapses in the cerebellum by GABA and thus to unmask inhibitory (hyperpolarizing) synapses. Other ω-amino acids (C_2 to C_5) block predominantly the depolarizing synapses, and longer amino acids (C_6 to C_8) block the hyperpolarizing synapses.[343] GABA is not very specific and can hardly be the inhibitory transmitter; however, it is probably one constituent of factor I extracts.

GIANT FIBER SYSTEMS

The preceding discussion of giant fibers (p. 596) as adaptations for speed indicated that there are several types of giant fiber system, that they have evolved several times, and are relatively specialized neural systems. The junctions in giant fiber systems have been considered as prototype synapses, and a survey of them shows a series of increasing complexity from through conduction, electrical transmission, to chemical transmission.[69, 71]

1. Earthworm giant fibers have oblique segmental septa, the two sides of which stain differently, and across which degeneration does not occur.[398] Electron micrographs show these septa to consist of double membranes with vesicles on each side.[178, 223] Transection of individual giant fibers of earthworms showed that the median fiber normally conducts posteriorly in the posterior region and the lateral ones, which are connected together, conduct anteriorly in the anterior region.[398] In isolated nerve cords impulses are conducted in either direction, indicating that the septa are not polarized.[120] The normal polarity results because the median fiber has sensory connections in the anterior end (first 40 segments), and the lateral fiber complex has sensory connections in the posterior part of the worm.[67] The septa impose no delay, no polarity, and show no block with fatigue; like intercalated discs of mammalian heart muscle, they are the remnants of developmental cell boundaries which impose no electrical barrier to conduction.[235, 236] Electrical records from intact nerve cords of *Lumbricus* sometimes show ꞏ repetitive responses of giant fibers to single shocks and also local graded synaptic responses; these represent re-excitation of giant fiber systems at their branches in the cord by small neurons.[235, 236]

2. In sabellid and serpulid worms (*Protula* and *Spirographis*), decussation of giant fiber impulses occurs in the midbody; on fatigue the crossing of descending impulses shifts toward more anterior decussations. These decussations show no facilitation, that is, they transmit one-to-one.[66] The fibers are well separated and no anatomical connections are known, but fine branches have been postulated[70] across which there could be electrotonic spread.

3. The lateral giant fibers of the crayfish (Fig. 266) show junctional connections (a) with sensory elements in the neuropile, (b) with the contralateral giant at a decussation in the cord, (c) with the lateral giant of the next posterior and anterior segments at regions of segmental overlap, and (d) with motor giant fibers of the next anterior segment.[451] The overlapping junctions of the lateral giant fibers are nonpolarized and normally conduct one-to-one, but when fatigued can require facilitation.[452] There may be re-excitation of the lateral giants by recurrent delay paths in the neuropile. The septal membranes have a much higher resistance than axoplasm, and local potentials are seen after each junction when the safety factor for conduction is low.[437] There appears to be through conduction with slight delay at the septa.

4. In the crustacean *Callianassa*, interaction occurs between the two giant fibers in the brain so that an ascending impulse in one fiber is "reflected" back in the other with delay of less than 0.5 msec; the junction can be fatigued, but shows two-way conduction.[421] In the polychaete *Protula*[66] similar reflection occurs, the junction following as fast as the fibers (160/sec). Junctional delay increases on fatigue, but there is no evidence of facilitation.

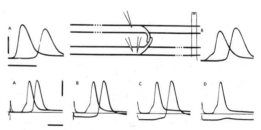

FIGURE 266. Potentials associated with electrotonic cross-excitation between the two lateral giant axons of crayfish nerve cord. Diagram shows top view of the axons and electrode arrangement. Right axon above, rostral end at left. Right axon was destroyed in rostral portion of segment and the left one in next caudal segment (broken lines). Caudal pair of stimulating electrodes shown. Recording microelectrodes inserted in each axon, also a polarizing electrode in left axon. Calibration 50 mv and 1 msec for each line.

Upper records: *A*, responses to stimulating the nerve cord rostrally. The initial, larger spike is in the left axon. The response in right axon arose by excitation through the crossed connections by processes in front of the oblique septal membranes. *B*, the right axon responded first to caudal stimulus. Its spike was preceded by electrotonic potential which is responsible for transmission across the septum.

Lower records: Stimuli through caudal electrodes as in *B* above. After control records *A*, the left axon was hyperpolarized with progressively stronger intracellularly applied currents (*B-D*). There was progressive delay of the spike in this axon (*B,C*) disclosing small potential ahead of spike. Strong hyperpolarization abolished the spike (*D*) but the initial potential was unchanged; this represents the electrotonic potential generated in left axon by directly evoked spikes in right axon. (Courtesy of A. Watanabe and H. Grundfest.)

5. The junctions of median and lateral fibers with the motor giants of the crayfish are polarized. When fatigued they show facilitation, and the excitatory synaptic potentials may sum on repetition.[451] The motor giants may give single large responses to single presynaptic impulses and then a series of small synaptic-type potentials, probably from recurrent small fiber systems. Intracellular records considered with transmembrane polarization show that the current from a presynaptic impulse is sufficient for transmission (see p. 600).[148] The motoneuron is activated also by branch fibers from the median giants and from small inhibitory axons of the nerve cord, and at these synapses transmission appears to be chemical.[451]

Similar junctional failure on repetitive stimulation occurs in some polychaetes at sensory-giant and giant-motor neuron synapses. When the junction between lateral giant and motor has failed, an impulse in the median giant restores the junctional responsiveness.[212]

6. The junctions between second and third order giant neurons in the stellate ganglion of the squid have long regions of overlap. Each postaxon, derived from many cell bodies, receives innervation from a large (200 μ) primary preaxon and a smaller (75 μ) accessory preaxon. In addition, a third group of accessory giant preaxons exists, some of which pass directly through the ganglion; others synapse.[61] Both primary and accessory impulses give rise after delay of 0.55 msec to EPSP's as recorded from a giant postneuron; spike responses arise at some critical height of the EPSP and the two prefibers can interact in spike initiation. The accessory synapse is more sensitive to fatigue and anoxia than the primary one; it appears to be an alternate path for exciting the mantle giant neurons.[61] Transmission is normally one-to-one, but facilitation occurs on fatigue, and the spike appears later on the EPSP.[68] Electrical transmission does not occur, but there is no indication of the nature of the chemical transmitter.

7. Giant neurons of ganglia of the gastropod *Aplysia* are activated by presynaptic impulses to give long spikes with considerable overshoot. The spike invades the cell soma. By appropriate polarization it is possible to separate EPSP, local potential, and spike. Some presynaptic fibers set up inhibitory synaptic potentials (hyperpolarizing)[407, 408] (Fig. 261).

8. In the last abdominal ganglion of the cockroach are junctions between sensory neurons from the anal cerci and large ascending neurons. Similar "giant" fibers have been noted in locusts and crickets. These junctions are polarized, they normally require facilitation or convergence, and they show some lability of response according to the timing of incoming impulses. Ganglionic delay is normally 1 to 2 msec, but it may be longer. The synapses block at 40 to 50/sec in roach and at 70 to 100/sec in cricket.[340, 360] The giant fiber system mediates the jumping reaction to a puff of air on the anal cerci.[362]

9. The Mauthner cells of fish and urodeles are giant neurons receiving multiple sensory input.[107, 395] Their thinly myelinated axons are large (40 to 45 μ) and mediate a rapid flip or escape reaction. Conduction is 38 to 63 m/sec in carp,[40] 18.5 m/sec in the lungfish *Protopterus*,[457] and 80 m/sec at 23° in catfish.[406] Antidromic impulses appear·not to invade beyond the axon hillock into the soma but do create large fields of extracellular potentials. Eighth nerve stimulation results in excitatory postsynaptic potentials and spikes, and stimulation of a collateral of the contralateral Mauthner cell elicits inhibitory responses.[147]

In the puffer fish *Spheroides* a cluster of 200 to 300 μ diameter cells occurs above the cord behind the cerebellum. The axons of these cells are large for unmyelinated fibers (5 to 15 μ) and are efferent in dorsal roots; they are not motor but may be autonomic, and the cells are excited synaptically by small sensory fibers in the dorsal columns. Each cell connects by a large process or neurite to much-branched processes in which synaptic excitation can occur. Synaptic potentials spread electrotonically to the soma and may become large enough to give a spike. The soma can be stimulated directly, but antidromic impulses do not invade the soma.[39, 174] Activity, particularly spikes, in one cell can be recorded in attenuated form in adjacent cells. This intercellular interaction favors synchronization by electrotonic spread.[39]

Giant fiber systems present a series of junction types; some are without any barrier to conduction; there are ephaptic-type junctions, polarized and nonpolarized, one-to-one conducting and facilitation-requiring; electrically transmitting and chemically transmitting; and complex plastic synaptic systems. None of the giant fiber synapses can be considered as primitive; rather their simplicity represents a recently developed specialization.

NERVE NETS OF COELENTERATES

A nerve net is a nonganglionic aggregation of interconnected neurons which conduct diffusely and which show integrative properties. A peripheral plexus permits spread of signals by local reflexes and conducts somewhat diffusely but more usually in a single direction. Nerve nets and plexuses comprise the major portion of the nervous system in coelenterates, ctenophores, enteropneustans, echinoderms, and ascidians; nets may be important in peripheral motor coordination in some annelids and molluscs; nerve nets provide for local integration in visceral musculature in animals of many phyla. Nerve nets have been best studied in coelenterates, where they constitute a primitive coordinating nervous system and show many of the integrative properties usually attributed to complex central nervous systems.

Early histologists pictured a nerve net of a polyp or medusa as a continuum of anastomosing fibers from multipolar and bipolar neurons. Considerable evidence[314] (Fig. 267) shows that the fibers do not usually fuse; the junctions are regions of apposition between fibers. Protoplasmic continuity is indicated in *Hydra,* and in *Velella* the fine net neurons are independent, but processes of the coarse net appear to fuse.[277]

Conduction in a coelenterate nerve net proceeds freely in all directions; impulses pass around corners and cross narrow bridges. The individual junctions are usually not polarized. In a mesenteric net of *Metridium,* for example, conducted signals go through 4 to 20 junctions in a centimeter distance in 10 msec. In *Hydra* the individual neurons may extend only 100 μ.[315] Possibly, in such a net of short neurons, local potentials (regenerative but not

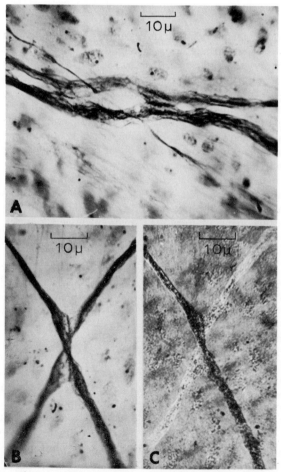

FIGURE 267. Portion of nerve net in mesentery of Metridium. Silver stain. *A,* parallel axons with four synaptic contacts showing lines of demarcation; *B,* parallel fibers photographed with ordinary light; *C,* with polarized light. (From Pantin, C. F. A.: Proc. Roy. Soc. London, B, vol. 140.)

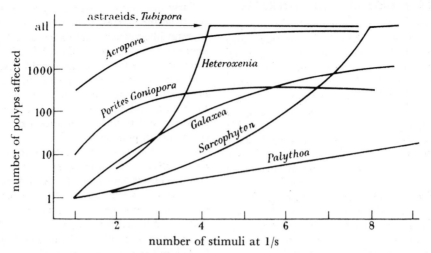

FIGURE 268. Relation between number of stimuli at 1/sec and number of polyps affected for a variety of corals. Whole colony active from first stimulus in *Tubipora* (top line). Accelerating slope in which wave eventually sweeps over whole colony in *Heteroxenia* and *Sarcophyta*. Decreasing slope by which response spreads to limited number of polyps no matter how many stimuli given—*Goniopora* and *Galaxea*. (From Horridge, G. A.: Phil. Tr. Roy. Soc. London, B, vol. 240.)

all-or-none) are adequate for conduction. In addition to the slow local net, there are regions of through conduction, faster than in the generalized net, 0.7 to 2.0 m/sec as compared with less than 0.5 cm/sec. The neurons of the fast net may be many millimeters long. In a medusa circular conduction by the marginal ring is fast; radial conduction over the bell is slow. In an anemone, mesenteric conduction is faster than in the column. The oral disc is 4000 times more sensitive to tactile stimulation than is the column.[319] A twitch-like contraction is mediated by the fast net. Slow contractions lasting many minutes are coordinated by the slow nerve net. In ctenophores, impulses in the nerve net initiating luminescence go in all directions; those for the comb beat go from aboral to oral ends.[91] Coelenterate nerve nets show a wide variety of facilitation requirements. In both anemones and medusae, repeated stimulation is necessary to elicit maximum response, and there may be little mechanical response of an anemone to a single volley. Experiments with drugs and regeneration show much of the facilitation to be neuroneuronal, part of it neuromuscular. An apparent decrement in transmission through a net can be explained in terms of decreasing facilitation at junctions as a wave spreads out from its point of origin. In *Aurelia* the individual nerve fibers show a single all-or-none impulse per beat of the bell, and the marginal ganglia are pacemaker centers. In the luminescent sea pansy *Renilla* nonpolarized, nondecremental conduc-

tion requires facilitation; facilitation drops rapidly at intervals greater than 1.5 seconds between impulses, but after tetanus some enhanced excitability lasts long, even out to 10 minutes.[303] *Metridium* may give a slow contraction to stimulation at one shock per 5 or 10 seconds, and an interposed extra shock may elicit a quick response; thus the infrequent shocks caused some facilitation.[366] The slow responses are much more dependent on facilitation than the fast ones.[300]

The refractory period of the slow net may be long—0.2 sec in *Renilla*,[303] 0.3 sec in hydromedusae;[208] in the fast net, refractoriness is much shorter (60 to 70 msec in *Cerianthus*).[210, 367]

Various corals show wide variation in dependence on facilitation.[209] For example, in the alcyonarian *Tubipora* a single conducted wave passes through the colony like the fast wave in the mesenteries of an actinian. In *Heteroxenia* the response increases on repetition until the whole colony is involved. In *Acropora* and *Porites* a single shock causes coordinated contraction of many polyps; the response spreads somewhat further on stimulation at 1/sec but not at 1 every 4 seconds. In *Palythoa* there is little spread on repetition (Fig. 268). Thus, nerve net conduction can be either incrementing or decrementing. In a quantitative analysis Horridge concluded that nonconducting synapses become conducting as successive impulses spread over a coral colony, that there is interaction among neurons, and that a critical density of active cells must be reached for a polyp to respond.[209]

Nerve nets frequently show repeated response as an after-discharge following a strongly facilitated response. A contraction wave, conducted by the nerve net in a doughnut-shaped ring from a medusa, may continue to circle for many hours or days. In leptomedusae a radial net is separate from the net of circular contraction, the radial response is slow and sustained, the circular response twitchlike, and both interaction between the two nets and double innervation of muscle fibers are indicated.[208] Reciprocal contraction of the circular and radial muscles occurs, and the radial system can inhibit the circular one but not vice versa.[208]

The marginal bodies of a jellyfish are ganglia, or neuron aggregations, and are responsible for rhythmic contractions of the bell and for some inter-net coordination. Intact sea anemones in darkness show spontaneous rhythms, some extremely slow (minutes and hours long); some nerve cells in the nerve net are capable of innate rhythmicity.[35] Food selection by coelenterates leads to complex behavior, rejection of some particles, acceptance of others, pointing of the manubrium in hydromedusae, expansion, elongation, defecation, swaying, and other postural changes in anemones.[35] The nerve net is capable of some plasticity of response.

If coelenterate nerve nets are taken as the prototype of central nervous systems, considerable complexity exists, as compared with the one-to-one relays of giant fiber systems. Facilitation must have been present in the most primitive nervous system; this guarantees that an animal does not respond to every stimulus but only to stimuli in significant number. The facilitation requirement may impose junctional polarity. After-discharge, spontaneity, inhibition, reciprocal innervation, and some flexibility of response are found in nerve nets.

PERIPHERAL VERSUS CENTRAL CONTROL OF LOCOMOTION

In coelenterate nerve nets some condensation of conducting pathways exists—there are through tracts, the marginal and circular oral rings of neurons. In sluggish animals a peripheral nerve net is adequate, but in those animals with greater speed and versatility, central reflexes take over locomotor control. Even in animals where locomotion is centrally controlled, visceral plexuses remain autonomous, e.g., the myenteric plexus of the vertebrate intestine and the stomatogastric system of annelids and arthropods. Integrating function in visceral plexuses has not been much studied.

The transition between peripheral and central control of locomotion is well shown in echinoderms and prochordates. The nervous system of echinoderms consists of a central oral ring which gives rise to five radial nerve trunks which contain nerve cell-bodies connected to the peripheral network which innervates tube feet, spines, pedicellariae, and other appendages.[386] In general, the central ring of echinoderms is directive in locomotion, the radial nerves are necessary for true locomotion and righting, but the peripheral system alone can permit a certain amount of coordination among locomotor appendages. In echinoids the peripheral net contains ganglion cells in local reflex centers at the base of the spines. In testing a fragment of living sea urchin, local stimulation by NaCl causes a near-by spine to bend toward the stimulus; if a cut is made between stimulus point and spine, no response occurs. If a spine is pulled, a near-by one bends; if a cut is then made between them, the excitation spreads between the two only if a third spine remains at the end of the cut. If a spine is held so that it cannot move, waves are not conducted past it. The ganglion cells at the base of each spine constitute local reflex centers; evidently the peripheral system is not a continuous net.[245]

If in a starfish a radial nerve is cut, responses to touch can be transmitted by the peripheral system to the ring or to other rays, and coordinated pointing of the tube feet continues.[227] A starfish with all radial nerves cut, if turned over, eventually rights itself but shows poor coordination. If all elements of the ring are removed, an isolated arm travels toward its base; if a bit of the ring remains, the arm moves toward its distal end; if the ring is cut in two places, the starfish pulls itself in two. Conduction goes in both directions in the ring and in radial nerves, and there is evidence for a "pointing center" for the tube feet at the junction of ring and radial nerve.[242] Tension on an arm also influences tube feet by local reflexes. Responses of tube feet to central stimulation show little effect of frequency (facilitation), but marked effect of intensity.[242] Similarly, in holothurians, there is little frequency-dependence of muscle responses to radial nerve stimulation. Conduction in the nerve ring is at 0.11 m/sec and in the radial nerves it is at 0.17 m/sec, at 20 to 23°C.[328] The ring is not so much a central nervous system as part of a peripheral one.

The nervous system of balanoglossids (Enteropneusta) consists of a subepidermal network, dorsal and ventral nerve cords, and collar connectives.[65] Unipolar neurons are abundant in the cords. The peristalsis of burrowing by *Saccoglossus* is controlled by the dorsal cord of the proboscis, and peristalsis of longitudinal body muscles by the main nerve cords.[248] Rapid contractions are mediated by giant fibers. In some species the proboscis lacks the cord and is coordinated by the subepidermal network. Responses of pieces of the proboscis to light seem to be peripherally coordinated.[248]

In solitary tunicates a single large ganglion lies between the two siphons. After the ganglion has been extirpated, intersiphonal reflexes are abolished in *Ciona* and *Ascidia,* or weakened (*Phallusia* and *Ascidiella*),[213] and body tonus lost. Local responses of single siphons and of the test remain; conduction may pass around the ends of a cut in the body wall. Responses of atrial and branchial muscles to stimulation of the test show marked facilitation (lasting to 10 seconds) and rapid fatigue on repetition.

In flatworms, nerve trunks (two to eight in number) run posteriorly from the brain and contain nerve cells not grouped in ganglia. A bit of one of these nerve cords seems necessary for spontaneous coordinated movement in planaria[32] and nemerteans; the extirpated proboscis is said to make feeding reactions.[241]

In annelids the balance between peripheral and central nervous control of locomotion varies in different groups. In earthworms a subepidermal plexus of branching fibers and scattered nerve cells lies outside the circular muscles; each central ganglion gives rise to three pairs of segmental nerves containing both sensory and motor fibers which connect with the subepidermal plexus. If the ventral nerve cord is cut or several segments of it are removed from an earthworm, peristaltic waves can still pass from one end of the worm to the other, although waves of mucus secretion may fail to pass. Peristaltic transmission occurs if two regions are connected by the nerve cord only, or if the two pieces of a transected worm are connected by a thread, or when a few segments have been anesthetized. If the nerve cord is removed from more than three segments and these segments are firmly pinned down so that no pull can be exerted beyond them, no peristaltic wave passes. Action potentials in the segmental nerves show that each nerve serves three segments with both sensory and motor fibers, the different nerves serving overlapping fields which are fairly discrete.[336] Spontaneous contractions of strips of earthworm body wall lacking nerve cord have been reported and also have been denied.[338] Deganglionated dorsal strips from posterior segments of *Allobophora* and *Lumbricus* (but not *Perichaeta*) sometimes show spontaneous movements. These may arise in the muscle rather than in the subepidermal plexus. Active deganglionated strips of body wall in posterior segments may contract locally to tactile and even to photic stimulation; hence there must be some connection between sense endings and muscle, yet the local nature of the response and its virtual absence from anterior segments show that it can hardly be of importance in behavior. There are many more sense endings in each segment than there are segmental nerve fibers; the subepidermal plexus is probably important as a distribution center, but not capable of independent integration.

In hirudineans transection of the nerve cord disrupts coordinated swimming.[233] In the luminous polychaete polynoids, transection of the nerve cord leaves only the posterior half able to flash.[302] Nereid polychaetes give little evidence for overlapping peripheral reflexes like those in the earthworm, that is, locomotion is more dependent on central rhythms. However, there are very few (only one to four) motor fibers per segmental nerve, and relatively few sensory fibers; hence there must be extensive peripheral relays. Innervation of body muscles is by second or third order motoneurons, and the histology suggests some peripheral short-circuiting between sensory and motor elements.[387] Physiological confirmation is needed.

In gastropod molluscs a subepidermal plexus has been described, particularly in the foot. Peristalsis and high tonus in a deganglionated foot have been attributed to release of the peripheral plexus from inhibitory control by the pedal ganglion.[232] Excised labial palps of *Anodonta* show autonomous responses to light and touch, possibly by a true net. There is no definitive evidence, however, by modern techniques for peripheral connections between sense cells and muscles in molluscs. Some molluscan nerves (e.g., *Helix*) show decremental conduction because bipolar cells occur along the nerve and the conducting fibers are not uniform.[375]

Nerve nets permit a rather diffuse slow response; they have been replaced in the course of evolution by centralization whenever speed and restricted responses became important. Nerve plexuses do permit autonomous coordination of a muscle system, which is not possible with central reflexes.

GANGLIONIC FUNCTION IN LOCOMOTION

Annelids. A number of segments of the ventral nerve cord of an annelid, isolated from the body musculature, can conduct a peristaltic wave to the region beyond. Normally, however, the wave is reinforced by segmental reflexes. A length of twenty to forty intact segments of an earthworm, suspended and mechanically balanced in a saline bath, shows no peristalsis, but a slight stretch or a tactile stimulus elicits persistent peristalsis[98] (Fig. 269). A tension-induced peristaltic reflex can be inhibited by vigorous tactile stimulation, particularly at the anterior end. The maximum frequency of rhythmic contraction is about one every 2 seconds, and if a weight is removed after a 0.5 second application, rhythmic afterdischarge may last for 2 to 3 minutes. Circular muscles contract while longitudinal muscles relax, and vice versa, and correlated reflexes control the setae. Peristalsis can be started also by electrical polarization with the anterior end positive.[158, 161] Earthworm nerve cords which have been isolated for several hours show bursts of impulses, but it is doubtful that this corresponds to a normal control of rhythmicity.[161]

In a leech not only tension and contact but also exteroceptive stimuli from the sucker are capable of eliciting peristaltic reflexes.[164] After removal of both head and anal ganglia the leech continues to swim.[233]

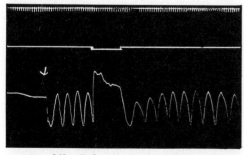

FIGURE 269. Reflex rhythmic contractions in an earthworm in response to tension applied at arrow and inhibited by tactile stimulation of dorsal surface. (From Collier, H. O.: J. Exp. Biol., vol. 16.)

In tube-dwelling polychaetes, feeding and irrigation cycles are centrally controlled.[442, 443] In *Arenicola marina* feeding is by rhythmic contraction of body wall and tail at a cycle of about 40 minutes. The nervous pacemakers of the two regions are separate, as shown by rhythms in isolated portions; however, their discharges may interact. In *Arenicola ecaudata* the isolated extrovert (proboscis and esophagus) shows continuous feeding movements; hence in this species the extrovert contracts cyclically only when under the influence of the supraesophageal ganglion.[442, 443] Luminescence in *Chaetopterus* varies according to the intensity and frequency of stimuli to the nerve cord, and facilitation of interneurons is indicated.[302]

Peristalsis in polychaetes is controlled by segmental reflexes and central rhythms. Motion pictures of *Nereis* in locomotion show parapodia moving successively in clumps of four to eight. Accompanying the wave of parapodial beat, the longitudinal muscles on the same side contract while those on the opposite side relax.[158] Thus *Nereis* crawls in the direction in which the wave travels over the body and not, like the earthworm, in the opposite direction.

Molluscs. In gastropod and pelecypod molluscs locomotor reflexes are mediated by four paired ganglia, cerebral, pedal, pleural, and visceral, which serve as local reflex centers and show some interaction.

In *Anodonta* the posterior adductor muscle receives motor impulses from the visceral ganglion; the anterior adductor, from the cerebral ganglion. The striated portions of the adductors show fast rhythmic contractions (twelve to twenty per hour) and the unstriated portions give slow rhythms (three to thirty per week). The rapid rhythm requires the ganglion nearest to the muscle; the slow, the cerebral ganglion.[33] In *Mytilus* the pedal ganglion permits the foot to creep and spin; the visceral ganglion controls the opening and closing reactions to changes in salinity of water.

Electrical responses in various nerves of *Mya* show that a single volley in any one main nerve may be followed by activity in all nerves; hence extensive ganglionic connections occur. There is much temporal summation and after-discharge. Fast-fiber systems (80 to 100 cm/sec) respond well at above ten shocks per second; slow ones (15 to 30 cm/sec) fail at above 4 per second.[211]

In gastropods the pedal ganglion innervates the foot; there is increased resistance of the foot to stretch after removal of the ganglion (*Helix*), suggesting that there may be both excitatory and inhibitory innervation. Removal of the cerebral ganglion from *Aplysia* increases locomotor activity; hence the cerebral ganglion may inhibit the pedal ganglion. Sensory fibers from the foot activate the opposite side of the foot reflexly through the pedal ganglion.[232] In the slug *Ariolimax* large neurons of the pedal ganglion can be activated via pedal afferents or from cerebral ganglia. The ganglion shows delay of 19 msec, convergence and summation.[423, 424] The pedal ganglion of a slug increases its "spontaneous" activity when the animal is dehydrated; hence the ganglion may be an osmoreceptor.[218]

In cephalopods the complex brain mass represents the fusion of several ganglia and permits extremely complex behavior. Each optic lobe is capable of some independent integration. Giant cells (in the lobus magnocellularis of the brain mass) receive impulses from various afferent nerves. Each has an axon which crosses to the opposite side and makes contact with second order giant cells in the palliovisceral ganglion; these pass to the stellate or mantle ganglia to activate the third order giant neurons at synapses described above (p. 616).[466] The mantle nerves contain giant axons and many small fibers, both sensory and motor. Reflex contraction of the mantle can be elicited over either of two pathways, primarily via the brain mass, traversing the stellate ganglion for both afferent and efferent fibers, secondarily via the stellate ganglion alone.[145]

Arthropods. Arthropod locomotion depends on segmental reflexes which are complex and precisely timed. Manton[280] has described the evolution of arthropod locomotor mechanisms in detail. Advances of the arthropods over the annelids are: the development of limb musculature, increased centralization of nervous control, and elaboration of jointed appendages. *Peripatus* presents the basic arthropod pattern[280] in which several gaits are possible. In "low gear" the paired legs move in phase, and legs make a long back stroke; in "middle gear" the strokes are equal; in "high gear" the back stroke is short, and the paired legs alternate. Diplopods have elaborated the bottom gear pattern, and they push by their legs; chilopods use the faster gear and tend to pull. In insects a continuous gradation of gaits makes use of various leg sequences.[280] In some lepidopteran larvae each segmental ganglion mediates reflexes of its own segment and the one ahead.[205] The stinging reflex of wasps and bees can be carried out by the last abdominal ganglion.

In animals which have developed a thorax the number of appendages is reduced, and thoracic reflexes control walking, flying, and breathing. Flight by insects is commonly initiated by removing support from under the legs, i.e., tarsal contact inhibits flight. When one or two segments—ganglion and limbs—are isolated (in scorpions, crayfish, beetles), reciprocal alternate contractions of flexors and extensors can be elicited. In the walking stick *Dixippus* each leg by its own motion has a reflex stimulating effect on neighboring legs. In the cockroach crossed inhibition has been noted, and the slow motor system (p. 445) responds reflexly to afferents from the same limb.[332] A "slow" nerve fiber to the extensor of the trochanter shows a steady rhythm at five to twenty per second, and a decrease in resistance to depression of the leg lowers the frequency; increasing resistance to leg depression raises the frequency.[332] Electrical polarization of a cockroach thoracic ganglion causes leg flexion or extension according to the direction of current flow; this indicates orientation of interneurons.[202]

Isolated arthropod ganglia show spontaneous activity (Fig. 264), and removal of a ganglion results in loss of tone in the segment it serves. By recording from segmental nerves and the central nerve cord and by stimulating various body regions, a functional map of the nervous system of an insect or crustacean can be made. In a crayfish, for example, the available central connections are multiple and many alternate paths are evident.[337] In circumesophageal connectives some 200 different units have been identified according to their sensory input, some of these with restricted "private lines," others activated from several sensory areas; some are direct sensory neurons and some are interneurons.[453, 454] Some small interneurons of crayfish abdominal ganglia may show irregular spontaneity and others may be activated by tactile proprioceptors or photic input via caudal ganglion photoreceptors (p. 371). Spikes of several amplitudes and forms, sometimes one superposed on another, can be recorded from fibers of the same interneuron in the neuropile. This suggests separate spike-initiating foci, much as in crustacean cardiac ganglion cells. These neurons are unipolar, with extensive dendritic branching, and apparently the soma is not invaded by spikes.[240, 330]

The variety of proprioceptive reflexes of locomotion and posture, the so-called plasticity of the arthropod nervous system, is shown not only by changes in leg rhythm according to gait but also by almost immediate changes after amputation; hence multiple connections in a ganglion must be available.[42] After two opposite legs are removed the remaining four legs of an insect show a diagonal rhythm.[217] A leg functions both in support and by protraction, and one leg cannot be protracted until support is provided by another leg. Each leg usually alternates with the contralateral limb of the same segment. After amputation of one or several legs, legs which previously alternated now work synchronously (Fig. 270), and pedipalps may function in locomotion (spiders, crabs, beetles, and the like).[205] Restraining a leg is not equivalent to removing it. Often the six legs of an insect form two alternating tripods and the leg most likely to step is the one bearing the least weight.[217, 226] Not only can changes in leg rhythm be brought about by amputation, but they occur with normal changes in gait. The mantis order[359] for quiet walking is L (left) 3, L2, R (right) 3, R2; when the mantis is excited and walking fast the rhythm is L2, R2; L3, R3; when climbing, L3, R1; L2, R3; L1, R2. In some insects the order of leg movement depends on kind of surfaces; the order is determined by proprioceptive and tactile reflexes. Locomotor reflexes are both segmental and intersegmental, and slitting one ganglion in the midline causes little disturbance, but slitting two is disruptive of locomotion. Transection between mesothoracic and metathoracic ganglia of a cockroach disrupts the rhythmic correlation between hind legs and those ahead.[217] In a caterpillar a peristaltic wave passes through nerve cord severed from lateral nerves faster than normally. Proprioceptive control would normally slow the wave.

The coordination of movements in capture of moving prey by mantids has been quantitatively analyzed.[292] When nerves to neck proprioceptors were cut, the proportion of successful hits on flies was reduced from 85 to 20 to 30 per cent; when the head was held fixed so that the eyes could not follow the prey, hits were reduced to 25 per cent; visual and proprioceptive (neck) cues could be added and subtracted by the normal free animal.[292]

In a cicada, posterior sensory stimuli cause synchronized reflex discharges of muscles of sound production; the right and left motor nerves alternate in their discharge irrespective of the side of stimulation, and central reflex time in the ganglion is 30 to 40 msec; hence the two motor systems must be controlled by

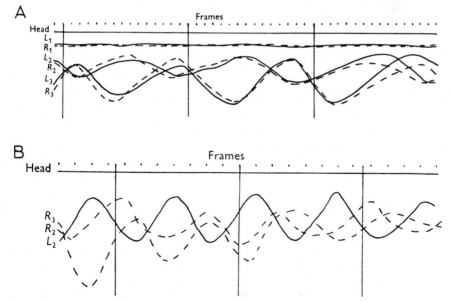

FIGURE 270. *A*, rhythm of leg movements during swimming in Dytiscus. Positions of left and right legs (L and R) plotted from successive moving pictures relative to head.

B, rhythm of leg movements following amputation of single hindleg (L3). (From Hughes, G. M.: J. Exp. Biol., vol. 35.)

one pacemaker. The motoneurons and muscle discharge at 100/sec; interneurons discharge at 200/sec; hence the rate determination is in interneurons, and right and left motoneurons respond to alternate impulses in interneurons.[176] A blowfly's feeding is controlled by a sequence of reflexes[106] (see p. 324, Chapter 11).

Other reflexes which have been analyzed are those of balance in flight and maintenance of flight (p. 446), spiracular control and ventilation (p. 174), righting, self-cleaning, and feeding. The self-immobilization reflexes (death-feigning) represent muscle tenseness maintained under rigid nervous control.

An important feature of arthropod nervous systems is what Roeder[362] calls "the parsimony of neurons." Each abdominal ganglion of a crayfish has 500 neurons; the subesophageal has 6000 and the brain has 10,000 cells, making a total of 28,700 neurons in "normal" layers plus an estimated 37,000 "small" nerve cells.[453, 454] This is to be compared with an earthworm (*Pheretima*) where each ganglion has 1100 to 1500 neurons and the suprapharyngeal ganglion has 10,800.[305, 419] Single interneurons of the circumesophageal connectives can represent several sensory fields; a few represent more than one sense modality.

Most insects have even fewer neurons. Considerable economy is effected by the small number of nerve fibers per muscle and the peripheral gradation of muscle contraction (Chapter 14). Paired giant neurons can control a complete startle response. Most insect neurons are small. The afferent axon from an abdominal stretch receptor of a crayfish enters the second root of a ganglion and sends one branch forward to the brain and another back to the caudal ganglion; most sensory neurons are shorter, but they frequently connect with interneurons in several segments.[219] The number of neurons in "brains" of cephalopods or vertebrates of comparable size or comparable behavior is many times the number in arthropods.

CEPHALIC DOMINANCE IN INVERTEBRATES

A stage in complexity of nervous function beyond local or segmental reflexes occurs with the increased importance of centers near the anterior end of the animal. Sense organs and the coordinative functions of the "brain" ganglia are concentrated at the front end of the animal.

Flatworms. In free-living flatworms the brain is associated with the eyes and other sense organs; in addition, this organ is needed for coordinated spontaneous activity. Some polyclads are inactive and less sensitive without the brain than with it, but they can be stimulated to swim. In others a rippling movement (ataxic locomotion) continues but extension, placing, and release (ditaxic locomotion), and peristalsis stop if the brain is removed or split. Planaria without brain may show extension of the pharynx and swallowing, but normal feeding behavior requires the presence of the brain.[32] In flatworms generally the directive function of the brain is important.

Annelids. An earthworm has sensory cells of various types—tactile, chemical, and light receptor—scattered throughout the epidermis, but most concentrated in the prostomium and anterior segments. Only those sense cells which are sensitive to dryness seem restricted to the prostomium. *Nereis* has fewer epidermal receptors; its effective chemoreceptors are on palps and tentacles, and instead of scattered photosensitive cells, it has several pairs of eyes on its head. After the brain is removed from an earthworm the anterior segments are lifted upward; it crawls normally, appears restless and active, it can right itself, can copulate, eat, and it burrows in a half hour as compared with the normal time of 1 to 2 minutes.[335] A nereid worm which lacks the brain no longer feeds, does not burrow, is hyperactive, and has lost its light sensitivity and most of its chemical sensitivity. After the subesophageal ganglion has been removed, there is no burrowing and nereids are nearly motionless. The brain, then, is a sensory center, and it normally has an inhibitory or restraining control over the motor centers in the subesophageal ganglion. Removal of the brain from a leech results in increased motor activity and sucking responses.[233]

An example of integrative cephalic dominance which has a simple morphological basis is found in the responses of an earthworm to light. Normally an earthworm responds negatively to lateral illumination, but after the brain is removed the direction of response is reversed.[190] If the ventral cord is transected a few segments behind the subesophageal ganglion, the anterior tip of the worm turns away from the light, but the region behind the cut bends toward the light. If one esophageal connective is cut, the worm tends to circus toward the normal side; when illuminated from the intact side it turns toward the light, but when illuminated from the operated side it turns away from the light.[334] Apparently, scattered photoreceptors set up a homolateral reflex in ventral ganglia, a positive response to light; the tracts from the prostomium and the first two segments, however, cross in the brain and elicit a negative response. The brain normally dominates, but at very low light intensities the response may be positive to light.

The brains of some polychaete worms are complex and have lobes corresponding to the specialized "mushroom bodies" of arthropods. Such lobes (corpora pedunculata) are best developed in free-swimming polychaetes which have cuticular eyes; they do not occur in oligochaetes.[180]

Arthropods. Complexity of the brain varies considerably in arthropods, but, in general, there are three regions: protocerebrum, deuterocerebrum, and tritocerebrum.[180] Most of the lateral portions of the protocerebrum are vision centers which are directly connected to the eyes; the middle and anterior portions contain the association areas: the protocerebral bridge, the central body, and the large cellular corpora pedunculata (Fig. 271). There are no corpora pedunculata in some of the lower crustaceans. The deuterocerebrum usually lies ventroanteriorly and may contain large antennal centers as well as "olfactory" lobes. The tritocerebrum lies behind and usually gives rise to nerves to the mouth parts as well as to the stomatogastric

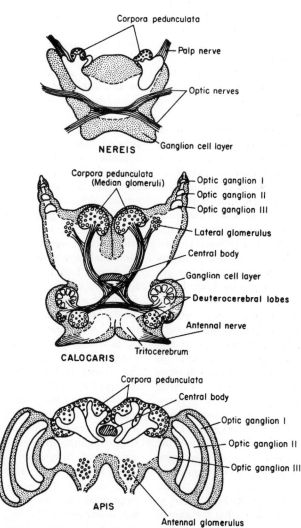

FIGURE 271. Sections of brains (supraesophageal ganglia) of several invertebrates with corpora pedunculata. Polychaete *Nereis*; crustacean *Calocaris*; a worker honeybee *Apis*. (From Hanström, B.: Vergleichende Anatomie des Nervensystems der wirbellosen Tiere. Springer.)

nerves; the tritocerebrum is continuous with the circumesophageal connectives. As in other parts of many invertebrate nervous systems, the central part of the brain is a fibrous neuropile, and a large proportion of the neurons are unipolar.

The brain is a reflex center for eyestalk and antennal movements. Optomotor reflexes of crustaceans result from a balance of sensory input, particularly from statocysts and eyes (p. 300). Maintenance of flight by flies requires wind stimulation of the antennae; hence, the ability is lost on removal of the brain.

The proportion of the brain occupied by vision centers is 0.3 to 2.8 per cent in arachnids and myriapods which have epithelial photoreceptors and ocelli, 2.9 to 9.9 per cent in lower crustaceans and insects with rudimentary compound eyes, and 33 to 80 per cent in those with highly developed compound eyes.[180] Olfactory centers are relatively less extensive in day-flying insects than in crustaceans and some night-flying insects.[180] In large insects the corpora pedunculata are larger relative to other parts of the brain than in small insects.[349]

The extensive literature dealing with brain operations in myriapods, higher crustaceans, and insects permits some general conclusions. Removal of any part of the brain which receives fibers from a sense organ is equivalent to removing that sense organ. An initial shock reaction of general incoordination usually follows an operation to the brain, but over a period of minutes or hours specific behavioral deficiencies appear. Many arthropods can compensate for removal of one eye or one antenna, but injury to the brain leaves a more permanent behavior deficiency. In insects an optic tract crosses in the midline, and there are also ipsilateral optic areas.[373] If both circumesophageal connectives are cut, reflexes of the head remain; spontaneous directed locomotion ceases although locomotion is possible under stimulation. Coordinated feeding is lacking; there may be chewing but not swallowing after brain removal. Righting and leg reflexes are unimpaired, and there may be excessive random activity of the legs. When one circumesophageal connective is cut or one lateral half of the brain destroyed, the arthropod circuses toward the intact side. Legs on the operated side tend to be flexed and low in tonus so that the animal leans toward that side.

Removing the subesophageal ganglion or cutting the cord behind this ganglion tends to stop spontaneous activity, but local segmental reflexes persist. The subesophageal ganglion is the principal motor center and is needed for coordinated walking, swimming, or flying, but the other ganglia are capable of reflexes of locomotion, autotomy, and the like; posterior ganglia are normally regulated by anterior ones.

The increased leg activity after brain removal suggests the release of ventral motor centers from inhibition by the brain. After the brain is removed from dragonfly larvae there is an increase in breathing frequency, whereas after the subesophageal ganglion is removed the breathing frequency is decreased. Death-feigning may require the brain (the spider *Celaenia*), or the feigning reaction may be present but more brief without the brain (*Ranatra*). Inhibitory action of the brain on ventral ganglia of crabs was shown by the cessation of circus movements on electrical stimulation of a transected circumpharyngeal connective.[231] Flexion of the abdomen of *Panulirus* and *Homarus* elicited by stimulation of the ventral nerve cord was diminished by simultaneous stimulation of the brain or circumesophageal connectives.

When one side of the protocerebrum of a praying mantis is removed the legs on the opposite side lose tone while legs on the operated side are more active and locomotor sequence is changed; circusing is to the normal side. After both protocerebral lobes are destroyed, leg tonus is lost on both sides, and there is locomotor restlessness; the mantis fails to avoid objects when it walks. After the protocerebrum is split, there is decreased leg movement, high tonus of neck and prothorax, and active visual following of moving objects. After the subesophageal ganglion is removed, there is no locomotion except in response to strong stimulation.[359] The subesophageal ganglion excites locomotor activity in thoracic ganglia; the protocerebral ganglion inhibits the activity of the subesophageal locomotor centers. The protocerebral centers are homolateral, are inhibited contralaterally by each other, and are strengthened by homolateral sensory input. Sometimes during mating, after clasping, the female mantis eats the male, head first, and copulation continues. If the brain only is removed from the male there is no sexual activity, but if the subesophageal ganglion also is removed copulation is completed.[359] The copulatory center in the last abdominal ganglion is inhibited by the subesophageal ganglion, removal of which releases copulatory activity. Some arthropods (female *Bombyx* and *Carcinus*) can mate although lacking the brain; others (butterflies) cannot. A hermit crab deprived of the brain will grasp a shell but will not enter it.[411]

The corpora pedunculata in arthropod brains are probably centers of complex integration; they consist of a cellular calyx and a stalk or peduncle connecting to α and β lobes. Removal of the cellular lobes releases motor activity in mantids. The percentage of the brain occupied by the corpora pedunculata is roughly correlated with complexity of behavior—none in isopods, 2 to 9.6 per cent in Odonata, Lepidoptera and Diptera, 10 to 30 per cent in decapod crustaceans, 40 per cent in worker ants.[180] However, the large size of corpora pedunculata (78.8 per cent of brain mass) in *Limulus* is not explicable by known complexity of behavior. The corpora pedunculata of bees and ants have both sensory and motor connections such that reverberating circuits are possible; β lobe to anterior motor centers and central body, α lobe to optic and antennal glomeruli.[226, 430] The electrical response in the α and β lobes of the corpora pedunculata to stimulation of the antennal nerve is a large synchronized spike of 40 to 70 msec latency, fatiguing at stimulation more frequent than 1 per second.[287] Those insects with well-developed corpora pedunculata are capable of conditioning, and conditioning is probably not limited to this part of the nervous system (p. 646). The cocoon of a *Cecropia* silkworm consists of outer and inner envelopes spun in a well-timed sequence of movements—reflexes and innate behavior. Anesthesia for one or two days by CO_2 abolishes or modifies the spinning without other evident sensory or motor impairment. Local destruction of cells or roots of the corpora pedunculata eliminated normal spinning of the two-layer envelope.[246] After local damage to the cell bodies of the unipolar or T-shaped neurons of the dorsal lobe of the brain of crabs, the branched fibers continue to function for a short time.[231]

Local stimulation of the brain of crickets can induce tracheal ventilation, locomotor movements, and sound production. Only in the corpora pedunculata is song initiated, and removal of both calyxes and protocerebral bridge and central body destroys the capacity for song; apparently the signals originate in the corpora pedunculata, the central body is the higher motor center, and the second thoracic ganglion the final motor center for song. The areas of initiation of other movements are more generalized.[215]

In summary: The brain of an arthropod is not only connected with the most important sense organs of the body, but it also exerts important integrative, particularly inhibitory, control of ventral motor centers. The comparative study of brains of arthropods should give useful information concerning interaction between environmentally and innately controlled behavior. It should be profitable to investigate localization of function within the arthropod brain and the mechanisms of interaction between brain and ventral ganglia and between subesophageal and other ventral ganglia.

Cephalopods. The cephalopod brain mass represents fusion of paired cerebral, pedal, and visceral ganglia, and it completely surrounds the esophagus. A respiratory center with regions for inspiration and expiration exists in the subesophageal portion of the brain mass.[62] Another center in the subesophageal portion regulates chromatophores.[51] The subesophageal portion of the brain mass contains brachial and pedal ganglia controlling arms and tentacles, a pedal ganglion controlling funnel and eye muscles, and a palliovisceral ganglion controlling mantle, fins, and viscera. In *Octopus* a center for pupillary closure is found in the subesophageal region.

The supraesophageal portion of the brain mass contains:[372] (1) Motor centers in the circumesophageal region—lobus basalis anterior, posterior, and lateralis, lobus pedunculi (Fig. 272C). Stimulation of these lobes elicits movements of large groups of muscles, and extirpation of one lobe results in circus movements which may be almost continuous. (2) Primary sensory centers such as the olfactory lobes, and optic lobes in the optic stalk. Stimulation of the optic lobe may result in reflex chromatophore expansion and mantle and fin movement. (3) The dorsal verticalis complex of three lobes. No direct motor responses are elicited by electrical stimulation of this region, which is evidently "associational." After removal of the verticalis complex *Sepia* can see, swim, steer properly, and capture and eat prawns, but fails to follow prawns as they disappear around a corner. Damage to the verticalis complex in *Octopus* interferes with its capacity to become conditioned (p. 646). The verticalis is similar in many properties to the associational cerebral cortex of mammals.[466]

Many locomotor reflexes of invertebrates

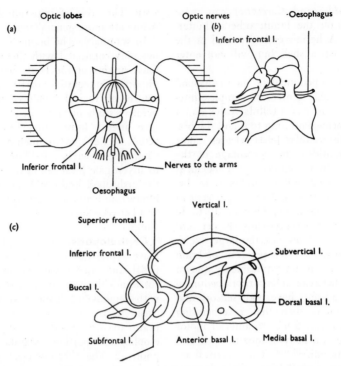

FIGURE 272. Diagrams of brain of Octopus. (*a*) brain as seen from above; (*b*) vertical longitudinal section through brain in midregion; (*c*) longitudinal section through supraesophageal lobe only. (From Wells, M. J.: J. Exp. Biol., vol. 36.)

can be described in terms of a direct relation between input and output and a switchboard type of coordination. However, locomotor reflexes show a certain amount of plasticity. Cephalic dominance is partly sensory and partly "integrative" in a sense that cannot be described by simple neuronal circuits. Complex stereotyped behavior must depend on genetically determined connections. In those centers with plastic reflexes and even more in those with modifiability and complex behavior there are central neuropiles of fine fibers usually associated with unipolar neurons. The small-fiber regions of the CNS have not been amenable to the sort of analysis which can be applied to giant neuron systems and locomotor reflexes.

SPINAL REFLEX CONTROL OF LOCOMOTION IN VERTEBRATES

The study of spinal stretch reflexes has contributed much to knowledge of synaptic transmission (see p. 600). The excitatory stretch reflexes are monosynaptic, their inhibitory phases appear to be disynaptic, that is, to have one interneuron. Two-neuron reflexes have not been studied except in mammals. In all classes of vertebrates, however, locomotion is mediated by complex multineu-

ron reflexes. During embryonic development, mass responses of muscle groups become differentiated into precisely localized responses. In phylogenetic development the spinal cord is less autonomous as the control of locomotion is pushed cephalad. Concurrent with cephalad development of reflex centers there appears more antagonism between regions of the central nervous system, cephalad regions usually inhibiting more caudal centers.

In general, each segment of the spinal cord receives two pairs of roots; the dorsal roots contain afferent fibers and a very few efferent ones; the ventral roots contain efferent (motor) fibers, both somatic and visceral (autonomic), whose cell bodies are in the ventral horn of the cord. In the many uniform segments of *Amphioxus,* dorsal and ventral roots alternate. In cyclostomes also the dorsal and ventral roots alternate; they unite and form mixed nerves in myxinoids but not in petromyzonts. From lower to higher classes of vertebrates there is a progressive reduction in number of spinal segments and in size of the caudal portion of the cord and an increase in the number of spinal tracts to and from the brain.

Cyclostomes have short-fibered ascending and descending tracts, principally of the reticular system, and ascending "Müller" neurons. In elasmobranchs and teleosts, ascending spinobulbar and spinomesencephalic tracts are present; in teleosts spinocerebellar tracts and sympathetic ganglion chains appear and also the descending vestibulospinal tract. As limbs appear, the cord enlarges in brachial and lumbar regions. Amphibians show a well-defined central gray H and great reduction in the number of spinal segments. In birds a tectospinal tract appears, whereas in lower vertebrates the tectum (part of midbrain) connects with the cord via the reticulospinal system. In mammals the corticospinals, particularly the pyramidals, appear as dominant ventral descending tracts; the spinothalamic tracts are differentiated, as are the long ascending tracts of the posterior columns. The dorsal spinocerebellar tract contains afferents from muscle spindles and tendon receptors.[276] In fish (e.g., the carp *Cyprinus*) the fastest tract (except for Mauthner fibers, p. 596) (58 to 63 m/sec) conveys tactile signals, mostly ipsilateral; the ventrolateral columns (18 to 20 m/sec) are descending motor tracts; the reticulospinals are slowest.[40] The cat spinocerebellar tract conducts at 30 to 80 m/sec in 5 to 14 μ fibers.[257]

The extent to which locomotor behavior is autonomous in the spinal cord or is determined by sensory input varies from animal class to class and from one related genus to another. The cord carries out more independent action in the lower vertebrates than in higher animals. Also the shock resulting from spinal transection is more transient in lower vertebrates. In higher classes the spinal cord is less sensitive to asphyxiation than the cerebrum.

In *Amphioxus* any local stimulus elicits a general avoiding response. Lesions to the cord show that propagation of strong undulations over the whole body and end-to-end startle responses require median giant neurons but that the rest of the cord can mediate superficial reflex waves. A swimming or crawling animal with many segments often locomotes by undulating waves which show remarkably precise timing. The nervous mechanisms of locomotion in fish have been reviewed by Healey.[185]

Spinal hagfish *Polystotrema* are inactive for long periods but upon stimulation they swim normally; undulating waves start at the anterior end, and the point of transection of the cord becomes a pacemaker for initiating swimming waves. When stimulation is vigorous, a wave may pass a cut by reflexly exciting the region beyond.

Similarly, a dogfish made spinal by transection behind the head swims much like a normal fish. Propagation appears to be by chain reflexes combined with pleurisegmental overlap of sensory and motor fields, and can proceed in an intact cord even through twelve denervated segments, although it stops at a cut in the cord. When a spinal dogfish is free from contact, a locomotor rhythm at about 40 waves per minute occurs; gentle tactile stimulation increases or inhibits this rhythm[269] (Fig. 273). The rhythmic movement of body and fins of a spinal dogfish is abolished by complete deafferentation, but the wave passes across a deafferented region of the cord, and about twenty-five segments must be intact to maintain the rhythm. Spinal dogfish also show a variety of fin reflexes, and a single segment of the cord can mediate homolateral and crossed responses.[160, 163, 269]

Spinal teleosts also show fin reflexes elicited from localized sensory areas. There appears to be much difference in autonomy of the cord from genus to genus. In the eel intrinsic spinal swimming rhythms have been postulated. Section of the cord interferes very little with undulations. The eel still swims after its skin has been removed, after muscles have been removed from a middle quarter of the body, and that region of the cord kept rigid by splints.[160, 163] In *Carassius* a reflex response of the tail shows more persistent rhythmicity after transection through the anterior medulla than after transection of the cord; hence there may be a medullary center for locomotor rhythms.[206] A spinal minnow, *Phoxinus,* blinded and free from contact with the substratum, shows spontaneous swimming movements for 8 to 10 days after cord transection.[109]

In summary: The spinal cord of fish permits complex chain reflexes, the transmission of coordinated wave patterns, and in some species may show inherent rhythms.

In amphibian evolution, after the transition from swimming to walking, the spinal cord retained much independence. A spinal frog jumps in coordinated fashion when stimulated, but not spontaneously; reflex responses, particularly of protractor muscles, remain coordinated.[162] If one or two legs are deafferented in *Bufo* there is little interference with coordinated ambulation; when three legs are deafferented, coordination is strikingly reduced. After deafferentation of all four limbs no locomotor movements occur, al-

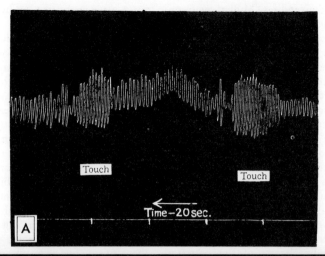

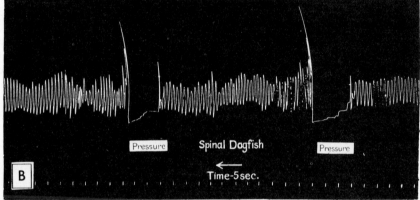

FIGURE 273. *A,* rhythmic undulations in dorsal fin of a spinal dogfish; rhythm increased when skin is touched lightly behind point of transection. *B,* rhythmic movement of dorsal fin in spinal dogfish; brief stimulation followed by inhibition when pressure was applied to body. (From Gray, J., and Sand, A.: J. Exp. Biol., vol. 13.)

though the toad can swim if labyrinths are intact. If only one leg retains both sensory and motor nerve supply and all other sensory nerves are cut, there are normal diagonal leg movements; if the motor root of the first leg is then cut, all ambulatory movements cease, and stimulation of this leg elicits only simple monophasic responses in the other limbs. In the toad, therefore, sensory and motor supply of one segment is necessary for the diagonal pattern of ambulation.[159, 162]

In contrast to the strictly reflex picture of ambulation in Amphibia is the concept of an inherent rhythm in the central nervous system which becomes established during development. Tadpoles' kept narcotized for several days show the behavior for their age without having performed the previous-stage motions. When in salamanders a supernumerary foreleg is transplanted to a position near a normal one, the corresponding muscles of the two legs contract simultaneously. If a transplanted limb is rotated 180 degrees, the grafted limb moves in perfect temporal coordination but in reverse direction to normal. The effects are similar when the limbs are deafferented. Each reinnervated muscle of the extra limb contracts synchronously with the corresponding muscle of the normal limb as if the spinal cord as a whole signaled a particular muscle.[441]

In mammals the spinal cord shows less autonomy, and shock following cord section lasts much longer than it does in lower classes.[146] When the spinal cord of a cat or dog is transected in the upper thoracic region in such a way that respiration continues, all motor reflexes are at first depressed. Flexor reflexes return in a cat in a few hours after cord transection; extensor reflexes, after several days. A spinal cat or dog cannot stand, yet when suspended it may make treading motions. A variety of intersegmental movements, both contralateral and ipsilateral, can be elicited, many obviously of primitive protective value. Single limb reflexes may coordinate many muscles, and the rhythmic scratch reflex is very complex. Visceral functions such as urination and defecation are elicited reflexly; when one leg is warmed, vasodilation may occur in the opposite one. Sexual functions such as erection of the penis, copulatory movements, and ejaculation can occur, and spinal bitches have been impregnated and delivered of puppies after a normal gestation period.[146] Deafferented sections of the cord show some "spontaneous" discharge, particularly in ventral columns. A single sensory volley may elicit rhythmic responses in the legs, even in deafferented hind limbs.

Spinal shock results from interruption of the corticospinal system, specifically of the pyramidal tract, and is greater in chimpanzees than in baboons and macaques, and less in monkeys.[146] In man, after spinal transection, reflexes are absent for 1 to 6 weeks, then flexor reflexes appear which may be flexor spasms and may be associated with defecation, urination, and sweating. Under good care, extensor reflexes return later and may become predominant over flexors.

The interaction between regions of the cord and between cord and brain increases with increase of ascending and descending columns in vertebrate phylogeny. As the brain gains importance, the spinal cord is less capable of independent control of locomotion.

The intrinsic pattern of the spinal network limits the range within which reflex control can operate. The physiological basis of the limitation is unknown, and there is a wide gap between our knowledge of two-neuron spinal reflexes and integrated locomotion. It is certain, however, that the spinal cord is much more than a complicated switchboard, and terms such as homologous function, resonance, and plasticity of the cord merely cover our ignorance of the bases of nervous integration.

EMBRYONIC DEVELOPMENT OF LOCOMOTOR COORDINATION

The sequence of development of locomotor behavior, both "spontaneous" movements and responses to stimuli, can be correlated with the development of sensory, central nervous, and effector structures. Usually, several gradients exist, the primary one from the cephalad end posteriorly, and a secondary gradient laterally from proximal to distal effectors.

Generally, a myogenic stage precedes nervous control of both spontaneous and evoked movements.

The extensive literature on embryonic behavior emphasizes a controversy over whether specific reflexes appear first and are later integrated, or whether an integrated pattern precedes the reflexes which individuate out from it. Diverging opinions result from differences in speed of appearance of adult behavior patterns in different species and from difficulties in comparing embryos which move first without appendages with those whose first movement is of appendages. The important generalization emerges, however, that reflex behavior is integrated from the beginning.

In the earthworm *Eisenia foetida* the first motile stage is a ciliated gastrula. Then follows a myogenic stage in which there are at first contractions around the stomodeum while the embryo swallows albumin; then, in response to mechanical stimulation there are peristaltic waves and local contractions. After nervous mechanisms develop, regular flexion of the head begins and the anterior end turns away from a point of stimulation. Head extension and flexion initiate the peristalsis of crawling, and withdrawal from stimuli develops and spreads backward until the whole animal is sensitive. The worm is capable of burrowing before it hatches.[333]

An extensive analysis of development of motility in the dogfish *Scyllorhinus* showed an initial myogenic phase when the myotomes of each side contracted independently, but there was some conduction along one side. At the next (neurogenic) stage, muscles were innervated but central connections incomplete, and stimulation elicited simultaneous contractions on the two sides; acetylcholine increased frequency of spontaneous contractions, but eserine and tubocurarine were without effect. Finally, the reflex stage appeared.[183, 184] A similar sequence of myogenic flexures, neurogenic movements, and reflexogenic activity is found in Salmo.[183, 184, 450] In the teleost *Aequidens* tubocurarine reduces but does not abolish body and tail contractions in early stages, but innervation appears just prior to hatching; from hatching until absorption of yolk, tubocurarine abolishes somatic motility.[55]

In embryos of the salamander *Amblystoma* Coghill[94] identified the following stages: a nonmotile stage when muscles of the somites contract in response to direct stimulation, a stage of simple flexure of the body in response to tactile stimulation, spontaneous bending into a coil and uncoiling, an S-stage, and finally a stage when the S-contractions effect locomotion. Motor and sensory neurons are present in the nonmotile stage, but bipolar commissural neurons do not appear until the coil stage. Limb and gill movements appear first in conjunction with trunk movements. Parts of limbs move first with the entire limb and later independently. The first movements are of gross regions; the total behavior complex appears early, and simple reflexes are individuated from it. In the axolotl there is a telescoping of stages, and early limb movements are independent of trunk action.[130] The anuran embryo general pattern is similar to that in *Amblystoma,* but there are marked differences in rates of development.

The development of behavior in birds and mammals likewise shows great species variability and has been summarized: chicks,[256] rats, sheep,[31] guinea pigs and rats,[84] cats, general summary.[31] Embryonic experience is combined with genetic makeup and immediate environmental stimulation in determining adult behavior.

In general there is an initial premotile stage when local contractions are elicited by direct stimulation of some muscles. The earliest definite responses to mechanical stimulation are gross reflexes of the neck (head movement) and then of the forelimbs. In the rat, limb movements occur first in conjunction with movements of the trunk; in cat, sheep, and guinea pig, limb movements appear to be independent of trunk movement; they are gross but integrated, and separate segmental movements develop later.

In the sheep fetus,[31] movements are at first (at 40 days' gestation) jerky, later smooth and sustained, indicating repetitive discharge of nerve cells. The latest movements to be developed are more sensitive to hypoxia than are earlier movement patterns. Brain transections show that the jerky movements are mediated by the bulbospinal system, are converted to sustained movement by the midbrain, and are inhibited by cephalad portions of the brain. In 1- to 2-day old kittens, reflexes are limited to neurons of the segment in which afferent impulses arrive, and no inhibition is observed. The earliest inhibition is at 3 to 5 days and has a long latency. At 6 to 12 days, after-discharge appears, and also inhibition initiated by antagonistic muscle afferents and at shorter intervals.[279] In newborn monkeys tonic innervation of muscles and grasp reflexes are dominant; then in a spastic stage limbs resist passive movement; finally discrete use of muscles appears. If in the adult monkey a premotor area of the cerebral cortex is removed, the grasp reflexes of the newborn return.

Knowledge of brain chemistry has not been sufficient to permit many successful correlations of biochemical development with neurological and behavior development.[432] In *Amblystoma* embryos, acetylcholinesterase is absent from the central nervous system in the myogenic stage and appears first in the spinal cord when the embryo begins to respond to tactile stimuli; acetylcholine appears then in progressively forward parts of the central nervous system.[50]

GROSS FUNCTIONAL EVOLUTION OF THE BRAIN

The vertebrate brain arises as an enlargement of the neural tube; the principal regions of expansion and the number of cranial nerves were established early, ten nerves in fish and twelve in mammals. There are marked differences in development of sensory regions, in elaboration of the neural core and its projections, and in the surface folding of cerebrum and cerebellum. In fish the number of visceral sensory and gustatory fibers in the facial nerve is large; in higher vertebrates the visceral centers are reduced, and in birds taste sense is atrophied. The lateral line is an important component of the tenth nerve from cyclostomes through aquatic amphibia; the cochlea is important from land amphibians through mammals; the vestibular nerve is important in all classes. Each of the sensory differences is reflected in medullary and midbrain centers.

Figure 274 shows diagrammatically the brains of animals of various classes of vertebrates. The cephalad shift in dominance parallels anatomical development, and as the cerebellum and cerebrum become more important, the opportunity for lateral connections and reverberating circuits is increased by surface folding and by projection bundles between the central core and the surface.

Medulla Oblongata and Pons. The bulbar region of the brain serves as the point of entrance and exit for most of the cranial nerves and provides way stations for their fibers in numerous sensory and motor nuclei. In addition to distributive functions, the hindbrain has many integrative functions, particularly those associated with visceral control. The hindbrain contains the respiratory center in all vertebrates; the motor outflow from this varies in different groups. Respiratory outflow in elasmobranchs is largely in the tenth cranial nerve, partly in the seventh; in skates the right and left halves of the hindbrain control respiration separately. In mammals, outflow is in the phrenic arising from the third to fifth cervical roots and in thoracic nerves to the intercostal muscles. Rhythmic electrical waves corresponding to breathing frequency have been recorded from the medulla of an isolated goldfish brain.[251] In the carp medulla, unit respiratory discharges occur 0.5 mm from the midline, 2 mm below the surface, and at the level of the acoustic tubercles.[459] The respiratory center is a swallowing center in adiaphragmatic animals, and its evolution is associated with movements of esophagus and glottis. In amphibians and reptiles, smooth muscle on the lungs is spontaneously active; contraction of this is inhibited in amphibians by the vagus during the swallowing act of breathing, while in reptiles the vagi are excitatory for the lung musculature but the vagal center is reflexly inhibited during breathing. In turtles there is evidence for

inspiratory and expiratory centers but not for a pneumotaxic (tonic) center. In mammals the respiratory center consists of lower inspiratory and upper expiratory portions. Farther forward, at the level of the pons, is a pneumotaxic center. The nature of respiratory movements and their reflex control is discussed on page 172.

The medulla contains also other regions which regulate autonomic functions. A vasomotor center is found in mammals in the anterior midmedulla, just caudal to the pons. The comparative physiology of vasomotor reflexes has been discussed previously (p. 391). The medulla of fish influences chromatophore expansion.

The most important function of the medulla through all classes of vertebrates is the control of equilibrium by the complex vestibular centers. If the eighth nerve of a dogfish is cut or the medulla injured on one side, the fish swims in a spiral, rolling toward the operated side; the eyes deviate toward the operated side, pectoral and pelvic fins are

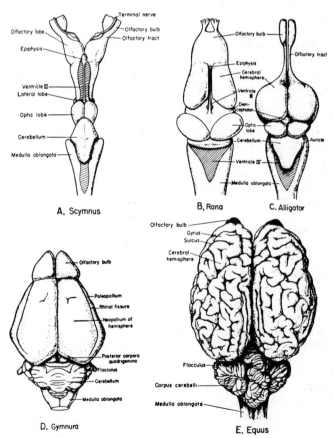

FIGURE 274.   Dorsal views of brains of a number of vertebrates: *A*, shark (*Scymnus*); *B*, frog (*Rana*); *C*, alligator, *D*, tree shrew (*Gymnura*), *E*, horse. (From Romer: The Vertebrate Body.)

elevated on the operated side and lowered on the normal side, and the dorsal fin is bent toward the intact side.[286] Electrical stimulation of the medulla dorsally behind the vagal lobes elicits downward movement of the homolateral pectoral fins and movement of the dorsal fins toward the side stimulated. Motor outflow is not only over many small neurons, but in teleosts and urodeles it is by very large neurons, particularly the Mauthner cells. The Mauthner apparatus in most fish provides for rapid flexion of the body and tail; it is not present in cyclostomes, elasmobranchs, tailless, and bottom-dwelling fish. The two Mauthner cells receive eighth nerve input both homolaterally and contralaterally; the latter is inhibitory, and one cell can affect the other.[350] Injury to the octavolateral region of the medulla of a toad causes flaccidity of homolateral limbs and extensor rigidity of contralateral ones.[2] Capacity to compensate for injury to the labyrinth by other sensory input varies; *Rana temporaria* compensates for labyrinthectomy in 6 to 8 weeks; *R. esculenta,* in 6 to 8 months.

Vestibular nuclei take on a special function with respect to posture control in birds and mammals. A dog or cat made decerebrate by transection in the lower mesencephalon shows enhancement of all extensor reflexes, diminution of flexor responses, and increased tone in all the antigravity systems of musculature. The exaggerated extension is reflex in nature and is reduced by cutting dorsal roots, particularly in the neck. Extensor rigidity also results when extrapyramidal tracts which normally inhibit the median reticular nucleus (at the vestibular level) are transected. Animals like the sloths and bats, which normally have a flexor rather than extensor antigravity response, show flexor rigidity when decerebrated.

In general, fish and amphibians transected just ahead of the medulla show nearly normal locomotion, while in birds and mammals no locomotion is possible with the medulla only; basic respiratory and cardiovascular reflexes remain. In lower vertebrates, e.g., salamanders,[188] sensory nuclei are less distinct than in mammals, and sensory fibers terminate widely in the neuropile.

Auditory nuclei in the medulla vary in complexity in different vertebrates. Electrical responses to auditory stimulation have been recorded from the acoustic lobe of carp[459] and cod.[124] In mammals, auditory nerve fibers synapse first in the cochlear nuclei; then the auditory tract continues, partly crossed and partly homolateral, via the trapezoid bodies to the inferior colliculus (midbrain); from there it passes in the medial geniculate to the acoustic cortex, which consists in higher mammals of three auditory areas.

Cerebellum. The cerebellum is an outgrowth of the dorsal lip of the fourth ventricle of the embryonic brain. Phylogenetically it is a region of interaction among afferents from vestibular and lateral line organs, descending fibers from the midbrain, and ascending fibers from the spinal cord, particularly those associated with posture and antigravity responses. The cerebellum is a small acousticolateralis commissure in cyclostomes; it shows much variation in relative size in fish, amphibians, and reptiles and has an extensively folded surface in birds and mammals. The cerebellum is concerned with fine gradations of posture and orientation in space. The archicerebellum appears as an outpocketing of the fourth ventricle in fish and amphibians and forms the posterior or flocculonodular lobe in mammals; it is primarily associated with vestibular input. The anterior portion or vermis (paleocerebellum) has extensive connections with the spinal cord, some with the tectum; it is greatly developed in birds. Laterally appear the hemispheres or neocerebellum, connected to midbrain and cerebrum via the pons, and most prominent in mammals.[253]

Removal of the cerebellum from dogfish fails to interfere with swimming, although when one half has been removed the dogfish tends to circus. In some fish (*Lophius,* flounder) there is a poorly developed cerebellum, but in others (goldfish) removal of the cerebellum leads to disordered movements, rolling from side to side, low tonus, and after unilateral decerebellation the goldfish has low tonus on the operated side and may roll toward that side.

Frogs and toads from which the cerebellum has been removed can jump and swim, although there may be symmetrical muscular rigidity. One side of the cerebellum can compensate for a defect in the other so long as vestibular (and to some extent visual) sense is unimpaired. A decerebellate lizard shows reduced spontaneity of movement and walks awkwardly. Electrical records from single Purkinje cells of the cerebellum of frogs show some high-frequency spontaneity and some responses via direct or indirect paths from other points of the brain.[285]

The cerebellum is highly developed in birds and is important in their sense of balance.

For some days after removal of the cerebellum a bird can hardly fly, walk, or stand; it falls readily to one side, but can eat and drink.[62] The vestibular centers in the medulla are normally inhibited by the cerebellum. Stimulation of the cerebellum in birds inhibits postural tonus homolaterally, and destruction of the anterior lobe produces extensor spasticity.

When the cerebellum is removed from a mammal, no single reaction is lost, but ability to balance precisely is impaired. Freshly operated-on cats and dogs may show some opisthotonus (strong extension of neck and head).[110, 111] Monkeys, after ablation of the posterior (flocculonodular) lobes, show disturbed equilibrium accompanied by tremor in volitional movement.[146] Stimulation of the anterior lobe of the cerebellum relaxes extensor muscles and diminishes decerebrate rigidity; removal of the lobe augments stretch reflexes.[391] Removal of the lateral lobes leads to muscle weakness and poor timing of movements.

Electrical activity of the cerebellum is characterized by the high frequency (150 to 250/sec) of spontaneous waves.[111] Responses from the cerebellum of mammals (mostly cats) show regions of projection of collaterals from sensory pathways—tactile, auditory, visual. In addition, stimulation of certain regions evokes motor responses, and points 1 mm apart may evoke different movements. The sensory and motor localization is not so precise as in the cerebral cortex, and there is some overlap of projection areas. There is also extensive interaction between the cerebrum and cerebellum.[388] Stimulation of specific sensory and motor areas of the cerebral cortex evokes potentials in areas of the cerebellum.[388] Stimulation of anterior and lateral cerebellum suppresses movements induced reflexly or by cortical stimulation; sometimes the cerebellum can facilitate cortically evoked movements. Diencephalic stimulation can inhibit cerebellar activity. Many of the cerebellar influences are transmitted via the bulbar reticular system. It is evident that the connections of the cerebellum are multiple and that it can regulate and be regulated by many parts of the brain, particularly those concerned with movement.

Lateral conduction on the surface of the cat cerebellum occurs at 0.35 to 0.5 m/sec for short distances (5 mm) in fibers of the molecular layer which can synaptically affect the Purkinje neurons.[110, 111] Strychnine, which blocks central inhibitory synapses, does not excite isolated areas of cerebellum as it does cerebrum; because there are fewer inhibitory synapses in the cerebellum, injected strychnine can stimulate the cerebellum only indirectly.[169, 171]

Midbrain. The midbrain (mesencephalon) is an important integrating center in lower vertebrates; it retains important nuclei of the optic system (superior colliculi) and adds auditory centers (inferior colliculi) in higher vertebrates. *Amphioxus* has a reticular mesencephalon. In cyclostomes, elasmobranchs, bony fish, and amphibians the dorsal portion is the tectum and receives terminal fibers of the visual system. In some fish the tectum has five cell layers; some of the cells resemble pyramidal cells of the mammalian cortex. By correlating electrical responses from the surface of the tectum of tench and carp with local stimulation of the retina, Buser[79, 81, 82] has mapped point for point the representation of the retina on the contralateral tectal cortex (Fig. 275). Electrical stimulation of the tectum (trout) elicits contralateral eye movements and movements of head and body; hence sensory and motor elements overlap.[8] In dogfish, eye movements elicited by midbrain stimulation are homolateral. A single shock to the optic nerve elicits fast and slow electrical responses from the fish tectum, the fast in incoming optic fibers, the slow in radial neurons oriented so that the polarity of the wave reverses in the midlayers.[79, 81, 82, 374] Rhythmic waves in the codfish and goldfish tectum increase in frequency on illumination of the eye, and responses may follow photic stimuli up to 40/sec; a thalamic contribution to this response is possible.[124, 374] The tectum also integrates other systems, such as the proprioceptive and exteroceptive systems of urodeles. Efferent tracts go from the tectum to cerebellum and to motor nuclei in the brain stem.

The ventral portion of the midbrain is the tegmentum, and in addition to ascending-descending tracts, this region contains the nuclei of the nerves to eye muscles. The tegmentum receives fibers from thalamus and forebrain and, beginning with reptiles, the reticular portion of it becomes differentiated as the red nucleus.

Motor function of the midbrain (optic lobes) in amphibia was examined by Abbie[2] using stimulation and lesions. In a toad, motor representation of the body is anteroposterior, movement of the optic bulb is elicited homolaterally, and a strong inspiratory response occurs on stimulation. After removal of forebrain and especially of cerebellum, stimula-

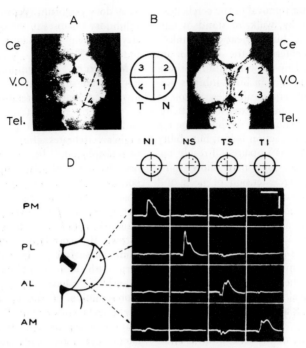

FIGURE 275. *A-C*, projection of retina (*B*) of carp (*A*) and tench (*C*) to optic lobes (*V.O.*) of brain: (*Tel.*) forebrain, (*Ce*) cerebellum; numbers *1, 2, 3, 4* correspond to lower nasal, upper nasal, upper temporal, and lower temporal quadrants of retina.

D, correspondence between response recorded from different portions of optic lobes and retinal quadrants. *NI*, lower nasal; *NS*, upper nasal; *TS*, upper temporal; *TI*, lower temporal quadrant of retina. For each region of stimulation there are four points of recording on left optic lobe; *PM*, posterior median, *PL*, posterior lateral, *AL*, anterolateral, *AM*, anteromedian. 50 msec and 200 μV calib. (From Buser, P., and Dussardier, M.: J. Physiol. Paris, vol. 45.)

tion of the tectum is more effective. Injury to midbrain results in hypertonia. Motor control by the midbrain in *Hyla* and *Lymnodynastes* is mainly crossed; in *Bufo* it is bilateral. Electrical records from the optic lobes of a frog show that the contralateral response to illumination of the retina is greater than the homolateral, but there is not so much crossing as in fish and birds.[348] Horizontal and vertical meridians of the retina of a frog are projected diagonally across the contralateral optic lobe.[151] An *Amblystoma* larva reaches a stage (Harrison's stage 40) when the bulbospinal apparatus loses its autonomy in controlling locomotion and the midbrain becomes essential; tectobulbar and tectospinal connections are then present.[108, 188] A center for the warning croak of a mating male frog is located in the base of the tectum;[18] a portion of the tegmentum is needed for normal spawning movements of male frogs.

In the pigeon tectum eight cellular layers are identified. Local photic stimulation of the retina elicits a response from projection areas of the outer three layers within 25 msec and from deeper layers in 50 msec.[179]

In mammals, reflex closure of the eye in response to flashes or approaching objects is mediated via the superior colliculi. Pupillary constriction requires the anterior midbrain, just ahead of the colliculi. Most visual responses, however, require the visual cortex, and the optic tract branches at the lateral geniculate (posterior diencephalon) to send some fibers to the superior colliculus, but the main tract goes to the cerebral cortex. A few cells of the lateral geniculate receive afferents from both optic nerves,[46, 47] and different layers of the optic tectum (superior colliculus) give characteristic responses to optic nerve stimulation.[308] The inferior colliculi may serve for some rapid auditory reflexes. A cat without its auditory cortex can discriminate tones and detect sound of low intensity; this ability is lost after the inferior colliculi too are removed.[413] When the brain is transected anterior to the midbrain, dogs and cats can right themselves and stand awkwardly, but primates are unable to stand. Local stimulation of the superior colliculus in cats elicits discrete eye movements. After the visual (striate) cortex is destroyed, cats and dogs show some visual discrimination; monkeys show less, and in man discrimination between light and dark seems to be lost.

The midbrain of fishes and amphibians is the region of highest integration and controls the most complex behavior which these animals show. In mammals the midbrain retains the regulation of restricted visual and auditory reflexes, and complex integration has moved forward.

Diencephalon. The importance of the thalamus, hypothalamus, and associated structures is increasingly recognized by neurophysiologists. In fish the thalamus has olfactory connections, and it connects the forebrain with the tectum; however, it is not well understood functionally.

In amphibians the thalamus contains several regions which may serve as relays to and from the forebrain hemispheres. The posterior part of the dorsal thalamus of a salamander receives many collaterals from the optic tracts. The posterior part of the epithalamus is the habenula, a structure characteristic of lower vertebrates; it has connections from forebrain lobes, thalamus, tectum, and bulbar regions; hence it must have important integrative functions. Frogs from which the thalamus has been removed are inactive and do not jump voluntarily.[62] Slow electrical waves are found in the thalamus, and stimulation of this region alters the intrinsic rhythm and initiates responses in the forebrain lobes.[86]

The thalamus of birds and mammals contains many sensory nuclei which, in mammals, are important relays to the cerebrum. In the ventral nucleus of the cat thalamus, for example, there is contralateral representation of cutaneous sense endings from tail, face, and extremities. Electrical rhythms recorded from parts of the thalamus can be of the same frequency as those of the cortex, and cortical rhythms seem to depend on reverberating circuits to and from parts of the thalamus. Stimulation of any of several reticular portions has a recruiting effect on the cortex and sets large association areas, also some motor cortex, into activity.[394] Stimulation of other reticular regions (lateral to the massa intermedia in cat) induces sleep, replaces the usual 8 to 10 cycle rhythm by a 2 to 4 cycle one.[9, 191] Still other areas, when electrodes are implanted, are favorable for self-stimulation by the rat or monkey.

The hypothalamus has important connections with the hypophysis and contains neurosecretory cells (p. 545). Some of the hormones stored and released from the posterior pituitary are produced in the hypothalamus, for example, the hormone regulating urine flow in amphibians and mammals (p. 45) and skin permeability in amphibians (p. 33). In the hypothalamus are the temperature-sensitive cells which constitute the "thermostat" of birds and mammals (p. 259). The hypothalamus also contains osmoreceptors which form the sensory side of the water-conserving hormonal arc. Stimulation of the hypothalamus (goats and sheep) induces drinking; stimulation caudal to the optic chiasma results in hyperphagia.[259] Stimulation of the supraoptic nucleus initiates the liberation of the hormone which causes the flow of milk.[15] Thus the hypothalamus is the neural seat of numerous autonomic and endocrine functions. It is important in regulation of emotional reactions, and it cooperates with certain parts of the forebrain (especially rhinencephalon) in complex instinctive behavior.

Telencephalon. The telencephalon is absent from *Amphioxus* but is present in all classes of vertebrates, where it has evolved in association with the paired olfactory nerves. In cyclostomes and elasmobranchs the primitive pallium (cortex) known as paleocortex contains secondary olfactory fibers, and the paleocortex is represented in higher vertebrates by the pyriform lobes (amygdala). The archipallium of teleosts contains tertiary olfactory neurons and becomes the hippocampus of higher classes. Birds have a limited, smooth cortex; the multilayered folded cerebral cortex occurs only in mammals. Inside the forebrain, beneath the cortex, are compact structures such as the corpus striatum which is present in fish and which in birds constitutes most of the forebrain. In mammals the neostriatum contains basal nuclei which are intimately connected with the thalamus. The nonolfactory neocortex is already well developed in primitive mammals. In higher mammals it contains six recognized layers, the sum of which may be as much as 100 cells thick in higher primates. From the monotremes and marsupials to higher mammals there is an increase in total surface by folding and formation of sulci between gyri. The total number of neurons in the human cortex has been estimated at 10^{10} and that of extrinsic ascending or descending neurons at 10^8. Most of the cortical connections are therefore within the cortex itself, horizontal or vertical from one cellular layer to another.

The function of regions of the cerebral cortex has been studied by various means: by ascertaining anatomical connections, by electrical and chemical (strychnine) stimulation and observation of motor and autonomic responses, by extirpation followed by observation of defects in behavior, by recording electrical activity of the cortex in response to sensory stimulation and excitation of other parts of the brain, and, in operated-on humans, by conscious responses to local cortical stimulation.

The forebrain (rhinencephalon) of fish is essentially an olfactory brain, and responses to chemical stimulation of the olfactory organs are superposed on spontaneous electrical rhythms.[7] Electrical waves from the telencephalon of codfish are slower (7/sec) and smaller than those from the optic lobes (8 to 13/sec alpha waves).[124] Spontaneous rhythms in goldfish cerebellum are fast (25 to 35/sec and 170 to 200/sec), from the mesencephalon 7 to 14/sec and from the forebrain 4 to 8/sec.[374]

Removal of forebrain from elasmobranchs and teleosts causes no readily observed disturbance of posture and locomotion. Fish without forebrains (*Carassius*,[224] *Phoxinus,* and *Gobio*) show nearly normal spontaneous activity, speed of locating and seizing food, and escape from disturbance; they do show less ability to react in a nonreflex manner, less variability in movement of opercula and eyes, less tendency to aggregation. *Holocentrus* lacking its forebrain can still learn to feed from the experimenter's hand. Removal of the forebrain from nest-building sticklebacks (*Gasterosteus*) caused no defects in posture, feeding, or swimming, but nests were not completed and building was erratic.[377] Sunfish (*Lepomis*) from which the forebrain was removed, were slow to learn and rarely initiated fighting although, once stimulated, they could show aggressive reactions. The ventricles of the forebrain of dipnoan fish are dilated; in amphibians some nonolfactory fibers enter the expanded hemispheric vesicles, but there is no superficial gray matter. Electrical stimulation of the forebrain of amphibians, as in fishes, elicits no motor responses.[2] The forebrain of a frog shows spontaneous electrical activity even when it is isolated. Removal of the forebrain from frogs, toads, and salamanders tends to reduce spontaneous movements and active feeding. Comparable reduction in foraging does not result when eyes and nasal organs are removed from amphibian embryos without brain interference.

Reports disagree as to whether local stimulation of the forebrain of reptiles can elicit motor responses. In the lizard *Lacerta* the motor responses caused by stimulation of the tectum are modified by simultaneous stimulation of the forebrain. After removal of the forebrain, lizards became lethargic and failed to explore, drink, or feed, apparently because they could no longer recognize objects.[329] Stimulation of the midbrain of lizards enhanced electrical activity in the forebrain and elicited seizure-type responses.[456]

In birds the existence of specific excitable areas in the cortex has not been established. Removal of the hemispheres from pigeons made the birds listless, but they could maintain postural equilibrium, could erect feathers, and maintain body temperature: the operated-on birds failed to feed initially and gave little attention to threatening approach. Without cortex but with the striatum intact some birds mated and reared young[333] and could be conditioned to lights and sounds.[420] Stimulation of the striatum elicited movements of the beak and other appendages; removal of large parts of the striatum caused severe behavioral defects,[364] and defensive conditioning was no longer possible. Tactile and auditory paths project to the striatum of pigeons, and responses there have twice the latency of the corresponding responses in mammalian sensory cortex.[126]

Mammals in the series from monotremes to primates show a wide range of cortical function, particularly in motor and sensory localization. The number of discrete movements that can be elicited by electrical stimulation is quoted as fewer than ten in monotremes and marsupials,[62] twenty-eight in an anteater, and several hundred in higher primates. The monotremes *Echidna*[155] and *Tachyglossus*[1] have a band of motor cortex with gross representation, from above downward, of tail, hind legs, trunk, forelegs, and head; the motor cortex activates a long corticospinal tract, there being no pyramidal tract. In *Ornithorhynchus,* however, a large portion of the cortex is excitable, with overlapping representation of forelimbs, head, and eyelids. In marsupials also the excitable areas are poorly defined, there is much overlap for different body regions, and hind limbs and tail are poorly represented.[1] Removal of the excitable area from the opossum causes temporary weakness of the forefeet; removal of cortex plus striatum causes contralateral paralysis and failure to climb and maintain balance, although the animal can eat if food touches the mouth. The opossum lacks a corpus callosum and connection between the two lobes is by anterior commissures, by the thalamus and other lower cross tracts.[293] In the hedgehog *Erinaceus* the neocortex is relatively small, electrical responses to olfactory stimulation are observed in the pyriform area and olfactory bulb, and the motor cortex is less well defined than in higher mammals.[17] In the porcupine *Erethrizon* quill erection can be elicited by stimulating the tectum but not the cortex; two-thirds of the dorsolateral surface of the hemispheres is somatic sensory and motor; auditory and visual areas are relatively small; three auditory areas occur.[261] Transection of the corpus callosum in rats has little effect, but in cats and monkeys it greatly impairs interocular transfer.[389]

In all higher mammals there appear to be two or three areas for each sensory modality, the primary, secondary, and tertiary regions

in decreasing magnitude of response[80, 461] (Fig. 276).

In rodents there are extensive motor areas, stimulation of which elicits movement of discrete groups of muscles. Rats lacking the occipital visual areas (striate cortex) show greater difficulty in a maze than when blind.[309] Decorticate rabbits can distinguish light and darkness. Dogs from which all of the cortex is removed show more severe deficiencies than rabbits; they are blind and nearly deaf although the pupils constrict to bright light; they lose conditioned behavior but are able to stand. Sensory areas of the cat cortex have been well mapped. The vestibular nerve projects to the anterior descending limb of the suprasylvian gyrus but overlaps the arm and face tactile areas anteriorly and the auditory area posteriorly;[239] removal of the vestibular projection area alone does not cause imbalance, but removal with the

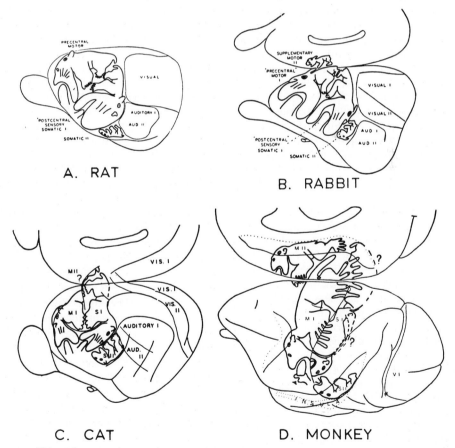

FIGURE 276. Diagrams of cerebral cortex of rat, rabbit, cat, and monkey showing localization of primary and secondary motor (MI and MII) and somatic sensory areas (SI and SII), and also primary and secondary visual and auditory areas. Orientation of body area representation shown as homunculus. Each brain outline corresponds to lateral surface of hemisphere; upper portion of each corresponds to mesial surface. (From Woolsey, C. N.: *in* Biological and Biochemical Basis of Behavior, edited by H. F. Harlow and C. N. Woolsey. University of Wisconsin Press.)

inferior colliculus as well results in serious equilibrium defects. Taste (chorda tympani stimulation) lies lateral and rostral to the tactile zone for the face but overlaps the tactile area of the tongue.[321] Tactile areas are extensive on the parietal surface in a mole.[228] The auditory areas are especially large in cetaceans, e.g., the dolphin.[255]

Localization in the cortex of primates has been extensively studied, but only a few examples can be mentioned.[193] The retina is represented point for point on the occipital cortex (striate area), with different amounts on the contralateral side in different species. Primary tactile areas are in the postcentral gyrus of the parietal lobe; secondary areas lie below and laterally. The tactile areas correspond in size to the more important sensory input; hand and face areas are large in monkey, mouth parts in rabbits, claws and forelimb areas in cats, and face area in dogs. The size of the tail area of monkeys corresponds to the prehensile use of this appendage in the series: $Ateles > Cebus > Macacus$.[193] Auditory areas in the lateral temporal lobes show projection from regions of the cochlea, hence of sound frequencies. In man the primary somatic sensory area is contralateral; the secondary, largely ipsilateral. In the somatic sensory cortex of the cat, individual neurons within a narrow cylinder respond to the same skin touch or pressure or joint rotation, and there is some overlap of 1 to 2 mm peripheral sensory areas in adjacent columns; hence a vertical organization of the somatic sensory cortex exists.[295]

Electrical stimulation of motor areas elicits responses of groups of muscles, exciting some and inhibiting their antagonists; delineation corresponds more to discrete movements than to individual muscles. The primary motor points in primates lie in the precentral gyrus with areas for feet and legs dorsally, then, progressing downward, for body, arms, neck, face, and tongue. Corresponding sensory points lie opposite on the postcentral gyrus (Fig. 276). Simultaneous proprioceptive stimulation reinforces cortical motor stimulation and changes the pattern of localization.[153] In rats the somatic face area overlaps the masticatory motor area, and in it responses are obtained also to stimulation of sensory fibers in the chorda tympani and ninth nerve.[36] Ahead of the motor cortex lies the premotor area (area 6) which effects movement by way of the motor area. Removal of premotor cortex from man leads to loss of acquired skilled movements. Also anterior to the motor area are regions regulating eye movements and respiration; distributed in the frontal lobes are regions concerned with autonomic function. The principal descending tracts are the pyramidals which go to anterior horn cells in the cord and are largely (85 per cent in man) crossed.

The extreme rostral portions of the cortex (prefrontal areas) are "association" areas, stimulation of which elicits no motor response.[284] Removal of this region by frontal lobotomy in humans results in "intellectual deficit" in respect to insight and foresight and reduces responses to emotional tension and the "worry tendency." Removal of the prefrontal lobe from monkeys causes hyperactivity and impairs performance in delayed-response problems.[431] The percentage of the cortex with specific extrinsic (sensorimotor) connections becomes less and intrinsic (intrathalamic) connections more in mammals with considerable "mentation"—primates, porpoises, elephants.[255, 331] Association areas which are silent to electrical stimulation occur in various lobes—occipital, parietal, and especially temporal. In human patients with psychomotor epilepsy, the epileptic patterns can be evoked by local stimulation on the superior and lateral surfaces of the temporal lobe.[322] "Interpretive cortex" occurs below the auditory portion of the temporal lobe (Fig. 277), and its stimulation in conscious humans calls up auditory and visual illusions, fear, disgust, and other emotions.[322]

The oldest part of the cerebral cortex retains some olfactory function but has assumed important autonomic regulation in higher mammals.[6] Cetaceans do not have olfactory organs or an olfactory cortex, but the paleocortex has assumed other functions. Olfactory stimulation of mammals elicits responses primarily in the olfactory bulb, amygdala, and pyriform cortex.[296] The hippocampus has some olfactory connections but, together with other parts of the limbic system, has important connections with the hypothalamus, hence autonomic functions.[166] Removal from monkeys of the amygdala overlying the pyriform cortex results in placidity and alters sex and feeding behavior.[165] Electrical stimulation of many parts of the limbic systems has autonomic effects—cardiovascular, gastrointestinal, pupillary, and other responses.[146]

Quadripedal vertebrates show a variety of placing reactions of their legs—hopping when feet are dragged laterally, foreleg placing on visual approach to a surface or on tactile stimulation of the throat. In cats, dogs, and monkeys, hopping reactions are lost when the contralateral sensory-motor cortex is removed and are retained when all but these gyri are ablated. In rats, placing reactions are controlled by a large area approximately one-third of the cortex, and hopping may be subcortical. In the alligator and lizard, proprioceptive placing remains when all of the brain ahead of the mesencephalon is removed, but placing fails contralaterally after removal of a lateral half of the midbrain (not tectum alone).

The cerebral cortex is also distinguished by a certain equipotentiality of function. Although there is point-for-point projection on the primary visual cortex, deficiencies in learned visual reactions occur in rats in proportion to the amount of cortex removed, largely irrespective of location.[260] Removal of visual cortex from monkeys may cause loss of a learned visual habit, but the habit may be relearned. Auditory learning can occur in

dogs when any of three auditory regions is intact.[11]

Such observations led Lashley to the concept of "mass action" in the cerebral cortex. Localization of sensory and motor function is not so precise as was formerly supposed; there are several sensory and motor areas for each body region, and "integrative" functions show ready cortical substitutions.

Intimate corticothalamic relations are indicated by changes in both cortical and thalamic electrical activity after undercutting a cortical area without disturbing the circulation. The alpha waves are lost although the slab of cortex may show some repetitive responses to direct stimulation[78] or may be spontaneously active.[222] In intact brains repetitive cortical responses due to corticothalamic reverberations can be elicited by stimulation of ascending tracts or by a click or flash stimulus.[90]

Alpha rhythms are at a frequency of 5/sec in rabbit, 7 to 8/sec in cat, 8 to 9/sec in

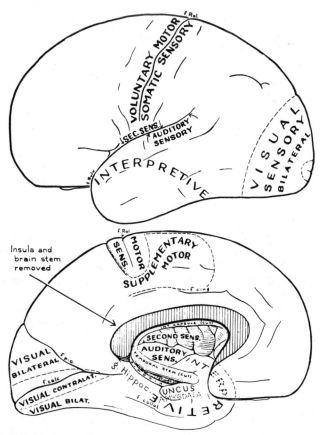

FIGURE 277. Left cerebral hemisphere of man. Lateral surface shown above and mesial surface below. In lower drawing the brain stem removed to expose inner banks of sylvian fissure and superior surface of temporal lobe. Interpretative cortex extends from lateral to superior surface of temporal lobe. (From Penfield, W.: Science, vol. 129.)

monkey and 10/sec in man. Brain waves are absent from human infants at birth, appear as slow waves (not true alpha) at about 3/sec at 3 months of age, are slightly faster at 1 year, and the slow waves are replaced by the normal 10/sec alpha at 10 years.[267] Puppies show some rhythmic waves at 18 to 20 days and stable alpha waves at 4 to 5 weeks.[92] The rhythmic cortical activity is interrupted by sensory stimulation, for example, by a visual pattern. This effect of visual stimulation first appears in children at about 3 years of age. Similarly, the slow rhythms of sleep are interrupted by arousal stimuli; the arousal reaction appears at about 5 years of age. By recording from the cortex by multiple electrodes it is shown that patterns of waves originate at certain regions and sweep slowly (0.5 to 0.36 m/sec) over the cortex, presumably involving corticothalamic connections throughout.[266] It is suggested that the alpha waves function as scanners, keeping the cortex alert for detection of ascending signals. Alpha waves regulate accessibility of cortex to incoming messages. In man, motor response to light has the shortest latency during the descending phase of an alpha wave.[268]

The threshold of a spontaneously active cell (frog brain) is 2.5 to 3.5 times lower than that of an inactive neuron, and the excitability is altered by feedback from interneurons connected to the one being stimulated.[399] Extracellular records by microelectrodes show in mammalian cortex spikes and slow waves, separable by anoxia or Nembutal. Slow waves at a depth resemble surface alpha waves and are not related to the spikes. Spikes are largest in the fifth layer where the largest nerve cells are located. Longer waves up to 100 msec may represent summation of 15 to 20 msec waves. Stimulation of the thalamo-cortical projection system elicits waves whose origin is at various depths. At the surface they are negative; those in unspecific terminals reverse at depths ranging from 0.4 to 1.5 mm; those in specific sensory bundles reverse at 0.6 to 0.8 mm.[90, 264] When the cortex is stimulated directly there is a surface-negative spike (in apical dendrites), then a prolonged wave; these conduct in the monkey laterally at 0.6 m/sec and in the cat at 1 m/sec. Below 1 mm the first wave is reversed.[323] A cut 1 mm deep weakens but does not abolish the surface-conducted response; a cut 3 mm deep does abolish it. Strychnine enhances the second or slow wave,[171] and D-tubocurarine blocks it. The slow wave is a synaptic-type potential from

dendrites, and it is postulated that it is caused by recurrent collaterals of pyramidal cells connecting via interneurons to dendrites of other pyramids and traveling at 0.5 to 1 m/sec. Convulsive responses are caused in cerebral cortex by strychnine, which blocks inhibitory synapses and releases excitatory ones, and inhibited by tubocurarine, which blocks excitatory responses. Inhibitory endings must be abundant in the cerebral cortex in contrast to the cerebellum, where strychnine is ineffective when applied directly.[342]

Reticulum. In addition to specific sensory and motor tracts, projection areas, and sensorimotor correlation centers and association areas of the brain, there is in the central neuraxis a network of interlacing small neurons and nonspecific conduction tracts known as the reticulum or neuropile or centrencephalic system. This constitutes much of the medulla, pons, tegmentum, and diencephalon, and receives collaterals of all sense modalities; it modulates lower motor activity, projects by nonspecific tracts to many areas of the cortex, particularly to the older regions.[165] It also receives descending impulses from the cortex. Stimulation of the bulbar or thalamic reticulum evokes cortical waves like those on awakening from sleep or in EEG arousal, and these recruited or arousal responses are recorded from various association areas of the cortex, with some motor overlap. General arousal results from stimulating anterior parts of the reticulum (thalamus); specific alerting, from posterior parts (pons and midbrain). In anesthesia the ascending reticular activating system is the first to lose its function; conduction in sensory tracts persists, but perception and sensory discrimination are lost along with reticular activation.[267, 268] Lesions in the various parts of the reticulum result in permanent sleep or coma. Electrical recording from reticular centers—midbrain tegmentum, red nucleus, median thalamus, subthalamus, lateral hypothalamus—gives responses to sound and to somatic nerve stimulation.[278, 394] Reticular activity is also modulated and often inhibited by stimulating the vermis of the cerebellum.[294]

Stimulation of the reticulum inhibits decerebrate rigidity; stimulation of the cerebral cortex may enhance some unit responses in the reticulum but inhibit others.[294] Stimulation of tegmental reticulum increases cortical potentials which are being evoked by thalamus or optic path stimulation but inhibits by occlusion if the test stimulus is to peripheral sense organs.[54] In man there is some projection from the centrencephalic system (reticulum) to the lateral surface of the temporal lobe, and stimulation of this part of the cortex in conscious patients calls up recollections or prior experiences, sometimes hallucinatory, often sequential in time. Penfield suggests that conscious integration occurs in the centrencephalic system combined with projection and reprojection to the temporal cortex.[322] The cortex (monkey) gives a single electrical response to two light flashes to the eyes less than 50 msec apart, but if the reticulum is simultaneously stimulated two cortical waves show that the two flashes are resolved. In addition, the time for choice in a visual pattern is less if the reticulum is simultaneously stimulated by implanted electrodes.[268] The reticular activating system is under the influence of corticofugal paths, and the cortex regulates excitation throughout the neuraxis[143] (Fig. 278). Perception of a visual pattern long outlasts the interruption of surface brain waves, presumably by involvement of the reticulum. When spontaneous activity in single reticular units is followed it is found that activation can be by a wide sensory (tactile) field and that spatio-temporal sensory patterns are reflected by alteration in spontaneous firing.[13] Reticular stimulation simultaneously with sensory stimulation may cause responses in further central regions.[270]

The seat of consciousness and memory is not precisely localized, but much cortical damage can occur without loss of consciousness; damage to the reticulum more readily interrupts a state of wakefulness. Interaction between cortex and reticulum and continuous sensory bombardment seem necessary for consciousness. The rhinencephalon, the older part of the neocortex, is an important part of the projection of the reticulum, and stimulation of the hippocampus can inhibit subcortical arousal mechanisms. This part of the rhinencephalon is closely related also to the temporal lobe. Stimulation of the hippocampus induces fear, rage, attention, and can inhibit subcortical arousal mechanisms. Hence the oldest part of the forebrain is concerned with olfaction, emotion, and memory. In hibernating animals awakening activity starts in the rhinencephalon which activates large subcortical areas. Animals (rats, monkeys) with electrodes implanted in reticular areas of hypothalamus and midbrain seem to "enjoy" stimulating themselves; there are a few regions in which they avoid stimulation. Regions which are favorable for self-stimulation lie in the rhinencephalon and basal ganglia of the forebrain, the hypothalamus, and tegmentum. The spots for negative conditioning or avoidance are more restricted than the positive or reward zones, but there is mutual inhibition between the "reward" and "punishment" regions.[266, 306] It is suggested that the cortex receives sensory signals, amplifies and encodes them, then feeds them back to the

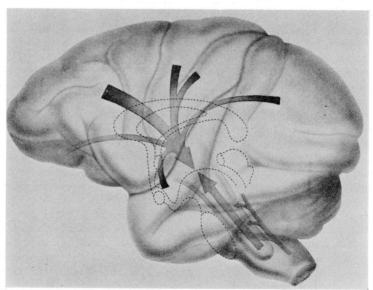

FIGURE 278. Schematic view of monkey brain showing ascending reticular system in core of brain stem, receiving collaterals from afferent paths, and also efferent connections from cortex. (From French, J. D., Hernandez-Peon, R., and Livingston, R. B.: J. Neurophysiol., vol. 18.)

older parts of the midbrain and paleocortex, that motivational and emotion-controlling regions occur in the rhinencephalon, basal ganglia, hypothalamus, and tegmentum.[307]

The reticular system has not been studied in any nonmammals although it constitutes a large part of the neuraxis in all vertebrates, and a comparable neuropile of fine fibers is present in invertebrate ganglia.

PERSISTENT PHENOMENA IN CENTRAL NERVOUS SYSTEMS

Study of two-neuron reflexes in mammals and of giant neuron synapses in squid and crustaceans has contributed much to an understanding of synaptic transmission. Analyses of multineuron reflexes and the mapping of projections of sensory and motor tracts treat central nervous systems as switchboards or, at most, as computing machines. The events of transmission, synaptic facilitation, inhibition, and even of reverberating circuits are transient, lasting at most a few hundred milliseconds. Much of taxic behavior can be explained by the switchboard view of the nervous system, yet the most adaptive properties of nervous systems are more complex and elusive. Among the most important phenomena of central nervous systems are variability and modifiability of responses, alterations of patterns which persist for long times —seconds, days, lifetimes.

Modifiability of Transmission. Posttetanic (postactivation) enhancement or increased responsiveness for some seconds or minutes following a repetitive activation occurs in many synapses and neuromuscular junctions. It appears to be an alteration in the presynaptic endings, sometimes referable to persistent electrical changes or to increased synaptic transmitter liberation. In monosynaptic spinal reflexes the excitatory postsynaptic potentials are enhanced; polysynaptic reflexes have greater amplitude; at motor endplates there is increased EPP and quantal liberation of transmitter. In partially curarized sympathetic ganglia the synaptic potentials are increased. Potentiation of the gastrocnemius monosynaptic reflex reaches a peak in 15 to 30 seconds after tetanus and persists for 5 minutes; the effect is primarily presynaptic.[271] Disuse of a spinal reflex center for a month following cutting of the dorsal roots is followed by reduced monosynaptic reflexes which can then be restored by tetanus.[113] Synaptic potentials are reduced by disuse or after the soma changes following cutting of a motor axon, and they are enhanced by exercise.[118, 119] Hence monosynaptic reflexes are modifiable.

Some types of facilitation may build up during periods of many seconds or minutes, e.g., in the nerve centers involved in copulation. In the mammalian cortex, response in one region may alter excitability in another region for some seconds, spreading depression.

Reference was made previously (p. 623) to the changes in arthropod coordination according to gait or number of appendages; these changes indicate flexibility in switching from one pathway to another. In a variety of transplantations of limb buds in amphibian larvae, of nerve exchanges, and reinervation of both muscles and sense organs from abnormal roots, normal function is resumed.[389] This suggests that each growing nerve, motor or sensory, receives specifications from its end-organ which determine its central connections. In similar experiments on adult mammals, and to a large extent on adult amphibians, no such functional alteration according to end-organ is attained. It is probable that neurons are plastic in their connections during embryonic development, and the stage at which specificity of a given neuron is established may vary in different regions and animals.

Another striking example of flexibility is the equivalence of many integrative parts of a brain, the mass action principle of Lashley[260] (p. 641). Cortical ablation in rats prior to or following training indicates that, within limits, defects in discrimination and maze behavior depend less on the region than upon the amount of cortex removed. Similar mass effects of the verticalis complex on learning by an octopus have been noted.

Conditioned Reflexes. The most extensively studied of persistent alterations in central responsiveness are phenomena grouped under the heading "conditioned reflexes." These constitute a large chapter in physiological psychology. Correlation of conditioned responses with level of organization of nervous systems may lead to an understanding of the nervous basis for learning. Conditioned behavior has been reported for animals of all the phyla where it has been carefully sought (see references 347 and 265 for references to older literature). Psychological theory has undergone extensive and continuing revision,[182, 186, 192] but little progress has been made in understanding the cellular basis of conditioning.

One ethological classification of learning recognizes the categories of habituation, conditioning, trial-and-error learning, insight learning and imprinting at an early age.[412] The following neurophysiological levels of modification of response may be recognized:

1. *Habituation.* Neural modification may result from repeated stimulation over one sensory pathway such that changes occur in the quantitative relationships between the intensity of a stimulus (S) and the size of response (R). The effectiveness of the stimulus may be either increased or decreased, for example, so that $\frac{1}{2}S \rightarrow R$, or $2S \rightarrow R$. Central modification must be distinguished from sensory adaptation by making sure that the altered response due to repeated stimulation is not in the sense organ. An example of decreased central excitability is extinction or "fatigue" of a behavior response on repeated sensory stimulation. Also, animals sometimes respond differently to different intensities of a stimulus, and the neural modification on repetition may consist in altering the range within which the response to the low intensity is elicited. One type of habituation, the "recognition" of irrelevance of extraneous stimuli may be a component in all higher levels of conditioning.[225]

2. *Sensitization.* The effect of one sensory pathway may be altered by messages over a second sensory pathway, even though the two are not presented in specific sequence. After repetition of $S_1 \rightarrow R_1$, a second stimulus, S_2, may elicit its own response, R_2, although, before the repetition of S_1, stimulus S_2 failed to evoke any overt response.

3. *Conditioning.* In classical conditioning one stimulus, the conditioned stimulus (CS), is usually followed by another stimulus, the unconditioned stimulus (UnCS), which by itself elicits a given response (RUnCS); after sufficient presentations of both stimuli in proper sequence, the first (CS) alone elicits the response (RCS). In negative conditioning CS may prevent the usual response to UnCS. If CS is applied repeatedly without reinforcement by UnCS the response to CS may become extinguished; recovery may occur spontaneously or as the result of some generalized stimulation, the phenomenon of disinhibition.

Several types of conditioning are recognized. In the simplest, the conditioned response is virtually identical to the unconditioned response in latency, amplitude, and form; persistence of the CS may be limited. Examples are conditioning of the knee jerk and of pupillary reflex. In classical Pavlovian conditioning the UnCs and CS are presented in definite temporal relation and they overlap one another. The RCS is a direct autonomic or motor response—salivation, change in heart-rate, leg lifting, or the like. However, the RCS usually differs somewhat from the RUnCS; it has a longer latency, differs in form, is anticipatory or preparative, and may persist for days unless extinguished. In instrumental conditioning the CS and UnCS need not overlap in time; the responsive action has reward value, either in stopping a punishing stimulus or in providing some satisfaction such as food. This is the basis for maze learning and problem-box solving. Trial-and-error learning is a type of instrumental conditioning. A further level of complexity occurs in sequences or chains of conditioned reflexes where the conditioned response of one reflex serves as the unconditioned response for the next.

4. *Cognitive Behavior.* Much behavior cannot be explained in terms of the taxes of switchboard reflexes or of conditioned responses. This is cognitive or insightful behavior where an animal reacts in the light of memory of complex past experience. Symbolism may be involved, and the use of tools, and what for man is called reasoning.

Distribution of Capacity for Conditioning. Differences in capacity for conditioned reflexes in animals must reflect levels of organization of the central nervous system.

"Conditioning" of Protozoa has been repeatedly described. A colonial peritrichous ciliate *Carchesium* is reported as conditioned to colored lights with accompanying mechanical prod. Paramecium "learns" to collect at a platinum wire where food is supplied.[152] The behavioral changes which have been reported for coelenterates and echinoderms on repetition of stimulation may be adaptations of sense organs or of sensory pathways.

Flatworms and annelids show reversal of a response to one sensory stimulus when this is presented with another which is normally more potent, for example, reversal of response to light with accompanying tactile stimulation. Specimens of *Neanthes* (Nereis) which normally responded negatively to illumination or to touch "learned" to come out of their tubes in the light by virtue of an UnCS of mussel juice presented at the time of the light or touch.[100] Earthworms stimulated repeatedly unilaterally by bright light (negative response), dim light (positive response), or by electrical or tactile stimulation on one side continued to turn in the "trained" direction in the absence of continued stimulation. This was not due to change in threshold (sensitization) of positive or negative phototactic responses.[254] Earthworms have repeatedly been conditioned to turn into one arm of a T-maze by using a shock in the other arm.[357] The turn habit was not lost after removal of the supraesophageal ganglion (brain), and worms from which several anterior segments had been removed could learn the habit. However, on brain regeneration the habit was lost. Planaria were conditioned with light as the CS and electric shock as UnCS. After training, the worms were transected and allowed to regenerate; worms formed from each half showed significant retention of the habit. Either the brain may be necessary for learning but not for retention, or when the tail regenerates a new brain the pattern of the RCS is built into it.[289]

Sensory adaptation is well known in molluscs, and the snail *Physa* has been conditioned toward tactile stimuli accompanied by lettuce as food. The cephalopods *Sepia* and *Octopus* learned not to eject their tentacles at a prawn behind a glass plate on which a white circle was painted while they continued to shoot at prawns not accompanied by glass and circle.[372] A normal sepia goes around a corner after a prawn which has disappeared behind a barrier; when the dorsal integrative portion of the brain mass, the verticalis complex, is removed, the sepia no longer hunts around a corner for a prawn. *Eledone* has been conditioned to give a chromatophore response with colored light as the CS.

In a variety of experiments *Octopus* have been conditioned to attack or not attack objects associated with food (a crab). Discrimination between different geometric patterns has been ascertained. Memory for preventing attack on a crab which is presented with a white square lasts 2 to 3 days if not reinforced, or indefinitely if the white square is shown three times daily. This memory is not lost after urethan anesthesia, but removal of the verticalis complex of the brain mass results in loss of memory not to attack, but memory leading to attack continues. However, after this operation it is possible to establish a brief (5 minutes) memory. The loss (not to attack) correlates with the mass of vertical lobe removed. The octopus can learn to attack (positive conditioning) without its vertical lobe, but it learns more slowly.[52] An octopus discriminates vertical and horizontal axes visually better than oblique figures and can generalize figure shapes to different sizes. This can be explained if the retina projects to an array of nerve cells in the optic lobe so that signals from horizontal rows are matched with those from vertical columns.[400] When a blinded octopus is taught a tactile discrimination, removal of the optic lobes causes no defect, but operation on the verticalis lobe causes loss in proportion to the amount of tissue removed. Some compensation can occur, and the defect may be indicated by decreased time of retention of the habit and the need for more trials to learn.[444, 445] If the verticalis is first removed and training then started, octopus is slower to learn than normally; if the octopus is pretrained and the verticalis then removed and the habit lost, fewer trials are needed for retraining than normally.[445] By training octopus to reject cylindrical objects by one arm and then testing with another arm it is shown that in the central nervous system functionally independent neuron fields represent the two arms, but that there is some spread from one to another.

The removal of the vertical lobe of the brain mass reduces efficiency of learning; then removal of the basal lobes causes no further decline in learning and does cause postural defects; when frontal and subfrontal lobes are then removed, learning is abolished. It appears that a few ten thousands of neurons in the lateral frontal and subfrontal lobes are enough for tactile learning in the octopus.[444, 445]

In arthropods, light has frequently been used as a CS associated with a prod or shock as UnCS, for example, in water mites, hermit crabs, prawns, and cockroaches. *Tenebrio* have been trained in a maze. Hymenoptera show complex behavior based on a combination of innate stereotyped patterns combined with short-term memory. Bees can be trained to come to specific colors, patterns, or odors, and they can then transmit information concerning distance and direction of food to bees in the hive.[144] The memory persists after a bee is anesthetized by chloroform[351] or cold. Some correlation exists between the proportionate size of the corpora pedunculata and complexity of behavior, for example, the elaborateness of cocoon construction, but there seem to be no reports of changes in conditioned responses after operations on the corpora pedunculata.

Fish have been conditioned in many experiments, particularly to color, shape, and sound as CS, and the habits have been retained for several weeks. Maze training has been used in olfactory conditioning, and this type of learning may be important in the homing of migratory fish. A goby can be trained with one eye covered, then perform with the other eye; hence the brain permits some interocular transfer; there are great species differences in the efficiency of this transfer.[390] There appears to be much variation in the function of the forebrain (principally striatum) in fish. Cichlid fish, for example, after loss of the entire forebrain showed sex recognition, learned new territories, but failed to deposit or fertilize eggs or to school. In the guppy *Lebistes,* mating persisted; *Hemichromis,* 19 months after a lesion to the striatum, failed to guard its eggs.[177] Removal of the forebrain from a stickleback resulted in no loss in behavior or in ability to learn color or form discrimination, and, after removal of the cerebellum, this fish learned and retained habits. Goldfish have been trained to second-order responses, i.e., first to a visual stimulus with food as the UnCS and then to the olfactory stimulus of amyl acetate with the visual stimulus as reward.[371] When part of the tectum was removed, the second-order learning was upset; hence the site of the conditioning was the tectum. Both the striatum and tectum serve for learned and complex behavior. In goldfish when heart rate was used as a response and light as CS, interocular transfer occurred (demonstrated by conditioning with one eye for conditioning and the other for testing), but when the response was avoidance behavior no transfer occurred; hence in goldfish there may be sensory transfer but not visual-motor transfer.[288] In mammals, interocular transfer of complex discriminations is possible for animals without prior binocular experience.[353]

Urodele and anuran amphibians have been trained in simple mazes and have been conditioned to visual and auditory CS. Associations are still formed with one side of the forebrain removed but not with both halves lacking.

Modifiability of reflexes can occur in spinal frogs[142] and mammals, but this may not be true conditioning. Motor responses of spinal cats and also of dogs can be altered by stimulus combinations and repetitions. The alterations are said not to follow a typical learning curve and to be variable. In chronically spinal rats multineuron reflexes can be extinguished after many stimulations at 15-second intervals, and these responses return (disinhibition) after general vigorous excitation. Responses which do not require cortical pathways, such as eyelid reactions, pupillary response, psychogalvanic and some other autonomic responses, and knee jerk, can be conditioned. However, there is indication that higher centers may be involved when these responses are conditioned. Conditioning of leg withdrawal in a dog requires the motor cortex and ipsilateral pyramidal fibers but not the reticulospinal or vestibulospinal tracts.[11] When a choice between a triangle and a circle is presented and their relative positions shifted and approach to the triangle is rewarded, solution is learned by fish, mice, pigeons, cat, dog, and primates. If circles and triangles are presented as three figures and the reward given for whichever is the odd one, the solution is not readily learned by any subprimates.[182]

Subcortical centers of the brain in birds and mammals can be conditioned. Decorticate dogs and rabbits as well as animals lacking the striate or visual cortex (rabbits, rats[22]) have been conditioned to light and sound. Even some responses acquired prior to decortication can be retained after the operation. The kinds of response that can be conditioned in decorticate animals are limited. After removal of the visual cortex responses to total flux of light, but not visual pattern discrimination, can be conditioned. Dependence on specific cortex decreases in the order: man, monkey, dog, rabbit. The midbrain appears capable of some generalized conditioning. The role of the reticulum in conscious behavior was emphasized above (p. 643). One function of the reticulum is local activation of the cortex, the arousal response pattern of brain waves associated with attention. Jasper[225] has suggested that local activation is the basis for habituation-selective responsiveness or unresponsiveness. A partially decorticate cat can be conditioned to give the arousal brain wave pattern in response to sound of 500 cps but not of 100 or 1000 cps.[225] The blocking of alpha wave activity by external stimuli can be conditioned.[267]

Hypotheses of Conditioning. All nerve centers show persistent changes in excitability, and many centers show modifiability, which cannot be explained in terms of "switchboard" reflex physiology. In mammals it is possible to substitute stimulation of the sensory pathway (spinal cord, sensory cortex) for the CS to the sense organ, but no conditioning occurs if the motor nerve or motor cortex is stimulated as the UnCS.[275] The overt motor response need not be made during the conditioning, as shown by training with motor nerves cut and response after their regeneration. Conditioning and extinction appear to occur not in sensory or motoneurons but in interneurons, particularly in the network of fine fibers in the neuropile. Those animals which show the highest degree of conditioning have an extensive neuropile—corpora pedunculata of hymenoptera, verticalis complex of cephalopods, reticulum of all vertebrates, and cortex of mammals.

New synaptic connections may be established during conditioning, yet when learning occurs at a single presentation there is little time for morphological change. Local volume changes might occur at synapses, and physical changes, such as slight shortening and opacity changes, have been noted in isolated axons.[415] Conditioning may start conduction in reverberating chains of neurons, and thereafter impulses pass continually around the circle; however, memory continues after deep anesthesia or inactivation by cold. Records from single reticular neurons show fluctuating excitabilities and convergence from many sensory inputs.[13] Other hypotheses of learning postulate excitatory and/or inhibitory mechanisms which strengthen or weaken earlier response tendencies.[182, 186] The neuropile must provide some means for first comparing temporal and spatial patterns of input and then relating these with previous similar comparisons. Spontaneous waves of activity may provide a scanning mechanism for comparisons.

Complex Sequential Behavior. Naturalists have long been impressed by what appear to be innate behavioral sequences. There is disagreement as to whether the concepts of ethology (the science of animal behavior) such as drive, release, behavioral inhibition, motivation, and imprinting have identifiable neurophysiological mechanisms. Recent evidence is that stimulation of certain regions of the brain, reticulum and other neuropile, can evoke complex behavior sequences. Examples have been mentioned above, chirping patterns during "brain" stimulation in crickets, brooding and territorial behavior in chickens, searching for drinking water after hypothalamic stimulation in goats, repetition of self-stimulation by rats and monkeys, memory recall on temporal lobe stimulation in man. Further evidence for localization of complex patterns comes from ablation experiments—defects in memory of recent events, changes from aggression to placidity and the converse. All of these patterns appear to require regions of interlacing small neurons where the organization may be

that of an analog computer with a continuous gradation of states rather than the digital organization which applies to sensorimotor mechanisms. It is probable that the next decade will see marked progress in analysis of the neuropile, whether in earthworm, honeybee, fish, or monkey.

The controversy over relative importance of inborn and learned behavior seems to be disappearing with recognition that the two are inseparable. Imprinting of specific reactions—to parent, food, or predator—occurs at very early and specific stages of development, and complex reactions are compounded from simple actions. Yet no imprinting or compounding of behavior can occur without some preexisting structure. Selective value accrues to those neurological structures which permit external stimuli to establish new reaction combinations. Animals differ greatly in their stereotypy of behavior, that is, in the modifiability which can be superposed upon patterns which were established early in development. Insects show more stereotyped behavior than fishes, which are more stereotyped than mammals. The neural organization up to some developmental stage is determined genetically, but transmission of an "innate" pattern of behavior from one generation to the next need not be genetic but often results by imprinting, for example, by the site of oviposition, the nature of parental care of the young, and by teaching. In animals the principal effect of conditioning is to determine where and when a given preestablished reaction will occur, i.e., to give approach and avoidance cues. In man, qualitative differences have emerged with the use of symbolization. Selective advantage comes from elaboration of innate behavior patterns in animals with marked stereotypy; this is surpassed in more complex animals by an increase in learning capacity and in man by the cognitive capacity associated with symbolization.[389]

CONCLUSIONS

Neurophysiology has undergone remarkable change during the past 15 years,[72, 74] in large part because of the use of unique preparations from a great variety of animals. An approach to understanding the ionic basis for the nerve impulse has been made possible by the introduction into the laboratory of giant nerve fibers, particularly squid giant axons, and by the invention of ultramicroelectrodes. These two technical advances have shown the relation between true membrane resting potentials and potassium equilibrium potentials, the overshoot of a nerve spike toward the sodium potential, and the sequence of movements of sodium and potassium (and the less understood calcium) during an action potential. The nature of the chemical changes in membrane conductance (ion permeability) remains to be elucidated.

A second important advance in neurophysiology has come in knowledge of synaptic transmission, and here large neurons have contributed much—squid third order giant fibers, crayfish giant motor synapses, *Aplysia* giant cells, and mammalian spinal motoneurons. The picture of junction potential, whether at synapse or at the neuromuscular junction, is of a short-circuiting and nonspecific increase in ion permeability under the influence of chemical transmitters. Electrical transmission has been established for at least one synapse (crayfish motor giant fibers) and has been ruled out for several others.

Efforts to identify chemical transmitters have frustrated many neurophysiologists. The role of acetylcholine in arthropod nerve impulse transmission is uncertain although the substance and its associated enzymes are present. Adrenergic junctions appear to be restricted to vertebrates, but 5-hydroxytryptamine may be more widely in use, and substituted amino acids are suspected as transmitters. It is probable that all synaptic transmitters are small molecules such as quaternary and other amines. Many neurons are primarily neurosecretory.

Not all nerve cell membranes are alike. The synaptic membranes of chemically activated synapses give local responses and differ in many respects from electrically excitable all-or-none conducting membranes. Membranes differing in excitability occur in different neurons and in different parts of a neuron. The soma may differ from its axon and each of these from the synaptic dendrites. An impulse can involve only part of a neuron, or it can be reflected electrotonically to other parts. There can be separate activities in two parts of a neuron, for example, in separated processes of large unipolar cells. Spike initiation can take place close to a synapse as in squid giant fibers, or at considerable distance as in cat motoneurons. The spike can invade the soma, as in *Aplysia* giant cells and cat motoneurons, or not, as in crustacean cardiac ganglia follower cells.

Not all nerve signals are all-or-none, and not all interaction between neurons is synaptic. Passive electrotonic spread of potential depends on the electrical constants of cell membranes and the surrounding medium. One cell within the electrotonic field of another has its excitability altered, and there can be electrotonic influences over low-resistance processes. An essential feature of nerve membranes is their nonlinearity of response, and the active process of membrane amplification can be either graded or all-or-none. Preceding a spike there is always a graded potential of one of the following kinds: pacemaker potentials in spontaneously active cells; generator potentials in sense cells; synaptic potentials in subsynaptic membranes; and local potentials preceding axon spikes. Some nerve cell processes and some short neurons may show only graded depolarization. The threshold of depolarization for a spike to occur (the critical firing level) varies with the neuron and with the region within a neuron.

Spontaneous activity is widespread in occurrence and may depend on oscillating local potentials or on electrical gradients between parts of a neuron. Groups of neurons may be synchronized in activity, as in vertebrate brain, or individual cells may fire independently of one another as in arthropod ganglia. Sensory input modulates preexisting central activity, either enhancing or depressing it. Many sense cells are spontaneously active and receive regulating efferent impulses. Neurons, either in reverberating circuits or individually, may be inherently rhythmic at intervals much longer than those determined by refractoriness, and sometimes the discharge is as infrequent as once in minutes or hours.

In animal evolution no precursors of nervous systems are known. If conduction occurs in intracellular fibrils (Protozoa), its mechanism must be different from that in nerve membranes. The primitive nerve nets of coelenterates show much specialization of facilitation, variety of conduction paths, and inhibition. Nerve nets provide connections from sense cells to muscles in coelenterates, ascidians, and echinoderms and are widely in use in higher animals in control of visceral musculature. Giant fiber systems have evolved numerous times, sometimes as fused axons, sometimes as large neurons. A number of adaptations related to speed of conduction are evident in electrical constants and morphology of nerve fibers—space and time constants, fiber diameter, presence of sheath and nodes. The transition from peripheral nets to centralized ganglia is apparent to different degrees in annelids, echinoderms, and molluscs.

The integrative properties of nervous systems are less well understood than are conduction and synaptic transmission. The simplest definition of integration is that mode of central nervous activity in which output is not equal to or proportional to input, and pulse-coded (all-or-none) sensory pulses are converted to analog (graded) signals, sorted out, and reconverted to pulse-coded signals to go out to effectors. Reflexes via switchboard-like circuits are common in control of posture and locomotion. Unisegmental and multisegmental postural reflexes of annelids, arthropods, and vertebrates are based mainly on proprioceptive, tactile, visual, and equilibrium input. Such reflexes commonly occur in chains, and their modifiability depends largely on the balance between several inputs. Antagonistic and synergistic reflexes do not sum algebraically as do neuron potentials, but rather selections are made from various inputs so that only one output response is made. All this involves switching and choice-making mechanisms which are not understood. There is balance between nerve centers, especially in the inhibition of lower motor centers by cephalic centers.

The integration which is the basis of complex behavior, especially that which is modifiable, occurs principally in neuropile regions of small neurons (central neuropile of invertebrate ganglia, gray substance and reticulum of higher vertebrates), where microelectrode recording, local stimulation, and ablation techniques are inadequate. At each level of morphological complexity new functional properties emerge, which could not be predicted from the simpler organization, properties differing qualitatively rather than quantitatively. Nonsynaptic interactions and synchronization of many neurons are added to reverberating circuits, delay paths, and capacity for persistent change in cell properties and connections. The response of a nerve center depends on its history, level of excitability, spontaneity, and general physiological state. "Recognition" and "decision" points occur in a hierarchy of integrative levels. At each level there are specific paths for given sense modalities, and nonspecific paths such as the corpora pedunculata of arthropods and the mammalian reticulum.

In insects and fish the stereotypy of behavior represents innate patterns of considerable complexity. Among invertebrates the octopus is outstanding in its modifiable behavior and massive nervous system. Arthropods are unique in the small number of neurons present to carry out varied behavior. Complexity of behavior is not proportional to number of neurons. Complex behavior is compounded from fixed patterns of action, and sequential reactions may have central nervous localization, as indicated by evocation of chirping from local spots in a cricket brain or the recall of visual and auditory experience by temporal lobe stimulation in man. In primates the storage of temporal sequences of experience appears more highly developed than in any other animal. During development of an animal the synaptic connections of neurons are more labile than in adult nervous systems.

Ethology, neurophysiology, and neuromorphology are merging as approaches to common problems.

REFERENCES—NERVOUS SYSTEM

1. ABBIE, A. A., Australian J. Exp. Biol. M. Sci. 16: 143-152, 1938; J. Comp. Neurol. 72: 469-485, 1940. Excitable motor cortex, monotremes and marsupials.
2. ABBIE, A. A., and ADEY, W. R., J. Comp. Neurol. 92: 241-292, 1950. Motor mechanisms of anuran brain.
3. ABRAMSON, H. A., and EVANS, L. T., Science 120: 990-991, 1954. Psychobiological effects of LSD on Siamese fighting fish.
4. ADEY, W. R., J. Comp. Neurol. 94: 57-103, 1951. Nervous system of earthworm Megascolex.
5. *ADEY, W. R., Ann. Rev. Physiol. 19: 489-512, 1957. Somatic aspects of central nervous system.
6. ADRIAN, E. D., Electroencephalog. Clin. Neurophysiol. 2: 377-388, 1950. Electrical activity of mammalian olfactory bulb.
7. ADRIAN, E. D., and LUDWIG, C., J. Physiol. 94: 441-460, 1938. Electrical activity, olfactory brain of fish.
8. AKERT, K., Helvet. Physiol. Acta 7: 7-28, 112-134, 1949. Visual function of optic tectum in trout.
9. AKERT, K., et al., Am. J. Physiol. 168: 260-267, 1952. Sleep induced by thalamic stimulation.
10. *ALBE-FESSARD, D., J. Physiol. Paris 49: 521-588, 1957. Sensory projections to the mammalian cortex.
11. ALLEN, W. F., Am. J. Physiol. 166: 176-184, 1951. Effects of pyramidal and extrapyramidal tracts on conditioning in dogs.
12. ALVORD, E. C., and FUORTES, M. G., J. Physiol. 122: 302-321, 1953. Monosynaptic myotatic reflexes.
13. AMASSIAN, V. E., and WALLER, H. J., Ford Hospital Symposium on Reticular Formation of the Brain. Boston, Little, Brown & Co., 1958,

* Reviews

pp. 69-108. Electrical activity in individual reticular neurons.

14. AMIN, A. H., *et al., J.* Physiol. *126*: 596-618, 1954. Sympathin, 5HT, substance P, in dog brain.

15. ANDERSSON, B., Acta physiol. scand. *23*: 8-23, 1951. Hypothalamic stimulation in sheep and goats.

16. ARAKI, T., and OTANI, T., J. Neurophysiol. *18*: 472-485, 1955. Responses of toad motoneurons to direct stimulation.

17. ARIENS-KAPPERS, C. U., *et al.,* Comparative Anatomy of Nervous System of Vertebrates, Including Man. New York, Macmillan Co., 1936, 1845 pp.

18. ARONSON, L. R., and NOBLE, G. K., Bull. Am. Mus. Nat. Hist. *86*: 83-140, 1945. Neural basis of sex behavior, male frog.

19. ARVANITAKI, A., Arch. Internat. Physiol. *49*: 209-256, 1939. Local responses in decalcified giant axons.

20. ARVANITAKI, A., J. Neurophysiol. *5*: 89-108, 1942. Ephapse transmission, local potentials.

21. ARVANITAKI, A., and CHALAZONITIS, N., Arch. Sci. Physiol. *3*: 547-563, 1949; *9*: 115-144, 1955; *10*: 95-128, 1956; Bull. Inst. Oceanog. Monaco *1143*: 1-30, 1959. Electrical activity in neuron soma and interaction between cells in ganglia of *Aplysia.*

22. ASCHOFF, J., Pflüg. Arch. *254*: 262-266, 1951; *255*: 189-196, 1952. Daily rhythms in mice.

23. VAN ASPEREN, K., Ent. Exp. Appl. *1*: 130-137, 1958. Kinetics of fly cholinesterase.

24. AUGUSTINNSON, K. B., Acta physiol. scand. *11*: 146-150, 1945; *15* (suppl. 52): 1-182, 1948. Distribution of cholinesterases.

25. AUGUSTINNSON, K. B., *in* The Enzymes, edited by J. B. Sumner and K. Myrbäck. New York, Academic Press, 1950, vol. 1, part 1, pp. 443-472. Properties of cholinesterases.

26. AUGUSTINNSON, K. B., and GRAHAM, M., Acta physiol. scand. *32*: 174-190, 1954. Choline esters in honeybee.

27. BABERS, F. H., and PRATT, J. J., Physiol. Zool. *24*: 127-131, 1951. Cholinesterase in housefly, cockroach, and honeybee.

28. BACQ, Z. M., Arch. Internat. Physiol. *42*: 24-46, 1935. Acetylcholine in tissue of invertebrates.

29. BACQ, Z. M., and GHIRETTI, F., Arch. Internat. Physiol. *49*: 165-171, 1952; Publ. Staz. Zool. Napoli *24*: 267-277, 1953.

30. BANISTER, J., *et al., J.* Physiol. *111*: 437-444, 1950. Acetylcholine synthesis, cat sympathetic ganglia.

31. BARCROFT, J., and BARRON, D. H., J. Physiol. *91*: 329-351, 1937; J. Comp. Neurol. *70*: 477-502, 1939. Behavior in fetal sheep.

32. BARDEEN, C. R., Am. J. Physiol. *5*: 175-179, 1901. Function of brain in planaria.

33. BARNES, G. E., J. Exp. Biol. *36*: 158-174, 1955. Neurophysiology of Anodonta.

34. BARRON, D. H., Biol. Rev. *16*: 1-33, 1941. The development of behavior in embryos.

35. BATHAM, E. J., and PANTIN, C. F. A., J. Exp. Biol. *27*: 290-301, 377-399, 1950. Rhythmic activity in Metridium.

36. BENJAMIN, R. M., and PFAFFMANN, C., J. Neurophysiol. *18*: 56-64, 1955. Cortical localization of taste, rat.

37. BENNETT, M. J., Biol. Bull. *107*: 174-191, 1954. Daily rhythms in clam activity.

38. BENNETT, M. J., *et al.,* Biol. Bull. *112*: 267-275, 1957. Tidal rhythms of crab activity.

39. BENNETT, M. V. L., *et al.,* J. Gen. Physiol. *43*: 159-219, 221-250, 1960. Electrophysiology of supramedullary neurons in puffer Spheroides.

40. BERKOWITZ, E. C., J. Comp. Neurol. *106*: 269-289, 1956. Function of spinal pathways in carp Cyprinus.

41. BERMAN, R., *et al.,* Biochim. Biophys. Acta *12*: 315-324, 1953. Specificity of choline acetylase.

42. BETHE, A., Pflüg. Arch. *224*: 793-835, 1930. Plasticity of arthropod nervous systems.

43. BIRREN, J. E., and WALL, P. D., J. Comp. Neurol. *104*: 1-16, 1956. Age changes in conduction velocity in sciatic nerve, rat.

44. *BISHOP, G. H., Physiol. Rev. *36*: 376-399, 1956. Natural history of the nerve impulse.

45. BISHOP, G. H., and HEINBECKER, P., Am. J. Physiol. *94*: 170-200, 1930. Fiber types and velocity, frog and turtle nerves.

46. BISHOP, P. O., Proc. Roy. Soc. London, B, *141*: 363-392, 1954. Synaptic activation of lateral geniculate cells, cat.

47. BISHOP, P. O., *et al.,* Science *130*: 506, 1969. Synaptic activation of single neurons in lateral geniculate, cat.

48. BLASCHKO, H., *in* Symposium on 5-hydroxytryptamine (Proceedings of a symposium organized by the coordinating committee for symposia on drug action), edited by G. P. Lewis. London, Pergamon Press, 1958, pp. 50-57; Arch. Biochem. Biophys. *69*: 10-15, 1957. Distribution of amine oxidase and the inactivation of 5-hydroxytryptamine.

49. *BODIAN, D., J. Comp. Neurol. *68*: 117-159, 1937; *73*: 323-343, 1940; Physiol. Rev. *22*: 146-169, 1942; Cold Spring Harbor Symp. *17*: 1-13, 1952. Structure of vertebrate synapses, particularly Mauthner cells.

50. BOELL, E. J., and SHEN, S. C., J. Exp. Zool. *113*: 583-599, 1950. Development of cholinesterase in nervous system of Amblystoma.

51. BOYCOTT, B. B., Proc. Linn. Soc. London *164*: 235-240, 1953. Nervous control of chromatophores in cephalopods.

52. BOYCOTT, B. B., and YOUNG, J. Z., Symp. Soc. Exp. Biol. *4*: 432-453, 1950. Learning in relation to the nervous system in Octopus.

53. BOYD, J. A., and MARTIN, A. R., J. Physiol. *147*: 450-457, 1959. Membrane constants, mammalian muscle.

54. BREMER, F., and STOUPEL, N., Arch. Internat. Physiol. *67*: 240-267, 1959. Facilitation and inhibition of cortical potentials.

55. BRINLEY, F. J., Physiol. Zool. *24*: 186-195, 1951. Effect of curare on activity of fish embryos.

56. BROCK, L. G., *et al., J.* Physiol. *117*: 431-460, 1952; *122*: 429-461, 1953. Intracellular recording from spinal motoneurons.

57. BROOKS, V. B., *et al., J.* Physiol. *135*: 655-672, 1957. Effect of tetanus toxin on inhibition of motoneurons, cat.

58. Brown, F. A., Jr., Am. J. Physiol. *178*: 510-514, 1954. Daily and tidal rhythms in oysters.

59. Brown, F. A., Jr., Shriner, J., and Ralph, C. L.: Am. J. Physiol. *184*: 491-496, 1956; Proc. Soc. Exp. Biol. Med. *101*: 457-460, 1959. Rhythms in rat activity.

60. Brown, F. A., Jr., *et al.*, Science *130*: 1535-1544, 1959. Hypothesis of a geophysically-dependent timer for activity rhythms.

61. Bryant, S. H., J. Gen. Physiol. *41*: 473-484, 1958; *42*: 609-619, 1959. Transmission in squid giant synapses.

62. von Buddenbrock, W., Vergleichende Physiologie, vol. I, Sinnesphysiologie. Basel, Birkhäuser, 1952, 504 pp.

63. Bulbring, E., and Burn, J. H., J. Physiol. *100*: 337-368, 1941. Acetylcholine on spinal reflexes.

64. Bulbring, E., *et al.*, Brit. J. Pharmacol. *4*: 290-294, 1949; Proc. Roy. Soc. London, B, *141*: 445-466, 1954. Acetylcholine in trypanosomes and in ciliated gill plates of Mytilus.

65. Bullock, T. H., Biol. Bull. *79*: 91-113, 1940. Organization of nervous system of Enteropneusta.

66. Bullock, T. H., Physiol. Comp. Oecol. *1*: 1-14, 1948. Mapping of giant fiber systems in polychaetes.

67. Bullock, T. H., J. Neurophysiol. *8*: 55-72, 1945. Function of giant fibers in Lumbricus.

68. Bullock, T. H., Nature *158*: 555-556, 1946; J. Neurophysiol. *11*: 343-364, 1948. Synaptic transmission, squid mantle ganglion.

69. *Bullock, T. H., Physiol. Rev. *27*: 643-664, 1947. Electrophysiology of invertebrates.

70. Bullock, T. H., J. Comp. Neurol. *98*: 37-68, 1953. Properties of natural and quasiartificial synapses.

71. *Bullock, T. H., Cold Spring Harbor Symp. *17*: 267-273, 1952; Fed. Proc. *12*: 666-672, 1953; Advances in invertebrate physiology, edited by B. Scheer. University of Oregon Press, 1957. Integrative functions of invertebrate nervous systems.

72. *Bullock, T. H., Science *129*: 997-1002, 1959. Neurone doctrine and electrophysiology.

73. Bullock, T. H., and Hagiwara, S., J. Gen. Physiol. *40*: 565-577, 1957. Intracellular records from giant synapse of squid.

74. Bullock, T. H., and Horridge, A., Anatomy and Physiology of Invertebrate Nervous Systems. In press.

75. Burgen, A. S. V., and Chipman, L. M., Quart. J. Exp. Physiol. *37*: 61-74, 1952. Location of cholinesterase in central nervous systems.

76. Burgen, A. S. V., and MacIntosh, F. C., *in* Neurochemistry, edited by K. A. C. Elliot, I. H. Page, and J. H. Quastel. Springfield, Ill., Charles C Thomas, 1955, pp. 311-389. Physiological significance of acetylcholine.

77. *Burn, J. H., Physiol. Rev. *25*: 377-394, 1945. Relation of adrenaline to acetylcholine in nervous system.

78. Burns, B. D., J. Physiol. *111*: 50-68, 1950; *112*: 156-175, 1951. Properties of isolated cerebral cortex, cat.

79. Buser, P., Arch. Sci. Physiol. *3*: 471-487, 1949; J. Physiol. Paris *43*: 673-677, 1951; Thèse. Paris, Masson et Cie, 1955, 162 pp. Electrical responses of the optic lobes of fish, mostly catfish, to visual stimulation.

80. Buser, P., J. Physiol. Paris *49*: 589-656, 1957. Neocortex of mammals: sensory, motor, and association areas.

81. Buser, P., and Dussardier, M., J. Physiol. Paris *45*: 57-60, 1953. Projection of retina to optic lobes of catfish, carp, and tench.

82. Buser, P., and Scherrer, J., C. R. Soc. Biol. *144*: 892-894, 1950. Electrical responses of the optic lobes of fish to optic nerve stimulation.

83. Cappel, C. H., Thesis, University of Illinois, 1960. Membrane constants, Mytilus muscle.

84. Carmichael, L., Psychol. Bull. *38*: 1-28, 1941. Behavior development in guinea pig.

85. Casida, J. E., Biochem. J. *60*: 487-496, 1955. Enzymology of insect acetyl esterases.

86. Caspers, H., and Winkel, K., Pflüg. Arch. *255*: 391-416, 1952. Relation between thalamus and optic lobes and forebrain rhythms in frog.

87. de Ceccatty, M. P., Ann. Sci. Nat. Zool. ser. 11, *17*: 206-288, 1955. "Neurons" of sponges.

88. Chadwick, L. E., *et al.*, Biol. Bull. *106*: 139-148, 1954. Kinetics of insect cholinesterase.

89. Chance, M. R. A., and Mansour, T. E., Brit. J. Pharmacol. *8*: 134-138, 1953. Effects of drugs on behavior of liver flukes.

90. Chang, H. T., J. Neurophysiol. *13*: 235-257, 1950; *14*: 1-21, 1951. Corticothalamic circuits and dendritic potentials in cerebral neurons, cat.

91. Chang, J. J., J. Cell. Comp. Physiol. *44*: 365-394, 1954. Nerve net control of luminescence in ctenophore.

92. Charles, M. S., and Fuller, J. L., Electroenceph. Clin. Neurophysiol. *8*: 645-652, 1956. Development of electroencephalogram of dog.

93. Clos, F., and Serfaty, A., Bull. Soc. Histoire Nat. Toulouse *92*: 205-217, 1957. Cholinesterase in fish.

94. Coghill, G. E., Anatomy and the Problem of Behavior. Macmillan Co., 1929, 113 pp.

95. Cole, K. S., and Curtis, H. J., J. Gen. Physiol. *22*: 649-670, 1939; *24*: 551-563, 1941. Resting and action potentials, giant axons of squid.

96. Cole, K. S., and Moore, J. W., J. Gen. Physiol. *43*: 961-970, 971-980, 1960. Resting and action potentials of squid giant axon.

97. Colhoun, E. H., Science *126*: 25, 1958; Nature *182*: 1378, 1958; J. Ins. Physiol. *2*: 108-116, 1958. Acetylcholine and choline acetylase in cockroach.

98. Collier, H. O., J. Exp. Biol. *16*: 286-299, 300-312, 1939. Central reflexes of earthworms.

99. Coombs, J. S., *et al.*, J. Physiol. *145*: 505-538, 1959. Electrical constants of motoneuron membranes.

100. Copeland, M., J. Comp. Psychol. *10*: 339-354, 1930; Biol. Bull. *67*: 356-364, 1934. Conditioned responses in *Nereis*.

101. Cragg, B. G., and Thomas, P. K., J. Physiol. *136*: 606-614, 1957. Relation between velocity, diameter, and internodes of trout nerve.

102. Creed, R. S., *et al.*, Reflex Activity of the Spinal Cord, Oxford University Press, 1938, 183 pp.

103. CURTIS, D. R., *et al.,* J. Physiol. *136*: 420-434, 1957. Pharmacology of spinal reflexes.

104. CURTIS, H. J., and COLE, K. S., J. Cell. Comp. Physiol. *19*: 135-144, 1942. Resting and action potentials, giant axons squid.

105. DEFFNER, G. B. J., and HAFTER, R. E., Biochem. Biophys. Acta *47*: 200-205, 1960. Ions and neutral molecules in squid axoplasm.

106. DETHIER, V. G., and BODENSTEIN, D., Ztschr. Tierpsychol. *15*: 129-140, 1958. Hunger in blowfly.

107. DETWILER, S. R., Neuroembryology, New York, Macmillan Co., 1936, pp. 167-181. Function of Mauthner cells.

108. DETWILER, S. R., J. Exp. Zool. *100*: 103-117, 1945. Forebrain lesions in Amblystoma.

109. DIJKGRAAF, S., Experientia *5*: 291-297, 1949. Spontaneous movements in spinalized minnows.

110. Dow, R. S., J. Neurophysiol. *12*: 245-256, 1949. Action potentials of cerebellar cortex in response to local stimulation.

111. *Dow, R. S., and MORUZZI, G., Physiology and Pathology of the Cerebellum. University of Minnesota Press, 1958, 675 pp. Action potentials of cerebellar cortex.

112. EASTON, D. M., J. Cell. Comp. Physiol. *40*: 303-315, 1952; Physiol. Comp. Oecol. *4*: 403-413, 1957. Excitability and other electrical properties of crab nerve fibers.

113. *ECCLES, J. C., The Neurophysiological Basis of Mind. Oxford University Press, 1953, pp. 236.

114. *ECCLES, J. C., The Physiology of Nerve Cells, Baltimore, Johns Hopkins Press, 1957, pp. 270.

115. *ECCLES, J. C., *in* vol 1, pt 1 of Handbook of Physiology, American Physiological Society, 1959, vol. 1, pt. 1, pp. 59-74.

116. ECCLES, J. C., J. Physiol. *101*: 465-483, 1943; *103*: 27-54, 1944. Action potentials in synaptic transmission in sympathetic ganglia.

117. ECCLES, J. C., FATL, P., and KOKETSU, K., J. Physiol. *126*: 524-562, 1954. Cholinergic and inhibitory synapses in spinal cord.

118. ECCLES, J. C., and LIBET, B., J. Physiol. *143*: 11-40, 1957. Effects of chromatolysis on mammalian spinal reflexes.

119. ECCLES, J. C., and McINTYRE, A. K., Nature *67*: 466, 1951; J. Physiol. *121*: 492-516, 1953. Effects of disuse and activity on mammalian spinal reflexes.

120. ECCLES, J. C., *et al.,* J. Physiol. *77*: 23P-25P, 1933. Two-way conduction in earthworm giant fibers.

121. ECCLES, J. C., *et al.,* Australian J. Sci. *16*: 1-7, 1953; J. Neurophysiol. *19*: 75-98, 1956. Cholinergic and inhibitory synapses in spinal cord.

122. ECCLES, R. M., J. Physiol. *117*: 181-195, 1952. Action potentials of mammalian sympathetic ganglia.

123. EDWARDS, C., and KUFFLER, S. W., J. Neurochem. *4*: 19-30, 1959. Inhibition of nerve cells by GABA.

124. ENGER, P. S., Acta physiol. scand. *39*: 55-72, 1957. Electroencephalogram of codfish Gadus.

125. *ERSPAMER, V., Pharmacol. Rev. *6*: 425-487, 1954. Pharmacology of indole alkyl amines.

126. ERULKAR, S. D., J. Comp. Neurol. *103*: 421-457, 1955. Tactile and auditory areas in brain of pigeons.

127. VON EULER, U. S., Acta physiol. scand. *28*: 297-305, 1953. Catechol amines in organs of fish and invertebrates.

128. *VON EULER, U. S., Noradrenaline; Chemistry, Physiology, Pharmacology and Clinical Aspects, Springfield, Ill., Charles C Thomas, 1958, 382 pp.

129. VON EULER, U. S., and ÖSTLUND, E., Acta physiol. scand. *38*: 364-372, 1957. Effects of 5HT, ACh, histamine, Adr on intestines of fish.

130. FABER, J., Arch. Neerl. Zool. *11*: 498-517, 1956. Development of coordination in urodele larvae.

131. FATT, P., and GINSBORG, B. L., J. Physiol. *142*: 516-543, 1958. Electrical constants, muscle membranes.

132. FATT, P., and KATZ, B., J. Physiol. *120*: 171-204, 1953. Electrical constants of crustacean muscle membrane.

133. FELDBERG, W., Arch. Internat. Physiol. *59*: 544-560, 1951. Acetylcholine, choline acetylase, and cholinesterase in mammalian nervous systems.

134. *FELDBERG, W., Pharmacol. Rev. *6*: 85-93, 1954. Pharmacology of central synaptic transmission.

135. FELDBERG, W., and GADDUM, J. H., J. Physiol. *81*: 305-317, 1934. Acetylcholine liberation at sympathetic ganglia.

136. FELDBERG, W., and VOGT, M., J. Physiol. *107*: 372-381, 1948. Acetylcholine synthesis in different regions of the nervous system.

137. FELDBERG, W., *et al.,* J. Physiol. *112*: 400-404, 1951. Alternation of cholinergic and noncholinergic neurones.

138. FERNANDEZ-MORAN, H., and FINEAN, J. B., Biochem. Biophys. Cytol. *3*: 725-748, 1957. Electron microscopy and x-ray diffraction of nerve myelin sheath.

139. FESSARD, A. E., *in* Brain Mechanisms and Consciousness, edited by J. F. Delafresnaye. Springfield, Ill., Charles C Thomas, 1954, pp. 200-236. Mechanisms of nervous integration and conscious experience.

140. FLOREY, E., Ztschr. vergl. Physiol. *33*: 327-377, 1951; Arch. Internat. Physiol. *62*: 33-53; Rev. Canad. Biol. *13*: 463, 1954; Canad. J. Biochem. Physiol. *34*: 669-681, 1956. Isolation of excitatory and inhibitory factors from mammalian nervous systems and their effects on invertebrates.

141. FLOREY, E., J. Gen. Physiol. *40*: 509-522, 1960. Distribution of an inhibitory factor and of acetylcholine in crustacean neurons.

142. FRANZISKET, L., Ztschr. vergl. Physiol. *33*: 142-178, 1951. Conditioned reflexes in spinal frogs.

143. FRENCH, J. D., HERNANDEZ-PEON, R., and LIVINGSTON, R. B., J. Neurophysiol. *18*: 74-95, 1955. Projections from cortex to reticulum in monkey.

144. VON FRISCH, K., Life and Senses of the Honeybee. London, Methuen & Co., 1954.

145. FRÖHLICH, F. W., Ztschr. allg. Physiol. *10*: 344-395, 1910. Function of mantle ganglion, cephalopods.

146. Fulton, J. F., The Physiology of Nervous Systems. Oxford University Press, 1943, 614 pp.

147. Furshpan, E. J., Unpublished data on Mauthner cells of goldfish.

148. Furshpan, E. J., and Potter, D., Nature *180*: 342, 1957; J. Physiol. *145*: 289-325, 326-330, 1959. Transmission at giant motor synapses of crayfish.

149. Gaffey, C. T., and Mullins, L. J., J. Physiol. *144*: 505-524, 1958. Ion fluxes in *Chara*.

150. Gasser, H. S., J. Gen. Physiol. *33*: 651-690, 1950; *38*: 709-728, 1955; *39*: 473-496, 1956. Properties of unmyelinated nerve fibers from dorsal roots and olfactory nerve.

151. Gaze, R. M., Quart. J. Exp. Physiol. *43*: 209-214, 1958. Representation of retina on optic lobe of frog.

152. Gelber, B., J. Comp. Physiol. Psychol. *45*: 58-65, 1952. Conditioning of behavior, Paramecium.

153. Gellhorn, E., and Hyde, J., J. Physiol. *122*: 371-385, 1953. Effect of proprioceptive stimulation on motor cortex.

154. Geren, B. B., and Schmitt, F. O., Proc. Nat. Acad. Sci. *40*: 863-870, 1954. Structure of Schwann cell and its relation to axon in invertebrate nerve fibers.

155. Goldby, F., J. Anat. *73*: 509-524, 1939. Motor Cortex, Echidna.

156. Gracobini, E., and Zazicek, J., Nature *177*: 185-186, 1956. Cholinesterase in single nerve cells.

157. Graham, H. T., and O'Leary, J. L., J. Neurophysiol. *4*: 224-252, 1941. Conduction in Mauthner-Müller fibers of catfish.

158. Gray, J., J. Exp. Biol. *16*: 9-17, 1939. Reflex basis of locomotion in nereis.

159. Gray, J., Symp. Soc. Exp. Biol. *4*: 112-125, 1950. Role of peripheral sense organs in vertebrate locomotion.

160. Gray, J., J. Exp. Biol. *13*: 181-191, 1936. Locomotor reflexes in eel.

161. Gray, J., and Lissmann, H. W., J. Exp. Biol. *15*: 506-517, 1938. Locomotor reflexes in earthworms.

162. Gray, J., and Lissmann, H. W., J. Exp. Biol. *17*: 227-236, 237-251, 1940; *23*: 121-132, 133-142, 1946. Locomotor reflexes in amphibians.

163. Gray, J., and Sand, A., J. Exp. Biol. *13*: 200-209, 210-218, 1936. Locomotor reflexes in dogfish.

164. Gray, J., *et al.*, J. Exp. Biol. *15*: 408-430, 1938. Reflex basis of locomotion in leech.

165. Green, J. D., *in* Ford Hospital Symposium on Reticular Formation of the Brain. Boston, Little, Brown & Co., 1958, pp. 607-619. The rhinencephalon and phylogeny of the reticular system.

166. Green, J. D., and Arduini, A. A., J. Neurophysiol. *17*: 533-557, 1954. Role of hippocampus in arousal reactions of mammals.

167. Gregerman, R. I., and Wald, G., J. Gen. Physiol. *35*: 489-494, 1952. Alleged occurrence of adrenaline in mealworm.

168. *Grundfest, H., *in* Evolution of Nervous Control, Washington, A.A.A.S., 1959, pp. 43-86. Evolution of conduction in the nervous system.

169. *Grundfest, H., Ann. New York Acad. Sci. *66*: 537-591, 1957. Drug action in bioelectric phenomena.

170. *Grundfest, H., Physiol. Rev. *37*: 337-361, 1957. Electrical inexcitability of synapses.

171. *Grundfest, H., and Purpura, D. P., *in* Symposium on Curare and Curarizing Substances, edited by D. Bovet. Amsterdam, Elsevier Publishing Co., 1959, pp. 394-445; *in* Handbook of Physiology, edited by J. Field. Washington, American Physiological Society, 1959, pp. 147-198.

172. Guyselman, J. G., Physiol. Zool. *30*: 70-87, 1957. Rhythms in crayfishes.

173. Hagiwara, S., and Bullock, T. H., J. Cell. Comp. Physiol. *50*: 25-47, 1957. Pacemaker and integrative neurons of lobster cardiac ganglion.

174. Hagiwara, S., and Saito, N., J. Neurophysiol. *22*: 204-221, 1959. Membrane constants of medullary cells of puffer.

175. Hagiwara, S., and Tasaki, I., J. Physiol. *143*: 114-137, 1958. Transmission across giant synapses of squid.

176. Hagiwara, S., and Watanabe, A., J. Cell. Comp. Physiol. *47*: 415-428, 1956. Discharges in motoneurons of cicada.

177. Hale, E. B., Physiol. Zool. *29*: 93-107, 1959. Forebrain function in maze performance of sunfish Lepomis.

178. Hama, K., J. Biophys. Biochem. Cytol. *6*: 61-66, 1959. Electron micrographs of giant nerve fibers of earthworm Eisenia.

179. Hamdi, F. I., and Whitteridge, D., Quart. J. Exp. Physiol. *39*: 111-119, 1954. Representation of retina on optic tectum, pigeon.

180. *Hanstrom, B., Vergleichende Anatomie des Nervensystems der wirbellosen Tiere. Berlin, Springer, 1928, 628 pp.

181. Harker, J., Biol. Rev. *33*: 1-52, 1958; J. Exp. Biol. *37*: 154-170, 1960. Daily rhythms, in cockroach activity.

182. *Harlow, H. F., *in* Behavior and Evolution, edited by A. Roe and G. Simpson. Yale University Press, 1958, pp. 269-290. Evolution of learning.

183. Harris, J. E., Ann. Acad. Sci. Fennicae ser. A, IV, Biol. No. 29, 1-11, 1955. Development of movements in embryos of dogfish.

184. Harris, J. E., and Whiting, H. P., J. Exp. Biol. *31*: 501-524, 1954. Development of movements in embryos of dogfish.

185. Healey, E. G., *in* Physiology of Fishes, edited by M. Brown. New York, Academic Press, vol. 2, pp. 1-119, 1957. The nervous system of fishes.

186. Hebb, C. O., and Silver, A., J. Physiol. *134*: 718-728, 1956. Choline acetylase in brains.

187. *Hebb, D. O., The Organization of Behavior. New York, J. Wiley & Sons, 1949, 319 pp.

188. Herrick, C. J., The Brain of the Tiger Salamander. University of Chicago Press, 1947, 409 pp.

189. Hess, S. M., Shore, P. A., and Brodie, B. B., J. Pharmacol. Exp. Therap. *118*: 84-89, 1956. Persistent action of reserpine on rabbit brain.

190. Hess, W. N., J. Morphol. *39*: 515-524, 1924. Reactions of Lumbricus to light.

191. Hess, W. R., *in* Brain Mechanisms in Con-

sciousness, edited by J. F. Delafresnaye. Springfield, Ill., Charles C Thomas, 1954, pp. 117-136. The diencephalic sleep center.

192. *HILGARD, E. R., and MARQUIS, D. G., Conditioning and Learning. New York, Appleton-Century Co., 1940, 429 pp.

193. HIRSCH, J. F., and COXE, W. S., J. Neurophysiol. *21*: 481-498, 1958. Cortical representation of cutaneous tactile sense in three monkeys.

194. HODES, R., J. Neurophysiol. *16*: 145-154, 1953. Relation between fiber diameter and conduction velocity in squid giant axons.

195. HODGKIN, A. L., Proc. Roy. Soc. London, B, *126*: 87-121, 1938. Subthreshold potentials in crustacean nerves.

196. HODGKIN, A. L., J. Physiol. *106*: 305-318, 1947. Membrane resistance of a crustacean nerve fiber.

197. HODGKIN, A. L., J. Physiol. *125*: 221-224, 1954. Electrical constants and velocity of nerve fibers.

198. *HODGKIN, A. L., Proc. Roy. Soc. London, B, *148*: 1-37, 1958; Biol. Rev. *26*: 339-409, 1951. Ion movements and electrical activity in giant nerve fibers.

199. HODGKIN, A. L., and HUXLEY, A. F., J. Physiol. *116*: 449-472, 473-496, 500-544, 1952. The relation between membrane current, ionic movements, and conduction in nerve.

200. HODGKIN, A. L., and KATZ, B., J. Physiol. *108*: 37-77, 1949. Effect of sodium ions on electrical activity of the squid giant axon.

201. HODGKIN, A. L., and KEYNES, R. D., J. Physiol. *138*: 253-281, 1957. Movement of calcium in squid giant axons.

202. HODGKIN, A. L., and RUSHTON, W. A., Proc. Roy. Soc. London, B, *133*: 444-479, 1946. Electrical constants and velocity of nerve fibers.

203. HOLMES, N., Phil. Tr. Roy. Soc. London, B, *231*: 293-311, 1942. Structure of giant fibers of prawn Leander.

204. HOLMES, N., et al., J. Exp. Biol. *18*: 50-54, 1941. Velocity of giant fibers of prawn Leander.

205. VON HOLST, E., Ztschr. vergl. Physiol. *21*: 395-414, 1934; Biol. Rev. *10*: 234-261, 1935. Ganglionic control of locomotion, lepidoptera.

206. VON HOLST, E., Ztschr. vergl. Physiol. *20*: 582-599, 1934; *26*: 481-528, 1939; Pflüg. Arch. *236*: 149-158, 1935. Reflexes and locomotor rhythms in fish.

207. HORRIDGE, G. A., Nature *171*: 400, 1953; J. Exp. Biol. *31*: 594-600, 1954. Conduction in nerves of Aurelia.

208. HORRIDGE, G. A., J. Exp. Biol. *32*: 555-568, 636-648, 1955; *33*: 366-383, 1956; *36*: 72-91, 1959. Properties of the fast and slow nerve nets and ganglia of medusae.

209. HORRIDGE, G. A., Phil. Tr. Roy. Soc. London, B, *240*: 495-529, 1957. Coordination of protective retraction of coral polyps.

210. HORRIDGE, G. A., J. Exp. Biol. *35*: 369-382, 1958. Coordination of responses of Cerianthus.

211. HORRIDGE, G. A., J. Physiol. *143*: 553-572, 1958. Ganglionic transmission in Mya.

212. HORRIDGE, G. A., Proc. Roy. Soc. London, B, *150*: 245-262, 1959. Analysis of rapid responses of Nereis and Harmothoë.

213. HOYLE, G., J. Mar. Biol. Assn. U. K. *31*: 287-305, 1952. Nervous control of responses in ascidians.

214. HOYLE, G., Nature *169*: 281-282, 1952; J. Exp. Biol. *30*: 121-135, 1953; *31*: 260-270, 1954. Potassium ions and insect nervous systems.

215. HÜBER, F., Verhandl. deutsch. Zool. Gesellsch. Freib. 1952, 138-149; Naturwissenschaften *20*: 566, 1955. Central nervous basis for song patterns of crickets.

216. HUGHES, G. M., J. Exp. Biol. *29*: 387-402, 1952. Effects of direct current on insect ganglia.

217. HUGHES, G. M., J. Exp. Biol. *29*: 267-284, 1952; *34*: 306-333, 1957; *35*: 567-583, 1958. Coordination of insect movements.

218. HUGHES, G. M., and KERKUT, G. A., J. Exp. Biol. *33*: 282-294, 1956. Electrical activity in a slug ganglion.

219. HUGHES, G. M., and WIERSMA, C. A. G., J. Exp. Biol. *37*: 291-307, 1960. Neuron pathways in abdominal cord of crayfish.

220. HUNT, C. C., J. Gen. Physiol. *38*: 117-131, 1954. Relation of function to diameter in sensory nerves, mammals.

221. HUXLEY, A. F., Ann. New York Acad. Sci. *81*: 221-246, 1959. Ion movements during nerve activity.

222. INGVAR, D. H., Acta physiol. scand. *33*: 151-168, 1955. Electrical activity of isolated cerebral cortex.

223. ISSIDORIDES, M., Exp. Cell. Res. *11*: 423-436, 1956. Ultrastructure of synapse in giant axons of earthworm.

224. JANZEN, W., Zool. Jahrb. Abt. allg. *52*: 591-628, 1933. Forebrain function in goldfish.

225. *JASPER, H. H., in Ford Hospital Symposium on Reticular Formation of Brain. Boston, Little Brown & Co., 1958, pp. 319-331; et al., Ann. Rev. Physiol. *18*: 359-386, 1956. Recent advances in understanding ascending activity of reticular systems.

226. JAWLOWSKI, H., Ann. Univ. M. Curie-Sklodowska C *12*: 307-323, 1957. Nerve tracts from eye and antennae of bee.

227. JENNINGS, H. S., Univ. Cal. Pub. Zool. *4*: 53-185, 1907. Behavior of starfish.

228. JERMÉ, R., Arch. Internat. Physiol. *61*: 35-40, 1953. Electrical activity of cortex of cat, hedgehog, and mole.

229. JOHNSON, G. E., J. Comp. Neurol. *36*: 323-374, 1924; *42*: 19-35, 1927. Structure and function of giant nerve fibers of crustaceans.

230. JOHNSON, M. S., J. Exp. Zool. *82*: 315-328, 1939. Daily rhythms in mice.

231. JORDAN, H. J., Pflüg. Arch. *131*: 317-386, 1910. Effects of lesions to nervous system on behavior of crabs.

232. *JORDAN, H. J., Allgemeine vergleichende Physiologie der Tiere. Berlin, Gruyter, 1929, 761 pp.

233. KAISER, F., Zool. Jahrb. Abt. allg. *65*: 59-90, 1954. Ganglion function in leeches.

234. KAMAMOTO, F. I., Science *125*: 351-352, 1957. Cholinesterase in a fresh-water nemertean.

235. KAO, C. Y., Science *123*: 803, 1956. Recurrent circuits in excitation of giant axons of earthworm.

236. KAO, C. Y., and GRUNDFEST, H., J. Neurophysiol. *20*: 553-573, 1957. Electrogenesis in septate giant axons of earthworm.

237. *KATZ, B., Electric Excitation of Nerve. Oxford University Press, 1939, 151 pp.

238. KATZ, B., Proc. Roy. Soc. London, B, *135*: 506-534, 1948. Electrical properties of muscle fiber membranes.

239. KEMPINSKY, W. H., J. Neurophysiol. *14*: 203-210, 1951. Cortical projection of vestibular and facial nerves in cat.

240. KENNEDY, D., and PRESTON, J. B., J. Gen. Physiol. *43*: 655-670, 1960. Activity patterns in interneurons, caudal ganglion of crayfish.

241. KEPNER, W. A., and RICH, A., J. Exp. Zool. *26*: 83-100, 1918. Reactions of proboscis of planaria.

242. KERKUT, G. A., Behaviour *6*: 206-232, 1954; *8*: 112-129, 1955. Coordination of tube feet in starfish.

243. KEYNES, R. D., J. Physiol. *114*: 119-150, 1951. Sodium content and exchange in cephalopod nerve fibers.

244. KEYNES, R. D., and LEWIS, P. R., J. Physiol. *113*: 73-98, 1951; *114*: 151-182, 1951. Sodium and potassium content and exchange in crab and cephalopod nerve fibers.

245. KINOSITA, H. J., Jap. J. Zool. *9*: 221-232, 1941. Conduction in sea urchin nerve nets.

246. VAN DER KLOOT, W. G., and WILLIAMS, C. M., Behaviour *5*: 141-156, 157-174, 1953; *6*: 233-255, 1954. Hormonal and nervous control of cocoon construction by Cecropia silkworms.

247. VAN DER KLOOT, W. G., Biol. Bull. *109*: 276-294, 1955. Control of neurosecretion and diapause by brain of Cecropia.

248. KNIGHT-JONES, E. W., Phil. Tr. Roy. Soc. London, B, *236*: 315-354, 1952. Nervous system of enteropneustan Saccoglossus.

249. KOECHLIN, B. A., J. Biophys. Biochem. Cytol. *1*: 511-529, 1955. Chemical composition of axoplasm, squid giant fibers.

250. KOELLE, G. B., J. Pharmacol. Exp. Therap. *100*: 158-179, 1950; J. Comp. Neurol. *100*: 211-235, 1954; *in* Progress in Neurobiology, edited by H. Waelsch. New York, Paul B. Hoeber, 1957, vol. 2, pp. 164-170. Histochemical localization of cholinesterase in the central nervous system.

251. KONISHI, J., Rep. Fac. Fish. Prefect Univ. Mie *2*: 347-358, 1957. Nervous control of breathing in fish.

252. KOSHTOYANTS, C. S., and KOKINA, N. N., Biophysika *3*: 422-425, 1958. Biopotentials in Opalina.

253. KRIEG, W., Functional Neuroanatomy. New York, Blakiston Co., 1953.

254. KRIVANEK, J. O., Physiol. Zool. *29*: 241-250, 1956. Habit formation in earthworm.

255. KRUGER, L., J. Comp. Neurol. *111*: 133-194, 1959. Thalamus of the dolphin.

256. KUO, Z. K., J. Exp. Zool. *61*: 395-450, 1932; J. Comp. Psychol. *13*: 245-271, 1932. Development of behavior in bird embryos.

257. LANCE, J. W., J. Neurophysiol. *17*: 253-270, 1954. Pyramidal tract in spinal cord of cat.

258. LAPORTE, Y., J. Gen. Physiol. *35*: 343-360, 1951. Conduction in lateral line nerves of carp.

259. LARSSON, S., Acta physiol. scand. *32* (suppl. 115): 1-63, 1954. Hypothalamic centers for eating; sheep and goats.

260. *LASHLEY, K. S., Am. J. Physiol. *59*: 44-71, 1922; Comp. Psychol. Monog. *11*: 3-79, 1935; Quart. Rev. Biol. *24*: 28-42, 1949. Neural basis of learning in rats.

261. LENDE, R. A., and WOOLSEY, C. N., J. Neurophysiol. *19*: 485-499, 544-563, 1956. Sensory and motor localization in cortex of porcupines.

262. LEWIS, S. E., Nature *172*: 1004, 1953. Acetylcholine content of blowflies.

263. LEWIS, S. E., and SMALLMAN, B. N., J. Physiol. *134*: 241-256, 1956. Acetylcholine content of various insects.

264. LI, C. L., *et al.,* Science *116*: 656-657, 1952; J. Physiol. *121*: 117-140, 1953; J. Neurophysiol. *19*: 131-143, 1956. Unit activity in various regions of the cerebral cortex, cat.

265. *LIBERSON, W. T., Ann. Rev. Physiol. *19*: 557-588, 1957. Recent advances in Russian neurophysiology.

266. LILLY, J. C., *in* Ford Hospital Symposium on Reticular Formation of the Brain. Boston, Little Brown & Co., 1958, pp. 705-721. Learning motivated by subcortical stimulation, monkeys.

267. *LINDSLEY, D. B., Ann. Rev. Physiol. *17*: 311-338, 1955. Recent developments, higher functions of the nervous system.

268. LINDSLEY, D. B., pp. 513-534 *in* Ford Hospital Symposium on Reticular Formation of the Brain. Boston, Little Brown & Co., 1958. Reticular system and perceptual discrimination.

269. LISSMAN, H. W., J. Exp. Biol. *23*: 143-176, 1946. Locomotor activity in spinal dogfish.

270. LIVINGSTON, R. B., pp. 177-185 *in* Ford Hospital Symposium on Reticular Formation of the Brain. Boston, Little Brown & Co., 1958. Central control of afferent activity.

271. LLOYD, D. P. C., J. Gen. Physiol. *33*: 147-170, 1949. Post-tetanic potentiation of monosynaptic reflexes, cat.

272. LORENTE DE NÓ, R., Am. J. Physiol. *112*: 595-609; *113*: 505-528, 1935. Responses of oculomotor nucleus, facilitation, and delay paths.

273. LORENTE DE NÓ, R., Stud. Rockefeller Inst. Med. Res. *131*: 496 pp., *132*: 537 pp., 1947. Relations between electrotonic and resting potentials.

274. DE LORENZO, A. J., J. Biophys. Biochem. Cytol. *7*: 31-36, 1960. Electron microscopy of ciliary ganglion in chick.

275. LOUCKS, R. B., J. Psychol. *1*: 5-44, 1934. Neurological delimitation of cortical learning.

276. LUNDBERG, A., and OSCARSSON, O., Acta physiol. scand. *38*: 53-90, 1956. Spinocerebellar tract of cat.

277. MACKIE, G. O., Quart. J. Micr. Sci. *101*: 119-132, 1960. Histology of nervous system of Velella.

278. *MAGOUN, H. W., *in* Brain Mechanisms and Consciousness, edited by J. F. Delafresnaye. Springfield, Ill., Charles C Thomas, 1954, pp. 1-20. The Waking Brain. Springfield, Ill., Charles C Thomas, 1958, 135 pp. The reticular system in the brain.

279. MALCOLM, J. L., *in* Biochemistry of the Developing Nervous System, edited by H. Waelsch. New York, Academic Press, 1955, pp. 104-109. Appearance of inhibition in developing spinal cord, kittens.

280. MANTON, S. M., J. Linn. Soc. London *41*: 529-570, 1950; *42*: 93-166, 1952; *42*: 299-368, 1954; Symp. Soc. Exp. Biol. *7*: 339-376, 1953. Evolution of arthropod locomotor mechanisms.

281. MARAZZI, A. S., *in* Annual Conference on Biology of Mental Health and Disease, Millbank Fund 1952, pp. 376-384; Science *118*: 367-370, 1953. Central nervous transmitters; effect of adrenaline in brain.

282. MARAZZI, A. S., and HART, E. R., Science *121*: 365-366, 1955. Effects of adrenaline in brain.

283. MARUHASHI, J., *et al.*, J. Physiol. *117*: 121-151, 1952. Conduction velocity in skin nerves, toad and cat.

284. *MASLAND, R. L., Ann. Rev. Physiol. *20*: 533-558, 1958. Higher cerebral functions.

285. MATTHEWS, D. B. C., *et al.*, Quart. J. Exp. Physiol. *43*: 38-52, 1958. Afferent systems to the cerebellum, frog.

286. MAXWELL, S. S., Labyrinth and Equilibrium. Philadelphia, J. B. Lippincott Co., 1923, 163 pp.

287. MAYNARD, D. M., Nature *177*: 529-530. Electrical activity in cockroach brain.

288. McCLEARY, R. S., J. Comp. Physiol. Psychol. *53*: 311-321, 1960. Interocular transfer of learned responses in goldfish.

289. McCONNELL, J. V., *et al.*, J. Comp. Physiol. Psychol. *52*: 1-5, 1959. Effects of regeneration on retention of conditioned response in planaria.

290. METCALF, R. L., *et al.*, J. Econ. Ent. *43*: 670-677, 1950; Ann. Ent. Soc. America *48*: 222-228, 1955; *49*: 274-279, 1956. Properties of insect cholinesterases, and insecticide action.

291. METZ, C. B., *et al.*, Biol. Bull. *104*: 408-425, 1953; *106*: 106-122, 1954. Electron microscopy of fibrillar systems of ciliates.

292. MITTELSTAEDT, H., *in* Recent Advances in Invertebrate Physiology, edited by B. Scheer. University of Oregon Press, 1957, pp. 51-71. Prey capture in mantids.

293. MORIN, F., and GOLDRING, S., J. Comp. Neurol. *93*: 229-239, 1950. Interhemispheric coordination in brain of opossum.

294. MORUZZI, G., *in* Brain Mechanisms and Consciousness, edited by J. F. Delafresnaye. Springfield, Ill., Charles C Thomas, 1954, pp. 21-53; pp. 269-286, 20th International Physiological Congress Proceedings, 1956. Electrical activity in brain stem reticular formation.

295. MOUNTCASTLE, V. B., J. Neurophysiol. *20*: 374-434, 1957. Unit organization of somatic sensory cortex, cat.

296. MOZELL, M. M., J. Neurophysiol. *21*: 183-196, 1958. Electrophysiology of olfactory bulb.

297. NACHMANSOHN, D., Bull. Soc. Chim. Biol. *21*: 761-796, 1939; J. Neurophysiol. *4*: 348-361, 1941. Cholinesterase in nervous structures.

298. *NACHMANSOHN, D., Chemical and Molecular Basis of Nerve Activity. New York, Academic Press, 1959, 235 pp.

299. NAYLOR, E., J. Exp. Biol. *35*: 602-610, 1958. Tidal rhythms of crab activity.

300. NEEDLER, M., and Ross, D. M., J. Mar. Biol. Assn. U. K. *37*: 789-805, 1958. Neuromuscular activity in sea anemone *Calliactis*.

301. *NICOL, J. A. C., Quart. Rev. Biol. *23*: 291-323, 1948. Giant axons of annelids.

302. NICOL, J. A. C., Nature *169*: 665, 1952; J. Mar. Biol. Assn. U. K. *30*: 433-452, 1952. Nervous control of luminescence in Chaetopterus.

303. NICOL, J. A. C., J. Exp. Biol. *32*: 619-635, 1955. Nervous control of luminescence in Renilla.

304. NICOL, J. A. C., and WHITTERIDGE, D., Physiol. Comp. Oecol. *4*: 101-117, 1955. Conduction in giant axon of Myxicola.

305. OGAWA, F., Tohoku Imp. Univ. Sci. Rep. ser. 4, *3*: 745-756, 1928; *5*: 691-761, 1930. Neurons in earthworms.

306. OLDS, J., J. Comp. Physiol. Psychol. *49*: 281-285, 1956; Science *127*: 315-324, 1958. Localization of brain centers for self-stimulation.

307. *OLDS, J., *in* Biological and Biochemical Bases of Behavior, edited by H. F. Harlow and C. N. Woolsey. University of Wisconsin Press, 1958, pp. 237-262; Ann. Rev. Physiol. *21*: 381-402, 1959. Adaptive functions of paleocortex and related parts of nervous system.

308. O'LEARY, J. L., and BISHOP, G. H., J. Cell. Comp. Physiol. *22*: 73-87, 1943. Electrical activity of optic tectum, duck and goose.

309. ORBACH, J., Proc. Nat. Acad. Sci. *41*: 264-267, 1955. Nonvisual functions of occipital cortex, monkey.

310. ÖSTLUND, E., Acta physiol. scand. *31* (suppl. 112): 1-67, 1954; Nature *172*: 1042-1043, 1953. Adrenaline, noradrenaline in invertebrates.

311. *PAGE, I. H., Physiol. Rev. *34*: 563-588, 1954. Serotonin (5 hydroxytryptamine).

312. PALAY, S. L., *in* Neurochemistry, edited by S. R. Korey and J. I. Nurnberger, New York, Paul B. Hoeber, 1956, pp. 64-82. Cytology of neurons.

313. PANTIN, C. F. A., J. Exp. Biol. *12*: 119-164, 1935. Properties of nerve nets, actinians.

314. PANTIN, C. F. A., Proc. Roy. Soc. London, B, *140*: 147-168, 1952. Histology of nerve nets.

315. PANTIN, C. F. A., Symp. Soc. Exp. Biol. *4*: 175-195, 1950; Pubbl. Staz. Zool. Napoli *28*: 171-181, 1956. Evolution of the nervous system in lower invertebrates.

316. PARDUCZ, B., Acta Biol. Acad. Sci. Hung. *8*: 191-218, 1958. Fibrillar system of ciliates.

317. PARKER, G. H., The Elementary Nervous System, 1919, Philadelphia, J. B. Lippincott Co., 229 pp.

318. PARKER, G. H., J. Exp. Zool. *31*: 475-515, 1920; J. Cell. Comp. Physiol. *1*: 53-63, 1932; J. Gen. Physiol. *1*: 231-236, 1918. Conduction in coelenterate nerve nets.

319. PASSANO, L. M., and PANTIN, C. F. A., Proc. Roy. Soc. London, B, *143*: 226-238, 1955. Mechanical stimulation of sea anemone Calliactis.

320. PATON, U. D. M., and PERRY, W. L., J. Physiol. *119*: 43-57, 1953. Synaptic blocking drugs in sympathetic ganglia.

321. PATTON, H. D., and AMASSIAN, V. E., J. Neurophysiol. *15*: 245-250, 1952. Cortical projection of chorda tympani nerve in cat.

322. *PENFIELD, W., *in* Brain Mechanisms and Consciousness, edited by J. F. Delafresnaye. Springfield, Ill., Charles C Thomas, 1954, 556 pp.; Science *129*: 1719-1725, 1959. The interpretive cortex in man.

323. PERL, E. R., and WHITLOCK, D. G., J. Neuro-

physiol. *18*: 486-502, 1955. Potentials in cerebral somatosensory cortex.

324. PERRY, W. L. M., J. Physiol. *119*: 439-454, 1953. Acetylcholine release in cat sympathetic ganglion.

325. PITTENDRIGH, C. S., Proc. Nat. Acad. Sci. *40*: 1018-1029, 1954. Temperature and daily rhythmic period.

326. PITTENDRIGH, C. S., and BRUCE, V. S., *in* Photoperiodism and Related Phenomena, edited by R. B. Withrow. American Association for the Advancement of Science, 1959, pp. 475-505. Hypothesis of an independent internal timer for daily rhythms.

327. PLETSCHER, A., *et al.,* J. Pharmacol. Exp. Therap. *116*: 84-89, 1956. Serotonin and reserpine action in brain.

328. POPLE, W., and EWER, D. W., J. Exp. Biol. *32*: 59-69, 1955. Physiology of nervous system of holothurian Cucumaria.

329. PRECHTL, H., Experientia *5*: 323, 1949. Function of forebrain of lizard Lacerta.

330. PRESTON, J. B., and KENNEDY, D., J. Gen. Physiol. *43*: 671-681, 1960. Activity patterns in interneurons, caudal ganglion of crayfish.

331. *PRIBRAM, K. H., *in* Biological and Biochemical Bases of Behavior, edited by H. Harlow and C. Woolsey. University of Wisconsin Press, 1958, pp. 151-172; Ann. Rev. Psychol. *11*: 1-40, 1960. Theory of interaction between neocortex, paleocortex, and reticulum in behavior.

332. PRINGLE, J. W. S., J. Exp. Biol. *16*: 220-229, 1939; *17*: 8-17, 1940. Reflex control of movement in cockroach.

333. PROSSER, C. L., J. Comp. Neurol. *58*: 603-630, 1934. Development of behavior in earthworm embryos.

334. PROSSER, C. L., J. Comp. Neurol. *59*: 61-91, 1934. Nervous mechanisms in reactions of earthworms to light.

335. PROSSER, C. L., Quart. Rev. Biol. *9*: 181-200, 1939. Physiology of nervous system of earthworm.

336. PROSSER, C. L., J. Exp. Biol. *12*: 95-104, 1935. Impulses in segmental nerves of earthworm.

337. PROSSER, C. L., J. Cell. Comp. Physiol. *4*: 185-209, 1935; *7*: 95-111, 1939; *16*: 25-38, 1940; J. Comp. Neurol. *62*: 495-505, 1935; J. Cell. Comp. Physiol. *22*: 131-145, 1943. Spontaneous activity, synaptic transmission, and neuron tracts in nervous system of crayfish.

338. *PROSSER, C. L., Physiol. Rev. *26*: 337-382, 1946. Physiology of invertebrate nervous systems.

339. *PROSSER, C. L., *in* The Nerve Impulse, Josiah Macy, Jr. Second Conference on Comparative Neurophysiology, 1950, pp. 81-107; *in* Modern Trends in Physiology and Biochemistry, edited by E. S. G. Barron. New York, Academic Press, 1952, pp. 323-336; Ann. Rev. Physiol. *16*: 103-124, 1954; *in* Evolution of Nervous Control, Washington, A. A. A. S., 1959, pp. 31-42. Comparative physiology of nervous systems.

340. PUMPHREY, R. J., and RAWDON-SMITH, A. F., Proc. Roy. Soc. London, B, *122*: 106-118, 1937.

Synaptic transmission in abdominal ganglion of cockroach.

341. PUMPHREY, R. J., and YOUNG, J. Z., J. Exp. Biol. *15*: 453-466, 1938. Velocity of fibers of various diameters.

342. PURPURA, D. P., and GRUNDFEST, H., J. Neurophysiol. *19*: 573-595, 1957; *20*: 494-527, 1957. Dendritic potentials and synaptic organization of cerebral and cerebellar cortex, cat.

343. PURPURA, D. P., *et al.,* Proc. Exp. Biol. Med. *95*: 791-796, 1957; *97*: 348-353, 1958. Synaptic effects of GABA and other active amino acids on the mammalian cortex.

344. QUASTEL, J. H., *in* Neurochemistry, edited by K. A. C. Elliot, I. H. Page, and J. H. Quastel. Springfield, Ill., Charles C Thomas, 1955, pp. 153-172. Acetylcholine synthesis in central nervous system.

345. RALPH, C. L., Biol. Bull. *113*: 188-197, 1957; Physiol. Zool. *30*: 41-55, 1957. Daily and lunar rhythms in salamanders and earthworms.

346. RAO, K. P., Biol. Bull. *106*: 353-359, 1954. Tidal rhythms in mussels.

347. *RAZRAN, G. H. S., Psychol. Bull. *34*: 191-256, 1937. Bibliography of conditioned reflexes.

348. RENSCH, B., Ztschr. vergl. Physiol. *37*: 496-508, 1955. Electrophysiology of optic lobes of frog.

349. RENSCH, B., Naturwissenschaften *45*: 175-180, 1958. Brain size, neuron number, and animal size.

350. RETZLAFF, E., J. Comp. Neurol. *107*: 209-225, 1957. Mechanisms of Mauthner cells.

351. RIBBANDS, C. R., J. Exp. Biol. *27*: 302-310, 1950. Effect of anesthesia on memory in honeybees.

352. RICHTER, D., and CROSSLAND, J., Am. J. Physiol. *159*: 247-255, 1949. Acetylcholine in brain in differing physiological states.

353. RIESEN, A. H., *et al.,* J. Comp. Physiol. Psychol. *46*: 166-172, 1953. Interocular transfer, visual conditioning, cats.

354. DE ROBERTIS, E. D. P., and BENNETT, H. S., J. Biophys. Biochem. Cytol. *1*: 47-58, 1955. Ultrastructure of synapses of frog and earthworm.

355. ROBERTS, S. K., J. Cell. Comp. Physiol. *55*: 99-110, 1960. Daily rhythms in cockroaches.

356. ROBERTSON, J. D., Proc. Soc. Exp. Biol. Med. *82*: 219-223, 1953; Exp. Cell. Res. *8*: 226-229, 1955; *in* Progress in Neurobiology, edited by H. Waelsch. New York, Paul B. Hoeber, 1957, vol. 2, pp. 1-22. Ultrastructure of invertebrate synapses.

357. ROBINSON, J. S., J. Comp. Physiol. Psychol. *46*: 262-266, 1953. Conditioning in earthworms.

358. ROCKSTEIN, M., J. Cell. Comp. Physiol. *35*: 11-24, 1950. Change in cholinesterase with age in honeybee brain.

359. ROEDER, K. D., Biol. Bull. *69*: 203-220, 1935; J. Exp. Zool. *76*: 353-374, 1937. Nervous control of sexual behavior, tonus, and locomotion in mantids.

360. *ROEDER, K. D., *in* Insect Physiology, edited by K. D. Roeder. New York, John Wiley & Sons, 1953, pp. 423-487. Physiology of insect nervous systems.

361. *ROEDER, K. D., Ann. Rev. Entomol. *3*: 1-18, 1958. Recent advances in insect neurophysiology.

362. ROEDER, K. D., Smithsonian Misc. Coll. *137*: 287-306, 1959. Startle and attack reflexes of insects.

363. ROEDER, K. D., *et al.,* J. Insect Physiol. *4*: 45-62, 1960. Endogenous nervous activity in mantis and cockroach.

364. ROGERS, F. T., Am. J. Physiol. *55*: 310, 1920; J. Comp. Neurol. *35*: 61-65, 1922; Am. J. Physiol. *86*: 639-650, 1928. Localization of function in pigeon brain.

365. ROMANES, G. J., Phil. Tr. Roy. Soc. London, B, *166*: 269-313, 1867; *167*: 659-752, 1877. Locomotion in medusae.

366. Ross, D. M., J. Exp. Biol. *29*: 235-254, 1952. Facilitation in sea anemones.

367. Ross, D. M., Nature *180*: 1368-1369, 1957. Fast and slow responses in Cerianthus.

368. Ross, D. M., Experientia *13*: 192-194, 1957. Effects of tryptamine and 5HT on sea anemones.

369. ROTH, L. E., J. Biochem. Biophys. Cytol. *3*: 985-1000, 1957; J. Ultrastructure Res. *1*: 223-234, 1958; Exp. Cell. Res. *14* (suppl. 5): 573-585, 1958. Ultrastructure and function of fibrillar system in Protozoa.

370. RUSHTON, W. A. H., Proc. Roy. Soc. London, B, *124*: 210-243, 1937. Electrical constants and velocity of nerve fibers.

371. SANDERS, F. K., J. Exp. Biol. *17*: 416-434, 1940. Second order learning in tectum of goldfish.

372. SANDERS, F. K., and YOUNG, J. Z., J. Neurophysiol. *3*: 501-525, 1940. Functions of higher nerve center, Sepia.

373. SATIJA, R. C., J. Physiol. *136*: 27P-28P, 1957. Visual paths in insect nervous systems.

374. SCHÄDE, J. P., and WECKER, I. J., J. Exp. Biol. *36*: 435-452, 1959. Electroencephalograph of goldfish.

374a. SCHALLEK, W., J. Cell., Comp. Physiol. *26*: 15-24, 1945. Acetylcholine in lobster nerve cord.

375. SCHLOTTE, F. W., Ztschr. vergl. Physiol. *37*: 373-415, 1955. Conduction in gastropod nerves.

376. SCHMITT, F. O., and BEAR, R. S., J. Cell. Comp. Physiol. *9*: 261-273, 1937; Biol. Rev. *14*: 27-80, 1939. Birefringence of axon sheath.

377. SCHÖNHERR, J., Zool. Jahrb., Abt. allg. *65*: 357-386, 1955. Brain function and complex behavior in stickleback.

378. SEAMAN, G. R., and HOULIHAN, R. K., J. Cell. Comp. Physiol. *37*: 300-321, 1951. Acetylcholinesterase in Tetrahymena.

379. SEDAR, A. W., and PORTER, K. R., J. Biophys. Biochem. Cytol. *1*: 583-604, 1955. Infraciliary fibrils in Paramecium.

380. SHALLEK, W., J. Comp. Physiol. *26*: 15-24, 1945. Acetylcholine in lobster nerve cord.

381. SHANES, A. M., J. Gen. Physiol. *33*: 57-74, 75-102, 1949; J. Cell. Comp. Physiol. *38*: 17-40, 1951. Electrical phenomena in squid, crab, and frog nerve.

382. *SHANES, A. M., Pharmacol. Rev. *10*: 59-273, 1958. Electrochemical aspects of physiological and pharmacological actions in excitable cells.

383. SHANKLAND, D. L., and KEARNS, C. W., Ann. Entomol. Soc. America *52*: 386-394, 1959. Properties of insect neurotoxins.

384. SHEN, S. C., *et al.,* J. Comp. Neurol. *102*: 717-740, 1955; *106*: 433-461, 1956. Distribution of cholinesterase in frog brain and chick retina.

385. SMALLMAN, B. N., J. Physiol. *132*: 343-357, 1956. Acetylcholine synthesis by blowfly.

385a. SMITH, C., and GLICK, D., Biol. Bull. *77*: 321-322, 1939. Cholinesterase in nerve, muscle, and cardiac tissues of invertebrate animals.

386. *SMITH, J. E., Phil. Tr. Roy. Soc. London, B, *227*: 111-173, 1937; Biol. Rev. *20*: 29-43, 1945; Symp. Soc. Exp. Biol. *4*: 196-220, 1950; Phil. Tr. Roy. Soc. London, B, *234*: 521-558, 1950. Nervous mechanisms underlying behavior and movement of tube feet and ampullae in starfishes.

387. SMITH, J. E., Phil. Tr. Roy. Soc. London, B, *240*: 135-196, 1957. Neuroanatomy of body segments of nereid polychaetes.

388. SNIDER, R., and ELDRED, E., J. Neurophysiol. *15*: 27-40, 1952. Cerebrocerebellar relations in monkeys.

389. *SPERRY, R. W., *in* Biological and Biochemical Bases of Behavior, edited by H. Harlan and C. Woolsey. University of Wisconsin Press, 1958, pp. 401-424; *in* Behavior and Evolution, edited by A. Roe and G. Simpson. Yale University Press, 1958, pp. 128-139. Physiological plasticity and brain circuit theory, developmental basis of behavior.

390. SPERRY, R. W., and CLARK, E., Physiol. Zool. *22*: 372-378, 1949. Interocular transfer of visual discrimination habits in fish.

391. SPRAGUE, J. M., and CHAMBERS, W. W., J. Neurophysiol. *16*: 451-463, 1953. Regulation of posture in intact and decerebrate cat.

392. *STAMPFLI, R., Physiol. Rev. *34*: 101-112, 1954. Saltatory conduction in nerve.

393. STAMPFLI, R., Ann. New York Acad. Sci. *81*: 265-284, 1959. Effects of external K^+ on resting potential at Ranvier node.

394. STAZL, T. E., and MAGOUN, H. W., J. Neurophysiol. *14*: 133-146, 1951. Diffuse projection of thalamic system to cortex.

395. STEFANELLI, A., Quart. Rev. Biol. *26*: 17-34, 1951. Structure and function of Mauthner apparatus.

396. STEPHENS, G. C., Physiol. Zool. *30*: 55-59, 1957. Daily rhythms of temperature sensitivity.

397. STERNBURG, J., *et al.,* J. Econ. Entomol. *52*: 1070-1076, 1959. Release of neurotoxins into insect blood on stimulation.

398. STOUGH, H. B., J. Comp. Neurol. *50*: 217-230, 1930. Polarized conduction in giant nerve fibers, earthworm.

399. STRUMWASSER, F., and ROSENTHAL, S., Am. J. Physiol. *198*: 405-413, 1960. Direct stimulation of single neurons in frog brain.

400. SUTHERLAND, N. S., Nature *179*: 11-13, 1957. Visual discrimination by octopus.

401. TASAKI, I., Am. J. Physiol. *181*: 639-650, 1955. Electrical properties of node and myelin sheath of frog nerve fibers.

402. *TASAKI, I., *in* Handbook of Physiology. American Physiological Society, 1959, vol. 1, pp. 75-121. Conduction of nerve impulse.

403. TASAKI, I., and BAK, A. F., Am. J. Physiol.

193: 301-308, 1958. Oscillatory responses of squid axons.

404. TASAKI, I., and HAGIWARA, S., J. Gen. Physiol. *40*: 859-885, 1957. Evidence for two stable states in membrane of squid giant axon.

405. TASAKI, I., and SPYROPOULOS, C. S., Am. J. Physiol. *193*: 309-317, 318-327, 1958. Oscillatory responses and membrane characteristics in squid axons.

406. TASAKI, I., *et al.*, Jap. J. Physiol. *4*: 79-90, 1954. Electrical responses from Mauthner cells, catfish.

407. TAUC, B., J. Physiol. Paris *47*: 286-287, 769-792, 1955. Intracellular responses and intercellular interactions of large ganglion cells from Aplysia.

408. TAUC, B., and FESSARD, A., J. Physiol. Paris *48*: 541-544, 715-718, 1956; *49*: 973-986, 1957; *51*: 162-164, 396-399, 1959. Electrical characteristics of cell membrane of large ganglion cells from Aplysia.

409. TAYLOR, C. V., Univ. Calif. Publ. Zool. *19*: 403-470, 1920; *in* Protozoa in Biological Research, edited by G. N. Calkins and I. M. Summers. Columbia University Press, 1949, pp. 191-270. Neuromotor system of ciliate protozoa.

410. TAYLOR, G. W., J. Cell. Comp. Physiol. *15*: 363-372, 1940; *18*: 233-242, 1941; *20*: 359-372, 1942. Relation between birefringence and conduction in nerve fibers of earthworm, shrimp, and cat.

411. *TEN CATE, J., Ergebn. Physiol. *33*: 137-336, 1931. Ganglionic function, invertebrates.

412. *THORPE, W. H., Symp. Soc. Exp. Biol. *4*: 387-408, 1950; Learning and Instinct in Animals. London, Methuen & Co., 1956, 493 pp. Concepts of learning and instinct.

413. THURLOW, W. R., *et al.*, J. Neurophysiol. *14*: 289-304, 1951. Neural auditory tract, cat.

414. TOBIAS, J. M., J. Cell. Comp. Physiol. *46*: 163-182, 1955. Conduction in giant axons from lobster.

415. *TOBIAS, J. M., Ann. Rev. Physiol. *21*: 299-321, 1959. Biophysics of conduction and transmission in the nervous system.

416. TOBIAS, J. M., and BRYANT, S. H., J. Cell. Comp. Physiol. *46*: 71-95, 1955. Velocity of conduction in giant fibers of the nervous system of lobster.

417. TOWER, D. B., and ELLIOTT, K. A. C., Am. J. Physiol. *168*: 747-759, 1952. Activity of acetylcholine system in cortex of a series of mammals.

418. TROUT, D. L., J. Pharmacol. Exp. Therap. *121*: 130-135, 1957. Action of serotonin and LSD in Siamese fighting fish.

419. TUGE, H., Tohoku Imp. Univ. Sci. Rep. ser. 4, *4*: 597-602, 1929. Neurons in earthworms.

420. TUGE, H., and SHIMA, I., J. Comp. Neurol. *111*: 427-443, 1959. Conditioning in pigeons.

421. TURNER, R. S., Physiol. Zool. *23*: 35-41, 1950. Function of giant fiber system in crab Callianassa.

422. TURNER, R. S., Physiol. Zool. *24*: 323-329, 1951. Conduction in stretched and unstretched Ariolimax nerves.

423. TURNER, R. S., J. Gen. Physiol. *36*: 463-472,

1952. Effects of temperature on conduction in the nervous system of gastropod Ariolimax.

424. TURNER, R. S., and NEVIUS, D. B., J. Comp. Neurol. *94*: 239-256, 1951. Organization and conduction in nervous system of gastropod Ariolimax.

425. TWAROG, B. M., and ROEDER, K. D., Biol. Bull. *111*: 278-284, 1956; Ann. Entomol. Soc. America *50*: 231-237, 1957. Effects of ions and drugs on abdominal nerve cord of cockroach.

426. UMRATH, K., Ztschr. vergl. Physiol. *34*: 93-103, 1952. Excitatory agents from sensory nerves.

427. UMRATH, K., and HELLAUER, H. J., Pflüg. Arch. *250*: 737-746, 1948. Excitatory agents from sensory nerves.

428. UZMAN, B. G., and NOGUEIRA-GRAF, S., J. Biophys. Biochem. Cytol. *3*: 589-598, 1957. Mode of formation of nodes of Ranvier in mouse nerve.

429. VOGT, M., J. Physiol. *123*: 451-481, 1954. Concentration of sympathin in different parts of nervous system.

430. VOWLES, D. M., Quart. J. Micr. Sci. *96*: 239-256, 1955. Structure and connections of corpora pedunculata in bees and ants.

431. WADE, M., J. Comp. Neurol. *96*: 179-207, 1952. Function of prefrontal lobes in monkey.

432. WAELSCH, H., Ultrastructure and Cellular Chemistry of Neural Tissue, *in* Progress in Neurobiology, edited by S. R. Korey and J. I. Nurnberger. New York, Paul B. Hoeber, 1957, 260 pp.

433. WAGMAN, I. H., and LESSE, H., J. Neurophysiol. *15*: 234-244, 1952. Conduction velocity in human motor nerve fibers.

434. WALOP, J. N., Arch. Internat. Physiol. *59*: 145-156, 1951. Acetylcholine, in crustacean nerve system.

435. WALOP, J. N., and BOST, L. M., Biochim. Biophys. Acta *4*: 566-571, 1950. Cholinesterase in crustacean nerve system.

436. *WALTER, G., *in* Handbook of Physiology. American Physiological Society, 1959, sec. 1, vol. 1, pp. 279-298. Brain waves.

437. WATANABE, A., *et al.*, Fed. Proc. *19*: 298, 1960. Conduction in crayfish lateral giant fibers.

438. WEBB, H. M., Physiol. Zool. *23*: 316-337, 1950. Daily rhythm of light sensitivity.

439. *WEBB, H. M., and BROWN, F. A., Physiol. Rev. *39*: 127-161, 1959. Review of activity rhythms.

440. WEIDMANN, S., J. Physiol. *114*: 372-381, 1951. Electrical characteristics of Sepia nerve.

441. WEISS, P., J. Comp. Neurol. *67*: 269-315, 1937; Comp. Psychol. Monog. *17*: 1-96, 1941. Coordination of transplanted amphibian limbs.

442. WELLS, G. P., J. Mar. Biol. Assn. U. K. *28*: 447-464, 1949; Symp. Soc. Exp. Biol. *4*: 127-142. Respiratory and feeding rhythms in Arenicola.

443. WELLS, G. P., and ALBRECHT, E. B., J. Exp. Biol. *28*: 41-50, 50-56, 1951. Oesophageal rhythms in Arenicola.

444. WELLS, M. J., J. Exp. Biol. *36*: 501-511, 590-612, 1959. Neural basis of tactile discrimination by octopus.

445. WELLS, M. J., and WELLS, J., J. Exp. Biol. *35*: 324-336, 337-348, 1958. Effects of lesions to the brain on learning by octopus.

446. WELSH, J. H., and HYDE, J. E., J. Neurophysiol. 7: 41-49, 1944. Acetylcholine in rat brain.

447. WELSH, J. H., and TAUB, R., Science 112: 467-469, 1950. Molecular configuration and biological activity of acetylcholine-like substances.

448. WELSH, J. H., and PROCK, P. B., Biol. Bull. 115: 551-561, 1958. Quaternary ammonium bases in coelenterates.

449. *WEST, G. B., Quart. Rev. Biol. 30: 116-137, 1955. Comparative pharmacology of suprarenal medulla.

450. WHITING, H. P., in Biochemistry of Developing Nervous Systems, edited by H. Welsh, New York, Academic Press, 1955, pp. 85-103. Functional development of nervous system of fish.

451. WIERSMA, C. A. G., J. Neurophysiol. 12: 267-275, 1949; J. Cell. Comp. Physiol. 40: 399-419, 1952. Electrical activity in giant nerve fibers of crayfish.

452. *WIERSMA, C. A. G., Cold Spring Harbor Symp. 17: 155-163, 1952; Physiol. Rev. 33: 326-355, 1953. Transmission in neurons of invertebrates, particularly arthropods.

453. WIERSMA, C. A. G., Acta Physiol. Pharmacol. Neerl. 6: 135-142, 1957; J. Comp. Neurol. 110: 421-471, 1958. Number of nerve cells and analysis of functional connections of sensory neurons in the central nervous system of crayfish.

454. WIERSMA, C. A. G., et al., J. Cell. Comp. Physiol. 46: 307-326, 1955. Central representations of sensory neurons in the crayfish.

455. WIGGLESWORTH, V. B., Quart. J. Micr. Sci. 99: 441-450, 1958. Distribution of cholinesterase in Rhodnius.

456. WINKEL, K., and CASPERS, H., Pflüg. Arch. 258: 22-37, 1953. Brain function in lizard Lacerta.

457. WILSON, D. M., Science 129: 841-842, 1959. Conduction in Mauthner neurons of lungfish.

458. WITT, P. N., Experientia 7: 310-311, 1951. Effect of LSD on web spinning by spider.

459. WOLDRING, S., and DIRKEN, M. N. J., J. Exp. Biol. 28: 218-220, 1951. Unit electrical activity in medulla of fish.

460. WOLFE, L. S., and SMALLMAN, B. N., J. Cell. Comp. Physiol. 48: 215-236, 1956. Properties of cholinesterase in flies.

461. WOOLSEY, C. N., in Biological and Biochemical Basis of Behavior, edited by F. Harlow and C. N. Woolsey. University of Wisconsin Press, 1958, pp. 63-81. Organization of somatic, sensory, and motor areas of cerebral cortex.

462. WORLEY, L. G., J. Cell. Comp. Physiol. 5: 53-72, 1934. Ciliary synchronization and reversal, Paramecium and Spirostomum.

463. WRIGHT, E. B., et al., Fed. Proc. 12: 160, 1953. Excitation constants and conduction in crustacean motor axons and giant fibers.

464. WRIGHT, E. B., and RUBEN, J. P., J. Cell. Comp. Physiol. 51: 13-28, 1958. Excitation constants and conduction in ventral nerve cord of lobster.

465. YAMASAKI, T., and NARAHASHI, T., J. Insect Physiol. 4: 1-13, 1960. Synaptic transmission in caudal ganglion of cockroach.

466. YOUNG, J. Z., Quart. J. Micr. Sci. 78: 367-386, 1936; J. Exp. Biol. 15: 170-185, 1938; Phil. Tr. Roy. Soc. London, B, 229: 465-501, 1939. Anatomy and physiology of the giant nerve fiber system of cephalopods.

INDEX